A Short Chronology of World Cinema

Dennis Grunes

For my mother,
Ana Grushinsky,
who kept taking me to the movies
even after I was born.

ISBN 9780955384318
© Dennis Grunes
First published 2010 in London by Sands Films Cinema Club.

Although great care was taken in preparing the first edition of this book, some mistakes and omissions may be present: please contact us by visiting our website:
www.sandsfilms.co.uk

Acknowledgements

My effort here has many parents. I wish to acknowledge those critics and historians I have read, including Andrew Sarris, Georges Sadoul (in Peter Morris's 1972 English translation of Sadoul's 1965 *Dictionary of Films*), Adam Garbicz and Jacek Klinowski, who authored the two-volume *Cinema, the Magic Vehicle* (1983), Eric Rhode, whose *A History of the Cinema* (1976) is never far from my desk, and Tom Zaniello, who authored *Working Stiffs, Union Maids, Reds and Riffraff: A Guide to Films About Labor* (2003); and many other individuals past and present. Above all, I wish to thank Mindy Aloff, a friend now for many years, not only for all her ready comments about hundreds, possibly thousands of films but also for her patient reading of and editorial help with my manuscript in one of its earlier incarnations. Many others, too numerous for me to list (and probably remember) them all, have variously assisted with pertinent remarks about film and films, among them Marty Cohen, Margot Fein, Brooke Jacobson, Jon Jost, Fannie Peczenik, Courtney Rojas, and Olivier Stockman, who has been the driving force behind the publication of this book—and who co-authored the script of *The Fool*, which is included in the list of outstanding films with which not a few of you will endlessly argue. That's what we all do when it comes to the movies.

Dennis Grunes

Portland, Oregon. May 2010.

Foreword.

In his book *Histoire du Cinema Mondial,* Georges Sadoul tried to put each film in its context; in an appendix, he added a chronology: giving for each year, from 1892 to 1966, a list of notable titles. Sadoul's list became the main inspiration for Sands Films Cinema Club and programming films by year of production.
The necessity of cinema clubs and film societies is demonstrated by the fact that many of Sadoul's 5,000 listed titles have not been seen since their original release; and when a film is lost, forgotten, or locked in the vault of a remote cinematheque, it ceases to exist: a film exists only when it is screened to an audience.

Searching for information about films I have not seen, I came across someone who seems to have seen everything. I then discovered that Dennis Grunes has written about almost each film he has seen during the last forty years or so. This massive work cannot be improvised nor even commissioned: it is a lifetime commitment. Taken individually each entry is, at the very least, an introduction to a film, but edited together and classified by year, these neat 300 word entries become a remarkable survey of the history of world cinema. Publishing this book became therefore the natural continuation of the club's activity and purpose.

Dennis Grunes is a sharp critic, opinionated and well informed, his passion and enthusiasm are contagious. Ironically, Dennis Grunes has never been to Sands Films Cinema Club, we have never met, we have never watched a film together and, perhaps, we never will: he lives and works in Portland, Oregon. Several thousand email messages exchanges supplied the material for this book, composed with care and discipline by an exacting writer.

Olivier Stockman

American English grammar and spelling conventions are used in this book, according to the author's instructions.

Foreword.

What follows is a chronological list of films, including brief entries about a number of outstanding ones, and twenty or so more extensive pieces. In the selection of these pieces, the vast majority of which are about 300 words each, I have tried to juggle a number of considerations: the briefest historical overview, the development of cinema as an art form, the degree to which films combine fictional and documentary elements, thereby nudging fiction in the direction of documentary and documentary in the direction of fiction, the challenge posed to film by political meddling, and insights into particular films and filmmakers.

I have tried to emphasize the expressive nature of films—those aspects that certify cinema as an art form rather than as a medium of diversion. Like most paintings, poems or whatever, most films aren't especially expressive; they simply fail as art. They may take as their primary aim the filmmaker's relationship with an audience, which the filmmaker tries to manipulate or entertain. A serious filmmaker places his or her primary interest elsewhere: in developing themes, which entails finding—by intellect or intuition, for different artists work very differently—the expressive means for doing this. Substantial films therefore require considerable focus for their creation, and they require, by us, scarcely less in their viewing and consideration. Diversions glide over us; art, on the other hand, makes demands on us—and rewards us generously when we meet those demands.

Dennis Grunes

Early Cinema

Begun as a mere transcriptive visual recording in the late nineteenth century, the "moving picture" had been exhibited as a novelty, a kind of freak show. Documentary, however, soon developed in the direction of fiction with the under-one-minute films of brothers Louis and Auguste Lumière in France (see "Exiting the Factory" in *The list* below). Beginning in 1896, Georges Méliès, also in France, opened his prodigious bag of camera tricks, retaining novelty, therefore, but shifting its character. In the 1910s, though, filmmakers in France, Sweden and elsewhere helped to define the emerging medium as an expressive art form; apart from telling a story visually, films conveyed ideas through a flexible variety of visual means. Therefore, the principal vehicle for content in an outstanding silent film, in conjunction with the silence itself, consisted of such elements as the composition of the frames (*mise-en-scène*), the modification of the appearance of the compositions as a result of the selected camera distance and angle, and the effect or idea achieved by editing, that is, the cutting from one image to the next. Not until the 1920s would camera *movement* become a comparable contributor to cinematic meaning.

Consider, for example, Swedish filmmaker Victor Sjöström's 1917 *The Outlaw and His Wife (Berg-Ejvind och Hans Hustru)*, which many regard as his masterpiece. In a key passage, the isolating height of the mountains where the "outlaw" couple hide projects the egotism into which their circumstance has pushed them. From this height, in order to protect their infant from police capture and contamination, Halla hurls down the baby; the subsequent cut away from her action—quick, startling—vividly conveys what brusque, desperate, incoherent, even lethal acts this kind of egotism enables. (Additionally, the abrupt cut shortcircuits any irrelevant sentimental response from us.) Both the shot describing Halla's deludedly protective act and the cut, then, conspire to reveal her harried mental state; we see the objective act she commits, but we also, in a way, see into her mind, gleaning from this subjective glimpse the *provocation* for her act: all that this innocent couple has been forced to endure that has led to the commission of infanticide. (A "cut" is the formal disruption of the visual field, either by a change of scene or by any noncontinuous shift in camera placement within the scene; a "shot" consists of any segment of film, whatever the length, between two consecutive cuts.) In effect, then, we become privy to Sjöström's feelings as well as Halla's, his outrage at the injustice targeting the fugitive couple. We are doing more than "following a story"; Sjöström compels us to think about what we see.

People have different tastes, and the list below of other films from 1895 through the 1910s does not include D. W. Griffith's 1916 *Intolerance*, which critic Pauline Kael once called the greatest film ever made. I consider this Hollywood production, like countless other mainstream U.S. films, an example of "visual storytelling"—the province of a hack, not of an artist. Like his *Birth of a Nation* (1915), Griffith's *Intolerance* brandishes an array of formal and technical means to no higher aim than narrative development; rather than visual expressiveness, the most it achieves is visual *impressiveness*. It underlines rather than Wife interprets the feelings of its characters, substitutes a "message" for ideas (the very selling of which invites skepticism as to its sincerity), and condescends to, by manipulating, its audience. In the case of *Intolerance*, one can certainly argue that the manipulation is at the service of a commendable social attitude; but surely one must distinguish between the film's lofty sentiment and crude technique. With the chauvinistic *Birth of a Nation*, one is at least spared confronting this task.

For a given year, films are listed in order of preference.

1895

EXITING THE FACTORY (France). The Lumière brothers provided a treasure-trove of under-one-minute filmlets, one of which, showing an ostrich leading a line of humans in their Sunday finest, surely influenced the satirical tone of René Clair's *Italian Straw Hat* (1927), and another that startles with its snowball fight in a wintry street because the participants, including ladies, are all adults. An especially beautiful example of early fresh, outdoor cinema is "La sortie des usines Lumière," shot right outside the Lumières' own factory as workers depart for the day through the main gate and an adjacent door. The silence of the silent film bolsters the sense of stiff formality that is actually the outcome of the documentary's "arrangement," the planning that has these workers pretending to do in the afternoon, when the light is right, what they will do for real at workday's end and the bit of direction that has been given them, that they should not acknowledge the camera's Wife presence, which increases their selfconsciousness. The slowness of their gait also contributes to an overall dreamy effect.

A few bicyclists dot the impossibly orderly pedestrian crowd (this orderliness is deliberate so that crowd-tangles do not wreak havoc with the filming time allotment), and with people moving offscreen to the right and others to the left, from implicitly confined space to spaciousness, an implication arises as to the reality of their lives, apart from work, in the directions in which they move: *home*.

Since all this is a presentation for the camera, however, it is the *idea* of home toward which the film tends. Indeed, this filmlet blends what its successors also will blend: documentary, fiction; objectivity, subjectivity; reality, fantasy; contrivance, spontaneity. In less than a minute the future of cinema is predicted, along with the audience's involvement in onscreen activity.

1905

THE BLACK DEVIL (France). We must take pioneering French filmmaker Georges Méliès at his word that he had no interest in turning film into art but, rather, wished to create theatrical scenes—but scenes containing camera tricks to conjure illusions that could not occur on stage. *Le diable noir*, called in the U.S. *The Black Imp*, is typical of his wee intentions. It is a kind of nonsense that has some affinity, perhaps, to the verbal kind that we associate with Edward Lear's verse.

In *Le diable noir*, a human-sized, black cat-like figure with a beard plainly considers a bedroom at an inn, especially the bed, as its domain. This "imp" disappears. Enter a guest (Méliès) for a night's lodging. Increasingly taxing the man's sanity, the invisible imp makes furniture suddenly appear or disappear, including a chair right out from under the guest; at another turn, the chair multiplies succesively. The series of quick cuts that creates these illusions—despite what some people seem to think, there isn't a single jump-cut in the four-minute film—is exquisitely timed to convey some sense of its own reality, which wars with the guest's rationality. When the mischief-maker turns visible and chases him, the guest has perhaps passed into a condition that represents the total opposite of the night's sweet rest which he had sought. Eventually, like a madman in a straight-jacket, he is escorted out of the room by the innkeeper and others, and the imp merrily reclaims its bed.

There is no serious consideration here of the guest's interiority, for instance, of the paranoid insecurity that might afflict someone away from home. The film aims only to delight with cinematic tricks.

Méliès made more than 550 films, in which he almost always appeared, between 1896 and the First World War.

1908

A FISH PROCESSING FACTORY IN ASTRAKHAN (Russia, France). In Moscow, in a small production studio owned by Charles Pathé and his brothers in Paris, Aleksandr Drankov initially made documentaries, thus helping to introduce the Russian people to cinema. Another Aleksandr, Khanzhonkov, also lit this path, beating Drankov at his own studio by releasing the first Russian feature film. Drankov himself likely directed the unsigned documentary "Zavod Rybnykh Konservov v Astrakhani," part of the *Picturesque Russia* series.

It opens with a startling moving long-shot surveying a dock where barrels of fish are being unloaded from boats; the camera itself is stationary, its simulated motion the result of its location: an out-of-frame motor boat.

The remainder of the eight-minute film consists of static shots. These, closer in, show workers weighing the catch, gutting the fish, delivering the salt with brooms, salting the fish. Gradually, the workers come to the fore, quite literally leaving the fish behind. The scene that effects this shift is a sustained shot showing the workers washing their hands; the degree to which they wash and wash conveys the effort involved in relieving themselves of the stink. It is also a practical preparation for the activity that follows: a communal meal in a room full of long tables. The image overflows with animated conversation and convivial atmosphere. The film ends jubilantly, with two woman workers, arms around each other, facing the camera and smiling with seeming sincerity and spontaneity.

Therefore, the film moves from a portrayal of labor as social contribution to the laborers themselves, their sparkling humanity and individualism. It is a case of putting the best face forward, for tsarist Russia was a place of terrible poverty, cruelty and oppression. Those who have work to do hide from view those who do not and starve.

Ironies abound.

1912

THE CAMERAMAN'S REVENGE (Russia). Born in Wilno, Poland, then part of the Russian Empire (and is, today, Vilnius, Lithuania), Władysław Starewicz is one of cinema's great animators. His animated short "Mest kinematograficheskogo operatora," from Russia, is a deft demonstration of marital hypocrisy and the double standard.

Two bourgeois beetles, a fat male and a plain-Jane female, have complacently settled into their marriage. Restless, taking off for a little excitement, the husband goes on one of his business trips, briefcase in tow. In the city, as is his wont, Fatso heads for The Gay Dragonfly, the nightclub where his mistress, a gorgeous dragonfly, performs. After her act, the two head for a room at Hôtel d'Amour, unawares they are being followed by the dragonfly's jilted spouse, a grasshopper, a budding filmmaker with camera in tow. Beginning with a keyhole shot, Grasshopper films his sweetie and her new partner bugopulating. Meanwhile, the fat beetle's plain-Jane wife is also having an affair, in her case, with a bohemian painter-bug—not just an artist, but an artiste, as telegraphed by his flamboyant gestures and big, floppy hat. Back home, Fat Beetle walks in on his wife and her lover bugopulating. He beats his wife and tries to kill Painter-Bug. With apparent generosity he forgives his wife, whose gratitude turns to rage when, taken by her husband to the movies, she sees the film of him and his mistress bugopulating. His forgiveness exposed as smug superiority laced with guilt, she whacks him with her parasol, and he takes off to kill Grasshopper, who is the projectionist for his own film. Both Beetles, husband and wife, end up in their new home: jail. Now they will know how the other half lives.

Most of the animation is intricate and brilliant—especially all the bugopulating.

1913

INGEBORG HOLM (Sweden). From Nils Krok's play, writer-director Victor Sjöström's Ingeborg Holm is one of cinema's earliest masterpieces, an overwhelming tearjerker about mother-love that strikes resonant chords of social commitment and consciousness. Its target is Sweden's poor laws; its tack, to expose their deviation from Nature.

Hilda Borgström is irresistibly moving as Ingeborg Holm, who plummets into bankruptcy after the death of her husband, Sven, and her unsuccessful attempt to keep the family business, a grocery, going. She ends up with an ulcer and a bed in the poor-house, separated from her three young children, the youngest of whom is "boarded out" (whatever that means), and the other two assigned to different foster households—an arrangement she agrees to, hoping to prevent their becoming beggars. (Her official identity has become "Ingeborg Holm, pauper.") When her only daughter, Valborg, falls gravely ill, with the system refusing to pay for her necessary operation, Ingeborg runs away and visits her dying child, whose foster parents live out in the country. Ingeborg's flight to Valborg's bedside visually connects her (for our eye) to Nature, much as her forced separation from her children assaulted a parent's natural bond with her children. Ingeborg is captured and returned to the poor-house; Valborg dies; brought in to visit, her younger boy no longer recognizes her. Ingeborg, shattered, drops into madness. Fifteen years later, Eric, her older son, a seafarer, who has held onto a photograph of his mother that she had once packed for her children, discovers her condition; but once he shows her the photograph, Ingeborg Holm is restored to herself and her sanity.

Each scene unfolds patiently and to the emotional full.

The same actor plays father and grown son, which may have influenced the casting of To Each His Own thirty years hence.

1914

HIS MAJESTY, THE SCARECROW OF OZ (U.S.). One of a number of silent films that the author of the Oz books wrote and produced, *His Majesty, the Scarecrow of Oz* was also directed by L. Frank Baum. Light and airy, it's pure enchantment. Unlike the lumbering, unimaginative *Wizard of Oz* (1939), *His Majesty* doesn't make us feel nostalgic for our childhoods; rather, it permits the adult viewer to enter a child's world of unfettered fancy. *There's no place like Baum, there's no place like Baum.*

The story, of course, is fabulous, and the filming, liltingly magical. Baum's cinematic guide is Georges Méliès, who in France had already taken his "Trip to the Moon" (1902) and made his "Impossible Voyage" (1904) and "Conquest of the Pole" (1912). These and other Méliès films helped fill Baum's wondrous bag of camera tricks. But Baum's sprightly humor is all his own. For instance, Scarecrow's squaring off and dance with Giant Crow in a field is hilarious.

There is a remarkable passage in which Old Mombi assaults Scarecrow and tears the Wife straw of life out of his chest as he lies on the ground. Seamless editing replaces the actor playing Scarecrow with a real scarecrow, permitting a scene of truly gripping witchly frenzy and scarecrowly vulnerability. More marvelous still are scenes on the barge as Dorothy and her companions pursue their plan to dispose of King Krewl. At one point Scarecrow is left behind, stuck on his pole in the water, and, looking for a way out, he goes into the depths of the sea, encountering a whole other realm. Later, the group on their barge goes up and comes back down the Wall of Water—one of the most deliriously beautiful passages in all of fantastic cinema.

There isn't a moment of this film that doesn't delight.

1915

LES VAMPIRES (France). Written and directed by Louis Feuillade, in its current abbreviated form running nearly seven hours, *Les Vampires* influenced the future architects of Surrealism (Aragon, Breton, Eluard), Fritz Lang, Carl Theodor Dreyer, Marcel Carné, Alfred Hitchcock, Luis Buñuel, Olivier Assayas. (The original *Mabuse* serial, 1922; two emissaries' walk through guests at a ball frozen mid-step on the dance floor in *Les visiteurs du soir*, 1942; the Cat Burglar in *To Catch a Thief*, 1955: much derives from Feuillade's film.) Blending airy naturalism and dark though entrancing intrigues bordering on fantasy, the ten-part serial finds contemporary Paris in the grip of a devilishly clever criminal gang led by The Grand Vampire and an eternally black silk-tighted Irma Vep (an anagram for *vampire*). Identities shift, as in a dream. The viewer appreciates the law (and their adjunct, a reporter investigating the crimes) but nonetheless holds dear the rogues, who oppose bourgeois literalism and sentimentalism. This is an intoxicating film—one that pirouettes off the murder of a Russian ballerina.

Shadows, kidnappings, killings, theft, chases, battles of wit—all this is here; but there are also ghostly imagery and set-pieces. In dusky daylight, her impossibly graceful figure-in-black stealthily making its way across a rooftop, Irma Vep is her own shadow—at once, reality and dream, charm and threat, athletic appearance and close-to-dissolving illusion. Aristocratic guests, gassed ("a delicate perfume floated through the ballrooms" at midnight), try desperately to exit a grand room, which they find impossible to do; slumped on sofas and in chairs, as fixed as the furniture, they are robbed by the gang, which weave around them in a radiant inadvertent mockery of their minutes-earlier turns on the dance floor: one of cinema's greatest passages.

The French love "their" Poe—and the Vampires have again escaped!

1916

THE DYING SWAN (Russia). Elegantly bourgeois, Yevgeni Bauer died months before Russia's October Revolution. He had made more than twenty films, perhaps the loveliest of which is *Umirayushchii Lebed*, written by 20-year-old Zoya Barantsevich before she turned to silent film acting. Denouncing it as decadent, the Bolsheviks banned the film.

It's a shame whenever live or recorded music is appended to outstanding silent films, a practice commercial pressure has been known to dictate. Silence is one of the most expressive elements in silent film and remains, even today, the grace of cinema. Musical attempts to heighten the emotional content of films strike me as barbaric and manipulative; as with other artistic elements, even in sound films the best music is analytical or distancing—not underlining, but aesthetically or thematically contributory.

Gizella (Vera Karalli, of the Bolshoi Ballet and Diaghilev's Ballet Russes de Monte Carlo) is a mute ballerina—and the silence of Bauer's silent film expresses this muteness, as does the muteness of two dream passages that, together, compose the spiritual and emotional vortex of Bauer's film: one is a waking dream—ours—in which Gizella performs (exquisitely) Anna Pavlova's signature dance, "The Dying Swan"; the other is Gizella's own sleeping dream, in which her fate is revealed to her should she continue sitting, in costume, for Glinskiy, the artist who, obsessed with the image of death that she projects in performance, is painting her. With its premonitions of the end of a class and a silken style in Russian cinema, Bauer's film begs to be read in terms of unfolding Russian history. (The earlier end of Gizella's romance with Viktor, whose unfaithfulness she discovers, creates a foundation for the principal theme.) Hauntingly, *The Dying Swan* mourns the loss that it anticipates.

And in silence! To paraphrase Shakespeare: Muteness is all.

A MAN THERE WAS (Sweden). From Henrik Ibsen's poem, Victor Sjöström's *Terje Vigen* is about a Norwegian sailor (Sjöström, robust, excellent), who, returning home, finds waiting for him, along with his wife, the fruit of his previous homecoming: an infant daughter. Terje Vigen "sobers down" as a result, rejecting a night of barroom comradery in favor of staying home. Implicitly, were his wife still his only companion, Vigen would scoot out in a heartbeat.

The land and the sea, family and himself: these polar forces tug at Vigen's heart. (In an amazing shot, Vigen stands at the open door of his cottage, looking out, his body indeed leaning out, the sea beckoning him.) A British blockade during the Napoleonic Wars leaves his family destitute, starving. Vigen will leave wife and daughter, but fortified with a rationalization capable of concealing his abandoning them: he will impossibly defy the naval blockade and procure food for his family at a safe port. On his way home the inevitable occurs; he is captured and imprisoned by the British. Part of the brilliant flexibility of Sjöström's film is its impassioned anti-war plea at the time of another European war; but *Terje Vigen* homes in on Terje Vigen. Returning home, he discovers that wife and child both died after he "fled." His denial that he did this provokes Vigen to seek unChristian revenge against the British captain who barred his reunion with homeland, wife, family. The sight of the man's wife and daughter, though, purges Vigen of this madness and confronts him with his own responsibility. The closing image is one of peace and redemption: the cross marking the shared grave of his wife and daughter.

Here facilitating his plans, there obstructing them, the sea suggests Vigen's tortured ambivalence, his convoluted psychology.

JUDEX (France). Wealthy Jacques de Tremeuse has an alternate identity: the caped avenger Judex—Latin, for Justice. He kidnaps and imprisons Favraux in a secret dungeon, leaving everyone to believe the Parisian banker is dead, after Favraux mistreats his elderly secretary, Vallières, and refuses to give half his ill-gotten fortune to the poor. But Judex has another, more personal motive: Once upon a time, Favraux financially destroyed Jacques' father, who committed suicide to avoid dishonor. Meanwhile, crooks kidnap, by turns, Favraux's widowed daughter, Jacqueline, whom Judex rescues and with whom he falls in love, and her little son.

Judex impersonates Vallières vis-à-vis Jacqueline, thus hiding from view his sexual interest. Here, the "good guys"—Jacques and his brother, Roger—kidnap as easily as do the greedy villains, Diana Monti and "Moralés" (another character assuming a false identity). Jacques' father did not live long enough to learn that a gold mine of his panned out; we keep wondering what sort of person Jacques might have been had he not inherited his father's wealth. Indeed, when kidnapped and marked for death he manages to substitute someone else, who is duly murdered, thereby becoming a kind of murderer himself. "Good" and "evil" fluctuate in this film, then, but love and forgiveness are ultimately triumphant, including the love of children, which turns a seedy character, private detective Cocantin, into a doting adoptive father, and an unexpected ally of righteousness.

In this dreamlike film, with its fluttering, mesmerizing flight of two white pigeons and Jacqueline, in mourning black, walking down a rural path followed by a pack of benign partly white dogs, one sequence finds Judex imagining Jacqueline, who is thinking about her son, from whom she is separated: a dream within a dream.

Louis Feuillade's *Judex* is the dream that is cinema.

1917

THE OUTLAW AND HIS WIFE (Sweden). *See above.*

1918

A DOG'S LIFE (U.S.). Charles Chaplin's *A Dog's Life* has three settings: the urban vacant lot where the homeless Tramp sleeps with Scraps, his cherished canine companion; the dance hall, where the Tramp meets the girl of his dreams, who is fired for not "putting out" for the male clientele (the place is named the Green Lantern—a wink away from its being the Red Lantern); the street outside.

When the Tramp desperately tries to get a job at an employment office, his attempts are thwarted by other applicants, who usurp his place on line. Used to being bullied, he rescues others who are bullied: Scraps, from a fight with other dogs; the girl. A thief chooses the Tramp's sleep-spot to bury a victim's bill-filled pocketbook—and, on all fours digging with his paws, resembling a dog in the process; Scraps digs up the find, which the Tramp takes as serendipitous—a redressing of the world's unfairness, which the fantastic presence of multiple vicious police officers conflates with the bullying. The thief steals back the money,

1918

but, fueled by a dream of sharing a patch of farm with the girl, the Tramp schemes to claim again the loot as *his*.

Writer-director Chaplin, en route to his masterpieces, devises a motif that symbolizes the Tramp's precarious existence: things with one or more holes in it. One example is the hole in the seat of his baggy pants, out of which Scraps's own tail spiritedly dangles after the Tramp has hidden her in his pants. In the dance hall, holes in a drape enable the Tramp to steal back the money from the thief by adding his own hands to the knocked-out accomplice across the table. Gunshot holes in a dish, with the Tramp ducking for his life, continue the motif.

1919

LEAVES FROM SATAN'S BOOK (Denmark). D. W. Griffith ponderously made *Intolerance* (1916) to prove he wasn't the sentimental racist that his *Birth of a Nation* (1915) showed him to be. For me, the film is soporific. My opinion hasn't prevailed. Filmmakers at the time, and since, have felt the film's enormous influence. Its collection of stories depicting different historical times and places within a loose philosophical framework informs Denmark's Carl Theodor Dreyer's *Blade af Satans Bog*.

I reject much of the film, for instance, the segments on the French and Bolshevik Revolutions, where his sense of decorum finds Dreyer siding with reactionary forces. Nevertheless, the first two segments, on the Christ's Passion and the Spanish Inquisition, are brilliant.

Naturalistic and unaffected, the Christ material has been surpassed only once, with Pasolini's *The Gospel According to St. Matthew* (1964). (At his death, Dreyer left unfilmed a long-planned film about the life of Jesus.)

According to *Leaves*, Judas is seduced into betraying Jesus by the argument that Jesus's death is preordained and necessary for the completion of his mission. But the segment on the sixteenth-century Spanish Inquisition is the film's most trenchant revelation of the workings of evil in our world. The terrifying opening shot is of torture devices in a dungeon. For a monk who is smitten with the aristocrat's daughter he is instructing, an image of a saint assumes her sensuous form. Satan, the "Grand Inquisitor," manipulates his unacted-on feelings, impressing the monk into service to the Inquisition, in which capacity he is ordered to condemn the woman he loves as a heretic—a rough sketch for *Day of Wrath* (1943).

For Dreyer, whose *The Marked Ones* (1922) is the most compassionate non-Jewish film ever made about Jewish suffering, religious persecution is unfounded in faith.

THE CABINET OF DR. CALIGARI (Germany). Made in Germany at the close of the decade and released at the dawn of the next, *Das Cabinet des Dr. Caligari* applies German Expressionism to a masked meditation on the distress Germany suffered following its defeat in the First World War. It remains among the most intriguing and harrowing of horror films.

Robert Wiene directed Carl Mayer and Hans Janowitz's script about an itinerant showman under whose hypnotic spell a somnabulist commits nocturnal murders. There is a narrative framing device: the chance encounter of two strangers leading to an extended flashback that discloses "the truth": the man who condemns this showman is, in fact, an inmate escaped from the insane asylum the man he accuses heads. No wonder, then, he loathes and fears Caligari! Only, can we not glean from the final fadeout—an ambiguous closeup of the "good" doctor—a likely germ of truth in the madman's ravings? The last shot pulls the rug out from under us, leaving our minds in a scramble to sort out the film's suggestions and insinuations.

To the sort of décor, in France, Georges Méliès had used in his curiously literal fantasies (among them, the *1902 A Trip to the Moon*), Caligari's painted backdrops, with their distorted perspectives, add an ambiguous subjectivism, helping film to become thereby a striking means of dark psychological probing. But that is not all. Here, proceeding from this probing are social and political implications that mine the national mood that eventually will give rise in Germany to Nazism.

History, then, would provide the lion's share of this extraordinary film's horrific aspect.

J'ACCUSE! (France). Unlike his own 1938 "remake," Abel Gance's silent *J'accuse!* is a great film, perhaps a masterpiece. Made during the Great War and incorporating actual combat footage into its romantic melodrama about two soldiers, both from the same village, both of whom love the same woman to whom one of them is married, *J'accuse!* has a real connection to the spirit of Zola, which the "remake" does not. Each version, while thematically similar, tells a different story. The silent version is one of the most massively moving antiwar films I have seen.

There are few, if any, decorous shots here; each shot instead is expressive, although one needs to be patient sometimes for this to become plain. A seemingly clichéd shot, when repeated, becomes haunting; a seemingly overwrought shot, when it also is repeated, becomes deftly ironical. The camera on occasion moves, following a character (humanity is at the center of *J'accuse!*); this surprises in a 1919 film.

But more surprising still is the inclusion of an instance of marital rape. Knowing that her husband wouldn't remember doing this (the rape scene is, incidentally, terrifying), Edith attributes her pregnancy to a German soldier's assault. Brilliantly, Gance accompanies her account with a seemingly expressionistic attack by German soldiers, all shadow and no substance—a visual indication that the pan-protective explanation is bogus.

War is initially folded into the romantic melodrama; gradually, the melodrama folds into the war, which shifts from background to foreground.

In the "remake" the dead rise up to warn people of the coming world war. In the original they confront the villagers with their sacrifice, to determine if that has helped in any way. They point out instances of ungrateful behavior, but commend the living anyhow: Christian sacrifice, Christian forgiveness.

The living owe the dead.

Films of the 1920s

To assert its modernity and to propagandize, the revolutionary Soviet Union seized upon the medium of film as though doing so would deliver another blow to the memory of Tsarist Russia. Thus Soviet cinema came to dominate the decade with superior examples of the summit of film art: the black-and-white silent film. The result: an explosion of energy and genius that cinema would not see again until the French New Wave in the late fifties.

In several ways Victor Turin's *Turksib* (1929), which arrived near the end of the decade, is the signature Soviet film: a pulsating documentary of the construction of a railroad linking north and south—an epic celebration of a young nation's determination to overcome and subdue Nature in order to better the lives of its people and to unify its vast territory. Taken together, the film's bounty of mostly brief shots composes a vibrant hymn to national purpose, the arduous, often piecemeal task of realizing a daunting enterprise and achieving a noble end. *Turksib*, then, is governed by metaphor (and, one might say, wish-fulfillment), for the construction of the Turkistan-Siberian Railroad everywhere suggests the building of the Union of Soviet Socialist Republics itself. Therefore, the film allows us, now that the nation in question has fallen and vanished, to glimpse afresh—amidst a good deal of snow and ice—the hope and spirit that the *idea* of the Soviet Union once brought to the world.

Nothing else of note apparently distinguished Turin's career. (Having seen no other film of his, I am simply repeating what I have always read.) Yet this fact, too, seems to contribute to the film's meaning, as if the immense achievements that the film relates, whether by direction or indirection, themselves pulled up Turin to a level of aspiration and artistry that otherwise he could not reach. In even this way, then, Turin's radiant film encapsulates the Soviet dream.

By comparison, its Hollywood anticipation, young John Ford's *The Iron Horse* (1924), seems to be rallying against fears of national decay. Here also is an epic about the construction of a transcontinental railroad; already Ford's vision, though, is tragic and complex. The film assigns the unification of the nation, east and west, to two individuals from Springfield, Illinois: a man whose son, once the father is murdered, adopts his dream of the railroad; Abe, the father's rail-splitting friend, who, later as U.S. president, signs legislation authorizing the construction, to realize the dream, against advice that the nation should spend all its money on the current war between north and south. With an eye on peace, Lincoln hopes to unify the nation. His offscreen assassination, however, merges with the death of the boy's father to suggest the awesome price that pursuing the dream exacts.

And there's more to pay: the exploitation of foreign labor to make the railroad construction financially feasible; the mass slaughter of buffalo to feed the workers; the incitement of Native Americans, who realize that the railroad, by consolidating white power, signals their end.

The film falls short of the first rank by admitting in too much melodrama and comic relief; visually, however, it astounds. The opening shot, with its peaceful mass movement of sheep, lends depth to the later, furious shot of buffalo being mowed down for meat. Ford's use of the moving camera, attuned to the movement of trains, is exemplary. But, above all, are the brilliant long-shots of the narrow pass between two huge mountains that will provide the means for the railroad's completion—a symbolical evocation of aspiration and vision, with erotic overtones besides: the pulsating train that will penetrate the Virgin Land.

"Ford's use of the moving camera": the 1920s indeed anointed this use as one of the most significant features of cinema. In particular, Germany's Friedrich Wilhelm Murnau helped make the tracking shot part of the artillery of Expressionism in cinema, which built on

Films of the 1920s

France's Feuillade's identification of cinema with dreams. Following the lead of Karl Grune's *The Street* (1923), Murnau discarded title-inserts to create an uninterrupted flow of images in *The Last Laugh* (1924). (The German title, *Der letzte Mann*, actually translates as *The Last Man*.) In this famous film, the camera moves a lot—and with purpose; for this study of a demoted hotel employee contains continuously moving shots that are ironic counterpoint to the toppled worker's disintegrated self-esteem.

Nevertheless, the film's high reputation has somewhat declined. While Murnau captures every nuance of his protagonist's fall from elegantly dressed doorman, a position of visible élan, to washroom attendant, he eschews every opportunity for probing analysis. Murnau skips by any consideration of the warped basis for the man's self-image. Like his protagonist, Murnau is fixated on the shiny-buttoned uniform. Why should status be determined by what a person's job is? The hollowness of such a yardstick could be connected to the capriciousness of the demotion. In some larger view that Murnau doesn't take, there may be food for thought about how employers jerk around employees, attempting to decide even their souls for them.

Still, the film fascinates, not only because of its use of camera, but also because of the towering performance that Emil Jannings gives in the lead role. The film's worldwide success brought both Murnau and Jannings to Hollywood, with Jannings winning the first best actor Oscar (for Josef von Sternberg's 1928 *The Last Command*) before returning to Germany to follow his Nazi heart.

The tacked-on happy ending in *The Last Laugh*, in which the crushed employee becomes rich: this has never bothered me. After all, it is thematically consistent, *organic*, because yet again the man's fortunes are beyond his control. I don't denigrate happy endings; I don't denigrate unhappy ones. I look for endings that suit the material they are ending.

Nevertheless, all serious filmgoers distinguish between truthful, artistic use of film and manipulative, commercial use of film—movies as art versus movies as industry. Vsevolod I. Pudovkin's *Mother* (*Mat*, 1926), a somber and militant Soviet masterpiece loosely taken from Gorky, provides an exemplary occasion for differentiating the two.

Mother's major motif consists of inserts showing the springtime breakup of river ice: a stunning metaphor for revolution's liberating sunlight following a long winter of tsarist oppression and constabulary cruelty. Pudovkin, a former physics and chemistry student, acknowledged his source; but, whereas the heroine's escape on ice floes in D. W. Griffith's *Way Down East* (1920) is just a sensational bit of plot meant to agitate and titillate, Pudovkin's motif is expressive and poetic—the visual rendering of one of *Mother*'s principal themes. Such is the difference between entertainment and art. One urges us, the audience, to consider what we are watching, to understand its meaning or thematic purpose; the other titillates, urging us to respond.

Coincidentally, both films are dominated by a superlative performance: Lillian Gish's in the Griffith; Vera Baranovskaya's in the Pudovkin.

Baranovskaya is tremendously moving as Pelageya Vlasova. An exemplar of Stanislavski's acting "method" devised for the Russian stage (where Stanislavski in fact directed her), Baranovskaya acted to the bone. Rather than playing scenes from whose sum an audience might induce her character, Baranovskaya acted fresh, holistically—out of a wholeness of characterization that she conceived and imaginatively drew into herself prior to performance. Moreover, she detailed the sort of archetypal role representation that populated the Russian stage by drawing on her own emotional history and life experience. (The misapplication of Stanislavski's method to naturalistic roles, coached by Stella Adler, Lee Strasberg and others, helps explain its artistic shortcomings in the U.S.) Thus in *Mother* was Baranovskaya able to play to the full both the Mother archetype and a highly specific individual.

Pelageya Vlasova is a quintessential instance of the Russian soul—a peasant who, trusting tsarist assurances, turns her son in for political pamphleteering but, when double-crossed by authorities by her son's kangaroo trial and imprisonment ("Is this justice?" she asks), becomes a revolutionary herself. Within its fictional framework, then, *Mother* documents the passing of the torch of commitment; revolutionary, implying generational equality, the torch in this instance is passed from offspring to parent rather than the other way around. Circumstances have *educated* Pelageya Vlasova to adopt her son's view of society and its power structure.

Baranovskaya's performance is one of the three greatest female ones in all of cinema. Another of the three can be found in the decade's greatest French film, *The Passion of Joan of Arc* (*La passion de Jeanne d'Arc*, 1928), made by a Danish visitor to France: Carl Theodor Dreyer—perhaps cinema's greatest artist. Dreyer moves us to contemplate history. Who was the chief architect of Joan of Arc's martyrdom? The English invaders, who imprisoned her? The French clergy, who tried and condemned her? God? The girl herself? The people, who identified with her and invested her martyrdom with political purpose?

Dreyer thus entered fifteenth-century France and collapsed the difference between present and distant past, not to construct an objective history, but to show opposing subjectivities at Joan's trial: her insistent faith; the heretic that her judges, at the behest of the English, felt compelled to subdue.

Using composition, camera placement and camera movement to isolate Joan within the frame, and a dissonant editing style wherein consecutive shots sometimes appear deliberately mismatched, Dreyer lays bare the politics of official persecution. Moreover, he plumbs a solitary soul's duress under this persecution and shows the transformation of the witnessing masses from an amorphous mob into a responsible voice—and fist—of moral protest. Transcending images of the exploitive circus that Joan's execution attracts, Dreyer's film achieves startling clarity.

Her unadorned face in varied closeup, at the center of the film is Maria Falconetti, who enrobes us in the silence of Joan's destiny, much as Dreyer enrobes us in the silence of silent film, with which added scores or orchestral accompaniments uncomprehendingly tinker. Falconetti's Joan helps make Dreyer's *Passion* a mystery there is no coming out of.

Among the decade's most notable misfires is Fritz Lang's half-mad, grandiose and largely frivolous science-fiction epic *Metropolis*. So long as it hews to Expressionistic representations of robotic mass labor, *Metropolis* is a great film. Alas, while these give the film its most memorable and trenchant images, not to mention social import, they make up only a small part of the film's broad design. Now that it is the twenty-first century, in which the film's futuristic action is set, *Metropolis* indeed seems especially lame. The grand joining of hands between ownership and labor is purely a matter of narrative neatness, the aesthetics of facile plot resolution. Capitalism's enslavement of the masses, currently deepened by globalization, and the harshness of industrial labor continue to convince; nothing else in the film, though, bears any ring of truth.

Addressing the twenties, one must mention *sound. There;* I've done it. It arrived late in the decade, was spottily embraced, and has proven over time to have been detrimental to the artistic development of cinema. It may have greatly assisted the industry, because unimaginative audiences came to rely on it, but it did little, if anything, to advance the art of the movies, which relied on the connection between cinema and dreams.

The list:

1920

THE PHANTOM CARRIAGE (Sweden). *Körkarlen* is often disparaged as an inferior example of Victor Sjöström's art, but it happens to be one of the few silent films of his that's widely available. Part of the problem, I think, is the film's immense popularity. Some take aim at it just because of that.
For me, it is a finely realized piece of work. Sjöström himself again stars, this time, as David Holm, who, like Scrooge, revisits scenes of his derelict life—but at the stroke of New Year's rather than on Christmas Eve. Through this narrative device, we ourselves become acquainted with Holm's character and life. Although he began as a hard worker, the temptation of alcohol took hold of Holm, costing him his job, undermining his marriage, and leading him to crime and prison. His agency of redemption becomes the death of a Salvation Army nurse who has vowed to save him.
The film's narrative is, in fact, convoluted in the extreme, but this becomes correlative to the tangle of Holm's life and the difficulty of his becoming free of it. (Therefore, this convolutedness is formally *expressive*.) The film is exceptionally gray, and this part of its visual aspect, as well as its detailed portrait of slum life, achieves a degree of observant realism that may strike Americans, at least, as Dreiserian. Holm's shabby existence is thus linked to an unwholesome social environment. But it is for its fantastic and expressionistic elements that the film is famous, in particular, its use of double exposures, and its images of Death, eerily nocturnal amidst fog and by the sea, riding its phantom carriage and making its collections. Without doubt, Dreyer's *Vampyr* (1931), the most magical and brilliant of all horror films, owes something to Sjöström's achievement here.
Sjöström's performance, incidentally, is tremendous.

THE PARSON'S WIDOW (Sweden). Carl Theodor Dreyer made comedies as well as tragedies, but none other so lunatic or fantastic as *Prästänkan*.
In seventeenth-century Norway, a young divinity school graduate wins an appointment to a parsonage that is intended to facilitate marriage with his sweetheart. Unfortunately, along with the parsonage comes the obligation to care for the previous parson's crone-like widow, whom he reluctantly marries, while passing off his true beloved as his sister. Hopes for the sturdy woman's demise end in disappointment, and doing away with her proves an impossible task, as she seems to possess supernatural powers. Can this all end happily?
Although very funny, *Prästänkan* is not without purpose. Dreyer shows (along two paths) that the course of true love never did run smooth, and plumbs the tension between self-determination and moral obligations to others, between self and community. It is the Protestant Christian balance that Dreyer pursues—a point his protagonist's résumé underscores. The resolution of the cleric's crisis ends the film on an unexpectedly warm, humanistic note.
Perhaps the film is most perceptive in its analysis of guilt—the rationalizations that allow good people (such as the parson) to do or to contemplate doing bad things. The young man proposes marriage to the parson's widow only when, inebriated from drink she has provided at dinner, he imagines her young and lovely—a fantasy suggesting his struggle to reconcile himself to his obligation to care for the woman. When, later, he dresses up as Satan in order to frighten her to death, we are, ironically, faced with his moral self-image for attempting thus to murder her.
With its touch of Boccaccio, *Prästänkan* is likely to expand anyone's narrow notion of Dreyer's range.

1921

DESTINY (Germany). We commonly call Fritz Lang's masterpiece *Destiny*, but the German title, *Der Müde Tod*, actually translates as *The Weary Death*. The most spiritually refined film ever made, its seemingly endless outdoor staircase, a symbol of aspiration, reappears (along with Lang himself) in Jean-Luc Godard's *Contempt* (1963).

The pastoral opening movement is both enchanting and full of foreboding. Two young lovers, so shy they cover their goose in order to kiss, are all of a sudden chilled to the bone by what appears on the road: a gaunt, seemingly ancient being entering a carriage as an elderly woman quits it. This is Death; and, while this image of it inspired Ingmar Bergman's in *The Seventh Seal* (1956), somehow Lang's is less susceptible to parody.

Soviet silent films rarely have much story or structural complication; German silents generally have a lot of both. The scene shifts from country to town, from outdoors to inn, and to an unspecified past. The topic of conversation among men at the inn is Death, leading to a flashback—a flashback, hence, within a flashback—showing a gravedigger's encounter with Death. Death, weary from its travels, buys a piece of land by the cemetery.

The main plot involves a woman's descent into the land of the dead in order to reclaim her husband. Three alternative destinies, however, all end with the same conclusion; but Death gives her another chance. She must find someone who is willing to die in her husband's place. When this also fails, she chooses death for herself so that she may rejoin her beloved. Thea von Harbou, Lang's wife, wrote the script.

No matter. It is its magical visual aspect—there is, in fact, a magician in the cast of characters—that makes the film a towering achievement. Alfred Hitchcock decided to become a filmmaker after seeing Lang's *Destiny*.

LA TERRE (France). Zola's 1887 *The Soil* transplants *King Lear* to rural France. In the novel, the earth is alternately described in erotic and cosmic terms, as a woman and the Mother Sea from whence we come and to which we return. At the close of André Antoine's silent film, naturalism rises to become the sheer organic poetry of Nature.

Too worn to farm it any longer, Fouan (Armand Bour, tremendous) gives each of three parts of his land to a son or son-in-law, but the younger generation's greed and betrayal eventually render Fouan homeless and starving. In the novel, each blow that the old man is dealt further erodes his sense of authority and importance, which is bound to his sense of patriarchic entitlement. Antoine's version simply has Fouan's material strength progressively deteriorate.

Nevertheless, the film is extraordinary. Visually, it interrelates wild and domestic animals, and humans, that is to say, the domesticators of animals; we are shown wild animals as they are being poached and farm animals as they contribute to farmers' lives. A transformative shot in this regard: a truck is opened at the back, with the camera facing this opening from inside the truck. The numerous sheep appear black because of the darkness of the truck's enclosure. They also appear wild in their haste to exit the enclosure. Below, on the ground, white sheep appear in an orderly procession. Within the same frame the dark sheep, billowy, formless shadows, reach the ground and, themselves white in sunlight, meld with the definable sheep, encapsulating domestication and metaphorically envisioning the process of civilization: disciplined by light, the emergence of humanity from dark, primitive impulses.

Fouan, a tiny figure beaten by downpour in a seemingly illimitable ground, dies as a young woman rises from bed to face the sunlit day.

1922

NANOOK OF THE NORTH (U.S.). Robert J. Flaherty is the "father of the documentary," not because he invented filmed documents (cinema's earliest incarnation, in fact), but because he invented documentary films—thematically unified works including instances of documented reality.

Flaherty staged things, having actual people in their usual surroundings—natives in primitive environments—"perform" what they routinely do or what ancestors did. His persistent theme is humanity in Nature—humanity endangered by Nature and by the intrusion of mechanical apparatus into their fragile world, including, ironically, the motion-picture camera that Flaherty brought in in order to document these disappearing cultures.

Shot in the Canadian Arctic, *Nanook* follows a family of Itivimuits (Eskimoes). The opening is unsurpassable cinema. From a boat, two tracking shots extend over stretches of water dotted by ice floes while a sterile sun illuminates a frigid no-man's-land. Nanook, a fur trader, appears to be standing guard at a lower corner of expository title cards, following which closeups introduce him and Nyla, his wife, prior to a thematic integration of all that we have thus far seen: Nanook in his canoe on the water, poised to provide for himself and his family—an Itivimuit in the wild.

Cultural anthropologists may gripe at Flaherty's "enactments," but in this "reconstructed reality" how wondrously Flaherty, as artist, shows humanity's resourceful adaptation to an almost inconceivably harsh environment. Indeed, Nature proves Flaherty's assistant in the savage snowstorm that threatens to engulf the Itivimuit family. Only luck saves them, in the form of an abandoned igloo—a set!—they supposedly chance upon on their way home. Upon their dogs outside the igloo, though, the snow falls and falls—this conclusive shot an associative reminder of the precariousness of the family's own existence.

NOSFERATU (Germany). Max Schreck is hideously made up as Count Orlock, the undead, in Friedrich Wilhelm Murnau's *Nosferatu*, based on Bram Stoker's *Dracula*. Make of this what you will: Kenneth Branagh patterned the movements of his Hamlet (1996) on the stylized walk of Schreck as Orlock/Nosferatu.

In order to save her husband, and to free Bremen from the pestilence Nosferatu has brought with it from the Carpathians, Eillen avails herself of the one proven way to destroy a vampire, submitting to its loathsome advances in her bed chamber, detaining the thing until the crowing of the cock, whereupon it dissolves into nothingness like a nightmare at the dawn's light. For Eillen, the necessary forfeit is her life.

Eillen's spouse, Hutter, seems "outside" his marriage, much as Nosferatu is outside life. In an "idyllic" early passage, Hutter rompingly gathers wildflowers; Eillen responds by longingly caressing the bouquet as though it were a baby—the child, the image implies, marriage to Hutter hasn't given her. Blissfully unaware, Hutter fails to respond to Eillen's heartache; acting more like a toy husband than a real one, he is draining her lifeblood. Her stunted marriage causes Eillen to desire Nosferatu, a husband-substitute, as much as Nosferatu desires her. But to submit to Nosferatu, even to save Hutter from also becoming the undead, is to betray her marriage, to admit its pointlessness.

The film achieves a captivating form in the phantomlike effects Murnau conjures. He locates, in imaginative space, a twilit blending of fantasy and reality, shadow and substance, death and life, and, following Kierkegaard, the twin components of dread, attraction and repulsion, revulsion and desire. In the same vein, Nosferatu's sea journey to Bremen impresses as a journey of the mind—Eillen's shrouded, twisted, storm-tossed unconscious to which the failure of her marriage has given birth.

1923

THE STREET (Germany). Karl Grune's captivating vision of Parisian nightlife dispenses with title-cards in order to achieve an uninterrupted flow of images.

A man, in a rut at home, dreams of the excitement of "the street." One evening, he leaves wife and home to pursue his dream but is lured into misadventure by a prostitute. He is arrested for a murder in her apartment he did not commit. As he is about to hang himself in his cell, he is released, the real killer having been inadvertently exposed by his toddler.

Three elements assist the film in transcending a melodramatic plot. One is the complex, intricate, at times expressionistic *mise-en-scène*, such as in the streets at night, with bristling human activity in the background while a car curves around in front of the camera in the foreground. To another element this *mise-en-scène* contributes: the blend of reality and artifice—the "streets" are detectably studio-bound sets—that moves the material toward abstraction and generalization. Finally, this method invites us to interpret the characters symbolically. The slinky, glamorous prostitute, the antithesis of the protagonist's stocky, fastidious wife, a bourgeois who sweeps clean a crumbless table, is his fantasy version of his wife—a dream that turns to nightmare. The man he is accused of killing is the protagonist's doppelganger, a revelation of his self-destructive tendency. The toddler is the child the man feels he is, unable to direct the course of his life. Released from jail, the man returns to his wife, setting his head on her shoulder as a child might when seeking consolation.

The wide-angle shot as the man walks home through the street at dawn is among cinema's most brilliant and heartfelt images

Die Straße, although set in France, reveals German defeatism and overreaching German idealism (dreams)—history would show, a dangerous combination.

THE PILGRIM (U.S.). Religious lunacy and hypocrisy in the American landscape: these are Charles Chaplin's targets in his sharp, satirical, refreshing *The Pilgrim*.

Charlie's introduction to us is his image on a wanted poster; Charlie has escaped from prison. His striped prison clothes are discovered by a bush. Hilarious cut: Next we see—or, I should say, first we see—Charlie walking down a street, feigning meditation, in his parson's garb. When he buys a train ticket, he grabs hold of the cage bars by reflex. Charlie will have to break bad habits in order to prevail in his current disguise. When an eloper approaches him to wed himself and his sweetie, Charlie, fearing capture, runs away. Ironically, his own awakened romantic heart is what will transform his "criminal" nature, moving even the sheriff who captures him to release him into Mexico at the Texas border.

It is in Devil's Gulch, Texas, that Charlie masquerades as the new pastor, the Reverend Mr. Pim, trying to steal the collection boxes and pantomiming a ridiculous sermon—but any more ridiculous than a real church sermon?—about David and Goliath, in which he identifies as David vis-à-vis the America that oppresses and incarcerates him. The congregation is confused by Charlie's antics, but a young boy who has been bullied throughout the service by his bourgeois mother applauds wildly.

"America is here or nowhere," British author Thomas Carlyle said when asked why, given his love of freedom, he did not move there. At the end of *Stagecoach* (1939) John Ford suggests that "America" is always somewhere else—in Mexico, as it happens. To Chaplin at the end of *The Pilgrim*, it turns out there *is* no America. Nearly thirty years later, this tragic insight proved prophetic in the writer-director-star's own political life.

PARIS QUI DORT (France). *Paris, Which Sleeps* (a.k.a. *The Crazy Ray*) is 25-year-old René Clair's attempt to grapple with the burden of mortal awareness. Another same-age Parisian begins his day at the highest level of the Eiffel Tower, where he is night watchman: a vantage fitting the seeming indomitability of youth. But Albert's life is undone by what he sees and hears: silence; peoplelessness; the absence of life. The silence of this silent satirical comedy contributes to our sense of what the boy suddenly experiences.

Albert wanders the deserted city. He finally encounters another working-class soul, one frozen in time, hunched over a public garbage receptacle; Albert pokes and laughs. Beneath the bravado, though, Albert is anxious, his existence, challenged. From the jacket pocket of a subsequent "frozen" figure, Albert pulls a handkerchief that he mockingly whips up and down in front of the owner's face. This mocking the man really mocks death, which suddenly terrifies Albert.

Our awareness of the economically depressed post-World War I conditions in Europe translates Albert's uncertainty, his discomforting bewilderment, into desperation. The scavenger at the trash can becomes a kind of mental image: a projection of the precariousness of Albert's own economic state. To stabilize his new, foundationless life, Albert, settled on a public bench, imagines the Paris he otherwise knows: a bustling metropolis. In this waking dream, cars in particular are in motion. A group of passengers who have flown in from Marseilles welcome him into their fold. Since their airborne altitude protected them from the "freeze," they seek to preserve their lives by mounting the Eiffel Tower. Amazing trick-shots of their ascent find the higher-ups going yet higher as a defense against the social standing they feel has slipped away.

The scientist who caused the problem reverses it. Magically, the world resumes.

THE RETURN OF REASON (France). Dada, an international movement begun in response to the horrors of the First World War, deemed itself anti-art, that is, opposed to those traditional, rigid, bourgeois forms of expression that reflected societal rigidity and, politically, had given impetus to the war. Dada persisted after the war, now opposing the social and cultural demoralization that the war had fostered, and was subsumed in other movements, for instance, Surrealism. U.S.-born Man Ray, photographer and painter, made films in France, the first of which, about two minutes long, is *Le retour à la raison*.

For Dada, war meant the loss of reason, but the images that Ray's film comprises—visual sensations of one sort or another—shift the emphasis to who has "returned to reason," and in what state. Purely abstract configurations (at first, of specks) yield to decipherable images from the known world, for instance, lights at night on a merry-go-round; however, the deep contrast of intense light and voluminous darkness, along with the motion (and invisibility of people), transforms a familiar image into something personal and highly subjective—a dream image. Geometric designs and real objects yield to a human form: a naked woman's torso, indoors, in bright daylight. Her round belly and breasts are the ground on which figures—shadows—generated by the natural light dance, assuming the curvature of her shape. The woman is introduced as a dancer in a title; or are the shadows thus being described? Regardless, their combination is incredibly sensual. The reality of the woman appears palpable, which stands in sharp contrast to the way the majority of female characters were portrayed in commercial films then (and still are now). This vivid sensual reality of hers may be what "returns" the one returning (for whom our eyes are surrogate) to "reason."

1924

STRIKE (U.S.S.R.). "The strength of the working class is organization . . . Organized, it is everything." — Lenin

Feverishly inventive, almost peerlessly dynamic, Sergei M. Eisenstein's second film, *Stachka*, testifies to a tidal wave of unity among nonunionized workers, at a locomotive factory in tsarist Russia in 1912, who strike once a fellow worker, accused by the foreman of the theft of a micrometer, commits suicide. Nothing good, though, comes of the strike, which triggers a brutal assault by authorities, a mass killing spree, in fact. Prior to this, we also witness the toll that the prolonged strike has on workers, depriving them of hand-to-mouth income, fraying tempers, causing marital discord. Management summons criminals, spies, soldiers—whatever it takes—to crush strikers and their families.

Of course, despair—here encapsulated by the suicide and the sympathy among workers it engenders—is a poor foundation for serious, committed action, almost guaranteeing a less than satisfactory result. True, it brings about worker unity, but rather more frenzied and self-indulgent than disciplined and organized. It is a fractious "unity." Moreover, so long as tsarism rules, such worker outrage may constitute little more than a futile gesture. Everything is rigged against labor.

Behind capitalists stands the Tsar. Rather than the strike, it is the Bolshevik Revolution in the future—which is to say, in 1924, the recent past—that will redress/has redressed worker grievances. In *Strike*, Eisenstein has conjured a feast of black-and-white images, often rapidly cutting between motion-packed shots. A stunning example of Eisenstein's visual artistry: outdoors, an angled overhead shot of a wasteland of depressed barrels, out of which human scum—"troglodyte lumpenproletarians," critic Anna Chen calls them—emerge. Superimpositions, constructivist compositions, reverse motion, traveling shots with the camera strapped on this and that: 26-year-old Eisenstein, flexing his flair for cinema, shoots the works.

GREED (U.S.). Erich von Stroheim's *Greed* was 9½ hours long. The version that MGM released, though, is two hours and twenty minutes. In 1957, after 33 years of suppression (to mark Hollywood's crucifixion of artists?), the excised footage was blithely destroyed by the studio. Stroheim died that same year. There is no possibility, therefore, of restoring *Greed* to any kind of fullness.

Based on Frank Norris's *McTeague*, the butchered *Greed* is nevertheless immense: a richly detailed, teeming canvas where highly specific yet almost primitive characters are enmeshed in a number of American landscapes, among these, at the last, Death Valley, where, shackled to one another, two greedy men unconsciously parody American myths: liberty, independence, rugged individualism. *Greed* holds up a mirror to America, clarifying, for instance, the parochial nature of American life, the dogged self-interest and tendency toward self-protection of those who are perpetually terrified of being cast adrift. The most memorable character is Trina (Zasu Pitts, tremendous), daughter of immigrants, whose luckily gotten loot—she wins a lottery—is her single anchor to a sense of being in a compulsively busy but essentially empty country that swallows up identities whole and spits out skeletal remains in a configuration of shibboleths: sanctified by manifest destiny, individualism amidst endless opportunity—all together, the great American hoax. Animating Trina are the gold coins she feverishly fingers in secret; her despair translates into hope, hope into despair—America's psychic seesaw negotiating between golden myths and shackling realities. Adding nothing and leaving her with nothing, the coins patch over a void of marital disappointment and absence of genuine community. Trina's mental and moral disintegration, echoed in the fates of Marcus and McTeague, the two men ultimately bound together in Death Valley, is America's story, which Stroheim, brilliantly alert, follows like a snake.

SHERLOCK JR. (U.S.). *Sherlock Jr.* is Buster Keaton's freshest, most captivating comedy. Keaton directed from an inspired script by Clyde Bruckman, Jean Havez and Joseph Mitchell. He also starred and edited. More than any other American film, *Sherlock Jr.* tests cinema's capacity, by tricks of editing, to delight audiences by seeming to obliterate confinements of space and time.

The character Keaton winningly plays—for want of another name, let's call him Buster—is a projectionist who seems flypapered by bad luck, including in romance. One day at work, in order to solve the crime in the movie he is running and thus prove his prowess, he walks into the screen and becomes part of the movie's action. Buster is now Sherlock Jr., master detective.

By skillful use of back projection, director Keaton zaps Buster from one setting to another in an instant. He has Buster, being chased, jump head-first into an outfit and emerge fully dressed, in disguise, as a woman; and he devises what remains to date the most exhilarating road chase in all of cinema.

Above all, Buster wants to impress his girl. What's an inexperienced boy to do when he wants to kiss his girl? At the close of the film, when Sherlock Jr. is back to being Buster in reality and Buster is running another film, a romance rather than a detective mystery, he gets timely help. A love scene in the film-within-the-film offers pointers and lends courage. As he makes his big move, Buster's eyes dart back and forth between the educative image onscreen and his beloved in his arms—for us, also a screen image. Art imitates life imitates art, and the movies have helped one more soul disclose his feelings and realize his dreams.

How to kiss? Sherlock Jr. has cracked another case!

DIE NIBELUNGEN, PARTS I & II (Germany). Dedicated to the German people, Fritz Lang's five-hour medieval epic is awesome. The first part, "Siegfried," remains the most starkly beautiful and darkly magical material Lang ever filmed. Siegfried, son of King Sigmund, is the apotheosis of the young hero, and his approach of the fire-breathing dragon through the dense, glistening forest is pure fairy-tale enchantment. In the lower foreground of one shot, a bifurcated trunk, in complete shadow, so frames the hero, who is in the background on horseback, that it appears the forest is giving birth to him—as indeed symbolically is the case. Siegfried slays the beast and bathes in its cascading blood, in order to render himself invincible. By soberly recording fantastic imagery at a middle distance with a fixed camera, Lang artfully nudges myth into a realistic realm while retaining fantasy's delight. Lang grasped what Peter Jackson, the director of the *Lord of the Rings* trilogy (2001-2003), failed to grasp.

Outdoors, huge rocks and trees, and expanses of sky, dwarf humanity. King Gunter's castle, where Siegfried goes to win Kriemhild, is another matter. The architectural designs project the fierce psychologies of the characters, who embroil "invincible" Siegfried in a plot that ends in his death, leaves Kriemhild insane in her bereavement, and sets the much more brilliant second part, "Kriemhild's Revenge," into motion.

Barbaric, dynamic, sweeping, the remainder of *Die Nibelungen* portrays Kriemhild's marriage to Attila the Hun and her terrible revenge against her brothers for Siegfried's death when they visit, and against her own court, because Attila, caught between his obligations as husband and host, refuses to join her in this effort. The resultant bloodbath would remain unparalleled in cinema until the Night of the Long Knives in Luchino Visconti's *The Damned* (1969)—another "Twilight of the Gods."

KINO-EYE (U.S.S.R.). As Dziga Vertov, Polish-born Denis Abramovich Kaufman pioneered the newsreel in two series: *Kino-Pravda* (*Cinema Truth*, 1922-25); *Novostni Dnia* (*New of the Day*, 1944-54, the year of his death). Committed to a cinema of fact, Vertov—with the assistance of his brother, cinematographer Mikhail Kaufman, and his wife, cutter Elisaveta Svilova—created *Kino-Eye*. Vertov's aim was to capture the myriad reality of the unfolding Soviet experience.

Largely following "Young Leninists," an educational troupe of activist children, *Kino-Eye* cross-identifies, in terms of freshness, wholeness, health and freedom, the following: the Soviet Union; the idealism that guides this revolutionary nation; cinema—cinema, that is, once it is liberated from its theatrical and reactionary origins. Vertov's work surely was far removed from the Russian heaviness that overtook Soviet cinema as the Soviet Union receded farther from claims to any sort of idealism. *Kino-Eye* in fact displays delightful camera tricks—for instance, passages of reverse motion that in the process of analyzing various activities and events suggest also sheer possibility and fresh beginnings, but with an ironic hint, too, of determinism. Indeed, no film in creation more seamlessly and unexpectedly darkens in complexion, shifting from being celebratory to exposing the threat to the collective welfare—a threat imaged in grotesque animated silhouette—posed by entrenched individual habits such as excessive drinking of alcohol and tobacco use! For Vertov, his new nation is not a done deal but remains vulnerable, and therefore he urges his audience to see analytically, to grasp causality and their joint responsibility in the Soviet adventure. Vertov wants to open eyes to everything good and everything bad that is happening, and he plans on keeping his own eyes open as well.

Discrediting plot-driven movies, Vertov also exhorted fellow filmmakers to show instead "the chaos of visual phenomena filling the universe."

ENTR'ACTE (France). Let's set aside whether it is more Dada or Surreal. Is it so bizarre, really, that it "could mean anything"? Do we think of René Clair in that way? Those who do not see that *Entr'acte* as a unified work of art are probably mistaking discontinuity—the origin of the Dada-or-Surrealism debate regarding the film—for disunity. Clair's wonderful satire—that's what Clair invariably is: *a satirist*—is thematically whole and scarcely esoteric.
What is this film about? War. (The film followed by six years the conclusion of a world war that devastated France and the rest of Europe; war's shadow still hung far and wide.) The film opens with a military cannon that is out of control; it moves around, apparently, on its own volition. Hm. Two men are playing chess, a board game that simulates war. Hm. At a fair, a man gets frustrated at a shooting gallery, perhaps the result of myopia; eventually, however, he hits a balloon, which suddenly turns into a real bird, reminding us how real war is. A twirling ballerina is shown from an overhead camera and from a camera looking up underneath a glass floor. In slow motion, her tutu reminds some viewers of a flower's opening. Perhaps I am perverse; I see a metaphorical image of aerial bombing. (The First World War was the first occasion for this activity.) A procession of people, in slow motion, follows a camel that is dragging a hearse. Hm. These people gather around a coffin from which a man rises. He is a magician. He makes all the men gathered around disappear one by one before he makes himself disappear. I know that different interpretations of visual data are possible. But whatever else this film is about, most certainly it is about war.

THE IRON HORSE (U.S.). *See above.*

THE LAST LAUGH (Germany). *See above.*

1925

BATTLESHIP POTEMKIN (U.S.S.R.). One would never guess that Sergei Mikhailovich Eisenstein heralded from the stage. Thrilling and kinetic, his *Battleship Potemkin* is purely cinematic.
The film re-creates the Kronstadt naval mutiny that triggered the doomed 1905 Russian Revolution—an event preceding the Bolshevik Revolution. In graphic detail, the film shows the conditions onboard that led to the mutiny.
Perhaps cinema's most celebrated passage is the Odessa Steps Massacre. In reality, this event never occurred, but, because of the power of Eisenstein's images, it is widely believed to have occurred. *Potemkin*, then, reinvents history, translating documentary and fiction each into the other—what has remained cinema's signature strategy for fathoming time and investigating social and political realities. It is important to note that Eisenstein's fiction remains true to political circumstance in Russia. His fabricated event captures the cruelty and oppressiveness of tsarist rule, creating for these a stark, fiercely lit metaphor. (Eduard Tissé is Eisenstein's essential black-and-white cinematographer.) In a rush of images, the masses, in enraged sympathy with the mutineers, are cut down by the police in the streets. Shot rapidly follows shot; but this ferocity gives way to another kind of passage later on—mysterious, meditative, lovely, one that is wrapped in silken darkness: dusk-cloaked sails on moonlit water—images that evoke the eternal note of sadness attending humanity's struggle to assert fundamental rights in the face of oppression. Somewhere, always, the battle continues.
Eisenstein's militant masterpiece is a national epic for his young nation, set a dozen years before its existence. It is a film full of anticipation—a look back for the courage to move ahead, united. The Soviet Union no longer exists. Today, *Battleship Potemkin* is cinema's most poignant elegy, and its most powerful expression of a now largely dormant idea: *the people.*

THE GOLD RUSH (U.S.). Charles Chaplin's *The Gold Rush*, about the 1898 Klondike gold rush, is humorous and serene—a wondrous light comedy in which Chaplin's persistent Everyman, cinema's signature icon, wins even at love.

But this is not to say that the film is free of anxiety. Amidst bewitching images of Charlie in the Alaskan wilderness, the American Dream gasps at a problematic final frontier. First cousin to Flaherty's *Nanook of the North* (1922), Chaplin's comedy eludes tragedy, it seems, by a single whisker. Snow burns intensely and, before he emerges from his ordeal triumphant, Charlie nearly starves, his imaginative and material resourcefulness, although great (consider the meal he concocts from boiled shoe and spaghetti-like shoelaces), a lame weapon against fierce Nature. A sublimely funny moment: Delusional from hunger, Big Jim, a fellow prospector and Charlie's cabin-mate, imagines Charlie as a giant chicken and promptly chases him for a much-needed meal.

Nor is Nature all that threatens Charlie, for he is searching out beyond its 1925 borders an already dwindling America, as the grandeur of America's terrain of hope yields to exploitation, population growth, and the cramping commotion of progress. Like many a comedy, then, this one teeters on the edge of disaster—like, unforgettably, Charlie's uprooted cabin slip-sliding away.

Everything—home, prospects, life, America—is perishable.

But Charlie at the last gets the girl!

THE JOYLESS STREET (Germany). If I were to make a list of the ten greatest shots in all of cinema, I would include the long tracking shot on the street outside the butcher's shop in inflation-beseiged Vienna: an irregular stream of defeated faces. Generally, the tracking shot consists of two contradictory aspects: the sense of extended, even limitless, space—here, ironically, correlative to bottomless human exhaustion; a hard limit, as the moving camera comes to a halt, if only by a cut to another shot—here, correlative to the butcher, who represents humanity's capacity to exploit the suffering of other members of the community.

If I were to make a list of the ten greatest performances in all of cinema, I would include Greta Garbo's as Greta Rumfort, the soul of innocence, whom economic hardship nearly drives into prostitution.

The film in question, Georg Wilhelm Pabst's *Die Freudlose Gasse*, is magnificent in bringing documentary realism to its portrait of the street, the beleaguered people's lives, their shabby tenement homes, the collapse of their middle-class existence and dreams. Dubious, though, is a good deal of the melodrama, and the ongoing comparison of Greta and another girl, who does become a prostitute and ends up committing murder, seems a little too patly engineered to suggest how easily the dire fate of one might have been the dire fate of the other. One may also quibble with the cinematography, which sometimes fails to do justice to the film's visual concepts.

Still, this is Pabst's first outstanding film, and Garbo, just about to leave her teens, is the first truly profound film actress, to be followed shortly by Baranovskaya (Pudovkin's *Mother*) and Falconetti (Dreyer's *The Passion of Joan of Arc*).

1926

THE GENERAL (U.S.). The American Civil War remains an emotional powder-keg, at least in the white South, which continues spiritually, and sometimes politically, to resist the idea of Confederate defeat. This may be why the one indisputable masterpiece about that war, Buster Keaton and Clyde Bruckman's *The General*, had to be a comedy.

Keaton has transformed an actual incident involving a Confederate engine driver, whose heroism helped score a victory against the Union army, into his signature theme of a boy trying hard to prove himself, in this case to the girl he loves, who rejects him as a suitor when she mistakes him for a coward. Johnnie Gray's attempts to enlist in the army are rejected because he can better serve the cause in his job as train engineer. But doesn't Johnnie pose a threat to the family inwardness that the girl's father and brother hope to remove by disparaging him, to keep him from making further romantic inroads while they are away at war, and doesn't this paranoia cast a sardonic light on the South's regional secession motivated by their desire to retain at all costs their "way of life"?

The girl tells Johnnie she won't accept him into her heart again until she sees him in uniform—translation: until he is more like Father and Brother. This grotesque failure of hers to fathom the horrible nature of war spins ironically throughout the film; and when, finally, Johnnie is indeed in uniform, it is left to us to grasp Keaton's closing irony, Johnnie's likely fate in a war that has only just begun. It is unlikely that Johnnie will come marching home again—and if he does, he will be transformed by the experiences of killing and defeat: the loss of everything that his beloved represents.

MOTHER (U.S.S.R.). *See above.*

THE ADVENTURES OF PRINCE ACHMED (Germany). Whether it is indeed the first feature-length animated film, *Die Abenteuer des Prinzen Achmed*, largely the work of avant-garde artist Charlotte ("Lotte") Reiniger, then 23, is certainly the most enchanting and gorgeous feature-length animated film. Carl Koch, Walther Ruttmann and Bertold Batosch co-directed.

In a series of *Arabian Nights* adventures Prince Achmed, finally with Aladdin's assistance, opposes the forces of evil. Two magicians are involved, one good, and the other wicked, assisted by tumbling-through-air, many-handed, clockwork-gear meshed "black demons"; but the featurelessness that the film's black-silhouette design gives its characters suggests a series of single identities that are, as in a dream, split into Manichean dualities. The two princesses function somewhat differently, with Peri Banu, with whom Achmed falls in love, functioning as a non-incestuous alternative to his sister, Dinarsade. In a film of such dreaminess, can Freud be far behind?

Reiniger's film thus reiterates the close connection between dream and cinema. Aladdin's dusky descent down, down mountains to retrieve the magic lamp creates an image of consciousness yielding by degrees to dreamy sleep.

The flying horse that Achmed is tricked into riding bridges dreamy fantasy and waking reality. It goes all one way: up; but Achmed finds the means to direct the horse earthward for a landing. Manageable, the horse becomes a figure of balance, of Achmed's moral centeredness.

The silhouette-technique, used earlier in Dziga Vertov's *Kino-Eye* (1924), involves intricately detailed cut-outs of various materials, with marionette-like intricate motion, set in front of illuminated glass sheets. The long- and thin-bearded silhouette of the evil magician would inspire cinema's most famous silhouette: Eisenstein's Ivan the Terrible.

Reiniger also draws upon Fritz Lang's magical films—and, for Aladdin's Genie, perhaps painter Marc Chagall's cosmos.

Amidst exquisite Islamic architecture, decoration, the film ends with morning prayers.

FAUST (Germany). F. W. Murnau's *Faust* opens with an unleashing of the forces of darkness, the evil dead, circling the earth. A subsequent shot will show the Devil (Emil Jannings, terrifying) as a looming, towering figure, his expansive cloak shadowing the City of Humanity. Early on, the Devil and either God or God's angel confront one another. "The Earth is mine!" Mephisto says. Its opponent, who, by contrast, appears feeble, counters, "Man belongs to God." Murnau employs the Faust legend to test the core Western assumption that Man possesses free will. Faust's mortal fear makes him a ripe candidate for the Devil's seduction and capture. Man is a battleground, with two grand adversaries claiming ownership —a sly metaphor for humanity's lack of self-determination. According to Murnau, it is irrelevant whether God or the Devil wins, because in either case Man—Faust—loses. Religion, superstition, mythology—these are determining Man's nature, depriving him of the free will that is his due.

Faust is preeminently a film of profound darkness eerily punctuated by diffuse, glowing light. Some will say it is the Devil's darkness, because the film conventionally identifies the Devil with darkness and God with light; but what Murnau's fantastic images repeatedly show is the systemic connection between darkness and light—a projection of the cosmic battle in which Faust is embroiled even before the Devil makes a move on him. What difference who owns Man? Murnau's masterpiece cries out against humanity's enslavement to restrictive ideas from the past, such as death's being a punishment that human actions draw.

A film of human trembling and brooding wonder (as in the phenomenal passage in which Mephisto transports Faust through the heavens across Europe), *Faust* was incomprehensible in the 90-minute version originally distributed in the U.S. Its restoration is triumphant.

MENILMONTANT (France). Estonian-born Russian emigré Dimitri Kirsanoff's *Ménilmontant* opens explosively. A grinning lunatic hacks to death a man and a woman with an ax, orphaning the couple's two daughters, whom we watch playing outdoors with a cat, lamenting their loss at their parents' graves, and walking together from the cemetery down a desolate path lined with a small number of bare trees. A dissolve shows the pair farther down the path all of a sudden; and, while it is likely he stopped filming in between the two points, Kirsanoff thus established the idea, the possibility, of a jump-cut. Mark Donskoi, moved and impressed, used Kirsanoff's lyrical method of transposing a human figure farther along in a significant foot-journey to conclude his *The Childhood of Maxim Gorky* (1938). Indeed, shards of *Ménilmontant*'s expressiveness would make their way into many other famous films. Alas, the two main characters, unlike Gorky, would remain anonymous—except to us. At some level, one cannot help but think, their orphaned fate is correlative to Kirsanoff's own separation from homeland, also instigated by violence, the 1917 revolution and the subsequent Soviet state.

Kirsanoff follows the sisters from the country to Paris, which electrifies amidst speedy tracking shots and use of handheld camera, correlative to the world of possibilities now seemingly before the girls. The world, though, shrinks; they begin and end working in a sweatshop. In between, a man comes between them, undercutting their one source of emotional support: each other. One becomes pregnant, while the other becomes a prostitute. Also, their parents' killer re-enters the picture.

As in Dickens, melodrama is a vehicle for social and psychological inquiry into the plight of the downtrodden. Kirsanoff's dazzling technical versatility—different camera angles and distances, superimpositions, dissolves—never overwhelms the sad, delicately spiritual human story.

THE CHESS PLAYER (France). Lithuanian Poland, 1776; patriots rise up against Russian occupiers and are crushed by Catherine II's tsarist forces. Boleslaw Vorowski, the rebels' young leader, is in love with teenaged Sofia Novinska, who is being courted by Prince Serge Oblomov, a Russian officer. Sofia is slow to realize her passion for the grievously wounded Boleslaw because their guardian, Baron Wolfgang von Kempelen, has raised them as sister and brother. Kempelen has also invented automatons—mechanical humans, one of whom he has invented in his own image. At the last, an army of his mechanical soldiers, in spurts of dreadful synchronized movement, descend upon a Russian villain as the Empress proceeds with what she believes is Boleslaw's execution.

Kempelen actually did tour Europe and the U.S. with "The Turk," a seeming automaton that beat opponents at chess, a board game based on war. Six years after Czech author Karel Čapek's *R.U.R.* introduced the word, Raymond Bernard's *Le joueur d'échecs*, based on Henry Dupuis-Mazuel's novel, dazzled with its robots. Visually, the film blurs the difference between its human characters and Kempelen's robots: Sofia, sitting for a portrait; musicians, absolutely still before they begin playing; Wanda, strikingly posed before she starts to dance; the jerky, "unreal" movements of soldiers in combat.

Marshaling cross-cutting, expressionistic shadows and superimpositions, and cinema's most sumptuous masked ball (with get-ups exemplifying both gender and racial crossovers), Bernard explores both machines as humans and—this was a prevalent eighteenth-century idea—humans as machines; this, combined with the many chess plays, suggests the idea of people as history's pawns. But for all the fascination of all this, the nobility of this electrifying silent film derives from its consideration of free will. Ultimately, at least three major characters commit themselves to actions that shine with distinctive humanity.

1927

THE END OF ST. PETERSBURG (U.S.S.R.). Commemorating the tenth anniversary of the Bolshevik Revolution, *Konyets Sankt-Peterburga* begins with a trenchant portrait of rural poverty in 1914 tsarist Russia. After the birth of a sister, "another mouth to feed," a boy leaves the farm and goes to the city to get a job. An uncle living there is a labor activist; his stingy wife (Vera Baranovskaya, superb) throws the boy out. When workers strike, the boy, hungry, becomes a scab. When he better appreciates matters, he assaults a boss, is thrown into prison and is sent to fight in the First World War. When he returns, he participates in the revolution that consecutively disposes of the tsar and Kerensky's provisional government, by which time his aunt's compassion and generosity have grown. St. Petersburg is now Leningrad.

Except for an overdone bout of crosscutting between suffering at the front and, back home, capitalists gleeful over war profits, Vsevolod I. Pudovkin and four assistant directors have wrought a perfect film. Along with Pudovkin's *Mother* (1926), it remains cinema's best study of radicalization. Its stark images stun—for instance, towards the camera in closeup, the scythe-like rotation of a windmill's fan on the farm: persistent, sharp motions that unsettle the frames, within the implied symbolism of life's tragic round. The image both conveys the harsh entrapment of poverty and signals the future growth of the peasant's political consciousness. Greed-driven, power-fixated St. Petersburg contextualizes images that prepare the boy for political maturation: dense factory pollution, amidst which overworked, underpaid workers toil, in contrast to the artificial lot of clean suits and straw hats—stock exchange participants, whose rat-like scurrying, shot from overhead, would be comical were it not for the connection to the plight of workers that the juxtaposition draws.

OCTOBER (U.S.S.R.). Commemorating the 1917 revolution, *Oktyabr'* is a "people's film." For the famous passage depicting the storming of Tsar Nikolai's Winter Palace, Eisenstein employed veterans of the actual event and borrowed details from the pantomimes of the seige that were annually staged by the people of Leningrad. These and other factors tend to collapse the difference between on-the-spot documentary and reenactment. The result is akin to faux-documentary.

Sergei M. Eisenstein pushed cinema beyond linear narrative, creating trains of images that figure forth ideas rather than "tell a story." One example: the officially ordered raising of the bridges, which unloads upon the water below—to which are added, for drowning, copies of the revolutionary newspaper *Pravda* (*Truth*)—a horse's heft and a girl's fresh, still sensuous corpse. In cinematic language, here is the tsarist establishment's attempt to break the spine of human ties to life, beauty, Nature and truth—truth, the passage implies, that is undrownable, so wedded to it are the hearts of the masses. The outrage that the tsarist act inspired, the passage suggests, called forth revolution.

When viewing it, one must constantly interpret *October*; it doesn't encourage, much less exploit, viewer passivity. Eisenstein had tremendous faith in the power of images—and in Soviet communism as liberator of the human spirit. But just his being Jewish drew Stalin's

1927

suspiciousness, and *October* became the first of his films to provoke official disfavor for its formalist tendencies—translation: too great an interest in art as something other than a tool of the state. Thereafter, Eisenstein's projects were monitored daily to hold these "tendencies" in check. At the last moment, moreover, *October* had to be hastily re-edited to delete from its cast of characters Leon Trotsky and others who openly opposed Stalin as betrayer of the Revolution.

BERLIN: SYMPHONY OF A GREAT CITY (Germany). Inspired by Mikhail Kaufman's *Moscow* (1926) and other Soviet documentaries by Vertov, as well as abstract German experimental films, *Berlin, Die Sinfonie der Grosstadt* is a rhythmic documentary. The idea for Walther Ruttmann's film came from Carl Mayer, who had scripted F. W. Murnau's *The Last Laugh* (1924). Shots were selected and edited to compose a day in the life of Berlin, from dawn to deep in the night.

The sweeping opening movement is the camera's approach to Berlin: over rolling water, across train tracks, including over a bridge. A montage of overhead shots portrays a dense metropolis; commercial advertisements on the sides of buildings perhaps introduce a disquieting note. Sewer; tall buildings. A solitary cat walks the street. A few people become visible, then more and more as the workday begins, with men in suits off to one kind of job, and laborers off to factories. Commuters enter Berlin (trains again); children are off to school. Here is a city that works.

Only, marching soldiers remind one of Great War defeat and Germany's subsequent economic hardship. Are there other clues of stress? Magnets for a crowd, two "respectable" men push one another on a street corner. On another corner, a rabble-rouser of some political stripe attracts his own crowd. In a blatantly staged sequence, a woman commits suicide from a bridge. Before she takes the plunge, we see her eyes bulging in horror and madness—the film's one closeup. A patron's-eye view of a roller coaster ride insinuates more stress, as does the quickened pace of the film's editing.

Most viewers, though, see Ruttmann's film as harmonious. My reading of Berlin's discontent may be wrong. It must be wrong.

Right?

THE WIND (U.S.). In his great Swedish films, Victor Sjöström had probably done more than any other artist to establish the expressive visual vocabulary of film. In Hollywood, he made two films with Lillian Gish, the brilliant star of *Way Down East* (1920) and numerous other films by D. W. Griffith: *The Scarlet Letter* (1926) and *The Wind* (1927). Gish, magnificent as Hester Prynne, is superb again in the latter film, playing Letty, a Virginian girl who moves in with a cousin of hers who lives in the southwestern prairie, a region beseiged by wind storms —a projection of the dissatisfaction with American life that in fact had prompted Letty's westward move in the first place. The piercing symbolism of *The Wind* addresses the paucity of choices available especially to women.

Wind and sand, sand and wind: Letty's turbulent soul, her sense of wanting self-determination, become startlingly visible in Sjöström's visionary work. Her cousin's wife bitterly resents Letty's intrusion into their home. Sjöström's portrait of their relationship glistens with thematic relevance. While the wife must cut a carcass for food, drenching herself in blood, Letty, neat and clean, wins the affection of the woman's children by leading their recreation. Implicitly, Letty's cousin's wife is also dissatisfied with her lot. Continuing the irony, when she tosses Letty out, Letty ends up marrying a farmhand whom she doesn't love—again, a reflection on the circumstance she and her cousin's wife share. What a concentrated, resonant film about American life this is.

Letty and her husband achieve genuine complicity as a couple only when he buries all traces of her having killed an attacker. He thus becomes his wife's buttress against the wind, underscoring her vulnerability and her reliance on marriage to help her navigate an inhospitable culture and nation.

THE ITALIAN STRAW HAT (France). Being bourgeois is a balancing act, and René Clair, adapting Eugène Labiche and Marc Michel's play, hilariously pricks that balance with his satirical needle in his most visually expressive, brilliantly edited comedy, *Un chapeau de paille d'Italie*. The indefinite article in the French title better suggests the film's light, casual air.

The nineteenth century is coming to a close. Clair has moved up the play from the 1850s; by evoking a time that some original viewers could recall, but only barely, he is better able to suggest how stuck in time are bourgeois notions of propriety and elegance, how stuck in trappings and property is the bourgeois mindset.

It's all about a woman's hat. While the married woman couples with her soldier-boy in the country, a horse chews up this hat. The horse is transporting Fadinard by carriage to his Paris wedding. Lieutenant Tavernier demands that Fadinard replace the Italian straw hat, or else he will demolish Fadinard's house: the ultimate bourgeois threat. One cannot blame Tavernier: Madame's husband might notice the hat and put two and two straws together. Madame is property after all—and all this reflects on the marriage about to happen. Meanwhile, someone in the bride's party can find only one glove to wear. An overhead shot revealing a plethora of women's hats taunts both the missing glove and the partially eaten hat. Apparel, appearances: these are what matter.

The film opens on the wedding announcement and immediately cuts to the wedding day, with all its attendant nerves and commotion. Thus Clair implies that the wedding brings to fruition the announcement, not the mutual love of those getting married. The adulterous woman faints a lot.

Pauline Kael: Clair's film "is so expertly timed and choreographed that farce becomes ballet."

THE FALL OF THE ROMANOV DYNASTY (U.S.S.R.). The first part of a trilogy the other parts of which I haven't seen, Esfir (Esther) Shub's *Padenie dinastii Romanovykh* documents the inequities promulgated by tsarist rule and the social unrest this fomented, which the First World War brought to a head. It consists of archival footage, some culled from hagiographic material that Tsar Nikolai II had ordered shot. Eisenstein's mentor in techniques of editing and montage, Shub is often described as a compilationist. Stalin and his ruling establishment considered her a gifted editor, not an artist, failing to grasp the difference between editing for continuity and editing to generate ideas and the feelings that attach to them.

Consider the film's opening. The Tsar's Kremlin palace is represented by three spires, suggesting the Holy Trinity. The next shot is of a cannon, which is made all the more fearsome by its filling almost the entire frame. The juxtapositon declares, "Religion makes war(s)." The next shot is of a long procession of Orthodox priests. They are an army. These priests do not participate in combat, but the juxtaposition of images generates the idea that, in tsarist Russia, the appetite for war is cultivated by the clergy and activated by the clergy's influence on power. The two shots that now follow are of the military. The first leaves an impression of messiness: officers are shown milling around. The juxtaposition with the previous shot makes unmistakable that the military, for all its elitist, aristocratic authority, remains under the thumb of organized religion—the military's tacit master. The next shot is of rank-and-file soldiers. Perfect. Interpreting the sequence, we realize that it is Shub's opinion that organized religion determines Russian military prerogative and this in turn determines Russian military activity: the fate of *real* people.

Fall is art.

UNDERWORLD (U.S.). A powerful melodrama of primitive emotions, Josef von Sternberg's *Underworld* launched the cycle of Hollywood gangster films.

Sternberg's own background of poverty—his family, which emigrated from Austria when he was eight, struggled in New York tenements—brings conviction to such tawdry settings as the Dreamland Café, where characters play out makeshift lives. Shadowed by death, which it attempts to block out by creating its own insular space, here is a world of much bravado but no real happiness.

An enormous clock, superimposed on the opening action, sets the time at two in the morning, when sleepless criminals are at work. It also conveys a sense of mortality's pressure. Later, a jewelry store owner is shot to death during a daytime robbery as he attends to a clock in his shop. The invisible phantom gunning him down is Bull Weed, gang leader, out to steal a bauble for girlfriend Feathers McCoy. The headlong shot (with Weed excluded) is framed to make the victim appear as his assailant's reflection. Time is also running out for Bull Weed.

McCoy is perpetually garbed in a gaudy mass of feathers, giving her her nickname. (This is a film of nicknames—symbolically, this cloaking of identity yet another attempt to elude death and the fear of death.) Throughout, the feathers slightly molt, this shimmering loss marking the transience of human life. A feather floating downward in space is, in fact, our introduction to Feathers, whose youthful sensuality, tarnished and endangered by her surroundings, comes to embody human vulnerability—a point punctuated by her near rape.

Underworld is beautifully acted, its three stars—Clive Brook as Rolls Royce (called so for his silence—his unwillingness to "squeal" and betray), Evelyn Brent as Feathers, and George Bancroft as Bull Weed—all giving their finest performances.

SUNRISE (U.S.). Friedrich Wilhelm Murnau's first American film, *Sunrise*, is cherished for its lyricism and transplanted German Expressionism. A critics' poll in the 1990s voted it the greatest movie ever made.

The marriage of a young farm couple, splintered by the husband's dalliance with a vampish visitor from the city, becomes whole again as the two become reacquainted—ironically, in the city. The film delights with its symphonic visual beauty and highly expressive technique. Murnau employs the liberated camera that distinguished *The Last Laugh* (1924) back in Germany, as well as accomplished subjective use of back-projection. As the couple walk, the background—their surroundings—magically transforms correlative to shifts in their feelings. There is also a tram ride they share that lyrically condenses the whole course of their relationship.

Even with its cribbing from Theodore Dreiser's much greater novel, *An American Tragedy*, and although a tad heavy, *Sunrise* is irreplaceable. (It directly adapts a story by Hermann Sudermann.) It seemed to predict Murnau's success in Hollywood. But the film, while applauded by critics, was a popular failure. The first year of the Oscars, *Sunrise* won for "artistic quality"—a category subsequently canceled, ostensibly not to confuse the American public with two "best picture" prizes (Wild Bill Wellman's *Wings* took the other, familiar one), although really so as not to encourage art over profitable entertainments. The fact that there were two such prizes in 1928 acknowledged the difference between art and manipulation, between individual expression and committee-determined commercialism. The dropping of the "artistic" prize was tantamount to a declaration of war on art and artists in the maniacal pursuit of quick, enormous profits. The industry ordained the sun should set on *Sunrise*.

Only it didn't. It hasn't. Who today, given the choice, would go with *Wings* rather than take in *Sunrise*?

NAPOLEON (France). Of the original 5½ hours of Abel Gance's silent *Napoléon*, the version produced by Francis Ford Coppola retains four. It is less than perfectly whole in another way. Gance was unable to continue the six-film series for want of funding.

Thin, grandiose, overloaded with technical flourishes that are less expressive than indulgently displayed: Is Gance's bio[-e]pic a real work of art? Perhaps—and one that fits Gance's profile as pacifist. Despite appearances, Gance's film may actually be critical of its historical subject. Its inflated style maybe suggests how Napoléon himself would want to be seen by future generations. Larger than life; destiny's child; heroic conqueror.

When the film opens, Napoléon is a schoolboy engaged in a play-military battle—a snowball fight where his side is greatly outnumbered. A military strategist even back then, he wins. "My boy," he is told by the one teacher who likes him, "you will go far." (Prescient!) He is thus described as being "made of granite heated in a volcano." (How gneiss!) Two schoolmates release his pet eagle to the stormy wilds one night, prompting Napoléon to beat up every boy when the actual villains do not own up to what they have done. The bird rejoins Napoléon in his solitary confinement by a cannon, both being creatures of "savage isolation."

Teary-eyed, this boy is mightily picked on; his future victories and accomplishments will settle scores, reconciling the grown Napoléon to his unhappy past. His shy courtship of Josephine and his curt, decisive hurry-up of their wedding ceremony also reflect how Napoléon wishes to be seen by posterity.

Napoléon's 1797 invasion of Italy is rendered in "widescreen," the result of three adjacent screens. The superimposed eagle has become a symbol of the man—the symbol that Napoléon has chosen for Napoléon.

1928

THE MAN WITH A MOVIE CAMERA (U.S.S.R.). Cinema began as a documentary enterprise, with the camera a purely objective recording device; but documentaries have also been subjective and personal.

Chelovek s kino-apparatom, by Dziga Vertov, employs a framing device: preparation for the screening, followed by the ceremonious screening, of the film itself. On the agile move, it follows the cameraman, the director's brother, Mikhail Kaufman, from dawn to darkness, here, there and everywhere, including bustling city streets in Moscow, Kiev and Odessa, as he tries taking in "life as it is being lived" from numerous perspectives while photographing the film we're watching. Two audiences complete this self-reflexivity: those attending the screening in the film; Vertov's audience—now, us. Both "half-create" what they see, as in life.

What's on screen is life then? Not so fast! What appears is full of camera tricks. In Vertov's earlier *Kino-Eye* (1924) the Chinese street magician's magic seems the result of his own sleight of hand. Now, however, the magic of life and the magic of cinema so continuously translate into one another that we cannot be certain whose "tricks" we witness: the magician's or Vertov's. The "factuality" that Vertov is after, then, isn't the sort that omits or discards the myriad ambiguities of human experience; his eclectic film displays various tones and moods, with beauteous lyrical inserts recalling poet William Wordsworth's visionary "spots of time," amidst highly descriptive passages, such as of people at work. The result places the adventure in the graciousness of eternity—although the film never quite loses hold of the here and now, even when, in a burst of ingenious animation, Kaufman's camera, onstage, comes to robotic life to confront its audience: a sci-fi image predicting a delightful Soviet future that was not to be.

THE PASSION OF JOAN OF ARC (France). *See above.*

STORM OVER ASIA (U.S.S.R.). *Potomok Chingis-Khan* is a little difficult to rank. While it contains the best material that Vsevolod I. Pudovkin ever shot, its level of achievement is far less consistent than that of either *Mother* (1926) or *The End of St. Petersburg* (1927) or of Pudovkin's outstanding sound film, *Deserter* (1933). Moreover, some viewers are likely to view as gratuitous the fact that the cheating fur trader in the film is an American.

An opening shot, however, is the single most awesomely beautiful evocation of sheer topographical remoteness in all of cinema. The shot, angled, captures what appears to be the top of the world as mysterious light shimmers across the curving horizon. Also, the film's portrait of the faces and nomadic lifestyle of Mongolians is indelible.

It is 1920, in Soviet Asia. *Potomok Chingis-Khan* charts the pilgrim's progress of a Mongolian boy, a fur trapper, who, descended from Ghengis Khan, is installed as a figurehead ruler but who matures to become an anticolonialist national leader. Lovely and leisurely until a rushed ending, the film occasions a stylistic lightness that accumulates into a metaphor for spirit, providing the hero with continuity even as he undergoes radical growth. The film is momentous for another reason. Early on, its highly specific detail and sense of spontaneous observation, while delaying the film's ability to take shape dramatically, succeeds in blurring the distinction between fiction and documentary. This blur, or blend, of elements stakes out one of the main trails—documentary nudged in the direction of fiction (see *Berlin: Symphony of a Great City*, 1927); fiction nudged in the direction of documentary —that authentic cinema has followed.

ZVENIGORA (U.S.S.R.). *Zvenigora* launched Aleksandr Dovzhenko as cinema's "poet of the Ukraine."

During the Ukrainian Civil War, a man tells grandsons stories of far away, long ago, including one about buried treasure. One boy as a result ends up fighting for the revolutionary cause. The other, identifying only with narrow self-interest, becomes a seeker of fortune and a counter-revolutionary. The latter, who has attempted to make a profit by advertising his suicide in a theatrical venue, ends up, later, an actual suicide.

One of the film's themes, then, is the power of art—for good or ill. The grandfather's story-telling, richly mining Ukrainian folklore, inspires both boys, providing a repugnant example of greed for one and a seductive example of it for the other. One boy affirms life; the other courts death. The two boys in Dovzhenko's *Earth* (1930), Vasili and the kulak's son who kills him, will be, in effect, transmutations of the grandsons in *Zvenigora*. In addition, *Zvenigora* questions whether Soviet ideology speaks to what is innate in humans. Does Communism express or seek to correct what is naturally human?

Zvenigora plunges us into images that correspond to the grandfather's stories rather than showing him reciting these stories. The first thing we see is a train of galloping cossacks in slow motion. Thus the film announced, for 1920s audiences, the remarkably original film they were about to view. *Zvenigora* is delirious with experimentation, including rapidly edited sequences and the fantastic use of double exposures.

But the film is also trenchant, as when a soldier directs his own execution, and real as well as fabulous, as in its industrial montage and in a majestic shot of men working in the fields, their unconsciously synchronized swings of the scythe creating an indelible image of the shared lot of laboring humanity.

UN CHIEN ANDALOU (France). A man (played by the director) sharpens a razor, walks out onto an upper-story balcony and, underneath the full moon, cuts straight across a seated, willing woman's eyeball. Director Luis Buñuel hated this idea of co-scenarist Salvador Dalí's. Good.

The 17-minute film jumps ahead eight years and bounds sixteen years back. In a summary shot outdoors, the woman seems displeased at what the man is showing her. All that's visible of him, alongside her face, is his wristwatch on his outstreched arm, with his opposite hand pointing out the time. Time! After a series of anticlimaxes suggesting reprieves from time's end, the film closes on a stunning image of the couple buried standing in the earth, their faces visible, dead.

It is the power and (still) surprise of the film's images, and of their collision and connections, that account for the film's reputation as an essential work of Surrealism. Many of the dreamlike images reflect the idea that sexuality is an obsessive defense against mortal awareness. A bicyclist falls down on a Paris street. The overhead shot, correlative to the woman's gaze from her upstairs hotel window, reveals the two wheels of his bicycle right below him—a displacement of his testicles. Mobility is power, sexuality, life; but this burp of temporary immobility connects to the image of permanent immobility at the end.

Another image: man groping woman's under-the-blouse breasts; in the next shot, he is blind, her groped top, naked; next, her naked buttocks have replaced her breasts. Many things appear in two's, including two nitwit priests, roped to a piano, being dragged across the floor.

At one point, the man's mouth disappears; next, there is a beard there. The woman checks an arm pit, but we know better the source of the displacement.

PANDORA'S BOX (Germany). Sensual, capricious, hedonistic, emotionally light-sensitive, but perhaps, really, only self-sensitive, Lulu is the main character of G. W. Pabst's finest silent film, *Pandora's Box*. A cabaret dancer who impresses her lover, Schön, into marriage after his fiancée catches the two of them together backstage, Lulu is the principal model for the behavior of Sally Bowles in Bob Fosse's flamboyant *Cabaret* (1972). A reckless girl (played by American dancer Louise Brooks, with luminous eyes and, initially, wearing bangs), Lulu does nothing to discourage her husband's son's ardent attentions the night after the wedding. When he catches the two of them together, Schön impresses Lulu into shooting him. Schön's dying words are a warning to his son that he may be Lulu's next victim—the conclusion of a superb performance by Fritz Kortner.

Lulu's misadventures after fleeing with the boy, following her conviction for manslaughter, account for the remainder of the plot. In London, where she barely survives as a prostitute, fate poignantly intercedes at Christmastime. Intersecting her life is the compulsive path of another outcast, Jack the Ripper, whose sympathy Lulu draws right before becoming his next victim—irony slashing irony.

One of the film's most brilliant passages finds Lulu the object of shipboard contemplation by those who would sell her as a sexual commodity to an Egyptian harem. "Worse than prison" is how she describes this looming possibility—a fate seemingly to be decided at a gambling table. Lulu, however, manages to escape, just as she had eluded imprisonment. Isn't she lucky?

Only sound would dispel Pabst's tendency toward melodrama. Still, this is preeminently a film of atmosphere, dizzyingly dense backstage, and haunting off-stage with a tragic sense of destiny. In ravishing contrasts of black and white, *Pandora's Box* is lively and heartbreakingly beautiful—like Lulu herself.

THE STARFISH (France). Everything is ambiguous in Dadaist-to-Surrealist Man Ray's—Emmanuel Radnitzky's—*L'étoile de mer*, whose very title finds the star of the sky in the "star" of the sea. Accompanied by a poem by Robert Desnos, Ray's silent masterpiece revolves around a man and a beautiful woman as they walk outdoors or otherwise unite. As its object, she embodies his desire—and the eternal mystery of this desire. But she is a tease. When we watch them as a seeming couple mount the stairs to her room, watch her undress and lie down in bed, we assume that he will follow; we assume that he *also* assumes this. No; the title card reads "Adieu." Obediently, he takes his leave. Or is it he who has said "Adieu" to cover his embarrassed disappointment? Or to tease *her?* In life's dance of desire, someone has to lead, someone has to follow. When they earlier seemed to be walking together, was one in fact leading the other?

Much of the time images are distorted, out of focus. (Ray, who cinematographed, had smeared his camera lens with vaseline.) At other times, images are supernally clear. Dream and waking, possibly—or do *both* sets of images belong to dreams, the latter belonging to a fever dream whose "distortion" is its brilliant clarity?

A starfish is encased in a glass jar; another, mysteriously, thrillingly alive in its vast sea-home, is as erotic as the rip in a paper curtain that invites us in.

"And if you find on this Earth a woman of sincere love." We expect a main clause to

complete this title, but it never does, unless it is this, a couple of title-pages later: "You do not dream."
But you *do*. All desire is dreamt, even as it is lived.

STEAMBOAT BILL JR. (U.S.). Home from college in Boston, Willie isn't the son his seaman father bargained for. He is wearing an unmanly hat (a beret) and totes a sissy musical instrument (a ukulele). On top of everything else, Willie falls in love with his father's rival's daughter. Can Steamboat Bill make a sailor out of his Willie? Can Willie somehow prove himself to his father?
Yet again Buster Keaton turns adolescent fantasy into brilliant cinema. It is Nature, in the form of a cyclone, that puts Willie to the test—and the boy succeeds with flying black-and-whites. Keaton's deadpan persona becomes the hilariously impassive eye of the storm as all sorts of destruction and devastation befall the boy, who remains oblivious when he is not seemingly unconscious of events, including the whole front of a house falling down on his location but leaving him unscathed. (The façade's open window miraculously falls on the spot on which Willie is standing.) No other comedy employs such wondrous special effects and requires from its athletic star such precision placement and timing to ensure his survival. Steamboat Bill Jr. drops the jaw and crashes the funny bone, achieving a degree of visual splendor worthy of the director of *Sherlock Jr.* (1924) and co-director of *The General* (1926). This film completes Keaton's trio of masterpieces.
However, Keaton, who co-authored the script, isn't—officially, at least—the director on this occasion. Charles F. Reisner is the one who is credited. But the film is Buster's from prissy start to flamboyant finish, where he saves his future father-in-law from drowning, as well as the preacher who will marry him and his girl.

GHOSTS BEFORE BREAKFAST (Germany). Faces of clocks assure us that we are witnessing time as we know it, but our eyes protest. Four bowler hats float through space, at one point becoming three, and then being a foursome again. Water flows back into a hose. But let's rewind for a moment. Starting his day at the mirror, which is to say, the camera, which is to say, us, a man is tying his tie, which won't stay tied, frustrating him, delighting us. Reverse motion keeps untying his necktie.
Ghosts must be afoot. In Hans Richter's playful, surreal *Vormittagsspuk*, getting ready for the day is a precarious act because one is submitting oneself to regulation, well-practiced order. No wonder that the Nazis, once in power, condemned the film and tried to destroy it.
You know the old joke: Mama will like this, but Dada will like it better. Richter's film pursues its own logic, setting its capricious poltergeists to rest. At noon, smashed teacups reconstitute and four fellows sit at table to have a lunchtime snack. Each of the free bowler hats finds its rightful place and lands on someone's head. Things work out, folding into time cosmic elements that seemed to be at war with time. Implicitly, war will once again interrupt the normal order, because that's what wars do; but this different kind of order, with its fantastical elements, bar the normal interruptions by granting delicious freedom to imagination. Yes, Richter's film is very, very funny; but it is more than that. It is a plea for peace ten years after "the Great War." It is a plea for order that derives from the chaos of imagination—an order from inside humanity rather than one imposed on humanity from the outside. It's a swipe at fascist evil.

L'ARGENT (France). "Money passed through like a cyclone."
Marcel L'Herbier's dazzling assault on capitalism updates Émile Zola's 1890-91 novel *Money*, part of the Rougon-Macquart series, from the 1860s to the 1920s and, alas, remains current. The plot turns on the rivalry between Saccard and Gunderman, two financiers. They operate in a world that reeks of money—wealth without bounds or taste; Saccard is a plump,

brutal speculator, a financial Id, and Gunderman a lean, cooler, more ultimately conniving and controlling financial Superego. (The reception area of Saccard's office sports a circular world map indicating his rival's holdings—an image of the world domination that both men pursue.) Saccard arranges a stunt to benefit his Universal Bank: Jacques Hamelin's flight to French Guyana (a parody of Lindbergh's 1927 solo flight from New York to Paris), where, engineer as well as aviator, Hamelin will exploit natives for the rigging of Saccard's oil drilling operation. Hamelin is a dupe, whose perfectly symbolical trouble with his eyesight helps get his signature on a document that ties his legal fate to Saccard's fraudulent schemes; meanwhile, in Hamelin's absence, Saccard pursues Hamelin's wife.

Inspired by Abel Gance's *Napoléon* (1927), L'Herbier has created a stunning, opulent spectacle that brings a rich variety of avant-garde techniques into mainstream filmmaking, as well as dynamic use of mobile camera (including cuts between different traveling shots), a breathtaking variety of camera angles, and a deliberate rushing back and forth between the prosaic and bursts of poetry. Many of L'Herbier's techniques, including point-of-view shots, amidst colonialist exploitation, showing Hamelin's foggy vision, destabilize frames to suggest the exploitative, self-delusional, sandcastle-building nature of money-pursuit and Mammonism.

Zola called money "the dung on which life thrives." L'Herbier: "Money was really the bane of all filmmakers, since we couldn't do anything without it."

1929

ARSENAL (U.S.S.R.). On the heels of his *Zvenigora* (1928) arrived one of the great films about war: Aleksandr Dovzhenko's *Arsenal*. It is set during the 1918 Russian Civil War, between the Reds and the Whites, communists and nationalists.

Some of the Ukrainian artist's images are indelible: amid combat, a soldier, eyes bulging amidst artillery fumes, his face a contorted mask; the mutineers' derailed train, from which drops an accordian, which collapses into motionlessness; an officer mechanically performing executions in rapid succession—arm up, fire, arm down, arm up, fire, arm down. In war's crucible, naturalism yields to Expressionism. Dovzhenko convinces that his impossible vision of war suits war's reality.

Yet this isn't the sum of *Arsenal*'s achievement, for Dovzhenko probes the politics and various casualties of war, from the competing civilian sides to the Social Democrats, to the soldiers in the field, to the starving peasants back home. (A farm horse drops to the ground in slow motion: starvation? or has it been shot, to appease human hunger?) War is shown, then, as an intricate mechanism in which everyone is impressed. There is, for instance, the agitated response of the bourgeoisie to a workers' strike in the munitions factory; and the coming to a halt of the arsenal, besides providing a brilliant image of revolt, weighs in with the dire consequences of nonproduction for the soldiers waging war and the war effort being waged by a fractured nation. The arsenal's stoppage would inform the heart-stopping stopping of the mill at the close of Dreyer's *Vampyr* (1931), much as the collapsed accordian would reappear in René Clément's *Battle of the Rails* (1945). *Arsenal* is an influential film, then, as well as a mind-boggling masterpiece—a part of our collective consciousness even if we have never seen it. stopping of the mill at the close of Dreyer's *Vampyr* (1931), much as the collapsed

REGEN (Netherlands). It is only minutes long, but *Rain*—now restored to completeness—is one of a kind. The year before, Dutch documentarian Joris Ivens launched his prolific, globe-trotting 60-year career with *The Bridge*; but, fine as it is, that film cannot predict the astonishing lyricism of *Rain*. Besides co-directing the film with Mannus Frånken, Ivens co stopping of the mill at the close of Dreyer's *Vampyr* (1931), much as the collapsed-cinematographed it with Chang Fai and edited it.

Dziga Vertov and Boris Kaufman shot material for their Soviet *The Man with a Movie Camera* (1928) over four years; another black-and-white silent, Ivens and Frånken's film also

1929

took time to compose. Several rainshowers in Amsterdam over many months were meshed into a single event encompassing darkened sky, splattered pavement below and, in between, radiant humanity busily in motion. The result is a luminous meditation on human stopping of the mill at the close of Dreyer's *Vampyr* (1931), much as the collapsed transience amidst Nature's volatility—if you will, permanent impermanence.

Time's rush, the passage of life—everything in the film contributes to the development stopping of the mill at the close of Dreyer's *Vampyr* (1931), much as the collapsed of this theme, including overhead shots of barges pushing through the frames, and scores of stopping of the mill at the close of Dreyer's *Vampyr* (1931), much as the collapsed people in the street hurrying away from the camera (to which they are oblivious) to get out of the rain.

Some insist that everyone is smiling in the film. I do not see this. It doesn't matter. Regardless, the film is not a lament. The metaphor for humanity's fleeting role in Nature is executed without selfconsciousness. Ivens and Fránken transcend the mortal condition they suggest—and we feel this transcendence. On one level, then, *Rain* is a film about the power of film, of art.

Among its accomplishments, *Rain* remains exemplary for its fluent use of handheld camera, which, on this occasion, seamlessly disappears into the viewer's captivated eye—a poor indicator of the technique's eventual agitato trademark.

Rain is the little film that could. It still can. It still does.

A PROPOS DE NICE (France). Crisp and exuberant, full of youthful iconoclasm, stingingly ironical, Jean Vigo's documentary *A propos de Nice* satirizes the resort crowd on the French Riviera. Its restless camera, both in terms of movement and the rapid-change variety of camera angles and positions that Vigo devises with the assistance of cinematographer Boris Kaufman (Dziga Vertov's brother), conjoins with the often frantic human activity to create a sense of exhaustion. Camera rotation, creating sideways and upside-down views of buildings, and a bit of fast motion only deepen the impression.

Vigo contrasts reality/Nature to human artifice. Beach hotels in the opening aerial view, real, could pass for a studio miniature. The first "guests" and "tree" we see are plastic, and this "outdoor" scene is really indoors; suddenly a croupier's rake removes the figures, and Vigo cuts to the rake doing its usual work, removing chips from a hotel gambling table. Subsequently there are shots of real trees, ocean, beach, sunlight.

A huge papier-mâché head is being painted—the gargoylish satire of a resort guest. Later, it is one of a host of such monsters in a parade, with rows of onlookers oblivious to the mirror-image of themselves that (at least in Vigo's mind) they are confronting. Conversations are "unnaturally" framed so that only one participant is visible. There is a montage of guests resting in the sun; their feet and legs are shot to seem strained and stressed. Guests aren't relaxed but posing relaxed—a part of their fakeness. By contrast, hotel employees are shown busily at work, efficiently doing what needs to be done, and other proletarian faces appear genuinely animated. Vigo also contrasts posh guests with the nearby poverty of locals. Closeups of a soldier's medals and a church-top cross expose some of the villains of the piece.

THE OLD AND THE NEW (a.k.a. THE GENERAL LINE) (U.S.S.R.). Jean-Luc Godard has said that the best way to criticize someone else's film is with a film of one's own. Among the most beautiful movies ever made, *Earth* (1930) was Aleksandr Dovzhenko's response to Sergei M. Eisenstein's *Staroye i novoye*. But Eisenstein's film is itself a magnificent achievement, despite the dismissive Soviet response it incurred in part because the two main characters were seen as being too highly individuated, and because Eisenstein's "formalism" countered what Stalin (through a critic) cited as the public's need for "simple, clear, realistic stories." One wonders whether something else weighed in: with its bare-chested farm boys, *Staroye i novoye* would remain Eisenstein's most aggressively homoerotic work.

1929

The film's most famous passage involves the maiden operation of a shiny new cream separator, on whose correct functioning the hopes of a struggling farm cooperative are pinned. The machine's fecund overspill exudes a sense of the collective release of the cooperative's members from both current want and past servitude—a discharge (with life-affirming erotic overtones) that symbolizes their (and others') becoming newly whole by returning to their generous, spontaneous natures, from which tsarism, as a matter of course, had endeavored to separate them. Intellectual montage? In this case, try *orgasmic montage*.

This time, Eisenstein lights on a representative heroine rather than hero, whose rise within the commune he traces. Marfa is full of initiative, acuity, and hope for the future. *Staroye i novoye* thus strikes a stunning chord of gender equality while balancing the integrity of this individual against group effort and aspiration. The film implies the necessity for such equality if the nation is to fulfill its mission.

How Eisenstein's films of the 1920s resonate with his faith in Soviet Communism as liberator of the human spirit.

HALLELUJAH! (U.S.). Although initially made as a silent, King Vidor's most vibrant achievement remains a splendid film musical. Its rich use of Negro spirituals and work-songs underscores an absorbing theme: the role of evangelism in exploiting and channeling pain, disappointment, unease in the American landscape—here, in the case of African Americans, who brought to the tent of salvation in the South a unique circumstance: the fact that Christianity had been the only "education" permitted slaves, with no other aim than to render them docile. Even if only unconsciously, therefore, a racist legacy confounds African-American Christian faith.

This underlying irony helps explain why *Hallelujah!* is at once jubilant and troubled, startlingly clear-cut and problematic. Through fantastic, hysterical religion, the Alabamans we watch, "free blacks," dance on invisible strings; still serving the motives of whites, their Christianity ties them to their slave past.

Vidor's grasp of such vastly implicative material is breathtaking; Vidor would return to a musical to direct, uncredited, the scenes in Kansas in *The Wizard of Oz* (Victor Fleming, 1939), including the one where Judy Garland sings "Over the Rainbow"—the only worthwhile scenes in an otherwise mediocre, unimaginative film.

Some Vidor "classics"—for instance, *The Big Parade* (1925)—are vastly overrated. Yet a Vidor film invariably includes *something* of value. Although *The Crowd* (1928) overall is a sentimental tearjerker bemoaning the dehumanizing impact of a modern urban environment, it contains a wonderful shot. John Sims, the protagonist, is born on Independence Day 1900; his father exults about what opportunities the newborn will have as we watch in a mirror—it is a somewhat faint reflection in an otherwise clear image—the doctor take the infant in the opposite direction: a disquieting anticipation of the father's death and of John's lost claim to his father's dreams for him.

FINIS TERRÆ (France). While every film exists on a sliding scale of expression whose opposite poles are documentary and fiction, Jean Epstein's *Finis Terræ* does more than combine the two modes; it anticipates generic (as distinct from stylistic) attempts—poetic docudrama; Italian Neorealism—to fuse them.

The initial action is set on Bannec, a Breton islet, during the summer. Two boys, dear friends, there to work, quarrel; Ambroise, whose cut finger results in infection, withdraws from Jean-Marie. Braving the elements, Jean-Marie attempts to row Ambroise to a medical doctor in Ouessent; meanwhile, the doctor is heading to Bannec to attend to the sick boy. Will the two vessels miss one another in the fog and tragedy result?

The story, then, is melodramatic and sentimental, and there are crude touches besides—and splendid poetry. Everyone notes the stark beauty of the harsh landscape and seascape in *Finis Terræ*. But consider also the objects that Epstein includes like loose beads in the brilliant opening movement: a disconnected wheel lying on the ground, seemingly enormous in the foreground of a shot; a broken wine bottle—it is this that becomes (along with a missing knife) the bone of contention between the boys; Ambroise's turned inside-out pants pockets; a large broken bowl smacked by the waves; stones. Combinately, all these also are correlative to the boys' (and others') hard lives, poverty, bleak prospects.

There is a heartstopping moment at sea where Epstein uses the silence of silent film to expressive and ironical intent. Jean-Marie sees the vessel that, as it happens, is transporting the doctor. He calls out. The shot, a closeup, magnifies the boy's effort to be heard, while the omnipresent silence reinforces our sense that all Jean-Marie's effort may prove fatally insufficient. The lives of both boys now hang in the balance.

TURKSIB (U.S.S.R.). *See above.*

BLACKMAIL (UK). From a Charles Bennett play, Alfred Hitchcock's startlingly brilliant *Blackmail* exists in a half-hour-longer silent version, but I have seen only the silent-sound hybrid. It opens with police action—a tight closeup of the mobile unit's wheel, seemingly spinning in place, then appearing to turn counterclockwise, hence a mirror-image and suggesting a rewinding reel of film. A long-shot confirms that the wheels are actually turning clockwise, the vehicle, advancing; but the opening shot throws into question everything that follows.

Self-involved Scotland Yard detective Frank Webber and petulant Alice White, a London shopkeeper's daughter, are going nowhere except, in lockstep, to the altar. Alice feels that Frank's job diverts his attention from her. Attempting to make Frank jealous, Alice ends up in an artist's studio apartment, and the artist ends up killed. To our eye, it appears that Alice *might* have killed Crewe (behind a curtain), with a cheese knife, after he attacks her, and she certainly believes she has; but it is just as likely that Crewe is playing possum and that someone else who ends up blackmailing Alice came in later and killed Crewe. Alice drops a glove before exiting Crewe's apartment.

Now, seemingly in a trance, traumatized, Alice makes her way through London streets at night. Others walk in either direction on either side of her, some diaphanous phantoms—a projection of how unreal everything now seem to Alice. The streets everywhere taunt her with evidence of her crime; for instance, a shaking neon mixed-drink canister strikes her eye as a neon knife stabbing down again and again. An upturned palm on an outstretched arm also repeatedly shows itself. And each hand of a "dead man" that Alice sees belongs in fact to someone who is alive, including a bobby directing traffic.

Frank retrieves the glove.

THE NEW BABYLON (U.S.S.R.). It is curious that neither of the two major films about the 1871 Paris Commune have come from French artists, but understandable, really, given France's suppressed memory of its painfully brief experiment with a just society. The second work, a masterpiece, was made by England's Peter Watkins: *La Commune (Paris 1871)* (2000). The first was made by the Soviet team of Leonid Trauberg and Grigori Kozintsev. Although the pair continued to make movies together, *Novyi Vavilon* was the final work of their avant-garde collective, The Factory of the Eccentric Actor, which Sergei M. Eisenstein's *Strike* (1924) had inspired to expand from theater into cinema.

The silent film (for which Dmitri Shostakovich composed live musical accompaniment—his first score) consists of broad strokes of heightened—sometimes, farcically exaggerated—reality. The opening movement portrays a frenzy of activity inside La Babylone Nouvelle (Zola's satirical *Au bonheur des dames* weighs in here), as the high bourgeois department store's vulture-like patrons descend upon bargains generated by the disastrous progress of the Franco-Prussian War. In a ferocious image, Prussian soldiers, in spiked helmuts, gallop towards Paris at night.

I don't buy the use of the shopgirl for a unique perspective on the unfolding events; the film's most famous aspect is, for me, its weakest. But the film delivers an engrossing portrait of the Commune's birth as workers and intellectuals come together; and the government's assault, and the street executions that followed, with merchants licking their chops, pierce. The Commune fell in less than two months.

The closing tone, so odd when one considers the historical tragedy involved, is justified in terms of the film's thematic motive. Trauberg and Kozintsev find in the crushed commune an unstoppable spirit that took political form in their own new nation—as can happen elsewhere besides.

PEOPLE ON SUNDAY (Germany). A documentary fiction, a fictional documentary: *Menschen am Sonntag, ein film ohne Schauspppieler*, written by Curt Siodmak and Billy Wilder, and directed by Edgar G. Ulmer, Robert and Curt Siodmak and, to a minor extent, Fred Zinnemann, is a notable late silent film from Germany—an experiment in which young filmmakers flex their love of cinema. It is indeed "a film without actors"; the five main characters are played by nonprofessionals, who, titles tell us, returned to their ordinary jobs the next day.

Cab driver Erwin joins friend Wolfgang, a wine merchant, and Wolf's new girlfriend (yesterday's pick-up on the street), Christl, at the beach, leaving behind live-in Annie, a model, with whom Erwin quarreled the previous day, the tension between them signaled by a dripping faucet in their apartment. (Great introductory shot: Annie, reclining and comfortably bent, filling the whole frame head to toe.) Christl has also brought best friend Brigitte, who sells phonograph records, whom Wolf seduces after Christl (in the water!) rebuffs his advances; but in front of all these girls, the boys take up with others. At the end of the day, Brigitte still hopes she will see Wolf again next Sunday. Monday, everyone is back at work in Berlin.

The brilliant cinematographer is Eugen Schüfftan, who would photograph seminal black-and-white films, including Marcel Carné's *Quai des brûmes* (1938). He and the filmmakers collaborate on a spontaneous air and fresh, crisp, exuberant, sometimes volatile images. Much of the framing surprises—and yet makes total sense: for instance, when Brigitte changes into her swimsuit she occupies a small lower portion of the screen and is surrounded by tall reeds that fill up the screen.

Charming: tots at the beach. Gripping: pans of tenement exteriors.

Films of the 1930s

For most, the greatest film of the 1930s is Jean Renoir's *The Rules of the Game* (more about which later); for me, it is *Earth* (*Zemlya*). Aleksandr Dovzhenko made this film in response to Sergei M. Eisenstein's *The Old and the New* (see 1929); he was expressing his *own* view of "the old and the new." Selfish peasants—kulaks—resist collectivization; seeking to retain exclusive ownership of land, they oppose Nature by violating the bond of sympathy that weds individuals to the common good. Here, Nature is shown as bountiful, ripe, nourishing, the source of moral truth, and an ennobling, humanizing force that the farm cooperative as a practical idea embodies. Nature also is the eternal witness in whose philosophical brea(d)th human mortality—the tragedy of life—unfolds. Whereas Eisenstein's *The Old and the New* points proudly, confidently ahead, *Earth* finds a solemn continuity, imaged forth by a vast ocean of waving wheat, threading past and present.

Dovzhenko's film is a different way of seeing, a different way of breathing air. *Earth* also misses—narrowly—having more history to take into account; for, while Dovzhenko was making it, Stalin's 1929 collectivization policy, which would soak the earth in human blood, had just begun. This tragedy was still unfolding when the film was released in 1930.

For all (at the time) Dovzhenko's acquiescence to Stalin's iron grip on the Soviet film industry, *Earth* was deemed suspect by Soviet authorities; as a result, Dovzhenko's father was expelled from his farming collective. Perhaps Stalin and those surrounding him found the silence itself of the film dubious (*Earth* was Dovzhenko's last completely silent film), as though sound might better promote the national interest by propagandizing more plainly and directly. In any case, the experience surrounding *Earth* pushed Dovzhenko into a near-suicidal depression.

Serene, meditative, transcendent, and more visually beautiful than any other movie in existence, *Earth* reflects none of this agitation. No other film so completely situates human mortality in the round of Nature. Indeed, *Earth* provides, early on, an instance of death outdoors on the ground, in the care and domain of Nature as it were, rather than with a conventional indoor "death bed" scene. The man is old, having spent, we learn, 75 years as a simple worker, a farmer plowing fields with his oxen. He is surrounded by family and friends of different generations, and by a harvested crop of pears lying on the ground: images certifying his status as farmer and, as such, his connection to Nature. The man's last act is to bite into a pear. The entire passage is interrupted by shots of oceanic wheat fields under a vast, still sky. Moreover, preceding it is the film's famous opening: a montage comprising shots of the wheat alive in breeze, a shot of her face as a girl stands next to gigantic sunflowers, and shots of apples, ripe, smooth, perfectly round. Following the old man's death are closeups of the sobered faces of those surrounding him; enjoying the fruit of their elders' labor, only children are untouched by this sobriety. One day, they too will harvest fruit. *Earth*'s opening movement has never been surpassed.

Dovzhenko follows this quiet, lovely scene of leavetaking with a family indoors in epileptic throes of excessive grieving. At first we assume that these people are responding to the man's death. Nothing of the sort, however; their selfishness is in sharp contrast to his selfless, unself-pitying departure. These kulaks are beside themselves over the news of collectivization! Rather than turn over his horse to the farming collective, one of them is prepared to kill the animal with an ax before a family member stays his hand at the last moment. Dovzhenko portrays these people as ridiculous in their resistance to change. Their selfishness has deformed them. In their insistence that the land is "theirs" rather than something they share with their neighbors, in this cutting themselves off from others, they have divided themselves from their own humanity.

Earth celebrates workers, and one of its most beautiful passages shows harvesters, at work in the fields, from every conceivable angle. (I'm not sure *how* I feel about the preceding part where urine cools the radiator of a newly arrived tractor.) There is such joy in their labor, for their being a part of Nature and close to the earth. Subsequent scenes show the mechanical threshing of wheat and, close up, the plowing of earth. A generalization arises as to the holistic nature of these people's lives.

With their selfish resentment, the reactionary kulaks are the serpent in the garden. Vasili (Semyon Svashenko, wonderful), who chairs the collective committee, has just spent a peaceful, romantic summer's night with his girlfriend. Walking home in the moonlight, full of joy for love of the girl, he breaks into dance on the road. Maintaining a fixed, implicitly documentary camera, Dovzhenko records an explosion of the boy's feeling: Vasili dancing and dancing, from long-shot to closeup to his being, finally, just out of camera range, with a subsequent long-shot sealing the integrity of the dance—a solitary boy's perfect enjoyment of a moment in his life. Suddenly Vasili drops; did he stumble? Did he fall? A horse reacts—to *what?* In the prime of his youth, Vasili has been shot dead by the embittered son of a kulak. He has been robbed of the long life of the old man whose death we earlier witnessed—robbed of the marriage he was looking forward to: robbed, as the kulaks themselves feel robbed of the property that collectivization threatens to turn over to general use.

Vasili's father Pyotr's grief and rage are vivid, and there is a stunning shot of Vasili's body, while being carried through the wheat fields, that is framed in such a way as to conceal the bearing hands of the living, creating a sense of the corpse's independent motion, ironically, in the direction of burial. A funeral has replaced the anticipated wedding. The funeral service is one of the great set-pieces of cinema, and the murderer's insane dance among the graves, replacing Vasili's joy in dance with inconsolable guilt, stresses the point that these two boys ought to have been comrades—friends; brothers. Earlier, the image of Vasili's intended bride, naked and in the throes of inconsolable anguish and grief, provides yet another dimension of the tragedy that has occurred.

Nature responds with lament: a downpour splashing fruit.

Dovzhenko's next film, *Ivan* (1932), is a transitional work between silent and sound films, and thus to be grouped with Sternberg's *The Blue Angel* and Clair's *Under the Rooftops of Paris* (both 1930), among numerous other works. (Clair on the subject of sound as it applies to cinema: "[A] redoubtable monster, an unnatural creation, thanks to which the screen will become poor theater.") For me, the most brilliant of these transitional films is, from Germany, Dreyer's *Vampyr* (*Vampyr—Der Traum des Allan Grey*, 1931), the greatest horror movie ever made. Like Lang's *Destiny*, it fully enters a magical world, in its case, a realm of sinister enchantment. Moreover, its images and sounds across a spectrum of fictional and nonfictional, and objective and subjective, suggestions are correlative to its attempt to bridge the worlds of sound and silence. The film's additions of sound effects and spoken dialogue, both sparse, interrupt and unsettle its silent or eerily quiet dreamlike state, helping the film to realize its central theme: humanity's anxieties as a result of (our species presumes) its peculiar awareness of its mortality. The dreaminess of *Vampyr* suggests more than an anxious dream, however; on one level, it is a desired or somehow willed dream whose aim is to relegate elements of anxious reality to the realm of dream so that the possibility exists of waking up and having these elements dissipate and dissolve. The film implies, then, a permanently objective world the fear of whose loss requires the landscape of a dream as a kind of safety hatch or escape route. The blend of elements is so complete that, throughout much of the film, there is, simultaneously, a quiet sense of stability and a disquieting sense of instability and loss. *Vampyr* exists within a dream, but, within that dream, it exists at the crossroads of possibility and impossibility, loss and the hope of defeating loss, subjectivity and objectivity, nonfiction and fiction. Not coincidentally, it is the grayest among all black-

and-white films.

The film opens with sound: the low, ominous strains of Wolfgang Zeller's musical theme, perfectly suited to the theme of mortal anxiety. Thus posited as a sound film, the film per se opens as a silent, or as a throwback to silent films, when a long title card appears, identifying the hero of the about-to-unfold adventure as young David Gray, whose study of evil and vampires from past centuries has rendered him a "dreamer, for whom the boundary between the real and the unreal has become dim." (The dream state of Gray's existence is reinforced by a subsequent reference to his "aimless journeyings.") In effect, we the viewer relate to this title card, and the one that follows establishing the setting, the village of Courtempierre in the nineteenth century, as though they are documents: documentary guideposts. This will later connect to a huge document about vampirism portions of which we will intermittently read over Gray's shoulder, as it were, as Gray himself reads it. On one level, this is an attempt by Dreyer to bring credibility to the fantastic, as Lang attempts to do by other means in *Die Nibelungen*. On a more pressing level, though, this is an attempt to use an element of silent films in order to stabilize the new anxiety-ridden territory of sound cinema (this was Dreyer's first sound film)—anxiety that is correlative to, and perhaps even representative of, anxiety related to human mortality. That the object of Gray's study is vampires makes the point perfectly, for vampires—the undead—are projections of this anxiety of ours over our finite condition. The peculiar nature of this printed language, however, is to encapsulate the anxiety that the language would seem to counter, much as, when a patient reads about a terminal illness he or she has, with the aim of mastering fear through knowledge, he or she may nevertheless be reinforcing the original anxiety. Facts about illness do not necessarily dissipate the fact of the approaching death. Attempts at objectifying often deepen a soul's subjectivity. To say the same thing in another way: One does what one can to reduce one's level of anxiety, but in reality, in certain situations, there is nothing one can do. The one possibility that is available is to go through the motions of doing *something*. Our fear of death stubbornly resists transcendence.

In the authentic kind of cinema in which Dreyer engaged, images take primacy over language, whether the language is spoken or written. After the two title cards, the film per se materializes; but it materializes in a kind of dematerializing way. Carrying against his shoulder a long-handled net, Gray appears walking up a hill with the sea in close proximity. Although he is fully dressed and dry, the shot is framed so that the "dream possibility" arises that Gray has just walked out of the water, and, in any case, because of what we have just read about his being a "dreamer," we immediately associate the water with the unconscious—a common symbolism predating Freud's naming of the unconscious. The complexity of the image speaks to the complexity of the film's tack: Gray is on land, which implicitly means he is firmly in reality, but the water, coupled with the butterfly net he totes, renders the image dreamlike, casting Gray symbolically adrift. He is, recall, an aimless journeyer.

The next images find Dreyer renewing this tack—as, indeed, will the entire film. Having mounted the hill, Gray arrives at the inn where he will stay. This is grounded in reality, for the event implies the mundane arrangements that must have been made in advance so that Gray would have a place to stay while in Courtempierre. Such arrangements counter the idea of a dream by suggesting a continuity of behavior on Gray's part. What we see next, though, counters the countering. Gray is at the door of the inn, but he finds no way of getting in. He knocks and calls to no avail; just when it seems that the implied "arrangements" have dissolved into nothingness, as things precisely do in a dream, a bespectacled woman opens an upstairs window, calls to Gray, and appears downstairs to let Gray in. Dreyer's choice to keep the camera on Gray rather than follow the young woman downstairs (the shot of Gray at the door is from inside the inn), though, deliciously holds us in suspense as to whether the innkeeper will in fact let Gray in or simply vanish. (Who knows what might happen in this film?) Meanwhile, a man who is carrying a scythe descends the hill and rings a suspended bell, with the water again in close view. The scythe, which traditionally is something that the figure of Death might tote, identifies the man whose face is invisible to us, because the camera is at his back, as Gray's reverse or contrary image: old instead of young, going down the hill that Gray has just ascended, and carrying the solid scythe instead of Gray's airy net. The tolling bell, too, replaces Gray's hello-ing, and, because of its visual juxtaposition with the sea, suggests the loss of human lives. Although the scene, and indeed the entire film, is wondrously light, there is an unmistakable presence here of human fear of death. This is reinforced to a stunning degree by a shot of the man, indeed old and now obliquely facing us with his scythe, shown against the quickly flowing water that now appears much closer than we have thus far seen it. We almost feel that it might carry us away.

The ridiculous plot of *Vampyr*, with its conspiracy to enslave a man and his daughters by a vampire and an evil doctor out of *Caligari*, comes from Joseph Sheridan Le Fanu's story "Carmilla" in *In a Glass Darkly*. The film's immense value owes little or nothing to its debased literary source. It's the magical quality of the film that matters, such as in those shots, in shadowy silhouette, where a man is digging a grave and we see, in reverse motion, the earth sail through space to the spoon of the shovel. What matters most is also the "not-quite-rightness" of the world that David Gray navigates, which achieves its culmination when he witnesses the movement of his casket towards burial, with himself, open-eyed, in it. It is the blending of anxious fantasy and objective reportage, subjectivity and objectivity, fiction and nonfiction that makes *Vampyr* cinema's preeminent (if uncredited) evocation of Edgar Allan Poe, the nineteenth-century American newspaperman and fantasist.

The decade's greatest U.S. film did not come from Hollywood and, in fact, cannot be said actually to exist. *¡Qué viva México!*, Sergei M. Eisenstein's never completed Mexican film, has remained cinema's most celebrated phantom work.

Its history is famous—a true legend, part of which unfolded in the U.S. Following *The Old and the New*, Eisenstein was invited to Hollywood to make a film of Theodore Dreiser's novel *An American Tragedy*. Eisenstein brought with him his indispensable master of light, cinematographer Eduard Tissé. Accompanying them also was Grigori Alexandrov, the "co-director" that Josef Stalin had assigned to Eisenstein to monitor his work, to hold in check those "formalist" tendencies of Eisenstein's that Stalin felt did nothing to serve Soviet interests. The Hollywood film, however, was not to be. Wishing to remain true to the sociological density of Dreiser's masterpiece, which included the novel's political underpinnings, Eisenstein reasonably sought to make a passionately anti-capitalist film; Hollywood had other ideas. (The mostly psychological film that eventually did get made—and a very good film it is—was made by Josef von Sternberg.) Eisenstein then turned his attention to Mexico, a country whose mixture of indigenous and Spanish cultures fascinated him, for another opportunity had come his way: socialist U.S. author Upton Sinclair (*The Jungle*) and spouse Mary Craig, along with some friends, agreed to bankroll an independent film by Eisenstein. This was to be Eisenstein's Mexican film. Unfortunately, Sinclair's group withdrew their financial support for the project once costs exceeded their expectation; a planned segment referring to the Mexican Revolution of 1910-16 was the principal casualty. Meanwhile, Stalin insisted on Eisenstein's return.

Assured by Sinclair that all the negatives would be sent to him so that he could edit what film there was, Eisenstein returned to Moscow. Fearing Eisenstein's political disloyalty, however, Stalin blocked the importation of these negatives, although officially the dictator blamed Sinclair. (Ironically, the processing ended up being done in Hollywood.) Further punished by being denied any new film assignment for five years, Eisenstein took up teaching at the state film school. Some of Eisenstein's Mexican footage, their use authorized by Sinclair, appeared in such films as *Thunder Over Mexico* (1933) and *Time in the Sun* (1940). Eisenstein died in 1948 at fifty, partly the result of stress caused by his conflicts with Stalin, who would not agree to "unshelve" the second part of Eisenstein's planned *Ivan the Terrible* trilogy or allow Eisenstein to film the last part. In the 1950s Sinclair deposited the Mexican materials at the Museum of Modern Art in New York, and in 1959 Stalin's successor, Nikita Khrushchev, freed from the vaults the second *Ivan the Terrible* installment as part of his program of "de-Stalinization." Twenty years later, his own career as a musical-comedy filmmaker long since finished, Alexandrov and another filmmaker, Nikita Orlov, edited and assembled the fifty-odd hours of Eisenstein's Mexican footage, at last in Soviet hands, interpolating the gaps from Eisenstein's own sketches and notes. Actor-director Sergei Bondarchuk (*Fate of a Man*, 1959; *War and Peace*, 1967) recorded (heavily!) a commentary consisting of Eisenstein's own written words. The result is what we have today, a silent film insofar as there is no spoken dialogue, but with music, sound effects and spoken commentary.

The film is episodic; some episodes are documentary, while others are acted-out dramatic vignettes. Even in its incomplete state, though, the film is unified as a study of mixed cultures, native and imposed, pre-Columbian and Spanish, the old and the new. But what more specifically unifies Eisenstein's film is its focus on the shifting role and importance of women in Mexico, in a downward direction. In this regard the film becomes a companion-piece to *The Old and the New*, which identifies the Soviet future with gender equality.

The grandeur of the opening predicts the film's larger-than-life style communicating Eisenstein's awe of the passion and mystery that he identifies with Mexico. The first shot is of the sunlit sky over the ancient sacred city of the Mayas, Chichén Itzá, in Yucatán, in southeast Mexico—a shot that fixes time into an eternal holding-pattern; as the film unfolds, the same unfiltered sunlit sky predominates, as though most of the shooting, if not all, was done within an identical range of time each day. A succession of shots of immense ancient pyramids, most of them huge closeups disclosing startling sculptural detail, accompanies commentary: "The time in the prologue is eternity. It could all be taking place today or have happened twenty years ago, or even a thousand years ago." We have entered a domain of myth. It will be Eisenstein's task to show the connection between this fabulous past, embodied in the stone faces of ancient gods, and the present. The commentary continues: "Stone. Gods. People." A long-shot of humans ascending a pyramid's steps yields to a series of closeups and medium closeups posing individual people amidst the sculpted stone at angles stressing the resemblance between them and the faces in stone. "Men and women with the features of their ancestors," runs the commentary; ". . . faces like those hewn in stone." Capturing an idea in a kind of mirror of the mind, Eisenstein thus simultaneously suggests both the living embodiment of Mexico's ancient past in her present inhabitants and the anthropomorphic basis of religion: a stunning distillation of far-ranging materials. He also selects one face, shown frontally in closeup, as what appears to be—it later reappears—a signature face for the film; it belongs to a beautiful young woman. Is she the future of Mexico? It becomes clear as the film unfolds that this is not the case.

We next see a (probably staged) funeral. Symbolically, it represents the historic suffering and oppression of the native Mexican people, hence, their romance with death. It is connected to the earlier part of the prologue with one of the film's eeriest shots: the faces of pallbearers, their chins on the lengthwise edge on both sides, set like stone over the open casket. (The corpse's bare feet are also visible in the foreground.) Eisenstein thus relates current religious ritual—the funeral—to the ancient religion of spectacular gods; once again the present incorporates the past, and here around the idea of death that will permeate the film to the degree that Eisenstein believes that this idea permeates human, and notably Mexican, consciousness. A long-shot of the funeral procession, by its explosion of the static shot at the open coffin, deliriously mixes life and death, merging (again, in a mirror of the mind) two ideas: death as part of the life cycle; and eternal life, represented by the movement of the procession, as a superstitious function of humanity's obsession with mortality. But something else quietly jars: the principal feminine element in the segment's *mise-en-scène* is the coffin, the faux-womb in which the dead man is "reburied." This contests the vibrance earlier identified with females through the closeup of the young woman's face.

The first episode, "The Sandunga," clarifies the dual, contradictory images of female power mined by Eisenstein in the film. An Indian girl, Concepcion, is the main character; the setting is Tehuantepec. But it is not with the girl that the episode begins; instead, Eisenstein essays the flora and fauna of the lush region: palm trees, monkeys, birds of various kinds. "Time flows slowly here," we are told, "linking past and present." (Ironically, this connects Indian life to the death movement of the funeral procession in the second part of the prologue.) The commentary refers to the natives' "regal indolence." Once again the sun is at its highest point, bathing everything in its wash of intense light; this segment displays the film's deepest, most ravishing contrasts of light and shadow. This isn't accidental, for the brightness striped by and riddled with darkness alerts us to the fact that "The Sandunga" is complex and ambiguous.

It's a love story, of sorts. Through palm trees, an overhead shot of boy and girl, both stripped to the waist and sharing a hammock, seems the height of directness and simplicity. A cut to two parrots in intimate closeness in a tree completes the benign portrait. A large, solitary wild cat, however, undercuts what just preceded its appearance. We are told: "Girls sing the Sandunga [whose lilting loveliness we hear on the soundtrack] as they dream of the future." The future they dream of is marriage. The necklace of gold coins that Concepcion pursues, coin by coin, will mean the realization of her dream; it is her necessary wedding dowry. The entrée into marriage that the necklace provides is part of a complex and ironical circumstance. Indigenous Mexico, native Mexico, Indian Mexico is matriarchic. We are told: "The woman works and chooses a husband for herself, and it is she who brings him into their new house." But what power accrues to the female by having to buy her "way to marital bliss"? Stop-gap photography tracks the necklace as, through sale after sale of one thing after another, coin after coin is added to it, and the visual trickery conveys a startling meaning: money not as power but as the *illusion* of power. Before the wedding, at a communal dance, the prospective groom is all smiles, but Concepcion is pensive, as though discordant notes were attending her anticipation of the "blissful" event. In dance, she is following his lead. The commentary reflects Concepcion's misgiving-riddled mood: "Isn't this what you wanted? What you dreamed about for so long?" Another shot pierces: the prospective groom lolling away in the hammock, one bare foot ostentatiously lifted up in a show of force amidst his leisure. This time the boy is alone. This time the boy's satisfaction—self-satisfaction— excludes Concepcion. And what are some matriarchs—mother and grandmothers of the prospective groom—doing? Studying the necklace, asking, "How many gold coins?" "Are they pure gold?" Matriarchy serving the interest only of the male is matriarchy undermined, undone. Eisenstein's film has caught the drama of one idea dimmed and tainted by another: an image of a powerful girl yielding to an image of a powerful boy.

The ringing of church bells signals the wedding day. The film cuts from an image of these bells to a shot of the bride in full blossom of gown. The irony is close to unbearable, for the bells belong to the patriarchic Catholic church, imposed on Mexico by her Spanish conquerors, with which the next episode, "Fiesta," will deal. Undoubtedly the wedding day belongs to the bride, making the cut from bells to Concepcion purposeful and transparent. But who will "own" the much longer "day" of the marriage itself? Will this day be equally shared? In the midst of the ceremonial joy of both bride and groom, amidst the native customs ironically governed, ultimately, by the non-native church, the groom, beside himself, takes the necklace off his bride's neck and at length, smiling, caresses it. Now there is an insertion: another shot of the two parrots in the tree—only, this time, while side by side, they might as well each be separate and alone, for no affection passes between them. An image of monkeys splashing through water becomes one of cinema's most unpleasant indications of sexual intercourse. Flash forward: Concepcion carries their son to the hammock to deposit

Films of the 1930s

him with his father, who is still occupying the hammock alone, in complacent glory. The *mise-en-scène* is principally this: father and son on the hammock in the foreground, Concepcion behind them, standing, attending to them. Devastating.

Huge, grotesque painted masks introduce "Fiesta," also set in pre-1910 Mexico. The withering hint of Spanish influence on native Mexican society and culture in "The Sandunga" becomes a blast of hot, oppressive air in "Fiesta," the closest Eisenstein has ever come to resembling Buñuel. This episode, the film's most disturbing, most trenchant, most brilliant, records the annual Feast of the Holy Virgin of Guadalupe—the dark-skinned translation of the Virgin Mary conjured to ease Aztecs, and the other Indian tribes that the Aztecs had conquered, into an acceptance of the Roman Catholic faith that the monks accompanying conquistador Hernán Cortés imposed on Mexico when Spaniards conquered her in the sixteenth century. These monks, the commentary informs, "wiped out the pagan cults," erecting Catholic churches on the very sites of the Aztec and Toltec temples atop pyramids, keeping constant the worshipful routes used for thousands of years, in this instance to facilitate the conquest of Indian souls. The celebration (like our Christmas celebration) dazzles with its mixture of pagan and Christian symbols and rituals. It is also, we are told, "an annual reminder of Spain's conversion of Mexico into a colony of bloodshed and suffering."

Eisenstein's contempt and hatred for Spanish clergy match his contempt and hatred for Russian Orthodox priests in his films at home. Consider this shot: human skulls huge in the foreground as monks—celebrants, that is, dressed as monks—stand in the background. This equation of religion and death conveys three interconnected ideas: one, the killing required to turn Mexico into a Christian country; two, religion's exploitation of people's fear of death to maintain its power and its hold on people; three, the romance with death, peculiar to the Spanish, that the Spanish conquerors and their clergy imposed on life-affirming Indians. As usual, Eisenstein's images are "packed"; they resonate with import.

The passion play annually reenacted reeks of suffering and death, and, yes, it utterly fascinates as colonial spectacle. It is Eisenstein at his most anthropological. Many men represent Jesus Christ crucified; the outstretched arms of each are tied to a cactus stem, the needles pricking the men's backs. These suffering Jesuses, here and there served water by women (Christianity, a male-thing, relegates females to the sidelines), walk up the pyramid steps; others laboriously, equally painfully, crawl up the steps, crouched, for hours. In long-shot, they resemble monkeys. At the mount, actual clergy, under the imposing head gear of patriarchic authority, cross themselves and bless the crowds. The celebration proper begins: "Masks of devils, pagan gods, and Spanish conquistadors side by side. The dance goes on from dawn to dusk. Without a pause, over and over, [celebrants] repeat the same steps in honor of the Holy Virgin of Guadalupe. Or perhaps—who knows?—of a more ancient goddess, the awesome mother of gods." This last suggestion, noting the Great Mother, pierces; Eisenstein is suggesting that the females participating in the celebration may be searching out from it not the degradation that it (and the "new life" it represents) imposes on them but some distant psychic or buried communal memory of a time in the sun when females walked proud and powerful. The dancing itself, joylessly ritualistic to Eisenstein's eyes, includes participants, solitary, spinning around: motion without advancement. (They are not really like Muslim dervishes because no trance, no higher consciousness, results.) This part of the religious event is as disconcerting as what has preceded it.

The episode is not yet finished. This part centers on the bullfight, the national sport and spectacle of Mexico that did not exist in Mexico until the Spanish conquerors introduced it. The bullfight, savagely depicted here, represents the masculinization of Mexico, the exiling of women, and the idea of women as powerful, to the sidelines.

The passage begins with the dressing of a matador for a bullfight that day. Part of this practical ritual—I say "ritual" because Eisenstein leaves no doubt that we are meant to connect this complicated dressing to the "fiesta" we witnessed in the previous part of the same episode—has the young bullfighter spinning around as his sash, his cumberbund, is wound onto him. Specifically, we are reminded of those dancing at the fiesta by themselves, twirling around and around. The boy may have an appointment with death. He and his younger brother, also fighting in the ring later that day, pay a ceremonial visit to their mother; this is the first of the episode's second half's two relegations of females to the periphery— and this, with respect to the mother who bore them. They kiss; they shake hands. In seconds the whole visit is finished as the mother sits amongst caged pet birds, each one in a separate cage, in fact, an image that strikes us as correlative to the woman's isolation, and her reduction in due importance. Think about it: She has been relegated to being the recipient of a *courtesy call*. Next stop for the boys: a statue of the Holy Virgin, at which they kneel—this, to Eisenstein's eyes, a symbol of female importance as permitted by the male power structure of the Church. This—this unreal woman—is now the female power in Mexico; actual women have been replaced in deference to the Holy Virgin's submission to patriarchal authority. At the bullfight, in the stands, the other reduced females appear: the "queens of the bullfight," who cheer on the bullfighters to kill the bulls. When the bullfighters do this, the sequence of shots makes the "queens" complicit in masculine savagery and killing, and the bullfighters, implicitly, no less complicit in the reduction of powerful females to their current ceremonial roles. Eisenstein is still not done with the episode. He has a final coup: not a man serenading a woman, as romance urges, but two women serenading the day's successful bullfighter. No one, however, informs the mother that both her sons are still alive. Commentary: "Mexico: tender and lyrical, and also cruel."

"Maguey," the next episode, and again set in the Mexico ruled by dictator Porfirio *Diaz*, is my least favorite. Melodramatic, it serves its purpose in the thematic development of the film. Provoked by the rape of one of their females, peons mutiny against their master, the landowner, and are viciously destroyed. Eisenstein knows what idea he is after, as those who assembled his film also understood: Woman as Victim, an occasion for the avengers' *machismo*. Indeed, Eisenstein will not permit us to sidetrack the point; the Indian boys rising up against the landowner for the rape of an Indian girl are equally shown, in their revenge and in the way they accept their fatal punishment, as acting out *machismo*. Whatever the stylistic excess of the presentation, this episode contributes memorably to the film's argument.

The episode that Eisenstein never shot, "La Soldadera," would have completed his portrait of the diminution of women in Mexican life and history. Men would be fighting the revolution; the central character of "La Soldadera," a soldier's wife, would be accompanying the revolutionary forces in which her husband was detached—a camp follower, as it were. Garbicz and Klinowski (in *Cinema, the Magical Vehicle*, 1975) explain: "Her husband is killed in battle at the moment when his child is born: the culmination of the motif of life and death intertwined, which for Eisenstein was the key to the essence of Mexico." No doubt; but *his* child? Doesn't my reading of the film also have a claim?

The epilogue returns the film to the present day (1932) and restores it to greatness. This epilogue centers on the carnival procession of the Day of the Dead, a holiday devoted to both mocking death and celebrating the dead. Here, dancing conveys the vitality of commonfolk. A stunning surreal image, that of a skeleton foot wearing a spur, promotes the deserved fate of one of the feudal "masters" torturing and killing peons in the previous episode. At the epilogue's conclusion, however, a child takes off his skull mask. The revealed face is that of a young boy. Think back: the face of a girl had once seemed the film's signature face. At the last the young boy's face is the face of Mexico's future. The symbolical triumph over death and the fear of death, therefore, is clouded by the real failure of the existing nation to pursue and nurture gender equality. To repeat myself, Eisenstein had ended *The Old and the New* with the heroine embodying the Soviet Union's future, a future he perceives to be dependent on gender equality; now, in his very next film, he finds a different story, a different future, in a foreign land. What we have of ¡Qué viva México! makes his case.

Or *somebody's* case, since, as I said, I am discussing a phantom film. The other edit of the Eisenstein material that I have seen excludes some of the material and includes some different material. It goes by the title *Eisenstein's Mexican Fantasy*; the filmmaker, or whatever, is Oleg Kovalov. While I have to admit that I would have had some difficulty following it had I not seen Alexandrov's reconstruction, this version is at least as wondrous, and probably more so. This "Fantasy" is less rigorous, less thematically particular, more associative, more poetic and dreamlike. The consecutive complete episodes of the Alexandrov reconstruction yield in this instance to luminous cross-cutting amongst the parts, releasing them from their narrative boundaries into an oceanic dream of Mexico. Moreover, the most remarkable passage of all doesn't exist in the Alexandrov reconstruction. The latter ends with the Day of the Dead celebration in brilliant sunlight. But Eisenstein also shot footage after the celebration, at dusk, as participants file out. You will recall Eisenstein and cinematographer Tissé's ravishing deep contrasts of black and white; this unfamilar passage is muted, shadowy, gray. Recall the passage in *Battleship Potemkin* of the shadowy, dusk-cloaked sails on moonlit water, with its note of the eternal? The passage in the "Fantasy" film is like that. With these ordinary Mexican celebrants leaving the amusement park on the evening of the Day of the Dead, Eisenstein conjures a dream of the spirits of the Mexican Revolution. It is soulful, thrilling, irresistible, *haunting*.

John Ford's *The Lost Patrol* also haunts. Based on a story by Philip MacDonald titled "Patrol," it is remarkable both for reasons often given and for others rarely, if ever, given—reasons that point to a far more intriguing piece that has been generally acknowledged. Most have been beguiled for so long by the stark adventure's splendid superficial aspects that they may have missed what in fact makes this a *Ford film*, a penetrating and highly suggestive work of art.

The story is too familiar to require an extended synopsis. During the First World War a British battalion, lost in the Mesopotamian desert, are being picked off one by one by the unseen enemy. "Where is your regiment?" the brigade commander, coming across the sole survivor, asks as this sergeant, overcome by unspeakable loss, points to a row of graves, each marked with a combatant's saber: an image Akira Kurosawa would famously borrow for the conclusion of his *Seven Samurai* (1954).

Ford's film mines two major themes: an identification of each side with the other; the religious basis of even such a "secular" war as World War I. One doesn't need to speak of the terrific suspense that the film generates; everyone—Fordians, non-Fordians, anti-Fordians—all agree on the film's high value as thrilling entertainment. Yet it is the film's analytical nature that draws attention here; for it is this that gives *The Lost Patrol* the depth and interest of Erich Maria Remarque's great novel about the same war, *All Quiet on the Western Front*—a depth and interest, I am sorry to say, that the largely sentimental Oscar-winning film version by Lewis Milestone (1930) lacks.

One of the combatants notes—the script is by Garrett Fort and Dudley Nichols—that there is no real reason for the Arabs who are killing them to be taking up arms against them. This is Fordian irony, for the soldier who utters this astoundingly casual remark fails to grasp what *we* readily do: that the truth of it cuts both ways. Ford's imagery couldn't be plainer: in a strange and provocative instant, another one of the soldiers, delirious from the heat and a protracted sense of danger, shoots at his own shadow in the sands only seconds before being shot by an Arab. This tragic mistake—it is the sound of the first shot that clarifies the target for the second and fatal shot—identifies each side with the other. In another incident, two soldiers are sent out to try to find the brigade that can rescue them while the battalion remains cornered at an oasis from which, at night while they fatefully tarried, exhausted, all their horses have been stolen by the enemy, which has also killed the sentry. When the two return from their failed mission, they are shot dead by their comrades who fatally mistake them—and, by extension, themselves—for the enemy. In effect, by killing two of their own, in what today is hideously and euphemistically called "friendly fire," the warriors have inadvertently consigned the distinction of opposing sides to the shifting sands of the desert. This hallucinatory environment consumes and obliterates such distinctions.

Psychologically, the identification has this basis: the Arabs killing the British are a projection of the British soldiers' fear of death. This possesses merit on its own as an idea for two reasons: it is this immediate fear of death, not ideology or patriotic principles, that in a war arena fuels the continuation of mutual combat; and it is the dehumanization of the enemy that this mortal dread excites and encourages that provides a compelling rational basis for the ongoing warfare, releasing it from the taint of what might otherwise be regarded as "unmanly," cowardly emotions. Thus in the context of identification that Ford provides, the invisible nature of the enemy becomes a Brechtian device for commenting on this process of dehumanization. Two additional strategies lead to this complex outcome: Ford refrains from any jingoistic generation of hatred targeting the Arabs, refusing to see in its pursuit a necessary means for engaging his audience by manipulating its basest emotions; and the film, principally through the agency of the battalion chaplain who notes the religious significance of the region ("This very spot is the Garden of Eden"), underscores that it is the British who are geographically the intruders. Indeed, the "invisibility" of the Arabs is possible only because of their familiarity with the desert, which the film continually stresses is alien territory for the British, who succumb to their detriment to its hypnotic monotony. All this in effect flips the film's perspective by providing a basis for our understanding the Arabs' dehumanization of the British. Something else contributes to this outcome, which an artist of less integrity than Ford would have regarded as unthinkable: the film's impartial tone and brisk style, both of which conspire to withhold any sentimental grieving over the serial deaths of the British combatants. Instead, it is their combinate death, at the end, that terribly and powerfully moves us (its index for us is the mute grief of the one shell-shocked survivor), by which point the emotion underscores rather than undercuts Ford's thematic intent.

Ford the New Englander takes up with issue the British class system that enforces itself even in a strange land far removed geographically from the British Isles. I remember as a child being totally baffled by the plot's point of departure: the lieutenant's refusal to share with the regiment, even his next in command, their specific orders, their mission and their itinerary. But this refusal, Ford suggests, is second nature to the lieutenant, a commissioned officer who thus holds rank of class in addition to military rank over the company's noncommissioned sergeant. He will, of course, share the orders on his own schedule, when he feels sufficient time has passed to remind the sergeant of his superiority and the sergeant's own inferiority; only, he is the first to be shot dead, leaving these orders undisclosed and consigning the regiment to abandonment and utter bafflement as to where they are and where they should be for whatever reason. (The sergeant, assuming command, makes the correct decision to keep due north in hopes of rejoining the British brigade.) There are two aspects to the lieutenant's arrogance: besides, obviously, his inbred feelings of superiority vis-à-vis the sergeant, the utter stupidity of assuming that his death isn't even a possibility for which the regiment must be prepared. Since the other deaths follow his, it is quite possible to find in *The Lost Patrol* a parable, a morality play if you will, in which all the other members of the regiment pay the consequences for their commanding officer's arrogance—this, one more working-out of Ford's refusal to make the Arabs the "villains" of the piece.

The soldiers are a various group, with at least one of its members, besides the (by now dead) lieutenant, seemingly belonging to the upper class: George Brown, played indelibly by Reginald Denny (*Of Human Bondage*, 1934; *Rebecca*, 1940), one of the finest character actors of the day. The chaplain refers to Brown as "a man of breeding," lest we miss the point, and Brown's own demeanor and personal stories seem to corroborate the fact. Upon his death, however, we learn that "George Brown" was not his real name but "the best he could come up with" when he enlisted: a note of ambiguity that re-establishes Brown's identity as either a member of the lower class or, more likely, a tainted member of the upper class who signed on for military duty, as many routinely joined the French Foreign Legion in order to flee some aspect of their former lives. Thus Brown becomes a touchstone in the film for considerations of class; the soldiers themselves reveal themselves to be less stamped by military discipline—they are repeatedly shown, and chided by their sergeant for, coming up short in this area—than by the reflexes of class that account for their military obedience.

The oasis the regiment stumbles across, giving them the chance to rest and refresh themselves and their horses, promises to obliterate the class references, much as the equalizing sands promise to do this. But the opposite occurs, as Brown and the chaplain's remark about Brown leave the impression that, wherever they find themselves, these British soldiers tote the baggage of the class system to which they are accustomed. The Irishman Quincannon Billy Bevan and the Anglo-Italian Morelli (lest we miss the point of identification, played by Irishman Wallace Ford) represent the "untouchables" of British society, the socioeconomic dregs. Ironically, the oasis is, by the chaplain's reckoning, the once Garden of Eden, the scene of humanity's original state of equality. The men's being trapped there suggests their failure to transcend the mindset of classism.

Ford suggests the contribution that classism makes to the generation of wars. It is with bitter irony that he passingly allows the realization to arise that these soldiers, fighting in the immediate to preserve their lives, are fighting in the larger scheme of things to preserve the British class system. Another theme, related to this, however, draws his greater interest: the religious nature of and basis for war—even a secular war such as the First World War. To me, his pursuit and development of this theme is the film's most remarkable achievement. Let us begin with a reminder of what we all know: among American filmmakers, Ford was the great atheist, a man steeped in the culture of Irish Catholicism who nevertheless never found a need to believe in God. Now let us admit at the outset that nothing in the demeanor of the soldiers or of their combat suggests in the slightest a holy war. Yet the film is saturated with religious overtones: the location, to be sure, and the chaplain's numerous attempts to impose a religious cast to the proceedings. This chaplain, Sanders, is generally described as a religious fanatic, but the film leaves open the possibility that his fanaticism is the result of the secular conduct of the war and of the men's refusal to bend to his religious leadership, both of which may conspire to enlarge his religious defensiveness. On the surface, then, the war that Ford shows us could not seem more secular, especially in contrast to the figure of Sanders. Indeed, for safety's sake the sergeant cuts short one of Sanders' services for the dead—or so the sergeant says, for we perceive, also, a certain distaste the sergeant feels for the religious intrusion that the chaplain's biblical reading represents. Ford stresses the point; when the young sentry is buried, someone suggests marking his grave with a cross made of twigs, but it is the sergeant who contrarily suggests the secular saber as a marker. "I think he would have liked that," the sergeant says. This may be so; it is no less true, however, that the avoidance of the religious marker likewise reflects the sergeant's *own* preference. The secular marker then becomes the standard for the subsequent graves of fallen soldiers—a marker honoring the soldier's life on earth, not Christ or the soldier's delivery to an afterlife.

The avoidance of the religious: isn't *this* what we see throughout the film, and isn't Ford's means for underscoring it the presence of Sanders, in whom religious feeling seems to reside in excess, as though the religious feelings of the others, whatever they may be, have been projected onto him so that they, the combatants, might better focus on their secular military duties? Yet the presence of Sanders continually reminds us of the opposite as well: that these soldiers are Christian, that the nation they represent and for which they are fighting is

Christian, and that theirs is a Christian incursion into a non-Christian place. (Militarily, Sanders' whole reason for being included in the mission is so that he can attend to the combatants' specifically Christian needs.) The implication is clear: what we are observing is a "holy war," like the Crusades, only one given the trappings of modern secularism. What Ford reveals throughout is the sublimation of the religious in modern secular war, which in turn implies the religious basis of modern war, which the British deny (are in denial over) because it threatens to expose the connection between the current war and the barbarous wars of the past likewise fought in the name of civilization. "Civilization," after all, always means *Christian* civilization. Ford's is a breathtakingly ironical approach; it's the absence of the religious from view that ultimately points to the religious basis of war for which the film argues. How I love the complexity of Ford's cinema!

Boris Karloff, in what is without doubt his greatest role, plays Sanders. The extravagant old-world style of his playing, especially in contrast to the restraint with which the role of the sergeant is enacted, helps Ford immensely in conveying what he believes to be the case: simultaneously, the piteous beauty and poetry of religious feeling and the vast danger that the irrationality of religious faith poses. But Ford is not done with Sanders, who contributes in another important way to his film's intellectual motive and design. For Sanders, the misfit too wrapped up in the rituals of death to embrace life fully, is an expressionistic reminder of another character: the lieutenant, so much in denial about the possibility of his own death that irony insists he must be the first to get killed. (The appearance of the Arabs at the last, when they are machine-gunned down by the sergeant, is another expressionistic touch, for Ford's image of them on top of a dune suggests the possibility that they are a mirage, a figment of the sergeant's heat-battered and company death-battered mind.) The identification of Sanders with the lieutenant is a master stroke underscoring how each is somehow apart from the group—the lieutenant, above; the chaplain, because the others to his frustration ignore him, below. It is Sanders' remark about Brown's "breeding" that prompts the identification, but it's the sheer lunacy that Karloff's acting conveys which forges it. Both these characters live perhaps only in their own heads. Alas, by implication, the class-structured Britain that the lieutenant represents may also be living, Ford implies, in a region of national ether and noxious gas. The larger point of the identification between the two disparate characters is that the nation's political class structure derives its authority from the nation's religious foundation and the hierarchic nature of that foundation.

Ford's film is exceptionally beautiful visually. Shot in the California desert on a shoestring budget, Ford and his black-and-white cinematographer, Harold Wenstrom, nevertheless are better able to conjure a (menacingly) bewitching landscape than David Lean and his color cinematographer, Fred Young, could manage with a humongous budget for the tepid *Lawrence of Arabia* (1962). The film is also superbly cut by Paul Weatherwax, who would win an Oscar for editing Jules Dassin's wonderful police thriller *The Naked City* (1948). Max Steiner's score, especially alert to Karloff's flourishes in portraying Sanders' insanity, is among his best.

Victor McLaglen appears in the lead role of the sergeant. His tremendous performance already deserves the Oscar he would win one year later for a completely different role for Ford: Gypo Nolan, in *The Informer* (1935). Indeed, McLaglen, the father of director Andrew V. McLaglen, would remain such an acting resource for Ford that he belongs with Henry Fonda and John Wayne in the pantheon of Ford's players. His detailing of the sergeant's trajectory from competent commander to broken man is utterly convincing and heartrending, and it is *The Lost Patrol*'s principal means for conveying Ford's abhorrence of war.

The list:

1930

EARTH (U.S.S.R.). *See above.*

CITY LIGHTS (U.S.). Still silent despite the advent of sound, Charles Chaplin now gave his most moving performance. Of course, he had the benefit of brilliant writing and directing: his own. *City Lights* is the seminal American movie about the Great Depression.

Chaplin's vagrant draws kindness from the girl he loves, a flower peddler whose blindness perhaps spares them both her judging his circumstance. Their lives are precarious. Charlie, homeless, routinely skirts starvation, and the girl, who supports her mother, with whom she shares a tiny apartment, is threatened with eviction. Charlie has crossed paths with a rich playboy whose life, luckily, he saved on the occasion of one of the playboy's frivolous suicide attempts—foolishness that stands in sharp contrast to the real hardship of others. Not so luckily, though, the playboy is generous only when drunk, which is also when he attempts suicide, but mean and stingy the morning after: a telescoping of society's ambivalent feelings about the poor. Charlie's goal to help the blind girl takes him from sweeping streets into the boxing ring, where he is hilariously ill suited, to committing a robbery in order to pay for a surgical operation that might restore the girl's sight. Released from prison, he chances across his beloved again. Now she is the proprietor of a flower shop, and she can see him for the first time. This is her benefactor—Charlie the Tramp. How he appears; her new status now dividing them: Will she be grateful only? Can she love Charlie? By dint of the film's closing fadeout, we will never know.

Thus Chaplin finds a perfect metaphor for the uncertainties of the time. Ambiguous, poignant, haunting, this celebrated ending releases such powerful, complex feeling as to give fresh meaning to the idea of the bittersweet.

THE GOLDEN AGE (France). A candidate for the title "the world's most incendiary film," Luis Buñuel's *L'Age d'Or* was withdrawn from circulation after its Parisian launch led to riots provoked by two fascist groups, the League of Patriots and the Anti-Semitic League. (The United States denied the film a commercial release for fifty years!) One would think that the passage of time would have relegated *L'Age d'Or*'s inflammatory nature to the regions of quaintness. Not so. The film's excitement remains intact.

This eclectic work opens with a brief documentary about scorpions that suggests the poison-tailed nature of another species of animals: us. Cave-dwelling bandits show that humans also do whatever they can in an effort to survive. This is the associative way the entire film works. Both the scorpions and the men, impoverished, have only themselves as resources—in addition to whatever they manage to take. Boats arrive; people mount the rocky terrain. They pay their respects to a grisly expanse of skeletons in religious garb—the surreal translation of a bandit's vision of mumbling clerics! The official ceremony is interrupted before it begins. A couple rolling in mud are pulled apart. Their coitus interruptus becomes the film's persistent motif. A shot of the woman, in agony while alone in her apartment, leads to the sound of her flushing toilet superimposed on a fantasy of "flushing" land that looks like a swamp, a slide, of shit. In the street, the man heartily kicks an object of bourgeois affection: a small dog. Buñuel, bless him, is really sticking it to propriety and domestic order.

The film's exhilarating social satire and liberated air, as well as its insatiable Jesus by way of the Marquis de Sade, astound.

Salvador Dalí contributed to the script.

THE BLUE ANGEL (Germany). The complex German personality, with its susceptibility to authoritarianism and idolatry, and its courting of humiliation and defeat: this is the theme of

The Blue Angel, which Josef von Sternberg, Viennese-born but who grew up in the Bronx, made in Berlin before returning to Hollywood. Its drama, effortlessly revelatory of the social psychology that helps explain the rise of fascism in Germany, covers the years 1925-1929.

Immanuel Rath teaches at a college in a small provincial town. He bullies his students, inviting them into his shabby living quarters for special chastisements, but harbors a sentimental streak; the one recipient of his affection, a pet bird that stopped singing long ago, has just died. An itinerant troupe of entertainers is at the club called The Blue Angel, and its star attraction, a sexy singer billed as Lola Lola, the professor feels, has been corrupting his students. He confronts her, having descended the corkscrew staircase from the club's stage to Lola Lola's temporary boudoir/dressing room, and, like a schoolboy, falls in love. Silently, the troupe's clown repeatedly taunts him, in full make-up, with forlorn and almost pitying looks. Professor Rath marries Lola Lola, forsaking the dignity of his profession to join the troupe. His wife proves unfaithful, and he replaces the troupe's painted clown.

The village sets, with their *Caligari*-like distortions, key us into the film's psychological nature. Equally discordantly non-realistic are the shifts between chaotic noise and sheer silence at The Blue Angel whenever the door to Lola Lola's quarters opens or closes. Highly expressive, Sternberg's aim is psychological realism.

As Rath, Emil Jannings is superb, and her phenomenal performance as impudent Lola Lola, which made Marlene Dietrich a star, grows richer and more ambiguous and provocative with each fresh viewing.

THAT NIGHT'S WIFE (Japan). Useless emotions: a father's shame; his arresting police officer's compassion. Stressing psychological elements (to which its use of German Expressionism is correlative), Yasujiro Ozu has made in *Sono yo no tsuma* a great film, one of his trenchant "dark" works in anticipation of *An Inn in Tokyo* (1935), *The Only Son* (1936) and *Tokyo Twilight* (1957).

Shuji and Mayumi are the struggling young parents of Michiko, who is bedridden with a high fever. The couple cannot afford a doctor. Shuji robs a concern, having tied up its employees at gunpoint, to get the money he needs.

He leaves behind a palm print—the mark of shame. Poor parents feel shame for a sick child: shame for their inability to keep their child well or make their child well. Demoralized by this shame, Shuji finds the robbery easier for him to commit; such shame illogically halts Mayumi's hand from adding expensive sugar to her tea as Michiko sleeps just feet away in their small, cramped apartment.

Hands. Shuji's bare hands are compared with the white gloved hands of the fleet of officers attempting to hunt down "the criminal." A pair of those gloved hands on the wheel of the "taxi" that Shuji takes alerts us that he is being shadowed home, is about to be caught, by the law.

The title (if accurately translated) makes sense only if it refers to the arresting officer, Kagawa, whose "wife" Mayumi becomes because Michiko becomes his "daughter" as all three adults await the doctor's arrival and news of the child's medical fate throughout the night.

At the last Shuji's shame trumps Kagawa's empathy and compassion because Shuji insists on his own arrest, depriving him of his daughter (and her of him) no matter the condition of her health.

WESTFRONT 1918 (Germany). François Truffaut once remarked even pacifist war films turn out pro-war because the battle scenes invariably prove the most exciting, undoing the intended message. He may have had in mind Lewis Milestone's stilted, poetical *All Quiet on the Western Front* (1930), which comes to life only in its spectacular tracking shots of combat, with rows of soldiers being mowed down—scenes whose aestheticism robs them of any sense of lost human lives. But had Truffaut seen Georg Wilhelm Pabst's *Westfront 1918*?

Based on Ernst Johannsen's novel *Four from the Infantry*, this account of four World War I soldiers, all of whom are eventually killed, is gray, unremitting, naturalistic, disturbing. The visual, aural and emotional tonalities of Pabst's first sound film coincide: dirt, artillery fire and explosions, claustrophobic trenches, monotony, madness, sudden death. At the original showing, patrons fainted at the sights and sounds of such realism on screen in portraying war. No conventional battle "excitement," sentimentality or aestheticism allowed the film to loosen its grip.

Pabst's long penultimate movement is in battle. At least twice Pabst fixes the camera and keeps it fixed, making us more eyewitnesses than film viewers. In one of these remarkable shots, a soldier falls to his death early on in the foreground while combatants rush across a field in the background, competing for our attention with only intermittent success. Stuck on the original anonymous corpse, we are frozen in horror.

The final passage is in a field hospital, a makeshift place of surgeries and insanity as soldiers bemoan the loss of sight, the loss of limbs; and, before our very eyes, one of the boys we've been following turns into a corpse, his mouth and the hollows of his eyes overtaken by darkness as in a grave: here, Pabst's single stroke of Expressionism.

THE BLOOD OF A POET (France). Near the beginning, a tall, slender chimney starts to collapse; the action completes at the end. In between, then, in a split-second, lies a dimension where time doesn't move forward but possesses depth.

According to Cocteau "a realistic document of unreal events," Jean Cocteau's *Le sang d'un poète* considers the sacrificial act of artistic creation. "It has a suggestiveness," Pauline Kael wrote, "unlike any other film."

Appearing in his palm is a speaking mouth/stigmata (inspiration), which at one point the poet tries shaking off but then transfers to the statue of a woman, which comes to life and directs him to enter the room's large mirror, which he does with a splash. He thus enters the theatrical hotel, with its many doors through whose keyholes he peeps; through one the poet espies the shooting death of a Mexican, which he (and we) then see in reverse slow motion that restores the mowed-down man to life. Eventually the poet re-enters his room through the mirror and smashes the statue that the woman has turned back into: his assault on the burden of being an artist—what a poet ought to embrace. As a consequence, he himself rigidifies into a statue in the snow. The snowball fight of oblivious schoolboys causes the statue to evaporate; out of another mouth—a fallen boy's—blood gushes.

With a cut, the same setting holds an "elegant gathering." The Angel of Compassion, a black boy, covers the dead white boy's body. Guests seated in theater boxes watch below a card game between a man and a woman. The latter, Death, wins but turns to stone and, ultimately, into a sketch: the immortality of art.

With its heady otherworldliness, this film is silly sometimes, a bit mawkish, and essential.

1931

VAMPYR (Germany). *See above.*

KAMERADSCHAFT (Germany). The title *Comradery* reflects the politics of its maker, Georg Wilhelm Pabst. The film is based on an actual 1906 mining disaster wherein Germans helped in the attempted rescue of trapped Frenchmen but is set some fifteen years later to draw contrast with what then would be the recently ended world war in which Germany and France were on opposite sides. In the silent era, "the universal language of film" had been a ubiquitous notion; now, with its fraternal border-breaking, Pabst's preeminent sound film encapsulated the hope that cinema might yet usher in a new era of international cooperation. Ironically, the film is set in the Saar Territory, which France administered under the League of Nations following the war, pending a plebiscite in 1935 that, as it happens, returned it to

Germany's control.

The claustrophobic condition in the coal mines is grim. When it appears that the French miners are doomed, a powerful sense arises of their being buried alive. It is a projection of the oppressive nature of common labor, for which the entrapment serves as metaphor. Sober and naturalistic, *Kameradschaft* eschews the giddiness and moody flights of Pabst's haunting silent *Pandora's Box* (1928).

Georges Sadoul, in his *Dictionary of Films*, describes the film's original ending, which by now may have finally crossed the Atlantic but which I have never seen: "After the rescue, the iron barrier between the French and German workers is re-established by the officials."

France applauded *Kameradschaft*; Germany dismissed it. One final mockery: Nationalism proved too strong even for Pabst, a Leftist, who chose to remain in Germany after the advent of Chancellor Hitler, in time assuming an elevated—he later insisted, minor—role in the Third Reich film industry. He never recovered either his artistry or his reputation.

DIE DREIGROSCHENOPER (Germany). Pabst's *The Threepenny Opera* portrays an impoverished Soho one hundred years after John Gay's *Beggar's Opera* (1728)—satirizing elitist high opera, the people's ballad opera that Bertolt Brecht's play updates. Its London reflects post-First World War Berlin, another hundred years later, exposing the social disease and discontent that had fomented the allure of National Socialism in the Weimar Republic. Pabst's film, like the play, is a musical *about* something.

It takes us into the criminal underworld. Mack the Knife, king of thieves, dandy and bully, preys on the weak in the dockside slums. He dumps prostitute Pirate Jenny (wonderful Lotte Lenya, wife of the play's composer, Kurt Weill) and marries Polly Peachum. When Mackie next visits the brothel, Jenny betrays him to the police. Will he hang?

Slow tracking and panning shots, and deep shadows, characterize the film's atmospheric visual style, along with sharp images of teeming humanity, such as when a street singer sings the most famous tune in the Weill-Brecht score, "Mack the Knife," and couples move toward the camera as it pans leftward across the backs of the large gathered audience—a separate shot places Mack himself at the scene!—and, also, during a beggars' demonstration at Queen Victoria's coronation. (In her pompous carriage, Victoria uses her bouquet to block her sight!) Veterans, whose "rags do not cover [their] wounds," are also demonstrating—against military wantonness and false promises. The film closes famously: at night, the camera at the backs of an army of the poor and the disenchanted filling the frames with foreboding—the dangerous raw edge of expectancy.

Brecht, unhappy with Pabst's film, unsuccessfully sued.

The Nazis destroyed the film's original negative and prints.

Die Dreigroschenoper remains cinema's most brilliant musical.

M (Germany). Giving birth to the police procedural, Fritz Lang's *M*, though talky, retains a grim fascination. It is about two city-wide hunts for the same man—one by the police, the other by the underworld, which hopes to put a stop to the police search of which their criminal business is running afoul. The hunted man is a pedophile and serial killer of little girls. When they wrongly suspect someone on the street of being the killer, people become an enraged mob and assault him, taking the law into their own hands, just as the criminals are doing. Moreover, they reflect something of the compulsive killer's own inability to control himself. Primarily, the film identifies the two investigating groups: police and criminals. Eventually, the latter group captures and tries the killer, occasioning a stunning pan shot of the massive "jury," and satirically pricking the modern concept of justice—trial by peers.

M is a pitiless film except regarding the mother of one of the victims, who waits for her child to come home for dinner, and the hunted man, whose sickness draws Lang's full measure of pity. Even children are casually monstrous. The film opens starkly, with an angled overhead shot of girls in a circle and one in the middle, who recites a gruesome variation on "eeny meeny miney moe" to determine which child is "it": something to do with a man in black who is coming to chop up whoever is chosen.

Humanity is often portrayed at a haunting remove: men are gesticulating shadows on a wall; the unseen killer is the tune he whistles from Grieg's *Peer Gynt* whenever he is about to strike. Indeed, this is how he is identified by the balloon seller, who is blind.

Young Peter Lorre is brilliant as the hunted man.

LE MILLION (France). Nothing could be lighter or more buoyant than René Clair's warm-hearted musical-comedy parodying operetta/opera, *Le million*.

The brilliant opening shot travels weightlessly along Parisian tenement rooftops; alternative lives to those in Clair's preceding film, *Sous les toits de Paris* (1930), will be shown to us. Romance is in the air—and revelry. Their sleep interrupted, two men slip and slide across the roofs to peer into the jubilant apartment. (Among those dancing, we fleetingly glimpse a bridal gown.) What is going on? "Haven't you heard what happened?" a reveler asks, looking up. "No." The revelers sing to the pair of insomniacs, beginning their account of the day that's now coming to a close. As the scene dissolves to an interior one that morning, we realize that we the audience are represented by the two men on the roof. Is this reality, or are we asleep, dreaming? Obviously a gorgeous fabrication (Clair's resident genius set designer, Lazare Meerson, at work again), the rooftops and windows had begged this same question. At the movies, are we not all dreamers?

Some "dreams" that we encounter in movie theaters are complex. Its string of dupings and misleading appearances slyly commenting on a frantic race to locate a winning lottery ticket inside a poor boy's lost jacket, *Le million* is about tenuous rather than assured lives. Heavily in-debt artist Michel (René Lefèvre, epitomizing the charm of youth) must find and hold onto that jacket of his! Among other things, this will lead to one of the funniest passages in creation: on the opera house stage, the mime of a rugby scrum.

We dreamers get the happy ending we want—ah, but we're ever mindful of the social reality from which we and our co-dreamer, Clair, have effected young Michel's escape.

LA CHIENNE (France). Jean Renoir's first sound film, a tragicomedy from a low-grade novel, is a magnificent social portrait and an embittered analysis of money's pernicious role in everyday life. Maurice Legrand (Michel Simon, perfect) is a full-time cashier; sustaining him through a miserable marriage is his passionate avocation: painting. Naïvely failing to recognize her as a prostitute, one night, walking home, he meets Lulu, who is being beaten by Dédé (Georges Flammand, both creepy and brilliantly funny), whom he fails to recognize as her pimp. They have an affair, Maurice doesn't know, so that he can underwrite Lulu and Dédé's existence. But Maurice's wife, taking all his money, gives him a tiny allowance; so Maurice steals at home, embezzles at work. Eventually Dédé connects with an art dealer and Maurice's paintings, with which he has gifted Lulu, make money, but none at all for the artist. Maurice doesn't even get the credit; Lulu has signed them as "Clara Wood," purportedly an American. Maurice doesn't mind the shortchanging, though, so long as he has his Lulu. When he discovers that Lulu and Dédé are lovers and she derides him, however, in an offscreen fit of rage he stabs her to death. Circumstantial evidence lays the rap on Dédé, who is guillotined. Meanwhile, Maurice, who has lost his job as a result of the scandal, ends up a homeless tramp, at the last watching his self-portrait being carted away by a posh buyer.

Dark, biting, hilarious, Renoir's film shines brightest on a Montmartre street as residents, including children, gather around a street singer and a violinist, perhaps his daughter, as the killing occurs upstairs. When he picks up his coins, the singer—another impoverished artist —embodies Renoir's theme.

Fritz Lang's Hollywood remake, *Scarlet Street* (1945), is thin, tawdry, sensational.

1931

PHILIPS-RADIO (Netherlands). Generally, there are two kinds of industrial documentaries: those that celebrate the factory; those that decry it. Dziga Vertov's *Enthusiasm* (1931) belongs in the first category; Robert J. Flaherty's *Louisiana Story* (1948), in the second. Joris Ivens's Philips-Radio, a.k.a. *Industrial Symphony*, is the first Dutch sound film; it was commissioned by the Philips Eindhoven company, branches of which refused to show it. This film is openly ambivalent about the factory whose activity it shows.

Glass bulb blowing exerts its usual fascination; the strenuously puffed cheeks are no worse than afflicts a musician playing certain instruments. The tone is moderate; most of the film seems neutral—although at length this in itself projects something of the dehumanizing factory monotony of Jean-Luc Godard's *British Sounds* (1968) and *Pravda* (1970). (It is in *Numéro Deux/Essai Titres*, 1975, that Godard, along with Anne-Marie Miéville, offers his most comprehensive analysis and criticism of "the factory.") Indeed, the assembly line in *Philips-Radio* echoes the sweatshop, the same year, in Josef von Sternberg's *An American Tragedy*, based on Theodore Dreiser's novel. (In another shot or two, the film echoes Fritz Lang's silent *Metropolis*, 1926.) Smoke fogs up the air outside, and inside the factory a machine is identified by number and addressed over a loudspeaker. Ivens keeps the camera focused on the inhuman loudspeaker, but, of course, it is the person who is manning the machine who is being addressed. Thus this unseen worker is equated with the machine that he is manning: a stunning instance of dehumanization exposed—this, one year prior to René Clair's *A nous la liberté* (1932) and five years prior to Chaplin's *Modern Times* (1936).

Ivens's film expresses the ambivalence towards the factory that most of us, consciously or unconsciously, feel. Such progress—at such a human cost.

AN AMERICAN TRAGEDY (U.S.). Theodore Dreiser's gigantic, moody, sociologically dense *An American Tragedy* is, for me, the greatest American novel of the twentieth century. Like another 1925 book, F. Scott Fitzgerald's *The Great Gatsby*, it is about the collision between an upwardly mobile heart, perpetually courting social acceptance, and realities that conspire against it.

Josef von Sternberg's beautiful film version is a small gem, not the tremendous thing that Dreiser wrought. It is, Andrew Sarris has noted, essentially psychological, not sociopolitical. With its lyrical dissolves, achy loon, and romantic swank, George Stevens's glossy adaptation, *A Place in the Sun* (1951), is closer to *An American Tragedy* had Fitzgerald written it.

Dreiser based Clyde Griffiths on Chester Gillette, who was electrocuted at New York's Auburn Prison in 1908 for the murder of pregnant girlfriend Gracie Brown. The "crime" in both Dreiser's novel and Sternberg's film, but not in Stevens's sanctimonious travesty, is ambiguous. Phillips Holmes contributes an unerring portrait of a youth overwhelmed by childhood want, thwarted aspiration, and class anxiety. The son of mission evangelicals, Clyde has been beaten down not only by the world's "misery and evil" but by the self-righteous example of his mother's "goodness."

Sternberg treats factory worker Roberta sympathetically, casting humane, exquisite Sylvia Sidney, the "proletarian princess," in the role. His film opens with a shot of water—say, lake water—being continually disturbed by a thrown-in pebble generating concentric circles. Thus three meanings coalesce from the outset: the rowboat trip during which the pregnant Roberta, who cannot swim, will fall overboard and drown; by its future tense regarding Clyde's outcome, the idea of Fate; Sternberg's psychological slant—the idea of Clyde's unconscious, where his own sense of guilt for Roberta's drowning will disastrously suit the official proceeding of his murder trial.

The die is cast.

1932

¡QUÉ VIVA MÉXICO! (U.S.S.R., U.S.). *See above.*

1932

LAS HURDES (Spain). Luis Buñuel's Spanish documentary, known in the States as *Land Without Bread*, is a portrait of backward lives barely surviving in abject poverty. The Hurdanos are mountain villagers in a remote, nearly inaccessible region of Spain near Portugal. This study in "human geography," though, isn't what it seems.

To reach Las Hurdes, Buñuel's expedition must pass through La Alberca, a village the front of whose church is uninvitingly decked with two human skulls, and where men engage in an annual ritual in which they tear heads off roosters. At the end of the film, an ancient woman tells us, "There is nothing better to keep you awake than to think always of death."

The contrast between monotonous voiceover and bold images of human stupidity, as well as dire poverty, alerts us to Buñuel's ironical method. When the commentary notes how religious the Hurdanos are, but Christian rather than barbaric, but Christian and *seemingly* barbaric, Buñuel discloses his thematic purpose. His target isn't the inhabitants of La Alberca and Las Hurdes, nor is he out and about to bleed willing hearts over the difficulty of their lives—although he certainly wouldn't disparage the amelioration of that as a collateral boon. His target is forward, not backward, non-primitive Spain, whose infatuation with Roman Catholicism, with all its attendant superstition and occult ritual, the more primitive existence of his ostensible subjects reflects. Call *Las Hurdes*, then, an unmercifully ribbing backdoor satire. It is part of the film's overwhelming greatness that not one jot of the humanity of the Hurdanos is sacrificed in the process. But part of its causal analysis is that Spain's allegiance to Christianity maintains its pockets of cruel poverty.

And what of those roosters that get their heads torn off? How does *that* reflect on civilization? Think: *War.*

I WAS BORN, BUT . . . (Japan). Yasujiro Ozu's great social comedy *Otona no miru ehon—Umarete wa mita keredo* was made during his prolonged, defiantly silent period.

Promoted, Chichi Yoshii has just moved to a Tokyo suburb, near his boss, whom he immediately visits, to pay respects, because that's "the way to get ahead." If only Yoshii could "read" images as well as Ozu can create them! For the film opens with a closeup of the moving truck's wheel, stuck, spinning—an instance of the undercutting that the film lobs at Japan's hierarchic social structure, the principal target. Yoshii applies this hierarchy from work at home; but it becomes clear that his (generally genial) rule of the family roost is also an attempt at compensation for the humiliations that he suffers at work. Meanwhile, his boys, ages 8 and 10, are bullied by peers, including the boss's son, at their new school—until, that is, they become the reigning bullies themselves. Whose father is the best? They feel they've won this contest hands down—until they espy their father kowtowing to his boss. Exposed, Yoshii explains to his children the facts of socioeconomic life—like the mother in Blake's poem "The Little Black Boy," promoting a false lesson by endorsing the status quo.

This is shrewd, brilliant, sometimes hilarious stuff—and with such an eye, especially outdoors. In one stationery shot, with the low-hung camera tilted upwards, Yoshii performs morning exercises while two trains pass in either direction, the symbolical outcome: stasis—an ironical undercutting of Yoshii's workday get-go. A traveling shot of the boys trailing their father on the path home expresses their awe of him and the security that they feel in his presence.

With added sound and color, Ozu's 1959 *Ohayô* is a partial remake.

IVAN (U.S.S.R.). To ensure the nation's future success, laborers must work not only hard and spiritedly, but also competently, efficiently, skillfully. Teenaged Ivan, unschooled, leaves his country village to participate in the Dnieper River dam-building project. Eventually, he is amongst countless other youth in a huge lecture hall—an indication of the "book-learning" that must precede his becoming a responsible crane operator. Thus former science teacher Aleksandr Dovzhenko ends *Ivan* on a note celebrating education and the trainability of youth.

At the beginning, the tracking camera glides, seemingly endlessly, along the river, capturing the reflection of sky and trees in the water; cuts indicating the redirection of the camera add complexity to the liquid beauty. This long, mesmerizing passage accumulates into an image of perfect placid loveliness, but also, ironically, of idleness and complacency; thus the camera finally shifts to a symphony of crashing water—the power that the built dam will harness, to fuel the nation's progress.

At the industrial camp, a mother covers the corpse of her son, who has just been killed in a construction accident. His name also was Ivan—our hero might as easily have been the casualty—and it is the name of another, studious boy: the kind that the hero will himself become. This woman tears from her son's body on the ground and starts running; amidst noisy industrial machinery, dodging cranes and other devices that, shot from the vantage of low cameras, appear to be attacking her, she keeps running. Her destination: the office of the man in charge of the dam-building operation. Safety precautions must minimize the risk to *all* workers. This grieving woman evolves into a transcendent figure: Mother of the Working Class. Her son shall not have died in vain.

Alas, Dovzhenko lets *Ivan* drop from poetry into prose.

BOUDU SAVED FROM DROWNING (France). Boudu: "Why didn't you let me drown?"

Michel Simon is hilariously anarchic as a homeless tramp—this may be his greatest role—in Jean Renoir's satire of bourgeois Parisians, *Boudu sauvé des eaux*, from the play by René Fauchois. Boudu is taken into the home of a conscientious bookseller who has rescued him after he tries drowning himself in the Seine. (Simon's Boudu doesn't fit in, wreaks havoc with his clumsiness, to which he reacts with obliviousness bordering on abandon.) Renoir changed the play's ending, where Boudu accepts bourgeois responsibilities. Renoir's Boudu seems headed down that path, but after he marries the maid he "drowns" again by accidentally falling into the river while sitting next to his bride, leaving her behind and reclaiming his liberty.

The immediate reason for Boudu's original suicide attempt is that he cannot locate his dog, a scruffy mess like his master. The police will not help him, but they help a bourgeois woman find her expensive lap pet—less a cherished companion than the lady's prized completion of her superior self-image.

Bookseller Lestingois rescues Boudu to maintain a self-image of virtue that offsets guilt over his bourgeois attainments—a guilt we also see when he gives an impoverished student two books behind his wife's back.

Everyone but me sees Renoir's revised ending as an occasion for unblemished joy: Boudu is himself again, a tramp at liberty. I look at this a little differently: Boudu knows only how to be himself, and that's not enough. Discarding his wedding hat is an extravagant gesture; but what does it mean that the hat is obstructed in the water, stuck? Before, Boudu needed his dog in order to survive emotionally. He still doesn't have his dog, and he may again try to drown himself.

KUHLE WAMPE (Germany). Despite its brilliance, Bertolt Brecht wasn't pleased with Pabst's film of *Die Dreigroschenoper*. Therefore, he entrusted an original script of his (and Ernst Ottwald's) to Bulgarian-born Slatan Dudow, who had directed his work on stage. The result is *Kuhle Wampe oder: Wem gehört die Welt?* The question the title poses is this: To whom does the world belong?

In Weimar Germany, not much belongs to the people, whom ever deepening unemployment affects. Dudow's film, first, shows a family whose integrity is undermined by this predicament, and then ever more satirically suggests the irrationality to which this family and other families are driven in a utopian quest to ease their hardship and restore some sense of wholeness.

The opening movement is stark. Youths bicycle all day through Berlin streets from one work site to another in search of employment. No job is available. One of these boys is castigated by his parents for being jobless for seven months. He doesn't care; he isn't trying hard enough; he is rude and incompetent. Only his sister insists there are no jobs. The boy, demoralized, commits suicide. A neighbor comments: "One less unemployed." In an extraordinary montage, Nature expresses its apathy.

The family, once evicted, heads for Kuhle Wampe, a settlement camp in the country—a commune of sorts. Now Nature is beauteous, idyllic—but this second montage, because it is accompanied by a song, the singer all the while invisible, suggests that rosy Nature is the result of human projection. When the bodiless singer is immediately followed by a verbal description of naked primitive dancers, the puncturing humor hits bone. Even more absurdly, but in the same corporeal vein, the camp becomes a gigantic outdoor gym class, with everyone exercising.

Nothing, it seems, can be done for the nation's poor economic health.

WOODEN CROSSES (France). From the 1919 novel by Roland Dorgelès set during the Great War, Raymond Bernard's *Les croix de bois* bears comparison with G. W. Pabst's *Westfront 1918* (1930), from Germany. Two things distinguish Bernard's powerful antiwar film. One is its absence of conventional, detailed narrative; in effect, the war, by disrupting the lives of the combatants, has put their "stories" on hold. In lieu of story, we are given scenes in trenches, others in combat, and a few respites. The other intriguing aspect is the film's melding of styles; Bernard adds haunting touches of Expressionism to the film's overwhelming documentary realism.

The opening shot consists of rows of soldiers standing at attention in a field. It is an illusion that they are the living, for the image of them fades and we are left instead with a vast graveyard—rows and rows of cross-marked graves. Similarly, as much as anyone else, law student Gilbert Demachy (Pierre Blanchar, magnificent) comes to occupy the center of the action. Surely he will survive the ordeal of the war; yet the film, like *All Quiet on the Western Front* (both Remarque's novel and Milestone's 1930 film), concludes with the death of its protagonist.

While Germans audibly rig explosives underneath, entrenched French soldiers must wait for orders to evacuate—an encapsulation of war's madness and the disregard for the lives of soldiers.

In another phenomenal passage, the solo singing of "Ave Maria" fills a church. This hopeful, restful beauty is an illusion, however; the camera moves to reveal the makeshift hospital in the church, and when the singing is finished the moans of wounded soldiers can be heard.

Charles Vanel is superb as a dying soldier who curses his unfaithful wife before forgiving her for the sake of their young daughter.

AMERICAN MADNESS (U.S.). Written by Robert Riskin, *American Madness*, a great film of the Great Depression, may even be director Frank Capra's masterpiece. Perhaps he could be so patiently and penetratingly objective about the times because, a right-wing Republican (who veered into fascism with *Mr. Smith Goes to Washington*, 1939, and *Meet John Doe*, 1941), Capra wasn't seduced by the sentimental mythology of F.D.R., whom he politically opposed, or of the New Deal, which he also opposed. Capra sentimentalizes instead a bank president, Dickson (Walter Huston, tremendous), whose generosity in approving bank loans is backed by an analysis of an applicant's track record and talent. Dickson reasons in the case of a formerly successful though currently failing businessman that greater economic damage will be done if, denied his loan, the applicant must consign his hundreds of employees to unemployment. Dickson was based on Amadeo Giannini, whose working-class bank in San Francisco, The Bank of Italy, looked ahead to today's Grameen Bank in Bangladesh. Dickson may have helped to inspire a later character: Fredric March's Al Stephenson, the postwar banker who "bets on America" by easing loan restrictions for returning soldiers in William

Wyler's very moving *The Best Years of Our Lives* (1946).
About half of *American Madness* is taken up by a run on the bank triggered by a grinding local rumor mill after a sizeable bank theft: this, the apogee of Capra's artistic attainments. In particular, overhead inserts of the bank-running mob grip and horrify. The combination of Stephen Goosson's stunning steely design of the bank vault, Joseph Walker's dark, deep cinematography, and Capra's marvelous *mise-en-scène* locates the housing of the money in the cultural recesses of a nation's collective unconscious.

Pat O'Brien is wonderful as an ex-con whom Dickson has given a responsible job and mentored.

MICKEY'S GOOD DEED (U.S.). A great American film of the Great Depression, producer Walt Disney's *Mickey's Good Deed* is both heartrending and sharply satirical. Mickey Mouse and faithful dog Pluto are homeless at Christmastime; while Pluto pathetically moans on cue, Mickey plays "O Come O Ye Faithful" on his bass fiddle as seasonally compassionate passers-by drop coins into his cup. At last Mickey and Pluto can have something to eat; but as they approach a restaurant, Mickey discovers that only nuts and bolts have been deposited into his cup—a ruse that allowed people to "give" without sacrifice. They merely *played* at having the Christmas spirit, and meanwhile Mickey and Pluto may starve to death.

By contrast, Mickey makes a real sacrifice, selling Pluto to a family of rich pigs, hoping that Pluto at least will be well taken care of. (Pluto instead is abused by the spoiled little pig who had wanted him—and part of the abuse is sexually sadistic. Pluto is summarily kicked back out into the snow.) Mickey uses the money to play Santa, bringing toys to an immense family of kittens whose mother Mickey earlier glimpsed, through the window of her shack, crying at kitchen table. In an incredible image, Santa/Mickey, leaving, peers again through the window; the simulated long-shot shows the innumerable kittens each at play with a toy. The intricacy of activity suggests Heironymus Bosch.

Mickey has money left over to eat outdoors, his companion a snow figure of Pluto; but the real Pluto replaces the fake, filling the hole in Mickey's heart.

In its fantastical and simplified way, *Mickey's Good Deed* recalls Chaplin's *City Lights* (1930)—and suggests on what shaky footing even the closest of relationships can find itself under economic duress and the convenient rationalization of charity.

1933

NEW EARTH (Netherlands). In 1920, Dutch workers embarked on a massive project of reclaiming fertile land from the sea, draining it for agricultural use, and closing off the Zuiderzee, an inlet of the North Sea, to prevent flooding. Largely fashioned from his own material, Joris Ivens created *Nieuwe gronden*, a hymn to both humanity's struggle against Nature and the combined efforts of engineering and labor that sometimes succeeds at this struggle. By 1932, "3,680 acres have been planted. Ten thousand workers working in two shifts, 12 hours a day for 120 months, have conquered new ground. . . . However, the wheat of the world is not raised for food but for speculating." This shifts the focus of Ivens's brilliant documentary from the harvesting of wheat to the withholding of wheat from the market, calculated to keep the price of wheat high. Newsreel testimony of the current worldwide hunger crisis arrives in the film's stunning final movement.

Headlines: ENORMOUS GRAIN SURPLUSES, GRAIN PRICES AT RECORD LOW, GRAIN MARKET COLLAPSES, MILLIONS OF TONS OF HIDDEN GRAIN LIE ROTTING." Ivens inserts a new shot to accompany the narration, "There is too much grain and not enough work": in long-shot, against a cloudy sky (symbolizing the Depression), a line of men walk in single file into an unseen future.

More headlines: CHEMICALS USED TO RENDER GRAIN INEDIBLE, DESTRUCTION OF HARVEST. This in effect mocks the long, hard efforts of the Dutch workers we watched earlier. The narrator notes: "We're bursting with grain! Thirty-one

1933

million unemployed are starving worldwide." There is a massive hunger march in the U.S., where greedy capitalism is up to the same tricks at humanity's expense. Ivens inserts a shot of a starving child into a litany of crops that are being burned or tossed into the sea.

Justice waits.

DESERTER (U.S.S.R.). Proletarian solidarity across borders: German shipyard workers delay striking in order to complete an order that will fortify Soviet defense needs. During the strike, a young dockworker, starving, disillusioned, strays from the cause, deserting the picket-line. Like the farmer in Vsevolod I. Pudovkin's earlier *End of St. Petersburg*, Karl Renn's class consciousness is embryonic. It develops in Moscow, where he is sent as delegate to an international conference and sees for himself a just society founded in worker solidarity. He returns to help seed such possibilities at home.

A young woman distributes leaflets about the strike on the street. Authorities descend, and she takes off. As she hurriedly walks, every now and then she looks over her shoulder. Intercutting her flight is a police officer's apparent pursuit of her; but when the sequence is resolved, he is in fact walking towards her, not after her. In effect, the woman's agitation and fear bring her into the arms of the law—the object of her fear. What seems at first clever becomes psychologically penetrating.

A rapidly edited montage of shipyard labor is strengthened by sound effects, *Dezertir* being Pudovkin's first sound film. Sounds burst out of silence and frequently, accompanying one image, derive from action shown in the next image. Based on a theoretical manifesto that Pudovkin and Eisenstein had devised four years earlier, Pudovkin's use of certain sound effects is based on models of dialecticism and point-counterpoint; asynchronous sound (con)tests rather than reinforces image, with the combination of the two, the tension between them, generating an idea wholly contained in neither the image nor the sound—rather than dialectical montage, dialectical sound-image within a shot. For instance, a striker's whistling accompanies a shot of another striker's eating a sandwich: a harbinger of the hunger ahead for the momentarily carefree whistler.

PASSING FANCY (Japan). In the opening scene of Yasujiro Ozu's first silent about the working poor, *Dekigokoro*, the camera moves backward across rows of people seated on the floor. The pervasive use of hand fans conveys oppressive airlessness and heat, thus fragmenting with shared discomfort a unifying shot. Someone's wallet, accidentally misplaced, makes its way through the audience, one shot showing someone's hand picking up the thing, followed by a shot of the person as he guiltily peruses the contents before tossing the wallet away, whereupon someone else's hand reaches for it. One man disrupts the continuity of this repetitive event: the film's protagonist, brewery worker Kihachi, who picks up, checks and tosses away the wallet, like everyone else, but then reconsiders, picks the wallet back up, empties the wallet's meager contents into his own, smaller purse, and tosses the other, so it makes its way back to the owner in this reduced state, before which we see again the hand-pickup routine until a foot rather than a hand enters the frame, a visual "difference" recalling Kihachi's. Suddenly it isn't a wallet that's passing from person to person but unseen mosquitoes or fleas. In a single shot audience members stand up and start scratching—visually, a scene of harmony (within a single static shot, people behaving identically) undone by the fragmenting nature of people's identical discomfort. We never find out what has occurred: wide insect attack or an outburst of contagious behavior. Either way, it's hilarious.

Two harmonious relationships of single father Kihachi's are tested by the appearance of a woman in the poor Tokyo suburb: with his young son, Tomio, and with co-worker Jiro. All works out affectionately for the best, with a touch of life's inevitable rue and disappointment, in the context of family and community.

1933

MADAME BOVARY (France). One hopes that a film version of Gustave Flaubert's *Madame Bovary* will have something of the excitement of the 1856 original, whose realism refreshed the art form of the novel. Jean Renoir's film is one of his string of 1930s masterpieces. The opening is jaw-droppingly brilliant: the camera—in this instance, Emma Bovary's soul—turns leftward, revealing a patch of trees, in Normandy, on the grounds of country doctor Charles Bovary, eventually stopping at a clearing that allows us to see and hear, in long-shot, farm animals close to the modest house. In a single shot wife Emma's sparkling dreaminess passes into her squawking/oinking marital reality, where the camera gets stuck.

Renoir's sensitivity to interior space maintains the film's great (because functional) beauty. We glimpse Emma at a distance through doorways; when Charles shows her the secondhand carriage he has bought her, even the outdoors is constrained by the open window frame through which we watch them. When her mother-in-law, who lives with the Bovarys, insults Emma, who orders her to leave the house, an archway frames the depth of blackness into which Charles's mother disappears—a void also threatening to absorb Emma, who stands right at its edge. Women are so vulnerable in this world—a point that the recent death of Charles's first wife underscores.

The downward trajectory of Emma's life (adultery, financial stress, sickness, death) is rendered in all its details without excess of melodrama. Thus we are able to see, calmly, the role that money plays in ruining people's lives. Valentine Tessier is superb as Madame Bovary—not an enigma, like Isabelle Huppert in Claude Chabrol's fine version (1991), or a sentimentalized, mouth-twitching neurotic, like Jennifer Jones, whose ineptitude reduces Vincente Minnelli's version (1949) to grating soap opera and inadvertent farce.

DON QUIXOTE (Germany). Georg Wilhelm Pabst filmed his *Don Quixote*, from Cervantes, in German, French and English versions. It was his last film as a committed Leftist before capitulating to German nationalism and joining the Third Reich.

Little of the novel survives. In the abbreviated edition I saw, Pabst doesn't make room even for Dulcinea, the creature of his imagination upon whom Quixote lavishes his outmoded chivalry but who appears in the film as little more than a walk-on—and as real.

Two passages, however, are brilliant. One, thrillingly edited, finds Quixote tilting at windmills, which he perceives as opponents—giants—that endanger the common good. When the jouster becomes trapped in one of the windmill's radiating slats, the camera angle and proximity help make it appear as though Quixote, having propelled himself into it, is stuck in the page of a book.

Once he is back home, what's to be done with all the books on chivalry that dazzled and misled his mind? They are ceremoniously burned. But for the viewer, *Don Quixote* itself is the most monumental book ever written on the subject of chivalry. In closeup, the camera catches a book that has been burned to a crisp. The single greatest shot Pabst ever devised shows the *un*burning of this book in slow motion and reverse motion until, page by page, the book is restored to wholeness. The film ends on the title page: Cervantes' *Don Quixote*. Symbolically, Quixote himself has been reclaimed from the fire.

Russian-born Feodor Chaliapin is superb as Quixote. He speaks softly and humbly at times, but some regret the actor's declamatory style at other moments. Not me. This element of selfconsciousness is perfectly in keeping with the idea that this Don Quixote is enacting a role—that this Don Quixote has read *Don Quixote*!

QUATORZE JUILLET (France). The title *Quatorze Juillet* refers to Bastille Day, the national celebration of France's freedom from oppressive monarchal rule, symbolized by the French people's storming of the state prison in Paris in 1789, and of the people's embrace of self-determination, the first instance of this on the European continent, in the republican form of government that was formalized on the same day one year later. René Clair finds in the fragile nature of Jean and Anna's working-class romance—its susceptibility to jealousy, youthful pride and (in the person of Jean's former mistress) danger from the outside—a reflection of how fragile are the hard-won freedoms France cherishes.

This episodic film unfolds lightly, casually, although its comedy is epic: an expression of the French people. This lightness of tone, because of the fullness of spirit it releases, brings especial poignancy to the romance. *Quatorze Juillet* is as warm as *A nous la liberté* (1932), for all its technical daring and formal brilliance, is cold.

Were it not for the economic depression gripping Europe, elements of *Quatorze Juillet* would be incomprehensible. Among these are Jean's participation in a robbery attempt, which he himself ends up foiling in order to protect Anna. When he chases away children who have gathered around and are touching his taxi cab, Jean isn't being mean-tempered or possessive; this vehicle isn't a showpiece but a necessary means to his livelihood. Above all, the volatility of the romance, as Jean and Anna come together, part ways, cross paths, part, and come together again, reflects the uncertainty of the economic and political moment. One's heart is stirred by the potential of the imaginary couple, as though the future of France depends on it.

An unseen singing chorus represents the collective wisdom of Paris on the subject of love.

DUCK SOUP (U.S.). "Hail, Freedonia!"

Duck Soup is the funniest, most anarchic of the zany comedies made by the Marx Brothers. Moreover, it is perhaps the most brilliant political satire in American cinema.

The same year as Hitler's appointment as chancellor in Germany, Rufus T. Firefly (Groucho Marx) is appointed Freedonia's ruler. Attending the ceremony in his honor in the national palace, he wakes up with a cigar in his mouth and descends from his bedroom via a firefighter's pole. His mistress is the widow of Freedonia's previous leader. Firefly is a fascist. He orders execution for anyone who is found displaying any sort of pleasure in public. As he puts it: And pop goes the weasel! (Patriotic American tunes and historical allusions reveal the real identity of Freedonia.)

Meanwhile, Harpo and Chico Marx play bumbling spies for Sylvania, with which Firefly goes to war.

In perhaps the film's greatest comical set-piece, a music hall standard, Groucho-as-Firefly finds himself facing another Groucho-as-Firefly in an empty space in the palace that, to shield himself from discovery, the mimic (Harpo) tries to convince him is a mirror. A series of duplicated gestures extends the illusion, which is, however, broken when the two mirror-images pass through and around the presumed barrier of the looking-glass. Thus conformity is deconstructed into individualism before our very eyes—one of many blows to fascism this hilarious film effortlessly delivers.

Nominally directed by Leo McCarey, *Duck Soup*, a financial flop, ended the Marxes' association with Paramount, which had allowed their inspiration freer range than timid, selfconscious M-G-M would. The American public, absorbed by the Depression, would not be interested in the issues raised by the film until it found those issues at its front door.

Today, *Duck Soup* is universally cherished.

OKRAINA (U.S.S.R.). In "the backwaters of tsarist Russia," life exists at a sleepy remove: ducks feed in murkily reflective water; a man dozes in his spindly coach as his horse shakes its head, the epithet "Good God!" seemingly coming from it, but as likely coming from its come-to offscreen master; a smiling girl, alone on a bench, noting couples—and an alternate possibility of her future: an unhappy unattached woman. From the outdoor leisure of strolling couples, the camera cuts to a shoemaking workshop: an unseen woman's foot is measured; the sounds and sights of speedy mass labor. Thus begins Boris Barnet's inventive, comical *Okraina* (literally, *Outskirts*, a.k.a. *Patriots*), an early Soviet sound film, and a brilliant antiwar film.

Two things rouse the town: a factory strike, compelling the cobblers to stop cobbling and join their comrades in solidarity; German invasion and war. The latter is a touchstone of the plot regarding the girl on the bench and her father, one of whose tenants is a German friend with whom he plays checkers. War sets them to bickering, the tenant moves out and they are friends no longer. Later, the daughter becomes infatuated with a German prisoner-of-war, stealing him into the boarding house before, roused from sleep, her father tosses him out. The boy, the one shoemaker in town willing (and eager) to work, is beaten up by folk, as though the town were the front. Meanwhile, the scenes *at* the front are trenchant, disclosing the horror of war. An extreme long-shot of one surrenderer and a man from the other side coming peaceably together, each followed by a flurry of soldiers, is surpassingly moving, as is the weary march of prisoners-of-war into town. Gorgeous lyrical inserts of Nature mark the 1917 revolution. Tsarist Russia is no more.

KING KONG (U.S.). "Blondes are scarce around here."
King Kong is a movie about the making of a movie titled *King Kong*. Carl Denham takes his Depression-era crew deep into Africa to locate the gigantic gorilla that is worshipped by natives as a God. Eventually he captures Kong, with his golden leading lady as live bait, and takes it back to New York City in chains, to display it in a stage show. God, as "another roadside attraction," as Tom Robbins would say: this is one of the themes of *King Kong*, to whose story Edgar Wallace contributed. The directors are Merian C. Cooper and Ernest B. Schoedsack, the documentarians who made *Grass* (1925).
The film explores the difference between the kind of wonder that inspires religious faith and the more secular kind associated with such technology as the motion-picture camera. Along the way, it takes us civilized folk back into the past, where the pterodactyls flew and the dinosaurs roamed. It provides a thrilling adventure. Everything resonates within the framework of its thematic intentions; even the film's semi-sensational nature reflects on humanity's appetite to reduce the irreducible to manageable, and manipulable, proportions. The image that gloriously encapsulates this is, of course, terribly ironic: the (relatively) tiny blonde goddess in Kong's enthralled paw.
This film is awesome in its power. When it was first released, my mother and her sister Estelle went to see it. My poor aunt! She screamed in such terror that the theater manager had the projectionist stop the show. Today, there would be no such accommodation for intense human emotion. Thus, the whole point of the film has been lost. This is not to the detriment of the film but to the detriment of the rest of us.

1860 (Italy). *Risorgimento*: the period, 1848-1870, when partitioned Italy was unified, provides the basis for Alessandro Blasetti's patriotic *1860*, which culminates in the Battle of Calatafimi. A Sicilian village, under oppressive Bourbon occupation, rebels. Carmine, a young shepherd, travels to Genoa to solicit support for the local cause from the movement's leader, Italy's liberator, Giuseppe Garibaldi. The location shooting, the nonprofessional cast, the focus on an ordinary villager rather than, say, Garibaldi, and the national portrait that Blasetti achieves through Carmine all look ahead to *neorealismo* and, specifically, Roberto Rossellini's *Paisà* (1946). But the artful finish Blasetti applies to his film and its grand historical sweep also look ahead to Luchino Visconti's two treatments of *Risorgimento*: *Senso* (1954) and *Il Gattopardo* (1963).
The opening is indeed worthy of Visconti: a bare tree, its branches knotted and twisted, symbolizes Italy in foreign hands before unification; soldiers on horseback imperiously gallop, the camera low and tilted upward, with martial music soft, insistent on the soundtrack; one soldier pokes with a pole a dead peasant on the ground; another drags a peasant, his prisoner. The camera surveys the desolate land and shows fire and then water: a rushing stream symbolizing hope. Suddenly, as if out of nowhere, villagers appear on foot and attack the mounted monsters. The rebellion has not been extinguished; the people have not been conquered. Perspective on village losses is given, though, by what follows: a tracking shot across the ground—a scene of slaughter. *1860*'s opening movement may even have inspired

Sergei M. Eisenstein in the making of *Alexander Nevsky* (1938).
As perhaps did the Battle of Calatafimi, the tree now in bloom, at film's end. *1860* isn't in all respects a great film (its middle is largely pedestrian), but it is bookended by two passages of gripping poetry.

1934

MAN OF ARAN (UK). One of U.S. filmmaker Robert J. Flaherty's works of "re-created everyday life," *Man of Aran* documents the harsh existence of island villagers thirty miles off the western Irish coast. Using sparely lit interiors and the rough sea outdoors to stress the isolation of the villagers, Flaherty further "isolated" them—not in space but in time, and even, existentially, from themselves—by immersing them in an elaborately staged shark hunt as it would have been executed a century earlier. The result is cunning and complex; for this ploy places the villagers at something of a remove from their own lives comparable to their remove, in the present, from us. The "performance" accomplished another feat: these nonprofessionals could portray their perilous circumstance with reduced selfconsciousness. Finally, Flaherty was thus able to commit to film a practice from the past—in its particulars, an activity that had vanished.

Even balking purists, whose literalism may prevent their grasp of an immense gain of truth at the forfeit of a bit of reality, should find exemplary the film's technical coup: Flaherty's use of the telephoto lens, by which, miraculously, he is able to stay, simultaneously, both "inside" and "outside" the action of the hunt—this ability itself a metaphor for his involvement in the life of the village, where he lived for a while in preparation for the film.

Flaherty's spouse, Frances, assisted him in cinematographing in starkly beautiful black and white (Flaherty had had a small processing laboratory built on the island), and his brother, David, was another member of his group. What, together, they achieved is Flaherty's most poetic film, a work of timeless, haunting visual grandeur.

A STORY OF FLOATING WEEDS (Japan). One of Yasujiro Ozu's last silent films is *Ukigusa monogatari*. "Weeds" refer to an itinerant troupe of stage performers currently lighting in a remote mountain village. The film opens with their "floating" in, and closes with their "floating" out, by train.

The group's leader is Kihachi Ichikawa. He visits Otsune (Chouko Iida, superb), the mother of his son, a postgraduate student, whom Otsune has raised alone. Much of Otsune's life consists of waiting for Kihachi's next infrequent arrival. The boy, Shinkichi, doesn't know Kihachi is his father. As they fish together, father and son, shot from behind, cast their rods in near unison. But revelations and tensions during this visit will undo the harmonious image.

Everything in this humane, humanistic film yields to flux, instability, incompletion. Even the absence of sound seems to contribute to this thematic result.

Both arthritic, Otsune and Kihachi testify to aging—the passage of time. Kihachi is proud at how big his son has become since the last time he saw him. Planning on staying put for a year, presuming that his show will be, as usual, popular, Kihachi hopes to see a good deal of Shinkichi on this go-round. But the troupe also has lost its luster, or perhaps tastes have changed, and Kihachi will be leaving sooner than he thinks. So will Shinkichi. Irony compounds irony: the family that never was is about to dissolve, and Ozu's comedy drifts into familial tragedy.

Wind-rippled banners outside; the ephemera of cigarette smoke indoors: Ozu orchestrates images of fluctuation, evanescence. We who do not travel for our livelihoods: we, too, are "floating weeds." It is the impermanent nature of existence. It is what makes the heart ache even as we hold onto those we love.

Ozu remade the film in 1959.

1934

THREE SONGS OF LENIN (U.S.S.R.). The tenth anniversary of Lenin's death inspired Dziga Vertov to make the lyrical *Tri pesni o Lenine* celebrating the "friend and liberator of the oppressed"—a masterpiece somewhat disfigured by state-added rushes of propaganda at the opening and the close. (A 1938 makeover purged purged officials and edited *in* Stalin!) It proved to be Vertov's final feature; for the next two decades, the Soviet film artist whose soul was most deeply wedded to the avant-garde was relegated to making cursory newsreels for the state. Vertov died before deStalinization could liberate him.

The prologue is elegiac: shots of Lenin's home; a gentle breeze animating surrounding trees, nearby river; a photograph of Lenin on his favorite bench; shots of the now vacated bench: all these accumulate into a portrait of Lenin's spirit, the *presence* of his *absence*, his ongoing influence. Thereafter, the film is in three parts. Located in the Soviet East, "My Face Was in a Black Prison" is the first song, in which the heavy veil that women traditionally wore functions as a metaphor for oppression. One woman after another lifts her veil, revealing a smiling face and new opportunities: education; work. As part of his legacy, then, female empowerment reflects Lenin's spirit. "We Loved Him," the second song, is an epic disclosure of love, reverence and grief; Vertov expresses his personal feelings about Lenin through female faces—the most powerful, sensitive closeups since Dreyer's *Passion of Joan of Arc* (1928)—and crowds gathered to bid Lenin farewell. Old photographs, newsreels translate the deceased Lenin into the living Lenin who helped forge the nation. Lenin's bench, empty, now is covered with snow. The final song, "In the Great City of Stone," continues to pay tribute. "Come look at Lenin, and your sorrows will disappear like water."

THE LOST PATROL (U.S.). *See above.*

TONI (France). Based on an actual crime dossier, Jean Renoir's *Toni* realistically depicts ordinary lives, thus departing from the theatrical or lyrically impressionistic styles that had dominated French cinema. Renoir filmed on location in Martigues, a village in southern France, blending local residents and professional actors and directly recording sound.

Immigrants from Italy and Spain have come to Martigues in order to work. Antonio Canova, "Toni," arrives by train from Italy, grateful for the opportunity to work as a quarryman but already homesick, as are others, as their singing suggests. Track laborers exchange remarks as the train passes, one expressing antipathy for these interlopers but the other noting that the men, like themselves, simply want to work in order to survive. Over the course of three years, a couple disintegrates and two bad marriages result. Toni, although innocent, is shot dead for an ensuing marital murder. Another trainload of immigrant workers and their families pulls in; in the closing shot, they are walking to their new lives, the children in particular appearing uprooted.

Some of the shots are extraordinarily complex, such as a deep-focus one in which Toni and a fellow worker converse high up in the foreground while in the background, far below, others are busily in motion: a two-person closeup and a long-shot, juxtaposing minimal movement (conversation) and considerable movement (work), within the same frame. Thus film historian Eric Rhode refers to the film's "socializing [of] space." The one gorgeously lyrical shot, as a woman rows across a lake, is cuttingly ironic: she is about to pretend a suicide attempt—a reflection of her unhappy marriage. Tracking shots of workers walking are typical of Renoir's liberating method.

Coincidentally, an Italian immigrant named Luchino Visconti assisted Renoir. Thus his *Ossessione* eight years hence, and the birth of Italian neorealism.

BORINAGE (Belgium). A silent Belgian companion-piece to Ivens's Dutch *New Earth* (1933), *Borinage*, co-directed by Ivens and Henri Störck, also shows capitalism run amok during the 1930s worldwide depression. "Factories are closed, abandoned, and millions of the proletariat go hungry." Food—coffee, wheat and milk—is destroyed—drowned, burned or spilled—so that lower market prices won't endanger the profits of capitalists. A different mindset is indicated on the placard that marching protestors carry: "God doesn't want death and starving children any more than women do."

A 1932 strike by coal miners is reconstructed, partly through the agency of a fifteen-year-old miner who is introduced walking above-ground in a traveling shot that teases us with what *should* be his condition: physical freedom; freedom from care. The reality is that this boy must work to support himself and his widowed mother. To cut costs, mine owners have reduced security measures; deaths of miners are the result. People are without water or electricity; homes are being dismantled for firewood. There are countless evictions; owners of the mines are also the landlords. Opposing this is the solidarity of ordinary people; by leaning on furniture, men prevent one woman's eviction "at least for the moment."

Ivens and Störck show the ruined barracks where mining families stay post-eviction; the diagonal perspective makes the row of units appear gloomily endless. These lightless "abodes" are like short mine tunnels.

A long pan of mounds of waste: "Enormous stocks of coal, estimated at four million tons, lie rotting ... The stocks grow, as does the number of the unemployed."

A demonstration that was staged for the film ignited the hearts of its regional participants, turning the show into the real thing and drawing a violent response from the police. Initially, the film was widely banned.

TWENTIETH CENTURY (U.S.). Frank Capra's wonderful *It Happened One Night* won 1934's best picture Oscar, but, that year, Howard Hawks made a sharper, nervier "screwball" comedy: adapted by Ben Hecht and Charles MacArthur from a Charles Bruce Millholland play, *Twentieth Century*. Hawks continued to excel in this genre: *Bringing Up Baby* (1938), *His Girl Friday* (1940), *I Was a Male War Bride* (1949) and *Monkey Business* (1952).

The plot involves an egotistical theatrical producer and his increasingly egotistical star, brilliantly and hilariously played by John Barrymore and Carole Lombard. Much of the film's most interesting material whirls around the lead characters, in particular, during a transcontinental trip aboard the train the Twentieth Century; for Hawks, in a darker vein than one might think that the plot would allow, explores issues of the Great Depression. For one of these, imperiled finances, the unpredictability of theatrical fortunes provides an apt enough occasion. But there is onboard the train, escaped from an insane asylum, a former corporate head who is now a pauper prone to writing bad checks and pasting onto windows and passengers' apparel, without their knowledge, a sticker that reads, "Repent! The time is at hand." This apocalyptic message reflects the uncertainty of the times and, also, the nutty allure of religion as antidote to this uncertainty. Two other passengers are European actors who star in a play based on the Passion of Christ; stranded in America, they beg for money because they want to go home. If they are to starve to death, they would prefer it to happen in familiar surroundings.

Twentieth Century, for all its frantic comedy, is as much a descent into torment as Hawks's gangland classic, *Scarface* (1932), two years earlier.

THE BLACK CAT (U.S.). Grim, remorseful, Viennese-born Edgar G. Ulmer's *The Black Cat* is a meditation on the human cost of the First World War in Europe. The war cast a psychic shadow, creating a group of survivors who regarded themselves as "the living dead." (Hence the spate of vampire and quasi-vampire films in Germany, France and the U.S. in the 1920s and early 1930s.)

The film unfolds in a mountainous stretch of Eastern Europe. Its protagonist is Hungarian psychiatrist Vitus Verdegast (Bela Lugosi, brilliant), a prisoner of war who, since his release from the Russian internment that—these are his words—slowly killed his soul, has been seeking his former commander, Hjalmar Poelzig (Boris Karloff); for Poelzig, a traitor to the Austro-Hungarian cause, sold his troop to the Russians in the war, and he also appropriated

Verdegast's young wife. Verdegast has tracked down Poelzig to the very site of the fort that became a field of slaughter because of Poelzig's betrayal. An architect, Poelzig has built a twisted, modernist mansion on the site, a projection of the tormented soul of Europe, in whose basement the beautiful women he has murdered for the religious rites of the satanic cult he heads are preserved, each suspended in a glass case. This transfigured catacomb— each case is lit from below to render the preserved corpse "spiritual"—becomes the film's most entrancing visual disclosure of Europe's doomed attempt to repress, transform and transcend a horrible past. The eerily forward-moving, seemingly floating camera as Poelzig takes Verdegast on a tour of this lowest level of the mansion, with Poelzig's disembodied grave voice directing the tour, precedes the disclosure of Verdegast's dead wife in one of the upright, transparent tombs.

Here is a horror film of profound import, climaxed by Verdegast's skinning Poelzig alive, shown in ghastly silhouette.

SONG OF CEYLON (UK). Commissioned to make travelogues publicizing the Ceylon Tea Propaganda Board, budding British documentarian Basil Wright made instead something else —just what precisely is debatable. Producer John Grierson thus defined the point of *Song of Ceylon*: "Buddhism and the art of life it has to offer, set upon by a Western metropolitan civilization which, in spite of all our skills, has no art of life to offer." Once a routine entry on lists of the all-time ten best films, Wright's *Song* is rarely sung anymore for its perceived chauvinism, although Wright may be ironically undercutting chauvinistic notions voiced in the late seventeenth-century text (by Robert Knox) that the film's narration draws upon. Everyone agrees that the film is lyrical.

The 40-minute film is divided into four parts: "The Buddha," "The Virgin Island," "Voices of commerce," "The Apparel of the Gods."

The opening tests the possibility of Wright's irony. Ceylon's "dark forest," which the narrator (quoting Knox) says existed "since ancient times," plants the land and its people in the symbolical "darkness" of ignorance, backwardness. But the accompanying tracking shot through forest is most striking for shafts of intense sunlight! The narrator proceeds to describe natives as making themselves "prostrate to the Devil" at night; but the accompanying image of grotesquely masked figures dancing in fire-lit darkness is sufficiently fantastic to suggest a dream, one perhaps lodged in the "civilized" Western mind that, we cannot help but note, presumes a literal belief in the Devil! In any case, the narration explains that Buddhism replaced such devil-worship as the film moves from night to day and from gaudy, pulsating closeups to orderly long-shots. We suddenly realize that the devil-dance is a performance, a reconstruction.

Wright's beautiful film is ripe for revisiting.

Ceylon today is Sri Lanka.

1935

THE CRIME OF MONSIEUR LANGE (France). When Jacques Prévert wrote for Marcel Carné (*Le jour se lève*, 1939; *Les enfants du Paradis*, 1945), the result would be fatalistic; but his one collaboration with Jean Renoir, *Le crime de Monsieur Lange*, is bursting with life and humanity. The son of Impressionist painter Pierre-Auguste, Renoir enjoyed his greatest period in the 1930s, when he was a sort-of communist. His masterpiece, Renoir's *crime* fits his politics—and soul.

Lange is an exploited young worker in a publishing firm. His alter ego is Arizona Jim, the adventurous, liberated character about whom he writes in his spare time. When his boss disappears, the boy and his co-workers transform the business into a cooperative. But guess who unexpectedly returns, disguised as a priest? What's to be done?

The workers' cooperative expresses the communard in Renoir. France's regrettable history on this score, her willed amnesia regarding her ill-fated 1871 political experiment in Paris, makes the cooperative in the film a thing to be cherished—an imaginary opportunity for France to redeem a part of the past. As far as movies go, the moral choice of the decade falls to those in the border town who must decide whether to turn in to the police Lange's loyal girlfriend and the fleeing "criminal," who dispatched (as Jules Berry plays him) a smarmily charming embodiment of evil, or let the couple go on their way across the border. It is remarkable how the situation predicts moral choices that persons in the same nation would face during the next decade. But even if one discounts this touch of prophecy, movies don't get more profoundly (as distinct from artificially) exciting than this.

With its fresh invention and moral vigor, *Le Crime de Monsieur Lange* anticipates the *nouvelle vague* by two decades.

AN INN IN TOKYO (Japan). Yasujiro Ozu's *Tokyo no yado* is a silent film about a homeless family—Kihachi, an unemployed father, and his two small sons—at a time of national economic crisis. His becomes an extended family when it unites with another homeless pair, a mother and her daughter. Kihachi ends up a thief.

The film opens on the road, in the industrial outskirts of Tokyo, the Koto district, as Kihachi, accompanied by his children, tries to find factory work. His wife has abandoned them, probably because of the family's poverty, and her dogging absence implies a kind of cosmic abandonment. With his meager resources, Kihachi must often choose between food and temporary shelter for himself and his children. Also, as Kihachi begs and begs for work, his morale is increasingly laid low. Moreover, tensions crop up between him and his sons, whose sense of entitlement to his taking care of them is frustrated by circumstances they minutely perceive but do not totally grasp. Ozu, then, shows us poverty in a depressed time and place and the resultant family dynamics.

As these circumstances press Kihachi towards crime, the film seems closer to Bresson's *Pickpocket* (1959) than to the postwar neorealism of Vittorio De Sica's *Bicycle Thieves* (1948), with which it is often compared. Still, Ozu's film is most expressive in portraying Tokyo's industrial hinterlands, a sunbaked wasteland with smoke-belching factories in the background. Gigantic spools lying on the ground, shorn of cables, encapsulate an expanse of land bereft of productivity. Their heightened, surreal tangibility, like the sights of factories that taunt Kihachi with the illusion of work possibilities, contrasts with a "family picnic" at which Kihachi and sons, pantomiming, pretend to treat their palates and fill their stomachs with imaginary food.

THE DEVIL IS A WOMAN (U.S.). "I kissed you because I loved you—for a minute."

Josef von Sternberg and Marlene Dietrich made seven films together. The best are the first and the last: from Germany, *The Blue Angel* (1930) and, from the U.S., *The Devil Is a Woman*, from a novel by Pierre Louys that Luis Buñuel would later film as *That Obscure Object of Desire* (1977). As Concha Perez in turn-of-the-century Seville, a woman who treats men as puppets on a string, Dietrich acts magnificently, giving a great comedy performance.

However, while Concha inhabits an ironical comedy, two of the men who love her, best friends, inhabit a different universe, one that veers between poles of melodrama and tragedy owing to their self-importance and self-pity.

Much of the narrative consists of Pasqual, a retired army officer, trying to convince Antonio, a young revolutionary fleeing authorities, not to keep his assignation that night with Concha because of his own bad luck with the woman, which flashbacks relate. Pasqual's wealth and self-involvement, though, distort aspects of his recollections. For instance, all the women in the sweatshop where Concha works smile at their labor in seeming contentment—a discrepancy underscored by the fact that Pasqual is part of an official contingent investigating labor practices at this cigarette factory. Similarly, Pasqual appears oblivious to the nature of the place where he later discovers Concha working: a bordello. All that concerns him is that Concha manipulates him to have him buy her way out of her contractual arrangement with the madam running the place. Sternberg creates a complex vision of how men easily discount female poverty and desperation, and of what women may be driven to do in order to survive. The devil is a woman—so long as a certain kind of man tells the tale.

THE INFORMER (U.S.). Dublin, 1922, during the Irish Rebellion. In with the fog is Frankie McPhillip, I.R.A. member on whose head the British have set a £20 bounty. He is informed on by Gypo Nolan, who, court-martialed out of the Organization months earlier, hasn't been able to earn money, the British and the Irish both mistrusting him. During the long, dark night, Gypo spends the money, leaving a trail of the evidence that convicts him at the secret court of inquiry into Frankie's murder.

John Ford's tremendous *The Informer*, from Liam O'Flaherty, generates compassion for Gypo, whose consignment to a no-man's-land prompts his betrayal of his best friend after his girlfriend wishes aloud for £10 so that they can book passage to America. Ford excels at his portrayal of a fear- and shadow-ridden police state and of the poverty and oppression that trample hope and encourage desperate, morally clouded acts. Redeeming Gypo is his guilty regret. Shot by the Organization to ensure his survival, he stumbles into church and confesses his crime to Frankie's grieving mother, who forgives him. With his last breath he addresses the image of the crucified Christ: "Frankie, do you hear that? Your mother forgives me!"—one of the most moving finishes in cinema.

Drawing upon German Expressionism, *The Informer* is highly poetic and, at times, almost dreamlike, as in the case of the blind man, propped up by his cane, whose path keeps crossing Gypo's, embodying both his shame and his doom.

Victor McLaglen is more than twice the right age to play Gypo, but his phenomenal acting won him an Oscar. Ford's direction, Dudley Nichols's script and Max Steiner's music also won Oscars. Because *Mutiny on the Bounty* won the top prize, Ford quipped, "They liked everything about the picture except the picture."

AEROGRAD (U.S.S.R.). A sequel to his astounding *Earth* (1930), Aleksandr Dovzhenko's *Aerograd* (a.k.a. *Frontier*) likewise assaults kulaks, Old Believers (Christians) whose selfish desire to maintain private ownership of land contests the right of the Soviet people, by virtue of the Bolshevik Revolution, to claim this land as their own. In *Earth*, land specifically refers to farmland, and the state's structuring of shared ownership is collectivization. *Aerograd* instead refers to the nation's eastward expansion, its (to use an American term) manifest destiny. The land in this instance is subject to conquest; the goal is to build a new city—the city of the future: Aerograd.

For once with Dovzhenko, none of the main characters is Ukrainian. One, a young soldier who embodies the "air city" to be built in the Siberian East, is guardian of the Soviet future. The other two are old comrades now divided by the Communist state; one is a frontier guard protecting the land from the infiltration of spies and the machinations of traitors, while the other is a hunter who is both spy and traitor. The guard eventually dispatches his old friend. Dovzhenko's feeling of betrayal by a revolution that produced a Russia-dominated nation, giving his beloved Ukraine short shrift, contributes a bleedingly personal chord in an otherwise largely impersonal film.

Two more elements are decisive in the film's favor. One is its black-and-white description of the Siberian *taiga*, especially shimmering forests below incandescent skies—images of unspoilt Nature that suggest the wholesome Soviet future to which the film looks ahead. Moreover, no other film has even remotely approached this one in the spectacular, stirring nature of its airborne scenes. Dovzhenko throughout, and especially at the close, creates visual symphonies of air flight that knock the legs out from under one and send the spirit soaring.

THE 39 STEPS (UK). The film that made Alfred Hitchcock famous, *The 39 Steps* is an espionage thriller in which the protagonist, who is being pursued by the police for a murder he did not commit, is an ordinary bloke rather than a professional spy. He is in pursuit of a villainous agent who is attempting to sneak out of Britain a complex series of technical specifications—the MacGuffin here—that will place the nation's security at risk. (Hitchcock: "[The MacGuffin] is the mechanical element that usually crops up in any story. . . . in spy stories it is almost always the papers.") They are stored in the brain of Mr. Memory (Wylie Watson, heartrending), a music hall performer who commits to memory an ever expanding wealth of facts.

The intrigue takes the protagonist, Richard Hannay, from his West End flat to Scotland; a visiting Canadian, he is thus doubly cast adrift. Visually, he often appears in the sites of those chasing him as a dot, in long-shots, fleeing across ravishing, dreamlike mountainous landscapes. Indeed, much of the film resembles a gorgeous yet distressing dream, complete with shifting or masked identities, where the villain, masquerading as a benign university professor, remarks, "I am not what I appear to be." Perversely, like Hitchcock he has a daughter named Patricia, and he is missing part of a finger: what identifies him.

There are vignettes of entrapment and escape along the way, including an unconvincing one involving a fanatically religious farmer who abuses his younger wife.

Fast-paced, the film is also a brilliant screwball comedy in which Hannay ends up handcuffed to a blonde who at first won't believe he is innocent. At the close, backs to the camera, they silently find each other's hand to hold: a powerful finish.

1936

GRETA GARBO (Sweden, Germany, U.S.). Grace, irony, gravity, timeless loveliness: Greta Garbo is cinema's most enchanting tragedienne—all in all, its greatest actress. From Selma Lagerlöf's 1891 novel, Mauritz Stiller's *The Saga of Gösta Berling* (1924), sparkling with feminism and romantic passion, is the Swedish silent that made Stiller's teenaged discovery a star. G. W. Pabst's *The Joyless Street* (1925) made her an *international* star as Greta, the soul of innocence vulnerable to corruption in economically depressed Germany. For the next dozen years the Swedish actress dominated the medium that grew in renown largely for presenting her. Hollywood beckoned. Sound arrived; "Garbo talks!" the studio advertised, and Garbo became a star again with her magnificent enactment of O'Neill's *Anna Christie* (Clarence Brown, 1930), a child already hauling a heavy past. She is brilliant as the stormy ballerina Grusinskaya in *Grand Hotel* (Edmund Goulding, 1932) whose near co(s)mic exhaustion—"I want to be alone!"—fresh romance reverses even as a bullet, unbeknownst to her, has canceled her happiness: stillness in heartbreaking constant motion. She is intricate, thrilling, deeply moving as "Maria," who insists on truth and others' believing in her in the midst of what may be an impersonation, in *As You Desire Me* (George Fitzmaurice, 1932), from Pirandello. Emphatic, overdirected, her *Queen Christina* (Rouben Mamoulian, 1933) intrigues nevertheless; and her solemn *Anna Karenina* (Brown, 1935) is superb. Rising to the peak of her gracious, captivating beauty and talent, she is transcendent as Marguerite Gautier, the Lady of the Camellias, in *Camille* (George Cukor, 1937), possibly cinema's greatest performance. *Ninotchka* (Ernst Lubitsch, 1939) proved her peerless at satirical romance. ("Garbo laughs!") Soon after, the world's most famous working woman retired. Europe, on whose box office returns her career profitability largely depended, was at war, and Garbo receded ever deeper into myth.

MODERN TIMES (U.S.). A comic strip of a movie, Charles Chaplin's *Modern Times* satirizes industrial capitalism and its mania for efficiency, and the dehumanization and exhaustion these foster. At film's end Charlie is on the road, accompanied by a gamin, searching for the home in America that hopefully lies somewhere ahead.

The film opens with a full-screen clock approaching six o'clock, the morning hour that sets American blue-collar workers into motion for the daily grind. An overhead shot of penned sheep forced through a chute dissolves into another overhead shot, of a pack of factory workers, on their way to work, moving up into the street from a subway station—a mechanical routine these souls passively enact.

Whether as factory assembly-line worker, shipyard worker, night watchman on perilous roller skates, or singing waiter whose "song" is utterly nonsensical, Charlie tries his hardest. It's on the assembly line—Henry Ford's invention—that we meet him. Electro Steel's maniacal surveillance and control of its workers define his workday. Charlie's single small job is to tighten nuts, with two wrenches, on every unit that passes him on the conveyer belt. Increased productivity has transformed the workplace into a torture chamber. Lunch is on the way out, given the Billows Feeding Machine that's tested out on poor Charlie: an automated system for speeding up workers' lunch time. Rather than providing him with a restorative respite, his "lunch break" now intensifies the degree to which Charlie is a slave to the factory's drive for profits, no matter the cost to employees. Having thus psychologically "merged" with factory apparatus, Charlie, back on the assembly line, ends up being "eaten up" by the machinery after falling onto the conveyer belt, becoming literally a cog in the gear-turnings: an hilarious metaphor for the mental battering factory workers experience.

A DAY IN THE COUNTRY (France). Light, tragic, Jean Renoir's *Une partie de campagne*, from Maupassant, is exquisitely ironical.

Townsfolk on a Sunday 1860 country outing, Dufour, a Parisian shopowner, noting carnivorous fish, and his employee look down at the river from a rowboat. Both speak of Nature as something separate; but the camera lithely dips down to catch their watery reflections, visually implicating them in the rapacious aspect of Nature they miss seeing in themselves. They agree that Nature remains a "closed book"; with gentle mockery, the camera slips back up—a book-closing gesture!—to the combined portrait of their complacency.

The employee is daughter Henriette's fiancé—a bourgeois arrangement. Intimately conversing, mother and daughter sit on the grass. Nature is achingly open to Henriette (Sylvie Bataille, glorious), engaging her tenderest sympathy—brimming feelings she cannot explain. Henriette asks Mme Dufour if she ever felt that way. "Sometimes I *still* do," her mother confesses, her foolish mask, hiding marital disappointment, briefly giving way to warm humanity.

Two strangers, working-class youths, pair off with mother and daughter while Dufour and his future son-in-law fish and nap. Alone in the woods, Henriette and shy Henri, emboldened by Nature, make tremulous love, fall deeply in love. Nature, adoring this new couple, sparkles before turning dark and stormy on a breeze; for the pre-existent marital arrangements, bound by class considerations and family-sanctified, cannot budge. In a one-year-later coda, both their lives shattered, boy and girl chance upon one another as each separately haunts the scene of their moment together. A scattering of words passes between them. They part, now for the last time.

Curiously, despite Renoir's professed intention to finish this film after the war, it already is complete.

Cousin Claude Renoir's beauteous cinematography is lyrical, light-sensitive; Joseph Kosma's music, enchanting wistful, piercing.

WE, FROM KRONSTADT (U.S.S.R.). The 1917 October Revolution did not settle smoothly into Russia; in 1919 civil war pitted the Bolshevik victors against counterrevolutionaries, the Reds and the Whites. The first decade of sound had already produced an outstanding film about the Russian Civil War: *Chapaev* (1934), by the (unrelated) team of Sergei and Georgy Vasiliev. *My iz Kronshtadta* was another.

A unit of sailors from coastal Kronstadt is mobilized to defend Petrograd from the White seige against it. This confrontation underscores the contemporary need for Soviet vigilance against current enemies.

My iz Kronshtadta was written by Vsevolod Vishnevsky, who at 17 had fought in the First World War and, as a Red, in the 1917 revolution and subsequent civil war. Efim Dzigan's strikingly beautiful film owes much of its authenticity to the experience that informed Vishnevsky's script. However, Dzigan's filmmaking also is wonderful. Consider the Baltic Sea approach of the White vessel to Kronstadt: three shots, beginning with a long-shot of the ship, followed by progressively closer shots of it. The ship appears to move effortlessly screen-right throughout the sequence; stealthy silence further renders the movement dreamlike. The camera does not move, and therefore the ship's progress becomes an invasion of *space*: an eerie and powerful evocation of *the idea of invasion* as well as an action suited to that idea.

Many other scenes are equally memorable: the Kronstadt detachment and other Red warriors sleeping on the floor and steps of the children's home, and they and the young children interacting the next morning; the advancing singing battalion, their voices struggling against the din of gunfire (thus associating the Reds with art and its affirmation of life), with the added poignancy of the death of one of them—a final stilling of his voice; the drowning murders of all but one of the captured sailors, each with a heavy rock tied to him and his hands tied behind his back, some pushed from a ledge into the sea, others electing to drop of their own accord; their caps washing to shore; dressed as a woman, the sole survivor's rowing to Kronstadt against a turbulent tide; the tracking shot of an expanse of slaughter; the Red band playing music as battle rages; the final battle, with Reds marching and cowardly Whites (in contrast to Reds earlier) leaping to their deaths into the sea.

The film ends as one marching sailor asks aloud of all Soviet enemies, "Who will take Petrograd now?"—a stirring finish to an irresistible film.

THE PLOW THAT BROKE THE PLAINS (U.S.). Various departments of the U.S. government routinely churn out documentary, propaganda and training films of one kind or another, but, for a brief spell during the Depression, thanks to documentarian Pare Lorentz, there existed what might be called a national American cinema. Heavily influenced by silent Soviet cinema, *The Plow That Broke the Plains* is nevertheless darker and more self-critical than that visual influence suggests. The film is too weather-beaten to be celebratory.

Its subject matter is land erosion; Lorentz's film might be called a deconstruction of the Great Depression, at least from the point of view of topography and agriculture. What can we learn from the crisis our nation and its people is currently enduring? Granted, aspects of the crisis were always out of our control; but what have we done wrong that has contributed to the crisis?—what might we have done differently?

The Plow That Broke the Plains is also a piece of poetry, finding in the topic of land erosion an implicit metaphor for America's torn, beaten, eroded spirit. Its awesome view of a ravaged Great Plains shows the need for remedial federal activism (the Leftist cause it is promoting), which would come in the form of the National Recovery Administration. Thus government, the repository of the people's hope and enlightened behavior, would help repair both eroded land and eroded lives. Responsive, coordinated federal action might make America whole again.

For all its measure of hope, however, this remains a bracing film. Through a succession of finely etched, powerful black-and-white images, Lorentz's *Plow* amasses an overwhelming record not only of Nature's assault on humanity but also of an irresponsible people's complicity.

LA VIE EST A NOUS (France). Commissioned by the Popular Front in anticipation of French elections, made by a collective of Leftist French filmmakers headed by Jean Renoir and including Jacques Becker, *La vie est à nous* (variously translated as *Life Is Ours*, *Life Is with Us*, *Life Is for Us*) combines newsreels, lectures, staged vignettes, and songs. (We hear at

1936

the conclusion the "Internationale.") Its agitprop directly influenced Jean-Luc Godard's filmmaking. The film was commercially released in 1969, that is, following the events of May 1968. During his postwar conservative makeover, to help ensure a viable renewed career at home, Renoir (who also appears in it) dismissed his involvement with the film—much as Pabst had downplayed his role in the Third Reich's film industry!

In one sequence, Jean Dasté plays a schoolteacher, as he had in Jean Vigo's *Zéro de conduite* (1933), who tells his class about the concentration of national wealth in the hands of a relatively few families and about capitalism's management of employment/ unemployment. Thus a real adult audience indirectly receives the lecture that the "stage" students directly receive—an attempt to educate French citizenry about sociopolitical forces arrayed against it, so that ordinary people can better oppose these on the basis of their own welfare *and the welfare of their children*. Brilliant.

Unemployment indeed seems to be the principal issue on which the Left focused for the upcoming French elections. In another vignette, an unemployed man considers joining a fascist group before another alliance, the Young Communists, rescues him from this fate. U.S. Americans will recall the comparable presidential claim that Robert F. Kennedy and, after his assassination, George Wallace made on identical segments of the disaffected American electorate. To ideologues, politics may be clear-cut. For ordinary voters, it can be up for grabs.

OSAKA ELEGY (Japan). Kenji Mizoguchi's first great film, *Naniwa erejî*, tells a complicated story, the through-line of which is this: Ayako Murai, a young telephone switchboard operator, becomes a kept woman in order to spare her father imprisonment after he has been caught embezzling, falls to being something in between a kept woman and a prostitute in order to pay her brother's college tuition, and lands in the gutter, becoming a streetwalker, after her family tosses her out because she no longer meets their standards of respectability. Men thus use women, and women pay the consequences.

Critic Michael Grost has noted the indebtedness of Mizoguchi's visual style here to Josef von Sternberg's. Richly layered black-and-white compositions; luminosity; the extraordinary complexity of visual tones within a shot; "outdoor" camera movements detecting characters, indoors, through windows—all these suggest Sternberg's influence, along with the feminist theme and the focus on, even obsession with, a female character. In place of Dietrich, Mizoguchi has Isuzu Yamada, whose performance as Ayako is brilliant.

But Mizoguchi eschews the glamorous closeups by which Sternberg tends to canonize female suffering. *Osaka Elegy* is a "distanced" film consisting of long-shots and longish medium shots—until the end when, joltingly and piercingly, Ayako, suddenly and forever a prostitute, seemingly walks into and through the camera: a shot to die for. What a contrast between this and another moment outdoors at night, with rows of tall, daunting buildings lining the street in depth, and a solitary soul walking across a cross-street in the distant background: a dot. Here, in the tiny figure, is the beseiged humanity that Ayako represents. The buildings—a superlative instance of realism yielding to Expressionism—represent the patriarchal and related forces arrayed against Ayako and others.

What gorgeous work Mizoguchi gets from his cinematographer, Minoru Miki.

SWING TIME (U.S.). Fred Astaire is Lucky, dancer and gambler, and Ginger Rogers is Penny, dance instructor, in their most brilliant musical, *Swing Time*.

Having been tricked by fellow performers, who don't want him to leave their show and cost them their jobs, Lucky misses his wedding; and he and his new girl, Penny, lose their first chance to dance together professionally—as it were, Lucky loses his new lucky Penny—through the fault of neither, although Penny, in denial over how unlucky Lucky (and, by extension, she herself) is, chooses to blame him nevertheless. Everything seems topsy-turvy. Once frowning, a wall portrait now smiles. What can be counted on? During the Depression, countless people felt the same way.

The film, of course, ends happily. Penny and Lucky are about to marry—"I guess so," is how Penny, laughing, puts it, upholding some piece of uncertainty to the last. The two then, in front of a vast, sky-high window, duet harmoniously as snow turns to sunlight in a heartbeat.

In *Swing Time*, the Astaire-Rogers cycle reached a luminous and—courtesy of Jerome Kern's music—melodious peak. The songs by Kern and lyricist Dorothy Fields, including "A Fine Romance" and the incomparably beautiful (and Oscar-winning) "The Way You Look Tonight," are magical—as are the dances, by Astaire and Hermes Pan. These include, intricate and deft, the "Waltz in Swingtime," and the glittering, dramatic dance to "Never Gonna Dance"—for me, also the best song. (When this dance lamenting hopeless romance quickly breaks into and out of a reprise of the hopeful "Waltz," it's a point through the heart.) Grounded, precipitous, delicate, robust, and shimmeringly mysterious, the "Never Gonna Dance" dance haunts with its grand passion, its soulful defenses against time. Astaire and Rogers astound.

George Stevens directed.

THE PETRIFIED FOREST (U.S.). Archie Mayo's film of Robert E. Sherwood's play *The Petrified Forest* is extraordinarily evocative of the loose-ended lives that the Great Depression wrought.

In the early morning light, a hobo, back towards us, walks down a dusty, seemingly endless road in the middle of nowhere. His protective hat underscores his fragility, vulnerability. A tumbleweed crosses his path; *both* are tumbleweeds, blown along either by wind or circumstance. The man tries thumbing a ride from a passing car; but the car passes him by. This is to be a film about unsettled, thwarted, disappointed lives. When the car pulls into a gas station-diner in the Arizona desert, a tumbleweed stumbles through the frame. The diner will turn out to be the hobo's destination as well. He will have his last meal there.

Gabrielle ("Gabby"), working as a waitress in her father's diner, dreams of leaving Arizona for Paris, as her French mother did years ago. Perhaps tumbleweeds blow through the hole in her heart. Gabby Maple feels as though her youth is being petrified into stone. Alan Squier, the hobo, and Duke Mantee (Humphrey Bogart, effectively mannered) drift into the diner.

Refined, learned, selfconscious, exceedingly kind, with a philosophical and at times fatalistic air about him, Alan (Leslie Howard, superb) is a gentle poet in a turbulent landscape —ineffectual Europe personified. Duke and Alan make a pact: the former agrees to kill the latter before his getaway.

Gabby knows she will never make it to France or see her mother again. Bette Davis, fetchingly lovely and fresh as Gabby, incomparably enacts heartbreaking innocence that's lightly dusted with growing experience. Before Mantee's arrival, Alan asks Gabby for a parting kiss. Gabby's wide eyes narrow just the slightest as she poignantly tells him, "I understand. It's just a kiss."

1937

LA GRANDE ILLUSION (France). Before the world changed its mind about *The Rules of the Game* (1939), *The Grand Illusion* was considered Jean Renoir's masterpiece. It is certainly the greatest "escape movie" ever made—but, here, the escapees aren't criminals but three First World War soldiers in a German prison camp: an aristocrat (Pierre Fresnay, Hitchcock's "man who knew too much," brilliant); a mechanic (Jean Gabin, wonderful); a Jewish banker (Marcel Dalio, himself Jewish, also brilliant). By its attempt to cast each class against itself, war is "the grand illusion"; but class also is "the grand illusion," because it wilts before the new alliances—ones not based on class—that war by necessity forges. To Renoir, then a communist, perhaps the most striking illusion is the belief that the world would not change. The world *must*.

In praising this widely cherished film, some slight its content—its visual expressiveness—in favor of its humanistic attitude. Consider: Comparing captors and captives in the prison camp, parallel tracking shots weigh nationalistic differences that class affinity among old-order aristocrats fails to cut across, clarifying the tension inherent in the whole idea and execution of a tracking shot: the obliteration of the boundaries of successive frames before a conclusive curtailment is finally, as it must be, reached—a tension between restriction, rigor (in Renoir's film, the past) and liberty, freedom of movement, aspiration (here, the future). Renoir thus explored and expanded his chosen medium, much as his father had done with his.

Perhaps only one other film, Robert Bresson's *A Man Escaped* (1956), expresses the idea of freedom as well as this one. Those who pay lip service to the idea but who hold no core allegiance to it will not be as moved as are others by *La grande illusion*.

THE SPANISH EARTH (U.S.). *Men cannot "act" before the camera in the presence of death.* — from Ernest Hemingway's commentary in *The Spanish Earth*.
Text and meta-text.
First, text.
The most moving American documentary ever, by Dutch filmmaker Joris Ivens, begins with two panning long-shots: a painterly sky; an expanse of parched earth. The scene is the Spanish village of Fuenteduena, between Valencia and Madrid. Two parallel themes will come together: a project to irrigate the land, to raise food to feed Republican soldiers opposing Franco's fascists and foreign cohorts—Nazi Germany; Fascist Italy—during the Spanish Civil War; the raging war itself, in and near Madrid, including the Republican effort to secure the bridge between Valencia and Madrid.

There are no reconstructions here. We see war—actual soldiers as they steel themselves for battle; fresh bodies of killed soldiers and civilians. The villagers succeed with their irrigation project; Republican soldiers secure the bridge.

Meta-text. Republicans, we know, will lose the war. How on earth can we watch this film today without bringing to it our knowledge of this bleeding history? Ivens made a hopeful film, but reality subsequently canceled hope. This cancellation, a gargantuan defeat for humanity in the twentieth century, is forever, now, a part of *The Spanish Earth*.

BEZHIN MEADOW (U.S.S.R.). Based on the 1852 story by Ivan Turgenev, Sergei Eisenstein's *Bezhin lug*, like his *¡Que viva México!* (1932), can hardly be said to exist. Stalin's story is that the film, production of which Stalin had stopped in 1937, was destroyed in a German bombing raid; others suspect that Stalin himself destroyed it earlier for his own reasons. The half-hour 1967 "reconstruction" by Eisenstein Museum curator Naum Kleiman and filmmaker Sergei Yutkevich was made from still images from the front and back of each shot that Eisenstein, according to his routine practice, had saved and his widow, Pera Attasheva, had kept. The original script and Eisenstein's storyboards and notes were used as blueprint.

The updated story is a return to the conflict of Dovzhenko's *Earth* (1930), another stab at the "the old and the new." Its protagonist is 11-year-old Stepok, a "Young Pioneer" who supports the collectivism that his father, a farmer, detests. This kulak, who has beaten to death Stepok's mother, is vicious. He is among those out to destroy the collective farm's harvest by incinerating it. After leading a collective action to combat this sabotage, Stepok is murdered by this monster. Like Lenin lying in state, however, the dead child reflects Soviet communism's abiding spirit and radiant future.

A montage of flowering trees: Eisenstein links this glimpse of gorgeous Nature to Stepok's mother, with whose burial the film opens. The face of her corpse is partially visible in the foreground; in the background, Stepok looks intently at it, bound in commitment to his mother's memory. His opposition to his father will thus be natural and moral as well as social and political: an indication of the crystalline condensation of Eisenstein's method.

THE RIVER (U.S.). Consisting of photographs he had collected and captioned, Pare Lorentz's book *The Roosevelt Year: 1933* established his concern with the social and political problems with which the New Deal in its first year had tried to grapple. Lorentz was also a political columnist for King Features until William Randolph Hearst pinkslipped him for a piece praising Henry A. Wallace, Roosevelt's secretary of agriculture. The Department of Agriculture, planning to make films to generate support for the administration's environmental programs, hired the thirty-year-old West Virginian in 1935, making him the New Deal's official documentarian. This led in 1938 to the formation of the United States Film Service under the auspices of the National Emergency Council. When Congress withdrew its funding two years later, Lorentz resigned as director. A commissioned officer in the Air Corps during the war, Lorentz produced training films for pilots. After the war, he directed the filming of the Nuremberg trials.

Produced by the U.S. Farm Security Administration, *The River* follows the Mississippi and its tributaries, disclosing land and people devastated by floods, in the process conveying their joint and inseparable destiny, and suggesting that "the river," properly harnessed, is the nation's unifying lifeblood. Moreover, the film extols the redemptive possibilities of federal action, here in the form of the Tennessee Valley Authority. Inspired by Dutch documentarian Joris Ivens's *New Earth* (1933), *The River* is a work of national purpose—hence, a kind of epic. Also, it's a thrilling record of humanity's struggle against calamitous Nature.

Lorentz's film represents the lyrical apogee of American cinema. His orchestration of the film's elements, including beautiful black-and-white cinematography by Floyd Crosby, Stacy Woodard and Willard van Dyke, and his own peerless editing, achieved a result that continues to indict the U.S. for failing to develop and maintain a national cinema.

ANGEL (U.S.). Whereas his *Cluny Brown* (1946) no longer seems as fresh as it once did, Ernst Lubitsch's *Angel*, a glorious sophisticated comedy teetering on the satin-covered edge of upper-class marital tragedy, is far better now that I grasp the stakes involved.

Marlene Dietrich is wondrously clear—crisp, delicately poignant—as Maria, the neglected wife of a conference-addicted English spouse intent on saving Europe from war's gathering storm. Herbert Marshall is at least as wonderful as this Sir Frederick Barker. Both are impeccable whether their characters are delighting or annoying us.

In Paris, while her husband is conducting important business somewhere else on the Continent, Mrs. Barker, incognito as Mrs. Brown, has a fling with a gentleman who pays her rapturous attention and calls her "Angel." Maria insists on their mutual anonymity. A Pirandellian breeze wafts through, as it must also the play by Melchior Lengyel on which the film is based.

History may be repeating itself, since during the Great War the two men shared a seamstress, and the lunch now shared by Frederick, who doesn't know that his Maria is his friend's Angel, Maria and her lover is a quietly upheaving event. Frederick catches on, and each character finds himself or herself in a deep moral quandary.

In Paris, in Grand Duchess Anna Dmitrievna's "salon" (the White Russian exile is a high-class—how shall I put this?—pimp), the three collide, and life-choices will have to be made. The entire film pours into the closing shot, which is perhaps the most brilliant one that Lubitsch ever devised. Two of the three walk out the door of Dmitrievna's waiting room side-by-side: a couple facing whatever lies ahead. It is a view from their backs encompassing not only the pair's future but also the odd-one-out's inconsolable loss. Devastating.

1938

ALEXANDER NEVSKY (U.S.S.R.). Eisenstein's films of the 1920s were like nobody else's. These highly analytical works combined his invention of intellectual montage (the juxtaposition of two images whose collision generates an idea neither contributory image wholly contains), dynamic, rhythmic image flow, the use of "types" to achieve bold, unvarnished "acting" that here and there pointedly slips into cartoonish caricature in order to skewer whatever the character represents (for instance, capitalism or religion), and a present-tense, immediate sense of history. But Stalin objected to the "formalism" of such techniques, and in the '30s Eisenstein found himself in the Soviet doghouse. *Alexander Nevsky* was supposed to get him back into the state's good graces.

Climaxed by Russian good's triumph over outside evil in the spectacular Battle on the Ice, possibly the most brilliant battle sequence ever filmed, the thirteenth-century struggle against Teutonic invaders served, after all, as a timely patriotic warning against current German ambition towards the U.S.S.R. Moreover, it is a stunningly beautiful piece of work, in black and white (the cinematographer is Eduard Tissé), thrillingly scored by Sergei Prokofiev, and starring, as the hero, the reigning titan of Soviet film acting, Nikolai Cherkasov. *Alexander Nevsky* is a fierce vision of cruelty and the noble response it incurs, with a ringing finale that also admits haunting, mournful accents: a celebration of victory in war on which duly weighs war's terrible human cost.

However, it is a different kind of film for Eisenstein, one more epic than analytical, and one less original, too, than his '20s work. The influence of Fritz Lang's *Die Nibelungen* (1924) hangs heavily over it.

Still, it succeeded in bringing Eisenstein renewed official favor—until, that is, Stalin's non-aggression pact with Hitler led to its being seized and shelved to prevent national embarrassment.

A PEBBLE BY THE WAYSIDE (Japan). About twenty years ago I saw Tomotaka Tasaka's *Robo no ishi*, from the novel by Yamamoto Yuzo, at the Northwest Film Center in Portland, Oregon. I have had no opportunity since to revisit the film, and I regret not having memorialized the occasion of my single visit by writing a piece about the film. As a result, while I vividly recall my response to the film, I do not recall the film itself, except fleetingly.

Tasaka's black-and-white *Robo no ishi* impressed me as one of the most powerful evocations of childhood in cinema. The protagonist, Goichi Aikawa, is an impoverished rural boy who dreams of a better life. In one indelible passage, with Goichi at play, I recall Tasaka's use of diaphanous superimposition to show the boy and—either in reality or dreaming thought: at this point, I'm not sure which—a passing train overhead. The train is achingly symbolic of the child's desire to escape his surroundings and poverty; but the superimposition also suggests the weight of this dream of his, the difficulty of its realization. I also vaguely recall a young man, a writer, I believe, who leaves the village for the city. Whether this is a character the course of whose hopes parallels Goichi's or, in fact, Goichi himself, grown up, my memory is too clouded to determine. It seems to me that failure envelops both characters—or the single character at two different times. While I associate the childhood passages with a spare, elemental visual style, I recall the city scenes as being visually intricate, busy and dense.

There isn't even a synopsis of this film currently on the Internet. The closest thing to this is a synopsis of an animated cartoon version of the same story.

THE CHILDHOOD OF MAXIM GORKY (U.S.S.R.). *Detstvo Gorkogo*, the first part of Mark Donskoi's trilogy about friend Maxim Gorky, the founder of Socialist Realism in literature, recounts the boy's hectic, impoverished childhood with maternal grandparents, in Nizhii Novgorod (later, Gorky), after his father's death.

Aleksei Peshkov's arrival by boat is preceded by two shots: an eternizing one of the Volga River, watched over by the sun in a white-clouded sky but for a single large storm cloud; another, of an irregularly shaped though orderly mass of men moving in something like unison on the shore, singing: Russian workers, the future author's subject and point of identification. Aleksei's grandmother, Akulina Ivanovna (Varvara Massalitinova, superb), is loving and nurturing; but Vasili Vasilyevich, his grandfather, is alternately cruel and tender.

Grandma teaches Aleksei to stand up to injustice; Grandpa provides occasions for his doing so. Their harsh existence makes some people harsh, others compassionate.

Grigori has been Grandpa's foreman in the dye works for 37 years. The daily combined assault of heat and chemicals has weakened Grigori's sight. Eventually he goes blind. Despite Grandma's pleas, Grandpa tosses out Grigori onto the street, consigning him to homelessness and street beggary. When the dye factory burns down, the Kashirins move and take in a lodger, a socialist whom a family member denounces, consigning him to a prison chain gang. Aleksei keeps observing. A same-named dying crippled boy deepens his love for society's outcasts.

It is time for Aleksei to leave. (In reality, Grandpa threw him out.) The final image is a rearward long-shot of the future Maxim Gorky on a winding road leading him to his destiny. The film ends with this Gorky quotation: "To live—to live—that there may be set free all that is good and human in our hearts and minds."

PORT OF SHADOWS (France). If nothing else, scenarist Jacques Prévert and filmmaker Marcel Carné's *Quai des brûmes* is momentous for launching two great movements in cinema: in France, poetic realism; in the U.S., *film noir*, which John Huston three years later invented by hardboiling poetic realism for *The Maltese Falcon*. Moreover, Carné's film gets better with each fresh viewing.

French poetic realism, whose shadowiness is indebted to German Expressionism and Josef von Sternberg's silents, is moody and violent, but withal suffused with a melancholy and sadness over doomed romance and constricted or blighted lives. Politically, it reflects France's fatalistic prewar mood as Germany's Adolf Hitler increasingly displayed his appetite for the rest of Europe.

The port is Le Havre. Bound for it, the trucker from whom Jean (Jean Gabin, brilliant), an Army deserter, is hitching a ride becomes the first one we see whom Jean enangers: Jean grabs the wheel to avert running over a lost little dog in the road. The eternally loyal creature adopts solemn Jean, becoming his playful shadow. Their poignant, though unsentimental relationship surpasses that of Baron Felix von Gaigern and his cherished dachshund in *Grand Hotel* (Edmund Goulding, 1932).

In Le Havre, Jean also angers Legardier (Pierre Brasseur), a small-time hoodlum whose face Jean publicly smacks (palm, backhand) after Legardier has manhandled Nelly (Michèle Morgan, 17, exquisite), Jean's love; furthermore, Jean angers Zabel (Michel Simon, wonderful), her guardian, who also has designs on Nelly. The one of these men whom Jean doesn't himself kill kills him.

Bereft of master at the last, the dog is at loose ends on the same road where he and Jean once came together. Hauntingly, the film has come full circle.

The entanglement of vice, in which Jean himself is no innocent, makes love, escape or freedom hopeless.

AMONG PEOPLE (U.S.S.R.). The second part of Mark Donskoi's *Gorky* trilogy, *Vlyudyakh*, finds Aleksei Peshkov—the future Maxim Gorky—out in the world. He tries his hand at a number of jobs, only to discover that some people will treat him as unfairly as had his grandfather, whom he now confronts, upon returning home for a visit, with a new, stronger voice. The form and texture of the film have changed. Whereas *The Childhood of Maxim Gorky* (1938) conveys life's rough, irregular rhythms, the tailored episodes of the second part suggest instead carefully reflected-upon incidents that have challenged the boy to take charge of his life. It is ironic, given his socialist destiny, that Aleksei becomes proficient as an apprentice Orthodox Christian icon maker.

Yet the second part has a kind of roughness, too: the discontinuous form of the narrative, which seems to jump from place to place, job to job, persons to persons. Thus Donskoi brilliantly conveys Aleksei's "shopping around" for a sense of his place in the world.

1938

Aleksei's imagination, motives and impulses are social rather than egoistical, and therefore the film's lack of attention to his individual psychology, or anyone else's for that matter, is true to the spirit and orientation of its subject. Donskoi shaped his material, and gave it such features, so that others might better know his late friend.

Above all, he made a heart-stirring film—as when, at the close, Aleksei's elderly peasant grandmother, watching the boy's boat leave, addresses him out of earshot: "You won't see me again. By the time you return, I will be dead. How wonderful the world is!" Fixed, the camera records what she sees: her grandson passing beyond her reach. Akulina Ivanovna's life has been hard; Aleksei's life may be better. How wonderful the world is!

THE CITADEL (U.S.). Robert Donat gives a brilliant performance—leagues beyond his Oscar-winning one the next year in *Goodbye, Mr. Chips* (Sam Wood, 1939)—as Andrew Manson, an idealistic young doctor who, investigating the linkage between silica inhalation and lung disease, is opposed by miner-patients and mining board members. After his research laboratory is deliberately destroyed, Andrew and wife Christine relocate to London, where the private practice he opens struggles until Andrew falls in with a crowd of mercenary doctors who minister to the self-indulgent rich, who cultivate hypochondria to make themselves the center of attention. On his way up, Andrew leaves more and more of his humanity behind. Whereas after he delivered his first baby, who seemed doomed but under his care survived, he said, aloud to himself alone in the street, "I'm a doctor," his eventual career poses this question: What is a doctor?

Intelligently written by Ian Dalrymple, Frank Wead, Elizabeth Hill and Emlyn Williams (who also enacts an important role), *The Citadel* (best film, New York Film Critics Circle, National Board of Review) is based on A. J. Cronin's popular 1937 novel, which in turn was partially based on Cronin's own experiences as a medical doctor beginning in his twenties. In 1924, Cronin was appointed Britain's medical inspector of mines, in which capacity he published research such as Manson pursues.

King Vidor directs—in spots, with bravura skill. Memorable indeed are Andrew's soul-searching walk at night, interrupted by piercing slivers of flashback, following the death in surgery of a dear friend, and Andrew's stirring speech before the medical board, both of which contribute to a coda of reintegration following a fissured narrative structure correlative to Andrew's moral disintegration.

The heart-walloping close consists of Andrew and Christine—*a couple*—walking toward us and their future.

BRINGING UP BABY (U.S.). Susan: Your *golf ball*. Your *car*. *Is there anything in the world that doesn't belong to you?*
David: *Yes, thank heaven:* You!

The "Baby" of the title is a leopard; this is a tale of two lookalike leopards, one tame, the other vicious. Embedded here in a "screwball" romantic comedy, they underscore the need of making the correct choice. David Huxley (Cary Grant), a fussy young paleontologist, is about to marry museum assistant Alice, who explains to him, "I see marriage purely as a dedication to your work." Upon meeting David by accident, though, Susan (Katharine Hepburn, dizzyingly hilarious, radiant, gorgeous), intrigued, cannot let this marriage happen. She wants David for herself and will go to any lengths, however risky, to get him. Susan's idea of marriage includes fun. She more or less kidnaps the boy, steals his clothes while he is showering and exquisitely torments him with her ardent pursuit. Meanwhile, Susan's dog has confiscated and hidden the rare bone that will complete the brontosaurus skeleton that David has been working on. This artifact of a stodgy past will be sacrificed so that David and Susan, who has exhausted his resistance, can face together a more interesting future.

Brilliantly written by Hagar Wilde and Dudley Nichols from Wilde's story, and directed by Howard Hawks even more brilliantly, this dark, dazzling, almost alarmingly funny film submits its two lead characters to considerable danger to underscore the degree to which reality constantly threatens romance. This is one Hollywood film where the final clinch isn't just a generic formality; it is an earned event. Susan has worked incredibly hard and adventurously to bag her David, and David deserves Susan more than he knows. In each other's arms: for the time being, both are where they belong.

1939

THE RULES OF THE GAME (France). Jean Renoir's *La règle du jeu* is the progenitor of 1960s mansion- or hotel-party films such as *La notte* (1961), *Last Year at Marienbad* (1961) and *The Exterminating Angel* (1962). The Marquis Robert de la Cheyniest (Marcel Dalio, terrific) organizes the weekend get-together at his country chateau. Among the guests are his best friend, his wife and her lover, who is a national celebrity, and his mistress. Intrigues unfold, including among the help. At the last, a bullet meant for one person finds a fatal home in another, occasioning a bracing, dignified speech by the host.

Classes intertwine and collide. The film bursts with both sharp and humane social observations, often achieving a rollicking sense of the emotions that drive us all, such as jealousy, no matter our station in life. Its most brilliant passage portrays a hunt on the Marquis's estate. The help prepare for the hunt, in which the aristocrats will participate, by whacking trees in the woods to set on the open run every lodging and burrowing creature. But, by dint of metaphor, might not the help also be the quarry? The methodical hunt is ghastly, with animal after animal shot from the sky or on the ground. Prey flutter and twitch in their death throes. It is a miniature of the war on whose brink the world at that moment stood, and the leisured warriors—the hunting party—project onto the animals they subdue their own anxiety. It is a denial—a displacement—of their dread of annihilation, as individuals, as a class. Sexual intrigue unfolds even in the midst of the hunt, and the animal that a guest espies may actually be a human one.

Life goes on until it stops—or is stopped by a bullet.

STAGECOACH (U.S.). John Ford's *Stagecoach* corrals American optimism while redefining the western genre as other than trivial or nostalgic. For Depression audiences, its weary past was recognizable, and they identified with the young outlaw couple's quest for peace, safety, financial security. While dangerous, the landscape, fresh and wild, offered hope of renewal.

The Ringo Kid has escaped prison to avenge the murders of his father and brother. A primitive character, Ringo acts gallantly towards Dallas, a prostitute who has been run out of town.

Ford's images engage the analytical mind. Twice, while haranguing about "law and order," a banker about to abscond with bank funds appears against a diffuse, shining cross on his office wall, the result of sunlight pouring in through a latticed window. Hollywood's most legendary atheist here scores a visual coup at the banker's expense. Touting "values," this pillar of society cloaks his corruption and greed in an upright posture and in staunch rhetoric, while the chance symbol of Jesus behind him slyly digs at his hypocrisy, reminding us how often those in positions of authority and power sanctify villainy with religiosity.

Later, the shadowy darkness that accompanies the ostrasized prostitute to her pitiful shack —the boy she loves is about to discover her trade—projects not only Dallas's shame but also society's tendency to relegate awareness of its exploitative nature to hidden outposts of the communal psyche.

Except for a plot-driven big Indian attack, *Stagecoach* is lustrous with meaning and thematic purpose—and irony. The action closes with Dallas and Ringo fleeing to another country, Mexico, in order to have a chance at realizing the American Dream.

Claire Trevor and John Wayne are wonderful as Dallas and Ringo, and John Carradine is superb as an elegant, morally complex gambler-assassin—a character presaging Paladin on television's *Have Gun, Will Travel*.

1939

THE 400 MILLION (U.S.). The 1937 Japanese invasion of Manchuria provides the background for Joris Ivens's film, begun in 1938, documenting one of the few aspects of resistance where the Chinese, the "four hundred million" of the title, prevailed against their aggressors. Narrated by Fredric March, it was financed by March, Dudley Nichols, who had written the commentary that March read, Ernest Hemingway and Luise Rainer, among others. With bitter irony, it was released a month prior to the disastrous outcome, in April 1939, of the Spanish Civil War, which Ivens had optimistically documented in his previous *The Spanish Earth* (1937).

Script refers to China's 4,000-year-old civilization, the imperialistic Japanese war machine opposing this, and Japan's alliance with "the Rome-Berlin axis." For Americans, the aerial strike that immediately follows portends Japan's attack on Pearl Harbor. But this is much worse; March runs through a list of bombed cities, citing statistics of Chinese fatalities for each before summarizing: "150,000 deaths, all civilians—not one soldier." Underscoring this is an image of precarious survival: a woman in grief on the ground, holding her toddler; the camera pans to reveal the dead body of (we presume) her husband and the boy's father. The film's silence but for the voiceover and sounds of fire—specifically, the woman's muteness—intensifies our sense of war as civilian nightmare. Bombers roar; people rush for cover; ghastly smoke and flames—destroyed homes; the quick insert of a horribly mutilated corpse; by another body, this time a man is in tears. Who was the dead man? His son? Grandson? Brother? More shots of mutilated bodies follow. And the living: "They leave the captured city . . . and move toward the interior of China."

The Great Stone Lions of China "look in the four directions of the wind."

LE JOUR SE LEVE (France). Written by Jacques Viot and Jacques Prévert, *Le jour se lève* would remain Marcel Carné's finest film. Its narrative complexity includes two interlocking romantic triangles and two different views of a single murder, one from outside the apartment in which the man is shot, the other from inside the apartment. Things indeed are paired in this film; two of its romantic characters, both orphans, are named François and Françoise. These pairings, as well as the pervasive atmosphere, suggest a dark dream. The film's signature poetic realism unfolds in the German shadow across Europe that's about to grip France. It evokes the fatalistic mood of a Europe which is increasingly left with only a soul to call its own.

The film opens with the camera looking down upon a horse-driven transport; the camera slowly moves up to find the window of the apartment in question. This combination of *mise-en-scène* and camera movement seems visually contradictory, dreamlike, impossible; when the camera moves upwards, it seems somehow to be moving downwards. Although nothing is reflected (as in water), we feel we have entered an inverted world.

Jean Gabin, tremendous, gives his best performance ever as François, the working-class mensch who is slowly dying anyway by what he must inhale at the factory where he works. François is the one who pulls the fatal trigger and is therefore cornered by the police. Despite his sturdy appearance, François is as vulnerable—as transient—as the rest of us. We well understand his dispatching the despicable Valentin (who else? Jules Berry) in a fit of rage.

François meets his fate in a world glistening with symbolism. For instance, he is survived by his ringing alarm clock. Perhaps he has woken up in a free, a more just Europe.

MY UNIVERSITIES (U.S.S.R.). Whatever its goals, Maxim Gorky felt that the 1917 Bolshevik Revolution would bring only heartache to Russia. He wrote: "Lenin and Trotsky have no idea about freedom or human rights. They are already corrupted by the poison of power." Gorky's death in 1936, officially from tuberculosis, motivated friend Mark Donskoi to make the Gorky trilogy and hid, many felt, Stalin's assassination of Gorky.

In the third part, *Moi universitety*, Aleksei Peshkov, now in his mid-teens, lives in a Kazan slum, hoping to enter university. A camera surveys open courtyard windows before lighting on his: a woman empties a wash basin; a woman howls as she is beaten; a hopeful singer practices. Aleksei, chastised for his awkward writing, curses the "oppressiveness" of grammar!

Tsarist police are making arrests. Aleksei joins an army of impoverished Volga dockers in rescuing cargo from a sinking barge: a joyous passage of humanity pulling together at hard labor. But the next job the boy finds is in a sweatshop bakery (the model for the work house in Lean's 1948 *Oliver Twist*). Aleksei shows compassion for fellow workers and stands up to their uncaring boss. "I feed forty people!" the latter boasts. Aleksei counters, "They feed you." Aleksei helps foment rebellion among co-workers, who realize dignity and strength in taking a united stand against the boss, who has endeavored to increase their work load beyond endurance: an extended dynamic passage.

Aleksei's suicide attempt, following the arrest of an underground journalist friend and the capitulation to their boss of the bakery workers, is an embarrassing hump for the film to get over. ("Hopeless dreams," diagnoses the doctor as he stands over the recovering patient at hospital!)

As ocean waves crash nearby, Aleksei helps a stranger give birth, restoring him to the path of his radiant destiny.

STORY OF THE LAST CHRYSANTHEMUM (Japan). Brilliantly acted by Shotaro Hanayagi as a Kabuki actor named Kikunosuke Onoe, Kenji Mizoguchi's *Zangiku monogatari*, from the novel by Shôfû Muramatsu, is one of the best films ever about actors and acting. Matsutarô Kawaguchi and Yoshikata Yoda wrote the script.

Kikunosuke gradually becomes a successful actor, thanks in part to the encouragement and counsel of Otoku, the family servant who loves him. Otoku's illness and death prevent their finally marrying.

Mizoguchi warmly conveys that theater and its illusions crystallize human vanities and yearnings, as well as the flux and frailty of life. Stage performances suggest the human spectacle we are part of. Such scenes are often introduced in long-shot, that is, at a vast distance, with great quantities of dark shrouding the top and bottom of the frames, so that the stage, with its appearing and disappearing screens and costumed players, appears as an angled strip of light converging three harmonious views: that of the spectator in the film; that of the spectator *of* the film—us; that of some cosmic spectator, the calm godly eye for which all human endeavor is a spectacle to be taken in.

These transcendent scenes are consistent with the visual tenor of a film that continually seems to be unfolding in darkness, with scattered light or white objects illuminating patches in the frames. Here is a film of small, cramped quarters with one light per room, of backstage areas, of streets at night—a film cloaked by night. Miraculous black-and-white cinematography, by Shigeto Miki and Yozio Fuji, renders this darkness vast, mysterious, profound, yet without ominous overtones or shrill accents. The cumulative effect is of a labyrinthine exploration, as though an eye—ours; the camera's; God's—were discovering particles of human light in an illimitable dark eternity.

THE LIGHT AHEAD (U.S.). Poetic, achingly spiritual, *Di klyatshe*, the third of four films Viennese-born U.S. filmmaker Edgar G. Ulmer made in Yiddish, is based on Mendele Mocher Sforim's 1873 story. (Sforim's real name was Sholem Yakov Abramovich; *mocher sforim* means *bookseller*.) Ulmer, the great director of *The Black Cat* (1934) and *Detour* (1945), filmed *Di klyatshe*—literally, *The Mare*—in Newton, New Jersey, which stood in for nineteenth-century tsarist Russia, outside Odessa. (Ulmer and wife Shirley wrote the script.) In the impoverished *shtetl* whose inhabitants the film portrays, young love has blossomed between Fishke, who is lame, and Hodele, who is blind. Fishke works in a bathhouse; Hodele plucks chickens.

The film is about compensation: "We Jews are supposed to have imagination to make up for the money we don't have." Blind Hodel "recognize[s] everybody's walk." Now Dropke, who took in and raised the orphan, wants Hodele to go door-to-door begging for money to compensate her. Won't Odessa, the city, replace the superstitiousness and hopelessness of the *shtetl* with possibilities? There is but one absolute: God—and derivative of that, the beauty of God's world. Man's world isn't always beautiful, however! In another of Ulmer's Yiddish films, *Green Fields* (1937), a boy notes, "Man couldn't create the world," to which the rabbi responds, "He can destroy it."

The *shtetl* faces the threat of cholera, but rather than address this the elders prefer to brandish their piety in religious activities. Following the book peddler's prayer for peace, so relevant in 1939, the film ends with a haunting long-shot of Fishke and Hodele walking away from the camera, side-by-side, to Odessa, where—who knows?—doctors may even be able to restore Hodele's sight. There's hope in the world; for the moment at least, there is a light ahead.

Films of the 1940s

War; postwar: the 1940s would prove an important decade, but, for the duration of the war, one necessarily dominated by U.S. films. The U.S. finally joined in on the fighting, after the Japanese attacked the U.S. Pearl Harbor military base, but the absence of combat in the homeland's 48 states allowed Hollywood to continue unabated. Orson Welles dominated the decade with works that are more highly regarded today than they were back then. Welles, whose genius inspired jealousy in the hacks and somewhat-better-than-hacks who were the majority of his peers in the industry, was booed each time his name or the title *Citizen Kane* was mentioned at the Academy Awards ceremony in 1942, where Welles actually won for the script, but only because its co-author was a popular figure in the Hollywood ranks. Welles's, then, was a sort of backdoor Oscar.

To some degree, the problem persists. *Citizen Kane* (1941) tops most lists as the greatest film ever made—a dubious, revolting distinction since its brilliance is often used by ignorant or vicious people, or ignorant, vicious people, to denigrate, even dismiss Welles's subsequent work, much of which is *also* brilliant (see list of outstanding films below). *Citizen Kane* does, however, provide a rare opportunity to watch something by Welles that isn't stressed by financial problems and studio interference. Throughout his career, Welles would remain the great "maverick" of American cinema, although his films often had to come from somewhere else in order to be made at all. When in the 1950s one of these, *Othello* (1951), took the top prize at Cannes, it did so as a Moroccan film!

The lives of famous persons are each a kind of living document, but one seen through a glass darkly—in part, the smokescreen of fictions that they themselves have invented and promulgated. They are, if you will, the authors of their own documentaries. With their passing, another document encapsulating their lives comes into play: the newspaper obituary —a document limited to the major known (or accepted) facts about individuals. This skeletal biography was written by others in advance of their death; it was filed in anticipation of their death. There you have it: say, the life of a famous former newspaper magnate fittingly poised to be included in the very newspaper he once owned. Its accuracy or certainty is not entirely unimpeachable. Questions might remain: *Did he really do that? Why, if he did, did he do that?* Nevertheless, this document, a reduction of the "document" of the man's life as he lived and half-created it, is poised to translate into yet another document, for this printed "life story" is apt to become, or contribute to, the man's extended epitaph. Now consider this: the man himself inadvertently throws a monkey wrench into all this planning by others by uttering something on his deathbed that casts doubt on the adequacy of his planned obituary. Say it is a single word: "Rosebud." He says this and expires. Nothing in what has already been written can account for what Rosebud is or was to this man, or what it represented to him. Yet whatever it is was obviously important to him; it expressed his dying, possibly summary, thought. The word then becomes a kind of challenge to newspaper detectives— reporters eager to investigate in order to unlock the secrets of the man's life.

This is the premise of *Citizen Kane*, which Welles directed from a script by himself and Herman J. Mankiewicz, Joseph L.'s alcoholic older brother. It is a film that begins with a man's death and proceeds, through investigative interviews by a dedicated reporter, to deconstruct the man's life. At least the reporter *tries* to do this; at least the film also goes through the motions of attempting to do this. If you (I believe, incorrectly) believe that the dying man held in his heart and mind a childhood sled at the point of his ultimate departure, you also (I believe, foolishly) believe that you, the viewer, succeed where the reporter himself fails. You may have then watched *Citizen Kane* without grasping it. But you are not wholly to blame. After all, Welles shows you the sled that Charles Foster Kane had had in his childhood, and as it is burned, along with other possessions of his, you witness that "Rosebud" was printed across it. Your filmgoing experience has taught you what such a circumstance means: the sled is *Rosebud*, hence, what Kane must have been referring to when he uttered the word before expiring. That is certainly how some other film than Orson Welles's might have worked. But Welles's film compels us to stop and think. Welles wants us to bring to bear what we humanly know and feel—and not let ourselves be led around by the nose, or the ears, or the eyes.

Welles starred in and co-directed his first film, "Hearts of Age," in 1934, when he was 19. (I haven't seen another short film, "Too Much Johnson," which Welles also co-directed.) Welles's third film, *Citizen Kane*, was his first feature and first studio film. For some reason, there exists the error in some minds that *Citizen Kane* was Welles's *first* film—a misstatement of fact most often used to exalt *Kane* to a superhuman level along the lines of this rhetorical question: *How could anyone's first attempt at filmmaking be this amazingly brilliant?* At least one reviewer, Pauline Kael, however, used the faulty premise, and more, in her self-serving attempt to besmirch Welles's reputation by discounting the idea that the film was even primarily *his*. The film was Welles's all right, but it didn't come out of the maidenly blue. Welles's experience as filmmaker preceded his experience as a director for the stage and for the radio.

Of course, it's amazing that *Citizen Kane* was anybody's *third* film. It would have been amazing had it been somebody's fifteenth or fiftieth film.

Citizen Kane is a nearly intolerably moving piece of work. It's a titanic, dark, dense canvas of American sociology, history and politics that sums up as waste the crammed life of a newspaper magnate (suggestive of William Randolph Hearst) who, disconnected from family and past, "buys things." Lots of things: sculptures, paintings, animals, bric-a-brac. With its infinite reflexivity, the hall of mirrors in the elderly Kane's vast and mostly empty mansion suggests his attempt to "extend" time and space, to defy mortality. This defiance, and the anxiety it implies, reveal the immense solitude that, since youth, following the withdrawal of familial care and love, Kane has been driven to fill with material things—"junk"—and with people whom he has also treated as though they were his possessions.

But life exhausts even these illusionary "extensions" of time and space; like the rest of us, Kane reaches a last deadline. It is here—at Kane's end—that the film begins, piecing together Kane's history as if it were a puzzle. Except for us, no one is present to hear "Rosebud," Kane's dying utterance, which becomes the springboard for enquiry. Those who cite this as a mistake, an oversight, miss the point, for this "inconsistency" signals the absurdity of any attempt to "solve" the mystery of a human life. What is "Rosebud"? At the last, one of the countless possessions of Kane's that is routinely shoved into an insatiable furnace is the childhood sled bearing that name and image. Rather than the sled, though, "Rosebud" probably suggests the accumulation of thought, feeling and memory that Kane attached to this discarded object. Ultimately, perhaps, "Rosebud" signifies loss, the motive (Welles may believe) of all human life, which Kane's egotism has monstrously enlarged into his own peculiar province, his Xanadu. Kane's losses—count them: in boyhood, a mother's care; all hope of political office; a business empire; two wives, and a son, his only child; life itself. Someone whom the reporter interviews notes that Kane was a man who lost almost everything.

Still, the word "Rosebud" explains nothing. At the end of the film "Rosebud" still is what it has always been—not the missing piece of a jigsaw puzzle, but an elusive clue in a mystery too vast to admit solution. Thus the film is self-critical, its zigzagging time structure at every point undercutting the straight line of inquiry that the reporter's investigation tries to impose. Welles's film isn't a search for the meaning of "Rosebud"; it's *about* the search for the meaning of "Rosebud." Until the distinction between these two things is made, and embraced, the meaning of Welles's film cannot come into focus.

Throughout, Welles's filmmaking is marvelous. With its see-through eye cavity, Kane's pet cockatoo—disingenuously, Welles told Peter Bogdanovich that this was a lab error—embodies the formal resourcefulness that is the film's hallmark while also encapsulating a major theme: the confusion with illusion that defines (and undefines) reality. No other American film so dazzles as *Citizen Kane* does, as in the vast visual pun, at the close, of a man's whole life going up in smoke, preceded by a sweeping crane shot surveying Kane's accumulated stuff—an apotheosis of American culture's material obsessiveness. Wedded to specifics of modern America, *Citizen Kane* nevertheless is like an ancient echo. Towering, it haunts and astounds.

The inspired creator of its black-and-white cinematography, Gregg Toland is Welles's chief collaborator here, Bernard Herrmann's music is essential, and the acting by Welles as Kane and George Coulouris as his nemesis, Thatcher, the banker whose ward Kane the boy becomes, is superb. Alas, although adequate at earlier stages as Kane's friend and Jiminy Cricket, Joseph Cotten fails to convince in old-man makeup. (Indeed, I for one would remain unconvinced by Cotten as an actor until Tony Richardson's 1973 film of Edward Albee's beautiful play *A Delicate Balance*.) However, all three of the film's actresses are wonderful: Ruth Warrick as his high-positioned wife, Dorothy Comingore as the mistress who becomes his second wife, and Agnes Moorehead as his determined, self-sacrificing mother.

Citizen Kane may be the most fascinating film ever made about the interplay between fiction and documentary, between "reality" and a more accurate reality, and the film's numerous inserts of newspaper front pages, and its nearly opening film-within-the-film, a documentary about the fictitious Kane that resembles a *March of Time* piece, deliciously rips, and riffs, across a keyboard encompassing "fictional" and "documentary" notes of expression. The tones combine to sound discordantly and be complex—a kind of *Rite of Winter* rather than of *Spring*, as correlative to the windy, winding echo that haunts Charles Foster Kane's empty yet suffocating domain. *Citizen Kane* is the *King Lear* of films—ancient, Renaissance, modern, postmodern.

It took a while for *Citizen Kane* to "catch on" as a great work. This is also the case with *Letter from an Unknown Woman* (1948), another Hollywood studio film, this one a result of the time that Max Ophüls spent in the U.S. Whereas Welles tears into the medium, using a vast range of tricks, and more or less announcing how important his film is, Ophüls proceeds more modestly and quietly. His is so exactingly sad a film, that one approaches it cautiously; one can get lost in its powerful moods—and then where is one? Upon sober reflection, one might even wonder, "Does this portrait of a woman's bottomless infatuation for a man—a man who woos her, impregnates her, discards her, and then, when their paths again cross, doesn't even remember her—warrant the weight of concern with which the film invests it?" I think it does, but my view encounters the film in a context quite apart from feminism, the genres of "woman's picture" and melodrama, and other issues and considerations that have been applied to the film in the past. I see the film with different eyes—my own eyes—and I feel its depth and passion differently. For me, the hopeless love of Lisa Berndl for her idealized concept of the womanizing Stefan Brand is due the tremendous feeling it attracts because of the historical—and, for Ophüls, highly personal—allegory it conjures. For me, the film is about so much more than it seems to be because its subjectivity, encapsulated in Lisa's emotions, is inextricable from the objectivity of European history.

The story, scripted here by Howard Koch, began as a 1922 short story, "Brief einer Unbekannten," by Stefan Zweig, an enormously popular and widely translated Austrian biographer and essayist with a psychoanalytical bent and, in his fiction, a penchant for combining delirious romance with unvarnished aspects of sexual politics. One takes Zweig seriously, literarily, at one's own risk, and doing so requires an adolescent cast of heart capable of digesting cynical nuts and bolts amidst an oceanic stretch of confectionary dreaminess. That his story's central male character is a writer—the film changes this to pianist and composer—perhaps suggests Zweig's identification with his creation's prodigious sexual activity: an author's prerogative.

The advent of Hitler in Germany and the banning of his books discombobulated Zweig, who wrote about the anti-Semitic course that Germany had taken, pronouncing it a national means of inflaming people in order to facilitate their subjugation: a breathtakingly prescient analysis. Zweig exiled himself to England in 1936, divorced his wife of eighteen years and married his secretary. Increasingly despondent over the course of a war that he had described as the suicide of Europe, he and his wife, Lotte, committed suicide together, in Rio de Janeiro, in 1942.

Ophüls also was a Jew, one who loved above all other cities Vienna, the city of Zweig's birth. It's turn-of-the-century Vienna that he re-created on Universal sound stages for *Letter from an Unknown Woman*. Two other events intervened between Zweig's death and Ophüls's film, both of which became essential underpinnings of the film. One was the heart-attack death in 1947 of Ernst Lubitsch, the Berlin-born Jew whose wonderful comedies, including *Ninotchka* (1939), *The Shop Around the Corner* (1940) and *To Be or Not to Be* (1942), Ophüls greatly admired. The other event, which began the year of Zweig's suicide and came to terrible light at the end of the war, is the Holocaust.

The tremendous feeling of Ophüls's *Letter* derives, I believe, from the weight on his heart of two (for him) inextricably connected matters: Jewish deaths—Zweig's, Lubitsch's, and those of the Six Million—and the destruction of the Europe he remembered, the Europe that Lubitsch had conjured, on an M-G-M sound stage, as the pre-war Budapest of *The Shop Around the Corner*.

Few of us are unfamiliar with the film's "plot." Three hours before he is scheduled to fight a duel, Stefan Brand, who has no intention of keeping the appointment, begins reading a letter he received in the post that day. It is from a typhoid patient at St. Catherine's Hospital, the wife, we will later learn, of the man whom Brand is supposed to face on the field of honor. We "hear" the letter as a bodiless voiceover, which begins: "By the time you read this letter, I may be dead. I have so much to tell you and perhaps very little time. Will I ever send it? I don't know. I must find strength to write now before it's too late, and as I write it may become clear that what happened to us had its own reason beyond our poor understanding. If this reaches you, you will know how I became yours when you didn't know who I was or even that I existed." This is Brand's letter from an unknown woman named Lisa, who recounts her love for him that began when she was a 14-year-old schoolgirl and he a keyboard prodigy whose music filled the Viennese apartment complex where Lisa and her widowed mother also were tenants. Lisa begins studying music so that she may "enter [Brand's] world." When Lisa's mother remarries, however, the family moves to Linz, a provincial Austrian town, thus interrupting what has become Lisa's devotion to a man who scarcely notices her existence as he enjoys his success on the concert circuit and, the fruits of that success, the bed partners who steadily stream into his bachelor apartment. Eighteen now, Lisa is courted by a handsome young lieutenant, an acquaintance of her stepfather, a military tailor. Upon his proposal of marriage, she blurts out as reality the fantasy of her engagement to Brand, and to make fantasy reality she forsakes home and family ties to return to Vienna on her own. She supports herself as a model in an exclusive dress shop; otherwise, her life is consumed with stalking Stefan Brand. Eventually he notices her and they become lovers; she is completely at his service and interested in him to the exclusion of herself. For his part, Brand is delighted by Lisa's devotion and, even more, by her insights into his life and his music. However, he never asks her her name. An unexpected concert tour interrupts their affair; she sees him off at the train depot but doesn't believe his promise that he will return to her in two weeks. Lisa knows he is sincere, but she also knows that his departure will snap for him the spell of their involvement; Brand's unmitigated self-absorption will reassert itself, other girls will beam to the flame of his prodigious charm, and Lisa, already a memory at the point of his leavetaking, will pass into the amnesia that overtakes all the romantic connections in Stefan Brand's existence. Lisa has their baby alone at the Catholic hospital. She fails to disclose Brand's identity for their son's birth certificate, intent on being one woman who doesn't ask Brand for anything. She alludes to a rough patch in her life, the implication being that she supported herself and her son by prostitution. But Lisa has come back from her degradation and oblivion and, although still in love with Stefan Brand, has married the well positioned Johann Stauffer for the sake of her son. She has been completely honest with him about Brand, and it's likely that he is genuinely in love with the beautiful, elegant woman that she has become. One night, with Stefan Jr. on vacation from boarding school and at home, Lisa and Johann attend an opera. Stefan Brand is also in attendance. Other theatergoers gossip about the downturn in his career; Brand is alone, unaccompanied by a date. Since his disconnect with Lisa, Brand has been, both as artist and man, without his Muse; and because he does not even remember her, he has been incapable of defining or explaining the emptiness that has overtaken his life. In the darkened theater, staring into her balcony booth from his, he cannot take his eyes off Lisa. Who *is* this beautiful woman? Lisa knows only that she feels her whole life slipping away—slipping back, that is, into the current of devotion for Brand that once was her life's sum and substance. She leaves her husband at the theater to go home without disturbing him. Perhaps Stefan Jr. is the antidote to the renewed claim she finds the boy's father suddenly and unexpectedly making again on her heart. Will all be lost? Outside, waiting for her carriage, she is approached by Stefan Brand. He can't help thinking they have met. Her ambiguous remarks pique his interest. When the carriage pulls up, Johann is inside. He knows Lisa didn't want this; he reminds his wife that there are such things as honor and decency. She has will to direct the course of her actions, he tells her; she doesn't believe this. Fate has delivered Lisa back to her passion, her obsession. Johann promises to do everything he can to deter the romantic course of hers that threatens to shatter the foundation of all their lives. At the train depot, where they have entered a compartment that should have been quarantined after the removal of a passenger with typhus, Lisa says goodbye to her son, who is returning to school so that she may rejoin his father. The boy doesn't mind because his separation from the mother he adores will last only a short time. "Two weeks!" he says. "Two weeks." The train pulls away, and Lisa goes to Brand's apartment to offer herself to Brand body and soul. He remembers her now—surely he remembers her now. But he doesn't, and his flippancy makes Lisa feel cheap. She leaves. She is sick. She writes in the letter that her one regret is that Stefan never knew their wonderful son. She has enclosed a photograph of Stefan Jr., who, she explains, has died of typhus. The boy died alone, before his mother could reach the hospital; perhaps, she muses, God will be merciful and take her, too. God has been merciful. The handwritten letter abruptly stops. There is a typed message from a staff member at St. Catherine's Hospital indicating the patient's death from typhus. Stefan Brand, perhaps for the first time in his nonprofessional life, has lost his superficial aspect; he is overcome with grief. He asks the one constant in his life, his mute manservant, if he recalls the author of the letter. On a slip of paper from Brand's desk the man writes "Lisa Berndl." Brand now utters the name with which he had never addressed the woman who so adored him: "Lisa, Lisa." It's dawn. The escorts for the duel between him and Johann Stauffer have arrived. Stefan Brand, fully human at last, will face his death after all. (Stauffer's reputation as "an excellent shot" leaves little doubt as to the outcome.) Before he enters the carriage, Brand looks back and sees, in his mind's eye, the girl and the woman who loved him. His belated discovery of all he had comes simultaneous with his discovery of his having lost all of it.

Memory is the repository of our humanity. This is one of the great themes of Sophocles' *King Oedipus*. Amnesia exacts the price of our humanity. In Ophüls's film, Lisa's letter to her beloved comes to embody memory, both hers and, ultimately, his as well. The letter transfers

Lisa's memory to Brand, replacing his amnesia. Stefan, then, is without memory; Lisa is *all* memory, even in the present where what she experiences is instantly transformed into memory: a point underscored by the fact that everything she experiences comes to us by way of her letter—her memory, in effect. In the end, through the anonymous letter—the film's extended flashback—she consummates their relationship spiritually by giving Stefan, from the grave, her own memory. This is the redemption of Stefan Brand.

The letter also gives us Lisa's memory. The letter's human weight never leaves us because of the voiceover and the imagery conjured, as it were, from that voiceover. It is the film, of course; but it's also Ophüls, who has his own losses to weigh and consider.

The continuity of Lisa's life is her memory of Stefan; even her love for Stefan Jr. is subsumed by her abiding, if at times dormant, love for the boy's father. The object of this love is the Brand she has made over in her mind. It is her idealized image of Brand that has sustained her emotionally. This is another way of saying that the unifying force of Lisa's life, what makes her life "continuous," is her imagination. Brand's, on the other hand, is a discontinuous life. It's a series of scenes: first, scenes of public attention and sexual conquest; later, scenes of abandonment and loneliness.

Self-absorbed, when he is about to seduce Lisa for the last time, Brand glances into a mirror in order to adjust the handsomeness of his appearance, unaware that Lisa perceives him not according to what his mirror reflects but according to her mental image of him, her idealization of him. When she is with him, she is still with her memory of him; but, living in the moment, he has no memory of her, of himself, of them as a couple.

With a turn of the screw, we can posit their relationship in slightly different psychological terms. The Stefan Brand whom Lisa perceives and loves is a projection of her desire for continuity in her life. Ophüls's Lisa isn't Zweig's masochistic creature; Ophüls has transformed Zweig's concept of the character, demoting her taste for degradation and stressing instead her drive for integrity. The Hays Office helped. Unlike Zweig's version, Ophüls's Lisa isn't given money by her lover. Prostitution isn't a motif in her life, in effect an agency of continuity; instead, it's one of several disruptions of that continuity that require the application of her imagination, her idealization of Brand, to remedy. For Stefan Brand, memory is something to shun or make a joke out of. There is an exquisite passage, in Vienna after Lisa has returned from Linz to find her Stefan, where the new couple take an imaginary trip together "visiting" sights throughout the world. Courtesy of Hale's Tours, the two sit in a railway car as, hand-cranked like an old camera, different backdrops—painted panoramic landscapes—appear through the window. The two "visit" the Swiss Alps and many other places, but eventually they exhaust the existing repertoire. But both of them want the date to continue; they want to prolong their romantic suspension of time amidst a pretended journey through space and time. Brand thus asks the operator to start over again from the first imaginary point of the worldwide tour; he says, "We'll revisit the scenes of our youth." This is an elegant throwaway line, a clever remark, a sophisticated joke—for Stefan Brand, that is. On the other hand, it's no such thing for Lisa. Lisa has been describing to Stefan how she and her father, when she was a small girl, countered their limited circumstances by going on imaginary trips throughout the world. Her "trip" with Stefan thus echoes her "trips" with her father, forging an imaginative connection. Moreover, as the letter itself demonstrates, she is not simply filling the present with Stefan but creating—perhaps, to be Wordsworthian, *half-creating*—future memories that again will assist her quest for a continuous life. Every moment that Stefan spends with Lisa is lightly taken, but every moment she spends with him attains a lifetime of importance. By encapsulating her love for Stefan, each moment contributes to her life's continuity.

Zweig's suicide is almost always described as a precipitous event; the course of the war would turn, after all, and Hitler would be defeated. However, I find Zweig's ultimate act prescient. Before the Holocaust had anything more than just begun, his suicide echoes it in advance—something peculiarly possible because the Holocaust itself echoes past devastations of the Jewish community—and the Holocaust's claim on the Six Million. Self-exiled to "safety," Zweig can be seen as another one of the Six Million. History can thus be seen as scarcely affording Jews safety, whether in biblical times or with the pogroms in Europe in (from Zweig's perspective) much more recent times. His suicide was, ironically, a way to assert his own will in a context where everything seemed to be out of his hands and to the detriment of Jews and other civilized elements of Europe. If nothing else, Zweig's death ended the torment of his anxiety and uncertainty about the fate of Europe and of European Jewry.

Ophüls yearned for his own disrupted life to be patched together into some sort of continuity. For him, Lisa embodies this quest, much as Stefan Brand embodies both the disruptions and the forces obstructing the quest. Lisa's quest for continuity, its agency her idealization of Brand and her imaginative memory, becomes the means by which Ophüls dreams himself, the European Jewish community to which he belongs, and indeed Europe itself whole again. Lisa's memory is Ophüls's own memory, and the passion that Lisa's memory contains discloses the passion of Ophüls's memory. The depth of Lisa's passion her own unfortunate romantic experience cannot really sustain; it's the depth of Ophüls's very different passion that sustains it. It haunts us with what haunts Ophüls; its music is Ophüls's lament for Zweig, Lubitsch, Europe, European Jewry.

The allegorical masks that Ophüls employs reveal by concealing his deepest emotions. Such is one of art's provinces and paradoxes.

Ophüls is legendarily famous for his tracking shots—continuously moving shots that formally express, in his use of them, the gracious imaginative elongation of time under the pressure that mortal consciousness exerts on humans, all of whom live in time. *Letter from an Unknown Woman*'s signature camera movement, however, is the panning, not the tracking, shot. Ophüls's pans in this film—rotations of the camera from a fixed mounting—are brief, poised, constrained; their cumulative effect, lending enormous delicacy and irony to both Ophüls's quest for continuity and lament for all he has lost, pointedly conveys a sense of imagination's limits. At one and the same time we feel his yearning to be whole again—his yearning for Europe and for European Jewry to be whole again—and we feel his utter sense of futility. What's lost is lost. Nothing can make his world whole or right again, ever. Nothing less than this can justify the immense sadness of this saddest of all Hollywood love stories. The love story gives us safe passage into an allegory of Max Ophüls's heart, to which each slight camera movement makes its poignant contribution.

The actors also contribute. Joan Fontaine's performance as Lisa is, of course, famous; it's a marvel of sensitivity and sensibility, achieving perhaps its most perfect tenderness in scenes between mother and son. Lit by black-and-white cinematographer Franz Planer (credited here as "Frank" Planer, much as Ophüls is credited as Max "Opuls") to make apparent the glow of Lisa's idealizing spirit, Fontaine beautifully conveys the high degree of intelligence that can sometimes guide the dreamiest of dreamers. However, no fewer than five other performances in the film are also superb. Louis Jourdan is heartrending as Stefan Brand at the moment of his awakened humanity; until then, Jourdan's entire performance is preparation for that moment. Mady Christians—her blacklisting a few years later would hound her to suicide—perhaps provides the film's finest piece of acting; in a relatively small part, and at that one seen largely around the edges of the film, she is possessed of ordinary bourgeois dreams as Lisa's highly sensible, materialistic mother. Lisa's mother is her daughter writ small and compact. Marcel Journet is appallingly correct as Johann Stauffer, who dismisses as "romantic nonsense" his wife's sense of having little power to direct the course of her life, and who perverts the spirit of "honor and decency" while hewing to their letter in his efficient pursuit of Stefan Brand's legalized murder. A closeup of carriage wheels suggests Johann's capacity to crush—the lethal egotism he hides behind a façade of impeccable manners. It also implies the inexorability of fate that his wife better grasps than he does. Leo B. Pessin is magnificent as Stefan Jr. Pessin makes this character so distinctive and interesting that the boy's death matters on its own, not just as it reflects the loss that his biological parents feel. Sonja Bryden is exquisite as Madame Spitzer, who owns the dress salon where Lisa works in Vienna.

John Ford's *My Darling Clementine* is another important postwar Hollywood film. An American classic, it is cherished by both camps: those who rightly regard the western as the richest and most important of all Hollywood genres; those who (for whatever foolish or pathological reasons) don't like westerns. Although it did little more than break-even business, the film was highly regarded in its own day, winning the best foreign-film accolade from Italy's film journalists; and, of course, it is even more highly regarded today, now that, courtesy of the University of California at Los Angeles film department, we have at our disposal a preview version of the film that's largely untouched by studio head Darryl F. Zanuck's heavy hand—meddling that includes the deletion of frames necessary for the mere comprehension of the film and its method or procedure, the substitution of emphatic music for Ford's silences, natural sounds and discreet music, and, most egregious, the changed ending, to which Zanuck's hack, Lloyd Bacon, blighted the film with the single worst shot in the entire Ford œuvre. It's a blessing to know, as we now do, that Ford had nothing to do with it.

By this time, Ford had won three directorial Oscars, for *The Informer* (1935), *The Grapes of Wrath* (1940) and *How Green Was My Valley* (1941). (He would win a fourth for *The Quiet Man*, 1952.) Imagine, then, the degree of studio meddling with which less firmly established Hollywood filmmakers than Ford routinely had to contend—at least if they felt compelled to go off in unconventional directions. Preview audiences insisted on a farewell kiss between Wyatt Earp and Clementine Carter that never would have happened, that makes nonsense of what the film has socially and psychologically disclosed about the two characters; so Zanuck the Hypocrite, while admitting that he thought Ford's own ending perfect, complied and had the kiss tackily inserted. (Earp wouldn't have given it; Clementine wouldn't have accepted it.) Nor can the moment be reconciled with Henry Fonda's otherwise superlative performance as the legendary lawman. (Fonda becomes hysterically goonish when he plants the roadside kiss on the new schoolmarm's face before leaving Tombstone.) And the shot is the worst lit thing I've ever seen, with the camera bewilderingly close, as is typical of Bacon's "contributions." As it is, the "preview version" is actually a hybrid; its opening movement includes, graveside, one of Zanuck & Bacon's too-close, too-sentimental post-preview "improvements." Nevertheless, the Fox DVD, which includes both versions of the film, allows us to appreciate, on the one hand, the depth of commercial depravity in Hollywood, and, on the other, the almost inconceivable beauty of one of Ford's most poetic and transcendent achievements.

My Darling Clementine is the film that, along with his later *Wagon Master* (1950), best captures Ford's dual sense of the fullness and the transience of human life. It is, among his westerns, the one that most closely approximates the elegiac emotion of his tremendous work knitting together sea plays by Eugene O'Neill, *The Long Voyage Home* (1940). It's Ford's first postwar western—his first western since *Stagecoach* (1939); and, rather than follow a story, it famously loses the thread of its narrative, risking to seem haphazard and diffuse, in order to concentrate on mood, feeling and character, and to express the tentative, drifting sense of life that his war service had made all the keener for Ford. *My Darling Clementine* is perhaps his most poignant western.

Just outside Tombstone, Arizona, the Earp brothers—Wyatt, who is famous for having been Dodge City's lawman, Morgan, Virgil and James—are running cattle to California when they come across their dark mirror-image: Old Man Clanton and his sons. The Earps, peaceable, turn to violence only when necessary and always reluctantly; Clanton disciplines his grown sons with a whip. (A sample of his fatherly advice: "When you draw a gun on a man, make sure you kill him.") Clanton offers to buy the Earps' cattle; Wyatt politely declines. Clanton lures the older Earps to Tombstone for a night of carousing; James, who is a teenager, remains behind, guarding the cattle. The Clantons murder James and steal the cattle. Wyatt, who declined the marshal's badge offered to him in Tombstone, a town as rough as its name, now accepts it so that he and his deputized brothers can track down James's killers.

A plot and the theme of revenge are thus launched, and if this were a film by Fritz Lang both would be lit into and unswervingly pursued. But Ford's larger theme is the flow of life that continues despite, and adding ache to, the losses of life we all suffer. Life goes on, ironically compounding our sense of loss and of life's frailty. Later, when a character who has been shot is precariously operated on, we hear outdoors men hootin' and hollerin'. Soon after, the patient dies. Ford releases the narrative thread of revenge—we watch the Earps become a part of the fabric of life in Tombstone, and they are eventually returned to their original mission only by a chance discovery—and creates a portrait of loose-endedness and open-endedness. The formal nature of his film correlates to this thematic portrait.

Lang would have made a film that seems to tighten like a noose; Ford's film, on the other hand, seems episodic, "loose." Its communal scenes especially—for instance, when a clamorous crowd is gathered in a theater to watch a visiting actor who is in fact off getting drunk at a bar, or the procession of wagons heading to a church consecration that quickly turns into an outdoor dance—seem to be passing before our eyes. The wild America of romance is passing into a civilized America that somehow seems fragile for the robustness it's endeavoring to hold in check and translate into a manageable form of life. Everything in this film is splendidly sculpted into light and darkness, fixing it in our eye; yet, at the same time, everything seems to be "unfixed" and in flux. The film is timeless in its rich visual poetry, but at the same time it captures the paradox of Ford's feelings as an American home from war: everything is at once more stable now and yet open, uncertain, fleeting, not least of all because everything now is imbued with the transience of life that war has taught. Ford's America, which he deeply, dearly loved, always had been a thing of reality interacting with myth, each settling and unsettling the other. Now this is truer than ever.

My Darling Clementine's night scenes—shot exquisitely, using day for night, by black-and-white cinematographer Joseph MacDonald—are among the darkest ever devised. The first long-shot of Tombstone as the Earps approach it on horseback amazes. The sky couldn't seem more voluminous and dark, and yet we can somehow make out the town's outline and contours, and the distant interior lamp lights create a haunting specter of evanescence. The town could be either emerging from the pitch darkness or disappearing into it, that is, being swallowed up by a vast void. Either way, the town seems, simultaneously, sturdy and delicate, solid and fragile. This is the way matter—buildings both inside and out-, as well as people—in the surrounding darkness appears throughout; Ford's visual principle, whether implied or explicit, is to have matter at once real and dreamlike, settled-in and dissolving. Moving like clouds, sheets of tobacco smoke inside the saloon and the theater seem correlative to this; ironically, the clouds outdoors appear too heavy to move. The visual effect—and it's a gorgeous one—is also ironic; one feels at times that the clouds alone, with their immense fullness and weight, are holding down Tombstone, keeping it in place, keeping it from vanishing before our eyes. Ford devises a wonderful moment that humanizes this effect before we see Tombstone. It occurs when his older brothers leave James Earp with the cattle before they depart for a night's entertainment in town. Ford holds the camera on the innocent boy as he bids each of his three brothers farewell. Ford holds the shot and holds the shot as if, knowing that James will be killed that night, he doesn't want to let the boy go. He wants to keep James alive as long as possible. However, the emotionally powerful shot also conveys, later, the Earps' desire to hold onto that last image they had of their younger brother. (This mental elongation of time predates by nearly a decade Satyajit Ray's extraordinary manipulations of time, including elongation, in *Pather Panchali*, 1955.) In context, in retrospect, James becomes like the diaphanous, fleeting tobacco smoke; in our mind's eye, or upon a subsequent viewing of the film, that long held-onto final image of James ironically translates into his passing into death's dust before our eyes.

As the night scenes are more deeply dark than one can imagine, so it is that several of the daylight scenes are extremely and very softly bright. Sometimes there seem to be auras of light flashing upwards from characters on horseback. Technical shoddiness? I don't think so, because Ford's use of too-bright daylight carries the same thematic weight as does his use of darkness. Before our eyes, substantial human beings appear to be dissolving into sunlight, as elsewhere they may seem to be dissolving into darkness.

The relationship between Wyatt Earp and John—"Doc"—Holliday is another element that contributes to the film's thematic development. After a strained beginning it solidifies, with Ford devising perhaps cinema's single greatest shot of male-male nonsexual intimacy as the men, side by side, await the lead actor's arrival in the theater, only to dissolve into Earp's erroneous suspicion that Holliday killed James. Once this is straightened out, Holliday joins the Earps for the shootout with the Clantons at the O.K. Corral. Holliday, mortally shot, leaves the world saving the life of an Earp by shooting to death the last Clanton. Indeed, throughout the film Holliday's bad health—he has tuberculosis—poises him for mortal departure. Moreover, the itinerant acting troupe provides a humorous instance of Ford's theme of transience, although not so funny is how the lead actor's loneliness and unhappiness provide an ironic index of the motives behind his audience's—the townsfolk's—hopes for a communal existence.

Ford's film is indeed full of humor, and it, too, is thematically relevant. At the Bon Ton Tonsorial Parlor, the town barber has difficulty managing his new chair, and thus, with blade in hand, he endangers his customers, one of whom, Holliday, gets grazed. (This happens offscreen; we see the result.) The barber also imposes an artistic haircut on Wyatt, and sprays him with cologne besides, providing us with a comical image of American hardiness passing into the civilized state of domestication bordering on dandyism. In an indelible scene that resonates, however humorously, with precariousness, Marshal Earp, seated outside, keeps the chair tilted back and, for balance, quickly alternates between placing left boot and right on the post in front of him. Earp is in control of himself and the town, but at any moment all may come falling down. (Wyatt's fancy footwork here, incidentally, releases a piercing charge of danger because it recalls that the murdered James, lying on the wet ground, still had one foot in the stirrup.) There is also character humor that helps enrich the film's portraits. Wyatt asks a bartender at one point if he has ever been really in love. "No," the man answers, "I've been a bartender all my life"—a line that Ford himself added to the script. (The screenplay, based on a story by Sam Hellman and the book *Wyatt Earp, Frontier Marshal* by Stuart N. Lake, is by Winston Miller, but the film's producer, Samuel G. Engel, bullied his way into the lead credit.)

The lively complexity of Ford's *mise-en-scène* in both the saloon and the theater translates as a human defense against the vast darkness right outside.

Many of the characters in this film are marvelously acted. Fonda is the quintessential Wyatt Earp, a man not given to jabbering but always shrewdly, and often sympathetically, taking things in. By a stroke of luck Victor Mature had bronchial pneumonia while enacting the tubercular Doc Holliday; even apart from his convincing coughing jags, this is the performance of his career. And what a contrast with Fonda!—monolithic Mature, in his usual dour Joan Crawford-vein, vis-à-vis the intricately deft Fonda whose acting, subtle and natural, remains largely invisible. Ward Bond and Tim Holt are Morgan and Virgil Earp; how I love Holt the two times Ford directed him—here, and in *Stagecoach*. Walter Brennan is frightening as Old Man Clanton, and it's easily one of his best performances, but Ford didn't succeed in realizing what I presume he was after: that we should feel over Clanton's loss of his sons, however rotten they and their father were, at least some of what we feel for the Earps' father's loss of sons, to which surviving brothers refer on at least two occasions. (Clanton murders both James and, later, Virgil, the next youngest.) Jane Darwell, who won an Oscar for her weak Ma Joad in Ford's *The Grapes of Wrath*, now redeems herself, giving her most interesting and touching performance, as the town madam—not that the character is at all realistically conceived. (I doubt prostitutes ever were so lucky as to be shepherded by anyone this nice.) Beauteous Linda Darnell—the Virgin Mary that b[r]atty Jennifer Jones "saw" in *The Song of Bernadette* (Henry King, 1943)—plays Chihuahua, the saloon singer who, Ford hints, was once part of the madam's gaggle of professionals. Chihuahua loves Doc Holliday to distraction. Jealous, pouty and spiteful, she is the film's most conventional character, and Ford applies purely conventional filmmaking to her that wittily stands out amidst the film's freshness. Like the madam and her whores, moreover, Chihuahua is almost exclusively shown indoors; she is the captive of her tempestuous though small emotions. Still, before and after the operation to remove a Clanton bullet, Ford gives her the Madonna-treatment that he once applied to Katharine Hepburn's Catholic Queen in *Mary of Scotland* (1936), probably to underscore Chihuahua's redemption through courage in the face of awesome pain—Holliday has nothing with which to put her to sleep—and likely imminent death. Darnell is often a terrible actress, but not here; she meets the small demands of an emotionally limited part. (Her *best* performance would come in Joseph L. Mankiewicz's 1950 *No Way Out*.) Cathy Downs also is perfectly adequate as Chihuahua's nemesis, Clementine Carter, Holliday's respectable girlfriend from a past from which he has severed himself in every detail. She is the bland sort that would seem heavenly to Wyatt Earp. Finally, Alan Mowbray is terrific as Granville Thorndyke, the itinerant ham actor for whom Ford has such immense affection that he would bring him back, as A. Locksley Hall (Tennysonians, take note!), in *Wagon Master* (1950), Ford's favorite among his westerns, from his own original story. Ford is typically fond of his characters, but somehow his embrace of this one provides an especially joyous index of his generosity. It's with real panache that Thorndyke skips out of town without paying his bill.

In Italy, a great movement, *neorealismo*, took shape during the war and after. The greatest exemplar of the movement would prove to be Roberto Rossellini, whose *Rome, Open City* (1945) and *Paisà* (1946), two beautiful works, are justly celebrated. However, the movement's singular masterpiece was his next film, *Germany, Year Zero* (*Germania, Anno Zero*).

Receiving French and East German financing, and filmed in German in Berlin with a nonprofessional cast, *Germany, Year Zero* was written by Rossellini and Max Colpet, with Sergio Amidei contributing to the dubbing script of the Italian version. The film took the top prize at Locarno in 1948. Its cool box office reception, though, helped move Rossellini into the arms of Ingrid Bergman, with whom he collaborated on a series of brilliant films blending neorealist and more personal elements.

To begin with, Italian Neorealism has literary roots in Zola's naturalism in France and, in cinema, can be traced to Luchino Visconti's apprenticeship to Jean Renoir, on whose *Toni* (1934) Visconti worked as a production assistant. Renoir thus described (in 1956) his approach in making this splendid film: "The cinema is based above everything on photography, and the art of photography is the least subjective of all the arts. Good photograph . . . sees the world as it is, is selective, determines what merits being seen and seizes it by surprise, without change . . . My ambition was to integrate the non-natural elements of my film, those elements not dependent on chance encounter, into a style as close as possible to everyday life. . . . There is no studio used in *Toni*. The landscapes, the houses are those we found. . . . The script was from a true story . . . No stone was left unturned to make our work as close as possible to a documentary. Our ambition was that the public would be able to imagine that an invisible camera had filmed the phases of a conflict without the characters unconsciously swept along by their being aware of the camera's presence."

While one must adjust these aims in the case of Rossellini to include a most highly visible camera that in fact becomes, perhaps, the principal "player" in *Germany, Year Zero*, one detects in Renoir's description the foundation of *neorealismo*, which came into being, enjoined to the fatalism of French poetic realism, with Visconti's *Ossessione* (1942). Rossellini, along with Vittorio De Sica, however, moved their neorealism away from literary claims and into rougher visual territory. Their on-location shooting eschewed the somewhat studied compositions and gorgeous aesthetics of Visconti's aristocratic method, connecting instead with the pulsating random energy of Dziga Vertov's documentary forays into Moscow streets in the 1920s. (In truth, De Sica's approach fell somewhere between Visconti's and Rossellini's.) Background and foreground, the latter occupied by nonprofessionals (Renoir, in *Toni*, blended professional actors and nonprofessionals, a procedure that Claude Chabrol would fall heir to beginning in the late 1950s), became in a sense interchangeable, the result an encapsulation of everyday life. In the case of Rossellini's film, this aspect befitted the juncture of a clinically observed case study, that of Edmund, a 12-year-old boy coping with the aftermath of the Second World War in a blasted and blighted Berlin, and the generalization of discombobulated life that the difficulties of his situation exemplify. *Germany, Year Zero* pursues the general, then, through the particular. Its first aim is immediacy—the immediacy of the boy's experience amidst the immediacy of his environment, each lending compelling credibility to the other and in a sense becoming the other, their interchangeability stressing, in addition to the causal connection in environment's shaping of the boy's actions, a sense of random character selection wherein some other selection—for instance, one of the other afflicted children with whom Edmund interacts— might have produced a thematically similar or identical result. The unpolished visual style, partly owing to the use of handheld camera, is of a piece with this aim of immediacy; indeed, this style, with its implicit banishment of studio tinkering and artifice, comes to encapsulate this immediacy. Nothing must derail this immediacy; hence, neorealism's use of post-synchronized sound so that the filming could focus on the visual recording of action and milieu without the claim on attention that simultaneous sound recording would impose. So much in *Germany, Year Zero* collapses figure and ground, theme and method.

To be sure, Rossellini imparts a heightened dramatic sense to Edmund's misadventures (something the music in particular stresses), but this, too, serves a thematic purpose, for Rossellini hopes to erase the possible complacent reaction that the commonplace of suffering contained in Edmund's example should reduce its claim on our social consciousness. The opposite is Rossellini's aim: that the common nature of such suffering should alert our attention to each and every example and to the task of remedying the conditions that generate so many like instances.

Rossellini's approach is too clinical, too objective, to admit sentimental notes of wallowing in some sort of guilt over Fascism or for the social distress generated by the collapse of Fascism. Critic Penelope Houston finds in Italian neorealism "the driving urge to rehabilitate the national reputation." I (happily) find nothing of the sort in *Germany, Year Zero*. Such an "urge" here would compromise the film's immediacy; backward-in-time recriminations would prove a distraction. On the other hand, Rossellini's own need to address his participation in his nation's recent derelict politics—his need, that is, to do this on his own time, not ours through the film—is another matter entirely. Rossellini, after all, did not share the Marxism of Visconti, De Sica and many other of his fellow neorealists.

About a child, *Germany, Year Zero* is dedicated to a child. The film begins: "In memory to my son Romano." This personal note becomes a part of the film, lending startling emotional depth to the film's clinical approach. In addition, the film's lack of manipulative sentimentality itself helps account for the pure consideration we as viewers extend to Edmund in light of his hopeless and tragic situation. Like all suicides, but especially those of children, his at the end of the film cannot admit our perfect comprehension, but at the same time it has none of the arbitrary quality of suicides in Hollywood soap operas. It makes perfect sense, even if the sense is too enormously painful to take in and clarify as to causality. Everything we have seen throughout the film, both in Edmund's own life and in the life everywhere around him, which I have said become in a sense one and the same thing, leads to his ultimate act, but the act itself retains an enormity with which cause-and-effect cannot cope. I know of no other film in which the death of a young child is so stunningly painful. Only one other film, Carl Theodor Dreyer's *Day of Wrath* (1943), leaves me with such inconsolable grief over the loss of a fictitious life. Surely it is part of the greatness of both these films that they find some way that other films don't to convey to the full the illimitable value of human life.

In a sense, Edmund is crushed by the burden of his milieu, the social panorama that war has wrought. In effect, he is a casualty of the war—a reminder that wars exact casualties even once they have officially ended. Thus the film, after proclaiming its aim to be "an objective assessment" so that the viewer, used to sentimental filmmaking, won't be thrown by its clinical approach, makes generalizations about Berlin and its children: the city is "almost totally destroyed"; there, "3.5 million people live desperate lives"; "German children need to relearn to love life." There is no point whatsoever for a film like *Germany, Year Zero* to be less than perfectly plain about its sense of reality; since the film's aim is to foster the kind of social consciousness that will search out remedies for appalling social conditions, the opening commentary is entirely justified. It orients viewers—a particular help here, since the actions that will unfold include events one is unlikely to anticipate: a boy killing his father with poison before dropping to his own death from a gutted neighborhood building. It becomes the film's immediate task following this introduction to locate Edmund in the milieu that will in effect crush him and urge his very young life to suicide. This is effected by a brilliant panning shot of the city that finds Edmund working at digging graves. We will learn that he is pretty much (besides government food rations) his family's sole financial support—a burden no set of 12-year-old shoulders can hope to bear. But the situation is worse than that, for he won't even be allowed to succeed in his attempt to bear such a burden. In this opening scene of hard labor—and labor, note, identifying Edmund with death at the outset, hence, indirectly, with his own death at film's end—he is fired from the job for being, officially, too young for it. Edmund is between a rock and a hard place.

The grave digging introduces two themes. One, because this school-age boy isn't going to school due to his family's need for support, is war's disruption and theft of simple childhood. Indoctrinated by the Nazi regime during the war, Edmund has yet to be returned to any kind of normalcy afterwards. The other theme is war's relegation of human life to the discardable and disposable. The course of Edmund's own life and death will bring this theme to fruition, but in the meantime its principal agency is Edmund's elderly, ailing father. "I'd be better off dead," he tells Edmund, his youngest child. "I have to watch all of you suffer without being able to help." The family's situation is stressed because Edmund's older brother, a soldier fearful of retaliation from Occupiers, has declined to apply for work or a food ration card for himself. Edmund also has an older sister. His mother is deceased. His family shares quarters with other families. One member of one of the other families helps Edmund when possible by donating a household item so that Edmund can sell it (for himself and his family) on the black market. But Edmund's father, who during the war hated Hitler, now is equally opposed to black marketeering, either having been or being, it is implied, an affront to his dignity and sense of lawfulness. He must rely on his small son to stay alive, but at one point he slaps Edmund across the face because of the child's shady associations and activities—because in their service he has stayed out all night. Again this is like Edmund's losing his grave digging job. It has been left to him to keep family intact body and spirit, but other paternal forces, whether nation or father, oppose this attempt. They have their standards; they have their guilt. But what is Edmund to do?

Edmund is in the process of being all used up. In a scene out of Dickens, he is used by other thieving children, who even confiscate the precious money he had made by selling an item that his neighbor has donated for that purpose. Nor is he safe from adults. A former teacher, whose sexual interest in him Edmund mistakes for pure affection, also uses Edmund. This teacher, a Nazi still, is involved in clandestine political activity in which he involves Edmund, who is unaware of the use to which he is being put. Edmund looks up to this man as a father; the teacher is indeed a father's age—in years, Edmund's own father could be Edmund's grandfather—and he is someone to whom Edmund feels he can confide, someone who seems to listen to him. One day, Edmund tells his former teacher about his father's hopeless remarks, his father's courtship of the idea of suicide. Distracted from his own political activities, the teacher thoughtlessly says things that Edmund interprets as meaning that killing his father, for his father's sake and the sake of the family, would be the right thing to do. Edmund steals poison from the hospital where his father stays for a spell. At home, once his father returns, he poisons his father, who dies. But when he tells his former teacher what he has done, expecting the approval, the gold star, he so desperately needs, the man, fearing political exposure and legal consequences for himself, turns on the boy. In killing his father, the boy has done a horrible thing. How could he do that? How can he now say that the teacher directed this act? The boy is left shattered. He has lost all three of his fathers: his nation; his actual father; his former teacher.

A child is lost before our eyes. We can do nothing to bring him back because we can do nothing to bring his father back. Some acts are irreversible, and a child especially is trapped in their emotional consequences. If you started from a point of barely coping with a burden that no child is emotionally equipped to bear, where do you end? What is Edmund to do? At the close of the film, the day of his father's funeral, we see Edmund for the first time at play. Searing irony. He is by himself on the pavement and then up in a bombed-out building, playing. Down below, his family, unaware of where he is, call out for him to join them. His eyes go blank, a train passes, taking all hope with it, and he takes his fall. A shot to the pavement confronts us with the result. Some acts are irreversible, and even if you are safely watching a film you are trapped in their emotional consequences.

Edmund: is he the lead character? Certainly the most dynamic "character" is Rossellini's camera—a darting, sweeping, probing, burrowing camera representing Rossellini's need to know about the consequences of War in a fallen foreign country. War is responsible—and Hitler. *Hitler.* In perhaps the film's most celebrated shot, the voice of Adolf Hitler, giving a rousing speech, plays off the phonograph record that Edmund has unwittingly transported at his former teacher's behest. (By symbolic association, Edmund is one of Hitler's children.) We hear that bodiless, empty, still shadowing voice, while what we see—what the camera shows—consists of the ruins of the Chancellery. What we see matches what we hear, and what we hear matches what we see.

But the conclusion of the film: How does something so tragic as Edmund's death become so satisfying, so beautiful to behold, and how does the beauty advance rather than detract from the tragedy? This is part of the majestic mystery of art that George Santayana attempted to explain near the turn of the century: "Art must not create only things that are abstractly beautiful, but it must conciliate all the competitors these may have to the attention of the world, and it must know how to insinuate their charms among the objects of our passion. But this subserviency and enforced humility of beauty is not without its virtue and reward. If the æsthetic habit lie under the necessity of respecting and observing our passions, it possesses the privilege of soothing our griefs. There is no situation so terrible that it may not be relieved by the momentary pause of the mind to contemplate it æsthetically." With Rossellini's neorealism, the beauty of his camera's eye consoles our grief even as the content, both releasing and containing our inconsolable grief, urges us to take social action. We are participants in that shot of Edmund face-down, crushed, on the pavement because it completes and invigorates our passion: our love for children; our love of life.

Edmund Meschke plays Edmund. *Germany, Year Zero* could have been Meschke's story. Acting it out perhaps spared him its *becoming* his story. This boy gives an indelible performance. It would remain cinema's most brilliant portrait of a boy for a dozen years, until Jean-Pierre Léaud's Antoine Doinel in François Truffaut's *The 400 Blows*.

A final note: *color*. Film color of one kind or another dates back to the late nineteenth century, when tinting and hand coloring were used. In the main, cinema's color experiment has failed since color so greatly restricts the range and diminishes the depth of visual expressiveness and emotional impact that are possible with black and white. On the other hand, commerce dictates the widespread use of color since the vast majority of filmgoers care nothing about films as art but only about films as superficial entertainment—mere television. (Today, most laboratories are set up to process only color film, and black-and-white film stock is rare to come by in any case.) However, a relatively small number of films in color provide instances where "the exception proves the rule." The 1940s produced the first outstanding film in color where the use of color actually contributed to the film's artistic success: Laurence Olivier's full-color *Henry V* (1944), which has remained the single most brilliant film from the United Kingdom.

The list:

1940

THE LONG VOYAGE HOME (U.S.). Drawn from four sea plays by Eugene O'Neill, here is John Ford's most poetic and affecting film—this, despite a slip or two into island native-exotica that, ridiculous, the original texts do nothing to discourage. Noble and humane, and rich with a sense of "the pity of war" (Wilfred Owen's phrase, not O'Neill's), *The Long Voyage Home* transcends (as Ford films often have to do) all manner of blemishes, including bad acting by John Wayne and Ward Bond, two normally reliable Ford regulars. (Wayne fumbles with a Swedish accent and doesn't seem quite dumb enough—a frightening prospect.) On the other hand, there is marvelous acting by Thomas Mitchell, Wilfred Lawson, Barry Fitzgerald and Arthur Shields, Fitzgerald's brother.

The film is set during the First World War but addresses the time in which it was made, reflecting Ford's unease over the world's then-current unsettled state, which for Ford and others the bombing of Pearl Harbor, less than two years away, would bring to a point of decision. The mood pervading *The Long Voyage Home* is of dispossession and homelessness, of irresolution, disquieting uncertainty. Sailors onboard the merchant ship Glencairn, like those in Ford's *Mister Roberts* (1955), inhabit a suspended state; a time-erasing fog envelops the Glencairn. This cargo vessel becomes a target of war; is *nothing* safe? Survivors and lost hands equally seem ghosts of the past: souls lost either to war or to time—souls "lost" in the very moment of their lives.

Incalculably aided by a virtuoso script by Dudley Nichols (which removes almost all of

O'Neill's use of dialect), Gregg Toland's shimmeringly beautiful black-and-white cinematography and Richard Hageman's haunting music, Ford thus distills an elegiac lament for us all. Especially in the last movement, his filmmaking achieves powerful, sweeping results.

THE GREAT DICTATOR (U.S.). Achingly funny, *The Great Dictator* finds Charles Chaplin belatedly letting into a film of his more than just a trickle of sound—and now, not to skewer a pompous politician (as in *City Lights*, 1930) or to ridicule the intrusiveness of sound in cinema (as with the nonsense song in *Modern Times*, 1936), but to excoriate Adenoid Hynkel's—Adolf Hitler's—messianic rants. At least on film, Hitler doesn't stand a chance.

Chaplin directs from his own script, and his double role here—as Tomania's anti-Semitic dictator who rules under the sign of the Double Cross, and, in the Ghetto, a polite, humane Jewish barber, a tad shell-shocked from his First World War experience (more or less, the Charlie who is familiar to us)—results in a split performance of sheer brilliance. There are any number of high points: the hilarious discrepancy between Hynkel's angry, vicious speeches in gibberish-"German" and their official translations into mild, conciliatory English; exposing megalomania, Hynkel's private ballet with a balloon globe of the world that he hopes to conquer, the ball bouncing off his head, arms, hip and buttocks; mistaken for Hynkel, the barber giving a speech that discloses his own loving heart rather than Hynkel's foul hatred. The last yields to an image of the barber's beloved Hannah (Paulette Goddard, irresistible), now in a concentration camp, perhaps telepathically hearing his words and looking up at the sky: a deeply moving finale.

Chaplin, the conscience of American cinema, could not fully imagine Nazi Germany's brutality or evil; the concentration camp here is a detention camp, not a death camp. But who knows what it cost the world that Franklin Delano Roosevelt, wedded to a policy of neutrality, kept Chaplin's film from being made for two years?

THE GRAPES OF WRATH (U.S.). During the Depression, the Joads and their extended family leave Oklahoma for California, the new Promised Land. Sharecroppers, they've been displaced by Nature and inhuman nature—dust bowl erosion and a foreclosing bank. They embody the hardships and aspirations of a people.

The Grapes of Wrath opens with young Tom Joad, paroled from prison, halted in the road on his way home. The film (apart from a sentimental scene the studio attached) also ends in the middle of things, with Tom having killed another man, a civilian "cop" who bludgeoned to death a friend of Tom's, a former preacher-turned-laborist who had been working to counter the local exploitation of homeless workers. In an eternizing long-shot, Tom walks across the horizon. Whatever in his journey on the lam he can do to help the oppressed, the downtrodden (". . . since I'm an outlaw already . . ."), he will do. But his solitariness will be less a political opportunity, which John Steinbeck's novel reduces it to, than endless heartache. Tom and his family will likely never reunite.

John Ford's imagery is brilliant. Superimposed Caterpillar tractors razing homes from which tenant farmers have been evicted appear alien, to underscore the unnaturalness of farm equipment's use against farmers—an instance of withering visual irony. Later, a traveling shot into a migrant camp finds faces and forms listlessly passing before the camera. They appear worn, depleted, ghostlike—a reflection of hopelessness among the dispossessed.

Henry Fonda's Tom Joad is insolent, embittered, selfish, loyal to family and friends, struggling to understand what is happening to himself and others, noble, unselfish and caring at times—a tangle of human contradictions. An Everyman precipitously poised at crossroads where great decency and great viciousness seem equal possibilities, he is the stirring quintessence of human possibility.

Chronology of World Cinema

1940

THE SHOP AROUND THE CORNER (U.S.). Having just made the heavenly *Ninotchka* (1939), highlighted by one of the greatest comedy performances in cinema, Greta Garbo's, Ernst Lubitsch now made a charming, funny, warm, delicate and, surprisingly, deeply moving romantic comedy, *The Shop Around the Corner*.

The setting is Matuschek's, a bourgeois gift shop in Budapest in the early 1930s. Two of the employees, Klara Novak and Alfred Kralik, constantly bicker. What Kralik doesn't know is that he is in love with Klara. They are anonymous pen-pals. Will the two come together in one another's arms or forever conduct their romance through the post office?

The title sets the universal tone of the piece. It also distances the time of its activities from the time when the film was made and released. The world that Lubitsch so lovingly details is just out of reach—"around the corner." The agent of change in Europe has been Adolf Hitler. In the guise of light romantic comedy, Lubitsch's *Shop* is his lament for the Europe that he remembers, the Europe that has vanished. A Berliner, Lubitsch also was Jewish, and this deepens his lament. The tenderness with which he gazes at the interconnected lives at Matuschek's is an index of the keen sense of loss he feels. They are a kind of family. This film is unique in Lubitsch's canon; it is emotionally full.

Actors are indispensable to Lubitsch. His star, sherry-voiced Margaret Sullavan, is wonderful as Klara, hilarious, poignant; James Stewart is good as Kralik; and the European-born Jewish actors in the supporting cast, Joseph Schildkraut, Frank Morgan and Felix Bressart, are excellent.

Along with Lubitsch, we all end up missing Matuschek's. And we miss his glowing film, until we pop it back in the machine and it breaks our hearts all over again.

POWER AND THE LAND (U.S.). *The bread we eat and the milk we drink depend on Bill and Hazel Parkinson . . . and their farm and how they're making out.*

Produced by the Rural Electrification Administration (REA), part of the U.S. Department of Agriculture, *Power and the Land* opens with a long-shot of rural America: a great expanse of sky beneath which trees and a house appear tiny. Birds fly through. Dutch documentarian Joris Ivens holds the shot long enough so that we take in the pertinent fact: No power lines interrupt this vast, open space. *Why?* Voiceover commentary—this is, otherwise, almost entirely a silent film—explains, "Power companies want a profit," and this they can make in cities but not in the country, where returns cannot overcome the cost to them for equipment and service. "The farms are left in the dark—[in 1940,] three out of four farms are left in the dark in this big, inventive country. Seems wrong somehow."

In 1935, the REA was set up to remedy this situation by offering low-interest loans to cooperatives of farmers, who then collectively own the means for generating power they themselves have bought and installed. An Ohioan family whom the film chronicles, the Parkinsons, become members of the Belmont Electric Cooperative. First, the film shows the daily hardships that the want of electricity imposes. A passage shows farmers in the area harvesting corn together; this spirit of cooperation at work leads to the formation of their electric cooperative, to make work easier. The film then catalogs numerous ways in which electricity makes life easier for Bill and Hazel Parkinson and their children.

Hearteningly, *Power and the Land* thus finds a space in American life (already inhabited by the U.S. postal service) amenable to socialist ideas.

PRIMROSE PATH (U.S.). Gregory LaCava's *Primrose Path* observes an impoverished family that today would be adjudged to be highly dysfunctional. The Adamses live in a shanty town, in a dilapidated house, by railroad tracks near, say, the Pacific coast. Homer doesn't work; his life has turned to despair, with gin his solace, in a country that places little value on his higher education and love of learning. Homer's wife, Mamie, supports their spotty, generally subsistent existence by prostitution although, for this field of employment, she is conspicuously past her prime. Her vicious mother, who is openly derisive of Homer, lives with them. Two children complete the family: proud, defensive Ellie May, a teenager (Ginger Rogers, achingly moving), and her unruly younger sister, Honeybell.

The film opens brilliantly, with the camera slightly panning to survey the tawdry environment where other poor children, to make themselves feel better, taunt Honeybell, on her way home from school, regarding her mother's line of work. Actually, this scene directly follows a written quotation from ancient Greek dramatist Menander that sums up Homer's (as well as LaCava's) philosophical resignation: "We live, not as we wish to, but as we can." Mamie also is living not as she wishes but as she can.

Ellie May falls in love with a burger-joint cook; they marry behind her screen of lies concealing her family background. Their eventual exposure busts the marriage. Another shock for Ellie May: her mother's shooting death at her father's hand as Mamie succeeds in foiling Homer's suicide attempt. Now it's Ellie May's turn to support the family; and, although a tacked-on Hollywood ending spares her a life of prostitution, LaCava has compellingly detailed the atmosphere and circumstances that seemingly lead Ellie May by degrees to a repetition of her mother's fortunes.

A trenchant anticipation of *neorealismo*.

THE LETTER (U.S.). Based on actual events upon which W. Somerset Maugham drew for his story and play, William Wyler's moody *The Letter* studies colonialist racism.

Robert Crosbie runs a Singapore rubber plantation. Wife Leslie (Bette Davis, staggering) had an affair with Geoffrey Hammond, whom she kills, and whose marriage to a Eurasian woman, once disclosed, turns the white British community against the deceased as they close ranks in defense of their own presence in Malaya. The film opens with a crane shot across the flimsy shacks of natives who work for the Crosbies, progressing to the shooting-death on the veranda of the Crosbies' posh bungalow. The piercing sound of revolver discharges is superimposed on images of the roused, frightened Malayans. The British, who don't belong in this environment, have nonetheless quite taken over.

Leslie's English lawyer, Howard Joyce (James Stephenson, superb), seems rock-solid, smooth as silk; his Malayan assistant, Ong Chi Seng, is an unctuous schemer: hatred seething almost invisibly beneath an accommodating smile. In the courthouse parking lot, Joyce leaves in his big, smooth-running automobile, revealing what it blocked from view: the Malayan lawyer's tiny, rickety, noisy vehicle.

Since Hammond's wife has in her possession a letter from Leslie to Hammond that could get Leslie hanged, her power over Leslie tests Leslie's sense of control. Leslie convinces Howard to risk disbarment by purchasing the letter, which costs Robert everything. "With all my heart," an acquitted Leslie shouts at him, "I still love the man I killed!"

At night, Leslie seems pulled outside by her own shadow, which is to say, the full moon, to her own death (symbolically, the British Empire being drawn to its extinction): while her "head boy" holds Leslie, Hammond's widow, executing her husband's revenge, stabs her through the heart.

Exquisite editing by Warren Low.

1941

CITIZEN KANE (U.S.). *See above*.

THE MALTESE FALCON (U.S.). By hardboiling French poetic realism, John Huston invented American *film noir*. The occasion was *The Maltese Falcon*, from Dashiell Hammett.

Here is a seedy, absurd world of intrigue, deception and betrayal played out, mostly by transients, in hotel rooms, dark, deserted streets, and private detective Sam Spade's San Francisco office. It's a blend of frayed and world-weary though persistent humanism, mordant wit, existentialism, cruelty and precise psychology, all unfolding in a landscape pitched between reality and nightmare.

Spade and Miles Archer are partners in a shoestring operation. Suddenly Archer is dead, the result of a tangled case of theirs involving a beautiful, slippery client, Brigid O'Shaughnessy. Spade seduces Brigid, whose character riddles, play-acting and tricky machinations intrigue and delight him. In her he has found his purest partner, someone as treacherous and dangerous as himself. Brigid falls in love with Sam but also plunges him into a whirlpooling abyss whose bottom is the gallows, in order to escape from which, at the last, Spade sacrifices her and, with her, all hope of love's redemption: the most shattering conclusion in American cinema.

Spade's "code of honor" is pure rationalization. Spade says a man must do something when his partner is killed. However, he himself wanted Archer dead. Thus O'Shaughnessy's mere presence would taunt Spade with his sense of complicity in his partner's death. Brigid might also murder him. Moreover, she has introduced him to a trio of homosexual adventurers who have tested the tight fist of his sexual discomfort. Sam Spade must destroy Brigid O'Shaughnessy to confirm, for himself, his heterosexual identity: a breathtaking analysis of American misogyny. He must feel a lover's pain, and to feel it he must sacrifice his beloved. He turns her over to the police.

Humphrey Bogart and Mary Astor give electrifying performances.

THE WHITE SHIP (Italy). The raising of a naval ship's three guns, along with similar flashes of militaristic rhetoric, recalls *Battleship Potemkin* (1925)—an odd thing, one would think, for a Fascist film to do. Things get stranger, for this Eisensteinian opening is immediately undercut by a warm-hearted, very funny scene among sailors composing letters to female pen-pals, the humanity of which in turn is undercut the next day by a call to posts aboard ship and a spate of officious, impersonal military conduct among officers as battle breaks out. A sailor, Augusto Basso, will not be able to meet Elena, the schoolteacher who is his pen-pal, after all. The filmmaker is Roberto Rossellini, and *La nave bianca* is the launch of his so-called "Fascist trilogy." Blending scripted fiction, beautifully enacted by nonprofessionals, and devastating documentary footage, it is one of the most moving films about war I have seen.

Young Basso is badly wounded in the engagement. He is operated on in casualty ward 3— and a shot of a surgeon's hand, gripping a scalpel and moving towards the patient as bombing shakes up the room, is far more compelling than anything in *M*A*S*H* (Robert Altman, 1970). Hemorrhaging, Basso is transferred to a Red Cross hospital ship for further surgery in an attempt to save his leg. His volunteer nurse, it turns out, is Elena, who keeps her identity secret from Basso since it is her duty to tend to all patients equally. The closing shot, a closeup of the cross on her uniform, follows heartrending scenes of injured sailors and soldiers, a singalong by patients on deck, and a mass. An Allied bomber flies overhead, honoring the inviolate space that a Red Cross ship represents.

Subversively antiwar and in humanity's corner, Rossellini's government-sanctioned first feature shines.

SULLIVAN'S TRAVELS (U.S.). *Hey, am I laughing?*

John L. Sullivan, heavyweight champion from Boston, met his match, decades after his demise, in another John L. Sullivan (Joel McCrea, wonderful), the successful Hollywood musical-comedy director in *Sullivan's Travels* whose masquerade as a hobo, intended to bring authenticity to his planned foray into socially committed cinema (*O Brother, Where Are Thou?*), reverses the boxer's ascension from poverty to celebrity. Our John L. ends up in a brutal prison while the nation thinks him dead. (His butler warned him this would happen!) That's life in socioeconomically topsy-turvy America.

Following his glorious romantic comedy *The Lady Eve* (1941), this time writer-director Preston Sturges gave romance a back seat, allowing it in at all only because "there is always sex in a picture," and dedicated *Sullivan's Travels* to clowns and buffoons—those who make us laugh. In turn, his Swiftian road comedy makes us laugh aplenty—until, that is, Sullivan's suffering becomes all too real. Sullivan's middle initial, we discover, stands for Lloyd, not Lawrence—a witty reference to Lloyds of London: as rich as this man is, his firsthand study of American injustice makes him uninsurable!

After his ordeal and resurrection, Sullivan decides against making a film about the beseiged underclass in favor of another hilarious trifle; the poor need to laugh more than anyone, he reasons. This lame conclusion—in truth, what the poor *really* need is more systemic justice so that they have less need for antidotal laughter—matters little, because the weight of the film documents Sullivan's descent into America's underbelly, where a tramp is mowed down on the tracks after robbing his play-acting surrogate. Critic Andrew Sarris nails the Social Darwinian metaphor: the derelict "is trapped in a metal jungle of switch rails, and is unable to avoid an oncoming train."

TOBACCO ROAD (U.S.). Written by Nunnally Johnson, John Ford's tonally complex, hilarious *Tobacco Road* restores the sympathy for the poor and understanding of poverty that distinguish Erskine Caldwell's 1932 novel, but which Jack Kirkland's long-running play replaced with condescension and theatricality. With the soul and eye of a poet, moreover, Ford has conjured a folk fable that lends to the material a sense of timelessness—or, rather, the sense of struggling humanity being constantly lost to time. One wonders whether Ford's haunting imagery of fall leaves blowing across the land owes something to Shelley's *Ode to the West Wind*.

Charley Grapewin gives the performance of a lifetime as Jeeter Lester, an ageing one-time tenant-sharecropper whose marginal existence has induced lethargy. He and his wife, Ada, have had sixteen children, five of whom are buried on the land that Jeeter used to farm for owner John Harmon, nine of whom have married and scattered or simply abandoned him and Ada, and two of whom, the youngest, Dude and Ellie May, still live in the family's dilapidated shack. Twenty-year-old Dude (William Tracy, frighteningly funny) abuses Jeeter horribly, brutally: this, for Jeeter, perhaps the ultimate blow.

The bank has foreclosed on the property and the Lesters must leave in days for the poor house unless Jeeter can raise $100 for annual rent that Harmon's son has negotiated with the bank. Dude has married a much older widow, Sister Bessie, a minister-minstrel whose husband's life insurance policy paid for the new car that means everything to Dude.

Ford, Hollywood's premier atheist, allows us to see the role of religion in these blighted lives without having to truck through extraneous religious affect and sentimentality. In so many ways, Ford is the man for the job here.

Sam Peckinpah declared *Tobacco Road* his favorite film by John Ford.

THE LADY EVE (U.S.). The sexiest romantic comedy ever, and also the funniest, *The Lady Eve*, brilliantly written and directed by Preston Sturges from a story by Monckton Hoffe, revolves around boy and girl. Charles ("Hopsy") prefers snakes to women and is heir to the Pike's Ale fortune, while self-assured con-artist Jean is out to fleece him. But the two fall in love, he finds out about her and turns on her (so far, so *Mr. Deeds*), and she impersonates the veddy British Lady Eve Sedgwick, one-upping him in society's ranks, getting him to fall for this lookalike and, this time, getting him to marry her. On their honeymoon trip to Niagara Falls, amidst stormy weather, Eve recounts numerous past marriages and affairs, scandalizing Hopsy, who slides into mud while hastening off the train. Her "sweet" revenge, though, depresses Jean, who earlier told Hopsy: "Good women aren't as good as you think they are, and the bad ones aren't as bad. Not nearly as bad."

Jean maneuvers another meeting—onboard a ship, like the first time, and—lesson learned—Charles throws his arms around Jean, who mutters, "Why did we have to go through all this nonsense?" Well, Jean also had a lesson to learn: that men aren't either chumps or snakes,

1941

or both. When these two come together as unprejudiced equals, it is tremendously moving. Charles confesses he is married; Jean responds, "But so am I."

Priceless: Jean, seated, "stalking" Charles in the ship's dining hall by looking into a compact mirror; Charles's intensifying sexual swoon as Jean plays, plays with his hair ("Why, Hopsy, you ought to be kept in a cage"); Charles's multiple falls at the dinner in Eve's honor; Charles's marriage proposal as the horse of one of them keeps interrupting by nuzzling him.

1942

THE MAGNIFICENT AMBERSONS (U.S.). Along with Erich von Stroheim's *Greed* (1924), studio-mutilated *The Magnificent Ambersons*, from Booth Tarkington, is one of the two great "lost works" of American cinema. It is still phenomenal, though: a dark, sober, penetrating meditation on a country in perpetual growth and transition. Nostalgia nearly coincides with experience, rather than waiting on the passage of time, amidst kaleidoscopic changes in fashion and—embodied in the "horseless carriage"—technology. An old-money family, the Ambersons, is tripped by these changes and, eventually, left behind.

Perhaps the most hauntingly beautiful sequence Welles ever shot is the Amberson ball. The camera follows guests in through the front door, winds of recollection rushing by; when guests dance in the echoing hall, an intricately choreographed long take discloses the last gasp, prior to bankruptcy, of the family's integrated high life. Later on, these exceptionally fluid shots reach an ironic impasse on the town's new, flat-sounding city street, where Welles's superimpositions of upheaval, denoting progress, find the insular family dream, along with the bones of its youngest, sturdiest member (Tim Holt, excellent), broken (by an automobile) into bits—metaphorically, the price exacted from those unable to adapt to growth's rapid changes. Welles's voiceover is grimly prophetic as a dollying camera—a pedestrian—tours a town that now consists of profuse power lines, new tall buildings and low, abandoned ones: "George Amberson Minifer walked homeward slowly through what seemed to be the strange streets of a strange city. The town was growing and changing. It was heaving up in the middle, incredibly. It was spreading, incredibly. And as it heaved and spread, it befouled itself, and darkened its sky."

The Magnificent Ambersons identifies America with stunted emotion. Consider George's frustrated Aunt Fanny, soul-sister to Trina in *Greed*, and powerfully acted by Agnes Moorehead.

OBSESSION (Italy). Aristocrat and also Communist, Luchino Visconti combines elegance and earthiness in *Obsession*, a languorous melodrama of adultery and murder involving a drifter (Massimo Girotti), an innkeeper and his wife (Clara Calamai, astounding). Visconti had apprenticed in the 1930s to Jean Renoir, whose liberated use of camera Visconti adopted, and whose *Toni* (1934) is an especial thematic influence. *Ossessione* is the first great work of *neorealismo*, here blended with the moody fatalism of French poetic realism.

Neorealism revitalized Italian cinema. Use of northern landscape, close attention to human behavior, a focus on the downtrodden, the human cost of poverty and economic marginalization: these supply neorealist credentials to *Ossessione*.

One of the contributors to the script, Angelo Pietrangeli, would write about it: "Ferrara, its squares, its gray and deserted streets; Ancona and its San Ciriaco Fair; the Po and its sandy banks; a landscape streaked with a rubble of cars and men along the network of highways. Against this backdrop are silhouetted the wandering merchants, mechanics, prostitutes and inn boys who have all the typical innocent exuberances, beset by violent proletarian love affairs, primitive anger, and the sins that flesh is heir to." The somewhat grandiose nature of this description perfectly suits Visconti's film, with its operatic sense of spectacle and its grand passions—all, here at least, given compelling form by Visconti's artistic rigor.

Unfortunately, trouble with censors and with copyright laws delayed the film's appearance worldwide, leaving the false impression that others were more instrumental in inventing Italian neorealism than Visconti, and helping to obscure Renoir's contribution. *Ossessione* is an "illegal" adaptation of James M. Cain's American novel *The Postman Always Rings Twice*, which Hollywood would badly film twice (1946, 1981), but which György Fehér, in Hungary, would again lift to the level of art in *Szenvedély* (*Passion*, 1998).

I WAS A FIREMAN (UK). Released in 1943 in the shortened version *Fires Were Started*, *I Was a Fireman* is a documentary reconstruction; actual firemen play firemen like themselves battling and quelling an enormous fire, the result of German aerial bombing of London during the Blitz. At Y substation, Precinct 14, men arrive from home and civilian jobs; the film spans 24 hours, dawn to dawn, siren alert to all-clear. These homefront warriors prepare for battle and do nighttime battle modestly, uncomplainingly, untouched by the bombast of a Hitler—or a Churchill. The film stays with the men, except for contextualizing snippets showing staff who are also in the system. No Luftwaffe plane is shown.

Detailed as to individual characters and firefighting preparations and procedure, this film by Humphrey Jennings shows British citizens united in labor and by a common cause: the war effort. Blending dramatic enactment and stock footage, the firefighting scenes are the most brilliant and thrilling of their kind.

But the film is also ironical. It opens on a frieze of ancient soldiers. Script introduces a backward glance—winter/spring 1940-1941. A new member of the squad, Barrett, who works in advertising, must be brought into the fold. Banter amongst the men, for the most part genial, occasionally lights on (and as quickly exits) an edgier note pertaining to class division. War brings these men together in both senses, but war reconciles their differences only in its own moment. Robert Browning: ". . . the good minute goes." Success: the warship moves out at dawn. Its immediate destination is combat; its ultimate destination, the past, leaving Britain to her future. How much at home will remain resolved after the war?

I Was a Fireman is a compounded epic, expressing at once the aspirations and the anxieties of a people.

FOUR MEN ON A RAFT (U.S.). This was part of the ill-fated, never completed Orson Welles documentary about Brazilian culture and politics, *It's All True*. It is a reconstruction of the voyage on a sailing raft that four impoverished fishermen had made eight months earlier from Fortaleza to Rio de Janeiro, then Brazil's capital, to present in person their grievances to President Getúlio Vargas. In the "feudal system" then in place, owners of rafts—*jagandas*—appropriated from such fishermen half their catch, imposing poverty no matter how hard the fishermen worked, while by law these same workers were denied the social service benefits available to other poor, *union* workers. Vargas initially renegged on his promise to remedy the situation but, perhaps pressured by Welles's filming, extended all normal benefits to *jangadeiros*, including housing, and medical and retirement benefits. During filming, the leader of the four men, Manoel Olimpio Meira, nicknamed Jacaré (Alligator), died. Welles's postscript haunts: "Jacaré and the others made their voyage by *jaganda* exactly as it is here filmed. They were sixty-one days in the open sea, without compass, and guided only by the stars. . . ."

The film is silent (given the equipment RKO provided, it could not have been otherwise), although sound effects and music were later added. This punctuation deepens the dreamy effect of the silence. The voyage is epic; the four men stop at various points along the way, mostly to interact with others (although in one scene they pray by themselves), affording cinematographer George Fanto opportunities to collaborate with Welles on gorgeously mysterious extreme long-shots of the men walking across sandy land, on the horizon or towards the camera, which is to say, us. The film is equally mysterious on water; a man will suddenly appear as a shade behind the sail.

1942

THE DEVIL'S ENVOY (France). This medieval parable about evil's attempt to destroy love on Earth refers to the present, to the plight of Occupied France. Jacques Prévert, who co-wrote the script, intended the Devil as a stand-in for Hitler. Director Marcel Carné's use of the past enabled him to get this film past Vichy censors.

Les visiteurs du soir—literally, *Evening Visitors*—captivates. The opening irises out, in a downward long-shot, on the Devil's two envoys masquerading as minstrels, Gilles and Dominique, who is masquerading as a boy, Gilles's brother. (Think Manda in Ingmar Bergman's *The Magician*, 1958.) The use of the iris, by its connection to silent cinema (for instance, D. W. Griffith's), underscores the sense of the past that Carné means to conjure. The camera's distance may also suggest cosmic observation, God's or the Devil's. In any case, a series of cuts makes our view of the riders increasingly accessible; we are being drawn into the past as correlative to our being drawn into the story. The envoys' destination: Baron Hugues's fairy-tale castle, which is celebrating the (loveless) betrothel of Anne, Hugues's daughter, and Baron Renaud, a figure so close to being satanic he may represent Pétain. The envoys aim to uncouple the couple; Gilles himself falls in love with Anne, and she with him, while Dominique sets sights on both barons.

The castle is ravishing white. Think painter Kasimir Malevich's *White on White*—but also, perhaps, Hitler's notion of Aryan purity. In the grand ballroom Dominique's strum of her lute gradually slows down the dancing couples to a complete halt so that the envoys can choose their partners for romance. The scene eerily anticipates the film's ending, where the Devil turns Gilles and Anne into stone, but their hearts—the soul of France—keep beating.

MEN ON THE MOUNTAIN (Hungary). István Szöts's *Emberek a havason* adapts stories by József Nyirö about poor, uneducated folk living and working near and in the Carpathian Mountains. One family is the focus: Gergely Csuták, wife Anna, and their son, Gergo. When the film opens, Gergo is an infant; at the close he is a toddler—and an orphan.

His parents early on introduce Gergo to the pristine beauties of Nature; water, trees and animals are also part of their primitive, primal faith.

Landowners sell the mountains and trees to the factory run by the Arbor Company. With his eye on Anna, the supervisor hires Gergely as a woodcutter, enticing him with substantial pay, giving Gergely hope he can provide better for his son, and sends him on a wintertime work-related trip during which time he tries to rape Anna, who, resisting, starts a fire that spreads and burns down the factory. Anna ends up gravely ill.

Gergely and Anna go on a pilgrimage to a monastic shrine. A monk directs the couple to a doctor. At Kolozsvár, a specialist explains it is too late. Anna's dying wish is to be buried in Rákos. Unable to afford anything else, Gergely takes his wife's body onboard a train.

After the burial, Gergely axes to death the supervisor and is sentenced to ten years' imprisonment. Even a full explanation of the context doesn't move the judge, who insanely asserts, "The law is the law." (Shades of Javert!) One of Gergely's neighbors counters this with simple truth: "The law is no good if it doesn't bring justice to the innocent." Gergo, now five, is consigned to an orphanage. Gergely is shot trying to escape. The wound proves fatal. The friend hiding him claims the reward for his capture and buys little Gergo new boots and clothes.

1943

DAY OF WRATH (Denmark). Although based on a play by Wiers Jensen, Carl Theodor Dreyer's *Vredens Dag* is apt to remind U.S. Americans of Nathaniel Hawthorne. Anne (Lisbeth Movin, wondrous), a parson's much younger wife, falls in love with her stepson. After hearing her heart's confession, her husband dies, and her beloved guiltily joins those denouncing her as a witch—a designation that she, broken, accepts.

Dreyer discloses a seventeenth-century world of dark, spare interiors, where, like the stiffly dressed souls inhabiting them, light appears molded, constrained. Outdoors, the young clandestine couple steal respites of fresh, sunlit air amidst beauteous Nature. The "Dies Irae," which opens it, also closes the film; on the latter occasion, the "day of judgment" is Anne's. To her public confession, before she is burned to death, we bring our memory of *The Passion of Joan of Arc* (1928). Whereas he showed us Joan's execution, however, Dreyer leaves Anne poised in the direction of hers; because she lacks Joan's sure consolation of a heaven-to-come, Anne is trapped and uncertain on eternity's brink. Like Occupied Denmark, which she embodies. Anne's unquarrelsome move toward her terrible end makes comprehensible, as nothing else in cinema does, the countless wartime acts of civilian courage and sacrifice committed by Europeans who, like Anne, felt certain that they also were on their way to the stake. Under their eyes, Dreyer took aim at his nation's captors; but refusing this as his own day of judgment, he managed to escape to neutral Sweden. Anne's fatalistic impulse to die, by its spiritual integrity, thus informed Dreyer's impulse to live.

Somber, spiritually radiant, almost unendurably moving, *Day of Wrath* is a work whose gravity and deliberate pace suggest human responsibility as it is perfectly weighed in the mind of God.

PEOPLE OF THE PO VALLEY (Italy). Released in 1947, Michelangelo Antonioni's *Gente del Po* is a documentary, some of whose material involving a woman's care of her sick young daughter feels scripted, possibly "reconstructed." Luchino Visconti's documentary-like, also nonprofessionally cast *La terra trema* (1948), about struggling Sicilian fishermen, surely was influenced by *Gente del Po*, which with its lyrical river barges itself looks back to Jean Vigo's *L'Atalante* (1934), and ahead to Antonioni's fictional *Il grido* (1957), also set amidst melancholy gray landscapes in the Po Valley.

Numerous shots divide the frame, such as the overhead one of a barge, center-left, proceeding forward, displacing water while still untouched water appears ahead. Humanity, even when invisible, is the key; we are conscious of the human activity involved in the barge's motion and use. In another "divided shot," a barge proceeds screen-right, with water below and land, including houses, above: a summation of the environment in which people, also excluded here, live and work.

Human figures appear in both long-shot and closeup, communally and as individuals. In an extreme long-shot from the vantage of the river, a solitary galloping horse projects an otherwise unavailable freedom and possibly reflects on the German occupation. In a bravura shot, the camera moves leftward like a barge, but on land, as women under large white hats rake the ground. Down below on the barge "Milano," the mother feeds her child medicine as an identical hat hangs on the wall.

The tremendous final movement depicts a gathering storm, with its dire potential for flood. People now move quickly to their homes, disrupting the rhythms to which the film has accustomed us. The storm subsides, but the impression of human vulnerability lingers. This conclusion owes something to the snowstorm in Flaherty's *Nanook of the North* (1922).

SHADOW OF A DOUBT (U.S.). Alfred Hitchcock's favorite among his films, *Shadow of a Doubt* peers behind the façade of an "average American family" and their small town. Uncle Charlie, Emma Newton's brother, visits her and her family. Unbeknownst to the Newtons, Charles Oakley is the serial murderer of wealthy widows, whose jewels he confiscates. Hitchcock views Oakley's sociopathic anti-materialism as the extreme reactive consequence of the social and corporate preoccupation with wealth and profit—*money*—that grips the land. The film's symbolical vortex, captured by a low-hung, upwardly tilted camera, is the BankAmerica tower that pierces the sacramental heavens, setting Mammonism above spiritual values even in Santa Rosa, California. When Young Charlie alone comes to realize that her uncle is a killer, he tries several times to dispatch her. Eventually, though, she dispatches him in a struggle, and the town, without knowing its source, is the beneficiary of the blood-soaked philanthropic fund that Oakley had established.

In a way, Oakley is the celebrated American loner and rugged individualist pushed to the extreme of dementia. He suggests the mortal fear that American cultural and political myth works mightily to suppress—a fear that also accounts for American eleutheromania and money-mania. His sister, who dotes on him, embodies those nostalgic ties that impose limits on our lives, in her case, setting limits on her marriage to which her spouse, Joe, has had to adjust. Meanwhile, Joe's dull, demeaning job in a bank inspires his hobby of imaginary murder.

Teresa Wright's Young Charlie is a fetching portrait of innocence as it stumbles into lethal experience. But it is Patricia Collinge whose inspired acting as Emma deepens *Shadow of a Doubt*'s undertow of melancholy, helping Hitchcock most of all to balance the beauty of kindness and affection against the tragic frailty of human existence.

1944

HENRY V (UK). Drawing visually on *The Book of Hours*, Paolo Ucello's paintings, and Eisenstein's *Alexander Nevsky* (1938), Laurence Olivier's *Henry V*, from Shakespeare, was his contribution to Britain's war effort against Nazi Germany: a pageant and a battle film full of patriotic fervor and stirring rhetoric. Ingeniously, it shifts from the Globe Theater in Elizabethan London to the fifteenth century and, at the end, back again, all the while reflecting on the present (1944).

In a stupendous performance, Olivier is the young king whose heroism we see in the calm he exhibits the night before the big battle with France, and in his rousing St. Crispian's Day speech to his battered troops, exhorting them to fight.

The 1415 Battle of Agincourt is the film's great set-piece: the cascade of English arrows given amazing flight to reduce the French army to a more manageable number. The day turns out to be Harry's; and, after the reading of the names of the dead, come the play's most poignant lines, rendered by Olivier with devastating irony:

> Let there be sung Non nobis and Te Deum,
> The dead with charity enclosed in clay.
> And then to Calais, and to England then,
> Where ne'er from France arrived more happier men.

At Agincourt, the camera passes through a palace window to survey, in one long tracking shot, conquered France: a bleak, inconsolable landscape punctuated by two lone persons, a girl and a boy. The shot is so achingly desolate that it chastises Harry for the flippancy of his remark to Princess Katherine, the French king's daughter whom he is wooing for a politically advantageous wife, that he loves France so much he will not part with a village of it!

Olivier brought us all "a little touch of Harry in the night."

IVAN THE TERRIBLE, PART ONE (U.S.S.R.). Sergei Eisenstein's *Ivan Groznyy I*, about the sixteenth-century Russian Tsar, owes some of its grand style to Josef von Sternberg's *Scarlet Empress* (1934), about Catherine II. Yet a far more instructive influence comes from Eisenstein's favorite American film, John Ford's *Young Mr. Lincoln* (1939), in which the future president, becoming infatuated with the crowd's infatuation with *him*, dons his hat inside a court room—a slip into arrogance and populist demagoguery. When in Eisenstein's film Moscow's archduke declares himself Tsar of all Russia, the camera behind him records this ascension in a Fordian gesture: Ivan's lowering the ceremonial cap onto his own head. Assumption of power; the *presumption* of power.

The palace, populated by plotting nobles (Boyars), is full of cavernous dark hollows and looming human shadows by torchlight; during Ivan's self-anointment, a shaft of light could be coming from the present, suggesting a unification of times as well as of Russian lands. The battle against the Tartars in Kazan (for access to the Azov Sea) suggests Stalin's war against the Nazis. A heart-piercing passage: the long procession of Ivan's warriors as they go off to fight, each in turn dropping a coin into a plate. Ivan explains that the coins remaining unclaimed following the campaign will provide the number of their fallen. The heap of coins symbolizes the high price that wars exact.

Enlivened by sometimes thunderous movement through the frames, the static compositions make thrilling each rare camera movement. Editing, particularly the inserted, often angled closeups, expressionistically destabilize the static compositions and the cumulative impression they convey. The poisoning of Tsarina Anastasia, Ivan's own near-fatal illness and recovery, his self-exile and triumphant return on the wings of public adoration: all this underscores the fairy-tale nature of the first part of Eisenstein's planned trilogy.

MEET ME IN ST. LOUIS (U.S.). Vincente Minnelli's musical *Meet Me in St. Louis* chronicles the Smith family through one seasonal cycle at the turn of the century. The most emotionally rich and turbulent of all his films (including the melodramas), it juxtaposes stability and flux—the things in our life, such as family, that appear to be rooted but are at constant risk for change, and the things, such as romance, that seem too fragile not to dissolve but which become the repository of our future hopes.

We never do discover whether Esther Smith (Judy Garland, glorious) marries her boyfriend. Uncertainty, anxiety, the inability of the strongest human emotions to stabilize our lives in the powerful current of time's passage: Minnelli has staked out a tremendous theme. Moreover, he explores its most problematic material. Lon, Esther's brother, and John, her boyfriend, resemble one another; their names rhyme. What is "the boy next door," after all, but a brother with an extra wall in between? Indeed, the inwardness of American family life, incestuous nostalgia, and the appetite of family to incorporate non-family all come together in a phenomenal set-piece. John is unable to take Esther to a Christmas ball because his tuxedo is locked up at the cleaner's; so her grandfather steps in as her escort, telling her how much she resembles his late wife. We see the dancing couple disappear behind the enormous pagan Christmas tree, but, when they emerge from behind it, Esther is no longer in her grandfather's arms. Miraculously, John, in the correct attire, has replaced him. Turn your mind around all the ramifications of *that*!

There is a reverse traveling shot to die for in the thrilling Halloween passage, and the songs are wonderful, especially "Have Yourself a Merry Little Christmas," with its profound melancholy.

DOUBLE INDEMNITY (U.S.). In adapting James M. Cain's novel, Billy Wilder, who directed, and Raymond Chandler created what may be the most brilliant American movie script ever. *Double Indemnity* is narrated—as a long confession into an insurance office Dictaphone—by a man who, having been shot, is as good as dead. Words, blood are pouring out of Walter Neff, an insurance salesman, who, along with the man's wife apparently, murdered a client. Neff's "confession" is as much accusation as confession. His target: his alleged accomplice and lover, Phyllis Dietrichson, whom he has just shot to death, in a clinch, at point-blank range, erasing the possibility of any airing of *her* side of the story.

Wilder riddles Neff's account with ambiguity. We learn that Neff's idea to commit a client-murder predated his meeting Phyllis Dietrichson! At the end of scenes Dietrichson is shown fixed in a cold, evil stare. This is Neff's characterization of Phyllis at moments *after* he departed the scene. Thus does Wilder expose the disingenuous, self-serving nature of Neff's confession. Because Neff is narrating, our minds and eyes are in his grip.

In their first encounter, Walter seems less interested in finding out about Phyllis than in making love with her. The indirection of his learning her first name through that "honey of an anklet" she wears suggests his attempt to entrap her in his particular view of women, who exist for him as potential conquests. The whole tone of this meeting fits Neff to a predatory disposition. Misogynistic Neff is ill-equipped to help navigate us through Phyllis's ambiguous humanity, which Wilder and phenomenal Barbara Stanwyck make profoundly, irresistibly moving.

Thus does Wilder, a Jew whose parents died in a Nazi death camp, move us to consider the cost of not believing in the reality of other people.

BLUEBEARD (U.S.). There is a point in the Seine underneath a bridge where "Bluebeard," the serial killer who is terrorizing Paris, especially its young women, and whose identity is unknown, drops in darkness the corpses of his strangled victims. The matte-shot—a sketch of the bridge is visually meshed with a studio tank shot—reeks of artificiality and reality, reminding us that the real Seine is an "engineered river," a conjoining of Nature and manmade construction. Much else also contributes to the confusion/conflation of reality and nonreality, the representation of reality and the thing being represented, subjectivity and objectivity. Ultimately, we are looking at a point in "Paris" that coincides with the killer's trapped and tormented mind, in which projectively we find ourselves also drowning; the recurrent shot is both exterior and interior, outside and psychological. Like the serial killer of children in Fritz Lang's *M* (1931), Bluebeard cannot help himself. He is driven to kill by impulses and forces beyond his control.

Edgar G. Ulmer, the director of *Bluebeard*, and Eugen Schüfftan, who also contributed (along with Jockey Arthur Feindel) to the film's eerie black-and-white cinematography, collaborated on the film's production design, evoking a nineteenth-century Paris of their own mind as well as Bluebeard's, where the "outdoors" of a puppeteer's nighttime show plainly is studio-bound, contributing to the overall effect and surrounding us with the killer's conscious mind and unconscious. "Poverty row" director Ulmer makes his meager means artistically count and thus triumphs over Hollywood.

Soft-spoken John Carradine, replacing Boris Karloff, Ulmer's first choice for the role a decade earlier, is memorable as Gaston Morrell, the sensitive painter-puppeteer who just cannot stop killing, and who for survival's sake must even assault Lucille, his beloved whom he had hoped would release him from his mental curse.

1945

SAN PIETRO (U.S.). Narrated by the director, John Huston's *San Pietro* documents the costly battle to capture and liberate a strategic Italian village forty miles southeast of Rome in 1943. The version we have, about a half-hour long, is one-third of the length of Huston's cut; the U.S. government slashed it for being antiwar. Huston's famous response to the American High Command: "If I ever make anything other than an antiwar film, I hope you take me out and shoot me." (Some of the censored material is included in the DVD of Huston's 1947 *Treasure of the Sierra Madre*.)

The film's opening surveys the valley at whose threshold San Pietro is located. It is a place of devastation and desolation because war has prevented the planting and tending of grapes and olives, which normally make the region lush. Huston explains that the elevated area beyond the valley had to be taken hill by hill. We glimpse American soldiers as Huston explains in detail the plan for taking San Pietro. The most ferocious, trenchant battle footage ever, some of it hauntingly shot through fluttering leaves of trees, is punctuated by montages of human death. A stunning passage: Soldiers wrapped in snow-white shrouds. A montage of enemy deaths also grips. More battle footage; more deaths. In all of the passages essaying American deaths, the corpses include soldiers we earlier saw alive, socializing with comrades. Huston informs us that many of the survivors of the Battle of San Pietro whom we are watching have since, in fact, joined their fallen comrades.

The film closes with wonderful shots of the liberated villagers. This conclusion is sober, heartrending—not exultant. Huston at least holds out hope that the children will rebound. I'm not so sure. See Roberto Rossellini's *Germany, Year Zero* (1947).

1945

BERLIN (U.S.S.R.). Yuli Raizman's celebrated World War II documentary is about the capture and defeat of Berlin by the Red Army after British and U.S. aerial bombardment had reduced the city to rubble. Most U.S. highschoolers apparently believe that their nation fought the Soviet Union in the Second World War. There may be some poetic justice here, if one recalls the non-aggression pact between Stalin and Hitler in the 1930s. But how about schools at least showing these kids *Berlin*?

This would also teach these students something about cinema. In one scene in the film, as the sound of bombing proceeds on the soundtrack, a Soviet soldier helps an infirm German across the street. Well, *perhaps*; for a trick of editing may have combined bombing from another time with the no-less-kind act. Sterling fellow that soldier, but not necessarily heroic.

The most oft-quoted documentary of all time contains bits and passages that are still being recycled, such as an aerial traveling shot of the ruined city. (The VHS box: "Over 40 Byelorussian and Ukrainian 1st Army cameramen contributed footage.") But perhaps what is most remarkable is Raizman's (and co-editor Yelizaveta Svilova's) correlation of Berlin-present and Berlin-past. Germany's official unconditional surrender is prefigured by a shot of white flags outside city window after city window. The next shot is a flashback showing the swastika-adorned flags that the white ones have replaced.

Some details are grisly—such as the scene of the charred corpse of Goebbels, the Third Reich's Minister of Propaganda, after his suicide. Yet this is followed by an incredible visual idea: the radio tower that no longer is broadcasting his propaganda. It is an "Ozymandius"-touch, but within a scheme of collapsed rather than extensive time, an ironical reflection on the sudden bankruptcy of German aspiration and phallic dreams of domination.

ROME, OPEN CITY (Italy). With Vittorio De Sica's *Bicycle Thieves* (1948), Roberto Rossellini's strikingly beautiful *Roma, Città aperta* is the signature work of Italian Neorealism. Like Rossellini's *Paisà* (1946), it is a national epic.

Rome, 1943-44; the Nazis are in control of the city. The opening shot is of German soldiers loudly marching in goosestep through the streets, singing. Its fearsome echo brings unexpected poignancy to a later shot of rambuctious boys loudly playing in the streets, symbolically juxtaposing the aspiration for freedom and the constriction of freedom that the occupation represents. The film focuses on resistance, both underground and above ground, on the Gestapo's dragnet efforts to capture members of the Resistance, and on the ordinary citizens of Rome, who embrace resistance fighters as their surrogates as well as countrymen by hiding them and otherwise lending support. Filming began while the Germans were still there; the film itself is a ringing act of solidarity.

"We shot [the film]," Rossellini would say, "in the same settings in which the events we re-created had taken place." The film's realism, its present-tenseness, is potent, demonstrating the affinity for documentary of a certain kind of fiction. *Rome, Open City* reminds us that fiction and documentary, although opposite poles on a continuum of artistic expression, intermingle and blend their elements in individual works. Even melodramatic chords (to which a Rossellini film at that time was never immune) become a part of the film's raw fabric —exposed nerves of heightened drama that stress the dire, distorted reality that the German occupation imposed.

The film is populated by nonprofessionals, but not exclusively. Two professionals contributed legendary performances: Aldo Fabrizi, as the priest, and Anna Magnani as Pina. Both characters, like so many others in the film, exemplify the heroism to which ordinary people can rise.

THEY WERE EXPENDABLE (U.S.). In the Philippines the attack on Pearl Harbor is announced. Based on John Bulkeley, Naval Lieutenant John Brickley has been promoting the war-readiness of motor torpedo ("PT") boats, which the U.S. Navy regards as too flimsy for anything other than message delivery. Once the boats start proving themselves, however, their crews are consigned to a no-man's-land of official concern. These sailors are "expendable." Sacrifice is war duty's calling, and the only realistic orientation for sailors and other soldiers is the presumption that they will be killed.

Based on William L. White's book, Frank Wead's script is brilliant; but John Ford's filmmaking raises the result to an even higher level. Dramatizing elements of the fall of the Philippines while the Second World War was yet in progress, Ford's *They Were Expendable* has its rousing, patriotic moments and its poetic, elegiac ones; it is a film of hope and of solemn tribute to lost warriors and those who will be lost. Flanked by *The Long Voyage Home* (1940) and *Mister Roberts* (1955), it occupies the middle position in Ford's seafaring war trilogy. It's an American masterpiece.

Hauntingly, Ford and his black-and-white cinematographer, Joseph H. August, create scenes where characters appear as shadows. The lighting achieves a suggestion of humanity drifting into mystery, myth. The scenes of military engagement, despite a necessary reliance on studio back projection interwoven with outdoor shooting, electrify and terrify; they impress upon the viewer the reality of war to a greater degree than any other U.S. nondocumentary does.

The acting is excellent—with one exception. As Brickley, Robert Montgomery is laconic, compassionate without being sentimental, sly, funny, worn and weary, resolute. In his greatest role he gives the performance of a lifetime.

To this tremendously moving film "We shall return."

THE SOUTHERNER (U.S.). Expertly written by Jean Renoir, Hugo Butler, William Faulkner and Nunnally Johnson from George Sessions Perry's *Hold Autumn in Your Hand*, *The Southerner* was Renoir's favorite among his 1940s Hollywood movies. (It was largely shot on location in Texas.) It is passionate, humane, beautiful.

Renoir evokes a famous scene from Aleksandr Dovzhenko's *Earth* (1930) as a cotton-picker, at work in the field, dies on the ground surrounded by other sharecroppers. With his last breath, he tells friend Sam Tucker (Zachary Scott, superb) to work for himself. The implication is this: Since work is going to kill you no matter what, you might as well at least have the dignity of being your own boss.

Sam indeed quits his job and moves with his family into a dilapidated shack—"nothin' extra" is how Nona, his wife (Betty Field, also superb), describes it—on a small piece of fertile land by a river. The Tuckers have two young children and "Granny," Sam's irrascible grandmother (Beulah Bondi, heavily made up but memorable). The film chronicles a year of their struggles against poverty, illness, an antagonistic neighbor (J. Carrol Naish, giving the film's most complex performance), and God and Nature, with a torrential rainstorm seemingly aiming at wiping them out.

Early on, Renoir uses inserted objective shots to stabilize traveling camera's-eye-view shots of the land and the approaching shack—subjective tracking shots recalling the Joad family's entry into the camp in John Ford's somewhat similar *The Grapes of Wrath* (1940). Renoir's integrated themes both refer to humanity's cooperative spirit: the socioeconomic need of country and city folk for one another; the bond that farmers should nurture. Sam describes this as "neighborliness."

The film took the top prize at Venice; the National Board of Review named Renoir best director.

LES DAMES DU BOIS DE BOULOGNE (France). Denis Diderot, whose belief that knowledge is power was the impetus for his *Encyclopédie* during the Enlightenment, also wrote novels, including *Jacques le fataliste* (1773; 1796), an episode of which Robert Bresson, updating the plot to the present, adapted as *Les dames du Bois de Boulogne*. Under a political cloud, Jean Cocteau, who contributed brilliant dialogue, was scapegoated by the press when the film proved financially unsuccessful. Bresson's first masterpiece—and his last

film to use professional actors—is nonetheless a stunning melodrama.
Either as a preemptive strike or to test his love, Hélène (María Casares, strikingly good) tells Jean she no longer loves him. The move backfires. Praising her for honesty, and noting how horrible it would be if either's love would outlast the other's, Jean pledges abiding friendship and suggests they may reunite as lovers somewhere down the road. When Jean leaves, Hélène pledges to exact revenge. Her elaborate scheme, involving the manipulation of others, culminates in respectable Jean's falling in love with and marrying a "tart" whom he mistakes for an innocent.

During the lovers' parting, we glimpse through Hélène's apartment door the living room, where a floor lamp burns brightly; by contrast, black-dressed Hélène is consigned to shadow. The implication is that the artificial light is what remains of Hélène's spirit. This launches a motif. For instance, her mother tells Agnès, with whom Jean falls in love, "Dancing changes you. You light up like a lamp."

The film closes on an ambiguity. Once Agnès's sordid past has been exposed, Jean rushes to his bedridden bride, who has collapsed, and begs her to fight for life. Agnès: "I will stay." The final image of her may be one of rest. It is just as likely she did not stay.

THE STORY OF G.I. JOE (U.S.). "[T]he best memorial for every ordinary soldier who fought in the war" (Gabicz & Klinowski), William A. Wellman's *The Story of G.I. Joe* is based on Second World War correspondent Ernie Pyle's observations as Pyle accompanies a U.S. Army infantry unit, first in North Africa and subsequently in Italy. Killed during the Okinawa invasion, the Pulitzer Prize-winning journalist would never see Wellman's film, in which Burgess Meredith plays him beautifully, largely silently.

After a spate of Hollywood films that "thrilled up" and sentimentalized war for homefront consumption, Wellman's came as a breath of fresh air; its realism captured the experience of soldiers and the world of sadness, loneliness, exhaustion and sudden death in which they dutifully waited or performed. Leaning on two of Pyle's four books, which themselves derived from his newspaper columns, Leopold Atlas, Guy Endore and Philip Stevenson fashioned a marvelous script consisting of small incidents (such as a soldier's repeated attempts to hear his child speak on a phonograph record that his wife has sent him), snatches of rumination and conversation, and Pyle's voiceover.

This script is episodic, and Wellman's principal contributions, in addition to the excellent performances he drew (playing Lt., then Capt. Walker, Robert Mitchum is unforgettable), are the unhinging of conventional narrative that honoring the script produces and the bone-weary tone he brought to the material. At various intervals Pyle is shown reconnecting with the same company when in fact he has never been shown leaving it. A major death occurs offscreen. In another episode, an awaited military order, rather than generating the presumed advantage for the U.S. infantry unit, maintains the status quo. What we have here is a discontinuous "road picture" in a dangerous foreign land.

One soldier, monstrously fatigued, falls asleep on his wedding night.

BRIEF ENCOUNTER (UK). David Lean's *Brief Encounter*, from Noel Coward's play *Still Life*, has seen its reputation slip. A complaint has been leveled against it: Just where do we find the affair between the man and the woman, both of whom are married but not to one another? We never see the couple make love; we see them only sneaking about, *trying* to be intimately together. It is an odd complaint, really, one that implies an endorsement of adultery and an indifference to the fact that arranged or semi-arranged marriages, as well as marriages of convenience, have momentously declined in the Western world. That world has passed by *Brief Encounter*. But our hedonistic culture need not be a barrier to our enjoyment of Lean's wonderful (and by no means moralistic) black-and-white film. One simply has to accept as convention the starting-point that Laura Jesson's guilt over the affair—the film, which largely unfolds as Jesson's flashbacks, penetrates her mental state—is what remains as residue. The affair has ended because her lover, Alec Harvey, a medical general practitioner, has moved to Africa—where *else?*—with his wife and family. And Jesson (Celia Johnson, sensitive and brilliant—best actress, New York Film Critics Circle) is securely back with her complacent spouse with his crossword puzzles, their measured, mutually considerate life, and their two annoying children. Because of the intrusion of a gossipy acquaintance, all Jesson got from Harvey at their parting was a hand on the shoulder.

Beautifully photographed by Robert Krasker, Lean's film is a fine, repressed study of middle-class doldrums, with condescending working-class colorfulness set at the fringes in a train-station restaurant. Something Laura says provides the key to understanding her, her moods and a segment of the wartime/postwar English mindset: "Not even life lasts very long."

1946

IVAN THE TERRIBLE, PART TWO (THE BOYARS' PLOT) (U.S.S.R.). *Ivan Groznyy II: Boyarsky zagovor* finds Ivan, back in Moscow, under "the burden of power." His increased paranoia is not without reason; in his absence the Boyars replaced him, and now their efforts to replace him permanently double. Cinema's greatest flashback shows that Ivan the boy's mother, like Ivan the man's wife, was poisoned by the Boyars, orphaning him. ("I am alone," he says, meaning, "I am alone again.") The Boyars had meant to replace his most trusted advisor with themselves. But even as a child Ivan opposed their schemes to sell Russian lands to foreigners; one day he will reclaim all Russia and unify it. This pact with himself shows his integrity of spirit. However, a brilliant shot underscores the limit that childhood imposes on his will: Archduke Ivan's feet do not reach their ceremonial cushion. Trust Eisenstein to show politics and sexuality converging.

The immense shadow on the wall, in the first part, of Ivan's bearded head projected the essence of Tsar Ivan's power, along with its burden of responsibility and loneliness — humanity beyond humanity. Ivan's boyhood past dictates his present for the sake of Russian history.

Lonely Ivan befriends a priest, conceding to him a measure of political power. Moreover, his behavior becomes increasingly erratic as the Boyars' plot expressionistically closes in on him—by a stroke of irony, a plot to replace him with a young idiot, a perpetual child whom the Boyars hope to manipulate as they once tried doing with him. Eisenstein's one passage in color reflects an insulated waking phantasmagoria.

Stalin, who felt reassured in his own power grab by the first part, now suppressed the second and terminated filming of the third. Eisenstein's unaccepted pleas contributed to his fatal heart attack at fifty.

BEAUTY AND THE BEAST (France). Jean Cocteau's *La Belle et la Bête*, based on the fairy tale by Mme Leprince de Beaumont, is both historical allegory and a hymn to freedom—an epic about the Occupation and the Liberation of France.

Embodying the Occupation, the majestic Beast is trapped between two modes of existence, those of free man and beast; its emotions as it pines for Belle convey the anguish of a fettered France recalling freedom and the enormous struggle by which this was achieved.

Belle, a domestic drudge, embodies Christian sacrifice aimed at bringing her father ease, comfort. While her sisters ask him for every nonsensical thing under the sun, Belle asks only for a thing of simple, natural beauty: a rose. Attempting to save their home and possessions (their bourgeois existence), the father is condemned to death by the Beast when he stops to snap off a rose from a bush on the grounds of the Enchanted Castle. Alas, Belle's *appearance* of virtue is inseparable from her sisters' bourgeois materialism. One props up and rationalizes the other. Belle is the victim that France has become under the Occupation. She is the still perfect appearance of France—sculpted, statuesque—cut off from the living, breathing, free *soul* of France.

Cocteau's magical film is formally wondrous, a visual poem: the castle's interior staircase indoors seems to appear from out of the darkness enrobing it just to guide Belle's light steps up or down; sensuous slow motion is applied to Belle's first entrance into the castle, transforming her heavy outfit into seemingly eternal waves and folds. The most ecstatic moment: at the end, the slight dip down to the ground and then the flight to the heavens as the Prince takes to his castle Beauty, now fully alive in his arms.

PAISÀ (Italy). Roberto Rossellini's *Paisà* (*Paisan*) is a composite film each of whose six episodes reflects on the Battle of Italy (1943-45) in a different region of the country, among them, Sicily, Naples, Rome, Florence and the Po Valley. The result is an epic national portrait. Was Rossellini influenced by the preceding year's *Battle of the Rails*, by René Clément, which consists of vignettes of the French Resistance—a rare French neorealist work? Regardless, *Paisà*'s final episode, which depicts a slaughter of partisans, achieves the sledgehammer force of Rossellini's *Rome, Open City* (1945), which very nearly ends with the execution of a priest sympathetic to the Resistance. *Paisà* shimmers with a tragic sense of the cost of Italy's struggle against the Germans before, during and after liberation.

The Naples episode involves an African-American soldier, a military police officer, whose boots are stolen by a shoeshine boy. When he goes to the boy's "home" to retrieve his property, the young soldier discovers the impoverished world the war-orphaned child inhabits. The soldier has told the boy that his American home is a shack to which he doesn't want to return; he, too, is familiar with desperate poverty. He leaves the boots.

Another episode also involves an American soldier. During the liberation of Rome, he meets an innocent girl, Francesca. Later, without recognizing her, he becomes her john. But the film reverses chronology, presenting the earlier time as a flashback, the soldier's reminiscence, when he is with the prostitute. He tells her how much he wants to meet Francesca again. She tells him she can arrange it—although, in a sense, she cannot. In any case, he doesn't show up for the arranged reunion.

Paisà is radical in its formal aim. Rossellini contests traditional "plottedness"; the film's episodic nature reduces "story" by multiplying it.

NOTORIOUS (U.S.). Alfred Hitchcock's *Notorious*, from Ben Hecht's script, is about how love blinds.

Two postwar U.S. spies, a misogynist and a dipsomaniacal libertine, are in Rio de Janeiro on assignment. The daughter of a convicted Nazi spy, Alicia Huberman has been newly recruited by the O.S.S. to keep tabs on Alex Sebastian, another Nazi spy. Alicia is in love with her operative, Devlin; Alex is in love with Alicia. Alex proposes to Alicia, who accepts, believing this is what Devlin wants, and not caring enough about herself to realize how "notorious" this will confirm for Devlin she is. When Sebastian discovers his wife is an American spy, he poisons her with arsenic.

Devlin has only to speak up, to protest the hellish intrigue into which the O.S.S. is prepared to plunge the woman he loves, to show her the depth of his feeling. Instead, he protests the assignment only behind her back. He is like stone to her, demanding she make up her own mind, oblivious to the fact that she isn't practiced, like him, in compartmentalizing duty and feelings. In effect, Devlin allows Alicia to become a whore for Uncle Sam in order to prove to himself she *is* a whore. He is blaming Alicia for her misguided attempt to please him, and she nearly loses her life as a result. The finale, when the two escape Sebastian's clutches, is sorely ironic. Devlin will likely prove a possessive mate. Moreover, Sebastian's tragic fate, implicit in the film's last shot, ruthlessly engineered by the film's ostensible hero, adds yet another wrinkle of moral ambiguity to the mix.

Hitchcock's liberated, expressive use of the camera is at a new peak, and Cary Grant, beauteous Ingrid Bergman, and Claude Rains all give the performances of their lives.

MY DARLING CLEMENTINE (U.S.). *See above.*

INDONESIA CALLING (Australia). During the Second World War, Japan occupied Indonesia; some Indonesians found refuge in Australia and fought with this ally against the Japanese. Prior to this, the colonial Dutch had ruled Indonesia for three and a half centuries, appropriating profits from the tin mines, oil fields and rubber plantations that Indonesians worked. After the war, presuming the applicability of the Atlantic Charter to the Pacific, Indonesians declared their independence; but the Dutch were poised to reconquer Indonesia. Documentarian Joris Ivens is himself Dutch; but, for him, Indonesia's right to freedom and self-determination trumps Dutch nationalism and imperialism. Produced by the film unit of Australia's Waterside Workers Federation, Ivens's reconstructive *Indonesia Calling* documents in particular the concerted effort by Indonesians and regional supporters to block the entry of Dutch ships that may have been transporting arms for use against Indonesians and the new Indonesian republic.

What filmmaking! Dockside, a pan of Indonesian faces composes an image of Indonesian determination and solidarity. From this, though, a wider anti-colonial brotherhood emerges. The "blacking" of Dutch ships succeeds except in one instance: the Dutch sneak in a ship by manning it with an Indian crew. A call-out to the Indians from a Federation spokesperson interrupts Peter Finch's voiceover narration: "Brothers: Indonesia's fight is *your* fight . . . Stop engines!" India's soul, as well as possibly Indonesia's fate, hangs in the balance. The crew proceeds but considers the plea; we see their troubled faces onboard. They stop the ship.

The film ends brilliantly and optimistically. Across a bridge and toward the camera, Indonesians and supporters from other nations, including China, march in solidarity. All the idle ships, we are told, lie below. Voiceover necessarily covers this complex instance of political causality; but our not seeing the ships actually enhances the impact.

TO LIVE IN PEACE (Italy). Wouldn't peace be wonderful? But Luigi Zampa's film takes place during the German occupation, and there is no real peace to be had. Tigna (Aldo Fabrizi, who contributed to the script, excellent), a farmer, somewhat reluctantly hides two American soldiers, one of whom is wounded, in the cellar. Drunk, the wounded soldier, who is black, one night reveals himself to Tigna's guest, a German official, who, himself drunk, mistakes what he sees as meaning *thank goodness! the war is over.* Discarding Nazi racism, the official takes to the streets with the American—two instant comrades and noisy celebrants. Their mood is contagious, waking up Tigna's neighbors; *thank goodness! the war is over.* Only, of course, it isn't, and eventually Tigna and the German, attempting to flee, are both murdered by the SS.

There is no escaping war and its effects. This idea is formally and tonally rendered in an ingenious way: the film's comedy passes into tragedy; hope for peace resolves into death by war. (Also, one might say that human simplicity is extinguished by the complications that war imposes.) Before this happens, the German expresses his kinship with the protagonist by noting that he, too, if he had his way would be farming back home.

One can see the influence of *To Live in Peace* in any number of war-set Italian tragicomedies, including Mario Monicelli's *The Great War* (1959) and Roberto Benigni's *Life Is Beautiful* (1998). But there is still more to Zampa's achievement—an irony beyond the scope of the action, provided by the world in which the film was first exhibited. The war is over now, but its ravages are residual. Ordinary postwar Italian citizens yet might sigh, *Vivere in pace.*

THE BEST YEARS OF OUR LIVES (U.S.). Written by Robert E. Sherwood from MacKinlay Kantor's blank-verse novella, *Glory for Me, The Best Years of Our Lives* is William Wyler's finest, most moving film, the one most infused with his humane sensibility

1946

and least compromised by melodrama. It essays the civilian readjustment of three soldiers upon their return home to Boone City somewhere in the corn belt. Their paths never crossed before the war, but they become friends on their flight back in a military transport.

One of these is Fred Derry, an Air Force captain and bombardier who returns to his prewar job as a soda jerk, which he summarily loses. Derry has returned also to the wife he hardly knew, who likes better her husband's impressive uniform than she does her husband, who for the moment seems without prospects. Homer Parrish (Harold Russell, best supporting actor Oscar), a sailor who lost both hands in the war, is terrified of reuniting with fiancée Wilma. Al Stephenson (Fredric March, best actor Oscar), an infantry sergeant, has returned home to Milly (Myrna Loy, best actress, Brussels) and two grown children. (Al, nervous, hopes to postpone having homecoming sex with Milly.) A banker, he is promoted to vice president in charge of loans; but, familiar with the courage and determination of the men he fought with, and wishing to bet on the future of America, he locks horns with bank management over his tendency to approve loans for returning G.I.s with little or no collateral.

The supernally clear deep focus that cinematographer Gregg Toland helped Wyler achieve suggests that the present contains a vision of the future. However, the most brilliant passage, in an airfield of retired B-52 bombers, finds Fred wandering into his recent past.

Oscars for best picture, direction, screenplay.

MURDERERS ARE AMONG US (Germany). *Murderers Are Among Us* had been the title Fritz Lang intended for *M*, but German censors rejected the implication of collective guilt. The first postwar German film, by Wolfgang Staudte, embraced the notion.

The script is contrived. Upon returning home to Berlin from a liberated Nazi camp, Susanne Wallner finds Hans Mertens living in her apartment. Because of the atrocities he witnessed as an army officer, Mertens drinks to excess, but, after initial sparring, the two fall in love. Mertens decides to kill his former commanding officer, who now runs a factory and celebrates at Christmastime with his employees. At Christmastime in 1942, in Poland, this same man ordered the execution of one hundred innocent civilians in response to a single anonymous shot fired at his company. In the nick of time, Susanne stays Hans's hand, saying, "We shouldn't pass sentence." Hans agrees, adding, "but we must make charges." At the close, the former captain is behind bars, vociferously protesting his innocence on the basis of war's requirements.

Thus was launched *trummerfilme*, the genre of fictional films amidst Berlin's rubble that dominated German cinema right after the war. But Staudte's entry was never surpassed; the pseudo-documentary shot of faces in the street that introduces Susanne is brilliant. A broken mirror, the broken windows, the bombed-out buildings: broken dreams; broken lives.

Indeed, this is a film of unforgettable shots, and none more so than the Langian one of Hans confronting his former captain, his shadow, the only part of Hans that's visible, expressionistically huge, in which the monster against the wall cowers and begs for life—but absent any recognition by him of his evil.

Mörder sind unter uns was East German before East Germany came into being.

LA SYMPHONIE PASTORALE (France). Michèle Morgan (best actress, Cannes) gives perhaps the most exquisite performance in post-silent cinema as Gertrude (with its soft *g*, an incredibly lovely name in French), a blind orphan who has been raised by Pastor Jean Martens and his wife, "Aunt Amélie," in a small late nineteenth-century village in Jean Delannoy's finest piece of work by far, *Pastoral Symphony*, from André Gide's story "L'aveugle." Distinguishing between "eyes of the body" and "eyes of the spirit," it is a study of divided hearts and the moral burden these incur. Amidst the Swiss Alps, which symbolically represent the spiritual aspirations of both pastor and Gertrude, Gertrude's fate directs her to a suicidal end once the surgical restoration of her sight pressures her to choose between the two men who love her, the married clergyman to whom she is bound in gratitude, and his son Jacques, who also loves her and whom she loves. The overwhelming burden of decision has tragically shifted to Gertrude, whose sudden sight has plunged her into adulthood following a sheltered existence; Piette, Jacques' fiancée, had pressed Gertrude's medical examination, hoping that her restored sight might press Jacques to choose between them. That everything turns instead on Gertrude's choice ironically reflects on the limited range of choices for women in a male-dominated culture.

This is a dark, somewhat claustrophobic melodrama—quiet and sensibly restrained, engrossing and deeply touching, in the main because of Morgan's sublime acting, but also Delannoy's sensitive direction from an excellent script by Jean Aurenche, Pierre Bost and himself. All the acting is top-drawer: Pierre Blanchar as Pastor Martens, who is blind to his own rationalizing and manipulating; Line Noro as his wife, who suffers mostly in silence and must ask him to be kissed; young Jean Desailly as Jacques.

1947

GERMANY, YEAR ZERO (East Germany, France, Italy). *See above.*

MONSIEUR VERDOUX (U.S.). Henri Landru had been guillotined for murdering eight women. Fifteen years later, in 1937, Henri Verdoux met the same fate, with a half-dozen more victims to his credit—or debit. From the grave, this "mass killer" speaks to us as disembodied voiceover, describing himself as having been "for thirty years an honest bank clerk until the Depression of 1930, in which year I found myself unemployed. It was then I became occupied in liquidating members of the opposite sex. This I did as strictly a business enterprise, to support a home and a family," that is to say, wheelchair-bound wife and young son. This modern Bluebeard, actually, juggled numerous marriages simultaneously, all to those whom he murdered for their money so that the only marriage and family that he cared about could survive in these "desperate times." Henri was too old to find other employment.

From an idea by Orson Welles, Chaplin's tartly funny black comedy, with slapstick interludes, reflects on the recently ended Second World War; looking ahead ten years past Verdoux's execution, it assumes the form of a political statement. Its centerpiece is yet another dazzlingly brilliant Chaplin performance, this time as a dapper, world-weary cynic who ultimately believes that he did not murder enough people, because, as he puts it (echoing Stalin), "[n]umbers sanctify." Through Verdoux, Chaplin is taking aim at war, in particular, the horrors of Hiroshima and Nagasaki. Relatedly, he is aiming at capitalism, which ruthlessly cuts employees loose when it has no further use for them. Business and war are combined in an unseen figure in the background of the plot: a munitions manufacturer.

"I've never had rum!" En route to his beheading, Henri thus has a new experience: Chaplin's quiet affirmation of the beauty of life.

RECORD OF A TENEMENT GENTLEMAN (Japan). Yasujiro Ozu's first postwar film, *Nagaya shinshiroku*, is as delightful as his comedy *I Was Born, but . . .* (1932) and twice as profound. Its makeshift family reflects Japan's shaken institutions, and its setting—the lower-class section of downtown Tokyo—reflects Japan's postwar economic hardship. What irony that the character who sets the plot into motion, Tashiro, is a fortune teller. Japan's future is clouded and indeterminate.

Kohei, the small son of an itinerant carpenter, attaches himself to Tashiro, who brings him home to his tenement to the dismay of his actor-roommate. They decide that Tané, their widowed neighbor, should take the boy in for the night. Tané wants no part of Kohei, but he is left there and, so, she complies. Attempts to find the motherless boy's father fail, and Kohei tries Tané's patience with his recurrent bed-wetting. But the two slowly bond, and Kohei becomes for a while a cherished part of Tané's life.

For a while; Ozu is cinema's great poet of transience, impermanence. A key shot consists

1947

of discarded newspaper pages blown by wind across the ground. The image, poignant, refers to Japan's postwar army of abandoned children. Can anything restore the nation's fortunes? Perhaps; but Kohei's young father shows up one day to claim his son, expressing charming gratitude.

Kohei and Tané: each wears a pudgy, sour face. Chouko Iida beautifully plays Tané. Thus Ozu's great pre-war tragedienne, best known for maternal roles, now plays a reluctant surrogate mother or grandmother—and she is hilarious when expressing disapproval of the boy, deeply moving once her heart opens up to him, and devastating upon her loss of him.

The film ends by showing anonymous young boys in a park. Two share a cigarette: the obliteration of Japanese childhood.

THE SILENCE OF THE SEA (France). Jean-Pierre Melville's (Grumbach's) stunning debut is an adaptation of the short story by Vercors, "Le silence de la mer." Static shots and short pans of a countryside village appear under a motionless, silent sky punctuated by cirrus clouds—on one level, the eternal "sea" of the title. It is 1941, and this is Occupied France. A German officer takes up residence in the home of an elderly man and his niece, who remain silent to him, the man at his pipe, his niece at her knitting, as the officer each evening fills the silence with his family history and professions of love for France. (He loves French literature as much as he does German music.) Even his appearance in civilian dress cannot shake the silence of the sea.

The uncle's voiceover turns the film into a journey into the recent past. The film is haunted by the humiliation of France's occupation and by the sheer exercise of historical memory, where individual recollection merges with the "sea" of national experience. Similarly, Melville haunts the past, shooting his film in the very house that Vercors chose as the setting for his story. The ticking of a clock and the officer's (in effect) monologues, by their interruptions, underscore the silence of the sea.

Appearing mute at middle-distance in a darkened doorway, the villager represents conscience, while his niece, whom the officer pointlessly loves, embodies the unyielding soul of France.

The naive officer believes that Germany's occupation of France is forging a benign connection between both countries. The film records his disillusionment. Melville anticipates this with a brusque cut: after the sentimental officer waxes about how "the city" opens the German heart, Melville shows the German assault on Paris.

Jean-Marie Robian and Nicole Stéphane beautifully play uncle and niece.

THE LADY FROM SHANGHAI (U.S.). The narration of Orson Welles's *The Lady from Shanghai* is ambiguous. One has no way of knowing the extent to which one should believe Michael O'Hara (Welles, excellent).

Welles's *film noir* claims two contexts: "waterfront agitator" O'Hara's participation in the Spanish Civil War; Welles's marriage to Rita Hayworth, which was already unraveling when Welles embarked on this project starring her. O'Hara's Leftist sympathies suggest his likely profound disillusionment, and indeed O'Hara at no time seems to fit into the current world. With its visual distortions, the celebrated fun-house sequence, including the Hall of Mirrors (inspired by Chaplin's 1928 *The Circus*) where Elsa and her husband try shooting one another dead amidst their countless deceptive images, may ultimately imply O'Hara's cockeyed view of reality. It is he, after all, who falls down the winding chute into the fun-house. It is even possible that the entire narrative consists of a madman's ravings. Welles, though, buys into the theme of human sharks in such a blood-frenzy they end up eating themselves.

Hayworth, of course, was the forties' most radiant star. For her role as Elsa, Welles cut her gorgeous locks and made them blonde, which, given her Hispanic complexion, works as strangely for her as it does for Olivier's Hamlet. Let's say it suits Elsa's ambiguity, as does the fact that she is a tsarist Russian descendant who speaks fluent (and thinks of love in)

Chinese. There's little hope of fathoming this predatory female, but, truth to tell, it has always seemed to me that O'Hara all but invites her to ensnare him in her deadly intrigue. Perhaps he seeks confirmation of how unlucky he is or how rotten the world is.

The end of the Welleses' marriage, which it symbolically incorporates, accounts for the film's unexpected poignancy.

TREASURE OF THE SIERRA MADRE (U.S.). Brilliantly written and directed by John Huston, who won Oscars for doing both, *Treasure of the Sierra Madre* begins in Tampico as a current of what appears to be good fortune launches an expedition for gold by three Americans, two young struggling laborers and old prospector Howard (Oscar-winner Walter Huston, John's father), whose eyes tell us he has seen *everything*, including "what gold does to men's souls." In the aftermath of the 1910-20 Mexican Revolution, the countryside is alive with mirror-images: murderous native bandits and their police opponents, the Federales. The trio of prospectors find and mine gold but run into trouble also from within. Heretofore a model of fairness, Fred C. Dobbs (Humphrey Bogart, riveting) comes to believe that the other two seek to cheat him out of his share of the gold; like Nixon, Dobbs takes to referring to himself in the third person as he mentally unravels. Tim Holt, still in his twenties, gives the film's most beautiful performance, one which perfectly captures an inflection of evil in a personality of resounding decency; his Bob Curtin is symbolically linked to James Cody, an outside prospector whom the trio decide to kill as a competitor (an expression of the novel's and Huston's hatred of capitalism), whose peaceful life home in Texas Curtin is prepared to take over once the bandits preempt the trio by killing Cody. The mysterious B. Traven (writer-director Huston), on whose book the film is based, appears dressed in white; he tells Dobbs early on, after giving him several pesos as handouts, "From now on, you will have to make your way through life without my assistance."

Poignantly, the prospectors lose all their gold to the winds of Fate—a cosmic joke and test of character.

ODD MAN OUT (UK). Abandoned to the streets and back-alleys of Belfast, to which he is doomed to wander as an exhausted outcast, Johnny McQueen (James Mason, phenomenal) is an I.R.A. chief on the lam from the police following a botched mill robbery ("funds for the Organization"), during which he has killed a man in order to escape. Already Johnny was a fugitive—an escaped convict, and now he is badly wounded, the loss of blood rushing his mind in and out of delirium. Along the way, some people help, others connive and betray. Meanwhile, Kathleen is trying to locate the dying man she loves.

Although a bit protracted and inflated, *Odd Man Out*, from F.L. Green's novel, is Carol Reed's best film. Johnny takes refuge in an air raid shelter, inside which Johnny's delirium takes over and he imagines himself back in prison; inflections of lighting and use of dissolves enable us to see the prison cell that Johnny *thinks* he sees. A ball bounces into the shelter, and Johnny perceives the child who enters to retrieve it as the prison guard. Johnny relates his killing the man at the mill offices, wishfully, as a dream; he is friendlier and more open with the guard than we've seen him be towards his own men in the Organization. *If only he had stayed in prison he would not have killed a man!* But his presence of mind returns, the prison cell becomes the shelter again, the guard is the child, and Johnny knows all over again he has probably killed a man.

A young couple enter; the girl hopes to marry the boy: a projection of Johnny's regret that he and Kathleen haven't married. His whole bleeding life is now one of sorrow. It ends tragically—and yet as a relief.

THE FUGITIVE (U.S., Mexico). Based on Graham Greene's story "The Labyrinthine Ways," John Ford's *The Fugitive*, beautifully acted by Henry Fonda, depicts the stumbling odyssey of a padre torn between duty and a desire to escape being killed now that the revolutionary government has outlawed the profession and practice of faith. The last cleric in a totalitarian state, his sense of duty wavers between selfless mission and pride in martyrdom. The priest opens wide the doors of his church; by delivering us the man's shadow, not substance, and by having this shadow hold the crucifixion pose a beat or two too long, Ford undercuts the padre's idealized, posturing self-image. The film charts his progress from would-be martyr to true servant of God, which for Ford and co-director Emilio Fernández means true servant of fellow humans.

Ford doesn't portray the regime in power in terms of its ideology or for political nuance; rather, he shows it to be a force that contests freedom, generates fear and creates outcasts. Its impact is omnipresent; accenting the military regimentation are the symmetrical design of numerous compositions, and the sound of horses' hoofs bursting through silence signals arrivals of police-soldiers. The villagers' fear reflects that which had overtaken the Hollywood community with, earlier the same year as the film, the start of the House Un-American Activities Committee witch-hunting hearings in Washington.

Cinematographer Gabriel Figueroa, employing ravishing, high-contrast black and white, intensifies the supernal quality of Ford's dignified, somewhat stylized imagery. Spare and essential, the images resonate with a heightened naturalism, helping Ford to achieve the level of abstraction that a universal parable requires. Thus the film's final image—a Cross of light —transcends particular religious meaning to convey something more general, more urgent: a persistent light of hope in the dark night of political oppression.

THE STRIKE (Czechoslovakia). Crude, sometimes clunky, always amateurishly acted, Karel Steklý's *Siréna*, from Marie Majerovà's novel, is also gripping and powerful. A corrective to much that goes haywire in one of John Ford's lamest films, *How Green Was My Valley* (1941), *Siréna* won the top prize at Venice and remains the only Czech film to have done so —although the outcome would likely be different today. Carl Theodor Dreyer's *Day of Wrath* (1943), from Denmark, also competed that year.

Steklý's film refers to an actual event: in 1889, in Kladno, a suburb of Prague, the strike by grossly underpaid workers in a metallurgical factory. The film focuses on a single family, although one other family in particular weaves in and out of it. The contrast between the industrialist's digs and the working-class lodgings seems crudely imagined, and the power structure that found the military police bending instantly to the industrialist's desire for the indiscriminate slaughter of his employees needs much more detailed contextualization. On the other hand, after one of their children is ruthlessly gunned down, the people's mob-rage against the industrialist's mansion—the trashing of musical instruments, other furniture, artwork, etc.—is enormously convincing.

Two more things help make the film great. One is its raw urgency, as though the filmmakers felt that the immediacy of the moral issues involved had to take precedence over period detail and evocation; the other is the dark, grimy visual poetry that Steklý conjures somewhere betwixt phantasmagoria and hard reality. Outstanding in this regard is the factory at night, a complicated complex of tall, looming structures heaving illuminated blasts of smoke.

The strike itself was crushed. Thus the film looks ahead to Communist Czechoslovakia, with indigestible utterances marking the way. But the real aim might lie even farther ahead: *social justice*.

BOOMERANG! (U.S.). Elia Kazan's stirring "docudrama" portrays a small-town Connecticut murder, that of a beloved Protestant minister, Father Lambert, and the trial of the young drifter, John Waldron, who is arrested for committing it. All the film's main elements aim at a restrained realism.

The actual murder of Father Hubert Dahme, in Bridgeport, Connecticut, occurred in 1924.

At the conclusion, voiceover reveals that District Attorney Henry Harvey is really Homer Cummings, F.D.R.'s first attorney general. But Kazan's film is contemporary; Waldron is a World War II veteran, whose being at-loose-ends, "lost," hence vulnerable to the criminal charge as a stranger in town, is meant to comment on the difficulty of Second World Warrior civilian readjustment. Moreover, the wrenching of chronology suggests another, subversive intent in Richard Murphy's brilliant script.

Harvey, Cummings's stand-in, risks career and angers the police by raising at trial more than reasonable doubt that the defendant had committed the crime. Harvey is the film's hero —the one for whom truth and justice are more important than playing by the rules. Cummings, still alive, needed his reputation rehabilitated because of his 1937 plan to pack the U.S. Supreme Court—a strategy aimed at preventing the Court from declaring New Deal policies and programs unconstitutional.

Because at trial Harvey circumvents the adversarial process by usurping the defense attorney's role, criticism accumulates as to the way trials are normally conducted with the adversarial system intact. *Boomerang!* doesn't vindicate the U.S. system of justice, as most commentators seem to think; rather, it questions it, ironically, much as Harvey questions all the evidence against Waldron. The implication is that truth and justice do not arise in U.S. criminal trials as they are normally conducted. One can go further: *Boomerang!* excoriates the adversarial system of U.S. justice for obscuring truth and compromising justice.

1948

CITY STREETCLEANERS (Italy). Rome, 1948. Night evaporates as dawn's light steals in. Human figures are dense shadows and anonymous. A train, marking time and infinity, passes through; substance translates into evanescence beneath a solemn sky. Slight camera movements suggest time's sweep. An angled overhead shot shows men sweeping steps in a public square. Influenced by Ruttmann's *Berlin: Symphony of a Great City* (1927), the delightful, rhythmic magic of Michelangelo Antonioni's *Nettezza urbana*, starkly photographed in black and white and jazzily scored by Giovanni Fusco, has begun.

With daylight, our view becomes clear. We see the faces of individual streetcleaners, as well as the faces of others in the streets. We also take in the integral role that streetcleaners play—their interaction with the rest of the city. Someone throws something out of her apartment window and it becomes part of what the streetcleaner sweeps up below.

In the course of the film, we see persons at other mundane work in the streets, with everyone contributing to the great symphony of Rome. Antonioni's film is poetic, associative, elastic. It purges its glimpse of laboring men of the overt socioeconomic context, relegating this to an invisible realm of inference—the maintenance we observe accumulates into a metaphor for Italy's postwar reconstruction—and thereby creating a complex double vision of (implicit) economic hardship in the present and (explicit) nuts-and-bolts activity that looks ahead, quietly and without fanfare or heightened rhetoric, to an employed, stabilized Italy in the future.

BICYCLE THIEVES (Italy). Once voted by critics worldwide the best film ever made, Vittorio De Sica's *Landri di biciclette* still retains a great measure of affection. Scenarist Cesare Zavattini and De Sica focus on Italy's postwar employment squeeze. In Rome, a poor man, Antonio, finally gets a job posting signs, for which he needs a bicycle to transport him from site to site. When it is stolen, he searches for the bicycle throughout the city, accompanied by his young son; spotting the thief, Antonio pursues the boy to his home. Epileptic, desperately impoverished, the thief is protected by family and neighbors. Outside a sports stadium, Antonio himself steals a bicycle but is caught and then let go. Ashamed, he holds on to his son's hand for emotional support.

Famously, the film's title, which translates in the plural, was changed in the States to *Bicycle Thief*, thus obscuring De Sica's social vision. This isn't an American film touting

independence and individual responsibility; poverty and desperation have turned Rome into a *city* of thieves and potential thieves, charlatans and prostitutes. Ironic: squabbling father and son are able to "steal" a rare moment of contentment dining at a black market restaurant.
Orson Welles marveled at De Sica's ability to make his camera disappear. Few today, however, would describe De Sica's camera as invisible. Rather, there is a gentle sweep of sadness to this mostly gray film, even a trace of melancholy, correlative to the plight of people doing their best to get by with dwindling resources. (It would be left to John Schlesinger, addressing hard luck and squalor in *Midnight Cowboy*, 1969, to inflate this style into grotesque sentimentality.) A memorable point-of-view shot, in a friend's truck as windshield wipers tackle rain, maintains De Sica's sensible aim even while departing from the film's stylistic procedure.

LETTER FROM AN UNKNOWN WOMAN (U.S.). *See above.*

SPRING IN A SMALL TOWN (China). Adjudged in 2005 to be "the greatest Chinese movie ever made," Fei Mu's blustery, black-and-white *Xiao cheng zhi chun* focuses on a "not normal" marriage that defines an historic space betwixt the Second World War, which in more ways than one has left China in rubble, and the Cultural Revolution up ahead.
Liyan, who is sickly, and Yuwen, his wife, sleep in separate rooms; Liyan's teenage sister sleeps elsewhere on the grounds. Yuwen is a dutiful though unloving partner. This Liyan cannot see because the vestiges of feudalism that are attached to him blind him to his wife's silent anguish and misinterpret her dutifulness. But everyone's consciousness is about to change as a result of Liyan's best friend's visit: Zhichen, now a medical doctor, turns out to be the boy that 16-year-old Yuwen loved ten years earlier, near the time of the Japanese invasion. A seemingly speedily rising moon in the nighttime sky is Fei's symbol for a breakthrough in understanding that occurs in each of the main characters.
The early part of the film is inundated with Yuwen's mundane voiceover ("I pushed away my own door and sat on my bed . . ."), for inside her head is more or less where she lives, not in the small town where, she laments, "nothing ever changes." (Irony.) The substantial erasure of this stream-of-consciousness voiceover once Yuwen has Zhichen with whom to interact comes as a jolt; from it, we feel the shift in Yuwen's mental and emotional life.
"I hope he dies!" at one point Yuwen says aloud to Zhichen about Liyan. She is properly aghast at this first-time notion. Individualism, once a refuge, has now become a source of decision-making and deeds.
The "decision" here is not to murder anyone.

LA TERRA TREMA (Italy). The Valastro family of Acitrezza are among Sicily's hardworking subsistent poor. The two eldest sons fish the sea, to which their father has been lost. They are exploited by *canotieri*, the wholesale fish merchants who maximize profits by conspiring to offer fishermen little for their catches. 'Ntoni, the eldest son, considers himself an enemy of injustice. He attempts to organize a strike and mortgages the family home to secure his own boat and become independent of the prevailing system. In a storm, he loses the boat; the bank evicts the family, and the *canotieri* refuse to hire him. When they acquiesce, the proud boy is unwilling to become again a "beast of burden." Eventually he capitulates, and life goes on; someday, he muses, workers will unite for the common good against such exploitation.
The Earth Trembles was shot amidst Acitrezza's rough land and rough waters using the inhabitants rather than actors; an actual *canotiero* plays a *canotiero*! They all speak in Sicilian dialect. (Luchino Visconti contributes voiceover commentary in Italian.) Visconti has created a sober, gritty, stormy, powerful Neorealist masterpiece about an environment as oppressive as the name of Mussolini on the wall at hiring headquarters. The film is based on a novel by

Giovanni Verga, *I Malavoglia*.
The imagery Visconti and his black-and-white cinematographer, G. R. Aldo, achieve is tremendous: long-shots of the rocky coast in which people appear as tiny and helpless; faintly luminous dawn, when the fishermen return after a night's labor; the black ocean at night, as vast nets are dropped and raised, each boat equipped with a lamp to attract fish; upon their return, the men on the ground, appearing trapped in the mesh, repairing the nets; 'Ntoni casting the *canotiero*'s scale into the sea, inspiring other workers to follow suit.

THE BLUM AFFAIR (East Germany). *Affaire Blum* is based on an actual case and trial in 1926 in Magdeburg. Working from Robert A. Stemmle's superlative script, Erich Engel investigates German anti-Semitism. A Leftist who had staged the original production of Brecht and Weill's *Threepenny Opera* but who nevertheless capitulated to nationalism and careerism and worked for the Nazi entertainment industry, Engel may also have considered the film an act of atonement.

The state will attempt to pin a murder on manufacturer Jakob Blum because he is a Jewish member of the political opposition. Blum is accused of murdering his discharged accountant, Wilhelm Platzer, presumably to conceal tax fraud. A subsequent investigation of his company, though, reveals no irregularities. The sole witness against Blum is the thief, captured with Platzer's checkbook, who in fact committed the murder. His guilt notwithstanding, the authorities convince their captive to accuse Blum. Justice isn't the state prosecutor's aim; silencing Blum is, along with covering up the mistakes the police have made.

The film evidences great visual fluidity and contextual elasticity. The police arrest Blum in his bedroom, forbidding him to speak to his wife—an encapsulation of worse state intrusions to come into Jewish lives. At the last, Stemmle and Engel allow themselves, forgivably because so hauntingly executed, a tad of rhetoric. In a restaurant, Sabine appears the happier at her husband's overdue exoneration. Jakob appears, by contrast, pensive, cautious, perturbed even. (The film is perfectly acted, but Kurt Ehrhardt, as Jakob Blum, gives a profound performance.) Sabine, having dismissed her own anxiety, notes that this triumph of justice was inevitable and that they are fortunate to be living in a free democratic state. From her husband's silent expression, however, we glean he has been impressed, instead, by how fragile German justice, freedom and democracy are.

MACBETH (U.S.). Shakespeare's play as *film noir*—medieval, though, not modern—and existential tragedy: a marvel that its studio, Republic, mutilated for no good reason. In its restored form, however, Orson Welles's first of three Shakespeare films seems to emanate from Macbeth's own mind (some of Macbeth's utterances emerge as somber voiceover), as if from his grave, and the witches—neither as ghostly as Akira Kurosawa's (*Throne of Blood*, 1957) nor as corporeal as Roman Polanski's (1971)—recall some ancient past and look ahead to an even gloomier fate. With its barren landscape echoing the inescapable outcome of grief, madness and power's pursuit, Welles's dark, barbaric fable takes us to the no-man's-land that projects Macbeth's eternally murder-damaged soul. (Like Shakespeare, Welles targets excessive rather than *all* ambition—an error that Kurosawa would have the boldness to correct.)

This film is full of powerful, grimly poetic images. The opening passage, which may have inspired the doll-making from chewed bread in Ilya Khrjanovsky's brilliant *Chetyre* (2005), is tremendous; the witchly formation of the clay figurine that embodies Macbeth and telescopes his destiny turns the Shakespearean inside-out, projecting instead of Shakespeare's secular gospel of individual responsibility Welles's own fatalism, a reflection of world horrors and personal calamities: the atomic bombings of Hiroshima and Nagasaki; the revelation of the Holocaust; the hour of footage that the studio had blithely ripped out of his final cut of *The Lady from Shanghai* (1947); the collapse of his marriage to Rita Hayworth. Welles, starring, proved an excellent Macbeth, and the dark, sweeping scene of Macduff's beheading him

1948

doubled as an authentic glimpse into Welles's own feelings vis-à-vis recent and current realities.
Welles's *Macbeth* is famous—unfortunately, for its vilified female lead. Agnes Moorehead, whom Welles had wanted to play Lady Macbeth, would have made the film perfect.

A HEN IN THE WIND (Japan). Postwar human devastation and national tragedy: Yasujiro Ozu's *Kaze no naka no mendori* mines a vein that looks back to his silent *Woman of Tokyo* (1933) and ahead to his *Tokyo Twilight* (1957). An upstairs boarder in Tokyo's bleak, industrial, working-class outskirts, Tokiko Amamiya (Kinuyo Tanaka, Kenji Mizoguchi's future star, wonderful) struggles to survive and support her toddler by making kimonos. When Hiroshi falls ill, Tokiko resorts once to prostitution to pay for his medical treatment. When he belatedly returns home from war, Shuichi, her husband, reacts to her "choice" with coldness, accusation and violence. When he rapes her, their son's ball—echoing Fritz Lang's *M* (1931)—drops to the floor.

Hiroshi's recovery, especially as recorded in a peaceful passage in the grass, constitutes a brief respite before the storm of Shuichi's reappearance. But, even here, Tokiko and a friend acknowledge the discrepancy between their younger dreams and current realities. Tokiko, exhausted, lies on the ground, and Ozu cuts to an ambiguous shot of the calm, cumulus-clouded sky.

At a "Time Life" workplace—a sign of the U.S. occupation—a friend comments on the inflation that is ravaging Japan and lends Shuichi money. Thus Shuichi sells off a bit of his dignity. We are reminded of his wife's earlier remark that she would "sell anything" to take care of Hiroshi.

In a stunning shot, Tokiko falls downstairs after Shuichi pushes her away—it turns out, in self-disgust. Tokiko crawls back up and begs forgiveness. Shuichi understands that she had no choice and says so. They will put this past "behind them." They tightly embrace. Ozu's closing shots, however, imply a circularity and enclosure as much as a moving ahead.

We realize that Shuichi's sense of shame is inextricably bound to Japan's defeat in the war.

BORDER STREET (Poland). Aleksander Ford's *Ulica Graniczna* is about resistance and German reprisal in the Warsaw Ghetto. Its opens with a montage of silent establishing shots of Warsaw. Often it is indeed a silent film with sound, giving it a poetic sadness. Transported back in time, we feel we may witness history taking a different course than it did. Only, it won't.

Beginning in 1939, Ford depicts the German invasion and occupation. There is a quadruple focus on neighborhood children, an impoverished Jewish family, and two Aryan families. When it is exposed that an Aryan family head, a doctor, is in fact Jewish, his daughter, Jadzia, is rebuffed by her Aryan boyfriend, whose father, a Polish military officer, on the run from Germans, escapes only because the elderly Jewish tailor, despite torture, refuses to denounce him—a fact that the fugitive, heretofore anti-Semitic, relays to his son. The weary, hopeless march into the Ghetto, despite (because of?) a certain impossible grandeur, is among the most trenchant passages in postwar cinema. After arranging for his daughter's safety, the doctor joins other Jews in the Ghetto; but Jadzia returns once she learns her father's fate. Partisans are rounded up and mass executed. David, a Jewish boy, and Jadzia attempt to flee through a Warsaw sewer. Witnessing resistance fighters heading toward the Ghetto, however, David heads back himself, to rejoin uncle and grandfather, pausing to wave goodbye forever to Jadzia (and us).

Ford sometimes applies an overly refined aesthetic, and some of the plot is melodramatic. In the main, though, he captures reality's rough textures, and his portrait of oppressed Ghetto life is vivid and terrifying. This haunting film, rich in symbolism, accumulates a spiritual air. Władysław Godik is unforgettable as David's devout grandfather—a man deep in prayer as Germans burn him alive.

Chronology of World Cinema

1948

THE QUIET ONE (U.S.). Ten-year-old Donald Peters lives in a Harlem tenement with his maternal grandmother. His father is out of the picture (dead, or just plain gone), and his mother, whom he adores, is busy with her new life—boyfriend and baby. Starved for affection, impressed by poverty, unable to read, Donald frequently skips school and takes to the streets, getting into trouble; his grandmother knows of no other way of dealing with him than with a belt. Donald is sent to a country school for delinquent boys, where his healing process begins. Gradually, after great effort by himself and staff, he ceases to be a baby, as the film puts it, and becomes a child.

The Quiet One, directed by Sidney Meyers, blends fictional and documentary elements. The boy and his family members are enacted roles, while the other detainees and staff members really belong to Wiltwyck School. The film is presented as a psychiatric case study, soberly, patiently; it is untouched by the sensationalism of the pseudo-clinical *Possessed* (Curtis Bernhardt, 1947) and *The Snake Pit* (Anatole Litvak, 1948). We do not see the actual psychiatrist, but we purportedly hear his account of Donald's homelife, case and progress. This voiceover narration, steady and restrained, was written by James Agee, no less, and is read by actor Gary Merrill.

One of the alleged liabilities of cinema is its inability to penetrate a character's interiority. Yet the combination of image and commentary accomplishes that task in relation to this boy. To an extraordinary degree, the film discloses Donald's spiritual constraint and disturbed emotions. It is also, visually, a starkly beautiful, intense, poetic black-and-white film.

Shot in 16mm on a shoestring, it inaugurated the New York school of filmmaking. John Cassavetes's *Shadows* (1959) exists in the shadow of *The Quiet One*.

YELLOW SKY (U.S.). In *Yellow Sky*, written by Lamar Trotti and directed by William A. Wellman (best direction, Locarno), "Stretch" Dawson leads a gang of bank robbers in Arizona. The Civil War's imprint is seen in the men's uprooted, restless, criminal lives. "The fastest growing town in the territory"—Yellow Sky, named for the gold that seized the imaginations of those who settled it, driving them to their delirious destiny in the desert—has turned into a ghost town. It represents the collapsed hopes of those who found in the surrounding hills only sand.

After robbing a bank, the gang crosses the parched Arizona saltlands. In extreme longshots, the men, moving very slowly, are black dots in the distance. Horses lose their footing in the salt and the sand; the men have to dismount and walk the distance, guiding their horses. One horse breaks a leg; the shot that kills the horse pierces the silence of this gorgeous, hallucinatory, deadly landscape out of a horrible dream. All the men are dying of thirst and hunger; Stretch sees in the distance something shimmering beneath the hot sun: a line of buildings that goes in and out of focus. A mirage? Stretch cautiously opines it's a town, with food, water and rest awaiting them. This is Yellow Sky.

The town isn't completely uninhabited. "Mike"—Constance Mae (Anne Baxter, wonderful)—lives there with Grandpa, an old prospector who lives one-quarter inside his head and three-quarters outside, rendering his talk wonderfully elliptical. Grandpa is a quintessential outsider, wary of whites but a friend to Apaches, who helped raise his proud granddaughter. After some sparring, Mike and Stretch fall in love. In this fairy tale for grownups, Stretch turns himself in, in effect "unrobbing" the bank, for Mike's sake and their life together: *the future*.

LES PARENTS TERRIBLES (France). Apart from *Beauty and the Beast* (1946), which is in a class by itself, *Les parents terribles*, which he adapted from his play, is Jean Cocteau's finest film. A highly versatile, intricately designed use of camera indeed makes it exemplary as a cinematic rendering of a play, one that is almost entirely restricted to the interiors of two apartments. The characterizations are Cocteau's richest and most complex. *Les parents terribles* is affecting, at times deeply moving.

1948

Young Michel lives with his father, Georges, his mother, Yvonne, to whom he is especially close—some would say, *too* close—and whom he calls Sophie, and Yvonne's sister, Léo (Gabrielle Dorziat, giving the best performance), the shrewdest, most worldly member of the family and the one who provides the household's principal financial support. Léo had been engaged to Georges but sacrificed her happiness for her sister's sake. She is still in love with Georges. Georges has a young mistress, Madeleine (Josette Day, giving the worst performance). Michel has fallen in love for the first time—with Madeleine. Neither he nor his father is aware of the coincidence. Aunt Léo surmises the truth; Michel brings his family to Madeleine's apartment so they can meet his sweetheart. The eventual result is the suicide of one of the characters.

Given this complicated nest of relationships, one may be amazed how uncluttered, calm and reasonable a film this is. Its theme is that of family sacrifices, the ongoing battle within its characters between selfishness and unselfishness, and the decisions they make to still the conflict one way or the other. One must add that this film is free of the artiness and the "ickyness" that often damage Cocteau's works.

Jean Marais, Cocteau's lover at the time, is wonderful as Michel.

1949

LATE SPRING (Japan). Every girl should get married, and every father is doing the right thing by seeing to it that this happens—in letting go his daughter. This conventional wisdom, though, does not describe how Shukichi and Noriko Somiya, in Yasujiro Ozu's *Banshun*, feel. Although no spring chicken (she is 27), Noriko has no interest in marriage and is as content remaining with her widowed father, a professor, as he is content in having her remain. But society takes a different view, and Masa, the professor's sister, is especially meddlesome in her determination to get Noriko married. If her getting married is the way things ought to be, Shukichi comes up with a scheme to push Noriko out of the nest: he will pretend that he is about to get remarried. Noriko, whose smiles conceal disappointment, finally accepts a suitor's proposal, and Shukichi ends up alone in his kitchen, peeling an apple. It drops to the floor. This, now, is the way life will be.

Based on a novel by Kazuro Hirotsu, *Late Spring* benefits from a brilliant script by Ozu and Kôgo Noda. Social comedy and familial tragedy brush across one another. Self-determination is hard to come by; disappointment results from the compromises one makes in the course of one's life. At the same time, however, Ozu hasn't made an adolescent film decrying how bad things are. His is a film of *acceptance*. Ozu's resigned acceptance, which is philosophical, not defeatist, derives from the contemplation that permeates his postwar films. As usual, Ozu is peerless at capturing another intersection: the rush of emotion; the passage of time.

And his two perfect actors give tremendously moving performances: Chishu Ryu as Shukichi, whose smiles conceal as much as his daughter's, and Setsuko Hara as Noriko.

BLOOD OF THE BEASTS (France). Along with Henri Langlois, Georges Franju in 1936 founded the world's most celebrated film archive, La Cinémathèque française. (Two years earlier they had co-directed a 16mm short, *Le Métro*.) After the war, Franju went solo, launching his career with the short documentary *Le sang des bêtes*, which surveys, in graphic detail, the routine inside a Parisian slaughterhouse, composing in stark images a freezing reflection on the violence that human existence may require in order to sustain itself. But it is we the viewer who are moved to reflection; we watch workers simply going about their killing business with apparent indifference to the bloody and lethal outcome, and as a result we watch hard for small signs of affect that might suggest the humanity that is being suppressed in order to put meat on French dinner tables. Franju's images combine the brutal and the lyrical, reportage and poetry; irony, too, becomes a prominent element of the director's distinctive style: one of the film's narrators describes sheep being led to their slaughter as "following like men."

We may say then that Franju's documentary unfolds in the war's hangover. The connection is elusive, but somehow its description of "normal routine" within so brutal a context suggests French accommodation to the German occupation, even collaboration. The soulless labor inside the slaughterhouse evokes wartime French activity divorced from the soul of France.

The hanging carcasses compose too complex an image to interpret easily. It evokes something more than the human slaughter that the war exacted. The routine labor surrounding these carcasses suggests the compelling capacity of war to draw humans into its killing reality. It is an image of war's dehumanization, both on the battlefield and at the homefront. It expresses horror that despite so much death "life goes on."

STROMBOLI (Italy). A pat, simplistic film in the version released in the States, in the version that Roberto Rossellini surreptitiously shot using RKO equipment, which was distributed in continental Europe, *Stromboli* is magnificent.

Again Rossellini took up the issue of postwar dislocation at the heart of *Germany, Year Zero* (1947), only, in this instance, powerfully mining its spiritual fallout. Ingrid Bergman, who had replaced Anna Magnani as Rossellini's muse, beautifully plays a cultured bourgeois who resists feeling humbled by her camp status as a displaced refugee after the Second World War. To exit her confinement, Karen opportunistically marries a simple island fisherman, and a process of humiliation and rehumanization is begun. Karen comes to embody a paralyzed Europe at a crossroads between selfish material survival and selfless spiritual survival, with no path in sight to strike a balance between the two. Rossellini essays class differences that, persisting even in a shattered Europe, make all the more elusive the task of making Europe "whole again." Thus the mesmerizing passages of the fishermen at work—it is not surprising that the first of the Rossellini-Bergmans should be the one with deepest Neorealist roots—disclose a world that Karen resists by bourgeois breeding as well as by temperament. The sea is an alien place for her—a fact Rossellini stresses when, making an honest attempt to bridge the gap between them, Karen briefly joins her husband for a work break.

Unlike Luchino Visconti in *La terra trema* (1948), Rossellini isn't driven by Marxist principle to ennoble Karen's spouse or the other fishermen; he sees them straight on, in ordinary light. Crisis can be a great leveler, and neither the traditional villagers nor Karen, who chafes under their conservatism, seem capable of prevailing over the stormy currents to which European lives have been tossed.

12 O'CLOCK HIGH (U.S.). Henry King's *12 O'Clock High* analyzes the stresses of military command and military service.

The 918 Bomber Group of the U.S. Air Force, stationed in England in 1943, are among the early participants in daylight bombing raids. The "boys" or "men"—two successive commanding officers, Colonel Keith Davenport and General Frank Savage, debate the distinction—are as a result being pushed to the limit in an effort to determine what that limit is. It is called "maximum effort," and the stress the combatants undergo is deepened by the near certainty of the ultimate sacrifice of each, eventually, in the service of the group. Without respite, constantly facing death, and pushed to the extreme of their physical and mental capabilities, the combatants are beginning to crack, and some may be attempting to evade their military duty. The high command feels that the combatants have a sincere though unwitting accomplice in Davenport, whose caring overidentification with them, in addition to further demoralizing the group and undercutting its military effectiveness, results in his own breakdown. He is thus replaced by the well-named Savage, a martinet who bullies and humiliates the men, for instance, by consigning those he deems delinquent to an airship renamed "The Leper Colony." Pushing ahead with mission after mission, Savage "sweeps his feelings under the rug" to the point that he, too, suffers a nervous breakdown.

The film's most absorbing, humane and philosophical character is the oft-inebriated Colonel Harvey Stovall, a First World War combatant who now does desk work, a role for which Dean Jagger won a richly deserved Oscar. After the war, haunting the country field where the group's missions were launched, Stovall is himself haunted by memories that form *12 O'Clock High*'s extended interior flashback.

KIND HEARTS AND CORONETS (UK). "He seemed a very pleasant fellow, and I regretted that our acquaintanceship had to be so short." — Louis Mazzini.

Brilliantly written by its director, Robert Hamer, and John Dighton, *Kind Hearts and Coronets* is a piercingly funny consideration of upper-class British arrogance. The aristocratic D'Ascoynes family has disinherited one of their own because in marrying an Italian singer she married beneath her station and—horrors!—she married for love. After his widowed mother's death, upon which occasion her dying request to be buried in the family grounds is denied, Louis Mazzini (Dennis Price, priceless) embarks on a mission to avenge her mistreatment by dispatching each and every D'Ascoynes, all of whom stand between him and a dukedom. Tried and convicted by the House of Lords for a crime he did not commit, Louis spends the night before his execution penning his memoir, inducing (for us) a flashback suited to his voiceover.

In Roy Horniman's 1907 novel *Israel Rank*, the mother marries a Jew, but the Holocaust argued in 1949 for his replacement, even amidst Edwardian sets and garb. The black comedy's unifying joke is that Louis, robbed of his birthright, mirrors the contumeliousness of those retaining the birthright. *Why shouldn't a man sniffle into his handkerchief if he must?* Yet when Louis laments the indignity of taking in a lodger (his mother and he are financially strapped), this inadvertent audible punctuation by the lodger becomes hilarious. Perhaps Louis's funniest line, though, simply indicates his Wildean wit. Louis tells the groom at a wedding, having spent the previous night making love with the bride: "You're a lucky man, Lionel. Take my word for it."

Alec Guinness (best actor, National Board of Review), beautifully plays eight different D'Ascoyneses including a doddering clergyman, a private bank president, a suffragette.

THE BATTLE OF STALINGRAD, PART ONE (U.S.S.R.). Although the second part (1950) is thinner and somewhat mechanical, even stilted at points, Vladimir Petrov's *Stalingradskaya bitva I* is tremendous, full of dark, turbulent poetry as a nation's survival, according to recent history, hangs in the balance. Perhaps this pressing danger helps explain why the first part is superior to the second, where the Soviet counteroffensive at Stalingrad ultimately succeeds, bleeding German morale and strength—the turning-point of the Second World War toward the Allies. (Adolf Hitler: "The God of War has gone over to the other side.")

In the main, three kinds of elements are interwoven: deep, deliberate voiceover—the voice of history; scenes of meetings between Stalin and others, very often Chief of the General Staff Vasilevsky, whose strategic contribution is slighted to flatter "Comrade Stalin"; generally at night, glimpses of battle. It is this last category of imagery, including fierce, frightening, profoundly melancholy tracking shots of city-as-battleground-and-bombing-field, that haunt and move the viewer's soul.

There is a striking contrast between Hitler, bug-eyed, yelling, threatening death to those who fail to deliver the military results he is after, and calm, steady, dignified Stalin. ("Good luck," he tells General Chuikov.) An old comrade—one he hadn't purged—visits: "Josef, you are tired." Stalin: "I'm not the only one." He is connected to the people in their joint danger, suffering, exhaustion. When he leans over his desk to consider his map of territory and troops, he leans down into the corner of the frame—an image of humble resolve; in a parallel shot, Hitler spreads his hands on *his* map: the image of a conqueror's ambition. (Chaplin's Adenoid Hynkel hovers!)

Like all epics, Petrov's is sublime propaganda; it "expresses" the collective spirit of a people in hopes of creating this.

WHITE HEAT (U.S.). *White Heat*, James Cagney's return to the gangster genre for the first time in a decade to revive his sagging career, is bookended by blasts of heat: from a steam engine, burning beyond recognition a member whom gang leader Cody Jarrett (Cagney, superb) leaves for dead, failing to recognize him as someone for whom he is responsible, a younger, alternate version of himself; from the blowup of an oil refinery, sending Cody up in flames: "Finally made it, Ma: Top o' the world!"

As a child, battling siblings for his mother's attention, Cody feigned headaches that have since become all too real, still requiring Ma Cody's soothing touch. Guilt-ridden, the woman has devoted herself to her criminal son's care, forsaking her other offspring. Viewers are simply wrong when they (ridiculously) say that Cody is "in love with his mother." Psychotic and infantile, Cody is incapable of loving anyone, including wife Verna; rather, perpetually afraid of losing his mother's love, he egotistically clings to her guiltily devoted image. After Ma's death (Verna plugs her in the back), his last attempted robbery conforms to the story of the Trojan Horse that his mother read to him as a child.

The emphasis on social context of 1930s gangster films—only Howard Hawks's *Scarface* (1932) stressed a criminal's psychosis—has been replaced by criminal psychology in a world upended by the war. (Cody's profits from theft are enlarged through the postwar European black market.) Moreover, *White Heat* is director Raoul Walsh's *hommage* to the cinema of Fritz Lang, whose determinism he relaxes a little, but whose geometrics (such as inside the prison housing Cody) and whose eerie otherworldliness (such as inside the belly of the empty oil truck—visually, a space ship; symbolically, Ma's womb) conjure images of science fiction.

I WAS A MALE WAR BRIDE (U.S.). Howard Hawks's *I Was a Male War Bride seamlessly* blends genres: screwball romantic comedy; postwar semi-documentary. Extensively shot in postwar Germany, it was based on an autobiographical story by Henri Rochard, the main character. Captain Rochard (Cary Grant, hilarious), of the French Army, and Lieutenant Catherine Gates (Ann Sheridan, even better), of the American, embark on Rochard's final mission, the unclear nature of which is correlative to their dizzyingly unclear personal relationship. Each apparently delights in making the other miserable, but only Gates, romantically swifter, is conscious of the delight; beneath a surface of bickering, the two are deeply in love. When both discover this, they wade through a dispiriting maze of bureaucratic U.S. Army red tape in order to marry and set off for America, their wedding night, at the mercy of rules and regulations pertaining to lodging, in a constant state of postponement. Categorized as Gates's "alien bride," Rochard must feign being a woman to be allowed on ship. They lock themselves into a cabin; the Statue of Liberty—France's goft to America—eventually appears through the port-hole: proof, after a series of humiliations, that Rochard's sense of manhood has been restored and that the Rochards' marriage has been consummated.

The outstanding script is by Charles Lederer, Leonard Spigelgass and Hagar Wilde. The Rochard-Gates union deeply affects us as a blossom growing from the rubble of war. All this couple is put through coalesces into one of the most forceful wallops to the heart that any light film has delivered, and it predicts the difficulties ahead for their marriage, given especially Rochard's cultural dislocation. The Rochards' ordeal also reflects on the considerable effort that may be necessary to reclaim Europe from the chaos that fascism and the war had embroiled it in.

Films of the 1950s

A curious trend in 1950s Hollywood cinema is the fusion of the western and *film noir* (Raoul Walsh's excellent 1947 *Pursued* may have started the practice), with a strong, even criminal woman at the center: Anthony Mann's *The Furies* (1950) and Samuel Fuller's *Forty Guns* (*The Lady with a Whip*, 1957), both starring Barbara Stanwyck; Nicholas Ray's *Johnny Guitar* (1954), starring Joan Crawford; and, above all, Fritz Lang's *Rancho Notorious* (1952), starring Marlene Dietrich.

Lang's best American film is propelled by a recurring ballad of "hate, murder and revenge." The images seem to elaborate on the song, "Legend of Chuck-A-Luck." Therefore, the song (with music and lyrics by Ken Darby) seems to attribute the film to a legendary domain, pointedly distancing us the viewer from the unfolding drama. This deepens the distancing achieved by both the remoteness of the western setting sometime in the 1870s and the use of color. (The cinematographer is Hal Mohr, whose specialty is dreaminess: *A Midsummer Night's Dream*, 1935; *Phantom of the Opera*, 1943.) Flamboyant yet elusive, convoluted in the machinations of its meanest characters, yet as persistent as a train going down a track, Lang's third and final western—the other two are *The Return of Frank James* (1940) and *Western Union* (1941)—altogether seems a dream existing in a dream.

Even the meaningless title, imposed over Lang's objections by RKO studio head Howard Hughes, fits the material perfectly. (Lang had wanted the film to be called *Chuck-A-Luck*.)

What sets the narrative wheel in motion is the rape and murder of Beth, a girl alone at the counter one day in her father's general store in a small Wyoming town. Set to marry her in eight days, cowboy Vern Haskell is left with a gaping hole in his psyche, which instantly is filled with hatred for the anonymous wrongdoer and a determination to exact revenge. Michael E. Grost, an Internet film critic, thus finds the film to be "deeply feminist, in taking with great seriousness the horrible crime of rape." This is certainly possible, so long as we admit that Vern's course of action divorces him from a feminist impulse. Vern's pursuit of "justice" objectifies the victim all over again, consigning her memory to the status of mere touchstone for his vicious, oppressive rage, and implying that the crime committed is one of a violation of his property rights. By extension, one may infer—although, of course, he himself would be incapable of such a formulation—that Vern felt that only *he*, as her husband had she lived, was entitled to rape Beth. There is a sourness to the tone of all this psychosocial complication that, while not excluding the possibility of frustrated feminism on Lang's part, suggests that other meanings may be more central. Indeed, the film's Langian sense of determinism all but requires the rape and murder of Beth—hardly a felicitous springboard for feminist inquiry. In addition, at some point the pun contained in Vern's last name, Haskell, likely kicks in: *has kill*, as in *has to kill*, may imply that Beth's fate is mere pretext—rationalization—for Vern's murderous impulses and vengeful mission, making the death of his beloved, in fact, a matter of convenience for him. Perhaps her end spares Vern the forfeit of his idealization of Beth; this cancellation of their wedding spares him the ordeal of embracing the reality of her with which marriage would have confronted him. Vern has been left with an image of Beth that he hopes to hold onto—and an image of himself, as her avenger, that may tighten the psychic grip necessary to accomplish the task.

Underscoring the theme of possessiveness is the glittering brooch that Vern pins on Beth at their last meeting and which her killer confiscates as a memento of the rape. In effect, Vern is after this prize to reclaim it as his own. This all but identifies Vern with Beth's (as yet) unknown rapist and killer. Certainly Vern's quest fails to characterize him as any sort of shining knight, for as the ballad tells us, " . . . deep within him burn the fires of hate, murder and revenge."

Different viewers will interpret Vern's tenderness toward Beth differently. Some may take it at face value. But, for me, what is so startling about that opening scene between the two on the threshold of their wedding is its unreality, its adolescent nature. It's a purely conventional moment between young lovebirds that's undercut by a curious remark Vern makes. When giving Beth the brooch, Vern boasts that the person who sold it to him said the brooch came all the way from Paris. Later, this ridiculous comment will connect the brooch to the world of an outlaw and gunslinger named Fairmont, who goes by the nickname Frenchy. Initially, though, it strikes us as juvenile that Vern seems to be unaware he has been the victim of a merchant's puffery; he seems to believe that the piece of jewelry crossed the Atlantic Ocean and the U.S. just to flatter his ego as gift-giver and to adorn his bride-to-be. This is a presumably grown man speaking, but his impossible innocence here reflects on the impossible purity and innocence to which he has mentally consigned Beth. It is *he* who has thus made her, at least symbolically, ripe for rape.

The exchanges between Beth and Vern are no less realistic for being giddily foolish. It is often the case that in wooing a girl, after all, a man is after a prize that marriage will suddenly convert into a flesh-and-blood woman—one who cannot help but contest the ego that her succumbing to his wooing previously nurtured and stroked. Weddings consummate the wooing; marriage is another matter entirely. The fact that *Rancho Notorious* is prevented from ever reaching Vern and Beth's wedding, let alone their nuts-and-bolts, two-human marriage, is one of the film's dream, even fairy-tale, elements. One is reminded here of *Much Ado About Nothing*, whose merry romp stops short of Beatrice and Benedick's wedding, sparing them (and us) the undoing of their love that marriage, according to Shakespeare, would likely have brought about. In tune with this idea, at the other end, is Ingmar Bergman's film *Scenes from a Marriage* (1974), which shows a couple who become friendly, finally, after divorce, after marriage.

Whatever its nature, Vern's quest involves the unravelling of a mystery: Who assaulted and murdered Beth? If, as I have suggested, in some sense (out of Sophocles's *Œdipus Rex*) the answer to this is "the quester, or detective, himself," then a significant motivation on Vern's part is to deny this truth by pinning the rap on somebody else. Like Œdipus and Hamlet, Vern Haskell looks outside himself to keep from looking too closely or carefully within. In part, the film's fatalism derives from the fact that, afflicted with a lack of self-knowledge, Vern cannot help but do this. All the while he is searching for the solution of the mystery at hand, he is venturing deeper and deeper into fantastic territory that removes him more and more from the truth about Beth's death, their planned wedding, and himself. Unlike Œdipus, Vern —and Lang's film along with him—will remain embedded in a dream. Vern will never face the truth because something in the American experience denies him tragic dimension and renders him, instead, cheap, evasive, dishonest. In many ways, *Rancho Notorious* is, thematically, the mirror-opposite of, four years hence, John Ford's *The Searchers* (1956), which also centers on a quest, but one that is tragic regarding its quester, Ethan Edwards, and the America he represents—a film in which Ethan's self-discovery and self-awareness result from his quest.

From an old man, the partner whom the rapist-killer (the projection of Vern's denial of responsibility) has shot in the back, Vern gets this clue as the man expires: "Chuck-A-Luck." This is the film's *Rosebud*, Grost notes; if only Vern can find out what *Chuck-A-Luck* means, he will learn, he believes, *everything*. Chuck-a-luck is a gambling game involving a wheel of fortune and bets placed on color-coded numbers on a board. The game was popular in the Southwest, into which Vern rides ever deeper and deeper in search of his solution. Instinctively, however, he knows that the dying man's utterance refers to something other than the game, to a place, perhaps, where he will learn the identity of Beth's assailant. It is worth noting that the game chuck-a-luck derives from the French roulette. Vern's trail is littered with things French.

As Vern questions people along the way, he encounters a series of recollections and accounts that come to us as dreamlike, exaggerated, borderline surreal flashbacks—dreams within the housing dream of the quest. They involve a fabulous woman of mystery, the powerfully alluring and unforgettable Altar Keane, who has seemingly dropped off the face of the earth. It turns out that, years earlier, with Frenchy Fairmont's help, Altar Keane, a saloon singer, right after being fired, made her fortune at the chuck-a-luck table in the saloon and has since retreated to her (relatively) palatial domain, a horse ranch which hills hide in its valley, and which is also called Chuck-A-Luck. Vern gains his entrance to this world-within-the-world by befriending Frenchy Fairmont, an outlaw, "the fastest gun in the West," and Altar's longtime lover, and by helping him escape jail. Vern's first distant view of Chuck-A-Luck, on horseback from on high, identifies it as a dreamlike vision—as glittering as the brooch that will reappear there, worn by Altar. The place, Altar's Xanadu, is a dream within a dream.

Indeed, the film questions its own reality, shifting its images to dreams. I noted the flashbacks that are conjured for us by people's recollections or accounts of Altar Keane. Are the images in these real? Dreams? How much is accurately remembered, how much exaggerated, how much wishfully invented? (In a deputy sheriff's account, for instance, Altar is lasciviously riding him, as if he were a horse, in a saloon race, in which she is wearing a fall, a golden faux-pony tail that rounds out an impossible portrait conjoining corruption and innocence.) Daniel Taradash's splendid script (from a story by Silvia Richards) pokes at us with these possibilities as some of those invoking Keane make comments such as the following: "I don't swear this is true, because I wasn't here. But this is how they tell it." "I was told a story . . . If you want to believe what you hear . . . I don't know if it's true, but . . . ." Those familiar with the rhetorical strategies of the trickster narrator in *Billy Budd* will recognize American author Herman Melville's method for throwing into question military officialdom and its pronouncements, as well as the instant history, the so-called truth, promoted by newspaper accounts. But Lang's aim in *Rancho Notorious* is somewhat different. Lang is questioning the reality, as well as the morality, of the rags-to-riches American experience that Altar Keane represents. Keane got her gains through Frenchy's cheating intervention, and she has used the money to build her own Chuck-A-Luck, a hideout for thieves 10% of whose stolen acquisitions she appropriates. The façade of American capitalism, that wealth is won by honest work, is a dream, according to Lang's film; the sordid reality lies underneath.

The night she met Frenchy Fairmont at Baldy's Palace, Altar, according to the flashback, was dressed in red and black. A wall painting is an abstract design consisting of red, white and black. The chuck-a-luck wheel is red, white and black. Moreover, when first we see Frenchy in his jail cell, he is dressed in these colors, and the same colors, in a more subdued incarnation, dominate Altar's residence and place of operations, Chuck-A-Luck. Without doubt, this color scheme is a parody of the red, white and blue of the American flag, but the virulence of Lang's parody fully kicks in only when we recall that red, white and black were also the colors of the Nazi flag, which was adorned by a swastika instead of a brooch. Half-Jewish, Lang fled Nazi Germany once Hitler came to power. Interestingly, his first stop on his eventual journey to the United States was France, the nation that produced Stendhal's (Marie-Henri Beyle's) novel *Le rouge et le noir*, in which the color red is identified with the military and black is identified with the Church. I don't know quite what to make of all this, but it's interesting, in this context, that Keane's Christian name is Altar. In another context, she is so named because she is a constant reminder to Vern of the wedding that did not take place owing to Beth's brutal death.

Lang's cinema had always been fatalistic; in light of the Holocaust, it could scarcely become less so. The nightmare of Nazism haunts *Rancho Notorious* as Lang addresses, and attacks, the dangerous nature of idealistic national myths, whether they are promoted in Germany or the United States. Vern's lack of self-knowledge is an index of the delusions that such myths

Chronology of World Cinema
Films of the 1950s

generate, and his grimly hilarious series of wrong assumptions as to who killed Beth from among the suspects at Chuck-A-Luck underscores his incapacity for self-criticism. Like the Nazis, this film implies, McCarthyite America pins its problems on "the Other." The Nazis had their Jews to scapegoat; the Americans, their communists. (Actually, the Nazis *also* scapegoated communists.) In the latter case, the film further implies, the scapegoating is a distraction from America's delusional foundation in myths about enterprise and financial success. Chuck-A-Luck, a parody of the American Dream, represents the nightmare of capitalism, which entraps human lives in a circle of luck and unfair competition, with its hidden or denied elements of advantage and disadvantage, and which promotes itself as providing fair, open opportunity. One shot is trenchant in this regard: Altar Keane, dressed in lavender, riding triumphantly in an open carriage, her black maid, dressed in black, sitting right behind her, shielding her from the sun with a black parasol.

Marlene Dietrich, who had had a brief affair with Lang a lifetime earlier, is stunning as Altar Keane, whose land, Vern roughly points out to her, is a graveyard. I worry that Americans are all, sooner or later, buried there.

The decade saw Vittorio De Sica's personal favorite from among his films and the end of *neorealismo* as a movement, although it still crops up as a *style* and progressive orientation in individual films from Italy and elsewhere. *Umberto D.* claims the most powerful opening of any Italian neorealist film. It begins with an overhead long-shot of a city street in daylight. From behind the cars that move up the street, steadily becoming the shot's focus, is an orderly mass of people, retirees who are demonstrating for a raise in the amount of their pensions. It's the next shot that discloses this intent of theirs: an upwardly tilted street-level shot showing, instead of the people themselves, the placards they carry. A frontal shot of the group reveals the fierce, wholehearted participation of the protagonist, Umberto Domenico Ferrari, a retired civil servant. (Umberto was the name of De Sica's father, a retired bank clerk to whom the son, in its opening credits, dedicates the film.) Police cars enter the scene, dispersing the protesters aggressively though nonviolently. Two of the shots here are key, one from the vantage of one of the slowly entering police cars as marchers run from it (subtly, De Sica has reversed the direction of the protesters in relation to the camera, to underscore their agitation at the arrival of authority), and the other from above: a tilted overhead shot—a disturbing glimpse of human panic. In sum, this passage, the most brilliant one that De Sica ever devised, not only launches the film, not only (as we shall see) connects with a later image to frame a consideration of the film's motive, but also permeates the entire film as a persistent theme of social concern for which the example we follow, Ferrari, strikes a single representative chord.

The scene following this opening is crucial to our understanding of the forces of authority arrayed against the protesters. Three of the marchers, including Ferrari, have taken cover from the police in an alley off the main street. Ferrari's companion, a mongrel named Flike, expresses his distaste for what the police have just done by snarling and barking, causing one of the men, who has just fearfully wiped his brow with a white handkerchief (a sign of surrender, at least a partial wavering in the cause), to shout that Ferrari should control his (actually, otherwise, perpetually gentle) animal. This man blames the organizers of the demonstration, who failed to secure the necessary municipal permit for the march, thus providing the legal basis for the police action in interrupting and disbanding it. Ferrari calmly explains that the organizers had applied for the permit but were denied. In this way, then, the municipal authorities had calculated in advance their basis for aborting the demonstration.

This provides food for thought, especially in the context of Italy's then recent history. Current civil authority clearly is at pains to differentiate itself from Fascist authority; cunning manipulation—bureaucratic shenanigans—has replaced brute force. Some of those marching, like the man now opposing the organizers, have adequate financial security; others, like

Ferrari, do not. About to be evicted for being in arrears on his rent, Ferrari is in a desperate situation that the 20% raise in pensions being sought would alleviate. The protest is, for him, a life-and-death matter. To be sure, the march is civilly disruptive; it contests the mundane order of things. De Sica shows the normal flow of traffic derailed by the marchers precisely to indicate this disruption. But what in this instance does restoring civil order precisely mean? By stopping the demonstration, authorities seek to isolate those demonstrating from their fellow citizenry, whom the demonstrators are trying to reach in their appeal for justice and whose support they need in order to marshal the political clout necessary to achieve their goal: the raise in their pensions. The authorities will claim as their support the "cause" of civil order so that the majority of citizens can have the uninterrupted enjoyment of their normal routine. This in effect seeks to contain the protesters within the status quo, without access to the means of remedying the problem besetting them. However, the disruption entailed by the march is *itself* contained; it's a limited disruption with legitimate aims. It gives a voice to a minority of people that the majority, whose sympathy they are attempting to engage, can also hear, on the street and through the media. Police interruption of this disruption is a way of shifting public attention from the message—the demonstrators' cause—to the fact of the disruption, which the police appear to be ending on behalf of the majority of the citizenry. It's a cloaked form of Fascism. The original message gets lost and another takes its place: the bogus issue of civil order—bogus, because the "disruption" of it was so deliberately contained and limited by the organizers and demonstrators themselves out of a need to strike a precarious balance between getting public attention and not irritating or enraging the public against their cause.

De Sica presents, then, an aborted demonstration, and the success of his method lies in the fact that we not only consider the cause of the demonstrators but also the motivation of the authorities who denied the permit in the first place, whom the police (obediently, professionally—in this instance, not maliciously) publicly represent. Almost all of the rest of the film will deal with a single individual, "Umberto D.," but so intelligently and cogently has De Sica established the social context of the financial needs of a group of people and the human, i.e., political forces intent on obstructing all remedy of the problem that this context accompanies the character throughout the film. This is a remarkable achievement, especially given the close attention that De Sica pays to the peculiar details of Ferrari's individual circumstance—details that speak to the humanity of the film no less than the social context that confers on Ferrari a representative identity.

The lion's share of De Sica's largely unsentimental film depicts the tragedy of Ferrari's circumstance. A pensioner, he is untouched by Italy's painful postwar economic recovery; he has, in effect, been left behind, consigned to anonymity in Italy's past, without recourse to his nation's future. But De Sica is careful not to pit one generation against another. He accomplishes this in two ways. One is to show how former colleagues of Ferrari repeatedly feign deafness to his overtures for financial assistance; all his better-off old friends appear too busy with their own lives to pause long enough even to provide substantive counsel. Written off by those who know him and should care, how much easier it is for the bureaucratic state to overlook or dismiss his right to live. Thus De Sica creates an implicit quarrel among the "war generation"; looking backward, even to an old bureaucratic comrade currently in dire need of help, is too distasteful, too demanding, too threatening in its capacity to awaken painful emotions that these individuals have smoothed over and suppressed, along with the political memories to which these emotions have necessarily become attached. Ferrari, like many others, then, has become a casualty to the national motive to move forward. The other way that De Sica spares the film a schematic competition between old and young is to make Ferrari's closest human friend a girl, Maria, who is his landlady's maidservant. Pregnant, not knowing which of two boys is the father (both deny paternity), she also lives a perilous existence, since exposure of her condition may at any point render her homeless as well. When Ferrari asks her if she might move back with her parents, Maria replies that her parents would beat her. Both on the verge of some sort of terrible beating from life, the old man and the girl have formed a deeply sympathetic bond. Maria is Ferrari's one steadfast friend, acting on occasion as intermediary between him and his landlady. The only other champion he has, of course, is Flike, for whose care part of his small pension must go.

The landlady couldn't care less about the ants in his studio apartment about which Ferrari, who has lived there for decades, complains. She wants the back rent he owes, which he cannot pay and which she is in no such economic fix as to need with any urgency. Indeed, she can do without Ferrari's money; what she really wants is for him to leave. During the day this viciously unkind woman—during the war, they had been friends—rents out Ferrari's room to extramarital couples, a violation driven home when we see one such couple leaving Ferrari's room as he is returning to it. At first, Ferrari is determined to remain in his home. He tries selling a watch, but like the hocked and stolen bicycles in De Sica's magnificent *Bicycle Thieves* (1948) watches abound; many others are trying to sell theirs to help make ends meet. By law Ferrari cannot be charged rent while in hospital, so he feigns illness in order to be admitted into this free institution, and the soul in the next bed charms a nun into extending his stay. This new friend counsels Ferrari to ask the nun for a rosary to show his good faith, and Ferrari, who it is implied doesn't even believe in God, much less practice Roman Catholicism, complies—one of several assaults to his dignity he reluctantly embraces in pursuit of a means of retaining his long-accustomed life. (Earlier, he practiced in the street extending his hand for a handout, but just when someone was about to deposit a coin he turned his palm downward, pretending he had been using his hand—on this sunlit day—to check for rain.) It almost seems that, lacking property of his own, he also lacks a life of his own. Self-determination is out of the question. But things are about to become much worse for Ferrari.

Once released from the hospital, Ferrari learns that his landlady had allowed his dog, under her maidservant's care, to escape into the street. Ferrari is beside himself. The most harrowing part of the film now follows: his desperate search of the municipal pound as massive cages full of dogs are delivered to their extermination. (This scene strikes an aural chord in my experience. At graduate school, daily could be heard the screeches of animals being experimented on and killed in science labs, in most cases purely to maintain for various programs a continuity of federal funding.) Ferrari finds his friend in time; however, the suspenseful experience has only intensified his already keen sense of vulnerability. Once he returns home with Flike, he is all but shattered by a further blow. During his absence, his landlady has had his room stripped of wallpaper and had one wall broken down in order to join its space to the adjacent room. Ferrari's home, if she has her way, will become part of a cocktail party room: the ultimate sign not only of this woman's inhumanity but of society's, insofar as someone's life is being discounted in favor of someone else's peripheral entertainment. Amidst his enormous sense of violation, Ferrari tries with all his might to hold on to his dignity; but the landlady, unswerving in her assaults, has finally broken his spirit. Ferrari decides to commit suicide. When he cannot find an adequate home for Flike, he decides they should both die together from the force of a train. At the last moment, Flike, unwilling to die, tears himself from Ferrari's grip, saving both their lives. Trust, though, has been broken; Flike will have nothing more to do with Ferrari until, by degrees, Ferrari wins back his companion, with the help of a pine cone, in a park. The film ends with children at play in this park as Ferrari and Flike reunite to face their uncertain fate. This image conjoining Italy's past and future, old and young, implies the single thread of humanity that society must acknowledge and appreciate if Italy is to survive with its character and morality intact.

De Sica admirably succeeds in keeping the landlady from becoming a villain; she is cold-blooded, not evil. She also has turned her back on the war and, in her own way, is in flight from her memory of it. (It helps, too, that Lina Gennari gives a crackerjack performance in the role.) Her evil, if De Sica had taken that route, would have constituted a sentimental touch, and since so much of the film is taken up by Ferrari's contest with the landlady this touch would have ruined the film. Moreover, her evil would have constituted a serious distraction, for our attention would have shifted from where it belongs, the evil inherent in the idea of property trumping humanity, to some monstrous flaw in someone's character. Instead, De Sica keeps us focused on the relationship between Italy's postwar present and recent wartime past.

Of course, there was another potential problem, a gaping sentimental hole lying in wait into which the whole film could at any moment drop. If a man so loves his dog, can Disney be far behind? With immense intelligence, De Sica again keeps his nimble directorial toes dancing over and around the hole. Closeups of the dog are mostly avoided, two-shots of the pair are given some distance, and shots even appear of his walking the dog where only the taut leash appears in the frame. We know the dog is attached to it; but De Sica understands we don't always have to see Flike.

Alas, there is a single point where, I feel, De Sica fails to avoid or transcend sentimentality, and it damages the film somewhat, although certainly doesn't ruin it. It's but a second or two, but it's a mistake. Back from the hospital, Ferrari opens his terrace windows as a zoom from behind his back, focused on the pavement below, discloses his suicidal intent. Ferrari looks appropriately transfixed afterwards, but the zoom lasts too long, if indeed such an attention-calling shot was necessary at all. Here, at least for me, the flourish of technical bravura slights the humanity involved: a man so full of hopelessness and despair that he would contemplate ending his own life. Indeed, the shot's "expressiveness" is even inexact, for when Ferrari then withdraws, shutting the windows, the viewer might reasonably assume that Ferrari has rejected suicide when in fact this is precisely the course he is about to pursue. The application of the zoom lens, especially at such length, cheapens and sentimentalizes an appalling moment in Ferrari's life and, in tandem with what then follows, possibly misguides the audience in terms of the direction of the narrative.

That said, *Umberto D.* did not deserve the treatment the Italian government accorded it. The film was roundly dismissed as being totally sentimental. The Andreotti Law, recently passed, codified state funding of Italian cinema, but only for popular entertainments, not the socially probing films that composed the neorealist movement. There are a number of reasons why Italy turned its back on the films that had been giving its cinema worldwide fame. For one thing, like many of the characters in *Umberto D.*, Italy wanted to put the past behind it, and Italian neorealism had become identified with wartime and just-postwar Italian cinema. Related to this, many neorealist films, especially the postwar ones by De Sica and Roberto Rossellini, addressed social problems besetting Italy, and the government felt that this was tantamount to airing their own dirty linen in public since Italian films were distributed to the rest of the world. Thus, while national pride dictated that such acclaimed films continue, national pride even more strenuously dictated that they cease, lest a certain kind of view of Italy, already negative from its connection to Fascism, be perpetuated. Italy's "problems" were behind it, Italy preferred to insist even at the expense of truth. Similarly related is the fact that these socially investigative films tended to proceed from a political and socioeconomic view either recognizably Marxist or quasi-Marxist, and both Roman Catholic and democratic strains endlessly worried over that. Finally, the conquering United States was extorting all sorts of favors as recompense for helping Europe, including Italy, to rebuild, and Hollywood, which had the federal government's ear, was flat-out unhappy that a few Italian neorealist films such as *Bicycle Thieves* and Giuseppe De Santis's *Bitter Rice* (1949) were cutting into its profits by drawing patrons away from Hollywood product. For all these reasons, then, Italy was determined to kill the movement that had elevated its cinema and given this a purposeful, progressive voice, and of this determination its cruel, dismissive reception of *Umberto D.* provided further testimony. Moreover, the film's unglamorous, noncommercial nature assured its popular defeat.

Cesare Zavattini and De Sica wrote the film's excellent script; Eraldo Da Roma superbly edited the film. The black-and-white cinematography by Aldo Graziati (G. R. Aldo) flawlessly blends De Sica's shooting on both streets and sets. Finally, the nonprofessional cast is excellent. Leading it is Carlo Battisti, the former university professor who memorably plays Umberto Domenico Ferrari, a role to which he brings just enough of a physical resemblance to Charles Chaplin to anticipate the latter's *Limelight* (1952). Like Chaplin's Calvero, Battisti's Umberto D. is a fully human characterization.

Let us permit De Sica to have the last few words on this very fine film of his. It is, he has remarked, "the tragedy of those people who find themselves cut off from a world that they nevertheless helped to build, a tragedy hidden by resignation and silence, but one that occasionally explodes in loud demonstrations or is pushed into appalling suicides. A young man's decision to kill himself is taken seriously, but what does one say of the suicide of an old man already close to death? It's terrible. A society that allows such things is a lost society."

Closer to *Anna Karenina* than any of the numerous film versions of Tolstoi's novel, *Madame de . . .* actually derives from a trivial novella, set before the Great War in the early twentieth century, by Louise de Vilmorin. In the opinion of most, it is the masterpiece of Max Ophüls, the German Jewish filmmaker, born Max Oppenheimer, who skipped from one country to the next in the 1930s and 1940s, eluding Adolf Hitler's grasp. Ophüls, of course, wasn't entitled to the nobility of his pseudonym (this was his invention, like the *von* that Erich Stroheim and Josef Sternberg adopted), but, when he confessed his ruse to the actual Ophüls family, which had made inquiries, they welcomed him into the fold with open arms. After all, he was no one to be ashamed of.

The title *Madame de . . .* refers to the film's main character. Her last name is not disclosed. Since her first name, like that of the author, is Louise, though, we may presume that she is the author's self-projection and complete the fictitious woman's name accordingly. Regardless, throughout the film we are teased into thinking we will hear or see the woman's married name, but we never do. This begins humorously, but by the end of the film, when the shot showing the name placard accompanying her final offering to her favorite saint at church is cropped sideways, allowing us to see only "Madame de," the result is tragic. This woman never found out who she is as a person, and now her life has been cut short. She will be identified henceforth with the man she really loved, not the one she was married to. All kinds of associations attend the aural and visual abortings of her married name. Finally, let us remember that the title plays on the old practice in newspapers of not identifying persons where scandal is involved so that legal reprisals could be avoided. Madame de . . . echoes Madame de—.

In the U.S., the title became *The Earrings of Madame De . . .* The U.S. is forever changing titles, distorting the meaning of films, corrupting audiences by thus guiding them to a misinterpretation of the films. The classic example is *Bicycle Thieves* (*Ladri di biciclette*), which became here *The Bicycle Thief*, as though the film were the portrait of an anomaly, a criminal individual, rather than a social portrait and protest. (More often, titles are changed to make the films seem more seductive.) But materialistic Americans might indeed believe that her jewels matter more than Louise does. This is a corruption of the whole intent of the film, in which Louise is infinitely precious and her diamond earrings have no intrinsic value to her. Her husband, the General, gave her the earrings as a wedding gift, but she secretly sells them in order to pay off debts that her extravagance has accrued—extravagance that in itself provides an index of her marital dissatisfaction. The jewels mean nothing to Louise because she isn't in love with her husband. Yet they become priceless to her when she is given them again, this time as a gift from the man with whom she has fallen in love. Louise's feelings deprive the jewels of value in one instance and confer value in the other. Only in America could people believe that the film is about diamonds and not about the woman. (Well, not quite: the Italian title translates as *The Emblazonments of Madame de . . . .*)

The time is early twentieth century; the place, Paris. (The film itself is from France; Ophüls settled there after the war.) Louise and her husband, André, come from two different though intersecting worlds. She is a *comtesse*—a member of the titled nobility; he is a general in the military, which in France confers great standing. The implication is clear: for Louise, this marriage was probably one of financial convenience. As a result of it, she lives as grandly as her ancestors had once been able to by virtue of family fortune and status. Although we may assume that André married Louise, at least in part, because of the allure of her nobility (throughout the film he praises her for her nobility), it is also unmistakable that he is very much in love with her. (We have no way of knowing whether this love of his predated the marriage; we do know that, by his own admission, he has been routinely unfaithful and that he tells her he loves her, in a voice too low to be probably heard by her, only when he is worried that he is about to lose her.) The Italian diplomat with whom Louise falls in love and who falls in love with her, Fabrizio Donati, is a baron. He and Louise, unlike André and Louise, in some sense belong to the same world, although the two men belong to the same club. When they come to fight the duel that will end in the death of one of them, André, the instigator, uses the pretext that the baron favors diplomacy over war—a *professional* division. In reality, the class division between the two is more relevant, because it adds salt to the wound at the base of their quarrel: the galling fact, for the General, that his wife loves Donati and not him. The humorous triviality of the pretext for the duel shelters André's pride and humiliation, then; indeed, this sketches in a method that Ophüls uses throughout the film, where a light touch masks a harsh, even a potentially lethal reality.

The film opens rapturously, with a seemingly perpetually tracking camera adopting a subjective point of view as Louise's hands ransack her finery and her jewelry box in search of the right thing to sell for money. Madame de . . . passes over the diamond earrings, saying, "If only my husband hadn't given these to me as a wedding gift!"—or words to that effect, the meaning being, these baubles mean little to me, but my spouse will notice their absence if I get rid of them. She returns to them, however, because everything else she owns holds more charm, more value for her. This long passage is accompanied by humming and singing on the soundtrack. At first we think it's the woman's own melodious voice. Then we're not so sure. We capture a glimpse of Madame de . . . as she glances in a mirror. We hear the lilting melody by Oscar Straus, both as background music and as humming or singing, but Madame de . . .'s lips aren't moving except when she speaks to herself. (Straus—one *s* and no relation to anyone with two *s*'s; nevertheless, the composer of the loveliest music that ever graced the movies.) This instantly fractures our sense of Madame de . . ., implying her lack of integrity and identity. It is an objective touch that pulls us in a direction opposite to the subjective camera in motion. Ophüls thus establishes irony as one of the methods of his film, as the fluent use of the tracking camera halts in long-shot with Madame de . . . at her mirror, and the casual, carefree air of the music is undercut by a debt-ridden woman's anxious search for something to unload for cash. Madame de . . . hurries down the stairs in her opulent home, headed for the jeweler's to strike her bargain, a deceitful woman about to sell her husband's most intimate gift. Only later do we realize that all she had to do is ask her husband for the money she needs; but this she could not do, out of pride (a woman of her station doesn't ask her spouse, who is of a lower class, for money), but also because to do so might stress the founding basis of their marriage and expose the marital dissatisfaction that has been driving up her debt. She and André have a genteel, delicately poised union in which she pretends that it isn't the case that she doesn't love him and he pretends not to know that she doesn't. Taking a cue from *Citizen Kane*, Ophüls may be implying, "It was a marriage like any other marriage"—at least regarding the limited choices that a woman at that time faced.

Films of the 1950s

Once one is settled into loveless security, though, love as a *second* option, as an extramarital option, may prove a necessity. Madame de . . .'s earrings light the path to this necessity. After Madame de . . . sells back to the original jeweler, behind her husband's back, the diamonds that the General gave her as a wedding gift, behind her back the jeweler resells them to the General, who can therefore well gauge how little his wife loves him. In turn, he gives the earrings as a parting gift to Lola, his mistress, who loses them at the roulette tables in Constantinople. The next time we see them, back in Paris, they are in the possession of Baron Donati, who explains at customs that he bought them in Constantinople. It is significant that Ophüls denies us a view of the purchase; by doing this, he undercuts the dynamic life that the jewels seemed to possess on their own. The truth is, Donati doesn't precisely know why he bought them; but when he falls in love with Louise, he gives them to her as a gift, and, because she reciprocates his love, the jewels that meant nothing to her as a gift from her spouse suddenly mean the world to her. Ophüls has seduced us with the idea of the importance of the jewels, but, really, it is love that matters. It is in this context, which André's jealousy eventually takes over and dictatorially directs, that the future course of the jewels, which pass through familiar and different hands, is best understood.

The two great loves of the childless Madame de . . .'s life are her Catholic faith and Baron Fabrizio Donati. To pay her debts, Madame de . . . might have chosen her exquisite cross rather than the earrings, but, talking aloud to herself, she rejects this because she "adores" it. Before visiting the jeweler, she lights a candle in church. Eventually, because of the duel about to be fought between her husband and Donati, the diamonds are her ultimate offering for a saint's protection of the man she loves. The General kills the Baron. The church is left in possession of the jewels. For all her allegiance to her faith, this faith is revealed to be a hollow thing; Madame de . . . gives to it adoringly, lovingly, and gets little or nothing back on her emotional investment. The implication is fierce and startling. Either God has nothing to give or, jealous like the General, does not wish to compete with another of Madame de . . .'s loves. It is impossible for me not to translate this strand of the film's import into the terms that decidedly shook Max Ophüls's Jewish, not Catholic, heart. Jewish love of God, not to mention God's alleged love of Jews, did nothing to prevent the Holocaust. (See my remarks on Ophüls's four-years-earlier *Letter from an Unknown Woman*.)

In a sense, this film is the subjective expansion of a patch of objectivity: the cut-and-dried newspaper account of Madame de . . .'s lost earrings, which invites a host of speculations, we are given to understand, from within her and the General's circle of friends and acquaintances. Irony is the method of this film, and it is ironical that the "facts" given in the printed news story are all untruths proceeding from Madame de . . .'s self-serving deception: innocent lies, if you will, intended to harm no one, just cover up her status of debt from her spouse. But the film shows us the emotional truths pertaining to Madame de . . ., including the course of her impassioned romance with Donati to which the situation to which the news story refers leads, behind the news account and lying in wait ahead of it. A sense of predestination develops, in contrast to the isolated snapshot of time that the news account represents. Everything pertaining to Madame de . . . comes to seem as though it is weighed upon by the pressures of eternity. Every one of Ophüls's signature tracking shots in this film, like all tracking shots, must come to an end, and our awareness of this contributes to their meaning. Every seemingly liberated movement of Ophüls's camera is constrained by the conclusion it will inevitably reach   a conclusion haunted by the inevitable end of Madame de . . . .

The film's most celebrated passage traces the course of Madame de . . . and the Baron's falling in love. The event is compressed from a series of public dances over time. The music is continuous as Ophüls and his cutter, Borys Lewin, shift from one dance floor to the next, one dance to the next between Louise and Fabrizio, their embrace tightening as they grow more and more dear to one another. The inspiration for the passage is undoubtedly the bravura passage in Orson Welles's *Citizen Kane* (1941) that charts the downward trajectory of Kane's marriage to his first wife, Emily, through a series of breakfast table encounters that show them growing progressively further and further apart. Some may find Ophüls's version a rapturous, upbeat version of the same technique, but, in reality, the dark nature of the Welles passage deepens the heartbreak of the Ophüls passage. Louise's and Fabrizio's whole lives now are played out on the dance floor. Their illicit love consists of nothing but stolen moments—moments that their increasingly tight embrace poignantly attempts to make private as they inhabit the space of their own emotions, oblivious to the other couples on the dance floor who, in the swirl of the waltz, often appear to our eye as Louise and Fabrizio's faint shadows. Their early incapacity to bring their mutual love to a satisfying state predicts the lovers' tragic end. It is the end that the General skillfully manufactures as, driven by offended pride, he divides the would-be lovers even though this separation drains the health and will to live from the woman whom he presumably loves. He finds no hypocrisy here, given his own extramarital affairs, because his heart was never in these while Louise is manifestly in love with Donati.

During Louise and Fabrizio's stitched-together, increasingly intimate turns on the dance floor that become one elongated dance over time, the immortal dance of love encased in the mortal dance of life, we see the couple as best we can. Our effort in keeping track of the couple is correlative to the painfulness of their circumstance, the dire nature of their impossible love. Ophüls teases the clarity and directness of our sight; other couples interfere with our line of vision, as do gigantic plants through whose bladelike leaves we espy the socially obstructed pair. The motion of the dancing itself dizzies and distracts our eye, as does the movement of the camera that keeps up with this motion; the two lovers cling to one another, then, in defense of our gaze, in defense of the motion and the movement, holding on to love, holding on to life. By implication, life is streaming out of the couple as we watch, a harbinger of their fates. Related to this is the beginning of the film, where we see Louise for the first time as a reflection in a mirror. (This is a film of gauze, silk, reflections.) This method of introducing her to us suggests the extent to which Louise's self-absorbed reality is determined by, while at the same time being a defense against, society's view of her. Her "reality" is at a remove, then; this seemingly willful creature lacks, in fact, self-determination. In a sense, Louise is at a remove from life. In following her, we follow a shadow, and her increasingly agitated circumstance becomes a reflection of our own mortal anxiety. Even if the specifics of this circumstance hadn't thwarted and in some cases ended their lives, the characters in this film, now more than fifty years earlier than the present (and longer, the later in time that we catch up with the film), all would have passed away by now—except for the boy, the jeweler's son, perhaps, whose cheerful, perfectly loving obedience to his father deepens our sense of the passage of time by suggesting a world that no longer exists. And the knowledge of this that we bring to the film contributes to its emotional texture and sense of tragedy.

Charles Boyer is a superlative actor on occasion, and the General is his most complex and fascinating creation. Danielle Darrieux is enchanting, as great as Garbo, as the vain, self-centered Louise, whose love for the Baron utterly transforms her. (Like Fanny Skeffington in Vincent Sherman's 1944 *Mr. Skeffington*, Louise has a flock of suitors with whom she flirts, all of whom the General tolerates. Only the Baron he cannot tolerate.) Vittorio De Sica, a wonderful actor as well as director, is dashing and passionate as Donati.

The script is by Ophüls, Annette Wademant and Marcel Achard. The lovely, limpid black-and-white cinematography is by Christian Matras.

Critic Andrew Sarris has called *Madame de . . .* the greatest film ever made. It is certainly a gracious portrait of romantic anxiety and the sheer grip of love. It's one of those rare films where the viewer keenly feels a rush of feeling and the passage of time.

Shot on location in black and white in his hometown of Sardent, mixing locals and as yet unfamous professionals, blending heightened drama and faux-documentary realism, and including autobiographical elements, Claude Chabrol's first feature, *Le beau Serge* (1958), was made outside France's film industry. It inspired the 1959 Manifesto that announced and launched the *nouvelle vague*.

Another film this decade became a signpost of this New Wave. With Sergei M. Eisenstein's *Battleship Potemkin* (1925) the most celebrated film ever made, and probably the more influential of the two, Jean-Luc Godard's *A bout de souffle*—literally, "out of breath"; in the States, irrelevantly called *Breathless*—helped establish and define, for themselves and others, the ripping movement that stormed French cinema, overthrowing the reigning "Tradition of Quality" and its academic, refined, meticulously crafted *objets d'art*. The movement denoted *freedom*: freedom from the constraints of conventional, worked-through and tied-up narrative, freedom of personal expression; the freedom of roving and penetrating inquiry— and formally encompassing all these, a freedom of camera motion scarcely seen since Dziga Vertov took to the streets in the '20s to record the pulsating synergy of Soviet life.

These young upstarts drew inspiration from Renoir's lifetime of personal expression, from Hollywood professionalism and (especially in screwball comedies, westerns and *noir*s) glints of anarchy, and from Rossellini's use of camera (for instance, in *Germany, Year Zero*, 1947) as character, even the main character, rather than as mere observer. Theirs was another French Revolution, sweeping out such "royalists" as Autant-Lara and Clément, who at the time were enthroned as arbiters of filmmaking form and taste.

Time doesn't march; it *sprints!* Now, fifty years after its arrival, *A bout de souffle* still astonishes; as in the case of *Potemkin*, its formal and technical excitement doesn't wane. Too, the film still exerts a zinging fascination with a theme whose currency hasn't faded: our dynamic relationship with the movies we watch. *How does the interaction between us and film shape and detail us?* While freeing us from some of the conventionalism of ordinary life, does it perhaps tie us to another set of conventions derived from films? Are we who we (think we) are? Or is our sense of self so informed by influences from films that who we (think we) are is a distortion we are either dimly aware of or unaware of?

Another related issue is the extent to which films have so conditioned our perception of reality that we sometimes address this perception as though it *were* reality. We may even lose ourselves in the discrepancy between our perception and reality.

Godard's *A bout de souffle* opens with Michel, a young hoodlum, standing on a street in Marseilles. Several times throughout the film he will repeat the gesture he now makes: in the manner of Humphrey Bogart, he rubs a thumb across his lips, announcing—to himself as well as to us—he's a tough guy. Once his accomplice gives him the all-clear signal, Michel steals a car; but before speeding away, despite her pleas (and her help), he blows off this accomplice, saying, "I'm in a rush." Michel is on his way to Paris to unload the car and be paid; he needs the money to beat it to Italy with Patricia, the American girl in Paris he loves (or says he loves because that's what guys say in movies). Driving, he talks out loud to himself; the image cuts back and forth among his mashed-in mug, the tree-lined road the car zips through, and the adjacent countryside. (A camera was inside the car, and two others were strapped to the car, one on the front, one on the side.) The sum is all of a rush; the title of the film, *Out of Breath*, begins to sink in. We're not passively watching this film; we feel we're in it for the ride. Still, we're caught up short when Michel turns to us to say, "If you don't like the sea, and you don't like the mountains, and you don't like the big city, then"—well, the English subtitle I saw smoothed out the French—"go hang yourself." Now we, too, have been blown off by this guy. But something subversive has just happened; Michel's addressing us reverses the roles of film and audience: briefly, we've become the movie that Michel is watching and (as adolescents of the day were known to do) is himself talking back at. *We're the show*, as Godard slyly makes his point that films and audiences mirror one another, become one another. (A film character's directly addressing the audience goes back at least as far as Maurice Chevalier's in Ernst Lubitsch's 1929 *Love Parade*.)

Having found a gun in the glove compartment of the stolen vehicle, Michel is not someone anyone else should cross. The cops are after him, and he's run off the road. An officer approaches; Michel blows him away. This kid is no longer just a car thief. Now he dashes across the countryside in the direction of the City of Lights. With a quick cut he is a backseat hitchhiker—this, the boy who, on the road, had disparaged two girl hitchhikers, refusing to stop for them. But Michel is full of tough-guy talk when it comes to girls. And now he's a cop killer.

My summary can't do justice to this marvelous opening movement which brings into play all sorts of ideas. Plainly, Michel's toughness is an act. But when the "act" is all one has, it can settle in, take over, and determine behavior even in the worst way. Now that he has killed, moreover, there may be no chance for Michel to come across anything new out of which he can fashion or re-fashion a persona. In other words, Michel may be stuck with the image of himself he has taken from movies. Now his whole young life will be a mad dash until he is literally out of breath—shot dead by the police who (we know from movies) must inevitably catch up with him. There is so much here that brilliantly interprets violent adolescent behavior—especially when one extends the textbook for creating one's persona to include venues of popular culture other than movies.

There is an even more intriguing dimension to the opening which resonates throughout the film. Godard uses the Hollywood gangster film and its conventions to provide a powerful sense of Michel's crisis of identity. The starting-point is again the boy's reliance on movies for the personality or self-image he has managed to compose. Let's face it: Michel is an aimless small-time hoodlum—a *punk*—who ends up shooting to death a cop for no better reason than he happens to stumble across a gun. Of course, he doesn't want to be caught and sent to prison; but the situation is absurd, nearly arbitrary, pointing up (for us) how unhelpful to him his reliance on movies may be. This boy has no script. In the old movies James Cagney was never clueless; he had a definite plot to locate, even fix him in a predictable sequence of events. But the off-the-cuff air of the movie Michel finds himself in more or less casts him adrift; and the "cool" he exhibits resembles not so much Keatsian negative capability as whistling in the dark. In this context, his nonchalance, even his apparent apathy, provides an index of his stress as well as a window on our own negotiations with film influences that may have insinuated themselves into our consciousness even more subtly and perhaps just as unhelpfully.

Godard may be suggesting, "In our brave new world the old ways have blown apart; it's a whole new movie, so don't look to the old rules for guidance." After all, no matter what consolation he derives from identifying with gangster movies, Michel is no gangster. His only connection to that world is a fence; certainly he belongs to no gang. How could he? Possibly anxious over their borrowings from the same movies, such associates might at any minute puncture Michel's mask, his patchwork of emulation and impersonation; then where would he be? His "cool" would become fodder for their ridicule—a fate adolescents can find worse than death. Michel's predicament is both comical and grotesque: on the one hand, by so poorly reflecting the image of a gangster that the old films project, Michel is effectively cut off from the genre that has formed and now feeds his posture and attitude; on the other hand, his continual reliance on this genre, besides distorting his view of reality, cuts him off as well from whatever possibilities exist that he might otherwise use to fashion another, more grounded sense of self. In this light, Michel's situation compares unfavorably with Godard's own. Godard can make a film, say, *A bout de souffle*, in order to discover—if you will, create—a sense of who he is that liberates him from the enormous influence of his filmgoing experience even while, bending it to his will, he draws from this experience; but Michel's "self-expression," stealing cars, is a poor substitute that in fact cannot help but deepen the rut the boy is in. May not Godard be looking at Michel and saying, "There but for the grace of making films go I"?

Michel's dream is to flee to Italy. There, of course, he would be an immigrant. This suggests another aspect of the '30s gangster film: Denied access to the mainstream, a despised immigrant resorts to the underground business of organized crime as a means of moving on up. By contrast, Michel—a *disorganized* criminal—is headed nowhere, not even to Italy, it turns out. Surviving him will be his girlfriend, Patricia, a visiting American student who will make it to Italy, her Italian surname, Franchini, suggests.

In some ways Patricia is Michel's mirror-image, someone incompletely formed as yet, in her case, rather than looking to films, looking to the girl in a (Pierre-Auguste) Renoir painting poster for guidance on her own appearance. Godard stresses this mirror imaging of the two main characters by having them on a number of occasions look into one another's eyes; the two even have a staring contest. Nevertheless, Patricia isn't nearly so adrift as Michel. For instance, she receives money from home that helps her sustain her existence abroad. Too, she is much more articulate than Michel, whose speech amounts to repetitive schtick—one more index of his juvenile insecurity. But these differences between them help us to understand them both. Because she is more verbal, for example, Patricia can articulate things about them both that Michel can't (or won't) articulate about himself. In effect, she speaks for him as well as herself.

Four of her pertinent remarks follow:
1. I want you to love me, but at the same time I don't want you to. I love my freedom also.
2. I don't know if I'm unhappy because I'm not free, or if I'm not free because I'm unhappy.
3. It's sad to fall asleep. [Falling asleep] separates. Even if you're lying together, when you're asleep you're alone.
4. I want to know what's behind that mask of yours.

Lonely, confused about themselves and others, desperate to know "the truth" about their feelings, the pair are in no sense adults, nor are they on any track that might get them to adulthood, no matter how many geographic moves they make. Right after she remarks about the sadness of separation in sleep, Patricia turns to us, showing the same need for us as Michel has shown. Why *us?* Because we, the audience, her reality, project her fantasy, her motive, of assuaging loneliness; and the self-reflexivity of the film corresponds in part to this sore selfconsciousness afflicting Patricia and Michel. This, in turn, may reflect some of our own feelings vis-à-vis the "reality" that films generally represent to us—but not *this* film, not Godard's, whose distancing devices permit us to see at work a process that other films make us a part of. Moreover, Patricia's utterances, including the four just quoted, often are pronouncements that sound suspiciously like movie dialogue—again, not a failure in the writing but a means of revealing the influence that movies have had on these two kids. At best this influence is a mixed blessing; for, while the films they watch, or the art they look at, or the pop music they listen to, help them to chart or invent themselves, because directed by a powerful force outside themselves this self-invention, or "self-discovery," may be a distortion of who they really are. At least, Godard and we worry this is so.

A bout de souffle projects an aching sense of *wanting to know*. Godard himself is trying to pierce the masks of his characters to sound out the reality, if any, that lies underneath.

Patricia's remark to Michel, "I want to know what's behind that mask of yours," is ironic in three ways: (1) Patricia herself often appears enigmatic; (2) it seemingly takes forever for her to decide that she loves Michel; and (3) standing over his bulleted corpse at the end, she adopts—by absorption? assimilation?—Michel's mask, as her duplication of his Bogart lip-rubbing gesture discloses. Her earlier remark now achieves brilliant clarity; she had also meant, "I want to know what's behind *my* mask." As do we. As does Godard. In terms of his *own* mask.

Some feel that they know what lies behind Patricia's front: a little bitch. This misinterpretation is based on two pieces of evidence: firstly, after announcing, "I hate squealers," rather than accompanying Michel to Italy she turns him into the police, who viciously kill him; secondly, Michel's own dying words seem to brand her as such, given the widely circulated mistranslation in prominent English subtitles. However, it would be a mistake in any case to view Patricia through the convention of the femme fatale when the film as a whole probes and pierces such conventions. The pertinent facts in context follow. One, the girl is confused and quite undone by Michel's lack of response when she finally declares her love for him. Two, yes, she phones the police, because she's in as thoughtless a rush to stay in Paris without Michel as, earlier, Michel had been to leave Marseilles without the accomplice who adored him. But she tells Michel that she has done so; it is *he* who tarries beyond the limit of his own safety, doubtless feeling hurt and betrayed and therefore summoning a full draught of his stupid adolescent bravado. (Make what you will of the fact that Godard himself plays the first soul to alert the police of Michel's whereabouts.) Three, Patricia is anything but heartless when she runs out after Michel during his final foot-run from police. Four, Michel's dying word, *deguelasse*, meaning *disgusting, filthy, vile*, is uttered neither angrily nor bitterly but *affectionately*—a fact that the police (as verbally fixated as some filmgoers are, rather than visually sensitive) fail to relay to Patricia when they translate for her. Five, yes, yes, the closing shot shows Patricia's face fully reflecting her feeling that she's damnable for what she did. So? Her capacity to feel remorse and guilt is proof of her humanity, not proof of a lack of it. Six, neither she nor Michel is an actual human being; they're characters in a film for gosh sake—and, at that, in a film whose distancing techniques constantly stress this fact. Seven, these characters are, as noted earlier, stamped with a basic likeness, a shared identity that makes them, according to the script, joint executors of Michel's fate and joint recipients of it. Michel's finish is Patricia's finish, too. No wonder the image with which Godard leaves us isn't a happy face.

Patricia and Michel are both, in some critical sense, one, making the gap between them an index of their incompletion and self-dissociation. Godard is saying that movies—in general, popular culture—help to create this cognitive and emotional gap while also, in complex fashion, functioning to negotiate and bridge the gap while at the same time, adding to the complexity, widening and deepening the gap. Thus he employs techniques which give form to the dissociation—this "gap." For instance, his use of unconventional narrative implies its discrepancy with the more conventional plot arrangements of most other films before his and since. There is also the discrepancy between how his characters behave, and why, and the relatively spelled-out ways that characters in conventional films behave. And there is another, electrifying technique that Godard employs (although doesn't invent) towards the same suggestive end as the others—a technique with which *A bout de souffle* has become all but synonymous: the jump-cut. Simply stated, the jump-cut is the visual jerk that results when consecutive frames are deleted from the imaging of a continuous action within the same shot and the same scene. Indeed, this technique formally embodies all the ideas I have touched on here, and it operates, also, as a Brechtian distancing device, stressing the film's analytical bent, by snapping us, the audience, into an analytical mode of attention.

The film's most moving shot is also its most famous: the traveling shot at his back when, bulleted by the police, Michel stumbles ahead to his end on a Paris street. Here, as elsewhere,

Films of the 1950s

Godard is invaluably aided by Raoul Coutard's fresh, light, unaffected black-and-white cinematography—see, for its antecedents, Vertov's *Kino-Eye* (1924) and, greater than even *A bout de souffle*, *The Man with a Movie Camera* (1928)—and by Martial Solal's quick, dramatic music. But the impact of this shot, and of the death scene that follows, derives most of all from the cumulative passion of Godard's humanistic vision and from young Jean-Paul Belmondo in his stunning, seamless, starmaking role of Michel.

Alas, Jean Seberg! Hounded viciously to her end by J. Edgar Hoover's F.B.I., Seberg, champion and fundraiser for the Black Panthers, left us long ago, at age 40. As Patricia, she is terrific; like Dietrich's Lola Lola in Josef von Sternberg's *The Blue Angel* (1930), with each fresh viewing Seberg's performance mellowingly grows in complexity and ambiguity. This performance of hers has since absorbed her own tragic finish, in no small part because reality, an ironist on this occasion, has seen fit to reverse her and Belmondo's fates in the film.

François Truffaut, whom we also have lost (to cancer, though, not politics—at age 52), is credited with the film's script. In fact, Godard himself prepared what script there was from a story idea that his friend culled from a news item. (Truffaut, whose celebrity shot up more quickly because of *The 400 Blows*, lent his name to give Godard's film a professional leg up.) These two would not remain friends forever. For us, an elusive measure of the poignancy of *A bout de souffle* derives from the film's absorption of the non-negotiable fate of a friendship that once seemed destined to last a lifetime.

The list:

1950

FRANCESCO, GIULLARE DI DIO (Italy). His films had been immediate, urgent, focused on the present; but, departing from the *neorealismo* of *Rome, Open City* (1945), *Paisà* (1946), *Germany, Year Zero* (1947) and *Stromboli* (1949), Rossellini achieved his masterpiece by looking to two places other than the present: the past; eternity.

Based on *I fioretti*, from the fourteenth century, *Francesco, giullare di Dio* (literally, *Francis, God's Fool*) essays the founder of the Franciscan Order in the thirteenth, Giovanni Francesco Bernardone—St. Francis of Assisi—and his followers, God's "little flowers." They exemplify Christian charity and devotion at the folk level; their legends, whether humorous or sober, place Francisco and his monks among the simple people they generally serve. This is in contradistinction to the insularity, haughtiness and corruption of the institutional Church, which foments poverty and strife in the country. Instead, Francesco and his nonmilitant band of brothers follow the path of Jesus.

Befitting an adaptation of a collection of stories, the film is given an episodic form. The result, a mosaic, unhinges linear narrative as decisively as had the episodes composing the national portrait in *Paisà*. Rossellini nonetheless achieves a unified vision—one of innocence, humility, tenderness and spiritual harmony. In drawing on the past in this way, he is able to suggest human possibilities and offers hope for Italy's postwar future. A reflection on the present (the usual reason for an artist to venture into the past), *Francesco* serves as antidote to Italy's then current disarray and political turmoil.

The final shot is among the most haunting in cinema: a skyward pan that seeks to restore uncertain humanity to a secure place in a continuity of time lost and timelessness—a thrilling imaginative gesture in a deeply humanistic work.

Federico Fellini contributed to the script.

GUERNICA (France). *Women and children have the same red roses in their eyes—their blood for all to see.*

On April 26, 1937, during the Spanish Civil War, Germany bombed Guernica, an ancient Basque town, burning it to the ground. The newsprint photograph of this outcome, with which Alain Resnais's 13-minute documentary opens, seems to be dissolving into dots. Working its way up to Pablo Picasso's commemorative painting made the same year as the event, *Guernica* shows, first, decades-earlier drawings and paintings of his that are especially suggestive, in this context, of innocence—an innocence that the Luftwaffe has now destroyed. Accompanied by sounds of bombardment, pieces of artwork, themselves seemingly targeted, partially disintegrate. Paul Eluard's script, heard as poetic voiceover, laments war as the destruction of innocence.

Resnais never shows Picasso's *Guernica* in its entirety, only bits and parts of it—isolated pieces, often given a blacked-out surrounding. The fragmentation again suggests bombardment while also creating its own kind of cubism. Hands are a motif that thread continuity between Picasso's *Guernica* and his earlier artwork: hands that are tenderly embracing, prayerful, stretched up in horror; hands of connection, and hands of inconsolable loss. The black-and-white film, exceptionally dark, marshals a somber use of negative space and as often invokes Goya (in his bleakest etchings) as Picasso. The elegiac refrain "Guernica" haunts.

A field of sculptures, in context suggestive of a graveyard that war has generated, replaces the painting, culminating in Picasso's 1944 bronze *L'homme au mouton*, which in contrast to *Guernica* is shown (frontally) whole. Its depth, in contrast to the painting's flat patches, appears to animate it; the sculpture is alive with hope, the lamb in the man's arms symbolizing the renewal of innocence.

Brilliantly edited by Resnais, *Guernica* is among his most powerful films.

DIARY OF A COUNTRY PRIEST (France). Robert Bresson's *Journal d'un curé de campagne* is, like *Mouchette* (1966), from Bernanos. It, too, is about human pain and suffering. This film inaugurated Bresson's use of nonprofessional actors to help achieve an anti-dramatic stylization. Bresson is after the essence, not a photographic copy, of human behavior—much as he pursues the essence of objects.

Claude Laydu is wonderful as the unnamed young priest who arrives in Ambricourt to assume parish duties and never fits in. He keeps a diary, whose entries we hear as voiceover, in an attempt to solidify the accuracy of his observations and sense of things; but he is almost always mistaken. The discrepancy between reality and our interpretation of things plays out in his experience, which is both distinctive and representative of our own.

Bresson's style is often described as spare and minimalist. Be prepared, therefore, for a gorgeous film; Bresson's *Diary* consists of his courageous first steps toward what would become his purer, more essential style, although already its materialistic details yield a store of spirituality.

It is impossible to resolve this brilliant film's ambiguities—and this is deliberate on Bresson's part. How much that we see, correlative to the experience that the priest records in his diary, is close to accuracy, exaggeration or wide of reality? (Simultaneously, the hostility he encounters from parishioners seems both unlikely *and* utterly convincingly provincial!) It is left for us to ponder whether the priest's stomach cancer is a projection of the crossroads of his self-pity and attraction to martyrdom.

Even this boy's death is ambiguous. The final, long-held shot of a cross: what does it mean? The boy's acceptance into heaven, or a perpetual barrier to his entrance? Is his earthly suffering still too much for heaven to bear?

WAGON MASTER (U.S.). John Ford's *Wagon Master* perfectly projects the idea that virtuous attainment in the American social and political landscape requires ordinary people to pull and work together. Indeed, another group joins the primary group so that both may successfully "go their own way." One group is Mormon; the other, a theatrical troupe. Both, ostracized, have been "invited out of town."

Wagon Master shows how difficult it may be for disparate groups to consolidate given their different agendas, and how much more difficult it may be for each to prevail because of the forces arrayed against them. Ford's conviction that consensus-building and activism are necessary helps make *Wagon Master* one of his most affirmative films.

Of all Ford's great films, this is the most formally relaxed and given over to (instead of rhetoric) naturalistic poetry; its characters seem to breathe the air of ordinary life as well as inhabit the space of myth. Morally rigorous and solemn in tone nevertheless, the film follows a band of Mormons as they trek westward, uprooted visionaries in search of a home. Ford is deeply sympathetic, but at the same time their religious certainty—recall Ford's bone-deep atheism—tellingly comments on the American "manifest destiny" that their mission in a diminutive and diminished form reflects.

The group is imperiled, by Nature and by the evil Cleggs. Contesting their adversaries, the Mormons draw their inspiration from their sense of community and their hopes for the future—the peace, bounty and liberty to which they feel entitled (the faith of Ford's own Irish Catholic ancestors) by surviving the ordeals of harsh terrain, bigotry, violence.

At his most accessible here, Ford beautifully balances history and mythopoiea, finding in the imaginative space where these merge perhaps his richest, most sustaining definition of America.

THE FORBIDDEN CHRIST (Italy). Stark, turbulent, poetic, *Il Cristo proibito* asks, "Why must the innocent always pay for the others?" In so doing it not only delivers a powerful blow to tyranny and the madness of war but also radically reinforces the tenets of Christian myth. The author of the script, filmmaker and composer of the score, Italian journalist, dramatist, novelist Curzio Malaparte—born Kurt Erich Suckert, but adopting early on a pen-name that, playing with Bonaparte, associated him with "a bad place"—had himself been a Fascist; but attacking both Mussolini and Hitler in the early 1930s, he was sent into exile. After the war, he became a Communist.

Il Cristo proibito—originally released in the U.S. as *Strange Deception*—centers on Bruno Baldi, who has just returned to his impoverished village, Siena, in Tuscany, after being released from a Russian prisoner-of-war camp following the Second World War. Bruno is dead-set on discovering the identity of whoever betrayed his younger brother, Giulio, a partisan who was fifteen or sixteen when the occupying Germans killed him. But no one, including his caring mother, is willing to disclose the villager's identity.

This is a searing, heartrending film. Bruno's friend Antonio arranges for a clandestine meeting between himself and Bruno; he "confesses" that it was he who betrayed Giulio. Upon hearing this, Bruno dispatches his knife into his dear friend's heart. Dying, Antonio *truly* confesses. No, of course it was not he; but now when Bruno discovers the actual identity of the traitor he will no longer be motivated to kill the person. Antonio declares Bruno innocent and dies.

Antonio, earlier: "Only in sacrifice is there Justice. . . . To suffer for others and to pay for others."

When Bruno confronts the traitor, his soul—and postwar Italy's—hangs in the balance.

SUNSET BOULEVARD (U.S.). Billy Wilder's celebrated *film noir* about the rapacious, destructive nature of Hollywood is, among other things, probably the funniest American film of the sound period. The comedy, though, is very dark, the laughs accompaniment to something close to horror.

Gloria Swanson's playing of Norma Desmond, a has-been former silent screen star who has deluded herself into believing she can make a comeback, may bewilderingly resemble Charlie Chaplin in drag, but the crux of the piece is William Holden's brilliant performance as Joe Gillis, the young scenarist who becomes Desmond's kept boy—a withering, nuanced portrait of a man sinking by degrees into prostitution and self-contempt: a metaphor for the price that the motion-picture industry exacts from people with talent and artistic ambition. The largest sphere of reference here is American capitalism.

Film critic Andrew Sarris has noted that *Sunset Boulevard* seems much more realistic than it did in 1950, when its Gothic elements came to the fore, like Desmond's servant's white-gloved hands on the organ, swollen in the foreground of one of the film's most chilling, brooding shots. (Desmond's servant, played by Erich von Stroheim, was once the first of her husbands—and the director who made her a star.) Indeed, the Gothic touches themselves are absorbed by the film's psychological realism because they are all correlative to Desmond's delusional world, into which Gillis is steadily drawn, his snappy cynicism, it turns out, insufficient protection against his Hollywood fate.

Gillis narrates from the swimming pool into which his corpse fell after Desmond shot him, twice in the back, once in the stomach. In effect, *Sunset Boulevard* represents Gillis's finest script. With different collaborators, Wilder's scripts for *Double Indemnity* (1944) and this film may be the two finest ones ever written for Hollywood.

LA RONDE (France). From Arthur Schnitzler's play *Reigen* Max Ophüls has created a rueful, wistful meditation on the transience of love, implicitly, life's transience. It is love's merry-go-round suited to a waltz—a haunting waltz by Oscar Straus. More: the film itself is a waltz, lovely, lilting, passing, passing into sadness and melancholy: the inevitable end to a waltz. Each romantic couple in turn dissolves; one partner moves on to another partner, while the latter's predecessor vanishes, having lost his or her place on the merry-go-round. (The film's soft grays, especially in faux-exterior shots, seem to encourage couples to dissolve and individuals to disappear—or, perhaps, are the result of these happenings.) However, the courtly Count and Army lieutenant (exquisitely played by Gérard Philipe), who leaves one partner to go off on a binge, ends up with the first character to get off the merry-go-round at the beginning of the film, Léocardie (Simone Signoret, nearly as haunting as the waltz), a solemn prostitute.

We are in Vienna at the turn of the twentieth century. In charge of the merry-go-round is the . . . well, what is he? Beautifully acted by Anton Walbrook, he is the storyteller, stage manager, film director, editor and projectionist. His job, I would say, is to hold back tragedy as best he can. He pops up in other guises: coachman, waiter, servant, etc.; and sometimes as the carousel operator he shares the same frame as one of the characters. This is Ophüls's delicately postmodernist film; and yet it dreamily conjures the past—a past the memory or dream of which it hopes to keep from dissolving. Opposing this attempt is recent European history: the war, France's Occupation, the Holocaust.

One is lost when watching a film by him if one forgets that Max Ophüls was Jewish.

SEVEN DAYS TO NOON (UK). Professor John Willingdon is England's chief scientist at its atomic research center. Now he has stolen a bomb, which he will detonate in a week's time, obliterating the seat of Government, unless the prime minister officially ends British manufacture of all such weaponry. Scotland Yard, convinced he is insane, works to find and apprehend Willingdon.

Adapting Paul Dehn and James Bernard's Oscar-winning story, writer-directors John and Roy Boulting pursue two themes. One refers to the peacetime dangers of such research as Willingdon is involved in. The Boulting brothers thus take a stand against the West's Cold War policy of courting universal destruction as a means of enforcing "peace" through terror. The other theme, more pressing and powerful, refers to Willingdon's "individual conscience" and the political misuse of his life's work. We see the folly of the law's position; Willingdon, as Barry Jones beautifully and humanely plays him, is in no way out of his mind. He is thoughtful and measured, but sees no other way of expressing an unconventional opinion for the cause of world peace. "Perhaps some of my fellow scientists," he reasons, "will understand and take courage from my example." The Boultings were reacting to assaults on free speech that they saw across the Atlantic in Washington. The police are incapable of acting responsibly in a political arena; the murder of Willingdon is unnecessary and, whether or not intended to do so, will silence through intimidation many more voices than his.

The entire film is Hitchcockian (*The Lodger*, 1926, seems an especial influence) and, anticipating Peter Watkins, the Boultings-edited evacuation of London, with its heightened documentary realism, is a stark and stunning passage. Who can forget the confused pets, on doorsteps, that people have been ordered to leave behind?

BACKWARD SEASON (France). Dimitri Kirsanoff's curve-around *Arrière-saison* is rigorous, forlorn, haunting.

The opening closeup shows the interior window of a spare, remote cabin. A woman enters the frame, looks out. In the forest, a tree falls; the ax whacking at another tree belongs to the woman's spouse. Outside the cabin, a dog runs in circles in a fenced-in pen, projecting the wife's feelings of desolation, entrapment. Her spouse works with other woodcutters; the woman feels all alone. At lunch, no conversation passes between them. This is a silent film (apart from music), and the silence conveys the couple's harsh, frustratingly secluded, noncommunicative life. A cut to outdoors shows leaves descending from a reflection of trees in a mirror-like pond—like all the shots of Nature here, the disclosure of a character's feelings and mental state.

The woman packs, leaves a note saying she will never come back. Before she departs, a panning shot of the stacked wood that her husband has cut extends her eye, suggesting what she feels stands between them: his labor; the geography and topography that this labor dictates.

The man takes his wife's parting letter in stride—we learn, because he has read these words on earlier occasions. The next day, he walks to work, ax on his shoulder; after a pan of an expanse of skeletal trees, as this image dissolves it opens up in the middle, to reveal the man at work, alone—a life's rupture. A shot of the dog running in circles in its pen now projects *his* feelings.

In the same frame, as the returning wife enters the door in the background, the dog still runs in circles. The film ends with her at the window, looking out, wearing the same clothes as she did at the beginning of the film.

VARIETY LIGHTS (Italy). Since he is credited first and his wife, Carla Del Poggio, co-stars, we may assume that Alberto Lattuada is the co-director of *Luci del varietà* who counts more heavily; but, since the hectic atmosphere surrounding the vaudeville troupe resembles that of a circus (Fellini came up with the story from which he, Lattuada, Tullio Pinelli and Ennio Flaiano wrote the script), and Giulietta Masina, *Fellini's* wife, is a prominent cast member, some may think of this beautiful, visually intricate film primarily as Federico Fellini's.

Eerily anticipating Chaplin's Calvero in *Limelight* (1952), Checco Dal Monte is the troupe's principal comic. Masina (superb—best supporting actress, Italian critics) plays Melina Amour, another careworn troupe member and Checco's caring partner. (At one point she asks Checco, "We will get married one day, won't we?" but so casually, fleetingly, it is more an expression of doubt than a question.) Del Poggio's Liliana insinuates herself into the troupe, by degrees taking over Checco, who takes over the troupe to advance her career. Lily, though, trades him in for someone who can be many more times helpful in making her a star. (Del Poggio is more realistic and complex than Anne Baxter in a similar although much more flamboyant role in *All About Eve*, Joseph L. Mankiewicz, 1950.) Checco, beaten, goes back to Melina; at a station, while Lily's train is headed for Milan, Checco and the troupe's train is headed in the opposite direction, toward another series of inconspicuous small towns. The film ends with Checco eyeing another girl on the train; perhaps she, too, will become a star.

Lattuada and Fellini create memorable shots: an angled one of a nighttime street suggesting phantasmagoria; a metaphor for the troupe and its tenuous existence: a goose in a straw basket.

1951

EARLY SUMMER (Japan). Postwar Tokyo; Noriko's family prevails upon her to marry, but she chooses a man of whom they disapprove. He is twelve years her senior, has a child, and is relocating to Akita. Noriko's family worries that she will not end up happy.

In the aftermath of war, with Japan's authoritarian ruler deposed and democracy dawning, the structured, stable Japanese family, as a social force, has devolved. A small child tells his grandfather (twice) that he hates him; her older brother (Chishu Ryu, superb) tells Noriko she is impudent to men—to which Noriko counters, "Men used to be too important." "Our family has scattered," the father will say once Noriko has left. "We shouldn't want too much," he tells his wife (twice). Is this the path to happiness—being content with what life gives rather than asking for more? Perhaps an attitude of acceptance provides the only consolation and relief for life's disappointments, and for life's transience.

Bakashû, delicately composed, is sensitive to light and to nuances of feeling; yet the accumulated result is overwhelming. No film more powerfully conveys the passage of time— here, a paradoxical, slow, inexorable rush. Sisters walk the beach, talking, the camera following, or the father and mother sit outdoors side by side, discussing family, the low, angled camera favoring their backs. Much of their anxious conversation is pressured by time —human time measured against eternity.

As ever with Ozu, human beings are paramount. In a beautiful long-shot, a loose balloon scales up the sky. "Some child must be crying," the father notes.

Ozu's characters experience happiness, when they do, not because of good fortune but from the way they engage life: with humility, and with their philosophical stance. This life is gently moving, always, imperceptibly, toward the last end.

THE IDIOT (Japan). We will never see the 4½-hour version of *Hakuchi*, Akira Kurosawa's version of Dostoievski's *The Idiot*, which, prior to its release, Shochiku slashed to 2¾-hours. What remains, though, is lyrical, captivating, haunting, precisely analytical.

The tragedy of soulful, honest Prince Myshkin, now called Kameda, has been moved from nineteenth-century St. Petersburg to wintry post-World War II Hokkaido. In front of a shop window, Akama (Dostoievski's Rogozhin—Toshirô Mifune, astounding) and Kameda stand looking at a portrait of the woman who will both come between them and enjoin their fates: Taeko (in the novel, Nastasya Filippovna). In one shot, camera at their backs, Akama and Kameda appear bodily real. In the next shot, though, the camera has been moved forward; the portrait appears flanked by the two male reflections in the glass. The men appear like specters, phantoms; the mere image of Taeko, by contrast, appears bodily real. The next shot reverts back to the camera placement and configuration of the first in this series of shots (a triangle of shots!). We are prompted by the visual evidence to consider that Taeko, the object of Akama's lust and Kameda's pity, has so taken possession of them as to drain them of their sense of existential being.

Hakuchi subtly envelops us, making us feel we are slowly succumbing to a strange, steady snowfall. Taeko's stabbing death happens offscreen. We aren't even shown her corpse— ironic counterpoint to the degree to which Taeko took hold of Akama's senses and, finally, directs him to his doom. At the last we see moments of fraternal intimacy between two men who began as strangers and will die together, huddled in a freezing shack. Having committed murder, Akama wants to bury himself in Kameda's purity and natural nobility. He is hoping for redemption.

BELLISSIMA (Italy). Maddalena (Anna Magnani, brilliant) enters little Maria in a contest for a movie role. There's no question who dreams of stardom. The day of the Roman cattle-call at Cinecittà, Maddalena is desperate to find her daughter, who has slipped away. At the initial interview, we see both standing in the same frame, each with her hand on a hip; just who is the one being interviewed? The joke is sealed when Maria gives the wrong family name and her mother steps in to set the matter right: "Cecconi." Indeed, Maria hardly speaks at all as Mama takes over.

The Cecconis make ends meet. Spartaco, a laborer, is a wage-slave (note the name). Maddalena herself gives insulin injections. These people aren't about to starve. But they live in a dreary, dilapidated apartment dwelling, where neighbors are fed up with the couple's vehement quarrels. While Maddalena plays stage-mother, Spartaco is trying to marshal financial resources so they can all move into their own place. *Bellissima* is about dreams and how their fervent attempt to remediate unpleasant reality seldom succeeds. Countless children audition for the one available role. *Bellissima* is an hilarious satire that segues into family—by extension, social—heartbreak before, happily, regaining its comedic footing.

Maria's screen test proves disastrous. The judges laugh at her appearance and inability, unaware that Maddalena is eavesdropping. Maternal instincts kicking in, Maddalena reveals herself and lambasts everyone. Now the men scurry to sign Maria to avert the PR crisis that would result if Maddalena went public with their mockery of the sanctity of Italian children and family; but Maddalena has come to her senses. Her daughter is not for sale.

Interweaving *neorealismo* and Maddalena's fabulous ambitions, sobriety and giddiness, nonprofessional and professional cast members, Luchino Visconti here made one of his greatest films.

THE RIVER (U.S., France). From Rumer Godden, Jean Renoir and color cinematographer Claude Renoir, his cousin, made their beauteous *The River*.

The setting is Bengal, in postwar India, although the film is structured as the reminiscence, years later, of Harriet, the eldest daughter in a British family. Harriet's father has one eye, and the American boy with whom Harriet falls in love, one leg, the maiming in both cases from combat. In the course of the film, three adolescent girls fall in love for the first time, a boy dies, and Harriet's mother gives birth to another child.

In numerous shots, the wide river on whose banks Harriet's family lives appears either at the fore or in the background. Fishermen fish in the river; people bathe in it. It is life-giving and eternal (it comes, the voiceover says, from the "eternal snows" of the Himalayas) and, symbolically at least, it also carries people away, to their ends (and rebirth).

Harriet and friend Valerie become rivals for Captain John's attentions. But it is their Anglo-Indian friend, Melanie, who falls for him hardest, although she keeps her feelings closeted. What can she give to a partner when she doesn't feel herself whole? Melanie feels she is straddling a fence each side of which is a different culture. "Why do we always *quarrel* with things?" she asks.

A great set-piece portrays Diwali, for five consecutive days in autumn the Hindu Festival of Lights. In this celebration of "the eternal war between good and evil," a candle is lit for each life that has been lost, turning each night, especially, into a great and grave spectacle. *The River* is a film about war. Melanie's father laments that the world isn't made safe for children: "We catch them in our wars ... and we kill them."

UMBERTO D. (Italy). *See above*.

EUROPA '51 (Italy). Following her son's suicide, an American living in Rome abandons an empty, wealthy lifestyle and, choosing to live among them, helps the poor instead, prompting her spouse to commit her to an insane asylum. Because Irene's pilgrimage ends rather than begins in confinement, *Europa '51* is a kind of *Stromboli* (1949) in reverse. Politically, the film confounds; for Roberto Rossellini finds the one possible solution, Communism, a fraud, thus implying for Europe endless tragedy.

Irene (Ingrid Bergman, superb) is a dauntingly independent, secular saint who falls in battle only from lacking the sanctioning armor of political and religious institutions whose own "good works" proceed from aims perhaps too divided to redeem a broken Europe. To be sure, Irene may in some sense prevail in her imprisonment, a sign of the cost of reactionary thinking, but Europe may prove the loser for marginalizing her and limiting her sphere of influence.

Rossellini may have made the couple American to reflect the Americanization of Europe that had begun as the United States helped to rebuild Europe. Also, this choice contributes to the film's persistent sense of Italy's—and Europe's—confusion of identity. What is "Europe" now, and what does it mean? How, if one is uncertain about this, can people aim at creating, or re-creating, Europe?

Moreover, the implacable cruelty of Irene's husband, an American businessman, implies America's incapacity to offer any kind of assistance except on its own calculating, self-serving terms. Indeed, underscoring the theme of American encroachment of Europe is the casting of, in the role of Irene's husband, Alexander Knox, the actor famous for playing Woodrow Wilson (*Wilson*, Henry King, 1944), the U.S. president who commandeered demands on Germany following the First World War that helped sow seeds of European discontent and economic ruin that contributed to the next world war.

HOTEL DES INVALIDES (France). War's hype and the legendary status that the state officially confers on warriors versus war's killing and maiming reality: Georges Franju's 23-minute *Hôtel des Invalides* assaults France's military mystique.

It is a subversive documentary, commissioned by the French government as a national self-advertisement; but Franju's cunning handling of the material created a powerful antiwar film, a model of how an insinuated level of meaning can undercut surface meaning.

The film begins as an innocuous tour of the French National Military Museum in Paris, which includes halls of military displays, a care facility for veterans, and a chapel. Holistically addressing the ideology that perpetuates war as a necessary, even noble endeavor, it takes institutional aim at both the military and the Church, and intellectual aim at such concepts as heroism and honor. We hear voiceover, sardonic for being disembodied, as well as trite guides, themselves disabled veterans, and we overhear the touring visitors on their tour, in particular, a deflatingly unimpressed young couple. Franju cuts between ghostly military exhibits, punctuating these with closeups of details (for instance, a medal for valor), and all-too-real mutilated men. A famous cut juxtaposes a statue of Napoleon with a veteran in a wheelchair. In effect, Franju is confronting the idea of war, so attractive to so many, with the horrific consequences of war for actual human beings. The guides are a reminder that war is in part perpetuated by stricken warriors who feel compelled to justify and validate their own sacrifices and the ultimate sacrifices of comrades-in-arms.

The film's subtle indirection accumulates into a quiet voice of reason and conscience revealing what individuals perhaps subconsciously feel about war in the face of its direct and official sanction and approval. The tour of L'Hôtel des Invalides unwinds somewhere in the mind of humanity.

THE THING FROM ANOTHER WORLD (U.S.). From the 1938 story "Who Goes There?" by John W. Campbell, *The Thing* is a terrifying blend of horror and science-fiction. It launched a cycle of fifties films involving belligerent creatures, linked either to atomic bomb use or tests or the Cold War being waged then between the U.S. and the Soviet Union.

The Thing centers on conflicts between the military and science. Specifically, an Air Force captain and a Nobel scientist, each the leader of his own contingent, lock horns over the discovery at an Arctic research center of an alien creature that, ejected from an alien spacecraft, has become frozen in a block of ice. The scientist wants to study the being; the captain wants only, instead, to follow orders. Each is, in his own way, monstrously extreme. The scientist embodies a reckless pursuit of knowledge; the captain, an utter lack of curiosity about anything beyond his ken. When the alien, a beast that has an insatiable thirst for human blood, accidentally is thawed, its danger challenges the capacity of the opposing camps to come together as a team. It turns out that, on whatever planet "the thing" comes from, plants have undergone an evolution similar to what animals have undergone on earth. The monster is a vegetable—a gigantic carrot, if you will.

Many interpret the film as a veiled allegory of Soviet danger to the U.S. Since the danger comes from a vegetable, however, the film seems to argue that we would do better to release our minds from the box that neatly identifies our current bogeymen. Ravishingly cinematographed in black and white, *The Thing* was produced by Howard Hawks, who probably worried about working in a disparaged genre. No matter the directorial credit given, every shot is Hawks.

LADY OYÛ (Japan). Meiji-period Japan; a marriage has been arranged for Shizu and young carpenter Shinnosuke. Accompanied by her widowed sister who lives with her young child with in-laws who prohibit her remarriage, Shizu visits Shinnosuke, who instantly falls in love with Oyû, mistaking her for Shizu. Shinnosuke and Shizu marry, but in name only—he, to be able to see Oyû; she, to sacrifice her happiness for her elder sister, who loves Shinnosuke. Soon, there is potentially ruinous gossip. After Oyû's child dies, the couple move away and make their marriage real, but Shizu still believes that her spouse loves her sister, Shinnosuke unable to convince her otherwise. When she dies in childbirth, which Shizu has more or less willed so that spouse and sister can reunite, Shinnosuke leaves their infant with Oyû, but without seeing her as he has vowed never to set eyes on her again. Unlike Oyû, he will remain truly wed to the deceased spouse.

From the 1932 novel *Ashikari* by Junichirô Tanizaki, Kenji Mizoguchi has wrought an exquisite melodrama of suppressed feelings and both the nobility and tortured ambivalence that often lie behind these. Mizoguchi expressed dissatisfaction with the result, probably in part because Tanizaki vetoed the idea of the proposed film's using the book's series of long flashbacks to relate the tale. But *Oyû-sama* transcends this obstacle with its brilliant final shot, which finds Shinnosuke, after depositing his child at his sister-in-law's place, standing amidst reeds and underneath a pale full moon, and then walking behind a tree and out of sight forever as the moon keeps haunting watch: an extension of Shinnosuke's silent reflection, which converts the linear narrative, retroactively, into memory.

Yuji Hori is wonderful as Shinnosuke, the memory of whose wife inspires him to sacrifice more than is apparent.

THE MAN IN THE WHITE SUIT (UK). Sidney Stratton gets moony-eyed when he imagines what he could do with "a modern laboratory—a proper laboratory." When the textile mill for which he works discharges him because of his unorthodox experiments, he steals into a rival's superior facilities and invents a fabric that repels dirt and never wears out. The mill's ownership and unionized labor unite against him since his discovery will curtail garment sales and cost workers jobs. In his luminescent white suit poor Stratton becomes a hunted man through Wellsburrough's nighttime streets.

Alec Guinness is heavenly as the young scientist whose tunnel vision banishes the claims of his fellow humanity, whose lives will be upheaved, even casually destroyed, by the obsessive "progress" that the twentieth century inherited from the Victorians as a secular holy principle. "What am I going to do?" a struggling neighbor, who takes in laundry to help her survive, asks him. Stratton's humane expression shows that he cares; but still he persists with his blasted science! Not to worry: Capitalism will suppress his invention as it does all "better mousetraps"—as it has, for instance, razor blades that never lose their edge.

Science's moral irresponsibility; the dogged pursuit of self-interest by both capital and organized labor; society's reluctance to depart from the status quo: it's all here, and with such visual fluency and grace one can hardly believe that Alexander Mackendrick's film derives from a play. The script is by the playwright, Roger MacDougall, John Dighton and Mackendrick.

This British marriage of satirical comedy and science-fiction recalls H.G. Wells's *The Man Who Could Work Miracles* (Lothar Mendes, 1937), but with an orientation more social than metaphysical. Here is one of the most riotously funny films in creation—a rival to Charles Chaplin's masterpieces.

ACE IN THE HOLE (U.S.). Kirk Douglas, normally not a favorite of mine, gives a finely judged and thrillingly intense performance as Chuck Tatum, an opportunistic newspaper reporter in one of Billy Wilder's most brilliant films, *Ace in the Hole*, former newsman Wilder's maiden effort after breaking with writing partner Charles Brackett. The hostile press and public reception to it instigated an artistic withdrawal and stylistic reconsideration like that which followed excoriating reactions to Alfred Tennyson's poem *Maud* and Claude Chabrol's *Les bonnes femmes* (1960). It's a pity that Wilder never did anything again that stuns and bristles like this blackest of *noir*s.

Based on a 1925 incident involving a man stuck in a Kentucky cave, its action updated and moved to the New Mexico desert, Ace finds Tatum manipulating reality to get the story he wants. Looting the "Mountain of the Seven Vultures" for Native American artifacts, Leo Minosa has been pinned by a partial collapse; he could easily be freed within a day, but Tatum arranges matters so that the rescue effort takes many days, milking the front-page story and bringing it national attention, and attracting a carnival atmosphere, indeed, an actual family carnival. Greed, political ambition, rank curiosity: all these are incited as Tatum pursues career advancement. Ultimately Minosa dies and, conscience-stricken, Tatum presses a train of events that ends in his own destruction.

The claustrophobic conversations between Tatum and Minosa through a hole, with Tatum performing a quasi-priestly role, reaches a point of withering irony when Tatum is replaced by an actual priest performing last rites.

Overhead long-shots of the camp's and carnival's dismantling after Minosa's death are among the most trenchant in the estimable Wilder œuvre: a vision of human folly and transience that recalls René Clair's in *A nous la liberté* (1932).

1952

MADAME DE . . . (France). *See above.*

IKIRU (Japan). Kanji Watanabe, an ageing civil servant, learns he has terminal cancer. Can he correct the insignificance of his life? Used to giving citizen complainants the runaround, city bureaucrats have dismissed the pleas of mothers who want sewage drained from a public park in a poor section of Tokyo. Watanabe takes up their cause and even gets a playground built on the site. At Watanabe's wake, though, the deputy mayor, up for reelection, takes credit. Alas, the drunken pledge of his co-workers, to follow Watanabe's example by doggedly pursuing the public interest, carries little weight against their complacency and the monotony of their workday routine. Children at play in the park, however, confer on Watanabe anonymous immortality.

Akira Kurosawa's greatest film suggests a melding of James Joyce and Frank Capra. *To Live* begins, though, poetically—with scant light shimmering in darkness: a full-screen x-ray of Watanabe's cancer-eaten stomach evoking the irreducible mystery of life and death. This static composition also sets the film's serene tone. Kurosawa's most meditative film, not surprisingly, is also his most quiet. Its evenness renders Watanabe's shafts of memory all the more painful; they pierce the quietude, admitting rushes of time and inconsolable loss.

Ikiru's most celebrated passage is magical. On his last night on Earth, Watanabe sits on a swing in the completed playground. Kurosawa frames the initial shot so that the swing's suspension is invisible; Watanabe seems suspended in air. In a children's area, he is lost in childhood reverie. Snow falls lightly on him as he sings, quietly, about life's brevity and the need to enjoy life. Earlier, the same song had been for him one of frustration and wistfulness —a song mourning the past and lamenting the future. Now a song of contentment, it closes an ordinary life to fullness.

THE LIFE OF OHARU (Japan). The opening shot is among the most famous in Japanese cinema: in darkness, the camera follows a woman as she walks diagonally through the frame, the slow, protracted nature of her movement along the street a metaphor for the difficulty of her life's journey.

Oharu, a seventeenth-century prostitute, is old: fifty. In a temple, perhaps she reminisces; as likely, the long flashback belongs instead to the authors of the script, Yoshikata Yoda and Kenji Mizoguchi, the latter of whom also directed. Oharu, a merchant's daughter, may have seemed destined for a better life. While serving at the Imperial Palace in Kyoto when she was young, she fell in love beneath her class, prompting her and her parents' exile and the beheading of her lover. (Indelible: the flash of reflected sunlight from the executioner's sword.) Over the years, many things happened, including her becoming a courtesan to pay off her father's debts, a brief marriage that ended when her husband was killed by thieves, and the rejection of her attempt to enter a convent when she was blamed for a sexual predator's use of her. Mizoguchi isn't taking aim at fate, but, rather, at the paucity of choices available to women in a world where their lives are dominated and determined by men. Mizoguchi regarded this theme of such importance that he returned to it again and again.

Here, he gave it exceptionally powerful form. *Saikaku Ichidai Onna*—novelist Ihara Saikaku's *Life of a Woman*—finds Mizoguchi at his most patient and precise; modern reflections deftly shimmer from his portrait of feudal Japan. In one passage, a puppet show features a female puppet in the artist's hand—a man manipulating a "woman" for the sake of male enjoyment while geishas also watch.

Kinuyo Tanaka is brilliant as Oharu.

RANCHO NOTORIOUS (U.S.). *See above.*

ÉL (Mexico). Whereas his *Los olvidados* (1950) focused on Mexico City's juvenile delinquent poor, Luis Buñuel's *Él*—in Spanish, the masculine definite article, but released in the States as *This Strange Passion*—addresses elite society. Mexican landowner Don Francisco is to be reckoned with.

Él opens in church. A priest washes and kisses a long line of boys' bare feet. A subjective camera discloses Francisco's interest: a string of female parishioners' shoed feet. The camera wittily backtracks to indicate the pair that wins Francisco's heart. They belong to Gloria.

Commentators often say Francisco becomes insanely jealous upon marrying Gloria. In truth, he is paranoid earlier in reference to his lawyer's (mis)perceived disloyalty. The guy has issues. Buñuel tracks Francisco's romance and *machismo*.

When poor Gloria seeks sympathy from her mother, we discover that Mexico itself romances *machismo*.

Here is one of cinema's great black comedies—until Alfred Hitchcock's *Psycho* (1960), its greatest.

Buñuel's film keeps going back to church because Buñuel finds the Church's patriarchic structure informing and buttressing *machismo* and sexism in Mexico. Francisco attempts to strangle Gloria in a bell tower—a scene that didn't escape the notice of Hitchcock (*Vertigo*, 1958), who declared Buñuel one of his favorite filmmakers. (Later, Othello-like, Francisco tries strangling Gloria in bed.) Francisco keeps apologizing to Gloria for his abuse because, while the Roman Catholic Church instills *machismo*, it preaches humility! In a phenomenal passage, at Mass, quick inserts—quasi-jump cuts—describe Francisco's delusion that fellow parishioners, altar boy, and even Padre Velasco are laughing at him!

It is time for Don Francisco to calm himself. He enters a monastery. In *Él*'s celebrated final shot, the poor guy, still batty in his holy trappings, walks zigzag down a path, away from the camera. Christian damage may be sublimated but never wholly taken away.

ROME, 11 O'CLOCK (Italy). The splendid Neorealist opening of *Bitter Rice* (1949) yielded to a flashy, melodramatic result, but *Rome, 11 O'Clock*, also by Giuseppe De Santis, is the last great work of Italian Neorealism.

The film is based on journalist Elio Petri's account of an actual 1951 incident—a tragedy resulting from Italy's postwar job squeeze. Some two hundred female applicants for a secretarial job crowd an old building waiting for an interview, causing the stairway to collapse. The film essays the fates of five: four of the injured, and the applicant, Luciana, whose rushing movement triggered the event.

De Santis stresses causality: the consequences of the disaster and its relation to capitalism. Burdened by guilt, Luciana contemplates suicide; her sense of responsibility, as grotesque as it is sincere, throws into relief what she herself is missing: the tragedy's underlying causes. The same analytical method is applied throughout as characters cope with the immediate hardship of their lives and we contextualize this in light of the film's argument. Three of the victims—victims of both the system and the event—are trying to "start over": a prostitute, a servant girl, the pregnant wife of an unemployed factory worker now striking out on her own. The remaining major character is not proletarian, but her marriage to an impoverished artist has set her relatives against her—an exposure of classism that reflects on the sociopolitical boat that all the main characters are in.

In 1949, Italy joined NATO and passed the Andreotti Law, which aimed to sweep its social problems—the meat and potatoes of *neorealismo*—away from international view and shift its filmmaking to the political right. In 1952, the effects kicked in, additionally pressured by the U.S., whose Hollywood raged against the financial success of a handful of Neorealist films.

THE CITIZEN (India). Although films from "Bollywood" are quite the fashion, nearly all outstanding films from India have been Bengali, not Hindi. Writer-director Ritwik Ghatak is the first great postwar Indian filmmaker. *Nagarik* is his first feature. Made when he was in his twenties, it was released in 1977, the year after his death. Satyajit Ray regarded Ghatak as "more Bengali" than himself.

The tragedy that is the foundation of *Nagarik* is the 1947 partition of Bengal (following the independence of India) that created countless refugees who flooded Calcutta, including Ghatak. The film opens with stunning irony: a freely roaming camera that captures trees and river, goes underneath a spectacularly intricate bridge, and finds rows of tall buildings: an encapsulation of the endless possibilities that the city offers. An overhead shot of a nicely dressed young man in the street, in conjunction with this sense of possibility, marks him for success. But we discover that Ramu has made another attempt at getting a job in borrowed clothes. Jobs are scarce, and his slum-dwelling family withers in poverty in cramped quarters, their lives at the mercy of the money they need and talk about. For now, Ramu is certain he will be successful. In time, the family's hopes evaporate.

Ghatak, a Marxist, has made a strong, evocative film that focuses on closeups of the faces of the family members and haunting long-shots, often with a single soul at least troubled, even defeated, in the frame. In a magnificent shot, a woman sits in front of a mirror. We see her and her reflection. Her eyes are closed. When financial stress consumes existence, there is scant existence; and, additionally, if you are separated from your homeland, there is scarce identity. It is like looking into a mirror with your eyes closed.

THE STRANGER'S HAND (Italy, UK). "Aren't we *all* fond of children?"
From a story by Graham Greene, who also helped produce it, *La mano dello straniero* pulsates with passion and humanity I find lacking in Carol Reed's *The Third Man* (1949).

The film's protagonist is mother-abandoned eight-year-old Roger Court, in a Venice hotel suite, expecting to reunite with his divorced father, British diplomat and anti-Communist spy Major Court (Trevor Howard, gripping), whom he hasn't seen in three years. En route to his son, Court follows someone he knows, who is being heavily guarded, who looks sick, drugged, and who no longer recognizes him. This results in Court's abduction by the sinister group. Roger roams Venice in search of his lost father.

Roberta, a sympathetic hotel secretary (Alida Valli, marvelous), helps. Torture during her interment in a Nazi camp has left this illegal Istrian refugee unable to bear children.

Mussolini had forced "Italianization" onto Istria's Slavic inhabitants; after the war, Tito's Yugoslavia took over Istria, its program of "ethnic cleansing" killing about 15,000 Istrians, with some 300,000 fleeing for their lives. Roberta was among these.

Roger, searching for his father, chances upon Dr. Vivaldi (Eduardo Ciannelli, giving the performance of a lifetime), Court's principal captor, who gleans whose son the English boy must be, tears a string, tying a piece of it around his finger and another piece around Roger's, to signify their friendship, assuage the boy's loneliness and give Roger hope. When Vivaldi dies from taking a bullet to spare Court's life, he lies face down on the ground. "Who is that?" Roger asks his father. The reply: "Nobody; just a stranger." It is Major Court who is the stranger to his son. The powerful closing shot reveals the bit of string still wrapped around a finger of Vivaldi's hand.

LIMELIGHT (U.S.). Self-directed, Charles Chaplin is deeply moving as Calvero, an ageing London music-hall comedian whose audiences no longer laugh at his routines but who is still capable of falling in love. The filmmaker is in an autobiographical mood; for Calvero loses his heart to a girl young enough to be his granddaughter (or, in Chaplin's case, wife), and Chaplin's own son, Sydney, plays the young man to whom Calvero loses her. Chaplin's grayest film, *Limelight*, then, is a faded, nearly rueful meditation on time's passing and on our gracious capacity to pass along with it.

Chaplin makes piercingly clear that in saving the life of the suicidal young ballerina (Claire Bloom, in her screen debut) Calvero is also saving himself; Calvero's exhortations not to give up on life are also aimed at himself. The Jewishness of the actress playing the ballerina helps invite an allegorical reading as to what people may gain by helping others of a different tribe. Indeed, *Limelight* can accommodate all kinds of interpretations. For instance, the resurrection of the crippled ballerina that returns her, after much hard work, to the dancing stage suggests the renewal of art despite humanity's limitations and mortal condition. For other artists, it is Nature that's eternal; for Chaplin, it is humanity's capacity to create beauty.

Two notes of regret attach themselves to Chaplin's last great work. One is that the sequence uniting Chaplin and Buster Keaton onscreen disappoints because director Chaplin allows actor Chaplin to hog the proceedings. Buster simply isn't given his due. The other exists outside the film per se. The U.S. government gave Chaplin's experience of making *Limelight* in his birth country a criminal coda; when he returned from England, Chaplin found himself barred from reëntering his long-since adopted homeland on fraudulent political grounds—no laughing matter.

MONKEY BUSINESS (U.S.). Written by Ben Hecht, Charles Lederer and "Izzy" Diamond, from Harry Segall's original concept, Howard Hawks's *Monkey Business* is a late "screwball comedy" showing, instead of romance leading to marriage, the hardship of romance *in* a marriage. In the U.S., it is an economically settled, socially complacent time despite a number of political agitatives current and upcoming (the Korean conflict, the McCarthy witch-hunts, the Cold War, the U.S. Supreme Court decision on school desegregation).

The highly commercialized suburban setting boasts fast, light sports cars and ugly advertising billboards—a nation glutting on success but, also, mightily suppressing ripples of discontent. Feeling pressured to make up for lost time, postwar Americans are newly obsessed with "being young." At an enterprising chemical company, Barnaby Fulton (Cary Grant, excellent) heads a team of scientists developing an elixir of youth. It's Barnaby's "baby"—a salient point, given that he and Edwina (Ginger Rogers, poignant, brilliant), despite a deep fondness for children, are an infertile couple.

Equally intelligent, stay-at-home Edwina makes do with her traditional role. However, she keenly regrets forsaking her own career path to support Barnaby's career. Moreover, Harvey Entwhistle still hovers about, hoping for a crack in the marriage that might allow him to reinitiate his suit. Barnaby's resentment about Harvey, Edwina's resentment over her might-have-been career: both lie repressed in their marriage, threatening to erupt.

The eruptions come, hilariously, triggered by the youth elixir that studious Barnaby mistakenly believes he has concocted. (Actually, lab test monkeys on the loose have willy-nilly mixed the potent Shakespearean brew.) Will the Fultons' marriage survive? Deeper, depressed chords solemnize the whacked-out humor; one episode, where age-regressed Barnaby enlists neighborhood boys playing Cowboys & Indians to kidnap, tie up and scalp Harvey, suggests a savagery beneath America's surface that curdles one's hysterical laughter.

CASQUE D'OR (France). Jacques Becker, Jean Renoir's former assistant, said that he had the paintings of Pierre-Auguste Renoir in mind when he made *Golden Helmet*. The film's vivid, bustling humanity, such as in scenes where working-class couples dance in close quarters at a riverside dance hall, recall, for instance, Renoir's 1876 *Bal du Moulin de la Galette*, or his 1883 *La danse à Bougival*, where the one couple shown dancing fills the tall, narrow canvas emphasizing the tightness of the space they inhabit—and possibly, given their different postures and facial expressions, the woman's feeling of being somewhat trapped. Becker's film also contains overpowering images of beauteous Nature, with which Renoir's paintings abound. Indeed, the gorgeous opening shot of a recreational row across silken river water recalls Renoir's 1873 *Canotier d'Argenteuil*, while the intoxicating lushness of trees recalls, for one, his 1874 *Sentier dans les bois*. While Renoir's paintings are bursting with children, however, there is only one child, in a walk-on, in Becker's film, which is set in both Paris and Joinville in the summer of 1898. This wan, surly boy, who delivers a note, is a world apart from Renoir's warm, vibrant girls. Their absence befits a film that ends bleakly with one half of a romantic couple watching, from a hotel window, as the other half is beheaded in the courtyard below for the crime he committed, in a sense, on her behalf.

Their relationship is doomed from the start because of the mob intrigue in which it is embroiled. The story, based on an actual turn-of-the-century murder case, provides a plot that intrigues with the ambiguous motivation of Felix Léca, the brutal dandy who also covets Marie (Simone Signoret, superb), who is being kept and abused by a member of Léca's criminal street gang. Killings await.

1953

TOKYO STORY (Japan). The Japanese family's postwar disintegration: this is the theme of a noble, massively humane work by Yasujiro Ozu, all of whose films bear the universal appeal of family (or surrogate family) concerns. The war's demoralizing outcome and the chauvinistic U.S. occupation that followed aren't mentioned in *Tokyo monogatari*, nor do they need to be. We grasp, as Japanese audiences certainly did, that what we are witnessing is, at least partly, fallout from what Japan endured over the previous decade.

An elderly couple visit their married son in Tokyo. Both the son, a pediatrician, and his wife work, leaving little time to attend to these guests; and their son is a disrespectful, unruly child. Only the widow of the elder couple's other son, who died in the war, is warm and attentive. Meaning well, the younger couple send the elder couple off to a spa, but thus being denied the company of those they came to visit only intensifies the older couple's loneliness and disappointment. At home, the doctor's mother falls ill and dies.

As it happens, the younger couple also are disappointed, but their sense of the traditional Japan that they've lost is less tangible. Ozu's film, then, is a study in disenchantment, disappointment, about a national mood as it affects the thoughts and feelings of individuals. Acting is key in such a film, and the performances are wonderful, especially those of Chishu Ryu as the father and Setsuko Hara as his compassionate daughter-in-law.

No film better portrays upheaved lives in a "society in transition." Moreover, Ozu's shots, such as those showing the backs of the elderly couple sitting outdoors, which convey their shared loneliness and suggest the world—the past—that is now behind them, are material and poetic, elegiac, mundane and transcendent.

UGETSU MONOGATARI (Japan). From Akinari Ueda's collection of stories *Tales of the Pale and Mysterious Moon After the Rain*, Mizoguchi's masterpiece is a tragic look into the human heart of war.

In sixteenth-century Japan, war ravages the countryside. A potter, a farmer and their wives are among those fleeing an overrun village. Both men abandon their wives, one in pursuit of wealth, the other in pursuit of military glory. Genjuro, the potter, sells his wares at market and falls under the spell of an exotic princess, into whose castle he moves. Both princess and castle turn out to be illusions. Genjuro goes home. Miyagi, his forgiving, devoted wife, tends to him lovingly through the night. The next morning, however, Genjuro learns that Miyagi, last night, was an apparition. Left unprotected, Miyagi had been killed in the war. The camera tilts upward from Miyagi's grave to reveal the whole peaceful village: yet *another* illusion. Beyond the village's borders, war rages on.

We surmise that Genjuro will remain haunted by Miyagi's memory and by questions: Did his intimacies with the phantom princess contribute to Miyagi's death? Whatever thing she is beneath her façade of seductive beauty—did the princess, out of jealousy, kill Miyagi? Or was the princess, in another form, Miyagi's ghost come to tempt him to abandon spiritually one he had already abandoned materially? At the end we hear, or think we hear, Miyagi's voice: Is this her spirit? The voice of Genjuro's guilt? Regardless, never again will Genjuro hold his wife in his arms.

Contributing to the visual poetry of this delicate, entrancing work is Kazuo Miyagawa's black-and-white cinematography; quiet, lovely, restrained, it projects Miyagi's sensibility and spirit. Thus Miyagi silently haunts frame after frame—a formal expression of the cost of war that is *Ugetsu*'s unifying theme.

VOYAGE IN ITALY (Italy). Ingrid Bergman is superb in husband Roberto Rossellini's *Viaggio in Italia*, which surveys a faltering marriage. Rossellini described its subject matter as "a couple's relationship under the influence of a third person: the exterior world."

Alex and Katherine Joyce first appear on a vacant, seemingly endless road to Naples. Only Katherine seems open to Italy. She tours alone a Neapolitan museum; ancient sculptures, which Rossellini's closeups and upwardly tilted camera angles invest with startling life, stir her soul. She visits ionized craters near Vesuvius in Pompeii, where the spark of a cigarette ignites a gorgeous expanse of voluminous smoke; must one "lose" oneself to (re)discover a truer self? Katherine also visits ancient catacombs stacked with skulls and, at Pompeii, other remnants of the past: human remains from the volcano's historic eruption. Molten plaster is poured into these so that the forms "come back to life." A couple is locked for all time in their last embrace: the act of love; the point of death. All this mortal evidence constitutes

Katherine's soul-turning "voyage in Italy"—a journey contested, however, by her worry that Alex no longer loves her.

At the volcano, the Joyces' agreement to divorce signals hope as the British couple concert their efforts to overcome the effect on them of the bubbling pit, a projection of their marriage's unsettled—*dormant*, not extinct—state. When a festive street crowd physically separates the couple, seemingly sealing the Joyces' marital doom, this separation in fact spurs the couple to reunite by providing them with an impediment they must push their way through. They have been roused from their lethargy, their dormancy, by the crowd's humanity —a reflection of the humanity of their own that, for fear of rejection and of being hurt, they had buried deep within themselves.

I VITELLONI (Italy). The twentysomething slackers in *I vitelloni* (literally, *The Overgrown Calves*) compose an affectionate portrait of provincial young maledom. The point isn't how bad, but how stunted, these boys are—perhaps for being cut off from The City. Only one, Moraldo, will make it out of Rimini.

This is Federico Fellini's most heartfelt film. It opens with one of cinema's most haunting images: four of the boys, then all five boys, arms around one another, zigzagging through Rimini's deserted streets late at night. Trust Fellini to come up with a long-shot that locates in imaginative space the point where documentary incident—if you will, *neorealismo*—yields to recollection and poetic reverie. The odd boy out who belatedly joins the others? That might be Moraldo—Fellini. Moraldo's being something of an outsider would foretell his singular escape.

The group's "leader and spiritual guide," brother-in-law Moraldo's voiceover tells us, is Fausto, who is forced by family into marriage and into a job of his father-in-law's choosing. Fausto, chafing under his conventional collar, will get fired, rob his former employer in retaliation, practice infidelity. We don't exactly blame him.

Carnival Time—Fellini Time—comes to Rimini. (Music therein links the film to Chaplin's *Modern Times*, disclosing Fellini's spiritual guide!) Alberto's sister, who financially supported the family, leaves, enforcing responsibility on her brother and evidencing the possibility of escape. Will Leopoldo, a budding playwright, also escape when, later on, a famous actor visits Rimini and reads his play? The whole strange episode invents the Felliniesque.

Moraldo's leavetaking by train is unbearably moving by one less jot than what follows: the boy—symbolically, the part of Moraldo that always will remain in Remini—balancing himself, sometimes falling off, as he walks a rail away from us, accompanied only by Nino Rota's poignant musical theme.

ILLUSION TRAVELS BY STREETCAR (Mexico). Juan and Tarrajas work for mass transit in Mexico City, where working people's "words and actions are always directed towards the realization of a dream, a desire, an illusion." The boys are chided for "too much efficiency" in repairing streetcar #133 in record time; the vehicle, "useless" despite being useable again, must be dismantled, which will put the two out of work. Drunk, they take out 133 for one last ride. They charge passengers nothing; some pay anyway. The sum of riders is a diverse portrait of humanity.

Distancing techniques urge an analytical approach to the material. Scenes of passengers shift to long-shots of the streetcar. Head-on shots show Tarrajas at the wheel and Juan standing alongside him, both framed by the car's square front window, creating the effect of a screen-within-the-screen. The Professor, a one-man Greek chorus, explains inflation to the depot watchman: More money is in circulation in the economy; prices go up; wages are stagnant; workers get poorer, while traders and businessmen get richer. Amidst the film's predominant naturalism, accompanied by deep shadows are phantasmagoric images of the bus at night.

Illusion travels by streetcar, the title of Luis Buñuel's film declares. Two superstructures, religion and capitalism, proffer an illusion of justice while disadvantaging and deceiving the working and nonworking poor. God will redress poverty in Paradise; in the meantime, so as not to miss out, people need to harken to what the Church tells them. The "illusion" that travels by streetcar is that things will improve for ordinary people when in fact they will stay the same or get worse.

Most everything in this marvelous comedy having to do with the streetcar and its passengers is imbued with spirit, and none of this spirit owes anything to the existence of God.

STATUES ALSO DIE (France). Alas, I have seen Alain Resnais and Chris Marker's *Les statues meurent aussi* only in the infamously truncated version that the French government permitted for forty years. Even so, it's a thing of passionate politics and dark, dazzling visual beauty.

The film opens in primordial darkness; a disembodied voice speaks: "When men have died they enter history. When statues have died they enter art. This botany of death is what we call *culture*."

Light appears, revealing public sculptures; even outdoors, these are objects of art such as one might encounter in a Western museum. A passage in such a museum that cuts between a piece of art and a patron gazing at it underscores the point; the reality of the piece relies on the patron's perception. This patron has entered the museum precisely to "see art"; seeing it is something she *does* in her life. It isn't a part *of* her life. The piece no longer belongs to the person who created it and that person's community.

African art is part of people's everyday lives. But by uprooting it, colonialism has usurped its identity. This is emblematic of colonialism's assault on African communities and human lives.

A tracking shot surveys piece after piece enrobed in darkness, but that is followed cuttingly by a montage of pieces, each one separate, isolated. Our eyes have replaced those of the patron. A montage of brilliantly grotesque death masks, intended to frighten away Death, now suggests labored curiosities: the impression on this art and its black African creators of Western museumitis. Elsewhere, scenes of Africans singing and variously working suggest the vitality from which African art has been cut off.

Statues also die when they aren't growing in the vibrant garden of a people's communal existence.

TOUCHEZ PAS AU GRISBI (France, Italy). Jean Gabin (best actor, Venice) is superb as Max, an ageing gangster in the Montmartre district of Paris, who has convinced himself, at least, that he wishes to retire, in Jacques Becker's razor-sharp, electrifying, ultimately wistful *film noir* of gangland warfare, *Touchez pas au grisbi* (*Hands Off the Loot!*). Gabin's final touch of secret gaiety in his complex role may owe something to the Mona Lisa-personality of Marlene Dietrich, with whom Gabin recently was involved romantically.

Becker's *mise-en-scène* dazzles with its intricate, dynamic activity. Contesting, moderating the film's intense realism is a dimension of theatricality and artifice nudged in by the opening of doors and windows, including interior windows on interior activity, that transform scenes observed by characters in the film as though they were playlets, emphasizing the degree to which these characters live well-rehearsed lives founded in well-rehearsed rituals. Hallways with progressive arches perform a similar function.

Max and pal Henri, nicknamed Riton, have made what they hoped would be their final heist: gold bars worth fifty million francs. But when the boss of another gang kidnaps Riton, will Max exchange the loot for Riton? Ultimately, no one gets the loot, and either Max or Riton loses his life. The fateful outcome follows something else that changes hands: Josy (Jeanne Moreau, strikingly young), once Riton's property, now the possession of the rival

gang boss, ironically named Angelo.
The shoot-out between gangs on a road in the dark of night may be the most thrilling passage in Becker's œuvre. The headlights of cars illuminate the determinism that these gangsters have interiorized; when the "good guys" subject a rival gang member to torture, the Resistance comes rushing back.
These men battle phantoms of historic memory, and the soul of France hangs in the balance.

THE WAGES OF FEAR (France, Italy). In fictional Las Piedras, various lives—people from all over—have reached their dead-ends. The area, somewhere in South America, is exploited and ruled by S.O.C.—the Southern Oil Company. Three hundred miles away, one of the fields is aflame; two pairs of drivers are offered $2,000 each by the U.S. company to drive trucks loaded with, combined, a ton of nitroglycerin to help contain the fire. Poverty is so deep, hope fragile, that applicants abound; the lucky four will have to transport their volatile cargoes over unpaved mountain roads in company trucks—this, a metaphor for capitalism—that do not even come equipped with shock absorbers! One of the four makes it.
From Georges Arnaud's novel, Henri-Georges Clouzot's *Le salaire de la peur*, which took the top prize at Cannes, is one of the most suspenseful thrillers ever made—a road picture where every bump—every obstacle—along the way may be fatal. The opening shot is of a backwater child tormenting with a stick cockroaches he has tethered. (Stringboarding.) Cosmos seems to be treating all adult humans in the same Shakespeare/Learian way.
The four men are a young Corsican, Mario (Yves Montand, strikingly good, sumptuously athletic), an ageing French gangster, Jo (Charles Vanel, terrific—best actor, Cannes), Bimba, a Dutchman embittered by his Nazi imprisonment, and an Italian, Luigi, whom a doctor has just informed has only months to live. Jo seems convincingly courageous behind his gun prior to the trip, and Mario slips under his wing; but he proves cowardly during the trip, confessing, "I'm not dangerous anymore."
Clouzot achieves turbulent, apocalyptic imagery involving black oil and black night, and raging fire. Fear had made the one survivor careful; stripped of that, he crashes and dies on his way back.

THE BAND WAGON (U.S.). Vincente Minnelli's glorious *The Band Wagon* is about preparations for a Broadway show. At least four of its characters refer to actual celebrities: Tony Hunter, a dancer back onstage following a long hiatus in Hollywood, suggests the actor who plays him brilliantly, Fred Astaire; Lily and Les Marton, who have written for Hunter a musical-comedy play, suggest the (unmarried) team of Betty Comden and Adolph Green, who wrote the script of *The Band Wagon*; Jeffrey Cordova, the egotistical director who transforms the play's light material (for us, hilariously) into a melodramatic modern-day rendering of the Faust legend, is a merciless parody of José Ferrer, who also had three plays running simultaneously on Broadway, with himself starring in one. (One of the musical numbers, "Triplets," with Hunter, Lily and Cordova appearing as homicidal infants, required the actors to have artificial legs strapped to their knees—as had Ferrer, as Toulouse-Lautrec in John Huston's 1952 *Moulin Rouge*.)
To their songbook, which the film summarizes, Arthur Schwartz and Howard Dietz added a new song for the occasion, "That's Entertainment!" Minnelli has made it and their old song "By Myself" the film's competing emotional coordinates. Will Hunter end up, as he began, solitudinous or part of a relationship and a community?
Cyd Charisse plays Gabrielle, the ballerina who selfconsciously stars opposite a selfconscious Hunter. Their walk-that-gradually-becomes-a-dance in Central Park, to the tune "Dancing in the Dark," is pure romance; it is imbued with both timelessness and a touch of melancholy transience. Their other magical number together, the Mickey Spillane spoof, with Hunter as a gumshoe and Gabrielle, in a flaming red dress, as the femme fatale out to ensnare

him, is darker magic—a mini-*film noir* with Astaire bending to Michael Kidd's muscular, sharp-angled choreography like a breeze.

GATE OF HELL (Japan). A fusion of melodrama and historical fairy tale, Teinosuke Kinugasa's *Jigokumon*, from Kan (Hiroshi) Kikuchi's play *Kesa's Husband*, enchants and, ultimately, deeply moves.

In 1159, the Heiji Rebellion is sweepingly underway; Lady Kesa volunteers to impersonate the Empress so that the latter may escape. Moritoh Enda falls in love with the imposter he is guarding. Upon discovering she is married, he impresses her into a plot to kill her spouse; Lady Kesa agrees, but, again play-acting, fatally substitutes herself for her spouse.

We have here, then, two competing versions of love, one selfish, the other unselfish—and, finally, selfless. Moreover, secretly, under the duress of the pressure that Moritoh applies (which includes, at one point, threatening her life as well as her husband's), Lady Kesa finds a way to carve a path of self-determination. Kinugasa's film reflects the concerns of its own time, the 1950s, when the outcome of the war wobbled Japan's traditional patriarchy.

Machiko Kyô's superlative performance as Lady Kesa drew commendation from the National Board of Review for its modernization of traditional Japanese acting. Moreover, Kinugasa and color cinematographer Kohei Sugiyama collaborate brilliantly. For example: the swordfight on the sand by the blue sea. Following a startling blow of the sword right into the camera and a quick cut, the victim falls face down, and with a dissolve the greenish waves, superimposed, cover the bloodied corpse: a momentary soothing of the violence; a consignment of the body, and of the conflict that took its life, to the lamentable history of Japan and the world. Time thus yields to timelessness, expressing—obliquely though fully— the hope that all the wounds inflicted on Japan in the Second World War, and on everyone else, will similarly wash away.

Top prize, Cannes; foreign-language film Oscar.

1954

ORDET (Denmark). From Kaj Munk's play, *Ordet* is cinema's finest expression of Christian faith.

In 1925, Morten Bergen lives on a remote farm with three sons: Mikkel, an atheist, whose wife, Inger, anticipates his return to the fold; Johannes, whose conviction that he is the risen Christ prompts him to chide "believers" for not believing fully enough; and young Anders, who has fallen in love with Anne, with whose father Morten has long been locking horns over their differing views of Christianity. Inger dies shortly after giving birth to a son whose wrong position requires the doctor to terminate the infant in an effort to save her life. Mikkel is left in inconsolable grief. Invoking Jesus Christ, Johannes resurrects Inger, bringing Mikkel to his wife's faith and reconciling both families.

Dreyer's sublime comedy accumulates the awesome power of his great tragedies. Its signature image is the family laundry, whites outdoors on a line, furiously flapping in the wind—perfectly mundane, and yet full of mysterious beauty that betokens spiritual possibilities. At Inger's funeral service, the sheer white curtains through which sunlight filters and the tick of a wall clock are transmutations of the laundry's sights and sound.

With a crystalline sense of the eternal, the mystery in our midst that gives rise to religious feeling, *The Word* encompasses, outdoors, an unsurpassed beauty of landscape and an almost palpable depth of air and, indoors, a miracle whose emotional power and depth of spiritual suggestion remain unmatched in cinema. Twentieth-century humanity's remove from natural sources of faith *Ordet*'s moment of rebirth shatters in a tidal wave of passion. Dreyer burns "religion" down to its ancient core of wonder, taking even nonbelievers to a summit of shared visionary experience where the pure air seems the very breath of God.

1954

SANSHO, THE BAILIFF (Japan). "Without mercy, a man is like a wild beast. . . . Men are created equal."

With these words to his young son, an 11th-century provincial governor who has contested the feudal order flees. En route to joining him in exile, his wife, Tamaki (Kinuyo Tanaka, superb), and their two children, Zushio and Anju, are kidnapped. Tamaki is sold to a brothel; meanwhile, her son and daughter are sold as slaves to Sansho, a brutal tax collector who balks at how unsuited to hard labor their small size makes them. Ten years hence, Anju helps her brother to escape so that he can search out their mother; to avoid punishment, she drowns herself. Zushio is appointed governor of the same province that his late father once governed. He abolishes slavery there and brings Sansho to justice. Freed slaves riot, and Zushio begins again to search for his mother, who has been branded, crippled and blinded, all to curb her repeated attempts to make her way to freedom.

Kenji Mizoguchi's *Sanshô dayû* is cinema's most powerful portrait of slavery, a slave uprising, and the will to freedom. It contrasts human cruelty and nobility, oppression and compassion. Mizoguchi and black-and-white cinematographer Kazuo Miyagawa have also made their film heart-piercingly beautiful: a natural reminder, nearly everywhere, of the equality to which, and the mercy for which, all of us have been born. The scene of Anju's suicide is unspeakably lovely; the sea into which she gracefully walks appears to enfold her as a mother might a child in need of comfort. Mizoguchi never made a more moving film.

It is the highly analytical nature of this riches-to-rags slave chronicle, however, that most decisively spares it the sentimental outcome of most other films that follow characters through travails throughout the years.

SEVEN SAMURAI (Japan). Akira Kurosawa's *Shichinin no samurai* is a powerful fable about the defense of a poor farming village in the sixteenth century. Dozens of bandits are poised to attack. The village leader suggests finding "hungry samurai" for whom payment in food is sufficient. Weary of fighting, Kambei Shimada (Takashi Shimura, magnificent) nonetheless consents to the task, recruiting six others, one of whom, brash, vulgar, boastful Kikuchiyo (Toshirô Mifune, turbulent, hilarious, heart-piercing—his greatest role), isn't really of the samurai caste, but, a farmer's son, provides a bridge connecting the simple farmers to the hired killers protecting them.

This film is elemental, intensely physical, and existential, with soaking rains, whipping winds, farmers in the fields harvesting barley, and a final ferocious confrontation between bandits and samurai. Too, there is one of the most gorgeous passages imaginable: amidst blossoms, the meeting of a boy, the youngest samurai, and the young daughter of a farmer. And one of the saddest: a prostitute's retreat into a flaming hut, to avoid facing her samurai-husband—the collateral cost of his protecting others rather than protecting his wife.

Robust, dynamic, *Seven Samurai* projects a harsh black-and-white world in which feudal wars have undermined order, inspiring criminals to prey on the vulnerable. Indeed, most everything conspires to threaten the survival of farmers. Someone says, "It is luckier to be a dog than a farmer." But it is far less fortunate to be a samurai. At the end of the film, only three of the seven are left standing. They face the graves of their four comrades, in each mound the warrior's sword as a marker—Kurosawa's glorious *hommage* to John Ford's *The Lost Patrol* (1934). One remarks: "Again we are defeated. It is the farmers who have won. Not us."

Bravery, honorable commitment, success—these say otherwise.

LA STRADA (Italy). Federico Fellini's *La strada* conveys life on the road and the rootlessness of lonely persons: Zampanò, a circus strongman (Anthony Quinn); Gelsomina, his assistant (Giulietta Masina, superb); the tightrope acrobat called Il Matto, "The Fool" (Richard Basehart, phenomenal).

Their itinerant world is worn and strange. Encapsulating it is an early image. Zampanò has abandoned Gelsomina for a night's pleasure. Sleepless, alone, she is on a dark, empty street down which inexplicably trots a horse, riderless, saddleless, the sound of its hoofbeats, interrupting silence, a measured clock of the soul. This haunting epiphany finds time forlornly blending into vacant eternity.

How have the three come to live on the road? His nature has led the boy there; his is the congenital homelessness of capricious spirit. Walking a tightrope for a living expresses The Fool's prescient grasp of human mortality. His flippancy, his main defense against mortal awareness, reflects also powerlessness to direct his own destiny. The selfish brute Zampanò —where *else* would he be but the road? Perhaps prison, for normal society dare not risk taking him in. Gelsomina's issue is poverty. With other, younger children to raise, her mother, a widow, has had to sell her to Zampanò, even though the rock-hard life Zampanò offers, coupled with his uncaring nature, will likely result in Gelsomina's death. All three characters lack the protection of material, familial and social enclosure, not to mention the comfortable myth of self-determination. Barely surviving in an inhospitable cosmos, they're driven "Still like the thistleball, no bar,/ Onward, whenever light winds blow."

What threads this odyssey? Two things: departing from dogma, the film's creation of its own myth of fall and redemption; Nino Rota's wistful trumpeted tune.

Otello Martelli's drab, faded black-and-white cinematography helps Fellini create the melancholy poetry that is the film's hallmark.

JOAN OF ARC AT THE STAKE (Italy, France). Ingrid Bergman is a miracle of sensitivity, giving a luminous performance, in Roberto Rossellini's *Giovanna d'Arco al rogo*. (Actually, I saw the French-language version, *Jeanne au bûcher*, but with Bergman's irreplaceable voice, not Claude Nollier's.) How can Bergman be brilliant here when she was dreadful in *Joan of Arc* (Victor Fleming, 1948)? Answer: Rossellini.

Like the earlier film, this one is based on a (different) theatrical piece Bergman did onstage (in a touring revival): the 1930s oratorio, based on a medieval miracle play, with music by Arthur Honegger and libretto by Paul Claudel. In contrast to the choral singing, Bergman's Joan is among the non-singing roles.

Jean Renoir's trilogy drawing on theatrical artifice had begun, starring Rossellini's former partner, Anna Magnani (*The Golden Coach*, 1953). (Bergman herself would star in the trilogy's concluding film.) Moreover, Bergman wanted another crack at the role. This Joan, surrounded by stage-night and blatantly artificial stars, bounds through space to no clear redemptive conclusion, glimpsing her history below, which is interwoven with the people of France, who have turned on her. The film nearly begins with Joan's being burned at the stake and nearly ends with that. Joan's existence is perhaps beyond Time. Is her ordeal recurrent and (as her noting the priest's absence) changing, as if to torture her further?

Indeed, the whole film is gloriously ambiguous. Consider the stage-lit wash of rosiness that may underscore Joan's identification with "the Rose of Innocence," but which jarringly draws our attention to Joan/Bergman's lipsticked lips and rouged cheeks.

Rossellini's Joan is repeatedly identified with circles—of angels, children, humanity. When last we see her she is heading up, chillingly alone. This theatrical rise, which questions God's participation, rivets our attention to Joan's own doubts about her destiny.

FRENCH CANCAN (France). Jean Renoir's *French Cancan*, the best musical film of the 1950s and his first film in France since *The Rules of the Game* (1939), occupies the middle of his Technicolored studio-bound trilogy, in between *The Golden Coach* (1952) and *Eléna et les hommes* (1956). It is about romantic entanglements in 1880s Paris and the launch of the Moulin Rouge, with its revival of the boisterous, bawdy cancan.

Films whose frames suggest Impressionist paintings tend to be academic. Peter Bogdanovich makes this distinction: Renoir's film suggests Impressionist painting, not specific paintings. Moreover, it coveys art and life's interaction, the continuous translation of one into the other, their common ground of creativity and humanity. Nini, the laundress who comes to lead the cancan dancers, an advancement that requires sacrificing her personal life, exemplifies another kind of creativity: someone's laboring on herself as though she were a work of art. We watch Nini re-create herself.

Jean Gabin is magnificent as Charles Zidler, the financially plagued impresario who founded the Moulin Rouge, who is here called Henri Danglard. We watch him in pursuit of his dream—a new way to please his soul and his beloved France: what *Renoir* wanted to do. Near the end, Danglard remains backstage on opening night as the cancan is performed, not watching, but listening and viscerally in sync, so that he can retain the dream.

Renoir immerses his camera in the dance so we feel we are a part of it—the dance of spirit on the floor, with its connection to all art, form releasing spirit, spontaneity, as in the birth of a child. The scene, more fragile than it seems, has passed, along with Renoir's father, Pierre-Auguste, who epitomized it. His son's final masterpiece gathers poignant affection for life's fleeting moment.

FEAR (Italy). Roberto Rossellini's stunning *La paura*, which updates Stefan Zweig's 1920 novella *Angst*, finds one kind of jealousy masquerading as another. Research scientist Albert Wagner knows that Irene, his wife, has been having an affair with Erich Baumann because Baumann's previous girlfriend, Johanna Schultze, striking out at the woman who replaced her, has told him this. Wagner thus impresses Schultze into a scheme whereby she torments Irene by blackmailing her for increasing sums of money, which Irene at first pays, hoping to keep her husband from finding out. Eventually Irene discovers her husband's plot against her and chooses suicide as a course of action rather than face him. Meanwhile, Wagner is himself consumed by guilt for what he has done, the deepest motive for which perhaps only we are privy to: Irene's business success with the research plant while Albert was a wartime prisoner. The villain here is the Second World War, whose shadows warp and riddle the Wagners' lives; in a great shot recalling silent German cinema's Expressionism, Irene's shadow looms enormously as, at night, she retreats to the laboratory in the abandoned plant in order to kill herself with her husband's experimental vaccine for counteracting paralysis, symbolically, the plague of the war's hangover, its residual moral numbing. In a sense, through his fiendish scheme, Wagner has indeed been "experimenting" on his wife.

Ingrid Bergman gives a phenomenal performance, among her three or four greatest, as Irene. At first, we may worry that the film abounds with too many fleeting allusions to other Bergman films, among them, *Gaslight*, *Notorious* and Rossellini's *Europa '51*, in which she played another Irene; but Irene Wagner emerges with especial force and clarity as a completely realized characterization, and with a lyrical beauty, attuned to Irene's increasing vulnerability, that is heartrending.

SALT OF THE EARTH (U.S.). During opening credits, Esperanza is shown, outdoors in a miners' residential camp, splitting wood for a boiling pot and boiling water. Post-credits, in the mine, a defective blasting fuse causes a near disaster. The new rule is that Mexican-Americans must work by themselves, denying them the precautions that have been extended to "Anglo" workers. Esperanza and her husband, Ramon, quarrel. Ramon insists workers' safety must be the union's priority, while Esperanza pleads for sanitation. When Ramon accuses her of selfishness, Esperanza replies, "If I think of myself it's because you never think of me."

Seeking economic justice, Mexican-American workers went on strike, beginning in 1951, against the mining company Empire Zinc in Silver City, New Mexico. *Salt of the Earth* brings documentary realism to its fictional reconstruction of the event. Perhaps its most electrifying aspect, though, is its portrait of the womenfolk, who crash the barrier of Hispanic *machismo* in their parallel quest for marital and communal equality. They join their spouses in the strike, take over the picket line when necessary and endure consequent incarceration.

1954

Anything but a reductive "message movie" of the liberal sort that producer Stanley Kramer periodically discharged, this is a remarkably holistic account of a community's multiple efforts toward equality.

The film, befittingly, is also an exemplary blend of objective and subjective, documentary and fictional elements. Playing Ramon, union president, Juan Chacon really was President of Local 890 of the International Union of Mine, Mill and Smelter Workers, other members of which populate the cast. Blending perfectly with these, in the film's central role, is superb Rosaura Revueltas, the Mexican actress who plays Esperanza.

Salt of the Earth was made by a cooperative of blacklisted artists, among them writer Michael Wilson and director Herbert J. Biberman.

LES DIABOLIQUES (France). Henri-Georges Clouzot's superbly acted thriller *Les diaboliques* (*Diabolique* in the U.S.; more accurately, *Fiends* in the UK) haunts with mortal awareness.

Clouzot had been plagued by poor health since childhood. During the Occupation, the Nazis found demoralizing elements in his provincial poison-pen melodrama, *Le corbeau* (1943), and halted his career; meanwhile, his countrymen suspected Clouzot of being a collaborationist. In 1947, officially exonerated but under a lingering cloud of political suspicion, he returned to filmmaking.

The setting of *Les diaboliques* is a provincial boarding school for boys. Michel, who runs it, has apparently recently ended an affair with teacher Nicole; Nicole and Christina, his rich wife who owns the school, discuss how they despise abusive Michel. Nicole convinces Christina they should murder Michel in a complicated plan that will conceal their guilt. Afterwards, signs point to Michel's having returned from the dead to taunt the homicidal co-conspirators.

Police Inspector Fichet's too-late intercession proves him an (unwitting) executor of justice. Christina, after all, was perfectly willing to kill her spouse. Nicole professes atheism; it is the devout Catholic Christina, who believes in Hell, who violates religious principles in order to kill. The public act of divorce would lead to her being excommunicated from her Church, but, on the other hand, if she can get away with murder—.

Clouzot poignantly contrasts the school's spirited, rambunctious boys and their worn, somewhat dissipated school masters. Also, he weaves into an otherwise sturdy presentation the haunting poetry of evanescence: one motor vehicle's tire disturbing while passing through a puddle; the reflection of passing trees on another vehicle's windshield; the playful energy of boys as they make their way down a hall; Michel's ambiguous photographic image—is it there or not?—in an upstairs window overlooking the school grounds.

CHIKAMATSU MONOGATARI (Japan). Seventeenth-century Kyoto; Japan's feudal moral code demands that two adulterous lovers, bound back-to-back, be driven by horseback through the clamorous street to the place of their double crucifixion. Ishun, a successful scroll-maker, is among the curious; but he is a philandering hypocrite. Osan, his decades-younger wife by financial arrangement, is wrongly suspected of marital infidelity with Mohei, Ishun's prize worker. The pair flee, intent on committing double suicide; but when Mohei confesses his love, Osan is given cause to live. They are caught, however, betrayed by Osan's "disgraced" family. Bound back-to-back, Osan and Mohei are driven through the street. This time, the camera is closer up; the abstract idea of the punitive code has been transformed into human reality. There's no need this time to show the crucifixions. We ourselves supply that image from what we saw earlier.

Based on a puppet play by Chikamatsu Monzaemon, Kenji Mizoguchi's intense, delicate love story and condemnation of social bigotry and the role money plays in determining people's fates is an exquisitely wrought film ranging from Kyoto's industrious bustle to the serenity of Lake Biwa, where, contemplating their doom, the fugitives already branded as lovers discover their love. There is no peace either behind or ahead of them; but in that moment, seemingly still while slowly moving across the misty lake, there is the otherworldly contentment of their feelings for one another. What we "see" is the interiority of their love.

On land, in rural hiding, Mohei recalls himself as a boy dreaming of his own future success in the city of Kyoto. Thus in the present he goes back to a past from which he looked ahead. The complexity of the psychological coordinates of time suggests the exhaustion of time— and the fates of the crucified lovers.

GOJIRA (Japan). Ishirô Honda's *Gojira* belongs to *kaijû*, the Japanese genre of "big monster movies." (The 1956 *Godzilla* is a slashed, English-dubbed version of the original, with an American reporter inserted to provide easy navigation amidst an unfamiliar culture.) Its 150-foot long reptile, with scorching radioactive breath, refers to the horror unleashed by the U.S. explosion of atomic bombs over Hiroshima and Nagasaki nearly a decade earlier. It has, we are told, "absorbed an enormous amount of atomic radiation."

Rising from its watery depths, Gojira is identified with oily black night, in which it majestically cloaks itself. It eerily, unfathomably emerges from Japan's collective consciousness. Its initial appearance is accompanied by a blinding blast of light, echoing Hiroshima. Soon afterward, it is also identified with torrential rain from above and upheaving sea below. Gojira suggests, at once, primordial Nature and Nature's interruption—unearthly silence, interrupted by bellows, moans and groans. It is elementally riotous, somehow both water and fire. It turns Tokyo, which it attacks, "into a sea of flames." Returning to the sea to regather its strength for a second attack, it leaves in its wake what looks like a bombed-out landscape: the outcrop of war. Hospitals are again filled with the burnt, the contaminated, the dying.

Although a radiologist pleads that Gojira must be captured and studied for its survival of such high doses of radiation, the nation is mobilized to down the beast, for instance, by a coast-long electrified fence and missiles launched from airplanes. Nothing seems to work; and Gojira's long assault on Tokyo, set to a measured pace, gives us time to contemplate the depth of its horror and not merely react to it. Here is one of cinema's great waking nightmares, profoundly realized by Honda and his principal collaborator, black-and-white cinematographer Masao Tamai.

REAR WINDOW (U.S.). From Cornell Woolrich's story, Alfred Hitchcock's *Rear Window* lays bare the postwar U.S. complacency that John Michael Hayes's brilliant, cynical script represents.

Photojournalist L. B. Jefferies, confined for weeks to a cast for a broken leg, has become a peeping tom. Each apartment window across the courtyard in his urban complex reveals another aspect of his own psychology, much of it having to do with his feelings of inferiority (buried under *machismo*), sexual unease, fear of marriage. He notes the downward trajectory, from hopefulness to dissatisfaction, of a pair of newlyweds, and the even more acrimonious longtime union of a knife salesman and his nagging wife. "Jeff" has been an outsider at home, living in a low-rent district because, always on the go, mostly out of the country, "home" is merely a pit-stop between assignments. Stella, his daily visiting nurse, remarks, "People should go outside and look into their *own* lives."

An early long-shot—in accordance with shots from the vantage of Jeff's confinement, this is a film full of long-shots—shows a cat scampering up courtyard steps, free to roam or go home, (unlike Jeff) unfettered by constraints, including his own and others' expectations. A neighbor's dog is murdered by the wife-killer (for sniffing about); the owner's cry of anguish at losing her companion, her principal defense against terrible loneliness, contests a rampant complacency that individuals feel (or at least practice) toward others. Wrapped up in the wife-murder, Jeff is temporarily distracted from his moral obligation to help the neighbor he has dubbed Miss Lonelyhearts, who is attempting suicide.

Meanwhile, Jeff's girlfriend, high-class model Lisa Fremont (Grace Kelly, giving the best, most complex performance), exploits Jeff's obsession with solving the murder mystery in order to counter his misogynism by proving herself a fit companion for him.

1955

NIGHT AND FOG (France). The subject of the Holocaust has generated countless documentaries, including outstanding ones as the twentieth century drew to a close: Harun Farocki's *Images of the World and the Inscriptions of War* (1989), Héctor Faver's *Memory of Water* (1993) and Dariusz Jablonski's *Fotoamator* (1998). But, closer to the event, Alain Resnais's *Nuit et brouillard* remains the finest.

Resnais's theme is the need to preserve historical memory—memory ever poised to slip away. At the sight of the Auschwitz death camp, careless green grass sways in the breeze, while black-and-white photos and newsreel snippets commit the reality of Auschwitz to flypaper. A long overhead shot of a blank field is held until the camera descends to reveal the surrounding barbed wire fence, with this ironical accompanying voiceover: "A placid landscape . . . An ordinary field over which crows fly"—author Jean Cayrol's reference to Van Gogh's symbol of matter's passage into ephemera.

The film's signature mode is the tracking shot. The camera surveys the camp, noting the massive fence, this time from the inside, and remnants of some of the abandoned structures. The film cuts from one tracking shot to another, edited to compose, seemingly, one mind's haunted journey, perhaps the return of a ghost. As the camera explores one of the barracks, we hear, "No description . . . can restore [the inmates'] true dimension: endless, uninterrupted fear." What we cannot grasp is already lost.

Intermittently, *Night and Fog* revisits human horrors—historical memory's overload: SS surgical experimentation on prisoners; the bulldozing of mounds of corpses into a mass grave. The commentary ends by weighing the matter of collective guilt ("War nods, but one has one eye open"), addressing denial and revisionism, and wondering aloud how much "the next executioners" will resemble ourselves.

Indeed.

PATHER PANCHALI (India). A record of the life of an impoverished family living in the Indian jungle, *Song of the Little Road* combines 1930s Indian literary realism, the influence of Italian cinema's *neorealismo*, and a commitment to the poetry of childhood as a filter through which to wring the poignancy of adult as well as much younger lives. From the 1934 novel by Bibhutibhusan Bandopadhaya, Satyajit Ray thus began cinema's most celebrated and heart-walloping trilogy involving continuing characters.

Ray had studied graphic art under Nobel Prize-winning Bengali author Rabindranath Tagore at Calcutta University and had apprenticed to Jean Renoir during the filming of the latter's beauteous *The River* (1951). He also was a Bengal—a fact that excluded him from official honor in India.

The family members are little Apu, his older sister, Durga, to whom he is devoted, as she is to him, despite their many childish quarrels, their mother, Sarbojaya (Karuna Banerjee, magnificent), whose daily routine of housework accompanies endless fretting wrapped inside a proud demeanor, the children's father, Har[har], a clerk and sometime priest who dreams of becoming a writer but who is too shy to ask his employer for back pay, and Indir[tharkun] (Chunibala Devi, brilliant), the frail, elderly aunt beloved by all—except Sarbojaya, who treats her like an unwelcome in-law.

The family dynamic is complex. For instance, Sarbojaya blames Indir for Durga's continual theft of fruit from the landowner's orchard: cherished gifts that make Auntie's starved, withered face light up. She fails to consider her own bitterness about the family's loss of the orchard—bitterness that she visits upon her spouse, who gave the orchard away to the landowner to pay (what the landowner at least claimed were) debts that Hari's late brother owed him.

No film more beautifully evokes playful childhood's suspended state. Or transience.

LOLA MONTES (France). *Lola Montès*, Max Ophüls's final, uneven, but intermittently most brilliant film, projects twentieth-century self-objectification and selfconsciousness back into the nineteenth to address the emergence of the idea of celebrity. Its case in point is an actual celebrity, Maria Dolores Eliza Rosanna Gilbert, a.k.a. Lola Montès, ersatz dancer, acrobat, and scandalous lover, including of King Ludwig I of Bavaria (Anton Walbrook, superb), who was dethroned by the 1848 Revolution.

The film's point of departure is a circus whose focus is Lola's life; Lola (Martine Carol, as untalented as Lola) plays herself. The ringmaster, knowing the public that his audience represents, describes her: "A master of cruelty with the eyes of an angel." A human being is thus reduced to a caricature, a "femme fatale." "Remember the past?" This question signals a "realistic" flashback; but is it reality or a reaction to the theatrical performance? Franz Liszt is the first of Lola's lovers to appear. Liszt leaves Lola by coach; cut to Liszt's coach departing from the circus stage. Similar confusions of theatricality and life ensue.

Lola's childhood is given short shrift—*another* reduction of her. Backstage, Lola asks the child who plays her, "Would you like to play the part for the rest of your life?" The implication is that "Lola" is just such a role for Lola. "I do as I please," she insists, but her unhappy marriage to a drunk was her way of escaping the marriage that her mother had planned for her.

With a weak heart poised to stop her life/performance at any moment, Lola ends, a caged commodity, as the camera withdraws and a new audience, our surrogate, moves forward to enter the tent. We who thrive on celebrity are the ones who have reduced Lola. The camera retreats into us.

LE AMICHE (Italy). Michelangelo Antonioni's first important fictional film is based on Cesare Pavese's 1949 story "Tre Donne Sole" ("Three Women Sun"). The considerable plot centers on Clelia (Eleonora Rossi Drago, wonderful), who has returned from Rome to Turin, her hometown, to manage a fashion salon. In the hotel room next to hers, Rosetta attempts suicide by pill overdose, drawing Clelia into Rosetta's circle of friends, which is dominated by sharp-tongued Momina, whose extramarital lover, it turns out, is the architect of Clelia's salon. Clelia herself falls in love with Carlo, the architect's assistant, while Rosetta has been stretched to the breaking point by her affair with Lorenzo, a painter who is jealous of fiancée Nene's greater commercial success. Nene (Valentina Cortese, brilliant) is a ceramics artist. Once Rosetta has recovered, Momina coldbloodedly encourages her pursuit of Lorenzo. (At one point she chides fragile Rosetta for the incompetence that her unsuccessful suicide attempt demonstrates.) Rosetta's next try at suicide succeeds. At the salon, Clelia "loses it" and publicly lambasts Momina. Clelia can work again for the firm back in Rome. Lorenzo ends back in Nene's arms. He asks why she puts up with him. Nene responds, with subtly devastating rue, "Perhaps because you come at so high a price." Clelia leaves by train for Rome as Carlo hides while watching her depart, fearful of exposing his broken heart.

What matters most here are the psychological inquiry, especially into the mental lives of the female characters (Suso Cecchi d'Amico co-authored the script with Antonioni), their unsettled spiritual state, and the shimmering poetry of Turin's deserted streets at night, which is correlative to this. As a result, for all its narrative complexity, *Le amiche* looks ahead to *Il grido* (1957), in which Antonioni radically continues Roberto Rossellini's experiments at unhinging plot.

IL BIDONE (Italy). In *The Swindle*, one of Federico Fellini's best films, Augusto fleeces peasants. The con man ends up alone on a hillside, beaten in every sense, after concealing money from accomplices that he intended to give his teenaged daughter so she could go to college and realize her dream of becoming a teacher. Augusto (Broderick Crawford, wonderful) has no dreams of his own.

His "original" accomplices, who abandoned him a year or two earlier, include Carlo, who is called Picasso because he paints; Carlo's wife, Iris, seems to want him to paint more than he wants to, perhaps to bring him back to an original desire that reflects the man she fell in love with. But it is principally fear that motivates the boy to quit his criminal connection to Augusto: fear that Iris will leave him, taking with her the light of his life, Silvana, their young daughter. Roberto, the other accomplice, dreams of becoming the Italian Johnnie Ray, the U.S. entertainer popular in the fifties for crybaby wailing aimed at overcoming deafness when he sang. Roberto's risking exposure by an application of light fingers at a New Year's party suggests another facet of his identification with Ray: Roberto also may be a closeted homosexual.

Augusto is sufficiently old that these "original" accomplices are themselves replacements.

Tonally, this is perhaps Fellini's most agile and complex accomplishment. Whether Augusto is bilking the poor posing as a monsignor or a housing commissioner, Fellini takes pains to aim ridicule at the Church, and the superstitious devotion it encourages, and postwar bureaucracy, not the poor. Fellini's ambivalence toward Iris (Giulietta Masina, his wife) may reflect pressures on him to hew to *neorealismo*!

Hauntingly, the film's action crosses that of its Fellinidom predecessor, *La strada* (1954), at least thrice.

SMILES OF A SUMMER NIGHT (Sweden). Eighteen-year-old Anne poses an odd question to Fredrik Egerman (Gunnar Björnstrand, elegant), her fortysomething husband, as he tucks her in: "Would you be jealous if Henrik started paying me more attention?" Henrik is lawyer Fredrik's studious son; the Egermans' marriage remains unconsummated. So the answer is "Yes." One-time wolf Fredrik patiently plays the part of a tender shepherd, owing to his love for Anne. But who can foretell the turns of plot in the romantic play of life? Not in this instance Fredrik, whose Anne soon elopes with Henrik.

Set in 1900, writer-director Ingmar Bergman's beauteous comedy *Sommarnattens leende* shimmers with twilit melancholy. Fredrik tells his "only friend in the world," actress Desirée Armfeldt (Eva Dahlbeck, haunting), about his two-year marriage. Fredrik's former lover, she finds the confidence odd. Soon, Desirée's current lover will return to his wife. But Fredrik will return to *her*.

Bedridden, Desirée's rich mother (Naima Wifstrand, brilliantly funny) hosts a midsummer's eve party at her country estate, to which four couples have been invited. It is there, in the Shakespearean air, that the romantic reformulations occur amidst wine, Mrs. Armfeldt's shrewdness, mother's milk, stallion's sperm and a little gunfire. The comedy teeters on the edge of disaster and Jean Renoir's *The Rules of the Game* (1939).

In a reversal of theatrical convention, early on Fredrik eavesdrops on his young maid, Petra (Harriet Andersson, bursting with life and allure), as she tells Henrik how she is drawn to her employer. Fredrik's smile, warm, without smugness, reflects instead his love for his son and the memory of his own callow youth.

The final shot proves that neither Pudovkin nor Hitchcock had the last word on windmills. Their radial vanes in motion suffuse life's sexual fortunes with a clock's mortal indication.

RICHARD III (UK). Now is the anytime of our great content whenever we revisit Laurence Olivier's *Richard III*.

It begins with a shadow-action: while attending the royal coronation, Richard of Gloucester (Olivier, brilliant throughout) lowers a crown on his own head, the materialization of his desire, as the actual crown is lowered on his brother Edward's head, the camera situated so we see both actions simultaneously. But the film's principal shadow, which at one point Richard conjures, is Richard's own: a suggestion that Richard is insubstantial, his materiality absorbed by his drive for the Crown of England, for which he murders everyone, including children, to set himself at the head of the line of succession.

Twisting his neck into the camera, Richard seems to be glancing at us, but with a cut director Olivier reveals that Richard is actually throwing a conspiratorial glance at his cousin, the Duke of Buckingham, inside the coronation chamber. This camera/editing strategy implicates us, as do Richard's soliloquies, which finds him finding us (and our hidden ambition?). When Richard bursts upon Anne and the corpse of her husband (more of Richard's handiwork), Henry VI's son, cuffs down a guard and gives him a gratuitous kick, Richard becomes an id-figure—Shakespeare's inspiration, surely, for Poe's Hop-Frog, another gleefully vicious hunchbacked cripple in a royal court, and actor Olivier's direct inspiration for Jean-Louis Barrault's Opale in Jean Renoir's Jekyll/Hyde film, *The Testament of Dr. Cordelier* (1959).

Richard becomes king, but as history turns against him he degenerates into a pathetic figure on the battlefield, his crown (literally) spinning away from him as he writhes on the ground in a shocking, moving animal death. Now we grasp his soliloquies: Richard's reach across time seeking the validation and exoneration from us that he knows we must ultimately deny him.

TALES OF THE TAIRA CLAN (Japan). *Shin heike monogatari*, like his earlier, uninteresting *47 Ronin* (1941), also done on an epic scale, contains the most violent material with which Kenji Mizoguchi had to contend since his postwar conversion to Buddhism.

Text summarizes the history involved. "In the tenth and eleventh centuries, the Fujiwara clan ruled Japan, but by the twelfth century its influence had begun to wane. Two imperial courts contended for power: the official one; the Cloister Court, headed by the emperor who had abdicated, which ruled behind the scenes. As temples, equipped with their own armies, sought to establish the primacy of their own power, both courts depended on samurai—paid warriors the use of whom exhausted them as a class. The Cloister Court employed samurai of the Taira clan." Thus "were sown the seeds of military government" that "dominated Japan for 700 years."

The opening crane shot, descending onto a crowded, contentious market replete with political debate regarding the two courts, homes in on Japan's past. Like most great art about the past, Mizoguchi's films reflect on the present, that is, the burden of the past that the present totes. *Shin heike monogatari* suggests that the Japanese people—an extension of the samurai that once represented their interests—remain at the mercy of national politics.

Mizoguchi's final masterpiece owes something to Sergei M. Eisenstein's *Ivan the Terrible* (1944-46) in its exploration of ruling court intrigue. Mizoguchi, though, is most interested in how individuals cope with the moral dilemmas that confront them. At the film's core is a twist of historical reality, as the heir to rule of the Taira clan discovers he may be, in fact, the son of either the ruling emperor or a monk. Mizoguchi is plumbing the ambiguous, uncertain waters of Japan's postwar identity.

THE GRAND MANEUVERS (France). Under the spell of Max Ophüls's *Madame de . . .* (1952), René Clair made his finest film since *Quatorze Juillet* (1933)—and his funniest since *Le million* (1931). Moreover, this film became his first in color—and *such* color: the cinematography by Robert Le Fèbvre and Robert Juillard achieved the loveliest, most gracious colors in all of cinema—restricted (as Garbicz and Klinowski point out) to one or two dominant hues per composition,—ones that were entirely appropriate to a period comedy-romance that slides into melancholy and worse: a heart shut to love; a premonition of war. Written by Clair, Jérôme Géronimi and Jean Marsan, *Les grandes manoeuvres* won Clair the best film prize of the French critics and the Prix Louis Delluc.

The subject is love as it collides with pride and poetic justice; the setting, a provincial town where a French army regiment is garrisoned prior to heading out for maneuvers.

Gérard Philipe is dazzlingly brilliant as Le lieutenant Armand de la Verne, who wagers fellow officers that he will seduce the first woman to appear at a ball to fall in love with him before the regiment leaves for maneuvers. Some reviewers mention names on slips of paper in a hat; but the hat spills its contents before Armand can choose, suggesting that the stars must align to get the *right* woman to be the choice: in this case, the one with whom the cad will really fall in love but who will break his heart (and her own) when she learns about the bet. This is Marie-Louise Rivière (Michèle Morgan, wan, tightly anxious), fresh from Paris, whose marital experience and divorce have made her wary of being hurt by men.

Poignantly, the time is sometime before the outbreak of war in 1914.

KOKORO (Japan). Drawn from Natsume Soseki's 1914 novel, Kon Ichikawa's deeply affecting *Kokoro*—called *The Heart* in the U.S., but *heart* in an expansive sense, including ideas of mind, spirit, love, sexuality—opens (after credits) and closes on the face of Shizu. At the beginning she has just quarreled with her spouse of thirteen years, Nobuchi, whom she (wrongly) suspects of having a mistress; at the end, she is a widow. Nobuchi's suicide comes shortly after the death of Emperor Meiji in 1912. Nobuchi, who had almost no contact with the outside world, suggested to Shizu that neither could move forward since Meiji's reign contained both their entire lives. The childless couple have forfeited the future.

A pre-credit sequence where sea is seemingly drowning us while splashing upward to obliterate nearly all the sky correlates to Nobuchi's death-wish. Nobuchi might have drowned, we later learn, but for the intervention of Hioki, a 23-year-old university student who befriends him, adopting Nobuchi as his *sensei*—his esteemed mentor and intellectual guide. But Nobuchi, who has never been employed, was once not so bookish and contemplative; that would have better described Nobuchi's close friend, Kaji, whose commitment to a path of spirit is interrupted by his apparent interest in Shizu—although this seems to strike out of the blue. Kaji—much of *Kokoro* unfolds in flashbacks—confides this to Nobuchi, who goes ballistic with jealousy, impulsively becoming engaged himself to Shizu. But of whom was Nobuchi jealous? Of whom was Kaji truly desirous?

By degrees we grasp the depth of Nobuchi's melancholy. Nobuchi has lost his dearest friend (for which Hioki becomes a temporary consolation until the same confusion as with Kaji reasserts itself), his peace of mind (he is racked with guilt for having destroyed Kaji's life), even his emperor.

1956

THE BURMESE HARP (Japan). About the effect of war's horror on a sensitive combatant in the Second World War, Kon Ichikawa's *Biruma no Tategoto* is the most humane of war films. Its eloquent simplicity befits its literary source: Michio Takeyama's postwar novel aimed at introducing Buddhism's tenets to children.

The film opens on a barren, desolate landscape. Dirge-like music; image and sound thus combine to suggest a vast graveyard. Titles appear—a kind of epitaph: "In Burma, soil is blood-red. So are rocks." A reflective voiceover replaces the titles: "It's such a long time since the war ended. The war has left many sad stories . . . By July 1945 the war was going badly." Memory of war becomes, then, the "life" of this film—life commemorating the lost and the dead.

The film's first movement introduces Inouye Company, the platoon including Private Mizushima, whose constant companion is his lute patterned after a Burmese harp. Captain Inouye, who studied music, has taught his men to sing. The beauty of their choral endeavors suggests the haven of humanity they perpetuate in the midst of their violent existence; their nostalgic, sentimental songs transport their souls to home. Similarly, the plaintive sounds of Mizushima's simulated Burmese harp are the repository of the men's embrace of life in the midst of so much death. Its soulful expression counters the imperialist motive of war, the power of governments that discounts the humanity of the ordinary people who become the

1956

soldiers and other victims of war. Mizushima goes AWOL and becomes a monk. The film charts his highly individual and transformative journey; but in some mystical sense, Mizushima is the extension of his comrades, including Inouye, whose love of music inspired him in the first place. Ichikawa's delicate, elegiac masterpiece inspires us all.

A MAN ESCAPED (France). Unsurprisingly, one strong nondocumentary about the Nazi death camps is Wanda Jakubowska's *The Last Stop* (1948), for which the filmmaker drew upon her own internment at Auschwitz. Robert Bresson was a prisoner of the Germans in Occupied France for a year. His *Un condamné à mort s'est échappé, ou Le Vent souffle où il veut*, is similarly authentic—and taken from actual events.

In Lyon in 1943, Resistance fighter Fontaine, based on André Devigny, is the prisoner of Germans, who have condemned him to die. Fontaine plots his escape. Long self-sufficient, he must cross a chasm of suspicion to an ambiguous cell-mate, a teenaged boy who may be a plant. Will Fontaine take the risk and include this stranger in his plans?

A Man Escaped is one of the great works of French Existentialism. It is also unmistakably Bresson, emphasizing the sights and sounds punctuating the routines inside the Gestapo prison. Throughout, subtle lighting implies, too, a gracious presence in the frames. When a fellow prisoner tells him that God will save them, Fontaine responds, "Only if we give him a hand." But *how?* All one can do is make personal choices and accept their consequences.

Fontaine, at the last, does the humane thing. We know the outcome, from what happened to Devigny. Yet each fresh viewing revives the suspense that Bresson's filmmaking, including Fontaine's voiceover, develops by bringing us into the young lieutenant's mind in the moment. And just as Fontaine is ultimately rewarded by escape, to execute which his companion proves absolutely essential (God at work?), we are rewarded with one of the most moving shots in cinema: the camera at their backs, the two men, side by side, walking their way at night, barefoot, to freedom.

The Spirit breathes where it will.

THE SEARCHERS (U.S.). The protagonist of *The Searchers* is Ethan Edwards (John Wayne, powerful), an embittered veteran of—from his vantage—the War Between the States. Edwards provides the occasion for John Ford's brilliant investigation of American racism; the film explores the darkest American terrain, where bigotry seems a primitive and instinctual birthright but is, really, a kind of insanity corrupting the moral landscape and tying all into a tangle American ideals, sentimentalism, territorial arrogance, loneliness, isolation, regional paranoia.

Ford sets the film's action, then, along the great divide of American racial consciousness and collision. In postwar Texas, Edwards searches for his niece, whose parents were murdered in a Commanche raid motivated by revenge following the murder of Commanches by whites. Over time, "tainted" by her sexual relations with Scar, a Commanche, the kidnapped child (Natalie Wood—the film's one piece of ineptitude) comes to draw her uncle's hatred, changing the complexion of his mission. At the last, with her, terrified, in his arms, the memory of his having held her in his arms years back restores a profound sense of family connection. But Edwards knows he has no place in the racially mixed U.S. future that she and his adopted nephew, Martin, represent. Dispossessed, although finally emptied of racist demons, Edwards must wander endlessly between the winds.

Ford astonishes with gorgeous seasonal imagery that ironically reflects on a cycle of madness in the American soul. Shot after shot appears to project a facet of Edwards's mental state: images that disclose the danger and desolation with which America is fraught—for the loneliness that connects Edwards with many other Americans isolates each of them.

Contributing to the film's ineffable sadness, its sense of monumental lament, is the haunting ballad that dominates Max Steiner's score, "The Searchers," by Stan Jones.

1956

THE SEVENTH SEAL (Sweden). *The Seventh Seal*, one of Ingmar Bergman's most powerful and spacious works, reflects on the first decade of the Cold War, the traumatized state of the world since the atomic bombings of Hiroshima and Nagasaki.

A knight has returned home from the Crusades. A shimmer of skeptical idealism is all that remains of Antonius Block's once strong religious faith. To what moral end have been these "holy wars"? The bubonic plague has struck, and the dying and panic-stricken litter roadways. Some, passive, defeated, accept the plague as divine judgment; others repent feverishly; still others seek psychic release in the scapegoating ritual of branding a child a witch and burning her. Everywhere, Block confronts a debacle whose enormity suggests the imminence of the Apocalypse.

Block challenges Death to a game of chess. He seeks reprieves for all members of his entourage, including a pair of wandering players, Jof and Mia (names derivative of Joseph and Mary), and the couple's infant son. He unsuccessfully probes his adversary for answers to eternal questions. Beaten in the contest, he returns to his castle. Death intrudes and claims everyone present.

Bergman achieves some of his greatest visual poetry—brooding, chilling, mysterious, barbaric. Lensed in fierce, haunting black and white, images express cosmic unfathomability. When Jof and Mia steal away at night in their wagon, for example, a very fine light blends earth and sky, the traveled-on ground and eternity, suggesting that such deliberate activity as the couple's flight is all the purpose and direction there is in the universe. As the wagon bumpily proceeds into darkness, its billowing cover eerily resembles a cloud entering the heavens, as if to suggest "eternal" images are composed of nothing but matter and man.

Max von Sydow's weary Antonius Block is one of cinema's greatest performances.

THE WRONG MAN (U.S.). Following eyewitness identifications, Christopher Emmanuel ("Manny") Balestrero (Henry Fonda, tremendous) is picked up by the police as an insurance office thief. The ordeal of his trying to prove his innocence, which the deaths of two alibi witnesses confounds, plunges wife Rose (Vera Miles, heartrending) into an abyss of psychotic guilt premised in the fear that her own financial demands triggered Manny's presumed crime. In *The Wrong Man*, Alfred Hitchcock once again is well understood as a Roman Catholic artist.

Frighteningly combining arrogance and stupidity, the police seize on every opportunity to disprove the latter but each time confirm it. The passage where Manny is booked, incarcerated and, after a long night, arraigned in court encompasses Hitchcock's most brilliant filmmaking. Almost pure pseudo-documentary, it is absolutely objective and, simultaneously, absolutely subjective—a profound revelation of Manny's shame, distress, fear. Throughout the film, Robert Burks's black-and-white cinematography blends documentary realism and dreamy *noir*ishness.

Beginning with a "chance" configuration of Manny a step ahead of, and visible between, two police officers on the street, the three-shot is a recurrent motif. It reaches its apotheosis in a psychiatrist's office: seated Rose, despondent, desk lamp, enormous from camera perspective, standing psychiatrist, face obscured by the lamp.

Finally, someone else is arrested for the crimes in question. There is a telling discrepancy between how much "the right man" is supposed to look like Manny and how little he actually does. Manny turns on him: "Do you know what you have done to my wife?" Ah! But there is as little reason to believe in this new man's guilt as there was to believe in Everyman Manny's guilt. The system, given its internal flaws, may have lighted upon another "wrong man."

Maxwell Anderson and Angus MacPhail wrote the terrific script.

THE RISING OF THE MOON (Ireland, U.S.). John Ford's *Rising of the Moon* opens with a sweeping shot of the Irish coast and ends heart-piercingly: in long-shot at night at the time of "the troubles," Sean Curran, having escaped a British hanging, leaves by moonlit boat, his standing silhouette facing Ireland rather than where the boat is headed, his soul forever to be haunted by the separation. Must I mention that Ford's first name is kin to Curran's?

Ford's film consists of three parts. The first, "The Majesty of the Law," derives from Frank O'Connor's story. A police inspector (Cyril Cusack, at 46 achingly young, and wonderful) arrests a close friend, allowing the old, poor, arthritic man the face-saving grace of reporting for imprisonment on his own. But should the arrest even have been made? In "1921," the film's final part, based on Lady Gregory's play *The Rising of the Moon*, a street officer permits Sean Curran's escape from the hands of the law despite the £500 reward being offered for his capture because his wife has stirred up in him a bit of revolutionary patriotism from their courting days long ago. As Sergeant Michael O'Hara, Denis O'Dea, who played the street singer twenty-one years earlier in Ford's *The Informer*, gives a beautiful performance.

The middle part is as intricately comical as anything by Jacques Tati. "A Minute's Wait" finds a train's departure repeatedly put on-hold for "a minute" that actually lasts a lot longer and into which momentous doings are crammed, including the forging of one marriage proposal and the cancellation by family of another romantic union. The shots of a mob either boarding or exiting the train for "a minute's wait" are gorgeously hectic, and the train's eventual departure haunts.

The cast comes from the Abbey Theatre Company.

THE NIGHTS OF CABIRIA (Italy). Federico Fellini's *La notti di Cabiria* is brilliantly acted by wife Giulietta Masina as the unselfpitying Roman prostitute Cabiria, whom they introduced in *The White Sheik* (1952). Cabiria tells co-workers she might not join them on a religious pilgrimage, but when a procession of singing pilgrims passes through the scene, moved by the example of their hopefulness, she follows.

Cabiria's path crosses that of a man who ministers to the poor who live in caves. At the time of the film's original release the Roman Catholic Church pressed for the deletion of this passage owing to the contrast it draws between the anonymous individual's mission and the nonsensical pilgrimage, a moneymaking operation exploiting people's hopes and fears, which brings participants to a pitch of hysteria in a packed, poorly ventilated church, and, as Cabiria herself points out afterwards, changes nothing and nobody. Fellini expresses outrage at the Church's exploitation of the poor and the sick. The stage hypnosis of Cabiria, which leaves her angry and humiliated, is a metaphor for the corrupt pilgrimage and the Church's manipulation of the masses.

Cabiria's fiancé steals her life's savings and abandons her. A high camera follows as she walks back, alone, through the dark woods. Suddenly young revelers playing musical instruments surround her—children who have thus crashed the barrier between artifice and reality, for the music we have been hearing on the soundtrack now has a visible, realistic origin. Weaving around her, the children are smiling; Cabiria also smiles, and for a quick instant finds us, anonymous humanity, by looking directly into the camera. We are complicit in her ambiguous fate. We have a job to do, and perhaps Cabiria will join us in this endeavor. The world is unjust, and people need our kindness and our help.

MAN ON THE TRACKS (Poland). Facilitated by the loosened Soviet grip on the Polish film industry resulting from Josef Stalin's death, Andrzej Munk's *Czlowiek na torze* is about Polish laborers. It begins with a man's death. A former railway conductor, Orzechowski (Kazimierz Opalinski, superb) haunts the local station post. He is run down on the tracks by the very train he used to engineer. How did this happen? Only one of two green lights showed, indicating—wrongly—safe passage for the train. Did Orzechowski remove one of the lights himself? If so, what was his motive? Was it political, because he was a member of the old guard? Was he nursing a grudge for having been discharged after decades of service?

Did he die attempting sabotage or committing suicide? A board of inquiry will determine the truth.

In 1950, a new program of railway efficiency has train engineers and crews competing to use as little coal as possible. However, older workers who resist the redefinition of their homeland as communistic must function under the deepest cloud of suspicion. Orzechowski, defiant, keeps burning coal generously. Younger workers have political memories that go no farther back than the German occupation; Orzechowski recalls another Poland. "Times have changed," stationmaster Tuszka tells him, trying to provoke Orzechowski's retirement. But Tuszka is also nursing a grudge. Years ago, Orzechowski reprimanded Tuszka for shoddy work.

The pitch darkness in which the black-and-white film begins, as the train inexorably proceeds until brakes are applied, is correlative to the mystery surrounding Orzechowski and his motives; the voluminous smoke anticipates the self-serving, murky testimony that those conducting the inquiry must navigate to arrive at the truth. Orzechowski, they find, sacrificed himself to protect fellow Poles. Boss, assistant; non-Communist, Communist; old, young: Munk instead stresses Polish identity under the political skin.

ALL THE MEMORY OF THE WORLD (France). "The [Bibliothèque Nationale de France] is a model memory, stockpiling everything printed in France." Alain Resnais's wondrous documentary, marred a bit by Maurice Jarre's jarring score, surveys France's national library, which Resnais depicts as a world inside the world, a prison for books. During the film's twenty-one minutes, voiceover narration indeed refers to the books as being "imprisoned" and as "prisoners." Library patrons, by taking out books and reading them, give them their freedom and in the process further liberate themselves. The opening comment that libraries are only necessary because humans have poor memories, coupled with the identification of books that are read with freedom as well as knowledge, surely refers to the recent publication of Ray Bradbury's novel *Fahrenheit 451* (1953).

But as a whole *Toute la mémoire du monde* relates in particular to Resnais's greatest documentary, *Nuit et brouillard* (*Night and Fog*, 1955), for which it provides an opposite image that nonetheless contains certain ironical links. The one-year-earlier short film, a postwar haunting of the Auschwitz death camp, is also about memory and also engages issues of confinement and release, and the card-cataloguing of books in the later film, the assignment of an identifying number to each book—no need to complete this sentence. But stark differences are also ironical. Whereas the Auschwitz film is in airy color, the Bibliothèque film is in oppressively underlit black-and-white; grass bends to a breeze at Auschwitz, while nothing visibly stirs at the library.

Memory in *Nuit et brouillard*, given official French assistance in transporting French Jews to their deaths, bears the burden of national shame; memory in Toute la mémoire du monde reflects richly earned national pride.

Indeed, human happiness is the destination, we are told, toward which the Bibliothèque is headed.

GERVAISE (France). From Émile Zola's novel *L'Assomoir*, *Gervaise* takes place in a nineteenth-century Parisian working-class neighborhood. Their gray, dilapidated, circumscribed existence makes inhabitants accomplices to one another's dreams, but also the jealous inhibitors and ambushers of these dreams. Disappointments deepen capacities to behave recklessly against oneself and others. Environment feeds disappointments, which in turn tighten the environment's grip on people's lives. Even when individuals seem most at the mercy of their foibles and failings, social environment is most decisive in determining behavior, however elusively.

Gervaise is a washerwoman whose lameness manifests as personal affliction this gripping environment. Her pride in her "handsome" lover, Lantier, overcompensates for her affliction and the restricted nature of her dream, to own her own laundry shop, which she pursues after Lantier abandons her and their two small sons. By this time she has married Henri Coupeau, a roofer whose drop one day to the pavement below breaks his spirit as well as a leg. Too proud to admit, post-recovery, his residual fear, that is to say, vulnerability, he drinks heavily and ends up stealing from Gervaise and demolishing her shop in an alcoholic rage. The closing shot is scaldingly ironic: Nana, their little daughter, seemingly carefree, heads into the neighborhood streets. Some say her future has been determined by her parents' past. It is more accurate to say that her future has been determined by the same environment that determined her parents' future.

René Clément has not made a "period film" per se; rather, inspired by Zola's naturalism and cinema's neorealism, he has made a fluent film that makes the past seem as though it were unfolding in the present. This is an exceptionally vivid, detailed film. Even so, its principal asset is Maria Schell's complex, devastating performance (best actress, Venice) as Gervaise.

FLOWING (Japan). Isuzu Yamada gives the performance of a lifetime as Otsuta (best actress, Kinema Junpo, Blue Ribbon, Mainichi Film Concours Awards), who runs a financially struggling, heavily in-debt geisha house in Tokyo as the custom fades into history, in Mikio Naruse's *Nagareru*, based on Aya Koda's novel. Yamada is highly particular, delicately nuanced, complex, forceful, sad and moving as Otsuta perseveres, becoming a figure of dramatic irony, like Garbo's searing Grusinskaya in *Grand Hotel* (Edmund Goulding, 1932), insofar as we know her fate when she does not.

Nearly as wonderful as Yamada, Kinuyo Tanaka, indeed a greater actress, plays Rika, who, mourning the loss of spouse and child, and fleeing the provincial strictures of her in-laws, becomes Otsuta's loyal maid. As such she is called Oharu—for us, Tanaka's greatest role (*The Life of Oharu*, Kenji Mizoguchi, 1952): beyond a postmodernist flourish, a distancing device by which Mika becomes the observant, caring outsider who flows in and (as Katsuyo anticipates) will flow out of Tsuta House, an embodiment of Japanese continuity.

Naruse begins and ends this beautiful film with shots of a flowing river, boats upon it, in long-shot, moving. Inside this narrative frame there is little movement, however; rather, static shots from a variety of camera positions accumulate into the suggestion of characters in a boxed-in domain, insulated from the tide of time working against them. Movement comes in dance: Otsuta's little granddaughter, practicing so that one day she can be a geisha; drunk, having just been jilted by her lover, a geisha brandishing bravado. And movement comes hauntingly: Tsuta House's former pet cat, on its own, walking a ledge at night.

Hideko Takamine plays Katsuyo, Otsuto's elder daughter, who practices using a sewing machine. One day she will have to support her mother and herself.

DIE HALBSTARKEN (West Germany). A distressing trend in Hollywood beginning in the 1950s with Nicholas Ray's worst, least interesting film, *Rebel Without a Cause* (1955), and reaching its apotheosis with *West Side Story* (Jerome Robbins, Robert Wise, 1961), grossly sentimentalized teenaged punks and antisocial youth. These films remain awash in whining self-pity, without any purpose apart from flattering its target audience: not juvenile delinquents, who were too busy committing crimes to go to the movies, but bourgeois aspirants to the label. It is difficult to process that the man who made such genuine films as *In a Lonely Place* (1950), *Johnny Guitar* (1954) and *Bigger Than Life* (1956) also made *Rebel Without a Cause*—although each of the worthy films by Ray here noted, and all of his others, including the remarkably sensitive *They Live by Night* (1947), admit mawkish accents.

Undoubtedly influenced by *Rebel*, *Die Halbstarken* (*The Half-Strong* perhaps?—a.k.a. *Teenage Wolfpack*), written by Will Tremper and beautifully directed by Georg Tressler, is different. It is hallucinatory though rivetingly real, totally unsentimental: a portrait of youth in stark black and white that captures their rudderlessness and recklessness in the absence of an authoritarian national figure such as Hitler, the blow to German patriarchy dealt by Germany's defeat in the war, and German preoccupation with pursuing the "Economic Miracle" that left West German youth in the streets on their bloody own. Like their elders, these kids go after money any way they can.

Tressler unerringly employs the atmospherics and techniques of *film noir* to suggest an American hand in guiding West German adolescent behavior and to suggest, for most of these youngsters, a comfort zone in the dead of night.

And Tremper and Tressler had a brilliant ace-in-the-hole besides: the ferocious performance that made Horst Buchholz, as gangleader Freddy, a star.

ON THE BOWERY (U.S.). There is a through-story in Lionel Rogosin's otherwise documentary *On the Bowery*, and its precise accumulation is like a first-rate short story by Ring Lardner or Ernest Hemingway. Ray drifts into New York's skid row, accompanied by his suitcase, which contains all his earthly possessions, including a pocket watch. Gorman, an older man, convinces Ray to part with clothes—the watch is off-limits—in order to pay for drinks for the both of them. When Ray passes out in the street, Gorman takes the suitcase, thus paying for himself a night in a flop-house rather than on the street. He sells the watch, giving Ray some of the proceeds, making up a story about the money's source.

Rogosin's tone is non-judgmental. In peerless black-and-white images, Rogosin captures the raucous, loose-ended lives of (mostly) men in Bowery bars, streets, a mission, a flop-house. The documentary and fictional elements seamlessly blend to create a penetrating series of observations—a piece of reportage anticipating *cinéma-vérité*, not to mention the documentary-styled fictions of John Cassavetes, who acknowledged Rogosin as his cinematic guide.

The richest aspect of this beautiful film is its embrace of down-on-its-luck humanity. In this, Rogosin may be indebted to John Huston, whose own earlier *The Asphalt Jungle* (1950) and later *Fat City* (1972) seem especially in tune with Rogosin's film.

1957

TOKYO TWILIGHT (Japan). Yasujiro Ozu's deeply affecting *Tokyo boshoku* illustrates the disintegration of family in postwar Japan. It makes explicit what is implicit in Ozu's exceptionally poignant *Late Spring* (1949), suggesting the bitter aftermath of the tenuously hopeful marriage with which the earlier film ends, and suggesting that the father's Prosperoic sacrifice there—his letting go of his daughter, who had been anchoring his life, into a life of her own—has turned up empty for them both. *Tokyo Twilight* joins *A Hen in the Wind* (1948) in being one of Ozu's bleakest works.

Shukichi Sugiyama's two daughters, college-age Akiko and older sister Takako, live with him. When Akiko was an infant, Shukichi's wife, Kisako, abandoned him and their children. Now Takako is conflicted for having left her spouse, an alcoholic brute, and her mother's reappearance in the neighborhood deepens her anguish. Father and daughters each lead a painfully lonely life.

This is a film of cold, wintry evenings; its dusky and darker grays are correlative to souls at loose ends, living lives they cannot take hold of. With Dreyer's *Vampyr* (1931), this is the grayest film ever made—*Vampyr*, light gray; *Tokyo Twilight*, dark.

Ozu's angled shots of a couple, backs to the camera, sitting side by side, generally intimate the couple's closeness and connectedness. Here, though, the couple aren't a comfortable pair of married folk. Akiko and her boyfriend, Kenji, sit on a pier, bound together by Akiko's news that she is pregnant, as fog and the moans of foghorns envelop them. Ozu cuts to a frontal view of the pair and cuts back and forth between them as they quarrel, now seemingly far apart. The couple disintegrates before our eyes.

Setsuko Hara, Ineko Arima, Chishu Ryu and Isuzu Yamada all give remarkable performances.

THRONE OF BLOOD (Japan). Akira Kurosawa's *Kumonosu jo* (*Spiderweb Castle*) transcribes *Macbeth* to medieval Japan.

The opening projects a sense of long-ago, by extension, timelessness; with formal rigor the camera's eye surveys mist-shrouded landscapes composing a wasteland and scans, downward, an ancient obelisk as a solemn, disembodied chorus chants the inscribed text warning against ambition. We feel we have entered the conclave of fundamental law.

In the forest's fog-drenched, convoluted maze, what can be clear or certain? There, two generals chance upon an otherworldly creature, an ancient, wraithlike spirit slowly, ceaselessly spinning silk—cobweb—at her wheel. In a voice so low it seems to emanate from earth, she announces that General Washizu will command, first, the insurgent's fort and, afterward, Lord Tsuzuki's castle.

Paradox: bold warrior, at home Washizu is a subservient mate. His battle prowess and military and political authority all enable him to hide from view his fear and trembling; he submits to wife Asaji's dominance and cynical, murderous promptings only because she points up those deceptive appearances of reality that imply the cosmic ambiguity that terrifies him and proposes such courses of action as might hold his fear in abeyance.

With tremulous bravado, Washizu rallies his troops. However, the forest, the opposing army's camouflage, appears to approach the castle on its own, its dark, billowing branches creating a magnificent sense of impending doom. Washizu's troops turn on him, savaging him with arrows, an awesomely protracted death, Washizu's eyes at the last bulging in animal horror at—*what?* The nothing that is?

Grave, powerful, eerily beautiful, *Kumonosu jo* depicts a world where humanity acts violently in hopes of stilling fear and distracting its eyes from impenetrable mists. Haunted by interminable echoes of slaughter, it is an ancient world—and the closer one of the Holocaust and Hiroshima.

WHITE NIGHTS (Italy). *Bellissima* proved to be Luchino Visconti's last Neorealist film. A purplish forbidden romance, *Senso* (1954), followed—a work of visual splendor that nonetheless leaves me cold. *White Nights*, based on the same Dostoievski story that Robert Bresson would film as *Four Nights of a Dreamer* (1971), was considered at the time a letdown. It remains one of my favorite Visconti films.

What Visconti described as "Neo-romanticism" resembles French poetic realism. But atmosphere, the correlative to European fatalism as Nazism threatened and devoured the continent in the real world, no longer is the repository of the film's urgency; this has shifted to Natalia and Mario (Maria Schell and Marcello Mastroianni, both tremendous), who meet on a canal bridge one night and begin to bond, on their date, the next night.

The romance is doomed from the start. Natalia haunts the bridge, awaiting the return of her lover, who failed to keep their rendezvous a year after his departure. Ironically, Natalia tries to duck her date with Mario in an unconscious replay of what her lover has done to her—an indication of how deeply her spirit remains embedded in the past with the man who has apparently ditched her. At first, Mario contests the unreality of Natalia's persistent hope for her lover's return but is then drawn into it, helping her compose a letter to him, just to keep her in his life. But Visconti's Marxist side lets us see another barrier between the two; Mario is a lowly clerk, while Natalia is a bourgeois whose family has devolved into genteel poverty.

Exquisite artificial sets, the painted sky, the voluminous darkness of Giuseppe Rotunno's superb black-and-white cinematography: all these shift reality to the young pair and to Natalia's oblivious joy when her lover returns at last, shattering Mario.

THE SEINE MEETS PARIS (France). After a decade spent making films in Eastern Europe, Joris Ivens went to Paris; *La Seine a rencontré Paris* won at Cannes. His East German *Song of the Rivers* (*Das Lied der Ströme*, 1954), with music by Shostakovich and lyrics by Brecht, composed a hymn to labor and international workers' solidarity along six rivers worldwide, to which the new film adds the Seine. "The Seine is a factory," Jacques Prévert's poetic commentary states; "the Seine is work." Much of the film is shot from measuredly paced river barges, and some of it indeed shows laboring humanity. But there is more than that. This river, runs the voiceover, "is a song from the headsprings. 'She has the voice of youth,' says a woman in love, smiling." This masterpiece conjoins French lyricism and Dutch sturdiness.

Silence, made all the more mesmerizing by Philippe Gérard's harpsichord music, explodes into sound: men at work excavating; a plethora of boys playing on a stack of logs; girls in a circle singing a song; the sights and sounds of traffic; the weight of a dog splashing into the river to retrieve a toy; a downpour of windy rain into the river (we see umbrella-ed souls in long-shot moving across an aqueduct), recalling Ivens and Mannus Frånken's great *Regen* (*Rain*, 1929).

Prévert's script: "A river like any other, and I'll be the first to lament her. And the Seine hears laughter and slips away like a cat." Images of and from the river accumulate an undertow of melancholy: three women walking together; against a tree, a girl asleep in her sleeping boyfriend's arms. A child's bicycle rises from the river, retrieved by a man wearing underwater goggles and an aqualung.

Prévert: "There once was the Seine. There once was life."

APARAJITO (India). The middle part of the Apu Trilogy begun with *Pather Panchali*, Satyajit Ray's *The Unvanquished* is a transitional work in which two different actors play Apu, one as a ten-year-old, the other as an adolescent. The family has relocated to Banaras, where pilgrims bathe in the Ganges, and Harihar, Apu's father, officiates as one of countless priests. Self-exile from his ancestral home following the death of his daughter signals Hari's defeat; he is farther than ever from his dream of becoming a writer, and his clock is set to borrowed time. Hari's death is marked by a rush of poetry: a burst of birds filling the sky. The fact that Apu at the time is bringing holy water from the Ganges to his dying father suggests the possibility that the course of Apu's life will be no better.

The financial struggles of the widowed Sarbojaya and her son, now drawn even closer by the deaths of daughter/sister Durga and their husband/father, ensue. Apu's paternal grandfather tries training the boy for the priesthood; is Apu's fate, then, set in stone? Perhaps not; Apu opts instead to go to school in Calcutta. Like his father, he has fallen in love with books. A scholarship helps, and Sarbojaya pays additional expenses by making sacrifices. Apu is drawn into life at the school and eventually must choose between attending his dying mother at home and taking final exams.

Aparajito is acute on the subject of the seductive force of education. However, its emotional centerpiece is the heartrending situation of Sarbojaya, whose separation from her cherished son while he is very far away contributes to her fatal illness. This heartache is in addition to the new gulf of learning between them. Karuna Banerjee's tremendous performance as Sarbojaya is almost intolerably moving.

THE HOUSE OF THE ANGEL (Argentina). Adapting her own novel, *La casa del ángel*, Beatriz Guido gave spouse Leopoldo Torre Nilsson an excellent script; but it is Nilsson's dark, precise, assured filmmaking that generated so memorably turbulent a result. The film also called *End of Innocence* sets 14-year-old Ana Castro's coming-of-age amidst the flux of Argentinean mores and manners in the 1920s. Ana (Elsa Daniel, the epitome of adolescent sensitivity and confusion—at once lyrical and achingly real) comes from an aristocratic family; her father is a scheming politician, her mother a puritanical Roman Catholic fixated on maintaining her youngest daughter's innocence. They live in a Wellesian/Amberson mansion that is beginning to decay; her ageing nanny, who sometimes fails to suit her behavior to Ana's mother's strict line, is principally charged with Ana's care. The back-to-back deaths of mother and nanny suggest a combinate loss for Ana—the loss of childhood.

Guido's intricate script meshes Ana's reminiscing voiceover and the events she recalls.

1957

Pablo Aguirre, a young, handsome colleague of her father's, shatters Ana's sheltered world. Drawn into a situation where he feels compelled to defend family honor, Pablo will fight a duel to the death, with pistols, on the Castros' grounds. At a dance in the mansion the night before his morning of reckoning, Pablo takes Ana into his arms—a phenomenal passage; afterwards, alone, Ana gazes into a mirror, attempting to search out signs of the utter transformation she feels. In truth, she has been infatuated with Pablo for quite a while.

The multiplicity of shots from a fractious variety of camera angles suggests memory's frustrated attempt to grasp an elusive, complex past.

An Argentinean of Swedish descent, Torre Nilsson creates haunting poetry as his camera, seeking light, roams the mansion's darkened rooms and halls.

LES MISTONS (France). Nice, France. Bernadette, about twenty, is the object of interest of a horde of schoolboys on summer holiday. The narrator, one of them grown up, explains, "She awoke in us the luminous springs of sensuality." The film opens on the open road as Bernadette, wearing a skirt, rides her bicycle towards a back-tracking camera.

Alas! Bernadette is "Gérardette"—with her fiancé, Gérard, half of an increasingly conjoined couple. The camera now withdraws to show Bernadette and Gérard riding bicycles side-by-side, holding hands, briefly letting go, holding hands again. The pair exacerbate the boys' sense of exclusion from something wonderful, mysterious: sexual experience; broadly, the adult world they ache to be part of.

A lateral tracking shot shows the boys, seated on the ground, smoking cigarettes: conformity in rebelliousness.

Gérard is young, muscular, sturdy. Looking at him, who would think about death? The schoolboys' attempts to torment the couple turn incredibly nasty when they send Bernadette a cruel postcard during Gérard's absence for a few-week bachelor excursion prior to his marrying her, the love of his life. Mountain-climbing, Gérard loses his footing, his life.

What do schoolboys know about death? We have seen them play shooting-death. One pretends to shoot another, who falls to the ground pretending to be dead. In homage to Jean Cocteau, the director of *Les mistons* (*The Brats*) applies reverse motion to the "fallen" child, restoring him to upright life, to express the schoolboys' innocence regarding death. François Truffaut's 17-minute film ends with Bernadette, widowed despite the wedding that never occurred, walking down a street towards the camera, which finally pans upwards to the sky. The narrator tells us this woman ceased to matter to him from that day forward—only, his reminiscence of her is haunted.

A lyrical, ironical black-and-white gem.

EROICA (Poland). Written by Jerzy Stefan Stawiński, directed by Andrzej Munk, *Heroism* consists of two parts. This external form—the yoking together of two World War II "short stories"—is correlative to the film's "split" attitude, its ambiguity and skepticism. Ultimately, Stawiński and Munk prick the concept of wartime heroism in order to deflate the whole idea of war.

The first part suggests Falstaff's "better part of valour." Gorkiewicz skips training for the Warsaw Uprising, the Polish resistance. But when a Hungarian officer engages him in wartime opportunism by employing him as a black marketeer selling armaments to Poles, Gorkiewicz becomes embroiled in the war, shaking off his indifference to his nation's fate. A comical figure, Gorkiewicz is Everyman. Ordered to carry an elderly woman's sack of belongings during the evacuation, he stumbles and falls under its weight. (Later he stumbles drunk fleeing a German assault and peeing—the stream of urine is a visual parody of the shooting and bombing!—behind a tree.) Gorkiewicz now engages the struggle, now tries escaping it. The "hero" is a coward is a hero, shirking responsibility yet affirming life amidst war's death and insanity. In a stunning shot, Gorkiewicz, barefooted by a stream, polishes off a bottle as a German tank slowly comes up behind him. The upshot, hilarious, leaves

Gorkiewicz shaking but intact.

The second part, grimmer, more sardonic, details life in a German P.O.W. camp. It might have been subtitled "Hell Is Other Polish Officers," as the close confinement takes its toll, redefining freedom and impelling one prisoner, Lieutenant Zawistowski, to escape. Or did he? Those left behind are united by his inspiring example. Reality or legend? Eventually we learn the truth, that the one good thing about the war experience shared by these comrades is a lie.

And so it goes.

IL GRIDO (Italy). Mechanic Aldo abandons lover Irma, taking their child, when she refuses to marry him upon news of her husband's death. Aldo drifts through gray industrial landscapes in northern Italy.

The Outcry's depiction of a man's life at loose ends finds Michelangelo Antonioni unhinging conventional narrative in order to invent a more flexible and poetic cinematic form stressing human behavior and the environmental factors contributing to it—Neorealist aims, but considerably less tied to the requirements of eighteenth- and nineteenth-century storytelling. Perhaps the melancholy landscapes may be too refined to counter with sufficient gusto the tyranny of plot (*L'avventura*, 1960, will complete the task); but the insinuative background of workers demonstrating against a proposed American airbase, not to mention the use of a poster advertising national integrity, doubles as a sly kick at the Hollywood way of pushing a plot line forward to connect a series of formulaic dots.

In retrospect, we see from whence Antonioni came; at the same time we grasp more fully at what his inspiration, Roberto Rossellini, was aiming with his composite portrait, in *Paisà* (1946), of a regionally varied national character. A brisk move away from traditional "plottedness," *Paisà*'s episodic nature reduces "story" by multiplying it—a method achieving especial grace and beauty in *Francesco, giullare di Dio* (1950), where the episodes are less like miniature stories or films, as in *Paisà*, and more like impressionistic brush strokes. Whereas *Paisà* resembles a completed jigsaw puzzle whose piece outlines remain discernible, *Francesco* is more than the sum of its parts, and a distinct whole that has thoroughly absorbed the pieces it comprises. This marks a formal departure from Neorealism that Antonioni, Rossellini's heir, brings to fruition even as his work keeps addressing contemporary themes and (for now) the lives of ordinary people.

ASCENSEUR POUR L'ECHAFAUD (France). "Julien, I looked everywhere for you." — Florence

In Louis Malle's electrifying, moody thriller *Elevator to the Gallows* (*Lift to the Scaffold*), Julien Tavernier commits murder. However, it is Tavernier's accomplice, the murder victim's wife and Tavernier's mistress, Florence (Jeanne Moreau, sensual, haunting, shattering), who is more likely to be guillotined as the criminal mastermind. The police captain predicts for the apprehended war hero ten years in prison.

Tavernier murders employer Simon Carala, a wealthy industrialist whose precise allegiance during the Occupation remains murky. Carala's last words: "You're not so foolish as to shoot. In war, yes, but not in more important things." His pointed response makes Tavernier morally shine by comparison: "Don't laugh at wars. You live off wars. . . . Indo-China; now Algeria. *Respect* wars; they're your family heirlooms."

Meanwhile, teenaged lovers Louis and Veronica steal Tavernier's car. Spotting the car and the passenger, Florence worries that Julien has betrayed her and run off with this younger companion. At a motel, Louis assumes Tavernier's identity (it goes with the car), pretending to have been a soldier, and ends up shooting dead two German tourists, using Julien's gun from the automobile's glove compartment. Determined to exonerate her missing lover of the motel double murder, Florence tracks down the kids. Alas, this exposes his murder of Simon Carala.

Thematically, Julien and "Julien," the real Tavernier and his impersonator, are precisely related. Too young to have fought in it, Louis now envies those like Julien who were able to prove themselves in the war in a nationally recognized way. In his unconscious, Louis imaginatively *becomes* a Second World Warrior by dispatching two Germans on French soil —with the real Julien's pistol, no less. Unifying the film, both Louis and Julien are homicidally directed in peacetime by the experience of war.

HE WHO MUST DIE (France). Connecticut-born Jules Dassin, blacklisted in the U.S., made his most powerful and personal film in France: *Celui qui doit mourir*, an adaptation of the novel *O Hristos Xanastavronetai—The Christ Recrucified*—by Greece's Nikos Kazantzakis. Formally, it resembles a Greek tragedy.

In 1921, the village of Lycovrissi is under Turkish control. Father Grigoris assigns roles to villagers for the annual Easter Passion Play. Manolios (Peter Van Eck, excellent), a shy, stammering shepherd, is chosen to play Jesus. "I'm not worthy," he protests.

Refugees—the film opens with a stark image of the burning of their village by invading Turks—swarm into Lycovrissi. They are dying of hunger; but, to generate sufficient fear so they will be locked out and sent on their way, Father Grigoris insists that contagious cholera afflicts them. Father Fotis leads the refugees; he beseeches Manolios to tell his people the truth, that hunger, not cholera, afflicts the refugees. Manolios counters that his stammer will disrupt and cancel whatever attempt he makes. Reminding him about Moses, whose stammer evaporated by the grace of God, Fotis tells Manolios: "[Y]ou won't stammer to your people because they need to hear you speak." Indeed, moved beyond measure, villagers make an instant collection of food and other items for the refugees; one villager even offers land. Alas, Grigoris draws battle lines, Manolios is arrested and, when he refuses to proclaim publicly his "error," he is beaten to death—inside the church. Forces approach to mow down with a thousand bullets refugees and their local supporters. Dassin's heart is in the way he ends the film. We are left with an image of fabulous courage—and the ironical certainty that if ever another Jesus should appear on Earth, he would be dealt the same fate as Jesus.

FORTY GUNS (U.S.). Shot in 1½ weeks, Samuel Fuller's anarchic black-and-white *Forty Guns* is one of the great American westerns. Set in and around 1881 Tombstone, Arizona, it revolves around complex, corrupt cattle rancher Jessica Drummond (Barbara Stanwyck, fierce, concentrated, brilliant), the landowning "lady with a whip," atop the throne of her white steed, leading an army of hired guns and headed for a fall to Earth, the resolution of her dark fairy-tale rule in the common clay of romance. What may seem like a tacked-on Hollywood ending is, in fact, the accurate reporting of Jessica Drummond's humdrum destiny in the American landscape: female subservience.

The gentleman who effects her, um, "emasculation" is irrelevant; he is one of three brothers precisely to suggest his irrelevancy as individual. Pointedly, he is played by a nondescript actor—one of those tortured fifties movie presences who possessed some vague, tenuous facsimile of minor stardom.

Fuller's film is famous for a stunning set-piece: an outdoor wedding ceremony that, interrupted by violence, with a collapse of time seamlessly turns into a funeral. This, the film's vortex, sums up the volatility of Fuller's America, much as the film's other major set-piece, a terrific windstorm, sums up his view of Nature's volatility, which helps form and inspirits human violence. The film suggests Drummond's connection to both, although she is unwomanned by each.

Making no sense, the central love story is a revelation of human absurdity, at least in part because of the causal connection between the American mindset's determination not to give Nature her due and its penchant for violence. Whatever its myth, American reality is a kind of madness.

Forty Guns is a fractured, half-baked piece of work, a near masterpiece, as stubborn as a tight knot yet as widescreen-elegant as something by Luchino Visconti.

1958

NAZARÍN (Mexico). Luis Buñuel's finest Mexican film of the 1950s is *Nazarín*, from the novel by Benito Pérez Galdós. A priest pursues the way of Jesus in Porfirio Díaz's Mexico.

Father Nazario, who lives amongst the poor, is pure of heart. He charitably gives away whatever is charitably given him. He is matter-of-fact about being repeatedly robbed. "The blessed one," as his landlady sarcastically calls him, is defrocked once he protects a wanted prostitute. When he works for bread as part of a road labor crew, his fellow workers, needing to be paid, oust him. The prostitute becomes his disciple, touting his ability to perform "miracles" even as he insists only "God and science" can save the life of a dying child.

Nazarín is a road film by foot. The pride Don Nazario takes in his humility and devotion is matched by the pride in arrogance the collusion of Church and State manifests. No matter how righteously Don Nazario's "saintly" virtue sets him apart, there is no "him" separate from the institutional influences his faith and lifestyle humbly contest. Social behavior, even the most solitudinous and outstanding, hence seemingly individualistic, is overdetermined. Like Fellini in *La strada* (1954), Buñuel challenges the fiction of self-determination. Beings must reach out to fellow and sister beings with compassion and equality—neither lowly nor in condescension—in order to be human.

The film is superbly written by Buñuel and Julio Alejandro, and shot after shot sets Don Nazario in a harsh landscape that is correlative to both his unconscious courting of martyrdom and the difficult road he needs to hoe in his pilgrim's progress. For now, he appears human only by contrast to the corrupt Church and Mexico's resident dictatorship, which conspire to maintain the poverty generating the miserable souls to whom Nazario ministers.

TOUCH OF EVIL (U.S.). When during a murder investigation in a U.S.-Mexican border town the "Anglo" police captain complains how tough his job is, a Mexican narcotics officer shoots back, "A policeman's work is only easy in a *police state*." Despite the misplaced modifier, this is one of the most compelling utterances in American cinema.

In *Touch of Evil*, his brilliant *film noir*, Orson Welles plays Captain Hank Quinlan, a corrupt detective with more than a "touch of evil." The title can refer also to Mike Vargas, the narcotics officer and "hero," who, in order to snare Quinlan, sinks to the level of his quarry.

Quinlan has framed a Mexican hoodlum for murder. Welles's outrage is such that even the actual guilt of the accused sharpens rather than blunts his civil libertarian point; and, when Vargas finally is reduced to secretly tape recording Quinlan's unwitting confession, Welles completes his argument that corruption corrupts. Vargas has been somewhat Quinlanized.

Quinlan's ethnic bigotry is matched by Vargas's class bigotry, which blinds him to the fact that, up from the ranks, Quinlan can hardly like being referred to as a la-de-da "policeman"—and, at that, by a nattily dressed representative of the Mexican government's elite. Welles, then, divides our sympathies, mixes things up. The morally clouded world in which both men function taints the whole idea of "justice."

Quinlan has already committed murder and framed a drugged patsy, Vargas's kidnapped bride, in order to discredit her spouse. It is the film's most riveting passage: tilted, clipped shots, some in swollen closeup; outside, neon flashing; a dead-dark, seedy hotel room disintegrating into waking nightmare: America, distorted—deranged—at reality's edge.

Helping to ensure its domestic commercial failure, Universal-International dumped the film on the market with scant publicity—another "touch of evil."

EQUINOX FLOWER (Japan). Yasujiro Ozu's first film in color again mines generational difference and conflict. At a wedding reception, businessman Wataru Hirayama notes the shift from arranged marriages to love matches. He approves, but at the same time Wataru deeply loves Kiyoko, his wife, who is present; how can he completely turn his back on the old ways that gave him a marriage that has been the principal blessing of his life, including its fruit, his daughters? Moreover, hasn't postwar culture also wobbled his sense of authority, hence, being? When a friend confides that his daughter is now living with a man without benefit of marriage, Wataru's confidence in the present is further eroded. He thus arranges a marriage for his elder daughter, Setsuko. Stubbornly, Wataru rejects the suitor of her choice, Masahiko Taniguchi, her co-worker, after the boy respectfully asks him for Setsuko's hand in marriage. Father and daughter become estranged as a result, and Kiyoko presses for their reconciliation.

Higanbana refuses to reduce its material to a study of hypocrisy; each character, including Wataru, is presented fully, as someone coping with contradictory, deep feelings. Unlike Akira Kurosawa in even his greatest film, *Ikiru* (1952), Ozu refuses to clobber one generation with another.

Perhaps the elegiac film achieves its most exquisite poignancy in the passage in a park. Amidst beauteous Nature (Ozu's cinematographer, Yuuharu Atsuta, contributes phenomenally throughout, even in interiors), the Hirayamas reminisce. Kiyoko speaks of wartime; she hated the war, but now, looking back, recalls how much closer people felt when the possibility existed that Allied bombing would cause them to die together. *Higanbana* is the rare film to analyze nostalgia rather than exploit it.

Higanbana is brilliantly acted: Shin Saburi as Wataru; Kinuyo Tanaka, Kiyoko; Ineko Arima, Setsuko; Keiji Sada, Masahiko; Chishu Ryu, Wataru's friend, Shukichi.

ENJO (Japan). Based on Yukio Mishima's 1956 novel *Kinkakuji* (*The Temple of the Golden Pavilion*), *Enjo* (a.k.a. *Conflagration* and *Flame of Torment*) unfolds as the unimpeded flashback of a stuttering boy, Goichi Mizoguchi, who has been apprehended by police for burning down Kyoto's 14th-century Soenji Temple, where he had apprenticed to the head priest, Tayama, after the death of his father, a provincial monk who revered the building. Tayama had seemed to the boy as pure as the temple itself; after a series of disillusionments regarding the temple either directly or symbolically (although the structure had eluded Allied bombing, U.S. occupiers defiled it by using it as an ad hoc brothel; the Japanese themselves commercialized it later on), Goichi learns that his mentor has a mistress and commits his irrevocable criminal act. If the temple proved too pure an ideal to exist in so tarnished a world, neither can Goichi sustain his own youthful idealism. Goichi commits suicide.

Something is rotten in the state of Japan; Goichi's arson assaults the betrayal of Japanese fathers and traditions. The boy bears his father's mark: the stutter, according to Goichi's narration in the book, that "placed an obstacle between [him] and the outside world." His father's death, then, has strengthened, not diluted, the filial bond. But his feelings are even more complex than this suggests, for the beauty of the temple makes Goichi feel that his own existence "was a thing estranged from beauty" (Mishima). Japan's betrayed past—its betrayed fathers—now taunts the youth, also contributing to his destruction of the Buddhist temple.

In the film, the temple isn't much to look at; this underscores its subjective beauty for Goichi. The whole drama is a thing of his mind. Ichikawa's austere, precise, analytical images are among the most beautiful in cinema.

AJAANTRIK (India). A dilapidated Chevrolet jalopy obsesses Bimal. The taxi driver has named it Raggadal. This work vehicle barely works, continually breaks down, requiring Bimal's constant mechanical attention and the reordering of expensive parts when Bimal's boss would prefer that the nearly forty-year-old car be put out to pasture. Because of Raggadal, Bimal is the village laughingstock. When a passenger complains that Raggadal "croaks," he and his companion get tossed out.

Raggadal *does* croak—and groan, and make all sorts of metallic sounds that are first comically and later pitifully exaggerated on the soundtrack. Bimal is continually talking to it, as though Raggadal were a cherished pet. Raggadal may be a symbol of technology that the times have passed by, a symbol therefore of the transience of successive technologies, but it is Bimal's lonely means of accessing some point in the lives of his fleeting passengers and an anxious attempt at a bulwark against his own transience.

Ritwik Ghatak's Bengal film *Ajaantrik* (a.k.a. *The Unmechanical* and *Pathetic Fallacy*), in black and white both stark and fluent, begins as a raucous comedy and slides into tragedy as we become increasingly aware of Bimal's unhinging soul. Comical obstinacy yields to the delusion that the past can be held onto.

Ghatak employs an artillery of visual techniques to accompany his stream of sound effects. Raggadal's headlights seem droopy eyes. In one shot the interior of the cab goes rapidly in and out of focus to suggest Raggadal's labored breath! In a winding shot giving Raggadal and Bimal's point of view on mountainous road, the same shot slides into objectivity when Raggadal itself, with Bimal, ends up coming toward the camera—a shattering glimpse of Bimal's dissociation.

Raggadal ends up scrap, with Bimal ambiguously smiling; on the ground, a toddler—the future—toots Raggadal's horn.

A DEADLY INVENTION (Czechoslovakia). John Huston and color cinematographer Oswald Morris had given their film of Herman Melville's *Moby-Dick* (1956) the look of old whaling prints; perhaps inspired by this example, Czechoslovakia's Karel Zeman and his black-and-white cinematographer, Jiří Tarantik, gave *Vynález zkázy*, their film version of Jules Verne's 1896 *Face au drapeau* (*Facing the Flag*), the appearance of the woodcut illustrations that accompanied the original publications of this and other fantastical fictions by Verne, which they set into motion. Zeman's intermittently brilliant film draws on other works by Verne as well: *Clipper of the Clouds*, *Master of the World*, *Mysterious Island*, *20,000 Leagues Under the Sea*. It was released in the U.S., English-dubbed, as *The Fabulous World of Jules Verne*.

Science and technology "toss aside outmoded ways of life." Among the futuristic sights in the film's opening late nineteenth-century setting is an aircraft being peddled by a lone gentleman! (Later, submerged, men unboard a submarine on individually peddled "missiles.") Professor Thomas Roche is investigating "pure matter," which will be used by villainous pirate Count Artigas, who kidnaps Roche and assistant Simon Hart, for the invention of a weapon of mass destruction. Reflecting on the superpower nuclear arms race of his own day, Zeman steers the film's course toward a pacifist message.

What sights Zeman conjures! For instance, there is a nighttime storm at sea: exploding waves of white amidst deep darkness. Much of the film combines live-action and both painted backdrops and charming animation: fish appear swimming by a submarine portal. The operation of the submarine reminds one a bit of the factory in Fritz Lang's *Metropolis* (1926). A gigantic white jellyfish provides a haunting touch to one scene; a sky full of flapping, chattering birds to another. In a projected film-within-the-film, men ride camels-on-roller skates!

TWO MEN IN MANHATTAN (France). Written and directed by Jean-Pierre Melville, who also took the lead role of a sanctimonious journalist, *Deux hommes dans Manhattan* is a procedural. Two men, journalist Moreau and photographer Delmas, investigate the disappearance of France's ambassador to the U.N. Their nocturnal search takes them throughout the electric city and into "darkest Brooklyn"—a reference that always cracks me up. *Two Men* looks back to a number of films, including two *noirs* by Jules Dassin, *The Naked City* (1948) and the London-set *Night and the City* (1950), and with its complex tone —a mix of journalistic objectivity, spooky mystery skirting luridness, macabre comedy—and tortured lonely lives, it looks ahead to Alfred Hitchcock's *Psycho* (1960).

It turns out that a heart attack killed the French diplomat in his mistress's apartment. His daughter shadows the investigative pair while her mother, the one most in the dark, waits for some word from her spouse. For her, it's another one of those nights.

The dead man had been a true hero of the Resistance. A quarrel ensues as to how to treat the "story"—sensationally, which will mean big bucks, or tactfully, which is to say, deceptively. Melville knows his *Fort Apache* (John Ford, 1948); Moreau and Moreau's boss insist on "printing the legend." Delmas, a cynic and the one struggling hardest to make a living, is slower to come around.

At one level, the two men are warring aspects of a similar job description; at another, they are both differently wrong. One adheres to the past; the other must cope with the present.

Widely regarded as one of his failures, even by Melville, this is actually one of his most brilliant, most moving works—and the black-and-white cinematography, by Nicolas Hayer and Melville himself, is peerless.

VERTIGO (U.S.). *Vertigo* is an hypnotic, richly colored dream of mirrored reflections, and of long passageways promising, just ahead, some flash of revelation and yearning's end. Steeped in Alfred Hitchcock's Roman Catholicism and, therefore, ideas of guilt, Original Sin, and ideal womanhood, *Vertigo*—on one level a psychological travelogue—follows the course of a man's obsession with a beautiful woman who (he believes) dies as a consequence of his weaknesses: acrophobia and the vertigo it induces; his inability as a rationalist police detective to grasp the mystery she is a part of, which is far more complicated than the murder-deception plot that she is also a part of, which he *does* unravel. When Scottie Ferguson (James Stewart, powerful) tries to make over (he believes) another woman into the image of his lost love, we confront Everyman's dream of attaining his ideal, whatever the cost. The object of Scottie's "second chance" risks exposure while hoping that Scottie will love her for herself rather than as a rekindled memory of who she once pretended to be. Still another woman loves Scottie; her "motherliness"—a threat because of the sexual confusion it engenders—has assisted in creating the platonic nature of their association, at a cost of great pain to her to which the Everyman-detective remains oblivious.

This darkly enchanted film leads to a redwood forest—most of the film's action unfolds in and near San Francisco—where trees loom as the material realities in which the detective is determined to believe and also as the mysteries of time that play a fatal role in his love life. The film ends with him, as it were, stranded on the ledge of a bell tower after his second beloved, exposed as the first, has fallen again to her death, now for the last time.

THE MUSIC ROOM (India). As credits roll, the opening shot of *Jalsaghar*, Satyajit Ray's study of fading Bengal aristocracy, social self-delusion, and pride, mesmerizes. In a pitch-dark room, only a heavy, ornate, grandiose chandelier is visible. The thing sways, like an erratic pendulum. The camera approaches gradually, until the gleaming fixture fills the screen. A dissolve replaces the image with a tight closeup of the pudgy face of a man, landlord Biswambhar Roy, from which the camera slightly withdraws. He is seated on his terrace. The blankness of his expression suggests eyes that have turned inward—not in contemplation, but nostalgia: Roy gluts on memories of wealth and position.

Roy's lands are being eroded by the river they embank. It is the late 1920s or early 1930s, and Roy is last in the line of feudal landlords that flourished in the previous century. In defiance of his reduced, indeed untenable, existence, Roy throws lavish parties—recitals in his jalsaghar, that is, music room. Much of the film is a flashback demonstrating his addiction to these ostentatious presentations that, indirectly, cost him the lives of wife and son. Despite his resolution to discontinue the events as a result, he takes them up again, both to take up where he left off and to fill the void of his loneliness.

Ray's film, highly analytical, takes up the collision of native and British colonial influences in modern India. A neighbor, a usurer, is insulted to Roy's detriment when Roy declines his invitation to a social event. Roy disdains the new order in which the neighbor participates and shuns the genuine wealth of this rival in order to cling to the delusion of his own continuing status. But the poetry of the film is what matters most: a spider that Roy sees crawling down his portrait.

ASHES AND DIAMONDS (Poland). What critics anointed as such, he has said, Andrzej Wajda never intended: the "war trilogy." Indeed, Wajda's next film after completing the trio of films—*A Generation* (*Pokolenie*, 1954), *Kanal* (1957), *Popiól i diament*—returned to the topic of World War II, albeit in color rather than black and white. This was *Lotna* (1959), whose hallucinatory atmosphere generates a sense of defeat and despair, over Poland's military backwardness, encroaching upon tenuous hope. *Lotna*'s centerpiece is a brilliant tracking shot that presents an almost surreal panorama of war's carnage and horror: the survey of a battlefield on which killed horses and killed cavalrymen lie bloodily equal. The inexorably slow pace of the camera evokes a seemingly endless stretch of slaughter. Nevertheless, *Popiól i diament* is the prize of the quartet.

Written by Jerzy Andrzejewski and Wajda from the former's novel, this film catches Poland at the very moment that fate cancels reprieve. On the day that war with Germany ends, two partisans, underground assassins, target the Communist district secretary, who represents the nation's new order of political woes. Prior to executing their mission, Maciek, the younger assassin, endures a long, dark night of the soul, during which, for once a bit lost, he questions the whole idea of Pole killing Pole. He also experiences fleeting romance. Soon after the assassination the next day, the boy himself is shot and dies an agonizing animal death amidst war's rubble.

The film's centerpiece is the tremendous acting by Zbigniew Cybulski as Maciek Chelmicki, which ensures the film's heart-piercing humanity. Adam Pawlikowski is likewise brilliant as Maciek's seasoned companion. Romantic, passionate, and grounded in Cybulski's legendary performance behind dark eyeglasses, *Ashes and Diamonds* is also famous for its stormy imagery and compelling symbolism—for instance, the upside-down Christ in a bombed-out church.

THE COUSINS (France). *Les cousins,* Claude Chabrol's second feature, co-written by Paul Gégauff, revolves around two college boys: naïve, plodding Charles from the provinces and cousin Paul (Jean-Claude Brialy, excellent), in whose Paris apartment Charles stays while attending school. Paul is insensitive and obnoxious; Charles, blind to his faults, idolizes him. But the *mise-en-scène*—relics of the jungle and the battlefield adorn the walls of Paul's apartment—hints at something restless, chaotic in Paul. This boy may not be what he appears to be. On the other hand, Charles seems transparent.

We glean that Paul is as much enamored of Charles as Charles is of him ("Oh, the famous cousin!" someone says upon meeting Charles), but he does a poor job of protecting him, even stealing Florence, the very girl for whom, he knows, Charles has fallen. Paul further exasperates his cousin by throwing a noisy party upon completion of his crucial final exam although Charles still has to take his the next day. (Charles, of course, plays the martyr by not studying elsewhere.) Unlike Paul, Charles fails, canceling his professional future.

Play-shooting at Charles with a pistol one chamber of which, he does not know, Charles has loaded for an earlier "play"-shoot at *him* while he slept, City Cousin kills Country Cousin. The whole world that Paul has staged in order to bolster a fragile ego explodes with the discharge of the bullet; Charles's body takes agonizingly long to drop, as though the suspension for both boys is disclosing their shared fate. The doorbell rings; cold reality is about to make a house call.

Set between the Indochina and Algerian wars (the latter probably erupted during the shoot), Chabrol's tart, brilliant film addresses France's gun-mania and military mystique, including Paul's inherited fascistic residue. And life's ambiguities—interminable; here, terminal.

BLIND DATE (UK). Trite, unrealistic, contrived: this is how Joseph Losey described the story of his film *Blind Date* (*Chance Meeting* in the States), adding that as a consequence he felt it necessary "that we give it as much interest in terms of observation and reality as we could, and that the characters be very rich." Losey succeeded, and the result is one of cinema's three or four most absorbing, most brilliant detective mysteries—one whose core element is not the identity of the killer but, instead, why the case so thoroughly baffles Scotland Yard Inspector Morgan. Beyond a whodunit, we have here a why-can't-he-solve-it.

As Jan, Hardy Krüger is wonderful, especially in his combustible working-class defensiveness; Jan is a precursor of the British Angry Young Man, except that he is a Dutch immigrant. The grandson and son of coal miners, he is a struggling painter who works in an art gallery. He becomes the prime suspect in the murder of his mistress, elegant Jacqueline Cousteau, but because we arrive on the crime scene in advance of the police, in tandem with Jan, we know that the boy has been set up. But by whom? Inspector Morgan wants to believe Jan but curiously finds his mind blocked from considering alternate suspects. He is Welsh; he is played by a Welsh actor, Stanley Baker, and the name of Morgan, given our recollection of the Morgans in *How Green Was My Valley*, both Richard Llewelyn's and John Ford's, teases us to consider the possibility that the inspector's ancestry also includes miners. Once he has undimmed his own working-class consciousness, Inspector Morgan solves the case.

Throughout, class-driven slights are gratuitously dispensed, not only with Jan as their target, but also Morgan.

What a fascinating film—by U.S.-born Losey, blacklisted at home, British immigrant.

THE USUAL UNIDENTIFIED THIEVES (Italy). When I was thirteen, my parents, Uncle Joe, Aunt Estelle and I wept with nearly nonstop laughter through a television viewing of Mario Monicelli's *I Soliti ignoti*, a.k.a. *The Big Deal on Madonna Street*. Uncle Joe, who was born in Italy, loved Italian films—even those whose politics and social mores were far more liberal than his own. But who doesn't love this heist spoof, a riotous send-up of Jules Dassin's somber *Rififi* (1955)?

Thieves begins with an attempted car theft in the wee hours. The horn gets stuck in its sounding mode. As the thief tries to vacate the scene, his coat gets caught in the door. Cut to prison, to what will become a visual refrain: a chain of incarcerated men in a military quick-step. Thief to lawyer: "I've got to get out right away. I have a job to pull that will get me sent up for life!" Solution: someone has to be hired to confess to the crime and take the thief's place. But it must be a first-time offender so he gets only six months. Does anyone know such an innocent?

Peppe, an inept boxer, gets into prison all right, but somehow the actual criminal isn't let out—and poor Peppe is sentenced to three years! Frustrated, the thief shares with Peppe the big job he has planned. Now in the know, Peppe tells the fellow the truth: he got a one-year suspended sentence. Released, Peppe recruits his buddies for the perfect, easy crime. But what bumblers they all turn out to be!

The splendid script is by Monicelli, Suso Cecchi d'Amico, and the team of Agenore Incrocci and Furio Scarpelli. And the cast is to die for: Vittorio Gassman, Marcello Mastroianni, Renato Salvatori, a luscious teenaged Claudia Cardinale, and Totò.

SUN SEEKERS (East Germany, U.S.S.R.). *Sun Seekers* didn't see the light of day for more than a dozen years after the Soviet Union suppressed it, ostensibly to keep details of uranium mining for its nuclear industry from the West.

The protagonist is 18-year-old Lotte Lutz, whose barroom misbehavior gets her and a prostitute-friend impressed into being forced labor at Wismut mines in Felsach—the peacetime equivalent of being sent to the battlefront. Indeed, memories of World War II hang over the 1950 mining community as socialists and former SS members mix. It's dark as a dungeon way down in the mine, and the film's overelaborated script, by Karl-Georg Egel and

Paul Wiens, presents numerous metaphorical instances of people being bereft of light. For instance, the Soviet engineer directing Wismut, one of three men who fall in love with "Lutz," is a widower, whose wife, a painter, murdered by the German army, was always "searching for the light."

Her youthfulness offers men hope of renewal, but her more or less imprisoned life, not to mention the fact that she lost both parents in the war, casts Lutz adrift in drudgery. Although she becomes pregnant by a young German miner, she marries instead the older pit boss, a former German army officer. Lutz, then, is herself tied to the past, although her husband conveniently becomes a casualty of a mine disaster, leaving her happily independent, holding Germany's socialist future in her arms.

Konrad Wolf's direction of the camera is dynamic and intricate, full of eclectic camera angles and movements, including sudden instances of subjective (point-of-view) shots, such as a seemingly freefalling descent into the mine. By contrast, many scenes in the mine are static, claustrophobic. Visually, Wolf suggests both a world of socialist possibilities and the "buried" past these must persist in overcoming.

1959

PICKPOCKET (France). Burdened by his history, a young pickpocket approaches us in voiceover in Robert Bresson's electrifying *Pickpocket*. Michel is poor, this, the principal reason for his stealing until the thievery becomes addictive, compulsive, thereby becoming its *own* motivation. Bresson does not reduce Michel's humanity by categorizing him as a criminal. Instead, the hinted connection between Michel and the lieutenant who escapes the Gestapo in Bresson's *A Man Escaped* (1956), both being in a constant state of anxiety, imparts to the pickpocket some of the Resistance fighter's heroic humanity. This largeness of spirit gives Bresson's film a religious aura, that and, on the soundtrack, the outbursts of quasi-religious music that either strengthen or tweak its religious identity. *You* choose.

On the other hand, though, Bresson *shows* dehumanization. At the racetrack, in the police station or the Metro, closeups focus on money and its movement from one hand to another, or from one place (such as a pocket or pocketbook) to another (such as a hand)—money taking precedence over humanity and directing the course of people's lives. Rock-bottoming out, however, Michel may be ultimately guided to his redemption by fellow humans or God's invisible hand.

Bresson emphasized pertinent elements once the resemblance between *Pickpocket* and *Crime and Punishment* struck.

Each shot is concise, passionate, radiant, and the dialogue is so minimal, elliptical, even cryptic, that we must invest ourselves imaginatively to bring a clear, continuous sense to the film. In the absence of much talk, we hear things wonderfully: footsteps; doors opening and closing; automobiles—all the sounds that Bresson has included and emphasized, translating each, along with each black-and-white image, into its essence. As ever, Bresson refreshes our sense of material life, which too often otherwise falls into jadedness and complacency by becoming detached from our sense of spirit.

A BOUT DE SOUFFLE (France). *See above.*

THE WORLD OF APU (India). *Apur Sansar*, the conclusion of Satyajit Ray's monumental Apu trilogy, from the novel *Pather Panchali* by Bibhutti-bhusan Badapaddhay, is cousin to Italian neorealism. The small boy from the impoverished rural family in the first part, *Pather Panchali* (1955), who went to school in Calcutta in the second part, *Aparajito* (1957), has now graduated from university and struggles to find work. In the meantime, he writes an autobiographical novel. He marries, but Aparna, his wife, dies in childbirth, estranging Apu from their son, Kajole, whom he abandons, and himself. The odyssey culminating in their reunion is the film's emotional crux.

Apu's reintegration comes after a great moment of loss and of moving on: from a hilltop, Apu, palms suppliant, lets loose—in a sense, sacrifices—the manuscript he has long labored on, which, given Aparna's death, has become a record of endless grief. When he reunites with his son, he gives the boy a toy train. Passing trains—memory's baggage—insinuate continuity throughout the trilogy; but it is a trail of loss, inaugurated by the childhood death of Durga, Apu's older sister, and (following the deaths of both parents) compounded by the death of his bride—a continuity that, the closing shots imply, Apu's reunion with Kajole, an image of his lost self, will reconcile him to and redeem. After Apu's failed attempts to win the boy over, the sight of Kajole at home on his father's shoulders overwhelms. But the trilogy is as circular as it is linear, with the first part as haunted by the future as the last part is haunted by the past. Still, the trilogy is open-ended. Where will the road of life lead that father and son end up on?

As Apu, Soumitra Chatterjee gives an eloquent, powerful performance.

THE 400 BLOWS (France). François Truffaut's *The 400 Blows* has drawn a measure of affection perhaps equalled only by *The Wizard of Oz* (Victor Fleming, King Vidor, 1939) and *La strada* (Federico Fellini, 1954). Some rainy days the head says Bresson but we pop *The 400 Blows* into the DVD player instead. Some of us grew up with this film and don't know where Antoine Doinel ends and ourselves begin.

Antoine, Truffaut's alter ego, is, of course, the world's most famous schoolboy. Priceless scenes take place in the classroom, reveling in the lively pupils' dear, quirky behavior. Truffaut once said the only reason to make films with children is to express your love for children. Few films are so full of love as *Les quatre cents coups*—this, despite the fact that it perfectly blends objective realism and personal commitment.

Here, Paris, the City of Lights, the City of Love, is also the City of Adolescence, rendered in gorgeous black and white by cinematographer Henri Decaë. A liberated use of camera is one of the hallmarks of the *nouvelle vague*. Like Jean Vigo's *Zéro de conduite* (1933), Truffaut's film is an anthem of freedom.

Antoine's troubled home life leads to his delinquency. His mother and stepfather have him put into a reformatory. Antoine's escape is unforgettable: the stirring, aching tracking shot of his flight through the countryside, resolved in the single most celebrated shot in all of cinema: at shore, a startling freeze frame of the boy, who, with no place to run, blindly faces us—we (frozen, too) who cannot reach him to comfort him.

Fourteen-year-old Jean-Pierre Léaud's monumental, heart-piercing performance as Antoine, is, along with Chaplin's in *City Lights* (1931), perhaps cinema's most cherished. And dear Jean-Pierre is still acting, confounding late '80s reports he had passed on.

RIO BRAVO (U.S.). Texas sheriff John T. Chance (John Wayne, gracious, wonderfully complex) stands against wealth, power, inhumanity, embodied by land baron Nathan Burdette, who wants to spring from jail his brother, who is being held for murder, and who terrorizes the town. Chance turns down help from townfolk, to spare them reprisals from Burdette, and confronts Burdette and his swarm of hired guns with three allies: his two deputies, alcoholic Dude and old, crippled Stumpy (Walter Brennan, brilliantly funny), and a teenaged fast gun, Colorado.

Howard Hawks's greatest western was a response to scenarist Carl Foreman's *High Noon* (Fred Zinnemann, 1952), in which Marshal Kane begs townfolk for deputies to assist him in standing up against a killer just out of prison. After every adult man turns him down, Kane faces Frank Miller and his men alone—except for his Quaker wife, who violates her religious principles by shooting Miller in the back. Kane may be described as a whining hero; Chance, as a man doing his job—and someone, however anxious, more at ease with himself than Kane.

The film begins with a nearly silent prologue that establishes two things: the plot (we witness the barroom murder); the relationship between Chance and Dude. Whereas *High Noon*'s characters are thinly conceived, those in *Rio Bravo* are richly human. Kane is fully formed, if along conventional lines; but Chance is still learning about life—as we see from his romance with Feathers, a younger gal with a past and, it turns out, an unwarranted bad reputation, and his exchanges with Carlos (Pedro Gonzales-Gonzales, marvelous), the town's Mexican-American hotel proprietor.

Chance and Dude's nighttime walks, to ensure the town's peace and safety, occasion passages of the utmost suspense and visual beauty—and a sense of pressing professional obligation: Hawks's American faith.

FIRES ON THE PLAIN (Japan). No film has distilled more hauntingly the sadness of war than Kon Ichikawa's *Burmese Harp* (1956). With *Nobi*, Ichikawa turned instead to war's savagery and cruelty.

It begins with a slap in the face—in closeup. The face belongs to Private Tamura, in the Philippines in 1945—the Imperial Army's raggedy last gasp. His squad leader is the one disciplining Tamura. The young consumptive was prematurely released from hospital; he should have stayed there five days instead of three, because who can be cured of tuberculosis in just three days? Moreover, food rations for five days had been sent along to the hospital for him. He is told to try to be readmitted; if that attempt fails, the squad leader continues, Tamura must fulfill his patriotic duty by blowing himself up with a hand grenade. He is no use to the platoon since he is constantly falling down on the job—at the moment, digging ditches.

Nobi becomes Tamura's odyssey—one punctuated by mysterious sightings of distant fires on the plain. The hospital is blown up, but Tamura survives to endure a series of incidents that encapsulate war's barbarism and the base impulses, such as selfishness, that it releases from humanity's Pandora's box. Patriotism, nationalism: these prove to be the bunk.

Eventually Tamura joins up with two soldiers who, without his realizing it, are cannibalizing human flesh. He dines with them. The two kill each other. When Tamura tries surrendering, an American kills him. Wilfred Owen wrote of "the Pity of war"; *Nobi* addresses the horror of it.

The fires on the plain are the illusion that war is productive or ennobling. Even Tamura, who had hoped to retain dignity and decency, is mauled by it. He dies for nought, with human meat in his belly.

BAD LUCK (Poland). Andrzej Munk's comedy *Zezowate szczęście*—in English, sometimes called *Cockeyed Happiness*—takes in a brace of Polish history, covering a quarter-century beginning around 1930. It follows Janek Piszczyk (Bogumił Kobiela, brilliant), a bumbling Everyman who tries fitting in. Jerzy Stefan Stawiński wrote the script from his own story.

In an extended flashback, Jan recollects a lifetime of "bad luck." He is a schoolboy in Warsaw tormented by peers, but his musical gift wins official favor—until a jealous schoolmate sabotages his band performance, causing him to be demoted back to an object of public derision. In college, when he attempts sitting in the part of the lecture hall reserved for Aryans—the front of the bus, as it were—he is beaten up by officials, who apologize once Jan produces identification certifying he is not Jewish despite his big nose. (Kobiela was himself Jewish; Munk, of Jewish heritage.) Lesson learned: "[H]ow important appearances are." Meanwhile, trapped inside narrow self-interest, Jan is oblivious to the worse luck befalling others.

Jan weathers German invasion, a German work camp, and a position in Poland's postwar Communist bureaucracy, all the while running on expedience and opportunism rather than conviction. Voltaire's eighteenth-century *Candide* informs Stawiński/Munk's satire of Polish temperament and politics; through his misadventures Jan might have learned that it's not the case that "all is for the best in this best of all possible worlds," but his self-centeredness precludes his taking responsibility for the consequences of his actions or his arriving at any philosophical generalization about the state of things. The plot's coincidences are correlative to Jan's sense that his life is out of his control, as are Munk's delightful bag of tricks: speeded-up motion, reverse motion, jump cuts, percussive sounds replacing voices, etc.

Was/Is God the progenitor of the *nouvelle vague?*

EYES WITHOUT A FACE (France). Based on the novel *Celle qui n'était plus* by Jean Redon, Georges Franju's *Les yeux sans visage* is a somber, poetic horror film. Plastic surgeon Génessier is its mad scientist (Pierre Brasseur, grim, concentrated, powerful). Encapsulated in his recklessness at the wheel of his car, his arrogance results in facially disfiguring his daughter, Christiane (Edith Scob, superb). Christiane wears a mask that shows two soulful eyes but otherwise hides where there no longer really is a face. Her widower-father performs operation after operation, each an attempt to graft onto Christiane another face. These surgeries are performed in secret, their privacy abetted by the fact that Génessier has declared somebody else's dead daughter as his own. In each case, Christiane's body—or, perhaps, soul—has rejected the grafted skin. These potential new faces for Christiane come from young women whom her father murders. Dr. Génessier, then, is a serial killer.

Contributing to the grisly horror is the dark, surreal chamber in which Génessier's dogs are kept locked up, each in its own cage; banks of cages flank both sides, receding into an empty, shadowy space. Strays, these dogs parallel the doctor's human victims; Génessier uses them to experiment on, in an effort to perfect his face transplant procedure. Finally, Christiane, fed up with her father's experiments on her, releases the dogs, which proceed to attack, maul and kill their master as though they are the avenging spirits of the murdered girls.

Once, Génessier must truly have loved Christiane; but the film commences after that point, when Christiane is his principal "guinea pig." The form of Génessier love for his daughter has eerily outrun any content of genuine feeling. In this light, Franju's intent may be satirical; *Eyes Without a Face* is a masked assault on reactionaryism.

ANATOMY OF A MURDER (U.S.). With *Anatomy of a Murder* Otto Preminger began a trilogy of films that questions U.S. institutions. The other entries would be *Advise and Consent* (1962), about government, and *In Harm's Way* (1965), about the military. But the first was by far the best. Through a sensational murder trial, it takes on the courts. The novel on which it is based was written by Robert Traver, the pen-name of John D. Voelker, a judge on the Michigan State Supreme Court.

Justice is hard to locate in Preminger's film. A palette of gray tonalities eliminates anything so harsh or glaring as that from an adversarial system of lawyerly points and parries. All that's determined is whether the man on trial, who admits to killing the man who (perhaps) raped his wife, is found by a jury "guilty" or "not guilty." As in Mervyn LeRoy's audacious *They Won't Forget* (1937), the crime depicted remains unsolved. Even the accused, whose "innocent" plea is based on a claim of "irresistible impulse," ends up making a joke about the trial's inconclusive outcome!

Preminger thus makes his spirited case against the inconclusive nature of American justice —and this, after skewering *conclusive* justice, in another time and place, in his *Saint Joan* (1957). Perhaps the financial failure of that (deadly) film helped dictate Preminger's inspired choice to direct *Anatomy* as an ironical comedy.

Skillfully represented by a wonderful cast, especially James Stewart as the cagey defense attorney, Preminger finds in the courts a metaphor for both representative government (the lawyers) and democracy (the jury). This is why the second entry in his iconoclastic series, *Advise and Consent*, which takes on Congress directly, despite fascinating sidebars, is superfluous.

THE LAMP (Poland). *Lampa* is a student film that Roman Polanski has somewhat disowned on grounds he hasn't chosen to reveal. It is nonetheless one of his most haunting works—and a clear influence on Steven Soderbergh's best film, *Bubble* (2006).

The title refers to the kerosene lamp by which a toymaker meticulously works in his shop, which is populated by dolls and doll parts, one with a conspicuously broken face, and punctuated by the sound of a cuckoo clock. There's no dialogue; Polanski draws us into a silent world where the toymaker, or Polanski, or we could be dreaming. It is *somebody's* chilling nightmare—likely, friend Mindy Aloff suggests, a metaphor for Polanski's wartime experiences.

We peer into the empty head of one of the dolls, into which the toymaker deposits something with tweezers. When he restores the doll's hair, we are surprised to discover that the doll is a girl-doll. The camera's eerie perusal of the dolls helps draw us into a sense of their being alive. This becomes especially true after the toymaker departs and shutters the shop. No longer does his presence compete for our attention. We are riveted to the dolls, perhaps ferreting out any sign of life.

Fire breaks out. We recall a cigarette with which the toymaker may have been careless. But what we see makes the origin of the fire impossible to determine. It seems to just happen. The incineration of the dolls is a horrible thing to contemplate.

Just as the camera had entered through sidewalk and road traffic at the beginning, it now withdraws without showing the ultimate horror. Therefore, we *must* contemplate the outcome. Although we glimpse consuming fire through slats, the people walking in either direction notice nothing. They don't look. Perhaps they dare not look.

THE VIRGIN SPRING (Sweden). Ingmar Bergman repudiated his sparkling medieval ballad *Jungfrukällan* on the grounds that it is essentially an inferior facsimile of Akira Kurosawa's *Rashômon* (1950), in which a rape and retaliatory murder are differently viewed by several characters. However, it is an exceptionally fine piece of work, at once lyrical and analytical.

In fourteenth-century Sweden, the proud teenaged daughter of a landowner insists on transporting candles to church by horseback. Along the way the virgin is raped by itinerant shepherds, against whom, including an innocent child, her father (Max von Sydow, wonderful) exacts murderous revenge. When he carries his daughter's corpse to the site where he promises God to build a new church, one that embraces Christianity's peaceableness as penance for his murders, a new spring bursts through the ground.

Bergman and black-and-white cinematographer Sven Nykvist have achieved the impossible: a world ravishingly pure and beautiful, yet full of dark foreboding and violence. The closeup of a raven in the foreground of one complex shot may remind the viewer of Charles Laughton's *Night of the Hunter* (1955), except, here, Nature isn't protecting the child on her journey but striking an ominous visual chord. The passage portraying the rape is brutally frank, unshakable. The scene where the young father bathes, steeling himself for his killing mission, is stunningly suspenseful, and his picking up the young boy and smashing him against a wall, heartrending. The array of the landowner's wealth against the shepherds' hardworking poverty adds another wrinkle of resonance.

But this isn't the sum of the film's tantalizing substance. The most interesting aspect of *The Virgin Spring* is that several characters religiously though variously interpret a natural occurrence, the spring's virgin gush—Bergman's probe of Christianity's mythmaking tendencies.

NORTH BY NORTHWEST (U.S.). In Alfred Hitchcock's fabulous comedy-adventure *North by Northwest*, appearances deceive. Roger Thornhill (Cary Grant, terrific) is a Manhattan advertising executive who is mistaken for a federal spy, George Kaplan, that the C.I.A. has fabricated as a decoy to divert attention from an operative who has infiltrated the inner circle of those chasing down Government secrets in the States.

Unsettling is the attitude of the C.I.A.'s polished The Professor, who lies, manipulates, and even permits the deadly pursuit of inconvenient—hence, expendable—innocents, and always nonchalantly explains afterwards, "Well, you see, I *had* to . . . ." With him, "the end justifies the means" has become "business as usual." The "good guys" and "villains" mirror-image one another.

Hitchcock sees the Cold War as pervasive, dispensing its cold snap even into the heated romance of the undercover agent, Eve (Eva Marie Saint, giving her best performance), and Thornhill. When he discovers that Eve, an impressed civilian who keeps tabs on the archvillain by sharing his bed, has set him up to be murdered, Roger turns against her; but it was to protect her cover—that is, her life—that Eve did this. Scenarist Ernest Lehman and Hitchcock have in mind the quandary that people in their own industry were put in when, under threat of losing their livelihoods and being imprisoned, they were asked to destroy the livelihood of others.

This film assaults the kind of programmatic nationalism that leads to state paranoia at the expense of ordinary people in their ordinary lives. Pursued, Roger and Eve heartstoppingly scramble on Mount Rushmore, their torsos and limbs jabbing, knocking, grabbing, sliding down sculpted national icons and symbols—the gigantic heads of revered U.S. presidents. We care here about the two Americans whose lives are at immediate risk. Nations don't matter; *people* matter.

KAGI (Japan). Kon Ichikawa's pre-Viagra *The Key* (called *Odd Obsession* in the puritanical States), from Junichirô Tanizaki's novel, addresses Kenji Kenmochi's problem: he can't much "get it up" anymore. The potency injections he has been taking on the sly aren't sufficiently helping, and having a younger wife, Ikuko, only deepens his discomfort. But Kenji lights on a plan: manipulate Ikuko and Kimura, a young intern, into a sexual relationship so that his (Kenji's) voyeurism can incite his jealousy and stiffen his, er, resolve.

The film begins with Kimura—and with poker-faced hilarity that eases into chuckling and a broad smile. Looking into the camera, prior to taking Kenji's blood pressure and giving him his virility shot in the hinterlands, Kimura pontificates on the swift degradation of the senses during the ageing process. Things start going sooner than we might have thought. Senility begins at ten years; at that same age, eyes begin to lose their "elasticity." Eros? Already at twenty we start suffering its decline. Being born hardly seems worth it!

Ichikawa has the good taste not to brandish Kenji's sagging buttocks, but what follows wittily underscores the concept of *backside:* Kenji's trip home is shown from underneath the streetcar that is transporting him! (It is very dark down there.) This purely visual comical passage resolves with unexpected poignancy: Kenji's unsteady walk after he has exited the vehicle.

Meanwhile, Ikuko is at her husband's doctor's office, sleuthing around in an effort to unearth what's what. She is slyly introduced with her back to the camera, suggesting that Kenji's marital partner primarily exists, in his scheme of things, as a touchstone for his feelings about himself.

Ichikawa's satire on Japanese ideas of masculinity is tart and terrific; the lead acting, by Ganjiro Nakamura, Machiko Kyô and Tatsuya Nakadai, irresistible.

HIROSHIMA, MON AMOUR (France). What are we looking at? The opening of Alain Resnais's *Hiroshima, mon amour* is beautiful and mysterious: in darkness, glistening forms. Out of this formless mass, with its primordial echo, two bodies gradually appear: a couple making love. She is a French actress, in Hiroshima for an anti-war shoot; He, a Japanese architect. The earlier glitter? Symbolically, the radioactivity from which nothing in Hiroshima can escape? Its indeterminate nature and that of the initial forms: the awful experience of Hiroshima that She cannot know about, no matter her investigation of the commemorative museum there, or She's awful experience at Nevers that He cannot know about, no matter how much She reminisces. Strangers, the two spend a day together, having sex, walking, having a drink together: passing time, emptying time, phantom/persons setting their souls to the rhythm of time.

Philosopher Henri Bergson wrote that human consciousness is a memory. Resnais's first feature is attuned to this suggestion. It is a complex fugue on the interplay of time, memory, history and intimacy, intricately edited, with slow forward trackings (through hotel, hospital, streets, etc., edited at the outset into a single movement) suggesting an ambling mind homing in on itself, with flashbacks giving the impression of a soft rainshower, and with Marguerite Düras's solemn, repetitive prose pitched somewhere between the articulate and the unspoken or unspeakable.

Exquisitely sensitive, Emmanuèlle Riva plays the actress who is searching somebody else's past, which is, at some level, really her own. Her fleeting affair with the architect triggers memories of her earlier "forbidden" love for a German soldier during the Occupation. Or is this memory a dream of history, the guilty personal rendering of a national shame?

Despite a patina of preciousness (French cinema's Achilles' heel), here is adventurous filmmaking.

Films of the 1960s

Much as the great films of Jean Renoir dominated the 1930s, those of Michelangelo Antonioni and Jean-Luc Godard—some might add Ingmar Bergman—dominated the 1960s. For me, the decade's supreme masterpiece, and Italy's greatest film ever, is Antonioni's *L'eclisse* (1962), which concluded his trilogy on contemporary alienation begun with *L'avventura* (1960), which is nearly as brilliant, and *La notte* (1961).

This visionary work tries "to see whole" a myriad of emotional, psychological and social currents, and it expresses these in vibrant, poetic visual and aural terms. One would have to return to silent cinema to discover another film equally original and complex.

Antonioni's cinema is essential to understanding the 1960s, a time of shaken identity and compensatory political radicalism. For a wrecked Western Europe, the immediate postwar period had been a time of terrible uncertainty about the future; many no longer knew what being European meant. It would seem that the progress which resulted in renewed economic viability would resolve this crisis, but instead it posed the overwhelming question, "What now?" The capitalism that had fueled recovery came under close, crabbed scrutiny, and an especial part of this was an examination of the extent to which capitalism intrudes on individualism and people's everyday lives. This included a keener awareness of others in the world—an examination of how, through colonialism, capitalism had intruded on other peoples' lives. For those in the West, these concerns seemed mooted in Eastern Europe by the imposition of Communist order; those in the West felt, instead, keenly afflicted by a moral and perpetual social disarray. They often felt terribly on their own. "I am the least speculative man on earth," Antonioni once said about himself. Such a soul was the right person for the job of tackling sixties unease at its tangled and in spots suffocating roots.

Something else qualified Antonioni. He had no need to contend personally with the ghosts of Fascism. Like Gillo Pontecorvo and Luchino Visconti, he had never taken even a turn on the national dance floor with Fascism. There was nothing for Antonioni to suppress. He would never be called upon to direct valuable psychic energy toward misremembering his own political history in an autobiographical film titled *I Remember* (*Amarcord*, Federico Fellini, 1974). Enlightened, humanistic, analytically probing, Antonioni arrived at his masterpiece with clear eyes and "clean hands." It is worth noting that much of *L'eclisse* takes place in the EUR suburb of Rome (Esposizione Universale Romana), whose postwar completion intriguingly wars with Italy's attempts at burying its ghosts. This new part of Rome had been conceived by Mussolini as an architectural and atmospheric monument to both modernity and Fascism, but the war, intervening, postponed its construction, which when taken up had of course lost its political impetus. Its futuristic appearance underscores the reality of inhabitants and identities unmoored and cast adrift. It implies an end to the world that has permitted a newer world to replace the former one.

L'avventura—*The Adventure* (and a more aptly titled film there never has been)—began the trilogy that *L'eclisse* completed. In this beautiful film that is sometimes credited with reinventing the language of cinema, two souls, Anna's lover, Sandro, and Anna's friend, Claudia (Monica Vitti, Antonioni's partner and muse at the time, phenomenal), search for Anna, who is missing from their party on an uninhabited island. In the course of this adventure, the two become a couple and lose the thread of their search. What had brought them together no longer matters—except to us, who miss Anna, who at first seemed to be the film's protagonist. Finding ourselves the projection of the pair's conscience helps make us a participant. *L'avventura* isn't the sort of film to wash over one.

The fragile nature of relationships; the ties that loosen and unbind: Antonioni shows the abstract way that modern humans live, giving themselves up to experience. These characters demonstrate self-estrangement and an inability to make emotional contact with others. Visually, *L'avventura* translates the concepts figure and ground into the relationship between humanity and landscape. Daunting Sicilian locations fail to do what we expect locations to do in a film: locate the characters and their story. Instead, they project the vast spaces, the disconnects, between, among and within characters who lack moral and sensitive rootedness. Here is a film, then, about will-o'-the-wisps.

Antonioni had mined the poetry of bleak landscape before, such as in *The Outcry* (*Il grido*, 1957), but never to such intoxicating effect. Used to their own abandonment, the landscapes appear to reveal (or mimic) the idle, empty, well-to-do characters. This is a film of long- and wide-angle shots, in which characters are often on the verge of becoming lost to the eye. It is about how, like Anna, we all can be lost in this modern world of ours—lost to ourselves and to others. Its overarching theme is the signature one of the sixties: alienation. But Antonioni investigates its character rather than exploiting a fashionable mood (as perhaps he does in *Zabriskie Point*, 1970).

La notte (1961) is the middle part of cinema's greatest trilogy. It occupies the dead-center between the hopefulness with which *L'avventura* ends and the utter desolation of *L'eclisse*, which begins and ends with the end of a relationship. It is a gray, weathered film that ends with a standstill in love that may yet be set back into motion. We certainly hope that life is still possible in Giovanni and Lidia's marriage, and we appreciate their courteous, civilized treatment of one another in this troubled time of theirs. Their humanity, then, forms the basis for our hope that the couple may yet prevail. In retrospect, the conclusion of the trilogy, although it deals with a different (and unmarried) couple, eclipses all such hope.

Giovanni (Marcello Mastroianni) and Lidia (Jeanne Moreau, wonderful) visit Milan to see Tommaso, a dying friend, in hospital. From this we can see their decency and compassion; few filmmakers have such fondness for their characters as Antonioni does. But, too, Tommaso functions symbolically to suggest the emotional and spiritual exhaustion that each of the marital partners feels. It is after Lidia learns of Tommaso's death that she tells Giovanni that she no longer loves him. She feels this way not because of anything that Giovanni has done but because of what he *hasn't* done; exhausted himself, he hasn't been able to pull her out of her doldrums. In Antonioni, a marriage isn't an island; Giovanni and Lidia are affected, severely, by the alienating modern world in which they find themselves. Antonioni wouldn't think of cheapening the moment with sentimentality, so it is all the more heartrending when he reveals that Giovanni, a writer, is so lost to himself that he fails to recognize the most intimate words he has written, in a letter, as his own.

Night may be Antonioni's most moving film.

L'eclisse begins with the end of one romantic relationship and ends with the end of another. The constant in both cases is the protagonist of the film, Vittoria (Monica Vitti, phenomenal yet again). Vittoria works as a translator, but the film doesn't show her at work. Translation connects people across languages and ethnicities. Our knowledge of Vittoria's work reminds us of the possibility of such connections, and indeed the film itself, viewed with subtitles outside Italy, brings this knowledge of ours to a kind of fruition. However, Antonioni's decision to withhold scenes of Vittoria at work helps establish a pull in the opposite direction, suggesting the limited capacity of translation to translate into connections between and among disparate cultures and individuals. At the beginning of *L'eclisse* Vittoria and Riccardo have lost their connection; near the end, as Vittoria and her new lover, Piero, commit themselves to a rendezvous, their faces silently reveal, cheek-to-cheek, that each has no intention of showing up for the date. They are losing their connection right before our eyes. The film ends with scenes of the appointed place of assignation, to which indeed neither has come. The film thus ends with an overwhelming impression of their permanent absence.

Absence is one of the things that *L'eclisse* is about. I stated earlier that the film opens with the end of Vittoria and Riccardo's relationship. However, I am not being entirely accurate. The film opens on the morning *after* the end of their relationship. It is a bravura passage of loose ends, with Vittoria, at Riccardo's place, already of the mind of being out of there. At some point, when after a very long silence she speaks, Vittoria says something to the effect that nothing more can be added to what was already said the night before. Perhaps last night Riccardo pleaded for Vittoria to sleep on her decision to leave him; if so, that decision hasn't budged. Out of breath and utterly helpless as a result of Vittoria's decision to end their relationship, Riccardo says to Vittoria, "Find something for me to do when you're gone." Riccardo's mind is already at the place where Vittoria is out the door. What terrible irony: their minds are at the same place, but that place is the imminent future when they are absent to one another because they no longer share a life in the present. They are no longer a couple, and their hopes for a life together are "out the door."

This opening passage consists mostly of the silence between Riccardo and Vittoria. Riccardo is waiting for Vittoria to speak, and Vittoria has nothing to add to what she presumably said the night before. It is the awkward silence of the end of a romance where both former partners know the irreversible score; one doesn't want to hear it, and the other, Vittoria, scarcely wants to repeat it, for to do so, however faintly, restores at the least the appearance of a connection, delaying yet again the necessary rupture. Antonioni's silence isn't a stylistic choice; it is the expression of what Riccardo doesn't want to hear and Vittoria doesn't want to say.

Vittoria makes herself busy filling the silence created by the lack of conversation between herself and Riccardo. (I don't want to be too clever, because *L'eclisse* is a devastating film, not a clever one, but in effect there is nothing left for Vittoria, a translator, to translate here.) Vittoria walks around the room; she touches this and that; she pokes her hand through a sculpture that resembles an empty picture frame, slightly repositioning a nick-knack on the same table. (Joseph Losey would joltingly adapt this concept in *Accident*, 1967, when something from outside unexpectedly sails through the "frame" of an open window toward the camera.) The implication is that the silence we hear (and see) expresses not only the end of the relationship but also the relationship's preceding petering out—the loss of meaningful conversation between Riccardo and Vittoria over time. The sounds we hear accentuate the absence of sound we otherwise "hear." A partially rotating fan—a simulated panning camera! —very slightly reverses the absence of air movement in the room; we see its slight effect on Vittoria's crown of hair. Another sound, that of Riccardo's electric shaver, eventually connects with that of the fan as Riccardo, both hideously and poignantly, attempts to impose a sense of order on the moment, as though this were any ordinary day. Later, the sound of a private airplane in which Vittoria is a passenger connects with the sounds of Riccardo's electric fan and electric shaver, stressing his absence by recalling Riccardo. In effect, noise punctuates silence, rendering it material and associating it with human relationships. Noise becomes a defense against a vast amount of silence that intimates human disconnection, loneliness and unease and ultimately, of course, mortality.

Antonioni delivers a shock to our ears. From the opening suburban silence in the early morning, interrupted by the humming sounds of fan and shaver and the blipping sounds of parting exchanges, he plunges his film, and us his audience, into the loud, cacophonous noise of Roman traffic, including honking horns, and the similarly dense, layered chaotic sound inside the Rome Stock Exchange, which is beset right now with human anxiety and intense trading activity. (Bergman drew upon *L'eclisse* for elements of *his* masterpiece, *The Silence*: the quietude, the hotel room fan, the fact that Ester is a translator, and Anna's plunge from the quiet hotel into noisy traffic.) Vittoria is there to find her mother, one of the army of those who, "playing the market," ironically identify Italy's gradual postwar economic recovery with an unsettled state of human affairs. Inside the exchange, everything human is suddenly in fevered motion and emotion, as though a series of cages of wild animals in a zoo had been rattled, eliciting a stark response. Antonioni isn't finished engineering the crash landing of hectic sound in silence; just as suddenly as he plunged us into noise, he plunges us back into silence—silence, that is, except for the stray ringing of phones. The occasion for this new sharp aural contrast is the moment of silence that is extended in memory of a broker who that day died of a heart attack. This unexpected shaft of silence associates silence yet again with ends, absences and mortality. Piero, who will become Vittoria's new lover, and who is a stockbroker himself, in fact Vittoria's mother's broker, explains to Vittoria that such silence as this costs millions of lira. His confidence and arrogance are breathtaking, but his inhuman remark, contrary to his intent, has the effect of exposing stock exchange activity as inhuman as well. It is another instance of us filling silence with noise to defend ourselves against the silence, and it casts a pall on the relationship between Vittoria and Piero that we already anticipate, because, well, she looks like Monica Vitti and he looks like Alain Delon and they're the two most gorgeous persons in the room. Even with Vittoria's mother as a linkage between them, they will prove a more short-lived couple than Vittoria and Riccardo, and in a time-bending prank that Antonioni allows us to invent in our heads we toy with the possibility that Piero is unwittingly mocking a moment of memorial silence for himself sometime in the future. In an elliptical way Antonioni swipes capitalism on the side of its head, and the impression this leaves is deepened once our recollection of the stock exchange passage in Vsevolod I. Pudovkin's *The End of St. Petersburg* (1927) kicks in. Piero's materialism and inhumanity are a match for the materialism and inhumanity of the economic/political system he toils in and represents. Both Riccardo and Piero come to mind when Vittoria tells a friend, "There are times when holding a needle and a thread, or a book, or a man are no different." (The brilliant script is by Antonioni and Tonino Guerra, in collaboration with Elio Bartolini and Ottiero Ottieri.) Antonioni achieves a shattering apotheosis of transience when inside the Rome Stock Exchange a siren signals the end of the memorial moment of silence and pandemonium noisily breaks out again. The man who died will never cross his colleagues' minds again.

Materialism is indeed one of the film's principal themes, and a signature concern of the 1960s. Materialism depersonalizes everything, even intimacy. Thus Antonioni shows huge columns at the stock exchange dividing future lovers Piero and Vittoria—a sign of the societal ill, capitalism, that will infect their relationship. Ironically reflecting Italy's flypaper past since it is obviously the case that an old building now houses the Rome Stock Exchange, the columns are orderly. But what now passes for order is divisive rather than integrative, an idea stunningly expressed in the film's conclusive series of bleak, underpopulated nightscapes —underpopulated in the main by the absence of Piero and Vittoria: a world of order with little or nothing left to order: *form* outlasting *content*. All this also relates to the theme of materialism by ironical indirection; Antonioni's minimalism, his spare exteriors as the film reaches its *fine*, counters Piero's compulsive greed—greed that is less voracious appetite than mechanical behavior, another something to fill up the silence with which modern society is loath to contend. (Sex-by-rote, without noticeable connection between partners, is still another such "something" to fill up the silence.) Capitalism itself is an example of form outlasting content.

Three passages in *L'eclisse* are among the finest in cinema. Two of these are the ones already noted: the early passage in the Rome Stock Exchange; the mostly vacant conclusive series of brief shots. Both these passages remind the viewer that Antonioni began as a documentarian; each is invested with an air of documentary realism. This is not the case, however, with the other great passage. Vittoria is visiting a colonialist friend of hers, a woman who is back from Kenya. This friend shows Vittoria a book of photographs of Africa; there is a photograph of a baobob tree. She explains: "Kenya has everything: Jungle, snow, savannah." Something is missing; once again, there is a particular absence. This friend of Vittoria's doesn't mention Kenyans, that is to say, Native Africans. By contrast, it is the photographs of black Africans that draws Vittoria's attention as she peruses her friend's book. Such people in Kenya were not a part of the colonialist's life; we find here the tragic circumstances of the West's failure to recognize, let alone embrace, its human connections to the rest of the world—a theme that Antonioni would bring to fruition in the film known in the U.S. as *The Passenger* (1975), where a reporter in Africa at a time of political upheaval fails to recognize any connection between himself and the people and events he is reporting on. In *L'eclisse*, the white European who has lived in Kenya is certain that no such connection exists. Vittoria, bless her, is not so sure; she is adrift between the moorings of Western culture and something else as yet undefined on the other side. In the ferociously nondocumentary-like moment to which I referred, she acts out her problem of identity; she does so at her friend's party, in pseudo-tribal dance. The electric moment is complex. This extreme performance of hers redresses the imbalance created by her friend's exclusion of African humanity from her experience and thoughts despite the time she spent living in Kenya. In a way, the get-up and the dance are a slight mockery of her friend's disposition and stance, that is to say, of the polite Europeanness that covers a basic inhumanity vis-à-vis "Europe's backyard." (Kenya was granted, first, internal self-government and, second, complete independence from British rule the same year as *L'eclisse*.) But, however unconsciously perhaps, Vittoria is also mocking herself, her performance of African tribal identity a reflection of her uncertainty as to who she is—this, an extension and reflection of Europe's uncertain identity that came about with the end of war, the turning of its back on its recent political storms, the confrontation with new economic hardship, and the African independence movements that further eroded its sense of control, superiority and destiny. Antonioni isn't resorting to literary allegory here; Vittoria comes to embody current European uncertainty and disarray from the inside out. Indeed, in this light (or dark), her friend and she seem to reflect a European attitude and counter-attitude, an insistence on past prerogatives and an embrace of the dashing of those prerogatives. Antonioni finds a gripping way to express this: at night, the two women venturing out into the streets to gather up the colonialist woman's fleet of escaped dogs—a scene lent a touch of the surreal by its association with a terrifying passage from Georges Franju's *Eyes Without a Face* (*Les yeux sans visage*, 1959), a masked assault on reactionaryism.

Perhaps the most phenomenal achievement of Antonioni's masterpiece is its visual form. Unlike the "flat," arid, expansive images in *L'avventura*, the frames of *L'eclisse* are composed in intricate, dynamic depth—a depth evoking modernity, where, rather than keeping hidden below, a now thoroughly and acutely known-about, hence objectified, unconscious so intrudes on the surface of human behavior and thought that, rattled and unsure of themselves amidst self-criticism and second guessing, people seem lost in their own lives—the problem of identity that Vittoria's frenzied dance, in African brownface, apotheosizes. The dense, teeming images inside the stock exchange, with its detailed gesticulations and grimaces, disclose a "civilized" ritual that masks and suppresses primitive fears of silence and vacant space—conditions that might press individuals to confront themselves. Instead, in this chaotic dance of sorts individuals seem to be confronting one another, as when Piero in the close background, facing the camera, grimaces and makes some incomprehensible point to someone else who has his back towards us in the foreground of the shot. All this is part of the scene just following the memorial moment of silence, during which Piero cannot even stay silent but must talk to Vittoria, his client's daughter. A tad farther back from the exchange floor than Piero, she is behind one of the huge columns, back and around of which Piero must twist his torso in order to address her. This seeming doubling or twisting of space has the effect of reinforcing our sense that Piero cannot leave the silence alone; he exudes a phosphorescent energy, like a marionette, that deepens the air of unnaturalness about what we see. The relative silence approaches the muteness of a dream, which throws into relief the selfconsciousness of all that we witness here, including the instant memorial, Piero's incapacity to cope with it for even a minute, and Vittoria's failed attempt to engage her mother's attention, let alone sympathy, following her breakup with Riccardo. Appearing calm and composed, Vittoria may be occupying the dead center of her own bad dream of modern times.

Even with, or perhaps because of, its documentary air, the closing series of shots showing (by their absence) Vittoria and Piero's failure to meet at night also suggests a waking bad dream. Over the shoulder of some anonymous passenger exiting a bus we read in his newspaper this headline: "Nuclear Arms Race . . . Fragile Peace." Piero and Vittoria have not kept their date. *L'eclisse* sharpens despair to a point of imminent apocalypse, signalling in the failure of two individuals to remain a couple the end of the world. By indirection, then, Antonioni touts the primacy of love. His film begins and ends in near silence—sheer silence but for sparse natural sounds—and with an overwhelming sense of vacancy, loneliness and abandonment. It is Antonioni's heart-piercing image of our modern lives.

Antonioni's trilogy was not the only famous one during the decade, and indeed I have already noted that Bergman's *The Silence* (1963), which as it happens concludes his own trilogy, draws upon the conclusion of Antonioni's trilogy for a number of its elements. Few of us love Bergman the way we do Antonioni, whose humanity, as disclosed by his films, is unassailable. Bergman has made many interesting and intriguing films, but most of us admire them more than we like them. Excepting *The Seventh Seal* (1956), which helped people of my generation (the post-World War II generation) fall in love with cinema, few of us think of Bergman's films as things even to enjoy. There is the bleakness of his vision, to be sure; but we do love the films of Bergman's fellow Scandinavian Carl Theodor Dreyer, and some of those (*The Passion of Joan of Arc*, *Day of Wrath*) are scarcely less bleak. The problem with Bergman, it seems to me, is his nasty tone—the surliness of his disposition. His films, which are deeply personal, allow this personality of his to come through unmistakably, to dispiriting effect. In these films Bergman reliably insists on his humanism, but the way he sets up one character to heap invective on another strikes some of us as *in*human. We are repelled at the psychodrama of it all and would rather not, with whatever mental scalpel we can muster, locate where Bergman's sadism leaves off and his masochism begins. In a Bergman film, when they are clear (in his "masterpiece," *Persona*, 1966, for me at least, they are not), ideas can be a godsend; they divert us from Bergman's nature to the nature of us all and of the universe, and this allows us to embrace the wisdom of the man without sinking into, and becoming lost in, his sourness.

One of the recognized great achievements of 1960s filmmaking, which Bergman both wrote and directed, is his trilogy on the nature of humanity's contemporary relationship with God. Bergman, the son of a Lutheran priest, approached this material from a unique perspective: that of an atheist—although, logically, one may wonder how Bergman could so hate what he believed didn't exist. For a humanist such as Bergman, however, the reconciliation isn't long in coming: Bergman hated God because *others* believed in God—others who discover in their hour of need that God isn't forthcoming with help or hope. Bergman hated the *idea* of God for its capacity to attract souls and betray them. Bergman despised his father for many reasons, including the memory of childhood whippings and the man's hatred of Jews; but most of all, I suspect, he did so because, as a hypocritical purveyor of Christian nonsense, his father seduced trusting parishioners and raped their minds and spirits. Bergman believed his father was one of God's pimps.

Bergman may have embarked on his trilogy, at least in part, to set the record straight after (bewilderingly, incomprehensibly) some reviewers misinterpreted *The Virgin Spring* (1959) as a work of faith. In the first of the three chamber dramas, *Through a Glass Darkly* (*Såsom i en spegel*, 1961—I have no idea how accurate any of the English translations of titles are), Karin, the schizophrenic woman who "sees" God, sees him in two questionable forms on the island where she, her husband (Max von Sydow), her father (Gunnar Björnstrand) and her 17-year-old brother vacation: as a spider; as the helicopter that will transport her to the insane asylum on the mainland. In a grotesque parody of the relation among romantic, familial and spiritual love, Karin's reception to God is predicated on her adulterous sex with Minus, her brother. After she has been taken away, Minus and the brother-in-law he has cuckolded speak of God's love; for the boy, the proof of this is pathetic: his aloof father has condescended to speak to him. *Crumbs. Through a Glass Darkly*, although good, is a somewhat dank film highlighted by Harriet Andersson's extraordinarily sensitive acting as Karin and Bergman's moody use of Bach's *Fugue No. 2 in F Minor.*

The second film, *Winter Light* (*Nattvardsgästerna*, 1963), again unfolds in a remote, isolated setting. It inherits Karin's concept of a "spider-God." It's surprising who holds this idea, however: the village pastor, Tomas Ericsson (Gunnar Björnstrand, exacting and powerful—tremendous). Since his wife's death, Tomas has lost his faith, and yet he continues in his ministerial duties as his congregation dwindles; it's his wife, not he, whom his parishioners loved. The village schoolteacher, Märta Lundberg (Ingrid Thulin, with luminous, spiritual eyes and a carnal mouth) is in love with Tomas, but Tomas holds her in contempt, nevertheless stringing her along because, he explains, he was raised to be polite. As pastor, similarly, he is a hypocrite clinging to the formality of his ministerial duties while failing to commit his heart to the emotional or spiritual welfare of his parishioners. (It's worth noting, perhaps, that Tomas's family name is Ericsson and Bergman's father's given name was Erik.) One devout member of the church, Karin Persson (Gunnel Lindblom), is the mother of two children and is again pregnant; she persuades her husband, Jonas (Max von Sydow), who is despondent over the state of the world, to seek counsel from Tomas. At their Sunday meeting, instead of trying to unburden Jonas, Tomas increases that burden by unburdening himself, gratuitously imposing on his fragile parishioner his own conviction that God doesn't exist, rendering the universe loveless. Jonas commits suicide that day. Tomas's self-involvement precludes his expressing even a trace of responsibility for Jonas's end, to which, trusting, Jonas's widow tells Tomas she is sure that he did everything he could to help her troubled spouse. After rebuking Marta, Tomas proceeds to church for evensong, taking her with him. She is present in church because of her feelings for Tomas; she has no religious motive. Nor do the organist, with ice water in his veins, and the sexton (Allan Edwall, excellent), a miserable little man with a hunched body crippled from a degenerative disease. Not one parishioner shows up for vespers. The church empty, as a matter of form Tomas nevertheless proceeds with the service. And why not? Everything about him reeks of form outlasting content or substance. His isn't an existential act willing some sort of individual heroic purpose in the midst of a meaningless universe; Tomas's own act is meaningless as well. It's an instance of religious decadence. Moreover, the style of the film, cold, precise and exceedingly dry, conveys the same intent on Bergman's part; it's as if Bergman had turned his human specimens upside down and emptied them of their life blood. Tomas has talked about the silence of God—the silence that overwhelms him (and others) with God's absence. The film, too, is very quiet, often silent; the images of snow outdoors, especially in long-shot, seem correlative to this. God seems to have abandoned these people; the only reasonable explanation for this is that God really hasn't abandoned anyone because he never existed in the first place. There's a fleeting second, as Tomas stands indoors near a window, when the winter light illuminates him; for this ripple of light breezing by is like the sudden spring in *The Virgin Spring* where the head of the raped and murdered girl is lifted off the ground: a natural occurrence inviting a false religious interpretation to be imposed on it. The winter light is just winter light; it's as bereft of meaning as the evensong that Tomas conducts and with which the film ends. Insofar as it bases existence in religious faith, the film argues, humanity lives lives of anticipation, not in-the-moment reality. Instead of looking around in order to tend to one another's needs, people are looking ahead for their own salvation. The problem isn't that God doesn't exist; the problem is that people believe, or pretend to believe, that he does. Enrobed in silence, like Robert Browning's Porphyria's lover they keep waiting and waiting for God to speak.

Winter Light is one of Bergman's most perfect, most brilliant films. Even Tomas's verbal assault on Marta is subordinated to the rigor of Bergman's thematic development. God does nothing because God doesn't exist; nonexistent, he can help neither the world nor anyone in it. The man of God's incapacity to return Marta's love is his following suit; God is love, and, since God doesn't exist, Tomas feels justified in mistreating Marta, whom he is certainly entitled not to love, but to whom he ought to be reaching out in sympathy to assuage the terrible loneliness and sense of being unloved that they both feel. As another son of a minister, English poet Alfred Tennyson once put it, translated into a social rather than an intimate context: "For merit lives from man to man, / And not from man, O Lord, to thee."

Much of the trilogy's conclusion, *The Silence* (*Tystnaden*), unfolds as though it were a silent film with sound effects—and therefore, as we shall see (or hear), every sound unusually counts. God's silence no longer allows the possibility that God is being reticent or has somehow been rendered mute; God is silent, the previous film established, because there is no God in reality. How fitting, then, that God isn't even mentioned in *The Silence*. *The Silence* is silent about God as a means of impressing upon the material both God's silence and the cause of that silence: God's nonexistence. When Bergman, like any artist, is at his best, form doesn't just convey content but helps determine it.

Its opening movement attests to the fact that *The Silence* is Bergman at his strangest, most concentrated and mysterious. Over the opening credits a ticking timepiece can be lowly heard. In the film proper, the silence is sheer except for the fainter sound of a moving train, which has replaced the ticking. We are in a train compartment—a world of black, grays and white. (The black-and-white cinematographer of all three films, and of *The Virgin Spring* also, is Sven Nykvist—here, doing his finest and most evocative work.) The first figure in the frame is that of a seated boy perhaps eight or nine years old; his dropped head is rising and waking up. The camera also rises to find a woman sitting to the left of him, presumably his mother, and another woman, who is as blond as the child, seated to the left of her. (Both women are dressed in white.) The woman we take to be the child's mother is attempting to wave away oppressive heat; her face and neck are covered by a film of sweat. How eerie that we can scarcely hear the train, as though it weren't traversing ground but moving through some other, alien dimension. The boy stands up and rubs his eyes. He faces us. Does he see us? This is Johan, and he's played by the same actor, Jörgen Lindström, who will play the Artist as a Young Boy in the experimental preface to *Persona* (1966). The woman we take to be his mother is Anna (Gunnel Lindblom); the other woman—who *is* she? Anna's sister? Anna's lesbian lover? both?—is Ester (Ingrid Thulin, in the performance of a lifetime). The boy breaks the silence to ask Ester, who is a professional translator, what is written on a posted card. Ester doesn't know this foreign language. Ester seems entirely free of the heat that's plaguing Anna; she seems cool and collected—just tired. Are these Swedes headed home from vacation, or are they off on vacation? Or is there some other reason for their trip together? The boy now sits between Anna and Ester, compounding the ambiguity of which is his mother and which is his aunt, or "aunt." Anna shifts her location to the bench on the opposite side of the compartment, and Johan lays his head in her lap. Without doubt Anna is his mommy; but we still don't know—we will never know—which of the two women, if either, is his biological mother. Anna darts a look at Ester, creating a sense of tension between them. Is Johan the bone of this contention? The reconstituted silence is broken again, this time by Ester, who coughs. She isn't as composed as we thought; she coughs blood into a handkerchief. Ester is sick, perhaps tubercular. Anna tends to her, gently shutting Johan outside the compartment. Ester lies down, in enormous pain, on the bench that Anna and Johan just occupied. Standing outside, Johan looks at Ester through the glass. When Ester raises her head, it overlaps with Johan's in the frame. Eventually Johan departs, sitting on the floor and yawning and trying again to sleep as a wave of light washes over him. He is disturbed by a foreign language: a train official opening each compartment to announce the destination that the train is pulling into. The boy stands up as alternating short waves of light and darkness roll over him. We are reminded of the flickers of a Magic Lantern or a silent film. Perhaps we also see the flickers as the visual translation of a heartbeat—a labored heartbeat. The sound of the train is now fully audible. Johan's eyes fall upon military men in their compartment; he leaps away not to be caught, standing at frightened attention. The men, now in the corridor, are oblivious to him. Johan's eyes now look out a window; darkness. After the tunnel the first images—like the images of a motion picture—appear. Darkened military tanks, one after another after another, in a seemingly endless line. Wherever the train is stopping either is in the process of being militarily occupied or is already occupied. What's happening? Johan is mesmerized by the phantasmagoric images on display, his eyes staying with one tank before repositioning to catch the next, his head moving back and forth. Johan is calm; but Anna has positioned herself behind him, and we see them both from the outside of the train through the window, and we see that Anna, the adult who knows about war, is deeply troubled. This is the place where the three of them are getting off. We do not yet know that one of them will never return home.

This is as good as Bergman gets. This is as good as *anyone* gets. In addition to suggesting and linking the two forms of human suffering that contest the existence of a loving God, mortality and violence, this opening movement locates in ambiguity the main principle of the Godless modern world. The death of God has deprived us of the clear, ordered meanings that our belief in God once allowed us to access. In a foreign country where even the expert among them is unfamiliar with the language, the trio of main characters have been plunged into ambiguity; and so are we, on other grounds, since we don't know, and will never know, the exact relationship between the two women, or the exact connection of each with Johan, or the nature of the military occupation that holds the unspecified country in its grip. The absence of God insists on a loss of clarity. The sum of *The Silence*'s enigmas is one of cinema's richest evocations of universal mystery—the mystery with which (according to Bergman) the invention of God had been a reductive attempt to deal. With the loss of this outmoded invention, this crutch, humanity is left to make do with the mystery that is reality.

From the train, the film is plunged into the honking horns and other sounds of traffic in the city below. The juxtaposition stuns: following the quiet, sheltered opening movement, this blast of exposed, noisy mundane reality. It lasts a second or two. The trio of main characters have exchanged one confinement for another, hotel room for train compartment. Anna will later have access to the city outdoors, where she will pick up a man; Ester, terribly ill, will pretty much remain confined to her hotel room bed. Johan will explore on his own the hotel corridors, chancing across a troupe of dwarfs staying at the hotel—circus performers. Somehow, these little people will come to seem a chiding chorus on the increasingly hostile and embittered outbursts between the two women in Johan's life. It has long been assumed that the two women are lesbian lovers, or have been lesbian lovers, no matter what else they are or aren't. (The mentioning between them of "Father" suggests that they might be sisters.) Those who make this assumption, though, seem to be engaging in the same sort of attribution of reductive certainties that once led to humanity's invention of God. We just don't know. For instance, Ester's anger when Anna has sex with a man in the hotel may have nothing to do with sexual jealousy; Ester may be enraged that Anna would thus abandon her, when Ester is deathly ill, for casual pleasure. The impermanent nature of Anna's sexual escapade may be rubbing salt into the wound of Ester's painfully sharpening awareness of her own impermanent existence. The women are certainly enrobed in a psychological mystery, for the two seem to be at once too close and yet out of touch. For some bizarre reason, however, the promotion of the film in the U.S. leaned on the titillating possibility that Anna and Ester are lesbian lovers. There is a coarse assertion behind this American "explanation": Oh, *that's* what they are. Oh, *that's* what the film's about.

The film's ambiguous nature, of course, argues against the narrative neatness and reductive certainties that viewers equipped with a low supply of Keatsian negative capability may wish to impose on Bergman's material. Without doubt, Bergman intends for us to follow Johan's exploratory example by becoming open and exploratory in our reception of *The Silence*. One can't appreciate the film's greatness if one is constantly attempting to reduce it to the dimensions of a more familiar kind of film. Bergman wants us to let his film *be* so that we apprehend the human mysteries that are a part of the universal mystery that draws him, moves him and holds him in awe. Shorn of the explanation of "God," the mystery tantalizes. It staggers the soul.

The sounds in this film are wondrously suggestive. For instance, there is the constant humming of the small fan that Ester has placed in her room. The complexity of this! Ester's aim is the modicum of comfort that the fan's cooling brings her, but at the same time, like the ticking of the timepiece with which the film opens, the sound of the fan's operation also suggests her mortal predicament—her intense suffering and imminent death. Too, I am reminded of the buzzing fly in the room of a bedridden woman who is dying—actually, the woman narrates the poem past the point of death—in a poem by Emily Dickinson. (In *Cries and Whispers*, some of Agnes's action unfolds past the point of her death.) Another sound in the film is the click of Johan's toy pistol. Nothing could be more mundane than this child's play were it not for the context: the military tanks outdoors. The tiny sound thus releases a flood of associations, including past European wars and current world turmoil such as the U.S. intervention in Southeast Asia, to which *Persona* will directly refer and to which *Shame* (1968) will indirectly refer. A child with a holstered pistol in itself suggests the impingement of American popular culture on Europe. Finally, the gun's click is another tick of Ester's and everyone else's mortal clock. Indeed, the sharp taps of Ester's typewriter keys seem to belong to the same cluster of mortal sounds.

Love is mysterious in this film, for it no longer can claim any derivation from or connection to God and God's love. Clearly, Anna and Johan love one another as mother and son; there's an image of the two napping together in the hotel that testifies to the closeness and contentment of their relationship. However, in that same image Ester is standing over the bed, almost aggressive in her attitude toward the two of them, a cigarette dangling from her mouth. What is she thinking? What about this portrait of mother and son asleep elicits her ambiguous response? In truth, Ester and Johan seem to have the closer bond—one more likely to retain consequence into the boy's future. Ester promises Johan to figure out some of the words of the language in whatever country they are in and to write these down for him. On her deathbed, she summons the effort to create this note—a selfless act in contradistinction to Anna's love for Johan, which is inseparable from the reciprocal nature of their affections. Ester gives Johan the note before he is taken away by Anna, who abandons Ester in this foreign country, where, presumably, Ester will die alone in a hotel bed. (The one person who may ease her passage as best he can is the Old World hotel attendant, a kindly elderly man—Håkan Jahnberg in a beautiful performance.) On the train back to Sweden, Anna interrupts Johan's private reading of Ester's short list of translated words and then sneers upon discovering its contents. But the boy is engrossed. Ester has left him everything she had, and he will cherish the gift and be inspired by it. Anna's meanness is part of the world with which Johan must learn to contend; but Ester's generosity—her keeping her word to a child by translating the foreign words for him—will lighten the load of his journey through life. Even if he forgets Ester (such things do happen), even if he loses the slip of paper with words as magical as the images of a great film, Ester's love for Johan will continue to educate his heart.

The joy of watching and listening to *The Silence* is in part the joy of heightened apprehension and reception. I only wish that more of Bergman gave me such pleasure. Perhaps the two other films of his that mine the same vein of ambiguity are *The Seventh Seal* and the one called in the States *The Passion of Anna* (*En passion*, 1969).

The Silence deserves the three top prizes it won from the Swedish Film Institute: best film, best director, best actress (Ingrid Thulin).

A co-production from France and Sweden, Godard's *Masculin-Féminin* (*Masculin, Féminin*, 1966) includes, as it happens, a parody of *The Silence* as a film-within-the-film that some of Godard's characters go see! His films provide sociopolitical snapshots of their particular day, but they also remain fresh, contemporaneous to the moment as well as to their own moment. Insofar as it explores the mysterious, ambiguous space where boys and girls interact, *Masculin-Féminin* retains its relevance—and, somehow, Godard's distinctive filmmaking remains cutting-edge. We used to be so particular in differentiating between "greater" and "lesser" Godard films, but the passage of time keeps shifting titles from the latter category to the former. *Masculin-Féminin*, however it may have once struck us, looks more and more like one of the *nouvelle vague*'s masterpieces. (I do not speculate when the "movement" "ended," although most set the date some time in the sixties.)

When asked if *Masculin-Féminin* was a film about youth, Godard described it instead as "more a film on the idea of youth. A philosophical idea, but not a practical one—a way of reacting to things. A young way, let us say." The narrative is disjointed. Throughout 15 vignettes, a boy, Paul, and a girl, Madeleine, try to penetrate each other's (and perhaps their own) image and defenses. The boy's death, which may be a suicide, aborts this ongoing attempt of theirs at communication. Before the end, the boy pursues his Leftist politics and, a documentary filmmaker, conducts interviews, and the girl pursues her career as a pop singer while working at the magazine for which Paul also comes to work, and both more or less pursue sex.

Little, if anything, then, strikes us as "finished" about this film. Godard doesn't make *objets d'art*. His films spill into our lives as much as our lives spill into his films, creating in fact a dialectic between life and art. Our own experience, including our reactions to both his films and what they show us, achieves the necessary synthesis. A Godard film doesn't numb us into passivity. *Masculin-Féminin* certainly doesn't. Alert, it keeps us alert; alive, it helps make us keenly, at times painfully, alert and alive.

Paul—dare I say Paul Baron? (more about which later)—is a 21-year-old who has just returned to civilian life, and Paris, after his stint in the army, which he describes in terms of deprivation: "sixteen months with no comforts, money, love or leisure." Military service interrupted his life, putting his growing up on hold; Paul must now strike out to define himself. The *cul* in *Masculin*—*ass*—suggests the urgent biological motive of his life, as males, at least young males, tend to hew to this path as a lifeline; but the *mask* that's also embedded in the word muddies the intent. Paul is (beneath antics) shy, as most boys in fact are, and just right now his priority is his radical Vietnam-era politics, a matter of deep conviction, to be sure, but at the same time another way for him to delay getting on with his life. Existing in a universe that's never either-or or this-or-that, Godard knows that one lives many lives behind different "masks," and one's individual existence, whatever that means, competes with one's social existence and political existence. Paul is a human work-in-progress; he plunges into activism and cinematic documentation because he knows precisely what he's doing and because he doesn't know what the hell he's doing. Like Godard; like us.

Godard is the film's scenarist. Nearly every film requires some sort of a script. Godard's loosely qualifies. Let me quote from Michel Vianey's *Waiting for Godard* about the "script" of this particular film: "The only working text [he] uses is a large sketch book . . . in which he writes a large series of notes, made up essentially of a summary of the principal sequences. . . Dialogue written the night before or improvised on the spot eventually fills out the summary." The film absolutely reflects this kind of preparation. It isn't something we watch in the usual sense of our being cozily settled. We catch it as it catches us.

Nevertheless, Godard's "original screenplay" has behind it, and presumably somewhere *in* it, two stories by Guy de Maupassant: "La femme de Paul" (1881) and "Le signe" (1886). Indeed, these two stories were supposed to be the film's original impetus, that is, from the standpoint of those bankrolling the project the reason for the film's being made in the first place. The time, the setting and the plot of these stories, though, claim little connection with the film that Godard did make; but something of their spirit contributes to the film's emotional texture and thematic development. The first story is about a young man, Paul Baron, whose mistress forsakes him one night for a lesbian encounter, prompting his suicide. "Paul's Wife" is the literal translation of the title, although, because Paul and Madeleine are unmarried lovers, the story has become known in English as "Paul's Mistress." Maupassant was a troubled man—syphilitic since youth and, as a result, increasingly unbalanced and eventually institutionalized (in 1892) after attempting suicide by cutting his throat; but he was no fool. Madeleine may not be married to Paul, but the point of the title is twofold: Paul's sense of commitment to Madeleine is already based on his assumption of their spiritual union; and Madeleine, who ends up being comforted by her new lover, at the last feels like a bereaved widow, as though she had been Paul's wife all along. Irony is the piercing delight of Maupassant at his best, here, the fact that sexual infidelity, given its unhappy consequence, can strengthen the girl's one-way emotional bond with the deceased even as she seeks solace in someone else's arms. (The oft-repeated comparison of Maupassant and North Carolina's O. Henry—William Sidney Porter—is ridiculous. There's nothing in O. Henry's stories to match the psychological complexity I have just described. His "ironies" are nothing more than plot twists.) The slighter "Le signe"—"The Signal"—turns on an irony of almost mathematical complacency. A woman notices from her window a prostitute who, from *her* window, is giving men down in the street the beckoning look that she, Mrs. Respectability, feels compelled to try for herself. This leads to an adulterous encounter whose moral offensiveness, a friend of hers, another "respectable" lady, counsels can be neutralized by using the ill-gotten money to buy the cuckolded spouse a gift. From "La femme de Paul" Godard draws the devastating sense of a non-negotiable gap between lover and beloved, despite all their intimacies, and from "Le signe," with its cunning exposure of bourgeois logic, he draws an equally compelling sense of the complacency into which lovers may retreat as a defense against both this omnipresent gap and the messy collision of their contrary impulses toward intimacy with their beloved and the maintenance of their own independence and individualism. "Le signe" also instances for him role-modeling, as one woman emulates and imitates another, even one of whom she is contemptuous, before in effect (by following her advice, it's implied) copying yet another woman. Godard surely doesn't seem to be paying Maupassant any notice, then, when in fact he is astutely engaging in literary criticism by drawing identifiable, interesting chords from the thematic heart of each story—chords that are, in the case of "La femme de Paul," deeply moving besides.

Pauline Kael, in one of her best reviews, noted that Godard "gets the little things that people who have to follow scripts can't get: the differences in the way girls are with each other and with boys, and boys with each other and with girls." Indeed, the differences between "masculine" and "feminine," as applied to these "children of Marx and Coca-Cola," as Godard describes them, is very much what the film is about. These differences still apply, no matter the distance now between us and the 1960s, and the moderation of gender collision into a more desirable gender companionability as a result of both the "sexual revolution" in that decade and the press for recognition of gender equality in the "second wave" of the feminist movement also begun then. However more amiably, each gender has remained "the other" to the other. "Men are from Mars, and women are from Venus," an American pop psychologist has opined, and although the schematic categorizing and the stereotyping point to oversimplification, an element of reality rings in the remark. Of course, such a statement presupposes the self-certainty, that people of either gender really have mastered issues of their own identity, which Godard's sophisticated film everywhere contests. Godard's characters slip into roles; they engage reality at the protective remove that one mask or another permits. As a result of its being implicit rather than sentimentally posited, vulnerability is shown the more exquisitely and poignantly to be at the core of human nature, but only fleetingly apparent.

Both Paul and Madeleine find role models in their popular culture, as young people still do today. When we first meet Paul he is seated in a café tossing and catching in his mouth a cigarette while composing a poem that seems (ambiguously) to anticipate his own death. It's possible that there's a slight hint here of the tradition of *le poète maudit*; but the much stronger, and contemporary, echo is that of the *nouvelle vague* itself, especially since the movement's signature actor, Jean-Pierre Léaud—François Truffaut's Antoine Doinel in *The 400 Blows* (1959)—is playing Paul. (In *hommage* to this glorious actor, another glorious actor, Keanu Reeves, thirty years hence does the cigarette toss in Steven Baigelman's *nouvelle vague*-ish *Feeling Minnesota*. Please note, also, that Claude Chabrol's 1958 *Les cousins*, like Godard's film, owes something to Maupassant's "La femme de Paul.") This self-reflexivity is itself New Wave; the upshot is that we perceive that Paul is in some sense Jean-Pierre, and vice versa. (This facilitates rather than hampers the film because what we really know about Léaud, from his films, doesn't measure up to what we *think* we know. The distance between us and Léaud, for all our movie-house familiarity, becomes correlative to the distance between Paul and Madeleine.) By the same token, Madeleine draws upon the popular culture for her ambition and her image—but from singing rather than cinema. The Bulgarian-born Sylvie Vartan, an actual yé-yé singer of the day, appears on a billboard in the film, her blank expression matched by that of Madeleine. Moreover, one of Vartan's fellow pop singers, Françoise Hardy, has a cameo in the film. (Brigitte Bardot, who starred in Godard's 1963 *Contempt*, has another.) Finally, the casting of Madeleine's role instances just as much self-reflexivity as does that of Paul's. The actress playing her, Chantal Goya, was herself a pop singer who would sustain a career by singing songs for children composed and written by spouse Jean-Jacques Debout.

Paul's death, again, is ambiguous. He may have taken an accidental spill off an apartment balcony. (That's the official story. He fell back over the balcony while taking photographs of the new apartment he had bought with money he inherited from his mother.) It may be a suicide—a leap to pavement. This fatal choice may be the only means, Paul feels, for negotiating the perpetual distance between himself and Madeleine. Another means would be for him to have murdered Madeleine; but Paul is a gentle sort and, possibly beneath his adolescent insecurities, not so egoistic as he seems. The other possibility is that Madeleine— or, I suppose, someone else—gave the boy a push. The close of the film finds Madeleine pregnant and responding to a police officer in a seemingly evasive and suspicious manner. She plays with her hair and alternately looks at the man questioning her and then off to the left, as though half in the shared routine world and half in some reverie of her own. The film ends with the word *féminin* printed on the screen, out of which the first and last two letters are selected for another word: *fin*. It is the end of the film, to be sure, but the shortening of the first word to the second suggests that Madeleine, the female, has always contained within her, somehow, the end of her lover, Paul—that women (as the saying goes) will be the death of men, in the sense of the frustrating effort men make to understand the women they love and to come together with them. (Of course, given the terms of this particular film, this automatically means simultaneously that men will be the death of women.) A shot pierces the soundtrack; this is the ultimate note of a film that had begun with two kinds of sounds punctuating the opening credits: gunshots; someone offscreen whistling the French national anthem, "La Marseillaise." We later assume that the whistler is Paul, and that the tune he is whistling bears three distinct and separate meanings. It is the residue of his just ended military service. It is irony, for the boy is opposed to the authoritarianism with which he identifies the state. It is heartfelt expression, for the boy loves the freedom with which he identifies France—the love of freedom he feels is ripe for betrayal by government. In any case, Godard, who I think to some degree identifies with Paul despite the objectivity of his filmmaking method, seems to have taken pains to give Paul a life beyond the limits of his onscreen character. We may say, perhaps, that Paul at least represents the spirit of restless, radical French youth.

But something else occurs to me of a deeply ironical nature. We never see the policeman; he is entirely offscreen, and as his questioning recalls Paul's own interviewing we may in some sense interpret him as Paul's reincarnation—to be precise, reconstitution—asking, for instance, about something wholly relevant to the deceased Paul, what Madeleine will do about the fetus she is carrying and nourishing. Her response is expressed in a coldly playful way: "curtain rods." In context, this teasing contemplation of abortion, besides assaulting the authority of the Catholic Church in France and therefore, by metaphoric extension, all other authority such as the government, expresses as well Godard's depth of concern for the future of France. Indeed, it is in this context that a part of the film's anti-Americanism is best understood. (Summarily I will take up two other parts of it.) The protests in the film against American involvement in Vietnam, far from facilely promoting French superiority over the United States, bears instead the deeply troubled memory of France's own quagmire in Indochina, that is, the mess there that the U.S. took over from the French, and more recently the Algerian War. Algeria had been colonized by the French in 1848, and Charles de Gaulle's election as France's president 110 years later was predicated on his keeping Algeria French. De Gaulle had his own contrary agenda, however, and he very slowly withdrew France from this bloody war, from Algeria, which became independent in 1962. This is my point: Paul's transcendence of the limits of mortal characterization has something to do with his coming after—that is, having eluded—the war; his military service was in 1965 and 1966. Yet his radicalism seems to come out of France's experiences in both Indochina and Algeria, the historical memory of which, borne as a subliminal burden, accounts for some aspect of his personal (psychological, behavioral) disarray. In a sense, Godard, nearly a generation older than Paul/Léaud, invests Paul with his own historical memory, thus making his own survival of Paul an indication of Paul's (somehow) survival despite the narrative of the film that posits Paul's death as a point of fact. (This death is never shown; we simply are told about it out of the blue, shortcircuiting our ability to attach to it any real emotional weight. Those put off by this Brechtian tendency in Godard betray the degree to which they are regrettably wedded to the manipulative sentimentalism of bogus Hollywood "filmmaking.") Related to this, we may also say, I think, that Paul in some sense embodies humanity's—and in particular Godard's—concern over war. Paul in voiceover can be heard among people at a bookstore asking, "Do you know that a war is going on between the Iraqis and the Kurds?"

One more point needs to be made about the ambiguity of Paul's death. In the Maupassant story, Paul's suicide is a given. This might have grated Godard, with its strong sense of omniscient narration, because human death is more often than not ambiguous and complex. It often only appears simple.

There are at least two more aspects of the film's anti-Americanism that are worth addressing. One again has to do with war. Why, it's often asked, does Godard toss into this film a bit of the American play *Dutchman*, by LeRoi Jones (later, Amiri Baraka). Consider the play's theme: waiting to explode, suppressed African-American rage against white America. Godard in passing gives voice to this black voice because he shares Jones's sense of white American oppression of black Americans. What does this to do with *Masculin-Féminin*? It deepens by association the protests in the film against the U.S. in Vietnam by suggesting the racist basis of this bloody involvement. I love Godard's coup of Brechtian Chinese boxes, for *Dutchman* itself is a play whose distancing techniques encourage thoughtful analysis on the part of the audience; the part that Godard selects likewise bears this Brechtianism, and the process of selection that takes out of context a part that can, as here, fairly and honestly represent the whole encloses the distanced material in another degree or dimension of distancing. Godard is never so difficult to understand as it is the case that certain viewers willfully find his work difficult to understand, although of course both their brilliance and open-endedness make his films inexhaustible—impossible ever to grasp fully, hence always ripe for fresh discoveries.

The other aspect of anti-Americanism in the film is its portrayal of that shallow and ubiquitous "pop culture" that's America's largest and most pernicious export. According to Kael, the film's unifying theme is "the fresh beauty of youth amidst the flimsiness of Pop culture and Pop politics." I agree in part. Godard takes a more generous view of youthful political activism than Kael's remark suggests; he distinguishes between the personality, if not the sanctity, of its idealism and the frequent immaturity of its expression. He finds it both "fresh" and "flimsy," as it were, and restless and messily groping. However, the classicist in him (which will especially come to the fore in the savagely satirical 1967 *Weekend*) finds it harder to accept a popular culture that, instead of forming a repository for a nation's, or a continent's, collective values, pursues consumerism in order to exploit a buying public and amass profits—although it just may be the case that greed is the only shared value of the corporate United States. Clearly, Coca-Cola is the symbol of this intrusion into France of American (pardon the pun) pop, and it's the perfect symbol, too: something insubstantial that seduces and addicts especially the young, at once, paradoxically, fueling and sapping their energy—and rotting their teeth. When Paul cries out, "U.S., go home!" it's clear, to us at least, that he wants the U.S. out of European, including French, culture as much as he wants the U.S. out of Vietnam.

Godard distinguishes between kinds of Americans and is, for example, in sympathy with those young Americans protesting their nation's vicious rampages of slaughter in Southeast Asia. Godard is against tyranny. Thus he has Paul sing against Hitler, Stalin and Lyndon Johnson, the then-current U.S. president, all of whom, he concludes, should be killed—a remark obviously targeting tyrants in general since Hitler and Stalin were already both dead. Reasonably enough, Godard takes aim, though, only at those elements of intrusive popular culture—a form of economic neocolonialism where the politics remain hidden—that serve the interests of tyranny. Thus he provides a scene in a café (just before Paul's merrily lethal ditty) where Robert, Paul's friend, speaks of Bob Dylan, about whom Paul is ignorant, describing him as a "Vietnik," a war protester being described by use of "an American word that comes from beatnik and Vietnam" and which, by the "nik" at the end, as in the case of the word "refusenik," implies (for the moment, two years before Soviet tanks rolled into Czechoslovakia) a pro-Russian bias. In short, the film distinguishes between two forms of "pop culture," the exploitive Coca-Cola kind, in pursuit of nothing but profits and control of markets, and what would become known at the end of the decade as the *counter-culture*, courtesy of Berkeley historian Theodore Roszak's book *The Making of a Counter Culture*. It's easy to see why the film implies that Madeleine's lightweight singing belongs in the former category. It's offensively inoffensive, this kind of pointless pop warbling, and, seducing girls to career ambitions facilitating political apathy, its sound seems wedded to the blank expression that so often occupies Madeleine's pretty face—the expression that convinces us at the last that Madeleine may have murdered Paul.

Even so dark a possibility as that—and that's all it is: a fleeting possibility—contributes to the openness and light-sensitive nature, if you will, the instability of youth from which Godard takes, creates the style of this amazing and irresistible film. This "style" brings together, mixes up and merges any number of styles, as is the wont of the *nouvelle vague*, whose films seek to share their possibilities with audiences rather than dictate to audiences what they should feel and how they should respond. There is romantic comedy, the behavioral comedy of the apartment scenes among Paul, Madeleine, Catherine and Elisabeth, the political patches including the political theater of the *Dutchman* episode, the sketches of friendship involving Paul and Robert, the screwball sexual-verbal sparring between Catherine and Robert, the parody of *The Silence* in a film-within-the-film throughout which Paul especially cannot stop talking and, of course, the lovely, open-ended incursions into *cinéma-vérité* in the interviews that Paul conducts. "Are you happy?" is the question that sociologist Edgar Morin asked passers-by in Jean Rouch's *Chronicle of a Summer* (1961), whose use of a lightweight portable camera—the "living camera"—has plainly inspired Paul, a budding Jean-Luc Godard. But certainly, through him, Godard has as much in mind *Le joli Mai* (1962), Chris Marker's marvelous vignette-crammed Parisian essay on the occasion of the end of the Algerian War, marking France's first breath of peace in nearly a quarter-century. Is there any "adult" event in (then) recent France as the end of this war that so matches the sense of possibilities that we and Godard's film identify with the young?

Indeed, Paul's inquiries, as the camera remains on his interviewee Elsa, draw together a stunning portrait of the openness and guardedness, the boldness and hesitancy, the certainty and uncertainty, the prosaic dullness and bewitching, all-flying lyricism and tenderness of the young. (Some of the conversations between Paul and Madeleine, incidentally, are shot in the same manner and arrive at the same effect.) Godard also, however, takes aim at what he perceives to be the imperiled nature of France's young people. Elsa, a friend of Madeleine, discloses that the magazine for which she works, *Mademoiselle 19*, has named her its representative 19-year-old for the year—Godard's witty and unexpectedly moving encapsulation of the lightness and fleeting nature of youth. Paul, typically off-camera, asks her why she wanted this title, and Elsa explains she *hadn't* wanted it; rather, it befell her as a stroke of luck. But the title has apparently reinvented her identity, for its "advantages"—trips; gifts—have persuaded her not to go back to college to complete her degree. Paul asks, "So you like having your car more than your diploma?" to which Elsa replies, "I'm happy because I have both," meaning a college degree is unnecessary now and her school diploma sufficient. (We later recall Paul's mention of the car because his acquisition of a private apartment—his revulsion at being co-opted unexpectedly by materialism—offers a possible motive for suicide, if indeed he did choose to end his life.) But what about the value of education? Paul presses, "For you, does socialism still have a chance?" "Oh, you know, I'm not very qualified to answer that," Elsa responds; "I don't know anything about it." She keeps dodging Paul's attempts to get her to think and speak, explaining, "I'll get confused," but Paul is like a hound on a scent, in part because Godard, through this encounter, is implying that the possibility of socialism in France may depend on Elsa and on all the nation's Elsas. Paul thus asks her about the difference between the American way and the socialist way of life, to which she expresses preference for the American way, preference even for the U.S. over France, because as Mademoiselle 19 she traveled to the U.S. and somehow found that women there "play the leading role, you know." Without losing a jot of his objective manner, Paul then asks her whether she knows what the word *reactionary*—implicitly, the word that sums up the U.S.—means, and Elsa says, "it's being in opposition, reacting against a lot of things, not accepting just anything that happens." But the astounding comment of hers comes after when she pronounces reactionaryism a good thing. Her explanation: "I don't like men who say 'Amen' to everything"—logic that scarcely supports or defends the position she has taken. Once we bring together these (and other) elements of the interview we are able to discern Godard's indictment of American corruption of French youth, given here the additional slant that, while being young is identifiable with openness and possibilities, American influence cancels these, destroying young people in France and thus threatening to rob France of its future. *Masculin-Féminin* unfolds as a mostly very gentle film. Neither its tone nor its style suggests the apocalyptic *Weekend* ahead, but the content, once you think about it, is strong stuff.

Léaud, who won as best actor at Berlin, gives a terrific performance as Paul. Two years hence his third whack at Antoine Doinel for Truffaut, in *Baisers volées* (*Stolen Kisses*, 1968), suggests a depoliticized version of Paul. (Both boys, just out of the service, are suddenly looking for themselves and for romance.) It has often been noted that Paul in *Masculin-Féminin*, not Antoine in *Stolen Kisses* with his bourgeois ambitions, appears the truer continuation of the troubled 15-year-old Doinel in *The 400 Blows*, the finest portrait of working-class male adolescence in all of cinema. In any case, this last film—the first of the three—had already secured Léaud's place in the pantheon of screen actors, but *Masculin-Féminin* elicited sighs of pleasure and relief: Léaud, it turned out, really could act; unlike certain other very young stars, he would have a career. And still does.

Those of the *nouvelle vague* admired Robert Bresson for artistically going his own way. From the 1937 novel *Nouvelle histoire de Mouchette* by Georges Bernanos, Robert Bresson's austere, elliptical *Mouchette* begins with a woman seated alone in a spare church who wonders aloud how her family will manage after her impending death. We hear her footsteps trailing as she exits the shot where she had occupied the foreground. The camera stays fixed; it is the steadfastness of God, perhaps, who oversees the exiting of mortals from the human scene. One might as well give God a name for this occasion. Call him Bresson. We are left with one thing in the frame, one thing in the church that is constant, that is to say, that we witnessed in the background of the shot even when the woman was present: a simple empty chair facing in the opposite direction from the camera as the woman had faced. Even though we have just met the worried mother who has just departed, the emptiness of the chair suggests to the quick of our hearts her soon-to-be-vacated life. We are implicated in her illness, her dying, her death and her family: three children, one of them an infant, and a spouse. The film will end with what appears to be, and may be, the suicide of her daughter, 14-year-old Mouchette. In fits and starts Mouchette rolls down a hill, entering and departing frames, the camera pausing to remain on the vacated scene rather than following her, just as it had done with her mother in the beginning in church. (Chords of Claudio Monteverdi's *Magnificat*—the two brief bursts, the film's only background music—further connect the opening and the close of the film.) We miss the point of entry when Mouchette tumbles into the river, but we note the evidence on the surface of the water. Some will say that Mouchette has fulfilled her mother's concern and apprehension. Others will think otherwise, saying instead that Mouchette has redeemed her mother's soul of part of the burden of her concern and apprehension. To know for certain which it is one would have to know the ways of humanity and the ways of God.

The setting is the provincial village of Saint-Venant in northern France. The pre-credit opening introducing us to Mouchette's mother raises an expectation that the first scene following the opening credits will show us the family over whose fate the unidentified woman has expressed such concern. This doesn't happen. The camera has shifted from indoors to outdoors, from inside the church to woods at the outskirts of the village. The intricacy of leaves in daylight has replaced the church's dark, spare interior. Three characters participate in this scene, two humans and an animal. We do not yet know the identities of the two men, just as we have yet to learn who the woman at the outset is. One, hidden from view from the other, is the game warden, Mathieu. Our surrogate as we also observe, hidden from view, he is silently watching—what we see of Mathieu, in silent inserts, are his eyes espying —Arsène, a poacher. We hear the rustle of the poacher's footsteps on the ground of the woods. Arsène is using a twig and looped string to trap a game bird by the leg. It works. The bird, caught, flutters desperately. After Arsène leaves, Mathieu extricates the bird from its "noose" and lets the bird go. The bird flies away, the sound of its flutter echoing its anxious flutter when caught, perhaps hinting that its vulnerability to capture renders constant its painfully qualified freedom. The juxtaposition of this passage with the pre-credit one may seem to associate the bird with the mother, presaging her death as freedom from sickness, but soon afterwards we finally see Mouchette as she is walking home, alone, from school. Now we associate the caught bird with her—Mouchette, whose name means "little fly." Her earthly freedom will come at the end: the moment of water covering her. Does God "test" and torture Mouchette, as well as the rest of us, before letting us go?

This suggestion would make *Mouchette* Bresson's most (Emily) Dickinsonian film. However, the ending, with its Godly suggestion, is not the only context that the film provides for the association of Mouchette with Arsène's trapped bird. Later, a drunken Arsène will rape Mouchette, after giving her shelter in a rainstorm, and then himself let her go. How does what we see early on in the film relate to Mouchette's fortunes and fate? Is it the case that we are complying with Bresson's clues leading us to the truth, Mouchette's association with the caught bird? *What if*—what if Bresson is challenging the whole literary notion of such symbolism on the grounds of its reductivism when applied to cinema? What if, in addition, he means to imply that the associations that we draw in reality are often a "misreading" of the clues that experience, or God, seems to leave for us to decipher? What if in fact Bresson is pressing us to attend to Mouchette's humanity rather than cobbling together an understanding of her from what in fact are random associations and meaningless clues? Throughout the film, Mouchette almost invariably will wear a blank, sullen expression. Perhaps this "mask" of hers reflects the burden of associations that have been projected onto her by the communal hostility that we will see in detail. Perhaps Bresson is prodding us to penetrate the mask, to see the humanity of the girl that lies behind it—the humanity that she keeps hidden as a means of self-protection. Or has Mouchette been thoroughly dehumanized by her environment? Bresson once said: "Mouchette offers evidence of misery and cruelty. She is found everywhere: wars, concentration camps, tortures, assassinations." Very shortly before her own death, Mouchette observes a rabbit on the ground in its death throes. Behind her own blank expression is she identifying with this creature?

I have long associated—at times, even identified—Mouchette with an animal myself: Balthazar, the donkey in Bresson's immediately previous film, *Au hasard Balthazar* (1966). At some level, this association of Balthazar and Mouchette is banal and incontestable; both lead lives of incredible challenge and hardship. Now I am no longer sure, though, that the association between them works at all levels of *Mouchette*. Bresson may also mean for us to test and contest this association.

It is certainly the case that Mouchette is an object of derision among her peers, her schoolmates, as well as among adults, whose cruelty that of the children likely reflects. Mouchette's family is poor, her father, who routinely smacks her, a drunkard (one piece of her mother's deathbed advice to Mouchette is to steer clear of men who drink alcohol); above all, it is the poverty that is most troublesome as a threat to others. The village is, overall, not one of means, and the poverty of one family threatens other families with its looming possibility at some point for themselves. However, I am struck by an interesting discrepancy between the derision with which we think that Mouchette is targeted and the actual amount that comes her way. Typical of this is a trenchant schoolroom scene in which the teacher torments Mouchette who perfectly sings a song but for a single off-pitch note. The teacher presses Mouchette's head down to the correct piano key, which she strikes again and again into Mouchette's face—an extraordinary pedagogical assault. We see what Mouchette, her back towards them, can't: her classmates are appalled by what their teacher is doing to her, fearful, perhaps, at their own vulnerability to such mistreatment. (Later in the film, Mouchette poignantly sings the song perfectly.) However, feeling humiliated before them, Mouchette assumes a solidarity among her peers and their teacher. Outside, Mouchette pelts classmates with dirt, which they do their best to ignore. Now we recall that, in an earlier scene at the end of another schoolday, a classmate had called out to her, "Mouchette!" and Mouchette ignored the girl and her likely friendly entreaty. Mouchette's alienation, Bresson wants us to understand, is partially the result of pride and of her own making.

Indeed, Bresson sensitively explores telling discrepancies as a matter of course. In *The Diary of a Country Priest* (1950), also from Bernanos, for example, the young cleric consistently misunderstands himself and others, and misinterprets reality in other ways. *The Trial of Joan of Arc* (1962) is largely constructed on the chasm between Joan's invisible interiority and various misperceptions of her. Two other "discrepancies" involving Mouchette also have to do with how this teenager is misperceived. The image of her as "dirty" floats about in the village; this is normal scapegoating procedure ("dirty blacks," "dirty Jews"), but it is undone by what Bresson actually shows us: a well-groomed girl whose mother has taken obvious care to dress her in clean, simple, handmade clothes. Certainly Mouchette stands out alongside the other girls in their store-bought clothes, but it is not for being dirty. (Nor can Mouchette make the *others* dirty; when she pelts classmates with clumps of dirt, none of the soil sticks!) Ironically, the more stylishly dressed other girls appear as a result more sexually precocious, but it is Mouchette who is branded a whore after she is raped. There is also a way in which we may misperceive Mouchette, assuming her incompetence as a maternal fill-in now that her mother, incapacitated, lies sick and dying. Although it is difficult to gauge at what emotional and mental price this is so, Mouchette is hugely competent at nearly all that she attempts to do. (At most, she gets a single note wrong here and there.) One example of this is her nearly simultaneous readying of four cups of coffee for her family and herself. Another is her feeding the baby milk, which she does in a manner both nurturing and efficient, at her mother's instruction from her deathbed. Mouchette may feel overwhelmed by the additional burden of responsibility she shoulders at home due to her mother's illness; but, to my eye at least, it doesn't show.

Mouchette is, after all, highly adaptable, and she takes what comfort and pleasure from her world as she can find. Consider her rape by Arsène, whose epileptic seizure so unmans him that this rape of a girl he had been helping and sheltering becomes his means of restoring a sense of command in the universe. During the rape, at first Mouchette resists with all her might; however, then she wholly participates in the sex, as we can see from the relaxation of her hand on Arsène's back and then her hugging him. Mouchette is drawing unaccustomed warmth from the experience, and the next day she even refers to Arsène, naïvely, as her "boyfriend." (Or am I the one who is naïve? Perhaps Mouchette refers to him as such only as a way to say "Fuck you!" to the world.) Earlier, at a makeshift amusement park, some kind soul places a coin in Mouchette's hand that allows her to participate in a car bombardment ride. It breaks our heart when we finally see Mouchette smile, and broadly too, as she gleefully throws herself into the event. On the other hand, her sensitivity and pride sometimes keep Mouchette from enjoying all she can in life. After her mother's death, one creepy adult acts "kindly" toward Mouchette, extending condescending charity from which Mouchette understandably recoils. But following that, someone extends genuine kindness to her, which includes giving her dresses that Mouchette will be holding onto during that ultimate roll of hers, and Mouchette treats the elderly woman unkindly, as though she were still reacting to the other woman who had treated her unkindly. (Sometimes we wrongly perceive unkindness as a result of *anticipating* unkindness.) Like the rest of us, especially when we are young, Mouchette isn't always fair, and this plays out to her detriment.

I cannot say why Mouchette commits suicide, or even if she *does* commit suicide. (Her "suicide" may be a misperception of her death; it is possible that volition is not among the elements which catapult Mouchette into the river.) There are unknowable things in Bresson's film, just as there are unknowable things in life. But one thing that makes Mouchette's death so shattering is precisely the fact that we never see her body enter the river. Let me explain. Like Bresson films generally, *Mouchette* is a thing of materiality; Bresson's film stresses objects, parts of bodies (such as the shot at the amusement park when the gift of the coin passes from hand to hand in closeup), and overall *thingness*. Mouchette herself is represented throughout the film by her clogs, which become a kind of synecdoche, as though these clogs aren't things she wears but are a part of her. We know her clogs by their sound, which Bresson has amplified as a disruption of silence correlative to Mouchette's sense, and the community's sense, that Mouchette is an irritant, somehow alien, someone who doesn't fit in. The shoes, like her outfits hand-made rather than store-bought, mark Mouchette's poverty and, to the ear, assume the aspect of a defiant child's curse. Late for her music class, Mouchette's disruptive entrance is summed up by the loud sound of the invading footwear, and we note the teacher's irritation, which erupts in cruelty once Mouchette is off-pitch in her singing; in effect, it is the discordant sound of Mouchette's wooden footwear that anticipates the bad note her voice hits. Why does Mouchette stomp one of her clogs as she, her older brother and her father are about to enter church? Possibly it is a respectful gesture clumsily executed, an attempt to rid herself of dirt for the sanctity of the hallowed building. Perhaps, too, it is intentionally disrespectful, an off-note of derision aimed at the notion of this sanctity and of authority in general. When her father assaults her in plain view for what she has done outside the church, it is clear that he believes that his daughter's act assails his authority. But, most intriguingly, the clog becomes a silent thing in another scene, when in the rainstorm Mouchette loses one of her clogs to the ravenous mud below and Arsène retrieves it for her, rescuing it as indeed he is rescuing her by providing her with shelter from the storm before, that is, the yonic symbol (a displaced vagina) that the clog also is (Bresson's Mouchette possesses affinity with Luis Buñuel's Viridiana from five years earlier) kicks into Arsène's unconscious an element of sexual provocation, especially when he feels compelled to redress the sense of imbalance between himself and the girl caused by the loss of control he incurred by his epileptic seizure on the floor of his cabin, with this pariah-child in humiliating attendance. The whole scene anticipates Mouchette's extraordinary end in reverse, the fits and starts of her hill-rolling unconsciously mimicking Arsène's fit, and her entrance into the river a purified visual echo of the temporary loss of a clog to the rain-soaked earth. In the cinema of Robert Bresson, the accumulation of materiality exerts a pressure on this materiality that yields an unexpected store, or discharge, or realization of spirituality.

Typically, Bresson's style is analytical rather than either lyrical or sentimental. Bresson rounds up the usual suspects: closeups of parts of people (eyes, hands, backs) and things (shoes, cups, bottles). The style of his editing is equally analytical, often enlivening our participation by short, quick shots, often in succession to illustrate the same action or event from different perspectives, whether physical or psychological, or both. It is this style, a breaking-down of things, that lends such overwhelming force to the second of the black-and-white film's two long-held shots, with the camera held back a bit (the first such shot is the opening one, as the dying mother expresses concern for her family in church): the close, as the surface of the river, glimpsed by us at an angle through and around a partial barrier of trees, records the drowning below of the dead mother's child and family surrogate. In this peaceful setting, Mouchette escapes the crash of her clogs, her father's slaps, the baby's cries that mimic her own inner cries—ironically, in the baby's case, for being wet. Perhaps Mouchette, for the first time, is going home.

The list:

1960

NIGHT AND FOG IN JAPAN (Japan). In 1958 Japan renegotiated its 1952 treaty ending U.S. occupation, whose original terms had impressed Japanese youth with a sense of futility, radicalizing them. Many felt the new security terms, which strengthened Japan's alliance with the U.S., betrayed its constitution, which had committed Japan to the course of peace. With its title referring to Alain Resnais's *Night and Fog* (1955), Nagisa Oshima's fictional *Nihon no yoru to kiri* haunts, instead of a Nazi death camp, Nozawa's wedding party, which is peopled by dimmed, compromised radicals. (As a student, Oshima had participated in the movement.) Withering, ghost-ridden, the film targets the nuclear-insane U.S., the insufficiency of Sovietism to provide a viable alternative, the collapse of Japanese radicalism and idealism. A wedding's new beginning occasions a renewed sense of betrayal, militant poses pointing to an empty nostalgia, and a catalogue of political post-mortems.

A seemingly black-and-white shot through a dark forest finds someone approaching the window through which we espy the groom and bride standing behind a table, flanked by others, and all so rigid we might swear we were looking at a photograph. Inside, all is in woody, earthen color; someone summarizes recent clashes between students and police. The camera moves back and forth, left and right, one camera movement ironically canceling the other; everyone stands perfectly still except for the one who is speaking, who is also standing. When he is finished, another man speaks.

In the same fluid shot, amidst constrained singing, the back-and-forth camera finds the man of the forest, the groom's friend, entering. Soon after, members of the wedding enter the past: voices and tableaux of student protest enrobed in darkness, ideological discussions, strategy sessions. Elegiac singing echoes: Where *are* we? Past or present? Among the living or the dead?

L'AVVENTURA (Italy, France). *See above.*

PSYCHO (U.S.). Marion Crane (Janet Leigh, marvelous) steals money from her Phoenix employer. On the way to lover Sam Loomis's small town, in the rainy dark she inadvertently slips onto a back road, finding a barely functioning motel run by Norman Bates. After chatting with Bates, Marion decides to return the money; but the boy's jealous mother kills her, and Bates unknowingly tanks the money in a swamp in covering up the crime. Bates's mother died years ago, it turns out, and Bates—in denial; schizophrenic—periodically "becomes" Mother to reverse her death and assuage loneliness.

Based on the case of Wisconsin farmer and serial killer Ed Gein, Alfred Hitchcock's *Psycho* essays American loneliness, which certain forces compel: rugged individualism as a character goal worthy of especially male pursuit; the suspiciousness, hostility and competitiveness this pursuit fosters; urban impersonality; rural isolation.

Marion steals because she sees no other way of translating her tawdry affair into the respectability of marriage. Bates also is in financial distress, the fortunes of his family enterprise having shifted with the California sands underneath when the main highway, whose traffic the motel once accessed, was moved, banishing the motel to a marginal existence. Sales of hardware should translate into sufficient income for Loomis, but his luck is adrift in the same desert. In the U.S., the unpredictability of survival is peculiarly accompanied by an official insistence that hard work always yields a solvent result and that a contrary outcome is the individual's fault.

Psycho sharpens its doleful black-and-white vision with wit, as when, from a tightly wound rotation on the murdered woman's face, the camera, abruptly, appears to float to the stolen money by her motel room bed—a parody of "spirit leaving body" pointing up materialism's place above spirituality in America's hierarchy of values.

DEVI (India). Formerly an assistant on Renoir's beauteous *The River* (1951), Bengali filmmaker Satyajit Ray achieved his most concentrated result with *The Goddess*, which charts a soul's disintegration. Subrata Mitra is Ray's peerless black-and-white cinematographer.

While Umaprasad, her husband, is away at school, Doyamoyee is destroyed when, believing she is the incarnation of Kali, the Great Mother, her father-in-law institutes a cult of worship around her. The girl, traditional, herself comes to believe she is no longer human, as processions of ailing individuals prevail upon her for blessings, and cures for themselves and loved ones. Tugged in opposite directions in a generational clash of males between father and son, Doyamoyee dissolves into madness.

Devi unfolds in dark, sensuous, dreamlike images that suggest the corruption of family relations by various forms of jealousy, including the father's against his becoming-higher-educated son, and by the past's legacy of religious superstitiousness, with its sublimation of eroticism. The boy away at university is the righteous hero—in his own eyes, at least. But he is oblivious to the contribution he is making to his wife's destruction by his insistence on India's future at the expense of its past. Unwittingly, Umaprasad sacrifices Doyamoyee to his "enlightened" stand. There are, in fact, no heroes or villains here; the situation is tragic, as India's past and future struggle without success to find common ground. Ray's powerful fable explores, then, different kinds of human blindness and pride; even Doyamoyee is ambivalent about the crippling designation—that of a goddess, after all—that is cruelly imposed on her. Doyamoyee loses sight of herself. In a shot of stunning irony, we ourselves lose sight of her in deep darkness as she loses contact with the last thread of her own identity.

Soumitra Chatterjee gives a tremendous performance as Umaprasad.

LES BONNES FEMMES (France). Written by Chabrol and Paul Gégauff, Claude Chabrol's masterpiece depicts the bleak, harsh world of four Parisian shopgirls. Along with *Que la bête meure* (1969), this is Chabrol's most personal film, as well as his starkest and most exacting. Its initial hostile reception found Chabrol (after a dip into rank commercialism) replacing its style with a silken, elegant one that yielded many beautiful results, but nothing to compare with the profound tragic disposition of *Les bonnes femmes*.

Chabrol signals his intent. The opening credit sequence, in gray daylight, shows Parisian traffic from an unsettling low camera angle. Immediately afterwards, blaring lights punctuate pitch blackness—a brusque shift to nearly lurid visuals that undoes the commercial come-on, "City of Lights." We hear an offscreen voice at the Grisbi Club huckstering naked women, commoditizing humanity and suggesting the vulnerability to economic and other forms of danger of close-by shopgirls Jane, Jacqueline, Rita and Ginette, who work together at an appliance store.

Chabrol expertly handles the individuation of the shopgirls and their participation in a group identity, a joint fate.

Empty workdays, off-hours fun, romantic connections and pickups: the moment of truth between Jacqueline and the man on a motorcycle who has been shadowing her, who is as lost and compulsive as G. W. Pabst's Jack the Ripper (*Pandora's Box*, 1928), who yet saved her from drowning in the community pool, brings things to a head in Federico Fellini's woods (*The Nights of Cabiria*, 1956).

Robin Wood has remarked that even the shopgirls' dreams have been constricted by their limited environment, debasing these dreams. Theirs is a life absent transport, transcendence.

A four-shot of three of the girls and Jane's fiancé, a soldier, "cages" them at the zoo.

Chabrol's closing passage is the most heartrending in cinema.

LATE AUTUMN (Japan). Yasujiro Ozu's *Akibiyori* is a lovely, humane, mostly comedic meditation on family matters, human existence and acceptance. It resembles Ozu's *Late Spring* (1949), but with a twist. Now it isn't a widower who courts greater loneliness by seeing a daughter through to her wedding, but a widow. While in *Late Spring* the professor feigns his upcoming marriage in order to release his daughter from a sense of obligation, in *Late Autumn* two friends of the widow's spouse concoct a rumor of the teacher's upcoming marriage toward the same end. Either parent chooses to remain solitary as a means of keeping faith with the past and embracing the natural course of life. "That's the way life is"—a summation of the Ozu spirit—is a recurrent line of dialogue in this film.

Ayako becomes enraged when she believes that her mother, Akika (heavenly Setsuko Hara), is planning to marry—a threat to the friendship that has deepened their bond since the death of husband and father. Misunderstandings, however, are corrected. Ayako marries. But the film ends sadly, with Akika alone in the apartment she shared with her daughter. Moreover, the marital match scarcely resolves itself into an image of bliss. The couple's dour pose for a wedding photograph suggests Akika's loving sacrifice for what will prove her daughter's unhappy union.

"Life is simple," someone says in the film; "It's people that make it complicated"—by their feelings. Ozu's is a cinema of transience, of stable life fluctuating, sometimes evaporating, in mortal breezes. Throughout, Ozu inserts shots of people walking—for instance, glimpses through alleyways. The haunting evanescence of such moments is extended through match-editing consecutive ambulatory movements of different characters, either from indoors to out (or vice versa) or from one indoor spot to another. Life passing by.

THE LADY WITH THE LITTLE DOG (U.S.S.R.). Based on Anton Chekhov's 1899 story (as in part is Nikita Mikhalkov's lumbering, inflated *Dark Eyes*, 1987), *Dama s sobachkoy*, by Iosif Kheifits, is an exquisitely wrought gem. With ravishingly lovely black-and-white cinematography (by Andrei Moskvin and Dmitri Meskhiyev), especially at Yalta, this film traces the meeting and the beginning, and possibly the end, of a love affair between two individuals, on holiday away from spouses at a seaside resort, and back home. Dmitri's marriage was arranged; Anna's, to a government official, is likewise conventional. Even their adultery is oddly straightjacketed by society's strictures, affording them little pleasure, only an anticipation of pleasure.

Kheifits has beautifully paced the film to express its Chekhovian stillness, its vertical sense of time. (I kept thinking of Emily Dickinson's marvelous line, "It will be summer— eventually.") Slow, gracious walks, with a pause to note the strange light on the water, contribute to an elongated poise. Each unfolding moment is crystallized by the downward pressure upon it of eternity.

The whole atmosphere, then, suggests that happiness is not in the cards for these two. On the other hand, there is nothing defeatist in their seizure of romantic opportunity, their making out of life's small opportunities whatever they can. They are the light upon the water.

There is one problematic detail: the dog—a nasty little thing. Its pampering, of course, reveals Anna's emptiness and loneliness. But providing an even greater index of her emotional predicament is that Anna holds on for some sort of balance to even so unpleasant a creature. The animal perhaps is a projection of how unworthy of love she feels herself to be because of the small amount of happiness with which she is supposed to make herself content.

Aleksei Batalov is piercing as Dmitri.

SHOOT THE PIANO PLAYER (France). François Truffaut's second feature, from David Goodis's crime novel *Down Here*, opens with a shot of the interior of a piano as the piano is being played. We do not see the pianist. We see the normally invisible apparatus attached to the keys. And we hear the result.

Tirez sur le pianiste nearly concludes with the same shot except that the camera then shows the small-town bar musician who had once been a famous concert pianist. This sadsack seems so passive and immobile that instead of his playing the piano the piano seems to be playing him.

Along with two of his brothers, Edouard-who-calls-himself-Charlie is stuck at the center of a fate that is especially hard on the women who love and are intimate with him. Each meets a violent end, as will happen, it is implied, to the braided young barmaid who is briefly introduced to him (and us) near the end of the film. A solution would be to "shoot the pianist"; he is either the source of or the magnet for the bad luck that lethally befalls his women. The symbolic suicide contained in his name-change is insufficient to undo his curse, and Edouard/Charlie apparently is lost in an aesthetic trance, too mesmerized by his fate to commit suicide for real.

Except that we know that we are peering into the interior of a piano at the film's beginning, near-end and periodically throughout, what Truffaut sets before our eyes would be indecipherable. For some, this film so mixes styles and tones that the result is chaotic, incomprehensible; but once we grasp the logic that connects the tragedies in Edouard/Charlie's life we perceive the sensible order into which the film's seemingly random pieces fit.

Truffaut's gray film is brilliant—and nearly confessional.

ROCCO AND HIS BROTHERS (Italy, France). Italy produces the most trenchant films about brothers. Among these are Valerio Zurlini's *Family Diary* (1962), Francesco Rosi's *Three Brothers* (1981), Gianni Amelio's *The Way We Laughed* (1998)—and, of course, Luchino Visconti's massive *Rocco e i suoi fratelli*, inspired by Giovanni Testori's novel *Il Ponte della Ghisolfa*, and a somewhat extravagant sequel of sorts to *La terra trema* (1948).

The film opens with the arrival by train of widowed Rosaria and four of her sons. Poverty has driven them from southern Italy to industrial Milan, where the family reunites with Vincenzo, a fifth son and brother, struggles, and two of the boys, saintly Rocco and obstreperous Simone (Alain Delon and Renato Salvatori, both wonderful), fall out over Nadia, the prostitute they both love. The atmosphere accompanying this last aspect of the film seems closer to Dostoievski than Visconti's earlier *White Nights* (1957), while the film's episodic structure formally embodies the family's disintegration.

"It's hard to find a job in Milan." Rosaria, Simone, Rocco, Ciro and Luca move into the basement of an apartment block, and the first work the boys do, shoveling pavement, is occasioned by a snowfall. Such fortuitous piecemeal labor, however, is insufficient to sustain them. Simone becomes a boxer; Rocco takes a job in a dry cleaner's. Eventually, after serving in the army, Rocco also becomes a boxer, signing a long-term contract, sacrificing himself in a complicated scheme of events for the sake of Simone, who would otherwise go to prison for theft. The burden of fraternal obligation undoes them both.

Visconti succeeds at describing, though not penetrating, a disastrous immigrant experience, adhering, rather, to Matthew Arnold's dictum, "Not deep the poet sees, but wide." The different degrees to which family members assimilate are fascinating to chart and compare.

PARIS NOUS APPARTIENT (France). Fascism continued after the war to be the principal shadow of murder (and self-murder) stalking the world and individuals in it; *Paris Belongs to Us*, written by first-time director Jacques Rivette and Jean Gruault, is the most terrifying political thriller ever made—one that expands the stalking shadow even while teasingly explaining it away. Encompassing a vast "organization" that may or may not exist, but certainly exists in the mind of Philip Kaufman, whom McCarthyism has driven to Paris from the U.S., this shadow remains a shadow and yet something substantial enough to affect and even determine several lives we see or hear about, leaving a trail of deaths whose final explanations are by no means certain, merely instead the *most recent* "explanations." The film's brilliant "conclusion" may confuse; but that's the point. "Evil has many faces."

Rivette evokes a stark and fluent black-and-white 1957 Paris, one that closes open-endedly on an elusive, haunting image of birds flapping across the Seine. Student Anne Goupil investigates the apparent suicide of Spanish radical Juan, whose death insinuates a spiritual or other connection between Franco and Richard Nixon, who (listen closely) is discussed in the background of one scene. In the process Anne takes up a role in a theater group's production of Shakespeare's *Pericles*, thus launching Rivette's delight in the interactivity of play and reality, artifice and life. The Shakespeare comes and goes, but the "reality" surrounding it is increasingly revealed to be, in a sense, "staged." Inward threats meet outward ones, or create them, or are created by them in a vision of floating paranoid realities complicated by a series of relationships, including romantic ones, but also Anne's relationship with older brother Pierre, which seems inordinately restrained but becomes the tragic center of her life.

1960

WHEN A WOMAN ASCENDS THE STAIRS (Japan). Mikio Naruse's *Onna ga kaidan wo agaru toki* opens with Tokyo bar hostess Keiko's voiceover accompanying shots of commercial streets: "On late autumn afternoons, bars near the Ginza [district] are like girls without makeup." Inside Bar Carton, Keiko's arrival is expected. She phones to say she will be late. Again, she is present only as a voice—and this time, a voice we do not hear. The next cut reverses the scene of the just-ended telephone conversation. We are with Keiko in her flat, and the sequence of shots implies that bar and home each extends the other. Two men are present: bar owner and business manager. The owner blames the business shortfall on Keiko's unwillingness to "go all-out." Translation: Keiko doesn't make herself sexually available to bar patrons, who therefore take their business elsewhere. Irony: before she materializes in order to be berated (rendered speechless, as it were), Keiko is merely a voice, underscoring how little voice she has in her own life.

Periodically Keiko's disembodied voice interrupts, expressing her own world-weariness or providing an objective overview of the lives of women and girls who work in bars: "Around midnight, Tokyo's 16,000 bar women go home. The best go home by car. Second-rate ones, by streetcar. The worst go home with customers."

Repeatedly we watch Keiko's feet as they ascend stairs. "After it gets dark," she says, "I have to climb the stairs [to the bar], and that's what I hate. But once I'm up, I can take whatever happens."

Keiko's attempts to find someone to marry fail. Meanwhile, her efforts to secure funding to buy a local bar also fail. All she can do is negotiate the hard, limited choices available to her. All she can do is ascend the stairs.

LOLA (France). With a tip of the hat to Marlene Dietrich's character in Josef von Sternberg's *The Blue Angel* (1930), Anouk Aimée dazzles as Cécile, a dancer who goes by the name of Lola at work, where she entertains American G.I.s, in Jacques Demy's first feature and enduring black-and-white masterpiece, *Lola*. Nervously breathless, this Lola is like a tremulous shadow flickering as gorgeous light across the screen; the essence of her presence is that Lola seems perpetually poised to take her leave.

Seven years earlier Michel, the love of her life, abandoned Cécile without explanation; she has sex with a sailor who reminds her of him. Frankie, headed home to Chicago, thinks he is in love with Lola, who crosses paths with out-of-work childhood friend Roland, who is definitely in love with her. But Lola's heart belongs to Michel.

The action unfolds in Nantes, whose streets and structures contribute—pardon the oxymoron—a dreamy realism to what critic Roy Armes has aptly called "a gay, lighthearted work, a sort of musical without songs and dances." Indeed, Demy has fashioned a *musical* film, one that is richly scored by Michel Legrand (and there is one sung song, and another melody that in the States is sung as "Watch What Happens"), and that has dancing around the edges. In anticipation of Demy's other masterpiece, *The Umbrellas of Cherbourg* (1964), the dialogue seems poised in the direction of being sung. At film's end, coincidentally, three characters are headed to Cherbourg.

Characters keep running in to one another, have "doubles" that constantly remind others of them and of heartache.

Lola's gaiety seems to encapsulate the comedy of human behavior, the ways in which we cope with longing, loss and practical responsibilities; it is the mask we wear amidst the tragedy of life.

THE CLOUD-CAPPED STAR (India). The first shot is of an enormous tree, the leafy crown of which is asymmetrical. The shot is held and held. A male voice is heard singing. A girl pops into the foreground of the frame. Across the river, a train chugs. The girl smiles, disappears. The camera moves, placing the singer into the frame's foreground. In a number of ways, this bravura opening suggests separation and out-of-jointness. Thus begins *Meghe*

Dhaka Tara, Ritwik Ghatak's turbulent, melancholy film about the misfortunes of a Bengal family from East Pakistan in a refugee village outside Calcutta. Ghatak himself fled to Calcutta as a result of the 1947 partition of Bengal. His film studies the effects of such an event on uprooted lives. It is a tragic anthem for all the world's displaced, dispossessed.

The protagonist is Neeta (Supriya Choudhury, wonderful), whose family, once middle-class, now struggles in poverty. A student, she sacrifices her education and postpones marriage in order to support parents and siblings after injury forces her father out of work. Rather than appreciating her efforts on their behalf, her family exhausts her emotionally and financially, and when her health fails—she is tubercular—her father tosses her out into a raging storm. Ghatak's film is indeed full of echoes of *King Lear*.

Perhaps *Meghe Dhaka Tara* could use a little more discipline; it is oversized, overripe. There may be a few too many trenchant closeups. But there are also beautifully layered compositions, to which foreground, background and the space in between contribute intricately and evocatively; and the film's main arguments, that being wrenched from one's homeland may loosen one's grip on one's humanity and that the family, as institution, may be insufficiently strong to shore up the weakening of these ties, compel. The film is half-baked, half-brilliant.

1961

VIRIDIANA (Spain, Mexico). Only Godard has made more superlative films than Spain's political self-exile Luis Buñuel, whose career spanned a half-century. Antifascist, surrealist, Catholic-turned-antireligionist, Buñuel is a withering artist perpetually applying a satirical razor blade to the eyeballs of the bourgeoisie, Catholic clergy, and other groups he deemed backward. The critical miscomprehension that attended his beautiful *Nazarín* (1958) found him giving many of its themes a more blatant treatment in *Viridiana*. For once, the less subtle rendering proved the greater work. *Viridiana* had to be smuggled out of Franco's Spain, to which Buñuel had returned just to make it, and completed in Mexico.

Dark, coarse, rough wool, black-and-white *Viridiana* is stylistically different from the teasing silk of Buñuel's later French work in color (*Belle de Jour*, 1967; *The Discreet Charm of the Bourgeoisie*, 1972). In it, altruism and idealism collide with mean, grubby reality and various forms of corruption. The film follows Viridiana, a girl about to take final vows at convent, the course of whose life is wrenched when the aristocratic uncle she is visiting lies to her before committing suicide, claiming that he violated her the night before while she was in a drugged state. Viridiana assumes charge of Don Jaime's estate, which she shares with his illegitimate son. Believing she can redeem them through prayer, Viridiana invites in beggars, resulting in the high point of the film's astonishing brio: a looting-rape celebration that visually parodies Leonardo's *The Last Supper* and is set to Handel's *Messiah*. *Hal-le-lu-jah!*

The closeup of a child's feet as she skips rope provides a sense of balance ripe for tragicomic reversal. Fernando Rey is marvelous as Don Jaime, whose chuckle right before he hangs himself with the jump-rope remains one of cinema's most enigmatic and haunting gestures.

LAST YEAR AT MARIENBAD (France). Alain Resnais's grand hotel in *Last Year at Marienbad*, in haunting black and white, is the Mansion of Europe housing France's memory. The twentieth century's traumatic events, beginning with the Great War, have emptied the mansion of inhabitants. Everyone now is a guest in what used to be a home. The place feels abandoned by history. No one quite knows anyone else because people do not quite know themselves anymore.

Resnais and scenarist Alain Robbe-Grillet share an irritation with conventional narrative, that is to say, plot, a lack of interest in character psychology, and a more flexible sense of time than chronology permits. Motivated to forget the century's horrors, can we be selective and retain the memory of love which once helped bring a sense of continuity to our lives?

Few films seem as hermetically sealed as this one, yet its insistence that it exists apart from our chaotic shared world only underscores its connection to that world. Hotel guests retreat into a fantastic realm where order can be (however unsuccessfully) imposed.

Fluid, upwardly tilted tracking shots through hotel corridors eternize human preoccupation with time. An elegant pair "reunite" in what may be, actually, their first meeting. How can one remember love when memory exists in time and in time's passing, but love exists, sublimely, outside time? At once this-worldly and otherworldly, Classical and Romantic, rigorous and at capricious liberty, Resnais's masterpiece is a compulsive yet unfettered dream that fulfills while yet confounding desire. The film's trackings are our eye's journey, the film's voiceovers the voice that the muteness of dream denies us. Like an epiphany, however mysterious, even unfathomable, *Last Year at Marienbad* is also crystal-clear—and cold, beautifully cold: the memory of love longing to be filled by the *feeling* of love.

LA NOTTE (Italy, France). *See above.*

JULES AND JIM (France). A vibrant, volatile bohemian in the first half of the twentieth century, Catherine (Jeanne Moreau, astounding) seeks to re-create herself in François Truffaut's Renoirian *Jules et Jim*. Dressed as a guy, she joins pals Jules and Jim for a spirited race through Parisian air—a lark to her playmates, but expressive of the recognition of her equality that she longs for. Truffaut doesn't disparage the men; he implies, instead, that if any two men could embrace independent, unruly Catherine as their equal it would be Jules and Jim. But telling of the projective fantasy to which this progressive pair is susceptible is that they both first fell in love with Catherine because she reminded them of a favorite statue; and so, from the start, despite their sincere atmospherics of gender equality, Catherine is the adored creature of their desire—and this she cannot bear. She marries Jules and takes Jim as a lover. Finally, having instructed Jules to watch, she drives off a cliff, with passenger Jim, into the sea, hoping to drown herself, along with her husband's behavioral mirror-image, Jim, in her husband's consciousness. Catherine feels she must alert Jules that his liberated self-image blocks him from seeing how gender-insensitive he remains; she sees no other way of improving the lot of their little daughter, Sabine; nor can Catherine otherwise resolve her feeling she remains tied to a variation on the traditional domestic scheme. Truffaut, then, reflects on his own time, the 1960s, when he thus rues the failure of gender relations to match their rhetoric of equality. A half-dozen years hence, therefore, he added a coda: *The Bride Wore Black*—a plea for gender equality as antidote to the destructive acts and behavior that in its absence both men and women are driven to.

SALVATORE GIULIANO (Italy). Francesco Rosi had been making films for a decade when he revolutionized cinema with *Salvatore Giuliano*, which drew upon Neorealism, purging it of sentimentality and didacticism. (Rosi began as an assistant on Visconti's *La terra trema*, 1948.) The film opens in 1950 with an overhead shot of the murdered corpse, in a courtyard, of Salvatore Giuliano, Sicilian folk hero and Mafia associate. A documentary inquiry, without guidance of voiceover or an individual investigator, creates a mosaic fleshing out the import of that shot. During the postwar fight for Sicilian independence, Giuliano is an activist whose partisans, the *pisciotti*, attack Italy's military police (which retaliates with equal brutality in the village of Montelepre) and massacre Communists at Portella della Ginestra. Giuliano eludes authorities, but Giuliano's close associate, Gaspare Pisciotti, is put on trial in Viterbo. Rosi's film, a painstaking reconstruction of events in Sicily and southern Italy, paved the way for Roberto Rossellini's present-tense histories and Gillo Pontecorvo's combustible *The Battle of Algiers* (1965), to whose script Franco Solinas again contributed.

Salvatore Giuliano eludes us as well as authorities; his face is rarely shown, and when the character is shown it is most often as a figure in white fleeing across white mountainous terrain. Beautiful pans of the landscape alternate between evoking the watchful eyes of partisans and searching for Giuliano. He is folk phantom and real boy, his mother's wailing over his dead body attesting to the latter. Using just two professional actors (neither plays Giuliano) in a sea of actual Sicilian villagers many of whom were reliving events in which they had actually participated, Rosi achieves a fantastic degree of realism. The scene in which a wailing mass of women floods the streets in protest to the military round-up of their men is exceptionally powerful.

NINE DAYS OF ONE YEAR (U.S.S.R.). "Now [war] supports science, because war needs science."

Bookending the collapse of the Soviet Union are two events that undercut people's faith in Soviet Communism: the Party's 20th Congress in 1956, where Stalin's successor, Nikita Khrushchev, denounced Stalin, whom the nation's propaganda machine had long elevated to the status of a Lincoln (an event that "happened twice," since the full text of the denouncement wasn't made public until 1989); the Chernobyl nuclear plant disaster, in 1986. Mikhail Romm's *9 dney odnogo goda* relates stunningly to both events. It could not have been made during Stalin's more repressive era, and (however obliquely) it prophesies Chernobyl by focusing on the dangers of nuclear radiation. Its protagonist, Grusev, is a scientific researcher, a nuclear physicist whose exposure to radiation is slowly killing him, unraveling his marriage as well as his life, and testing his resolve to press on for the greater good of humankind—the contribution his experiments is making to Soviet military strength. In one poignant interlude, Grusev visits his father's farm; this dying man's trip to his past is also a collective journey to the agricultural roots of Soviet Communism, suggesting the rift between its idealism and current reality, in however large measure the latter is the result of the Cold War that the U.S. impressed upon the Soviet Union and the rest of the world following World War II.

Starkly composed shots and editing, the film's dark grayness (punctuated by white lab coats), and one other recurrent technique contribute to the film's pervasive fatalism. Low, upwardly angled cameras in Soviet films once showed human forms and faces against the eternal sky, implying a lyrical, progressive Soviet destiny. What irony! Romm uses this camera position and tilt in claustrophobic indoor shots.

A lean, analytical film, this.

(THESE ARE) THE DAMNED (UK). Joseph Losey's science fiction-horror film is a withering piece of prophecy. Children who have been born radioactive as the result of countless nuclear "accidents" are raised underground, by remote control dictate and interaction with adult authority, and studied as models for survival for the "inevitable" event of a nuclear holocaust that will affect everyone. In the process of their captivity, they attempt to escape, guided by adults who have chanced upon them. These orphaned children are the British casualties of World War II ally America's atomic "experiments" involving Hiroshima and Nagasaki. In its broadest scope, *The Damned* is a stinging antiwar film.

Losey, who forsook the U.S. for England in the 1950s after being blacklisted, and Arthur Grant, his black-and-white cinematographer, have devised a series of stark images suggesting a near end of the world to which its inhabitants have reasonably adjusted, as though their whole lives are an evasion of the evidence of imminent annihilation already in their midst. Waves crash against rocks in a seaside setting. There, a sculptor, Freya (Viveca Lindfors, superb), the most decent human being imaginable, sculpts seemingly primordial forms of animal life and fantastic human forms that, by harkening to long-ago beginnings, anticipate life's end. The children's government program is hidden almost in Freya's backyard.

Freya is a friend to Bernard, who runs the program. When she learns about the program and objects to it, he has her killed.

Unlike Stanley Kubrick's glib *Dr. Strangelove or: How I Learned to Stop Worrying and*

Love the Bomb (1964), *The Damned* is genuinely concerned about the fate of humanity. It decries the web of authoritarianism in which societies ensnare children and all the rest of us. Losey doesn't love the bomb or the nuclear nightmare it plunged us into. He cares about the children.

THE EXILES (U.S.). London-born Kent MacKenzie's *The Exiles* begins with Edward S. Curtis photographs: the Native American Past. Cut to the present, on a Bunker Hill, Los Angeles street; through this shot, which initially appears to be another photograph, a trolley moves. This first, unexpected bit of motion establishes a tension with the preceding stasis, motionlessness: moving in time; frozen in time. Homing in on a community of young Native Americans, most of whom have moved off reservations, the film provides this glimpse in a café: the camera pans leftward across a group of seated patrons, and then moves rightward as, standing, one Native American, cornering her, presses another for a date. This passage again combines instances of motion and stasis, creating a tension between them. This isn't haphazard; it is thematic, to the point.

In lustrous black and white, *The Exiles* covers a period of twelve hours, one Friday night and Saturday morning. Three of the characters provide stream-of-consciousness voiceover that they themselves wrote; all the "actors" play themselves. Yvonne's partner, Homer, who routinely abandons her for a night on the town, drinks and doesn't hold a job. Pregnancy, expectancy, possibility: "He might change when he sees the baby," Yvonne tries to convince herself. "He does like children"—although her remark that Homer especially wants a boy introduces a note of uncertainty. Later, when we see Homer in a bar observing other patrons as sharply as MacKenzie observes people in the film, we think: *Ah, Homer might have become a filmmaker, too.*

On Hill X, the men end their day by beating tribal music on drums. At dawn they go home. Tomorrow will be the same. The men know they are not really "off the reservation," and they also know they have no place else to go.

BRUTALITY IN STONE (West Germany). Five years earlier than his feature debut, *Parting from Yesterday—(Anita G.)*, which launched one of the most important film movements, the New German Cinema, writer-director Alexander Kluge, with Peter Schamoni, co-directed a 12-minute black-and-white documentary short anticipating the movement-to-come. *Brutalität in Stein* gathers historical testimony to puncture his nation's attempt to overlook its recent Nazi history and just get on with its "economic miracle." The year after this stark work, Kluge helped write and signed the Oberhausen Manifesto, which announced the need for the movement that would shortly arrive.

Influenced by Alain Resnais, especially his *Statues Also Die* (1953), which Chris Marker co-directed, *Night and Fog* (1955) and *Hiroshima, mon amour* (1959), *Brutalität in Stein* relies on our capacity to analyze tone. On drawings and images of German architecture at and around a Nazi rally area in Nuremberg, it superimposes recordings of speeches by Hitler, Hess and others to suggest that the buildings themselves have retained the memory of this Nazi history. An occasional zoom electrifies the film's series of very briefly held stills, as does a sweeping camera up grandiose front steps. Hauntingly, by stately, silent forward movement—ghost steps—in symmetrical interiors, the film suggests a German crematorium and the connection among German political speech and spirit (as art embodies it), and the Holocaust. Discolorations on the outside of stone buildings double as reminders of spilt human blood. Another influence: Roberto Rossellini's *Germany, Year Zero* (1947); but one must also note that Kluge and Schamoni's film helped inspire Jürgen Böttcher's tremendous *The Wall* (1990), where the Berlin Wall, while it is being dismantled, is transformed at night, by voice recordings and flickering film images from the past, into a sadly vanishing repository of a brace of German memory, history.

1961

MINT TEA (France). The setting is a Parisian café at lunch time in the midst of the Cold War and towards the end of the Algerian War that would trounce French colonial power. A civil defence siren sounds, and through the café's expansive glass we see a flock of people hurriedly responding to the warning or drill. In English on the radio, a commentator speaks of U.S. homeowner shelters and the "possibility of shooting your neighbor if he tries to get in your shelter."

The film contains no other English. The cosmopolitan nature of Paris is certified by the range of languages we hear spoken in the packed café. A young man sits by himself at a small round table, but others are seated in sociable pairs and groups. A dedicated observer, the young man notes an elderly man who enters the café alone—himself, he may think, years hence. Soon, though, the old man is joined by a younger one who shows him books. Clearly this is an arranged meeting, not a chance encounter, and the old man is either a buyer or seller of books. Later, he leaves by himself, and the young loner remains absorbed by the projective self-image; but a stylistic rupture of the subjective camera—a very high shot of the old man outdoors—implies that he, unlike the younger one, has somewhere else to go, that is, a life outside the café.

Pierre Kafian's *Le thé a la menthe* is full of surprises. An apparent bachelor eyeing the ladies is abruptly joined by his young daughter and her mother; a seemingly alone young woman, one of the anonymous crowd, leaves with Zbigniew Cybulski, possibly playing himself. Kafian's brilliant short film looks ahead to Chantal Äkerman's *Toute une nuit* (1982) and Jon Jost's *Oui non* (2002).

THE FAT AND THE LEAN (Poland, France). Roman Polanski acts in the two-character, dialogueless 14-minute film he made in France right after graduating from film school, "Le gros et le maigre." He is "le maigre."

The opening sideways shot outside a wealthy fat man's rural house places the skinny, barefooted servant in the foreground, his master in the background. "Le gros" sits, rests; the servant is busy, beating a drum with one hand and playing a flute with the other: a one-man band performing for the pleasure of his master, for whom he dances in the field: ordered self-expression, art under duress—a metaphor for the warping of spirit that human relationships predicated on vastly unequal power constitute.

The boy anticipates, and hops to. When the master starts fanning himself with his hat, the boy runs inside, bringing out a feather broom to do the job more effectively; when the master takes off his shoes, the boy runs inside, bringing out a basin of water so that the master can cool and soak his feet. Birds fly overhead—a snapshot of the boy's wistful wish for freedom; but no sooner than they appear, the boy runs inside, bringing out his master's rifle, with which the master shoots down a bird that the boy must take indoors to cook for the master.

Sights of Paris in the distance deepen the boy's desire for freedom, but his attempted escape is punished. A goat is chained to his ankle, hobbling the boy, who now dances less Isadorably than earlier. Worse: he is being seduced into feeling grateful for whatever the master does, in fact, for his own benefit. The master unchains the goat, and the boy kisses his hand (he does this often), the Eiffel Tower behind him—in *our* view; not his.

ONE, TWO, THREE (U.S.). *One, Two, Three* is Billy Wilder's most consistently hilarious and most gorgeous comedy. Partly drawn from Ferenc Molnár's 1929 play *Egy, ketto, három*, the film received a monkey-wrench from history when the Communists put up the Berlin Wall during the on-location shoot, requiring that the film, whose action freely passes back and forth between the non-Communist and Communist sectors, be converted into a year-earlier flashback. This cataclysmic political change, however, perfectly suits the transformational nature of Wilder and co-scenarist Izzy Diamond's thematic material.

Hoping to secure a promotion (and therefore linked to rat-racing C.C. Baxter in Wilder's previous *The Apartment*, 1960), C.R. MacNamara, a Berlin-based Coca-Cola executive, is hosting his boss's 17-year-old daughter, Scarlett. A deal he is pushing to have Coke distributed behind the Iron Curtain causes MacNamara to be a lax substitute-guardian; Scarlett, pregnant, drifts into marriage to poor, unkempt Otto Piffl, an East German Communist beatnik. With Scarlett's folks flying in from Atlanta, MacNamara frantically attempts to remake Otto into an image of both enterprising capitalism and titled nobility.

The breakneck pace conforms to the instruction that heads the script: "This piece must be played *molto furioso*." The underpinning delight, on the mark (a double-meaning there), is how Otto's ideological resistance flows into complicity with the effort to turn him into a rich capitalist. Horst Buchholz is spectacularly funny as Otto.

Communism takes all sorts of jabs from MacNamara, who mercilessly verbally assaults Otto, "the Kremlin Kid," whom he instructs, when the boy threatens to agitate Coca-Cola workers into rebellion, "Pull up your pants, Spartacus." But MacNamara is a sleaze who cheats on his wife and is perpetually driven by self-interest. For him, democracy is synonymous with corporate profit.

James Cagney, as MacNamara, gives one of his best performances.

IL POSTO (Italy)—literally, *The Job*, but released in the U.S. as *The Sound of Trumpets* to discourage, for commercial reasons, the notion that the film has anything to do with work. But writer-director Ermanno Olmi's film has *everything* to do with work.

Domenico, 15, is out in the job market because his younger brother is in school and the family needs whatever it can get. In their apartment in Meda, a village in Lombardy, Domenico sleeps in the kitchen and his brother does homework at the kitchen table. This is not a family of means.

Domenico applies for a clerical post at a large company in Milan. With a host of others, he is taking a general examination including an aptitude test. His father has told him that a job at this company, however little it pays, is a job for life.

The film, wonderfully acted by nonprofessionals, resurrects a Neorealist line. The key is subdued, and the style, rigorously documentary. There isn't even a score on the soundtrack.

The film is divided into two parts, one in which Domenico tries to get the job, and one in which he holds a job. The enormity of the palace of employment, coupled with the practiced subservience of those who work there, suggests that employment is a gift. It turns out, despite job advertisements, nobody will be hired as a clerk; because he did well on the tests, Domenico is hired as a messenger—a position too low to bolster the shy boy's confidence to pursue Magali, who has been hired as a typist. (Oh my!) A fortuitous death, probably the result of work monotony, opens a clerical position that Domenico gets to fill, thus becoming one of a roomful of robots. Few films slip so easily from realism into satirical Expressionism.

ACCATTONE (Italy). Pier Paolo Pasolini's first film is a portrait of young males in a Roman slum. Its aim isn't to contextualize poverty but to describe the pervasive mood of a subculture, one of meager opportunities, cynicism and despair. The title character, ferociously and at times lyrically played by Franco Citti, pimps Maddalena, whose arrest by the police divests him of income, sending him into a downward spiral. Eventually he resorts to petty crime. He dies as anonymously as he lived.

Pasolini based this remarkable film on his novel *A Violent Life*, where the protagonist is a homosexual rather than a pimp; the substitution suits and deepens the material. It is silly and heartless to insist that the boy might do more to lift up himself. As with Gregory LaCava's *Primrose Path* (1940), with which this film has much in common, we see while watching it how environment and personal despair feed one another, and how, here, that environment sucks Vittorio Accattone in. In a way any "way out" for him is impossible; he is mired in the whole atmosphere and process of his hopeless existence. He tells Stella, the innocent peasant with whom he falls in love, upon meeting her, "You're lucky not to know things." Vittorio knows *too many* things.

Gut-wrenching: the scene in which watching his toddler play in the dirt (Accattone abandoned wife and infant), out of his son's earshot he apologizes aloud for being a bum. With Citti in the role, there's nothing rhetorical about the moment; it is bone-deep and soul-shaking.

The bursts of Bach on the soundtrack are intended as ironic counterpoint to the film's desperate, messy lives—a reflection on the order and beauty missing there. This music doesn't work, coming off instead as a bone to the culture-vultures.

CLEO FROM 5 TO 7 (France). Writer-director Agnès Varda's *Cléo de 5 à 7* begins in vivid color with a direct overhead shot of two pairs of women's hands across a table where client Cléo, a singer, and Madame Irma are seated. Cléo's hands select the tarot cards that Madame Irma turns over and interprets. When the camera alternates between the women's faces, the color is gone; we see gray and white. When the view shifts back to the cards on the table, though, there is color again: an indication of the unreality of the "reading." Madame Irma assures Cléo that the "Death" card indicates a transformative experience, not necessarily, literally, death. After Cléo leaves, by which time the film has entirely passed into black and white, Madame Irma tells her spouse that Cléo will surely die shortly of cancer: as she awaits the results of her biopsy, the very concern of Cléo's that brought her to Madame Irma.

Varda's film proceeds in patches, each of which is captioned with a start and end time. To the usual reading that Cléo becomes increasingly aware of how superficial her life is, let me add this: rather more importantly she becomes increasingly aware of time and its passage, and of life's transience.

Varda's film is touted as being in "real time"—an odd thing, given its subjective nature, its revelation of Cléo's interiority. (Walking down after leaving Madame Irma, Cléo is shown in quick cuts taking the same step three times, resulting in an impression of her discombobulated state.) Despite the title, the film lasts ninety minutes—an overarching indication that time now for Cléo is a function of her perception of it, and that part of this perception of hers is that time is shorter than heretofore she had imagined it.

1962

ECLIPSE (Italy). *See above.*

THE TRIAL (France, Italy, West Germany). Orson Welles, who wrote and directed *The Trial*, from Franz Kafka, considered it his best piece of work. I concur.

Certainly it is Welles's most haunted film. It satirizes bureaucracy by promoting it to an almost cosmic level of authoritarianism, as Kafka had done in order to portray humanity's sense of cluelessness in the vast, impersonal modern world; but Welles also lends great sorrow to the satire by infusing it with a specter of the Holocaust. (Kafka's novella preceded the Holocaust by about twenty years; the film came about twenty years after.) This brings to fruition the full horror of totalitarianism that Kafka had only begun to imagine. To be sure, the film dazzles with its kaleidoscopic maze of ambiguous black-and-white images and visual cul-de-sac, its use of chiaroscuro, its urgent sense of parable; but it is the film's phantomlike repository of historical memory, an omnipresent insinuation, that accounts for its inexhaustible power of emotion.

Not everyone who loves Welles loves this film. Critic Andrew Sarris, who places Welles in his pantheon of great American filmmakers, finds *The Trial* "hateful," "repellent," "perverted"—or did so at the time of *The American Cinema* (1968), where he writes: "Welles asserts in his prologue that his story has the logic of a dream, but Welles on Kafka, like Modigliani's white on white is less logical than superfluous, less a dream of something than a dream of a dream of something." Bound up in memory, Welles's film *is* the dream of a

dream. It is Welles's nightmare of an historical waking nightmare that we all share.
The Trial is Welles's great lament for humanity's inhumanity. It is a film mourning a world of justice and reason that it nevertheless knows existed in mind but never in time.

THE MAN WHO SHOT LIBERTY VALANCE (U.S.). James Stewart and John Wayne are magnificent in John Ford's last great film, which addresses the foundation of lies and myths sustaining ideas of national destiny, frontier and progress in the U.S. "The man who shot Liberty Valance" doesn't refer to the man who actually shot and killed the embodiment of Old West lawlessness but to the gun-shy lawyer who, given the credit, builds upon this celebrity a lofty political career that is about to allow him, as U.S. senator, to bring irrigation to Shinbone, thereby turning vast, open desert into a fenced garden, and consigning anarchy to the discipline of rules and boundaries, all of which entails, along with some reluctant modification of individual liberty, the loss of an elusive quality of romance.

Here is Ford's most intricately composed yet grayest, knottiest, thorniest western—his most highly analytical film. (German filmmaker Jean-Marie Straub has called Ford "the most Brechtian of all filmmakers, because he shows things that make people think . . . [and that make] the audience collaborate on the film.") Like Ford's *My Darling Clementine* (1946), also in black and white, the film seems to emanate from some dark collective mind, the historical imagination where myth and truth, shifting in and out of one another, are phantoms of the night. Senator Ransom Stoddard's marriage is also founded on the error that he dispatched Liberty Valance; Hallie, his wife, originally loved Tom Doniphon, who really did kill Valance, and who, losing Hallie to Stoddard and gleaning his nation's future, chose to pass into oblivion. Divided, like America, Hallie loved the dashing substance of one man in the righteous form of the other.

What an enduring, frightfully weighted haul is here—America's baggage of memory, regret, contradiction, political disillusionment.

THE FIANCÉS (Italy). *I fidanzati* is about the strain on an engaged couple, Giovanni and Liliana (Anna Canzi, trenchant), once Giovanni relocates from Milan, where he works as a welder in a petrochemical factory, to his new job at the company's new plant in Sicily. Writer-director Ermanno Olmi clarifies the extent to which work directs the course of working-class lives—including working-class love.

Giovanni's time in Sicily, intended by its job advancement to facilitate his marrying Liliana, proves very lonely. For the first time, the alienating nature of his work isn't mitigated by any family or social life away from work.

I fidanzati includes a shot of showers of sparks from Giovanni's worksite set against the dark sky. The image is sorely ironic. Its black-and-white beauty is something that *we* see; the workers who are inadvertently creating it do not. Through no fault of their own, the beauty does not touch their lives. A related image consists of mounds of salt—eerily lovely to our eye, but also encapsulating the backbreaking labor that created them.

Giovanni's off-work wanderings through a bleak landscape show the influence of *L'avventura* (1960). Disconnected from Milan and all that is familiar to him, Giovanni has no place to go and therefore drifts. Is his life "going nowhere"?

His relationship with Liliana takes a terrible beating. The separation, letters unanswered, wayward thoughts that seize her agitated imagination: all this helps make Liliana feel that she is losing Giovanni. Indeed, Giovanni succumbs to loneliness to the detriment of the bond between them. (Absence makes the heart grow fickle.) The context that Olmi provides takes these matters out of the realm of moralistic or (primarily) psychological consideration. What *we* see is the extent to which Giovanni's work determines the rocky course of the relationship.

1962

THE TRIAL OF JOAN OF ARC (France). Basing his script on the fifteenth-century trial transcripts and, as is his wont, casting nonprofessionals, including in the central role, Robert Bresson's spare, stunning *Le procès de Jeanne d'Arc* is modern, intellectual, Existential. Cinema's original minimalist stresses Joan's solitude; defiant in court but really at a loss, Joan prays privately for the best answers to give her inquisators so that she may best represent God. Dreyer's instinctual folk Joan acts according to her feelings, which are immense (*The Passion of Joan of Arc*, 1928), while Bresson's Joan acts according to conscience, which at any point is precise but which fluctuates, given her uncertainties; overcompensating for these in public, she is, actually, reluctant to embrace martyrdom. Dreyer's Joan is, along with the masses supporting her, us; in Bresson's film, the spying eyes through a peep hole into Joan's prison cell—jailers; priests—are us, as we attempt to observe a depth of spirit in one who seems so imperviously matter-of-fact. Bresson's Joan, observed from the outside, evidences a solitary's resolution of her crisis of ambivalence.

The film is full of visual echoes. Joan's hands, for instance: cross-chained in closeup she lays these on a bible to take her oath in court, and she is made to do this again in another trial session, yielding the same winged effect in closeup. At her execution, her hands, now tied behind her back, reappear in closeup. When doves appear, shot from below, we are reminded of Joan's "winged" hands to haunting effect. An image of confinement has become one of ultimate liberation.

The film begins with two sounds: the ringing of church bells, followed by a drum roll. It ends only with a drum roll: Joan the individual's silencing of the Church that has put her to death.

KNIFE IN THE WATER (Poland). Roman Polanski's *Nóz w wodzie* opens with an unhappy couple on the road, like Roberto Rossellini's *Voyage in Italy* (1953). These two, however, are at home, although they are headed for a weekend's yachting, and no landlubbers are ever "at home" on the water. Along the way they pick up a hitchhiker, a college student, and invite him along after nearly running him down. The nasty, professorial man, who hardly talked at all to his wife, jabbers away with the kid, playing a "game" of domination with his mind. Onboard the boat, rigging ropes cut across a three-shot of the couple and their guest. Once they set sail, the camera slips into erotic attention, noting the woman's breasts, the boy's buttocks, and the bare feet of both. The husband looms as an overseer, an orchestrator of we-don't-quite-know-what. We know this, though: Nothing good is going to come out of this threesome.

Polanski scripted his masterpiece with Jerzy Skolimowski and Jakub Goldberg, but it is the visual realization that sparkles, marshaling a kaleidoscope of camera angles and distances, and punctuating the elemental, acrimonious drama with symbols, such as the knife in the water—a dropped penis; a lost male advantage. The boy is no innocent, but when compared with his jaded elder and adversary he is precious for his youth and we root for him painfully, terribly. We become the surrogate parent that the man in the film ought to have been.

Polanski's visual invention onboard the boat, recalling Alfred Hitchcock's in *Lifeboat* (1944), accumulates into a metaphor for quietly desperately wrought possibilities within a restrictive framework that suggests Communist Poland itself. The Party's leader in Poland announced this: Polanski's film displays "the kind of thinking for which there is no place anywhere in the Communist world."

THE EXTERMINATING ANGEL (Mexico). We all know the feeling; we're at a party and we want to leave, but can't. Luis Buñuel employs this premise for his black comedy *El ángel exterminador*, in which guests find that they cannot leave their host's music room. As hours stretch into days, something of a *Lord of the Flies* degeneration takes hold. Sheep wander in, which the guests eat. After a mind-boggling moment when they realize that they have all inadvertently assumed the exact same positions they occupied some time earlier, the guests are cleared of their paralysis. They attend church. Upon leaving, they are gunned down. Many strange, surprising things happen. Early on, for instance, all the posh guests save one have gathered in the music room. The one who has remained in the dining room throws a glass, breaking a window, the sound of which the others hear. Someone tersely explains: "Probably a passing Jew." Here is the phenomenon of something "outside," and an outsider, being blamed for what has happened from within. But more: the seemingly crazy explanation, proffered so matter-of-factly, reminds us how irrational sometimes is the basis for social and political statements and actions that the powers that be make appear perfectly rational. In this instance, a shared hatred of Jews makes nonsense seem feasible to the two conversing guests.

Bristling with irony, like so much Buñuel, *El ángel exterminador* is hilarious. It is also a harrowing satire on authority—authority, apparently, that feels threatened by even the most trivial and inadvertent deviation from the norm. Moreover, the film is a cunning allegory on Buñuel's encounter with Franco over *Viridiana* (1961).

Dark, dense, *El ángel exterminador* is like a dream. "Its images, like the images in a dream," Buñuel said, "do not reflect reality, but themselves create it."

ALONE ON THE PACIFIC (Japan). May 12, 1962: Kenichi Horie, 23, in the dead of night steals out of Nishinomiya Harbor in a small sailing craft. Ninety-four days later, the social dropout and perpetual worry for his parents reaches his destination: San Francisco. Back in Osaka, his father publicly apologizes for his son's individualism and pesky independence.

Working from wife Natto Wada's brilliant, intricate script, an adaptation of Horie's account, Kon Ichikawa has created a massively moving masterpiece, a hymn to the human spirit. Ichikawa's film is also highly analytical, especially in its fluent interweaving of Horie's experience at sea, which is interrupted by flashbacks prior to his departure from home, and his voiceover. What we see as the present is the recent past; what we *hear* as an echo of this past is, actually, closer to Horie's present. Different tenses, time frames: Ichikawa is exploring the unfettered, integrative nature of the human mind. "I wonder if I'll ever reach America": one must be alert as to what Horie visibly says, as here, and what he discloses in recollective voiceover. Horie continually speaks aloud to assuage his loneliness.

"You know what it's like, Dad, pushing and shoving your way through life, trying to survive": a flashback shows the reconstituted conversation in which Kenichi says this. Kenichi's adventure, which a number of times nearly kills him, shows the boy honoring tradition and the past—in effect, his father—even as he seems to be rebelling against them. For instance, Kenichi's making it to America symbolically reverses Japan's defeat in the Second World War; when he crosses a spot where twenty years earlier the Japanese navy suffered losses, Kenichi offers a silent prayer. At different junctures, we see (a decade after the U.S. occupation) America's continuing pernicious grip on Japan.

... A VALPARAÍSO (France, Chile). Three brilliant documentarians worked on the French and Chilean... *A Valparaíso*: its maker, Joris Ivens; in his twenties, Patricio Guzmán, Chile's future premier political documentarian, who assisted Ivens; Chris Marker, who wrote voiceover commentary suited to Ivens's images.

Valparaíso, Chile, evidences landmarks from as many countries as have come to port there through conquerors and ordinary seamen. It is a city, we are told, "created, forged, peopled by sailors." A montage shows buildings designed and constructed to resemble ships and boats.

It must have been the Valley of Paradise prior to development; now it is something else. Down below is the commercial city; at various tiers above, built on hills, is a "cluster" of 42 residential villages, one per hill. It is a system of ramps and stairs. It is a kind of Hell, where the poorer that people are the higher up they live, the farther away they are from the sea, which is the city's "truth," and the closer they are to the sun, which is the city's "lie." There, considerable effort is required to bring water up from down below. Life's a struggle.

A one-legged man is shown climbing 121 steps. Marker: "One needs a strong heart and a good memory." An overhead shot shows another man struggling up different stairs. Nature as well as geography mocks him, for the next thing we see is a chicken springing up the steps.

It's easier for children—but also damaging. Their lungs, their breathing, are stressed, and they need to work at their play. Their profusion of kites in the sky—a visual echo of seagulls—may be expressing an unconscious dream for themselves of lightness and flight.

A posh woman prods a penguin with her parasol.

Artwork memorializes centuries of Spanish colonial rule.

THE LOVERS OF TERUEL (France). Graced by the most delicately mournful musical theme imaginable (by Mikos Theodorakis), which we first hear plucked on a guitar and then played on a harmonica, Raymond Rouleau's beauteous *Les amants de Teruel* exists in a haunted space betwixt theatrical grand passions and a ballerina's dreams of erotic reunion with Diego, her lost love. The gypsy dance troupe to which Isa belongs—Ludmilla Tcherina, strikingly beautiful and achingly bereft—features her in a ballet that translates her turbulent grief into dance. For now, art's sublimation of her torment helps keep Isa alive as Manuel, the troupe's leader, having bought her from her father, nags her to become his own.

One expects this of feet in a dance film, but, here, hands are equally eloquent. Isa privately caresses a photograph of her and her lover; in the same shot, Manuel snatches the keepsake, crumples and drops it as Isa's hand, curbed by fate, takes a tiny step or two toward saving it. In a ghostly dream, Isa's outstretched hands, seemingly belonging to a blind soul, seek out Diego. She finds him and kisses his face, which turns out to be a mask. Now they are making love, and on the bed beside the couple is the mask, upside down.

Diego's return after three years ends in tragedy, thanks to Manuel's jealousy; "reality" replays the dance about "the lovers of Teruel." Rouleau's Cocteau-kissed, experimental musical interweaves a number of avant-garde techniques while never letting go of the humanity at the film's core, the piercing reality of feelings of love, hope, despair, bereavement.

Cruel, possessive Manuel is played by the film's choreographer, Milko Sparemblek. Diego by his absence also has been "possessing" Isa—this, the male principle that the film decries.

Claude Renoir's color cinematography is to die for.

KANCHENJUNGHA (India). Satyajit Ray's first film in color is, like the later black-and-white *Days and Nights in the Forest* (1969), a "holiday film"; Calcuttans are vacationing in Darjeeling, a hill station with Kanchenjungha, one of the highest peaks of the Himalayas, beyond—except that, for the duration of their stay, fog has blocked their view of the mountain's reality, inspiration and hope. On this, their last day there, will the fog lift?

The expectancy is correlative to the suspension of the Choudhurys' lives—in Darjeeling, of course, but also back home: the lives they have brought *with them*. Indranath, the industrialist-patriarch, is too expectant of a transformation that can come only from within. He more or less gently tyannizes his family, while his wife, Labyanya, must contest his authority out of his view, for instance, in the matter of the marital match he is engineering for one of their daughters. Their other daughter is adulterous in *her* marriage, a reflection of the level of success in family matters that follows from Indranath's authority. Now someone, a young stranger, directly challenges this authority, signaling a breakthrough. Indranath discovers his own humanity. The fog lifts.

This beauteous film unfolds in real time, but judicious editing helps prevent this from becoming a stunt. Ray, working for the first time from his own original (Ibsenian) script, captures everyday reality, and yet achieves, also, a lyrical result. His is a film of walks and conversations, full of long-shots of resort guests walking and of guests watching *others* walking. Kanchenjungha looms in the background, struggling for breath to cross our line of sight full and clear. We are not just responsible for what we do. We are also responsible for

1962

what we see.
These people who walk: where are they going? Their "Limited" view might be: "Omaha."

MEMORIES OF MY MOTHER (Japan). Based on the 1931 kabuki play by Shin Hasegawa set during the Tokugawa period, *Mabuta no haha* is a piercing, melancholy remake of Hiroshi Inagaki's silent classic. Writer-director Tai Kato's electrifying, moving version, a national allegory of Japanese self-sacrifice, adds color as well as sound to the original.

Banba no Chutaro, a young blade-ready yakuza, travels to Edo in search of his mother, who abandoned him and his father, who abused her, when he was five years old. (His father died when Chutaro was 12.) Should she be impoverished, Chutaro hopes to provide his mother with money he has saved for her; he also hopes to liberate himself from his violent life, which has flourished in the absence of their bond. He treats kindly two different women even when he discovers neither is his mother; but what does he do when he finds his mother and she is suspicious and dismissive?

Kato fills his frames with dynamic activity and action; but Chutaro's search for his mother weaves through this with soulful calm and purpose, achieving more than a contrast: an emotional complexity. Kato's fine *mise-en-scène* stresses, depending on the scene, either Chutaro's brashness or bereftness and humility. Enhancing it are two outstanding contributions: the pulsating main theme of Nakaba Takahashi's score and Osamu Furuya's cinematography, which especially at sundown achieves tremendous poetry: dim, gray-blueish cloudiness correlative to Chutaro's lack of moral clarity as a result of the missing familial bond.

In locating his mother, Chutaro discovers he also has a younger sister, who overturns their mother's rejection of him, sending mother and daughter, ironically, out in search of *him*. However, Chutaro hides; he closes his eyes, sacrificing even a loving sister to retain the mother "under his eyelids"—the dream that surpasses reality.

TRANSPORT FROM PARADISE (Czechoslovakia). Written by the director, Zbyněk Brynych, and Holocaust survivor Arnošt Lustig from Lustig's book *Night and Hope*, *Transport z ráje* (best film, Locarno) imaginatively takes us into the Terezin Ghetto in Germany (the opening shot, from inside an SS officer's entering car, ironically sets us in the front passenger seat), the model "town" devised to hoodwink the International Red Cross and the rest of the world into believing that the Nazis were treating Jewish prisoners humanely. A documentary like the one being shot in the film's first movement actually was made, and in his quick, precise direction of the camera Czech New Waver Brynych distinguishes between his own film and this film-within-the-film, catching closeups of spent or fearful faces amidst the general pretense at comfort and ease. One of his gripping techniques is to create pseudo-photographs or freeze frames of the people being filmed, which with only the scarcest motion then come eerily to not-quite-life. Thus the false impression of benign circumstance is invested with a sense of horror. Partially whistled upbeat music adds dark ironical humor.

An underground group within the Ghetto operates a printing press; the discovery of some of its handiwork—posters saying "Death to the Fascists!"—invites retaliation: thousands will be ordered selected, and transported to Birkenau, for extermination. When he refuses to sign the deportation order, the head of the Jewish Council of Elders is arrested and replaced with someone compliant. At his moment of brave refusal the man is surrounded in blackness, his sewn-on Star of David lustrously prominent. Throughout this stark black-and-white film, closeups of faces withstand backgrounds of pitch darkness or are half-lost to the darkness.

A Kafkaesque image—one that becomes a visual refrain—consists of a vast expanse of tagged suitcases in a chillingly dark room.

LE DOULOS (France). The title of Jean-Pierre Melville's *Le doulos* translates as *the finger man*—in American parlance, the stoolie or rat. The film is an ambiguous descent into a morally clouded world of hoodlums, cops and, treading a line between the two, informants. Here, people may not be what they seem in either direction on the moral scale. An "underground" of rootless, subsistent, hunted criminals recalls the wartime Resistance, while more posh criminals, assorted turncoats and squealers, and the police authorities to whom they squeal, recall the collaborationists.

During Maurice's incarceration jewel-heist accomplice Gilbert "silenced" Arlette, Maurice's girlfriend, to insure against her defection to the police. Maurice shoots Gilbert dead. He had to, he explains, because Gilbert, turning around, had seen the gun—"and you don't point a gun at a friend." This tortuous logic may be hiding shame and fear of reprisal.

Thérèse, Maurice's current girlfriend, may be treacherous. Is Thérèse also sleeping with and working undercover for policeman Salignari? Maurice's one friend, Silien (Jean-Paul Belmondo, terrific), is also *Salignari's* friend. Salignari is killed. Does Silien know it is Maurice, during a bungled heist, who killed Salignari? Is Silien loyal to Maurice?—or to Salignari's memory? Has he fingered Maurice? From his prison cell Maurice arranges for Silien's execution. When convinced of Silien's devotion, Maurice tries frantically to subvert the arranged hit. *Too late.*

This deeply affecting work is full of embittered sorrow, regret. Underlit interiors; the collision of small light and vast dark along the metaphysical line where life passes over: flashlights illuminating stretches of interior space; street lamps seemingly exhaling tenuous breath. Nothing is quite clear, in an atmosphere of suspiciousness, betrayal, ever possible betrayal: an evocation of the Occupation that also describes its legacy: France, coping with her memory.

Keep your eye on Silien's hat.

FAMILY DIARY (Italy, France). From Vasco Pratolini's autobiographical novel (Pratolini contributed to the script), Valerio Zurlini's *Cronaca familiare* follows Florentine brothers Enrico and Lorenzo Corsi. Zurlini emphasizes universality, in particular, the grandmother's love for the boys (Sylvie's performance is tremendous), and the elder brother's contemplation of the eternal mystery, for him, of Lorenzo's nature—a mystery ultimately sealed in the latter's youthful death from an ailment itself so mysterious that it comes to seem a projection of Enrico's limited capacity to fathom Lorenzo.

The film opens in 1945, in a newsroom in Rome, where Enrico (Marcello Mastroianni, deeply affecting), a struggling journalist, is informed that a piece of his will be published. But news he receives by telephone robs the moment of joy: Enrico's younger brother, in his twenties, died yesterday. The different course of their lives consigned Lorenzo to relative wealth and Enrico to poverty and squalor. Tubercular, why isn't *he* the one to have died? In an outdoor long-shot, slowly moving down a street against a continuous backdrop of immense buildings on both sides, Enrico seems like the narrowly entombed walking dead.

When Enrico returns to his meager accommodations, Zurlini slips into using a subjective camera. The emptiness confronting Enrico (empty chair, unpopulated desk) reflects his vacant feeling. He is separated forever from the treasure of his brother's company and love. He has finally caught up with Italy's postwar mood of bereavement, exhaustion, defeat. He withdraws into memory, the years of the boys' separation owing to their father's war-wrought absence and their mother's death, the baby's adoption by another family, contrasts (example: Lorenzo, Fascist; Enrico, anti-Fascist), and then unlikely reunion and gradually reignited love.

The film is literary though heartrending. The jury that awarded it the top prize at Venice: "delicious, powerful evocation of feelings filtered by memory."

SHIRO OF AMAKUSA, REBEL (Japan). "We have started a battle we can never win." Reflecting on the collapse of the radical protest movement that followed Japan's 1958 treaty renegotiation with the U.S., which threatened to divert Japan from its constitutional course of peace, Nagisa Oshima for the first time dipped into the distant past. *Amakusa shiro tokisada*, one of cinema's starkest studies of official oppression, thus becomes a companion-piece to Oshima's masterpiece, *Night and Fog in Japan* (1960).

In 1637 Shimabara, the shogunate is determined to wipe out Christian peasants revolting against it. Cunningly, Oshima advances the age of the young boy who led the actual uprising to that of Jesus, to capture the conflicted position of one who is prompted to mount a bloody assault when his commitment to Christian principle prohibits this course of action. Moreover, his astute judgment tells Shiro that his side isn't yet strong enough to prevail. All hell breaks loose, and Shiro's mother and sister are among the fatalities. The film's postscript refers to the wholesale massacre of Christians in 1638.

Early on, twelve peasants are subjected to "straw dancing": a pack of straw is attached to each and set on fire. In the foreground of a great shot encapsulating cruel oppression, mounted samurai, enforcing the group execution, look ahead to the blazing, "dancing" victims. Later, the literally crucified are burned to death. All total, in battle some 37,000 Christians died.

Oshima takes two visual tacks. One consists of nearly out-of-body closeups of suffering peasant faces that inevitably recall Dreyer's *Passion of Joan of Arc* (1928). The other is deep night: symbolically, the earthly Christian ordeal. In one interior shot, luminous peasant faces are like candles in the dark.

Numerous images are variations on a visual theme: ascending flames in pitch darkness.

THERESE DESQUEYROUX (France). Updating François Mauriac's 1927 novel, Georges Franju's *Thérèse Desqueyroux* shifts its sphere of thematic reference from sin and expiation to a woman's interiority, from Roman Catholicism to a fusion of the existential and the lyrical.

Accompanied by her solemn voiceover, Thérèse Desqueyroux's flashbacks account for much of the film. Thérèse is acquitted of her real attempts to murder her husband, Bernard, by poisoning him, and that her acquittal follows Bernard's perjured testimony at trial ironically underscores his control over her. As punishment, Bernard banishes her from their mansion, imprisoning her in separate quarters on his country estate; but even he is moved to discover, when he finally can bring himself to look upon her, that she has deteriorated almost to the point of death. Suddenly his coldness melts; but this unexpected about-face yet again shows how dependent Thérèse is on *him*.

Pauline Kael thinks that Thérèse poisons Bernard because he is dull. He is complacent, self-absorbed, overbearing. He gulps down soup and wine, and then turns the back of his chair to Thérèse to nod off facing the fire. He cares nothing about his wife's feelings. Facing her, he holds a bird by both legs as it flaps and flutters wildly; Thérèse feels she is looking into a mirror of their marriage. She poisons Bernard to see, for once, uncertainty in his eyes.

What filmmaking! A pan of the grounds comes to a stop that Franju holds—an anticipation of Thérèse's feeling of imprisonment. In her husband's prison an open window provides Thérèse with a draught of freedom: the wind singing through the trees. When Bernard releases her to Paris, another shot of these trees dissolves into a shot of bustling Parisian humanity.

Claiming here her greatest role, Emmanuèlle Riva (best actress, Venice) is phenomenal.

BARREN LIVES (Brazil). The highwater mark of Brazil's *cinema nôvo*, Nelson Pereira Dos Santos's black-and-white *Vidas Secas* derives from Graciliano Ramos's 1938 novel about an impoverished young family—Fabiano, wife Vitória, their two small sons, and Baleia, the family dog—attempting to survive in the sun-seared *sertão*.

The film opens on endless, open land. One bare tree punctuates the dry landscape. Distant dots to the tree's right move. As the camera moves left very slowly and the figures advance, tree and humans are each associated with the other. First to burst into full view is Baleia, running ahead. The skeletal tree is a figure of looming death; the implication arises that the dog, leaping between family and tree beyond the frame, protects the family from extinction. Soon after, Baleia barks to alert the others of a family member's distress and, a proficient hunter, helps keep all from starvation.

Almost as soon as they arrive close to a shack that cowhand Tomás has vacated, the landowner, imperious on horseback, armed with a whip, orders them out but relents when Fabiano offers to work for next to nothing. Even so, "Boss" cheats Fabiano, who chooses family survival over personal pride. Fabiano is whipped and jailed for no offense.

Eventually they all must move on. Baleia is sick, so Fabiano first must kill their protector —a protracted passage presaging the family's own imperiled fate. A few amazing shots illumine the dog's consciousness as she dies: a zoom-out from the cabin; animals that Baleia won't be hunting down. The family is on foot again, this time without certain destination. Vitória wonders aloud, "Will we ever be human?" The camera behind them this time, rather than appearing out of the distance they disappear into the nothingness stretching in front of them.

1963

IL GATTOPARDO (Italy, France). Following an engrossing, brooding *Rocco and His Brothers* (1960), about a rural peasant family's demoralization and disintegration after their move to industrial Milan in order to better their prospects, Luchino Visconti made his most celebrated work: *The Leopard*, from Giuseppe Tomasi di Lampedusa, about an aristocratic Sicilian family's demoralization and disintegration under *Risorgimento*, the unification of Italy begun with the revolution of 1848.

Prince Fabrizio of Salina is an intelligent, enlightened man; and, although the nationalist movements point to the end of his influence and the death of his elegant way of life, his feelings about the changes are divided. Like Lampedusa, who based Don Fabrizio on his great-grandfather, Visconti was an aristocrat deeply committed to social and economic justice. (He was a Marxist.) Both author and filmmaker, then, identified with the larger-than-life character at the center of their epic accounts. The film's expense required a considerable star to make it bankable; enter Burt Lancaster, who had never given the slightest indication of acting ability. Here, superlatively dubbed, he impresses, as does Alain Delon as Tancredi (so different from Delon's Myshkin-like Rocco), Don Fabrizio's dashing young nephew, who comes to embody *realpolitik*, beginning as an impassioned enlistee in Garibaldi's people's army, and then switching to the cause of Camillo di Cavour, the aristocrat who succeeded at unification where Garibaldi failed, but only by ruthlessly assaulting regional cultures.

A grand ball and, for Don Fabrizio, its ambulatory aftermath: in the last movement, the tracking camera witnesses the proud patriarch's self-aware eclipse in a lofty world that is losing political ground. Detailed, sweeping and, like the rest of the film, objectively toned (a surprise from Visconti), this phenomenal passage suggests history meditating on itself. Nearly an hour long, it brings Visconti's masterpiece to a stunning close.

LES CARABINIERS (France, Italy). Across cultures, with twenty-four years dividing them, Roberto Rossellini and Jean-Luc Godard, *neorealismo* and *nouvelle vague*, unite: cinema's dream collaboration of the decade. *Les carabiniers*, a brilliant antiwar film, was adapted, from Beniamino Joppolo's play, by Rossellini, Godard and Jean Gruault, with Godard directing. Perhaps Godard and Gruault translated and amended Rossellini's adaptation. It would be interesting to know how this film evolved.

Reversals of fortune in war sum up war's futility. Two brothers are recruited to be soldiers. In the service of their king they do their duty; they rape, kill and plunder, only to be put to death themselves by revolutionaries opposing the king. Critic Roy Armes describes the film as a Brechtian fable.

In black and white, hastily shot without concern for compositional refinement, repetitively punctuated by gunfire on the soundtrack and by abrupt cuts and title cards on the see-track, raggedy, minimalist and blessedly free of all "entertainment value," *Les carabiniers* prompts us to analyze what we see and hear rather than seducing us with attractive surfaces. (The film begins with a voice summoning military music—music that we then hear as the opening credits roll.) Moreover, the film is nonprofessionally cast; there isn't a Bardot or Belmondo in sight. Newsreel inserts of war footage and a montage of nondescript photographs further contribute to the correctly highly distanced result. This style is compelling; it suits the film's thematic assault on the dehumanizing properties of war. Doubtless, Rossellini, Godard et al. were motivated by the Western world's then-current tour of duty in Vietnam, but the masterpiece they wrought, which approaches the force of Dovzhenko's *Arsenal* in addressing war, the worst idea that we have borrowed from lower species, has universal and, appallingly, persistent application.

THE SILENCE (Sweden). *See above.*

PASSENGER (Poland). Andrzej Munk was not quite forty when he died in a car crash in 1961. At the time, he was filming *Pasazerka*, which his friend Witold Lesiewicz completed, using stills and voiceover. The narrator tries to fathom the stills that piece together the drama aboard a cruise-liner. In effect, the narration hopes to recover Munk's original intent. This comports with Munk's own theme: the recovery of historical truth from memory's distortions and denials. Rather than intruding on Munk's vision, this approach deepens the work's haunting quality and chill beauty.

The script is by Munk and Zofia Posmysz-Piasecka, from the latter's novel. Aboard an ocean liner a German passenger sees another woman passenger whom she thinks she recognizes: a prisoner at Auschwitz, where she was an SS guard. The sight of this possible face from her past prompts the German to disclose to her spouse, for the first time, her role at the death camp. But are her memories accurate? The film pursues discrepancies between past events at Auschwitz and the former guard's guilty reimaginings of them. One flashback shows the guard protecting the prisoner; a subsequent flashback exposes the "protector" as tormentor. Anyhow, is the glimpsed passenger the same person from Auschwitz? Is this even possible?

Munk employs a camera of unsurpassed sensitivity; it seems as light as air—in 1961, it wasn't—and quick as light, correlative to the hard to catch-at nature of truth. Moreover, this lightness and speed are attuned to each fluctuation of feeling, and each real or perceived reversal of power between guard and prisoner. The women's relationship is complex and volatile, and the film explores with fascinating results the guard's structure of rationalizations designed to keep her from identifying with monstrous evil.

Such mental adjustments we make for the harm that we do.

WINTER LIGHT (Sweden). *See above.*

L'IMMORTELLE (France). In Istanbul, N is sexually involved with L, who disappears, for whom he searches, who reappears and is killed in an automobile accident in which he, her passenger, grabbed the wheel, consigning him to become—or continue to be—the prisoner of his labyrinthine mind, which the streets of Istanbul project.

Robbe-Grillet's *L'immortelle* explores the relationship between interior and exterior, thought and experience, mind and matter. It has a reputation for being esoteric, even pretentious, but in reality (hm) it is burrowing, clear as clean mirror, and intriguingly and appropriately, not irritatingly, elusive. Misogynistic, as some claim? No; rather, it explores the extent to which the objectifying male mind makes over a woman's reality into its own projections, with all the attendant neediness and ego. (The film is *about* what inattentive viewers mistake it for being.) Shot on location, author Robbe-Grillet's stunning filmmaking debut is from Turkey, Italy and France.

Robbe-Grillet establishes the parameters of both the film's method and concerns at the get-go. A roadway travelogue tracking shot, accompanied by a woman's voice in foreign song (I immediately thought of Wordsworth's poem "The Solitary Reaper"), yields to the sound of a crash—the automobile accident. A photograph of L, an exotic beauty, freezes life into death. N looks out a hotel window. The blinds open, revealing the photograph right outside behind them. This yields to dreamy shots of L alive but silently posing: on the beach, looking at the sea; inside N's room, slowly turning to face him. Following the repeated shot of N at the window, the blinds close on L's photograph. We are glimpsing, Robbe-Grillet's train of images reveals, N's haunted and tormented mind.

Fragmented time forms a mosaic—even a kaleidoscope—of the present that N's mind contains.

Prix Louis Delluc.

REVENGE OF A KABUKI ACTOR (Japan). "I swore I would find a way for you to avenge [your father]."

What does it mean to live life at such a remove that its motive becomes to achieve the revenge for your parents' suicides that somebody else wants more than you do? When Yukinojo Nakamura was seven, his father hanged himself, driven to this by warlord Sansai Dobe, who had ruined him. It is the family's servant boy who swore revenge. Twenty years later, Yukinojo calls this servant "Master" and carries out a scheme that ends in the deaths of the men who had conspired against his father, including Dobe and Dobe's innocent daughter, Namiji, whom Yukinojo had ensnared by pretending to love her—that is, before he really fell in love with her. He addresses her corpse: "It is as if you were born only to be deceived."

Yukinojo is an *onnagata*, the female impersonator in a kabuki theater troupe, in Kon Ichikawa's beauteous, utterly fascinating *Yukinojo henge*, a remake of the same-titled 1935 film that Teinosuke Kinugasa directed and in which Kazuo Hasegawa starred. Nearly thirty years later, Hasegawa brilliantly reprises the effeminate role. The revenge plot means that Yukinojo performs offstage as well as on-, and Ichikawa expressionistically has spaces of interiors go dark, in addition to framing both interior and exterior shots, to suggest a theatrical performance.

Actually, Hasegawa reprises a *double* role, for he also plays the robust, virile thief Yamitaro, who shadows his image, as though watching a play, and announces at the end that he will give up thieving to become Yukinojo's servant.

Set during the Tokugawa period, Ichikawa's film, a Pirandellian meditation on acting and selfconscious role-playing, teases us into awareness of ourselves as audience by dotting the soundtrack with inapposite music.

LE JOLI MAI (France). Following Jean Rouch's *Chronicle of a Summer* (1961), Chris Marker's 3-hour *Happy Month of May* is dedicated to "the happy many" (Rouch had asked people in the street, "Are you happy?"), whose numbers, and whose happiness, prove elusive to find in Paris despite the end of the Algerian War, which has given France an unaccustomed taste of peace.

In the first of two parts, those interviewed are bound up in their own lives. This is a Paris "made up of solitudes," as in the case of a woman who grows flowers for no other reason, she believes, than that she loves flowers. When she reveals she grew up in the country, we realize (although she does not) that the motive behind her favorite activity, and possibly her whole life, is one of separation and loss. A couple of 21-year-olds anticipate their marriage. When they were fifteen, they met at a wedding; so Marker interrupts the interview and shows a noisy, chaotic wedding dinner before returning to the couple. The boy, in the military, is about to leave for Algeria. Politics have nothing to do with them, the two say; they don't think about politics, and in any case they are powerless to influence events.

The darker second part is social; it is about *shared* Parisian lives, although the "sharing" sometimes is a matter of conflict. The opening event, though, is a sharing of grief: a funeral march in the streets, attended by more than 500,000 people, commemorating eight of their lives lost in February: people demonstrating for an end to the Algerian War. The police unnecessarily fired on the crowds; fleeing to a subway platform, eight "were crushed and bled to death."

Marker's tremendous documentary combines smooth classical long-shots and in-the-rough *cinéma-vérité*.

HANDS OVER THE CITY (Italy). In Naples, disaster strikes. How closely adjacent to a slum building is the new apartment building that was being constructed? The former has collapsed, killing two and robbing a boy of his legs. The real estate developer responsible for the new construction, Edoardo Nottola, sits on the City Council. The public land had been sold to him, and his development of it ignored urban planning law, including safety regulations. With the next municipal election one month away, an investigation is launched into governmental responsibility, but each agency admits to only the narrowest handprint on the project, declaring itself innocent of all irregularities. Someone else is to blame; but, as a both-serving political alliance is forged between Nottola's right wing and the center, all responsible hands are absolved and Nottola, following re-election, is made City Commissioner! One cover-up covers up another.

With documentary realism and poker-faced satire, former journalist Francesco Rosi's *Le mani sulla città* achieves brilliant, absorbing, sometimes thrilling results. It is a film of hands. Hilariously, after the accident, city councilmen—and at this point in patriarchic Italy they are all men—throw up their hands as a sign of having hands that are *clean* of the building disaster. Other shots involve a sea of hands; in another, in the street, they belong to impoverished tenants who have been evicted as the city poses as though it were conducting itself responsibly. Where will these people—and in this group there are *countless* women—go?

Toward and at the end, two shots of epic withdrawal, one inside the City Council chamber and the other outdoors, as another construction project is christened that will make Nottola even richer, one by dollie, one by reverse zoom lens, challenge us: Step back, and see what's going on!

MURIEL OR THE TIME OF A RETURN (France). Written by Jean Cayrol and directed by Alain Resnais, *Muriel ou Le temps d'un retour* takes place during two weeks mostly in early October 1962, that is to say, after Algeria's achievement of independence in July following war between France and its colony that had begun in 1954. Information about the French military's widespread use of torture on Algerians had also come to light. With its topical brace of history, Resnais's film is a haunted repository of ongoing relevance.

Delphine Seyrig gives a beautiful performance as Hélène, a widow who sells antiques in Boulogne. She lives with stepson Bernard, who is haunted by memories of Muriel, an Algerian girl he tortured and killed while soldiering in Algiers. Hélène remembers love: her first love, Alphonse, whose visit (with his current mistress, masquerading as his niece) is ostensibly the "return" to which the title refers. Moreover, Alphonse keeps "returning" to his fifteen years in Algeria, where he may never have actually been. Bernard keeps returning in his mind to Algiers, and as a result (possibly) kills again: this time, Robert, with whom he tortured and killed Muriel. Or is the memory of Muriel an oppressive phantom encapsulating for individuals a national burden of guilt? The substance to which our memories allude is elusive because it is dispersed throughout our sensible lives.

Resnais's trademark intricate editing creates a mosaic of past, present and, implicitly, future—lives fractured by war, even on the homefront. Humanity breaks down when memory is either attached to or dissociated from traumatic experience.

The titular "return" refers also to Cayrol and Resnais's return to their previous collaboration, *Night and Fog* (1955), a documentary survey of the history that haunts Auschwitz and another previous Resnais film that is also in color.

THE ORGANIZER (Italy, France, Yugoslavia). In late nineteenth-century Turin, at a textile mill laborers clock in 14-hour days, increasing risk to life and limb, for little pay, no benefits. Organized by a socialist, a former schoolteacher from Genoa who is fleeing authorities, the workers strike. Professor Sinigaglia is certain the strikers will prevail. He sees righteously; but the Professor is blind without his eyeglasses.

Mario Monicelli's long, atmospheric chronicle *I compagni—The Strikers*—benefits from a number of things: his excellent script, co-written by the team of Agenore Incrocci and Furio Scarpelli; his outstanding widescreen compositions, especially in powerful long-shots of humanity en masse; gorgeous black-and-white cinematography by Giuseppe Rotunno; Marcello Mastroianni's fiery lead performance.

The Professor thus identifies himself: "I have no home, no family, no friends." He is at the service of his political ideals. Paradoxically, Monicelli's film is a fractious epic—like John Ford's *The Searchers* (1956). It encompasses national divisions: city vs. country, North vs. South, management/ownership vs. workforce. The Professor comes in on a train, as later, from Saluzzo, scabs do; at the end, with a touch of Fellini, a young laborer, on the run like Sinigaglia, who has been caught and jailed, leaves by train. Perhaps he will "organize" elsewhere. Here is a film about national dislocations and relocations, a gradual, cumulative diaspora.

Monicelli aims to create "a Visconti film"; actors Renato Salvatori and Annie Girardot remind us of *Rocco and His Brothers* (1960), with another family's relocation in search of work. But when the Professor flexes and scratches himself, we think *Yojimbo* (Akira Kurosawa, 1961).

Management always confronts labor with the same veiled threat: "Do you know how many unemployed there are?" Translation: "You do not matter. You are nothing."

Carted around in a wheel chair, the mill owner carries, uses a switch.

1964

GERTRUD (Denmark). An Ibsen's *A Doll's House* without agenda, *Gertrud* is Dreyer's refined, rigorous valedictory—a last work of such nobility and clarity that it transports the viewer to astonishment and grace.

Adding a haunting coda to Hjalmar Söderberg's play, *Gertrud* shows the consequences of choice for a woman who, in the early twentieth century, leaves the security of a stifling marriage and ends up—calmly, with dignity—alone. Gertrud's responsible life discloses her great spirit, releasing it from the distortion of a too highly placed wall mirror in her husband's vast, cold, empty house; her exercise of free will, and her unquarrelsome acceptance of the disappointing results, help compose her integrity. Austere, poignant, mature, *Gertrud* is the patient revelation of the gravity and weight of a human life as it incrementally advances—moment by moment, choice by choice—in the direction of eternity. Bergman's atheism seems crabby alongside Dreyer's massive faith.

Gertrud's measured pace; the measured pace of the characters' speech; the camera's tactful distance in so many instances; the beauteous black and white; the solitude; the sheer calm: even in the exalted œuvre to which it belongs, *Gertrud* seems like nothing else. It captures life as life is measured against eternity. It is Dreyer as he prepares himself for God. For us, too, the film seems like some sort of momentous preparation—if only for our next viewing of this inexhaustible masterpiece. *Gertrud* is a movie to live by.

1964

Nina Pens Rode, as Gertrud, is sublime. Who can forget Gertrud's final gaze, from her apartment door, as she bids farewell to a guest? Her sight seems to turn inward, approaching private reverie. What is it at the last that she sees? I think I know—perhaps the film that the rest of us have just seen. *Gertrud.*

IL DESERTO ROSSO (Italy, France). A coda to his titanic trilogy, Antonioni's *The Red Desert* continues his consideration of alienation, the signature theme of the sixties. In Ravena, in northern Italy, the film follows another unsettled soul, Giuliana (gorgeous Monica Vitti, superb), a plant manager's wife, this time peripatetic in an industrial landscape. For whatever she is searching, at one level a sense of self and integrity, Giuliana won't find it in her extramarital affair with an engineer who, passing through, is already poised to abandon her. In her drab, cold, rainy milieu, the only bright colors are from paint on walls and plastic products. Thus Giuliana dreams of another, radiant space, one of sand, unpolluted ocean, clear sky—and of freedom and escape.

Giuliana's "sickness" is the modern condition. What the eye takes in reflects our ambivalence toward the modern world. Outdoors, lakes are polluted and polluted air assumes a terrible grandeur, while at home a helper-robot hints the high technology to come—which, while easing work, marginalizes people, as does all the manufactured stuff that turns a home into a house: a circumstance at which Giuliana's agitated care of her sick child at one point levels a furious assault.

The film's celebrated use of color as a means of expression rather than decoration contributes to Antonioni's vision of a world out of joint. (Carlo di Palma is his cinematographer.) It is the world of products that Antonioni will blast into space in *Zabriskie Point* (1969)—things that take over our lives, sapping our strength, cutting our humanity off at the knees.

Antonioni has always insisted he isn't a political filmmaker, and I take him at his word. However, his *Red Desert* delivers a blow to capitalism the force of which few ideological films can match.

DIAMONDS OF THE NIGHT (Czechoslovakia). But for sound effects a nearly silent film, Jan Němec's *Démanty noci* is the greatest work of the Czech New Wave, which, along with much else, fell to Soviet tanks in 1968.

Based on co-scenarist Arnošt Lustig's story "Darkness Has No Shadows," it is about Czech boys on the run, two "diamonds of the night": Jewish teenagers, pursued by authorities and hostile locals, after they escape from a train transporting them from one death camp to another. (Lustig spent years in various camps, himself escaping on the way to Dachau.)

All the "actors" are nonprofessionals, and the agitated use of handheld camera mimics documentary filmmaking. Despite this foundation in at least the appearance of objective reality, *Démanty noci* proceeds subjectively, its camera sensitively attuned to the boys' flight and feverish attempts to remain alive. The repetitive circular mosaic that constitutes the film's method, with its flashforwards and shafts of memory, and perhaps dreams, records the flight as a doomed, fear-fraught standstill. Němec and the magnificent dark, dusky black-and-white cinematography by Jaroslav Kučera move us inside the boys' consciousness.

As if in a fairy tale, the flight takes the boys to a forest that they must penetrate. They collapse on the ground before their brisk walk into utter darkness, during which, one boy behind the other, their arms, like insects' antennae, bound out to navigate though the thicket of branches attacking them. Later, one boy enters the home of a villager, who, wary, gives him bread and, on his return entry, milk. The boy imagines killing the woman. His not doing so leads to his and his companion's capture and murder.

"Well, the boy should have killed the woman": the film's humanity may lie in its refusal to submit to this facile conclusion.

IL VANGELO SECONDO MATTEO (Italy). When Pier Paolo Pasolini's *The Gospel According to St. Matthew* was first released here, it disappointed my sister-in-law. All the buzz about a Marxist filming of the Christian gospel had her expecting what today we would call a communist "spin" on the material. This she did not find; this, no one would be able to find. Indeed, the film doesn't impose a communist complexion onto the Gospel. Rather, by allowing the text to speak for itself, in the context that the images provide, Pasolini's film shows that, translated into twentieth-century political terms, Jesus *was* a communist. Humanistically and non-ideologically, the film presents the character that the Gospel indicates.

Pasolini came from the right country to accomplish this. Christianity, humanism and *neorealismo* all converged to enable this son of Italy to make this particular film. Beautifully shot in gritty black and white over rough terrain (the cinematographer is Tonino delli Colli), the *Gospel* does complete justice to the hardship endured by those whom history would anoint as the first Christians. Here is the finest, most profound film about Jesus, perhaps surpassing even the wonderful material about Jesus included in Carl Theodor Dreyer's *Leaves from Satan's Book* (1919). It may also be, apart from *Francesco, giullare di Dio* (1950), cinema's finest instance of applying *neorealismo* to the past—and without the addition of fabulous elements that partially shift Rossellini's (greater) film to somewhat different expressive territory. In its attempt to unite Marxism with his deep religious feeling, moreover, it may also be Pasolini's most personal work.

The *Gospel* is nonprofessionally cast. I do not quite know what to make of the fact that Pasolini gave his own mother, Susanna Pasolini, the role of Mary, the mother of Jesus. For the record, though, her performance is wonderful.

FATHER OF A SOLDIER (U.S.S.R.). Sergo Zaqariadze gives a titanic performance as Georgy Makharashvili, an ageing Georgian farmer who ventures beyond his rural village in search of his son, Goderdzi, a tankman and army lieutenant who has been wounded. ("Do not come back without our son!" Goderdzi's mother tells her husband right before his departure.) Along the way, Georgy dons a soldier's uniform and suffers the loss of comrades, including a boy who might have been his son. In Berlin, at its fall, he reunites with Goderdzi. Briefly. Freshly wounded, Goderdzi dies with his father beside him.

This humanistic tragicomedy—its Georgian title is *Djariskatsis mama*; Russian, *Otyets soldata*—was written by Suliko Zhgenti and directed by Rezo Chkheidze. His trek across Soviet land identifies Georgy with this land; he is Soviet—but not Russian. Even his name reminds us he is Georgian, as do his interactions with Russians throughout. Politically, Russia dominates and controls the nation; ethnic republics have the paradoxical status of being quasi-satellites within national borders. Yet it is Georgy Makharashvili who, by film's end, has accumulated the iconographic texture of Soviet spirit. Deepening this irony, Georgy vaguely resembles another man from Georgia: the Soviet Union's leader at the time the film is set.

The black-and-white film's visual style derives from Soviet silents. For instance, low, upwardly tilted closeups of this *Father of a Soldier* show humanity mediating between Earth and the eternity of sky, between Soviet reality and (poetically) Soviet destiny. In context, such shots become sorely, and subversively, ironic; for, by taking us back to an earlier Soviet Union, these familiar shots now imply the national destiny that the Soviet Union has since failed to achieve.

Another passage likewise draws upon the fierce immensity of silent Soviet filmmaking: at night, a train of tanks looming phantasmagorically.

BLACK GOD, WHITE DEVIL (Brazil). Gláuber Rocha's *Deus e o Diabo na Terra do Sol*, literally, *God and the Devil in the Land of the Sun*, opens with an overhead shot of the sunbaked *sertão* in northeast Brazil. Impoverished Manuel rides home. En route to landlord

Moraes, half the cattle die, for which Moraes demands that Manuel pay. When Moraes whips him, Manuel cuts down Moraes with a machete. Manuel tells wife Rosa they must pilgrimage to Monte Santo. Manuel follows Sebastião, a black mystic preaching rebellion. Manuel, "sick with hope" in her eyes, leaves "faithless" Rosa behind, but she follows. As Sebastião walks alongside him, Manuel, on his knees, hauls a boulder up to Sebastião's church. Rosa murders Sebastião at the altar; Antônio das Mortes, a gun hired by the Church and landowners to kill Sebastião, massacres his followers, sparing Manuel and Rosa, who, led by Julião, a blind singer, end up following Corisco, a white bandit, whom Antônio eventually kills, releasing Manuel yet again from the grip of a deleterious social or religious influence. Manuel and Rosa, in a spectacular long-shot, flee across the land; when Rosa falls down, she is again left behind. Manuel reaches the sea—this final passage an *hommage* to Truffaut's *The 400 Blows* (1959), much as Sergio Leone's westerns will pay homage to Rocha's allegory.

A seminal work of *cinema nôvo*, Rocha's black-and-white film refers to actual events, combining these with shifting chronology, magic realism (a Latin American form of surrealism), *neorealismo*'s humane concerns, and the *nouvelle vague*'s formal freedom—elements of *cinema nôvo*, to which Eisensteinian imagery (*¡Qué viva México!* is an especial influence) has been added. Rocha shifts from sound to silence and inserts Godardian gunshots into the soundtrack, as well as haunting songs, resulting in a somber yet delirious mix.

CHARULATA (India). Bhupati Dutta's publication of a political newspaper in the late nineteenth century limits the attention he pays to Charulata, his lonely wife, in Satyajit Ray's film based on Rabindranath Tagore's 1901 novel *Nashtanir* (*The Broken Nest*). In their wealthy mansion, a caged bird projects how Charu feels. Charu fills her time with unrewarding activities such as embroidery; we see her hands at such work—an image of alienation—as the opening credits roll.

In a way, *Charulata*—the film of which Ray himself was most proud—recasts his tragic *Devi* (1960) as social satire, creating in this instance an undreamy and claustrophobic result. (One glorious shot outdoors, in homage to Jean Renoir's 1936 *Une partie de campagne*, underscores by contrast the sense of confinement that Ray imposes on the rest of the film: Charu, uncharacteristically smiling while swinging on a swing, the apparatus of the swing nowhere visible, the resultant image one of joyous, if brief freedom and motion.) Charu in this film, unlike Doyamoyee in *Devi*, is painfully aware of the male domination being leveled against her; but her recourse, a fixation on Amal, her cousin by marriage who encourages her interest in the arts, compounds her crisis rather than emancipating her. Will Charu's marriage survive her deeper connection to her husband's younger, handsome relation?

While *Devi* is a powerful fable, *Charulata* comes closer to a detailed realism; while *Devi*, the greater work, can stand on its own, *Charulata* gains strength and conviction when viewed as the earlier film's companion-piece. Both marvelously address the individual need for gender equality. With *Mahanagar* (1963), which addresses a social need for this as well, a loose trilogy thus emerges.

Charulata's finest performance comes from the brilliant star of *The World of Apu* and *Devi*: Soumitra Chatterjee, who plays Amal.

THE UMBRELLAS OF CHERBOURG (France). Jacques Demy's experimental musical in which the dialogue (all written by him) is sung, *Les parapluies de Cherbourg* invests the bittersweet with great power. The action itself, covering more than a decade, falls entirely within France's delusional stand in defense of her colonialism in the Algerian War. Its constant singing expresses the lock that conventionalism has on people's lives.

In Cherbourg, Geneviève, the daughter of a widowed shopowner, and Guy, who works as a garage mechanic, are passionately in love. The army drafts Guy; Geneviève finds herself pregnant with his child. Pressured by her mother, Geneviève marries a rich suitor. Believing that Geneviève would wait for him, Guy is devastated upon returning home; his guardian-

1964

aunt's legacy moves him to accept her caregiver's solace and helps him to open his own garage. Visiting Cherbourg, Geneviève, accompanied by their child, pulls into Guy's garage; married now, Guy also has a child.

Geneviève is caught between her heart and the bourgeoisism that her mother embodies, whose notes of aspiration, convenience, complacency and betrayal Demy links to France's (then, ongoing) military engagement. Seriously wounded, Guy nearly lost his life; having made the choice she did, one of class to boot and the choice that her mother also had made in marrying Geneviève's father, Geneviève has relegated both herself and Guy to an emotionally compromised existence.

It is her mother's "practicality" that Geneviève invokes when, discounting her own feelings, she decides to marry Roland if he proves his love by still wanting to marry her after learning she has been "knocked up."

"It is strange," Guy writes Geneviève from Algeria, "how sun and death travel together," with its echo of Camus's *The Stranger*. But Cherbourg's raininess is redolent with its own kind of death.

The glorious music is by Michel Legrand.

BEFORE THE REVOLUTION (Italy). "Those who didn't live in the eighteenth century before the [French] Revolution will never be able to know the sweetness of life." — Talleyrand

At 22 Bernardo Bertolucci made *Prima della rivoluzione*. Fabrizio, his young protagonist, concludes there's no escaping his bourgeois past, no matter his Leftist political leanings. The oppressed whom he would help liberate aspire to be members of the middle class! Meanwhile, he has an affair with Aunt Gina, whom as a little boy he enjoyed watching dress. "I always laugh, I always cry," says this encapsulation of Mother Church. She breaks down after being taunted by a child—I presume a Puckish image of herself—obliviously singing up in a tree. "You are happy," she says aloud as Fabrizio (whom we glimpse through a window) dances in the street. "But it won't last . . . you'll forget me. You'll hate me." At Fabrizio's wedding send-off, Gina (Adriana Asti, terrific) is tearfully showering with kisses a younger nephew.

Inspired by Godard, and Resnais's *Marienbad* (1961), Bertolucci tries everything: zooms; a moving car camera, attached either to the front or the side; dissolves within a scene—if you will, "soft" jump-cuts; hard jump-cuts; misty lyrical poetry by a lake. This movie is in love with movies and movie-making.

It is also one of the most important films for understanding the sixties. Its lovely incest (seven years before Louis Malle's *Murmur of the Heart*) reaches for a synthesis derived from thesis (family, structure, order) and antithesis (the pleasure of doing one's own thing). In the States we knew on the basis of this reconciliation that revolution would never happen here.

Or, perhaps, anywhere else in the postwar West. A schoolteacher tells Fabrizio, "[Y]ou can argue only with people who have the same ideas."

Devastating; irreplaceable; phenomenal.

CULLODEN (UK). Peter Watkins was not yet thirty when he revolutionized the genre of historical documentary, thus becoming one of the most influential serious filmmakers, with *Culloden*, whose form expands the creative and expressive possibilities of the genre, for example, by its interviews/testimonies of participants in the 1746 battle at Culloden between rag-tag Highland Scots, French-supported Jacobites attempting to restore the House of Stuart to the British throne, and the well-heeled Hanoverian English army and Lowland accomplices. *We are there*; we see for ourselves and keenly feel the horrible suffering that war, that armed confrontation, entails. Equally vivid, gut-wrenching in fact, is the post-battle slaughter of Highland families, including women and children.

Impoverished clansmen have been forced into, for them, the "suicidal" Battle of Culloden with threats by landowners of losing their rented homes and other meager property. Some leaders, though, are motivated by the fact that Charles Edward Stuart is, like them, Catholic; they hope he replaces Britain's Protestant king. ("God is on our side," Stuart insists, thus believing he will prevail despite the fact that his army is outnumbered, out-armed.) After his defeat, we are told, Stuart abandoned his cause and those who had fought for it, numbers of whom awaited his return indefinitely, creating a glowing legend around "Bonnie Prince Charlie."

Voiceover—Watkins?—provides a wealth of factual detail. Soldiers and their outcomes—deaths; maimings—are identified. We discover for ourselves how the winning general, the Duke of Cumberland, King George II's son, acquired the nickname "Butcher."

Surely this black-and-white film owes something to John Huston's on-the-spot World War II documentary, *San Pietro* (1945), but, set in the past with unknown actors in the roles of combatants and other victims of the English massacre, *Culloden* is also unlike any film I know of before it.

KAIDAN (Japan). An early twentieth-century Japanese folklorist of Irish and Greek descent, Lafcadio Hearn wrote the "strange tales" that Masaki Kobayashi's *Kaidan* samples. This tense, spooky, stylized, painterly quartet of ghost stories transports us to another world in order to return us to human nature.

In "The Black Hair," a samurai abandons his devoted wife and marries a governor's daughter for the sake of career advancement, eventually abandoning her for his first wife, citing his thoughtless youth. But, as in *Ugetsu monogatari* (1953), the reunion is illusory, and the man here is punished for continuing selfishness; for doesn't this motivate his abandonment of his second wife also? To underscore the point, the segment ends in a freeze-frame of his horrified face as he fails to exit a world of caustic memory and avenging ghosts.

"Woman of the Snow" features a supernatural snowstorm—trees dance in its thrashing winds—and culminates in the abandonment of a woodcutter by his wife over a broken pledge he made to a spirit in the storm. "Hoichi, the Earless" includes a ferocious battle at sea under a blood-orange sky and horrific revenge by ghosts of its warriors exacted against a blind musician for favoring pride over his sacred obligations to art and to the past. "In a Cup of Tea," about a man who sees a stranger's reflection in his cup of tea, is introduced by voiceover narration speculating on why some tales are left incomplete. After the cup falls to the floor, claiming being "wounded," the stranger mysteriously appears in front of the man, de-materializes. The same thing happens to the aborted story! The author has vanished, too, leaving it to others to complete it so that he doesn't disappoint. For us, the man has replaced the stranger at the bottom of the cup.

INTENTIONS OF MURDER (Japan). Shohei Imamura's snowy black comedy *Akai satsui* revolves around Sadako, the uneducated common-law wife of Riichi, who hasn't married her because of her inferior status; Sadako had been housemaid to Riichi's family. Masaru, the couple's kindergarten-age son, was registered to his paternal grandparents for the same reason. (Sadako's persistence officially corrects this.) Riichi, a university librarian with a long-term mistress, repeatedly addresses Sadako as "stupid," and indeed she isn't adept at following orders. But this may reflect resistance to being unfairly ordered about or the partial internalization of put-downs Riichi and his mother, Tadae, routinely inflict. Note that Sadako is finally adept at using the knitting machine which initially seems beyond her capacity to master.

When Sadako is alone in Riichi's shack near commuter train tracks, a thief breaks in; dying of heart disease, Hiraoko needs money for medicine. He rapes Sadako, whose ambivalence is ignited by this departure from Riichi's condescending uses of her. (Hiraoko leaves money, making a joke of Tadae's later remark, "Being a woman doesn't pay.") Sadako's "intentions of murder" are "honorably" aimed at herself; but her attempt at hanging herself only drops her to the floor. Hiraoko's bothersome obsession shifts Sadako's murderous intentions to *him*. Caged white mice dominate the foreground of shots; one, hungry, Masaru muses without affect, eats the other. Sadako also testifies to this survival instinct, which Japanese society and its moral injunctions paper over. In another stunning shot, Hiraoko threatens to burn Sadako with a steam iron. We simultaneously see Sadako and her reflection in the iron's mirrorlike underside: an image of passivity against which she will henceforth react.

A startling dream sequence throws into question the objective reality of much else. Both Riichi, who often wears a pollution mask, and Hiraoko have labored breath.

LEMONADE JOE (Czechoslovakia). Cinema's premier western spoof is manic, gorgeous, technically dazzling: *Limonádový Joe aneb Konská opera*. Directed by Oldřich Lipský from his and Jiří Brdečka's script, it slyly riddles with bullets, and douses with lemonade, some of the evil and a few idiocies of capitalism.

Lemonade Joe rides into an Arizona town—Arizona, because of the Arizona Kid in Jacques Prévert and Jean Renoir's 1935 *The Crime of Monsieur Lange*?—and struts into the Trigger Whiskey Saloon and, with an hilarious show of his miraculous sober shooting, exacts the substitution of Kolaloka Lemonade for hard spirits. Dressed in white, he is the transformative hero, the all-American fascist, and two women fall instantly in love with him: the saloon singer, who hopes Joe will make her "new, different," and a temperance activist, who recognizes in him a kindred spirit. Unbeknownst to the hoodwinked town, Joe's father owns Kolaloka Lemonade. (Note the brand name.) In this context, his promise to "return with the law," that is to say, federal marshals, takes on a darker meaning: the collusion between big business and government.

Lemonade Joe is huckstering a good product, one capable even of raising the dead. A battle ensues between the liquor faction and the lemonade faction, ripping apart the town before the arrival of a compromise that cloaks a brutal abdication. Here also is a reminder, at the time of the Vietnam War, of the wars upon which U.S. capitalism depends—for additional resources, but also, more simply, to brandish its capacity to kill and maim "to show the world," all under the cloak of some strategic nonsense (for instance, fighting Communism).

With jump-cuts, sped-up motion, shift from objective to point-of-view shots, smoke-ring signals (whole letters!), blackface disguise, lemonadey color tinting and, in one breathtakingly beautiful segment, blue tinting.

1965

THE ROUND-UP (Hungary). Every film exists on a continuum of expression governed by opposite poles of objectivity and subjectivity, documentary, fiction. In *Szegénylegények* (*The Round-up*; *The Hopeless Ones*), the *mise-en-scène* is objective; the camera, subjective. One presents material; the other interprets it. The film's creator, Miklós Jancsó, is, like Chabrol and Eisenstein, a master formalist. Viewers breathe according to his shots and their tempo. He is also a minimalist.

Szegénylegények is about state terrorism. In 1848 Hungary tried unsuccessfully to overturn Austrian rule. The failed revolution—echoed by the crushed 1956 anti-Communist revolution —plunged the country into residual turmoil as guerrillas kept up the cause. In 1868 Austria concentrated into a stockade captured rebels and anyone else they suspected of supporting a free Hungary. Outside the camp, farmers were encouraged to denounce neighbors. Those officiating at the camp go about their business grimly, sometimes even remorsefully.

In a harrowing passage, peasant women will be made examples of in an open field. The women flee, but mounted soldiers take off after them, into the background of the frame. The next shot returns us to the compound, where the women undress. Two rows of soldiers face one another. The first woman is made to run back and forth four times between the two rows of soldiers. Eight times, therefore, the soldiers' whips strike the woman's back. In outrage and sympathy, male prisoners drop to their deaths from the roof of the compound, aborting the procedure below.

Jancsó is an ironist as well as a formalist. Having been rounded up, Hungarian rebels are interrogated, tortured, killed, all of which is recorded by an intricately choreographed camera whose fluent, relentless trackings and backtrackings thread an impartial noose around oppressed and oppressors alike—those, unaware, who share small breathing space in history's tightening grip.

PIERROT LE FOU (France). The most tender and most troubled of love stories, Godard's musical-satirical-tragicomedy shimmers with the beauty of love's and life's volatility and transience.

At a party, Ferdinand (Jean-Paul Belmondo, wonderful) passes through a funny series of monochromatic tableaux, each one with a different group of guests whose "conversation" consists of lines from TV commercials. This commercial vampirism, wherein people's personalities have been taken over by consumerism, motivates Ferdinand to run off with his children's babysitter, Marianne (Anna Karina, perfect), abandoning wife, job, home—in sum, his bourgeois life. Ferdinand is also in love with Marianne. He sets out with her, then, to follow his heart.

On the run, the lovers sleep in the wilds in complementary fetal positions, as though possessing a single body and soul; yet they remain separate and distinct. "We never understand one another," Marianne tells Ferdinand; "You talk to me with words, and I look at you with feelings." Their romance, she prophesies, will be short and sweet.

They put on a show for a docked American sailor. Marianne, in Vietnamese makeup, protests fiercely; Ferdinand, wearing a naval officer's hat, spouts Americanese ("Sure"; "Yeah"). Fire and a wooden stick, the latter a prop bomber, assist the pair's makeshift portrayal of the Vietnam War. Explosions, gunfire fill the soundtrack. "That's darn good," the American sailor says about this evocation of American slaughter. The U.S. has moved on to other atrocities; but nothing else in cinema so brings back the horror of that moment in time when America sold whatever shred of soul it possessed in the name of fighting communism.

The final shot of *Pierrot le fou* casts the by-now dead lovers' disembodied voices against an illimitable nighttime sky.

Throughout, Raoul Coutard contributes the most gorgeous color cinematography I have seen.

SIMON OF THE DESERT (Mexico). Its shooting aborted, apparently, when the producer ran out of money, Luis Buñuel's Mexican *Simón del desierto* is set in the past. The film skewers organized religion and laments the gap between one man's asceticism and the grubby self-interest of those purportedly enthralled by him.

Simon emulates St. Simeon Stylites, the fifth-century fanatic, by standing on a gigantic, narrow column in the desert—on one foot, even, when he feels obliged to do penance. He has been at it for six years, six months, six days when Satan, in the form of a temptress, pops up to taunt and seduce him. At the end s/he takes him by airplane to 1960s Manhattan, where his column has been multiplied into skyscrapers; in a swinging nightclub, when he half-heartedly announces he is going home, s/he informs him that he has already been replaced on top of the column—the implication being, with nobody, including the priests, any the wiser.

In one of the vignettes way below Simon in the desert, a former thief asks for the restoration of his hands—they were lopped off as punishment—so that he can farm again and support his family. Simon prays while one of the large gathering quips, "Maybe today we'll see one of Simon's miracles." Indeed, the hands are suddenly back on the man, whose nonplussed response, however, wittily robs the moment of the miraculous. There is also the implication that, if need be, he will steal again.

Buñuel visually plays with the question mark of whether Simon's being so far above other humans sets him any closer to God, and the turbulent, windswept black-and-white images of

Simon recorded by an upwardly tilted camera, beautifully cinematographed by Gabriel Figueroa, suggest an unsettled soul for all Simon's air of confident faith.

VAGHE STELLE DELL'ORSO (Italy). *Misty Stars of the Great Bear* (called *Sandra* in the U.S.) took the top prize, the Golden Lion of St. Mark, at Venice. It is Luchino Visconti's starkest film and among his most brilliant ones.

Claudia visits Volterra, in Tuscany, with her American husband. The occasion: a ceremony honoring her Jewish father, who perished at Auschwitz. She and her brother, Gianni, suspect that their still-living mother and stepfather denounced their father. They determine to pursue this and extract justice. Their own close relationship, the subject of a novel he is writing, constitutes a memory that Gianni cherishes, but Claudia is perplexed and nearly traumatized by it. Just what happened so many years ago, on *both* fronts?

As he did in *Il Gattopardo* (1963) and would do again in *The Damned* (1969), Visconti explores the decay and collapse of an aristocratic family as a reflection of national history. Both Claudia and Gianni feel driven to connect the dots of family history. Their stirring up a cauldron of secrets and suspiciousness ultimately shatters one of them, who commits suicide. Mourning may become Electra, but Claudia heads back to America—in its simplicity, heartlessness and obliviousness (qualities represented by her spouse), a refuge from her obsessions with father, brother, Italy, the past.

We have, then, a skeletons-in-the-closet film, one that generates ancient echoes through its absorption and delicate rendering of the Electra myth. Italy has made many haunted films about its Fascist past and the German occupation, but this may be the most gripping. Armando Nannuzzi's black-and-white cinematography encompasses claustrophobic darkness and sorely ironic ravishing light. It befits an operatic mood-piece about unsettled and unsettling events, both familial and national.

Claudia Cardinale and Marie Bell memorably play daughter and mother, while Jean Sorel functions lamely as an Alain Delon-substitute.

ALPHAVILLE (France). Jean-Luc Godard looks ahead, from the past and from his own vantage; a futuristic application of themes from poet Paul Éluard's 1926 *La capitale de la douleur*, *Alphaville, une étrange aventure de Lemmy Caution*, operating under budgetary restrictions, uses present-day Paris, without tricks or prefabricated designs, to suggest a city of the future, Alphaville. (We know it isn't Aerograd by the number of cars.) It is run by computers, of course, and it is on some other planet. Assisted by Raoul Coutard's gorgeous black-and-white cinematography, Godard creates a vast, mysterious nighttime vision of chill beauty, where individual freedom is verboten and dehumanization reigns—an expression of Godard's concern for the Western world circa 1965. *Alphaville* is Godard's *1984*.

Alphaville is haunted by memory. It reeks of totalitarianism, under whose weight of political oppression humans can no longer project themselves ahead but can find traces of freedom only by entering the illimitable space of memory and imagination. Dead-end Alphaville, encapsulated by a mechanized voice, accompanied by teeming lights in voluminous darkness, including flashing neon, signals the luminous rebirth of human emotion: romantic love. The film persuades by leaving no doubt that Godard would go to the end of the cosmos for his enchanting spouse, Anna Karina. Will she and the hero escape Alphaville and make it back to Earth? And is this possible to do in a Ford Galaxy?

Godard fuels his sci-fi marvel with images, not plot. His surrogate in what story there is is secret agent Lemmy Caution, who, having indeed strayed from the confinement of plot, the pages of pulp detective fiction, has entered Alphaville in order to assassinate the city's fascist architect, Professor von Braun. Caution's destiny's also in the stars.

A companion-piece to Chris Marker's *La jetée* (1962), this immemorial film dazzles and delights.

THE LION HUNTERS (France). Lion hunting, by tradition, is the province of the Gao people. Members of the Fulani, nomadic shepherds in northern Niger and Mali, whose herds are being attacked by lions, approach the Gao for help through the proscribed intermediary of the Songhai, whom the Fulani pay in cattle.

The distribution of tasks and their performance for mutual benefit suggest a social correction to "survival of the fittest." But killing lions is serious business. Passages documenting the processes by which the Gao forge arrows and brew poison for these arrows index, ironically, the spiritual weight of the life-taking that will result. In a sense, each group represents the precariousness of African life. The shepherds will be lost if the lions continue to devour their animals; the Songhai and the hunters will be lost if they fail to perform functions that tradition has assigned to them. In the mortal realm of Darwinian survival, a cosmic order is being heeded and worked out. Experience has given the Gao an exhaustive understanding of the terrain over which the hunt will proceed; they are presumably connected to the spirits of the grass, trees and water. France's Jean Rouch thus brilliantly shows the rationalization involved in killing—by implication, in men killing men as well as animals. Killing must be *more* than killing; it becomes "sanctified," elevated by its connection to God or to spirits.

How perfectly the Gao understand—that is to say, believe they understand—their prey, to the extent that they can decipher which lion has committed which offense and therefore warrants the proper dispatch. *Scape-lioning.* Their reward comes from the sale of proofs of their slaughtering: skin, skull, etc.

In Rouch's ethnographic *La chasse au lion à l'arc*, the primitive casts a light into the heart of darkness of civilization.

FISTS IN THE POCKET (Italy). In perhaps the most stunning debut in Italian cinema, 25-year-old writer-director Marco Bellocchio tackles the contemporary Italian family, suggesting the perverted mindset of Fascism, which, the film implies, proceeded from an obsession with family to the detriment of individualist consciousness and behavior. Augusto's fiancée, Lucia, has received a threatening anonymous note from, they believe, his sister, Giulia, telling her to back off because she is pregnant with his child. The presumed motive: to keep Augusto at home, in part to help take care of their blind mother. Meanwhile, Giulia has received a love letter from Alessandro, their brother, who (perhaps having read *Of Mice and Men*) gets miffed when their other brother, Leone, feeds the pet rabbits he considers his own. Who and what belongs to whom?: What *isn't* mixed up now, twenty years after the war?

Ale—Alessandro—is the main character. He and Leone, who is mentally slow, are epileptic. We know things are just not right with Ale by the way he is introduced; he falls into the frame from above, presumably out of a tree. One of cinema's greatest black comedies is in full gear.

Indeed, Ale owes something to the protagonist of cinema's *greatest* black comedy, Norman Bates in Alfred Hitchcock's *Psycho* (1960). Ale kills, too—also from a surfeit of family feeling, you understand. Augusto, who at least seems normal, should not have to put up with this ratty family of his. One by one its members meet a horrible death, starting with Mom.

Lou Castel's remarkable performance as Alessandro highlights this hilarious and frightening film. Paola Pitagora also is memorable as Giulia.

Castel's Alessandro not only looks back to Bates but also ahead to River Phoenix's heartrending narcoleptic Mike in Gus Van Sant's *My Own Private Idaho* (1991).

MAN IS NOT A BIRD (Yugoslavia). Belgrade-born writer-director Dušan Makavejev's first feature, *Čovek nije tica* shows Godard's influence while staking out a distinctive artistic signature. Jan visits an eastern Serbian industrial town in order to assemble heavy machinery in the local copper factory. The factory, which is real, reminds that Makavejev is a former documentarian. But there are also "scientific" passages of faux-documentary—a Makavejev specialty.

One of the factory workers, Barbulović—"Barbool"—tyrannizes his wife, whose favorite dress he has given to his mistress, causing his wife to assault the other woman publicly. Barbool explains to the police that he bought the dress for his wife and therefore has the perfect right to give it away. Providing for her, he adds, he also has the right to beat his wife —which the gradual blackout of an earlier domestic scene suggests he has done. His crude, cruel behavior becomes comprehensible when we see Barbool at hard labor at his job—an extensive passage, before a fixed camera—while, with withering irony, upbeat voiceover notes how much easier industrial work is now than before the war. Periodically Makavejev shows an expert lecturing an audience about hypnosis. The gentleman hypnotizes audience members, having them, once under, flapping like birds. But "man is not a bird," and the totalitarian state is hypnotizing the masses, in the process dehumanizing them. "That's how we live, believing everything," Barbool's wife tells Barbool's mistress, newly an ally, adding, "You do everything [my husband] says." "No more hypnosis!" the wife protests.

Jan and Raika (Milena Dravić, vibrant, sensuous) become lovers. Their scenes together in bed are both erotic and melancholy, sex—well, intimate human contact—being necessary to navigate an unfriendly world encapsulated in a searing overhead shot: the couple walking across a desolate expanse of dried, cracked mud.

GOLDEN RIVER (India). With *Subarnarekha*, Ritwik Ghatak completed the trilogy he had begun with *Meghe Dhaka Tara* (1960) and *Komal Ghandhar* (1961) about the human upheavals, strife and all-out war, famine and dire poverty created as a result of the 1947 Partition of India, the arbitrary line that the British drew on a map as its farewell colonialist act, dividing India into a secular state and Islamic Pakistan. Ghatak's saga over many years focuses on a family of Bengal refugees from East Pakistan (now Bangladesh) trying to establish new roots.

It is a work structured by coincidences; but its melodramatic material everywhere gains resonance by references to Partition. The film opens, for instance, with a lower-caste mother pleading for her little son's admission into school, only to be told that the line dividing school districts cannot be crossed. Suddenly regional conflict ignites and the woman is snatched away, leaving Abhiram orphaned; the child is adopted by Ishwar Chakraborty, whose little daughter, Seeta, Abhiram grows up to love. (Seeta commits suicide when her brother solicits her as a prostitute.) Meanwhile, the Subarnarekha River flows near the refugee colony on the outskirts of Calcutta—the beautiful illusion that division can be peaceably adapted to. ("Subarnarekha" literally means "golden line.") The surrounding dull, daunting rocks taunt the illusion.

As with *Meghe Dhaka Tara*, Ghatak has fashioned a piece of powerful yearning—the desire of people to lead settled lives. An upwardly tilted shot suggests that sparsely adorned branches of a tree are reaching hopefully with all their fragile might into the heavens: a piercing image. "All year I've been yearning to come home," Abhiram, who has been away at school, tells Seeta at the edge of a forest. Without realizing it, the boy is giving voice to the hearts of a shattered people.

THE MAN WHO HAD HIS HAIR CUT SHORT (Belgium). Senne Rouffaer gives a beautifully modulated, pitch-perfect performance as Govert Miereveld, who keeps working as hard as he can (his surname means "field of ants"), in André Delvaux's film *De man die zijn haar kort liet knippen*, from Johan Daisne's Flemish novel. Govert begins as a teacher at a girls' high school, proceeds to being a lawyer, but gives that up and becomes a court clerk; but one can hardly be sure of this chronology. Since he ends up as a patient in an insane asylum, we cannot separate delusion from reality or fix relative dates in time. It is his obsession with a beautiful student that presumably sets Govert's course in the direction of derangement; but what is he remembering, imagining or reimagining? How does one know what parts, if any, of this narrative happened or are happening?

I am not sure that he even meets this student, Fran, at a hotel years later. Does he really shoot her? Heck, I'm not sure that there ever was such a student! And I am *not* complaining; Delvaux has fashioned a fascinating study of mental distress and delusion.

The grisly autopsy that so discombobulates Govert constitutes one of the most brilliant passages of surreal horror in cinema. We do not see into the raised coffin where the autopsy is being performed, but we see hands going in with all sorts of implements, we hear stabbing and cracking and see organs lifted above the rim. It is after this ordeal that Govert presumably chances upon Fran, now a famous actress, at a hotel. There, also, he casually suggests to the doctor who performed the autopsy that the human soul may be lodged in the appendix.

Belgium's Delvaux, like Govert, studied law.

MAHAPURISH (India). *The Holy Man*, Satyajit Ray's brilliant comedy about religious conning and chicanery, is the funniest such satire since Chaplin's *The Pilgrim* (1923). Even believers may find themselves wetting lower garments by laughing so hard.

Birinchi Baba (Charuprakash Ghosh, hilarious) takes up court with his young companion-disciple in the residence of a widower, retired lawyer Gurupada Mitter, who is having a devil of a time finding a suitable match for his younger daughter, Buchki. Homeward-bound following a pilgrimage, accompanied by Buchki, Gurupada met the con artist onboard a train; he was immediately taken in by the Hindu "holy man," while Buchki was silently derisive. (Birinchi had offered his deformed foot for good-luck touching to the masses and made a big show of causing the sun to rise.) Buchki decides to get suitor Satya in line by pretending to consider becoming Birinchi's disciple. Satya implores friends to help, and they hatch a plot to expose Birinchi. But the greater con artist is Buchki herself, who knows her heart and will get her Satya to propose.

Birinchi professes to believe there is no present, only past and future, and he twirls a finger of one hand clockwise and the corresponding digit of the other hand counterclockwise and touches the two to express his profound philosophy. He also name-drops worse than Baba Wawa, for instance, Jesus, whose crucifixion he apparently attended, which he can thus attest was not "cruci-fiction" but "cruci-fact." He goes into trances in front of his audiences in addition to dispensing his religious nonsense, but promptly halts everything every night at 7 p.m. The timeless fellow is obsessed with time, and this proves his Achilles' heel.

With popping eyes and painted lips, the holy man is quite a sight, and his hirsute back completes the outrageous portrait.

THE BATTLE OF ALGIERS (Italy, France). Gillo Pontecorvo, as a teenager, was a leader in Italy's anti-Fascist underground movement. As a filmmaker, though, he proved dull and unadventurous (*The Wide Blue Road*, 1957). Although derivative of Francesco Rosi's *Salvatore Giuliano* (1962) and Nanni Loy's *Four Days of Naples* (1962), *The Battle of Algiers* marked his immense improvement.

The Battle of Algiers, which ended in 1957, began the Algerian rebellion, 1954-1962, against longtime French colonial rule. Soldiers, dispatched to crush the rebellion and given a blank check in their methods, tortured and murdered, including vast numbers of innocents, claiming as many as a million Algerian lives. Pursuing their people's independence, the FLN (Front de Libération Nationale) used violent means that today would brand them as terrorists.

Pontecorvo's reconstruction of the street war, shot with handheld cameras on black-and-white newsreel stock in the actual locations, has such raw urgency that the film announces upfront—boasts, really—that no newsreel or documentary footage was used. The brilliant cinematography is by Marcello Gatti.

Commissioned by the ultimately victorious FLN, the film is passionately anticolonialist. There is a passage that shows an FLN member, a young woman, coolly blowing up a restaurant, before which she and the camera survey innocent French Algerian patrons, including children; some viewers go with this and other moments to claim for the film a "balanced" approach. The tone of the film admits no such possibility. Clearly, Pontecorvo feels that the situation—colonialist rule, now exacerbated by military terror—gives the African Algerians a moral blank check in their pursuit of independence. It is the French whose catalogue of terrorism, in the service of the status quo, overwhelms with its viciousness.

President Jacques Chirac, a soldier in Algeria, thus counseled George W. Bush against repeating, in Iraq, France's mistakes.

1966

CHIMES AT MIDNIGHT (Spain, Switzerland). Banished by Hollywood, Orson Welles made movies where he could. *Chimes at Midnight* is primarily wrought from *Henry IV, Parts I* and *II*, although *Henry V*, *Richard II* and *The Merry Wives of Windsor* are also drawn upon. The film, then, patches together appearances of Shakespeare's most beloved character, Sir Jack Falstaff, whom Welles himself beautifully plays. Welles described the film as a "lament for Merrie England"—in effect, a lament for all that's past. Apart from Kurosawa's *Throne of Blood* (1967), it is the greatest film derived from Shakespeare. Welles was proud of it on another score: No horses were injured or killed during filming. Unlike countless other U.S. filmmakers shooting abroad, Welles did not take advantage of laxer laws regarding the (mis)treatment of animals.

In particular, Welles considers Falstaff's fatherly tutelage, in taverns and brothels, of Prince Hal (Keith Baxter, brilliant), young heir to the British throne. Alas, their close alliance as fellow carousers does not spare Falstaff royal dismissal once King Henry IV (sonorous John Gielgud) dies and the prince takes his place. By noting from the start the emotional distance between the boy and Falstaff, which the former imposes and the latter ignores, the film makes Hal's subsequent rejection of his surrogate father less a betrayal of familial love than a signal for the collapse of illusions.

With its melancholy, absurdism and rich comedy, the whole film amazes. One of its sequences, though, is often anthologized as clearest proof of Welles's genius: the Battle of Shrewsbury. With Falstaff's armored bulk darting about ("The better part of valor . . .") lending the film one of its touches of the absurd, the passage becomes a massive, near abstract spectacle of muddy, flashing death—Welles's stunning portrait of war's enormity.

ANDREI RUBLEV (U.S.S.R.). The episodic nature of Andrei Tarkovsky's most famous film accommodates not only a panorama of fifteenth-century Russia but also the time's incapacity to see itself in coherent terms. The experiences of the actual icon painter who serves as the black-and-white film's protagonist (Anatoli Solonitsyn, wonderful) are signposts directing the viewer's journey through an historical landscape. "Not deep the poet sees, but wide," England's Matthew Arnold wrote. The aborted balloon ride with which the film opens corroborates this, implicitly adding, parenthetically, "imperfectly" right before "wide." Tarkovsky's wintry *Andrei Rublev* begins at a place of religious faith and proceeds to another, different place during the long odyssey that the film recounts. Medieval man ultimately anticipates modern man, with Robert Browning more than Arnold the Victorian poet who ultimately weighs in most resonantly.

Like Shakespeare, Tarkovsky throws everything into his epic mix. At turns he shows the madness and barbaric cruelty of war. Early on, the slow motion that is applied to a horse that has fallen down a flight of stairs announces the influence of Dovzhenko, whose famine-stricken horse from *Arsenal* (1929) seems to have merged with *Arsenal*'s collapsing accordian. Tarkovsky collapses the difference between medieval and modern, and between 1918 civil war and Soviet reality nearly fifty years later.

The film's most moving segment centers on a boy who to escape execution feigns the requisite knowledge for engineering the making of an enormous Orthodox church bell, during which process he comes to embody, for us at least, Russian heart, resourcefulness and resilience. So much has always been necessary, Tarkovsky is implying, just to survive.

Andrei Rublev closes on a color coda of Andrei Rublev's art. Terrible irony, this, that art (such as Soviet silent cinema) remains the region's principal legacy, and people, implicitly, the principal sacrifice.

MOUCHETTE (France). *See above.*

AU HASARD, BALTHAZAR (France). A very strange and moving film, *Au hasard Balthazar* is the pilgrim's progress of a saintly, downtrodden donkey in rural France. Indeed, Robert Bresson's austere black-and-white film shows our world, or some segment of it, from Balthazar's perspective. This world, the scene of the animal's serial suffering, is cold, spiteful, cruel and criminal. Most people do not behave in ways worth emulating. One only hopes that the note of grace that Balthazar interjects reveals a more hospitable eternity beyond our world's borders.

The donkey, which is expressionless, has been described by critic J. Hoberman as "pure existence." We follow the course of its life, from birth to death, as it passes from hand to hand, and sometimes back again, in what might be described as a portrait of perpetual orphanage. Briefly, Balthazar is featured in a circus, but the rest of its existence is an anonymous, hidden ordeal. The human characters, who also are inscrutable and expressionless, treat one another poorly, too, and may in some sense be kin to Balthazar.

Formally, the action is conveyed through a lightning series of elliptical scenes that suggest a depth of experience beyond our capacity to plumb—or do I mean, beyond *Balthazar's* capacity to plumb? In any case, only Balthazar demonstrates the perfect humility of Jesus that Christianity calls upon its members to emulate.

The same year as *Au hasard Balthazar*, Bresson also made *Mouchette*, from Georges Bernanos, a wonderful film about a human Balthazar, an abused rural teenager, who, experiencing rare liberty, rolls off a hill into a river and drowns herself.

Both are exacting in their vision of human nature and among the most compassionate films ever made.

HUNGER (Denmark, Norway, Sweden). *Sult*, by Henning Carlsen (who also edited), is based on the great 1890 first-person novel by Norway's Nobel Prize-winning Knut Hamsun. The most phenomenal aspect of this crisp black-and-white film is its lead performance. As the starving, hallucinating writer, Per Oscarsson gives what is possibly the most brilliant film performance ever. What tremendous acting!

Sult opens on the street—actually, a bridge—and mostly takes place there or just off it. In Kristiania, with his back to the camera, a man is bending over, seemingly observing something below, or spacing out. Tinkly music evaporates into silence. The camera approaches the man slightly, sideways. A flock of birds flies upward past him—a suggestion of his crumbling sanity. On a street, the man bursts into inappropriate talk at a sitting stranger. In a subjective shot, now he is in conversation with his dilapidated shoes, explaining they must attend to one another because he is too busy to chat. With an acquaintance he chances upon, he inspects publicly posted want ads. The acquaintance offers him lunch; famished but proud, the protagonist just sits with him in the restaurant and watches him eat. Both are struggling to be published, but only the protagonist is barely holding on at the frayed end of his life.

His belly is hungry. He also hungers for the feeling that life matters—that *he* matters.

The film is a pilgrim's non-progress, then, within a narrow range of incidents, such as ducking and confronting the landlord who wants to evict him.

Where is the vessel bound that he boards at the end. Home? Eternity?

Our hearts cry out for his future, but we know better. He is moving on to some other nowhere. We barely hold on at the frayed end of our own lives.

THE RISE TO POWER OF LOUIS XIV (France, Italy). Ingrid Bergman behind him, Roberto Rossellini made the documentary *India* (1958) and then *Il general della Rovere* (1959); the latter was named best film at Venice, and the Italian critics named him best director. But, according to daughter Isabella, all this created a moment of crisis for Rossellini. He knew his World War II drama lacked the urgency of his 1940s work; the passage of fifteen years had given it a stylish gloss. Would prizes and renewed commercial success seduce him into continuing in the same vein? For a few years, it did; but then Rossellini decided to resurrect himself as an artist and strike out on a new, unchartered path. French television provided the means. Rossellini's film about France's Louis XIV's coming into his own, eighteen years into his 72-year reign, brought a present tense to events three hundred years earlier. It applied *neorealismo* to the distant past.

With the death of his godfather, Cardinal Mazarin, in 1661, Louis, who had ascended to the throne when he was four, took real power—governance of France and Navarre as well as ceremonial rule. Rossellini's film portrays the royal court as "a maze of intrigue," as Eisenstein did in *Ivan the Terrible* (1944-46), but it does so in an unemphatic, "be there, watch this" way so different from Eisenstein's Expressionism. Perhaps Rossellini also sought to flesh out the reality of a figure who, thanks to the *Man in the Iron Mask* romance of Dumas père, had entered the domain of myth.

In effect, his film answers this question: How did Louis-Dieudonné become the Sun King? Rossellini's film amazes because it demystifies royalty in order to clarify, not debunk it.

It would also clarify Chinese monarchy when Bernardo Bertolucci applied Rossellini's method to *The Last Emperor* (1987).

MASCULIN-FEMININ (France). *See above.*

WAVELENGTH (Canada). Michael Snow's experimental *Wavelength* is legendary. Across a vast loft, sparsely populated with office things (chair, telephone, file cabinets), our eye travels to part of the far wall between two of the high, enormous windows. The agency of this journey is often described as a forward zoom, but throughout the filming Snow has minutely repositioned the camera, in effect creating the appearance of a single shot, including a jump-cut near the end that puts us into a photograph of ocean waves—this, one of a cluster of pictures that, unlike the other two, had been featureless, blacked-out. Enhancing our perceptual capacities, *Wavelength* is an eye-opening experience.

Urban street sounds are replaced a bit in by a sine sound that grows ever louder; sometimes, sound is layered. We hear an explosion. Gunshots? Construction? Drilling? Later, a young woman enters—intermittently folks enter and leave the room, evoking a sense of transience that complicates the forward journey—and she phones someone and speaks of a dead man outside. "What should I do?" she asks before leaving and waiting for an ambulance. Is our eye sharing the end-of-life journey that the dead man is making? Snow himself has stated that *Wavelength* expresses his "religious inklings."

Snow's pieced-together "road picture" through interior space marshals delightful visual artillery: shifts between black and white and monochrome (simulated color tinting: pink; orange/beige—colors suggesting "white" flesh), different film stocks and exposures, etc. The jump-cut relates less to Godard's in *A bout de souffle* (1959) than to the woman's opening eye in Marker's *La jetée* (1962), a film otherwise consisting of stills. It's revelatory. The waves filling the screen transform the mundane into epiphany. Much as the simulated zoom has exhausted the room's length, these waves may signal something spiritual, momentous.

And now . . .

1966

YESTERDAY GIRL (West Germany). With parentheses around her name suggesting (in addition to her imprisonment) how bereft of context Anita G., a Jewish East German migrant, is left by the "parting from yesterday" that she is constantly impressed to pursue, writer-director Alexander Kluge's *Abschied von gestern—(Anita G,)* launches the New German Cinema, which confronted West Germany's attempt to deny the past its due, including Germany's recent Nazi past, in favor of starting afresh with the "miracle" of economic recovery. Important, astounding, exhilarating, Kluge's first feature drew inspiration from the *nouvelle vague*, especially Jean-Luc Godard's films starring Anna Karina, whom Kluge;s Anita G. is often shot to resemble.

The film also contests the tyranny of linear narrative, proceeding by shots rather than novelistic scenes, and displaying (delightfully) tracking shots, jump-cuts, sound erasures and comebacks, cartoonish insert, a bit of war with toy soldiers, absurd banter, the time-condensation of romantic relationships through montage, etc. Perhaps casting his sister, Alexandra, in the lead role (which she enacts beautifully) helped Kluge to maintain the film's human(e) focus in the midst of his dazzling technical devices.

One of the principal events is the theft of a co-worker's cardigan sweater, for which Anita G. stands trial. It is the judge who, after asking for Anita G.'s personal history, dismisses this ("the events of 1943-44") for having no relevance to the course of her conduct. (Her Jewish family's property, of course, has all been confiscated by the Nazis.) Why *did* she steal the sweater, the judge asks. "I was cold." He reminds her it was summer. Anita G.: "I get cold even in summer." The defendant thus enrobes (or ensweaters?) a pertinent joke in the appearance of courtroom responsiveness, for her remark implies the verboten past.

Gorgeous black-and-white photography by Edgar Reitz and Thomas Mauch.

THE PORNOGRAPHERS: INTRODUCTION TO ANTHROPOLOGY (Japan). "Subu" Ogata is an illegal artist, a skinflickmeister making two films a day, who reasons he is making a valuable social contribution. (Discussions amongst Subu and collaborators, such as his cutter, convey their absolute seriousness about their work.) He lives with Haru, who, believing her dead husband, reincarnated as a carp, disapproves, is herself ambivalent about their relationship. Subu finds himself increasingly attracted to Haru's daughter, Keiko, whose surrogate father he has been since she was little, and whose flirtatiousness summons all Subu's powers of resistance. Meanwhile, Subu must hide from the law and the mob.

Shohei Imamura's wickedly funny black comedy *Jinruigaku nyumon: Erogotshi yori* satirizes both sides of the coin of sexual impulses: the government, for denying their existence in attempting to sanitize art; Subu, for yielding to them, at home and at work. It also addresses the human capacity for self-examination that results in transforming existential life into an object of study featuring "meaningful" symbols (camera; carp). Imamura additionally weighs humanity's voyeuristic preoccupation, which helps explain all these matters as well as cinema itself.

It is structured as a film about a film (the interior one being Ogata's personal story), an early image showing a window within the screen populated by those viewing the film; they could be looking at us. (Subsequent images feature another window, populated by someone else, inside the frame.) Thus Imamura adapts realism for his purposes. Elsewhere, images are surreal dreams punctuated by freeze frames. They mine Ogata's history, psyche.

Ogata has his priorities, and all hell breaks out when he spends Haru's savings to save money by setting up his own film processing laboratory. To quote Seiko: "Everything is about money."

Except for some floor-level shots, one would never guess that Imamura's mentor was Yasujiro Ozu!

MADE IN U.S.A. (France). Jean-Luc Godard's *Made in U.S.A.* provides this summary prophecy: The Right and the Left, although an "outdated formula," will continue because the

Right is too mean to change, the Left, too sentimental to do so.
The film, Godard himself explained, "worked a marginal episode of the [Mehdi] Ben Barka affair into the main theme." This leftist Moroccan politician was presumably assassinated in 1965 by French and U.S. intelligence agents. Godard: "My idea was that [Georges] Figon[, called Politzer in the film,] was not really dead, but had fled to the country and sent for his mistress to join him." Figon, a small-time crook, claimed to have witnessed Ben Barka's assassination by General Mohammed Oufkir, formerly Morocco's minister of defense, and himself suspiciously died before he could testify at Oufkir's second trial. Godard: "[Figon's mistress] comes to the address given her and finds him really dead this time."

Two hit men are veterans of the Moroccan war, Morocco's invasion of Algeria having followed right after Algeria's war of independence from France. Spilt blood's visual echoes mark and fragment the *mise-en-scène*: red backdrops, bricks, cars, flowers, walls, doors, shirts, socks, tie, notebook cover, etc.

Sartrean to the core, Godard has Paula (then-wife Anna Karina), who plays detective, to utter the creed he himself embraced: "Whatever I do, I cannot escape responsibility for others." Paula: "Always blood, fear, politics and money."

Jean-Pierre Léaud plays Siegel, a thug shadowing Paula. In a commercial garage, Paula, offscreen, asks Siegel, the only one visible in the frame, "If you are about to die, would you like to know in advance?" Siegel: "No." But, facing Paula and her pistol, Siegel *does* know; there is no real choice here. Gunshot; Siegel's death—a series of horrifyingly comical stumbles and rolls, limber, painful, protracted. Shattering.

CUL-DE-SAC (UK). Roman Polanski recently won the directorial prize at Berlin for his exhilarating, humane *The Ghost Writer* (2009); but more than forty years ago a film of his took the top prize, the Golden Bear, at the same international festival. This was the black-and-white *Cul-de-sac*, Polanski's second film after exiting Communist Poland.

Two wounded criminals invade a castle on Holy Island, off the coast of Northern England; Dicky, armed, terrorizes the occupants, a couple, nervous George and his much younger, nervy French wife, Teresa.

Cleverly, quite beautifully, Polanski creates images of expiration: in a point-of-view shot, Albie, Dicky's dying partner, watches Dicky walking away from him, to explore the castle, from inside their stopped vehicle, framed by the open passenger-side door; Dicky espies (what turns out to be) Teresa's beachside adultery through slats whose restricted vision correlates to restricted breath; the camera facing him, ulcerous George is forced by Dicky to drink a cup of something alcoholic, the cup covering his nose and mouth—a metaphoric asphyxiation. (This moment echoes one in which Teresa has sexually humiliated George by compelling him to wear her negligee.) When Albie dies, moreover, Dicky has George bury him in a scene that somewhat suggests the gravedigging scene in *Hamlet*; but, given its publication two years earlier, one must plead the mediation of Warsaw-born literary critic Jan Kott's *Szkice o Szekspirze*, especially since Polanski's entire film is cloaked in absurdism, which some call Pinteresque, forgetting that Samuel Beckett's *Waiting for Godot* had been a major influence on Polanski's work since his student days at Łódź Film School.

Tables turn, and George shoots Dicky dead. The final shot, "existentializing" Antoine's final run in François Truffaut's *The 400 Blows* (1959), finds George running furiously toward an ever withdrawing camera.

Brash. Brilliant.

WINGS (U.S.S.R.). Larisa Shepitko had been mentored by fellow Ukrainian Aleksandr Dovzhenko. Her first feature, *Krylya*, is one of the three or four most wonderful Soviet films of the 1960s. Shepitko was 28 and would die in a road accident at 41, widowing Elem Klimov.

The protagonist is Nadezhda Petrukhina (Maya Bulgakova, superb), a former Great Patriotic War pilot who is now headmistress at a provincial school, where her pedestrian duties make her feel as though her wings have been clipped. Middle-aging, Nadya finds other things feeding her mid-life crisis: her daughter has moved out and married; she herself is only mechanically attached to her gentleman friend. Nadya is lonely. However, it is her soaring memories of having been a State-valued fighter pilot that express the core of her dissatisfaction with life. Yet, also, a part of her life ended with her wartime lover, also a pilot, whose death on a mission she witnessed while likewise airborne. Perhaps Tanya, whom Nadya adopted, was meant to be the child that she might have had with the boy she loved with all her heart.

Nadya imagines airplanes and the experience of flight. The first image Shepitko gives us of a "steel bird" is momentarily ambiguous; Nadya could be dreaming, but it turns out that the plane is real. Thereafter, Nadya imagines herself flying, and the film ends with her up in the clouds in a cockpit—a long-shot and an objective one; but by this point these visual indicators of reality might not apply. (Signaling the closing ambiguity is Nadya's having quit her job offscreen.)

Nadya had headed the school in a somewhat capricious, borderline authoritarian manner; she had found the adolescent pupils unruly. One particular boy, who righteously opposes her, gets suspended "for nothing," as another pupil puts it.

THE HAWKS AND THE SPARROWS (Italy). Pier Paolo Pasolini's rambunctious comedy *Uccellacci e uccellini* is an ideological fable.

An old man and his son are walking down a vacant road. They pass through a slum punctuated by billboards, each identifying an individual but also a widespread problem: an unemployed man; a child who ran away. Down the road they meet a black crow, a self-described Leftist intellectual. The crow says his parents are Conscience and Doubt. The crow accompanies the pair.

Suddenly the men are transported to the thirteenth century, where they are friars. St. Francis charges them with preaching God's love to hawks and sparrows and converting the birds to Christianity. This they do amidst hilarious chirping; the hawks convert to consolidate their power, while the sparrows convert out of desperation. When the sparrows explain they need wheat and millet, they are told to fast! But the friars burst into tears when a hawk assaults and kills a sparrow. God's love, apparently, is insufficient to counter class warfare. The two report back to St. Francis, who chides the friars for misunderstanding history and foretells the Coming of the Messiah: Karl Marx!

Back in the present, the father utilizes an outhouse for a bowel movement. He and his son are told to take their shit with them. They refuse; they are shot at. Ownership and property lead to strife and battles.

Now the two are a landlord and his goon. They invade the shack of an impoverished couple and threaten to confiscate their home for nonpayment of rent. For four days running, the woman has convinced her children to stay in bed because she has nothing to feed them. She is cooking a bird's nest for her spouse. So recently victims themselves, our pair are unmoved.

Food for thought.

DAISIES (Czechoslovakia). The most beauteous flower of the Czech New Wave, *Sedmikrásky* is a fresh, anarchic romp combining elements of French New Wave, social satire, slapstick comedy, science fiction, *Alice in Wonderland*.

Gal pals Marie I and Marie II decide to be bad—spoiled, mischievous, heedless—because this is how they find the world. Since it is beyond their means to set the world right, they will go along with the world as it is. Thus the teenagers spring into a hedonistic world of their own unfettered imagination, where they dance, vamp, manipulate men, and (beginning with an apple from a tree in the Garden of Eden) mercilessly devour food and drink. Věra Chytilová and Ester Krumbachová wrote the script, creating, among other things, a feminist fable of liberation. In this, the film follows a negative procedure; while we watch the two Maries do lots of things they ought not to do, *Daisies* argues that they ought to be sufficiently free in society to choose on their own not to do such things. These rebels might restrain themselves were they not under social constraint. Society should not limit female autonomy and freedom. Doing so helps make the world bad, pushing the girls to misbehave.

Chytilová imbues her film with the liberated air of Buster Keaton's wondrous *Sherlock Jr.* (1924). Indeed, she adopts one of that silent film's techniques: discontinuous cuts that plunge a character into a new scene from one instant to the next. Here, too, an impression is given of unbridled cinematic possibilities.

The girls burn their apartment, wage a food fight, trample a formal festive spread. But the film is bookended by documentary footage of war, reminding us of the worse things that happen in the male-directed world. The Czech government, feeling its ox gored, promptly banned the film.

A REPORT ON THE PARTY AND THE GUESTS (Czechoslovakia). Written by himself and then-wife Ester Krumbachová, the latter of whom originated the story idea, Jan Němec's *O slavnosti a hostech*—literally, *The Festivities and the Guests*—is a cunning, quirkily funny, cumulatively chilling satire showing the atmosphere of persecution with which citizens who live in a totalitarian state must contend. It joins sharply observant behavioral comedy to darker currents. Czech authorities banned the film "forever."

The plot revolves around the classical motif of the failed feast. A casual, carefree picnic is interrupted by a cruel, sadistic, charismatic stranger and his impressed followers. The picnickers are invited to a more formal event, an outdoor banquet. Their various rationalizations, delusions, ambitions facilitate both their passage from one "feast" to the next and their adjustment. There, they evidence the conformism that the original followers demonstrated; when one of the guests takes off on his own, they, the remaining guests, disrupt the second "feast" to hunt him down. At the end, the screen goes black, accompanied by the sounds of vicious dogs. While this finish predicts the price that individualism costs in the kind of society that is being depicted, it is also a summary metaphor for what the entire film has shown: the devolution of humanity into a regimented mob that keeps itself from being tagged as the prey by doing the state's bidding. What Czech audiences cannot see at the conclusion becomes a kind of dark mirror in which they were invited to confront the nothing that they themselves were under communist rule and to hear what constant fear could make them become. One failed feast leading to another, the narrative progression encompasses a bankruptcy of hope and of people pulling together toward positive social developments.

The U.S. title yields an apt, ascerbic pun.

THE HUNT (Spain). Three businessmen go rabbit hunting one day thirty years after being fascist compatriots in the Spanish Civil War. They start bickering from the get-go, kill animals, and end up shooting and killing each other.

With Carlos Saura directing from a brilliant script by himself and Angelino Fons, *La Caza* revolves around the metaphor of the hunt as a revival of the war from the vantage of Franco's winners, disconsolate men burdened somehow by the past despite victory. Another of their old group, Arturo, became an embezzler and committed suicide—an act they cannot comprehend; yet doesn't their new bloodbath comprise their own suicides by proxy? Many shots show trapped animals: caged pet ferrets; a rabbit attacked in its hole by one of the released ferrets; a beetle, in closeup, transported to a wall of rock, where it's shot to smithereens. But the hunters themselves are trapped in that earlier time, when they hunted Loyalists instead of rabbits, and they can't escape. One has brought along his brother-in-law, Enrique, who is way too young to have fought in the war; but he, too, it turns out, chokes on the symbolic noxious fumes that are the result of the war's tragic outcome. Sardonically, Saura traps him in a conclusive freeze frame in mid-flight from the scene of carnage.

In one of the close mines a skeleton resides—as one of the hunters explains, a likely veteran of the war. Are any of these men really alive, or do they creep like guilty things in the shadow of blood they long ago shed? The infected rabbits symbolize the sick Spain that the war's outcome consolidated. The desolate black-and-white landscape: the radio's rock 'n' roll desecrates this hallowed ground.

Enrique is warned: "Be careful. Aim at the rabbits."

MODESTY BLAISE (UK). A spy spoof based on a comic strip, Joseph Losey's exhilarating, hilarious *Modesty Blaise* revolves around a former thief (Monica Vitti, dazzling), an icon of "girl power" in anticipation of postmodernism, who is ostensibly engaged by the British government to foil a diamond heist when she is actually an unwitting decoy for a British Secret Service diamond transaction.

Men and male-dominated societies consign females to limited power or no power whatsoever. When a former lover praises her "woman's intuition," Modesty feels sufficiently annoyed to start busting up his apartment. An Arab sheikh has the antidote for his normal disrespect for women when it comes to his honored Modesty. He refers to her as his "son"!

Modesty Blaise is full of circular things: globular light fixtures, concentric circular floor design, circular openings, balls, umbrella tops, gun barrels, men's hats, a circular mirror, a cooking pot, scoops of ice cream in an oversized cone, cars turning and turning around, binoculars, etc. All these yonic symbols—displaced vaginas—resonate, alas, contradictorily: as female power, but in a fantasy world, with the subordination of females triggering the wish for freedom, power, completion. The circle suggests, also, confinement, imprisonment. (Example: the room aboard his cargo ship to which Gabriel Fothergill confines Modesty—with its red-painted corkscrew staircase leading to *his* quarters).

Indeed, Modesty herself everywhere skirts a line that implies the collision of the fantastic and the real. For instance, she possesses the power to change at will her hair color, makeup, clothes, accessories. But this exercise of power is illusory, always leaving Modesty just as vulnerable underneath her changed appearance.

Gabriel, her nemesis, hurls derisively this epithet at Modesty: *suffragette*. Losey's aim throughout is to inspire thought and activism to make the recognition of gender equality part of the *real* world.

BLOWUP (UK, Italy, U.S.). The coolest, most happening movie of the "Swingin' Sixties" was made by someone in his mid-fifties.

A self-absorbed London fashion photographer (David Hemmings, wonderful) snaps photographs in Maryon Park, prompting a woman (Vanessa Redgrave, anxious, vibrant, haunting), apparently with her lover there, to demand the roll of film. The boy refuses. After successive blowups of portions of the developed photos, he comes to believe that the assignation preceded murder. In the park at night, he locates the corpse. But both photos and the body subsequently show up missing.

Michelangelo Antonioni's brilliantly directed *Blowup*, inspired by a Julio Cortázar story, claims a mesmerizing first half that follows the photographer about, including into an antique shop, where he buys an airplane propeller; when the mystery plot kicks in, though, the film turns feeble. However, the contrast created by black-and-white photos in a (beautiful) color film is surprisingly powerful, and the photographer's gradual slippage into his humanity convinces. Moreover, the return to the park and the finale are fabulous, with the protagonist, embracing the illusionary nature of reality, tossing an imaginary ball to a couple engaged in pantomiming a tennis match.

Sound is as exquisite as image in *Blowup*: the rustling of tree leaves in the breeze; accompanying a closeup of the boy's face as his eyes follow the ball, the sound of this imaginary ball as it strikes opposing racquets. The boy's face registers the loss of innocence —the loss of the safe, insulated, egotistical world in which we first found him. This conclusion is wry, satisfying and deeply moving—the equal of the finish of Alfred Hitchcock's *Vertigo* (1958).

One thing more: *Blowup* contains the best movie line ever. "I thought you were in Paris," the photographer tells a model at a party. Zonked, she replies, "I *am* in Paris."

CHELSEA GIRLS (U.S.) The exclusively interior scenes of Andy Warhol and Paul Morrissey's *Chelsea Girls* largely take place, shot by Warhol, inside apartments in the Chelsea Hotel in New York City. Its cast members, consisting of friends and acquaintances of Warhol, play themselves, improvising along the episodic route of Warhol's script. The original version ran 6½ hours, but a second version cut this length in half by splitting the screen and running two titled episodes simultaneously. The result, occasionally lame, is much more often brilliant.

One paired episode is always mute; sometimes both are silent. Zooms startle the one with a fixed camera; on the other side, the camera may be intensely moving about. Earlier on, both screen halves are in black and white, but one may be relatively dark in complexion while the other is relatively light. (Changes occur in both actual lighting and exposure levels.) Later on, color is introduced to one side of the split screen and then both sides.

Sometimes it appears, quite by accident, that human images on both sides of the dividing line merge, like pieces of glass in an Italian kaleidoscope; sometimes sound seems to correspond to the drama on the other side of the dividing line as well. "Stand up!" someone screams here, and there, on the other side, the camera drops, giving a seated person the appearance of rising up. Although such visual and aural connections between left screen and right screen catch us by surprise, after a while we also look forward to them; we imaginatively try integrating the two screens. However, for mental focus, we also try keeping the screens separate and distinct. Each is dominated by someone who is quite a character.

We eventually feel we are watching our mind processing this miraculous film.

1967

WEEKEND (France, Italy). A savagely satirical take on "modern times," *Weekend*—or *Week End*—is one of the signature films of the sixties. (A gloriously agile performance by Jean-Pierre Léaud helps certify this.) A typical bourgeois couple take a weekend drive to visit the woman's mother, whom they murder for her money. The woman later joins the band of revolutionaries who have murdered her spouse, whom they eat for lunch. An alternative title might be: *Ties That No Longer Bind*—including patriotic ties to nation.

Godard lays claim here to the most celebrated tracking shot of all time: a massive, seemingly endless, corpse-strewn traffic stall revealing the enormity of human folly as disparate, blindly self-contained fates are headlong-prone to one explosive end. Pitched complicitly and elegantly between determinism and documentary discovery, the sunlit shot proceeds gradually, shifting from a straight, rigid course to a course slightly, subtly more relaxed, and catching about the honking metal hulks belligerent confrontations and witty scenes of resourceful recreational activity. What a shot!

Scarcely less remarkable is a later shot that likewise discloses Western civilization's bankruptcy: a fixed, rotating—continuously panning—camera, flattened by its slow pace, and thus adding inexorability to the noose-like circle it draws around a pianist, encapsulating Western culture, who plays Mozart in a farmyard—a scene both lovely and incongruous. With great love for the music and an appreciation of the irrelevancy of Mozart to so many oppressed lives, Godard can lament the passing of such perfect beauty while yet keenly feeling the need to erase the social and political inequities that have enabled high culture to exist and that still seek to sustain it. Were Godard not tugged in these opposite directions at once, his apocalyptic *Weekend* would not be the heartrendingly beautiful thing that it is.

CHRONICLE OF ANNA MAGDALENA BACH (West Germany, Italy). A woman recalls how she met the man she married and their sad life together, including the deaths of numerous children and his own illness and death. Her voiceover is our guide into the past, and the images she recovers have a formality that befits the film's subject. We are listening to the second wife of Johan Sebastian Bach.

Written and directed by the marital team of Jean-Marie Straub and Danièle Huillet, *Chronicle of Anna Magdalena Bach* had its funding withdrawn at the last moment, but an angel, Jean-Luc Godard, stepped in and saved the project. Since the film consists mostly of performances of Bach's music (with Bach—that is, harpsichordist Gustav Leonhardt—conducting), some viewers are stymied. Why isn't there domestic or other melodrama here, as in Hollywood biographical films? In truth, there is sufficient "drama" to illuminate the music's sublime nature, and Bach's music was central to his life. By contesting the convention of pushing an artist's art to the periphery of his existence in portraying his life, Straub and Huillet achieve a measure of truth and purpose. They aren't interested in "humanizing" Bach by reducing him to a facsimile of ordinary viewers whom they hope will identify with him. They represent Bach's genius and its musical accomplishment honestly—and effortlessly. In the process, they suggest how this music expressed Bach's emotions by heroic containment and concealment, and created astonishing rigor and harmonious complexity in the midst of a tragic life. This is no cozy *Rhapsody in Blue* (1945).

Godard himself is an influence; Straub and Huillet draw upon his elegiac sensibility. Another influence is Roberto Rossellini's austere *The Rise of Louis XIV* (1966), a film about a king that actually shows the monarch's activities.

And the music is glorious.

PLAYTIME (France). On the loose in Paris, Monsieur Hulot must stay the night to roam the streets because the official he is supposed to meet is too busy to see him. Hulot's delayed entrance gives advance hint of his invisibility when he appears since he is a silent figure in a sound film—well, at least a film that's full of sounds. Percussive music accompanies the opening credits, while mellifluous music ironically accompanies the opening shot of Paris. The irony is doubled by the silence inside the airport terminal—except for the exaggerated sounds of people walking, including two nuns; one man's shuffle sounds like a soft gallop. These everyday noises fix the alienated state of people, including their alienation from a modern urban environment overloaded with "thingamajigs."

Suggesting a satirical fusion of Chaplin, Federico Fellini and Heironymus Bosch, Jacques Tati's tribal *Playtime* may be the most detailed, visually intricate comedy in existence—disclosed almost entirely in long-shots, a "modern times" of glass walls, metallic gadgetry, and people at business and leisure (including a flock of American tourists herded from plane to hotel by bus), all befuddling Tati's signature Hulot, whose pantomime and unfailingly polite air prevail, even when he is, understandably, mistaken for a door. Hulot maintains the fiction that he can remain himself in a world where no one is anyone any longer. Hulot isn't one to "adapt"!

In *Playtime*'s summary image an obstinate glass door, given a good shake by Hulot, disintegrates. On a posh nightclub dance floor each couple acquits itself in its own style as part of a canvas of human frenzy rendered with documentary calm, which elevates the filmmaker's vision to a phenomenon that is hilarious and, cumulatively, very moving.

Both glass and open night air expose Hulot's vulnerability and our own.

I WAS NINETEEN (East Germany). Konrad Wolf's *Ich war neunzehn* is autobiographical. Nineteen-year-old Gregor Hecker, a lieutenant in the Russian Army as it advances on Berlin in April 1945 in the war's waning days, is German-born, his parents having moved to Moscow, fleeing Hitler, when Gregor was eight. Gregor encounters various German soldiers, officials and ordinary citizens. One of these encounters is with a death camp guard. In one way or another, all these encounters are with himself.

His voice amplified over a desolate landscape, the lieutenant beseeches German soldiers to surrender. "I am German," he strategically tells them. Throughout, he alternates between speaking Russian and German, depending on the situation, and this continually underscores the complexity of his national identity. At the end, he repeats, "I am a German," this time with understanding. His vehicle disappears into the distance of another hauntingly bleak black-and-white landscape that sums up a wearyingly enlightened life's journey.

In 1965, East Germany had passed a law prohibiting filmmakers from viewing the nation's current situation—social, political, economic—in a negative light. Therefore, Wolf deviously wrought a work that addresses the past as a way of addressing the present because of the weight with which the past impresses the present. We are in Gregor's "present" twenty-odd years earlier; but the pensive, disembodied sound of his voiceover transforms this "present" into a poetic generalization touching on matters of time, memory, separation from home, separation from oneself, and a search for wholeness.

Early on, road signs tell Gregor he is in his homeland. He has a job to do, to help secure the region militarily, and he is also a wanderer in the unchartable, elusive regions of identity building. "I was nineteen," he will tell us at the last, shifting his perspective to the past. Now he knows what *being German* is.

THE RED AND THE WHITE (Hungary, U.S.S.R.). Apparently *The Round-up*'s being set in the past sufficiently masked its contemporary relevance that the Soviet Union helped finance *Csillagosok, katonák*—and subsequently banned the result! *Csillagosok, katonák* is the middle part of Miklós Jancsó's black-and-white trilogy that *The Round-up* opens (1965) and *Silence and Cry* concludes (1967).

Set around the Volga River in 1919, in the second year of the Russian Civil War (between Soviets and tsarist counter-revolutionaries), Jancsó's film follows in part a Hungarian regiment in support of Bolsheviks and envisions war as a continuous wheel of fortune, where, first, one side holds sway over the other and then, with a reversal a moment later, the other side does, and so on, back and forth. (Fittingly, an abandoned monastery takes turns being either side's headquarters and hospital.) Sometimes, someone turns against someone else on the same side; thus, each side's spinning wheel of reversals is contained within the larger wheel of opposing sides. His lenses and cameras attuned to each of these shifts, Jancsó achieves a paradoxical (and brilliant) result. On the one hand, his long-shots, especially, capture war's dehumanizing aspect. On the other, a sameness is enforced on both sides, divesting the conflict of opposite causes, and thus underscoring, without sentimentality, the human dimension and the human cost of war, especially as one participant after another falls. Eschewing flatfooted realism, Hungary's master formalist has thereby found a way to show war's mercilessness, analyze the mechanism of war, and take aim at the very *idea* of war.

One interlude encapsulates war's absurdity: a White military band playing a waltz in the woods for which nurses have been dressed up and impressed—a respite that reflects on war's war against the loveliness of life that humanity's soul finds necessary for existence.

JAGUAR (France). *Cine-fiction*: France's prolific Jean Rouch coined this term for ethnographic documentaries that are launched by a contrivance. Shot in 1954-55 and edited more than a decade later, Rouch's *Jaguar* casts three young African non-actors as three African men who journey from rural, impoverished Niger, along the Ivory Coast, to robust cities in Ghana in search of seasonal work. Their migration is the launch, but the film is the product of Rouch's research into actual activities and social customs in areas at both ends of the journey and along the way. *Jaguar* contrasts country and city, the primitive and the more advanced. We may say that the camera follows countryfolk to where people take the camera's presence—modernity—in their stride.

The slight narrative was improvised by Rouch and the trio, and the soundtrack, consisting of remembered dialogue, ruminations and questions, was improvised post-production. At the time the film was shot, the portable equipment that might have recorded synchronized sound did not exist.

Jaguar is dazzlingly cut and assembled, with perhaps more shots per length than any other film in existence, to convey the complex experience of the trio on their city adventure. This diamond-faceted, restless, highly analytical visual style—Resnais out-Resnaised, and without the long trackings to add countervailing lyricism—is correlative to the real adventure going on: the social elasticity of the protagonists, their Keatsian negative capability, their ongoing need to process the unfamiliar experiences bombarding them, and the mental and emotional agility that allows them to readjust and reinvent themselves as a result. To turn around a famous remark by Tennyson's Ulysses, all that they have met becomes a part of them. Back home three months after they left, they are partial strangers to themselves and others. *Jaguar* is a model of technical form analyzing humanistic content.

THE STRANGER (Italy, France). Albert Camus, who wrote the 1942 novel *L'Etranger*, had been born to pieds-noirs in Algeria. His protagonist, a clerk, is a Frenchman who also lives in Algeria. In Luchino Visconti's film, Meursault is played by Marcello Mastroianni, who was a dozen years too old for the part and way too emotionally accessible: a fortuitous stroke of monumental miscasting, for Mastroianni seems to be showing us Meursault (simultaneously) both outside and in-. In book and film, Meursault reminds one of Herman Melville's Bartleby the Scrivener, whose ready response to any instruction or possibility of behavior is, "I prefer not to." Meursault's unintended assault on bourgeois sensibility when he fails to cry at his mother's funeral is why he is tried and sentenced to beheading for the shooting death of an Arab man in the desert. His explanation for the act is the blazing, dizzying sun. The way Visconti shoots the scene is fiercely literal; it locates the absurdity of the act in the metaphysical conjoining of the death's finality and Meursault's casual, throwaway (though not quite flippant) explanation. Visconti is enormously convincing here.

Indeed, Visconti is close to brilliant throughout, succeeding in making both the Arab victim and a neighbor's loved/hated, talked-about scabby dog somehow seem broken images of Meursault himself. It is a broken world, in fact, in which Meursault endeavors to rely on himself for integrity.

Lo Straniero reminds one how incredibly funny Visconti can be. The scene where Meursault's avowed atheism causes the Prosecutor to go ballistic is hilarious. The film's greatest shot, though, is anything but funny: the camera surveying Arabs in the dark holding cell after Meursault, arrested, answers, "I killed an Arab," when asked by someone there what crime he committed. Here, we are very far from the ambiguating sunlight in the dunes.

LE SAMOURAI (France). Alain Delon claimed his most melancholy role, and a brutal one, as hitman Jef Costello in Jean-Pierre Melville's electrifying *Le samouraï*. Jef doesn't make mistakes; his careful arrangement of details, including alibis, makes him arrest-proof. But his murder of a nightclub owner generates unaccustomed eyewitnesses, one of whom, the club singer, got a *good* look. After the police take him in, and let him go because the woman insists he is not the killer, he becomes a target for both the police and the one who had hired him.

Jef has little life apart from work. He lives in a spare, small apartment with one companion: a caged bird. This pet possesses a joyless, one-note chirp, but he or she is the essence of loyalty. When he returns after his place has been bugged, the animal's agitation alerts Jef that something is amiss. The bird, at first little more than his or her sound, initially seems a projection of Jef's solitude and forlorn, vampire-like existence; as the film progresses, we wonder whether this companion, along with Jef's loyal girlfriend, is all that keeps Jef sane; and, at the end, when Jef meets a heart-piercing end that reveals *his* capacity for loyalty, we worry about the bird, who has now lost his or her one friend.

Delon is superb; but equally brilliant is François Périer, who plays the police inspector

determined to bring Jef down. Both fatalistic and sadistic, as remorseless as Jef, and fleetingly human, compassionate, this cop believes that the end justifies the means.
"What sort of man are you?" the singer asks Jef when he tells her that he killed the club owner, whom he didn't know, for money.
"Why, Jef?" she asks when he turns his gun on her.
But wait!

WE STILL KILL THE OLD WAY (Italy). Caustic, terrifically exciting, Elio Petri's *A ciascuno il suo*—literally, *To Each His Own*—finds a plethora of rumors at a funeral and a wedding addressing a Sicilian tangle of politics, corruption, Mafia, murders, extramarital sex, incest, and the Church. Anything-goes in its dazzling variety of shots, electrically paced and beautifully acted, the film is an adaptation of Leonardo Sciascia's novel. Petri and Ugo Pirro took the best screenplay prizes at Cannes and from the Italian critics, who also named Petri best director and the film's superlative star, Gian Maria Volontè, best actor.

Volontè plays thirtysomething Paolo Laurana, a university professor, bachelor and, like Petri himself, former Communist who, suspicious of the official arrests, takes upon himself the investigation of the murders of two men, both of whom he knew, during an early morning hunt in the hills. The "felling" of the pharmacist, who had been receiving anonymous death threats in the mail for weeks, and Dr. Roscio following the gun-blasting of one bird after another from the sky is both frightening and hilarious—like much of the film. Paolo slips ever deeper into paranoia, a reflection of Italy's mood in the mid-1960s.

Americans are apt to chuckle (nervously!) when someone compares Sicily, because of the violence, to U.S. cities, specifically, Chicago and Dallas.

Co[s]mic fate, we realize, may have had a hand in the mayhem inasmuch as Dr. Roscio's grieving father, a former eye doctor, is blind now.

Paolo, although slow on the romantic draw, falls for Roscio's widow, Luisa (Irene Papas, stunning—and uproariously ambiguous), is warned away from her by Luisa's cousin, a powerful attorney, and starts getting death threats himself. *Oops.*

The approaching darkening mass of people turns bride's white to widow's black in the closing shot.

LAND IN ANGUISH (Brazil). "We live with death inside us. . . . As we advance, we retreat."

Using the device of a long dying flashback, Gláuber Rocha's *Terra em transe*—literally, *Earth Entranced*—is a major work of Brazil's *cinema nôvo*, the movement that rejected Hollywood-type escapism in favor of native forms and political hot topics. The film's journalistic, feverishly surreal, and operatic qualities suggest also the influences of Francesco Rosi, Luis Buñuel, Luchino Visconti.

Shot by military police, Paulo Martins is a journalist and poet, and a thread of continuity throughout is his heavy Russian-sounding narration and his speech within the flashback, which is often delivered in the exact same way. Paulo, who finds himself at the vortex of opposing political currents, is based on Rocha, who is thus able to express his ambivalence as to what political course Brazil should take. (The fictional Eldorado, where the film is set, stands in for Brazil.) Through Paolo, Rocha considers the situation of artists and intellectuals following the U.S.-backed military coup that sent Leftist president Joao Goulart fleeing Brazil in 1964.

The film opens with a bravura helicopter shot that entrances us with Brazil's "entranced earth." The film is dotted with bizarre, baroque images: on top a hill, a fascist madman, holding a crucifix in one hand and a flag in the other, proclaiming, "I want a new sun"; Paulo, armed, on his back, struggling his way up a long series of steps. When in a street demonstration he says, "I am the people; I have seven children and no place to live," a peasant is seized and (along with others) strangled with wire on the spot. Immediately the crowd is assured there's no hunger or violence in Eldorado.

Woven into *Terra em transe* is documentary footage from Rocha's *Maranhão 66.*

ACCIDENT (UK). Adapting titled Nicholas Mosley's novel, Harold Pinter wrote an excellent script, with his signature terse, pointed yet almost cryptic dialogue, for *Accident*, the second of his three extraordinary collaborations with Joseph Losey. This is one of Losey's best films.

Britain's class system daily twists a knife in Oxford don Stephen's social wounds as he tutors students above his station, in especial bonding with William and William's Austrian girlfriend, Anna (with a "von"). What motivates William's befriending Stephen? (Is his calling this philosophy tutor by his first name amiability or condescension?) Against his knowing better, why does Stephen allow himself to be reeled in?

"*Don't! You're standing on his face!*"

In the dead of night, outside his house in the country, the automobile crash occurs, killing William, disorienting Anna. As Anna lies asleep, Stephen, who is standing, watching her, is snapped to attention by a flashback: Anna's spiked heel, in closeup, digging into William's face as she frees herself from the crashed, mangled car. *Don't!* Hearing his own cry in his head again, Stephen flashes back and we get the whole story leading up to the accident, which will transform (perhaps invisibly) the rest of Stephen's life. It brings to a head all of his suppressed emotions: his self-dissatisfaction; his sense of his marriage as a compromise (Vivien Merchant is marvelous as Rosalind, Stephen's perpetually pregnant wife); his jealousy of best friend Charlie, a fellow don who is also a novelist and TV personality.

The film is almost fiendish in finding a teeming sexuality lying in wait in beauteous Nature, and hilariously funny—this *is* Pinter—as Stephen courts a TV job himself. Far less convincing is a Resnaisian subplot, artily done, as Stephen rekindles an old romance with his college provost's daughter (Delphine Seyrig, no less).

CHINA IS NEAR (Italy). The dysfunctional family in Marco Bellocchio's second feature, *La Cina è vicina*, which Bellocchio co-wrote with Elda Tattoli, is a whole lot funnier than the dysfunctional family in his first one, *Fists in the Pocket* (1965). Glauco Mauri is beautifully bedeviled as Vittorio, a political science professor who is guiltily entrenched in aristocracy and massive family wealth. He has traded in his Communist credentials to run as the Socialist candidate for a municipal position, inviting the ire of his activist teenaged brother, Camillo, whose Maoism and brattiness compel him to regard Vittorio as traitor to their far leftist cause. (U.S. Americans who regard liberal Democrats as members of the far left will have to rearrange their insanity in order to grapple with Bellocchio's narrative premise.) Their sister, Elena (Tattoli, excellent), although politically conservative, is sexually promiscuous.

There are also two working-class characters: servants and lovers Carlo and Giovanna, whose appetite for financial advancement suits their sexual pursuits of Elena and Vittorio. They covet a bit of the high life that they also hypocritically decry. Additionally, Carlo himself wanted the Socialist Party candidacy that Vittorio has drawn.

Bellocchio orchestrates a brilliant satire of politics and sex, religion, abortion, class, class envy, marriage and incest, taking aim at everyone's hypocrisy, compromises, secret and unconscious motives. Consider Camillo's exalted self-image as heroic revolutionary. He eventually blows up the toilet at the Socialist Party headquarters! In an elusive and surreal way this act underscores the family identity that Camillo is denying inasmuch as we were earlier introduced to Vittorio as he prayed for release from constipation while sitting on a home toilet. Indeed, this is a film full of oblique connections and echoes.

Apparently, the grip of institutions like family and Church helps keep Italy's Left in disarray.

(I EVEN MET) HAPPY GYPSIES (Yugoslavia). One of the founders of *Novi Film*, the Yugoslav New Wave, Aleksandar Petrović made a tragicomedy about the Roma—"Gypsies": *Skupljači perja* (literally, *Feather Buyer*). Bora trades in goose feathers in northern Serbia, as does Mirta, whose stepdaughter, Tisa, Bora is after despite being married. Mirta also desires Tisa and eventually tries to rape her. Bora and Tisa, who has fled Mirta, marry. Mirta goes to

Belgrade at the suggestion of her husband's other wife, discovering there that her people are consigned by bigotry and poverty to slums. Hitchhiking home, she is beaten nearly to death by a driver whose advances she rejected and, when found, is returned to Mirta. Bora confronts and kills his rival in order to reclaim Tisa, and the two disappear. United, the Roma tell outside authorities nothing about the couple's whereabouts.

Feathers, a lyrical motif, encapsulate the heartaching beauty and transience of Romany existence. Both Bora and Mirta are associated with feathers, and therefore their less than admirable traits are counterbalanced by this association and its implication that the two men's volatile, violent and selfish natures are to some extent the result of the mistreatment and marginalization of the Roma, whose males cling desperately to a kind of *machismo* as a bulwark against the sense of inferiority that the larger society imposes on them. After scoring a bounty of feathers, against his own economic interest Bora slits open one sack after another to watch the wind turn feathers into "birds"—facsimiles of the Roma. Bora and Mirta have their decisive combat in the latter's storeroom of feathers, disappearing into its depths before only one of them emerges to wipe the blood off his knife. It happens to be Bora. It could as easily have been Mirta. Hence, the title's ambiguity.

SILENCE AND CRY (Hungary). Hungary, 1919. The First World War has ended, as has the Communist rule that briefly followed. Patrols of the nationalist Royal Gendarme are hunting down soldiers of the Red Army, one of whom, István Cserzi, hides in a farmhouse on the plains.

In Miklós Jancsó's black-and-white *Csend és kiáltás*, the young revolutionary continually has to weigh competing values: historical imperatives versus humane alternatives; his own survival against the survival of others. What does he do, now that he knows that those who are protecting him are also poisoning the farm's legal owners? War had kept him warm, obliterating the need to make moral choices. In hiding, though, he is back to being human. Or *is* he? István's exhaustion overwhelms not only his moral judgments but even his notable attempt to leave the area. Escape may be impossible.

Visually, Jancsó draws from Michelangelo Antonioni's *L'avventura* (1960) and John Ford's *The Searchers* (1956), setting his human figures in vast, bleak landscapes and moving his camera from inside to outside the farmhouse, enlarging by perspective the expanse of land, but, ironically, only to reflect on István's limited, perhaps exhausted possibilities. As in *The Round-up* (1965) and everything else, Jancsó employs long takes in which characters walk and walk, this way and that, their movement vis-à-vis the movement of others as sensitively, precisely choreographed as are the camera movements. Often, the net result is that open space is divided, narrowed, restricted—correlative to the crucible in which István finds himself. As startling as in films by Robert Bresson, sounds also weigh in: footsteps; the clatter of carriage wheels; howling winds—history's circling, echoing winds.

That Communists are being ferreted out and executed adds another wrinkle of irony, for surely Jancsó's target is in the present: Hungary's Communist rule circa 1967.

HOUR OF THE WOLF (Sweden). A horror film, Ingmar Bergman's black-and-white *Hour of the Wolf* is creepy and terrifying. It draws on stories by E.T.A. Hoffmann and, like Thomas Carlyle's *Sartor Resartus*, it purportedly and playfully derives from its fictitious protagonist's diary. Its store of anxieties is perversely comical.

Johan (Max von Sydow, excellent), a painter, and his pregnant wife, Alma, share a cottage on a remote island. Johan barely sleeps, and his sketchbook documents nightmares: a beaked "bird man"; an ancient woman who pulls off her face. Wealthier inhabitants of the island, suggesting these creatures, may be figments of his imagination, in which Alma shares. Eventually, at night, while Alma watches helplessly at a distance, they attack Johan and cannibalize him.

Bergman's poker-faced reaction shots of Alma secretly reading Johan's diary are hilarious, as is the suggestion that the painting by Johan adorning the wealthy couple's bedroom—it is a portrait of a past mistress of Johan's—hangs upside down. Bergman's camera doesn't show the painting, only Johan's and Alma's reactions; it's left to our imagination, in this case prompted by dinner conversation about some other artist on whom the derisive joke had been pulled. Sometimes the humor is retroactively associative. If Johan is eaten up at the end, earlier, in one of the film's starkest passages, he is bitten, while fishing, by an imagined boy whom he bludgeons to death, the corpse hauntingly reemerging from the sea's depths—Johan's subconscious—into which he had tossed it.

Johan the Artist is bound to his imaginings, and even Alma, who apparently survives him, may be imagined. We, the audience: Has Johan, or Bergman, imagined *us* into existence? Or is it we who have imagined the Artist into existence, the better to negotiate the hour of the wolf between midnight and dawn?

LOVE AFFAIR, OR THE CASE OF THE MISSING SWITCHBOARD OPERATOR (Yugoslavia). Can humans sufficiently "reform" to fulfill the Stalinist aspiration of a new political order? Writer-director Dušan Makavejev's gray, very funny *Ljubavni slučaj ili tragedija službenice PTT* opens with an elderly sexologist who asks this while lecturing us. From time to time he returns to address us again—such as at a farm hen house, outside which he marvels at a freshly laid egg, which he calls "the most highly developed female reproductive cell." Izabela Garodi, a young switchboard operator, is pregnant with his child (unbeknownst to him) when, after she cheats on him, devastated and jealous, Bušatijia Ahmet, a sanitation engineer (translation: rat catcher), kills her by accidentally pushing her down a well. This "modern girl" precipitates this outcome by clinging to him, not permitting "Meho" the time alone he needs to process her betrayal of their love affair and master his feelings of dejection, disgust and rage. Meho is still governed, it seems, by his old-fashioned sex organ.

Dazzlingly, Makavejev's tragicomedy is full of indications of the "newness" toward which the joint protagonists (beautifully played by Eva Ras and Slobodan Aligrudić), as well as society, strive. Both characters have relocated to become part of the Yugoslavian adventure (while maintaining a Communist dictatorship, Tito split with Stalin following the Second World War): Izabela, from Hungary; Meho, from Albania. The city is under tumultuous construction. Both Izabela and colleague Ruza get their feet scraped of dead skin! Makavejev lets Izabela's autopsy reflect satirically on Communist aspiration. The final struggle between Meho and Izabela as they move through dark, dank tunnels, the camera dogging them, suggests a descent into a mindset that may be more a part of human nature than adherents of the "new order" grasp or care to admit.

THE FIFTH HORSEMAN IS FEAR (Czechoslovakia). The four riders of the Apocalypse appear in the Book of Revelation. Our scourges, they are identified as Death, War, Hunger, Pestilence. And the fifth rider, according to Zbynek Brynych's film (from Hana Belohradska's story "Bez krásy, bez límce"), is Fear: . . . *A páty jezdec je Strach*.

Ostensibly in Prague during the war (soldiers do not wear German uniforms), the film admits a double focus: Braun, a Jewish doctor; inhabitants of an apartment building the Germans are occupying. The film's expressionistic visual style helps unhinge the moorings of specific time and event. What emerges is a Kafkaesque parable about fear in the crucible of whatever the form of totalitarianism or political tyranny may be.

Braun, preferring not to be invisible and safe, must be persuaded to remove a bullet from a Resistance fighter; in a waking nightmare, he desperately roams Prague in search of morphine for this patient. A kind of double life overtakes his, moreover, as he moonlights as the custodian of a warehouse crammed full of confiscated Jewish possessions headed for a museum that the Germans hope will commemorate an extinct people. Other sights, such as a belching chimney glimpsed through a window, also remind us of the Holocaust.

Fear: posters throughout the city and newspaper advertisements encourage Czechs to safeguard themselves by calling 44811 to inform on one another's suspicious behavior. On the soundtrack, military music inexplicably starts up without there being a soldier in sight. Jewish persons, we are told, are committing suicide in Prague at the rate of twenty a day. Black-and-white compositions are stark; a human figure or an object, such as a clock, may appear against the sheer backdrop of a blank wall or looming building. The space warehousing Jewish property suggests a kind of slaughterhouse.

1968

THE HOUR OF THE FURNACES (Argentina). "Latin America is a continent at war: for the ruling classes, a war of oppression; for the oppressed peoples, a war of liberation."

In their manifesto "Towards a Third Cinema," Fernando Ezequiel Solanas and Octavio Getino argued that Latin American Third World countries should enjoin their political struggles for liberation with the power of images, creating a democratic cinema by "giving cameras to the people." Nearly 4½ hours long, *La hora de los hornos: Notas y testimonios sobre el neocolonialismo, la violencia y la liberación* is a collectively-made "guerrilla" documentary. Voiceover narration highlights Latin American dependency—economic, political, cultural. Historically, European colonialism has been replaced by U.S. neocolonialism in collusion with oppressive elements at home; "educational colonialism," for example, "molds minds" suited to neocolonialism. Argentinean, the film devotes specific attention to Argentina.

Into this eclectic, dark, pulsating black-and-white film are crammed on-the-spot documentary, newsreel borrowings, *cinéma-vérité*, reconstructions, Godardian visual sloganeering, you-name-it, generating a richly contradictory result. Moreover, subsequent events rendered it additionally problematic. Student uprisings led to Perón's return from exile and assumption of the presidency in 1973. (Perón had ruled Argentina from 1946 to 1955, when a military junta removed the Laborist who had focused on improving workers' lives and whose wife successfully campaigned for women's suffrage.) Perón eventually purged his administration of Leftists, lending Solanas's *Hour*, retroactively, a coda of disillusionment.

Encompassing both (first-wave) Perónist and post-Perónist Argentina, *Hour* is perhaps most trenchant in documenting the heartrending poverty and miserable work conditions (in the fields, mines, factories) to which ordinary Argentines are consigned, and in contrasting this with the high life of the ruling oligarchs. It remains a massive document of oppression whose energetic radical propaganda reaches into historical testimony to forge a kind of national epic.

INNOCENCE UNPROTECTED (Yugoslavia). Dušan Makavejev's *Nevinost bez zaštite* draws upon fictional and documentary materials, either contemporary or from a quarter-century earlier, during the Nazi occupation of Belgrade. One of these, cut, rearranged, noncontinuously presented, is a whole other film: *Nevinost bez zaštite*—the same-titled film by and starring Dragoljub Aleksić, a Serbian athlete and celebrity. At his postwar trial Aleksić insisted he had made the film without German knowledge, much less support, and indeed the Germans had banned the film as deleterious. Aleksić was exonerated. His film is trite and melodramatic, and clumsily framed and shot; but Makavejev provides a last word, subtitling his film *A New Version of a Very Good Old Film*. Although Serbian himself, Makavejev isn't functioning as a nationalistic archivist. His own film contextualizes Aleksić's.

Makavejev, whose film is in color, applies color tinting to some frames of the old black-and-white film, at one point creating the effect of a flashing traffic light by alternating between the tinted and original Aleksić material. Other materials Makavejev employs include ones contemporaneous with the Aleksić film: newsreel snippets; German propaganda film snippets; newspaper headlines. Disparate elements either fuse or collide with one another, establishing coordinates of implied unity and explicit disunity, the latter correlative to military bombardment. Aleksić's film is escapist, apolitical, while Makavejev pursues the political context (including Nazi atrocities) that Aleksić ignored or avoided.

Makavejev's collage transforms everything in it into documentary materials, including pieces from two fictional films, Grigori Aleksandrov's *Circus* (1936) and Aleksić's. Within an analytical context, then, anything can become "documentary." All Makavejev's distancing techniques—among them, shifts among different kinds of material and the disparate length of elements (some, quick inserts—like bullets ripping continuity)—direct us to analyze the whole, making Makavejev's film a veritable "textbook" on how to "read" a film.

SAYAT-NOVA (U.S.S.R.). "My songs alone will not desert me."

Harutyun Sayatyan is the seventeenth-century Armenian poet who was known as Sayat-Nova, "King of Songs." He, his life and the culture to which he contributed inspired Armenian filmmaker (of Georgian ancestry) Sergei Parajanov's *Sayat-Nova*, a.k.a. (in re-edited versions) *Red Pomegranate, The Color of Pomegranates*: a Soviet attempt to short-circuit any stirrings of independence among its ethnic republics. Parajanov was himself imprisoned in a Soviet labor camp five years hence for his sexual orientation.

Grouped into chapters corresponding to different stages of Sayat-Nova's life, Parajanov's series of tableaux resonates with cultural symbolism, Armenian Orthodox Christian rituals, Armenian costumes and artifacts. An introductory shot consists of a trinity of pomegranates which, although apparently intact, "bleed" their ruby-colored juice on the sheet of parchment underneath them. Pomegranate red punctuates many of the film's gorgeous images.

Numerous images are exquisite and exotic, exerting for us foreigners a heady fascination. Others, seemingly impossible, startle. One powerful shot shows the love of reading —"Without the written word, ignorance would rule the world"—that Sayat-Nova has been introduced to in childhood. A high camera looks down high outer walls of a structure into a courtyard below, where the boy thumbs through the pages of a book. The ground around him is covered with books, their pages flipped through by the wind. The walls are inundated with windows, but in place of each window is a book, its pages flipped through by the wind. In a single image, therefore, we see at once the young reader and the lifetime of reading (and, implicitly, writing) in store for him.

Increasingly, intimations of mortality seep into the frames, deepening their mystery, referring to an afterlife. Posterity provides a temporal mask for eternity: the poet's sacred words and the undying myth of the poet.

MANDABI (Senegal). "Stop killing us with hope!" one of Ibrahima's two wives says as the postman delivers a money order from Ibrahima's nephew in Paris. (Most of the money is meant for the nephew's mother, but Islamic tradition requires that a male handle business transactions.) In their husband's absence, armed with the gift, the wives buy food and water on credit—a bit of independence for which their spouse will later castigate them. Meanwhile, Ibrahima hasn't worked in four years, and his small Dakar abode includes seven children. Senegal became independent in 1960, but the removal of colonialism hasn't given it much success, and the money order, in a way, makes the Diengs once again reliant on France.

Ousmane Sembène's *The Money Order* is a satirical comedy that follows Ibrahima's manifold attempts to convert the money order into cash. A convoluted bureaucracy confounds these attempts—a series of intersecting runarounds. Will any of the gift's value remain as Ibrahima's wives keep making purchases on credit, as Ibrahima himself borrows and borrows while trying to get the necessary documentation to be able to cash in the money order, and more and more people prevail upon him for handouts or money owed? Hope indeed is the measure of what France has left the Senegalese—and contentiousness and suspicion. Everyone assumes that Ibrahima is "selfish"—and *why?* because his wives rule his house. Someone remarks: "There is no solidarity anymore."

Along the way people either overcharge Ibrahima for helping him or rob him outright.

Eventually one of the film's few "haves" succeeds in turning the money order into cash only to steal the cash, giving Ibrahima instead a bit of rice, which starving neighbors descend upon. The film ends with their testimonies of poverty—and Ibrahima's conviction that it's a sin to help others.

RAMPARTS OF CLAY (France, Algeria). Concentric circles of oppression structure the main action in *Remparts d'argile*, French filmmaker Jean-Louis Bertucelli's beauteous, sun-bleached adaptation of Jean Duvignaud's novel. In a Tunisian village in the early 1960s, a strike by salt mine workers, which is set off when they are paid only half their wages, inspires a young villager to assist in their cause. However, she is deemed by village elders to be somehow possessed for discarding her traditional garb and modest demeanor and for behaving rebelliously, and the women attempt to bring her back to her senses by subjecting her to purifying rituals. But there is no turning back for her; her mind has already touched the border of freedom and self-determination.

Seamlessly mixing actual villagers and professional actors, Bertucelli translates documentary into fiction and fiction into documentary. It is amazing how thoroughly the film absorbs viewers into its reality—an outcome that the sparseness of dialogue facilitates. When villagers spatter the protagonist with fresh animal blood to drive demons out, one is unlikely to ask, "What were these superstitious people thinking in relation to the actress that they were treating as though she were one of their own?" They are simply maintaining their way of life; and one wonders only after the film has ended what parallels are to be drawn between the intruding filmmakers and, in the film, the intruding mining entrepreneur and the thugs he brings in to intimidate the strikers.

Banned in Algeria, where it was filmed, and in Tunisia, *Remparts d'argile* is a powerful feminist fable portraying a brave, solitary soul's rebellion against both primitive local custom and intrusive neocolonialism. The workers' strike helps crystallize both her sense of exclusion and her radical dream of real, not nominal, independence. Her desire is to shed *two* African pasts.

THE IMMORTAL STORY (France). Orson Welles, working in color for the first time, made *Une histoire immortelle* for French television. This rueful, exquisite erotic fable comes from a story by Isak Dinesen.

In order to actualize an ancient legend and experience sex vicariously, a wealthy Macao merchant hires a teenaged boy to make love with his "wife," whom the merchant has also hired for the occasion. The man's voyeurism turns out to be a lethal mixture of too much cold and too much heat. The film addresses romantic idealism, which is in bloom for the youth, is faded for the woman and, for the merchant, is long gone—till suddenly it brightly flickers before extinguishing his life. The fact that the man is rich enough to buy the event and its participants, including his surrogate, implies a causal connection between the way he has chosen to live his life, in pursuit of money and material comfort, and the emotional bankruptcy of that life.

Playing the merchant, for whom the pain of being alive, after such long denial, proves terminally intense, Welles is magnificent, giving probably his greatest performance. As the merchant's play-wife, beauteous Jeanne Moreau is even more remarkable. She projects the most poignant eroticism in all of cinema.

THE UNFAITHFUL WIFE (France). Claude Chabrol's rigorous *La femme infidèle* is about delusional bourgeoisie willing themselves into a facsimile of sexual love simply to complete the jigsaw puzzle of their self-image. Hélène and Charles Desvallées participate in a token union. Charles (Michel Bouquet, superb) walks in on Hélène on the telephone taking such time at sending a presumably wrong number packing that we instantly know Hélène is speaking with her lover. "Do you love me?" Charles uneasily asks Hélène at dinner one night. Hélène doesn't know what to say; Charles presses, and Hélène answers "Yes," but dismissively, not reassuringly. Angled and off to one side, the camera composes an image of the pair's seeming closeness in bed, but a shift in camera position reveals that they are widely apart. Charles hires a private detective and confronts Victor Pégala, the man cuckolding him. Unhinging Charles, Hélène has gifted Victor with the cigarette lighter that he had given her for their anniversary. Charles bludgeons Victor to death to reclaim this item.

Chabrol's film, co-written by Paul Gégauff, shifts from Charles's to Hélène's point of view. Hélène is disconsolate that Victor no longer phones to arrange a tryst. When she discovers in Charles's jacket a photograph of Victor with contact information, she makes the necessary calculations and destroys the evidence. Accomplices in a murder, the couple is finally, though silently, united.

The police come walking down the path to their secluded home in the country; Charles goes to meet the police; Hélène watches. The camera withdraws, correlative to Charles's being taken away, in tandem with a forward zoom, correlative to Charles's aching desire to remain. We see all he is losing through a luxuriant growth of trees.

Both characters are thus removed from the image of marital contentment they have managed to recompose.

ARTISTS AT THE TOP OF THE BIG TOP: DISORIENTED (West Germany). From the New German Cinema, which addressed contemporary issues and Germany's right-wing past, the first outstanding West German films emerged. Alexander Kluge's *Brutality in Stone* (1961) and *Yesterday Girl* (1966), his first feature, were among these. His *Artists at the Top of the Big Top: Disoriented* would remain among the movement's most brilliant entries.

Inspired by Jean-Luc Godard's methods, Kluge's film is a collage juxtaposing fictional, documentary and pseudodocumentary elements. Its protagonist is Leni Peickert, who runs a political circus. She is the anti-Riefenstahl Leni, whose aim is, through entertainment, to urge Germans to confront the recent past that most Germans would sooner forget. Because this is also Kluge's aim, the circus-within-the-film and the film enrobing it, a kind of bigger circus tent, combine to direct our attention to a consideration of the political role of art in general. But Kluge is unsettled as to what this role should be. His film weighs possibilities.

A point of departure is how Germany's Nazi past influences current art. The past is simply there, so Kluge juxtaposes the circus operation with shots of a Hitler rally. The fact that performers actually die in this circus, as in any other, reflects on the discussion that Leni's team encounters at a writer's convention: "Can there be art after Auschwitz?" Kluge's answer would seem to be: there *must* be—if for no other reason than to honor the dead. Moreover, by assisting audiences in confronting the past, art provides a therapeutic means of dealing with national trauma.

The film opens with footage of a Nazi "festival of the arts"—something Riefenstahl might have devised—and, later, achieves its symbolic apotheosis recollecting zoo elephants that died in a fire: the past that "won't forget" and won't let *us* forget, either.

IF . . . . (UK). Lindsay Anderson's *If* . . . . examines the culture in a British boys' school dedicated to training the cultural elite and tomorrow's political leaders. It seamlessly blends naturalism and fantasy, realism and surrealism, and its cautionary prophetic tone seems to argue that reality itself is headed for a dive into errant, disastrous fantasy. The school's oppressive atmosphere triggers a murderous rebellion by a few students that's as hilarious as it is terrifying. *If*. . . . launched a trilogy that Anderson continued shakily with *O Lucky Man!* (1973) and completed brilliantly with *Britannia Hospital* (1982).

The film combines traditional and classical elements with wild, surprising ones. One set of elements is correlative to the school's history, the self-seriousness of its mission, and its religious underpinnings; the other, to the boys' wildness and their wish to spring from the fetters that the school's discipline imposes on them.

The senior rebels, headed by Mick (Malcolm McDowell, terrific), disrupts an assembly in church by pelting the school with artillery and opening fire as officials, guests and students rush out. The film shows the reactionary intertwining of Church, military, and traditional schooling, whose aim is to maintain the illusion of the global importance of the waning British Empire.

Anderson uses the school's dense homoerotic atmosphere to imply one poisonous social outcome. Won't graduates contribute to their nation's homophobia in an effort to suppress and deny the homoerotic aspect of their formative school experience? Anderson contrasts this atmosphere with the warm, gentle, mutually supportive sexual relationship that develops between one of the rebels and an underclassman.

The achingly lovely, powerful strains of the "Sanctus Chorale" from the Congolese Mass *Missa Luba* perfectly express the film's stylistic and thematic conjoining of liberation and formal restraint.

TEOREMA (Italy). Pier Paolo Pasolini's Marxism, religious feeling, gayness and penchant for startling visual poetry combine for a heady brew in *Theorem*, a surreal allegory about a handsome no-name stranger (Terence Stamp) who inexplicably visits a bourgeois Milanese family and proceeds to seduce maid, son, Mom, daughter and Dad before departing. This is *The Gospel According to Sinner Pier Paolo*. The Vatican condemned it, and Pasolini was actually tried for obscenity. Thank God he prevailed!

Dad (Massimo Girotti) owns a factory. He gets it in the behind last because he is the *pièce de résistance*. Upshot: Dad turns over his factory to the workers. Well and good; but Pasolini reflects upon a possible adverse consequence: that the working class itself might turn bourgeois. Pasolini: "[A]nything done by the bourgeoisie, however sincere, profound, and noble it is, is always on the wrong side of the track."

The opening shot is of an expanse of seemingly ancient barren land, upon which is superimposed a quote from Exodus to the effect that God led the people by way of the wilderness. This is followed by shots of the factory complex, followed by the owner's chauffeured entrance into the complex. Shots of the wilderness are interspersed. The factory owner thus appears as the modern diminution of God, while the factory, "civilization," has replaced the wilderness. A shot of the owner with his family at the dinner table implies that "home" is an extension of "factory." With its touch of wildness/wilderness, the anonymous stranger's pansexuality is bound to shake things up.

The stranger's first conquest is the maid (Laura Betti, brilliant), who simply adores him. She ends up, miraculously, suspended in air, arms outstretched, herself an object of adoration.

Despite efforts to condemn Pasolini, his film is chaste: bare male buttocks—no genitalia.

LE GAI SAVOIR (France). Over three years, partially lit by the interior flame of their radicalism, two young militants, Émile Rousseau, a descendant of Jean-Jacques, and Patricia Lumumba, Patrice's "daughter," meet after-hours on a bare stage in an otherwise pitch-dark television studio and discuss politics and filmmaking. As witnesses, we receive from this discussion, and from accompanying recent and contemporary images and sounds, an enlightened education. The young pair teach themselves and one another, and we are collateral beneficiaries—along with writer-director Jean-Luc Godard, whose ambivalence over violent revolution is given a projective debate. The film's title translates as *Joyful Wisdom*.

Godard set this film aside in 1967 but picked it up in 1968, after the May student uprising and strikes. Initially caught up in the Leftist waves of *La Chinoise* (Godard, 1967), *Le gai savoir* emotionally expanded to include a sense of Leftist turmoil, disarray. We hear a rewinding tape recorder and recorded moments from 1968 street rallies. A substantial part of this film shows a kaleidoscopic collision of images and sounds outside the studio, testing their relationship, how they are politically manipulated, when they are "false" or "true." Brechtian distancing devices compound Brechtian distancing devices, threatening to lose all sense of argument or coherence in a barrage of sights and sounds. But this never happens, primarily because of the actors, Jean-Pierre Léaud and Julie Berto. Léaud in particular gives an astonishing performance, which includes a simulated tightrope walk, under a clear plastic umbrella, while singing (beautifully!).

Richard Brody is plain wrong that the "images" of them "matter little." One of Godard's themes is the relationship between sex and politics, and the intimacy between Patricia and Émile, with their various close arrangements vis-à-vis the camera and the lustrous brown of their heads of hair, speak to this.

DEATH BY HANGING (Japan). Nagisa Oshima's *Koshikei* is the blackest black comedy. A Korean boy, hanged for raping and killing Japanese girls, survives his execution, throwing the Japanese legal system into mortification. The restricted oxygen to his brain has rendered R— the name by which the boy is known—amnesiac, and he is "re-educated," to make him civilized, acceptable, "Japanese," and ready for another execution. However, the process reveals how well R eludes Japanese stereotypes of Koreans and how easily the Japanese elude their own exalted self-image. Thus the film's objective first movement, by patiently observing the procedure of capital punishment both in rehearsal and execution, indicts state murder for its inhumanity, while the wilder second movement indicts Japanese society for arrogance, self-delusion, and ethnic and racial bigotry.

Implicit throughout is the brilliant theme that will later inform Oshima's *Empire of Passion* (1978): that "modern justice" is, in fact, an unwitting repackaging of *ancient* "justice"—a means by which modern society projects its enormous burden of guilt onto select individuals: a process sufficiently unsatisfying that it needs to be performed again and again. R's survival of the state's attempt to put an end to him reflects society's failure to face and subdue traumas gnawing at its collective unconscious. R's poise despite becoming the system's pawn provides an ironical index of the chaos of the Japanese character, even as it strives to affect a composed self-image. R blindfolded, facing the noose, erases his distinction as non-Japanese; he becomes an instrument by which Oshima studies the people he knows best. Japanese humanity would seem to depend on how R is treated; but, blindfolded themselves, in their case by the self-image rattling inside their collective head, Japanese officials refuse to consider their own behavior and bent. To quote Nietzsche: "We are all murderers."

THE CREMATOR (Czechoslovakia). Juraj Herz's *Spalovač mrtvol*, from Ladislav Fuks, is a very dark Czech comedy about Nazism, occupation and the Holocaust. Karl Kopfrkingl (Rudolf Hrusínský, superb) is in charge of daily operations at a Prague crematorium. He is obsessed with the rapidity with which corpses can be turned into dust. A Jewish neighbor, Dr. Bettelheim, assures Karl that ashes, whatever a human's ethnicity, are identical. When Prague is occupied by Germans, a Nazi friend informs Karl that his wife Lakmé's mother was Jewish, making Karl's son and daughter quarter-Jewish, and that terrible suffering is in store for Jews. After denouncing the crematorium director, Karl ascends to his post and oversees Lakmé's cremation, having tricked his wife into hanging herself. He bludgeons their "effeminate" boy and stuffs his body in with someone headed for cremation. Daughter will be next. Meanwhile, Karl is invited to apply his skills to a secret program of Jewish extermination. Karl's mind collapses into the insanity that such mass murder will liberate Jews from death's alternative in their case: insupportable suffering.

Kopfrkingl appears in every scene and nearly every shot; this helps Herz draw us into the film's revelation of an increasingly unhinged mind. But Kopfrkingl was strange to begin with. The spotless bathroom is his favorite room in his house. We know that he is planning to kill his bespectacled son when he applies a comb briefly to the boy's scalp and then, just as quickly, to his own—his habit with laid-out corpses. His talk is endlessly about the wonderful state of death.

Herz's Kafkaesque black-and-white film is loaded with paranoid closeups, especially eyes, including the eyes of "mute" animals at the zoo. Dvorák, who prepares the bodies until Karl denounces him and he hangs himself, works to the largo of Dvorák's "New World Symphony."

LUCÍA (Cuba). Ten years after the Revolution deposed Batista, *Lucía*, by Humberto Solás, expressed hopefulness of the future. Depicting progressive changes in Cuba over more than half a century, the film's formal design—three episodes, each in its own visual style, showing the role of Cuban women at three different times—implies quantum leaps in political consciousness. *Lucía* adheres to the dictum that a woman's lot reflects a nation's value.

In the case of Cuba, that lot is marked against entrenched patriarchy and socially rampant *machismo*, one source of which is Spanish culture. The first Lucía is embroiled in a well-heeled romantic melodrama in colonial times, their late nineteenth-century romance at the mercy of her lover's whims, and the period sets, costumes and florid attitudes—betrayal and madness figure in—correlative to the entrapment of history. In the next, tragic episode, romance strikes out at another Lucía's insulated world as the political ground underneath the Caribbean island begins to shift. Society-maiden Lucía falls in love with a guerrilla fighter and joins Cuba's war of independence from Spain. The idea of independence resonates on different levels as the personal and the national cross, resulting in the kind of "intimate epic" that *Gone with the Wind* (Victor Fleming et al., 1939) failed to achieve due to its intellectual vacuity and sentimental compromises. In the final episode, a third Lucía yet more sociopolitical distance to cover. After the Castro revolution, *then what?* Progress is being made throughout the island, but Lucía's spouse, who at times keeps her (literally) locked up, is resistant to any tampering with his male prerogatives. For Solás, "revolution" must be an ongoing thing, and education is the key.

The lukewarm mush of Solás's recent *Miel para Oshún* (2001) begs the question: Is the Cuban Revolution dead in the water?

JE T'AIME, JE T'AIME (France). Written by Jean Sternberg (hm), *I Love You, I Love You* is Alain Resnais's most daring attempt to use images and editing to suggest thought processes. Claude, recuperated following a suicide attempt, is recruited by scientists who are researching time in order to verify their experiment with a mouse, which they believe they succeeded in transporting to a moment in its past before bringing it back to the present. But something goes awry with the human version of the experiment, and Claude is stuck in the past, not only recapturing a lost moment of time, but also reliving seemingly random fragments of the past, many revolving around his conviction that he has murdered a woman, Catrine. Among the events that Claude relives is his attempted suicide.

An astonishing essay on how the human mind organizes time elements thematically, achronologically, this science-fiction poem gives Claude a companion for his time-travel: his predecessor, the mouse—a perplexed image of himself, it turns out, straining for breaths in the cage, in this instance, the belljar of time that proves its eventual home.

Wry dialogue includes the delightful possibility that the cat was created in God's image, and that man was created to be the cat's slave and caregiver. By extension, time's relation to humanity is a cat-and-mouse game. A cab driver casually asks Claude, "Have you got time?" Really, time has us.

Resnais's film can seem a fiendishly desentimentalized version of Frank Capra's lugubrious *It's a Wonderful Life* (1946); but its ultimate effect recalls the powerful last shot of Alfred Hitchcock's *Vertigo* (1958): Everyman, on a ledge, all but falling, fixed in helplessness, guilt, loss, regret.

Moreover, this haunting film, especially given its themes of time, loss and memory, anticipates another great work of science fiction: Andrei Tarkovsky's *Solaris* (1972).

THE DEEP DESIRE OF THE GODS (Japan). Shohei Imamura's *Pornographers* (1966) is chiseled in black and white; most subsequent Imamura films, however, are messy and in color: a better indicator, perhaps, of his vision of overflowing humanity. *Kamigami no Fukaki Yokubo* was Imamura's first film in this mode.

Kariya, a Tokyo engineer, visits an island south of Japan, planning for the construction of a sugar refinery. But the gorgeous expanse of water he must traverse to reach this practical destination shimmers with the collective Japanese unconscious. Kariya is thus sailing out of himself *into* himself; for the primitive community inhabiting the island mirror-images him. Tied to the past, these natives are fascinated with the modernity that Kariya brings and represents; for his part, Kariya is fascinated with the island customs that seem to have veered very little from an ancient past. One of the norms on the island appears to be incest. Nekichi spends his days chained in a gigantic pit: paternal punishment, not for the incest he committed with his sister—his father also is incestuous—but, rather, because he mixed modern with tradition by fishing with dynamite. Nekichi's predicament evolves into a subtle metaphor for Kariya's ties to the mainland. Nekichi's incest reflects modernity's repression of familial sexual instincts and of the human nature red in tooth and claw that the islanders freely, voluminously exhibit.

Kariya is deigned a deity by the islanders for the technology (and the Coca Cola) he brings. Nevertheless, his denial of basic connectedness to the natives, which he represses beneath a screen of objectively studying them, assists in his becoming an instrument for the destruction of island culture. Kariya reflects on how advanced he and postwar Japan are. Imamura reflects, instead, on how little Japan has progressed, how basic and instinctual human nature remains.

THE 17TH PARALLEL: THE PEOPLE'S WAR (France, Vietnam). "[The U.S.] destroyed everything. The rice was so beautiful. The tanks crushed everything."

A somewhat more formal on-the-spot documentary than his phenomenal *The Spanish Earth* (1937), Joris Ivens and Marceline Loridan's black-and-white *Le 17e parallèle: La guerre du peuple* is the best movie ever about the Vietnam War. During the two months of its making, Ivens and Loridan lived with Vietnamese peasants under frightening U.S. bombardment; the U.S., you will recall, had militarily intervened in a civil war that had come about because South Vietnam, under Ngo Dinh Diem, refused to permit democratic elections in the country in 1956 as indicated in the 1954 Geneva Accords, which had temporarily split Indochina into two halves along the 17th parallel, with a demilitarized zone (DMZ) in between.

"Ngoc's home was bombed again." For the third time.

Looking into the camera, a man speaks: "Some villages were hit by 5,000 shells in three days. Others received 70 to 80 bombs per inhabitant. . . . The Americans pushed the war to the edge of the Ben Hai River. They violated the demilitarized zone. . . . Our anger and our hatred for them are deeper than the river."

Farmers at work in the rice paddies are fully armed. The winding tunnels of the subterranean shelter include a hospital. A panning shot in sunlight surveys the bodies of dead children. Boys play at war as preparation for the real thing.

The peasants persevere. "We prepare to greet the Americans," someone says, sardonically meaning with "thunderclaps"—*firepower.*

A nine-year-old child's into-the-camera monologue haunts. Inside the tunnels, defying the B52s overhead, a group exits away from the camera to attend a performance of political theater. What visual irony! We can see "the light at the end of the tunnel."

ORATORIO FOR PRAGUE (Czechoslovakia). In 1968 Alexander Dubček, its new leader, instituted a series of reforms that transformed Czechoslovakia's tenor and political landscape, including freedom of assembly, speech and worship, and the release of all political prisoners.

Chronology of World Cinema

1968

As Mikhail Gorbachev would discover twenty years hence, such a process creates its own dynamic, one that Dubček, likewise remaining a committed Communist, also refused to rein in. In summer 1968, in Prague, filmmaker Jan Němec began documenting a vibrant national celebration in the city square—a people's tribute to new freedoms and a discussion of their nation's future. When Soviet tanks invaded, trampling Dubček's liberalization, Němec and crew, at great risk, kept filming. The material was smuggled out, shifting moral winds in the Cold War, and providing recyclable material about the event thereafter. In *The Unbearable Lightness of Being* (Philip Kaufman, 1988), from Milan Kundera's novel, not only was it visually quoted, but Němec played himself filming it!

The first fallen patriot's blood on the street; a blood-stained flag; the Soviet seige of the radio station that had been the invading Nazis' first target; a Soviet soldier hiding his face; street fires; Czechs appealing to the soldiers, one of whom, in secret, is glimpsed reading a Czech pamphlet; etc.

Clocking in under a half hour, *Oratorio for Prague* is one of the most soul-battering documentaries ever made, one that captures the jubilant, hopeful Czech spirit, Czech national pride (the passage on Czech Jewry wipes one out), the delusional dismissal of the cloud gathering against Czechoslovakia and, alas, the Soviet crush (Dubček: "a crime against the fundamental rights of man"). One instantly realizes why Němec continued filming, beyond the desire that the world should see what happened. It is all that he *could* do. We also feel helpless, vulnerably raw, watching this irreplaceable film.

1969

FATA MORGANA (West Germany). Werner Herzog's hallucinatory *Fata Morgana* is a non-narrative work, filmed in different places in Africa, including the Sahara Desert and Kenya, its mesmerizing shots, including many traveling shots, pieced together into a visual poem of an alien visit to scenes of a mysterious world, heretofore unknown to Herzog, his crew and, likely, us. Many shots include, on the distant horizon, "fata morgana," that is, mirages: visible things—water, islands, vegetation, moving automobiles, etc.—that, although capable of being photographed, are not really there: phantasms originating in reflections and refractions of light transporting images of actual occurrences to the eye over vast intervening space.

Comprising three increasingly sardonic sections, "Creation," "Paradise," "The Golden Age," *Fata Morgana* is, according to Herzog, a science-fiction film with the story—for, originally, a story had been planned—removed. Accompanied by readings from the *Popol Vuh*, the sacred text that includes the Mayan myth of creation, the images of "Creation" suggest a primordial wasteland, a vast region of hills and sand dunes at some dead-end of civilization. Strewn over the landscapes are the carcasses of vehicles and other things abandoned by European soldiers in World War II. Tracking shots disclose empty gasoline drums in the dunes—more evidence of Western intrusion. We see Ground Zero, where the French, performing atomic tests, exploded a bomb. The juxtaposition of the creation myth and these sullied images, which hint invasion and appropriation, accumulates an aura of sadness, resignation, defeat. Africa is thus portrayed as "Europe's backyard" or dump—the scene of Western colonialist and neocolonialist presumption.

Europe used Africa but did little or nothing to alleviate African poverty. The pianoed parlor of a Western-style brothel provides an example, post-"Creation," of what Europe did give to Africa. Europeans in Africa were the ultimate fata morgana.

THE MILKY WAY (France). According to Luis Buñuel a "journey through fanaticism," *La Voie Lactée* follows two poor pilgrims in the present, one young, one old, an atheist and a believer, through southern France to Santiago de Compostela, Spain, where St. James the Apostle's bones are presumably interred. Their various encounters, along with a stream of historical vignettes, compose a surreal landscape of Christian dogma, heresies, hypocrises, blasphemies. There are also visions and miracles. This brilliant comedy is as fluent as spun silk.

At a village inn, where the pair stop, a priest and a police officer genially converse. Painstakingly the priest explains the dogma of transubstantiation to the officer: The body of Christ is not contained in the wafer, but in the sacrament of the Eucharist the wafer becomes Christ's body—actually; not symbolically. When the restauranteur mildly asserts that the body of Christ is in the Host like the hare is in the pâté he is serving, the vexed priest counters that in the sixteenth century the Pateliers were burned for that heresy. Now the priest has a revelation: the restauranteur is correct! When the officer expresses surprise at this contradiction, the priest, really vexed, flings hot coffee in his face. Men in white cart away the priest. Thus Buñuel exquisitely mocks religious dogmatic "thinking" (such as currently afflicts Islamic and U.S. Christian fundamentalists). A subsequent argument, about grace versus free will, between a Jesuit and a Jansenist leads to a duel.

Jesus—he spits on the blind and they can see!—and the Marquis de Sade are among the cast of characters. Sometimes, historical characters cross paths with our twosome.

Buñuel: "Bourgeois morality, for me, is immoral and to be fought[—t]he morality founded on our most unjust social institutions, like religion, patriotism, the family, culture."

Buñuel!

DAYS AND NIGHTS IN THE FOREST (India). Conjuring an atmosphere both Shakespearean and Chekhovian, and borrowing Antonioni's signature theme of alienation, Satyajit Ray achieved a complex, poignant result with *Aranyer Din Ratri*—like Ray's *Kanchenjungha* (1962), a "holiday film."

Four young, unmarried men from Calcutta spend the weekend at a wooded resort in Bihar, in the Bengal countryside. They bring their arrogance with them, disdaining the locals, except for two young women, members of a cultured household: sisters-in-law, one of them widowed. A fish-out-of-water comedy thus deepens into something else: an urgent opportunity for the boys, amidst their cranky leisure, to come out of their complacency and respond to the two girls and to unspoilt Nature in the beauteous surroundings, and transcend their usual rat race of urban careerism, gender and class bigotry, and monkey-mimicked Western ways. Perhaps they do not entirely miss the boat, that is, the forest. However, their whirlwind intrusion far more profoundly affects at least one of the young women.

Ray's apprenticeship to Jean Renoir is richly evident here; *Une partie de campagne* seems an especial influence. Like Renoir, Ray portrays Nature as a moral force one can either resist or submit to; unlike the men, their pair of picnic partners already seem to have taken Nature into their lives, perhaps along with their joint loss (brother, spouse), but, as likely, steadily, gradually. The sparkling forest in *Aranyer Din Ratri* exudes the mystery that would elude the Mirabar caves fifteen years hence in David Lean's *A Passage to India*.

The mystery is something the men, in their disparate lives, may yet respond to. Or suppress.

This ravishingly beautiful black-and-white film is quietly momentous about love—few films are so driven by erotic undertows—and about the ways we open up to others and the ways we stay shut.

ARMY OF THE SHADOWS (France). Jean-Pierre Melville, born Grumbach, was a member of the Resistance during the Occupation of France. Three wonderful films of his address this period during the Second World War: *The Silence of the Sea* (1947), *Leon Morin, Priest* (1961) and *L'armée des ombres*—although his *film noir*s also refer, symbolically, to the Resistance. Joseph Kessel, the author of the novel on which the film is based, was also a member of the Resistance.

This is a nuts-and-bolts film, rigorously detailing Resistance activities, including planning sessions, brutal interrogations, and executions, in which endlessly lonely, solemn participants, almost sleepwalking in the oppressive atmosphere of the times (to which the film's repressed tenor is correlative), often seem divided from their own humanity as well as their nation, which they are relentlessly trying to reclaim and restore—although at times they also seem to be *all* mission, without memory of motive. A dark, somber film much of which unfolds in hidden, confined spaces, it is as psychological as historical. Its soldiering civilians in constant fear of death might pass for villains in another film. This is an unvarnished look at the French Resistance, and one doesn't doubt for a moment its authenticity.

The protagonist is one of the movement's leaders, but the most unforgettable character is Mathilde, played beautifully by Simone Signoret. A loyal, committed member, she finds herself between a rock and a hard place courtesy of the Gestapo, which threatens her with her teenaged daughter's consignment to a Polish brothel unless she betrays the cause. Like other traitors, she is dispatched—one of the most emotionally bleeding moments in cinema.

There's no question as to what must be done with her. There is endless question, though, whether the world can ever be made right after it's done.

MY NIGHT AT MAUD'S (France). Jean-Louis Trintignant is terrific as Jean-Louis, an unmarried engineer in his mid-30s, who knows his ideal woman when he sees her. Writer-director Eric Rohmer's astonishing *Ma nuit chez Maud* opens with him in contemplation over a balcony on a Sunday morning; a sporadically devout Roman Catholic, should he attend Mass when what is really drawing him to church is a beguiling blonde parishioner? He goes and takes his glimpse, which is how in retrospect we are able to figure out what he had been contemplating. We "feel" his eye on this stranger by her uncomfortable looks back at him.

Jean-Louis runs into schoolmate Vidal after fourteen years. Over dinner they discuss Pascal's Wager, the probabilities game of getting oneself in line for Eternity, whether one is a believer, just in case God exists. Jean-Louis finds many grounds on which to dispute Pascal, including the philosopher's eventual repudiation of mathematics, upon which Jean-Louis's professional life is based, but Vidal, a Marxist, dazzlingly applies Pascal's Wager to history. And then he proceeds with yet another application, replacing Eternity with temporal bliss, by introducing Jean-Louis to Maud (Françoise Fabian, fabulous), a fresh divorcée with a quick intellect to match Jean-Louis's. Jean-Louis spends his night with Maud but marries Françoise, the blonde from church, whom he meets after departing from Maud, and who, unbeknownst to him, may have participated in the adultery that precipitated Maud's divorce. Like Maud, the couple have a child, and in a five-years-later coda, for all his intelligence at math and science, Jean-Louis is distinctly lagging understanding of his own wife and their marriage, the conventionality of which he clings to as to a life preserver.

Rohmer, a devout Roman Catholic, witheringly ponders Jean-Louis, who naïvely asserts, "Religion adds to love."

Captivating, devastating comedy.

QUE LA BETE MEURE (France). Claude Chabrol's heart-piercing *Que la bête meure*, in color, is based on the 1938 British novel *The Beast Must Die* by Nicholas Blake—the pseudonym that poet Cecil Day-Lewis used when writing popular mysteries. Charles Thenier, the protagonist, is also an author—of children's stories. He lives with young son Michel, whom we see at the beginning at the shore toting two fishing nets, one of them empty. When Michel becomes the fatal victim of a hit-and-run road accident, Charles sets out to identify the killer and dispatch him. We see (presumably) the child's mother, Charles's arms wrapped around her, in black-and-white home movies that Charles, haunted, revisits.

A number of correspondencies identify Charles himself with Paul Decourt, Michel's killer, including a piece by Brahms. In some sense, Charles is searching, like Œdipus, for himself. Both men live in Brittany. Hélène, Paul's sister-in-law, was once Paul's mistress and becomes Charles's mistress. Michel and Philippe, Paul's teenaged son, look alike. By film's end, Paul has been murdered and Charles may be headed toward suicide.

Chabrol's film embraces ambiguity; we cannot determine who murders Paul: Charles, in his son's name, or Paul's own son, Philippe. Each in turn confesses, either telling the truth or sacrificing himself for the other's sake. Charles's mission to punish his son's killer appears to memorialize his parental dedication. But the home movies where we alone see father and son together are idealized, idyllic—not the realistic documents they purport to be. What about the all too plainly real grief we observe when Charles picks up his dead son off the street, holds him in his arms and carries him off? Could Charles's grief be driven by guilt for the missed opportunity of being a good father, with which Charles is now left?

FELLINI SATYRICON (Italy). Inspired by Petronius, Federico Fellini's *Fellini Satyricon* followed the swank and soap opera of *La dolce vita* (1959) and the vacancy of *8½* (1963), in which a filmmaker who has just had a stupendous hit—read in *La dolce vita*—is given lots of money and freedom to make another film; but about *what?* Some find beguiling the idea of a film with nothing to say about the making of a film with nothing to say. I have nothing to say. *Juliet of the Spirits* (1965) was better though somewhat diffuse.

Fellini described his *Satyricon* as a science-fiction film, but one about the past. It's a kaleidoscope of humanity.

The film's barbaric first-century Roman odyssey follows young Encolpio through a phantasmagoric landscape of gods, goddesses and grotesques, a false minotaur and a real hermaphrodite, homosexuality and public sexual humiliations, carnival-like revelry, and fierce punishments. It opens with the student wailing against solitude and life's injustice in front of a blank wall. Shit happens. On the same stage where a theater-piece is being sensually performed, a poor soul gets a hand axed off for real. The writer Eumolpo is tortured for plagiarizing and finally cannibalized by relatives. The film ends mid-sentence (as did Petronius's uncompleted original), with the film's assorted characters visually translated into the completed fresco—the once blank wall with figures frozen in time yet hauntingly alive, eternally.

Blending harsh reality and mysterious legend, Fellini's masterpiece posits humanity's hapless existence. It is also a film about the artistic process by which the past is given form and its characters, finally, direction and purpose—humanity's redemption. A part of this form is the film's interrupted quality; narrative threads are abruptly dropped, and interruptions are themselves interrupted by other stories envisioned as flashbacks: an expression of life's uncertainty, richness, unfathomability.

EVEN DWARFS STARTED SMALL. (West Germany). *Even Dwarfs Started Small*, the first film since *The Terror of Tiny Town* (Sam Newfield, 1938) to be populated by midgets, is an amazing saga of rebellion. It's a horrific, hilarious meditation on the suppression of freedom and the nature of violence. A favorite film of David Lynch's and perhaps the favorite film of a deceased friend of mine, it confirmed the evidence of *Fata Morgana* (1969) that West Germany's Werner Herzog is a cinematic genius—and, also like Lynch, quite an oddball.

At a remote post, dwarfs have been virtual prisoners at "the institution" until they take over one day. The instructor in charge, feeling surrounded, has locked himself in the principal's office, along with Pepe, one of the inmates; the inmates outside raucously laugh down all his pleas to be "reasonable" and resume their passive existence. Lighthearted acts of rebellion progressively take a turn for the worse as inmates, feeling increasingly imperiled, go on a rampage of destruction, arson and violence, some of it directed at "Mother Nature" in the form of animals (including a crucified monkey)—a protest against the beleaguered human condition.

Twisted trees and dead animals litter the setting, a patch of desert beyond which loom volcanic hills. Thus Herzog's *mise-en-scène* resonates with a sense of humanity in its most imperiled form, in the most extreme conditions imaginable. The brutal overcompensations of the dwarfs are constantly measured against their physical limitations, composing a metaphor of our frustration and desperation vis-à-vis the forces arrayed against us, including, at the outermost limit, our mortality. The film urges us to consider the various ways in which our own lives are confined and regulated by natural conditions, schooling, employment and the state.

Blending fantasy and documentary realism, Herzog's black-and-white *Even Dwarfs* shocks, amuses, devastates.

THE FRUIT OF PARADISE (Czechoslovakia). *Ovoce stromu rajských jime*, Věra Chytilová's follow-up to *Daisies* (1966), is prefaced by an experimental film based on Genesis. Superimpositions (to which are applied quick camera zigs and zags) evoke an Eden through which a naked pair make their way to the forbidden Tree of the Knowledge of Good and Evil. But did this opulent Eve come from that scrawny Adam's rib (or whatever), not vice versa? Colors are rich: deep, woody greens; orange fruit; red petals—everything (including Man and Woman) appears to be rotting to earth. Satan lurks about, and when the man and the woman lean in, it is an equal coming together, and sad, full of the kind of self-aware regret one associates with humanity after the Fall—a flip of the dogmatic mythological telescope, perhaps, wherein our original parents sacrificed their suspension of time in order to deliver us, their future, into life and death. Overall, the long-shots identify the point of view; Chytilová gives us a God's-eye view of our mythical fall into humanity, mortality, selfconsciousness.

After this dazzling opening movement, a modern pair sits under a tree on the grounds of a resort. The guy, lazy, is unfazed by his environment; he has assumed God's authority, self-righteousness. The gal is curious about everything, having assumed God's endless curiosity in his own creation. The postal carrier brings letters—symbolically, connectedness to others and institutions. All the mail is for the guy. Meanwhile, a Satanic figure in red rides a bicycle (which he keeps falling off) and pursues the gal. While pleading for gender equality, Chytilová invokes *Alice in Wonderland*, *La coquille et le clergyman* (Germaine Dulac, 1926), *Un chien andalou* (Luis Buñuel, Salvador Dalí, 1928), Jean-Luc Godard's *Pierrot le fou* (1965), and quotes Aleksandr Dovzhenko's *Earth* (1930).

THE DAMNED (Italy, West Germany). The indispensable contribution that industrial capitalism made to the madness gripping Germany in the 1930s: this is the theme of *Götterdämmerung* (*La caduta degli Dei*), the first installment of Luchino Visconti's trilogy targeting German decadence. In light of the corporate fascism that currently defines "globalization," Visconti's film now has about it an awful air of historical prophecy as well.

The Damned revolves around the aristocratic Essenbecks, who are bound together by their steel works factory. The family head, Baron Joachim von Essenbeck, holds the National Socialists in contempt. Nevertheless, he allies his company's future to their fortunes, and this entails providing whatever is necessary to build up the German war machine. Meanwhile, the Nazis are burning the Reichstag (the democratic Weimar Republic's lower body of governance), blame for which they will succeed in laying at the doorstep of Communists, giving themselves the pretext—to "restore order"—for gaining control of the country.

Aristocrat and Communist, Visconti has created a harrowing, haunting portrait of Nazi evil. He applies to his exacting *mise-en-scène* a dark, infernal Expressionism. His reconstruction of the Night of the Long Knives shows what a gifted artist can do to make an historical event come alive. The whole passage sustains a grim, nearly intolerable intensity.

Visconti elicits two superb performances: eyes darting, muscular shoulders flexing, Ingrid Thulin's Sophie, widow of one of the baron's sons; and young Helmut Berger's Martin, Sophie's drug-addicted, pedophiliac son, to whose revenge on his mother, for manipulating and (psychologically) abandoning him, Berger brings a springing edge of terrible sorrow. Moreover, Berger finely charts Martin's transformation from fearful pervert to fearsome Nazi —neither growth nor regression, just a spiraling out; and it is this pathological odyssey, indelibly etched, that helps keep *The Damned* from collapsing into an array of sumptuous, somewhat too elegant fragments.

THE STRUCTURE OF CRYSTALS (Poland). In a remote, rural outpost, Jan, trained as a physicist, lives with ebullient wife Anna, a local schoolteacher, and functions as a statistical meteorologist—a scientific hack. A former colleague visits. Marek, an urbane researcher, is a scientific star who travels widely and drives a sports car. Marek chides Jan for wasted potential, withered ambition. But Marek fails to take into account "the structure of crystals"—internal forces that compel individual "choices." Ironically, given his freer time, Jan, it turns out, has maintained the richer, more committed intellectual life. Jan reads, studies, thinks, while busy Marek laments how little spare time he has. Jan discusses the nature of infinity; Marek notes he saw Marina Vlady in a Chekhov play in Paris.

With *Struktura kryształu* Krzysztof Zanussi brought a distinctive signature to cinema. The physicist and philosopher's first feature weighs the disparate professional and personal lives of these two scientists in a Communist country, Poland, where a person's contribution to society, from the national political perspective, trumps everything else. This is the film's foundation, but there is no message-mongering. Yet no other film more forcefully conveys the situation. In truth, both scientists have been reduced to the state's use of them.

Employing black-and-white bleakness, where snow projects aridity (with the couple's childlessness, accentuated by the scores of children with whom Anna works, adding an almost subliminal note of poignancy), Zanussi pursues momentous themes with mathematical precision and deep irony. (En route to a nearby city, the couple shows Marek a desolate fertilizer factory; but we never see anything grow.) Molecular drawings somehow disclose Zanussi's fascination with the human condition. Zanussi's love of cinema is equally apparent. Standing in front of a framed wall mirror, Jan and Marek miraculously suggest a celebrated shot from Ingmar Bergman's *Persona* (1966).

BOY (Japan). By the mid-1960s Japan has miraculously recovered from the Second World War, defeat, military occupation. Or had it? Writer-director Nagisa Oshima's *Shonen* detects a residue, a social warping, an appalling degeneration. His is a precise and burrowing film.

The focus here is on a criminal, renegade family. Father is a wound-riddled war veteran. Chillingly, Mother is absent; we never learn her fate. But Stepmother is on hand: the Boy's Stepmother, that is, and the infant boy's biological mother. Father has impressed his family into a routine of grifting in order to earn a living. Either Boy or Stepmother rushes into the course of a moving car, sustains a hopefully limited injury, and Father on that basis extorts money from the driver. But the authorities aren't insensible, one of the patsies turns out to be a savvy garage mechanic, and the family is on the run, northwards. The color film passes into and out of black and white.

This film really ripped at my heart. Boy: "I don't think anything about anything"—and Boy's general demeanor suits the disposition of this remark. Father is a nasty, raging bully, partly to rail against the loss of his traditional authority as a consequence of the war; Stepmother, reflecting the same assault on the Japanese family, believes that Boy is out to get her. She casually tosses away the one thing that Boy holds onto as his own: his cap. Compare Oshima's analytical treatment of this cap and the sentimental treatment Peter Bogdanovich affords another boy's cap in *The Last Picture Show* (1971).

Is it possible Oshima knows his *Little Caesar* (Mervyn LeRoy, 1930)? "Is this the end of Japan?" Boy asks. He is referring, of course, to geography; but the line reverberates beyond this ten-year-old's intent.

A beautiful film.

ANTÔNIO DAS MORTES (Brazil). A reworking of the myth of St. George and the Dragon,

O Dragão da Maldade contra o Santo Guerreiro—literally, *The Dragon of Evil Against the Warrior Saint*—is Gláuber Rocha's sequel to his *Deus e o Diabo na Terra do Sol* (1964), a.k.a. *Black God, White Devil*. Hired assassin Antônio das Mortes reappears, this time allying himself with oppressed, exploited peasants, whose protector and avenger he becomes. The setting again is the sunbaked *sertão*. Full of ritual, steeped in folklore, rich in song and dance, this brilliant example of *cinema nôvo* suggests a heady Brazilian mixture of Francesco Rosi, Miklós Jancsó and Jean-Luc Godard.

Indeed, Rocha presents a landscape of shifting loyalties and betrayals amidst the constants of feudal and colonialist legacies. But the central shift proceeds politically forward: the villain, the Dragon Antônio das Mortes, slays the Dragon Slayer, becoming himself the *cangaceiro*, the people's bandit, whose personality suggests the dimensions of guerrilla fighter Che Guevara, whose 1967 death fully released the legend. The film's formal theatricality, both distancing and visually flat, stabilizes the circus-like shifts, creating a tension that is correlative to the hero's divided nature, which encompasses the degree to which he is haunted by his past. In a way, like Ethan Edwards in John Ford's *The Searchers* (1956), he ends up "wandering between the winds," a solitary figure in a landscape at once both alien and familiar.

The film's amazing final movement finds the hero moving in and out of remoteness, timelessness and immediate, time-specific traffic, while the film itself moves in and out of sound, in and out of silence. The closing shot finds the hero walking down a deserted road away from the camera, with a Shell Oil station up ahead—a mark of exploitation: post-colonial colonialism.

HIGH SCHOOL (U.S.). Frederick Wiseman's contentious documentaries investigating various institutions constitute one of the most important bodies of work by an American filmmaker.

High School was shot in a Philadelphia area public school, Northeast High, whose academic reputation is esteemed. The film orchestrates various school processes and activities. The occasional snippet of classroom instruction reinforces the overarching theme that the primary function of the American high school isn't education but, instead, socialization and indoctrination. (If anything, today, more than 40 years later, this is even more so the case.) An early encounter between a student and the vice-principal in charge of discipline is exemplary. The boy's attempts to explain that the detention time a teacher has imposed on him is unwarranted, that the teacher literally misidentified the culprit in a classroom incident, are frustrated by the administrator's inflexible position that the boy should accept his punishment, regardless of his guilt or innocence, as a way of proving himself a man and showing he can obey orders. Respect for authority is the school's administrative mantra. The film ends with the reading of a letter, by a teary-eyed teacher or administrator (it hardly matters which), from a former student grateful to be fighting in America's Southeast Asian war. Indeed, the woman obscenely opines that the feelings expressed in the letter constitute proof that the school is succeeding in doing its job.

Along the way Wiseman's camera exposes a plethora of absurdities: an administrator explaining to an irate parent that her daughter's outstanding achievement in written work for a course can't overturn the justice of her having received a report card grade of F; a moonily condescending teacher passing off a fatuous Paul Simon lyric as poetry worthy of study; an endorsement by NASA of the school's simulated aeronautical program.

Wiseman produced, directed, edited.

THE WILD BUNCH (U.S.). The same year as the glib, intellectually vacuous *Butch Cassidy and the Sundance Kid*, Sam Peckinpah's *The Wild Bunch* portrayed the twilight of the Hole-in-the-Wall gang. In 1969 I disparaged the film on the basis of the version that its producer had butchered, but the richly restored "director's cut" is a coherent achievement—one of the westerns (a few others being Samuel Fuller's *Forty Guns*, 1957, Howard Hawks's *Rio Bravo*, 1959, Robert Altman's *McCabe & Mrs. Miller*, 1971, Jim Jarmusch's *Dead Man*, 1995, and Michael Winterbottom's *The Claim*, 2000) to approach the greatness of John Ford's best westerns.

In 1913 Texas, a bunch of bank robbers pull off a job for which, in fact, they have been set up by their nemesis, a railroad baron. The failure of the robbery, in which they are all nearly killed, causes the younger members to question the ageing leadership of Pike Bishop once the gang reaches their Mexican hideout. Meanwhile, the baron has among the bounty hunters in his employ Deke Thornton, who used to ride with the gang—a projection of Bishop's world-weariness and self-disgust. For many reasons, the gang is falling apart and coming to an end; a harbinger of this is one of its youngest members, Angel, a Mexican Indian with revolutionist sympathies because of the brutal oppression of his people.

Peckinpah's embrace of the humanity of his lead characters combines with complex, dusky images, beautifully color cinematographed by Lucien Ballard, to achieve something like the dimming of reality into elegy. A fit of nervous applications of the zoom lens provides a few hiccups in what is otherwise a trenchant, austere vision less indebted to Ford than to John Huston. William Holden and Robert Ryan, as Bishop and Thornton, are superb, giving lived-in, concentrated, unsentimental performances.

WHY DOES HERR R. RUN AMOK? (West Germany). In this explosive, powerfully affecting film, co-scenarists, co-directors and co-editors Michael Fengler and Rainer Werner Fassbinder employ a *cinéma-vérité* style to explore the nature of bourgeois insecurity.

The R.s live in Munich. Herr R. works long hours as a technical draughtsman. At home, he has migraines, in part work-induced. The R.s seem a smooth-running family.

Only they aren't. Intensely selfconscious, the R.s perpetually feel the need to justify themselves and their existence. Herr R. is never exactly settled at work but always eyeing the promotion, and even the most minimal salary increase, just up ahead.

Fengler and Fassbinder show the extent to which, when they help their son with schoolwork, the R.s act according to how they believe they should behave. However much they love their child (and, of course, they do), nothing in the assistance the R.s provide Amadeus seems to flow spontaneously from parental affection. Everything is modeled, part of a plan. After a coffee klatch where one of Frau R.'s neighbors notes Herr R.'s rapid weight gain, Frau R. throws this up at him, her neighbor's apparent disapproval motivating her "concern" for her husband's health.

In this peculiarly unsettled film, middle-class people fill the void of their identity with the self-importance of alleged "responsibilities" and "obligations." Generally, the mundane content of the human behavior on display, which is both reinforced and probed by the application of handheld camera, stresses the dissatisfaction of the R.s beneath their consciously/unconsciously modeled façade. Eventually Herr R. implodes, creating a massive scene of violence that turns the ordinariness of everything we have witnessed inside out. We are left with the legal reportage of a criminal event, an objective series of facts for which the whole film provides an explanation rooted in the protagonist's suppressed emotions.

LE BOUCHER (France). One of Claude Chabrol's warmest, most elegantly ambiguous films, *The Butcher* seamlessly blends actors and locals in the provincial village of Trémolat. A wedding and the bride's funeral are two key fictional events largely attended by villagers, while the lead actors, in character, weave in and out of the workday world of the village.

Popaul, like his father, is the village butcher. At the wedding he meets Hélène, a poised, middle-class schoolteacher, with whom he falls secretly in love while respecting her withdrawal from sex and romance following a disastrous breakup. A serial killer is on the loose targeting women. By one of the corpses, while picnicking with her innocent young pupils, Hélène finds the cigarette lighter with which she gifted Popaul, or one just like it.

While painting her flat, Popaul discovers the lighter inside a drawer; Hélène has not turned it over to the police. Popaul "confesses" to her that he is the killer before stabbing himself, bringing her to the point that she gives him a first and last kiss.

How one interprets this series of events probably depends on whether one believes that a mere butcher, upon finding the lighter and recalling Hélène's nearly hysterical relief upon seeing it (after the murder) in his hand, could figure out what's afoot in Hélène's mind and how impossible their relationship therefore is. He *is* that intelligent. His confession is the lie he must tell to move Hélène's heart towards him. Much of the exquisite ambiguity comes from the film's veering towards Hélène's subjective view and by keeping the murders hidden from view.

Both characters are related to humanity's primitive past: Popaul, at war in Indochina; Hélène, by her enforced celibacy—a suppression of something essentially human.

Stéphane Audran and Jean Yanne are superb.

MEDEA (Italy). "I have a dim foreboding of grief." — Medea
The first half of Pier Paolo Pasolini's anthropological *Medea* contains his most brilliant work; when the part corresponding to Euripedes's tragedy kicks in, the film is less satisfying, partly due to the inadequacy of opera diva Maria Callas, whose striking poses do not add up to a performance.

But the first half! The film opens with his adoptive father, Chiron, talking to Jason, who is, first, an infant, then thirteen, then an older teenager, then grown, as the centaur continues, telling the boy the boy's family history and, ironically, contrary to the passage's continuity over time, registering a changing viewpoint, beginning with a belief in the gods and that "everything is holy," and ending in disbelief in any god's existence.

But we know the story of the Golden Fleece, and that is partly why Pasolini doesn't spoil his solitudinous vision of Medea's barbaric culture with intrusive dialogue. In an extraordinary passage, a virgin is sacrificed—a boy this time—so crops will grow. His neck broken, the boy is communally slaughtered, his blood and body parts imbibed and devoured. Haunting pans of the barren land are correlative to the primitive madness we everywhere see. The hard edge of the film's fiercely sunlit images collapses the distance between reality and ancient myth.

Medea's relationship with Jason is an instance of cultural collision. The barbaric sorceress Medea: can her marriage to civilized Jason prosper? No. He betrays her, and to punish him she murders their sons and Jason's new bride, bringing to fruition what we first see as her premonition or dream. "Nothing is possible!" she cries out at Jason.

The tenderness with which Medea tends to each of her children right before dispatching them is a highlight of the second half.

UNE FEMME DOUCE (France). In Robert Bresson's first color film, *Une femme douce*, based on Dostoievski's story "Krotkaya," Luc loses his beautiful young wife (Dominique Sanda, brilliant), who drops from their bourgeois balcony to the classless street. Indulging his complacency, Luc impresses Anna, the maid, into listening to his half-hearted flashbacking attempt to piece together the puzzle of the girl's suicide. But what of human feelings can a pawnbroker understand, one who trades daily in drops of human misery? (It's easy to be generous with *my* money, he tells his wife. "Perhaps," she counters, "but that doesn't mean you own me.") Luc is spiritually bankrupt, having missed the chance for redemption that his wife offered him. "I want to pray," he confesses, "but I can only think." He insists how she tormented him; we only see him tormenting her. Another confession: "I enjoyed our inequality."

Bresson has updated the story to the present and moved it to Paris. The "gentle wife" goes unnamed, suggesting both her husband's domineering and the girl's vacated identity. All three main characters—the wife, Luc, Anna—are anonymous in a sense; Bresson delays shooting their faces, showing instead Luc's pacing shoes, Anna's hands in prayer, and the back of the suicide's head as she lies on the blood-splattered pavement below the apartment. This last image—in sequence, actually the first—brings to a hard close the girl's descent, which is rendered in mysterious, poetic, transcendental terms. From inside the apartment we view a chair rock and a table tumble on the balcony; cut to outside, where a heavenward camera captures amidst sounds of traffic the girl's white shawl alive and floating downward, buoyed, caressed, kissed by air. It never lands.

Footsteps; doors opening and closing. Cool, wry, sad, hilarious—and erotically brushing Buñuel.

SALESMAN (U.S.). A bleak black comedy, *Salesman* follows door-to-door four Bible salesmen in their holy quest for an unholy buck. (Such laborers, capitalism's dogged foot-soldiers, have been replaced by telemarketers and by pitch-people on televised infomercials.) An example of *cinéma-vérité*, *Salesman* was shot in black and white by Albert and David Maysles and brilliantly edited by Charlotte Zwerin.

The four men—The Badger, The Rabbit, The Bull and The Gipper—have a lonely job: walking and walking through abandoned streets, often in the dark, knocking on doors, and trying to convince strangers they need what nobody needs: a fancy, expensive Bible. The target group is the devout, but this group also coincides with the less-than-affluent, in general, the working class, the lower middle class. The Badger, Paul Brennan, is the principal character, a loony sadsack of a man, who becomes an ironical reflection of those his employer is aiming for him to bilk. The circle of exploitation is complete.

Salesman is well understood, perhaps, as a coda to Alfred Hitchcock's *Psycho* (1960), cinema's preeminent study of American loneliness, financial insufficiency among the rank and file of its citizenry, and desperation. Each of the salesmen is another Norman Bates, and another one still may lurk behind each door to which they raise a fist or at which they ring a bell. Life is passing these people by, and the Bible represents the illusory possibility of some sort of an anchor, for salesman and prospective buyer alike. Otherwise, they are all drifters, even given the apparent stability of a home. Offering an implicit critique of religion's role there, the Maysles brothers have composed a devastating portrait of ordinary American life.

Films of the 1970s

With *A bout de souffle* (1959) Jean-Luc Godard gave the *nouvelle vague* its most formative practical definition and, as time has shown, made the single most influential film of all time. In the 1960s Godard came up with one brilliant work after another, including the fierce, stunning *Weekend* (1967). Expanding on the experimental nature of *Le gai savoir* (1968) and *Wind from the East* (1969), his finest achievement in the 1970s is *Numéro Deux/Essai Titres* (1975), co-written by Anne-Marie Miéville. (Some sources list Miéville as co-director; some do not.)

Numéro Deux proceeds in sections, mostly domestic vignettes, with rolling letters giving each a title—an alternate title, it turns out, for the whole piece. The film essays three generations of a family (un)settled under one roof. At the outset, two children, siblings, appear by a window, staring out. "There was a landscape," Nicolas says, "but they put a factory in it." The image cuts to Grandpa who, steeped in nostalgic socialism, touches on the horrors of The Factory's workaday reality; in a chemical factory, he notes, women's fingers are being eaten by acid. His remark sets two themes into motion: industry's disregard of workers as anything other than replaceable tools—a part of the machinery, as it were; the exploitation of women.

Both themes find a domestic application. Pierre, the children's father, home from work at The Factory, belittles Sandrine, his wife, who keeps house, raises the kids, copes with fragments of inherited radicalism, envies Pierre that he gets out of the house, and wonders aloud to her spouse why he always gets to decide when (and how) they have sex. A small domestic triumph comes when Sandrine proves capable of repairing the washing machine despite Pierre's contrary interruptions; but, overall, her sense of stasis/incompletion is summed up by the fact that she hasn't had a bowel movement in weeks. (Trust Godard to find a metaphor that gets to the nitty gritty.) Through all this runs oppositions: landscape and factory; Nature and capitalism. Everyone is damaged. Even Grandpa, whose heart is rooted in the politics of equality, marginalizes Grandma, whose own stopped-up feelings she can share only with us and the filmmakers. From Grandpa, the image returns to the grandchildren at the window. To her older brother's statement, "There was a landscape, but they put a factory in it," Vanessa, perhaps trying to emulate Nicolas, says, "There was a factory, and we put a landscape around it." Out of the mouths of babes; we *do* adjust ourselves to the unnatural, the inhuman, so that even capitalism can come to seem natural—and inevitable. Vanessa's innocent remark connects later with something Grandpa recalls: the camouflaging garden planted around a wartime weapons factory. We also hide The Factory, where we toil for others, even from ourselves. This is the only way we can make peace with the unnaturalness we are buying into.

Godard shows capitalism—ideologically, its tenets; temperamentally, its coldness and coarseness—penetrating our lives, shaping our behavior. (The Factory is the God in whose image we've been remade.) For instance, in one of their domestic vignettes Nicolas is watching a sports event on TV while his grandfather very much wants to see the Soviet film that another station is broadcasting. The boy, rude and defiant in his selfishness, very much like his father vis-à-vis Nicolas's mother, tells Grandpa, "I don't care if you're happy." Thus the way Papa gets treated at work has made its way down to how a child addresses his grandfather. Nor is that all; offscreen, Pierre further lights into Grandpa, defending his son's selfishness as he would his own: "Get your own set," he says. Grandpa, defeated, responds: "Selling price. Buying price. I have no savings." (This is probably the reason he is permitted to stay in Pierre's house.) The family has thus been reduced to the tone and dimensions—the power coordinates—of commerce. The home's new "hearth" is The Factory.

Another set of images finds, superimposed one on the other, Pierre and Sandrine having anal intercourse and Vanessa's watching it; the dominance of the two simultaneous images shifts between them back and forth. Why not use the more conventional method of crosscutting?

That way would not have so fully conveyed the child's absorption in the parental spectacle. In turn, Godard's presentation more fully conveys the spectacle's impact on Vanessa. Finally, the degree of abstraction that the superimposed images affords suggests that the spectacle that Vanessa's eyes take in belongs to a whole series of such events she has glimpsed. She indeed tells her brother, "Sometimes I think what Mama and Papa do is pretty," sufficiently piquing his curiosity (and annoyance that baby sister has seen more than he has) for Nicolas to ask their mother if he too can watch her and Papa in bed. (He isn't the independent explorer his sister is!) Sandrine replies, "Perhaps," after admitting that it sometimes hurts when Papa touches her breasts. Later, in a section ironically titled "Brotherhood," Sandrine in fact invites both children into the bedroom—not to watch their parents make love but to discuss with them parental lovemaking. She and Pierre are both naked. On one level the scene couldn't be more charming—and, for the children, instructive; and Pierre's one contribution, the remark "When it's over, Death lays a finger on our lips," touches.

But the context that the film provides unearths in Sandrine a glint of unexpected motivation. Earlier, before questioning why Pierre always gets to decide about sex, she asked him, "Should we make love tonight?" "We'll see." Sandrine's return: "Thanks, boss." Coupled with the preference of Pierre's with which their lovemaking is stamped, this suggests a (maybe unconscious) reason why Sandrine lets the children into the parental inner sanctum. For doesn't doing so give her in effect some sense of being in control of her own sexual existence, as compensation for Pierre's otherwise unyielding dominance? Moreover, her calling him "boss" is pointed; it connects their bedroom to The Factory. In turn, this interprets Pierre's "bossiness" at home as compensatory for work where he is a wage slave constantly at the beck and call of others. Thus, marvelously, the film shows how The Factory has intruded upon two very private, presumably sacrosanct areas of the couple's life: their sexual intimacy; the raising of their children. And another ominous dimension also insinuates itself; Pierre's added remark about death, intended to draw a precious line linking life and sex, finds an echo later in Grandpa's most solemn utterance: "Every night Death enters The Factory." The sum of these linkages finds The Factory emerging as institutionalized despair.

All this is typical of the film's brilliant method. Things connect; echoes accumulate; meanings emerge.

Often, the result deepens what at first may seem a chance line or image. In one vignette, Sandrine bathes Vanessa. Looking down at herself, the child asks her mother whether memory comes out of her "hole." In response to the affirmative she receives, Vanessa then asks, "Where does [memory] go?" Sandrine's answer deepens to sadness her son's opening statement, "There was a landscape, but they put a factory in it": "[Memory] vanishes into the landscape—only, there's a factory there now." Just what do we lose when memory has nowhere to go, nowhere to abide and exist? Our connection to the rest of humanity? A significant connection to ourselves? Godard—recall *Alphaville* (1965)—finds memory at the very core of our humanity; and in the shadow of The Factory, he suggests, the future capacity of children to remember their own untutored experience, in addition to what we've attempted to pass on to them as important, already is being dulled and diminished. (*Numéro Deux* seems to some a dry experience in the viewing; but when you think about the film, *remember* it, it moves you.) For Godard, capitalism opposes the very idea of humanity, the foundation of what it means to be fully human: *memory*—and the sense of continuity and interconnectedness this provides. Capitalism blots all this out, creating instead a self-referential system that boxes workers and their families into a repetitive present (see Godard's *See You at Mao*, a.k.a. *British Sounds*, and *Pravda*, both 1969), and thus cuts them off from past and future.

This film which is so full of echoes, then, is on the side of memory. It isn't driven at all by ideology. It plainly announces, in fact, "This isn't a rightest or a leftist film. . . ." Like all of

Godard, it's humane and humanistic. Godard succeeds in keeping the film both away from the abstractness of political dogma and connected to accessible human experience.

This is also a film about film and video, about the technology through which film artists are obliged to express themselves. This technology, in effect another part of The Factory, also places humanity—*humanity's* humanity—at risk. Seducing the artist towards impersonality and the dehumanization of others (the artist's human subjects; the artist's audience) as well as of oneself, this technology both assists the artist's creativity and constantly tests the artist's connectedness to others. This technology—filmmaking as process—distracts and abstracts the artist, then, facilitating his or her doing as much to fellow humans. Those familiar with Thomas Carlyle's concerns in nineteenth-century Britain regarding possible consequences from the intrusion into people's lives of technology brought about by the Industrial Revolution—his disciples, Charles Dickens and John Ruskin, registered similar prophetic warnings—will best appreciate the thoughtful and passionate tradition to which *Numéro Deux*'s anxiety belongs.

The film's masterful *mise-en-scène* manifests in order to convey this danger; technologically overloaded, it reminds us of the challenge we all face, artists and audiences alike, to keep a grip on our humanity in a world of increasing utility and gadgetry. Many of the images include a TV screen, that is, a screen-within-the-movie-screen. Moreover, numerous times one or two monitors become the medium through which information is conveyed. (If one views the film on television, therefore, it becomes a little like cut-open Chinese boxes.) Sometimes the monitors are of equal size; at other times, one is prominent, the other recessive. Sometimes the monitors are all we are given; at other times, there is aural accompaniment—a voiceover, or a natural soundtrack (bird chirps and the like). Sometimes both monitors display the same image; more often, they display different images—two perspectives of the same scene, perhaps, or two different scenes purposefully juxtaposed. (Eisenstein's dialectical montage, updated.) Slow wipes in any possible direction may be used to transition from one image to the next. Et cetera, et cetera. This highly technical *mise-en-scène* continually implies those pieces of the "film" itself that we see Godard, appearing as himself, carefully reviewing, not only to settle on a final form for *Numéro Deux/Essai Titres*, but also to grapple responsibly with these materials and their themes, and to keep them (and himself) connected to human experience. (The material, actually, wasn't filmed at all but videotaped and later transferred to 35mm film—still more of the wizardry which the artist may tap into and with which he or she must contend.)

Godard once said that the best way to criticize a film is to make a film of one's own in response. Toiling in The Factory of the commercial movie industry, François Truffaut two years earlier made *La nuit américaine* (*Day for Night*, 1973). It also showed at work a filmmaker played by the film's maker, and it drew fulsome bourgeois praise. Compare the two works, and no wonder the gulf between the two former *Cahiers du Cinema* critics and *nouvelle vague* compatriots. Whereas Godard shows the filmmaker dealing thoughtfully, searchingly with his visual material and, also, sensually with sound levels (Godard's hand on the sliding controls becomes a breathtaking erotic refrain), Truffaut instead shows the filmmaker as a director of actors, a massager of on-set egos, a reviewer of mood music—in short, a hack. The film each man made corresponds to the image of the filmmaker his film presents; and while Godard's video-within-the-film is fresh, riveting, Truffaut's film-within-the-film is even sillier and more conventional than *La nuit américaine*.

It is Sandrine who characterizes Godard's film, explaining: "This isn't a rightest or a leftist film—but a before and behind film. *Before*, there are children. *Behind*, there is the government." This identification of The Factory with government, and vice versa, implies what has come to be termed corporate fascism, that is, the consolidation of power in moneyed big business at the expense of citizenry and democratic processes—the capacity of ordinary people to direct the course of their lives and their nation's moral spirit. In this regard Godard finds in his France a parallel with Hitler's Germany, and it chills him to the bone. Sandrine's voice adds: "[Godard's is] a film you can look at. Quietly." The adverb *quietly* stakes out the humanism of the film's venture; it shows our importance as audience, the respect the filmmakers here gladly give us. Quietly. We the film's viewers aren't to be pushed, pushed around or exploited; rather, the film quietly, thoughtfully shares things with us—quite unlike the disposition of Truffaut's film, which assaults us with its aim to please and win us over, to make up for Truffaut's unhappy childhood, or the even nastier disposition of (released the same year as *Numéro Deux*) Steven Spielberg's *Jaws*, which coldly manipulates us so that the filmmaker—absent a soul, as time (and *Schindler's List*) has proven—can feel omnipotent at our expense. (Truffaut dropped to the bottom of his moral standing by appearing two years hence in a Spielberg hoax, *Close Encounters of the Third Kind*.) Godard has never made films so that he can be liked, feel powerful, use people or let himself be used by others; for him, filmmaking is neither exploitation nor self-exploitation nor therapy but, rather, using sound and image to make discoveries about the human condition and about the contribution that art can make to this. Nor will he practice sleight of art on us, his partners-in-film. We are told up front, "Images are manufactured"—a confession implying that no one's hands, certainly not *his*, are perfectly clean of The Factory's influence. As always, Godard's honesty is a bracing tonic. But this film of his isn't just proffering an antidote to a grubby kind of cinema he (hopefully with our support) despises. It's registering a different way of interacting with others than The Factory and corporate fascism embody. It is a humane, respectful, sharing way.

In sum, The Factory represents everything that institutionally attempts to subordinate humanity, separate or segregate humanity, or turn humanity against itself. Since this extends beyond manufacturing it should come as no surprise that Pierre doesn't literally work in any facet of industry. He isn't even a manual laborer. Indeed, the work he does isn't even particularly taxing. Apparently his voice possesses certain natural qualities that make it ideal for testing a new kind of microphone! The work, then, isn't hard; what's hard, what's debilitating, is the character of the work, and the marketplace and the power structure enforcing it. For the job Pierre is being paid to do is atomizing, dehumanizing and self-objectifying; a mere part of him, his voice, is continually called upon to function apart from the totality of his being. What had Pierre done before? Before teaching jobs dried up, he taught children. Not only is he now, in order to survive, forced to do something wide of what he wants to do, what indeed he has been trained to do, but this current employment of his, foolish and empty, falls gallingly short of his calling. Whereas once his job found him interacting with fellow humans and helping them, now he primarily relates to equipment; whereas his former job confirmed and enhanced his humanity, his current one divorces and alienates him from it. The "explanatory" material about the new microphone that Pierre brings home exposes his present job as ridiculous; he is the one being ridiculed by it, slowly crushed by it, when in fact he is capable of nourishing, nurturing, satisfying work.

The fact that Pierre feels diminished—*is* diminished—by his employment doesn't dissuade Sandrine from desiring work of her own outside the house. And she finds it. But she quits one job because it gives her no contact with people; and she plans to quit another—as a pharmacy clerk—because the contact it permits is fleeting and superficial. The Factory may be vast, but it lacks depth; and it's spreading. Says Grandpa: "We came from the Internationale that represented the world's proletariat . . . Now it seems Europe has opened lots of factories [elsewhere] because of the cheap labor." What does this mean for us? Those who toil in The Factory—and, in one way or another, most of us must—accrue no value from either our effort or our sacrifice; we're all as replaceable as machine parts. And when we *are* replaced, the web of exploitation only widens simply to reduce The Factory's expenses and thereby enlarge, cancerously, its profits. It's all impersonal, mechanical, inhuman.

Sandrine—wonderfully played by Sandrine Battistella (the nonprofessional cast lend their first names to their characters)—at the last speaks of Godard. Is it scripted? I don't know. But what Sandrine says corresponds to Godard's own need to keep at himself (like the rest of us) to retain his humanity in the face of The Factory that would divest him of it. However, her remarks also ironically reflect on the yet lower status of theirs that finds women yearning to attain, in The Factory, even the low, debased level that their male counterparts, however tenuously, have already attained. Here are some of her words: "Suddenly [the film's] over. Something happens. My role ends. What are we playing at? [Godard] interprets me, but he shouldn't . . . , Always men like him say: 'Wash the dishes . . . , Go on strike . . . , Come fuck . . . , Go on vacation . . . , And him in my place, working. . . , Letting others tell you things about yourself is a crime. . . .'"

Powerful. Perhaps Sandrine would like to make her own film; if so, she should be able to. She should be able to respond, in film, to *Numéro Deux* just as Godard was able to respond to *La nuit américaine*. But will The Factory allow it? Collaborators on this film, though, Sandrine and Jean-Luc are on the same side, the side of memory; but The Factory wants to get them both, to turn one against the other, person against person, group against group. This isn't paranoia; it's Western history since the Industrial Revolution. Until she does make her own film, if she wants to, however, Sandrine is here for us to see and listen to. And this moves Godard, one of the world's greatest artists, his soul perpetually humbled by the burden of being human, by his sense of responsibility to *stay* human. The film's final image shines— and pierces: Godard seated, his head, in his hands, bowed.

The list:

1970

IL CONFORMISTI (Italy, France). The quality of Bertolucci's films is all over the map, but it is universally agreed that, from Alberto Moravia, *The Conformist*, about Fascism's ghosts, is exceptionally beautiful.

For many of us, when we were in graduate school or college, *The Conformist* was *the* film to see. When two glamorous young women danced together in a working-class dance hall, incongruity deliciously compounding incongruity, a heady intoxicant of perversity overtook our senses. *The Conformist* has remained one of the films of our dreams.

Mild-mannered Marcello Clerici's mania to appear "normal" and to disappear into the crowd drives him into an ill-suiting marriage and into becoming a Fascist assigned to assassinate a former professor of his, an antifascist activist. The film begins in the 1930s and ends after the war, by which time Clerici appears to embody Italy's determination to deny its political past.

The Conformist dazzles with its bits and pieces juggling the present and different degrees of the past. Vittorio Storaro's color cinematography—at a level of achievement beyond what he contributed to the films that account for his three Oscars—deepens the impression that everything in the film is haunted by memory. Italy's past is flypaper; but in the disposition of the Clericis' marriage at the last Bertolucci also summons echoes of John Ford's *The Man Who Shot Liberty Valance* (1962).

Bertolucci is famous for eliciting superlative performances: Adriana Asti, *Before the Revolution* (1963); Marlon Brando, *Last Tango in Paris* (1972); Ugo Tognazzi and Anouk Aimée, *Tragedy of a Ridiculous Man* (1981); John Lone, *The Last Emperor* (1987); Keanu Reeves, *Little Buddha* (1993). On this occasion, with Jean-Louis Trintignant, Dominique Sanda and Stefania Sandrelli, however, Bertolucci broke the bank. *The Conformist* may be the most brilliantly acted movie ever made.

1970

THE DECAMERON (Italy). Pier Paolo Pasolini's episodic masterpiece springboards off Boccaccio's crammed 14th-century text to reflect on modern times.

Shamelessly wealthy Andreuccio is tricked by thieves into an archbishop's sepulchre to hand up costly garments, presuming his cohorts will share with him; but they lock him inside with the corpse. But who is the biggest thief? The Church, whose fabulous wealth comes at the expense of feeding the poor. Doesn't the Church *know* the tomb will be robbed? This letting the poor think they're getting away with something helps maintain Church authority. Similarly, by controlling the distribution of wealth, capitalism sets workers to low wages, the constant threat of unemployment, hence starvation, keeping them in tow. Again, redress waits upon some egalitarian afterlife.

Pretending to be a deaf mute, a poor boy becomes the gardener at a convent, happily servicing the sisters' long-suppressed sexual needs until his cock is worn to a frazzle. Masetto cuts off sex with Mother Superior and tries negotiating a more humane arrangement. Upon his hearing and speaking, Top Nun proclaims a miracle. "Independent" at the convent's whim, Masetto is reduced to being Church property, as indeed workers in factories and businesses become owners' property.

When Elisabetta's three brothers, wealthy merchants we never see do a stitch of work, discover that she and Lorenzo, a hardworking Sicilian laborer, are lovers, they murder Lorenzo. She severs his head and plants it in a pot of basil in her bed chamber.

A master artist surveys the gorgeous work he and his crew have wrought in a cathedral. He muses: "Why create a work of art when dreaming about it is so much sweeter?" *To reach out; to share something of the dream with others.* Pasolini's delight at doing this counters the religious hypocrisy and capitalistic mean-spiritedness his *Decameron* condemns.

BEWARE OF A HOLY WHORE (West Germany, Italy). The "whore" is Hollywood. Rainer Werner Fassbinder's *Warnung vor einer heiligen Nutte* is one of the best movies about the making of a movie. Or about *not* making a movie, since cast and crew are gathered at a Spanish hotel awaiting the arrival of the director, a script, and money from Munich so that they can all begin work on a gangster film starring Eddie Constantine, no less. Some couple uncouples; some chat; some get on each other's nerves.

The protagonist is Jeff, the director. A yelling egotist and face-slapping bully, Jeff occasions Fassbinder's witheringly funny self-parody. To compound the comedy, Fassbinder himself plays Jeff's assistant. Both characters are remarkably self-contained and ungiving. Lou Castel is superb as Jeff. Born Ulv Quarzéll, in Bogotá, Colombia, Castel is the great star of Marco Bellocchio's *Fists in the Pocket* (1965) and Philippe Garrel's *The Birth of Love* (1993).

Formally, the film is very beautiful. Achieving the tenor of a generalization and an artistic credo, a panning shot of the hotel lobby patiently surveys a vacancy of space before stopping on Jeff engaged in conversation. But the shot's poignancy derives from the fact that its populated destination cannot overturn the loneliness of the transport. The camera moves to what only seems resolution. Fassbinder's cinema is one of intense emotion—and of little hope for humanity's lot.

Fassbinder's characters connect without bonding. François Truffaut, in *Day for Night* (1973), emphasizes his love of movie-making; Fassbinder, his accuracy and integrity, as Jeff explains to a cameraman the shot he has in mind to film the next morning. Although one approaches a genre piece with caution, one could sit through what Jeff has up his artistic sleeve. This is not the case with *Meet Pamela*, the film-within-the-film in *Day for Night*.

DÔDESUKADEN (Japan). Shugoro Yamamoto's *The Town Without Seasons* includes the stories upon which Akira Kurosawa drew for *Dôdesukaden*, one of his most trenchant and haunting achievements. The film, Kurosawa's first in color, is set in a Tokyo slum. The title is a word that Yamamoto coined; it is the sound of the imaginary streetcar that a feeble-minded boy, Rokkuchan, repeats over and over as he trots and shuffles along, circumventing piles of garbage, going through the motions throughout the area of being the car's conductor. Thus Rokkuchan copes with both his limitations, mental and socioeconomic, in the same way: by imagining himself beyond them. This makes life bearable; at least he can pretend—and *believe*—that he is a productive worker, and in a respectable position. Otherwise, all that sustains him and his careworn mother, with whom he lives, are their Buddhist prayers—another version of his trolley-chant!

An antecedent to this film is Kurosawa's *The Lower Depths* (1957), from Gorky's play. *Dôdesukaden* also weaves a tapestry of assorted impoverished human lives. Imagination ameliorates the trauma of poverty for Rokkuchan but falls against hard limits for others. The imaginary dream-house that a beggar builds for his son, with the boy's own input, cannot protect the child from painful illness and death. Ocho's single lapse of infidelity, more an imaginative leap out of the poverty with which she identifies her marriage than out of the marriage itself, becomes unforgiveable to Hei; he also is striking out at her as a way of striking out at his status and struggles. He is consumed with anger; she, with guilt—and her trek when, tossed out by Hei, she wanders off amidst a bleak landscape signals imagination's suicidal end.

The final shot is heart-piercing: pictures of trolleys adorning the walls of Rokkuchan's hut. Hopes, dreams, delusions.

THE CLOWNS (Italy, France, West Germany). *I clowns*, we've been told, is "minor Fellini." Perhaps; however, it is a minor masterpiece. Made for Italian television, with additional support from France and West Germany, Federico Fellini's phantasmagoric celebration of circus clowns provides, also, a valedictory for them. At the last, the death of a clown signals the loss of childhood, which signals the "last end" for which life prepares all of us "clowns."

A boy wakes up in the wee hours at noise outside his bedroom window in Rimini; the big tent is being raised, for the circus has rolled into town. A haunting camera adopting young Fellini's point of view enters the dark, sheltered domain of the tent. Someone smiles at the boy—at us, too, for we've entered the tent along with young Fellini. Seamlessly, this hours-early event is transformed into that evening's performance. A midget-clown annoys a big clown, who plants an ax in his noggin: the circus as waking nightmare, the little clown an encapsulation of Anychild's vulnerability, fears. (We're reminded of childlike Gelsomina, strongman Zampanò's "clown"-companion in Fellini's *La strada*, 1954.) Flash to the present: dressed in a gray suit punctuated by a mortally red tie, the adult Fellini plans a documentary to answer this question: What has happened to the great clowns? The pseudo-documentary that follows introduces us to the different historic types of clowns and to actual reminiscing clowns. It dramatizes Fellini's—and *our*—denial of childhood through serious inquiry, research, documentation. Yet it draws us close to what we have lost.

A clown, vanished, is presumably dead. His companion-clown trumpets the wistful tune that the other clown used to play, to summon him. Dressed in black, the missing clown appears to take the white-dressed clown with him: the end that either was born for.

VLADIMIR AND ROSA (France). ". . . . all those people locked up in that factory-prison all day long. . . . well, they're *people*."

Vladimir et Rosa is a film about the making of a film—by Vladimir Lenin and Karl Rosa, played by the filmmakers, Jean-Luc Godard and Jean-Pierre Gorin—about the Chicago Eight trial. (Eight became seven when Bobby Seale, disruptive and black, was separated out and sentenced to four years' imprisonment for contempt of court.) Following massive protests at the 1968 Democratic National Convention against U.S. involvement in Vietnam, the defendants were charged with conspiracy and with crossing state lines with the intent to incite a riot. They were found guilty of the second and lesser charges. This film predated the defendants' largely successful appeal.

Chronology of World Cinema

1970

It "[talks] about the rain before the clouds gather." The Seale-character has a gun pointed at his head by a hand that his own hand is chained to. His back is up against a wall; the gun's shadow is on the wall. Now *two* guns are each pointed at an opposite side of his head. Shadow has become substance, completing the metaphor by clarifying the political reality that informs the metaphor!

"Godard and Gorin as performers," according to Godard biographer Richard Brody, "suggest new forms of political cinema: the two men walk side by side on a tennis court, on opposite sides of the net . . . They are wearing headphones, which are connected to the tape recorder that Gorin is carrying as Godard points a microphone at whichever one is speaking: the momentary tape delay with which they hear themselves, a sort of feedback, impedes their ability to speak clearly."

His "dishonor" Judge Himmler hilariously stands in for Julius Hoffman. Signed by Groupe Dziga Vertov, this probing film ends powerfully with a call to unite for equality and justice.

PERFORMANCE (UK). James Fox gives a scalding, brilliant performance as Chas, a vicious East London enforcer hiding in a faded rock star's mansion following a killing that his boss had warned him *not* to commit, in Donald Cammell and Nicolas Roeg's *Performance*. Chas becomes unexpectedly helpless as he more deeply enters the drugged, delirious, androgynous realm of Turner, the rock star (Mick Jagger, okay—and riveting when he sings). Each young man is forced to confront subconscious elements of personality that test his survival. The experience proved discombobulating for Fox, who left acting and fled into religious retreat for nearly a decade before (thank God!) regaining his sanity and resuming his career.

"I know who I am," Chas tells Harry, his boss. But, like the rest of us, he only *thinks* he does. Before being picked up and escorted to his finish, Chas is drawn into a transformation of himself—including wig, costume, makeup—that blurs the distinction between him and Turner, and between him and others—females—in Turner's house. Chas's face becomes Turner's; a small hand mirror attaches a woman's breast to Chas's naked chest. Indeed, this is a film full of mirrors and reflections off glass. Fleeting confirmations of identity ironically underscore the vast terrain of human mystery always gaping below one's idea of oneself. At a point when he still believes he may elude mob capture and death, Chas, masquerading as a juggler, pleads with Turner to rent him the basement room: "I'm determined to fit in. I've *got* to fit in, Mr. Turner." (Cammell wrote the script.) But this will not be possible based on who he "knows" himself to be.

This kaleidoscopic film suggests the piecing together of a puzzling identity—and the disintegration into chaos of Chas's preëxistent role.

TOKYO SENSO SENGO HIWA (Japan). Dazzlingly directed by Nagisa Oshima, *Tokyo senso sengo hiwa*—called in the States *The Man Who Left His Will on Film*—revolves around Motoki, a member of a cell of young activists who document by filming public protests and official abuse. In its fated, circular narrative domain, the film opens on a day of demonstrations with Motoki armed with the group's camera, which is apparently taken from him by someone else after a considerable tussle, only to be used for the purpose of filming "landscapes" irrelevant to any political events just prior to the confiscator's leaping from a rooftop to his death. Motoki has been observing this opponent; when he tries reappropriating the miraculously undamaged camera, however, the police intervene, appropriating it as "evidence," and (offscreen) beating him up. The condition of the presumed "suicide" seems to be in doubt, with Motoki sometimes believing he is in pursuit of this nemesis, catching quick glimpses of him throughout Tokyo streets. (Other times, Motoki insists, the man doesn't exist.) Yasuko, the other's former girlfriend, is now *Motoki's* girlfriend. At the last, we learn that Motoki and the suicide are indeed one and the same soul—a heart-piercing moment. Their quarrel, then, was always within Motoki and pertained, at least partly, to the best uses of film, the best way to contribute to Japan's postwar development.

Oshima moves his camera through a dynamic variety of perspectives; its mode shifts between objective and subjective. In the latter category is cinema's most powerful depiction of rape, in the back seat of a moving car, with Motoki closely observing as Yasuko, the victim, is "numbing out" on the "landscapes" whipping past the car window. Yasuko also imagines the highway transport upside down. Yasuko contemplates suicide; partly, Motoki's suicide is responsive.

THE AMERICAN SOLDIER (West Germany). Concluding writer-director Rainer Werner Fassbinder's early gangster trilogy, *Der amerikanische Soldat* is a near-masterpiece whose continual reference point is Jean-Luc Godard's *Alphaville* (1965). Likewise in gorgeous black and white, Fassbinder's film creates a *noir*ish landscape; although its Munich necessarily fails to be as romantic as otherworldly Alphaville, a futuristic Paris-and-beyond, it, too, is a place of dark, semi-delirious dreams. Ricky, its protagonist, has a German mother, an American father; after serving in Vietnam, he has come for a visit. Hired as an assassin by three cops, he continues doing what the U.S. military trained him to do. One of his hits, at point-blank range, is the woman in his arms: a stunning *hommage* to Billy Wilder's *Double Indemnity* (1944).

Ricky briefly visits his mother and infantile younger brother, whose homosexual infatuation he brushes aside—*again*, the feeling is. But we can see, even if Ricky cannot, that Ricky perpetually denies his own rigidly suppressed gayness as he cuts a ridiculously exaggerated heterosexual figure. With Ricky, misogyny could be either the odd element "in" or "out," the behavior either insisting upon or contesting his heterosexuality.

The final shot is brilliant. Ricky is shot to death at a train station when the unexpected appearance of Ricky's mother and brother, to say goodbye, distracts him, giving his two captives a chance to turn tables. In hilariously, painfully protracted slow motion, Ricky falls, whereupon—the slow motion continues—his brother descends upon Ricky's corpse with a brace of embraces. Because Ricky's mother remains absolutely still in the background of the shot (visually, her son's death has frozen the life out of her), the slow motion possesses the illusion of belonging, being *intrinsic*, to the action to which it was subsequently applied.

Time, it appears, has the last image.

CLAIRE'S KNEE (France). The crisis for a man of turning forty is the theme of writer-director Eric Rohmer's *Le genou de Claire*, an elegant, richly ironical comedy, the fifth in his series of "moral tales." Rohmer himself had just turned fifty.

Jérôme (Jean-Claude Brialy, brilliant) is a French foreign diplomat, just weeks before his wedding, alone on holiday in the countryside near Lake Annency. There he runs into an old friend, a writer also on holiday. In an effort to break through writer's block, Aurora (writer Aurora Cornu, sophisticated and sexy) concocts with Jérôme an amusing episode for him to act out: a gentle flirtation with teenaged Laura (Béatrice Romand, smashing). Jérôme and Laura do become friends, but romance between them fizzles. Jérôme, however, pursues a sudden attraction for Laura's pretty half-sister, Claire, the epitome of promising adolescence on the verge of dull womanhood. Agreeing with Aurora that his pursuit must be chaste for the "story" to be interesting, Jérôme becomes obligingly fixated on the girl's knee, which in order to caress he is determined to find, or contrive, a fitting occasion.

Early on, the camera, at this point subjective with Jérôme, catches sight of someone else's hand on Claire's knee: that of boyfriend Gilles. How dare this boy possess the youth Jérôme not so distantly remembers! Jérôme's innocent "pursuit" of Claire, then, aims at replacing Gilles's hand on her knee with his own in an attempt to reclaim his own lost youth.

Rohmer uses Nestor Almendros's color cinematography to underscore the extent to which self-involved Jérôme does not quite fit into these beauteous surroundings of his youth. We also glean that Jérôme's upcoming marriage has been unduly pressured by his mid-life crisis.

Louis Delluc prize; top prize, French critics; in the U.S., best film, National Society of Film Critics.

ICE (U.S.). Writer-director Robert Kramer's futuristic Orwellian *Ice* refers to the present. The "Old Left" was bugabooed by the disastrous Spanish Civil War and buoyed by the example of the Soviet Union—until Czechoslovakia 1968, the final straw that eliminated Stalin as the explanation of all things bad there. The "New Left," bugabooed by the Soviet Union, was buoyed by the example of Cuba and those independent African nations liberated from colonialism. *Ice* wittily shows a battery-operated "Empire" descending upon the Third World prior to a shot of actual Third Worlders raising their hands in political victory. But weighing against this image are numerous references to the oppression of African Americans in urban U.S. ghettoes.

New Leftist Kramer envisions his own castration by the state. His 16mm film, shot like *cinéma-vérité*, propagandizes for "interactive collaboration," the forging of a national revolutionary effort from regional political activities. Its focus is a New York City cell that looks ahead to a national spring offensive. Currently, it is rife with internal arguments.

Much comes up in this nuts-and-bolts portrait. For instance, the government controls the media, characterizing the results of the organization's activism—an industrial fire, for example—as something *non*-political. National revolutionary activity must seem meaningless, unconnected.

Remarkably, Kramer shows inequities in the organization and its "puppet-like," "unfeeling" aspects—the cost of its necessary divorce from Soviet mythology. This film is blissfully bereft of self-pity and paranoia.

After the spring offensive, there is an official retaliation, and the film becomes discontinuous—form expressing content. Kramer plunges us into political discussions without providing an establishing context. In the absence of such cues, we have to listen hard and sit tight.

Ice visually reverses Pudovkin's *Mother* (1926) while corroborating it: "Ideas [are] not your own ideas but [are] part of the movement of things."

THE GARDEN OF THE FINZI-CONTINIS (Italy). "I am happy I made [this film] because it brought me back to my old noble intentions . . . All my good films . . . made nothing. Only my bad films made money. Money has been my ruin."

Vittorio De Sica's *Il giardino dei Finzi Contini* is based on Giorgio Bassani's 1962 autobiographical novel. Bassani escaped Italy in time to avoid the fate of other Italian Jews who were rounded up by Germans in 1943.

In 1938, Italy's "race laws" barred Jews from public schools and libraries. Jewish life and death no longer existed in the eyes of the law; Jewish obituaries were prohibited. In Ferrara, Giorgio was a bourgeois boy in love with Michol, a member of a wealthy, aristocratic family that lived behind a great wall, which couldn't finally protect it from the tumultuous history unfolding outside. Too attached to a family mystique, Michol doesn't reciprocate Giorgio's love. For Giorgio, love between them was always doomed because Michol and six million other Jews were doomed. There is no recollective narration; rather, the whole film is saturated with a sense of Giorgio's memory, and this memory has made Michol prescient of what was to happen to so many.

The two Jewish families live in different worlds; Giorgio's father even questions the Jewishness of the Finzi-Continis. Others make no such distinction, consigning members of both families to the same assemblage, the same fate of deportation. The film ends with an overwhelming sense of a single Jewry.

The soft, airy, gorgeous images of this eternally sad film dissolve into a haze of sunlight—conjured memories of the nation's past too shameful, too tragic, to bring into sharper focus lest they prove unbearable. They achieve an elegiac tone, the visual equivalent of a distant tolling bell.

1971

MEXICO: THE FROZEN REVOLUTION (Argentina). Raymundo Gleyzer's pulsating, deeply moving *México, la revolución congelada* is a brilliant documentary about the "stillborn" 1910 Revolution that failed to bring economic and social justice to Mexico, but, rather, maintained the desperate poverty and hunger of the country's indigenous peasants. Gleyzer, 34, was kidnapped and murdered by Argentina's ruling military five years after this film. (His films are usually about Argentina.) Gleyzer won for it a special prize at Locarno for Third World production.

The film combines historical documentation, consisting of voiceover and old photographs and newsreel footage in sepia or black and white, as well as footage from the Tlatelolco Massacre in Mexico City during the 1968 Summer Olympics, which claimed 400 lives, many of them students, and freshly shot material in color. The latter includes material from the 1970 presidential campaign—at least I think at least some of it is fresh—and interviews with rural peasants, for instance, Mayans.

The materials are dazzlingly assembled; the result, trenchant. Gleyzer explores the reasons for the Revolution's failure, its departure from socialist principles, its co-option by reactionary forces, including middle-class business, and so forth, and the effect of all this on the lives of actual people. At the outset of the Revolution, 1% of Mexicans owned 97% of Mexico's land; nominal ownership expanded to about 50%, wherein persisting feudalism kept crops that these "owners" raised, on the land that they worked, nearly entirely out of their hands and their children's mouths, prompting their further victimization by usurious lenders. All this also entailed the collaboration of Mexico's exploitational neighbor to the north.

The nobility of starving Mayans is apparent in their faces, their willingness to work, their love of family—and their great ancestral stone carvings, which this peerless film also encompasses.

LOVE (Hungary). It is a cold, wet spring in Budapest. Luca (Mari Törőcsik, astounding), a schoolteacher, loses her job and is assigned apartment co-tenants; her husband, János (Iván Darvas, unshakably moving), is the cause. He is in prison over politics. Meanwhile, János's old, bedridden, ill mother (Lili Darvas, Ferenc Molnár's widow) believes that her son is in the United States making a film. The woman's servant, Irén, has joined Luca in spinning this compassionate web of protection from the truth. Luca even writes letters to her mother-in-law that are presumably from János. What harm? The old woman, who has already lost another son (to war), will not live to see her János again.

Written by Péter Bacsó from a novel by Tibor Déry, *Szerelem* is a work of poetry and great humanity. Witty and spirited, Luca has a complex relationship with her mother-in-law, whom she visits every day, with flowers. Her own problems she keeps to herself, not even burdening Irén. She wonders whether her husband is alive. The lies with which she comforts her mother-in-law, who possibly knows more than she is letting on, help Luca keep her husband's spirit alive and cope with loneliness and her sense of hopelessness.

The filmmaker is Károly Makk. His black-and-white film revolves around Luca's reality and her mother-in-law's difficult present, which is infiltrated by slivers of memory, including of her very long-ago past, and imaginings. The film's rhythm and events do not conform to time; one scene to the next can represent, well, who knows? A week, a month. In this way Makk is able to convey both certain routines and uncertainty, fear, unpredictability. A glimpsed bench later reappears as a memory—or was it a memory in the first place? Bits of film create a haunting mosaic of gray existence.

BLAISE PASCALE (Italy, France). "[Pascal] was a very boring man, who never made love in his life." — Roberto Rossellini

One of the most beautiful of Roberto Rossellini's unsentimental, highly analytic, deeply

1971

moving present-tense histories, *Blaise Pascal* examines seventeenth-century Europe from the perspective of a scientist, philosopher and mathematician who helped change the world by advancing the cause of reason. Among his many accomplishments, Pascal invented the mechanical adding machine.

The film begins matter-of-factly, in the middle of a conversation in the street, and ends on the threshold of eternity. Pascal's painfully difficult life ended before he was forty.

The first movement is extraordinary. Pascal is a young man under the wing of his father, a Parisian official. Pascal's father is dedicated to reason. He is one of the judges at the trial of a maidservant who has been accused of witchcraft. Stubborn, she would not confess to her pact with Satan until her legs were broken; she is in court on a stretcher. Badgered, she declares, "I'll confess to everything," meaning, whatever charge is leveled against her. Her wish now is to be burned so that she might reclaim her soul. Rossellini's method enables us—in my case, for the first time—to penetrate a facet of the establishment mindset from the inside, as well as be objective; we get to see irrationality as it is most rationally pursued—by men, that is, who cannot imagine their own irrationality. Pascal, who is sitting in, remarks to his father afterwards he is bewildered by what he saw in the courtroom.

Pascal's life is consumed by his struggle to know God. But *how?* "To penetrate infinity," he tells Descartes, "we need a multitude of methods." Subtly, mystically lit, Pascal's death scene intimates Rossellini's, if not God's, mercy across time—a sober, stunning, luminous passage.

LAND OF SILENCE AND DARKNESS (West Germany). Fini Straubinger has been deaf and blind, the result of a fall, since her teens. She is the principal subject of Werner Herzog's documentary *Land des Schweigens und der Dunkelheit*.

Film began as an artless visual recording device. A camera captured human activities in the range of its sight. As soon as the documentary became an art form, however, it invited carps and quarrels regarding its purity. Documentarians staged events, blending non-fiction and fiction, objectivity and subjectivity. Herzog wrote some of the lines that interviewees, including Straubinger, speak. Horrors! What else might such a control-freak do? Direct a film for which the actors have been hypnotized? (Herzog, in fact, did this: *Heart of Glass*, 1976.)

Documentary and non-documentary are not separate and distinct categories, but, rather, opposite poles on a single continuum of represented reality. Herzog's camera is smart, not dumb; as artist, Herzog participates in whatever we see in his films. Like *Fata Morgana* (1969), *Land of Silence and Darkness* is drawn to an extreme of human existence. It is about the terrible isolation that deafness-blindness imposes and about Straubinger's attempt to help others like herself. She overcomes her sense of isolation by helping others overcome theirs. This glorious film moves us to measure our own participation in the human community.

Four passages: Fini's and a companion's childlike delight during their first air flight; feeling Nature's textures at a botanical garden; representing the League of the Blind, Fini greets a stranger, "Hello, my sister of destiny!" and tries communicating with her; a trip to the zoo, during which a monkey reaches out and pulls open the gate of the camera—a (staged?) metaphor for Fini's risky barrier-crashing in her world and between hers and ours, with all its sights and sounds.

IN THE NAME OF THE FATHER (Italy). Surpassing Jean Vigo's *Zéro de conduite* (1933), Henri-Georges Clouzot's *Les diaboliques* (1954) and Lindsay Anderson's *If....* (1968), the other titans of boys' boarding school films, *Nel nome del padre* is also Marco Bellocchio's most savage and caustic work, one eviscerating both the bourgeois institution of the Italian college and the Church that runs it. The film is an assault on patriarchy and paternalism, which proceed from the father's being the family head, which proceeds from God the Father's being the most authoritative member of the Holy Trinity. The film also assaults Fascism, the political translation of the nation's paternalism.

If the film is Buñuelian in content, it is also so in form: a black comedy in which human experience is heightened to the nearly surreal, and interwoven into whose fabric are flights of the fully surreal. The school morality play whose staging is usurped by the most rebellious among the students, who lend to it its bizarre tone, exemplifies fantasy's invasion of reality. Variously fantastic images of the Madonna also contribute to Bellocchio's form and style while at the same time suggesting the distorted images of women with which a patriarchic society is likely to become obsessed. Fascism, with its military trappings, exemplifies political fantasy's invasion of reality. For all the wildness of its presentation, Bellocchio has wrought an intellectually coherent work.

The Jesuit-run school at its center is no place any boy would want to be—a point hilariously underscored by the film's opening, in which a father and son assault each other as the former drags the latter to the school to enroll him. The pupils, then, have already chafed at authority. But the film's anarchic spirit contests such an outcome as beating them back into line.

THE TRAIN ROLLS ON (France). Perhaps Chris Marker's masterpiece, *Le train en marche* has three distinct parts—an unwieldy structure for a half-hour film. The film opens and closes with a silent train in motion, but this Cocteauan sandwiching only underscores the film's split quality. This "splitness," however, serves Marker's overarching theme.

The first part is the most identifiably Markerian, a tone poem haunted by hypnotic voiceover: "Soon after October [the 1917 Revolution] the trains begin to roll, and through the trains surges the blood of the Revolution.... Through the trains the voice of Lenin was heard across the Soviet Union as far as the republics of Asia, where young Communists were bringing literacy to women in shackles."

Archival materials also dominate the second part, which refers to the 1930s. A different voice introduces Aleksandr Medvedkin's CineTrain, by which "cinema was to become something created out of contact with the people."

When the film flashes forward by forty years, Medvedkin speaks directly to us, recalling the CineTrain's traveling film studio. The object was to "film our people, show these films to our people, and thereby help them construct a new world." Faults at a steel works, for example, were shown so that workers themselves could devise a plan to correct these.

Medvedkin now is old. (Of the CineTrain's 32-member crew, only eight are still alive in 1971.) Not a single shot from the films remains. The Soviet Union, tarnished by Stalinism at home, Hungary and Czechoslovakia in the fifties and sixties, no longer encapsulates the world's hope. Now, nothing does.

But, like the peasant in Medvedkin's satirical *Happiness* (1934), one must persevere to come close to happiness. "The biggest mistake would be to believe," Marker says, "that [the train of revolution, of history] had come to a halt."

LA RÉGION CENTRALE (Canada). With the help of technician Pierre Abbeloos, Canadian filmmaker Michael Snow mounted a camera on a programmable mechanical arm and set it on a plateau in winter in the wilderness somewhere in Quebec. Some have theorized about Snow's eliminating the human eye from the experience of filmmaking, but Snow himself has suggested instead its simulated replacement. What we see, in effect, are images as an alien might process and transmit them back to Mars or wherever. Here we have, if you will, an original filmmaker.

The camera turns in every direction; there are complete rotations. The opening movement, recording stones on the ground, seems perfectly objective. However, increased camera speeds later on, as well as literally fantastic imagery (the camera seemingly moves from ground to sky and back to ground in a single one-directional move), suggests the emotions attached to whatever "eye" is taking in the strange environment. Several upward movements away from the Earth might be interpreted as homesickness, a longing to get out, yet at the same time later shots of the landscape seem more conventional, less sporadic, atomic and impressionistic, and more integrated and familiar. One might take the experience of Snow's "alien" from another world as a metaphor for the human process of being born into a new environment, to which one must adjust and where one must assimilate. One's odd perceptions coalesce into the place one calls home.

This is a long, slow, mesmerizing and deeply moving film—except for blips and electronic sounds synchronized with the awesome images, a silent one. It is a dream of the dream that we call reality, and a reminder of how we constantly work to bring new, jarring perceptions into the domain of the familiar.

I process images, therefore I am.

THE WORKING CLASS GOES TO HEAVEN (Italy). "A man has a right to know what he is doing, what use he is."

"Use" and "use": the contribution one makes to society through work, or the use to which one is made through institutional exploitation—in other words, how one is used.

Ludovico Massa, nicknamed Lulù the Tool, operates a lathe in a factory. He is a thorn in the side of co-workers because he is so damned efficient. He sets the inhuman standard by which others are fined for failing to keep pace. He is most at home in the grinding monotony of his work. He has become a machine.

Recalling Fritz Lang's *Metropolis* (1927), a shot of workers factory-bound suggests the perspective that Lulù, captivated by his labor, lacks. The appeals by Communists for workplace justice fall, in his case, on deaf ears. Then one day a workplace accident costs him an index finger, and the loss of this displaced cock, in which his sense of manhood is bound up, sets the stage for an even more unmanning blow: Lulù is laid off. The one-time tool of capitalists becomes the tool of Communists.

Writer-director Elio Petri (Ugo Pirro co-authored the script), himself a Marxist, shares in the critique of industrial capitalism; but the point of his satirical comedy lies elsewhere. Petri is targeting institutions—as he did in *We Still Kill the Old Way* (Mafia, the Church; 1967) and *Investigation of a Citizen Above Suspicion* (the police; 1970). Lulù's absurd switch of allegiance underscores his continuing status of being owned—by this group or that, one ideology or another. Lulù remains locked up, albeit in a different institution—like his friend, Militina, whose experience in the military, another gripping institution, has resulted in his confinement in a mental institution.

THE GOALIE'S ANXIETY AT THE PENALTY KICK (West Germany, Austria). *Anxiety* doesn't measure up to *angst*. West Germany's Wim Wenders' first feature is more existential than psychological. The kick the distracted goalkeeper, Josef Bloch, lets through in a soccer match gets him benched after he protests the call. His sense of ordinary reality threatens Josef's sense of being, which demands he see himself as hero. In town, he picks up different women on two consecutive nights. He is mugged in the street before spending the night with the second of these. Violence has become accessible for Josef B.—an omnipresent possibility. In the morning, after she playfully mock-strangles him, he strangles the woman, seemingly out of the blue, and takes off. The film follows him to a provincial town, where he visits a single mother he knows and blends in with residents, occasionally pausing to keep current on the police search for the killer. A more imminent search is also under way; a mute child has been missing for days.

Based on Austrian-born Peter Handkë's novella, the script is by two former seminarians: Handkë and Wenders. The film, a crystal-clear, unfathomable meditation on visible life and hidden dreams, weighs the consequences for humanity of a world unstructured by faith, in which self-involvement struggles to fill the void with meaning and purpose. The monotonous, insistent chords of Jürgen Knieper's musical theme encapsulate the forces arrayed against our secret, futile dreams of heroism, and the filthy American coins in Josef's pocket, a legacy of his team's tour of the States, suggest the assault on the human spirit leveled by the voracious appetite of American wealth, culture and influence.

Die Angst des Tormanns beim Elfmeter comes as close as any film can to being essential for understanding a segment of the world at a particular time.

THE CEREMONY (Japan). Masuo's flashbacks and present-time experiences allow us to view the fortunes of the Sakurada family, to which Masuo belongs, and all this in turn reflects on postwar Japanese history: such is the ambitious intent of Nagisa Oshima's *Gishiki*. It is a convoluted and, in its tenor, a nearly subterranean film, one that in fact ends in the brief, fleeting present-time coda to one of Masuo's childhood flashbacks—to a baseball game he sees but can no longer enter: a cousin to the elusive tennis match with which Antonioni ended *Blowup* (1966). The shards and fragments of memory that sadly drift somewhere within Masuo's tormented soul—one of these is a family suicide that may have been a family murder—mask a life of losses and humiliations, and collisions with the patriarchal power, the spirit of Japan's past long before Masuo's birth, that his grandfather, Kazuomi, continued and represented, testing the capacity of Masuo and his generation to liberate Japan from this past.

The color schemes of both interiors and even exteriors suggest entombment. The film mainly proceeds through a series of family weddings and funerals; but these are ghostly, pale events. (It is Grandfather's death, leading to his funeral, that sets the plot in motion.) The ghoulish wedding in Luchino Visconti's *The Damned* (1968) is done one better by Masuo's "brideless" wedding in *Gishiki*, where the bride, whom Masuo has not met, pleading appendicitis, declines to show up, but Grandfather, committed to form and ritual above all else, as a means of exercising and securing his own power, insists that the ceremony continue. Masuo feels the perfect fool at the altar—although he does intriguingly improvise on his brideless wedding night.

Kenzo Kawarazaki is excellent as the grown Masuo. Kei Sato's graceless Grandfather, however, grates.

AUGUSTINE OF HIPPO (Italy). In the time of the Roman Empire's waning, decadent, self-indulgent days, the Algerian-born Catholic convert Augustine was appointed Bishop of Hippo in Roman North Africa. Seeing his own time, with its widespread poverty, greed, materialism, and the Vietnam War, reflected in this fifth-century world, Roberto Rossellini turned his series of present-tense histories to the figure of Augustine, the splendid result being *Agostino d'Ippona*.

Rossellini portrays Augustine, whom the Church will declare a Saint, as a roly-poly man, but also an austere one without Rabelaisian appetites. His former rambunctious, libertine nature, which we know about from the *Confessions*, has passed; when he notes, "[Y]outh is worshipping a cult of the senses," he is applying analysis to the present while also measuring the extent of his own spiritual advancement.

The conflict between Augustinians and the Donatists takes up much of the film. These punk-heretics constantly inflict violence on the meek, non-violent Augustinians. But then Rome falls, *all* Christians are deemed responsible, the Donatists themselves are targeted with violence, and Augustine takes them in, providing sanctuary.

Augustine exhorts his gathered flock to war against materialism, poverty and social iniquity—and *power:* "All that regards power is like a river after the rain. It is born, it swells, and it is lost in the sea." The destruction of Rome by the barbarians is a case in point; Rossellini's Rome, Rossellini worries, may be another.

To which city does each belong? "If you are a citizen of Babylon," Augustine says, "tear the greed out of your heart." Become instead a citizen of Jerusalem, the City of God. But what of Rossellini himself, whose humanism has set him against Babylon but kept him from embracing faith?

Passionate, intensely personal, Rossellini's film proceeds, like Augustine, with the analytic calm of reason.

1972

AGUIRRE, THE WRATH OF GOD (West Germany, Peru, Mexico). Werner Herzog's *Aguirre, der Zorn Gottes* is the highest attainment of the New German Cinema, a Leftist movement, begun in the sixties and reaching fruition in the seventies, which disdained any sweeping under the rug of Germany's role in the Second World War or possible German cultural predisposition to fascism. Like Ford's *The Searchers* (1956), *Aguirre* is about a madman, not as a case study, but as a revelation of cultural presumption, cultural insanity. It takes on Western "civilization."

Based on the Spanish quest for El Dorado, this richly colored work—the cinematographer is Thomas Mauch—follows a conquistador who imposes his will on a splinter group of Pizarro's army in Peru, in a mad effort to re-create the world in his own image: shorn of rationalization, the colonialist impulse. The film begins and ends loftily, in both instances with an extreme long-shot suggesting an implacable God's-eye view of human endeavor: first, in the beginning, ordered, united, intoxicated by dreams of glory, questers on a steep mountain of aspiration; at the last, amidst taunting monkeys, deprived even of his daughter, the one soul capable of calming his paroxysms, only the conquistador left alive, on a raft in the Amazon River. Herzog, a bit mad himself, committed those making the film—himself, cast, crew—to a daunting experience paralleling the one that the film depicts, perhaps hoping, like his protagonist, to validate both his own existence and the existence of God. He achieves, if not enlightenment, suasive fear and trembling, especially from the contribution of his "best fiend," lead actor Klaus Kinski, whose ferocious, nearly intolerably moving performance gives the conquistador the massive emotions of Goya's *Saturno*.

RED PSALM (Hungary). "The land belongs to those who cultivate it."
People, circling in dance, are themselves encircled by mounted soldiers. An 1890s peasant uprising is about to be put down.

The entirety of Miklós Jancsó's *Még kér a nép* unfolds in a field—and *unfolds* is the right word, because it is a scene of constant and immediate motion—dancing, walking, shooting, falling down dead, horses trotting—and motion in all directions, and lines of motion interweaving, or one encircling another: continual movements; continuous motion. Cinema's greatest post-silent formalist is at the top of his art, choreographing humanity more deftly, more intricately than ever—and, as in *Winter Wind* (1969), in color. Irony compounds irony; for the heartless nineteenth-century autocrats whose soldiers kill find Jancsó taking aim, in his own time, at ruling communists. *The People Still Ask* translates the Hungarian title; dressed in different ideologies, hiding behind different political masks, the powerful still oppress the masses, who must still ask, therefore, for change. Early on, a soldier shoots a girl's hand; the bleeding is magically replaced with a red ribbon. One of the film's final images: a panned mass of workers, a palm of each of them marked by a red ribbon.

Defying socialist realism, Jancsó creates entrancing abstractions to accompany the film's wealth of folk songs and dances and other movement. A church burns, but we aren't shown the arson; people are killed, but we aren't always shown the killing. The idea emerges that people are in the grip of historical forces; Jancsó focuses on outcomes rather than individual actions. Jancsó exhorts his audience to organize and oppose injustice and oppression en masse.

Jancsó puts few objects into his long, fluid takes. Rather, he invests his frames with movement, motion, humanity—a moving redefining of *mise-en-scène*.

SOLARIS (U.S.S.R.). Andrei Tarkovsky's *Solyaris*, from Stanislaw Lem, opens with tentacles of grass swaying in a stream—an insinuation of the unconscious just below the surface. The image is part of a lush landscape whose natural beauty is nourished by falling rain: *water*. The land is attached to the dacha of Kris Kelvin, a psychologist still mourning the loss of his wife, Khari, seven years earlier. Kelvin is recruited to join the Solaris mission, one of whose cosmonauts has committed suicide; he is to investigate what is happening. "What am I expected to find there?" he asks. The response: "That may depend on *you*."

The planet Solaris is "out there" somewhere; but the vast, churning sentient ocean covering it, above which the space station hovers,—more and more water,—connects outer space to Earthly cottage, the mind of the ocean to Kelvin's mind. The remaining two cosmonauts have already grappled with the ocean's capacities; the ocean can birth forms—false appearances rooted in an individual's deepest wish. His "wife," Khari, now appears to Kelvin—only, he knows it/she isn't *really* Khari (but how can one be sure?), as does it/she know. "Khari" is a phantom conjured by Kris's heart's desire. Is the ocean tempting Kris to the flood with his own yearning? Or is the ocean a projection of this yearning? Kris and "Khari" fall in love. Or *do* they? Is it his wife's death that has conjured Kris's memory of love?

Tarkovsky's space station is as (elegantly) sterile as the one in Stanley Kubrick's *2001: A Space Odyssey* (1968), to which many think *Solyaris* is providing a humane, humanistic response. Just below the surface, though, is Tarkovsky's critique of Soviet totalitarianism, which taints everything, including the most intimate aspects of a person's existence, turning even love into a question mark.

OUT 1: SPECTRE (France). Originally made as the 13-hour *Out 1: Noli me tangere*, Jacques Rivette's subsequent 4¼-hour version (which is what I have seen), involving two theatrical troupes, is his most entrancing multilayered "created reality" to draw us into a self-referential dream of doubled and parallel existences. It duplicates its cast (including marvelous Jean-Pierre Léaud, who, when first introduced, plays a deaf-mute playing a harmonica in search of handouts and some sort of recognition from café patrons) while going back and forth between a mystery narrative of sorts and improvised lunacy, thus having contrivance and free form, Old Wave and New, transparency and nontransparency (although it isn't always transparent which is which) imaginatively collide. *Out 1: Spectre* is cinema's great haunted-house comedy.

It is infused with intellectual spirit, and Rivette's bag of tricks riddles the certainty of action and conversations into ambiguity, magic, possibility. There are long takes, and those that are reflections in mirrors put us in the position of engrossed mirror-gazers searching out strange others in ourselves; brief blackouts may interrupt a scene, reviving the discontinuity of Godard's jump-cuts in *A bout de souffle* (1959) and again suggesting a revealing mismatch-up of person and persona, being and constructed image or self-image; sounds intrude to mask and obscure dialogue; and so forth. Rivette likes to keep us on our eyes and ears.

The film's self-divided, self-analytical nature creates a delicious air of expectancy. Some of the film hints an experiment in real time, but in fact, like it does much else, the film *approaches* real time, and it's the approach from which we infer psychological reality, including our own, as we begin to sense the degree to which actions in our own lives fail to coincide with our consciousness of these actions, our minds normally up ahead, *anticipating*.

THE MATTEI AFFAIR (Italy). Again Francesco Rosi applies documentary and fictional elements to an actual set of circumstances: the life and death of oil industrialist Enrico Mattei (Rosi's indispensable Gian Maria Volontè, superb), whom *Time* magazine called "the most powerful Italian since Cæsar Augustus." The film takes the form of a journalistic investigation, especially into the matter of the ambiguity of Mattei's death in a plane crash in 1962, for which it offers alternative explanations as though trying to get to the truth by finding the most suitable script. One way or another, whether by dint of mechanical failure or of a conspiratorial something-else, Mattei was taken down. This becomes the take-off for a consideration of everything surrounding Mattei and what he represents: Italy's past hopefulness and national spirit (during the war Mattei had fought in the Resistance), a growth of experience in capital investment in public companies, and the corruption into which Italy's postwar economic recovery summarily fell, and the exploitation of Third World oil resources that the new global fascism required. Rosi and his writers, including Tonino Guerra, take their largest aim at capitalism and the means by which it prevails. What, if anything, lay behind Mattei's death? None of the film is idle speculation, because the analysis it ultimately provides illuminates Mattei's life, not death, and his corporate empire-building (in what the state intended to be its own operation).

This piecing together of a man's life owes a debt, of course, to Orson Welles's *Citizen Kane* (1941) as well as Rosi's own past work, all the while aiming at a nation-as-pilgrim's progress. Rosi's communist heart weighs the price to Italy's soul of postwar economic upturn. *Il caso Mattei* is the ultimate *Invasion of the Body Snatchers*. The patient has recovered; but is the patient now the same person?

CRIES AND WHISPERS (Sweden). Ingmar Bergman's *Cries and Whispers* is, like many of his films, both beautiful and cruel.

Ravishingly cinematographed by Sven Nykvist, this one is in color. Reds, blacks and whites dominate the *mise-en-scène* as the film weighs the commitment of two estranged sisters to a third sister, Agnes (Harriet Andersson, heart-piercing), past the point of her death; waiting for the soul's release, Agnes's corpse pleads for comforting, which her sisters refuse to give her now that they can no longer bask in the glow of her living gratitude. Overmatched by ovarian cancer (the realism of Andersson's performance is immense), Agnes cannot draw their compassion across the line of mortal trembling; but, ignorant of this rejection-to-come, in a flashback that accompanies the reading of a diary entry of hers at film's end, she voices perfect contentment at her sisters' loving company. Placing the other sisters beyond the pale of forgiveness (their contrast is the maidservant, beautifully played by Kari Sylwan, who does comfort Agnes in her darkest hour of need), Bergman's contempt for them is unmistakable—this, the self-righteous posture of a man who, past 50, a year earlier refused his father's dying request for audience on the grounds of bitter childhood memories and the fact that his father, a Lutheran priest, had been unbendingly Christian and anti-Semitic. (Does some regret, if not guilt, over his refusal to comfort his father beat behind the *Cries*?)

The film is precise. The camera is often placed to follow characters into a confined space; the rigorous *mise-en-scène* contains Bergman's familiar overload of clocks, their ticking presence made even more oppressive from being "enlarged" by use of closeups and amplified sound, in ironic counterpoint to the secret purpose for clocks: to manage and "contain" time —humanity's defense against an overwhelming opponent.

FRENZY (U.S.). An airborne camera swoops down along the Thames River, creating an impression of grandeur and pristine beauty. It is the Thames Alfred Hitchcock fondly remembers. The closer the camera comes, though, the more reality overtakes memory. The Thames is polluted. Bank side, an official explains to a gathered crowd that industrial discharge is the cause; he promises a cleanup. Suddenly someone shrieks at the discovery of another kind of pollution surfacing in the river: the strangled naked corpse of a woman. The Necktie Murderer has struck again.

Frenzy provides a variation on Hitchcock's theme of the "wrong man." Circumstantial evidence convinces Scotland Yard Chief Inspector Oxford that Richard Blaney is the Necktie Murderer. Blaney's ex-wife and current girlfriend are among the victims. However, someone else is the real killer.

Oxford represents the myopia of the British establishment. He says the case against Blaney is "uncomplicated" by the existence of any other suspect. Rather than pursue the possibility of other suspects, then, Oxford fits pieces of evidence into his preordained jigsaw puzzle assigning guilt to Blaney—apparently, normal police procedure. The film implies it's amazing that the police ever get the *right* man.

1972

Oxford dismisses his wife's gourmet dinners (which express her frustrated creativity) with the same breathless arrogance with which he dismisses the possibility of Blaney's innocence. But Blaney's conviction, based on the case Oxford built against him, turns this innocent man into someone who escapes from prison to kill the person he realizes is the *real* killer. By the end of the film, his transformation into a murderer (morally, though, not literally) is complete. The law has had its day, reminding us that "civilization" provides a thin veneer to cover the ancient scapegoating process that modern criminal investigation and prosecution essentially remain.

Frenzy, beautifully acted by Vivien Merchant as Oxford's wife, is Hitchcock's last great work.

THE DISCREET CHARM OF THE BOURGEOISIE (France). Luis Buñuel's *Le charme discret de la bourgeoisie* is a title worthy of this beautiful satire. Its members of the French upper middle class, along with a South American ambassador, keep having their meals interrupted and aborted. It's a crisis of culturally elevated *coitus interruptus*.

First, a group arrives for dinner, only to have their hostess explain that it's the wrong night. Inviting the hostess along, they next check in at a nearby eatery; but a solemn wake going on in the back room—the establishment's manager died that afternoon—bankrupts their appetites. Another day it is lunch, but the host and hostess, who are having sex (eventually, outside in the bushes), are late in joining their guests, who by that time have left. Another day it's lunch in a restaurant, and a stranger, a young army lieutenant, invites himself to the group's table to relate his tragic childhood, which we see as one of the film's marvelous dream episodes. And so the film goes, giving us a lot to chew on, but very little to its characters, for which a dream cast has been assembled (Stéphane Audran, Jean-Pierre Cassel, Delphine Seyrig, Bulle Ogier, Fernando Rey—with Ogier, in particular, screamingly funny as a girl who can't hold her liquor).

Of course, since it's Buñuel, the comedy is serious. There is a gripping vignette showing the torture of a young radical. The theme of the film is the complacency by which the middle class abets fascism, and at one point one soul awakens from another's dream, suggesting a lack of individuality among this group. Periodic inserts of the group walking down a vacant road, seemingly sure of where they are headed but going nowhere, suggest a dangerous absence of self-criticism and self-awareness.

ILLUMINATION (Poland). Writer-director Krzysztof Zanussi's *Illuminacja* is autobiographical. Its protagonist, Franciszek Retman, is a graduate student in physics because he wants to know "things that are certain, unequivocal." Zanussi himself studied physics at the University of Warsaw before proceeding to loftier intellectual ground, studying philosophy at the University of Kraków. (He studied film at the Łódź Film School.) His "illumination," the wisdom he attained as "an enlightenment of the mind" (St. Augustine), required redirecting the course of his life.

Retman's experience reflects this. Transforming him are a turbulent romantic relationship and the death of a friend during their mountain-climb—and something else: the responsibility that scientists are loath to embrace. Early on, Retman remarks, "I don't feel responsible for the A-bomb," on the grounds that he hadn't participated in its invention. Another student, though, wins their argument by exposing Retman's evasiveness, self-absorption, self-delusion: "But [the inventors] were physicists, too." Retman's journey, then, is in the direction of responsibility.

Most decisive for the movie's brilliance is the form Zanussi has given it. It's a mosaic, a kaleidoscope of pieces in which one set of snippets of film sometimes is interrupted by another set of snippets. This "piecing together" opposes complacency; we viewers are compelled to approach this film in a mentally active way. One cannot "go with the flow" when there *is* no flow.

1972

At one point Retman interrupts his contemplation of cosmos to have his palm read. He is curious to see how inaccurate the palm reader will prove herself! She tells him he doesn't like himself. She is saying this to a most self-satisfied creature! But, of course, Zanussi's prick of wit eventually turns around and aims itself at the boy whose self-satisfaction has been an evasion, a delusion.

Hacks do not spare others. Artists do not spare themselves.

THE ASSASSINATION OF TROTSKY (Italy, France, UK). Despite its reputation for being god-awful, *The Assassination of Trotsky* is one of Joseph Losey's moodiest, most powerful films. Trotsky's assassin, Ramón Mercader, here rechristened Frank Jacson (Alain Delon, excellent), and not Trotsky, is the central character. Internet critic Fernando F. Croce has drawn the main contrast between Jacson and Trotsky, saying that Jacson is "as confused in his identity as his redoubtable prey is embalmed in his." Early on, on the sidewalk of the Mexico City street as the May Day parade passes by, Jacson turns his back to the procession, facing a wall, to light a cigarette. Symbolically, that blank wall measures up as two things: Jacson's cluelessness as to who he is; the monolithic, fixed nature of Trotsky's self-certainty. "Who *are* you?" a policeman asks after Jacson has ripped open Trotsky's head with a pick-ax. He has found his historical, fabled identity: "I killed Trotsky."

Jacson is a mercenary who is racked by ambivalence as he sets up and approaches the kill. He doesn't know what he wants to do. The man who has hired him tells him more than once that he is free, that he can walk away without assassinating Trotsky; but three women, unwittingly, bind him to the darker choice. Gita, the idealistic Communist he has made his lover for access to Trotsky's barricaded Coyoacán villa, where she works; how else to hide the shame of his having thus used her but to complete the job? "I've seen your mother," the hirer casually mentions; "She's well"—a veiled threat. And Natalia (Natasha here; Valentina Cortese, marvelous), Trotsky's wife, remarks that Jacson is the same age as their son who was assassinated in Paris.

Jacson must *not* be him.

Nicholas Mosley and Franco Solinas principally wrote the script.

THE CULPEPPER CATTLE CO. (U.S.). Beautiful, incisive, *The Culpepper Cattle Co.* follows an 1866 cattle drive from Texas that doesn't make it to Fort Lewis, Colorado. The sole survivor of the battle between a landowner and the cowboys is fifteen-year-old Ben Mockridge, the recruited "Little Mary," that is, cook's assistant, who inspired the others to take up the cause of protecting a religious commune from the landowner's wrath. "There are more important things than cattle," the teenager advised his elders, alone staying behind to defend the pacifist group before his fellow cowboys followed his lead. Now the commune members decide they cannot stay where so many have died, for the land is "soiled with blood," God led them there only to test them, and they must move on. So must Ben, who adds his gun to the corpses on the ground before going his own way. In the shadow of the Civil War, America finds itself in moral disarray—a reflection on the present and America's misadventures in Southeast Asia.

The sharp story by Dick Richards led to his even more brilliant filmmaking. The first shot is a freeze frame that comes to rousing life; retroactively it provides an index of Ben's haunted soul, immersing the entire action of the film in the regions of Ben's painful memory. Ben's mother's parting words to her son as he leaves to join the drive, "Be a good boy," are a delayed attempt to say *something*; but Ben holds fast to them nevertheless. What unfolds is war predicated on theft (cows, horses, guns, "God's land")—a series of bloody encounters suggesting that Ben is not where he ought to be. Wherever he is, this fatherless boy—one wonders if his father died in the Civil War—must now become his own father.

1973

THE AGE OF COSIMO DE MEDICI (Italy). Roberto Rossellini's tripartite examination of Florentine society and culture in the fifteenth century begins with a banking family. Aligned with merchants and the explosion of European trade, the Medicis embody a new pursuit of wealth and power. In its style, this 4-hour film is heir to Rossellini's sober, immaculate *Rise to Power of Louis XIV* (1966), which inaugurated his series of minimalist present-tense histories treating figures such as Socrates and Pascal. According to critic John Wyver, the world that Rossellini reveals in his Medici film "is both patently artificial and startlingly real." Stately formalism and documentary roughness balance each other, creating a secular vision in which the religious, more primitive world of *Francesco, giullare di Dio* (1950) still hangs lightly about, a ray of residual simplicity in a new world of immense complication.

Leon Battista Alberti, philosopher, painter, sculptor, musician, architect, embodies the humanistic impulse that is also integral to this world. "What use is beauty?" a merchant asks as he peruses art. Art reflects humanity. Masaccio's painting of Jesus gives scientific attention to human anatomy at the expense of a more traditional, "spiritual" approach. Its linear approach applies principles of mathematics. Art, then, incorporates a range of knowledge and attainments—including the financial, with the couple who paid Masaccio to paint the portrait themselves appearing in the piece!

We see Masaccio's painting as it is discussed from various perspectives. Indeed, this amazing film contains many conversations on a wide range of matters, including the Florentine tax code. It is especially steeped in architecture and certain organizing ideas: freedom; "the city" as being based on families; the marriage of art and science, which have in common "the progress of mankind." Alberti is referring to architecture, but, surely, Rossellini also has cinema in mind.

DISTANT THUNDER (India). The "forgotten holocaust": the Bengal Famine (1943-44), engineered by British prime minister Winston Churchill—Britain ruled India at the time—and abetted by Hindu trader-profiteers, that exacted the lives of 3.5 million Bengals to help keep World War II British soldiers clothed and fed. The price of rice soared beyond the means of rural people to feed themselves and their families; British imports to India were slashed as exports from India increased. Satyajit Ray's tremendous *Ashani Sanket* commemorates the tragedy.

Gangacharan Chakravarti (Soumitra Chatterjee, superbly charting a selfish soul's gradual shame, humbling, enlarged humanity) has moved with wife Ananga to Natungaon in Bengal and, a Brahmin, has taken charge of the rural village because of his higher caste and education. He becomes priest, doctor, teacher, and opportunist, extracting payments when he and Ananga are already much better off than their neighbors. Meanwhile, the rice shortage takes hold, eventually reducing residents to privation and the sway of their basest instincts. It is another front of the war. (The Famine accounted for 90% of British fatalities in the Second World War.)

The film's phenomenal opening: Grass; sky; trees—pristine Nature, suffused with melancholy. The closeup of a hand in the river: Ananga, bathing. A formation of war planes flies overhead, its drone drowning out the chirps of birds. The planes "look like a flock of cranes." The intrusion of war; the illusion of war's distance and normality.

A leper or, possibly, burn victim offers Chutki rice in exchange for sex. She chooses life.

The first village corpse—an *untouchable*. In closeup, Gangacharan's hand holds her wrist, to check her pulse.

The celebrated closing shot: an old man and his seven dependants approaching the Chakravartis, to be taken in; the camera pulls back, revealing all the starving Bengals they represent.

1973

THE MOTHER AND THE WHORE (France). "By the time a guy realizes he is in love, the woman has decided she doesn't love him." — Alexandre, referring to Gilberte

Alexandre (Jean-Pierre Léaud, tremendous) is enamored of three women: current partner Marie, former partner Gilberte, and Veronika, whom he picks up one day and tells Marie about because, he says, "I can't keep anything from you." Actually, Marie loves Alexandre more than he loves her, and Alexandre desperately wants to believe he and Gilberte might come together again sometime in the future. He himself relates this wish to the loss of political hopefulness among the French Left following May 1968. Alexandre illustrates lines by nineteenth-century English poet Matthew Arnold: "Wandering between two worlds, one dead,/ The other powerless to be born."

Writer-director Jean Eustache's script is brilliant, hilarious. For 220 minutes his *La maman et la putain* thoroughly engages with its loose-ended young lives. Alexandre, despite a disadvantaged background, is learned, intellectual; he explains, he stole books as a child because poverty shouldn't limit anyone's education. Alexandre doesn't work. Veronika, a nurse, is proud of her salty language and forthright discussions of sex. She anticipates the end of a relationship.

In a great passage, Alexandre and Veronika are walking at night to the Seine—"the water," Veronika, who is Polish, calls it. She tells him she could walk with him all night. Earlier, at a restaurant, Alexandre began their date by monologuing, pontificating; Veronika finally joined in, gently asserting herself; and then the two connected, interacted, shared. We get to see the nervous date become a shared, breathing, equal thing.

Eustache's film is tragic, its primarily lighthearted tone making it all the more heartrending, and very raw in portraying its characters' sex lives and feelings. Its style resembles *cinéma-vérité*.

THE SOCIETY OF THE SPECTACLE (France). Guy Debord's *La société du spectacle* conjoins powerful images with voiceover reading from his own book. Some of these "autonomous" images, either photographic or filmed, are familiar: the assassination of Lee Harvey Oswald; a moon walk. Others are generic—familiar as a *type* of image: aerial bombing; Castro giving a speech. "All that was directly lived has moved away," we are told, "into a representation." This "Spectacle is not a collection of images, but a social relation among persons, mediated by images." In this brilliant documentary's first coup, an overhead image of a massive crowd expresses simultaneously this "social relation" and the mediation, draining the implication of proletarian power almost as quickly as positing it. Debord's book preceded the May 1968 revolt, which his own group of "Situationists" helped foment, but the film, coming after, all the more locates *the people* in a state of disadvantage.

Production and consumption determine images. The Spectacle is "the affirmation of appearance," "the negation of life." A scene of factory labor yields to a militaristic shot—missiles, poised for discharge from a vessel—and we hear about the economy's role in forcing workers' "total submission"; "[the Spectacle] is the faithful reflection of the production of things, and the unfaithful objectification of the [workers]," whose alienation from the world reflects their alienation from work that accumulates capital—in "such abundance" that it becomes an image—for others.

Power is at the ancient root of the Spectacle. A parliamentary image yields to police in riot gear violently confronting a street demonstration; "[The Spectacle] is the diplomatic representation of hierarchical society to itself, where every other form of speech is banned."

By the Spectacle, "one part of the world represents itself as superior to the rest of the world."

TOUKI-BOUKI (Senegal). Shimmering in heat waves, a wide-angle shot shows a boy mounted on a zebu leading a herd of oxen towards the camera. Theirs is a single destination that therefore applies, at least metaphorically, to both beasts and boy: the slaughterhouse.

What follows is graphic and gory—stuff so discombobulating (for us, in our safety) that we think: No child should be part of this. But no matter how young he is, this village child, Mory, must do what he can to survive. Djibril Diop Mambéty's *The Hyena's Journey* has astonishingly begun.

The next shot is point-of-view; the stylistic rupture corresponds to the fact that time has passed. Mory is a young man now, and he is riding into Dakar—the city—on his motorbike. How do we know this is Mory, only grown up? The horns of a zebu adorn the handles of his motorbike. This is how Mambéty's masterpiece proceeds: elliptically, expressively.

Mory and college student Anta dream of fleeing to Paris, and much of the film records the couple's attempts to get the money to do so however they can. (Mory, the hyena, still pursues survival—mental, now, as well as material.) French singing, some of it by U.S. expatriate Josephine Baker, dots the soundtrack. The confusion of Western and French icons and emblems reminds us that Senegal had been a French colony. But the point is, the Senegalese *need* no reminding. Mambéty's film is about the people's confusion of cultural and national identity—a legacy of Senegal's colonization. The dream to escape to Paris reveals the need for a resolution to this confusion.

References to French films—Franju's *Blood of the Beasts* (1949), Godard's *Pierrot le fou* (1965), Truffaut's *L'enfant sauvage* (1969) among them—suggest the ironical allure of *more* confusion as some sort of resolution!

THE LONG GOODBYE (U.S.). During the seventies, Robert Altman made a series of "revisionist" films testing the assumptions of familiar genres. Perhaps the most brilliant of these is *The Long Goodbye*, from one of Raymond Chandler's Philip Marlowe private detective novels.

Let me give an example of the film's method. One of the assumptions of the genre is that the detective is a lone wolf, drawing strength of purpose from his version of rugged individualism. But, instead, Elliott Gould's updated Marlowe is an hilariously pathetic loner, more unhappily lonely than ruggedly alone, and very nearly terrorized by his cat, who claws him and rules the roost before abandoning him after Marlowe fails to buy the desired cat food. Other generic assumptions meet a similar prodding and twisting, with the surprise of a lifetime befitting this procedure awaiting those who have read the book: a different murder solution than Chandler devised—and one that fits just as nicely. Here is, perhaps, the most entertaining American movie-movie of the decade.

Richard Nixon, nowhere mentioned, had been reelected U.S. president. He, along with related aspects of American political, social and cultural life, represents the entrenchment of generic assumptions—the accepted clichés, the way things are supposed to be. Altman combatted reactionaryism by refreshing our whole sense of what's going down.

In one of the film's most powerful scenes, a mobster disfigures his mistress's face to threaten Marlowe, explaining that if he would do this to someone *he loves* . . . ! This not only turns the assumption of misogynism, as part of the fabric of the world which detectives and criminals share, on its ear (again, hilariously) but also suggests the irrelevancy of love in a reactionary world—unless, as Nixon would insist when he resigned office, one's mother was a saint.

THE HOURGLASS SANATORIUM (Poland). It opens a bit like *Dracula* (Tod Browning, 1931). In slow motion, a black bird, like a bat, flaps in the sky, without lateral movement, amidst a tangle of bare tree branches against a sunless sky. (Lines from Paul Kesler's poem about Caspar David Friedrich's painting *Abtei im Eichwald*: "Branching,/ the roots of agony/ climb to the heavens;/ the broken husk/ of autumn/ lingers in their veins. . . .") The camera slowly pans leftward to follow this symbol of death as it finally flies; but the bird is lost from view as the camera withdraws, entering the window of a dilapidated train whose passengers seem on the verge of mummification. One man, though, is young; Jozef is en route to visit his dying father in a remote sanatorium. "How will I find it?" he asks the conductor. The reply: "You will have to do that yourself."

Wojciech J. Has's *Sanatorium pod klepsydra* is based on stories by Bruno Schulz, whom the Gestapo murdered in 1942. Jozef's father is still (technically) alive because time has been slowed inside the sanatorium, which reeks of dying and decay. In all probability it is Jozef who is dying; what we see unfold is a fantasy of expiration. One Jewish death is *all* Jewish deaths; all Jewish deaths are *one* Jewish death. In Polish, *klepsydra* means both *sandglass* and *obituary*. At film's end, Jozef crawls out of the earth. Back to life? To death?

Has's strange, darkly wonderful film somehow manages to be, visually, both spare and luxuriant. It follows Jozef's odyssey, which may be to the underworld or the past. Jozef is immersed in a Hassidic community whose vibrance and reality, fragile, are measured against time. He sees his father young; down the rabbit hole, he becomes an archaeologist of ethnic memory.

Ours.

THE SPIRIT OF THE BEEHIVE (Spain). Victor Erice's *El espíritu de la colmena* reflects on fascist Spain. Two sisters, Ana and Isabel, eight and ten, live with their parents in a rural Castile community in 1940, shortly after the defeat of decency in the Spanish Civil War. Their parents are each in their own lives: their father intently experimenting with bees, having transferred a colony to an artificial structure that unconsciously projects the political environment; their mother, consumed by solitude. (In a warm, fleeting scene, however, the mother combs Ana's hair.) The girls are largely on their own; at night, they whisper back and forth between beds. Ana and Isabel are also cocooned, not as a matter of withdrawal from fascist reality, but in childhood's innocence and ignorance. Now a stray wounded Republican soldier, whom Ana finds in an abandoned barn (she gives him her father's coat for warmth), is about to be murdered. At night, in long-shot, it's a massacre; so many bullets for one debilitated man. Ana's world will be disturbed even worse than by her sister's "dead" act on a floor of their home.

An itinerant projectionist has brought a movie to town: James Whale's *Frankenstein* (1931). Ana, who cannot understand why the townsfolk kill the creature, relates the soldier to it before his disappearance. There is little speech in this mesmerizing film, and only silence—sweet solidarity—between Ana and her secret friend.

The stone well, the barn, the schoolhouse, wild mushrooms, the father's musical pocket watch: in long-shot or closeup, things are simultaneously mundane and mysterious. A passing train, in long-shot, is immense compared with the sisters.

Brown, beige, gray, white, black, occasional reddish brown, dark green, pale amber: Erice orchestrates colors of repression, with glimmers of life: the spirit of the beehive.

THE MIDDLE OF THE WORLD (Switzerland, France). Paul Chamoret, a French Swiss engineer running for political office, thinks he is in love with Adriana (Olimpia Carlisi, terrific), a northern Italian emigrant who works as a waitress at the railway station café not far from where Paul was born. Rumors pertaining to his extramarital affair cost Paul the election; relieved, he anticipates a new life with Adriana. But she leaves him.

Sensitively written by the director and John Berger, Alain Tanner's brilliant, feminist *Le milieu du monde* portrays a park in winter, trimmed trees in the background, each the exact same height, with snow falling diagonally on the cold grass, providing the illusion that we can see each individual flake. The trees represent Paul and this self-made man's "perfect" life; but the snow suggests Adriana, who later remarks to Paul in bed, "Everyone always is alone."

A widow, Adriana comes by this conviction easily. When she is with Paul, which is often, it is especially easy for Adriana to feel alone. When she suggests that their relationship may change each of them, Paul counters, "Why should I change?" "You never listen," she later tells him. "If you don't listen, you never get to know people. . . . You don't know *me*." She is right; Paul knows only what he wants. One time they are about to make love, Adriana counters, "I'm cold," after Paul stupidly remarks, "Whores undress only below the waist." Cut; Paul and Adriana are fucking, both entirely naked.

Across their divide of differences (Swiss, Italian; male, female; bourgeois, working-class), this couple presumably illustrates "normalization," post-ideological détente, a middle of the road at the middle of the world. Paul gifts Adriana with a movie camera. She explodes; but isn't she perhaps filming right now the story of their unequal relationship?

1974

CARTESIO (Italy). Ironically, seventeenth-century mathematician and philosopher René Descartes had to be coaxed into publishing, and no sooner had he done so than he was in political trouble. He took his time in order to allow for the greatest measure of reflection before committing himself to his convictions; but, in reality, the times weren't ready for him no matter how much time he took.

One of Roberto Rossellini's present-tense histories, *Cartesio*, which is phenomenal, brings its in-the-momentness to an open-ended point by leaving its subject in the middle of things. Descartes, beautifully played by Ugo Cardea, describes himself as a pilgrim journeying through his own thoughts; the film becomes torrentially moving once we realize that Descartes also is journeying from the Middle Ages to the Renaissance. He insists on clear, honest thought in a world plagued by religious dogma—for which Rossellini devises the most gripping metaphor: as Descartes walks a street, conversing with a friend, those collecting victims of the plague in wheelbarrows are also going about their business.

Descartes contested the falseness of knowledge, the conforming of science to inherited prejudices, including those of faith. For him, Rossellini implies, "original sin" is whatever one has been taught that constructs a barrier between oneself and the truth. Descartes devises a list of twenty-one rules for the mind's right use, one of which requires a methodical approach to testing hypotheses, observations and evidence that circumvents bias, prejudice. He is quintessentially his own man. Descartes is "attracted to mathematics," he explains, solely for the "metaphysical truths" that can be accessed through its study.

Rossellini's frames are elegantly restrained yet bursting with human activity. One series of shots confines people to the lower half of a room, with vast blank walls above them: interiors suggesting humanity's place in the cosmos!

MIRROR (U.S.S.R.). "And I can't wait to see this dream/ In which I'll be a child again/ . . . everything will still be ahead/ Still possible." — Arsenii Tarkovsky, Andrei's father

Andrei Tarkovsky's *Zerkalo* interweaves three time frames, the 1930s prior to the Second World War, wartime, and the 1960s, color and black and white, waking reality and dreams. Margarita Terekhova, superb, plays Masha, young Aleksei's mother, and Natalia, the grown Aleksei's wife; one actor plays young Aleksei and the grown Aleksei's son, Ignat. This double imaging conforms to the metaphor of mirrors, which accumulates a sense of transaction, at times a quarrel, between past and present. An elderly woman appears to be approaching the camera, which is to say, us; approaching her is the young mother, who has just been abandoned by her spouse. When the two face one another close-up, young Masha smooths the mirror right in front of her, revealing that she is—or we are—glimpsing her future self. Aleksei dreams he is watching his mother wash her hair as his father leaves the frame; the day the father walks out, a barn burns down—a borderline image, one as real as it is dreamlike. Throughout, shots of successive doorways suggest mirrors that characters pass through. Even a television screen appears to Ignat as a kind of mirror.

The abandoned Aleksei becomes an abandoning father; the grown Aleksei, kept offscreen, has become a disembodied voice, absent even when present. (Tarkovsky's actual father, another disembodied voice, reads his poetry, and the film has an unseen narrator besides.)

Tarkovsky's haunting evocation of childhood and time-elastic symbolical autobiography blossom into a meditation on Soviet history, implying an antitotalitarian dialectic between personal and national histories wherein individuals become the prism through which a society is best understood and judged, thereby reversing the Soviet dogmatic telescope.

CONVERSATION PIECE (Italy). *Gruppo di famiglia in un interno* finds a retired science professor nearing life's end when the intrusion into his life of a contentious family of strangers shakes it up. Professor has long since settled into a quiet, studious and very private existence in his art-heavy, Mozart-filled Roman palazzo. Suddenly, Marchesa Bianca Brumonti insists on moving her daughter and son into the upstairs of the mansion, along with her young lover, Konrad Huebel, a mercurial Leftist. Only her right-wing industrialist husband dislikes Konrad, and he eventually delivers his wife an ultimatum: Find some more suitable lover, or divorce. The marchesa chooses the latter, but Konrad is wearying of his wealthy mistress—and, perhaps, of life. His death, which may be a suicide, triggers the end of an arrangement that may have been holding back Professor from his own end.

Conversation Piece moves from old landlord-unruly young tenants absurdist comedy to a profound meditation on various collisions—between classes, intentions and the aspirations bolstering them, young and old, classical and modern. Everything has its place downstairs, secure; but, upstairs, Konrad is none too competently expanding the bathroom, and water is seeping down the downstairs walls, threatening Professor's high-hung paintings. Against all odds, the boy and the professor become friends; the former's vulnerability, cloaked in cynicism, touches the latter, and their politics, we eventually discover, aren't so far apart. A ripple of latent homosexuality may even be drawing the old man to Konrad. More than anything else, Professor becomes Konrad's surrogate father.

This beautiful piece about the outdated remnants of selfish aristocracy (to which the disintegrating Brumonti family is correlative) is the penultimate film by Luchino Visconti, who draws superlative performances from Burt Lancaster, Claudia Marsani as the marchesa's daughter, and his last lover, Helmut Berger.

STILL LIFE (Iran). *Tabiate bijan*, by Sohrab Shahid Saless, is a minimalist study of lonely, isolated existence. Mohamad Sardari has spent thirty years at a remote outpost raising and lowering a gate to keep road traffic from crossing tracks when a train passes. He lives with his wife in an unadorned shack; a few bare trees dot the threadbare landscape.

The railroad brings in the son, who is in the army, for a night's visit. His mother asks why he hasn't written; he insists he has—*once*.

Father, mother, son assume stilted poses; when the three eat, each on the floor is isolated in a separate shot. The son, who takes over the one bed, his father's, is almost too big for it. He tells his mother a button has come off his coat, takes off the coat and hands it to her as she, a beat behind, says, "Give it to me to sew." He has already done this. The timing discloses the son's male presumption and prerogative, to be sure, but also an all-round awkwardness that undercuts the idea of family as bulwark against a formidable outside world.

An official, dropping by, buys a rug that the woman has woven—one adornment in the shack. Mohamad, given ridiculously little money, is told, "You don't have to sell it if you're not satisfied"; but the rug has already been rolled up and is headed out the door. "I've been dismissed," Mohamad says over and over again, as if trying his best to adjust to the shocking news, once he is informed of the fact. His last act before vacating the shack and heading for nowhere in a horse-drawn cart is to remove the shack's other adornment: a small wall mirror that reflects back at him a disposable existence.

KARL MAY (West Germany). *What does the fate of one individual matter when one is dealing with the vast and lofty issues of the whole of humanity?*

1974

Filmmaker Helmut Käutner gives a bone-deep performance as Karl May, the nineteenth-century German author of cowboy stories and exotic adventures, whose extreme popularity came under attack by his insistence on their basis in actual experience, his alleged immorality, and his long-ago imprisonment for theft. May, defending himself against slander, became embroiled in an exhausting series of lawsuits.

Beautifully written and directed by Hans-Jürgen Syberberg, *Karl May* opens with a flourish of artifice: a miniature village poured upon by fake snow; it is an "exterior" moment in a work whose subsequent interiority we must intuit from a series of domestic and public vignettes. Syberberg investigates the tension between the public and private May, who anticipating the modern era applied imagination to make of himself a work of fiction—life as an extension of art.

The film's second part, "The soul is a vast land into which we all flee," presides over the disintegration of May's marriage into a minutely contentious divorce, during which accusations of homosexuality and lesbianism are inflicted. At his final trial May is branded a compulsive liar and criminal, but much more than this draws parallels between him and Adolf Hitler, who himself was inspired by the heroic mold of May's writings. Syberberg exonerates May, branding Hitler (who appears in a flashforward) as the one who is responsible for Hitler, noting that no artist can bring up anything in any individual that isn't already there. Here, Syberberg also takes aim at the masses who anointed Hitler their "hero."

The woman who loves May tells him, "You were at the limits of human endurance . . . in the Rocky Mountains."

ELEKTRA, MY LOVE (Hungary). Working from László Gyurkó's play, Miklós Jancsó finds a folk use for the ancient Greek Oresteia myth in *Szerelmem, Elektra*: a representation of the Hungarian people and their historic suffering.

It has been fifteen years since the death of her father, Agamemnon, and Elektra (Mari Törőcsik, claiming yet another terrific role) still burns with hatred for Aegisztosz, who conspired with Elektra's mother to kill him. "I do not forget," she announces; Elektra is historic memory in search of justice. After a line of candle-holding women turns toward a wall, Elektra walks between rows of corpses on the ground, which then, in sync, roll off out of sight—but not out of Elektra's mind. Meanwhile, Aegisztosz rules as a tyrant ("People are content if they know what to fear"), inducing Stalinist terror, and Elektra waits upon brother Oresztész's return for the enactment of justice. (A line of whip-wielding guards embodies state terror's constant threat.) Aegisztosz teases Elektra with the thought that Oresztész is dead—a way of trying to convince himself, perhaps, that he has no retribution to face; but the people rise up against their tyrant when Oresztész does return. The siblings exact their revenge, killing Aegisztosz and killing themselves, thus passing into inspirational myth to counter future tyrants. The history of Hungary is just such sacrifice. "Cursed be every tyrant," Elektra has said, "and blessed be everyone who resists tyranny."

Jancsó's measured style expresses itself in delicate singing and slow, stylized mass dancing —a people's mournful though determined self-expression—in long, intricately choreographed takes. For instance, a long, winding line of women dance down a hill that is dotted with candles marking tyranny's victims.

The intrusion of an anachronistic helicopter makes plain that Jancsó is reflecting on his own time, his own Hungary.

EVERY MAN FOR HIMSELF AND GOD AGAINST ALL (West Germany). In 1828, a teenaged boy appears in Nuremberg. He can barely do simple things: speak, walk, eat or dress himself. He grew up locked in a dark cellar, apart from other people. A local doctor attempts to socialize and "civilize" him. Werner Herzog's film is based on fact.

The actor playing Kaspar Hauser, Bruno S., was beaten by his prostitute mother when he was three, leaving him deaf and leading to his institutionalization, as a mental case, for a quarter-century. Cruelty traverses time, and *Jeder für sich und Gott gegen alle* is a disguised biography of its star, who shares his character's fate.

The film opens, close to Aleksandr Dovzhenko's *Earth* (1930), with a silent scene of oceanic grass. This visual poetry associates the boy, in his innocence, with Nature and, more disturbingly, projects the "screaming silence" of his isolated, nonsocial existence. When he learns to play music, Kaspar finds it "strong in [his] heart" and feels "unexpectedly old." The naïf questions what he hasn't been socialized to automatically accept. He asks why women are allowed only to cook and knit—and, failing to appreciate society's approved division of gender roles, takes up knitting himself!

We see Kaspar's dreams. They pulsate with light, like flickering silent films. In one, a blind man leading a caravan in the desert redirects course away from the mountains he, unlike the sighted, identifies as illusions—a reference to Herzog's *Fata Morgana* (1969). The entire film may be interpreted as a coda to Herzog's *Land of Silence and Darkness* (1971), and this summary work also includes references to other Herzog films. Kaspar Hauser is Germany, whose cultural load Herzog now totes in his art, giving the unfortunate boy fresh tragedy and new spirit, new life.

EDVARD MUNCH (Norway, Sweden). *Edvard Munch* essays the Norwegian painter, focusing (in flashback) on his impoverished childhood, and on his Expressionism and bohemian lifestyle, including his friendship with Swedish playwright August Strindberg in Berlin. The film, by Britain's Peter Watkins, blends scripted elements (such as voiceover narration) with improvised dialogue from its nonprofessional cast, and applies a documentary style to its biographical account. Characters, presumably being interviewed, speak directly into the camera, collapsing the difference between past and present, both in terms of time and technology.

Watkins is interested in context. The cramped, overflowing quarters beset with family sickness in which Munch grew up constitute the initial element that Watkins shows contributing to Munch's dark, brooding, interior art. Munch is often shown painting, and one of the film's most thrilling aspects is its sense of all the unconscious elements, in concert with those of conscious artistic purpose, that come together to help determine what Munch creates as paintbrush touches canvas. Watkins has made a film about the complex nature of the creative impulse, and Munch's nearly compulsive scraping away of colors on his canvases becomes like a perpetual child's—forgive—scream at the edge of a void only an adult can perceive.

Watkins also depicts, in detail, a time and place: the café society frequented by European artists and intellectuals toward the turn of the century. Watkins has correctly balanced Munch's solitude, including his inner demons, and the rich social life, the community of artists and others (such as anarchist Hans Jaeger) to which he belonged, that fleshed out Munch's existence. Again, the film argues that an artist's creativity springs from both the mind and soul and the environment in which the artist's life unfolds, and Watkins's patient, cumulative and eclectic method does brilliant justice to this idea.

EFFI BRIEST (West Germany). Rainer Werner Fassbinder is full of surprises. For his film version of Theodor Fontane's 1895 novel *Effi Briest*, he employs a classically pure style in exquisite black and white. Beginning in 1880s Prussia, it's a period piece.

Or is it? Henning Carlsen's *Hunger* (1966) avoided becoming this by focusing on the humanity of its protagonist and by finding visual correlatives to the first-person narration of Hamsun's book. Instead, Fassbinder's dry, distanced, muted approach tends to abstract the material out of place and time. Fassbinder certainly doesn't "milk" the costumes and décor. Rather, his precise method locates the action in particular milieus that help determine it, while simultaneously resisting any attempt by us to consign its exposure of marital and familial cruelty and narrow-mindedness to the past. Fassbinder achieves something akin to a universal parable. An idea that might never have occurred to me were it not for this film is how arranged marriages, with all the peril these entail, still sometimes exist in the West— only, instead of being parentally arranged, "arranged" by the marital participants themselves. Even today, love isn't always the principal motivating factor.

For Effi, her husband's conviction that she has been unfaithful deprives her of her parental home, as refuge, as well as her marital home, suggesting that the latter, always, was an ideological extension of the former. Effi never was anything but property—property that changes hands.

In her first great performance, Hanna Schygulla makes Effi a portrait of intense loneliness and feeling useless. Effi is between a rock and a hard place, prevented from becoming a self-determining individual and cut off from the family ties that might have ameliorated this alienated state. Nineteenth century? Without a doubt—and very much closer than that for the rest of us.

FEAR EATS THE SOUL (West Germany). Rainer Werner Fassbinder's *Angst essen Seele auf* opens with a great deep focus shot, from which we infer that Emmi Kurowski, a dumpy, middle-aged widow (Brigitte Mira, marvelous), is the object of considerable attention when she walks through the door of a bar that Arab immigrants patronize. Emmi is looking to get out of the downpour outside, but she is also drawn by the Arab music that is strange to her playing on the jukebox. She strikes up a conversation, and a friendship, with Ali, who is from Morocco. Ali and Emmi are lonely, he, because he is separated from family, she, because her family—three married children—"live their own lives" locally, ignoring her except on holidays.

Emmi is without prejudice, but, apparently, she is the only one. Her growing relationship with a younger black man invites disdainful comments from neighbors, co-workers, and family members, who are suddenly concerned about Mother now that she and Ali plan to marry. Upon hearing the news, one of Emmi's sons kicks in the television set.

Inspired by Douglas Sirk's *All That Heaven Allows* (1955), Fassbinder's tragicomedy shows how little we sometimes care about others and "live and let live." Why should people busy themselves with obstructing the happiness of others? Perhaps they are terrified that the world should in any way not reflect what they are most familiar with. Perhaps they feel so bereft of power and autonomy that they must intrude where they can, even at the expense of others.

Bigotry is exposed as a security blanket, a means of asserting some bit of control over a vast reality, a way of countering, however tentatively, the fear that eats the soul. But Emmi chooses another way of doing this: *love*.

LANCELOT OF THE LAKE (France). Robert Bresson's Arthurian *Lancelot du Lac*, from Chrétien de Troyes, was meant to follow immediately *Diary of a Country Priest* (1950); by the time Bresson realized his dream project nearly a quarter-century later, his work had passed from black and white into color—color, here, rich, mysterious, hauntingly beautiful.

Still, this isn't a period film in which viewers "lose themselves." One always *hears* a Bresson film as much as sees it, giving it immediacy. This time, it isn't jangling jail cells or shuffling clogs or street traffic that we hear. It is alienating clanking armor, clashing swords, pounding hoofbeats. The film opens at night in the forest, and two armored men are wielding swords at one another—doubtless with skill, but also with difficulty. This is heavy combat. One prevails by slicing off his opponent's head. Bresson creates, amplifies the sound of gushing blood, which we also see soaking the ground. Hero? Villain? Which is which? The two men look identical, and life is over so quickly. War's trappings have changed; war has remained constant. King Arthur's reign is coming to a sad, bitter close.

Some of us learned about adultery, before we had a word for it, from Arthurian tales and films. Adultery absolutely fits in a world geared for war. Corrupt, it is, ironically, a reach for some antidote to corruption. Knights wear armor indoors in Bresson's film to convey not just their vulnerability but also the burden of bloodshed into which they are locked. They hide their corruption, deceiving themselves, others, no one. Poor Gauvain so wants to continue revering Lancelot and Guenièvre and disastrously keeps defending them.

Time passes all by. But these characters are also right *here*, along with their legacy: the disastrous confusion of idealism and corruption.

CELINE AND JULIE GO BOATING (France). *But, the next morning* . . .

Sharing a sense of the dramatic and the spirit of adventure, librarian Julie (Dominique Labourier, hilarious) is the more imaginative and occultish, the one who believes in real magic, while nightclub magician Céline is the more practically intelligent. They come to share Julie's Paris flat. Except that Jacques Rivette's *Céline et Julie vont en bateau* isn't at all schematic, one might consider the two of them complementary aspects of a single personality, especially since each substitutes for the other on an important occasion (one involving romance, one involving work). Their zany, fun-loving, free-flowing relationship owes something, as does the film, to Věra Chytilová's Czech *Daisies* (1966). The film also alludes to Lewis Carroll's *Alice's Adventures in Wonderland* and stories by Henry James.

What is it about that odd abandoned mansion at 7 bis, rue de Nadir aux Pommes, where Céline says she once worked as a nanny and where Julie may even have lived as a child (she describes the girl there as having been "the same age" as she)? Each day one or the other visits the place, the scene of the same recurring set of events involving a perplexing family and the murder of the child; but no sooner is Julie or Céline outside she is able to recall nothing (except in teasing incoherent flashes) until the magic candies that don't have to advertise "Eat me" help provide some continuity. Both women find a way to enter together this parallel universe to solve the murder, reverse it and rescue the child. Finally, the three go boating—although Céline and Julie have been figuratively boating on the lake of their intertwined unconscious from the start.

Airy enchantment, this recovery of one's lost inner child and harmonious integrity.

1975

THE PASSENGER (Italy, France, Spain). Written by Mark Peploe, Peter Wollen and the director, Michelangelo Antonioni's *Professione: reporter*, a baleful, delicately mournful mystery, tests assumptions about identity, responsibility, authority. Antonioni also prods our perception to the full—for instance, by setting critical action just beyond the camera's range so that we must listen carefully to *hear* what is going on.

David Locke, a fatigued, jaded journalist, starts anew by exchanging identities with a corpse in a North African hotel. Maintaining professional distance, seeing detail but always missing the larger picture, Locke has held himself aloof from the revolutionary upheavals he has been covering, discounting their relevance to his own life. Now his new identity places him dead-center in the opportunistic, politically non-committed world of gunrunning.

Professione: reporter critiques the assumption that the only connections the West can have to the Third World are colonialist, insisting instead on a shared humanity that links all people's fates. As reporter, Locke stresses the eye ("Tell me what you see now . . ."); as artist, Antonioni stresses the soul.

Antonioni's penultimate shot resolves his material. (To be precise, it's a gyroscopically "smoothed" meshing of shots whose outcome gives the appearance of a single slow camera movement.) From inside to out, through a close-barred window in a Spanish hotel, the (seemingly) steadily moving camera draws connections among disparate humans, including Locke, and elements of geographic and political space—indoors, outdoors, indoors again (now using a doorway instead of a window)—before the camera returns to Locke, dead, in his room. Failing to perceive all the connectedness that the camera has just elegantly drawn, Locke has taken a circular stroll into the arms of his own defeatism, uncovering the death lurking beneath the mask/metaphor of the original identity-exchange in Africa: for us, a cautionary rendezvous.

1975

THE PHARMACY (France, China). In the years just before Mao's death and the arrest of the Gang of Four, which signaled the end of the Cultural Revolution in China, Joris Ivens and wife Marceline Loridan took their cameras into Pharmacy No. 3 in Shanghai, which in addition to dispensing drugs manages an outreach program of medical services (after attending to peasants, pharmacists work in the fields alongside them), an extension of the pharmacy's in-house medical care center.

The employees have developed five rules for themselves: to show the same concern for both steady customers and transients, for those who buy and those who simply want information, and for those who buy a lot and those who buy a little; to be equally attentive to customers no matter how busy the pharmacy or whether it is day or night. Their goal is to wholeheartedly serve the public.

There is a fascinating discussion of the competing motives of profit and service; at a weekly employee meeting, one of the participants reconfirms, "We should be concerned [above all else] with people's needs." This has nothing to do with dictate ("The customer is always right") and everything to do with what the workers themselves feel should be motivating them.

La pharmacie N° 3: Shanghai keeps widening, eventually integrating the employees and patrons into the bustling life of the port city. The opening shot at dawn evokes a Turner painting; the closing one, a long-shot of Shanghai citizens under umbrellas in the rain, Ivens's *Regen* (1929), to "de-exoticize" the Chinese.

This documentary is more relaxed and fluent than other brilliant documentaries by Holland's Ivens; the difference may be Loridan, born Rosenberg, a teenaged survivor of a Nazi death camp. There are no tirades against capitalism, only a warm embrace of Chinese humanity.

HARVEST 3,000 YEARS (Ethiopia). "The father grew maize. His son sowed bullets. That black bull will charge if sufficiently provoked."

Mirt Sost Shi Amit is a Brechtian parable about class division and revolt. Based in the U.S., Haile Gerima returned to his native Ethiopia to shoot this massive, staggering reflection on Ethiopia amidst the collapse of Haile Selassie's uncaring regime prior to the military takeover.

Tenants work in various capacities on a farm riddled with echoes of feudal colonialism. Mostly silent, the film is punctuated by distancing naturalistic sounds: mooing cows, squawking chickens, dripping water—this last, a sign of something ominous steadily growing. Work is treated neutrally; it isn't sanctified, in the silent Soviet manner, or identified with oppression. Rather, it is the landlord, equipped with an absolute sense of entitlement, and the social structure he represents that attach oppressed lives to the farm laborers. Indolent (he even has to be shoed by a servant to be ready for church), the landlord berates the shoeless farmers for indolence—a charge that images of their field and other labor piercingly refute. However, this rural situation is metaphorical for all Ethiopia, including urban Ethiopia: "The rich live in high buildings while we, who have worked hard, live in graves." Someone also says that an Ethiopian without money in a bank in Addis Ababa is out of luck, nowhere.

Political conversations, both veiled and blatant, dot the film. More dramatic are instances of that earlier drip-drip coming to an accumulated point of satiation. One is ironic: the cowherder dying in a flooded-over stream trying to retrieve a cow after the landlord has promised death if she loses any of the cattle. Another: the landlord's own lethal pummelling, to which conditioned peasants respond as if he were one of their own.

THE BATTLE OF CHILE: THE STRUGGLE OF AN UNARMED PEOPLE, PART I (Venezuela, France, Cuba). On-the-spot documentaries can capture the most unshakable things. *La insurreción de la burguesía*, the first part of *La batalla de Chile: La lucha de un*

1975

pueblo sin armas (top prize, Grenoble), the immense tripartite film directed by Patricio Guzmán and produced (and partially shot?) by Chris Marker, ends with a stunning moment. Democratically elected Salvador Allende, a Marxist, aimed to bring social justice to his nation. One of the soldiers opposing a crowd of Allende supporters after Augusto Pinochet's September 11, 1973, military coup faces one of the film's cameramen. Guzmán freezes the frame in which the soldier takes aim at the cameraman; the restoration of motion thus finds the Argentinean, whose camera falls into darkness, recording his own death.

This 3-hour-plus installment spans the election of Allende's Popular Unity government and its legislative and military opposition. (The U.S. had backed the right-wing Christian Democrats, one of the political parties opposing Allende's election.) The black-and-white film is blessed with clear, soft, mostly gray cinematography by Jorge Müller Silva that moderates the pulsating handheld camera work, much as Abilio Fernandez's measured, soft-spoken narration moderates the political turbulence we watch unfold. Guzmán's tack is to bring meditative calm to the material so as not to exploit and cheapen this material. The purity this tack cumulatively achieves astonishes; the result is deeply affecting.

One of the most complex passages addresses a copper miners' strike whose organizers aimed at undermining the government following Allende's nationalization of the mining industry. Guzmán presents here an unusually sensitive portrait of individual versus national interests that freshly illuminates familiar material.

Guzmán's cameras, everywhere, record everything, including individual faces and an electrifying overhead view of massive humanity.

JEANNE DIELMAN, 23 QUAI DU COMMERCE, 1080 BRUXELLES (Belgium). A sometime (and brilliant) documentarian, Chantal Äkerman remains a documentarian of sorts even in her fictions, seamlessly blending the two modes, for example, in her first masterpiece, *Jeanne Dielman, 23 Quai du Commerce, 1080 Bruxelles*. In addition, the particularity of the title yields to a generalization on the modern human condition. Äkerman's minimalism assists this process and the other, collapsing forms of expression at opposite poles into a common essence. Similarly, sound yields to nearly total silence.

In her greatest role, Delphine Seyrig plays Jeanne, a widow who belle-de-jours in her own home to support herself and her son. Here is a soul, it is implied, without better options, and her twin activities, domestic and remunerative, have much the same character. Äkerman, then, has collapsed the difference between these also, wittily/tragically reflecting on the cultural assignment of "woman's work." Both are driven by necessity, in one instance, psychic, for the sake of imposed order, and in the other, financial. At the same time, Luis Buñuel's film (*Belle de jour*, 1967) reminds us, the motives for becoming a prostitute may be ambiguous and complex. For Jeanne, it is a routine that both extends and takes her out of her domestic routine and connects her with her son by elusively paralleling his school attendance.

This powerful film's 3¼ hours cover three days. They are three routine, repetitive days like countless others in Jeanne Dielman's life. The routine and the repetition are in effect anchoring Jeanne, shielding her from the unchartable, indefinable void of modern existence; their rupture triggers calamity, exposing the lack of structure and cohesiveness for which the routine was compensation and cover-up. At the end, isn't Jeanne's apparent explosion really an *im*plosion?

Äkerman's feminism yields an across-gender social critique.

NUMERO DEUX/ESSAI TITRES (France). *See above.*

XALA (Senegal). Ousmane Sembène looks back to Senegal's independence from France. People rejoice in the streets—perhaps prematurely. Fifteen years later, Sembène implies, Senegal still hasn't come into its own.

1975

The protagonist is El Hadji Abdou Kader Beye, a food merchant who, like other members of the government-connected businessmen's group to which he belongs, routinely diverts funds intended for the poor, for whom he has contempt. Enamored of power and influence, and having adopted the French colonialists' smug sense of superiority, he exploits black Africans. He is, after all, a capitalist.

Each group member has been given a stash of cash for business use, but El Hadji uses his for a lavish wedding. His young bride looks miserable at the ceremony, though, and Wife #2 counsels patience to Wife #3. What a hard limit, it turns out, #2's patience really has!

El Hadji defends his status-seeking third marriage for its "Africanity"—its revival of traditional black African practice. "I am the master here!" he shouts at daughter Rama, a socialist and feminist, after striking her for telling him that all polygamists are liars.

Plainly El Hadji needs to be taught a lesson. The lesson is not long in coming. El Hadji cannot "perform" on his wedding night. His penis, we are informed, "crumpled like a wet piece of paper"—an allusion, perhaps, to the new nation's Constitution. Has someone put a hex on him a xulu, a curse of impotence? El Hadji tries everything to undo the "curse." Finally a traditional "healer" succeeds, exacting a capitalist's price: El Hadji's full purse.

Overextended, El Hadji goes under financially. Not having been paid, the healer reinstates the curse. Beggars El Hadji once had hauled away by the police now occupy his home and dish out just desserts. Sembène knows his *Viridiana* (1961).

NASHVILLE (U.S.). "I saw a leg sticking out. . . . I need something like this for my documentary! It's America: all those cars *smashing together*." —Opal, BBC reporter

As a friend recently reminded me, I used to not like Robert Altman's most celebrated film. The passage of time, though, has helped me see that I was wrong. *Nashville* really is a masterpiece.

Altman's *Nashville* zigzags among different stories involving performers and "civilians" at a particular time in Nashville. Someone with a loudspeaker attached to his vehicle is a presidential candidate seeking to abolish the Electoral College and "The Star Spangled Banner" as the national anthem, and a self-involved Brit is on hand making a documentary about America for the BBC. But the wonder of *Nashville* is its tightly woven fabric of somewhat peculiar American lives. Like Alfred Hitchcock in *Psycho* (1960), Altman finds the American mainstream full of human aberration.

Perhaps the most remarkable contributor to this composite portrait of American behavior is Tom Frank. Frank, part of a trio, is narcissistic; he makes love while tape recordings of his songs play. Yet, when a performer (not in the trio) is shot down on stage from the audience, he is there, helping however he can—*instantly*. Keith Carradine, as Tom, gives the film's finest performance. He also wrote and composed the film's two best songs. Carradine won an Oscar for "I'm Easy"; but how many realize he also wrote "It Don't Worry Me," the anthem by which another character, beautifully played by Barbara Harris, rallies the shaken audience after the (likely successful) assassination attempt? *Nashville* is Altman's, but also Carradine's —a step in his becoming one of his generation's most interesting American film actors.

Nashville includes Altman's best shots: closeups of the American flag rippled by a disconcerting breeze.

F FOR FAKE (France, Iran, West Germany). *F for Fake*, also known as *Vérités et mensonges* (*Truths and Lies*), is Orson Welles's exquisite documentary about trickery and fraud—something the world's most famous amateur magician should know something about. Indeed, the film nearly begins with a cloaked Welles delighting two children with a magic trick at a train depot. It exactly begins with just the sound of his voice beginning this trick against a blank screen, a reminder of how Welles convinced countless Americans during the Depression of a Martian invasion through the simulated news bulletins in his radio broadcast of *War of the Worlds*. All's Wells that ends Welles.

1975

Welles uses the form of a film about the shooting of a film. Deceptively, we will find out, he assures us at the outset, that his film is entirely true. This is one of his most playful films.

Among the "practitioners" of fakery it documents are Elmyr de Hory, the art forger, Hory's biographer, Clifford Irving, who also wrote a fraudulent biography of recluse Howard Hughes, and Welles himself, whose sleight of artful hand, besides juggling old and new documentary elements and sly reenactments, creates a structure of Chinese boxes among which Welles cuts back and forth with dizzying, delightful rapidity.

Eventually, the film pulls its Persian rug out from under us, exposing how it has succeeded in fooling us. This isn't errant manipulation because it clarifies Welles's thematic intent: a bravura demonstration of our inclination to cede to seemingly authoritative information and to authority itself. *F for Fake* is, ultimately, an anti-fascist work. This serious purpose, then, accounts for its complex tone, which includes notes of profound melancholy. Too often we have been fooled by dangerous political ideas and leaders.

CRÍA CUERVOS (Spain). *Raise ravens, and they will pluck your eyes out.* — Spanish proverb

Carlos Saura's *Raise Ravens*—nonsensically in the U.S., *Cria!*—is, like his *Garden of Delights* (1970), a political allegory about Spain under Franco, who died sometime around when production began. It is also a sensitive evocation of a nine-year-old's childhood, but this childhood, described by the adult Ana as "sad" and "indeterminate," itself suggests the imprint of fascist Spain.

The film opens with black-and-white photographs of Ana and family. Color photos follow —also snapshots of the past, but, in juxtaposition with those preceding it, also suggesting the present. Finally, the appearance of both color and black-and-white photos within the same shot, intermingling time frames, suggests memory. Ana's mother, Maria, is dead; Ana's father, in bed with his mistress as Ana listens outside his door, is about to be, from a heart attack.

Ana's father was a military officer—one of Franco's soldiers. The night of his death the camera moves through the darkness of his house; emblematic of Francoism, he is the darkness in the house. Maria might have been a concert pianist, but her husband's rigid authority denied her this. He had translated the home into Francoism.

Geraldine Chaplin plays (beautifully) two roles: Maria, as the adult Ana recalls or reimagines her; the adult Ana. The film is surrealistic, so there is really no way to determine whether or when Ana the child is imagining herself as a grown-up or remembering her mother, or whether or when the adult is Maria or Ana, or a conflation of both. In the same frames, both child and adult appear; but who is comforting whom? Daughter bereft of mother reflects mother bereft of daughter, and fascism has tightened the tangle of experiences and memories entrapping both Anas.

THE LOST HONOR OF KATHARINA BLUM (West Germany). Brilliantly written and directed by Margarethe von Trotta and Volker Schlöndorff, *The Lost Honor of Katharina Blum, or: How Violence Develops and Where It Can Lead* is an assault on the contemporary West German yellow press, showing the dire, even fatal consequences for innocent lives wrought by tabloid smears. From Heinrich Böll's novel, it reflects the author's own run-ins with Bild Zeitung.

Katharina Blum, a young maid who is completely apolitical, spends the night with a man she meets at a party. He is an anarchist. The police storm into her apartment the next morning and, in the absence of their main target, arrest her instead. A tabloid, *The Paper*, does the rest, smearing her as a politically motivated slut. Von Trotta and Schlöndorff intriguingly connect the police and the press, showing how the latter's inapt democratic claims of "freedom of the press" distract from the former's fascistic tactics and their own deutsche mark-chasing opportunism. Here, in the States, we speak of the media's "feeding frenzy," its steamrolling appetite for more and more "news" to keep a "story" current, which is to say, solvent. However, the monstrous activity this film portrays, however frenzied it may appear in the aggregate, is too calculatedly cruel and vicious to justify the term. Blum herself remarks that her ordeal, to which the authorities and the press contributed, robbed her of her honor. She ends up in a frame of mind that her existence previous to the ordeal could not have predicted.

Angela Winkler is wonderful in the lead role, especially when Katharina's mother pays the ultimate price for her daughter's misfortunes. Indeed, the entire cast, which includes a superb Heinz Bennent as a sympathetic lawyer, is flawless.

1976

IN THE COURSE OF TIME (West Germany). Apart from Herzog's *Aguirre*, the most magnificent West German film of the 1970s is *Im Lauf der Zeit*, Wim Wenders' nearly three-hour road movie about an itinerant film projectionist, Bruno, who, along the West-East German border, visits expiring cinemas in small villages—a reflection of a culture evaporating as a result of changes wrought by time, current collusive film distribution practices, and American popular culture influence. Along the way, Bruno gives a ride to Robert, a pediatrician whose marriage and own vehicle have collapsed. They encounter a suicide's widower, precipitating certain decisions of their own and eventually contributing to the dissolution of their growing bond. Like Federico Fellini's great road movie, *La strada* (1954), Wenders' signature epic is about will-o'-the-wisps, uprooted and rootless humanity amidst a mesmerizing landscape under an illimitable sky that, especially at night, sparkles with an omnipresent sense of eternity. Misleadingly, in the States and Britain the film is called *Kings of the Road*.

Wenders' film is imbued with two dual senses: the frailty and infinite worth of human lives; aimlessness or restlessness, and mission or purpose—improvisation amid the playing-out of individual destinies. One episode that crystallizes both these dual senses finds Bruno and Robert conjuring a clown act for raucous schoolchildren eagerly anticipating their annual movie.

Few films more beautifully captivate with a tragic sense of the passage of time. The film's deceptively leisurely pace conveys the weight of humanity's persistent mortal awareness. Time is the "king" of this road, and everything that happens happens in the course of time.

Wenders' most important collaborators for his most heartfelt and inexhaustible ride are his black-and-white cinematographer, Robby Müller, and his lead actor, his patient Everyman, Rüdiger Vogler, who plays Bruno.

ASCENT (U.S.S.R.). With Esther Shub, Larisa Shepitko was one of two outstanding Soviet woman filmmakers. In 1979, while scouting locations, Shepitko and four members of her crew were killed in a road accident. Shepitko was 41 years old. Elem Klimov, her widower, made two films in tribute to her: the documentary *Larisa* (1980) and the film that his wife did not live to complete: *Farewell* (1981).

The film of Shepitko's that's most widely available in the U.S. is the most famous: *Voskhozhdeniye*. With its foot journey doubling as a journey into the snowy depths of self-knowledge and spirituality, *Voskhozhdeniye* depicts in stark black and white the German occupation of Byelorussia during World War II. Two Byelorussian soldiers venture ever deeper into occupied territory in search of supplies for their beleaguered troop. Captured, they face their certain fate differently, in ways corresponding to the historic conflict between humanity's mind and soul.

Based on Vasil Bykau's story "Sotnikov," Shepitko's final work testifies to her profound religious feeling and the breadth of her philosophical engagement of experience encompassing universal truths regarding what might be described as the endless dialectic of life and death. *Voskhozhdeniye* achieves a serene contemplation of chaotic circumstance, avoiding both defeatism and bogus inspiration. It is a just consideration of both the reach and hard limits of human possibility.

In an extraordinary shot, a blank screen is held for what seems an eternity. From below the screen, heads finally bob into view: partisans being marched uphill to their executions— humans headed for the eternity from whence they came.

Ukrainian, Shepitko was mentored by Aleksandr Dovzhenko, cinema's "Poet of the Ukraine," whose final film, *Poem of the Sea* (1958), she assisted his widow, Yulia Solntseva, in completing. Shepitko was fond of quoting Dovzhenko: "Approach each film as though it were your last."

PASTORALI (U.S.S.R.). Otar Iosseliani's *Pastoral* is the Georgian's first truly signature work. It opens in the city—Iosseliani's own Tbilisi—where arrangements are being made for a string quartet to spend the summer in the country. Whatever the reason for their visit, they end up as cultural anthropologists by recording the singing of *kolhozniks*.

This is a film about work, including farm work: chopping this, hauling that, shepherding animals, etc. Upon arrival, one of the musicians kicks aside a bottle that had been upright in the road. A farmer lugging a huge hill of hay pauses at the spot in order to reset the bottle to a standing position—work inside work, and a very human interruption of seemingly animal labor. Women are shown endlessly cooking and cleaning. Moreover, everyday activities are shown to be work; for instance, a local teenager who has taken a shine to one of the musicians grooms her hair while looking into a mirror. Her earnest concentration turns this ordinary task into pressing work.

Pastoral is mostly a black-and-white silent. Dialogue is minimal. We hear musical instruments, voices in song, and farm, domestic and wild animals' squawking, mooing, oinking, barking, chattering. A large herd of sheep crosses the road. A bus disturbs part of the orderly procession up ahead, while another part of the herd, closer to the camera, remains uniformly intact, all this mirroring humanity: lives structured and controlled by the work they must attend to; boisterous lives bursting out of this controlling structure.

Iosseliani shows great affection for his characters, who come in all ages, sizes and shapes. With the musicians, it avoids fish-out-of-water material; neither city nor country gives the other a comical beating. There is no bogus feeling of regret when the musicians are back in Tbilisi.

Pastoral is a beautiful comedy.

JANA ARANYA (India). The final part of his Calcutta trilogy (the first two parts being *The Adversary*, 1970, and *Company Limited*, 1971), *The Middleman* is Satyajit Ray's bleakest film, its satire on capitalism ending in tragedy.

On a year-end college exam, many students cheat. Honest, ethical, bright, well-prepared, Somnath Banerjee does not. Somnath passes, but without honors, because the grader, needing stronger eyeglasses, cannot read his small writing. What's the point then? The boy quits school to enter the workforce. He has no luck despite countless interviews—the result of the pointless questions he is asked. ("What is the weight of the moon?") A friend, though, offers him work as a "middleman"—someone who fills orders for business clients at a markup while also fulfilling other expectations. It's corrupting work. Somnath's cultured father feels disgraced by his son's wallow in the muck of business. Meanwhile, Somnath's friend Sukumar, struggling against poverty, has finally found a job as a cab driver, but the income is insufficient to keep Kauna, his sister, from becoming a prostitute. Somnath delivers Kauna, prepaid, to a potential client—a violation of his closest friendship that gets him a big contract.

I have read that *Jana Aranya* drew upon Ray's despair over the corruption and anti-civil libertarianism of prime minister Indira Gandhi's administration. The long passage during which Somnath reluctantly moves from brothel to brothel in search of the right girl for the client he is courting suggests his gradual collapse into shame, compromise and moral equivocation. He tells Kauna she does not have to go through with the meeting, but Kauna's insistence on an alternative work identity—Juthika—to dissociate herself from her sordid secret life is irreconcilable with any failure to service a client. The closing image is of Somnath's father feigning happiness at his son's "success."

THE MARQUISE OF O . . . (West Germany). Eric Rohmer ventured outside France for the West German *The Marquise of O . . .*, from Heinrich von Kleist's 1808 novella. It is a civilized, exquisitely ironical comedy about a woman's rape, a meditation on the limits society imposes on a woman's right to self-determination.

During the Franco-Prussian War, Julietta, who has been faithful to her deceased husband's memory, is saved from rape by a Russian officer, a Count, who, unbeknownst to her, takes advantage of her himself when she is asleep. Once she is pregnant with her third child and can offer no explanation, her parents dismiss the Marquise's claims of abiding virtue and toss her out.

Structured as a flashback, the film opens with men in a tavern discussing the Marquise's newspaper advertisement soliciting her unborn child's father to come forward and marry her, to undo some portion of her estrangement from family and to moderate her family's shame. The Count, who has already guiltily pressed his marriage proposal several times, shows up to confess his crime and claim his bride.

Given this conclusion, how do we know that Rohmer appreciates the horror of rape? The shot of Julietta, passed out on her bed, as the Count enters her boudoir to violate her derives from the most horrific fantastic painting of sexual assault imaginable: Henry Fuseli's 1781 *The Nightmare.* (A shot of the nape of Julietta's neck, projecting both sensuality and vulnerability, derives from Fuseli's 1800 *Nude Woman Listening to a Girl Playing upon the Spinet.*)

Edith Clever and Peter Lühr, as daughter and father, are brilliant. Those who cherish the paintings of Caspar Friedrich, moreover, prepare yourselves for a visual feast, courtesy of Rohmer and his color cinematographer, Nestor Almendros.

COMMENT ÇA VA? (France). Twice during Jean-Luc Godard and Anne-Marie Miéville's very beautiful *How's It Going?*, we see graffiti on an outside wall consisting of a swastika and a circle—an expression of fascism. Or is it? The circle, on top, makes a target out of the swastika; this, then, is *anti*-fascist. But this presumes that the swastika preceded the circle. Might not the fascist symbol instead be obliterating a conventional symbol for harmony? Or perhaps the closed circle indicates the closing off of democratic debate, and the superimposed appearance of the swastika may be glossing commentary—to this effect: *such "closure" invites fascism.* Images bewitch with their ambiguity and possibilities. (One wonders: did Godard himself sketch the graffiti?!)

An editor of a Communist newspaper (based on *Libération*) and Odette (Miéville), a typist, together watch the former's "videofilm." Thus, for a good deal of the film, we watch these two watch the film-within-the-film, with Odette probing the interior film's maker out of his clichés and complacency. Here is a film about two photographs, one of confrontation between protestors and the police in Portugal, and the other of a similar scene in France. Perhaps the most striking aspect of the Portuguese photograph is that a young man on the protesting frontline grips the raised fist of an opposing officer. In any case, wipes ever more rapidly flip back and forth between the two photos until both images are superimposed. Correlative to this is a political pronouncement in the editor's voiceover, a call for one solution to more than one problem: not "equal labor, equal wages," but "unequal labor, equal wages"!

Odette hits her manual typewriter's keys: sometimes the sound is erased while we watch her hands at work; sometimes we hear the sound combined with other images.

PRIVATE VICES, PUBLIC VIRTUES (Italy, Yugoslavia). Neil Burger's *The Illusionist*

(2006) is the thinnest, dullest, most inconsequential film to touch upon the "Mayerling affair"; Hungarian master filmmaker Miklós Jancsó's *Vizi privati, pubbliche virtù*, from Italy and Yugoslavia, is the liveliest, most intriguing, most passionately moving. (This assessment takes into account Max Ophüls's estimable *De Mayerling à Sarajevo*, 1940.) Among young royalty and others, amidst marvelous classical, folk and martial music, dancing and laughter, and assassination passed off as murder-suicide—this last incident is among the film's numerous "what ifs"—Jancsó addresses "people and the masks they wear," historical figures who have "a face for every occasion." In one extraordinary party sequence, during which Crown Prince Rudolf learns that his father, Franz Joseph I, Emperor of Austria, King of both Hungary and Bohemia, has stepped down, giving him, Rudolf, those positions, we see a mask of Franz Joseph covering a girl's vagina, suggesting the repressiveness and tyrannical nature of Franz Joseph's rule, and, in an even more stunning shot, a lateral view of Rudolf removing from his face an identical mask of his father. This is heady stuff.

Indeed, there is much intoxicated revelry, illicit and group, and even incestuous, sex, an astounding degree of nudity, including frontal, both male and female, all played out with sensual abandon at the Mayerling estate following a failed assassination attempt against the Emperor, in which his only son and heir played a part. It isn't merely a contest of power; Rudolf, here, despises everything his father stands for. In Jancsó's film, liberated sexuality denotes opposition to and contempt for tyranny, and surely reminds one of the heavy, puritanical Soviet hand that was part of the package of oppression that Jancsó's own Hungary was enduring.

The film, in Italian, was written by Giovanna Gagliardo.

ILLUSTRIOUS CORPSES (Italy). The same year that the U.S. produced its middling, indifferently acted *All the President's Men* (Alan J. Pakula, 1976), another film exemplified the conspiratorial political thriller at full-throttle. While police inspector Rogas (Lino Ventura, in his finest performance) investigates a high court murder, other judges, prosecutors and magistrates continue to be killed. Dark, convoluted, blurring the line between paranoiac perception and a reality suited to paranoia, Francesco Rosi's *Cadaveri eccelenti* makes its way through a sludge of suspects, beginning with the Mafia, before lighting on right-wing assassination squads—the sort (though not in Italy) that the U.S. government is routinely fond of supporting.

Rosi once described the film as "a journey through the monsters and monstrosities of power," and along the way both Left and Right are in for close examination. But the particularity of such actual case studies as Rosi's *The Mattei Affair* (1972) yields here to a more unbounded, featureless province, that of the waking nightmare. *Illustrious Corpses*, based on a novel by Leonardo Sciascia, is Kafkaesque.

This kind of film hews to a line of unearthing the truth. Fittingly, this one begins in catacombs, amidst mummified corpses, suggesting the shadow of mortality dogging us and pressing our activities, including insane political acts, and introducing a permeative claustrophobic sense. We feel "buried alive"; Rogas becomes buried in the case.

As assassinations mount, Rosi investigates their cost to society. Indeed, the horror of the unfolding event threatens to sweep away society's institutions. Like a cancer, the conspiracy has a life of its own—a power to effect social consequences beyond the grasp of all its members.

Rosi risks Kramertosis by casting Charles Vanel, Max von Sydow and Alain Cuny as legal V.I.P.s, but his taut control, not to mention gifted actors, keeps this a burrowing, enveloping film.

MOTHER OF KINGS (Poland). "A person may give his life for some undefined hope because he does not control his fate."

From Kasimierz Brandys's novel *Sons and Comrades*, writer-director Janusz Zaorski's

Matka Królów charts the life of Łucja Król (Magda Teresa Wójcik, tremendous), a Polish washerwoman, the widowed mother of four sons, from the mid-1930s through 1956, when deStalinization permitted a rehabilitated Władysław Gromułka to be elected president of the Polish Communist Party. Unlike Gromułka's, the political imprisonment of one of Łucja's sons, Klemens (Bogusław Linda, superb), resolves itself in his death. Uninformed of this, Łucja awaits Klemens's release and return. "You've had a hard life," an old friend notes. Łucja: "Others have had a harder one."

Łucja is apolitical, but the family is Communist and possessed of an eventually important Communist friend, a lawyer, who (unbeknownst to her) betrays her lest the Party turn on him. Zaorski compellingly shows the impact of Stalinist oppression on ordinary lives. Indeed, his vision is more widely applicable, for a connection is drawn between the juvenile robbery in which Klemens's youngest brother participates and the unfairness, cruelty and paranoia of the state.

Private lives are at the mercy of the state's convoluted politics. Klemens, whom the Gestapo had imprisoned at Auschwitz during the war, marries afterwards Marta, whom he chides for being "Miss Bourgeoisie." But he teaches her to believe in the Party. When Klemens is arrested on unwarranted charges of disloyalty, Marta is determined to wait for him; but she eventually abandons that cause, reasoning that the Party doesn't arrest people without cause. We begin to see Stalinism as a configuration of fear into which people's lives are powerfully impressed.

Zaorski's black-and-white film seamlessly incorporates newsreel clips. It is as if we have lit upon Łucja in an actual crowd in the street.

THE KILLING OF A CHINESE BOOKIE (U.S.). Ben Gazzara, an excellent actor, claims the role of a lifetime as Cosmo Vitelli, hands-on owner of the strip club the Crazy Horse West, in one of the ten best U.S. films of the 1970s, *The Killing of a Chinese Bookie*. Writer-director John Cassavetes has created a moody, atmospheric, tense, ultimately heart-piercing melodrama about Cosmo's laconic navigation of a tawdry milieu largely populated by lowlifes. Cosmo himself maintains a facsimile of emotional balance by skipping from gambling debt to gambling debt, doing his best to pay one before moving on to the next. By no means is Crazy Horse West making him financially flush. Cosmo is in a grip of trouble.

Color cinematographers Mitchell Breit and Al Ruban help Cassavetes evoke a subterranean seediness which surpasses that of Martin Scorsese's *Mean Streets* (1973). Indeed, Cassavetes conjures an infernal realm of barely penetrable darkness, as thick as smoke. This is correlative to moral cloudiness. For a gambling debt he is tardy in paying off, Cosmo, a veteran who killed men in the Korean War, is forced to take out an elderly importer-exporter, the Chinese bookie of the title, in order to lose the debt. In reality, he was set up for this outcome and another one to follow: his own execution.

Strangeness and corruption are pervasive. Commandeering the stage at Crazy Horse West is Mr. Sophistication, a weird, rotund crybaby who sings to the audience "I Can't Give You Anything but Love, Baby" and nurtures jealousy against the girls. This mess of a performer encapsulates the reduction of Cosmo's aspirations, the dead-end that his life has become.

Cassavetes' uncompromisingly pessimistic film more convincingly invokes the Watergate scandal, however elusively, than either Roman Polanski's *Chinatown* (1974) or Alan J. Pakula's *All the President's Men* (1976).

1977

THE SEALED SOIL (Iran). Marva Nabili's *Khak-e sar beh Morh* revolves around 18-year-old Rooy-Bekheir, beautifully played by Flora Shabavis. The rest of the cast consists of actual inhabitants of a small Iranian village. By her age, her mother had borne four children, but Rooy-Bekheir has declined all matches arranged for her. She cannot explain her reluctance to marry. That would take a voice in a place where women unroll a rug so men can sit and decide things—although social upheaval is contriving to undermine even their authority. Rooy-Bekheir is given to tarrying in the woods, deep in thought. One day, shown from the back, she is alone there, seated in silence except for luminous rain. She undresses from the waist up and breathes deeply, her shoulders delicately inflecting as she steals a liberated moment. Soon after, she hysterically kills a chicken. Someone is summoned to exorcise her "demons." The rituals may have worked, for at film's end Rooy-Bekheir seems resigned to marry.

We watch sewing, meal preparations—daily routines. Outside the family's primitive home, squawking chickens and unseen wild birds both interrupt and underscore the quiet. All the shots are static, many with Rooy-Bekheir either walking towards or away from the camera—sometimes alongside a road outside the village, generating incongruous images of the traditionally clad girl and a few motor vehicles in the same frames. The cumulative result of the fixed camera set-ups is an exquisite stillness ironically also denoting, for Rooy-Bekheir, a straightjacketing existence.

The Sealed Soil suggests a more meditative version of Jean-Louis Bertucelli's powerful *Ramparts of Clay* (1968). Like that film, Nabili's ran into political trouble. Once Islamic fundamentalists came to power, the film's rough cut had to be smuggled out of Iran. The remaining work was done in the United States.

NEWS FROM HOME (Belgium). Belgium's greatest filmmaker ever is a Jewish woman and (as some of her films make explicit) a lesbian. This is Chantal Äkerman, whose masterpiece, *D'Est* (1993), I named one of the world's ten best films in my 100 Greatest Films List.

For a spell, Äkerman lived in New York City, where she made, at a hotel inhabited by elderly persons, the haunting documentary *Hotel Monterey* (1972). She returned to the city to make *News from Home*, about her relationship with her mother during the time of her first stay away from home. The New York she documents along the way isn't Woody Allen's elegant haunt scored to Gershwin (*Manhattan*, 1979) but a teeming, colorful metropolis correlative to the explosion of possibilities in her (then) young life.The film counterpoints soft, vibrant city images with her mother's lonely letters from Brussels, which in effect the images drown out, their "voice"—Äkerman herself reads the letters aloud—trailing to an inaudible whisper to suggest the normal separation from family of a grown offspring and her passage into an irresistible life of her own. Her mother's gingerly expressed pleas for companionship, to maintain the security of their familiar bond, the film doesn't caricature as manipulative stratagem, nor are we likely to mistake daughter's neglect of parent for abandonment. Rather, the film records a life-process whose enveloping warm irony is the fact that Äkerman, now independent, through this film of hers, shares with her mother her own "news from home," thus making possible between them a new, more appropriate, no less loving relationship. (Äkerman's mother would appear in her daughter's next film.)

Two of the hallmarks of Äkerman's great art are her humanity and minimalism, both in evidence in *News from Home*. Although stylistically elliptical, the film is emotionally direct —and immensely satisfying.

THE BATTLE OF CHILE: THE STRUGGLE OF AN UNARMED PEOPLE, PART II (Cuba, Chile, France). We hear the tumult in the street in Santiago before we see it; the opening credits of *El golpe de estado*, the second part of *La batalla de Chile: La lucha de un pueblo sin armas* (top prize again, Grenoble), are blocking our view. The first part begins similarly, but in this instance the procedure formally resonates; for, with the launch of "el golpe"—the coup—against him, Salvador Allende does not quite "see" *the people*—about a third of the electorate had voted for him—who are so willing to defend his presidency at ultimate personal risk to themselves. Rather, he focuses on the Chilean legislature in pursuit of a course for resolving the crisis that would not "de-legitimize" his presidency nearly three years after his historic election. Ironically, the U.S.-backed Christian Democrats, who continue to oppose him, meet with Allende, to give the appearance of underway negotiations, only after the Catholic Church publicly prays that such meetings take place. Politics are merely forestalling the inevitable military ousting of Chile's democratically elected Marxist president.

As with the first part of Patricio Guzmán's monumental black-and-white documentary, light gray predominates; but this time there is at least one jolting scene in which the faces of people in the street are dimmed to darkness.

Speeches and public pronouncements by all sorts of individuals and groups, including media, now become the film's principal mode of content; this, added to the continuing voiceover narration, creates a stream of talk that eventually makes the announcement of Allende's death a seemingly slipped-in thing. Ironically, one might almost miss the momentous news: Augusto Pinochet has seized power.

Cumulatively, the second part is overwhelmingly sad, tremendously moving.

CEDDO (Senegal). Banned by his nation, Ousmane Sembène's *Ceddo* is set in Senegal's past, when the Ceddo—*the people*; those who resist—were forced to convert to Islam by occupying Islamic forces. The film, by turns a mythical and grimly realistic epic, reflects on the African need to retain native cultural roots against whatever outside forces oppose this: Christianity, colonialism and neocolonialism, as well as Islam. A Catholic priest and a white trader crop up as figures of oppression and exploitation.

Ceddo is a film of revolt, a cry to rise up against foreign invaders. (It is worth noting that Sembène, "the father of African cinema," studied film in Moscow under Mark Donskoi, the director of *The Rainbow*, 1944, about a Ukrainian village occupied by the Nazis.) Its style is minimalist and, at times, semi-abstract; derived from ideas embodied in its images, the film's force owes nothing to sentimental manipulation.

Like nearly all of Sembène's films, this one is feminist, gleaning a connection, a mirror-imaging, between tribal patriarchy from within and oppression from without. The principal agency of this feminism is the character of Princess Dior Hocine, whose kidnapping is the result of her father's, King Demba War's, alliance with the Islamic invaders. Communal debate ensues. Ultimately the princess shoots dead the Imam occupying her father's throne.

Throughout, the distancing techniques that Sembène marshals do even more than make us think (Brecht); they are correlative to the cultural self-dissociation that Islamic and other oppressors seek to impose on native Africans and which the latter, Sembène feels, must do their utmost to resist. His film is graced with long-shots of *the people*, and it's reasonable to assume that he was partly inspired by one of the three greatest shots of the 1970s: the closing one of Satyajit Ray's *Distant Thunder* (1973).

CAMOUFLAGE (Poland). A summertime graduate student linguistics competition is underway. Philosopher-physicist Krzysztof Zanussi's satirical comedy *Barwy ochronne* (literally, *Protective Colors*) largely consists of exchanges between two academics, an assistant lecturer and the associate professor who presumably is trying to educate the former as to the realities of human nature and university politics—out of boredom, he maintains. The boy, Jarek, is an insufferably rigid, self-righteous soul who ascribes to notions of rules, justice, honesty, morality, ethics. These concepts, his self-appointed mentor points out, do not exist in nature. They deny humanity's animal being and make sense only in the service of an individual's pursuit of survival. Jakub argues seductively; Jarek parries. The similarity of their names suggests we are witnessing a dramatic translation of a debate between opposing forces in the human personality. On the other hand, Jakub's example may predict Jarek's own necessary evolution.

Actually, Jarek is doubly mentored, for he was hired by the school's vice chancellor, who has put the boy in charge of the contest, although a panel, headed by Jakub, selects the winners. (Jakub claims to have ghost-written the book that launched the vice chancellor's career.) Against Jakub's advice (advice that may be calculated to prod Jarek to take the contrary action), Jarek allows a submission into the competition that arrived a day late—and from a student at a school of which, Jakub claims, the vice chancellor disapproves. The author of an inferior paper is given first prize; at Jarek's insistence, the late paper's author, "honorable mention." When the vice chancellor hands the latter his certificate, the student bites the vice chancellor's ear. Meanwhile, Jarek's scholarship to London hangs in the balance.

With Andrzej Wajda's *Man of Marble* (1977), *Camouflage* helped found Poland's "kino moralnego niepokoju"—cinema of moral concern. It did so sparklingly, delightfully.

JULIO BEGINS IN JULY (Chile). Torrentially dynamic, in terms of bold, sharp camera movement and a high degree of human and other motion energizing the *mise-en-scene*, *Julio comienza en julio* is an astounding film from Chile. Well written by Gustavo Frias, beautifully directed by Silvio Caiozzi, and brilliantly cinematographed in high-contrast sepia by Nelson Fuentes (although I thought I saw a green-leafed tree), it condemns Chile's then-current rule, and gets away with it, by suggesting parallels between Pinochet's military dictatorship and, in 1917, a doomed feudalism.

Wealthy landowner-cattle rancher Julio Garcia Castano, a widower, has three interconnected worries: the nearby Franciscan monastery is claiming ideal grazing land as its own, embroiling him in a legal suit that is taking the courts forever to resolve; Europe's Great War may wind down, which would deflate the market price of his beef; his son, also named Julio, is turning 15, and he wants to "make a man" of Julito and compel him to "face reality." To his son's grand birthday party, Don Julio has invited the local madam, who has brought with her every one of her whores so that Julito has a wide pool from which to choose. Julito chooses Maria, whom he ardently pursues thereafter. Until it reaches a blatant , predictable finish, Caiozzi's film pirouettes across a turbulent tangle of politics, family and other human relationships, spinning the theme of ownership—who owns what and whom. Don Julio's expansive ownership, which includes his lawyer and Julito's live-in-tutor, trumps everyone else's—but an unexpected rebellion changes this.

Surveying family portraits, the opening movement has us waiting for each pair of eyes to blink.

Felipe Rabat is magnificent as Don Julio; Juan Cristobal Meza, his father's son—a contumelious shit.

Possible influences: Tomás Gutiérrez Alea, Haile Gorima, Luchino Visconti.

GRIN WITHOUT A CAT (France). A massive journalistic essay on the post-colonial failures of Leftist radicalism and revolution in the 1960s and 1970s, *Le fond de l'air est rouge* (literally, *The Base of the Air Is Red*), by Chris Marker, a Leftist, marshals a wide range of archival materials, including newsreel excerpts and interviews. The titles of its two parts, "Fragile Hands" and "Severed Hands," chart the direction in which the thing moves. The launching perspective is the rupture of political tissue connecting socialism and communism in France.

The first part addresses the 1968 university student protests in Paris, in particular, unionism's co-opting of these by assigning strikes to their tail. Unions perhaps perceived a relationship between these protests against societal oppression, citizen apathy, and the Vietnam War (the colonialist Indochina War that the U.S. had taken over from France) and their own interests, or simply an opportunity to impress these high-profile protests to their own ends. Thus Marker challenges the myth of Leftist coordination and solidarity, finding little political potential in the heady revolutionary atmospherics in which Paris had become immersed. Ranging the globe (the Congo, Bolivia, Chile, etc.), his film proceeds to deal with numerous events, such as right-wing assassinations and the confrontations between citizens and police throughout Europe.

Alas, I saw the U.S. version, which is reduced by an hour—and not by the editor, Marker himself. Rather than collating different examples of the failure of radicalism and revolution, this version sometimes lurches forward from one example to the next, with only a sentence of narration forging a connection between them, and no mention is made of a country's revolution's becoming mired in pre-revolutionary history, culture. Moreover, a wan British voice has replaced narrators Yves Montand and Simone Signoret, whose disllusionment with Sovietism after Prague '68 was bone-deep.

LAST CHANTS FOR A SLOW DANCE (U.S.). *Last Chants for a Slow Dance*, Jon Jost's "Gary Gilmore film" (metaphorically, not literally), proceeds by set-pieces, switching between color and black and white, sound and silence, static and moving camera, realism and moody dreaminess, script (by Jost and Peter Trias) and improvisation. A haunting evocation of some interior male American landscape, the film follows Tom (Tom Blair, excellent) throughout western Montana in his truck, with lonely stops along the way. Tom, out of work and luckless in his attempts to find work, is chewed out by Darlene, his pregnant wife, for failing to support her and their children. We watch both cede to their roles as defined by U.S. myths: rugged individualism; personal responsibility; effort, hard work = success.

Tom is often not quite what he seems. In his conversation with a young hitchhiker he appears to be a misogynist (aren't working-class adult males supposed to be that?), but a subsequent conversation with someone in a café suggests otherwise.

A teasing refrain accompanies the postal sheets Tom's hand flips through: ". . . should be considered armed and dangerous." These people matter; they are "wanted." "This is all I have left," Tom says, referring to his gun. He has stopped on the road, perhaps with the initial intention of helping the motorist whose car has stalled. Playing the Good Samaritan is a possibility, but starting fresh depends on retaining his anonymity. The motorist recognizes him. After confessing he is jobless and broke, Tom robs the man in a middle-distance shot and shoots him dead in long-shot, the camera distance in the latter case perhaps indicating his not having wanted to do this. At the last Tom is back on the road; his first victim may not be his last.

Jost cinematographed, edited, sings(!).

PADRE PADRONE (Italy). In *Father and Master*, based on Gavino Ledda's memoir, Paolo and Vittorio Taviani portray Ledda's coming out of the shadow of his father, a Sardinian shepherd whose severity is dictated by overwhelming poverty, harsh terrain, hard work, and Italian patriarchy. Until he is 18, Gavino works (as his mother puts it) "alone alone" in his father's pasture, guarding sheep and tending to crops.

The film opens with the actual Ledda, age 35, now a linguist despite having been illiterate for the first half of his life, stripping a tree branch and handing the result to the actor playing his father, saying, "My father always carried a stick." The actor graciously thanks Ledda, but this graciousness instantly evaporates as the actor slips into his role and into the schoolroom from which he will remove little Gavino. This concise opening ironically reflects on the extent to which environment contributes to human behavior; but for their different circumstance, the father might have been like the person who is playing him. In mimicking his father by fashioning the stick, moreover, Ledda makes the kind of implement with which his father punished (and, once, nearly killed) him. Because Ledda betrays no emotion, we fill in by imagining how Ledda must feel amongst his private memories. The Taviani brothers have drawn us into their film.

There is the slow, trotting journey to the distant, isolated pasture where Gavino must stay, and the father's moving attempt to educate his son as to the sounds of the pasture. Conjoined with images of Nature, the father's voice becomes disembodied, creating a haunting echo of the past.

The first part of the film is brilliant; the second part, charting Gavino's victory over his past through education, should have been condensed into a page or two of script.

ELISA, MY LIFE (Spain). Geraldine Chaplin, Carlos Saura's companion and Charlie's daughter, haunts in *Cría cuervos* (1975), but she gives her finest performance in another one of Saura's most wonderful nonmusicals: *Elisa, vida mía*. Again Chaplin plays two parts: Elisa, and Elisa's mother. One must also note that Fernando Rey, tremendous here as Elisa's father, also delivers his greatest performance.

With its analytical flow of time, memory, reality, illusion, *Elisa* mesmerizes and succeeds in making surrealism as much the content as the method of the film—though what we can glean of the psychological narrative also is extraordinary: an elderly writer, ill, secretly writes a book about his grown daughter, Elisa, but from *her* viewpoint—autobiography by imaginative proxy—in order to secure their bond. Once this daughter reads the manuscript, also secretly, however, his sometimes inaccurate view of her view of reality creeps into and begins replacing her own. Thus an ironical Saura posits patriarchal authority and imposition in an elusive, circuitous way fully capable of suggesting their social and cultural pervasiveness; and sharpening the point is the unresolved ambiguity that the father may have left the manuscript in sight in order to entice his daughter into reading it. Saura worries here, as in *Cría cuervos*, that fascism in Spain is not finished as a result of Franco's death, that the social and cultural features that helped install Franco may survive his political rule.

Saura's method also enables him to explore the impingement of one psyche on another—one of the great modern themes—without reviving nineteenth-century overtones of vampirism that somewhat cloud, for instance, Ingmar Bergman's *Persona* (1966).

A SPECIAL DAY (Italy). Sophia Loren is superb as Antonietta, who stays behind rather than join her husband, Emanuele, and their six children on May 8, 1938, when Adolf Hitler, heralded on the radio as "a man of peace," rolls into Rome for his first meeting with Il Duce, Benito Mussolini. Yet it turns out to be *una giornata particolare* for her also; Antonietta meets for the first time Gabriele (Marcello Mastroianni, excellent), her smart, bookish neighbor from across the courtyard, who treats her with respect despite her lack of education, who is as lonely as she, and whose homosexual orientation disqualifies him as a patriarch of any kind. "I'm none of those things [that a man must be]: a husband, a father, a soldier," Gabriele says, to explain why neighbors have warned her away from associating with him. The two spend the day learning to care about each other in defiance of the cold-blooded dance of tyrants outside—and of Antonietta's autocratic spouse, who "doesn't talk," Antonietta confides; "he just gives orders." (Perhaps worse is that her eldest son treats her so snarkily and dismissively.) At day's end, authorities take away Gabriele, delivering him to political exile—the current fate of "subversives" and "perverts." From her window, Antonietta witnesses the event.

Ettore Scola (David di Donatello Award, best director; along with Ruggero Maccari and Maurizio Costanzo, the screenplay prize of Italy's film journalists) here creates a film of such bone-deep melancholy as to qualify it as a quiet, microcosmic epic. Early on, down in the apartment complex courtyard the camera, looking up, rotates; there are human stories through each of these windows. This stressing of individuals runs counter to the fascistic disposition, which Scola's later *La famiglia* (1987) summarizes: "The will of everybody becomes the will of one man."

1978

OUR HITLER (West Germany, France, UK). Hans-Jürgen Syberberg's 7½-hour *Hitler—ein Film aus Deutschland* bombards eye and mind with a staggering vision of Nazism. The non-narrative film fuses Wagnerian opera, political cabaret, wax figures, German film references and fairy-tale mythology ("the World Ice Spirit . . . rebirth . . . master race"), starry heavenly vistas, paintings, speeches, songs, lectures, voiceover, assorted set-pieces to penetrate the fascist German psyche.

Imagined interviews of "men in the street"—those who "elected" Hitler—collapse time and blur the line between history and imagination, finding Hitler at their crossroads. Hitler filled a need for faith in one's discredited, demoralized nation; he loomed as a god demanding self-sacrifice that appealed to the German appetite for self-debasement.

One remarkable segment: Does it correspond to actuality by dint of metaphor or historical accuracy? What revelation either way! Dressed as Caligari (1919), an actor lectures us, describing the schools for boys that the Nazis instituted. Hitler loved birds, he tells us, and, because cats eat birds, as part of their "education" schoolboys gouged out the eyes of cats. Darwin's Nature is thus translated into politics "red in tooth and claw," and self-pity and cruelty, both monstrously enlarged, become indistinguishable. Syberberg's Caligari proceeds to draw the Nazi identification of Jews with rats.

Another segment draws upon past German cinema: Syberberg redoes the scene in Fritz Lang's *M* (1931) in which Peter Lorre's child-rapist/killer breaks down, explaining to the court that he cannot help doing what he does, that he is in the grip of a compulsion beyond his means to resist. In the new version, the man is a Nazi protesting his inability to resist his own politics! On second thought, though, we may wonder whether this constitutes a reimagined *M* or a critical analysis of *M*. What revelation either way!

HYPOTHESIS OF THE STOLEN PAINTING (France). Perhaps the two most dazzling and brilliant works of Victorian literature are Thomas Carlyle's *Sartor Resartus* (1834) and Robert Browning's *The Ring and the Book* (1868-9). One is a convoluted piece of autobiographical prose; the other, a long, complex modernist poem about a Roman murder trial two hundred years earlier. As springboard, each work incorporates a synopsis of its remarkably similar genesis: the coming into the author's hands of a book or facsimile—in Carlyle's case, an esoteric unpublished manuscript by a German professor, Diogenes Teufelsdröckh; in Browning's case, an account of the trial that has come to be known as the *Old Yellow Book*. In the latter case, Browning did purchase such a book at a Florentine flea market in 1860; but in Carlyle's case, the discovery was an elaborate ruse that allowed him to stretch and snap the traditional style of narrative autobiography and to address all manner of social, political and religious subjects at stormy and frequently hilarious liberty.

L'hypothèse du tableau volé, by Raúl Ruiz (in France, Raoul Ruiz), a political self-exile from Pinochet's Chile, is a film approaching the level of wit and invention of Carlyle's first masterpiece.

Written by Ruiz and Pierre Klossowski, it's presented with a poker face as the studious tour of a cache of discovered paintings. Their purported discoverer lectures us; if we don't grasp that (in subsequent parlance) we're being punk'd, we may be inclined to bend to his expertise. The film's bizarre "explanations" of *tableaux vivants* based on the bogus series of "discovered" paintings, in fact, throw into question all such self-involved, convolutedly rational, dictatorially arbitrary exegesis. Soft, dim, in rarefied black and white (the cinematographer is Sacha Vierny), its bewitching visual aspect suggests the self-reflective interiority of Edgar Allan Poe.

IN THE REALM OF PASSION (Japan). A companion-piece to the swooning, painfully immediate *Ai no corrida* (*In the Realm of the Senses*, 1976), *Ai no borei* (*Empire of Passion*) again involves a passionate illicit couple, but is distanced and lacks the oversaturated colors of its predecessor, not to mention the slicing off of an erect penis.

Again, Nagisa Oshima (brilliantly) directs. In a rural village in the late 1800s, a young man convinces his mistress that they should murder her spouse, a rickshaw driver. They dump the body down a well and continue their clandestine affair. But the husband comes back in two ways: as a communal memory, as the villagers wonder how he could stay away in Tokyo year

1978

after year; as a ghost, haunting the killers. The latter might be a guilty projection; or it *could* be a ghost.

The former possibility is in keeping with the film's understanding of human behavior. Oshima's ghost story relates individual acts to communal justice. This "justice" suppresses its own real motives, sublimating these, much as the ghost may be a sublimated form of the couple's guilty regret. Oshima already explored the possibility that capital punishment echoes ancient barbarism in *Death by Hanging* (1968). *Empire of Passion*, in this instance ironically referring to society as it metes out what it has convinced itself is justice, involves a painfully protracted punishment for the offending pair. Oshima goes further, suggesting (compellingly) that society desires, even requires, hideous crime for the sake of both the cathartic release and the reassuring sense of its own justice that the brutal punishment of wrongdoers provides.

But, above all, it is the form of this burrowing work that captivates: dark, mysterious, eerily beautiful color images exquisitely lensed by Yoshio Miyajima, the cinematographer of Masaki Kobayashi's *Kaidan* (1964).

NORTHERN LIGHTS (U.S.). *Northern Lights*, co-directed by John Hanson and Rob Nilsson, attempts to blur the line between its historical fiction and documentary. Blending actors and nonprofessionals, it brings an achingly beautiful black-and-white immediacy to the American past and creates a stirring ode to the American labor movement.

In the fierce North Dakota winter clime of the 1910s, farmers find themselves discounted by politicians and set upon by foreclosing bankers. The grain they work hard to harvest—in a snowstorm, no less, in one of the film's most amazing passages—is sold for processing to grain elevators; the banks and railroad that control these pay exceptionally little. Thus the farmers unionize, in the Nonpartisan League. One of the organizers envisions their cooperatively owning their own grain elevators and becoming shareholders in state-chartered banks. *Northern Lights*, then, depicts the daunting circumstances the farmers face and the countervailing efforts of these new pioneers. It documents the retaliation they endure from the current institutions arrayed against their attempts at social change. It finds in dark, drafty rooms sparse though glowing light—a persistent symbol of hope.

The narrative unfolds as the reminiscence of one of the League's organizers. It is framed in the present. Sadly, the ringing optimism of the tail-end of this narrative frame would soon be erased by the pathological presidency of Ronald Reagan, and so, in our minds, we must add another coda to *Northern Lights*, however much doing so breaks our hearts.

There is a spirit to this film that's irresistible—and, in the extended context of the crippling of unionism in America, which Reagan launched but which considerable mismanagement by unions themselves abetted, this joyful spirit assumes a tragic dimension.

PROVINCIAL ACTORS (Poland). Among Poland's most exceptional films, Agnieszka Holland's *Aktorzy prowincjonalni* revolves around a provincial theatrical troupe outside Warsaw. They're rehearsing something called *Liberation*. The play is historical (". . . 100 years in fetters"), but it reflects the Communist state of Poland. It is a dark tragicomedy that early on gives us the possible suicide of a cat and, later, has an elderly man right before he also falls, or jumps, to his death from an apartment building window describe Poland as "a country in which anyone can insult an old man." He could not secure help for an assault by a dog inside a café because the police official he approached sided with the dog owner, a personal friend. Someone remarks, "Our future is written in nothingness." Is he speaking about the theater company or Poland? Since one represents the other, it doesn't matter.

Krzysztof Malewski and Anka Malewska's ten-year marriage is falling apart as Krzysz locks horns with the visiting director who aims to avoid controversy and whose concern about the play's length finds Krzysz's role, while remaining the leading one, losing lines and scenes. Meanwhile, Anka has lost all standing in the troupe. Krzysz hasn't noticed that Polish women have even more cause for anxiety than Polish men. A troupe member finds female employment reliant on male connections: "Do you think our actresses would get so many parts if their husbands weren't directors and managers?" In a long scene between Anka and a school acquaintance, which is underlit (like numerous scenes) and punctuated by bursts of stressfully discordant music, the latter recalls how confident Anka had always seemed. We see that that confidence has evaporated.

Two conflicting impulses drive Holland's and co-author Witold Zatorski's characters: the freedom of self-determination; security—freedom from constant worry, fear.

LES RENDEZ-VOUS D'ANNA (France, Belgium, West Germany). Parisian Belgian-born Chantal Äkerman's most emotionally exacting film, *Anna's Meetings*, centers on Parisian Belgian-born filmmaker Anna Silver. Her arrival in Germany to show a film occasions the static, symmetrical, long-held opening shot of a vacant train station stairwell. A train finally pulls in at the opposite platform; eventually, before the train continues, out of the right-hand lower corner of the screen a swarm of humanity appears and descends the stairs. Patient, orderly, by contrast with the platform's rigid design these people are a teeming mess! They disappear down below, eventually followed by the independent filmmaker, all alone in a foreign country. Äkerman's stand-in speaks French slowly, Germans speak French haltingly to her, both to be understood.

Anna has come together with a soul for the lonely night: Heinrich Schneider (Helmut Griem, heart-piercing), a schoolteacher. In bed, Anna aborts their awkward foreplay ("We don't love each other") but visits Heinrich and his five-year-old daughter on her birthday in Bottrop, during which time Schneider reports his wife's abandonment, a fellow schoolteacher's denouncement and discharge for being "anti-social," and laments Germany's twentieth-century history: "What will become of [my country]?" We add our own perspective and answer: "Reunification."

It grates that Heinrich doesn't acknowledge the Holocaust. In Cologne, Anna next visits Ida, a Polish Jewish friend and war refugee, who remarks: "We have no family [in Germany anymore]. They're either dead or all scattered." Holocaust, diaspora. Äkerman herself is Jewish.

For all the solidity of subway station stairs, this film is about transients, transience: the bluish landscape fleeing outside the window on the train to Cologne.

In this episodic film denoting a fractured Europe, Anna cannot commit romantically as she tries coming to grips with her lesbianism. "In transit"—which much of the film is—translates into transience.

DOSSIER 51 (France, West Germany). Brilliantly written by Gilles Perrault and the director from Perrault's novel, Michel Deville's (by far) best film unfolds entirely from the viewpoint of a subjective camera, befitting the relentless surveillance of Dominique Auphal, a young French diplomat, by a foreign government's secret service that is shadowing him (perhaps with French governmental assent), amassing a dossier of information about him, seeking the critical vulnerability of his that might be used to compromise him and thus undermine his organization's aim of providing economic counsel and assistance to African nations. Gathered data, once analyzed, yields the conclusion, possibly accurate, possibly not (it hardly matters), that Auphal is homosexual. "Exposed," he commits suicide.

This is not an obtuse, inflated melodrama, like Francis Ford Coppola's similarly inclined *The Conversation* (1974), but, rather, a clinical, burrowing, harrowing achievement. The anonymous voiceover that accompanies the spying camera—in effect, the film itself is the visual equivalent of "dossier 51"—suggests the inhumanity of the spies' activities; in addition, the loneliness of their surveillance comes to seem a mirror-image of the loneliness of Auphal's life. Human connections have been lost in a chilling atmosphere where privacy is routinely and perniciously invaded by political forces too daunting and powerful for targets to withstand. The student protests in Paris in 1968 seemed to predict a progressive future through organized activism; less than a decade later, a progressive individual seems hopelessly alone, while reactionary forces are as organized as ever, and technologically advanced.

The film's dry, distanced style, then, reflects the efficient detachment of the snooping agents, but there is also to it a margin of irony that subtly admits wit and compassion in order to put the dossier compilers, and their activities, in perspective. Moreover, the wonderfully wounded performance by Françoise Lugagne as Dominique's grieving mother breaks the viewer's heart.

BEAUTY AND THE BEAST (Czechoslovakia). Juraj Herz, whose brilliant *Cremator* (1968) is a very dark comedy about Nazism, wartime occupation, and the Holocaust, ten years later would make perhaps the most beauteous film ever that's drawn from fairy-tale material. This is *Panna a netvor* (*The Virgin and the Monster*), from Mme Leprince de Beaumont's eighteenth-century "La Belle et la Bête." It is not, like Jean Cocteau's great 1946 version, a thrilling allegory of the Occupation and Liberation of France; it is Czech, after all. But there are flickers of political symbolism all the same—these, pertaining to the shadow of Communism hiding behind, ironically, Julie's father's financial ruin: the destitution into which a burning bridge tosses the widower and his three daughters. Julie, the Beauty of the piece, pays the price to liberate her father and sisters; in the main, however, she falls in love with the gigantically bird-headed monster who instantly fell in love with her and is keeping her in his dark, labyrinthine castle in hopes she will take the leap of faith that will free the handsome prince from his monstrous "imprisonment" and make them both a human—well, fairy-tale—couple at last.

With the glow of soft candlelight and other golden visual punctuation, this is a very dark film that is also warm, sensuous and mysterious because it is so full of the possibility, promise and, finally, reality of love. Julie has free will and, exerting it, passes through a castle door to the instant alternative reality currently occupied by the rest of her family. It is, of course, this freedom that makes falling in love with the beast possible. Here, too, Herz is reflecting on Communist Czechoslovakia.

Jirí Macháne's gorgeous, dreamy color cinematography, sometimes showing voluminous mists of gray, is the year's best.

THE TREE OF WOODEN CLOGS (Italy). I must have a cruel streak, for once upon a time I dismissed this film with this witticism: "De Sica, and ye shall find." Over the years Ermanno Olmi's peasant epic *L'albero degli zoccoli* (Palme d'Or, Cannes) has grown on me, although I still question its reputation as a masterpiece.

The theme is ownership: property rights versus natural rights. Near the turn of the century, families struggle to survive in a Lombardy farm district whose landowner takes three-fourths of the fruits of their harsh labor, paying them a measily amount based on their comparative productivity. One daring, devout family decides their son will go to school, for which he must walk many miles going and returning. When his shoes give out, the boy's father fells a poplar tree to make him a pair of new shoes. This is deemed stealing, sealing the family's fate.

The richest part of this long film, which Olmi wrote, directed, (gorgeously mutedly) cinematographed, and edited, is the rhythm of life it conveys, at work and socially, portraying life's events, including detailed studies of people hard at daily work, measured against a breathtaking sense of eternity. Shortly after Roberto Rossellini's death, the spirit of his humanistic *Francesco, giullare di Dio* is evoked (1950), here given the political context of tumultuous Italian history that, unbeknownst to these farmers, will help determine the course of their families' future.

Beautifully acted by nonprofessionals, the film mixes documentary realism, authenticated by the recollections of his own family's elders upon which Olmi drew, and selfconscious, hifalutin art, such as the explosions of Bach on the soundtrack. De Sica, Rossellini, Pasolini!

If some of us once dismissed it in reaction to the fulsome praise it received, it may be time to give this film a second chance.

PERCEVAL (France). *Perceval le Gallois* is not in the mold of writer-director Eric Rohmer's contemporary romantic comedies. After all, it derives from a 12th-century work by Chrétien de Troyes! (Rohmer's farewell film, however, returns to medievalism.) Highly stylized and studio-shot, with minimalist sets and gorgeous color (cinematographer, Nestor Almendros), the film purports to show the Middle Ages as it appeared to those living then—whatever *that* means. It's a spare film of poignant innocence, the poignancy lying in the loss of innocence knowledge of which we bring to the film. Paradoxically (and brilliantly), *Perceval le Gallois* immerses us in its distancing, giving us a double sense of time correlative to innocence and the loss of which we are selfconscious. Some of us may even feel we have "fallen" into a better place.

Rohmer's theme, the arrogance of entitlement or of the sense thereof, sounds a cautionary note for the Western world of Rohmer's day. Perceval, the young Welshman with "noble bearing," is an ugly little snot who takes what he wants. (The peasants working his mother's land "shook with fear" at his presence.) When he crosses a tent occupied with an unattended damsel, he steals a kiss and her ring. He demands of poor King Arthur that he be made a knight—and not just any knight but the Red Knight, whose armor he covets, and whom he kills with a spear through the eye just to make that armor his own. Perceval's (itself half-hearted) attachment to his mother underscores his incapacity to feel for anyone else.

The presentation is complex. Quartets of singers tell the story that we watch unfold, and Perceval's own monologues assist the story's onward course. One might say that Perceval's tale of knightly accomplishment is *over*told, reinforcing the stress of his sense of entitlement.

WE SPIN AROUND THE NIGHT AND ARE CONSUMED BY FIRE (France). "Order reigns but does not govern."

Perhaps inadvertently, but nonetheless a virtual companion-piece to Chris Marker's *Grin Without a Cat* (1977), future suicide Guy Debord's *In girum imus nocte et consumimur igni* is a documentary on the state of things in France, socioeconomically, culturally, politically. Debord provides caustic commentary throughout a series of stills and film clips, with photographic inserts of himself as he responds to reactionary reaction to himself and his work. The statement with which he begins is the credo of all genuine artists: "I will make no concessions to the public."

Debord's sober, massive documentary takes on "commodized society," the "chemistry of adulteration." The working class comprises marginal existences that society has trained into the habit of spending. The cinema to which they flock is "a deranged imitation of deranged life." Its "existing images reinforce the existing [sociopolitical] lies." To say the least, the film is far-ranging.

Like Marker's film, Debord's addresses a divided Left, referring, for example, to ". . . those flourishing political and labor-union functionaries [who are] always ready to prolong the grievances of the proletariat for another thousand years in order to preserve their own role as its defender." More often, Debord addresses governmental corruption.

His is a dry, ascerbic attitude—humanistic though not necessarily humane, at times cynical, even misanthropic. For Debord, Marcel Carné's immensely popular *Children of Paradise* (1945) has been appropriated by a reactionary culture, turning its egalitarian spirit from living principle to sentimental complacency. The people of France have been divested of the idea of *the people.*

It is not unusual for French documentaries to hew to a strictly analytical line. But this is a noble work, and Debord confesses, "The sensation of time's passage has always been vivid for me."

1978

LA CHANSON DE ROLAND (France). Frank Cassenti's gorgeous *Song of Roland* is not exactly an adaptation of the French medieval epic. Rather than taking place in the tenth century, as the eleventh-century poem does, it takes place in the twelfth. Peasants on a pilgrimage to a holy site are accompanied by a band of travelling players who enact the exploits of Charlemagne's soldiers. Their journey is upheaved by a peasant uprising, costing the lives of some members. However, Klaus, the actor playing Roland des Roncesvalles (Klaus Kinski, splendid), becomes a hero himself by taking up the peasants' cause.

Cassenti's film is a meditation on life and art, but also one on time and history. Filled with song and in-the-momentness, the pilgrimage seemingly suspends time, with its religious motive granting it an eternal component. The performances, though, enact a French history of war and betrayal. But in the present it isn't foreign invaders that are the concern, but injustices stirring up homegrown rebellion. All this looks ahead to France at the time of the film's making, when it was enjoying a respite of peace following wars of the 1950s and 1960s, in Indochina and Algeria, and mindful as well of the upheavals at home in the late sixties. It is time for France to tend to its people rather than obsessing on dangers from without. By way of meta-text, alas, France would again find itself worrying about a form of Islamic "invaders"—immigrants—up ahead.

In the course of this enchanting film, both peace and violence are shown—but "peace" as a rarefied realm that exists apart, and aloof, from righteous agitation. It provides a glimpse of heaven, perhaps, but there is raw and necessary work to be done here on earth, to bring justice as well as poetry into people's lives.

MESSIDOR (Switzerland, France). Referencing the crime spree of two French teenaged girls, writer-director Alain Tanner's dark, corrosive *Messidor* begins with an aerial tour whose gaze shifts upwards—to the soprano accompaniment of a Schubert song. *Freedom; aspiration.* Cut to Earth. Marie Corrençon, an 18-year-old Moudon shop clerk, looks out her window onto the street, the camera behind her; down below, everything is particular, distinct, while she is a blacked-out blob. Similarly, Jeanne Salève, a bespectacled 19-year-old college student, looks out her window in Geneva and sees hectic activity, hears urban noise. Marie lives with her separated mother, with whom she constantly quarrels, and her mother's lover —"an asshole"; Jeanne lives with her boyfriend. Both bolt, meet while hitchhiking, get tossed out by a middle-aged rider who seems frustrated that girls (including his daughter) are college-educated. Visiting where Marie grew up, the girls camp out—"city girl" Jeanne for the first time—in a dark forest. Ride by ride, they tour Switzerland. Their money runs out; they scrounge, beg, steal a ride's gun—initially, only to brandish, encounter much help, even after/because of becoming wanted fugitives.

We watch the friendship forming, the distance between the girls narrowing; they kiss, caress. When the police stop them, Jeanne identifies them as sisters: Thalia and Clio Messidor. But Marie may be more in control of the relationship. When they spend a night in a motel, Jeanne cannot read in bed after Marie announces she can't sleep with a light on. Tanner charts the pair's progress from complementarity to symbiosis. Neither, we come to realize, would have committed to her downward spiral without the other. (The first violent act is with a rock, one girl protecting the other against rape.) By extension, violence assuages their alienation, desolation, loneliness.

Jeanne: "We're moving through empty space."

1979

CHRIST STOPPED AT EBOLI (Italy). Among the twentieth century's greatest works, *Cristo si è fermato a Eboli* (1945) is Carlo Levi's account of his forced exile in Gagliano, an impoverished southern Italian village in Luciana province, after his arrest for antifascist activities—Levi was a Jewish socialist—in 1934. Levi wrote this account in the form of a novel, bringing into concert his use of the past tense and the spontaneity of stream-of-

1979

consciousness. With its clarity of detail, suffused poetically by melancholy, the book is glorious. So is Francesco Rosi's deeply moving film of it, in its 228-minute version available in North America, on VHS and perhaps (transferred from VHS) DVD. The 145-minute DVD version is less satisfying.

Somber, mysterious, Rosi's film mines the nostalgic properties of memory. We go back in time, guided by an elderly Levi's haunted memory. This will be a secular man's last testament. His memory will become our own.

The strangeness of the village customs; because of his medical training, Levi's acceptance by the villagers; his witnessing of petty politics; the mistreatment of the alcoholic village priest with a past: the film provides a vast, rich canvas of humanity. The title refers to the villagers' sense of isolation and wretchedness, which they explain by the fact that Christ never visited their village, stopping short of it.

Rosi captures the sense of a pause in one's life, with its opportunity to observe and learn. This "pause" is two-fold: the temporary derailment of Levi's political activism; forty years hence, Levi's facing natural death. This is a reflective and humanistic film. Everyone whom Levi has met, including the peasants of Gagliano, has become a part of him. This helps explains why he never returned to the village.

Gian Maria Volontè, as Levi, gives the performance of a lifetime.

STALKER (U.S.S.R.). Adapted by Arkadi and Boris Strugatsky from their novel *The Roadside Picnic*, Andrei Tarkovsky's *Stalker*, like much futuristic science fiction, reflects the present day. The anonymous city where the stalker lives: call it Moscow—here, some grim future police state. At dull dawn the stalker rises to do his illegal work: sneaking out and leading others into and across the Zone (Oz, degenerated), the wasteland that a meteorite created by wiping the previous place off the face of reality. This time, the stalker has two clients: a self-doubting writer; a truth-seeking scientist. Their destination is The Room, where the two men have been led to believe they will be granted their wishes. En route, they question themselves and dread the possibility that their wishes will come true. Suggesting the danger they are in is the history of the Zone. Others who have entered it have disappeared entirely. The man who trained the stalker lost his own brother, whom he had led into the Zone, and committed suicide days after his return.

Like Tarkovsky's *Mirror* (1974), *Stalker* translates into a symbolical journey into the past —that is, from the current Soviet Union back to the original Soviet promise, which at best is now bankrupt, and which may have always been a delusion or a hoax. Images turn up of an abandoned faith. One hallucinatory passage, for example, finds Orthodox Christian symbols, among other discarded artifacts, stirring remotely in deep, rank, sluggish water. Tarkovsky masterfully orchestrates elements—drab, drained color, an extremely slowly moving camera, mystical lighting—to evoke the "fallen meteor" of a state where religious and other practices it has expelled nevertheless survive underground and in the collective memory, holding out hope for their eventual revival.

Tarkovsky himself left family and home. *Stalker* was his last Soviet film.

WAYS IN THE NIGHT (West Germany). The year before making his masterpiece at home, *Constans*, Poland's most brilliant filmmaker, Krzysztof Zanussi, wrote and directed *Wege in der Nacht* for West German television.

During World War II, a German officer falls in love with a Polish baroness whose castle his unit is occupying. The woman remains scornfully nonresponsive until she begins manipulating the young man toward her own ends. In truth, they are both occupied—she, literally, as a Pole at the mercy of German invaders; he, by the Nazi programme he represents, however much it grates against his decency.

Zanussi, who would go to Monument Valley to conclude his *Year of the Quiet Sun* (1984), knows his John Ford, whose *The Man Who Shot Liberty Valance* (1962) provides the structural model for *Ways in the Night*. A contemporary narrative frame encases the wartime material, each in a sense occupying the other, each releasing into the other a store of import and feeling. The flashback correlates to the memory of none of the characters; it is objective and historical, and yet it projects all the turbulence of war, invasion, occupation and thwarted love. On the other hand, both abstracting (that is, generalizing) and sharpening the irony of a German's loving a Pole who cannot help but despise him, the present-day frame shows a future generation, while resolute in its indifference to the past, sleepwalking in the might-have-been couple's shadow: the war is *not* over.

The rich, spectral darkness of the nighttime images in the extended flashback, with their prussian and other deep blues, creates a double sense familiar to Fordians: a haunted past now populated by ghosts and the past haunting the present.

Despite Zanussi regular Maja Komorowska's bravura performance as the baroness, Zanussi's preeminent collaborator is his phenomenal color cinematographer, Witold Sobocinski.

THE MARRIAGE OF MARIA BRAUN (West Germany). Rainer Werner Fassbinder's *Die Ehe der Maria Braun* evokes West German history—from its state of rubble under an obtuse, hypocritical American occupation to its rise from the ashes of defeat—through the upward mobility of an independent woman armed with wit, business savvy, perseverance, and prodigious promiscuity. Hermann, her husband, was a Russian prisoner of war who is presumed dead.

Cunning, painstakingly crafted, Fassbinder's rich canvas includes oblique, discreet *mise-en-scène*, and faces reflected in snatches of mirror: the portrait of an extended family fractured and burdened with national guilt. A black marketeer provides an ambitious Maria Braun (Hanna Schygulla, ravishing and brilliant) with the low-cut dress that will set her fortunes amidst Americans, one of whom becomes her lover and teaches her English, knowing which helps ensure her success. When her husband unexpectedly returns, Maria kills her lover. Hermann takes the fall when the occupation court insults his wife by translating her precise German expressing her powerful love for him into cold, unfeeling, indiscriminate English. It's a "bad time for feelings."

While Hermann languishes in prison, Maria proves indispensable to a German company doing international business, becoming the owner's partner at work and in bed. Maria becomes rich. "I'm a master of deceit," she says during management-union negotiations; "a capitalist tool by day, by night an agent of the proletarian masses. I am the Mata Hari of the 'economic miracle.'" She embodies the opportunism greasing its wheels.

After Hermann's prison release, at least Maria, perhaps both, go up in smoke from a kitchen gas explosion while the radio raucously announces Germany's victory (against Hungary) in a world championship soccer match. Maria Braun's flaming fate, with its echo of wartime bombing and the Holocaust, underscores the suffering and anguish, buried, supporting West German socioeconomic progress.

WISE BLOOD (U.S.). "Sin is a trick on niggers. . . . Jesus is a trick on niggers. . . . There is no peace to the redeemed." — Hazel Motes, in *Wise Blood*

The legacy of Christianity in the South is this: It was a method for drawing obedience from African slaves. It promoted the obscenity that such obedience (to the overseer's lash, for instance) constituted a kind of discipleship to Jesus, holding out hope for an eternal reward no matter the hardship of the slave's mortal lot.

Flannery O'Connor's novel about the early twentieth-century son of a preacher man becomes a powerful film thanks to a good ol' atheist, John Huston. This was the director's own favorite among his films.

Hazel Motes, the protagonist, is also an atheist. This isn't theology; this is *human*—a reaction against his preacher-grandfather. But Motes can't escape the family business. A cab driver mistakes him for a preacher because he *looks* like one. Motes starts up his own church: The Church of Truth Without Christ Crucified, because Christ's blood redeemed no one. This becomes The Church of Truth Without Christ.

Through a series of stark color images, Huston achieves a vision of an ordinary world whose religious underpinnings render it, first, absurd and, finally, tragic. It remains cinema's finest exploration of the role of religion in the culture of the United States, especially in the Bible Belt.

Brad Dourif beautifully plays Motes. Shame on us! Despite his Oscar nomination for *One Flew Over the Cuckoo's Nest* (Milos Forman, 1975), we haven't permitted this gifted actor the career we needed him to have. Nor have we been honest about the cruelty of Christianity in the American landscape.

THE PREFAB STORY (Czechoslovakia). Written by Eva Kacírková and herself, Věra Chytilová brilliantly directed the satirical *Panelstory aneb Jak se rodí sídliste*—*Panelstory*, in short. The setting is a vast apartment building complex just outside Prague; the complex is partially occupied, partly still under construction, with all the attendant machine-noise, mud and debris due to the latter. The overflowing, mostly unpleasant humanity, mostly within flats and in the outside mess, contrasts with long-shots of the solid, sterile edifices. As though battering these buildings, Chytilová's camera dynamically pans, whips around and across the sides and windows, its zoom lens highly active both forward and back. Chytilová's film is the most extreme application of *cinéma-vérité* camerawork to a fictional film that I can recall, lending the material, for all the film's zaniness and slapstick comedy, a stunning degree of realism.

The suburban complex of cold, hideous high-rises is a dead-ended descendant of the old Soviet farming commune; but most everyone we see living and working there is out for himself or herself, untouched by any group identity or goal. Doubtless, Czech authorities feel good about providing this housing (having waited for five years, one unapproved woman simply moves into an unoccupied flat); but nothing we see conforms to anything ideal, least of all human behavior. Someone at some point remarks, "Man reflects his surroundings." A young boy who lives with his mother there, perpetually off (and both dangerous and in danger) on his own, is constantly digging through garbage receptacles.

An elderly man, who has just arrived, notices that an elderly woman, visible on her way-up terrace, isn't moving; everyone counsels him to mind his own business. Eventually, a black African climbs up to see. What follows is a note of anxiety followed by a note of serendipity and bliss.

MANHATTAN (U.S.). Visually, writer-director Woody Allen's *Manhattan*, co-written by Marshall Brickman, is a romantic dream of the city, gorgeously photographed in black and white by Gordon Willis—but a dream into which Allen's anxious psyche intrudes, as though Allen, in the persona of Isaac Davis, cannot help playing chicken with his dream. Isaac's adolescent cynicism borders on defeatism, and *Manhattan*'s comedy and romance teeter on the brink of evaporation. Manhattan ought to be locating Isaac, stabilizing his wobbly ego, but instead he projects upon it his own self-doubts. Matters in his life reflect the self-uncertainty his cynicism covers: Jill, his more recent ex-wife, left him for a woman and is now writing a book smearing their unfulfilling marriage; Tracy, his current girlfriend (Mariel Hemingway, sensitive, sublime), is 17 ("She does homework!")—Isaac is 42—and therefore cannot possibly, he says to her exquisite face, really be in love with him. But she *is*; Isaac, open your eyes! Before you trample something fragile, *wonderful!*

Isaac breaks off with Tracy and settles in with Mary (Diane Keaton, close to sublime) after this "high-strung" journalist guiltily breaks off with Yale, Isaac's married best friend. But Mary, still in love with Yale, dumps Isaac for Yale, confirming Isaac's cynicism. The Manhattan that Isaac loves is disappearing (some of it is literally being demolished);

relationships are evanescent. Tracy must lose the quality of innocence—narcissistically, for Isaac, her *teachableness*—and everything else also must change. How does one hold onto things when the world keeps turning?

One thing one can do is insist on one's own moral authority. When Isaac jiminy-crickets him, Yale explodes, "You're so self-righteous. You think you're God!"—to which Isaac explains, "I've got to model myself on *someone*."

Beneath all the wit and hilarity, there is an irresistible undertow of melancholy.

THE TIN DRUM (West Germany, France, Poland, Yugoslavia). Günter Grass helped with the script for Volker Schlöndorff's film of Grass's 1959 novel about Oskar Matzerath (David Bennent, son of Heinz Bennent, superb), who, fully intelligent since birth, decides on his third birthday not to advance beyond that age, to remain a "gnome," given the state of the world. (Oskar takes a deliberate tumble down stairs, injuring his spine, in order to achieve his goal.) The setting is Danzig in the 1920s, where Germans and Poles live together in hostility, presaging Europe's future. The shadow of the world war recently ended portends another horrifying world war as Nazism gathers political steam.

So, Oskar is a loveable blighted innocent attempting to withstand the tide of the times? No; he is a perfect terror, alternating between sullenness and aggressive obnoxiousness, practicing occultish gifts and, on occasion, fiercely resembling a little Nazi himself. He bangs on his tin drum in protest of the corrupt, nasty world he sees (but doesn't his possessiveness of the drum mirror the bourgeois values that irk him?) and shatters glass with his scream. Who can resist being stamped by political currents and cross-currents? Our imagination and conviction are inadequate to keep any of us from being a child of our place and time.

Schlöndorff's *Die Blechtrommel* is a marvelous, colorful allegory, a rich symbolical tapestry of surrealistic weirdness and fantasy, farce and tragedy, constituting a pilgrim's non-progress of perpetual protest as no one listens to Oskar and the world around him sinks ever deeper into social and political insanity. Of course, *we* listen—Oskar narrates his life-story—but, already knowing that his concerns are prophetic, we are as powerless to change history as Oskar is to avert it.

In a huge supporting cast, Charles Aznavour pierces as a Jewish toy store owner.

MALUALA (Cuba). The final entry of a trilogy begun with *The Other Francisco* (1975) and *Slave Hunter* (1976), *Maluala* is in the mold of Gillo Pontecorvo's *Queimada* (*Burn!*, 1969) —but without the Brandopiness. Fiercely beautiful, Sergio Giral's film fictionalizes slave revolts in Cuba in the latter part of the nineteenth century. Its protagonist, called Gallo, leading an army of runaways, petitions the Spanish colonial government for freedom and land; he and his followers are met with brutal reprisals. Their settlement tucked away in eastern mountains, Gallo and the others come to presage Castro, "Che" Guevara and their anti-Batista guerrilla forces in the 1950s. The film suggests that the latter revolution has brought to fruition the earlier movement by Cuba's most oppressed individuals—a connection that Giral, a black Cuban himself, draws with heartfelt conviction. Indeed, the film ends with a freeze frame that perfectly expresses the historical weight that Giral wishes to bring to bear. After engineering a massacre of blacks, the colonial Spanish general— Gallo's nemesis—is shown surrounded by a taunting crowd of the dispossessed. They represent the future as much as the present, and the freeze frame captures the general's howl and bulging eyes, slyly anticipating the end to the power upon which the colonial forces then so ruthlessly relied. This man embodies injustices perpetrated against the Cuban people; with hindsight, then, the film looks forward to his getting his comeuppance. The film's heightened style—its rich colors, music and touches of primitive folklore—helps the connection drawn between the black slave revolt and Castro's later defeat of the Batista government appear almost mystical. In this, the film owes something to *Battleship Potemkin* (1925), where a failed Russian revolution looks ahead to the successful one that has already since occurred. Like Eisenstein's masterpiece, *Maluala* is a national epic.

THE THIRD GENERATION (West Germany). Rainer Werner Fassbinder's Godardian/ doubly Melvillian *Die Dritte Generation* dazzles with slapdash brilliance while hilariously pursuing its satirical aims. The title refers to a post-Baader-Meinhof group of Leftists terrorizing West Berlin. A bunch of bourgeois bumblers led by a mercenary, they plot the kidnapping of Peter Lurz (Eddie Constantine, parodying Yves Montand in Costa-Gavras's *State of Siege*), an industrialist the sale of whose computers has fallen off. Unbeknownst to the ersatz radicals, Lurz himself manipulates matters behind the scenes, engineering his own kidnapping. He can taste the outcome: refreshed profits.

A Leftist, Fassbinder nonetheless stands against terrorists, not least of all because their tactics fortify, not undo, the reactionary power structure. He thus stated the film's theme: "terrorism is an idea generated by capitalism to justify better defense measures to safeguard capital." It is as if he had in mind Bush/Cheney, for whom the word *democracy* would always mean *capitalism*.

In the opening shot in Lurz's office, two screens-within-the-movie screen appear: a turned-off computer monitor (a sign of the magnate's business malaise); a turned-on television, which secretary Susanne, a member of the terrorist cell, watches. This profusion of screens sets off its aural equivalent, Fassbinder's use of layered sound almost throughout; while people converse, either movie dialogue, conversation or music emits from a TV set. This overload of distraction helps explain how the times undercut the terrorists' hewing to a political course of action. Along the way, Fassbinder suggests that identity is largely imposed on individuals rather than being the result of self-discovery.

Very late in the film, on "the last day of carnival madness," the kidnapping finally occurs, with the terrorists dressed up as clowns. As he is videographed reading (and re-reading) the text his kidnappers have prepared for him, Lurz is most obliging.

Films of the 1980s

"I thought we would grow old together." — film critic Stanley Kauffmann, reflecting on the death of François Truffaut

A decade of blows: Hitchcock, Fassbinder, Truffaut, Welles, Tarkovsky—1980, 1982, 1984, 1985, 1986.

The list:

1980

THE CONSTANT FACTOR (Poland). For whatever reason(s), Krzysztof Zanussi has participated in obscuring his artistic signature by doggedly trying to make films that are different from one another. *Constans* is perhaps his most personal film.

Witold is beset with difficulties. He is his dying mother's caregiver; at work his idealism collides with the inwardness, rigidity and corruption of an entrenched bureaucracy that mounts a plot against him; and he longs to scale the Himalayas, as his father died doing. Witold's life appears bleak at the crossroads of his own character and things beyond his control. Finally, he withdraws from the world and becomes a window washer—a grotesque parody of mountain-climbing. The son will never become his father. The integrity to which he aspires must forever elude him.

Witold places his faith in mathematics, believing it can explain his apparent bad luck, and the film's precise, almost mathematical style is suited to this faith and Witold's perception of the world. Something human, though, is ever poised to drop into or out of such a view of reality. As a result, Witold unwittingly contributes to a tragic outcome. *Constans* is breathtaking in its irony.

Zanussi, a former student of physics and philosophy, has fashioned a rigorously intellectual work about self-determination and other-determination. *Constans* elegantly locates a man's emotional life in a complex social and political environment. It demonstrates the struggle for survival by an individual whose resilience and intelligence would seem to offer more hope and better prospects. Of all great films, this may be the bleakest, not least of all for its portrait of daily existence in a joyless, programmatic Communist state. Throughout, its cold colors appear on the edge of colorlessness.

Zanussi has made an uncompromising film about an uncompromising man. The implied self-criticism is devastating.

BERLIN ALEXANDERPLATZ (West Germany). Expressionism and naturalism inhabit different universes, but in Arthur Döblin's 1929 novel *Berlin Alexanderplatz*, and in Rainer Werner Fassbinder's moody, underlit 15½-hour film version originally made for West German television, they intersect. Chronicling the struggles of an Everyman, Franz Bieberkopf, to survive in depressed 1928 Berlin after he is released from prison for killing his girl, Fassbinder's masterpiece finds humanity mirroring the disintegrating social order.

His landlady perceived sufficient goodness in Bieberkopf to hold his apartment for him for the four years he has been away. Bieberkopf isn't after the moon. He wants to get a decent job ("I'm not much of a guy for luxury"), but this proves impossible. Tempted by the satanic Reinhold Hoffmann (Gottfried John, brilliant), Franz pimps, steals, and distributes pamphlets for a lunatic fringe group now gathering political steam: the National Socialists.

Loss of an arm, the result of his being pushed out of a car into traffic by his criminal compatriot, sums up Bieberkopf's fate as a continual subjugation to forces one can neither predict nor control. Bieberkopf is a faithless, criminal Job enduring life as best he can—what humanity has been reduced to. Promise of happiness, though, comes in the form of Mieze

(Barbara Sukowa, heartrending), a prostitute whose sweet devotion calms Bieberkopf's emotional storms; but then Mieze also is taken from him, by the same fate that took away his arm.

Günter Lamprecht, as Franz, gives a titanic, seamless performance, showing in this unpleasant man's experience the plight of the downtrodden.

Fassbinder's achievement may be most trenchant in the chapter "A Handful of People in the Depths of Silence." On the other hand, it is weakest in a superfluous coda, the homoerotic phantasmagoria with which Fassbinder concludes his complex, absorbing vision. But by that time, he can be forgiven *anything*.

CONFIDENCE (Hungary). Budapest 1944 is a bleak place. People are disappearing, in some cases on their own in order to escape Nazi capture. There is an Hungarian underground, but there are also Hungarian collaborationists. "János Bíró," a burnt-out member of the resistance, is in hiding, along with Kata (Ildikó Bánsági, tremendous), whose spouse also has gone into hiding. Kata and János, who is also married, are pretending to be a couple as cover while renting a room from an elderly couple. János is full of fear and lacking confidence; "our only chance [for survival]," he tells Kata, "is to prepare for any and every betrayal." Kata is impatient with what she calls her companion's "cowardice." Gradually the pair become lovers. When the war ends, back in her husband's arms, Kata is full of fear at the prospect of unending separation from a man whose real name she doesn't even know, while János, newly hopeful, tries to find his pretend-wife, hollering "Mrs. Bíro!" along a line of refugees in the street.

Budapest-born István Szabó's *Bizalom* is an existential study of risk and trust so cleverly enfolded in a detailed, almost documentary depiction of wartime survival that the insertion of black-and-white archival material causes not the slightest stylistic rupture. Szabó's and cinematographer Lajos Koltai's color scheme, in which browns and grays dominate, conveys the sense that fear and suspicion have squeezed the life out of people, making patches of light haunting and precious in a film that unfolds mostly in darkness.

Szabó is at his most ironical when a former schoolmate, who has had her nose changed and hair dyed, begs Kata for a night's hiding. She is convinced that Kata is only pretending not to recognize her; but Kata really does not recall her—when you think about it, a harsher circumstance.

THREE BROTHERS (Italy, France). The three Giuranna sons have gathered for their mother's funeral in a Puglia village, in Francesco Rosi's *Tre fratelli*. Nicola, the youngest, works in a factory in Turin and is an activist for workers' rights. He and his wife are divorcing. Single, Rocco works at a boys' reformatory in Naples. The eldest, Raffaele, happily married with a grown son, is a Roman judge, whose current case involves terrorists, making him a potential target for assassination. In the country, the father, Donato, interacts with his granddaughter and reminisces about himself and his wife when they were newlyweds.

Rosi's film opens on the exterior wall of the institution where Rocco works: concrete and orderly windows. In terrifying closeup, rats lurk on the grounds outside; the cut to Rocco waking up suggests this is a dream. Donato's lush rural surroundings contrast with Rocco's milieu. What different times and lives—a point ironically underscored by the fact that Vittorio Mezzogiorno plays both Rocco and Rocco's father as a young man. Charles Vanel is excellent as Donato.

But father and sons are each now a stranger to the three others. Nicola remarks, "My hometown is no longer a part of me, nor I of it." In a wonderful shot, Rocco is upstairs, in the foreground, back towards us, looking out the window, and in the courtyard below his siblings are both walking very far apart. Rocco begins to cry. During the funeral, a flock of birds flutter; we see their shadows on an outside wall. Each of the sons is at loose ends in his life, although Raffaele (Philippe Noiret, in one of his greatest roles) is best at concealing this. About the delinquents, from poor families, whom Rocco helps, Raffaele tells him, "It would have been better had they not been born."

HOUSE (Israel). As abrasive as stone, brilliant in stark back and white, the documentary *Bayit*, which launched a trilogy, I understand, consisting of two more stop-bys to the same house in West Jerusalem, first announced Amos Gitaï as Israel's greatest filmmaker. After commissioning it, Israeli television suppressed the film for its unblinking view, in miniature, of the Israeli-Palestinian conflict and its suggestion that tragic history poisons the foundation of the modern state of Israel. (U.S. Americans should be able to relate.) Until the 1948 war, the house that is the subject here was home to a Palestinian doctor (Dr. Mahmoud Dajani, who speaks impeccable English, returns for a visit in the film's last movement), with Israel's government taking over the property and renting it, in 1956, to Jewish Algerian immigrants; the university professor who eventually bought the property—he is complacent and overstuffed, like one of Eisenstein's caricatured capitalists—is now having it expanded. Thus the house doubles as a metaphor for Israel itself. Interviewing various individuals including owner, contractor, the original builder and a Palestinian stonemason who, at work on the expansion, voices hatred of Jews, Gitaï turns the partially demolished solid house into a phantom that's differently viewed by different pairs of eyes rooted in different histories within the same history.

Bookending the film are shots of intensive labor: Palestinians breaking down rock in a quarry with pick axes because security concerns prohibit their using explosives. The harshness of the sound suits the Palestinian predicament and the sterility of the Israeli-Palestinian conflict: an aural metaphor.

Startlingly, an interview may abort the material preceding it, intensifying the suggestion of conflict; a Palestinian refugee camp intrudes upon the contractor's nostalgic reminiscence of his youthful socialism.

Deeply moving: the humility of an Algerian couple who once lived there.

MY AMERICAN UNCLE (France). Alain Resnais's *Mon oncle d'Amérique* blends documentary and fictional aspects. Evolutionary biologist/behaviorist Henri Laborit, who appears as himself, had selected Resnais as the logical person to direct a documentary in which he, Laborit, would present his views about human behavior on the basis of experiments with rats. Resnais brought in Jean Gruault to expand the concept, however, by devising a script about fictional characters to accompany Laborit's science lectures. A female and two males, these characters whose lives intersect come from different backgrounds; they are a one-time radical who subsequently pursues careers in acting and business, a factory middle-manager who anxiously faces corporate downsizing, and a public radio news manager who leaves wife and kids for the actress. Their autobiographical voiceovers extend a documentary air to the fiction. Depending on one's point of view, the film conforms to a point-point model, in which fictional characters illustrate Laborit's ideas, a point-counterpoint model, in which the characters' actions and behaviors ill match Laborit's ideas, or a more elusive and ambiguous thing that falls somewhere in between these two models—if you will, a partial illustration.

Among the issues addressed: inhibited behavior; uninhibited behavior/"defensive violence"; circumstances under which one turns aggressive behavior against oneself or others; the relationship between social conditioning and nervous system functioning; competition; domination; "what we call 'mental illness'"; group and individual survival; the cultural, political and geopolitical applications of all these, including war and racism.

Laborit: "Language convinces the individual that in serving the group he is serving himself."

The title refers to an illusory ideal of happiness. What one of the characters says: "America

doesn't exist. I know; I lived there."
Wonderfully, characters at certain points wear rat heads!
The film ends with a montage of building bricks, a metaphor for human "personality" and the unconscious.
Fascinating film!

1981

DIARY FOR MY CHILDREN (Hungary). Writer-director Márta Mészáros's autobiographical *Napló gyermekeimnek* is highly specific and detailed about daily life under Communism. Juli, 14, is brought back to Hungary from Soviet Russia, along with adoptive relations, by her "grandfather"'s sister, Magda, an editorial office Communist Party official. We see rebellious Juli at 16 and 20; as Juli grows to responsible womanhood, Magda rises to a position of punitive power. Juli and her foster-mother, who are constantly locking horns, lose much along the way: Juli, her fierce pride; Magda, all idealism and hopefulness. Bit by bit Magda has had to accommodate Hungary's political reality in order to justify her lifelong commitment.

The film opens with an airplane's descent into Budapest: a gray, bleak landscape. Mirrors and mirror-images dot the *mise-en-scène*, suggesting lives led at a remove from reality and the need to confirm one's existence. Magda, who has suffered imprisonment and torture, wants to be loved, but Juli recoils from Magda's attempts to touch her. After Yugoslavia's Tito declares independence from the Soviet Union, Magda says, "There are enemies everywhere." She decides one such enemy is her oldest political ally, whom she wrongly feels is encouraging Juli to abandon her. She has János imprisoned. When Juli and his son visit János, they are separated by screens on either side of a pathway up and down which an officer walks while the three try to converse.

Searing flashbacks show Juli as a child with her loving parents. Her father "disappears" after authorities take him away. Typhus does the same to her mother at hospital. Her father, a sculptor, is shown amidst sheafs of sparkling white stone; is it a marble quarry or the moon?

The gorgeous black-and-white cinematography for this "diary for my children" is by Niyika Jancsó, Mészáros's son.

BLUE PLANET (Italy). Franco Piavoli's *Il pianeta azzurro* compresses a cycle of the four seasons into a day and a half in a rural setting. Time passes, bringing changes; indeed, the film is about the passage of time.

Fields, trees, sand, river; the effects of wind and rain on all these; flora and fauna: others have catalogued the sights and (amplified) sounds that Piavoli, working as his own color cinematographer, has conjured for this gorgeous film. But to describe it, as some have, as a "Nature documentary" is to miss the point. The natural landscape affects the humans, the farmer and his family and neighbors. People remain unseen so long as the "blue planet" is to their liking, representing hope, possibility, an easy breaking through of obstacles. But the long-shot of the family house at dinnertime, with doors and windows open, revealing reddish light indoors confronting the darkness outdoors, hollowing it out, carries a suggestion of anxious blood in addition to humanity's precarious accommodation with Nature. One can go further: the reddish glow intimates human sacrifices.

Earlier, Nature is portrayed as wet, overflowing, erotic, fecund, and a frolicking couple, in the throes of youthful passion, seems to suggest harmony between humanity and Nature. If one isolates a segment of the seasonal cycle, one can believe this. But Piavoli's theme runs counter to this. His film exposes this alleged harmony as humanity's delusion. Anticipation of the culminating winter invites lonely regret for one woman alone in her bed at night and quarrels among people during the day; its arrival chills the landscape, replacing the earlier balmy breeze with a blast of cold wind that turns the landscape into a metaphorical graveyard. The blueness of life has progressed through prussian blue to the cold blue of a corpse. Nothing grows.

1981

BLOOD WEDDING (Spain). Federico García Lorca's 1932 play *Bodas de sangre* was based on an actual murder involving feuding families; for Alfredo Mañas's 1974 musical adaptation Antonio Gades devised choreography suited to Emilio de Diego's music. Flamenco ballet is —yes, this is possible!—both flamboyant and austere, as is Carlos Saura's film version, again choreographed by and starring Gades. It is the most exciting dance film I've seen.

It reminds me of Laurence Olivier's *Henry V* (1944), which begins with the backstage preparations for a performance of the play at the Globe Theater, and then gradually draws us into the play's medieval action before returning us to the framing device representing Shakespeare's day. Saura begins and ends his film with the same sepia photograph: at the outset, perhaps of Andalusian villagers; at the close, of the dancer-actors in costume posing as them—yet a photograph haunted by the reality the villagers represent. At the beginning, there are preparations for a performance, including the thoughts of dancers as they apply makeup. Elvira Andrés, artistic director of Ballet Nacional de España, who worked on the film: "Saura wanted to see what happened when the dancers arrived and their preparations for the day[,] and he made wonderful photography from it. The images are memorable because they are authentic."

This is followed by the performance—a rehearsal set against enormous windows in a barebones rehearsal space. The drama passionately unfolds: a bride takes off with her former lover, and a knife duel to the death ensues between the two men. By that time, we have been so fully drawn into the action that our hearts are poised to burst.

In a way, then, the film is about us, the audience—about our willingness to suspend disbelief. We embrace the human reality a performance represents.

DO YOU REMEMBER DOLLY BELL? (Yugoslavia). Emir Kusturíca's *Sjecas li se, Dolly Bell* is about the Zoljes, a Sarajevo family in Tito's Yugoslavia in the early 1960s. It is especially about 16-year-old Dino, whose coming of age involves a blonde-wigged stripper and prostitute who goes by the name of Dolly Bell. Kusturíca, a Bosnian Muslim like the Zoljes, has said the film is partly autobiographical.

Maho (Slobodan Aligrudic, phenomenal), the family head, bears indignities well. While endlessly waiting for decent state housing, he and his family live in a one-room apartment dominated by a kitchen table. Maho, wife and daughter sleep in one bed, the three boys in the other. A true believer, Maho keeps waiting for true communism to kick in and transform all their lives. When Maho is dying of lung cancer, Dino helps roll him over for the nurse's injection. Maho's face at that moment reflects a lifetime of disappointment, humiliation, forbearance.

Like his brothers, Dino is forbidden to smoke, but you know kids. Anyhow, Maho is on the threshold of death; Dino, on the threshold of maturity. The two are seated alone, and Maho is smoking a cigarette. He invites Dino to smoke one, too. "I don't smoke," Dino says—not out of fear of punishment, but gallantly, out of filial respect. However, the father's gallantry exceeds his son's. "I know," Maho says, giving Dino a cigarette and lighting it with his own. Well practiced, Dino doesn't cough, and the two share a piece of eternity together that may calm prodigious misfortunes ahead.

Kusturíca's rich, lovely comedy is sufficiently elastic to incorporate life's tragedies. "Every day, in every way, I'm getting better": this is the self-hypnotic mantra that Dino ritualistically repeats to counteract life's bleakness for youth in Sarajevo.

And then there is Dolly Bell. . . .

MAN OF IRON (Poland). From a brilliant script by Aleksander Ścibor-Rylski, Andrzej Wajda's sequel to *Man of Marble* (1977), *Człowiek z żelaza*, is about a Polish labor strike and its organizer, Maciek Tomczyk, whom a radio newsman, at the behest of the Communist Party, investigates in order to discredit, only to become an admirer. The strike refers to the actual massive one in the summer of 1980 that gave birth to "Solidarność" ("Solidarity"), a

1981

federation of some fifty trade unions whose president, Lech Wałęsa, a Gdańsk Shipyard electrician, was (along with other labor leaders) imprisoned by the government, which had declared martial law. Other events past the film's time frame: Wałęsa's winning the presidency in a partially free 1989 election, the collapse of Communism in Poland, the collapse of Communism in the Soviet Union. Wajda's film references as far back as the student protests of 1968 and the brutally repressed strikes of 1970 (Tomczyk's father, the hero of *Man of Marble*, was a fictional casualty)—events that appear in interwoven documentary footage—but, in retrospect, also embraces future history. One may say that the film's aim is the same as that of "Solidarity": to oppose and undo Poland's communist incarnation, as well as expose the myth of such a dictatorship's being a "workers' paradise."

Wałęsa appears in a contemporary documentary insert in a montage accompanying a reading of the 1980 strikers' (most reasonable) demands. Jerzy Radziwiłowicz is magnificent—impassioned, direct, intelligent, complex—as the Tomczyks, son and father, with whose memory the former has quarrels. But the heart of the film may belong to Irina Byrska as an elderly woman, a strike supporter, whom the reporter interviews about the Tomczyks. The woman's legs prevent her from demonstrating, but she has been reading Polish history. Her conclusion: "[T]here *has* to be justice."

LOOKS AND SMILES (UK). Barry Hines's novel *A Kestrel for a Knave* provided the source material for the film that put director Ken Loach on the map: *Kes* (1969). With *Looks and Smiles*, Loach kept Hines's title. (Hines also wrote the script, which won a prize at Cannes.) This film goes way beyond what Loach and Hines achieved with *Kes*.

Chris Menges contributes grim, grimy, black-and-white photography of a higher order than the pretty color work that would win him two Oscars later in the decade. It reflects, as do the writing and the filmmaking, the hopelessness that Margaret Thatcher, elected British Prime Minister in 1979, had unleashed on the United Kingdom. Her principal targets were the struggling working class and labor unions, and national industries and utilities, which she privatized.

I repeat what I have oft said: every film exists on a continuum whose opposite poles are documentary and fiction. This fictional film of Loach's exhibits documentary realism. Unflinchingly clear-eyed, it admits no sensationalism or sentimentality.

There are three main characters, about 17 or 18 years old: Mick, with dreams of becoming a motorcycle mechanic, who cannot find work in the recession; Alan, who joins the Army and loses his soul policing Belfast, and who clings to an oversized plastic bullet to justify his brutality against Catholics—and to punish himself with his awareness of it; Karen, Mick's girl, who works in a shoe store, negotiates warfare with her mother, with whom she lives, and more or less is shell-shocked from her parents' divorce. Karen and Mick, beautifully played by nonprofessionals Carolyn Nicholson and Graham Green, have their ordinary girl-boy quarrels, even a patched-up breakup, all of which, like everything else here, are deepened by the bleak environment and the toll it takes on drifting, unsettled lives.

LE BEAU MARIAGE (France). The second of Eric Rohmer's six "Comedies and Proverbs," *Le beau mariage* is the most brilliant comedy of the 1980s.

Fed up with his wife and children phoning him, art student Sabine dumps Simon. "I'm getting married," she announces to Clarisse; "It's an idea!" Clarisse has an unmarried cousin, Edmond. Introducing them, Clarisse announces, "You make a great couple." Clarisse indeed convinces Sabine that Edmond is interested in her, and Sabine pursues the busy lawyer. Sabine wants Edmond to desire her, to suffer. "Is that necessary?" her mother, who works in a bank, asks. After she meets this potential son-in-law at her daughter's birthday party, she pronounces him "too grand," warning Sabine, "Don't get too worked up over him." However, she can see that Sabine already is. Meanwhile, Edmond is also being tactful by declining to declare his lack of romantic interest in Sabine. Cornered, he finally tells her, "I'm not available, even as a friend," but does he know his own mind? Why when dumping her does he tell her, "I'm attracted to your type of woman. That's why I must defend myself against you"?! A lot of male egotism tumbles out when he adds that he should have been permitted to think of marriage first—or "at least at the same time"! "He's not my type," Sabine announces to Clarisse; her romance with marriage is over. On a train one day she sits opposite a boy, and each steals looks at the other. At the beginning of the film, on the train, the same boy noticed her with interest, but, en route to Simon, Sabine didn't notice him.

"Can any of us refrain from building castles in Spain?" (La Fontaine). Perhaps not; but we may finally settle for something closer to home.

FAREWELL (U.S.S.R.). Elem Klimov is responsible for nearly all that we see in *Proshchanie*, which Ukrainian-born Larisa Shepitko did not live to complete. Based on Valentin Rasputin's 1976 novel *Proshchanie s Matyoroy*, Klimov's labor of love for his wife, who died along with crew members in a road accident, is a tremendous achievement—even though Klimov indulges his penchant for weirdness, caricature and cruelty, thereby disturbing the film's delicate spiritual roots. Klimov felt he had sacrificed his style for Shepitko's, but her superstititousness, which Shepitko shared with her elderly protagonist, Darya, created a bond with the material that her widower could not duplicate.

Matyoroy is a remote Siberian island village. The state has determined it must yield to progress; the island will be flooded for the sake of the construction of a hydro-electric dam, the villagers uprooted and relocated to impersonal urban apartments. Some, however, choose to stay behind.

The opening movement is phenomenal. At night the tree-cutters traverse the dark, moon-dappled water to reach the island. We do not see these strangely garbed invaders, only the water with its play of light; the angled camera fools us into thinking that the camera is directly—flat—overhead. The journey thus seems, visually, a climb, an ascendency—but isn't. At dawn, when the invaders arrive, the perspective also makes the crude dock seem like something that the camera is scaling. These distortions provide commentary on the unnaturalness of the invaders' mission. Their obscene laughter as they later tackle the job of felling an immense tree perhaps goes too far. Indeed, it is annoyingly convenient that Darya's own son is charged with the responsibility of directing the crew that prepares the island for its "progressive" fate.

Memorable: Darya in the forest, running her hands along the ancient ground.

THEY DON'T WEAR BLACK-TIE (Brazil). Brazil's military dictatorship, in place since 1964, had entered a period of liberalization when Gianfrancesco Guarnieri and director Leon Hirszman adapted the former's 1958 play, *Eles Não Usam Black-Tie*, in response to industrial strikes occurring in São Paulo, to where they reset the play's action (from Rio de Janeiro). Both Guarnieri, who also assumed the principal role of union leader Otávio, and Hirszman, whose Polish parents eluded the Holocaust by moving to Brazil, are Marxists committed to workers' rights and social progress.

At the center of the film are a father and son. Both work in the same metalworking factory that also employs the boy's pregnant girlfriend, Maria. But while Otávio helps organize the strike at work, Tião opts for a more immediate, practical future, one that entails providing for Maria, whom he wishes to marry as soon as possible, and their baby. In the service of this priority, he becomes a scab, deepening the divide between himself and his father, which his mother, Romana (Fernanda Montenegro—Oscar-nominated for Walter Salles's 1998 *Central Station*, but here giving a much more complex and valuable performance), painfully does her best to moderate. Ironically, Tião's stance also damages his relationship with Maria, who is more in tune with Otávio's activism.

One of the accomplishments of this fine example of *cinema nôvo* is the distinction it makes between Romana and Otávio's modest working-class home and the poorer, more cramped quarters that Maria's family occupies.

Each one of the characters is admirable in his or her own way, including Tião, who steps up to the plate of quite overwhelming responsibility. The film's generosity in this regard helps lead to a humane rather than a schematic result. At the same time, there can be no mistaking where the filmmakers' political heart lies.

1982

CAMMINA CAMMINA (Italy). Hauntingly beautiful, Ermanno Olmi's masterpiece is cinema's greatest foray into biblical territory—and its least dogmatic. A commemorative reenactment by peasants of the journey of the magi to witness the birth of Christ drifts into the actual event, triggering again for the first time King Herod's rampage of slaughter in Bethlehem. A "road picture" by caravan and foot, *Keep Walking* questions the faith of the faithful, the distinctions to which they cling in order to certify their faithfulness, and the disparities they often ignore between their behavior and professed beliefs. It's a restless film.

One of the opening events is little Rupo's denunciation of Mel[chior], one of the magis, for ritually sacrificing a lamb, the boy's sweet, innocent companion and, symbolically, The Lamb —Jesus. By film's end, the three "wise men" and their entourage will have furiously withdrawn under threat from Herod, leaving Mary and Joseph and the newborn infant in peril. A lamb will prove the sole survivor of Herod's raging fear of prophecy that this baby, not he, will prove to be the King of Kings. Did the infant Jesus, then, perish? Did he survive, or did only the *idea* of him survive? Is the grown Christ's summary crucifixion a projection of the earlier event? In her brilliant analysis, critic Susan Doll asks, "What are the implications of building a religion based on the savior's death?" In the film, his translator warns Mel that he will end up celebrating not Christ's coming but Christ's death.

The film also conflates Testaments, identifying disparate humanity in its overwhelming aspiration. Doll points out that Olmi's version of the magis' journey suggests the Israelites, "who escaped Egypt to wander across the desert in search of the Promised Land." Wanderers all, we are searching for home.

Olmi wrote, directed, cinematographed, edited.

(ON) TOP OF THE WHALE (Netherlands). By the late twentieth century, the United States and the U.S.S.R. have appropriated Europe—the Soviet Union, for instance, the Netherlands. This conceit imagines the transformation of familiar nations into states of exile. Chilean surrealist Raúl Ruiz's own European exile was prompted by the military coup against Allende, whose cinema advisor he had been. *Het Dak van de Walvis* is one of his most delirious and ambitious hoax-like fictions.

A Dutch couple, anthropologists, visit the retreat of millionaire communist Narcisso, presumably in the wilds of Patagonia. There, the woman, Eva, digs up tribal artifacts on the grounds with her bare hands and her husband painstakingly interviews Adam and Eden, two surviving members of the Yachanes Indians, whose language (concocted by Ruiz) he attempts to decipher and record. Meanwhile, five other languages are also spoken: Dutch, Spanish, French, German and English.

Linked to one in Eva's dream, Narcisso's remote house admits realistic interiors, although sparked by the magic of shadow-plays and mirrors, while the exterior, in long-shot, exists in the landscape of a dream. While her husband clings to his identity of scientific outsider, appropriating discoveries as his neocolonialist own, Eva chooses to remain behind when he leaves. In the course of the film her child's gender slides from boydom into girldom; even more so than her mother, Anita fits in in her new surroundings.

This wonderful film is ill-served by critical attempts to seize upon a remark here or there for the comfort of a reductive meaning. Ruiz illuminates the distances that the familiar, outside world creates when it deludes itself into believing that it is closing these distances. Some feel that the film is esoteric; rather, it is gravely mysterious, gorgeously distilling the sadness, longings and emotional disarray of political exile.

FANNY AND ALEXANDER (Sweden). Although lame in its 188-minute version, his *Fanny och Alexander* is one of writer-director Ingmar Bergman's most wonderful films in its complete form, which runs 312 minutes. The latter comes from Swedish television; Bergman himself trimmed this version for theatrical release. He did so reluctantly: "I had to cut into the nerves and the lifeblood of the film." The complete version, critic Stig Björkman has accurately written, "is, without a doubt, Bergman's most richly orchestrated work."

Symbolically rather than literally autobiographical, the film chronicles the Ekdahl family in the early part of the last century, especially two children, brother and sister, who lose their father to death and their mother to their stepfather, a strict Lutheran bishop, who replaces their liberal, luxuriant existence with a spartan one. Among the restored elements is initial expanded coverage of young Alexander's colorful, haunted imagination, his waking visions and dreams, which connect with the mysticism into which the film eventually passes. The stepfather is primarily based on Bergman's clergyman-father, whose dogmatic Christian beliefs and virulent anti-Semitism divided the two of them; indeed, the film presents something of a dream world, one in which a Jew, assisted by magic, rescues the children from their new, inhospitable home and hides them away in his pawnshop. (He is their Grandma's long-ago lover.) Especially for Alexander, this signals their renewing immersion in the kind of inspiring love of art and imagination that the children's father had instilled in them. The film thus comes full circle, but "outside" the Christian life that Bergman, an atheist, considers anything but life-affirming. Bergman's religion, the object of his faith, is art—classical music, Expressionistic theater, cinema.

Fanny och Alexander achieves the spirit of a fairy tale—a spirit that shimmers its way through a naturalistic narrative, transforming everything.

SHEER MADNESS (West Germany, France). Margarethe von Trotta's brilliant, coolly analytical *Heller Wahn* explores the relation to society of the connection between two women: divorced university professor Olga (Hanna Schygulla, at her peak) and painter Ruth (Angela Winkler), who lives with spouse Franz—following her suicide attempt and breakdown, a watchful, solicitous near-guardian. Franz objects when Ruth replaces him as her confidante with Olga. Having determined a pecking order of relationships based on male domination, which Ruth's new friendship challenges, society also objects.

Initially, Franz must overcome Olga's resistance in his solicitation of her to become Ruth's friend. A flattering self-image as being loving, caring, unselfish: Franz is free to enjoy this while "setting up" the friendship, but how quickly it empties, leaving him unexpectedly defenseless, once Ruth and Olga's friendship passes out of his control and assumes a life of its own. Insisting it is Olga who is a threat to her, the man protecting his spouse now becomes her unprotector. Franz's sense of well-being, unwittingly, has always depended on Ruth's *lack* of well-being and on her total reliance on him.

Von Trotta uses a subjective camera when Ruth has disappeared from the country place where she and Olga have just met. What appears to our eye is a fluent roaming exploration of a labyrinthine darkness. In fact, the camera is recording Olga's search for Ruth, which indeed locates her. We may even say that Ruth hides in order that Olga might find her.

Olga and Ruth visit Egypt. It is an interlude they share away from the male-biased social strictures that normally contain and disadvantage them. They are on holiday, a spiritual quest entirely of their own, unfettered by male carping, crabbing and disruption. This journey runs a stream of quiet poignancy through the center of the film.

IDENTIFICATION OF A WOMAN (Italy, France). Niccolo, a filmmaker, has difficulty focusing on the woman he is with. Mavi has detached herself from family; nevertheless,

Niccolo obsesses on them. With Ida (Christine Boisson, superb), Niccolo obsesses on the past —on Mavi. Niccolo takes up his nephew's suggestion to make a dumb *Star Wars*-level piece of escapism, which finds him (on film) star-trekking toward (the newspaper says) a dangerously expanding sun, to jolt himself out of space and time and into the moment.

Niccolo and Mavi take a motor trip into the country, where they get lost, and stuck, in an immense fog. By providing a kind of protective cover, this fog, a projection of their anxiety and ambivalence, releases the couple's worst mutual behavior. When Ida accompanies Niccolo to Venice on holiday, the other great set-piece seems to evoke this alternative couple's stability and shared contentment. But it *turns*. On the water, in a canoe, Ida and Niccolo find themselves in a vast floating fog, the measured sound of lapping water adding to the melancholy to which the lovers differently respond: she, with her whole spirit; he, analytically. Ida and Niccolo float apart, together. At their hotel, Ida learns by phone she is pregnant, and the relationship drowns. Is Niccolo able to live with someone else's past— Ida's, or the child's father's?

What a joyous tonic Michelangelo Antonioni's *Identificazione di una donna* is for all the strident, empty stylizing, sociologizing, politicizing and manipulation that take up so many screens nowadays. Mysterious pressures invisibly weigh in on his characters, leaving us to wonder whether our own lives, too, are an elusive fine thread whose course is best picked up somewhere unexpected, uncharted, far, far beyond our familiar sensible or emotional galaxy, in the direction of the sun's perfect (if dangerous) clarity—somewhere beyond the clouds.

BRITANNIA HOSPITAL (UK). *Britannia Hospital* completes Lindsay Anderson's satirical trilogy about the state of Britain (*If...*, 1968; *O Lucky Man!*, 1973). Fiercely funny, darkly prophetic, it is a transmutation of Mary Shelley's *Frankenstein; or, The Modern Prometheus*. Scenarist David Sherwin notes collisions between classism and democracy and between imperialism and other problems of equity—social welfare problems—at home. Everyman Mick Travis (Malcolm McDowell, marvelous) now completes his life's journey, achieving his tragic destiny as a subversive, surreptitious documentarian. Anderson's behavioral blend of humanism, anarchism and mordant wit, and his stylistic blend of realistic and fantastic elements, stamp again the final instalment.

Britannia Hospital is beset with the problems besetting Britain's healthcare system and, indeed, British society in general in the mid-1970s. Workers are on strike; for example, the kitchen cooks won't cook, and the oranges being served for breakfast can't appease the luxuriant appetites of the hospital's upper-class residents. Also, the hospital is under seige because of one of the hospital's visiting patients, whom demonstrators want removed: a cruel, oppressive and rather infantile African dictator reminiscent of Uganda's Idi Amin. Meanwhile, Dr. Frankenstein, rechristened Professor Millar, has frozen assorted human body parts and is planning on electrifying into existence their composite. Oh, dear: the head, defrigerated, has wilted; a replacement today must be found. Exceptional guests, including the Queen Mum, are expected on the occasion of the hospital's 500th anniversary, and Millar has a surprise demonstration in store.

A number of labor leaders pursue personal power in the film, a corruption and distortion of their representative mandate. Anderson was one Leftist who thus understood why his nation took the corrective course of electing Margaret Thatcher in 1979—this maniacal Rightist and upholder of all the privilege that disgusted him.

WÊND KÛUNI (Burkina Faso). The first film from Burkina Faso is wonderful—a beauteous, visually unaffected pastoral about a 12-year-old boy. It takes place in the early nineteenth century, before the white man's intrusion, along with his Christianity, before Islam's intrusion. The film is quiet, tranquil, as rhythmic as a river. The baa-ing of sheep and chirping of birds are recurrent sounds.

The father apparently abandoned the mother when the boy was an infant. At ten, the latter and another child in the village fell ill, causing his mother to be branded a witch. Mother and son were driven out, their hut, burned. That day, his mother died, and he ran for hours, dropping down from exhaustion and nearly dying himself. The film opens as an itinerant merchant gives him water, bringing him back to life, and takes him to the nearest village on his way, depositing him there. The boy cannot speak. Tinga and Lale adopt him, naming him Wênd Kûuni, "God's Gift." This is his second rebirth. A couple's domestic quarrel leads to the husband's suicide, which Wênd Kûuni uncovers. This restores his voice—his third rebirth. With this voice he discloses his history to his sister, Pognere, thus becoming a storyteller: another rebirth.

Gaston Kabore's film consists mostly of the family's daily life. The boy's adoptive mother hardly ever seems to stop working; she is shown performing numerous tasks. (The village men, by contrast, seem on perpetual holiday.) Wênd Kûuni shepherds the family's flock. In one shot, he is walking towards the camera in the tall, dry grass in the fields. The animals in front of him become visible later than he—a magical moment. In another passage, we watch Wênd Kûuni make a flute.

Kabore's *Bûud Yam* (1997), which I haven't seen, catches up with Wênd Kûuni's life.

THE PREFAB PEOPLE (Hungary). Highlighted by his curve-around narrative form and long takes, but not imbued with his later Euro-lyricism, Béla Tarr's Hungarian, Cassavetesian *Panelkapcsolat* essays the disintegration of a marriage. It opens with Róbi packing and leaving as his unnamed wife (Judit Pogány, phenomenal) becomes increasingly hysterical. At the door she begs, "If I get fed up, where can *I* go?"

The next scene is a past anniversary; the "flashback" is Tarr's. A failed feast results when Róbi turns a deaf ear to his wife's pleas for a chance to work outside the home. (The couple have an infant and a small child.) She kvetches, he forbears; but the force of her protest is something we take in.

A scene at the hairdresser's cuts between the woman and a friend, both under dryers, and the loss of the long take underscores how odd such a sociable exchange is for the woman. The club scene that immediately follows explains the hairdo. Another failed feast results as Róbi ignores his wife, not even dancing with her (but dancing with some other woman!), as his wife retreats behind a mask of boredom before, unnoticed, dissolving into tears. In the next scene the couple quarrel. A job opportunity would take him away, alone, for two years. "It looks like we'd have a car inside a year," he says. She responds, "The point isn't how soon we'd have a car."

An imperfect narrative circle occurs when the earlier scene of stormy abandonment is reached, but begun earlier, reenacted rather than duplicated, and moved beyond. Soliloquizing, the woman says: "The only thing that might bring him back is the children. But it wouldn't be the same."

They are back together, and it *isn't* the same. Quarrel-free, they buy a washing machine. No conversation passes between them.

TOUTE UNE NUIT (Belgium, France). Compressed into the course of a single night in Brussels, various couples interact, some of them strangers, many of them grabbing at each other across a gulf of loneliness or fear—perhaps fear of loneliness. In *All Night Long*, Belgian minimalist Chantal Äkerman gives the impression of having cut into a series of dramas, each at its highest point, when someone is leaving with someone, someone is leaving someone, or someone is returning to or reuniting with someone. Each drama is unique, and yet each is structured by similar emotional imperatives that consign it to an identical pattern of behavior. We may not see our lives in the film's vignettes, but we see our longings and concerns, feel them refreshed, and find them clarified by the intensity of their expression.

Instead of a safely potted narrative plant, Äkerman gives us a plethora of seemingly random narrative shoots. These bits of life reflect how we experience our own lives.

1982

Characters are let go of for a while and picked up again. While her husband soundly sleeps, a woman noisily packs her bag right on the bed and leaves him, goes to a hotel, but returns home at dawn defeated, gets back into bed just in time for the ringing alarm clock to presumably awaken her, as well as him. For years I took exception to this artificial aspect, this miniature story, but now I find that it underscores by contrast the different method of the rest of Äkerman's formally rigorous yet open-ended film.

Äkerman's characters aren't an exclusive bunch. They represent a range of ages, live in houses and apartments, include same-sex couples (a volatile pair of gals, a tender pair of guys).

Encapsulating the passion of *Toute une nuit* is a recurring Italian pop tune, "L'amore perdonera."

MOONLIGHTING (UK). Poland's Jerzy Skolimowski co-authored the script for Roman Polanski's masterpiece, *Knife in the Water* (1962), and worked in English for the first time with his own brilliant, tragicomical, working-class *Deep End* (1970). *Moonlighting* is a patient, haunting comedy-drama about Polish workmen who are providing cheap labor on a remodeling project for a Polish official in London. In effect, the Polish team is undercutting their British brethren, whose union-negotiated minimal fees are higher than their fellow Pole wishes to pay. Meanwhile, back home, the Communist government is crushing Solidarity, the democratic Polish labor movement, one upshot of which is that the workmen are stranded in England on their tourist visas. The contractor leading the group, who alone reads and speaks English, however, isn't telling anyone anything.

Largely a silent behavioral comedy, *Moonlighting* showcases Jeremy Irons's dazzling performance as Nowak, the Polish contractor, who keenly misses his family. His loneliness in London is palpable. Nowak must eventually steal in order to keep the workers in his charge fed, and a vision accumulates as to how effortlessly ordinary workers are exploited. Trying to contain the restlessness and questioning of his crew, Nowak finds himself between a rock and a hard place.

Moonlighting draws empathy. What would it be like to be stuck in a foreign country when your own country is in upheaval and who knows when, if ever, you will be able to return? The film also has a critical edge, showing how workers are pitted against workers for the benefit of greedy bosses who care about none of them. As a comedy, it's frequently hilarious; but its political bite turns the film into a radiant beast.

It is also gorgeous, thanks to Skolimowski's cool, observant eye and color cinematography by Tony Pierce-Roberts (*A Room with a View*, 1986).

FLIGHT OF THE EAGLE (Sweden, West Germany, Norway). This chronicle of Swedish engineer Salomon August Andrée's 1897 North Polar expedition using a French hydrogen balloon, available in the States only in a trimmed, dubbed version, is Jan Troëll's greatest achievement—an epic account of three men's tragic attempt to make history for their nation. "There will always be a risk," Andrée concedes to an assembly of colleagues before the launch. "But let me ask that you weigh the risk against Sweden's glory." Troëll's theme of insane European aspiration—the colonialist impulse—becomes clear when someone likens the imminent flight of The Eagle, to conquer the North Pole, to southern Europe's conquests in Africa.

To begin with, what a fresh approach to such material—what a boon alongside so many uncritical, most often adulatory films about humans trying to be the first here, to accomplish this, that or the other there. Andrée and his crew persevere and show phenomenal courage as they wither away and die amidst freezing cold and ice, in image after image of ghastly beauty. (Troëll is the color cinematographer.) But none of this (if you will) heroism distracts us from the madness of the mission in the first place. Recently, the United States was having a hard time distinguishing between the valor of many American soldiers in Iraq, often expressed as the homefront obligation to "support our troops," and the incredible wrongness and vileness of the American invasion. Troëll's stunning film refreshes our capacity to make the distinction.

"God and Country," "Long live Sweden!": these are the mantras we hear from the crew that seal their doom. Shafts of memory—flashbacks—poignantly reflect on what these pioneers have forsaken.

Max von Sydow is wonderful as Andrée, and it's his irreplaceable voice we hear in the English-dubbed *Ingenjör Andrées luftfärd*.

TIME STANDS STILL (Hungary). Lucid yet also elusive, Péter Gothár's *Megáll az idö* presents a social vision of a Soviet satellite. Its focus is a Budapest family. The father flees during the 1956 Hungarian uprising rather than face prison, or worse, as a "counterrevolutionary." His wife chooses to stay behind with their two sons. The film covers the next ten or twelve years.

One brother, Dini, loses his girlfriend, Magda, to his older brother, Gábor, after a teacher convinces him that sexuality, which he is profaning by his adolescent interest in it, is "sacred." A more liberal new order replaces that teacher with one who encourages class participation—a ploy to catch them in a political trap, their father's understandably paranoid comrade, released from prison, insists. The boys' struggle with adolescence, then, is compounded by issues of political authority: a state too repressive for their ache towards freedom and independence; the quarrel between different "orders" of Hungarian communism. Indeed, the attitude of the entire high school comes to a head when the kids openly deride the school head's solemn "patriotic" speech. Paul Anka singing *"You are my destiny . . . "* is for them both a sexual and a political anthem.

Connections must be courted, state favor curried, to ensure a professional future. Because of their father's politics, the brothers are stuck in a black hole.

The opening movement, in 1956, blends fictional and documentary elements; thereafter, the film's style veers toward a nostalgic, and heartbreaking, Expressionism. Tight frames; pans and tracking shots that inevitably come to a hard finish; backlighting that darkens human faces, their individual features indistinct or blotted out: various elements contribute to a palpable portrait of oppression. Even in the streets, Gothár and color cinematographer Lajos Koltai convey a world in which people draw only quarter-breaths.

1983

L'ARGENT (France, Switzerland). We tend to think in boxes. Materialism is one thing; spirituality, quite another. Yet in the cinema of Robert Bresson, materialism yields a store of spirituality.

From a story by Lev Tolstoi, "The Forged Note," Bresson's final film is titled *L'argent*—that is, *Money*. A schoolboy uses a counterfeit 500-franc note at a shop whose owners just as knowingly pass it on to a young laborer who is servicing them with an oil delivery. It is he who, using the phony note at a restaurant, is tried criminally; the charges are dismissed, but this boy, too proud to reclaim his job, descends a chute into crime, including murder, for which he never seemed destined. He loses wife, toddler, home, himself—all the upshot of that note whose forgery he never guessed. One might say that the bill was passed from hand to hand, but Bresson shows the transactions otherwise. The bill instead passes from hand to hand while finding at last its home. Money has a life of its own here, controlling everyone and everything in society, contested only by the free will that the boy, in the grip of need, fails to summon. However, the film will end with his redemption, by which time Bresson will have dismantled the fragile barrier between providence and individual, between apparent universal direction and the messy groping and stumbles issuing from the mind and spirit of this accidental criminal.

Bresson typically isolates and amplifies sounds to emphasize materiality: footsteps; objects being set down on a table; ringing cash register; doors opening and closing; screeching mopeds. It is an impersonal world in which humans impassively disadvantage fellow humans —a world seemingly without mystery, out of which Bresson precisely sculpts the dusky, illimitable mystery of the course of a human soul.

THE BALLAD OF NARAYAMA (Japan), The opening shot of Shohei Imamura's *Narayama-bushikô* (Palme d'Or, Cannes) is cunning. Accompanying a caption that sets the action in nineteenth-century northern Japan, the camera reveals vast terrain: miles of snow-covered trees. It's a helicopter shot!—and the visual implication of this modern contraption draws our attention to something else that might otherwise have remained "invisible": the camera it is transporting. All this has the effect of wittily collapsing the distance in time of about a hundred years. Imamura's study of greed, the sex impulse and the survival instinct in a remote, wintry, primitive community thus will be, in reality, a reflection on how these elements still structure human behavior and activity.

Orin is 69. At 70, elders in this villagre trek to Mount Narayama to die, thereby relieving the impoverished community of their burden. It is time for Orin to put her hut in order. Son Tatsuhei must get a wife!

The hard work of farming, as well as other aspects of life in this community (such as Tatsuhei's sexual encounters), are interrupted by inserted closeups of Nature: bugs and snakes copulating; a snake, later an owl, devouring a rodent. The villagers are always one bad harvest away from disaster, but winter keeps some of them warmer than others. Food, scarce, is precious, and when one of them steals crops the village comes together as an avenging mob, burying alive the offender and his entire family. Otherwise, "we will get no sleep," "he will steal again."

The film's last movement enchants. Orin has turned 70, and Tatsuhei carries her, piggyback, to her last end. She accepts this, as she must; wild animals cross their silent path. Spirits animate a tree, bringing it to sparkling life. It is the spirit of Orin. It is the ballad of Narayama.

AND THE SHIP SAILS ON (Italy). Bettered only in the Federico Fellini canon by *Fellini Satyricon* (1969), *E la nave va* is a meditation on the persistence of war and its ravages on humanity set against time's passage. It is among Fellini's most moving works. Like his masterpiece, it comments on human folly.

A celebrated opera singer's ashes are onboard a luxury liner that sets sail days after the assassination of Archduke Franz Ferdinand by a Bosnian Serb. The ship is transporting her friends to an island where her funeral service is to be held. Among the other people onboard are Orlando, a journalist and the humorous guide who speaks to us directly between attempts at interviewing guests, and Austria-Hungary's Grand Duke.

The film begins scratchily in sepia and silence; this bravura opening depicts the dockside activity, a good deal of it involving playful children, prior to the ship's departure. The intricacy of this activity, especially since it's captured primarily in long-shot, evokes allegorical paintings by Hieronymus Bosch. The artifice of the studio-bound details (cellophane ocean, solid, material smoke, etc.) likewise prepare us for an allegory, or at least a parable. The boiler room, with men working below as elaborately dressed guests espy them from on high, may even remind us of Dante's *Inferno*—although guests sing for the workers, who applaud. (But do they really enjoy this zoo patron-like intrusion into their workplace?)

Color is itself distancing: browns, white, black, and a touch of red.

When Serbian refugees are brought onboard, spirited peasant dancing augments the plentiful operatic singing. (This film is full of wonderful music.) What is the captain to do when an Austro-Hungarian battleship demands that the refugees be turned over? The Grand Duke intervenes, but only so the funeral service can proceed.

Heart-piercing finale.

1983

ZELIG (U.S.). Woody Allen's track record has never been consistent. An eyesore, and onanistic, *Annie Hall* (1977) represents the scenarist-director at his worst—or appeared to, until winning Oscars for it plunged Allen into the dank family melodrama of *Interiors* (1978). A lovely *Manhattan* (1979) was followed by two inferior works. *Zelig* therefore came as a revelation. In gorgeous black and white (*Manhattan*'s Gordon Willis, the cinematographer), it is both Allen's *Sherlock Jr.* and *Citizen Kane*—a humanistic piece of such wit and dazzling invention that it accumulates into a metaphor for creative possibilities. As such, Allen can separate himself from the protagonist that he plays, who keeps changing without, somehow, contributing to these changes. At the same time, worked on by Allen's imagination, this protagonist, Zelig, reflects both his creator and their volatile home: the twentieth century.

Zelig is egoless. Starting in the 1920s, he appears to take on the aspect of whomever or whatever group he happens to be with, and because none of these authentically define him he happens, or seems, to be *everywhere*: at a ticker-tape parade of heroes, at a Scott Fitzgerald party, at a Nuremberg Hitler rally, and so forth. Reflecting the uncertain sense of self at America's core, this "chameleon man" becomes a freak celebrity and a subject for medical study. In truth, nothing can be learned from him, because he can scarcely be said to exist. Were it not for Mia Farrow's inability to portray her sympathetic character as a mature woman (hence, the role is uncomfortably split between Farrow and another actress), this would be a perfect film.

Contesting obsessive American myths (individualism, independence, work ethic rewards), *Zelig* is, come to think of it, also Allen's *Greed*. And it's riotously funny—of the high satirical order of Mark Twain's literary masterpieces.

UP TO A CERTAIN POINT (Cuba). In an interview being filmed, a Cuban explains: "It's right that men and women should be equal. But only up to a certain point."

Machismo dies hard in Castro's Cuba—and maybe, truth to tell, in Castro himself; but at least it finally dies, however slowly. In another of this film's pseudo-documentary inserts, a Havanan says that her man gave her a choice: him or work. No fool, she chose her job, asking where she would be if he decided to leave her someday. No film I know of better links gender equality to personal destiny and social necessity than *Hasta cierto punto*.

Tomás Gutiérrez Alea's most captivating comedy looks back to *De cierta manera* (1977), which Alea helped complete upon the death of Sara Gómez Yera, and looks ahead to Carlos Saura's Argentinean *Tango* (1998). Alea's film draws similar thematic and stylistic concerns from Gómez's film, and in fact pays tribute to it, and, like *Tango*, is a film about the making of a film—but here the protagonist of the film, Oscar, wrote the script for the film-within-a-film, not directs it. However, there is a similar thematic back-and-forth playing out between Alea's film and Oscar's. Oscar's documentary exposes *machismo* and consequent Cuban difficulty in realizing gender equality; his romance with Lina, the activist dockworker who appears in the film, suggests the need for cameras to be turned on him. But wife Marian's friend Flora, wife of the film-within-a-film's director, counsels a kind of cynicism about men that reflects the men's own *machismo*. This *machismo*, along with labor issues of the dockworkers, Lina included, undermine the Oscar-Lina relationship. It seems that the male sense of entitlement to adultery links new Cuba to the old.

Well, that's true *up to a certain point*.

AMADA (Cuba). *Beloved*, one of cinema's great love stories about thwarted passion, is a visual feast served up by legendary Cuban filmmaker Humberto Solás—some sources cite co-scenarist Nelson Rodríguez as co-director, some do not—and exquisite color cinematographer Livio Delgado and composer Leo Brouwer, the main theme of whose score sweeps one up in its gigantic mood of melancholy. Conjuring memory, its echoes of Tolstoi's *Anna Karenina* and Vittorio De Sica's *The Garden of the Finzi-Continis* (1971), from Giorgio Bassani's autobiographical novel, and even a bit of Orson Welles's *The Magnificent*

Ambersons (1942), from Tarkington, suit its historical location between Cuba's War of Independence from Spain and the Castro Revolution. It begins in 1914, with the outbreak of the First World War, which drove up the price of sugar, Cuba's signature export; the previous year saw the election of President Mario García Menocal, who favored both corporate business and Cuba-U.S. ties to the needs of ordinary Cubans and ran a deeply corrupt administration. Solás's focus is an aristocratic family, the Villalosas, whose wealth derives from past slave-trading. Amada's unfaithful spouse, Dionisio, uses her prestigious family to pursue political ambitions. Amada falls in love with her young cousin, journalist Marcial, who at first resists forsaking his revolutionary principles and running off with her, and later, when he capitulates, because he is in love with her, finds her unwilling, or unable, to do this. The beating that Dionisio gives Amada exposes his double standard when it comes to adultery—and his pride.

Amada's appearance of sepia substitutes reddish-brown for beige and brown, hinting the spilling of national blood; the sculpted images, including the constrained light inside the cavernously dark Villalosa villa (Amada's one surviving parent, her mother, is blind), bespeaks an insulated existence stored in closets of the past.

THE PIT, THE PENDULUM AND HOPE (Czechoslovakia). Stop-motion animator Jan Švankmajer's *Kyvadlo, jáma a nadeje* is an eerie, powerful live-action adaptation of Poe's story "The Pit and the Pendulum." Sweeping back and forth as it descends to his heart, a sharp blade in the form of a clock's pendulum measures the mortality of a man who is strapped to a table in a dark dungeon, a victim of the Spanish Inquisition.

We never see the prisoner's face. The face of a thickly garbed and hooded cleric we *do* glimpse, in closeup, before he blows out a candle—an indication of the death sentence that has been dealt the heretic. This is followed by the subterranean journey leading to the torture chamber, a place of fear and dreadful execution. The camera shows the bumpy ceiling of the passageway; the heretic may be flat on his back, being carried to his fate. We hear the moans of the tormented in other rooms. A second closeup is of the heretic's hand chafing against its confinement. The gears of the torture apparatus break the silence; out of the mouth of a painted skeleton the blade starts its descent.

Another credited source is French symbolist Villiers de L'Isle-Adam, with whose work I am unfamiliar. But the Poe source is completely recognizable, with a few exceptions. For instance, whereas the narrator/protagonist is rescued in the original, here he ingeniously effects his own escape, enlisting the aid of the numerous rats about. Is it a trick of my eye? The animals' faces, shown in closeup, resemble the face of the hooded monk. The black-and-white camera records the heretic's flight by showing his scurrying bare feet. Outside, his face covered, a robed figure like that at the outset enfolds the escapee in pitch darkness.

Is there any hope?

1984

THE HOME AND THE WORLD (India). From a novel by Rabindranath Tagore, *Ghare-Baire* is Satyajit Ray's most majestic and splendiferous film. The protagonist is Bimala Choudhury, who recalls her marriage in the early twentieth century. Nikhilesh, her spouse, a wealthy Bengal landowner and merchant, encourages her education and departure from traditional Hindu ways. Bimala eventually has an affair with an old college friend of his, Sandip Mukherjee (Soumitra Chatterjee, brilliant), a leader of the incendiary nationalist movement Swadeshi, whose first female member she becomes. Nikhilesh opposes Sandip's politics, which he foretells will further divide Hindus and Muslims in a region that the ruling British have partitioned in order to short-circuit an alliance between the two groups. Sandip's call for a boycott of British imports, Nikhilesh contends, will further impoverish Muslim merchants who are already struggling to survive. When his local agitation falls flat, Sandip organizes and unleashes a terrorist response.

This is no facile *Reds* (1981), *Doctor Zhivago* (1965) or *Gone with the Wind* (1939), where history supplies a sweeping backdrop for soap opera. Ray, instead, creates a rich tapestry in which British imperialism, Indian nationalism, the Choudhurys' marriage, Bimala's tentative moves toward a liberated modernism, and her extramarital affair are tightly interwoven, generating a complex vision of a society in upheaval. Bimala is portrayed as existing uncertainly between two worlds, while the two men in her life, political opponents, are each certain of himself but only in partial possession of the truth. Have you ever wondered what it would be like to see the political views of others apart from the prism of your own views? Ray's late masterpiece enables us to take in a myriad of sociopolitical shades and inflections in a complex, combustible situation. Moreover, it concludes with a devastating shot telescoping a devastated life.

CLASS RELATIONS (West Germany, France). Franz Kafka's posthumously published *Amerika* is faithfully rendered here, even to the point of being left unfinished, by the married writing-directing-editing team of Jean-Marie Straub and Danièle Huillet. Straub and Huillet aren't as funny as Kafka and are working from a text that Kafka would have tightened (and perhaps filled in) had he returned at some point to this early fragment of his, but they achieve a transcendent result, exploring the class- and status-determined politics of human relations in pristine black and white. Their *Klassenverhältnisse* blends realism and surrealism, documentary and fiction.

"Amerika" is an America of the European imagination. Kafka himself never visited the country in which his story, without reference to specific time, is set. Police officers there look like silent Hollywood's Keystone Kops.

The protagonist is teenaged Karl Rossman (Christian Heinisch, excellent), who has immigrated from Kafka's own Prague to New York, where he is eventually tossed out by his uncle (ubiquitous Mario Adorf) and cast adrift in a chaotic, cruel, capricious world based on capital and power. Like the book, the film is absurdist, enmeshing the youth, another one of Kafka's self-projections, in a seemingly endless puzzle of disadvantage and uncertainty.

This pilgrim's progress is eventually Oklahoma-bound, where, with a nod to Pirandello, a theatrical troupe awaits Karl—as in Bergman, a dream within a dream.

In a sense, Karl is lost somewhere in his own mind, and even this most private aspect of existence is heavily imprinted by the politics and economics of the world outside. Dissolved is the barrier of sanity—where one can get one's bearings—betwixt interior and exterior worlds. Whereas Kafka (like David Lynch) is more intuitive than intellectual, Straub and Huillet are more intellectual than intuitive. This rounds out the Kafka, in effect completing *Amerika* without extending the story.

A SUMMER AT GRANDPA'S (Taiwan). Based on co-scenarist Chu Tien-wen's childhood, Hou Hsiao-hsien's *Dongdong de jiaqi* revolves around Tung-Tung, an eleven-year-old boy who, along with Ting-Ting, his four-year-old sister, spends a summer in the country with maternal grandparents and his teenaged uncle, while Mother is in hospital. This is the first part of Hou's Coming-of-Age trilogy.

The film admits a wealth of incidents, and only the scarcest amount of plot, as Hou patiently, unhurriedly reflects on how children often feel lost amongst adults in the adult world, where they are rarely listened to and largely inhabit a shared world of their own. We watch a turtle race they conduct. They set loose wild birds a neighbor has caught and caged. They swim in the river. A boy tells Ting-Ting, who is watching, to go away: "Your eyes will grow germs!" Left out (*again*, is the sense of it), Ting-Ting retaliates by silently gathering up the boys' clothes bank side and tossing these to the current—this, after observing the motion of a train.

Dim-ma, "madwoman" with a tattered umbrella, is mentally slow. She is introduced in a high overhead shot from the perspective of boys in a giant, leafy tree: a projection of Hou's wish to protect her even as one of the boys scorns her. Dim-ma snatches Ting-Ting in the nick of time from railroad tracks, carrying her piggyback to safety. Dim-ma has been raped and is pregnant. Adults discuss what needs to be done.

Uncle, once he is tossed out by Grandpa, lives with the girl he has impregnated. The couple marry. Respect in marriage, the one officiating explains, is a building block of society.

Numerous themes come together in this complex, beautiful film. One is this: for Chu and Hou, the birth of their feminist consciousness.

PARIS, TEXAS (West Germany, France, UK). Lost in the desert, a man wanders without history; but this comes to him in the form of his brother, who asks: "What the hell happened to you, anyhow? You look like forty miles of rough road."

Written by Sam Shepard and brought into reality by L.M. Kit Carson, *Paris, Texas* is another of Wim Wenders' "road pictures"; and, while it falls short of the brilliance of his *In the Course of Time* (*Kings of the Road*, 1976), also from West Germany, it has something of the same appreciation for gaps in people's lives, the spaces that separate people, a sense of drifting, the heartache of disconnected lives. Wenders and cinematographer Robby Müller find in the American landscape an infinite expanse of loneliness—and the possibility to irrigate its aridity with wellsprings of love, self-sacrifice and reaching out. At last, here is a film that mends one's heart after breaking it.

The protagonist is Travis (Harry Dean Stanton, at his best), a man who brutalized his wife, Jane (Nastassja Kinski, phenomenal), abandoning their three-year-old son, Hunter, who has been raised by his brother, Walt (Dean Stockwell, giving as beautiful a performance as an ordinary man as he elsewhere gives playing freaks), and Walt's French-born wife, Anne. Travis assumes custody of Hunter, in the end returning the boy to his mother, who currently works in a peep-show parlor, before returning himself to the desert alone—as John Ford's *The Searchers* (1956) puts it, forever riding between the winds. American cinema's only comparably moving reunion of mother and son would come two years hence, in David Lynch's *Blue Velvet*.

The strains of Ry Cooder's score suggest the fragile nature of human lives that the film poignantly essays.

MEMORIES OF PRISON (Brazil). Nelson Pereira dos Santos's *Memórias do Cárcere* is based on Brazilian author Graciliano Ramos's posthumously published account of his year long incarceration in the mid-1930s simply for being a suspected communist. No charges were filed against Ramos; there was no trial. Ramos was recently discharged as Director of Public Education of Alagoas.

The film sketches the family life of Ramos's about to be disrupted and his southward journey to prison in Rio de Janeiro, during which a military officer asks for his autograph. The rest of the film details the culture and daily life at the prisons where Ramos was confined.

It is clear at the point of Ramos's first arrival that political imprisonment is routine in Brazil. In a heartrending shot, the camera moves across an expanse of cheering male anti-fascists behind bars in countless cells and ends in the female part of the prison, where spirit and nostalgia, expressed in song, is equally strong, and where a cut, disrupting the shot, reveals a peeping male eye. The inmates are in solidarity. The incipient deportation of two female inmates to Nazi Germany provokes outrage in both parts of the prison. "There is no justice nowadays," Ramos tells his wife on one of her visits. Ironically, Ramos's incarceration seems to clarify his previously uncertain politics.

Ramos is relocated to the brutal Ilha Grande Correctional Colony. Arruda, the white-outfitted despot at the colony, unmercifully beats a black prisoner for no reason. Arruda asks Ramos, who has been helping fellow inmates with their Portuguese, to write a speech for him; Ramos declines, although permission for his own writing hangs in the balance. Ramos is

shipped back to Rio.
Carlos Vereza gives a tremendous performance as Ramos, whose novel *Vidas Secas* Pereira dos Santos filmed some two decades earlier (1963).

YELLOW EARTH (China). "Of all us poor folk, girls are the saddest."
Reputedly the first work of the "fifth generation" of Chinese filmmakers, *Huang tu di* is gorgeous—Zhang Yimou is the color cinematographer—and poetic. Chen Kaige captures a dream of national unity under the threat that the Japanese pose in the late 1930s. Qing Gu is a young revolutionary soldier who visits the northern wilderness in order to collect folk songs to inspire comrades and bind them to the common folk. Staying with a peasant farmer, he discovers that the songs, all sad, wed haunting melodies to lyrics such as "Suffering is forever, sweetness is short." Gu inspires Cuiqiao, the widower's 13-year-old daughter, who wants to join the Communist army to experience the equality with men that "Brother Gu" from the south has told her about. In the world with which she is familiar, marriages are arranged for girls, whose singing gives them their only voice of freedom—the "freedom" of lament.

Chen combines captivating lyricism and a documentary-style attention to the harsh conditions of the peasants' lives. (Stunning: amidst drought, the communal prayer for rain.) The flowing Yellow River interrupts the mostly static shots of daunting terrain. In one radiant shot, Cuiqiao's carrying buckets of water from the river appears to extend the river's motion. Nature is arrayed against the people, but they are also a part of it.

Qing must rejoin his outfit. "Take me with you," Cuiqiao pleads. It is against "the rules." "Can't the rules be changed?" she asks. "We depend on rules for our cause." But Qing does promise to return. "I'm afraid I shall not see you again," Cuiqiao sings out as he leaves, a pair of reverse long-shots recording the vast distance now between them. She is right, of course.

PIEMULE (Czechoslovakia). "Pigs will eat the corn, but we'll go hungry."
Piemule is an ethnographic documentary by Jana Sevcikov. It explores a community of rural Romanians, descendants of Czech immigrants in the 1820s. This is what the forefathers found: "Bare hills, sky, impenetrable forests." "Dreams of a better life," says the narrator, "ended in grief and despair . . . [and b]itter disillusionment." In the mid-1980s, a woman unsteadily leading a horse smiles good-naturedly: "This wasteland is where we live. Why did those Czechs land us here?"

This film shows people at work. Steep, rough hills, along with outdated tools and equipment, make the farm work nearly impossible. Heavy mists cast a veil of irony over scenes of plowing, hoeing, etc., consigning labor to the province of insubstantiality and illusion. Nicolae Ceauşescu, Romania's Communist leader, at the time exported nearly all agricultural and industrial production in an effort to pay the country's massive debt. Hunger and poverty gripped Romania. By decade's end, Ceauşescu was overthrown, tried, executed.

Sevcikov shifts among sepia, color, and black and white, here again suggesting illusion and wobbling the distinction between past and present. Ordinary people's singing fills the soundtrack; faces, the frames. The camera pans in a church, observing the faces of children as this captive audience is indoctrinated in the dogma of Original Sin. (A parallel scene at school shows children being taught allegiance to the State.) These faces disclose a vast variety of attitudes and personalities in contrast to the stricture of the priest's instruction. Sevcikov is a master ironist.

The subject of her most heartrending interview is a handsome boy in his twenties who prefers pop music to waltzes and yearns for a less harsh life. He writes to foreign girls but isn't permitted to leave Romania. He dreams of immigrating to Czechoslovakia.

THE ELEMENT OF CRIME (Denmark). The first installment in his dark "European trilogy,"

1984

Lars von Trier's *Forbrydelsens element* is among the most sorrowful crime detection works in cinema—a film in which murder weighs heavily as the loss of human life, not as an entertaining occasion for crime-solving ingenuity. Summoned by Osborne, his mentor, ex-cop Fischer investigates the serial murders of young girls selling lottery tickets. Proceeding "by the book," in this case, Osborne's treatise on criminal behavior, and assisted by hypnosis that projects him into the killer's mind, Fischer retraces the steps of a suspect based on past police surveillance of him.

The suspect's name is Harry Gray, an amalgamation of David Gray, who investigates vampires in a remote seaside village in Carl Theodor Dreyer's—Trier's idol's—*Vampyr* (1931), and *The Third Man*'s (Carol Reed, 1949) postwar opportunist, a black marketeer in penicillin, Harry Lime. These influences suggest the weird, hallucinatory, post-apocalyptic world of bombed-out buildings, scrounging children, and sleepwalking souls through which Fischer moves as in a nightmare. It's Noir City. Also, partly because something again is rotten in the state of Denmark (or in whatever Scandinavian post the action unfolds), *Hamlet* is in the heavy air. After all, what is Fischer doing but trying to vindicate Osborne, his surrogate father?

Trier, who enacts the hilarious role of the Schmuck of Ages, and his color cinematographer, Tom Elling, have given the film a strange, haunted look, partly the result of saturating the negative with gold. A glimmer of light may insinuate itself into a bottomlessly dark frame. We feel we are looking into the end of the world, a disintegrating society populated by desperate lives. How can anybody be killing all these children?

Stay tuned. Trier's brilliant trilogy has only just begun.

KARIN'S FACE (Sweden). Ingmar Bergman's short film about her begins with a photograph of his mother, Karin Åkerblom Bergman, taken for a passport only days before her death. The old woman, a former nurse, is beautiful—as beautiful as Bergman's love for her can imagine her. We all know all about her, because we have seen her history, beginning with Lutheran priest Erik Bergman's courtship of her, in Bille August's *The Best Intentions* (1982), Ingmar's son Daniel Bergman's *Sunday's Children* (1992) and Liv Ullmann's *Private Confessions* (1996), all written by Bergman. We care almost deeply about this woman we have never in actuality met.

Karins ansikte slips into Bergman's family album, for the camera to visit, in some cases scrutinize, old photograph after old photograph, the earlier ones in sepia, a few more recent ones in black and white. There she is, and there is Bergman's father, whom we know his son hated, and we can see this here; and we can identify which of the babies and the children is Ingmar by those ears of his. This film contains no speech, only faces; it possesses the muteness of a haunting dream.

There is a photograph of Karin at work, and another of her smiling facing a cat. There aren't too many smiles in the Bergman family album. Perhaps this one is the only full-fledged smile—although the hint of another in the new passport photo, with its utterly relaxed composure, suggests that Karin herself is anticipating the irony that her final journey, only heartbeats away, will render this photograph useless.

We return to that photo, which a series of other photos that we have seen earlier deconstructs—for Bergman, the eternal mystery of the human face.

The spare, delicate piano score is by Käbi Laretei, Daniel's mother.

THE HOLY INNOCENTS (Spain). From Miguel Delibes, Mario Camus's *Los santos inocentes* is an incisive, haunting portrait of the political connection between Franco's fascism, the Church, and the feudalism of land barons in Spain's countryside in the 1960s. Impoverished peasants Paco and Régula work for Pedro, who manages a vast rural estate. Their problems are real, unlike those in the mansion that can be credited to high-born vanity and indolence.

Paco and Régula have three children: a sick, bedridden child, her older sister, and Quirce, their son who resists the status quo encapsulated in his mother's by-rote utterance, "We're here to serve." This boy, serving in the military, delays using his leave to go home. The film alternates between him in the present and his and others' flashbacks. There is one other member of the household cramped into small quarters: Azarías, a simple man who as a result of washing his hands in urine to keep them from chapping was discharged after sixty years of service, causing him to move in with Régula, his sister. Régula desperately wants her older children somehow to get an education.

Paco believes that his relationship with Ivan, the landowner's son, is special. Ivan avidly hunts birds on the estate, and gamekeeper Paco is his guide, assistant and strength; but when Paco breaks a leg after falling from a tree, Ivan shows a total lack of concern. Quirce's insolence prompts Ivan to speak of the need for "hierarchy." Paco's tumble to the ground visually suggests the potential for a collapse of hierarchy, and something else later drives this home: when he is perched on a tree branch, Azarías's roping Ivan below and hanging him because the latter, frustrated that without Paco his hunting sucks, shot to death Azarías's pet goshawk from the sky.

ANTONIO GAUDÍ (Japan). Japan's Hiroshi Teshigahara: I dislike his fictional films. But his documentary *Antonio Gaudí*, about Catalan architect and sculptor Antoni Plàcid Guillem Gaudí i Cornet, is exceedingly beautiful and adventurous. Teshigahara, assisted by color cinematographers Junichi Segawa, Ryu Segawa and Yoshikazu Yanagida, has created a nearly silent waking dream, with one "talking head" who (very late) speaks for only a few minutes. We listen carefully.

Gaudí (1852-1926) derived his forms, he said, from the Book of Nature, and indeed one sees in his work the influence of honeycombs, spiraling seashells, the luxuriant growth of rough-textured trees, and regional caverns with their stalactites and stalagmites. Gaudí's prolific work, which rambunctiously pursued curvilinear lines, especially turned Barcelona into a breathing, overflowing garden of public art. All this art still stands. One shot is framed so that a child glides backwards amongst columns that Gaudí designed—Teshigahara's evocation, perhaps, of Cocteau's use of reverse motion in the Underworld in *Orphée* (1949). But here it is daylight, the child is happy, alive, and a dip of the camera reveals she is on roller skates. She is unaware of the "art" she is maneuvering her way around, but in a sense those columns were designed and constructed for her, and the structure belongs to her by her use of it. Increasingly religious, Gaudí's art is, at its best, splendiferous and mysterious.

Teshigahara's slow camera movements in every conceivable direction, including inwards, take us on a journey. (Teshigahara edited—brilliantly.) We see connections in and influences (besides Nature) on Gaudí's art: in the medieval past, the Romanesque that evolved into the Gothic; in the present, Art Nouveau. (Gaudí himself influenced Surrealism.) Thrillingly, we journey into a portion of the mind of humanity.

Antonio Gaudí is what Kubrick hoped his *2001* would be.

1985

A TIME TO LIVE, A TIME TO DIE (Taiwan). The second part of Hou Hsiao-hsien's Coming-of-Age trilogy is based on Hou's own childhood. *Tong nien wang shi* begins with Hou's voiceover recalling that his father relocated from Mei County, Kwangtung Province, in mainland China to Taiwan shortly after his birth, with him and the rest of the family following a year after. Hou, in effect, knew only the new country; his difficult adjustment, therefore, was to his family, whose difficulty adjusting to Taiwan exceeded his—although, because of his connection to them, he also experienced an acute sense of loss of homeland.

Tong nien wang shi comprises incidents—recollections, to which Hou has added imagination, especially regarding his mother, who is seen explaining things to the family that goes beyond what she must have said at the time. One infers from this Hou's greatest need for reconciliation with the memory of the woman who spunkily spanked him and kept the family together. However, it is Grandma whose wanderings keep her searching for Mekong Bridge and the way home. Eventually Grandma returns to the mainland.

We know the name of Hou's father from her cries at hospital at his death. *Fen-ming!* A laterally moving camera records the children's faces of grief. Ah-hsiao, or Ah-ha, as his peers teasingly put it, is bathing in an adjacent room when he hears his mother's piercing lament.

We watch the boy and other children at play and getting into more serious trouble. It is the portrait of a great artist as not yet a young man.

Tong nien wang shi is a gently melancholy work, full of a sense of lost cultural moorings that Hou now can grasp as an adult. The film is his brilliant attempt to fill in the blanks of his aching heart.

FACES OF WOMEN (Ivory Coast, France). Désiré Ecaré's *Visages de femmes* shows a society in transition. Framed and punctuated by a street festival providing linking all-female choral commentary, two overlapping stories address the status of women as this evolves from patriarchal oppression—the residue of both tribal organization and colonialist imposition—to newer demands for equality. The past, deeply entrenched, opposes either protagonist.

Brou suspects his wife of committing adultery with Kouassi, his brother; he barks at N'guessan: "You are my slave . . . I own your body." The adultery eventually materializes, prompting Brou to respond with brute force. By compounding N'guessan's voice with several likeminded voices ("Men never trust us. . . . [Brou] deserves to be deceived"), the chorus implies the political strength in numbers necessary to uproot the idea of ownership that Brou professes.

In the second tale, another, older woman has succeeded in the marketplace. Her fish-smoking operation employs 200 women and supports herself, spouse, family. For all this, her husband's position of authority within the family hasn't budged. The woman decides to open a restaurant, hoping that making more money will help.

However, the banking system she must approach for the loan needed to launch her new venture hews to its own patriarchic logic. The woman finds herself facing an obstructive kid —an educated banker young enough to be her son. Therefore, she now frames her loan plea in familial terms, hoping a son would not turn down a mother. Humiliatingly, the strategy fails. Despite his youth, the banker stands in for a husband who discounts his wife's ambitiousness (she has "too many plans," he tells her). This husband also exemplifies patriarchal form taking precedence over what should be the tender, egalitarian substance of marriage.

Ecaré's marvelous comedy concludes with women dancing by themselves. They can rely only on themselves.

VAGABOND (France). Sandrine Bonnaire, excellent, is Mona Bergeron, a backpacking dropout and drifter who appears in farmland country. She comes from the city; or (although dry) she walked out of the sea, according to one legend. Legends, gossip, interviews; a wide glance at the girl is pieced together by police after her corpse one morning is found in a ditch.

Beautifully written and directed by Agnès Varda, *Sans toit ni loi*—literally, *Without Roof or Rule*—is constructed as a curve-around narrative, its flashbacks and testimonies proceeding from the ditch and ending there; but the circle is incomplete. Whereas the film begins with Mona's death from exposure to the elements, it ends with her still alive. She has stumbled into the ditch for what she may think is a night's sleep. She cannot muster strength to raise herself and in any case has no place else to go.

Abrasive, defiant, solitudinous even when pretending to be sociable, Mona has turned off with her attitude everyone with whom she has come into contact. She hasn't revealed herself. But the construction of the narrative, which leaves Mona alive even as we know she has already died, lays responsibility for her fate, at least partly, *on us*.

We needed to make more of an effort to get to know this child. We should have done more to protect her. Kids are too busy being themselves, or who they *think* they are, to know when they need our help, and too stubborn and proud to ask for it even if they do know.

When they callously manipulate us, they are doing what they need to do in order to survive. If we respond defensively, moralistically, we are putting them into the ditch.

Varda's indefatigably humane film won the top prize at Venice.

COME AND SEE (U.S.S.R.). Byelorussia, following the Nazi invasion. Partisans come for a 12-year-old recruit, Florya, in his shack, where his mother, a widow, has pleaded for him to kill her and his siblings if he is going to leave. Can a boy, though, resist the call of the Great Patriotic War? What the partisans want, however, is what Florya is required to bring with him: a gun. Florya is certain to be killed. No matter. He will leave behind the gun he worked so hard to dig up.

Only, Florya doesn't get killed. He lives and witnesses the horrors of war. Unsentimental, Elem Klimov's *Idi i smotri* is among the most powerful films about war.

Klimov moves desaturated colors into stunning near black and white; the carcass of a cow, a casualty of war, lies in a vacant field. Separated from his group, a solitary Florya passes the corpse that might have been his. His contorted face has lost its innocence. Its title from the Book of Revelation, Klimov's masterpiece beckons us to look at what one of the twentieth century's Four Horsemen of the Apocalypse has wrought. In stark, hallucinatory images, we along with Florya, his face transfixed in horror, witness the extermination of a mass of people. There are deep trenches in his brow. The village is torched. The air is filled with German cheers, shrieks of the burned-alive and, on the soundtrack, yodeling. German soldiers pose for a photograph, having grabbed Florya and put a gun to his head. On his knees, Florya, alone again, falls upon the ground, recalling the cow.

A black-and-white storm of reverse motion, highlighted by documentary footage of Adolf Hitler, marks Florya's slide into the freezing of his humanity.

The Byelorussian holocaust: 628 villages burned, and all of the people in them.

THE TIES THAT BIND (U.S.). Su Friedrich's black-and-white documentary is two films in one: her much admiring biography of her mother, a longtime political activist, to whom she is bound in familial love; her own autobiography, centering instead on her difficulties, even now in adulthood, vis-à-vis so formidable a role model, to whom her own sense of identity is inextricably bound.

Friedrich's mother, Lore Bucher, was born in 1920 in Ulm, Germany, where she lived until 1950 before moving to the U.S. with her American husband, Paul Friedrich. Bucher had been vocally anti-Nazi, refusing in school, even, to raise her hand and say "Heil Hitler!" Neither she nor other family members would give up Jewish friends, causing her father's horticultural business to suffer, and culminating in their family's being "written up" in *Der Sturmer*, the Nazi paper. Throughout, Bucher's voice is the one we hear; Friedrich's questions to her mother appear as intertitles.

The Ties That Bind thus becomes Friedrich's antidote to both rigged family melodramas (like Robert Redford's 1980 *Ordinary People*), where a parent is conveniently and gratuitously cast as the villain, and trash television talk shows where whining grown-ups confront a parent to "resolve issues" between them. Her film is a coming-to-terms with a larger-than-life parent, but Friedrich accomplishes the task lovingly, admiringly, humanely.

Nevertheless, whenever (like Little Red Riding Hood vis-à-vis Grandmother-Wolf) Friedrich isolates in closeup this or that part of her mother (such as a foot), as though the whole of her mother were too much to take in at once, we glean how daunting a marker to measure up to Friedrich finds this woman—how in her presence Friedrich still feels like a small child.

At times in this tremendously moving film, Bucher's blazing decency and no-holds-barred courage make us feel a little as her daughter does.

THE OFFICIAL STORY (Argentina). During the 1976-1983 military dictatorship in Argentina, thousands of citizens were tortured and murdered; they simply vanished, never to return to families who had no idea what had happened to them. Additionally, the children, including babies, of these *desaparecidos* were turned over to military and other right-wing families. Once the dictatorship fell, mothers of *desaparecidos* organized, protested and searched for their missing grandchildren. Luis Puenzo's *La historia oficial* approaches this material from the opposite dramatic perspective: in Buenos Aires, Alicia Marnet de Ibáñez (Norma Aleándro, in the performance of a lifetime), a high school teacher and the wife of a lawyer, begins to suspect that their five-year-old adopted daughter, Gaby, was one of these state-abducted children. Alicia's relentless search for the truth sets her on a collision course with her spouse and their bourgeois existence.

For quite a while, Alicia herself wears political blinders. Ironically, she teaches Argentinean history, but it is her students, unruly, self-righteous and inquisitive, who press her to learn more about what has been recently and is now going on in their country. Alicia cannot believe that such things happened as did happen. A Leftist colleague challenges her: "It's always easier to believe it's impossible, right? Because if it *is* possible, this would require complicity." Her husband, Roberto, lied to Alicia about the adoption at the time; now Alicia must accept her own complicity in the unfolding national nightmare of which she had been ignorant. Of course, both she and Roberto adore little Gaby.

Eventually Alicia meets a woman who may indeed be one of Gaby's birth grandparents.

By the film's end Gaby has mastered the song that she has been attempting to learn throughout. This is part of the lyric: "In the land of I-don't-remember,/ I take three steps and am lost."

MALA NOCHE (U.S.). *Mala Noche* is a pseudodocumentary study of the border between tiers of minimal subsistence in a U.S. urban environment—here, Portland, Oregon. Gus Van Sant evokes the hard-luck milieu of a neighborhood of transients. Existentially, his is a world of days and nights rather than events.

Walt, a convenience store clerk, pursues Juan, a teenaged Mexican boy sharing a skid row hotel room with a *compañero*. Walt explains, "I only want to caress him—hold him." He is settling for the curbed freedom of something less than one's heart's desire. In the last gasp of youth, he hopes to stretch his monotonous place in life into a realm of interest and of the heart.

By misadventure Walt ends up with Juan's friend, Roberto. Walt and "Johnny" have boyish get-togethers, which, "for some reason," Walt notes, always include Roberto. Walt thus knows his one arduous coupling with Juan-by-proxy, which sent him to the bathroom for vaseline,—his *mala noche*, his "bad night"—is as close to heaven as he is likely to get.

When Roberto is shot dead for no reason by the police, Juan turns on Walt—this, the final revelation that theirs was always a threesome. His and Walt's impasse, it turns out, was simultaneously negotiated from *both* sides.

Van Sant's film is enamored of night. Darkness is profound, and spurts of light exist to show the dark and draw us into it. Van Sant's characters feel their way in and around the dark, the home their lives inhabit. It is America—the "bad night" those born to it have long since adjusted to, believing (mostly on the basis of testimonies from immigrants like Juan) that, however "bad" America is, things elsewhere are worse. The American Dream has turned into a nightmare about the rest of the world.

HOUR OF THE STAR (Brazil). "I'm not much of a person," 19-year-old Macabéa tells boyfriend Olimpico, and her self-evaluation is accurate. She lives with three other renters in a single small, squalid room. Both Macabéa and Olimpico are impoverished, socially and academically uneducated rural migrants in the city; she, the protagonist of Suzana Amaral's *A Hora da Estrela*, which is based on Clarice Lispector's novel, is nicer, though. When Olimpico dumps Macabéa for someone who is more (obviously) attractive, he tells her, "You are a hair in my soup."

Macabéa, like Olimpico, is an orphan. She works ineptly and painfully slowly as a typist, and is constantly on the verge of being fired. (Olimpico is a factory worker.) Macabéa continually asks Olimpico questions, often about unfamiliar words she has heard used on the radio. When she asks what *culture* is, he typically hides his ignorance behind a brusque, dismissive response: "Culture is culture." Macabéa wants to better herself, but she doesn't know how, and her attempts to do so are routinely blocked.

Yet Macabéa perseveres. She succeeds somewhat in coming to terms with herself in a largely inhospitable environment. For the most part, no one sees her. In a crowded fast-food restaurant, Macabéa is pleased when she thinks a man is noticing her, but as he leaves she realizes he is blind. Throughout, we see her looking at her image in mirrors and windows, and the reflecting surface usually is vague, smudged or given to distortion. At first, she is trying to see herself as others see her; later, she is trying to see herself more clearly, more kindly than others do. Amaral's at times almost documentary-like film cries out for us also to see Macabéa and people like her.

Profoundly engaging, sometimes radiant, Marcelia Cartaxo is superb as Macabéa.

1986

HORSE THIEF (China). In the tradition of Robert J. Flaherty's *Nanook of the North* (1922), Tian Zhuangzhuang's fictional, objectively toned *Dao ma zei*, nonprofessionally cast, documents an end-of-the-world existence, in Tibet, amidst an incarnation of Nature that is as fierce as it is gorgeous to behold so long as one doesn't live in it and have to cope with it. The prevailing silence, especially in terms of the sparseness of dialogue, is correlative to the primitive life of the film's protagonist, Norbu (Tseshang Rigzin, wonderful). His is an elemental life—and an awesome odyssey. Norbu is devout; despite this, due to his harsh existence, he steals from his Buddhist temple and, as a result, when he is caught, he, his wife, Dolma, and their son, Tashi, are banished from their clan. Stripped of communal protection, they are at the mercy of the elements. Tashi dies. Another son is born, steeling Norbu's determination to ensure the newborn's protection, no matter what this may take.

Here is the masterpiece of the Fifth Generation Movement in Chinese cinema—a portrait of such human hardship and impossible life choices as to unsettle viewers' complacency and expand their sympathies. Tian has created an ordeal of enlightenment, a celebration of unearthly beauty—his astonishing color cinematographers are Zhao Fei and Yong Hou—that is perpetually disrupted by assaults on the human condition from within and without. His *Horse Thief* is also a piercing meditation on social organization, on the family unit within the larger group. We are moved to ponder issues of social responsibility in either direction, between family and community, divorced from the prism of ideological prejudice. *Horse Thief* is heartrendingly humane, as also would be, in a more conventional narrative mode, Tian's epic of China's Cultural Revolution, *The Blue Kite* (1993).

DUST IN THE WIND (Taiwan). The conclusion of Hou Hsiao-hsien's Coming-of-Age trilogy, *Lianlian fengchen* draws upon (with Chu Tien-wen) co-scenarist Wu Nien-jen's youth. It follows the fate of two highschoolers in love in a small mining town.

The film opens with a fleck of white in cavernous darkness and appears to be in black and white. It turns out that the growing speck is the exit of a tunnel through which (from a train's-eye view) a passenger train moves into light that's banked by leafy trees, in rich color, and into another tunnel. Cut to a car, which Wen-yuan and Huen, standing, alone occupy, their forms captured by dark as the train enters a tunnel. The two are silent until Huen confesses difficulty with a math assignment. Wen-yuan asks why she didn't tell him sooner and ask for help. Wen-yuan is an excellent student; but the train forcefully conveys that life isn't in his control. Train movements in and out of tunnels become a motif. Delicate guitar strains pluck the heart.

Wen-yuan quits school—his father, a miner, tells him, "If you want to be an ox, there will always be a plow for you"—and moves to Tapei, where he works for two years in a printing shop and attends night school, with Huen, having followed, working as a seamstress. At first, Wen-yuan recalls, homesickness had made him "cry out of [his] pants." In the city, the pair are cast adrift. Wen-yuan enters military service. Huen marries someone else. "It's fate," Wen-yuan's Grandpa says.

Trains; transience; tears: *Lianlian fengchen* may be the most achingly sad, wistfully contemplative of all Hou's works. Its characters seem to be flickering in memory, renewing their haunting grip. The memories of youth are a tunnel there is only the illusion of coming out of.

ROSA LUXEMBURG (West Germany). The co-founder (with Karl Liebknecht) of the movement that two years hence, in 1918, evolved into the German Communist Party, Rosa Luxemburg was murdered en route to prison in 1919. Jewish, Russian Polish, and middle-class by birth, and German by marriage, Rosa was a Marxist journalist and lawyer committed to worker activism and worker rights, believing that socialism required democracy. In turn, Lenin and Stalin repudiated her no less than the German establishment did, and part of the legacy of her death was the weakening of her Party, thus facilitating the rise in Germany of Adolf Hitler, whose National Socialism courted the economically disaffected, many of whom might otherwise have gravitated toward her message and cause.

Margarethe von Trotta's film about Rosa's political struggles is sober, restrained, and cumulatively very powerful. It also adheres to a conventional form, eschewing the addition of cinematic controversy to its already incendiary subject matter. The film begins in 1916, in Wronke Prison, and flashes back to 1900, with socialists anticipating a century of achievement to follow a previous century of hope. It essays in spirited, if not quite probing detail Rosa's intense involvement in socialist causes. It shows Rosa as being, as she puts it, hard on herself and others.

The film is particularly adept in portraying the volatile relationship between Rosa and her longtime lover, Leo Jogiches, who arranged for the publication of her collected works before also being murdered in 1919. It shows Rosa's disdaining martyrdom because she found it sentimental and bourgeois. It makes perfect sense out of Rosa's opposition to World War I yet ceaseless advocacy of mass labor strikes and proletarian violence inside and outside Russia.

Von Trotta's chief asset is her star. Barbara Sukowa's Rosa Luxemburg is among cinema's most intelligent and passionate performances.

DEVIL IN THE FLESH (Italy, France). Marco Bellocchio's bewitching *Diavolo in corpo*, from teenaged Raymond Radiguet's 1921 novel *Le diable au corps*, relocates the story from Great War France to present-day Italy. The woman is now engaged, not married. Her intended isn't, literally at least, a soldier; he is a terrorist who yet hopes to live a free, "normal" life. At Giacomo's trial, Giulia befriends Andreà, an eighteen-year-old schoolboy. Giulia, shaky, realizes that a relationship with Andreà might divest her of her sanity. Her attempts to warn him away, though, fail. They become lovers.

The opening passage mesmerizes. Onto a rooftop in the square connecting an apartment building and Andreà's school a distraught girl ventures. A hot breeze turns her hair into oceanic drifts; her enormous eyes disclose distress. The child speaks in some other language than Italian. Giulia, her neighbor, responds with compassion. Bellocchio's patient, placid gaze alternates between Giulia and the foreign girl, recording their mysterious communion and interjecting glimpses of Andreà's appreciation of the revelatory and redemptive act he is witnessing. Snapped out of her trance, pleading for help, the girl is safely rescued. Into Andreà's tormented adolescent world the possibility of tenderness has been introduced. He is seduced by it.

Giulia's relationship with Giacomo is conflicted. Her father was the victim of terrorists; on her way to Giacomo's trial, Giulia stops by her father's memorial with fresh flowers. Now Giacomo has recanted and "repented," thus inadvertently mocking his fiancée's painful reconciliation to his cause, and thereby exacerbating her sense of guilt over betraying her father's memory.

With Andreà, Giulia seeks to reconfirm her humanity; but Andreà seeks to *confirm* his identity. At times their disparity of needs puts the couple emotionally out of sync. Inevitably, Giulia will be sacrificed at the altar of Andreà's burgeoning ego.

THERESE (France). Like Tennyson's "The Holy Grail," *Thérèse* studies the religious impulse as sublimated sexuality—or, for one of the cloistered Carmelites, a socially accepted retreat from the "ugly [world] outside." Alain Cavalier's brilliant film marshals Rembrandt lighting and earth-tones for its portrait of Thérèse Martin, who was canonized as St. Thérèse of Lisieux in 1925, less that thirty years after her tubercular death. When she marries Jesus, the girl speaks proudly of her unworthiness, and it is just this sort of contradiction that renders her personality complex throughout. When she is waning, she remarks: "I see nothing after this life. A wall rising to the stars." Shortly after, she decides that her doubt is Jesus's own devious doing. "He is most handsome when he hides."

The film's centerpiece is the Christmas celebration inside the convent. Exchanging small gifts on their "husband-child's birthday," the sisters hug and kiss each other while taking turns cradling in their arms a clay baby Jesus; the sound of an actual baby's cries underscores the delusional nature of the event. A gift of champagne leads to singing, swaying, dancing—a mellow group ecstasy. Cavalier emphasizes the sisterliness of the sisterhood (Martin's own sister is another member of the cloister)—a state that includes whispers, bonds, intrigues, little conspiracies, jealousy. Cavalier's minimalist shots sometimes show nuns in groups of two or three; a good many shots consist of closeups of hands, such as at labor or of one soul's hand wrapped inside another's.

"I love wide-open spaces," Thérèse writes in her diary. "But is there pure love in my heart?"

Who can say such love exists? Encapsulating the ambiguity is the closing shot: following her death, Thérèse's cloth slippers, touching one another, on the floor by her bed—material scraps of an unfathomable life.

GINGER AND FRED (Italy). There are films by Federico Fellini that I wouldn't wish on my worst enemy (*8½*, for instance); but *Ginger and Fred*, about a dance team reunited for a Christmastime television special after a thirty years' separation, is wonderfully entertaining and deeply affecting. Compounding its rich nostalgia is the casting of the two lead roles: Giulietta Masina, Fellini's wife, as "Ginger"; Marcello Mastroianni, Fellini's longtime onscreen alter ego, as "Fred."

Apart from the act, "Ginger" is Amelia Bonetti; "Fred," Pippo Botticella.

Their dance steps on the televised stage more or less creak; but the two are dressed in silken charm and lit with humanity. Of course, the actual lights all go out just as "Ginger and Fred" start their routine, and the two consider crawling away. "We're phantoms," Pippo whispers to Amelia; "We rise from the darkness and vanish." The lights do return, and Pippo embarrassingly falls down, but, professionally persevering, the couple complete their modest routine.

Fellini's glowing film looks back but is also alert to what's going on in the present. It spiritedly rakes over Italian pop commercialism. Billboards and television commercials reek of bad taste and ridiculousness. Backstage at the show, a girl sticks out her rump as the inventor of the panties adorning it pontificates on his product: aromatic, edible panties "in eleven fruit flavors, plus tuna and onion." The team of Ginger and Fred represents the humanity that this sort of commercial dehumanization has replaced. Indeed, the TV special itself is a cheesy affair, and the celebrity who follows the pair onstage is an even older soul than our dual protagonists. The past is being trotted out with little appreciation and even some derision; but at least some audiences—*we*—respond very differently. *Warmly.*

Masina is heavenly; Mastroianni, brilliantly funny.

THE SACRIFICE (Sweden, UK, France). It is Alexander's birthday. On his luxuriant grounds the journalist, accompanied by his toddler, whom a sore throat has rendered temporarily mute, plants a tree to mark the occasion, all the while chattering on, as much to himself as to his son. A friend, dropping by, asks, "Do you know that Gandhi had a day each week when he didn't speak?"

At his party, bombers overhead signal the fact that World War III has broken out. Alexander will offer his newly planted tree and himself as an offering to God for the safekeeping of his family and—dare he hope?—civilization, represented here by family and friends (and, by extension, us), Bach's *St. Matthew Passion* and Leonardo's *Adoration of the Three Kings*, a reproduction of which adorns one of Alexander's walls.

Ingmar Bergman and Andrei Tarkovsky, atheist and religionist, were a mutual admiration society. For his third film outside the Soviet Union, which he had fled, Tarkovsky went to Bergman's island refuge, borrowed Bergman collaborators, including cinematographer Sven Nykvist and Erland Josephson, who plays Alexander, and made his most Bergmanian film. Befitting a work by Tarkovsky, though, *Offret* is deeply spiritual as well as moral and psychological. It includes anguished "chamber" scenes that might belong to either artist, but also slow, solemn, profoundly moving tracking shots and pans, outdoors, that are unmistakably Tarkovsky. Mud, water, discarded objects: to these familiar features of Tarkovsky landscape the lush green of the opening scene eventually yields. The shot of a small, abandoned chair haunts and devastates.

Tarkovsky knew he was dying of cancer when he made this film. He worried about the world he was leaving and hoped for its salvation. Artistically, *Offret* is his heartfelt last will and testament.

MELO (France). *Mélo*, from Henri Bernstein's play, finds past haunting the present and thus helping to determine future. The situation: a married woman's adultery with a friend of her husband and the guilt this engenders, which finally drives her to commit suicide. Despite the conventional plot and straightforward (linear) treatment, *Mélo* provides an index of Alain Resnais's filmmaking brilliance.

In 1926, a dinner at a couple's home; host and hostess entertain one guest: the host's friend, a violinist who has a concert career while the host toils modestly in an orchestra and gives lessons on the side. But Pierre, however, has one thing that Marcel doesn't: Romaine (Sabine Azéma, best actress César). At least until tomorrow. As the friends talk, the camera records something extraordinary: the new couple, Marcel and Romaine, gradually taking shape from the clay of the married couple and their guest, with the host none the wiser. It simply occurs, with only a minimum of subtle flirting on Romaine's part, and a corresponding bit of vacant loneliness on Marcel's part. While compositions stress the trio's interconnectedness, the camera moves to isolate Marcel, enrobing him in the darkness of the failed romantic past he seems fixated on, to suggest the possibility of his upcoming betrayal of Pierre. It is Romaine, however, whose guilt will prove the most corrosive—and, in an odd way, Pierre's, whose subsequent illness reflects the double betrayal, by spouse and friend, that he doesn't quite know about but also, unconsciously at least, doesn't quite *not* know about. Pierre is heartsick, and Romaine may be trying to bring things to some sort of conclusion by poisoning him on the side.

Its title suggests the melodramatic genre to which the plot belongs—and the line along which marriage and adultery themselves conform to the nature of melodrama.

1987

LONG LIVE THE LADY! (Italy). Written and directed by Ermanno Olmi, *Lunga vita alla signora* is Italy's most brilliant film comedy. The "lady" in question, decrepit though still holding on, represents capitalism and wealth. She is her own guest of honor at an elaborate formal dinner/business celebration. Closed-circuit television sets are rolled down the in-between path of the U-shaped dining table to broadcast record high profits.

Her Ladyship wears a veil because, if ever breathed on directly or exposed to too much light, she would disintegrate. She doesn't attend the opera, because culture might kill her, but she espies distant dinner guests through opera glasses from underneath her veil. Infantile, her Ladyship drinks wine through a straw.

Yet she is not the protagonist of Olmi's intricately edited, combustibly funny satire. Boys and girls from a cooking school who have been brought in to serve the wine and dinner are the focus. (Cooked by the lady's own chef and staff, the unusual meal begins with frogs and reaches a climax with an unidentifiable sea-beast—those familiar with Federico Fellini's *La dolce vita*, 1959, will savor the joke—whose skeleton, when it is ceremoniously carted away, is picked-clean and bone-dry.) A flashback-insert shows the working-class youths' instruction and preparation: *Don't turn around suddenly. Don't look bored,* etc. A flashback is inserted inside the flashback, showing one of the boys being similarly instructed years ago in church: "Beware of impure thoughts!" Libenzio's "career path" has been this: church; school; job. This path of obedience reflects the patriarchal structure that capitalism now dictates more essentially than the Church.

Poignantly, Libenzio and his truck-driver father steal a private moment outside the mansion. After dinner, a guest tries to impress the waiter sexually, but, come dawn, Libenzio flees the maze of Her Ladyship's domain.

THE DEAD (Ireland, U.S.). Some literary works are untranslatable into cinema, and *The Dead*, from James Joyce's 1914 collection *Dubliners*, is probably one of them. However, Irish-American John Huston long had nurtured the dream of turning the most beautiful short story in the English language into a film. He was in his eighties and working from an oxygen tent when he did this, from son Tony's script, and the result is overwhelmingly moving. *The Dead* was Huston's last completed film.

With its bristling life, irresistible humor, sharp observation, and glow of melancholy, *The Dead* is Huston's most deeply felt and beautifully composed film. One problem, though, did intercede. Joyce's story unfolds through an omniscient narrator, some of whose gravest reflections are, now, unsuitably given over to Gabriel, the protagonist. Otherwise, though, the film is bliss. With guests dancing lightly around their persistent awareness of "the last end," the film gives us afresh Joyce's buoyant, captivating comedy of life written in his twenties to acknowledge "all the living and the dead." Approaching his own end, his legendary sourness gone, Huston transforms this young man's piece into a serene contemplation of a universal mystery whose depth of secrets only now he is on the verge of discovering. This hauntingly lit and gloriously acted film—Donal McCann, Anjelica Huston (Huston's daughter) and Donal Donnelly are the Gabriel, Gretta and Freddy of our dreams—bears the sense of a gracious last testament freely given.

Huston's is one of the most substantial careers in American cinema, and some films of his that once seemed failures or overly commercial, such as *Key Largo* (1948) and *The Misfits* (1961), are of greater interest today.

DAMNATION (Hungary). To begin with, the opening shot is documentary: coal-mining cable cars, against a bleak sky, move through space. Sound and image, in basalt-and-gray black-and-white, create an image of monotony. Almost as a reverse of the penultimate shot of Antonioni's *Passenger* (1975), very slowly the camera withdraws through a window into an apartment as barren as the landscape, withdraws, shifts screen-right a tad to show the glass's vertical frame-divide, and withdraws steadily until it captures in darkness a back view of the occupant, who is staring out the window. Thus a shot that began as objective has crept into a realm of interiority, the subjectivity of someone's frayed-end feelings. Documentary has pulled back into fiction, wordless stream-of-consciousness, suiting Karrer's consciousness to his environment, suggesting possibly a causal connection, at least a spiritual interactivity. A monotonous routine, shaving, breaks the monotony, as in a mirror—thus at a remove—we finally see the face of the man whose mind we have just glimpsed. Outside, in long-shot, someone gets into a car in front of an apartment building. The camera withdraws again to reveal Karrer observing. We assume it is more pointless glaring on Karrer's part, but we discover that Karrer has been waiting for the man to leave so that he can pop up to see the man's wife, his mistress, who through a crack in the door gives Karrer his walking papers. Karrer, loath to relinquish the one bit of intrigue in his life, haunts the bar where the woman sings and eventually denounces her shady spouse to the police. In so doing, however, he only deepens the extent to which his humanity is lost to the dead-ended environment.

Béla Tarr's Hungarian *Kárhozat* confronts state communism through a non-ideological backdoor, condemning the grinding, desperate, dehumanizing existence it fosters.

WINGS OF DESIRE (West Germany, France). A shimmering, ecstatic, poignant embrace of the joys and sorrows of being human, *Wings of Desire* provides an unusual perspective on the matter. Above postwar, divided Berlin, Damiel and Cassiel, two angels from the beginning of time, hover and invisibly descend, floating about and through buildings and people, penetrating people's thoughts, including their deepest worries, at one point laying a gentle hand on the shoulder of a young man who is contemplating suicide—and who *does* commit suicide. Each in its sphere, human or angel, is limited, but angels at least do not die.

But one day Damiel (Bruno Ganz, wonderful) espies a beauteous circus acrobat and becomes a dissatisfied angel. Now he wants to be human, to experience human love. Becoming mortal would be worth it. Born to the human round, we better appreciate the gift of life and death through Damiel's fresh eyes and senses. And the world is more magical and spiritual than we imagined, because Damiel isn't the only former angel among us. Another one, for instance, is Peter Falk playing himself—and giving his finest performance.

"I wonder if she is Jewish," Falk muses as he sketches an elderly woman. Falk is himself Jewish. For all we know, the Holocaust survivor whose thoughts the angels hear might also once have been an angel. Great suffering, as well as great happiness, comes with the human lot.

The universe the angels perceive is in austere, timeless, blue-tinted monochrome, suggesting silent cinema; the world that humans see, in full color, is sensual and vibrant. Henri Alëkan (Cocteau's *Beauty and the Beast*) contributes astonishing cinematography.

Wim Wenders beautifully directed from one of cinema's finest scripts, by himself and Peter Handkë—two former seminarians who know a thing or two about angels who have risen to earth.

THE LAST EMPEROR (Italy, France, UK). "Don't you *ever* like films that win best picture Oscars?"

The Last Emperor, the first part of a trilogy that gets progressively more lost (*The Sheltering Sky*, 1990; *Little Buddha*, 1993), is one of the two or three best "best pictures," and maybe the best. For the record, though, if Academy voters had grasped its politics, they never would have given Bernardo Bertolucci's film its Oscar, nor given it eight additional prizes besides, including those for direction and cinematography (Vittorio Storaro).

1987

This is a mesmerizing, if dubious, biography of Pu Yi, China's last emperor, whose humbling and rehabilitation by the Communists is heart-piercingly symbolized by the release of a cricket from long captivity. *The Last Emperor* is the richly detailed drama of the liberation of a soul from the decadent lifestyle and the arrogance that misled him to believe that the common lot of humanity was beneath him. Communism enables Pu to learn, by difficult degrees, to be human.

It is (especially in the hour-longer version now available on DVD) one of the most passionate and splendiferous movies ever made. It is a work, also, of cool irony, for Pu's enforced obscurity and humility mirror his confinement behind imperial walls during a terribly lonely though exalted, endlessly pampered childhood. Pu's existence remains solitary. From start to finish, his is the life of one of history's unluckiest pawns.

The film is formally indebted to Roberto Rossellini's *The Rise to Power of Louis XIV* (1966), whose objective humanism Bertolucci moves toward a more sensual romanticism. However, the film's most gripping scenes, perhaps, are those describing Pu's imprisonment and re-education. These are spare and austere.

As the grown Pu, John Lone is superb.

PLAIN TALK & COMMON SENSE (UNCOMMON SENSES) (UK). Jon Jost's holistic films interrelate a series of humane, social and political concerns. *Plain Talk*, a British documentary Jost wrote, directed, cinematographed and edited, addresses U.S. myths and realities. It reminds us that we reside on confiscated land.

The film's opening is lyrical, as a shot of sturdy wild grasses changes to one of a pulsating river superimposed over which a hand tries grasping the U.S., which Jost's voiceover poignantly explains always eludes him. American tourists are shown at a topographical point where New Mexico, Arizona, Utah and Colorado meet, accompanied by an inscription in stone: "Four states meet here in freedom under God." Playfully, compulsively, families take photographs, unwittingly reducing the experience of place to *things:* snapshots—commercialized "memories." People are thus deftly divided from their humanity by a commercial(izing) culture. They are also being divided from Nature, for, Jost's voice reminds us, states' boundaries, artificial, were drawn by politicians.

The film itself becomes a kind of tourist in its attempt to take hold of America. A segment presents overlapping voiceovers reading from a plethora of American documents and utterances, accompanied by gorgeous abstract designs that compare the U.S. to a vast cosmic mystery. Jost then analyzes America, initially in terms of European perceptions of it and, later, in terms of demographic facts and figures. (Examples: 1% of the population owns 33% of the nation's wealth; 31% of eligible voters elected Ronald Reagan president in 1984.) A chamber of commerce-type promotional film about Colorado Springs yields to a frightening consideration of the Strategic Air Command and its role in overseeing prospects for World War III.

In this "essay from the margins," Jost addresses U.S. nuclear obsessiveness, the military-industrial complex, marketplace tyranny, and the pernicious nature of the nation-state. It's edifying stuff.

MEDEA (Denmark). Pier Paolo Pasolini's *Medea* (1969) is barbaric, fantastic, political, anthropological. Its theme is cultural collision. Lars von Trier's version has to contend with an anxiety of influence other than that of Euripedes (or Marx). It is based on a script that fellow Dane, Carl Theodor Dreyer, Trier's idol, left unfilmed at his death. Moodily poetic and psychological, it shows the influence of Andrei Tarkovsky, especially his *Nostalghia* (1982). To the eye and the soul, in whatever connection, it's a beautiful film.

Here is perhaps the world's most famous tale of a woman's revenge—in ancient Greece, Medea's murder of their sons after Jason abandons her and them and takes another wife. Medea's magic brought Jason riches and fame, and the Golden Fleece. But he is "moving on" with his life, as cranky, restless spouses sometimes do. Medea gave Jason stature but relinquished much of her own in the process. Now it is her day to inflict sorrow. By Medea's design, Jason will be married to a corpse, and his children, hanged with their mother's tender assistance, will be corpses as well. Medea must settle for nothing less than Jason's devastation.

But, of course, the overwhelming tragedy is Medea's. The children do not deserve to die, but cosmic justice, for which Medea is mere agency, demands these deaths. The one constant is Medea's suffering—a mother's pain as well as a wife's.

Trier's visual poetry stresses Medea's—a mother's—continuing connection to Nature. Nonsensical interpretations, to the effect that Medea, a mother, errs by destroying her children, need not apply. It is self-righteous Jason who alone acts contrary to Nature. Only death can bring Medea peace.

Judgments against Medea fade in the vast marsh and fog in which Trier locates/loses her. She is lost along with the rest of us.

YEELEN (Mali, Burkina Faso, France, West Germany). I am not familiar with Mali myth.

Soulaymane Cissé's medieval *Brightness* helps us out with this mythological orientation: "The two worlds, earth and sky, exist through light." This film is about light—but the light of understanding as well as of material illumination. Instances of both abound.

When does a boy become a man? Let me ruminate. As I was growing up, being neither Jewish nor Christian (or, possibly, by dint of my parents, both), I wondered that Jewish males were ritually declared adults at 13 while the Christian demarcation of male maturity was the christological age of 33—a twenty-year difference. How does one reconcile this discrepancy? I decided this: Judaism in this regard is projective, setting maturity as the consequence of a boy's admittance into the adult community; Christianity, however, focuses on the individual boy's relation to Jesus. In short, while some religions are primarily social, others are solitudinous.

To confront the person who abandoned them both, the boy here abandons his loving mother. Additionally, the country's survival is at stake. Soma, the father-king, feels obligated to vanquish son Nianankoro lest his own existence be the forfeit. Nianankoro beds his father's new, young wife; but the whole to-do is less Oedipal, that is, psychological, than individual/emotional. Nianankoro's motive and the outcome are less relevant than the journey that takes him to the confrontation with his father and better determines his adult status.

Cissé's beauteous film speaks its own truth. However, Nianankoro becomes "adult" by dint of experience, not mythological fiat. It is a cumulative process, which we watch unfold. Moreover, we question everything we see, including "the terror" that Nianankoro's mother indicated that Soma was and would be, but who also plays his part in helping his son realize the full benefits of identity: hopefully, Africa's future.

THE EMPEROR'S NAKED ARMY MARCHES ON (Japan). Based on an idea by mentor Shohei Imamura, Kazuo Hara's *Yuki Yukite shingun* is a confrontational documentary. Haunted by Japanese military behavior in New Guinea, where he himself served in his youth during the Second World War, Kenzo Okuzai is on a mission. Okuzai has spent time in prison for various offenses, including slingshooting with pinballs Emperor Hirohito (known as Shōwa, since his death, in Japan) for war crimes. Okuzai's attempts to redeem both his nation from the wrappings of historical lies and his own reputation coincide. Given Okuzai's search for truth and ongoing anger, Hara's procedure combines *cinéma-vérité* with a more sensationalist aspect that had previously been applied only to exploitative documentaries. This befits the film's grotesque revelations of Japanese wartime murder and cannibalism in the New Guinea jungle. Japanese officers leveled against select soldiers false charges in order to justify having them executed to provide meat for the rest of them to eat. In Ichikawa's *Fires on the Plain* (1959), cannibalism is a metaphor for war; here, it is grislier: an aspect of war that represents the *whole* of war—a kind of synecdoche.

Hara's camera follows Okuzai, who, his car equipped with a loudspeaker, rides around visiting relatives of those who were cannibalized and confronting responsible officers. In a way, Hara is recording an historical-archaeological "dig." It may be that the camera's presence now affects some of Okuzai's behavior, which can be seen as being self-aggrandizing at times; but it is far more important to the film's implied argument that the absence of cameras at the wartime scenes in New Guinea may have contributed to the ruthless outcome. Perhaps it is hyperbole, but Hara's bracing film resonates with the idea of the camera as a guardian of civilized behavior.

1988

MORTU NEGA (Guinea-Bissau). Drought has dried the village's wells. Guinea-Bissau's war of independence from Portugal has been won, and those guerrillas to whom death has been denied have returned home. Fractious, selfish interests war against the unity for which ethnic groups strive. A woman who secured her free allotment of oil before the commodity ran out is selling it in portions. Her rationalization for exploiting others, "I am doing it for my children," is punctured by the sight of children—the new nation's future—celebrating en masse, first, war's end and, finally, the end of the drought.

Underwritten by the Guinea-Bissau government, Flora Gomes's *Death Denied* is an epic, that is, an expression of the aspirations of a people. The first part, which follows a contingent of guerrillas who have just been resupplied with artillery, is a great, gripping mini-film about war. Instantly the guerrillas are humanized as Diminga participates in the struggle in hopes of reuniting with her husband, Sako, whom she hasn't seen in years. Almost as soon as they do (most tenderly, most movingly) reunite, an aerial attack wounds Sako, who orders Diminga back to their village, out of greater harm's way. When Sako himself returns after war's end, his health is most vulnerable, it turns out, from an earlier war injury, in his foot, that has reopened and become painfully infected. It refers to many things: historical pride, hence, vulnerability; the loss of his children that war exacted delicately, Gomes mentions this loss only in reference to Diminga); his disillusionment on the heels of victory. Collapsing time, Gomes includes a song in which Diminga has passed into legend even as she tends to Sako's needs. The future will commemorate her past; in the meantime, Diminga lives in the present.

And the struggle continues.

ARIEL (Finland). A tragicomedy of the discontinuous lives of the working poor, *Ariel* is the second part of Aki Kaurismäki's "proletarian trilogy." Taisto Kasurinen's unhappy lot in life, we are given to understand, was set prior to the film's action and will continue beyond its completion. At the outset, the closing of a coal mine deprives him and his father of their jobs; the latter gives Taisto the keys to his convertible and announces his intention of committing suicide. Taisto doesn't believe he will do this, even after he brandishes a gun, for the simple reason that he has not *already* done this in a perpetually hard, unfair life. But we hear the offscreen shot and see Taisto looking down at his father's body, which remains out of camera range. What we see reflects what Taisto sees, because we see *him* and his fate reflects his father's.

Taisto, on the road, is beaten and robbed. He becomes a day laborer and sleeps at night in a mission flophouse. Nights are as black as oil. He meets Irmeli Pihlaja, who gives up her job monitoring illegal parking ticketing cars in exchange for dinner, and has sex with him. "I hated [my ex-husband] from the start." Taisto: "That's unusual." Irmeli: "That's what *you* think." The two, along with Irmeli's self-sufficient young son, become a family. Irmeli takes a factory job cutting meat.

But the law puts Taisto in prison after he runs across one of the men who robbed him and he tries taking back some of his money. With Irmeli's help, he escapes, and the three plan on fleeing aboard the Mexico-bound Ariel under a mockingly gorgeous, dusky blue sky. We hear

"Over the Rainbow" sung in Finnish and recall Percy Bysshe Shelley's ill-fated schooner, Ariel.
Poignant. Devastating.

EPIDEMIC (Denmark). Save *Vampyr* (1931), by another Dane, Carl Theodor Dreyer, Lars von Trier's *Epidemic* may be the greatest horror film ever made. It is certainly one of the most playful and visually fetching horror films.

It's pseudo-*cinéma-vérité*—a film-within-a-film the boundaries of whose Chinese boxes bend and blur. A film director named Lars (endearingly played by Lars von Trier himself) and his scenarist, Niels (played by Trier's actual co-scenarist, Niels Vørsel), dream up a medical horror movie, in the dream of which Dr. Mesmer (Trier again), an epidemiologist, battles a disease that in fact he unwittingly spreads. Both films are in black and white; but the objective framing film is shot in 16mm, while the interior dream of a film is shot in luxuriant 35mm. The phenomenal cinematography is by Henning Bendtsen, who photographed Dreyer's *Ordet* (1954).

The dream is a nightmare of reality; talk of "mass graves" invokes specters of two world wars, the Holocaust, and the threat of annihilation imposed on us all by the examples of Hiroshima and Nagasaki. Indeed, the framing film, in which the plague ultimately erupts with the assistance of hypnosis, seems to be catching up with the interior film.

Irrepressibly funny and absolutely terrifying, *Epidemic* locates individual imagination in the grip of shared political realities. We cannot get away from our worst dreams, our worst imaginings, because they are real and because the paranoid U.S. is ever poised to drop at a whim another stupendous bomb. Art, our principal defense, only returns us to reality. Something is rotten in the state of Denmark because something is rotten elsewhere in the world. Europe exists in a colossal shadow.

This is the second entry in Trier's "European trilogy" begun with *The Element of Crime* (1984).

DEKALOG (Poland). Written by lawyer Krzysztof Piesiewicz and the director, Krzysztof Kieślowski's ten-hour *Dekalog* consists of ten episodes, each of which reflects on one of the Ten Commandments. The action involves residents in a Warsaw apartment complex; another point of unity is a sad, silent observer who, appearing in most episodes, suggests a surrogate for Kieślowski or God, or both. Kieślowski's moody, somber entries compose a probing portrait of humanity caught in moral dilemmas. The Ten Commandments aren't always the guide by which human behavior can be morally measured. In the initial episode, a scientist unwittingly sacrifices his son by the faith he places in computers and calculations—a faith, though, that had helped father and son to bond. Often, the commandments seem a codification of moral standards that's too rigid to provide much guidance through the complex maze of modern realities. Profound mystery permeates most everything we see in the film; but Kieślowski is a secularist, not a religionist, and certainly not a fundamentalist. His *Dekalog* never degenerates into judgmentalism or pat irony.

In the second episode, Krystyna Janda brilliantly plays a woman with a lover and a hospitalized sick spouse. She is pregnant, and her husband cannot be the father. Should she have an abortion and choose her husband, or keep the fetus, banking on the fact that her husband will be dead soon, and choose her lover? She defers the impossible choice to her husband's doctor—a marvelously elusive application of taking the Lord's name in vain; but the doctor's "decision" comes out of the complex of his own conflicted life, and the patient's fate confounds everyone's "choices" anyhow. All this is typical of the film's rich procedure.

Another episode finds the stricture "Thou shalt not kill" falling equally on the killer and the state.

1988

DAYS OF ECLIPSE (U.S.S.R.). Aleksandr Sokurov paid tribute to Andrei Tarkovsky with *Dni zatmeniya*, which is loosely based on *Billion Years Before the End of the World* by Boris and Arkadi Strugatsky, on whose *Roadside Picnic* Tarkovsky had based his *Stalker* (1979). Like Tarkovsky's film, its futuristic vision actually refers to Soviet totalitarianism—or, rather, its emotional legacy.

A young Russian doctor in a remote Asian outpost, Dmitri Malianov lives disconnected from family, locals, himself. He attends to patients who may be plagued by something from outer space. Piles of papers and photographs infest his flat; unwanted intrusions and visits abound; he keeps losing friends. His off-hours research into juvenile hypertension among believers underscores his own lack of religious faith. When he tries engaging the outside world, it is likely to be with children. He breaks up a street quarrel between two small boys, who turn on him instead, in an hilarious long-shot. With another boy, who mysteriously shows up on his doorstep asking to be taken care of, he develops a close, affectionate relationship (actor Aleksei Ananishnov speaks to the child with the same tender cadences he would enlist in Sokurov's 1997 *Mother and Son*); but then one day bodiless arms snatch the boy up away into the sky. This glorious *hommage* to the subjective balloon passage in Tarkovsky's *Andrei Rublev* (1966) suggests that the child, rather than real, is Dmitri's childself. Their separation is the most painful evidence of Dmitri's alienation.

Fear is pervasive, with people constantly admitting "I am afraid" or asking, "Are *you* afraid?" Yet, this masterpiece is nimble, playful, very funny. Formally, the film amazes. To its sepia-like frames and abundance of wide-angle shots Sokurov has applied a stroboscopic slightly stalled, hiccuping motion that distances us as correlative to Dmitri's distance from a satisfying life.

A TALE OF THE WIND (France, China). Ninety-year-old Dutch documentarian Joris Ivens's last film, which he co-wrote and co-directed with wife Marceline Loridan, is set in China. Ivens died the following year.

Une histoire de vent mixes various elements, including encounters, travelogue, dreams of childhood, film allusions, conjurings of Chinese myth, as Ivens pursues his lifelong attempt to film the invisible wind—a "foolish plan," he admits.

From a radio—think Cocteau's *Orpheus* (1949)—Ivens hears about floods and fires worldwide, and about "a Mexican woman [who] was carried 100 meters by the wind." Other scenes suggest Cocteau's *Testament of Orpheus* (1959). Ivens himself appears in what had seemed a Méliès clip, one of a handful of black-and-white passages. Ivens also reconstructs the waves and cross-waves of wheat in Dovzhenko's *Earth* (1930), only in color instead of black and white.

Asthmatic, Ivens has half a lung's capacity with which to breathe. For most, breathing represents life. An old man tells Ivens, "For you, breathing represents death."

We follow Ivens into a dark tunnel. When he emerges from the tunnel, he is coming toward us. "We've been expecting you," he is told by two different souls. Indoors, a case is opened, promising the wind. There is a mask on the case. Cut to the mask-maker, young and strong, who tells Ivens, "May this mask give you the strength to carry on."

Beauteous and haunting is the imagery accompanying this text: "One drunken night, when he wanted to touch the moon, a rebellious poet drowned."

The wind is given voice: "Van Gogh went mad trying to paint me."

A woman in the desert says she can draw a magical figure in the sand that will call up the wind. It all happens.

Somewhat disjointed; captivating; mortality, masks, ritual, magic.

THE LEGEND OF THE HOLY DRINKER (Italy). Because it has an air of fable or legend about it, *La leggenda del santo bevitore* somewhat resembles Orson Welles's *The Immortal Story* (1968) or Roberto Benigni's *Life Is Beautiful* (1997). Some may even be reminded of

1988

Vittorio De Sica's *Miracle in Milan* (1951).
Written, directed and edited by Ermanno Olmi, the film derives from Joseph Roth's 1939 novella, his last work. Roth was an Austrian Jew who exiled himself to Paris with the rise of Hitler in 1933. Roth, who wrote about Jewish life (for instance, in *Job*, 1930), suffered from chronic alcoholism, like Andreas Kartak (Rutger Hauer, beautiful), the protagonist of *Legend*, who, impoverished and homeless, sleeps under bridges in Paris in 1934. One day a stranger gifts Andreas in the street with 200 francs, explaining a debt he (the stranger) owes to St. Thérèse of Lisieux, and Andreas promises to repay the 200 francs, when he is able, to a nearby church. But each Sunday something comes up, including pleasant distractions or shards of painful memory from his haunting past; and, even though the 200 francs lead to more and more money coming his way, Andreas doesn't repay the debt he owes. Olmi's enchanting film is a study of loss, shame, perseverence and redemption.

In the opening shot, the solidity of the outdoor stairs down which Andreas walks is wobbled by falling leaves, which evoke transience. The whole "legend" that unfolds may be Andreas's dying fantasy; doubtless, much of what Andreas "sees" are apparitions or delusions induced by chronic drinking. Holding the pocket watch they gave him years earlier when he set out on his own, Andreas "sees" his parents in a bar. He passes out at table; when he awakes, the elderly couple are gone.

Everything evaporates.

THE THIN BLUE LINE (U.S.). For a while, one of the unfortunate legacies of *The Thin Blue Line* is that its use of reconstructed events, corresponding to witness testimony, was adopted by television news shows. Now that that practice has subsided, if not entirely vanished, Errol Morris's beautiful documentary can be appreciated afresh.

On one level driven by narrow agenda, the film sets out to show that a man then serving a life term for killing a Dallas police officer was most likely innocent. Indeed, the attention Morris's film drew to this likely miscarriage of justice helped get the man released. This is no small thing for a film to accomplish, but, of course, this speaks not at all to the merits of the work. This *does:* an eerily engrossing mosaic of interviews, reportage and dramatic reconstructions, with fugue-like repetitions and a both burrowing and meditative temperament, and all of it enriched by steely, somber color and by Philip Glass's hypnotic music, *The Thin Blue Line* achieves the aspect of a tone poem on human ambiguities. All this, moreover, combined with the Dallas locale, elusively insinuates the mystery surrounding President Kennedy's death. The result haunts.

And one thing more: Like Orson Welles's *Touch of Evil* (1958), Morris's film inconveniently rattles us, in this instance, with racist testimony helping to exonerate the imprisoned man.

ASHIK KERIB (U.S.S.R.). "In the temple of cinema, there are images, light and reality. Sergei Parajanov was the master of that temple." — Jean-Luc Godard

Shortly after Andrei Tarkovsky's death and shortly before his own, Sergei Parajanov made *Ashug-Karibi*, dedicating it to Tarkovsky, who died self-exiled from Soviet Russia. It is based on a story by nineteenth-century poet Mikhail Lermontov, from his period of exile in the Caucasus. Lermontov had had problems with his tsar; Parajanov, with the Soviet state. Imprisoned for five years for homosexuality, Parajanov spent fifteen years in exile. *Ashug-Karibi* is about a poor minstrel who must wander for a thousand days and nights in order to make enough money to marry Magul, a rich merchant's daughter. Its piercing wail of poignancy derives from its spiritual biography of Lermontov and Tarkovsky and its spiritual *auto*biography. It is a Byronic romance of exile deepened to the quick by the dream of going home.

Back home, Ashug-Karibi's romantic rival offers stolen clothes as proof that Ashug-Karibi river-drowned. Magul weds herself to widow's black; dressed in her own widow's garb,

Ashug-Karibi's mother goes blind. (Believing her son dead, the light has gone out of her world.) Eventually, with a saintly sorcerer's help, Ashug-Karibi travels back from "there" to "here" in one day, accompanied by the purse the sorcerer has given him, his faithful lute, and sufficient magic to restore his mother's sight—the restoration of his own light and life.

This richly ornamented film, with its exquisite tableaux, includes Islamic folk art: frescoes, dances, songs, garments, prayers. Parajanov finds the past exiled from the present, and he aims to bring it home. Successive shots home in on the blue bell tower, moving us from architectural form to sculpted detail. Characters speak in Azeri, but the translating voiceover brings the Georgian film home.

A STORY OF WOMEN (France). Adapted by Colo Tavernier and the filmmaker from a book by Francis Szpiner, Claude Chabrol's fascinating, powerful *Une affaire de femmes* is an account of Marie Latour (Isabelle Huppert, complex, brilliant—best actress, Venice), who thrived as an abortionist during the German occupation, lifting herself and her family out of poverty, even managing to connect her husband to a job, as a dockside lookout for Allied invaders, through her lover, a collaborator. It is with perfect sincerity that Marie identifies herself nonetheless as being "for the Resistance." Marie is an actual person at the center of a fictional film; throughout, Chabrol has created an elastic form that permits a sophisticated blend of fictional and documentary elements.

Marie's remark to her son that having a boy baby is always "right" refers to a patriarchal society and culture—what in fact will determine her guilt and have her guillotined. Chabrol's film, made when abortion was no longer illegal in France, passionately defends moral and political progress against its reeling back into the beast of twisted priorities, religious barbarism, and the subordination of women's reproductive rights to the laws and authority of men. Latour, though, is no feminist herself. She provides abortions to better her own life economically and that of her children, snapping from the sidelines of her essential powerlessness Greek chorus commentary ("Lose a war, and a man's like a wounded bull!"). Unusually happy, she is dancing by herself to a record that plays on an unseen phonograph: an image of independent female humanity. But when, with withering irony, the camera withdraws, we discover that Marie is *not* alone. Her lover is in the room with her. Marie is dancing on an invisible male string, not just for herself. What conjoining of camera movement and *mise-en-scène*.

HERDSMEN OF THE SUN (France, West Germany). Before the precipitous decline in the quality of his work that began in the 1990s, Werner Herzog made a very beautiful film for French television: *Herdsmen of the Sun*, a documentary about the Wodaabe people who live at the southern edge of the Sahara Desert. Herzog's opening commentary claims that the expansion of the desert has radically decreased the Wodaabes' living space, imperiling their existence. In addition, a recent drought has devastated their numbers.

Herzog's claim that the Wodaabes consider themselves the Earth's most beautiful people is followed by a continuous handheld shot of a long line of Wodaabes, their faces bedecked in colorful makeup, their eyes and smiles widened and pronounced (presumably to enhance the Wodaabes' beauty, according to their own concept of beauty), accompanied on the soundtrack by Gounod's "Ave Maria"—one of the weirdest shots in creation. These are *male* Wodaabes! This shot is followed by a similar one of a line of Wodaabe women, who appear, by contrast, unadorned and subdued.

A long passage—is it real, or is it Herzog?—depicts an annual festival in which eligible young men make themselves up into what they consider painted images of beauty to attract women who choose whom they want for mates. We feel we have entered a parallel universe headier and more fascinating than that in *The Matrix*.

Perhaps inspired by Robert J. Flaherty's films, Herzog suggests at the last that the African nomads are a fragile group poised for extinction. However, this nearly elegiac note may be a sentimental add-on; the particularity with which Herzog has portrayed these people and their sometimes exotic customs either imputes to them a terrific resilience or, by doing so, ironically deepens the poignancy of what may be their imminent doom.

COMMISSAR (U.S.S.R.). Aleksandr Askoldov's gripping *Komissar* is most famous on other than artistic grounds. Based on the story "In the Town of Berdichev" by Ukrainian Jewish author Vasili Grossman, it is writer-director Askoldov's only film. Made in 1967, it was suppressed by the Soviet government for twenty years, appearing, after finally being completed, only with the liberalization of *glasnost*. It took the international critics' prize at Berlin in 1988; Askoldov also won at Flanders.

The film, in part about an impoverished Jewish family in 1922 during the Russian Civil War, takes aim at anti-Semitism. It brought reprisals: Askoldov was banned from Moscow, his place of birth, and banned from making movies for the rest of his life.

Cultural collision is at the heart of *Komissar*. Klavdia Vavilova (Nonna Mordyukova, tremendous) is a Red Army cavalry commissar who is stationed in a small town. When a military dalliance results in her pregnancy and abandonment, she is placed—that is, strategically hidden away—in the cottage of Yefim Mahazannik (Rolan Bykov, best actor Nika), a Jewish tailor and mender of pots and pans, his wife, Mariya, and their six children. The close-quartered interactions between the formidable Klavdia and this warm, somewhat stereotypical Jewish family that weighs in on her help to move her to higher human ground.

Stunning transition: pregnant Klavdia, naked, indoors, alone, taking a bath; heavily, officially clothed, ordering the execution of a boy who may not even have been deserting—just going AWOL for a while, lured by the temptation of seeing *his wife*. As the execution is recorded in slow motion, a surrealistic pitcher of milk falls from the boy's grip—a reflection of how much at war with her suddenly maternal aspect Klavdia's military behavior is.

The Mahazanniks will raise the baby that Klavdia must leave behind.

LITTLE DORRIT (UK). The financier Merdle is a secular God in *Little Dorrit*, which marked Charles Dickens's second step, after *Hard Times*, toward more baleful fiction. It was fully accepted and expected that Merdle would buy up the whole of England to extraordinarily beneficial effect, so highly he was seen as having the most enlightened social and political aims. Perversely, Christine Edzard in her film of *Little Dorrit*, a dark and glowing tapestry, banishes Merdle to brief background appearances until his suicide, while underscoring the patriarchal element he represents by the ironical indirection of having had his wife constantly speaking for and representing *him*. In effect, Merdle ultimately appears only to vanish, leaving us to contemplate his invisible influence in most everything we have seen, and exposing the riotous lack of appreciation of the deleterious effects of capitalism throughout various strata of Victorian society. Marshalsea, a debtors prison, keeps collecting people who had been marked by great expectations but who end up, for all their airs and ambition, as the disposable property of creditors. Amy Dorrit—"Little Dorrit"—was born in Marshalsea, where her father is incarcerated.

In "Nobody's Fault," the first of the six-hour film's two parts, responsibility for widespread poverty is taken up by no one; someone or other declares "Nobody's fault!" so often it comes as a shock when someone says "My fault!" over a trivial accident. Following Dickens, Edzard also undertakes a satire of bureaucratic runaround, propelled by Arthur Clennam's desire to secure a patent for a safely operating machine for his business. The second part, beginning with her birth, follows noble Amy's pilgrim's progress. Before Edzard concludes her calmly feminist work, we see a number of scenes we have already seen in the first part, but with the events shifted to poor, noble Amy's perspective.

1989

IMAGES OF THE WORLD AND THE INSCRIPTION OF WAR (West Germany). The objective nature of photographic images is probed in this brilliant West German documentary by Harun Farocki. Such images, Farocki's cinematic essay suggests, bear the subjectivity of the political uses to which they are put at one end and the subjectivities of human reception and perception at the other. Indeed, something else predates either of these mediations: manipulations of reality that generate those appearances which images then proceed to memorialize. In wartime, factories producing necessary equipment, for instance, are camouflaged to fool aerial reconaissance into generating photographs in which the factories appear to be ordinary residences.

Such photographs were inadvertently taken of Auschwitz during the last world war. This was April 1944, when Allied reconaissance was searching instead for factories, chemical plants, etc., that is, bombing targets in order to fell the Nazi war effort. The aerial photographs were ignored as revealing nothing relevant; only in the mid-1970s, when they were discovered in C.I.A. files and scrutinized from the vantage of considerable knowledge of the death camps, were they correctly deciphered. Farocki compares this "outside," "objective" view with an "inside," personal view aiming at objectivity: drawings of Auschwitz by Jewish prisoner Alfred Kantor. The photographs are also compared to Nazi photographs of Auschwitz.

We may fetishize the photograph—and, more generally, technology. Farocki mockingly prefaces the Auschwitz material with the case of Albrecht Meydenbauer, a nineteenth-century architect who, in order to safely deduce measurements of a church, relied on still photographs from which a scale model presumably could be constructed.

Farocki's associative method may seem at times to want coherence, but his stunning *Images* is tightly constructed without appearing to be—a strategy to avoid imposing on the viewer just the sort of quantifiable "truth" the film seeks to penetrate.

HISTOIRE(S) DU CINEMA (France, 1988-9; 1998). "The image/ will come/ in time."

Nothing could be further from a public television documentary about the history of the movies than Jean-Luc Godard's eight-hour *Histoire(s) du cinéma*. It is, after all, a work by Godard. It's playful, penetrating, Brechtian.

It's a collage—a trebled, quadrupled kaleidoscope—of sounds, voices, and images drawn from film, literature, social commentary, painting, especially French Impressionistic painting, photography. Curiously, though, it fails to impose an overload; rather, it's an inexhaustible complexity inspiring one's continual return to it, much as Godard (and some of the rest of us) are continually drawn to cinema.

There are stills and snippets from films (to which Godard applies his own camera movements and speeds), superimpositions, voiceover, sounds, music, and the rush of references is so intense that often I recognized an outstanding image but couldn't recall from what film it came. (More often than not, one film will be noted while a clip of some other film is being shown.) I couldn't identify, either, countless photographs of doubtlessly important filmmakers.

One ever darker segment begins by questioning what cinema is and takes a train ride through the period of France's Nazi occupation—a train ride to Auschwitz. There is mention of a "broken memory." A flash of Monet's *Camille on Her Deathbed* is the perfect interruption: the shrouded image of a mistress who became a wife and died as a result of giving birth: the fate of cinema. Godard proceeds to consider U.S. cultural colonialism following the war—French cinema's second occupation. ("The American cinema made advertisements.")

Unsurprisingly, Godard is peerless in addressing the *nouvelle vague*, and his back-and-forth between snippets of Truffaut's *The 400 Blows* (1959) and Hitchcock's *Vertigo* (1958), two films he loves, revolves around the difference between Nature's water and a studio tank.

WHY HAS BODHI-DHARMA LEFT FOR THE EAST? (South Korea). The title is a *koan*— a Zen riddle whose refusal to yield a material solution helps move the seeker along the path to Enlightenment. Bodhi-Dharma is the South Indian or, possibly, Persian monk who introduced Zen Buddhism to eastern Asia in the fifth century. Bae Yong-Kyun wrote, directed, cinematographed and edited *Dharmaga tongjoguro kan kkadalgun*, South Korea's greatest film.

The opening shot projects the distracting nature of the contemporary urban world. Most of the balance of the film unfolds at a secluded monastery amidst gorgeous Nature. An elderly Zen Master instructs two disciples: an orphaned boy; a young monk, Yong Nan, whom the Master calls Kibong. The child asks Kibong why they have left the world. No peace or freedom is there, the monk answers after a pause so long we feel it will not be filled. The Master comes up behind them and immediately adds that the world is too full of Self. Another day, the monk continues the lesson: the world is a place of passions and possessions —enslaving ties; pain. We glean that the monk is recalling personal history. He is betwixt the Master, who has transcended such, and the child, who is bereft of ties and memory of ties.

On the other hand, while the monk has much to learn, the child has much *more* to learn. Inquisitiveness stirs the child. Yearning—to leave the past behind; to achieve Enlightenment —stirs the impatient monk. He must learn "the roots of the Way." Toward this end the Master gives him *koans* upon which to meditate. As he counsels the monk, a shot sets the back of the Master's head against the freely flowing river.

In turmoil, against a tracking shot of desolate woods, the monk asks, "Isn't Enlightenment a dream?"

NOSTOS: THE RETURN (Italy). Call him Nostos. The name of the ancient Greek who attempts to make his way home after many, many years at war in Franco Piavoli's astonishing *Nostos: Il Ritorno* means *homecoming*. Call him Odysseus if you like, or Ulysses.

Nostos's single-minded aspiration to get home accounts for the film's unity; its continuity, though, is in disarray, in pieces, conveying what war has done to the soldier's spirit. A tremendous storm wrecks the ship carrying Nostos and surviving comrades. Or Nostos was the sole survivor among his group of middle-aged warriors, the storm perhaps being an image, a symbol, of a war that can never be left behind. Piavoli, who cinematographed and edited, cuts from the storm to a solitary Nostos on land. Nostos howls with grief for his lost comrades. A beautiful young woman swims naked; they make love. Do they? Isn't Nostos alone on that island (as the establishing extreme overhead long-shot suggests)? Isn't the girl a fantasy recollecting his Penelope at the age when he left her to go to war? We see Nostos floating in the sea, struggling to reach home. (At one point, he appears to be swimming across a gigantic moon.) But isn't this emblematic of his endurance of what war demanded of him? As he floats, memories interrupt—for instance, of childhood, of a child pursuing an endlessly rolling hoop. When, having washed ashore, Nostos is at last home, the hoop rolls into the frame and finally comes to rest.

Piavoli doesn't show the couple reuniting. Instead, Nostos's wife is shown in long-shot, waiting. The couple's separation, the passage of time, and Nostos's experience of war—a form of exile—have made them different persons than when they were lovers long ago. Not all gulfs can be bridged.

BERLIN-JERUSALEM (Israel, Netherlands, Italy, France, UK). Amos Gitaï is Israel's premier filmmaker. His *Berlin-Yerushalaim* follows two actual Jewish women who meet in Berlin and separately emigrate to Palestine in the 1940s: German Expressionist poet Else Lasker-Schuler (Lisa Kreuzer, magnificent); Russian revolutionary Mania Shochat, who helped found Israel's Kibbutz and Labor Movements. The film cautions that these lives "inspired" the film; both women are represented as being much younger than they were at the time.

The film opens with a screen-leftward traveling shot of the future nation of modern Israel: a sweeping expanse of rocky desert—an aching vision of possibility crying out to people as the Holocaust coalesces in Europe. Gitaï crosscuts between this place and Berlin, with Shochat's uprooting preceding Lasker-Schuler's, the death of whose young son seals her decision to move. An upwardly tilted, screen-leftward traveling shot through bony, bleak trees accompanies her voiceover: "There is a lamentation in the world/ As though God himself were dead." In the new land, Shochat suffers a tragic loss to regional violence; Lasker-Schuler's adjustment is worse. Hers is a cosmopolitan soul. What will be Israel is more hospitable to laborers and laborites—nation builders—than to artists.

But Lasker-Schuler tries to unite her son's memory with the future of her new homeland by envisioning a place where children can play in peace. Dressed heavily in black, she is walking outdoors, and the camera keeps apace with her as she walks, walks screen-leftward amidst sounds of the Israeli-Palestinian conflict in the streets. Cain is killing Abel again, she thinks. Buildings, traffic, radio reports—all these, circa 1989, surround her. No longer do we see her. The camera that has been following her now is completing her long, long walk across 45 years: a stalking spirit of national disappointment. Here is the single greatest shot in Israeli cinema.

THE JUNIPER TREE (Iceland). *The Juniper Tree* is less macabre and far less violent than the Grimm Bros. fairy tale upon which it is based. A film from Iceland (*Einitréð* is its Icelandic title), but one in English, its creator was an American filmmaker and teacher, Nietzchka Keene, who somewhere is a bird now, having died of cancer in 2004. Transaction between the worlds of birds and humans is at the heart of both the story and the film. Keene wrote, directed, edited.

Keene has wrought a haunting, solemn, black-and-white medieval ballad. Her film, which is ghostly, quiet, shivering, claims some affinity with two films by Ingmar Bergman: *The Seventh Seal* (1956) and *The Virgin Spring* (1959). It is equally naturalistic and dreamlike.

Björk plays Margit, one of two sisters who flee their village after their mother is burned as a witch. Margit herself "has visions," and Katla, the bold one, presses her younger sister to acknowledge these visions. Meanwhile, the two move in with a young farmer, with whom Katla has fallen in love, whose wife has just died and whose young son proclaims Katla a witch upon advice, he insists, from his departed mother, whose place in his home, he feels, Katla is attempting to usurp. The boy, Jónas, insists that his mother's spirit is still protecting him, allowing Katla to goad him into jumping off a cliff to prove his contention that his mother will change him into a bird so that no harm comes to him. Mother doesn't come through, and the fall kills the boy.

Very strange, very beautiful, this minimalist piece locates an imaginative space where spiritual and (subsistent) material worlds touch. An image of a huge, fierce bird—a human who has passed into spirit—dominating a humble juniper tree *amazes*.

FREEZE, DIE, RISE! (U.S.S.R.). Vitaly Kanevski's first feature takes its title, *Zamri, umri, voskresni!*, from a children's game. Valerka, based on Kanevski, is an impoverished boy in Suchan, a mining town in the Siberian wasteland in postwar Stalinist Russia.

The film opens with Kanevski, invisible, singing on the soundtrack as he readies the shoot. He has "risen." The first shot per se is of boy miners exiting a mine. The next shot is of children, mostly kerchiefed girls, at play, with Valerka hurling profanity at and chasing one of the girls. All these children are "frozen" in their place and time, suffering the consequences of whatever "crimes" their parents have committed that resulted in this forced relocation. In the course of the film, Valerka will descend into crime and "die." The film closes with Kanevski shooting a scene that quotes Dovzhenko's *Earth* (1930). His film testifies to Soviet oppression, hardship and resurgence.

Valerka lives with his mother. When he asks her in the street, "Where are you going?" she reminds him he should ask instead, "Are you going far?"—an index of the weight of suspicion she feels is upon her. Valerka at play has gotten his coat dirty. "Now I'll have to clean it again." Valerka assures his mother that at the next snowfall he himself will clean it. Like Edmund in Roberto Rossellini's *Germany, Year Zero* (1947), Valerka is set on doing his utmost to shoulder much more than a child's load of responsibility.

Apart from his pet, a piglet, Valerka has one friend: Galiya, a playmate, a rival at selling hot tea to miners, a companion eyewitness to their bleak, debilitating surroundings populated by desperate individuals, including forsaken veterans. Without realizing it, the pair are gathering evidence against Stalinism. Photographs of the executed cross their line of sight.

DRUGSTORE COWBOY (U.S.). Filmed in Portland, Oregon, Gus Van Sant's *Drugstore Cowboy*, from James Fogle's novel, is without agenda—an unsentimental account of a young man's dogged attempt to lift himself out of a makeshift lifestyle composed of drugs and theft. The film ends ambiguously, with Bob (Matt Dillon, trenchant) perhaps about to die as he is rushed to hospital in an ambulance. If he survives, despite his dedicated reforming, he may be en route to becoming the wasted, homeless, "fat as butter" Bob of Van Sant's lyrical, devastating *My Own Private Idaho* (1991).

Despite a foray into commercial filmmaking he has since repudiated, Van Sant has emerged as perhaps the premier American filmmaker at taking on American myth—for instance, the fiction of self-determination, in which, collectively, many Americans deludedly believe; for, at best, all Bob can do in *Drugstore Cowboy* (as he ultimately discloses in his unselfpitying voiceover) is try his best and see what comes. His life is so far out of his hands that it nearly seems to be somebody else's life, which, as it happens, he is constantly, curiously observing.

If, unlike *My Own Private Idaho*, where Falstaff-Fagin-Bob bitterly dies, *Cowboy* ends open-endedly, with tentative hope, there is a key passage that hints at the oblique sequel to come. In the woods we see leaves in whose green color neither blue nor yellow predominates; the woodsiest, most insulated green imaginable, it images growth bereft of a sunlit spark of life: an epiphany of Bob's fate, which, for all his countervailing efforts, an insurmountable environment will execute against him. The fact that he is in the woods burying the corpse of a compatriot who drug-overdosed completes the symbolism.

Drugstore Cowboy is a haunting achievement.

ANGANO . . . ANGANO . . . (Madagascar, France, U.S.). In Brazilian-born César Paes's *Tales from Madagascar*, a highly original ethnographic documentary, we hear storytellers recount founding myths of Malagasy culture; rather than these folk historians, who appear only in occasional inserts, or dramatic enactments of the tales they tell, we see instead people in the here and now, principally, at work, myths flowing through them, informing who they are and what they do in their everyday lives. Their myths continue to explain their environment.

We begin at the beginning: the Malagasian creation myth—voiceover set to images of sky, sea and earth. Thunder and lightning—war—was the result of conflict between the Gods of Sky and Sea, both of which coveted Earth. The sight and sound of the matching meteorological display obliterates the difference in time. Past is present; all, eternal. Earth raised mountains to attack Sky, but both Gods struck an accord, inventing peace, and decided on a joint project: the creation of the human—shaped from mud, invested with spirit. Set to this voiceover is a long-shot of a boy running towards the camera. Once created, humanity became a bone of contention, reviving conflict between the Gods and within their human creation.

Bored and lonely, humanity made fire, hence, smoke, so God of Sky sent down his daughter to keep Man company. But she missed the taste of rice, so she and her mate visited her father, stole some of his rice and returned to earth, planting the rice. Set to this voiceover are images of rice harvesting. We see, for instance, women chattering away at work, up to their waist in muddy rice paddies—like the original boy, creatures of the mud themselves now, but also part of a sociable community.

Myth and reality flow as one river throughout Paes's radiant film.

YAABA (Burkina Faso). Idrissa Ouédraogo's *Yaaba*—Mooré, for *Grandmother*—is about acceptance of responsibility. Although its focus is a village, Ouédraogo's concerns are clearly national, regional, continental.

Someone has ignited the grainary. Eyewitness testimony is discounted because it comes from "a drunk"—the role to which villagers have relegated the man. Discounting his testimony, then, confirms their accuracy in assigning him the role, thus blocking any need to take responsibility for their error. But a voice of reason among them remarks that the drunk drinks largely because the community so ridicules and routinely dismisses him.

The village blames the arson on Sana (Fatimata Sanga, wonderful), an elderly woman who also has been categorically defined—in her case, as "a witch." The communal superstitiousness isn't purely a matter of ignorance and backwardness; another component is the (false) sense of security that its familiarity imparts. However misguided, however much the practice converts neighbors into outsiders and pariahs, it reassures villagers to maintain faith in the roles that they have assigned others. It enables them to evade responsibility for what happens in their midst. The earlier arson burns with especial irony in our minds when the villagers, scapegoating Sana just as ridiculously for something else (a child's illness), burn down her hut.

The main characters are young cousins Nopoko and Bila. The boy, Bila, befriends Sana; both children are shown as being skeptical of the idea that Sana is a witch. When Nopoko falls ill, her cousin, at Sana's instruction, makes a journey in order to bring a healer to Nopoko. In this way the boy is taking responsibility for the outcome of Nopoko's illness—an act that stands in contradistinction to how the village generally functions.

Indeed, the children represent a more hopeful future, one of responsibility rather than blame.

Films of the 1990s

Among the decade's major filmmakers is Iran's Abbas Kiarostami, whose work was championed by Antonioni and Godard, and whose *A Taste of Cherry* (*Ta'm e guilass*, 1997) shared the Palme d'Or at Cannes with Shohei Imamura's *The Eel*

A Taste of Cherry applies to an engrossing instance of life and death cinema's signature mediation between documentary and fiction. Kiarostami both wrote and directed this complex film; his narrative, though, is a simple thread. Having decided to end his life this very night, Badii (a younger ringer for Kiarostami himself) spends the day driving around the outskirts of Tehran in his Range Rover. He is a (relatively) well-off pilgrim in what, were it not for his imminent suicide, would be called the middle of his life. But he resembles Dante less than he does Robert Browning, who, in the most brilliantly conflicted of all English love poems, "Two in the Campagna," can't quite latch onto an elusive evolutionary thread teasing him throughout Rome, a city of ruins haunted by ancient, shifting ghosts. Badii also finds his finite grasp falling short of his infinite passion. He is trying to locate someone who would be willing to assist him in the grim task he has committed himself to. Therefore, he picks up, in his expensive motor vehicle, one stranger after another, interviewing each in turn. His plan is to offer a substantial sum of money—his life's savings—to whoever will agree to visit the outdoors death site he has chosen in order to make certain the following morning that his pill overdose succeeds in ending his life. This accomplice would also be charged with burying him—unless, of course, the plan, having gone astray, has left Badii still alive, in which case the stranger would have to help him to his death before burying him. Iran clearly isn't America, where hardly anyone would turn down a proposal that brought in a buck, so Badii is having a devil of a time finding his Good Samaritan. But, after a few rejections, he gets lucky; his willing ad hoc gravedigger finally appears—a man older than himself and stably employed, but in great need of money owing to his child's grave illness.

Badii's course isn't subject to revision. By providing no explanation for Badii's death wish, and by so intriguing us that we don't require one, Kiarostami relieves us of the distraction of weighing whether the "causes" justify the irreversible decision. The decision is self-justifying. The effect of Kiarostami's economy in the matter also is to situate Badii firmly and wholly in the present, not in some contrived past where he was dealt this blow, and another, and so forth. Such a past, whatever it was, could only obscure Badii's reality as a character in a film rather than in life. And this *is* a film; it isn't *life*. Now and then Kiarostami insinuates the camera's presence by his use of windows in the *mise-en-scène*; but his boldest device—it is the key to the film's purpose—is his use of a startling ellipsis: Badii's consenting Angel of Burial isn't shown, like previous candidates for the job, being stopped for and being picked up; he just pops up in the cab of Badii's vehicle, seemingly out of nowhere. Nothing so drives home as this that we are watching a film; some of us may even wonder whether we momentarily nodded off and missed the picking-up.

Still, in the course of watching the film, we may do what (even sophisticated) audiences tend to do; by mentally contesting the filmmaker's distancing strategy, we may "make real" Kiarostami's fiction—with Kiarostami's own slyly seductive help, in fact, as he increasingly involves us in Badii's anxiety-ridden quest to find a burial agent. In short, Kiarostami plays us, moving us the audience in opposite imaginative directions at once. He may deny us access to Badii's explanatory past; but he nonetheless encourages us into projections of Badii's possible future. For, eventually, Kiarostami has us wondering whether Badii's suicide attempt will succeed. If we are mind-locked Spielbergians hopelessly prone to mistaking fiction for reality, we may even wonder whether Badii's money "saves" the other man's sick child! Most of us, however, will not go that foolishly far; but we will wonder how things will pan out for someone—a character—who (1) could not be dissuaded from suicide in any case and therefore has no future; and (2) isn't real to begin with and *therefore* has no future. Indeed, the resolution of Kiarostami's "plot" seems to turn on whether Badii ends up alive or otherwise, and our (however misguided) desire for such resolution may prompt us to relax, rendering moot, whatever distancing Kiarostami supplies. We audiences can be a stubborn, silly and wayward crowd.

Up to good even if we the audience aren't, though, Kiarostami at the end of his film re-distances us. We witness Badii's pill-taking and, just before sound vanishes and the screen goes black, we see Badii lying in his "grave"; but, instead of our learning his fate in the next image, we next see something we could scarcely have anticipated: a sequence purporting to show the shooting of the film we have just been watching. Thus Kiarostami implicitly completes a framing device that in fact had no beginning other than the reflection of sunlight off a camera lens—something we, as audience, take for granted. These last images lack clarity; they resemble something on television that is being shot off the television screen. In short, the images are deliberately debased; and jolting us further out of our accepting the film we are watching as "reality" is the appearance of Homayoun Ershadi, the actor who plays Badii, whom we naturally enough mistake, momentarily, for Badii, prompting us to wrongly think, "Oh, he's *alive*; the suicide attempt failed," until we realize that no word or image is coming to resolve the question of Badii's outcome, leaving us instead—gratefully or irritatedly, depending on whether we love movies—to gauge our dependence on cozy, conventional, pedestrian narrative.

Like Orson Welles's marvelous *F for Fake* (1975), another Iranian film that jerks its (Persian) rug out from under us, Kiarostami's film can justify its prank by the thematic purpose that the prank serves. But Kiarostami isn't satisfied with merely demonstrating how film audiences may buy into a plot at the risk of forfeiting their sense of its unreality. He is also exploring the fluidity of a line of representational reality that defines the very essence of cinema; for the margin of anxiety that attaches itself to Badii, and sticks to him even after he connects with his morning-after burial assistant, provides us with an emotional correlative to the discrepancy between documentary and fiction with which this film so earnestly plays.

Most of the film, hypnotic, is taken up by Badii's determined journeying through stretches and turns of barren vacancy—a landscape pitched between somewhere and nowhere, between life and death—and by his conversations-in-motion with various candidates for the job he is offering. Badii's highly specific motivation, therefore, intrudes a fictional premise in what otherwise might seem an observational record. Suggesting *cinéma-vérité*, the exchanges between would-be employer and might-be employee indeed take the form of documentary inquiry and response. Whereas, though, the pertinent question in Jean Rouch's *Chronicle of a Summer* (1961) is "Are you happy?" the question here becomes, in effect, "Will you bury me?" Is there a difference? I think so. The *Chronicle* question is objective; interviewer Edgar Morin asks it because he and Rouch are interested in how others will respond to it—and because Morin wishes to socio-analyze the respondents. On the other hand, Badii solicits comments only as a means to an end, and that end—the help he is after—aims at his own benefit (although there is also ancillary financial benefit to whoever becomes his helper). All this makes Badii seem more fictional, less documentary, than Rouch. Additionally, if we were to construct imaginatively a documentary-fiction continuum, we might place Badii's patently rehearsed inquiry more to the fictional end and the responses he receives, which are made to look spontaneous and unpredictable, more to the documentary end. At bottom, of course, it is all Kiarostami much as, with its (marvelous) pseudo-documentary inserts, *The Passion of Anna* (1969) is (brilliantly) all Ingmar Bergman. On the basis of appearances (and what *else* is cinema?), we may nevertheless describe the generic compound to which Badii belongs as fictionally compromised documentary—a *nouvelle vague*-like blending of these two opposite modes of expression, flexible and dynamic, where in their back-and-forth exchanges the more-fictional interviewer is nudged in the direction of documentary and the more-documentary interviewee is nudged in the direction of fiction. To me, this is astonishing.

Kiarostami has found a way to humanize and dramatize what in fact is the fluid nature of cinema as it fluctuates between its two signature modes of expression.

Thus the gap between the two men—Badii and whoever his current passenger happens to be—is at once a mediating area of conversation and mutual influence, transference and transformation, and a kind of submerged battlefield between determined opposites. Relating this gap or, if you will, chafing space between documentary and fiction back to its emotional correlative, Badii's anxiety, we may discover that those whom Badii interviews are more fully documentary because they fail—more often than not, refuse—to conform to his mental "script." As such, they represent some aspect of reality that fiction cannot suppress or totally control. In this light, however they respond, his pickups constantly confront Badii with his own anxiety.

But what is Badii so anxious about? Not death; for he faces by choice his imminent end. His demeanor, moreover, suggests he has arrived at his choice—that was the journey preceding the journey we are shown—calmly, carefully, thoughtfully; the steadiness and patience with which he conducts his search reveals the opposite of an erratic soul prone to making a hasty decision. If not death, then, what brings him such anxiety? *Life*—its manifold uncertainties, which he hopes the single uncertainty of death will put to rest. How fitting, then, that once Badii has actually found someone to bury him he nevertheless retains his anxiety. Before, it might have seemed that eliciting at last a positive response would relax his anxiety in anticipation of his final rest. But life—reality—isn't so accommodating. Once the desired response comes, it's conflicted, after all, because the man whose help he enlists, although desperate for money, must find Badii's request odd and disconcerting, and because one soul's needs never suit another's exactly. Loudly accompanied by reluctance and disapproval, in fact, the last interviewee's assent is riddled with equivocation. Thus is Badii's anxiety *extended* rather than removed; and because of this he follows this recruit—embarrassingly! disruptively!—into the man's workplace and entreats him for more and more confirmation. The man can only say—it's one of the most ambiguous utterances in all of cinema—"I will keep my word." Such a statement can do nothing for Badii. After all, the man's sincere intent isn't in dispute; rather, Badii's intelligence tells him that this man's ambivalence might yet dissuade him from showing up the next morning. Even as he prepares for a departure from life, then, Badii must continue—and continue—to face life's uncertainty.

All this gives human, dramatic form to the conflicted nature of cinema as it perpetually fails to resolve itself fully into either fiction or documentary. But more: Kiarostami thus posits anxiety over life as somehow at the very heart of the art form—perhaps even the impulse behind a wider range of art. Our own anxiety answers Badii's and Kiarostami's. How ironic that we ourselves feel this uncertainty most keenly when we are forced to face Badii's unreality; for the film's blatant refusal to follow Badii as far as the next morning leaves us, to the extent that we insist on his reality, unsure about his fate. Thus are we, presumably (as real people viewing reel happenings) by definition pure documentary, irresistibly nudged in the direction of fiction as it absorbs our consciousness and helps structure our perception of what's on the screen and what's off, including ourselves.

Our participation as audience in the quarrel, tension, contest, what-have-you between documentary and fiction, sealed when we momentarily mistake the actor playing Badii for Badii the character, is the film's ultimate point of investigating its theme. In effect, after the (unreal, fictional) fact, we ourselves become implicated in the "human" exchanges that were made in the cab of Badii's Range Rover; we ourselves have been drawn into that imaginative mediatory space where fiction and documentary interact. We find ourselves, as it were, at the crossroads, left to wonder whether the film has put us there or, by its exploration of a theme, discovered us there. We are not there alone. Incorporating these crossroads of documentary and fiction, and life and death, is an image that the film repeats and repeats; in imaginative space, it represents the precise point of mutual influence, mediation, transaction. It is a cherry tree. It is the film's key image. On one level the tree, in tune with Freud's cigar, is simply a tree—that is, an instance of absolute thingness. But because it also represents the material reality that Badii plans to give up, the tree becomes by extension a symbol of life. We do not have to reach far for this identification, for one of Badii's passengers even refers to the cherry tree as a tree of life, the sum of all reasons for rejecting suicide. Thus the tree is both objective (thing) and subjective (symbol)—although such a widely agreed-upon symbolic interpretation of tree as tree-of-life blurs the distinction, crossing over from one realm to the other, one world to the next. If we (reasonably enough) identify objectivity with documentary and subjectivity with fiction, then we find in the tree the very flux between alternate modes of expression that is at the heart of the film—of *all* films, Kiarostami would say. The way he shoots the tree also supports this; for, framed by the camera at a middle distance, with the screen containing the entire above-ground portion of the tree but almost nothing surrounding it, the tree seems to exist at some medial point, between solid earth and the human mind, as a tree of death as well as a tree of life—a kind of natural gravestone; a floral epitaph. As such, it is not only an enticement for Badii to stick around by keeping himself alive but also an intransigent emblem of hard, sturdy, confining limits very much worth getting out of.

Here, as throughout the film, Kiarostami is abetted by his "third eye," his color cinematographer, Homayoun Payvar, who resists touting the cherry tree's loveliness and suggests instead an intriguingly ambiguous embodiment of the film's play between opposite chords and genres. Payvar is also instrumental in helping the filmmaker devise a purposeful *mise-en-scène* where the landscape outside the Range Rover, in juxtaposition to the fixed tree, breezes by, providing persistent, nearly subliminal visual evidence of the growing pressure of time on Badii, and of the fleeting nature of life. One other contribution to the film's excellent result must be noted: the cutting, executed by Kiarostami himself. In particular, there is the popping up in the vehicle of the soul whose child is ailing; this constitutes an audacious rupture of the film's smoothly continuous flow. On some level, surely, this circumstance is related to the several appearances of the cherry tree.

How roots of this film reach out! Because of its ambition to interrelate numerous strands in a complex analytical fabric (like Antonioni and '60s Alain Resnais, Kiarostami selfconsciously elects to make masterpieces), however, the film falls a tad short of being the stunning, unified achievement that, say, Kiarostami's *Life and Nothing More* (1992) and *The Wind Will Carry Us* (1999) are. Possibly the filmmaker places too much store in the image of the cherry tree's ability to pull the film's argument and diverse elements together. But *A Taste of Cherry* is a towering work nonetheless by one of cinema's most burrowing and philosophical artists.

From the 1970s on, while Hollywood pursued profits by creating action-adventure blockbusters like *Jaws*, *Star Wars* and the Indiana Jones films, as well as inflated soap operas and melodramas like *E.T.* and *Schindler's List*, cinema was given fresh air and fresh blood by the contributions made by two expanding groups: black Africans, who often reflected on their countries' colonial histories or the difficulties that persisted despite independence; women, whose liberation movements found more and more of their ranks interested in shining a camera on the world around them. The survival of serious cinema is in their debt.

One such example from Africa, specifically, Senegal, as well as Switzerland and France, is Djibril Diop Mambéty's *La petite vendeuse de Soleil* (*The Little Girl Who Sold the Sun*, 1999) —a play on words, *The Sun* being a daily newspaper. (Please note below how often French funding helped a recent outstanding film into existence.) Dedicated to street children and their perseverence through incredible hardship, it is a Third World story whose tone is complex and highly ironical. Mambéty imparts a sunny complexion to the 45-minute film in order to stress profound social and economic shadows. *Little Girl* is what used to be called a "message movie," and it packs a considerable punch.

It's a film about town and village. The city, in Senegal, is Dakar, an urban environment whose sun-baked streets teem with children hustling newspapers and adults begging or trying to earn money by selling from stalls. The film opens in Dakar, and it's not a pretty sight. A merchant accuses a woman of having stolen some unknown thing from him, and three officers, at his behest, violently arrest her while she protests her innocence and neither merchant nor policemen bother to inspect the bucket she is carrying for the alleged pilfered item. We see her behind bars—in a masterful shot that likens the woman to a caged animal, the camera is pressed against the outside of the bars, which seem enormous—and it appears she has been driven insane by the humiliation and rough treatment. The implication is clear: she was fragile to begin with, poised for the breakdown we witness. *She isn't a thief but a princess*, she shouts to the still air.

The film's title, which refers to a child, not a woman, dissuades us that the prisoner is the protagonist. Rather, we see her as representative of a social vulnerability. Perhaps she is the woman who the girl of the title is in danger of becoming.

Indeed, the scene shifts from city to village, where Sili (Lisa Balera), the film's main character, appears, and the juxtaposition implies the seemingly indomitable girl's shared destiny with the mad woman. (The village may be Colobane, Mambéty's own birthplace near Dakar.) It's either dusk or pre-dawn, and long-shots bathed in a lovely, diffuse blue establish the village where Sili and her family live. By all rights, Sili should be securely asleep, at home, in bed. However, she is on a mission; she must find a way to earn money so that her family can survive. We see her emerge from shadows into the dawn's light: a girl on crutches, each step a hardship. She reaches the highway, whose few cars at this early, otherwise quiet hour suggest the connection between the village from which Sili, if you will, is commuting and Dakar, her determined destination. One other sound interrupts the silence: that of a man pounding rocks into smaller pieces, to sell for construction work. A closeup of his labor is followed by a more distant shot revealing the mound of broken-up rock that the man has been creating for hours—all night, probably. His making do as best he can, with what's available to him, becomes a metaphor of the harshness of ordinary existence in this part (and other parts) of Africa (and beyond). Globalization has brought construction, including workers, while those who are native to the region can break up rock. Sili is no less connected to this silent man than to the raving prisoner. He represents where she is starting from, a point of ingenuity, adaptability and resilience, while the woman who has been wrongly jailed as a thief represents where Sili may be headed. In Dakar, Sili also is wrongly arrested as a thief, and, self-assertively, she manages the release of both herself and the strange woman. But Mambéty leaves little doubt that this plucky victory is challenged by the odds against either of these individuals prevailing.

A pattern is established early on with the boy who transports Sili in the direction of Dakar. For all her apparent independence and self-sufficiency, Sili is reliant on others. She continually requires rescuing, for instance, when one of her crutches is stolen. Sili's smiling optimism—she is a little like Federico Fellini's Cabiria—covers a terrible vulnerability. Sili mentions that her knee was recently injured, hinting that her crippled state hasn't been of long duration. We speak of people not knowing their own strength. It is possible that Sili doesn't know yet her own weakness.

In Dakar, Sili's blind grandmother sings on the street for the coins of passers-by. But what can Sili herself do to earn money? The sight of swarming boys huckstering newspapers points her in the direction of what she interprets as her immediate destiny. However, Mambéty prefaces this revelation of hers in a disquieting way. The boys nearly knock her down as they go about their business. There are several shots of animals in the film; the animals always appear either passive or tranquil. But these newsboys are like a pack of wild animals.

Hyenas. They resent this new seller on their turf, who is a girl, besides. Their first violent encounter with Sili is thoughtless and accidental. All subsequent encounters will be deliberate and confrontational, and even accompanied by death threats. Sili's vulnerability, encapsulated by her handicap, will prove a magnet for their vicious assaults. They compete energetically with one another, but the competition that Sili poses is something of which they want to rid themselves. Their attitude and actions toward her transform them into a metaphor of unbridled competition—to paraphrase Tennyson, *human* nature red in tooth and claw.

Mambéty portrays the whole competitive atmosphere as a cauldron of madness. Human beings are debased by this environment; they become beasts or the prey of beasts. The issue isn't precisely globalization, the integrated global economy, but rather the mechanism of this integration as globalization is currently constituted: *capitalism*. The part of the world that Mambéty shows cannot withstand the onslaught of forces that competition for survival has unleashed. People should be pulling and working together for the benefit of all (as the kindnesses that a few persons extend to Sili imply), not feverishly working against one another for the sake of the illusion that many, or any, of them will come out on top. Indeed, Mambéty implies, no matter their illusions, the Senegalese are doomed from the start. Those who prevail exist outside the borders of the Third World. They are foreign capitalistic entities, not the hapless individuals whom we see scrambling on the streets of Dakar. (A silent Greek chorus of sorts is the legless boy in a wheelchair who constantly observes, seemingly searching out the truth in everything he sees, but ultimately powerless to weigh in effectively.) Mambéty succeeds in conveying a sense of the manipulation of people's lives by forces originating outside the upheaved community. The beneficiaries of foreign investment do not appear to be the Senegalese, whose suspiciousness, even hostility, towards one another provides an index of how all their worst impulses are being stirred up. Not that this will help any one of them. We become witness to the destruction of a people's sense of community and common interest. They no longer seem to inhabit their region but only to rent space there. The "landlord" is the aggregate of corporate interests impinging on the region. According to Tom Zaniello, the author of *Working Stiffs, Union Maids, Reds and Riffraff: A Guide to Films About Labor*, "it is France's collusion with the World Bank that keeps former French colonies at the mercy of economic forces they cannot control." "The street market in Mambéty's world becomes," Zaniello writes, "metaphoric for the world market."

Sili ends up selling copies of the newspaper *The Sun*, thirteen at a time, because—this is one of numerous indications of her naïvité —she mistakes 13 for a lucky number. She begins her endeavor in a golden dress that visually puns on the loftier sun, but on her second day of labor she is wearing a different dress, green in front and blue in the back. Mambéty thus characterizes his heroine as, unbeknownst to herself, self-divided as she copes with the reality with which she must contend. Perhaps the green represents the financial growth she seeks, while the blue suggests a lingering connection to the sun in the sky. However, the composite —the appearance that she is wearing two dresses at once—is an exacting visual irony: Sili only *thinks* she knows whether she is coming or going. Even as she succeeds in making a little money, she is losing ground because her persistent optimism is making her increasingly blind to the vulnerability of hers that she is failing to recognize. (The film's devastating final shot has her disappearing into the distance as a blur; this is correlative, I'm afraid, to her disconnect from reality—an anticipation that she, like the woman at the beginning, is headed for madness.) From the outset, she exudes a sense of being charmed, especially when someone who recognizes her from the village buys all thirteen of her newspaper copies, paying in fact a lot more than they are worth, as an act of charity. (This is the source of her delusion that 13 is a lucky number.) Therefore, she hasn't really *earned* the money, and the implication is that her survival remains mostly predicated on luck. It's part of the capitalistic delusion that the efforts of individuals bring them just compensation; rather, capital goes to capital—that is, to corporate capitalists. Sili is able to sustain her cheerful disposition largely because of her faith that her efforts will pay off. She has no knowledge of the forces that are arrayed against her.

A boy whom Sili befriends sells a rival newspaper, *The Nation*. At one point she asks him why his newspaper sells so much better than hers. The boy explains that *The Nation* is "the people's paper" while *The Sun* is the government paper. Employing a child's illogic, Sili says she will stick with selling *The Sun* because that "will bring the government closer to the people." The irony is that even the government is powerless, powerless to govern, that is, now that the nation's destiny is determined by decisions made outside the country by global capitalists.

Finding themselves in an unexpected pressure cooker, the Sengalese who are portrayed in this film are losing their identity, their ties to their culture, which, by definition, is homegrown. They are becoming part of a global village that derives from a vastly different outlook, to say the least. The ties within the community by which people might help one another are being thinned and stressed, and financial (and other) help from the larger outside world now comes as part of a complex package that postpones individual access to benefits until some indefinite future. The world's poor are getting poorer—most certainly, culturally and spiritually. The unhappy message of Mambéty's film is that, for all her hard work and positive attitude, Sili doesn't stand a chance of prevailing.

Message movies occupy an honorable place in cinema. They are disparaged when the examples considered are largely rhetorical (such as films by André Cayatte or Stanley Kramer), not analytical. Italian neorealism, on the other hand, largely consists of message films whose analytical aspect prevails over the rhetorical. While stylistically different, Mambéty's film follows the latter model. Indeed, it is very nearly free of rhetoric, as befits a film the target of whose message consists of those forces that are mostly invisibly underpinning the scenes that the film depicts.

A film that takes its zestiness from the lead character's innocent, can-do personality, Mambéty's *La petite vendeuse de Soleil* was released posthumously. Mambéty, 53, died before he could complete the trilogy to which this film belongs. The first part of the trilogy is *Le franc* (1994); the third would have been *La tailleuse de Pierre*. The umbrella title of the trilogy was *Tales of Little People*.

The most brilliant film from anywhere in the 1990s, *D'Est* (*From the East*, 1993) is the work of Belgian-born Chantal Äkerman. Along with Iran's Abbas Kiarostami, Äkerman is cinema's reigning humanist, and for more than thirty years she has been going back and forth between documentary and fiction, although her documentaries are highly dramatic and her fictions sometimes seem documentary, and she often lands in some magical space in-between. Like Vertov's *Three Songs of Lenin* (1934), *D'Est* is a photographic essay, a visual survey, of humanity.

Although Äkerman's masterpiece defies categorization, it is a kind of "road picture." For it, Äkerman herself took to the road, traveling from Germany to Poland to Moscow, shortly after the collapse of the Soviet Union. She explains that she had always wanted to make a film about "the diaspora of the Eastern European Jews," and that, in a transfigured form, *D'Est* became for her that film, for, in each human face she encountered along the way, she felt the history with which she was investing it—a history including the Jewish ordeal of Hitler and the death camps and of Josef Stalin, the former candidate for priesthood whose anti-Semitism was actually more authentic (by which I mean less politically motivated) than Hitler's. Road pictures are drifty things reflecting the impermanence and uprootedness of human lives, and in the sustained ironical technique by which Äkerman's film proceeds it's the "impermanence" and "uprootedness" of her own traveling and tracking camera that, destabilizing figures in often stationary positions, transforms them into a metaphor for lost and scattered Jewry—the most moving use of a moving camera I have encountered. Äkerman also films people walking, and this motion of theirs contributes to the same thematic result. It doesn't matter how few, if any, of these people are actually Jewish, for Äkerman's own Jewishness, and her reflections on the historic plight of European Jews, invest what she sees as a visionary with the thematic import she pursues as an artist.

Another aspect to this is the darkness of night in which Äkerman films much of what she sees, for instance, in Moscow streets. Headed for home carrying packages that imply rootedness and deliberation, people seem by the determination of their stride to be doing their best to push their way out of the darkness that nevertheless dogs them and is enveloping them. If one is of a literal mind, one can watch this and see little or nothing; but, once drawn into the film's metaphorical, which is to say, spiritual life, one is overwhelmed by a circumstance so enormous it's as if one were "feeling history." The black of night in this film resonates with a sense of the eternal tragedy of Jewry: the home or even the life always being taken away—the nothingness to which the rest of the world is ever poised to consign Jews by scattering either them or their ashes to the winds. Äkerman's irony embraces the idea that those whom she films here, who are seemingly hewing to a sure, steady course, are contesting their fate as wanderers or are in denial that this is their fate and their history. Closer to the surface, the Soviet Union has ended but its former citizens, apparently unfazed, go on with their mundane lives. They also are scattered to the winds, and therefore the continuation of ordinary existence cocoons them from this sea-change while Äkerman's camera penetrates and deconstructs the event of their survival.

For the most part, Äkerman employs two kinds of shots in *D'Est*, tracking shots and static shots. Her long tracking shots, among the most beautiful I have seen, are correlative both to her own (topographic, emotional, spiritual) journey and to the uprootedness of her camera subjects, which, by ironic dint of her travels, she shares. Äkerman tracks through railway depots and through streets, alternating between humans in a kind of limbo, between their lives, as it were, and people, as Carl Sandburg would have it in his great American poem "Limited," who are certain they are headed, by train, for Omaha, which in fact is only their most immediate destination. Perhaps the most piercing element in these trackings arrives very late in the film, on a Moscow street, when the camera passes a young boy (at one point the boy stretches back from the extreme right of the frame as if unsure about continuing on his way screen-left), finds him again, alongside a woman we also have seen before, and then loses him forever as we strain in anticipation to see him again, as if his future and ours depended on our reunion. Nothing so crystallizes the sense of impermanence that permeates this film than this little drama which is embedded in the flux of urban pedestrians all making their way to Sandburg's Omaha. *D'Est* is a film populated by ghosts whose substantial reality provides an index of the depth of humanity that, metaphorically, has been lost.

Most of the static shots are interior shots, in people's homes, and some of these find people, including children, in fixed poses, while others are engaged in repetitive activities. One such scene recalls similarly obsessive kitchen scenes in both Äkerman's *Je tu il elle* (1974) and her tremendous *Jeanne Dielman, 23 Quai du Commerce, 1080 Bruxelles* (1975): a woman, seated at a kitchen table, slices a salami and some bread, slicing and slicing, and intermittently eating only a little bit (but with relish!). Do people do this? Perhaps rarely, if at all; but much of what we do amounts to doing this and things like this, and in all these interior shots Äkerman captures a sense of the routines and compulsive behaviors that people employ to curb frustrations and uncertainties and assuage loneliness. In line with this, a television set, usually playing, appears in these interior scenes.

One of the earliest static shots in *D'Est*—it comes close to opening the film—shows a boy in his late teens or early twenties seated on a roadside bench, presumably waiting for a bus. He is wearing a red tank top, and behind him, on the vertical slats of a wooden fence framing his head, are painted red markings. Throughout the film, dabs of red punctuate nearly every shot, appearing quite often as an item of apparel, for instance. (In the film's rural scenes, fluttering trees, in long-shot, evoke the ephemeral and evanescent nature of existence.) Late in the film, the seemingly purposeless boy has been replaced by a concert cellist, who, after her seated performance, is gifted from the audience with bouquet after bouquet of red roses. Numerous nighttime shots in the film are bathed in a reddish glow, while others favor dusky blues that stress the film's twilit sense of the eternal. (The film's two principal color cinematographers are Bernard Deville and Raymond Fromont, and their work is wondrous.) On one level, Äkerman's repeated use of red suggests the lifeblood of the people she essays, their determination to persist and survive, if not quite their ability to prevail. This is another way of saying, perhaps, that red is armament against the drabness and crushing oppressiveness of life. On the other hand, in ironic counterpoint to this, red evokes a sense of spilt blood, suggesting as much the forces arrayed against humanity as humanity's quickened response to these. And, of course, red throughout, by its association with Communism, continually reminds us of time and place, and the end of the Soviet Union.

Time is a strange thing in this film. Some visual points of punctuation disclose the time in which the film was shot, the early 1990s, but for the most part there is washing over everything a sense that the human lives we see haven't budged from the 1930s. *D'Est* is saturated with a sense of the past, implying that a connection with the past has in some sense held people back from their future. On the level of Soviet reference, this may suggest an ideological nostalgia contesting a nation's ability to adapt and grow. On the level of Jewish reference, a more dire suggestion arises: the extent to which, by isolating and targeting Jews, the world has helped create a community whose insularity became a defense against eradication. On the other hand, some moments vividly juxtapose time references. In one scene, for instance, a pop singer, wearing a mini-skirt, performs on stage with a band while couples below dance in tentative rock fashion, among them a woman whose very long skirt seems to belong to a time of long-since abandoned modesty. In *D'Est* time yields to unspecified time yields to intimations of timelessness.

There is almost no dialogue in the film. It's a solemn world we enter, one certainly not without joy, but a world caught somewhere in between earth and eternity, hope and hopelessness, despair and fortitude. It's a world of sounds and background noise, but the camera records the silence of faces—the gap between what they show and what they hide. On Yasujiro Ozu's tombstone, American maverick filmmaker Jim Jarmusch has informed us, Chinese characters appear whose "rough translation" is "the space between all things." Äkerman's camera captures the space between all people, even when they are jostling one another in a crowd, as well as the space between all things that make up a person, an identity, or the elusive, perhaps illusionary appearance of identity. There is no rhetoric of humanity in Äkerman's films; somehow, like Ozu, in fact, Äkerman is peculiarly capable of showing us in each person whom her camera passes over the individual's silent participation in the aggregate of humanity. There is a universe in each grain of humanity.

Äkerman's extraordinary use of camera would appear to stylize the humanity that her camera discovers, but, to an unprecedented degree, her human subjects react to the camera in their midst in all kinds of self-dramatizing ways. The net result is a film that is, at once, pure cinema and pure humanity. Post-*D'Est*, no one can be so foolish as to think that one precludes the other. Perhaps the fullest measure of the humane film that Äkerman has wrought is this: we keenly feel the loss of each face, each soul, the camera passes by, and, because there are so many of these souls in the film, we are never passive in watching the film, for we are always catching up with it.

D'Est is from Belgium, France and Portugal.

From France, the beguiling, haunting *Olivier, Olivier* (1992) is Polish filmmaker Agnieszka Holland's companion-piece to her *Europa Europa* from the year before. Both, fact-based, center on an adolescent boy whose life is unimaginably rough—in Salomon's case, in *Europa Europa*, because he is a German Jew impersonating a Nazi to elude imprisonment and death; in Olivier's case, because, a runaway from home where he was sexually abused, he ekes out a perilous existence as a prostitute. Olivier, also, leads a "double life," once he expediently slips into the role of Elizabeth and Serge Duval's son, who disappeared, at age nine, six years earlier. And, like Salomon, he gets away with it, convincing even the parents. Indeed, some of his behavior argues that he *must* be little Olivier six years hence, even though, eventually, the child's remains are discovered in a neighbor's basement. We have, then, a mystery of time and identity, of the kind of Krzysztof Kieślowski's *The Double Life of Veronique* (1991). And we have one film mirror-imaging the other; for, if *Europa Europa* is the story of a boy with two identities, then *Olivier, Olivier* is the story of two boys with the *same* identity. How different their fates, though. Salomon Perel's impersonation—his double being—rescues him, reuniting him with the one other family member of his to survive the Holocaust; but, bound by guilt, Olivier sacrifices his search for his own mother in order to adopt permanently the role of the Duvals' lost son.

Informing the film is Charles Perrault's "Little Red Riding Hood." When nine-year-old Olivier takes off from his parents' country home, on his sister's bicycle, he is wearing his red 49ers cap and is headed to his ailing grandmother's house with a basket of food that his mother prepared; en route, he is lured off the path by a "wolf"—Marcel, whose sexual overtures precipitate the child's death down a flight of stairs. (For an even more bizarre and terrifying updating of the story, consult Nicolas Roeg's *Don't Look Now*, 1973, from Daphne du Maurier.) In a silly, later version of the tale, the child, ripped from the wolf's belly, survives. Holland's film, then, encompasses *both* versions; by impersonating, or replacing, the dead boy, Olivier is—to apply Elizabeth's phrase describing her son's miraculous recovery from his almost fatal premature birth—"born twice."

Little Red Riding Hood's vulnerability is encapsulated by her namelessness; her only "protection," symbolized by the cloak her grandmother made for her, is the family identity that contests her right to an identity of her own. This child exists solely as a family extension; the family permits her none of the individuality or independence that might save her. In Holland's splendid film, both Oliviers are likewise victims of "family": the nine-year-old, whose dependence on her his mother, almost hysterically fearful of losing him, has fostered, whose neglected, jealous sister, Nadine, terrorizes him, and whose surrogate father, Marcel, tries molesting him, causing his death; the fifteen-year-old, whose mother, ignorant of what was happening under her own roof, failed to protect him from the stepfather who raped him. Moreover, the latter boy ends up appropriated by the Duvals, with whom he remains in order to console them and keep them on an even keel and to assuage his guilt for having pretended to be their son in the first place. In perhaps the most radical reading possible, the film implies that the pressure that family members feel to flesh out the form and features of a myth makes any family, in effect, "surrogate," the non-surrogate "reality" becoming the fantasy ideal every family must fail to realize. In the meantime, Olivier's life is destroyed. It misses the point completely to suggest that, since "Olivier" has found the Duvals and the Duvals have found him, everyone benefits from the arrangement because none of them will ever be lonely again. Like Little Red Riding Hood, "Olivier" ends up having no name or identity except what "the family"—here, the Duvals—self-servingly confers on him. His life is over before it hardly began.

The film opens with what in retrospect is bleak irony. The screen is black. We hear a plaintive tune. Marcel, the young man whistling it, bicycles through a field; it is the tune he later plays as a trumpeted lament the fateful morning Olivier bicycles by his place on the way to Grandmother's. For now, though, the camera slowly picks up Olivier safely playing with sister Nadine elsewhere in the field. Leading the play, Nadine, who is older, conjures a fantasy of alien intrusion that she and her brother must guard against. Of course, the real danger to them both is much closer to home. Nadine crushes a beetle—a show of force, invincibility. As Marcel pedals through, she raises to her eye a tube and makes a noise that magically translates into a beebee that knocks Marcel onto the grass. Undetected, the children giggle over his tumble. But it is Marcel who will decisively end their childhoods. Their power over him is illusory. It is adults who hold final power over children. Later, "Olivier" relishes manipulating the Duvals, all the while unaware that it is he who is helpless in their tightening grip.

Olivier's disappearance clarifies the painfulness of the Duvals' lives. Their "powers," mental or imaginative, always come up short. Initially, Nadine believes that she herself wished Olivier out of the family for being their mother's favorite; yet she cannot wish him back, even to relieve her own enormous pain. All she can do with her "mind" is perform parlor tricks: topple things; extinguish light bulbs. True, her initial guilt over Olivier's disappearance gives way to gladness over having her mother, now, to herself; but her depth of love for her brother, which Holland is careful to show, becomes a retroactive index of her pain over his loss. Her mother can do even less to alter reality. Holding herself responsible for Olivier's leaving home, because she failed to provide him with a "normal" environment, she is haunted by his image. After the boy's "return," when Nadine abruptly exits while she and Elizabeth are quarreling, through the outside door, flung open, Elizabeth "sees" her nine-year-old happily at play on a backyard swing, and she "hears" his giggling. But the visitation charts their non-negotiable separation; Olivier occupies a child's world-of-his-own which his mother can "look at" but not enter. Even forging a continuity of identity between the two Oliviers cannot restore her cherished child to her aching arms.

But Elizabeth's desire for this, plainly, is what leads her to accept this other boy as her lost son, despite the fact that he is missing Olivier's round face, long eyelashes, freckles. Each point of similarity she can find, such as the "new" Olivier's appendectomy scar, she clings to in defiance of the more considerable evidence of dissimilarity. Serge joins her in this, but for another reason as well; for this "return" of their son has meant the restoration of their marriage following a separation caused by Elizabeth's appropriation of their loss as entirely her own—much as, previously, she had nurtured a closeness with the child that effectively had shut this father out. And why does Inspector Druot accept "Olivier" as Olivier, despite the physical dissimilarities between the two boys, despite the fact that the correct answers to his questions that "Olivier" provides—mostly, family names—the teenager could have gleaned from the case folder lying open on the policeman's desk? Guilt. The boy's disappearance had been his first case, which in the absence of productive leads he had had to close—but only after promising Elizabeth and Nadine that he would find their son and brother. Having failed to do this, he must come up with "Olivier" no matter what. Also, Druot's career has stagnated under the stigma of this beginning failure of his—a situation he is motivated to reverse.

Why, however, does the boy himself say he is Olivier? Well, he never really *does*, although he craftily says enough to let others believe what they want. When interrogated, the boy is defensively glib. (From his eye movements and body language, it's clear he is afraid of a beating.) Of the mother he is in Paris in search of, he says: "She is a Baltic empress. She was dumped by the Emir of Kuwait. Now she's a maid at the Swedish embassy. Her father's Scandinavian." This cocky mixture of fairy-tale romance and real-world degradation reminds us of the childhood this "toilet hustler" has been robbed of; its riches-to-rags reversal of a fairy tale, in fact, implies a longing for childhood in one too steeped in a sordid world to hold out much hope of regaining it. More: his search for his mother suggests a specific fantasy that the teenager may be holding close to him. Might he not dream of rescuing *her* from whatever brutal fate his sudden departure from home may have provoked? When asked for her name, the boy restores her to a pedestal by replying, "Greta Garbo." His ambivalence regarding her is simple to fathom but very painful to take in; he wants to protect his mother, but he also wants *her* to have protected *him* and to continue to do so—a crisis of confusion as to whether he is, or should be, a grownup or a child. This is heartrending stuff.

The adolescent's fierce independence, though, kicks in to curb his pretense at being someone other than who he is. When he shifts tone to declare,

I'm telling you the truth. *No kidding:* My name is Sébastien Blanche,

there is no doubt he is being truthful. However, it isn't the truth that Druot is desirous of. When Sébastien asks what will happen to him now, Druot, instead of offering help to find the boy's mother, presents three choices: being returned to his miserable, ugly life, being sent to reform school, or, if only he "admits" to being Olivier Druot, being sent home to an environment whose protective warmth and happiness Druot greatly exaggerates. In effect, Sébastien's "choice" is made *for him*. Also, he "confesses" to being Sébastien because he aches to please, which he likely associates with not being hit or hurt. Later, he confesses (again) to being Sébastien; this comes after he exposes Marcel as a child molester, in order to protect a boy littler than himself, and offers a solution to the real Olivier's disappearance. "Why did you pretend?" Druot asks. Sébastien replies: "It's what you wanted. It suited everyone. To make you happy."

By "becoming" Olivier, Sébastien makes Elizabeth happiest of all. But when she takes him "home" by train the scene is fraught with a sense of the emotional danger he is being drawn into. Elizabeth rushes into their compartment with enough sandwiches for a family picnic, all for "Olivier"—feeding as a form of consuming. Already the boy is asleep by the window, utterly passive, vulnerable. Elizabeth cannot resist; she sits beside him. Fearing forgiveness isn't possible, she pleads, "You'll forgive me?" (Later, she explains, "It isn't blackmail—but if you disappear again, I won't be able to survive it.") She starts to caress the boy's cheek. His nervous system revulses; asleep still, he throws up his hand at her. Holland sharply cuts to the landscape fleeing, as if in terror, past the train window. Sébastien's fate seems sealed. He will not be permitted *not* to be "Olivier."

The one Duval who doesn't believe him, who isn't willing to pretend that he is Olivier, is Nadine. Since her brother's disappearance and her father's departure, she has had her mother all to herself. Even if correct, then, her skepticism about "Olivier" is as self-serving as everyone else's *acceptance* of him. Her waking dream-world is disintegrating, revealing the extent to which she also has been crippled by "family." To be sure, Nadine is unusual (as a scene showing her, in bed, stroking her pet lizard drives home), but she isn't "her own person" as much as she thinks she is, for she has been shaped by her mother's obsessive attachment to Olivier. This is why, although she dearly loved her brother, she bullied him and wished him, literally, out of a family picture in the first place. Now Nadine unreasonably expects Elizabeth to decline to have sex with her husband for the sake of some unspoken pact of sisterhood between mother and daughter. Like "Olivier," Nadine is caught up in a tangle of blurred family roles. Her making love with Sébastien adds to this—although, for us, this humanizes her. In the midst of his deception, it also exposes Sébastien's essential honesty. When Nadine (oddly) notes she hadn't expected such pleasure from sex with a man, Sébastien replies, "But I'm not a man—I'm a boy." It would seem that their having sex should keep Nadine fortified against accepting Sébastien as her brother; but the incestuous implication doesn't deter, or apparently even faze her. Now she believes Sébastien *is* Olivier. It is as if "incest" has moved her to openness to the possibility, perhaps as a rebuke to the whole idea of family. But the actual point of revelation waits for the next day. Through the window she sees "Olivier" merrily engaged in a "peeing contest" with Paul, the neighborhood child he will later rescue from Marcel's grip; this is what Olivier and Marcel used to do, and "Olivier" is singing the same song that they used to sing together. Nadine's initial hold-out lends credence to the idea that Olivier and "Olivier," if not one and the same, are somehow connected—this, the core of mystery contributing to the film's quality of elusiveness.

The film's final scene argues best for this mystical connection between the two boys. Immediately preceding it, the dead child's body is dug up in Marcel's basement. Only Olivier's wristwatch is shown, its face missing, suggesting a stoppage of time, to prepare us for a drift from reality to fantasy. Serge faints; Nadine spits in Druot's face; the screen goes black.

The final passage consists of six shots. The first is the longest. Night: Nadine stares out the window, presumably at Olivier, at play, in her mind's eye. The camera pans left, from Nadine's reflection to her person—the effect is that, somehow, we have passed through a looking-glass,—and proceeds to follow her as she turns to serve her father coffee. Grim, he says: "You got your truth. Is that what you wanted?" The camera dips to Elizabeth, seated, looking stark, spent, almost in shock; behind her, Nadine continues to walk screen-left across the room's length and then, with a turn, screen-left halfway across the room's width, in advance of "Olivier," whose parallel walking, in an adjacent room, we see through an archway. The camera proceeds left, passing a halted Nadine, to show "Olivier" entering through another archway and, before penetrating the room, smiling at Serge, from whose face, transformed, all care seems to have fallen away. Thus this single fluid, intricately choreographed camera movement creates an invisible thread connecting all the family members, including "Olivier" and, at the outset, by implication, the actual Olivier. We are about to reach a cut, concluding this extraordinary first shot.

Rather than fluid and extensive, the next shots are short, static. The cut beginning the second shot of the sequence occurs when "Olivier" sits down beside Elizabeth, who is, as she has been before, in a trance. (This reverses the shot, on the train, where Elizabeth sits beside the sleeping, dreaming "Olivier.") As Olivier had done as a child, and "Olivier" except for somehow "being" him could not have known, "Olivier" waves his hand in front of Elizabeth's face, saying, as another cut brings us a closeup of her face, "Back to Earth, Mom; I'm here." And, just like six years earlier, this snaps Elizabeth to. Like Serge's, her torment dissolves. Smiling, she turns to "Olivier" and says: "Olivier. You're here?" Cut three; shot four is a closeup of the boy's tearfully smiling face. Elizabeth continues: "You came back?" Cut four; shot five is a closeup of Elizabeth's reciprocally tearfully smiling face. One more cut delivers the final shot, mysterious, sad, haunting: through the window, amidst blowing rain, the vacant swing. "Olivier," the replacement, must forever remain an index of inconsolable loss.

This closing desolate shot sweeps away whatever might be mistaken for a happy family reconstitution. Rather, what has tragically occurred indoors, at least on one level, is the completed projection upon Sébastien of Olivier's identity. To be sure, Sébastien himself chose to return to the Duvals. However, he was really driven back by a combination of guilt, confusion and compassion. However we come to make them, though, our choices have psychological consequences. Tactfully, Holland declined to pursue these in her powerful *Europa Europa*, which passes over the mental and spiritual costs for Perel, not only of denying his Jewishness for survival's sake, but of masquerading as one of the killers committed to destroying Jewry. By contrast, *Olivier, Olivier* fully intimates the toll of its aftermath. For Sébastien, there is neither freedom nor redemption; there will be no Israel where he can start afresh. For this boy ends as a sacrifice to stabilizing the Duvals. His mystic connection to their son clears the pathway to the altar, where the boy Sébastien is as lost to himself as his actual mother is lost to him. All loss, Holland suggests, is permanent. The empty swing evokes Olivier's fate and, it turns out, Sébastien's.

Films of the 1990s

Holland has made an authentic film, one where each character, even Marcel, is probed and found to be behaviorally rich and complex. Holland is analytical; she has no interest whatsoever in providing a comic strip of victims and villains. She embraces the humanity of her characters in order to embrace her own humanity.

Holland directs actors wonderfully well. The acting in *Olivier, Olivier* is in fact perfect. Brigitte Rouan and François Cluzet as Elizabeth and Serge Duval, and Frédéric Quiring as Marcel, are all excellent. Three of the other cast members are, however, superb. Jean-François Stévenin, a director himself, is brilliant as Druot, who, unaware of his psychological kinship with Marcel, seems to be turning away from himself when, in disgust, he turns away from Marcel after the digging up of the dead child. Faye Gatteau, as the six-year-later Nadine, and Grégoire Colin, who plays Sébastien, are memorable, too. Of course, in the decade following his exquisitely sensitive performing in this film, Colin became one of the world's great actors (*Before the Rain, Fiesta, Nénette et Boni, The Dreamlife of Angels, Beau travail*). This adds an unexpected note of pleasure to Holland's film, for providing us outside France with our first long look at Colin's amazing talent, and his chiseled face and haunted eyes. Sébastien's eyes.

The list:

1990

THE WALL (Germany). The final days of the Berlin Wall dividing East and West Berlin, East and West Germany: this is the subject matter of a tremendous work, perhaps the last important East German film, by painter-filmmaker Jürgen Böttcher.

Die Mauer is without commentary, music, "talking heads." It is pure cinema. It opens with a series of panning shots of dismantled pieces of the wall, their graffiti broken up. A skyward pan discloses a flock of birds; the camera descends to the wall—solid, but in the process of being deconstructed and memorialized by cameras. Pans to the right, pans to the left: the eerily deserted Postdamer Platz subway station encapsulates the moment of transition: everyone, except two subway workers, is aboveground, witnessing history.

Celebratory fireworks light up the sky, echoing the time when Allied bombs rained upon Germany.

Intermittently presented, the film's most haunted/haunting material also unfolds in the darkness of night. Black-and-white newsreels—Böttcher's film is in color—are projected onto a still standing portion of the wall. There is Emperor Wilhelm riding through the Brandenburg Gate; there are the Nazis again, in a torch-lit procession: the Wall has become a repository of German history leading up to it. People smiling in the street at the end of the war: Böttcher segues from this, startlingly, to the current, more youthful celebration.

Through a hole in the wall, people test the air on the other side. Into the next night, heavy equipment continues the job of creating an uncertain future.

The Wall is becoming part of the history the film projector projects onto it. The past possesses insufficient allure to contest the sensationalism of the moment, in this case, fueled by a media frenzy to which the young are highly susceptible—ironically, an echo of the Hitler phenomenon.

OPEN DOORS (Italy). Former documentarian Gianni Amelio's *Porte aperte* is cinema's most electrifying study of judicial process. In 1937 Italy, Tommaso Scalia, a former compliant Fascist accountant, murders within minutes the employer who fired him and the man who replaced him as a result of pervasive corruption for which he was scapegoated, and then rapes and murders his nagging wife, whom he had forced into prostitution to pick up some of the slack of their vanished income. The death penalty is almost certain for this "Beast of Palermo," except that one of the three judges presiding in the case, Vito Di Francesco (Gian Maria Volontè, brilliant, at times manically so), who is opposed to capital punishment on the grounds it politically serves State interests, turns the trial into a probing investigation of the defendant and the complicated context of his actions in hopes of unearthing a mitigating circumstance that might justify a sentence of life imprisonment. It's a tough patch to hoe. Even Scalia desires a prompt dispatch.

Based on a novel by Leonardo Sciascia, the script by Amelio, Vincenzo Cerami and Alessandro Sermoneta, among the dozen or so finest scripts ever produced, encompasses vibrant exchanges among the judges, between Di Francesco and the enraged widow of one of the victims, between Di Francesco and the young boy whom Scalia's execution would orphan, between judges and jurors. No film better demonstrates how human personalities, grounded in both common and widely differing individual experience, weigh in on legal process. Without resorting to the theatrics of rhetorical statement, Amelio has made a witheringly anti-fascist film, its visual aspect keyed to its profound humanism and analytical bent.

If I had to choose one film, had he lived so long, that Roberto Rossellini would have embraced as beautiful kin to his own work, this would be it.

WILD AT HEART (U.S.). "Seems we broke down somewhere on the yellow brick road."

Among cinema's most passionate romances, David Lynch's southern "road picture" *Wild at Heart* (Palme d'Or, Cannes) tests a number of assumptions and activities, their interactivity and mutual compatibility, in the American landscape: individualism, personal freedom, social compassion, violence and other antisocial behavior (including ultra-liberated sex), medieval European chivalry, the baggage of violation and haunted memory, popular culture as represented, for example, by Elvis Presley and *The Wizard of Oz* (Victor Fleming, King Vidor, 1939). Lynch thus adapted the first of the Sailor-Lula novels by Barry Gifford, who would co-write with Lynch *Lost Highway* (1997). Despite an unhelpful inserted bit here and there, *Wild at Heart* is Lynch's first masterpiece.

The tenderness of the young lovers (Nicolas Cage, Laura Dern—he is okay; she, electric) gives Lynch's film its beautiful ache, while the interference of Lula's murderous mom (played brilliantly by Dern's mother, Diane Ladd), Marietta Fortune, who fears Sailor Ripley's knowledge of her role in Lula's father's fiery dispatch and who, in some twisted way, loves Sailor as much as despises him, turns the young couple's dreamy partnership into a horror stamped with her own witchly image. Something else intrudes, turning nighttime to nightmare: a horrific road accident. Here, Sailor and Lula witness the death of a girl, awakening their caution and compassion. Lynch's film embraces the agony of life and death, including the memory of an abortion that Mom forced upon Lula, which impacts Lula's current pregnancy.

This wonderful film, which includes irreplaceable performances by Harry Dean Stanton and, underneath an ill-fitting wig, Isabella Rossellini as Johnnie Farragut and Perdita Durango, treats hot-button issues in purely human, humane terms and wallops the heart with an ending that always moves me to pure joy.

DREAMS (U.S., Japan). *Yume*, by Akira Kurosawa and Ishirô Honda, may be the most gorgeous film in creation. Laying out a panorama of concerns pertaining to responsibility, war, the environment, art's irreplaceable value, its segments are best understood as waking dreams, poetic visions. One protagonist proceeds across them from early boyhood to adulthood.

In one segment, spirits of a felled peach tree orchard appear to the boy, who shares their sorrow at this assault on Nature. Magical: the stationary spirits come into motion in slow, stylized dance to show their appreciation. To the boy's poetic eye, the dance culminates in the orchard's full restoration; but when he rushes up the hill, again there are only stumps—except for a single branch of blossoms: *hope*. A freeze frame captures the budding environmentalist's troubled look. Two segments address war, while two more enjoin the antiwar and environmental themes by summoning holocaustic visions of nuclear radiation.

One of the war segments is brilliant. Learning that his entire platoon, except for him, was wiped out, a soldier confronts his comrades, explains their fate, and orders them to march through a dark tunnel to the Land of the Dead. When he attempts to leave, he, too, is confronted—by a dog, with grenades strapped around its radioactive torso, eyes like burning coals, barks aggressive, ferocious: the Beast of War.

The last segment is sublime. Chishu Ryu beautifully plays the Old Man of the Village of the Watermills, who lives in harmony with Nature. There is a ritualistic funeral march, in which all the villagers participate, led by the Old Man, that exemplifies acceptance of death as part of the life cycle. With stunning clarity, *Yume* suggests that war—competitiveness *in extremis*—is grounded in the quarrel that too many of us have with Nature and with death.

LETTERS FROM ALOU (Spain). Looking for more bountiful economic opportunity than Senegal, his African homeland, can provide, Alou (Mulie Jarju, marvelous) becomes an illegal immigrant in Barcelona. There, Alou connects with fellow illegals, variously interacts with the natives—this includes his romance with a Spaniard—, finds work, finds other work, tries to legalize his status, mourns (uninhibitedly) the death of a roommate, eludes the police, all in an unhurried narrative that finds him, rather than sullen, both disappointed and perplexed by the racial hostility he encounters. Eventually Alou is caught and sent home; but the end of the film finds him, undaunted, on his way back to Spain. He has grown used to white people, he explains; and he isn't about to leave behind the woman he loves.

Las cartas de Alou is without rancor or self-pity; its tone instead resonates with Alou's youthful "Let's-see-how-we-can-negotiate-this" attitude, a disposition of adaptability aiming at assimilation—finding a way to "belong" on foreign shores. Except elliptically, Montxo Armendáriz's film doesn't assault intolerance; it isn't a smug, one-dimensional, self-righteous diatribe. Rather, in an engaged and engaging way the film observes Alou's engagement of racial intolerance and other hardships with which life challenges him and his compatriots. Alou is in Spain as a matter of choice; he is committed to the experience, including all its turns, that this choice has brought on him.

The film's naturalistic acting helps Armendáriz reach a captivating middle ground between fiction and pseudo-documentary—a region of expression that neither overcontrives content nor forces upon it a rigid shape, but nevertheless meets the formal requisites of art. At times evoking the dark, rich though subdued colors of Goya, but without enforcing on the frames a sluggish, painterly selfconsciousness, the film's visual aspect (enriched by Alfred F. Mayo's beauteous color cinematography) is incomparable.

TWILIGHT (Hungary). A dynamic remake of the Swiss *Es geschah am hellichten Tag* (*It Happened in Broad Daylight*, Ladislao Vajda, 1958), based on Friedrich Dürrenmatt's novel *Das Versprechen*, the Hungarian *Szürkület* opens with a long, continuous shot scaling upwards a dark expanse of the Black Forest until forlorn light is encountered above mountains. A serial killer, on the loose, seduces young girls with chocolates shaped like hedgehogs. Like much else in the film—nearly everything, in fact—the gorgeous opening is ambiguous. Is the light to which the camera comes with agonizing slowness the clarity for which the police investigators strive: the identity of the killer? Or is it a projection of the killer's own tortured mind, struggling to reach in its isolation a calming quiet? Justifying the ambiguity, *both* possibilities apply. Throughout, György Fehér's brilliant, fluid filmmaking identifies each side with the other. Ultimately both cops and killer pose equal danger to a village girl.

The slow, deliberate camera movements, the deep shadows into which Fehér sets principal faces, the indeterminate content of certain frames, the gradual slippage into point-of-view shots (in an amazing one, we end up seeing through the killer's eyes), the not-quite-point-of-view shots, where we see (in the same frame) people looking at something and the something they see: these and other elements create a dreadful, elusive vision. Mournful choral music that accompanies repeated shots of soft light above mountains contributes to a lament for the child victims, including the yet living ones whose innocence has been intruded upon.

A caustic example of *mise-en-scène:* after a misguided interrogation drives a suspect to leap to his death, the investigators talk over the corpse about what to do next, one stepping over it, the corpse's twisted, broken hand in the foreground silently commenting on their cold-bloodedness.

THE MATCH FACTORY GIRL (Finland). The conclusion of Finnish writer-director-editor Aki Kaurismäki's "proletarian trilogy," *Tulitikkutehtaan tyttö* opens with a brilliantly edited passage recording working-class dehumanization. Various machines, each alienatingly noisy, are shown operating at a match stick factory; not a single worker is visible. (Sounds throughout the film are preternaturally loud.) Finally we see Iris (Kati Outinen, wonderful), alone, performing quality control on an assembly line conveying boxed matches. When she leaves, no conversation passes between her and the one co-worker we see. Home, Iris cooks for Mother and Stepfather; no words pass among them. The human voice we finally hear belongs to a television news anchor noting the Tiananmen Square massacre. A man sings a rather hopeless love song at a dance, where Iris, unpicked, remains alone on a bench. She sleeps alone. "A small beer": before silently reading magazines, including at a laundromat, Iris makes this modest purchase.

Kaurismäki's suspenseful, bleak, concise, very funny comedy finds Iris turning over the remainder of her paycheck to her parents after buying herself a red dress and black shawl. Her stepfather slaps her resoundingly across the face; her mother instructs her to return the dress. She looks adorable in the outfit at a nightclub, though, where a man, Aarne, mistaking her for a prostitute (despite her restrained makeup, unassuming demeanor), silently dances with her before taking her home. He leaves money; she leaves Aarne a note, signing it "Iris." We now know her name.

Iris writes Aarne, who is white collar, a long, warm letter informing him she is pregnant; he sends a check along with the note, "Get rid of it." Accidentally she does—when (offscreen) she is hit by a screeching car. At hospital, Stepfather evicts her. Iris buys rat poison, exacts revenge all around.

Essential.

NOUVELLE VAGUE (Switzerland, France). *But I wanted this to be a narrative. I still do. Nothing from outside to distract memory.*

The futuristic voiceover of Jean-Luc Godard's *Vertigo*-film *New Wave* confounds; its statement opposing interruption is itself an interruption. Roger Lennox's hard-luck life is interrupted by an automobile heedlessly driven by Elena, a rich businesswoman. "Are you in pain?" she asks. A hand of each reaches through spacious sky (and time?) to touch the other. Elena might as well ask, "Are you in the moment or memory? Alive or dead?" She as easily could be asking herself these questions.

Characters walk back and forth. In this film, people pace that way outdoors. Indoors, the camera itself tracks back and forth between different sets of characters, the conversation of one set superimposed on the image of another, and the voices of different sets interrupted—or united?—by voiceover. Roger challenges Elena (who has taken him in and become his lover) with the reality of other people, including his, that her self-absorption keeps her from believing in. "Is my brother real?" has replaced "Am I my brother's keeper?" as a central moral question.

In a way we *also* wonder, given Roger's restrained voice and philosophical detachment.

Did Roger actually die as a result of the road accident? (Elena confesses, to him, "remorse.") Eventually Roger is goaded into mountain water by Elena, who knows he cannot swim and watches him drown. Whose consciousness this water?: his; Elena's; ours; Godard's; Roger's brother Richard's? Richard, his brother's identical twin, proves the more aggressive, volatile. He takes over the business. Inserted shots of the Swiss drowning lake haunt the film, which includes another outstretched hand, another drowning.

Or does it? Resurrection? Second chance?

We do not "live life." We navigate its competing claims. Or drown.

SONG OF THE EXILE (Hong Kong, Taiwan). "Life at every point might have been different. Isn't life strange?" — Aiko

Written by Wu Nien-jen, Ann Hui's autobiographical *Ke tu qiu hen* folds the relationship between a Chinese-born daughter, who has just returned to Hong Kong from the UK, and her Japanese-born mother into both Chinese history, including the Sino-Japanese War and Communism, and prospects for China's future. Hueyin (Maggie Cheung)—in effect, Ann Hui—also pieces together her own identity by revisiting her childhood and accompanying Aiko/Kwei Tzu, her recently widowed mother, to Japan for a visit. Their conflicted relationship yields to reconciliation, and Hueyin's integration, as Aiko opens up to her 25-year-old daughter and Hueyin, lost in a strange country where she does not even understand the language, finds her own experience touching on her mother's years earlier in Macao and Hong Kong. The film is light-sensitive and exquisite, and haunted by the passage of time. Its point of departure is more than fifteen years in the past, and from there it flashes back, in snatches of time rather than in sustained recollections that would establish their own quasi-present. Memories circulate inside memories, piercing the present while clarifying emotional states, family quarrels, a depth of family love. There is a bravura withdrawal of the camera from a glimpsed moment of the past that perfectly expresses the passage of time and our inability to hold onto such scenes; the counter-pull of the present will not allow it.

The film's two intimately connected personal odysseys are also mutually connected to *one* of the most beautiful love stories in all of cinema: that of Hueyin's parents. This alone is worth any price of admission. Given the war and xenophobia, Aiko's in-laws weren't loving.

Life gives—and takes away everything.

SINK OR SWIM (U.S.). Paul Friedrich, anthropologist, poet, linguist, university professor, regarded daughter Su as a substitute for his adored sister, for whose childhood death he has (unnecessarily) blamed himself. We may infer from his cold withdrawal from this daughter's life, especially after he leaves and divorces Su's mother, disappointed expectations. In becoming herself, Su increasingly departed from the identity that her father had imposed on her.

The title of Su Friedrich's *Sink or Swim*, a companion-piece to her film about her relationship with her mother, *The Ties That Bind* (1985), refers to the serendipitous mystery of conception addressed by the film's first three chapters, "Zyglote," "Y-chromosome" and "X-chromosome." (The first letter of chapter titles reverses the alphabet, Z to A; the film ends with a recitation of the "ABC"-song accompanying a doubled, hence destabilized, image of Su as a child.) Also, "sink or swim" summarizes the attitude informing both how Paul taught his daughter to swim and his parenting generally. Friedrich's black-and-white film includes snippets of home movies, scientific films, TV shows, newly shot reconstructive material, etc. The haunting silence of the opening movement is pierced by the voiceover of a young girl representing Friedrich as a child.

Paul, competitive, taught Su chess. He never played again with her following the first time she won.

The clanking of typewriter keys trails off into silence as we watch (in stark photographic negative) "Su" type a letter explaining the family hardship post-abandonment: "P.S. I wish I

could mail you this letter."
Father and daughter travel together to Mexico, but Paul sends Su back home, alone, as punishment. Su: her tears were not those "of an orphaned child but those of a frustrated teenage girl who had to pay for a crime she didn't commit."
Delicate, profoundly moving coming-of-age documentary.

TILAÏ (Burkina Faso, Switzerland, UK, France, Germany). Set in the pre-colonial past, Idrissa Ouédraogo's *The Law* attributes a harsh injunction to an authoritarian/patriarchal bias and the need for social order.

Saga is returning home after a long voyage away, planning on marrying Nogma. Before he can enter the village, Kougri informs him that Nogma has married their father in his absence. It was a "forced" marriage. Nomenaba desires Saga's acceptance of Nogma as stepmother. Defiantly, Saga remains at the village outskirts, where the pair consummate their adultery and incest. It falls to Kougri to kill his brother. "I'm sorry," he says to Nogma before informing her that her disgraced father has hanged himself. "You bitch! You made me a widow," her mother shouts at her daughter at her husband's burial. "I never want to see you again!" Meanwhile, his life spared by Kougri, Saga is again a wanderer—as is Nogma, in search of him and pregnant, after she learns the truth. A troubled conscience afflicts Kougri, who selfishly followed his heart rather than honoring tradition. News of his mother's illness splits the reunited couple. Upon Saga's reappearance, Nomenaba exiles Kougri, who, before leaving, finally kills his brother.

If Ouédraogo's film is Wagnerian in its observation of the role of sex in familial and communal discord, its intimacy and minimalist style are otherwise. The opening identifies Saga as a solitudinous figure, a solitary moving slowly by mule across a barren landscape, in order to suggest Nogma's contrary need for social existence that helps explain her acquiescence to a loveless marriage—in effect, a symbolic one to Saga at a generational remove. For Nomenaba, the marriage symbolically made him his own son, whose youthful existence he envies.

"The law"—both men's laws and "the way things are"—exiles all men from civilization.

SURE FIRE (U.S.). With David Lynch and Gus Van Sant, Jon Jost is one of the three great U.S. filmmakers currently working. *Passages* is my favorite 2006 film, and *Over Here* is at least my favorite 2007 U.S. film. (*Homecoming*, for which Over Here is a companion-piece, is my favorite 2004 U.S. film.) But Jost has been at his calling now for four decades and, prolific, *many* works of his shine.

Sure Fire shows us a family as it disintegrates—combusts, really—principally as a result of Wes (Tom Blair, riveting), husband and father, a Utah businessman whose gaping insecurity is masked by a complex of bullying, egotistical postures. Wes is the soul of American optimism, like Ronald Reagan, as he pursues his latest get-rich-quick scheme: the sale of retirement and vacation homes in Utah to wealthy Californians. But the desert surrounding Wes suggests the shifting sands beneath his unsteadying feet. The capitalistic rat-race is a hole in which Wes is in free fall. His marriage is cracking from the stress that he daily brings to it, and his teenaged son fatefully tells Wes that he plans to stay with his mother if she leaves Wes. On a hunting trip, a rite-of-passage for his son, Wes shoots the boy dead before committing suicide.

This stunning film, about two interlocking families, marshals an array of avant-garde techniques to convey the inner turmoils of its characters. (More than any other American filmmaker, Jost refutes the idea that interiority is off-limits to cinema.) Yet, Jost also brings documentary realism to *Sure Fire*. It's a visionary work that fashions a metaphor for American dismay and desolation out of what may seem initially an unhappy case far afield from our own (presumably) solid, secure lives.

Jost wrote, directed, cinematographed and edited.

THE FOOL (UK). Henry Philip Mayhew's journalistic four-volume *London Labour and the London Poor* compiles interviews of members of the lower class on downwards, of both genders, all ages.

Drawing upon Mayhew's tome, Christine Edzard's colorful *The Fool*, from her and Olivier Stockman's script, is an unsentimental satire of scandalous cross-classing by the clerk of a theatrical booking agency, who in effect has booked himself for a long-running gig in Victorian society, where his appeal principally lies in his presumed wealth and apparent financial wizardry. Sir John is lowly Mr. Frederick's lofty persona.

A posh after-theater party is contrasted with the backstage activities at the theater and interactions between the humble individuals there and other common folk. A blind man movingly speaks of his love for *Hamlet*, which he has committed to memory, noting with irresistible humility that blind people have a relatively easy job of memorizing voluminous material. Another poor soul savors a small piece of buttered bread. Ironically, Mr. Frederick/Sir John enters atop a descending platform stage—a visual lowering of the fraud into his more humble reality.

Alternating between passages of the high and the humble, the film, set in 1857 London, presents a vision of a fractured society. Especially in the "humble" passages, Edzard evokes a richly detailed Dickensian milieu.

Even some who are well-heeled perpetually worry about money. Such anxiety indeed helps account for the susceptibility of the rich to be deceived and bilked by frauds masquerading as peers or as financial wunderkinds. Greed certainly plays a part, but money-based society *engenders* such insecurity, prompting the haves to pursue the promise of windfalls.

Mr. Frederick/Sir John embodies "transactions" between high and low. His fraudulent impersonation, which risks his psychic disintegration, suggests the social danger for a nation —for a world—divided into haves and have-nots.

KORCZAK (Poland, Germany, UK). "An ancient Jewish myth ... has it that there must live on earth at one time thirty-six righteous people. Only the existence of these righteous ones justifies humanity's continuation in the eyes of the Lord ... [In our own time, one of these, Jewish physician and educator] Dr. Janusz Korczak, [head of the Jewish orphanage in Warsaw,] steadfastly rejected many offers to be saved from extermination in the death camps. He refused to desert in extremis the orphaned children to whose well-being he had devoted his life. As he said to those who beseeched him to save himself ... 'One does not leave children in a time like this.'" — Bruno Bettelheim

Written by Agnieszka Holland and directed by Andrzej Wajda, *Korczak* is sober, spare and very gray (it is a black-and-white film), and absent the bug-eyed theatrics and sentimentality of self-acknowledged admirer-in-chief Steven Spielberg's *Schindler's List* (1993). How does one find the courage to perish at Treblinka? One doesn't "find" it because one isn't looking for it. One is instead looking at other things—in this case, *people:* children, for whom the prospect of abandonment could only worsen the dire situation they faced. It isn't courage that Wajda's film has us contemplate; rather, it is decency, dedication, the love of children, humanity. How ironic; but for the monstrous historical context, Janusz Korczak might pass for an ordinary man.

Jewish or non-Jewish, many of us put little store in ancient myths. Yet I do believe that Korczak justified our continuation—in the eyes of God, if one chooses to put it that way. The beauty of Wajda's fictional film is that it demonstrates this justification. Inseparable from this accomplishment is the towering performance that Wojciech Pszoniak gives as Korczak—this, the same actor who brilliantly, and frighteningly, played Robbespierre in Wajda's *Danton* (1982).

1991

EUROPA (Denmark, Sweden, France, Germany, Switzerland). The conclusion of Lars von Trier's stunning "European trilogy" that began with *The Elements of Crime* (1984) and *Epidemic* (1988), *Europa* is like some ghastly prophetic warning that's couched in such elusive, ambiguous terms that you don't exactly know how to protect yourself. As Welles did in *The Trial* (1962), Trier captures, in a stream of highly suggestive, potent black-and-white (and, also, color) images, the helpless way many of us felt in our Century of Sorrows, the twentieth, which indeed may have predicted the twenty-first as its unearthly continuation.

Defeated in the war, 1945 Germany is occupied. Leopold Kessler, an American of German descent, relocates to Germany, where an uncle gets him a job as a sleeping car conductor on the Zentropa train line. Soon, Leo becomes the pawn of two competing sides, the Hartmanns, who own the line, and the occupying forces ferreting out former Nazis. Leo's neutral position becomes untenable once he falls in love with Katharina Hartmann (Barbara Sukowa, giving the decade's most brilliant performance—as she had done in the previous decade, as Margarethe von Trotta's Rosa Luxemburg). Post-war, then, eerily feels like pre-war and wartime, with Nazism still an able, if, now, creepily insinuating force. Max von Sydow's disembodied narration looms as a voice of doom: European history, which is repetitive, compulsive, tragic. The Holocaust, in particular, strikes Trier as a nightmare there is no coming out of.

One of Trier's darkest films, *Europa* (called *Zentropa* in the States) wraps one up in its grim, gorgeous images (Henning Bendtsen, Edward Kłosiński and Jean-Paul Meurisse are Trier's cinematographers), tightening the folds until one feels like a mummy. The glorious impish comic of *The Idiots* (1998), Trier's Dogme 95 masterpiece, isn't in evidence here. He shouldn't be.

GERMANY YEAR NINE ZERO (France, Germany). A sequel of sorts to his 1965 *Alphaville*, a futuristic rendering of Paris in the grip of fascism, Jean-Luc Godard's *Germany Year Nine Zero* takes its title from Rossellini's film about Berlin in World War II's aftermath (*Germany, Year Zero*, 1947). The film also looks ahead to Godard's masterpiece, *In Praise of Love* (2001), about habitual memory—the completion of this unofficial trilogy.

Back on Earth from Alphaville, Lemmy Caution (Eddie Constantine again) visits Germany. The occasion is the fall of the Berlin Wall. Godard surveys the past and worries about the future, both (geo)politically and cinematically, now that borders are blurring and transnational corporate interests are emerging as the decisive power in determining the course of people's lives and what art can be produced.

The film alternates between color and black and white. One black-and-white shot portrays a wasteland from which smoke seems to be rising—Time's exhalation. Another shot shows a discarded street sign on the ground: Karl Marx Street. The Wall's fall represents, Caution explains, Marx's triumph: "When an idea trickles down to the masses, it becomes a physical force." This irony collapses, though, amidst black-and-white inserts of Nazi Germany, including a massive pro-Hitler street demonstration. It is history—the connections between Germany's Nazi past, the postwar division of Germany and the Wall's construction—that may vanish from the tearing down of the Wall. Goethe: "Out of darkness you cannot create light."

Godard weighs the current world's Faustian bargains. At what price of historical memory come the dismantling of the Wall and Germany's reunification? At what price comes the worldwide tyranny of commercial cinema?

Blending fictional and documentary elements, this amazing film is stamped with haunted memory, the exquisite elegiac sense that has become an indefatigable part of Godard's signature as humanist artist.

RAISE THE RED LANTERN (China, Hong Kong, Taiwan). "Isn't it the fate of women to become concubines?" Songlian more tells than asks her mother, in 1920 China, when yielding to her mother's pressure to marry a rich man in order to alleviate their poverty. Thus the educated girl becomes Fourth Mistress to Chen Zuoqian, a Lear-aged lord who encourages competition among his wives suited to his choice each night of one over the others for his sexual pleasure. The symbol for this is the lit red lantern that is placed outside the separate home of the chosen one. From Su Tong's novel *Wives and Concubines*, *Da hong deng long gao gao gua* has remained Zhang Yimou's most outstanding film.

Two things distinguish Zhang's feminist howl. One is Gong Li's powerful performance as the rebellious Songlian, who descends into madness over her lack of autonomy. The other is the *mise-en-scène*. Shots of the courtyard banked by parallel buildings in the complex, as well as meticulously symmetrical interior shots, generate an increasing sense of claustrophobia and oppression. It is as though Songlian's mind and spirit have been consigned to a vise.

Curiously, while lighting and use of color are exquisitely restrained, there is a sense of psychological glare that helps define Songlian's disaffection. Her first night with Chen, she complains of the profusion of lit lanterns in her boudoir—this, celebratory of her arrival. But she will not be permitted to hide from her arduous circumstance under cover of nighttime darkness. Chen responds, "I like to keep things formal and bright." And that's that. In everything, Chen is the one who has the final say. Even the ceremonial foot massage that Songlian is given isn't for *her* pleasure. Chen explains to her, "When a woman's feet feel healthy, she is better able to serve her master."

CABEZA DE VACA (Mexico, Spain, U.S., UK). An outgrowth of his earlier ethnological documentaries, Nicolás Echevarría's most celebrated film is based on explorer Álvar Núñez Cabeza de Vaca's 1542 report to Charles V about a 600-man expedition to the New World—the mission was to claim Florida for Spain—that only four others survived. In particular, the film explores the relationship between Cabeza de Vaca and, once separated from his shipwrecked group, native tribes he encounters. But the film departs from what Cabeza de Vaca wrote to the King; Echevarría pursues instead a *what if?* approach to the historical material. Indeed, Cabeza de Vaca weighs aloud the prudence of telling the King lies, so unbelievable has been the course of his adventures, against a desire to tell the truth.

When indigenes take Cabeza de Vaca away, his comrades assume that he is headed for the roasting pot. Rather, as the fairest of the group, he would perhaps make the best slave. However, the tribe's shaman takes the white man under his wing, and the Spaniard proves his worth by restoring the sight of a blinded chieftain. When Cabeza de Vaca, thus allowed his freedom, departs, the eyes of Malacosa, the armless dwarf who had once derided him, well up in tears.

Cabeza de Vaca searches throughout America for his comrades. Eventually they reunite. The cannibalism that had seemed to be his destiny proved instead to be theirs, on the other end of the ladle. One of the group attributes his man-eating to "a Christian's hunger"—an indication of how easily the "civilized" rationalize their own barbaric behavior.

Echevarría's wild, hypnotic, at times deliriously magical film ends with one of cinema's most searing wide-angle shots: a gigantic Cross being carried across the landscape—colonial presumption, and the enslavement of indigenes and destruction of their cultures.

PROOF (Australia). In Jocelyn Moorhouse's comedy *Proof*, Martin has been blind since birth. Celia (Geneviève Picot, delicious), his housekeeper, in love with him, is mischievously obsessive because of Martin's rebuffs to her overtures. Now Celia is jealous of Andy (Russell Crowe, charming), Martin's new friend. What to do? To expose his unworthiness, she makes Andy her lover.

All three seek "proof" of something. Raised by his mother, Martin, mistrusting his mother's descriptions, began using a camera in childhood to record a verifiable reality. A blind photographer still, Martin now amasses symbolic "proof" that his mother was a liar who so didn't love him she even feigned her final illness and death in order to rid herself of him. His and Celia's relationship operates on reciprocal torment. By contrast, the basis of his friendship with Andy is trust, although there's scant evidence this drifter and dreamer merits such approbation; and the lonely intensity of their sudden friendship, especially after they're perilously mistaken for a homosexual couple, confounds Andy's simple feelings, urging quick confirmation—proof—he is what he is: heterosexual. Thus the boy is ripe for succumbing to Celia's scheme to seduce him. To expose Andy as untrustworthy surely isn't Celia's only motive for seducing him, however. Her continual battle with Martin has been losing and bruising. Celia needs confirmation—proof—she is what she is: a sparklingly attractive woman.

Moorhouse's film is spirited, fresh and very funny. It is also poignant, the result of Moorhouse's having structured her material to intrude gorgeously lit shafts of the past, involving mother and son, on a largely comical present. These flickers of childhood pain key us into a somber undertow, which deepens *Proof*'s humanity.

DANZÓN (Mexico). Julia Solórzano (María Rojo, radiant, heartachingly good), a single mother who works as a telephone operator in Mexico City, relaxes by dancing the highly formal *danzón* with Carmelo, an older gentleman whom she meets only on the dance floor. (The wide-rimmed white hat Carmelo always wears denotes his cheished privacy.) One night Carmelo doesn't show up, and Julia uncharacteristically takes time off to go to Veracruz in search of him. While not finding him there, Julia experiences what working-class persons, especially women, rarely, if ever, get to experience: liberty. This includes friendship with a cross-dresser, whom she teaches to dance, and a love affair with a hardworking boy.

Written by sisters Beatriz and María Novaro and directed by the latter, a former documentarian, *Danzón* opens with a closeup on Julia's and Carmelo's feet on the dance floor and ends quietly, jubilantly, with the pair dancing again. In between, the film follows Julia only, sparking their reunion with both wistfulness and a sense of new possibilities. How important Carmelo is to Julia doubtless reflects how important she also is to him. Novaro suggests how important all kinds of people are to us, both inside and outside of romance.

The film pairs Julia in heartfelt conversation with other women and girls, including co-workers and Julia's teenaged daughter, whom Julia helps adjust to her new job as operator while retaining a mother's worry. (In San Juan, a phone operator was raped at her worksite.) Novaro's delicious comedy owes something to Antonioni in its open sense of adventure and pays (in the tarot-reading scene) homage to Agnès Varda's *Cleo from 5 to 7* (1961). It expresses our need for both structure and liberty, showing how structure can liberate, and how liberty, so hard for so many to come by, can enrich our lives.

MY OWN PRIVATE IDAHO (U.S.). Gus Van Sant vividly observes the milieu: streets at once teeming and vacant; chop suey joints; rooms of sexual trade. Documentary interviews reveal what street kids daily have to deal with, and with what few defenses.

Mike, a narcoleptic street hustler (River Phoenix, to-the-bone), and Scott Favor (Keanu Reeves, showing from the start the something cold as ice at Scott's narrow core) try to find Mike's mother; but Mike remains motherless and even loses what "family" he has when Scott, his protector, abandons him. Earlier, he seemed conjured by an Idaho road "with a fucked-up face" from which flamboyant images return when he is back there at film's end: rushing time-lapsed skies; upstream-leaping fish—like the road, projections of Mike's aspiration, the soul behind the seizures. Form is ironic, for the initial sequence "pieces together" a glimpse of Mike's fragmented nature. The one "continuity" is Mike's *yearning* for integration.

In Italy, Scott turns Mike from the door in order to make love with the girl, Carmella, whom he will marry. The couple embrace, striking a stand, causing water in a basin to whirl, sway, touch the rim. The dynamic, erotic sensation cannot carry over and emotionally animate what follows: short, static shots—the actors holding poses—showing the naked couple variously intertwined. Mike's exclusion likewise suggests that his quest for wholeness is doomed.

In numerous ways, the film resists coming together, most strikingly because of the undigested intrusion of Shakespeare's Henry IV-Falstaff-Prince Harry fathers-son triangle. Although we may swallow whole Scott's rejection of the Falstaff figure, the accompanying rejection of Mike, shortly after Scott has told him, "You're my best friend," shatters coherence. For Van Sant, a smooth, worked-through wholeness would obscure, even deride, the fractured young lives he portrays in *My Own Private Idaho*.

THE CABINET OF DR. RAMIREZ (France, Germany, U.S., UK). David Lynch executive-produced for the BBC writer-director Peter Sellars' *The Cabinet of Dr. Ramirez*, a brilliant remake of Robert Wiene's silent horror classic *The Cabinet of Dr. Caligari* (1919). It, too, is a kind of silent film—at least insofar as there is neither any dialogue nor diegetic sound. There is abundant music, however (more about which later), although this also vanishes here and there to create perfect, and perfectly frightening, silence. Generically, the film exists betwixt parody and horror. Sometimes funny (or do we chuckle purely as a release?), it is also one of the most terrifying movies ever made.

Weird camera placements and angles, including low angles applied to tall city buildings, provide facsimiles of the Expressionistic distortions in the stark, black-and-white sets in Wiene's masterpiece. Sellars has made a color film, flat and underlit, but, within that visual framework, also gorgeous (the cinematography is by David Watkin: *Chariots of Fire*, 1981; *Out of Africa*, 1985, for which he won an Oscar). The whole thing plays as a dream that encompasses the "reality" of a sterile office environment. The new Cesare—Mikhail Baryshnikov: inspired casting—is no longer the *one* somnambulist; everyone in this version, to varying degrees, seems to be sleepwalking. Peter Gallagher, who is terrific, plays a character who sometimes seems to be desperately attempting to fight his way out of "the dream." His character, which the credits identify as "Matt," is the protagonist here—hence, likely, the dreamer.

Nearly all the superlatively used music in the film—pulsating here, slashing there, even gnawing at times—comes from John Coolidge Adams's 1985 orchestral composition, *Harmonielehre*. Its union with the imagery generates an intensity rarely matched in cinema.

Sellars' final movement overwhelms.

1992

DON QUIJOTE (Orson Welles, Spain, Italy, U.S., 1992). A "medieval dreamer in a sixteenth-century post-medieval world," Don Quijote confronts present with past. His head full of books and in the clouds, trying to right the world's wrongs, this noble knight is grounded by the humanity of his devoted squire, Sancho Panza. "I must follow my path despite all the world," he says. Orson Welles might have said the same about himself.

Welles began shooting his film of Cervantes' seventeenth-century novel in the mid-1950s. He died in 1985. In 1992 a version appeared in Spain, completed by horror filmmaker Jess Franco, who had assisted Welles on *Chimes at Midnight* (1966).

One of Welles's most massively moving, gorgeous works, the stark black-and-white *Quijote* begins in the style of a Soviet silent; low-hung, upwardly tilted cameras frame bony Quijote on horseback against eternal sky, here, of legend, myth, literature. Ironically, this repeated camera ploy has the effect of destabilizing the image of Quijote, wobbling it, as though only his horse could manage to keep a nearing-fifty Quijote upright. Quijote has endured, we are later told, obscurity, repression, tyranny—a reminder that Francisco Franco (until his death in 1975) ruled Spain.

The first time Quijote, on horseback, confronts his Dulcinea, the creature of his imagination upon whom he wishes to lavish his chivalry, she is a present-day woman riding a motorcycle! Thereafter, periodically the past and the present intermix, as do the Cervantes film and Welles's own stay in Spain while shooting it—a postmodernist delight, but again underscoring how out-of-place Quijote always was in time. Quijote concludes that humanity's choice to be enslaved by machines, not progress, is modernity's problem.

Missing is extraordinary footage wherein, watching his first movie in a theater, a battle epic, Quijote charges the screen, cutting it to shreds.

LIFE AND NOTHING MORE (Iran). In 1990, northern Iran experienced a devastating earthquake. The warm, humane comedy of Abbas Kiarostami's film precludes condescending rhetoric of noble suffering. His surrogate, an unnamed filmmaker, accompanied by his young son, Puya, tries driving to Koker; the main road is backed-up with traffic, and another road is impassable because of landslides. Their mission: to locate two young boys who appeared in the director's *Khane-ye Doust Kodjast?*, in which one fails to find the house of a school friend in a neighboring village. Will the director have more luck now? Did the Ahmadpour brothers survive? The director comes armed with a poster for the earlier film prominently featuring the starring Ahmadpour boy's face. En route, father and son learn that the earthquake razed every home in Koker.

Kiarostami is documenting his own attempt to find the boys. A camera strapped to the side of his surrogate's vehicle records the devastation. In addition, beautiful extreme long-shots of the vehicle's upward trek through mountainous terrain suggest the struggle of mortally aware humanity to push onward, to keep afloat—what Tennyson described as "ever climbing up the climbing wave."

A woman on the road relates she has lost home and family—eighteen persons. She declines a ride, as though too much mitigation of hardship would break faith with the dead. But elderly Mr. Ruhi, from *Khane-ye Doust Kodjast?*, gets in. He tells Puya that if the dead could return they would appreciate life more. He was made to look "older and uglier" for the 1987 film. "That's not art," he humorously opines. "If you make an old man young and handsome, *that's* art."

Puya is receiving an education of the heart. The film stops mid-journey.

Zendegi va digar hich: And life goes on . . . .

DREAM OF LIGHT (Spain). Portrait of a man at work: Victor Erice's *El sol del membrillo*, also known as *Quince Tree of the Sun*, is among only a handful of Spanish film masterpieces. At once dreamy and realistically particular, *Dream of Light* is a documentary hybrid, and even when its elastic nature expands to include scripted elements it captures life.

There is a lush, fruit-bedecked quince tree in Antonio López García's courtyard. García, a realist artist, plays himself. We watch him recommence his autumn ritual of painting the tree. The process begins with the preparation of the canvas indoors and the meticulous engineering, outdoors, involved in determining the painting's center, the direction of light, the staking of the painting stance. Whenever it seems that calculations might demystify the creative process, the subject of the painting, the tree, is there to remystify it.

Over time, we watch García paint his tree—and life goes on. His wife, who is a fellow artist, family members, including offspring, friends and neighbors, and even strangers such as a visiting Chinese artist: all sorts of people drift in to converse with García as he goes about his work. In time, the work and this other activity all become part of *one* thing, García's openness, his humanity, a rhythm of life. Eventually inclement weather intercedes, canceling the project before it can reach fruition. What is the point then? *Possibility*—and García still communes with his cherished tree. Shifting gears, he begins drawing it.

What a glorious film this is, radiant with life, finely realistic and yet punctuated with mysterious shots of the moon that suggest the infinite and eternal regions of imagination and inspiration. Assisted by rich color cinematography by Javier Aguirresarobe and Ángel Luis Fernández, Erice has created a moving meditation on the passage of time.

1992

A TALE OF WINTER (France). In Eric Rohmer's *Conte d'hiver*, Félicié (Charlotte Véry, most felicitous) makes passionate love with Charles, a cook, with whom she falls out of touch, having given him a wrong address, before he leaves the country. Five years later, Félicié is raising their daughter, Elise. In Paris, she has two lovers: Maxence, for whom she works, and Loic. By not choosing one of them over the other Félicié has preserved the memory of Charles's romantic preëminence. But now Félicié *must* choose. Maxence has decided to leave Paris for his home town. Leaving Loic behind, Félicié goes with Maxence. After experiencing a "lucid" moment in church, however, Félicié returns to Paris. One night she and Loic, now just a friend, attend a performance of *The Winter's Tale*, from which Félicié concludes that Hermione is brought back to life by faith. This in turn leads her to anticipate Charles's miraculous reappearance. Then one day, sitting opposite her and Elise on a bus . . . .

Félicié, note, does not even "own" her choice of Maxence over Loic; her decision to accompany Maxence is forced by his decision to leave Paris. (Indeed, Maxence's decision is partly motivated by his desire to force this decision.) This in turn makes easier Félicié's opting out of her "choice" by returning to Paris. The first in a series of romantic dodges, self-deceptions and equivocations, Félicié's "slip" of giving Charles a wrong address was also an unconscious way of giving herself a way out of a relationship in order to keep from becoming bound to an uncertain choice. Rohmer shows that Loic and Maxence are similarly rattled by responsibility in romance.

Like Shakespeare, Rohmer finds sexual love a grand—a *necessary*—subject. His *Winter's Tale* is a blissful descent into its ambiguous depths.

THE MEMORY OF WATER (Spain, Argentina). The disembodied voice is of a Russian man, Joseph Gruferman, during his last moments; images of trees, child and water are ancient memories of himself before his mother and he fled Stalinist Russia for France after his father's "disappearance" at the State's hands. Scenes of mother and son follow, but they are to be separated from one another, just as they have already been separated from husband and father, and homeland. "At what grave will I kneel, Mother," the voice asks, "if I don't know where you are?" Now an exhumed voice: that of Ivona Gruferman, Joseph's wife, who died thirty years earlier. She reads from journals she kept to redeem her "anonymous existence." She recalls her own separation from parents and sister—the time she spent in a Nazi death camp. The images accompanying her voiceover are images of death camps; the scene of one's liberation is populated by an indistinct procession of ghosts. Ivona did not understand what she was being punished for. She never saw her father, her mother or Lea again. Ivona is fearful "it" could all happen again, endangering Myriam, her and Joseph's daughter. Indeed, the springboard for this creative Spanish documentary is an event that occurred only two years into the past: in southern France, the desecration of Carpentras Jewish Cemetery—part of an outburst of like incidents in the 1990s throughout the world, including the United States.

Argentinean filmmaker Héctor Faver, working from his and Eugenia Kleber's script, patiently, poetically explores a plane of existence haunted by memory. Two other essential collaborators are black-and-white cinematographer Gerardo Gormezano and Lito Vitale, who composed the plaintive score. *La memoria del agua* may be the most lyrically sad movie ever. It is about two Holocaust survivors who came together and created hope.

GUELWAAR (Senegal, France, Germany). Barthelémy, now a French citizen, has returned to Senegal for his father's funeral. Pierre Henri Thioune, "Guelwaar" (meaning, Noble One), was a district leader whose especial cause was foreign aid, which he inveighed against for costing people dignity. Senegal won its independence from France in 1960, but assistance since then has kept Senegal dependent on the outside world. Yet Ousmane Sembène tweaks the political underpinnings of this psychological concern by showing how reliant on others

Guelwaar remains even in death. Someone's inability to read French(!) has resulted in Guelwaar's burial in a Muslim cemetery. Guelwaar was Catholic, as are those now mourning his suspicious death. It falls to Guelwaar's sons to get officials to unbury his father's corpse so it can be buried where it belongs.

But things happen slowly in Senegal. Part of the painful comedy of this glorious satire hinges on the pace at which things move. This pace suits the film's exquisite formality and rigor, as well as the delicate issues involved. The majority Muslim community must be convinced by officials and politicians, all variously motivated, of what's what. Even the imam initially believes that pesky Catholics are looking for an excuse to violate the Islamic cemetery's sacred ground. The Muslims insist that the right person, one of their own, is buried in the grave where they are being told Guelwaar is buried. They are poised to shed blood as a result.

"When a vulture attacks your enemy, that could have been you," the imam concludes, "so do something to get the vulture off him."

A truckload of charitable commodities is discarded. Catholics pass back their cross as they proceed to the truck; the cross thus recedes, releasing irony's undercutting. The mass activity we see is a tribute to Guelwaar, not a decision.

OLIVIER, OLIVIER (France). *See above.*

THESE HANDS (Tanzania). Dedicated to women everywhere struggling to survive in poverty, Flora M'mbugu-Schelling's documentary *These Hands* shows women from Mozambique in a sunbaked Tanzanian quarry relentlessly cracking rock into bits with stone hammers. With conversation among the laborers, but without voiceover or other commentary, that is to say, contextualization, the film thus proceeds until its last breath, at which point script appears to inform us that these refugees work for themselves. This is heartening insofar as they aren't being directly exploited, yet worrisome as well, for, given the harshness and monotony of their toil, it seems evident that they would be doing other things instead if a choice were available to them. These immigrants and pioneers are starting at the bottom—a familiar kind of place for those in an unfamiliar land.

The opening is extraordinary. A barefooted woman is sitting in a space of rock, hammering, both raw material and results in piling abundance between her separated legs: a complex image resonating with equal suggestions of barrenness and fecundity, stasis and productivity. Meanwhile, we hear a cacophony of the hammering, the sound of which continues as the camera follows another woman carrying a basket of stone chips on her head. A wide-angle shot shows an army of the refugees at work as the sound that their labor generates continues and continues. M'mbugu-Schelling's film condenses a single day's work, but it also conveys the impression that the activity is endless, that, for the moment at least, it defines these women's whole existence.

It does not. At one point, asserting her personality and her autonomy, one of the women stops working and breaks into dance, triggering a hand-clapping community of joy in the quarry. Spontaneity; humanity—and then, back to work. Not a regulated factory break, but *their own* break.

THE BLUE EYES OF YONTA (Guinea-Bissau, France, Portugal). Portuguese Guinea won independence, becoming Guinea-Bissau, in 1974. Vicente fought for it. In Bissau, the West African nation's capital, he struggles to keep solvent his fish-exporting business, both for himself and the local fishermen who supply him with their catch. Vultures circle in the sky. One day he looks up and sees himself as one of the vultures.

For Vicente's generation, disillusionment isn't hard to come by. The struggle for independence has passed into nostalgia; the dream of progress for everyone has failed to become reality. Electricity is a sometime thing in Bissau, threatening to rot Vicente's stored fish; people and their possessions are being evicted from longtime homes. Meanwhile, a wedding celebration shows the pluck of the younger generation, who may be, however, whistling in the dark.

A high school dropout who helps support her family, Yonta is oblivious to how she has had to adjust her own dreams in order to accommodate reality. Like Vicente, she keeps busy in order to nurture blindness; but the pathos of her vacancy as she sits alone by the sea, waiting for someone who will not show, sums up the wistfulness she suppresses. (She is too young yet to be able to name it.) Yonta's parents are old comrades of Vicente's, and Yonta is in love with her romantic notion of Vicente. In turn, Yonta has an unknown admirer who sends her love letters that wax poetically on the subject of her blue eyes. Yonta's eyes are brown. The boy's feelings are as idealized as once were Vicente's hopes for his country.

Flora Gomes's *Udjua azul di Yonta* is concentrated and easy, jubilant and heartbreaking. Gomes is of Vicente's generation. He finds that looking ahead casts an eye backward.

Blue is the color of sky, sea, dreams.

WE ARE GOING TO AMERICA (Russia). Drawing inspiration from stories by Sholom Aleichem, including "Boy Motl," and paintings by Marc Chagall, Efim Gribov's *My yedem v Ameriku* is a tapestry of present and past, hardship and hope, reality and reverie, humanity and ghosts. An impoverished Jewish family, along with neighbors, commit to a rough odyssey from their nineteenth-century Russian shtetl to America. Along the way they encounter a carnival of folks, trials, adventures. This is not an immigrant saga, focused on the group's arrival at their destination; it is all about the journey, what moves it ahead and holds it together. There are discussions. Two children address what a pogrom is. Two other characters, before breaking into song and dance, discuss when the Messiah will come. Part of this part of the journey is by train; part of it, by foot. The group is robbed twice. "All Jews are rich!" one of the assailants insists.

Heading the family is the widow of a cantor, who was killed. However, the film's protagonist is 11-year-old Motl, her younger son, to whose heightened perception its surrealism and sense of wonder are keyed. This boy, who seems to inhabit both material and spiritual worlds, is associated with equally gentle wild birds. We watch him feed one seeds from his lips; we later watch him let the bird (or another) go. The bird's *upward* translates into the boy's *onward*, and the moment achieves a poignancy both light and momentous.

The mostly sepia palette makes the film a continuous animated photograph—a richly populated memory. We bring to the film our own historical memory—of the pogroms, for instance. At the odyssey's outset, when the family begs its way onto the train, we brave the terrible irony.

We Are Going to America honors Jewish losses, Jewish survival.

HYENAS (Senegal). In German, Swiss playwright Friedrich Dürrenmatt's tragicomic *The Visit of the Old Woman* (*Der Besuch der alten Dame*, 1956) is a modern masterpiece. Its action, necessarily modified, has been transposed to a Senegalese village in Djibril Diop Mambéty's *Hyènes*. Colobane, dried up after a run of prosperity, represents Africa beseiged by poverty, drought, exploitation, communal and regional strife, lack of enterprise. When Linguère Ramatou (Ami Diakhate, brilliant), a former resident who is now filthy rich, visits, the townfolk are enticed to help her in her plan of revenge against shopkeeper Dramaan Drameh in exchange for the wealth and goodies, including refrigerators and television sets, that she dangles under their noses. When she was a girl, Dramaan jilted her.

Mambéty's darkly comical fable brandishes the mirror-imaging of a parched landscape and Linguère's parched soul. Colobanians are only too eager to allow their human folly to tumble out. Environment clarifies their conduct. In addition, the film's satirical edge administers appropriate cuts to Western materialism. The embittered, withered hag that Linguère has become should discourage anyone from following her; but it doesn't.

The opening shot sets the humorous tone: a closeup of an elephant's front feet moving at a lumbering pace. This image of African indolence yields to a wide-angle shot of the herd, with its suggestion of herd mentality. (School children being led in group recitation reinforces this impression.) A red monkey swaying to the beat of a village band's music—what an image!—rounds out a portrait of defeatism: everyone and everything fiddling, as it were, while Colobane burns.

It is fitting that enterprising, steadily contributing Dramaan should become the one that his neighbors rally against—neighbors, already quarrelsome, who need a target to give themselves some sense of purpose, unity and communal identity, however false that sense may be.

QUARTIER MOZART (Cameroon, France). Jean-Pierre Bekolo's dazzling *Quartier Mozart* is set betwixt farce and fable. In Yaounde's working-class district, various characters, both real and magical, interact. We begin with a schoolgirl called Queen of the 'Hood. "Which would you rather be?" she asks the local witch, "a man or a woman?" The sorceress responds, "A woman in the body of a man." To help Queen learn Mozart's gender politics, the witch zaps her into the husky body of Myguy, and, for a little impish humor, zaps herself into the form of a folk figure, Panka, who is able to divest men of their penises with a handshake. All this is fabulous; but underpinning the transformations are the indeterminate relations in a post-colonial society—a context that the name of the neighborhood, in addition to the French language that we listen to, underscores. (De Gaulle's likeness also pops up on a woman's tee-shirt.)

Mad Dog, the bull-headed, pot-bellied police chief, is an arresting figure. Tied to the ways of the tribal past, he wields power in the present, mimicking oppressive colonial rule while enforcing a continuity of male domination. He is laughably, although dangerously, irresponsible. Since taking a second wife, he fears his first wife, whom he wants nowhere near his bed but still around so that he can keep a watchful eye on her. (He has her tossed out, though, when the television set turns up missing.) How she has changed, he laments! It never occurs to Mad Dog that this "change" in her is his doing, a result of the second marriage that the local Catholic priest—like Mad Dog, wishing above all to retain authority—blesses. Meanwhile, Mad Dog has hired Panka to bolster his authority at home, and Queen, as Myguy, dates Saturday, Mad Dog's independent young daughter.

DEAR EMMA, SWEET BÖBE—SKETCHES, NUDES (Hungary). After *Confidence* (*Bizalom*, 1980), perhaps the best István Szabó film I have seen is *Édes Emma, drága Böbe—vázlatok, aktok*, a heartrending study of the chaos into which freedom following the collapse of the Soviet Union plunged Hungarians. The film, written by Szabó and Andrea Vészits, centers on two schoolteachers, who have moved themselves from the country to Budapest, and who switch the subject they teach from Russian to that "damn English," which they themselves struggle to learn. Emma (Dutch actress Johanna ter Steege, raw, powerful—and dubbed by Ildikó Bánsági) and Böbe share a bedroom in the "teachers' hotel" near the airport, where the disturbing sound of airplane engines tauntingly reminds both women of the freedom that at least some others seem privy to. Emma is having a nowhere-destined affair with their married headmaster, while Böbe gets sacked once she is arrested for prostituting herself with a long string of foreign men.

Emma and Böbe do not feel free despite evaporated Soviet bossiness and influence. Early on, by ambiguously overlapping one's invisibly uttered romantic words to a man with an image of both roommates, Szabó makes us feel for a heartbeat that the two women are lovers and, when we discover this is not the case, that perhaps they *ought* to be, or *want* to be, or do not consciously *know* they want to be. Whatever the political change of guard, freedom has limits. Ultimately, one woman ends up in a pool of blood while the other caresses her cheek.

Throughout the film, Lajos Koltai's rich, underlit color photography deepens the intimacy between the two while ironically dimming into uncertainty the prospects of countless Hungarians. There are two things to do: persevere; give up. Emma does one; Böbe, the other.

1993

D'EST (Belgium, France, Portugal). *See above.*

WHISPERING PAGES (Russia, Germany). *Tikhiye stranitsy*, which is called *Whispering Pages* in the U.S., translates more accurately as *Silent Pages*. Anticipating his *Russian Ark* (2002), Aleksandr Sokurov's beauteous film journeys into the cavernous Russian soul, this time by way of literature rather than history: primarily, Dostoievski's *Crime and Punishment*, scenes from which settle into the context of a peripatetic Raskolnikov (Aleksandr Cherednik, wonderful), weaving in and out of street crowds, boisterous and turbulent humanity, that appear from nowhere, a troubled dreamer slowly making his way at night through an impoverished, dilapidated part of a mid-nineteenth century city situated on lapping water that perpetually suggests the unconscious. The final encounter between him and Sonia, a Bergmanian two-shot in which the boy with fleeting poignancy smiles this one time, pierces.

With *Mother and Son* (1997), this may be Sokurov's most poetic, most humane and moving film. Slow pans and tracking shots create with their aura of deliberateness ironic tension with the boy's lostness and apparent aimlessness, his suspension in a place both in and out of time. The film flows imperceptibly back and forth between black and white and a trace of color, with at least two stunning bursts of Turneresque lighting—one of the visual methods that the film employs to suggest a hovering spiritual presence poised to redeem the boy if only he will notice it as we do. Sokurov creates such long takes, measured and fluent, here, static, more often in motion, that when a cut arrives the bewitched viewer isn't certain what has come and gone—whether there even *was* a cut. Watching this film, we also become a dreamer. Its silent pages whisper to us.

This is a moody, entrancing, melancholy piece of work attuned to sung bursts of Mahler and Raskolnikov's endless youth.

THE PUPPETMASTER (Taiwan). Taiwan was ceded to Japan in 1895 under the Manchu treaty; the end of World War II, fifty years later, brought liberation. Parallel to this, Li Tienlu is required to address his biological parents as "aunt" and "uncle," and to adopt his mother's name. He becomes a renowned puppeteer. In his eighties, the actual Li, on-screen and off-, narrates his life story, while Hou Hsiao-Hsien's *Xi meng ren sheng—In the Hand of a Puppet Master*—re-enacts episodes from Li's life. The title refers to both Li's profession and Taiwanese history under the Japanese, who appropriated Taiwanese puppetry for their own propagandistic purposes and who otherwise impressed their own culture on the Taiwanese, making puppets of them. It refers also to Hou, vis-à-vis us.

Sometimes Hou's history of Li doesn't match Li's own account. It is impossible to tell at these points which, if either version, is accurate. Memory falters; history is revisionism. Ironically, it is Hou's images—brilliantly color cinematographed by Lee Ping-bing—that create their own reality, while Li functions as "storyteller"—artist, that is, like a puppeteer. But Hou also is artist. Sharp and clear, his images sift reality, becoming shifting sands. Extreme long-shots, in which people appear as dots amidst vast landscapes or seascapes, further tweak the notion of absolute substantiality.

Hou's film, both majestic and intimate, expansive, humane, shows reality/human history resisting being pinned down in another way. Throughout, our comprehension of what occurs lags behind the film's sights and sounds; subsequent shots provide the basis for our understanding of what we have already witnessed, placing us in the position of historian as well as audience.

The exquisitely formal, decorated puppet shows exert great fascination—and some discomfort, as we gradually accept that we ourselves are puppets. Puppets of nations, puppets of war, puppets of Time.

THE BED YOU SLEEP IN (U.S.). Set in Oregon timber country, Jon Jost's *The Bed You Sleep In* studies a family within the context of regional economic downturn in the mid-1990s. The opening image, of a lumber mill's smokestack belching out smoke into the air, conveys both productivity and pollution. Logging cranes in operation, resembling gigantic metal insects, suggest both useful labor and something amiss.

Ray owns and operates the mill. In addition to a timber shortage wrought, in part, by stringent environmental laws, the mill must contend with the housing slump wrought by an overall ailing economy.

Ray and Jean's marriage is happy and affectionate. However, Jean is Ray's second wife, and their affair began while he was still married to his first wife. A lingering knowledge of Ray's capacity to lie convincingly is thus further compounded by Jean's own guilt for having contributed to this long-ago lie. Overcompensating, Jean has loved Tracy, Ray's child from his first marriage, as her own. Nevertheless, her repressed guilt has erupted periodically whenever she and Ray quarrel, as accusations against *him*.

Disaster awaits the two, triggered by freshman Tracy, whose women's support group at college has convinced her her father sexually abused her as a child. Memories are popping up in her head—not "memories" exactly, but "images," she writes Jean, explaining she doesn't know when, if ever, she will be able to return home.

Driven to believe Tracy to assuage her own guilt, Jean demands Ray tell her "the truth," which is impossible for him to establish, and which Jean is incapable of accepting because of its indeterminableness. The marriage unravels; each family member, between a rock and a hard place emotionally, commits suicide.

This film brilliantly charts the intersection of family and socioeconomic stress—a long problematic American history that's taking its toll.

THE BIRTH OF LOVE (France, Switzerland). *"Do you love me?"* This question involving friends Marcus and Paul encapsulates contemporary egotism and self-doubt. Marcus must ask this of his partner, who may have initiated their love affair but who is now exhausted by her lover's need for reassurance, which losing his job has only deepened. On the other hand, Paul receives the question from the mother of his teenaged son and infant daughter. He loves family for whatever reassurance it provides against the uncertainties of life; but her in particular? He is more emotionally giving in succession to two mistresses. At one point, their son relays his mother's question to his father, and we understand that the boy also wonders whether Papa loves him. Paul has returned home only to abandon his family again; "Papa! Papa!" the boy cries out into the street as Paul, suitcase in hand, once again leaves in the midst of his middle-age crisis.

Incisively written by the director and Marc Cholodenko, Philippe Garrel's *La naissance de l'amour* is a film about two men who are "wanderers" even when they stay relatively put. It is about life's loose-endedness, its incapacity to provide fulfillment for its artistically gifted members who aren't runaway successes. Paul acts; Marcus writes.

Assisted by Raoul Coutard's peerless black-and-white cinematography, *The Birth of Love* is Godard's *Alphaville* (1965) long since come back to Earth with heartbreak. It is domestic indoors, except in the bedroom, where it is achingly lonely and reaching-out; outdoors at night, as Paul and Marcus walk together, it is lyrical and endlessly dead-ended. Finally, the film takes to the road as Paul delivers Marcus to Rome.

Subtle use of handheld camera becomes a part of our eye.

Lou Castel gives a lived-in, career-capping performance as Paul; Jean-Pierre Léaud is a wonderful Marcus.

THE BLUE KITE (China). Beijing, China, 1953. Comrade Stalin's death postpones Lin Shaolong and Chen Juajan's marriage. Their son's voiceover notes the delay. Like David Copperfield, he refers to time even prior to his birth. At the ceremony, his future parents first pay respect to the wall portrait of Mao Zedong. Mao's image, actually, falls between them—the iconography of pervasive political power. A year later, the narrator is born. First he is called Lin Dayu—"Big Rain"—because of the weather that day; thereafter, Tietou—"Iron Head"—for the strength it indicates by way of compensation for that weather. This is normal stuff regarding parental names for children. But everything, including this, takes on a different meaning when symbolical power must be drawn to compensate for the everyday autonomy one isn't allowed. In this context, I differ with most commentators as to the (gorgeous) visual punctuation that Tian Zhuangzhuang, the filmmaker, provides with shots of the blue kite sailing in the open sky. Freedom and hope, others say. I say: compensation for the lack thereof, and implicit defeat and resignation. Of course, I and everyone else are both right.

This is a narrative film—hence, one that is highly reliant on Mao Xiao's script. This is a family and community saga, but one in which Tian's patient, incisive filmmaking counts most heavily. Politics determine everyone's life, including the lives of those who deny the importance of politics.

Nothing inherent in communism as political ideology helps explain the constraint under which ordinary people's lives are put. This isn't a negative film, only a particular, sharply observant one. The boy grows up and passes on the kite.

Critic Andrew Sarris has called *Lan feng zheng* "the most amazing act of political courage and defiance I have seen in the cinema."

Could be.

THE GREY WOLVES (Russia). Perhaps cinema's most brilliant political thriller, Igor Gostev's *Serye volki* depicts the ouster of Soviet Premier Nikita Sergeyevich Khrushchev (Khruschyov) in October 1964. Among the conspirators participating in the coup are Khrushchev's replacement, Leonid Brezhnev, and the head of the K.G.B., Vladimir Semichastny. Unlike most films of this kind, this one finely details the surreptitious process by which the coup was formulated and executed—and this is fascinating stuff. Khrushchev finds out about the plot against him and blames himself for relaxing his vigilance. Despite all his great liberalizations (deStalinization, the freeing of political prisoners, and so forth), it never occurred to him to dismantle the K.G.B.; or, to put it another way, he still found the terrorist state police *necessary*. Ironically, Khrushchev ended up their prisoner, living a secluded life of retirement under their watchful eye.

Khrushchev—Rolan Bykov caps his career with an amazing performance—is enormously complex: pure steel beneath a warm, folksy, humorous persona. One highlight occurs when he explodes over the fact that Sweden—Sweden, for gosh sake!—was a socialist country while more than 45 years after the Bolshevik Revolution the U.S.S.R. still wasn't. (At the time of the coup Khrushchev was rewriting the national constitution.) Another highlight: Khrushchev remarks to First Deputy Premier Mikoyan, "We're the last people to remember why this nation was created!" Khrushchev says repeatedly that he needs ten more years in office to accomplish his goals.

This terrifically suspenseful film, to whose script Khrushchev's son contributed, suggests a more intricate, more visually graceful instance of Constantinos Costa-Gavras's cinema. It also suggests Luchino Visconti's *The Damned* (1969), but with the body politic substituted for family. Gostev's zooms, though, are petite. It is as if Gostev were telling us, "Lean in and watch and listen."

BELLS FROM THE DEEP: FAITH AND SUPERSTITION IN RUSSIA (Germany, U.S.). Munich-born Werner Herzog has made brilliant, beautiful documentaries (*Fata Morgana*,

Chronology of World Cinema

1993

1969; *Land of Silence and Darkness*, 1971; *Herdsmen of the Sun*, 1988), incompetent, worthless ones (*Lessons of Darkness*, 1992; *The Wheel of Time*, 2003), and ones of intermediate quality. *Glocken aus der Tiefe—Glaube und Aberglaube in Rußland* belongs ringingly in the exalted first group. It is also, perhaps, his most insane film since the fictional *Heart of Glass* (1976), for which Herzog had his cast members hypnotized. It is, also also, insanely funny.

This poker-faced "documentary," accompanied by Herzog's own poker-voiced voiceover narration, opens with two men on all fours on a frozen-over river—presumably pilgrims in search of a lost holy city or otherwise involved in some prayerful ritual. In reality, they are a couple of drunks whom Herzog hired to crawl about on the ice. "Poker" Werner, justifying his method, has explained: "I think the scene explains the fate and soul of Russia more than anything else." (Could be.) The film includes the following: the Messiah, whose Second Coming has "quietly" arrived in Siberia, and who preaches against the superiority of any nation to any other (a notion with which Jesus-Werner likely agrees); a mass exorcism inside an auditorium; choral singing that is, in fact, profane rather than sacred; and all sorts of other bogus testimonies. I have long insisted that each and every film exists somewhere betwixt the poles of documentary and fiction, but this particular film tugs the line the hardest away from its documentary label and category.

Oh, did I forget to mention the born-again bellringer who used to be a movie projectionist?

In one gorgeous transition, the frozen river comes to life as Werner-as-camera subjectively moves into humble, peopled abodes.

SANKOFA (Ghana, Burkina Faso, Germany, UK, U.S.). Ethiopian-born, U.S.-based Haile Gerima's bewitching *Sankofa* begins with African drumbeats and chants as the camera curves around the bronze sculpture of a bare-breasted mother looking down at the child who is cleaving to her: Mother Africa and her offspring, who will be stolen, put in shackles, taken away. An invocation follows: *Lingering Spirit of the Dead, rise up and possess your Bird of Passage*. With cunning irony, the lamentable past of enslavement shall impress itself in this instance on a chic visitor wrapped up entirely in herself: Mona, an African-American fashion model in Cape Coast, Ghana (because once a major slave post, now sacred ground), on a shoot. *Sankofa*, in Akan, means "We must go back and reclaim our past, to know how we arrived at where we are, so we can move forward."

Gerima's film, then, resembles *A Christmas Carol*, where the "offender," instead of failing to heed the humanity of others (and losing his own in the process), has failed to embrace her heritage and therefore is stuck in an inhuman routine that passes for accomplishment. White Americans are loath to imagine the depth of anguish and deprivation that slavery wrought, reducing it to a mere past fact that black Americans should simply "get over"; but black Americans also have been loath to embrace the knowledge of this horrific experience, and their not doing so extends their victimization. *Sankofa* will remedy this in Mona's case by sending her back in time so that she, as Shola, can experience her own slavery on a southern plantation. (When she is captured, she screams: "Don't you recognize me? I'm Mona! I'm not a black African!") The majority of this film is with Shola—a letter away from Shoah—in hell.

THE MAN BY THE SHORE (France, Canada). Haitian-born Raoul Peck's *L'homme sur les quais* draws upon Peck's memories, as an eight-year-old, of a frightening, brutal place, dictator François ("Papa Doc") Duvalier's Haiti, where Peck's father was arrested twice and many others contesting the government were murdered. The better to emphasize childhood vulnerability, Peck has chosen an eight-year-old girl as his protagonist. Through Sarah, we take in an environment of daily political terror. Showing one of Duvalier's vicious Tontons Macoutes, Janvier, terrorizing Sarah, Peck declines to sensationalize the scene and thus brutalize the character himself. Peck grasps he cannot credibly show how regimes dehumanize ordinary people if he himself dehumanizes the characters who represent these people.

We watch Sarah hide a pistol on her person, knowing that her father has taught her how to use it. She and her older sister ride to the shore on their bicycles, luring Janvier to mess with them. When Janvier pulls her sister by the hair in order to rape her, Sarah retaliates, her armed hand in closeup. There is a click; no discharge. A second click; discharge. Janvier falls to the ground dead. The camera moves screen-left to record the stunned girls' escape; the camera now moves screen-right, revealing that someone else, Gracieux, the girls' godfather, whom Janvier earlier sexually brutalized with his thick stick, delivered the lethal shot. Gracieux, as gentle as Sarah and nearly as innocent, has been perverted into becoming a killer, as Sarah herself might have been. The passage is structured so that not a drop of glee rises in our hearts over Janvier's end. Implicitly punctuating the scene are the realizations that we bring to it: this death's human cost to the innocent; the fact that Duvalier will promptly replace Janvier with another of his soulless army of Tontons Macoutes.

LATCHO DROM (France). Written and directed by Tony Gatlif (born Michel Dahmani), a Frenchman of Romany and Algerian descent, *Latcho Drom* is one of the ten best musical films of all time. With visual grandeur, it traces the combinate journey of the people we familiarly call Gypsies, from Rajahstan (India) to Egypt, Turkey, Romania, Hungary, Slovakia, France and Spain. In each location, Gatlif stages scenes of performance—folk dance, song, instrumentals (including an utterly dazzling instance of dueling guitars)— employing local Gypsies. The resulting documentary is a truly epic musical.

The title means "safe journey." The irony turns on the discrepancy between the commemorative "journey" that Gatlif films and the real original circumstance. In the desert, a child is dying of thirst; suddenly the image explodes, water is plentiful and the trekkers are joyful. Now they are aboard an ocean liner, but in the same water are tiny, flimsy, imperiled boats.

The Romany people were doomed to their nomadic existence by white European hostility, which at one point is crystallized—in a film which elsewhere expresses great love for animals —by snarling, barking dogs. A passage of Kusturícan exuberance is followed by a tracking shot along barbed wire and somber singing about Auschwitz.

The glorious music takes center stage. It is as though Gypsy music burns off impurities, leaving the essence of Gypsy history, community, suffering, joy.

Adaptation, endurance, survival: "We Gypsies are like lost sheep," a ubiquitous boy sings. "No one will change our way of life."

A grown woman: "Why does your evil mouth spit on me? So what my skin is dark, my Gypsy hair black?"

Latcho Drom is undiluted by explanatory public television voiceover. Watching it, you see and hear in song and dance what you need to know to experience the film to the full.

BOATMAN (Italy). Shot on the Ganges River at Varanasi (formerly Benares) in northern India, a center of Hinduism, Sanskrit learning and Buddhist pilgrimage, the black-and-white *Boatman*, in Hindi and English, follows boatman Gopal Maji and takes in a plethora of sights both tranquil and troubling. Directed and photographed by Eritrean-born Gianfranco Rosi, this superlative film possesses current and enduring interest, addressing Hindi-Muslim tension.

But the film's two intertwined main themes lie elsewhere. One has to do with the contradictory nature of the Ganges: a polluted sacred river. The source of much of the pollution accounts for the other theme: the accumulation of the cremated and uncremated remains of the dead, which are routinely and ritualistically consigned to the river. All this occasions another consideration: who are permitted to employ the river for this purpose; who can afford to do this. Sometimes the financially destitute cannot mark a burial with the traditional funeral pyre.

Rosi, offscreen, asks questions of Maji and others, and all the responses become part of the fabric of the river as we watch. On land, by the river, Rosi immediately establishes the river's potent symbolism. He invests the camera with continuous motion through crowds of people, thereby conjuring the sense of a flowing river even before we are in Maji's rowboat on river. In this way, the river is associated with people's bustling lives. Once we leave land for the river, another association accumulates: the river as embodiment of the continuity of life and death. Indeed, few films more openly address death as a part of life.

Rosi's film is full of fine images—for instance, the parallel rows of huge shadow-casting drumlike thingamajigs between which Maji rows and halts his boat. It turns out these are anchors, and the image provides a powerful presentiment of death.

1994

SÁTÁNTANGÓ (Hungary, Germany, Switzerland). The doctor in Béla Tarr's 7¼-hour *Satan's Tango*, from László Krasznahorkai's novel, sits and observes the people in his rural Hungarian village, a prisoner of alcoholism, his fat body, the isolated community itself and, stumbling outdoors in pursuit of another bottle, of the drenching autumn rain that, in conjunction with the mud below, fills his soul and the souls of his likewise impoverished, desperately unhappy neighbors: entrapment from the inside out. A herd of cows has slowly made its way away; but the human characters are stuck. Progress is an illusion: steps forward, steps back—like the steps of a tango.

In that dance, a performance of which holds the black-and-white film's imaginative center, the couple's steps also occur simultaneously and even overlap; similarly, activities in Tarr's film are parallel and overlapping, like its 12 "chapters." Another such image is the dance by which spiders weave their entrapping webs. But not all animals have it better than the people here. A young girl, cheated out of money by her older brother and denied consolation from even her mother, a prostitute, murders her cat and, appalled by the loss of this one companion of hers, kills herself with the same poison.

Expectation, betrayal; canceled trust: such events keep cropping up. The promise of financial riches for the villagers empties. Formally, long, fluid takes are betrayed by an eventual cut, brusquely signaling a new shot. Tarr's narrative sometimes curves around, showing an event from another perspective—a compounding of subjectivity and complexity, but bereft of advancement: *another* illusion of progress.

Communism has yielded to capitalism: six steps forward, six steps back, for the hope proffered has been taken back, and the film ends poised on the verge of a possible commune —a step forward into the past. Gray lives; cosmic betrayal.

LAMERICA (Italy, France, Switzerland). Communist Albania has fallen. Two Italians arrive armed with a scheme to pretend setting up a shoe-making concern; the interests they represent will pocket the grant money. They recruit from detention Spiro (Carmelo Di Mazzarelli, poignant), a presumed Albanian, to chair the fake company; but when Spiro takes off right before he can be presented, young Gino (Enrico Lo Verso, tremendous), one of the con-artists, searches him out. In the process, the boy is immersed in the poverty and deprivation of ordinary Albanians; for the first time, his humanity is tested. It turns out that Spiro, an army deserter from World War II, is Sicilian, like Gino; the fraud of an Albanian identity was to keep the Communists from executing him when they took power from the Fascists, who had imprisoned him. When both are "fired" from their crooked jobs, Gino and Spiro try returning to Lamerica, that is to say, home. Arrayed against this attempt are the authorities who wish to keep Albanian refugees from entering Italy.

Amelio's *Open Doors* (1990) is cool, analytical, precise; Amelio's *Lamerica*, his masterpiece, though, is sweeping, volatile, passionate. No less political, however, it is cinema's most stinging indictment of the "new capitalism," for which the exploitative scheme is both an instance and a metaphor. The color film opens with black-and-white Fascist newsreels, circa 1939, boasting the end to Albanian poverty, which nevertheless continued unabated, with new "invaders" now poised to exploit Albanians afresh, promising jobs and livelihoods, but only to line their own well-stitched pockets. In a dire form, the beleaguered Albanians become emblematic of all pawns of capitalism. Italy, like the United States earlier in the century, sparkles with promise; but will refugees fare better there than in Albania?

The montage of human faces aboard the crowded ship: *heartrending*.

THROUGH THE OLIVE TREES (Iran, France). For *Where Is the Friend's House?* Abbas Kiarostami recruited locals from the rural northern Iranian village of Koker, among them, the Ahmadpour brothers. In *Life and Nothing More* (1992), an earthquake has razed Koker, prompting the director—Kiarostami's stand-in—to return to Koker to see if the boys are alive. The film ends without resolving the matter. In *Zire darakhatan zeyton*, a different actor is playing the director, who has returned to Koker to make—well, *Through the Olive Trees*. One of the most joyous moments in cinema occurs when whose faces should pop into the car window: the Ahmadpour brothers, on their way to school. This is handled offhandedly, but how momentous in terms of life and death.

The film opens with Kiarostami's surrogate conducting a casting call outdoors to find among the young female villagers the right girl to play a leading role in the new film. The one selected is named Tahereh; she will play the bride, Tahereh. The wedding is supposed to have occurred right after the earthquake. The first actor chosen, who stutters, proves impossible. A local bricklayer is the next boy chosen for the part; but Tahereh won't speak to him, because Hossein really has been proposing to her, and her parents won't give their consent. Faced with her obdurate silence, Hossein hopes to glean a sign from Tahereh that he has her heart despite his disqualifications: being poor and unschooled, however hardworking; having no home to provide for whomever he marries. The making of the film, then, is a comedy covering the tragedy of life—"covering," as in concealing, documenting, however "inadvertently," and building upon: this, a metaphor for Koker's year-after renewal in the wake of the quake.

Will there be a wedding? Will there be a film?

RICE PEOPLE (Cambodia, France, Switzerland, Germany). Rithy Panh's rhythmic *Neak sre* revolves around a family, Poeuv and Om (Peng Phan, phenomenal) and their seven daughters, and the Cambodian village community on the Mekong Delta to which they belong. These are "rice people"—people whose subsistent lives derive from planting, growing, harvesting rice.

Poeuv's death leaves Om and their eldest daughter, Sakha, hardest hit. Om, in fact, goes insane under the burden of having to provide for her family. Sakha takes her mother's place in the paddies while Om unsuccessfully undergoes treatment in an urban hospital. When Om returns, the magnitude of her concern for her children's survival means there can never be enough rice now. From her naturally poetic soul comes this utterance: "The sun has taken our rice field into its grave." She also says: "I worked and worked. I plowed with all my strength. I sowed. I replanted, I harvested. But it's all the same: I don't see anything. Where's my rice?"

There are sacks and sacks, but Sakha had to give some away to help repay the loan that paid for Om's hospital stay. Now she is mother to six sisters and her own mother.

Documentary realism is folded into the fiction. We see a family's reconfiguration after the double jolt of one parent's death and the other's mental illness; and we also see how the community tends to the stricken family that is a part of it. The closing long-shot shows Om running back and forth across her patch of land, perhaps shooing away sparrows. Now and again feeling useful is as much as she can hope for.

Panh, who dedicated the film to his own family, ends by quoting Rilke: "We dare not see through pain and distance . . . ."

We dare not do otherwise, either.

1994

EL JARDÍN DEL EDÉN (Mexico, Canada, France). On the Mexico-U.S. border, Tijuana is the principal setting for *The Garden of Eden*. Written by sister Beatriz and herself, María Novaro's masterpiece follows a range of lives there.

A corrugated steel fence spans the area, attempting to keep Mexicans out of the U.S. Baleen whales, though, migrate into Pacific Baja waters, causing a Mexican child to wonder at such unfettered liberty. Frank, who is obsessed with the graceful gray creatures, relocated there long ago. His sister, Jane, visits; a would-be writer, she hopes to delve into Mexico. Jane's friend Elizabeth is also there, trying to reconnect with her Mexican roots. Jane romances Felipe, an impoverished farmer making continual attempts to get to the U.S., "the other side." Felipe has befriended Julián, a teenaged shutterbug, whose mother, Serena, recently widowed, has come with her children to start afresh. Only Frank seems past hope.

Felipe returns from the other side beaten to a pulp by thugs policing the barrier. The sight of Felipe in bed takes Julián back to the scene of his father's death at hospital.

Felipe's friendly habit of referring to Julián as "brother" misleads Jane, who sneaks both of them across the border in the trunk of her car. (Language and cultural confusions between characters abound in this film.) When the boy turns up missing, Jane and Felipe search for him, wandering into a funeral. There, Jane infuriates Felipe by contributing money to the pot to help get the body back to Mexico for burial. Felipe: "We may be poor, but we don't need your charity!"

Novaro surveys the border with documentary attention both sweeping and minute. Her eye achieves great visual poetry, especially in long-shots.

"Garden of Eden" turns out to be less than Paradise. It's a motel on the other side.

JOAN THE MAID, PARTS I and II (France). "Give me some time," Jeanne asks so she can turn a seeming military defeat into a victory against the British in the Hundred Years' War. (She helps lift the Siege of Orléans.) Time is of the essence in Jacques Rivette's stunning two-part, four-hour *Jeanne la Pucelle*. Early fifteenth century; minimalist scenes. As Sandrine Bonnaire beautifully plays her, however, Jeanne could not be more modern if we are to go by demeanor. (Indeed, *postmodern:* Jeanne knows God's script; Bonnaire, the film script.) Rivette's Jeanne is out of her own time and in-the-moment—this, correlative to Rivette's procedure: uncluttering the past, hauling it forward, securing it in the present. We can envision only an invention of the past; for the moment, this keeps our own time from dissolving *into* the past.

Slow pans, slow tracking shots. In long-shot, Jeanne on horseback and others move screen-left, passing a leafy tree, the camera keeping apace. When the tree is about to pass out of the frame, a cut takes us into the woods. We may have been thinking: *Is the tree God? Jeanne's spirit?* The abrupt cut aborts this idle speculation.

The coronation ceremony of Charles VII, with its solemn pace, Latin, gorgeous Church costuming, culminates in the lowering onto the Dauphin's head of the "holy crown." But England's Henry VI likewise claims France's crown, and Charles betrays Jeanne; among major players, perhaps only God is taking her side. Rivette's film *assumes* the rehabilitation of Jeanne's reputation and the Enlightenment's debunking of the sixteenth-century codification of the Divine Right of Kings. Present *illuminates* past.

Incidentally, Rivette moves Jeanne's trial as a heretic to the out-of-doors. Incidentally, God's instruction to Jeanne mimics the instruction given the magical horse in Cocteau's *Beauty and the Beast* (1946)!

THE SILENCES OF THE PALACE (Tunisia, France). We were taught one rule: *Silence.*

The death of an ex-bey who may have been her father brings Alia to the palace where she grew up in the 1950s. Tunisian filmmaker Moufida Tlatli creates a masterful blend of Alia's own flashback and a more generalized and objective reclamation of the recent past touching on Alia's life. Intermittently returning to the present ten years later, the film's richly detailed, solemnly paced backward look focuses on young Alia and her mother, Khedija, one of the poor downstairs servants and a favorite, because of her beauty, in upstairs bedrooms. Eventually both Khedija and infant die in childbirth, orphaning Alia, who never learns her father's identity.

A Twainian coincidence of births, Alia's and the palace's legitimate daughter, who is her playmate, has given Alia a precarious existence in two worlds. Khedija (Amel Hedhili, superb) worries that her teenaged daughter, as she has been, will be impressed into sexual slavery. Tlatli portrays the supportive community of women downstairs, but something else exists above. When Khedija is serving dinner, she is rebuked—an index of female discontent: fallout from the interest that she generates in the princely men. Upstairs women dare not speak against their husbands, so they take everything out on Khedija—an arrangement the men, guilty cowards, tolerate. For women, it appears, *silence* is the rule both downstairs and up.

With withering irony all this occurs as nationalists beyond palace walls rattle the French colonial cage for independence. The bey, we are told, gets flak from both sides: from the French, for listening to nationalists; from nationalists, for ceding to the French. Someone observes, "There are no strong men in the palace anymore."

Samt el qusur views the oppression of women with profound melancholy. Tlatli is an Arab woman.

WOYZECK (Hungary). Based on Georg Büchner's great unfinished play, János Szász's film is dark, cold, fastidiously brilliant. Updated not so much to the present as to an abstraction of an industrial time that could be the present in some backward stretch of Eastern Europe, the play exists as a point of reference for the film. Woyzeck is, for instance, no longer in the army, or a barber, yet he shaves his boss and addresses him as "Captain."

In the railway yard where Woyzeck now works as low-wage janitor, the tracks do not appear to have anywhere to go. *Woyzeck* is a dead-end piece, at the end of the world, a film of bleak days and nights suggesting the dark night of Woyzeck's soul. Society is too apathetic and oblivious even to cast out Woyzeck, who, after all, has his uses. Monitoring his body's responses during hard-driving push-up sessions and endlessly analyzing samples of his urine, "The Doctor" makes of Woyzeck an encapsulation of dehumanized humanity. "The Captain" also is constantly at Woyzeck, interrupting his quiet work, summoning him for "reports," and lecturing him about his low morality. (Woyzeck lives with girlfriend Mari and their bastard infant son.) We see Woyzeck seething with resentment—a rare expression of feeling to which Szász applies slow motion, the better to anticipate the Captain's end many shaves hence. Pushed and pulled and constantly called "stupid," Woyzeck is a slave perpetually on the edge of revolt.

Woyzeck sees odd shapes in the billowing smoke from trains that suggests to us, in an overhead shot, the clouding over, the pollution, of Woyzeck's mind and sensibility—the consumption and extinction of possibility. Constantly reading his bible, Woyzeck talks to God, even hears him. "Go on, go on," God tells him, urging Woyzeck to kill again and again.

1995

BEYOND THE CLOUDS (Italy, France, Germany). Based on his short story collection *That Bowling Alley on the Tiber*, Michelangelo Antonioni's *Al di là delle nuvole*—with assists from Wim Wenders—is a spacious, summary work, a mystery of sorts, that gathers up moods and images, ghostly echoes, from the filmmaker's past. Its theme is the gap (wherein the human heart is most guarded and secretive) between desire and attainment, imagination and reality. What the enchanted eye takes in, the flesh can't hold; even as love overwhelms with powerful emotion, it shifts, confounds, remains elusive.

In the film's final episode, suddenly captivated by a girl he catches sight of (Irène Jacob, sublime), a boy pursues her for the balance of the day and into the night, only to be told by her that he cannot see her again because she is entering a convent that morning. He asks, "What if I fell in love with you?" She: "You would be lighting a candle in a room full of light." The boy's flaming moment of impossible love reflects the girl's love for Jesus; for, by intensifying her glow, this pure devotion of hers, with its effortless capacity to still the boy's exaggerated mortal anxiety, proves an irresistible force of attraction for him, although it is precisely, also, what makes her unsuitable for him. The boy has not been fooled or victimized, either by girl or cosmos; rather, he simply doesn't grasp—as so often we do not—the impetus behind his falling in love and, as a result, lights upon a partner who must abandon him. Piercingly, the "relationship," stillborn, ends before it has begun.

Always Antonioni urges on us and on himself a fuller view of things; and the fuller the view, the less knowable and more mysterious humanity and life itself show themselves to be.

GOOD MEN, GOOD WOMEN (Taiwan, Japan). Three time-lines span more than a half-century of Taiwanese history in Hou Hsiao-Hsien's *Hao nan hao nu*. Liang Ching is an actress playing Chiang Bi-yu in a film-within-the-film titled *Hao nan hao nu*. Chiang Bi-yu and her husband, Chung Hao-tung, and three others were among Taiwan's "good men, good women," who contributed to the mainland Resistance movement against Japanese invaders-occupiers. Ching, through the experience of playing the politically committed Bi-yu (Annie Shizuka Inoh, searing, plays both parts), gropes for a surer sense of herself and her nation's identity. The actual Bi-yu, hospitalized, also participates in the film, but offscreen, only through Ching, who sadly informs us of Bi-yu's death prior to the film's premiere.

Music or voiceover may slide from a bit of one time-line to a bit of another.

The film opens in the past. In long-shot the five idealistic young patriots move across a field to join the anti-Japanese cause. The image is monochromatic, like all the images in the film-within-the-film, whose camera remains invisible. The film ends with the same image, but in color, like the other present-day and relatively recent material. The past has been brought to the present that it helped shape. Static camera recording walking (and singing) souls who at the last pass out of the frame: stillness; transience; recollection; loss.

Ching is haunted by her past as a drug-addicted bar hostess, a gangster's mistress, his death—a mirroring of Taiwan's tragic history.

Postwar, in the 1950s, Bi-yu and other reformers opposed to the continuation of feudalism were arrested; many, including her husband, were executed as Communists. If you have forgotten how evil Chiang Kai-shek was, or the role that the U.S. played in his reign of terror, this film will remind you.

Rigorous, complex, haunting.

UNDERGROUND (Federal Republic of Yugoslavia, France, Germany). Belgrade, 1941. Ivan, the young, simple zookeeper, tends to his animals. Luftwaffe bombs litter the ground with dead and wounded creatures. The animals, along with everyone else, are frantic. Ivan closes the eyes of a ripped-open chimpanzee and rescues Soni, another chimpanzee. (Soni will later blow up a wedding with heavy artillery, frightening himself, causing him to flee, causing Ivan to search for him for fifty years!) It is the German invasion; and, for animal lovers at least, Emir Kusturica, following Dušan Kovačević's story, has found a fresh, heartrending way to portray war's horror.

Bila jednom jedna zemlja—Serbo-Croatian for *Once Upon a Time There Was a Country*—covers regional history over more than five decades: Yugoslavia, to which Tito's iron-handed communism brought stability following the war; the dissolution of that federation, unleashing ethnic and religious conflicts; the Bosnian War.

In the main, Kusturica's sprawling, boisterous, rambunctious, intermittently surreal tragicomedy follows two black marketeers and romantic rivals, who begin by selling the arms they produce to the communists, but whose motive is profit, not politics. One is somewhat more humane than the other; but the participation of many other characters besides, some of them idiots, form a portrait of chaos, tumultuousness, and moral rudderlessness. It's the insane twentieth century, a world of contentiousness and cinema (there is a film-within-the-film about the two men, and a collision between the films that results in murder), one punctuated by celebratory get-togethers, continuing on into heaven.

Some note a Serbian bias in Kusturica's view of history. He has explained: "My father was an atheist, and he always described himself as a Serb. . . . we were Muslim for 250 years, but we were Orthodox before that, and deep down we were always Serbs. Religion cannot change that. We . . . became Muslims [only] to survive the Turks."

ULYSSES' GAZE (Greece, France, Italy, Germany, UK, Federal Republic of Yugoslavia, Bosnia-Herzegovina, Albania, Romania). Poised between calm survey and piercing elegy, a slow, measured camera sleepwalks as its trackings—a fusion of ancient and modern wanderings—follow a filmmaker (Harvey Keitel, magnificent) who, separated from his Greek homeland—hence, his family; hence, himself—for 35 years, returns from the U.S. to research a documentary on Miltos and Yannakis Manakis, brothers and pioneering Greek filmmakers, the film claims, who began their own documentary recordings in 1905. Death interrupted elderly Yannakis, who was shooting a blue ship of hope sailing across the ocean; we ourselves "see" the solemn image as it haunts the American's speculative mind's eye—this, a part of Yannakis's ultimate work, although none of the film stock was ever developed. Death, politics, war, indifference: all these have marked the passage of the missing three reels that the American, commissioned by the Athens Film Archives, has come over to locate. One of several guides is his brother, a journalist; and, eventually, this search brings the American to Sarajevo, the fog-enshrouded, bleeding heart of the Balkans, a war-targeted city of civilians in a region steeped in and torn apart by long, terrible conflict.

"In the end is my beginning," the American has said of this "personal journey." And, persevering, he reaches "the end"; for he does find Yannakis's missing reels and even views the developed footage. But this "end" only begins his burden; for amidst war's rubble and ripped or canceled lives, he discovers that his heart—which he had thought belonged to cinema, career and mid-life malaise—admits the prior and transcendent claim of humanity.

In *To vlemma tou Odyssea* Theodoros Angelopoulos has passed the 1900s through a prism of family, art and politics, achieving a monumental vision of Western civilization in disarray, trauma, sorrow—broken idealism, bleak prospects, partisan strife—and undying hope.

SPIRITUAL VOICES: FROM THE DIARIES OF WAR (Russia). *Dukhovnyye golosa. Iz dnevnikov voyny. Povestvovanie v pyati chastyakh* chronicles a troop of soldiers that Aleksandr Sokurov and his two-person crew accompanied to a frontier post on the Tajikistan-Afghanistan border in 1994. Russia had inherited the Afghanistan conflict from the Soviet Union, whose dissolution has now rendered the conflict meaningless, providing Sokurov with a stunning metaphor for the absurdity of war. Boys and men go through the motions of soldiering in a remote place seemingly out of time, their Taliban enemy mostly lost to the eye amidst a primitive landscape of blowing sand and dust. "War is hideous," Sokurov tells us in voiceover; ". . . There is nothing but dust, the smell of burning, stones, hot shrapnel, blood, and the hint of fear."

This 340-minute film is absorbing for every shot of its length. Its immaculate, haunting first "episode" consists of an angled long-shot of frigid terrain in St. Petersburg before Sokurov has embarked on his documentary mission. (Of course, it may actually have been shot afterwards.) As the time-lapsed image very gradually transforms, at times with a burning fire in the distance, Sokurov guides us through an aural tour of classical music, including bits of Mozart and Beethoven, encapsulating the "civilization" Sokurov is about to leave behind for war. The final episode shows him packing for his return to Russia, leaving behind, in their monotonous, dutiful existence, soldiers who cannot return, and who have toasted with champagne, in their commander's quarters (a cave), the coming of the new year—a point of withering irony. In between the bookending episodes, long takes and slow camera movements à la Andrei Tarkovsky, enjoined by a rocky terrain bleached of color, associate war with a dreamlike No-Man's-Land. When snipers attack, though, the event is all too real.

1996

ARISTOTLE'S PLOT (Zimbabwe, Cameroon, France). Jean-Pierre Bekolo's *Le complot d'Aristote*, a satirical gangster film indebted to early Godard, turns on a plea for postcolonialist Africa to come more fully into its own.

Gangsters gathered at the Cinema Africa bug out their eyes and brains on nonstop-action movies. Their leader is called Cinéma. Cinéma's opponent is Cinéaste, who wants African films to liberate itself from cultural neocolonialism and express African cultures, not Hollywood, not U.S. popular culture. Hilariously, the government investigates the reappearance of characters who have already died in previous movies. Clearly, films can usurp, redirect and reinvent reality—a capability all the more dangerous when the "reality" that films serve is of the Hollywood sort, where the values, implicit or explicit, almost invariably support economic exploitation of the Third World.

Can Africa emerge from the shadow that made it "the dark continent" in Western eyes?

The scene of crossing railroad tracks that frames *Aristotle's Plot* equally suggests African possibilities and African confusion, with the "civilized" Western view of Africa opposing a homegrown African view or, even, impulse toward such a view, inhibiting the latter from achieving clarity.

Bekolo's film resists the narrative tyranny that charts a plot for complacent audiences. (Thus the film opposes complacency.) Things unfold in *Aristotle's Plot* in a haphazard way. This tack accomplishes two seemingly contradictory things. One, it reflects the uncertain, ambiguous nature of existence, the absence in our day of clear definitions and categorical boundaries. At the same time, it contests rigidly plotted films in their seduction of viewers into accepting the most outrageous confections as reality. Like Godard's, Bekolo's filmmaking, indebted to Brecht, is much about distancing one's materials in order to spur thought. Nothing ingratiates in his method, nor is there much that is likeable about this brilliant film.

WEEKEND STORIES (Poland, 1996-2000). An octet of works about individuals facing moral dilemmas, writer-director Krzysztof Zanussi's *Opowiesci weekendowe* probes contemporary Polish life and the human condition.

"Woman's Business" ("Damski interes," 1996) claims two protagonists: Zofia, a scientist whose life was ruined when her opposition to Communism led to the revocation of her passport, separating her from her French lover; Lukowska, the Party secretary who ordered the punishment largely out of spite. Since Communism's fall, Lukowska has become a successful businesswoman; driven by selfishness rather than ideology, she remains as cheerful as Zofia is unhappy. Two of Zofia's woman friends kidnap Lukowska, forcing her to confront Zofia, her own past, her nature, affording Zofia at last some measure of relief.

"Little Faith" ("Slaba wiara," 1996) is about a married couple. Tomasz is an engineer; Olga is devout. When preliminary tests indicate their young boy's high white blood cell count, Olga, dreading leukemia, imagines that God's indifference to their son's fate is meant to punish their indifference to God; meanwhile, she pushes her spouse out of his shy passivity in pursuit of more tests and clearer medical results. We come to see Tomasz's rationality at loving work as he employs it to enter Olga's mindset in order to calm her fears. Zanussi, the former physics and philosophy student, creates a gorgeous ode to reason.

In "Unwritten Law" ("Niepisane prawa," 1996), a married chauffeur having an affair with his high-powered business boss must decide whether to risk his marriage by exposing his boss's crooked deal. In "The Soul Sings" ("Dusza spiewa," 1997), a neighbor begs a music teacher, the night before a public performance that could change his fortunes, to go out in bad weather to take her sick pet to a veterinarian. Should he risk losing his voice to help? Great stuff, beautifully acted.

GOODBYE SOUTH, GOODBYE (Taiwan). Taiwan's rudderless young underclass is epitomized by two low-level criminals—their criminality eventually gets politically connected upwards—and the girlfriend of one of them. These are Kao (played by Jack Kao, who with King Jieh-Wen wrote the story that Chu T'ien-wen turned into a brilliant script), Flathead and Pretzel. In the opening shot they are onboard a train; Flathead and Pretzel appear in the background, seemingly unconnected with Kao, the perpetual schemer on his cell phone in the foreground of the shot. There is a train's-eye rear view of fleeing tracks indicating the train's movement, followed by an objective shot of the train moving ahead. What we haven't been shown is the trio getting off the train, but there they are, together, or kind of together, at the stop. This encapsulates the film's elliptical style as well as the sense of there being no real destination for these folk. Showing the train stop and the three passengers getting off would have implied that they at least had a temporary destination.

Hou Hsiao-Hsien directed *Nan guo zai jan, nan guo*. There are scenes at gambling tables (an early one erupts into a fight) and of other sitdown occasions, but these scarcely can be said to weigh the film down. Rather, they fail to ground or stabilize the "road" shots: cars, trains, motorcycles. On the contrary, the latter continually destabilize the former, setting the rootless lives of the trio at dangerous liberty. The film ends wide-angle with a stalled car in a field.

Exactingly lit and somewhat greenish, the film's *mise-en-scène* overflows with painfully loose-ended lives. The direction of the dialogue sears. "What's with Pretzel? Slit her wrists again?" Kao asks so casually that we struggle to focus on the rest of the scene.

BRIGANDS, CHAPTER VII (Georgia, France, Russia, Italy, Switzerland). Otar Iosseliani made his hilarious black comedy *Kachagebi, tavi VII* in his adopted France but mostly in his homeland of Georgia. Charting a continuity of ordinary human misery, it follows Vano in three different time periods, including the present, which weaves in and out of the medieval period, when King Vano has the Queen's head chopped off for adultery and his attempted murder, and the 1930s, when Vano was a hooligan who becomes a Stalinist official. Currently Vano is among the dispossessed in an upheaved post-Soviet society. It is possible that the earlier "times" are actually the vagrant's own dreams. If so, reality and fantasy intersect; at one point, today's down-and-out Vano confronts his royal image in a painting.

An especial influence is another French immigrant, Luis Buñuel, whose *Discreet Charm of the Bourgeoisie* (1971), with its gunning down of dinner guests, is paid homage to.

In one of Iosseliani's Stalinist passages, a schoolteacher is hanging a picture of a Communist hero on the wall. Oops! The thing drops, glass shatters, and one of the schoolteacher's heels tears the print. Espying this, a student denounces her, and she and her spouse are carted away by the police: a precise evocation of a terrorist state.

An elderly woman is literally carried away by the Stalinist police. For a bit her vacant wheelchair follows the truck that is transporting her before veering to the curb and falling over—an echo of the 16th-century Queen's lopped-off head.

In a contemporary passage, explosives are attached to an automobile's right rear tire. The owner gets in and drives out of frame. Explosion; the wheel, on fire, rolls back into the frame.

Beautifully, fluently edited, the film is also full of heartache for oppressed humanity—for instance, in the singalong among the homeless.

BLACK KITES (U.S.). Written and directed by performance artist Jo Andres, the spouse of Steve Buscemi, who co-produced and (beautifully) acts in it, *Black Kites* draws on 1992 journals, as well as drawings and collages, by Alma Hajric, a Bosnian artist holed up with her spouse and child in a basement during the seige of Sarajevo. Alma is divided into two distinct incarnations: Alma, wife and mother, played by Mimi Goese, whose family interactions appear against a rich black backdrop, to suggest that these reenactments have been reclaimed from the dark recesses of memory; and Alma the artist, whom we hear narrating the film (Mira Furlan provides the voiceover), and whose "text," the journals contemporaneous with the ordeal, suggests the agency of this reclamation.

The film is dreamlike, a fusion of simple human activities and ambitiously complex technique. The result suggests the pared-down Anne Frank existence—a minimalist life—that Alma and her family eked out of the chaos, cruelty and insanity of the war raging around them. Father, mother, son—the Buscemis' adorable 3½-year-old son, Lucian, plays the boy—appear luminous against the black backdrop. Andres marshals also an array of experimental techniques, partly to convey the mental and spiritual resourcefulness at the core of Alma and her husband's resilience. (Andres herself describes her aesthetic style as "perceptual mischief.") This is risky procedure, to say the least, especially in light of the oppressively busy result Peter Greenaway, for instance, manages by the profusion of visual techniques he applies to his *Tempest* film, *Prospero's Books* (1991). But Andres prevails; her *Black Kites* is free of all blot of technical fancy or visual overload. Indeed, the piece achieves a sense of intimacy and gracious solitude, becoming a near-meditative experience. Startlingly humane, *Black Kites* seems spare, burrowing, endlessly mysterious.

NUN VA GOLDOON (Iran, France). Called *Bread and Flower* or *A Moment of Innocence*, Mohsen Makhmalbaf's film, like Kiarostami's films, revels in self-reflexivity. Makhmalbaf plays himself.

Twenty years earlier, in Shah Pahlavi's repressive dictatorship that incited the Islamic Revolution, Makhmalbaf was a 17-year-old activist who was imprisoned for stabbing a 20-year-old police officer, Mirhadi Tayebi, whose pistol he tried to steal. Now he has reunited with the former officer to film the incident, since which time Tayebi has had an unlucky life. That long-ago day, he had been trying to work up the courage to present a flower to a girl who was in the habit of passing by during his street watch. There she was, asking him for the time; then the attack. Now, after years of pining for her, he learns that that girl is in fact Makhmalbaf's cousin and was part of the plot!

Both men advise the boys who are playing them. Tayebi, bitter, instructs his surrogate to shoot the girl before he is stabbed. But the boy playing Makhmalbaf breaks down; how can he stab anybody? There must be a better way of "saving the world." Makhmalbaf gets the boy back on track. As one boy approaches to commit the assault, the other boy fails to shoot the girl peremptorily. At the point of decision, two things suddenly, unexpectedly, happen involving the bread (under which the gun is hidden) and the flower—a new moment of innocence that perhaps, just perhaps, redeems the past.

Thus the puppetmaster-filmmaker discovers he cannot control his puppets—although it is deliciously impossible to determine just what Makhmalbaf has predetermined as the author of the (brilliant) script. The original event slips into a new reality, affecting the young actors as profoundly as the original event affected its actors on Iran's political stage.

TIRED COMPANIONS: FIVE STORIES FROM THE WAR (Federal Republic of Yugoslavia). Episodic, correlative to the fragmented former Yugoslavia and fragmented Balkan lives, Croatian-born writer-director Zoran Solomun's *Müde Weggefährten: Fünf Geschichten Aus Dem Krieg* shows disparate refugees heading to and trying to survive in Germany.

A young Bosnian named Jimmy, who is always after a buck until at the last he feels compelled to recapture his soul, is a recurrent "through"-character. But each character is fresh and each segment heartrending.

The film opens at the Serbian-Hungarian border in 1993, a year into the Bosnian War. Two women, along with Jimmy and others, are expelled from a crowded train of refugees for having either no passport or an "expired" one due to the war. Jimmy makes his way to Germany, illegally, on his own. There, Croats, Serbs and Bosnians of varying durations in Germany meet and clash, sometimes within the same ethnic group.

In one segment hustler Jimmy and a refugee who spent time in a Serbian concentration camp try peddling the latter's "story" to a Berlin newspaper. But the young former Yugoslavia-editor, having just published such a story only weeks ago, proves deaf to the two men's entreaties. Jimmy will find another way to score a deutschmark, but the older man badly needed the money to help support his family. Besides, the editor makes plain that the man doesn't really exist, that his story does not matter. He hangs himself. In the last segment, someone who earlier transported illegal refugees into Germany is transporting the coffin back to Bosnia, along with Jimmy and the suicide's wife and daughter. (Caption: "We've got a corpse, but its papers are in order.")

The war, which is over, "destroyed everything." In a bar, Simple Simon-instructions freeze patrons mid-dance: a metaphor for political pliability and acquiescence.

DRIFTING CLOUDS (Finland). A sharply funny deadpan comedy, Aki Kaurismäki's *Kauas pilvet karkaavat* shadows the fortunes of a married couple, Ilona (Kati Outinen, brilliant) and Lauri, when both lose their jobs, one because the business for which she works is sold, the other because of company downsizing. Will clouds drift apart enough to admit new shafts of sunlight, keeping the once happy, loving couple intact?

Kaurismäki proceeds elliptically and minimalistically, like a Bresson gone comedic. Almost everything in the film is delivered in a comical fashion, and often the delivery comes in the form of an aural piece of punctuation, such as a drunk Lauri's body falling unexpectedly to the floor. Kaurismäki's method is sufficiently flexible to include so devastating a moment as when, while Ilona waits for Lauri to return home one night, the camera catches her standing by a photograph of a young child—the couple's child, we glean from her still, haunted look, who has died.

Some people are put off by the film's happy ending. Doesn't this ending blunt Kaurismäki's socioeconomic point, how close to poverty hardworking members of the working class can be? No. The film's method makes this fact movingly clear. If Kaurismäki had adopted a naturalistic style, the film's hopeful ending would likely ring false; but Kaurismäki's style has already established, deftly, how much survival in a capitalist society depends on luck. Good luck is the flip side of *bad* luck.

Much of the film is shot in a restrained, sober visual style that color cinematographer Timo Salminen punctuates with scenes of exquisite beauty. This contrast becomes another of the film's artillery of distancing devices. One never "enters" a Kaurismäki film, losing oneself by dint of a filmmaker's manipulations; rather, one observes and locates, in oneself, the point where critical analysis crosses humane emotional engagement.

THREE LIVES AND ONLY ONE DEATH (France, Portugal). Chilean emigré Raúl Ruiz had been living in Paris for about twenty years when he made his surreal, intricate *Trois vies & une seule mort* about split identity and various forms of separation. It consists of three episodes, in each of which a major character looks identical (Marcello Mastroianni, captivating) while living a different life; a fourth episode, or coda, with another such identical twin, suggests that all four men occupy a single body, each immersed in his own role and reality.

The film begins as a radio-broadcasted story that becomes what we see, which is structured as a story-within-the-story as told by Mateo to Andre, a stranger in a café. Mateo, the first husband of Andre's wife, left María twenty years earlier to live in a nearby apartment, "the proportions" of which "were deceptive." Resident Time-eating fairies trapped Mateo in an alternate reality of their own conjuring: a story-within-the-story-within-the-story. Mateo brings Andre to this apartment; failing to convince Andre to swap places with him so that he can reunite with María, Mateo plants an ax in Andre's head, buries the body and heads home. The arrangement of mirrors gives us triplicate views of both man and former wife. María presumes that Andre has abandoned her and welcomes Mateo with open arms. Here using Nathaniel Hawthorne's story "Wakefield" as a springboard, Ruiz and Pascal Bonitzer's brilliant script starts spinning its delightful web.

In subsequent episodes Georges Vickers, seemingly on a whim, trades in his respected role as university professor to become a beggar and Butler, a butler, is actually the anonymous benefactor of the poor young couple he is slowly poisoning. In the coda, Luc Allamand is a banker and arms dealer exploiting and "poisoning" more than a couple of us.

PRIVATE CONFESSIONS (Sweden). Written by Ingmar Bergman and directed by Liv Ullmann, *Enskilda samtal* continues the Bergman family chronicle begun with *The Best Intentions* (Bille August, 1991).

Bergman's theme is Ibsenian; how necessary is truthfulness in light of its often stark consequences? His script explores the line between truth and falsehood, responsibility and irresponsibility. Ullmann's theme, though, is more psychological: the shifting nature of both truthfulness and deceit—the more blurred line between the lies we tell others and the lies we tell ourselves. Ullmann wants to show how we achieve a sense of balance by believing our own lies. Ullmann sees this as a process quite apart from any moral considerations. Her perspective completely transforms the material.

The film proceeds achronologically, as a series of five "confessions" involving Anna (Pernilla August, superb), her spouse, Henrik, and Uncle Jacob (Max von Sydow, in a towering performance), both Lutheran priests. In one of these, Anna devastates Henrik by confessing her adultery.

The final "conversation" is a thirty-year-ago flashback. On the eve of confirmation, Anna confesses to Jacob her religious doubts. Is Anna being honest about her feelings? or is she merely creating an opportunity to be alone with Uncle Jacob, her heart's desire? Could what we see be a lie of memory—a strategic lie by which Anna's mind hides from her the truth? Did Jacob seduce Anna that fateful day, right before her confirmation? Did he then confess this to his wife, Maria, whose forgiveness is the basis of Jacob's later counsel to Anna that she confess *her* adultery to Henrik? Has Anna been, secretly, the love of Jacob's lifetime? All we know for certain is that Anna proceeds with her confirmation—and spends the rest of her life estranged, if not quite divorced, from God.

Human nature: fascinating stuff.

CRASH (Canada, UK). Steven Spielberg's *Empire of the Sun* (1987) was an unmitigated disaster, both artistically and financially. Some felt, therefore, that J.G. Ballard, on whose autobiographical novel the film is based, was unfilmable.

Canadian David Cronenberg, however, tackled *Crash*; and, while it falls short of Ballard's gorgeously poetic science-fiction novel, it's a poignant film.

James and Catherine Ballard aren't hedonistic sexual experimenters. They're a married couple who love one another to the limit and who keep hoping to add sexual compatibility to the mix of their intimacies. Rather than go separate ways, they will try anything to achieve orgasm with one another, including preparing for the hoped-for event by having sex with other partners and, while making love with each other, or trying to, sharing the details of their adulteries as a mutual excitement. I don't consider this a brilliant reading, only a necessary one, given the bizarre attempts to characterize this heartrending love story as an exercise in near-pornography.

It is certainly wrong to take Vaughan, into whose cult the Ballards fall after James is involved in a traffic accident, as a guide for determining the Ballards' motivation. Vaughan, obsessed with the connection between traffic collisions and sexual excitement, arranges reenactments of such collisions and attempts to arrange, also, new collisions. He rationalizes his obsession as a scientific interest in how modern technology is reinventing the shape of the human body. What we see, by contrast, is the mangled appearance of automobiles as a result of crashes, correlative to which is not only human injury but also death. A man dies in the collision that leaves Ballard bruised, broken and shaken.

It's the human heart that Cronenberg cares about, to which his star, James Spader, contributes in full, humane measure, giving one of cinema's most moving performances.

SOMERSAULT IN A COFFIN (Turkey). Dervis Zaim's *Tabutta rövasata*, a humane comedy, follows Mahsun, an impoverished Turk living on Istanbul's streets. To survive emotionally and spiritually, as well as materially, he does what he can—which, always illegal, gets him repeatedly beaten by the police. No defeatist, Mahsun creatively holds onto life. This requires awesome effort. Mahsun is a down-on-his-luck Everyman whose humanity we instantly recognize. By contrast, Mahsun's official tormentors seem robotic.

Working on a fishing boat, Mahsun makes almost no money. He feels trapped. He *is* trapped. So, in his way a gentleman, Mahsun borrows parked cars, neatly returning them when he is done going wild behind the wheel. Thus he is able to steal self-validating moments of self-determination and freedom. Mahsun's girlfriend uses heroin; Mahsun's joyrides are *his* fix. They're what keep him going.

When Sari, Mahsun's closest friend, dies on the streets, the precariousness of Mahsun's situation is brought home to him. Early on, Zaim applies an impressionistic style, consisting of stark, short scenes, to jolt us into the harsh immediacy of homelessness. Also, Zaim inserts sharp closeups—for instance, of the fire that people light to warm their hands. Zaim discards this tack before it can drift into mannerism, adopting a more naturalistic style (punctuated by fleeting moments of expressionism) while retaining the previous edginess.

While street folk scramble to find what cover they can, gorgeous Iranian peacocks roam an ancient castle—the city's well tended anachronism. These birds, though, speak to Mahsun's heart; he somehow draws a line of kinship between their pampered confinement and his comfortless plight. Nearly starving, he makes a meal of one of the birds—a self-assault; an act of utter desperation. The crime's oddness attracts television reportage; but Mahsun's pointless celebrity, however, is unlikely to alleviate the poverty that's killing him.

PRISONER OF THE MOUNTAINS (Russia, Kazakhstan). This extraordinarily moving tragicomedy updates Tolstoi's 1822 children's story "Prisoner of the Caucasus"—the film is identically titled: *Kavkazskiy plennik*—to the Chechen War. Its protagonists are two Russian soldiers, a young conscript and a seasoned veteran; the only survivors of a massacre, they are chained together at the ankle and held as hostages by Abdul-Murat, a villager who wishes to exchange them for his captured son.

The film portrays a cultural collision between the Russians, who are played by professional actors, and the Muslim peasants, who are played by Muslim peasants, inhabitants of the remote village where the film was shot, some twenty or so miles from actual fighting. (All the acting is excellent.) Needless to say, the Russians have nearly as much trouble with each other, in a more playful, antic, and also deeper version of *The Defiant Ones* (Stanley Kramer, 1958). Much of the film is hilarious; its most explosively funny moment involves the unintended, inopportune discharge of a stolen rifle after the Russian prisoners have made their escape.

Still, director Sergei Bodrov keeps our attention on the surrounding conflict. The Russian boy's mother journeys to the area, hoping to effect the necessary trade that will free her son. Meeting with Abdul-Murat, she notes that she is a teacher, like his son. His response is precise: "That doesn't matter now. We are at war." When his son is shot dead trying to escape, what is there left for Abdul-Murat to do but execute the woman's son? Ah, but he has now met the woman, and his own 12-year-old daughter also pleads for the boy's life.

Bodrov once claimed that President Boris Yeltsin, who had ordered the invasion of Chechnya, withdrew forces after being moved by Bodrov's film. Isn't it pretty to think so?

EASTERN ELEGY (Russia, Japan). Gorgeously photographed by Aleksei Fyodorov, Aleksandr Sokurov's *Vostochnaya elegiya*—gray, muted green, eerily *slightly* out of focus—is a dream of death, perhaps the dream of a dream. Low constant wind suggests the echo of a sound which is vaguely recollected. Faint music; distant bursts of song. Sokurov is the dreamer, a gently inquisitive wanderer who finds himself in an old Japanese town on a remote island that is blanketed by layer and layer of swirling fog and mist. "All is a dream," we hear the dreamer's low voice say; ". . . nothing weighs on my heart." Moonlight palely glimmers on water—a reflection; perhaps, rather, the reflection of a reflection. The dreamer's hand lights on the sign of an old tobacco shop.

"Am I in Paradise?" the voice, now sad, asks. Is the garden sculpture a Buddha? The dreamer's voice is still accompanied by wind: "The houses are as if they have turned to stone. I do not hear my steps at all. In this fog, I am like a fish in water. But I feel a chill, as a human would. . . . There is a light in a window. For *me*, perhaps?" Enrobed in dark space, the face of an elderly woman dimly appears; she is seated, alone. Then elsewhere, the face of an elderly man, who also is seated alone, also dimly appears. The man reminisces. The voice of the dreamer asks, "Do you know how men change after death?" The reply: "They become more tender." Dreamer: "Why is there such sadness in poetry?" Silence.

Revisiting the old woman, the dreamer asks, "What is happiness?" Almost nothing in life, she says, made her happy.

The dreamer's voice: "It seems I am welcome here, and this island is enough for all my dreams. I will stay."

SHAMAN (Russia, France). Home: What *is* it? Is it where you come from, to which you try with all your might to return? Or is it your destiny, to find which you must go *somewhere else*? One of the most mysterious, beautiful Russian films of the post-Soviet era, *Chamane* doesn't disclose the full import of its title until the last minute. Only then do we grasp the journey we have been watching unfold.

The action begins in a Siberian gulag before the collapse of the Soviet Union. Two prisoners escape using Yakut horses: wily Anatolia, a shaman with a Jew's harp, who knows the *taiga* and its spirits; Dmitri, a Muscovite with a violin, who wants only to go home. When Toli dies, or appears to die, this is something that Dmitri must try to do on his own.

A series of adventures takes the violinist out of his comfort zone and ever deeper into unfamiliar natural and human terrain, an exquisite realm of frozen light. To get back to Moscow, Dmitri ends up selling his horse; to become for the first time a whole, free person, he ends up selling his violin for another horse. At the last, riding off alone, he is playing a Jew's harp—like Anatolia; like John Ford's Young Mr. Lincoln (1939).

Simple, clear, rapturous and unfathomable, *Chamane* was made by Bartabas, founder and director of the Théâtre Équestre de Zingaro just outside Paris. Indeed, it is a film full of gorgeous horses, one imbued with the spirit of a circus. In it, the transport becomes the destination; hope, the shoes in which one is most comfortable. Life is a Gypsy caravan sparking grave delight in the spirit world; if we let go of the past, we can enter the quiet, illimitable beauty all around.

1997

THE SALTMEN OF TIBET (Germany, Switzerland). Ulrike Koch's *Die Salzmänner von Tibet* documents elemental, nomadic existence. Four tribal men—Old Mother, Old Father, Lord of the Animals, the Novice—journey to a lake in northern Tibet in order to extract salt to sell for grain. The day before, there is a communal discussion; the price of salt currently being very low, how many yaks can they spare, if necessary, to sell for barley? (Seemingly offhanded; actually, life-and-death.) The trek itself is punctuated by religious rituals, singing, cooking, meals, conversations, and recollections spoken into the camera. A bus passes the quartet on a nearby road, disrupting our sense of theirs being a world unto itself. Indeed, a tribal woman earlier prayed for world peace.

Because it is packed with purposeful activity (including startling shots of people's hands at work), the tribe's existence, as represented by the salt-traders, seems sturdier than that of Werner Herzog's *Herdsmen of the Sun* (1988). It isn't. Koch and Pio Corradi, her intense color cinematographer, thus conjure images of ephemera. The camera rises to capture voluminous smoke rising from a cooking pot; shadows shimmer across the ground, their substance—yaks—lagging behind. We see the immense shadow from an overhead airplane, whose substance we only hear, its engine's sound shattering silence. These saltmen shared their experience with the filmmaker, in fact, precisely because they fear that theirs is a vanishing life.

Koch details the arduous labor of raking the salt and collecting it into mounds for the gathering, sacking, and transport by yak. The conclusive shot of the return home, the longest take in a film full of long takes, evokes not only the slow, steady rhythm of tribal existence but also, powerfully, the hope of survival contained in the saltmen's patience, tenacity, perseverance.

MOTHER AND SON (Russia, Germany). *Mat i syn* is about the familial bond between a dying mother and her grown son, who is her caregiver. It is a visual poem, spare, spiritual, intense.

The setting is one of sublime isolation: a remote country home amidst ravishing landscapes and skies of pristine, unearthly beauty. (Outdoor space was shot by reflection in gigantic mirrors, giving the film a haunting glow.) These formidable surroundings set off the intimate humanity at the movie's center. Enfeebled, the woman receives from her son the care she once gave *him*. He carries her outdoors and "walks" her in his arms.

Aleksandr Sokurov and his cinematographer, gorgeous colorist Alexei Fyodorov, have applied special lenses that appear to collapse space and remove depth, converging the two characters and thus distilling their close connection; as a result, their relationship seems to define rather than fill space.

Exhausted, the mother must take her leave; now her son must let her go. A peculiarly Russian form of irony—it soothes rather than pricks—translates the son's assurances into the very comfort that the mother needs to pass freely from Earth. Son lays down Mother for her last nap. A butterfly lights on her hand. Walking outside, in sympathy and exhaustion, the son also lies down, while land and sky—rolling-off mists; in the distance, a train's passing—relate to him his mother's passing, her journeying out. He rejoins his mother; the butterfly hasn't quite left her hand. Gently stroking her other hand, he whispers to her spirit, which is to say, himself, "Be patient, Mother; wait for me at the place we agreed on"—this, his final loving assurance.

Humane, mysterious, bathed in tenderness, *Mother and Son* evokes the stillness of a poet's soul amidst the silent, steady passage of time.

THE PRINCE OF HOMBURG (Italy). Marco Bellocchio's films blend fantasy and reality in pursuit of an analytical outcome. Dark and dreamy, like Kleist's play, *Il principe di Homburg* departs from Kleist's (conscious) intent and accumulates into an indictment of war.

The protagonist is the titular young German general who is fighting the Swedes in the Thirty Years War. Swept up in romantic reverie centering on his beloved Natalia, he leads a cavalry charge prematurely. The offensive action succeeds; but his unintended disobedience of military orders requires his death. The Grand Elector, Natalia's uncle, orders this after a trial; meanwhile, Natalia must marry the King of Sweden. Brave and heroic on the battlefield, the Prince disintegrates into fear at the prospect of execution. Natalia's pleas on the Prince's behalf win the Elector's retraction of the death sentence—with this caveat: the Prince must agree to this outcome in writing. Honor and military code preclude his doing this; but before going to his death, the Prince secures the undoing of the planned political marriage for the sake of his and Natalia's undying love.

War, then, is at war with human feelings. It distorts, falsifies much that is human. Masks replace humanity: Hohenzollern may not be comrade of the Prince that he appears to be; the Grand Elector, anticipating Melville's Captain Vere, is certainly not the loving surrogate father that the Prince believes him to be. Even the Prince's cowardice turns out to be a mask! —irony of ironies.

Bellocchio conjures images that intercept a voluminous dream. Outside a window in a dark room, soldiers on horseback pass; they appear as an expressionistic regimented train of ghastly silhouettes—a war-haunted European history, a revelation of the Prince's tormented soul, a harbinger of his death: the convoluted suicide *preceding* his dreamt wedding.

LOST HIGHWAY (France, U.S.). David Lynch's *Lost Highway* proceeds from the Western mind's split into competing selves by dint of Darwinism and Freudian psychology, systems that objectified us for ourselves. The result has been nearly constant self-awareness, which can quickly turn to paranoia, which as quickly creates the need to justify the paranoia, even if this means bending reality to it. Our self-objectification led, politically, to the twentieth-century birth and growth of totalitarianism. In retrospect, Lynch's *Blue Velvet* (1986) seems a gloss on Reaganism and related outcrops of reactionary thought and feeling.

Lost Highway's opening movement is bone-crunching—spare, concentrated, almost intolerably intense. Minimal lighting, deep colors, the suspenseful use of negative space, inexorably slow camera movements, an ominous soundtrack: these and other elements collapse naturalism and surrealism in order to evoke, as if from within his tormented mind, a club musician's suspiciousness regarding his wife. Videotaped evidence has him murdering her savagely—or is it an *image* of himself murdering an *image* of her? The man is tried, convicted, locked up. One morning, inexplicably, someone else is occupying his solitary cell. The law must release whoever has "replaced" him, on the grounds that this someone else must be occupying another life.

Working intuitively from his morbid yet salutary imagination, Lynch proceeds (with lowered ferocity) to interpret selfconsciousness through a crisscrossing pattern of lives where any soul can be instantly replaced by a "double"—sometimes a different mask, sometimes a different life. Brilliantly acted by Patricia Arquette in homage to Barbara Stanwyck's phenomenal performance in Billy Wilder's *Double Indemnity* (1944), *Lost Highway* remains elusive where it isn't unfathomable. The film suggests some anxious, violent, weirdly funny cousin of Jacques Rivette's self-referencing "created realities." It also suggests Poe and Pirandello.

Watching *Lost Highway*, I thought I had died and gone to hell.

THE TANGO LESSON (UK, France, Argentina, Germany, Netherlands). Londoner Sally Potter's exuberant *The Tango Lesson* draws on three of her passions: humanity, film, dance. Sally the character goes about making a film that becomes, in effect, *The Tango Lesson*. The film breathes. It's aglow with life and spirit.

Central to the film is the Argentinean tango—a sensuous, intricate dance where the woman must be like water to a minutely nuanced breeze; sensitively alert, she must respond to the man's lead in less than a heartbeat.

But this dance raises an issue that Potter feels compelled to address. Is there a way to reconcile the dance's beauty with its subordination of the female to the male?

The dance is new to Sally, whom Potter herself (wonderfully) plays. Sally isn't simply, passively trying to learn a dance. She is also trying to teach *it* a thing or two about her and about gender equality. The "tango lesson," then, is a matter of who should not always be leading whom. By thus striking her own perspective against the rock of a traditional male prerogative, Sally also helps to objectify, for herself, a dilemma of opposite impulses—at once, her desire to "do" the tango, which is, after all, a dance where the male does decisively lead, and her desire somehow to change this in order to make the dance her own. Is there a way of tossing out the bathwater and not the baby?

Not according to her dance instructor, who becomes her professional dance partner. The dance's masculine bias suits him fine; in one way or another, he "tangoes" onstage and off. Sally's love for him coincides with her love of the tango.

The Tango Lesson is as playful as its underpinnings are solid and serious. Unerringly, Potter holds in balance its gravity and lightness.

THE EEL (Japan). In Shohei Imamura's *Unagi*, mild-mannered Takuro, suspecting infidelity, catches wife and lover in bed together and stabs her to death. Blood sprays the camera. Thereafter, red periodically indicates Takuro's persistent guilt.

In prison, an eel becomes Takuro's pet. Robotic from his regimen of incarceration, Takuro can yet find an image of his submerged humanity in his sleek, slithering companion. Released, Takuro rescues Keiko after she attempts suicide. Keiko's people skills make a success of Takuro's barber shop, which his shyness was prepping for failure. Keiko falls in love with Takuro. Incensed that Keiko has retrieved money that he appropriated from her insane mother, her former mobster boyfriend is hell-bent on revenge. A young man who has befriended Takuro, genially obsessed with U.F.O.s, has constructed in their remote outpost an elaborate display to attract aliens. When the mobster is about to savage Keiko and Takuro at the shop, this friend realizes that aliens have landed, and they're unfriendly, and he gets help. The result: an hilarious barber shop frenzy out of the Keystone Kops. Before Takuro is returned to prison for violating parole, Keiko tells him she will wait for him. Takuro is mum.

Keiko is a dead ringer for Takuro's wife. (Misa Shimuzu splendidly plays both women.) This is why Takuro was attracted to her; it is his wife whom he still loves. By now having twice brought Keiko back to life, Takuro has resolved his crisis of guilt. He will not return to her.

Or *do* the women look alike? Perhaps we see this resemblance because of the connection that Takuro has subjectively drawn between them. We are seeing what *he* sees, regardless of what is objectively the case.

Imamura: "Above and beyond anything else, working as an artist means having a limitless curiosity about human beings."

A TASTE OF CHERRY (Iran, France). *See above.*

WHO THE HELL IS JULIETTE? (Cuba, Mexico, U.S.) Argentinean-born Carlos Marcovich made ¿*Quién diablos es Juliette?* in Cuba, Mexico, and the U.S. He co-wrote (with Carlos Cuarón), produced, directed, (gorgeously) cinematographed, and edited the film, which fuses documentary and scripted material. Yuliet Ortega is an ebullient 16-year-old Havana prostitute. The film runs parallel/intersecting courses, attending also to Fabiola Quíroz, a Mexican model with whom Yuliet appeared in one of Marcovich's music videos—in a sense, Yuliet's alternative, better existence, though one hiding considerable misfortune. Marcovich records remarks by both and family members of theirs. Film scholar Brooke Jacobson has perfectly described the film as being all the more heartrending for being so lightly presented.

The film opens with a visual tweak: Yuliet's wiping the camera that's filming her as she addresses us. The gesture passes quickly; it may be meaningless—or does it show that Yuliet wants us to see her clearly? It possibly confirms Yuliet's reality (for her, for us) by confirming ours. Its poignancy perhaps derives from its emotional location between both possibilities. Rather than interpenetrating, documentary and fiction in this film exist where either may be the other or is on the verge of becoming the other, underscoring the elusiveness of Yuliet's reality even as she discloses specific facts about herself, such as her family's abandonment fifteen years earlier by her father, an electrician whom we meet in New Jersey. (Yuliet's younger brother, without irony, explains that their father is "slow in returning.") Yuliet's mother committed suicide. Yuliet's phone call to her father brandishes anger and hatred that her brother describes as hiding love. The father and others very differently recount his killing the family dog after it attacked one of his sons. He feels that his wife abandoned him by not coming along with him.

Reality: unresolved, ambiguous, complex.

DRANCY AVENIR (France). Descriptions of writer-director Arnaud des Pallières's extraordinary meditation on the Holocaust, *Drancy Avenir*, say it consists of three "tales" or "narratives." Commentators ferret out the few narrative details that exist and exaggerate them; what may be a narrative springboard somehow becomes a structuring narrative, and this obscures the film's essentially poetic nature. This is not a "narrative film." Another point on which everyone seems to agree is that the disembodied voice that launches the film is an elderly—in fact, the oldest—survivor of the Holocaust who regrets not having written an account of what he witnessed and experienced in a death camp. He does say all this; but how does *that* make it so? Everywhere the film insists on the conflation of time elements, with the Holocaust's being a still unfolding event; is it not possible that the disembodied voice we hear actually belongs to a Holocaust fatality that must roam, lost, in a confusion of time and circumstance, a soul cast adrift in "the silent wilderness"?

Correlating visually to the voiceovers are extended Resnaisian tracking shots—of buildings along a street, streets seen from a bus, a tree-banked river. Survivors/nonsurvivors speak, referring to "truth stripped of the cloak of time," the long-ago "suspicion of not being human." "The victors control the truth," a history professor tells his class, referring to the fact that de Gaulle after the war did not commemorate the Jewish dead, and asks, "At what point does the Final Solution really end?" As his students file out, the professor is seated at his desk, behind which the erased blackboard projects a melancholy blotting-out.

Many trains pass at a juncture, observed by a fixed camera. Thunderous and screeching, the sound obliterates time: the distance between the living and the dead.

ROSTOV-LUANDA (Angola, Mauritania). Raised in Mali, Abderrahmane Sissako returned to his homeland, Mauritania, in 1980. Nearly twenty years later, he proceeds on a quest, which *Rostov-Luanda* documents. The adventurous road takes him much farther south, to Angola, also on Africa's western (Atlantic) coast. Accompanied by his elderly former nanny and armed with an old photograph, Sissako is in search of a friend, Afonso Baribanga, a fellow student in Moscow whom he hasn't seen in seventeen years. *Rostov-Luanda* is about the people Sissako meets along the way—and about Africa. Since gaining its independence from Portugal in 1975 (fifteen years after Mauritania had gained its independence from France), Angola has been beseiged by civil war. Sissako's journey is into the heart of uncertainty—the difficult reality that replaced Africa's post-colonial hopes.

Outside Biker's, a brasserie, a man looks at Sissako's class photograph, shrugs and declares, "One should speak only of what one knows for certain." If Sissako had been missing, the man says while facing Sissako, then he could be sure, because Sissako has that kind of face. Inside, Sissako interviews cook and customers. One of the latter also was in Soviet Moscow. His conclusion: If he weren't someone else, he could be the one for whom Sissako is searching. He, too, is "lost."

An orphaned boy describes his war-disrupted life. He is determined not to run away from school again, not to be homeless again. A woman explains why she became a teacher. A man

decries Soviet influence in Africa.
An older man looks at the photograph, shakes his head and, referring to Baribanga, muses, "I will probably meet him someday."
Could be. Sissako learns that his friend is coming home, from the former East Germany.
Part of the film's silent broken melody is the Soviet collapse.
Abbas Kiarostami's "road"-influence is everywhere.

VOYAGE TO THE BEGINNING OF THE WORLD (Portugal, France). Prolific Manoel de Oliveira, who at 101 is still making movies, was a mere octogenarian when he wrote and directed the autobiographical *Viagem ao Princípio do Mundo*. The film opens by quoting Nietzsche: "To master the chaos of oneself"—the object of being and a proper aim of autobiography. Another aim is to grapple with the mortal implications of time's passage. The film is dedicated to the memory of Marcello Mastroianni, who (achingly) plays filmmaker Manoel and who died prior to the film's release. The first shot—this is a road picture—is of white lines on a highway rushing by.

In the car are Manoel and French actor Afonso, both of whom have been drawn to Portugal by memories—aging Manoel, by his own; Afonso, by his deceased Portuguese emigré father's, shared with him when he was a child. De Oliveira achieves a sense of "pastwardness" by shooting road from the back of the moving vehicle and cutting to inside, where Manoel reminisces. Visually, we are being pulled forward into the past.

The statue of a man shouldering a beam: Manoel recalls it; Afonso recognizes the mustache as the model for the one he wears in Manoel's film. The two men, accompanied by two other crew members, are now on foot, exploring the area. A looming lateral view suggests that the four visitors are taking their leave of the statue even as, pausing, they are studying it. The group locates Afonso's elderly aunt (Isabel de Castro, phenomenal), with whom Afonso cannot communicate in Portuguese. María Afonso's impoverished life in a rural area of haunted darkness: here, Afonso and the others have entered the past. They will emerge from it transformed.

Life continues; de Oliveira's *Voyage* finds fresh memories being formed.

1998

FLOWERS OF SHANGHAI (Taiwan). We do not expect a "period piece" from Hou Hsiao-Hsien, but *Haishang hua*, an exquisitely wrought film about the hapless lives of prostitutes, is set in China in the 1880s. We follow a number of prostitutes in elegant, richly upholstered "flower houses"—brothels—as they try to eke out a bit of self-determination in claustrophobic surroundings, where their destinies are at the whim of madams, clients, and their own schemes and anxieties. The entire action of *Flowers of Shanghai* unfolds within windowless brothel walls.

Beautifully lit, the film is formally brilliant. The rigorous sculpting of each image is correlative to the restricted lives of the "flowers," but it also, ironically, consigns the men to a structured existence—this was colonial China—in which the women who serve them become an index of the men's also limited possibilities. The central relationship is a long-term one; but Wang (Tony Leung Chiu Wai, superb), taciturn and in the grip of melancholy, is tiring of Crimson and dallying with Jasmine, who is younger, much to Crimson's dismay. The bonds that tie these individuals together are what they have in lieu of love, and their temper-tossed intrigues play out against another prostitute's circumstance: Emerald buys her freedom from the brothel where she works. It is a meticulous arrangement.

Austere, relentless, nearly merciless, *Flowers of Shanghai* lacks the tenderness and overflowing ordinary humanity we associate with much of Hou's work. It is a portrait of blighted lives. Behind their polite, efficient veneer, the brothels hide beatings and instances of sexual sadism. It is hard to believe that Hou isn't groping for a metaphor for Communist China. (Artists often venture into the past to comment on the present.) In any case, Hou's least typical film is devastating.

THE IDIOTS (Denmark). Dazzling, brilliant, hilarious, poignant, Lars von Trier's *The Idiots* is the masterpiece of Dogme 95, the movement Trier helped found that chooses naturalism and realism over artifice or technical manipulation in order to contest what its adherents see as the falsifying tendencies of individual and technologically obsessive cinema. Thus, location shooting is in, studio shooting, out; films, which must be in color and video recorded, can use no special lighting apart from a single lamp attached to the camera, nor can filters be used, nor can optical work of any kind be applied; no sound can be used apart from sounds that correspond to the images being presented; the camera must be *handheld*; the action, contemporary. Trier's creation of both Dogme- and non-Dogme films suggests he may have been putting us all on (that is, acting like an idiot), but the movement continued a while. Impishly, Trier's offscreen voice can be heard "seriously" interviewing his fictional characters as though this film is a documentary. Indeed, few films collapse so decisively the difference between fiction and documentary.

The Idiots portrays a commune whose members in public pretend to be mentally challenged—for instance, in a restaurant, at a home insulation factory they tour, at a public swimming pool. Each is searching for his or her inner idiot; idiots, one opines, are the people of the future.

These young persons are having a blast with their antics. We, however, also get to see the responses they provoke—and, in some cases, the responses ordinary people keep themselves from having. Trier skewers the reactionary social tendency that in the U.S. goes by the name "political correctness"—"liberal" fascism.

It's exhausting acting like an idiot. Eventually, commune members test the waters of the mainstream. Some make it; some are left behind.

PASSION (Hungary). Pre-title, a threadbare kitchen is glaringly lit by a naked lightbulb. In the foreground, two men sit facing each other at table. On the left, the older man, light shining off his naked brow, silently faces down the younger man, who, underneath a hat, is submerged in darkness. The man on the right is under the thumb of the man on the left, for whom, it turns out, he works. In the background, visible between them, her back towards us as she washes dishes in the sink, is the garage owner's wife (Ildikó Bánsági, magnificent). The owner rises, turns music on, and (literally) throws together wife and employee. The future lovers, under duress, dance. Like the employee the wife is shorter, younger; the owner separates them by pulling his wife by the hair; when he walks up the stairs to bed, she obediently, quickly follows.

Written by the director and Béla Tarr, György Fehér's *Szenvedély* adapts James M. Cain's novel *The Postman Always Rings Twice*. The grainy, volatile black-and-white film, set in the 1930s, evokes a clouded universe in which a pair of lovers who have murdered the woman's spouse seem to get away with what they have done, the moral weight of which, however, pulls them apart.

One is reminded of Robert Browning's brilliant Victorian poem "Porphyria's Lover," whose titular narrator, having strangled Porphyria with the "wedding band" of her long hair, contemplates with wonder God's failure to intercede.

Fehér's long, hypnotic takes suit a film whose characters remain anonymous, elementary figures—"the wife," "the man," etc.—in a dream. Reality, minutely observed, becomes *non*reality, almost entirely interior, a negative glimpse of all that the lovers' unbridled passion shuts out. Light appears hysterically overexposed, blindingly flashing distortions amidst so much darkness: an unbalanced world.

ETERNITY AND A DAY (Greece). *What is Time? Grandfather says it is a boy playing jacks on the beach.* — the voice of Alexandre as a child, now coming back to him.

It is routinely claimed that Roberto Benigni won the 1998 Palme d'Or for *Life Is Beautiful*. That year, in fact, the world's most prestigious film prize was unanimously awarded to

Theodoros Angelopoulos for *Eternity and a Day*, the loveliest Greek film in creation.

Writer, widower Alexandre, convinced he is about to die, is full of aching memories of childhood and of Anna, his wife, while family members cannot quite fit what may be his last hours into their schedule. He therefore befriends an eight-year-old street child, an illegal immigrant from Albania whom he rescues from being kidnapped and sold. One is an exile; the other is about to be.

One leg of the pair's odyssey is across the border to the boy's village, razed by war and populated, in a ghostly long-shot, by erect, unmoving male bodies. In the eerie fog and snow, are these prisoners corpses? The child has lied; no grandmother awaits him. Alexandre takes the boy back to Greece, where the white of a bride's gown, in contrast to dingy yellow buildings and street, electrifies a wedding procession.

Derivative of Ingmar Bergman's *Wild Strawberries* (1957), the film has the pair walk through a scene from the past that Alexandre tells the boy about. Before Alexandre visits his ancient, bedridden mother, they find Selim, the child's friend, dead in the harbor. The boy visits Selim in the morgue and burns his clothes underneath a building under construction, with other refugee children in attendance. It is a ceremonial farewell to friend and homeland —an acceptance of exile.

A passenger appropriates a bouquet of flowers left on a bus.

LIFE ON EARTH (Mali, Mauritania, France). In anticipation of the Millennium, Mauritanian filmmaker Abderrahmane Sissako contributed *La vie sur terre* to the 1999 French-Swiss television series *L'An 2000 Vue Par* . . . .

From busy, decorative Paris, on the verge of ebullient millennial celebrations, Sissako, playing himself, returns to his father's rural Mali village to welcome the epochal event. A long tracking shot of an infinite number of cheeses in a Parisian supermarket dominates the film's opening; thereafter, in Sokolo, life is simpler, and the year 2000 demarcates nothing new or noteworthy. One isn't overwhelmed by nonsensical choices. Instead of the ether of consumerism, one experiences there "life on Earth." "I'll arrive there," Sissako writes his father, "fresh and young."

A measured zoom on the intricate network of a baobob tree's bare branches against the sky marks the shift in geography. A cyclist's upside-down image in the river goes one way; a paddled rowboat, carrying a passenger and her bicycle, goes the other way. The human result is mathematical: *stillness.*

Getting back to basics, though, isn't all a Godsend. The one telephone, at the post office, doesn't always connect. ("It's hard to reach people. It's a matter of luck.") A local radio station is the only other technology. (A photograph of Princess Diana and Prince Charles adorns the wall.) Cameras are ancient. But the rhythm of life is set to the beating of the human heart, and the place is gorgeous beyond belief. Sissako's film is gently satirical regarding both sides of human existence: the artificial and bourgeois; the natural and impoverished.

A boy kicks a soccer ball up a street of sand; heads of cyclists appear above stone walls. Expectancy attaches itself to more pressing matters than the Millennium. "We'll be harvesting soon."

PHOTOGRAPHER (Poland). In 1987, in a Viennese antique shop, some four hundred color slides were discovered of activities inside the Lódź Ghetto, where Jewish men, women and children were held and put to work while Nazis determined their fate—if you will, a productive halfway concentration camp. The first voice we hear in *Fotoamator* (literally, *Amateur Photographer*), Dariusz Jablonski's probing documentary, belongs to one of the 877 survivors from the 230,000 Lódź Jews, to which, during the course of the war, 25,000 others were added. This is Dr. Arnold Mostowicz, whom we actually see, who immediately informs us that the photographs do not show the truth. Rather, they compose a documentary record skewed by the outlook of their amateur photographer, the Ghetto's chief Nazi accountant, Walter Genewein, an Austrian from whose written records an actor reads. Genewein explains that the purpose of the photos is to demonstrate the Nazis' "achievement" in civilizing subhuman Jews. The camera used? Confiscated from a Jew.

One principle of the film's methodology is the discrepancy between the innocuousness of the slides and the horror of the Holocaust. "The Ghetto was not a death camp," Genewein's words insist. There, in the courtyard, children with a wheelbarrow! Mostowicz explains their fate: deportation; extermination. Moreover, Mostowicz vividly recalls sounds and odors— things that photographs cannot communicate.

The role of Chaim Rumkowski, the Jew who orchestrated the Ghetto's work ethic at the Germans' behest, is exactingly addressed. Steven Spielberg (*Schindler's List*, 1993) whitewashes Oskar Schindler, failing to note Schindler's selection for extermination of people on his labor "list"; Jablonski gives us Rumkowski's rationalizations, how the "limb" of Ghetto children had to be "sacrificed" to save "the body."

In the process of its investigation Jablonski's film uncovers different strategies for coping with very different involvements in the enormity of the Holocaust.

LATE AUGUST, EARLY SEPTEMBER (France). Life is fragile and fleeting, along with everything in it—and that includes male friendships as well as romantic relationships. Writer-director Olivier Assayas has created a complex masterpiece with his brilliantly scripted tragicomedy *Fin août, début septembre*, one whose especial focus consists of two relationships in which Gabriel participates. Gabriel is a young man who doesn't quite know how to use his literary interest and expertise in terms of employment. He is at loose ends also in romance, leaving one partner, Jenny, for another, Anne (Virginie Ledoyen, marvelous), whom he is slow to realize he deeply loves and whose challenging forwardness covers her insecurities. Gabriel is friends with Adrien, a few-times published novelist whom he admires. They are scarcely in sync. Gabriel is selfconscious but not really self-aware, while Adrien is keenly self-aware but not selfconscious. Adrien also lacks self-confidence, while part of Gabriel's self-confidence derives from his knowledge that Adrien lacks it. The high intelligence of either allows him to negotiate the gap between the qualities he possesses and the ones he lacks. Adrien falls deathly ill, coalescing his philosophical disposition while Gabriel, with so much in his life remaining unresolved, fails to respond adequately to this friend of his. Indeed, it is eventually revealed how competitive Gabriel is with Adrien. We see this, but it is doubtful that Gabriel does.

If one grasps their implications, the film's final few moments overflow with stunning, heart-piercing revelation.

Assayas's quick, light use of handheld camera is correlative to the quick, light mortal breeze permeating the lives of his characters, except for Adrien's secret 15-year-old mistress middle-aging men and women who are constantly taking the pulse of their lingering youth and promise.

Mathieu Amalric plays Gabriel. His tremendous performance is among the greatest in cinema.

OUTSKIRTS (Russia). An extremely dark, mordant satire of post-Soviet Russia, and of the political ties that bind this present to the Communist past, Pyotr Lutsik's black-and-white, Dovzhenkonian *Okraina* is one of the best excoriations of privatization and capitalism I have seen.

Near the Ural Mountains, the collective farm "Homeland" has been taken away from farmers and is being drilled for oil. Who is behind this? The farmers need their farmland to survive; now, their necessity has been trumped "legally," at their expense, by pursuit of profit. A group of villagers sets out to discover what's going on. Their long, difficult odyssey eventually takes them to Moscow, where they execute the callous oligarch behind their misery. Instead of lab jars filled with preserved body parts, this facsimile of Dr. Frankenstein is backed by banks of oil samples: a projection of his soullessness.

Along the way, the band of comrades tortures (to elicit information) and kills, and sees its own number diminished. Lutsik's deadpan attitude—even as one of the farmers slowly gnaws at a victim in a deep, dark pit—prompts reflection on the folk feelings that Sovietism channeled and that are now boiling beneath the surface. *Okraina* has been banned from view in Russia as being "too dangerous," according to Raissa Fomina, who works for the film's Russian distributor. "They say it will cause a revolution." The film leaves Moscow in flames.

Outskirts ends in a mock-elated mode, with the Homeland back in the care of the tractor-riding farmers smiling cheesily. Lutsik is sarcastically asking: Was Stalinism so good? Isn't there something better for Russia than what we had then and what we have now?

Blackness—ironically, the blackness of oil—is the film's predominant shade, and faces are hard to see in it: the dehumanizing reality of the new Russia.

BULLET BALLET (Japan). Dazzling, gorgeous, pulsating, visionary, Shinya Tsukamoto's black-and-white *Bullet Ballet* fuses social criticism, ultra-violence, *West Side Story*-street gangery, Tarkovskian science fiction, and *film noir* to wrestle a stunning life-affirmation from a compelling description of the nihilism of young Tokyoans who see violence, including murder and suicide, as the logical extension of what they perceive to be dead-ended lives. Wrongly, some commentators have said that the film itself is nihilistic. Tsukamoto, the cult favorite who directed *Tetsuo, the Iron Man* (1989) and *A Snake of June* (2002), wrote, directed, cinematographed and edited this fantastic film.

Goda, beautifully played by Tsukamoto, seems to scurry through a dark, occasionally deadly dream. The point of departure is girlfriend Kiriko's unexpected suicide with a gun the calibre of which only the police use. How did she get this gun? Was her death really a suicide? Goda himself investigates, descending into a gang underworld not only to discover the truth, which proves elusive, but to secure his own gun of the type that killed Kiriko so he can strike out at some portion of a dizzyingly immoral world. The mystery police gun suggests that Tsukamoto had in mind Akira Kurosawa's swooning postwar *noir Stray Dog* (1949), thus laying Japan's current moral chaos at the doorstep of the U.S. occupation that stressed capitalism at the expense of Japan's religious foundation and family orientation.

This is a dank film (another touch of Tarkovsky), with a leaky faucet and dripping corridors, and a rush, with flights across streets and bridges in pursuit of confrontation's clarity. *Handheld* camera rules. The production design, as in a dream, makes inside Goda's never-locked apartment one step away from some bizarre, leaky subterranean world that accesses the outdoors. People run while urgently using their cell phones.

Futuristic; contemporary.

JEW-BOY LEVI (Germany). In the mid-1930s, young Benjamin Levi, cattle trader, is making his annual work visit to a remote Black Forest farm village, hoping also, this time, to ask Andreas Horger for his daughter Lisbeth's hand in marriage. Lonely in his itinerant life, he aches for her companionship. But there has been a sea-change in Germany. Angrily, Andreas now flashes an epithet at Benjamin: "Killer of Christ." Benjamin mutters, "Killer of Christ, yeah, yeah."

Also visiting is a Nazi from Berlin, a railway engineer, accompanied by workers, sent to repair worn train tracks and a collapsed tunnel. He tells Benjamin, "You are nothing."

In the restaurant where Lisbeth works as a waitress, and where the community normally gathers after the day's work, one by one, those who haven't yet fully turned against Benjamin do so—except for Lisbeth. Two of the workers twist Benjamin's ears, ordering him to sing a song of hate against Jews. Everyone but Lisbeth points the finger at Benjamin, declaring him the source of the social disharmony—a modern age's pestilence—with which the village has become infected. We see the dynamic of scapegoating, the process of hate, calmly exposed.

In the film's mesmerizing final shot, a long shot, the rear light of the motorcycle on which "Jew-Boy" Levi leaves, alone, in the deep darkness of night recedes and recedes. The scene is the opposite of the daylight one of Benjamin's arrival, where he joyously sings in anticipation of his Lisbeth. The world lay all before him. Now he is disappearing into the silent dark, becoming a "nothing" before our very eyes: the most haunting intimation of the Holocaust in all of cinema.

From Thomas Strittmatter's play, Didi Danquart has made a totally unsentimental film. It sinks into the brain like a collapsed tunnel.

1999

THE WIND WILL CARRY US (Iran, France). In *Bad ma ra khahad bord*, a fish-out-of-water comedy, a man from Tehran arrives, along with a crew, in Siah Dareh, a small, backward village in Iranian Kurdistan. While he waits to record the anticipated death of a 100-year-old resident, Behzad encounters strange people and customs, and copes with the failure of modern technology in so remote a place, encapsulated in his ringing cellular phone, which compels him to seek ever higher ground to try to find the signal that will enable him to hear whoever is calling him. This running gag befits a film that keeps significant action offscreen; very often we must glean what we can from the sounds that we hear. In this, the film is indebted to Antonioni's *The Passenger* (1975), whose method, however, writer-director Abbas Kiarostami extends, alienating even more decisively passive viewers who demand plots with the dots connected.

Kiarostami is as sensitive to the arid landscape as to the animals crawling across it; but what engages him most is humanity. One of the characters whom Behzad encounters is a ditch-digger. We hear the ditch-digger's voice; that's *it*. Eventually, the hole the digger is digging collapses on him, and Kiarostami's unorthodox presentation—not only no closeups of the man, but no shots whatsoever—conveys a searing sense of the victim's reality. Pursuing fresh milk, Behzad also meets this man's fiancée, deep down in a dark family cellar, where she is milking a cow—a stunning visual descent into the very idea of how people, how whole peoples, remain hidden to us, invisible.

The Wind Will Carry Us moves us to believe in the reality of other people(s). Once we do, we can better grasp that their lives are no less important than our own.

THRONE OF DEATH (India, UK). One of the most brilliant satirical films in recent memory, *Marana Simhasanam*, from Kerala, India, in the Malayalam language, is Murali Nair's first feature. It won Nair the Caméra d'Or at Cannes.

Along with his wife, Krishnan has one more day of seasonal low-caste/subsistent-pay employment to go. The film opens with him in the throes of hard physical labor; when he takes a cigarette break, no one will doubt he has earned it—and thus he ekes out the extra day. Years of hard work and deprivation have made the couple look prematurely old, and the introduction of a young boy as their son comes as a shock.

"How long can we starve?" his wife asks Krishnan. That night, Krishnan attempts to divest the landowner's tree of some coconuts, but his timing couldn't be worse. Somehow, miraculously, perhaps by dint of higher caste, the landowner knows what Krishnan is up to beforehand; as he reaches for a coconut, there comes the posse already, by water, to apprehend Krishnan. Also, it is election season, and poor Krishnan becomes everyone's pawn as candidates and supporters eke out what electoral advantage they can. The party in power adds an unsolved murder to Krishnan's criminal résumé, while a Communist opponent goes on a hunger strike on Krishnan's behalf so that Krishnan, rather than being hanged, can experience the "blissful death" delivered by the U.S.-invented "electronic chair" whose widespread distribution the World Bank is planning to underwrite! The end of the hunger strike and Krishnan's execution each prompts a public event, with fanfare and grandstanding speeches. At the former, amongst a flurry of faux-documentary interviews, a villager says:

"While I'm sorry he is going to die, I am happy that Krishnan's death will be blissful."
Media influence!
Grim, hilarious.

ADWA (Ethiopia, Italy, U.S.). A nation, a people: this identity often coalesces around the memory, the history, of a monumental shared ordeal—if possible, victory. In 1996 Ethiopians celebrated the centennial of their ancestors' defeat of the foreign army that invaded so that Italy could colonize Ethiopia. Haile Gerima decided to document the commemoration. (Gerima is currently working on a second part to this project.) The decisive Battle of Adwa is the focus of both the celebration and, hence, this film.

There are no live-action reconstructions; Gerima made this masterpiece on a shoestring—and an Ethiopian-born artist's soul. Having learned about the Battle of Adwa from his own father, he interviews other Ethiopians, some elderly ones whose fathers fought in it, others who provide historical, cultural and political (both geopolitical and pan-African) perspectives. He surveys the terrain leading to and at Adwa. Children keep the memory alive, making it their memory, in rich song. Above all, Gerima sets his camera on extraordinary artwork—paintings, engravings, early photographs that depict the battle and the soul of a people. *Adwa* is among the greatest films to absorb art treasures into their being and make these come alive, both to the eye and the soul of the viewer. Gerima has made, in effect, a spiritual documentary.

Emperor Menelik may have seemed the hero, but it was always *the people:* vast numbers that gathered from distant communities to face their well-armored, well-weaponed Goliath with a stone and a sling—whatever they had. Those who had nothing took weapons from fallen Italian soldiers. Their victory grew into the sunlight of legend, inspiring movements—Pan-African; nationalist ones; the U.S. civil rights movement. In 1935 Fascism took its revenge by invading Haile Selassie's Ethiopia (then called Abyssinia) on a "civilizing mission," resulting in guerrilla resistance that made Italy's life hell.

HUMANITY (France). In Bruno Dumont's nonprofessionally cast *L'humanité,* an eleven-year-old girl, dropped off by her school bus and on her way home, is raped and killed; the force of the intrusion shreds her vagina. We see none of this. Very briefly we see the aftermath. Not the child's face; everything else.

The small town police superintendent who investigates is deeply affected by the crime. Two years earlier he lost both girlfriend and baby in a road accident. Pharaon De Winter suffers lost children; he embraces humanity, feels complicit in the suffering of others. The film largely unfolds in Bailleul, the northern town in France where Dumont is from. De Winter could be Dumont.

Pharaon, unorthodox, sniffs a suspect, "inappropriately" hugs and kisses suspects and others. He isn't above suspicion himself. He is sexually frustrated; a grown man, he lives with his mother. He has a temper. He throws himself on the ground sobbing before an official report of the crime even reaches him.

Some reviewers suggest that Pharaon doesn't solve the crime. Certainly he takes no credit. When at last he confronts the contrite confessed killer, he remarks, "Surely it isn't *you.*" And, in a way, it isn't. It could be any one of us, including Pharaon himself. But in his seemingly slow-witted way it is Pharaon who has moved the investigation along to the point when the killer must reveal himself. This is Pharaon's humanity; however, it's also his way of playing God. For Pharaon, since there is no possibility of glory in raping, murdering and mutilating a child, neither is there glory in solving such a heinous crime. This also is Pharaon's humanity. He does his job in such a way as to allow others to take credit; but with all his heart *he does his job.*

THE ROAD HOME (China). Gorgeous, lyrical, poignant, *Wo de fu qin mu qin* is framed by the fierce, wintry, somber black-and-white present, with the past, in between, in lush, vivid color. (Hou Yong cinematographed.) A cosmopolitan businessman visits his northern rural home, where his father, Changyu, who has just died, was the beloved village schoolteacher. Although he is certified to teach, Yusheng has never taught and has never married (the film implies the sterility of an increasingly capitalistic China); his parents, by contrast, were mutually devoted for forty years. Their romance occupies the film's middle, as an old family photograph shifts Yusheng's mind to his parents' meeting and falling in love, as Yusheng has come to "travel" these events. Yusheng's steady, solemn voiceover enters a domain of love and sweeping feeling; some trouble Changyu experienced with authorities—offscreen, because this wasn't discussed—led to his "restriction" and temporarily separated the pair. (The life he has lived vicariously may have become more vivid to Yusheng than his own.) Bound in love to his mother, Di, and his father's memory, Yusheng helps arrange for the traditional funeral march that his mother insists on despite its disfavor since the Cultural Revolution.

Zhang Ziyi and Zhao Yulian are superb as the young and older Di. Working from a fine, haunting script by Shi Bao based on his own novel, director Zhang Yimou applies tracking shots to 18-year-old Di's dashes through landscape to capture glimpses of the boy she is in love with, wringing from the moving camera powerful emotional mileage. Di's meticulous decoration of Changyu's schoolroom, her sitting alone inside the empty classroom: intense sexual sublimations. The final color coda freezes a long-shot of young Di on the road home; in its stasis we experience the heartaching rush of time.

CLOUDS OF MAY (Turkey). Nuri Bilge Ceylan's *Mayis sikintisi* suggests Chekhov's *The Cherry Orchard*. Like Abbas Kiarostami's *Closeup* (1990) and *Through the Olive Trees* (1994), it is a film about the making of a film. Ceylan's surrogate, Muzaffer, has returned from Istanbul to recruit his cast from family members. Meanwhile, Muzaffer's father (played by Ceylan's father, Emin) is trying to save his land from state appropriation; in particular, he doesn't want trees to be clear-cut. Despite Muzaffer's contrary efforts, his film bends to his actors' concerns, including his father's wish to protect some of the natural beauty whose enrichment Muzaffer, who remains fixated on his film, seems to have forgotten.

There is a Chekhovian density of family relations, the tension between family cohesion and the concerns and aspirations of individual members. Ceylan evokes in the country landscape the stilling of time that discloses, ironically, time's rush that the stillness tries holding back. Muzaffer's father's endeavor to save the trees is also an attempt to hold back time.

Muzaffer's blindness to Nature's beauty makes him like his little cousin, whose aunt, Muzaffer's mother, promises him any present he wants if he keeps an egg in his pocket for forty days. On his way home from school, the diligent boy is handed a basket of tomatoes to deliver to someone. The woman warns him not to rock or crush the tomatoes. En route, though, a tomato falls out of the basket, and when the boy bends over to retrieve it, we hear *crack*. The egg! He drops the basket; the tomatoes go tumbling down a hill towards the camera—sheer beauty, to which the boy, fixated on his anticipated gift, is oblivious. He is rewarded anyhow, with a musical watch: time rendered delightful.

Both boy and uncle learn and grow.

THE CARRIERS ARE WAITING (Belgium, France, Switzerland). A brilliant, painfully funny tragicomedy about family in a suburb within sight of a grimy industrial landscape, former documentarian Benoît Mariage's *Les convoyeurs attendent* beautifully mixes naturalism and surrealism.

The Clossets live on Impasse Jaunet. (Note both names: family; street.) A newspaper photojournalist, Roger runs to each newsworthy event that's reported on his police band radio. His wife, Madeleine, is plainly patient, tolerant, long-suffering. Her stoicism is matched by the couple's 8-year-old daughter, Luise, whose shyness is matched by her sensitivity to what goes on around her. Her teenaged brother, Michel, is sweet on Jocelyne. Félix, a reclusive neighbor (Philippe Grand'Henry, giving the best performance), works in a factory but lives for the competitive carrier pigeons he raises. Like Luise, who befriends this kindred spirit, he is shy, quiet, gentle, kind. A greedy local bully fancies Félix's prize pigeon, Napoléon.

Roger yearns for a bit of status in his bleak life. To win a car to replace his demoralizing scooter, he orders Michel to beat the current Guinness record for door openings, walk-throughs and closings in a 24-hour period. The lone standing frame and door that he sets up outside, for Michel's tortuous training, is out of Magritte; the contest itself unfolds in a boxing ring. Many superlative shots situate Roger in the foreground while in the background Michel practices—a projection of Roger's desire to find a door to success that is getting him nowhere. Roger bullies his son to distraction, leading to a self-destructive (and car-destructive) act that leaves Michel comatose. It is in such a state that Michel and pregnant Jocelyne participate in the weirdest wedding ceremony since Luchino Visconti's *The Damned* (1969).

His insecurities erupting into violence, Roger reminds me of my father. Now, may both of them know peace.

JOURNEY TO THE SUN (Turkey, Netherlands, Germany). Yesim Ustaoglu's *Günese yolculuk* addresses Turkey's mistreatment of Kurds. While not Kurdish, Ustaoglu comes from a largely Kurdish area of Turkey near the Armenian border. Former spouse Tayfun Pirselimoglu's story revolves around the friendship that develops between two young men who have relocated in Istanbul from western Turkey. "Dark-skinned," Mehmet becomes a police target. Berzan is a Kurd; the village massacre that killed his father has radicalized him. When Mehmet loses lodgings and employment after being mistakenly jailed and tortured as a Kurdish rebel, Berzan takes him in. After Berzan is clubbed to death by police during a Kurdish street demonstration, Mehmet takes his friend's body, in a cumbersome coffin, on a long, difficult journey home, to Zorduc: a watery wasteland now. Mehmet commends his friend's coffin to the deep. The film's timely release followed the capture of Abdullah Ocalan, who had led Turkey's Kurdish armed rebellion.

A former architect, Ustaoglu has a clear eye for the dim details of Istanbul's slums. She impressively films spontaneous group street dance as a defense by Istanbul's young against the crushing monotony of urban existence. Nothing short of devastating, though, is the related scene of Mehmet alone in their apartment after Berzan has been killed. (A brain hemorrhage is the official finding.) The boy begins tossing himself around the room, hitting this, banging that, until his moves coalesce into a discernible dance—a dance aiming to relieve the pressure of his anger and grief.

But the film's crowning achievement is Mehmet's "journey to the sun," which completes the emotional and spiritual identification as a Kurd that began when the police mistook Mehmet for one and therefore mistreated him. Every fleeting glimpse of vacancy in land and sky and abandoned impoverished homes resonates as metaphor for the devastated Kurdish population.

GENESIS (Mali, France). *The world is torn asunder . . . Each devours his neighbor's flesh.*
Although *La Genèse* will proceed in the Bambara language, it opens wittily with biblical text in French; France's colonizing of Mali thus implicitly launches Cheick Oumar Sissoko's stunning film loosely based on chapters 33-37 of the Book of Genesis. Its ancient drama, transposed to the vast Mali desert, reflects on contentious post-colonial Africa. We impute to Sissoko's dedication, to all victims of fratricide, however, the widest possible reference.

Everyone's complaint is rendered suspect. Exhorting himself, Esau shouts, "Do not forget to take revenge." Having returned from exile with an army, he is referring to his brother, Jacob, whom he feels robbed him of his birthright; a later flashback shows that, exaggerating hunger, Esau sold his birthright to Jacob for a bowl of soup. Meanwhile, Jacob's protracted mourning for son Joseph, reportedly torn apart by wild beasts, has reached ridiculous proportions, causing Jacob to ignore his other sons, who are in need of control, as well as daughter Dinah. We later learn that Joseph is in fact alive. Meanwhile, Dinah crosses camps to bed Shechem, Hamor's son; on no apparent basis, their sex is reported as rape. No one thinks to ask Dinah, since Jacob and sons feel that the relevant issue is family honor. The sons massacre the males of Hamor's tribe (Hamor survives in this telling), including Shechem, causing Dinah to lose her mind.

Repeatedly Jacob is shown inside his dark tent indulging his mourning while sunlight dazzles outside; visually, the nighttime massacre thus becomes an extension of his mindset, holding Jacob responsible. During the dark night of his soul, Jacob later does his celebrated wrestling—in this telling, *with God*. The final rush of reconciliations is moving beyond belief. It expresses hope for Africa.

THE COLOR OF LIES (France). "In a small town, people talk. You just need to listen."

Claude Chabrol's *Au coeur du mensonge*—literally, *At the Heart of the Lie*—is an amazing portrait of marital complexity, jealousy, the infliction of past on present, as well as a suspenseful mystery. Its launch: after she leaves the home of art instructor René Sterne (Jacques Gamblin), the rape and murder of ten-year-old Eloïse Michel in the woods of St. Malo in Brittany. Gossip identifies outsider René as the prime suspect, and he loses his pupils one by one. Chief Inspector Frédérique Lesage (Valeria Bruni Tedeschi, marvelously exasperating), another former Parisian and out to fit in, tells him, "You're either the last or next-to-last person to see the child alive."

René, who paints, hasn't had a show in twelve years; he is lame, a victim of one of the 1986 Hezbollah bombings in Paris—and a victim, too, of the depressed art market. Discombobulated, he forsook painting portraits for landscapes; his wife, Vivianne (Sandrine Bonnaire, brilliant), holds him together. They met when she was his nurse after the explosion that has variously crippled him. Vivianne commits adultery with neighbor Germain-Roland Desmot, a successful author of whom (though he denies it) René is intensely jealous. René suspects the adultery. Meanwhile, his jealousy is matched by that of Inspector Loudun (Bernard Verley, terrific), the local who plainly feels that Lesage's job ought to have been his. The point-of-view shot encapsulating Lesage's realization of this is a devastating insert.

A great cut: from an overhead shot of Eloïse's coffin in the ground to a whispering Vivianne and René in bed that night, themselves mentally trapped in that coffin.

Chabrol and Odile Barski wrote the complicated script. Barski's son, Rodolphe Pauly, plays a very strange teenager!

THE LITTLE GIRL WHO SOLD THE SUN (Senegal, France, Switzerland). *See above.*

BELFAST, MAINE (U.S.). For four fascinating hours, Frederick Wiseman surveys the mid-sized bayside town of *Belfast, Maine*—its (gorgeous) natural environment, its people, its institutions. People are shown at work, such as in a sardine factory, where each step is shown in the process that ends with the tinning of the fish; there are also social workers, ER receptionists, police officers, and so forth. People are also shown in social activities and more highly personal exchanges. Here is a massive sociological work.

It is also a summary work, recalling other Wiseman films. For instance, *Belfast, Maine* returns to the American high school. As in *High School* (1969), the results are bleak. Here, the English teacher is neither fatuous nor incompetent; he teaches Herman Melville's *Moby-Dick* with intelligence and passion, but he must persevere, which he admirably does, through a sea of student otioseness and indifference that drowns all hope for America's future. In many details, the film is an apocalyptic work. On the other hand, patience and kindness are also shown, such as in the care of the elderly, implying a community spirit that defies the fact the town has many more good years behind it than ahead. With thematic rigor and a sense of completion, the film ends in church.

Wiseman's films observe, absent voiceover guidance. One watches as scenes accumulate into a rich, full vision of existence. Wiseman's method enables viewers to feel they are half-creating Belfast, Maine; they aren't just looking at the town's inhabitants but imagining their unspoken thoughts and feelings, perhaps challenged by the degree of strangeness in the people on view, perhaps beckoned by the complicity they themselves feel in the shared American experience—or both.

If Wiseman's New Englanders are going down for the count, so are the rest of us.

MALAISE (India). Doctors, baffled, have been unable to diagnose the illness that has hospitalized Geeta, who, exhausted from blood drawings and injections, has lost her will to live. Her daughter, movie star Rohini ("Runu"), has left a shoot to attend to her mother and her father, Sudhamoy, with whom she is constantly short. Sudhamoy is concerned about his daughter's irritated eyes and habitual use of sleeping pills, and he is sufficiently concerned about Geeta to have supplied the hospital with disposable needles to use on her. Also, his pride is delicately strained by his famous daughter's financial support.

Bengali writer-director Rituparno Ghosh's *Asukh*, which is headed for an emotionally overwhelming finish, may be regarded as the dramatic translation of music's *basso profundo* —except that its somber tone and quietude are continually interrupted by the screech of ringing cellular phones! This is a film of interruptions, including those caused by Geeta's mystery illness, and perhaps encapsulated by a poem by Rabindranath Tagore, which Geeta knows by heart, which she read to Runu as a child to help her sleep, but which Runu now struggles to recall. Slivers of the past interrupt the present; a little girl pops up in the parents' home—and in a staggering moment, what first seems Sudhamoy's reminiscence of his daughter in childhood almost immediately, with a shift in camera perspective, seems the grown Runu's reminiscence. Here is one of the most moving films in creation about family.

Ghosh punctuates single-color scenes (sepia, pale blue-and-white, etc.) with exquisite bursts of delicate color.

Soumitra Chatterjee is tremendous as Runu's quiet, shuffling father—forty years past Satyajit Ray's *The World of Apu*, and still at work. Poignantly, Debajyoti Mishra's score teases with echoes of Ravi Shankar's for *Apu*.

India's National Film Award; International Critics' Prize at Bombay.

MUNDO GRÚA (Argentina). In Argentina, the disparity between rich and poor is deepened by a global economy that impoverishes much of the middle-class and sacrifices the poor to enhance the wealth of transnational corporations. This new eco-colonialism contextualizes Pablo Trapero's (mostly) black-and-white *Mundo grúa* (*Crane World*).

Divorced, in his forties, Rulo (Luis Margani, wonderful) does odd jobs in Buenos Aires such as selling tires and fixing trucks. Torres, a friend, gets him a job in construction operating a crane. The day that Rulo is to start work, however, he is let go in favor of a younger man, ostensibly because Rulo smokes and is fifty pounds overweight. But one wonders; in what may be a flashforward, the film opens with Torres, who is slim and fit, being fired from his construction job for not being "dressed right." Intrusive impersonal forces, rationalized by "rules," apparently determine employment. After Rulo is fired, shots of dormant equipment project his banishment from the work site.

Torres secures Rulo another crane job, as an excavator in Patagonia, in the southern desert. This means leaving behind friends, mother, teenaged son Claudio, and girlfriend Adriana, whose once profitable sandwich kiosk struggles against a backdrop of prodigious construction.

Fellow workers provide the only companionship in Rulo's new environment. When one day food that the "bosses" are supposed to provide doesn't arrive, in a spontaneous show of solidarity the workers refuse to work until it does. Later, their pay stops. Is the company that was bankrolling the construction pulling out? Everyone's job evaporates. This time, static shots of abandoned equipment occupy a wasteland of vast sky and of sand composed of volcanic white shells. Each worker heads back to wherever he came from. Makeshift lives; transience.

Trapero: "I wanted a film that was like a hidden camera filming snatches of reality."

BEAU TRAVAIL (France). First things first. Her gorgeous, brilliant *Beau travail*, whatever Claire Denis may think, has nothing to do with Herman Melville's even more brilliant *Billy Budd*, which questions our allegorizing tendency, as well as our ready submission to various kinds of authority (military, media, biblical, political, etc.), and does *not* involve any allegorical confrontation between good and evil.

Certainly Denis's Sergeant Galoup, the foreign legionnaire patterned after Claggart, is tainted with unMelvillean literalism. Launching the voiceover narration, he admits that "[different] viewpoints count"; but he is no match for Melville's trickster narrator, whose unreliability tosses everything we "see" and "hear" into question. (Or is it that Dénis Lavant's performance is so dreadful?) On the other hand, her Billy Budd, the enlistee called Gilles Sentain, is a more striking presence. (Or is it that Grégoire Colin is titanic and heartrending in this role?) One's jealousy of the other, as Sentain draws away from Galoup the fatherly attention of Commander Bruno Forestier (Michel Subor, in the performance of his life), is among the misinterpretations with which Melville's trickster narrator tries to distract the reader from more relevant matters, such as the discrepancy between reportage and truth.

Hypnotic chanting on the soundtrack; the camera pans across half-naked young men, white and black, their arms stretched up. When the camera lights upon Sentain in the intense sunlight of East African desert, its angle suggests a crucifixion, as of Jesus, and the boy's angular face and muscular torso cede to a dreaminess: superimposed pulsating gray water. Denis is conjuring a dream—actually, a dream-within-a-dream: the subconscious homoerotic one of military calisthenics, obedience, comradery, conflict, inside her own waking, antimilitary, artistic one, the dreaminess that releases the poignancy of her inability to control her characters and divert them from their tragic fates.

AIMÉE & JAGUAR (Germany). "Aimée" and "Jaguar" are code names for two women living in Berlin during the latter part of the war, 1943-1944. Aimée's real name is Felice Schragenheim; she is Jewish and a Resistance fighter, her risky cover, working for a Nazi paper under an assumed identity. Jaguar's real name is Lilly Wust; she is married to an officer at the front. The two become lesbian lovers—verboten activity in Nazi Germany. Begun triflingly, their love affair becomes all-consuming. Co-written and directed by Max Färberböck, from a book by journalist Erica Fischer, who interviewed the real "Lilly," *Aimée & Jaguar* is structured as Lilly's reminiscence. Lilly is in her 80s now; the love of her life, we surmise, perished in a death camp.

Here is one of the saddest, most fear-fraught films in creation—reckless passion in a maelstom, recollected in poignant tranquility. The exquisite nature of the visuals, their rich, dark colors, suggest things burned in the memory—atypical ghosts contributing to the haunted memory of a nation.

Some commentators quibble about this or that. For instance, how realistic is it that the Nazi newspaper's editor would help protect Felice's cover? I take this as an index of how decadent Nazism had become by this late date; its form had outlasted its fervor. What about Lilly's husband's frequent trips home from the war? I take this as being emotionally expressive—an index of how intruded-upon Lilly felt her affair with Felice to have been. Where either history or memory is concerned, literalism may not be the best interpretive tack to take.

Impossible love affairs happen. In Nazi Germany, lovers of any kind would have had to

retreat into their own world—and all the more so with this pair.
Maria Schrader is extraordinary as Felice.

GHOST DOG: THE WAY OF THE SAMURAI (France, Germany, U.S., Japan). Forest Whitaker gives a titanic performance—his finest—as Ghost Dog, a Mafia hitman in Jim Jarmusch's *Ghost Dog*. It was shot mostly in Jersey City, but the setting is even more anonymous than Ghost Dog, whose adopted name reflects his allegiance to his guiding text, *Hagakure*, based on actual eighteenth-century conversations with a former samurai, who was prohibited from committing suicide after the death of his master—a tome nostalgic for the "old days," when a samurai really was a samurai. Near the twenty-first century, Ghost Dog is himself even more of a throwback, as is the Italian-American Mafia. When he was eight, the life of the boy-who-would-become-Ghost Dog was saved by Louis, who became his master. Ghost Dog, who lives in a rooftop shack amongst pigeons, uses a carrier pigeon for contact about a job—another throwback. Now there is a contract out on *him* because of who witnessed one of his hits; but Ghost Dog is fighting back, doing all he can to eliminate those who would eliminate him.

Whitaker's role makes full use of his sensitive hands and disparate eyes, one of them droopy, the other alert, mischievous. He is a figure of ambivalence, a warrior in peacetime, an African American in a white man's world. We see the full draft of his humanity, though, in his friendship with Pearline, the young girl with whom he shares a love of reading books: a version of himself once upon a time.

The young protagonist of Jarmusch's mystical *Dead Man* (1995) is dead to begin with; his journey allows his lagging consciousness to catch up with the fact. Who knows? Perhaps "Ghost Dog" lost his life on that fateful day when he was eight years old.

HEROD'S LAW (Mexico). *Herod's Law: Fuck people over before they fuck with you.*

Luis Estrada's brutal, brilliant film satirizes the Institutional Revolutionary Party (PRI)'s stranglehold on Mexico's politics and Mexican lives since the Revolution. The government succeeded in suppressing the film until adverse publicity compelled its release. The following year, the opposition candidate (National Action Party), former Coca-Cola manager Vicente Fox, was elected president.

Mild-mannered, naïve Juan Vargas, a junkyard custodian, becomes mayor of a tiny rural patch, San Pedro de los Saguaros, whose non-Spanish-speaking indigenes have already lynched a number of his predecessors. Vargas begins idealistically and compassionately, intending to bring social justice and erase poverty, but the Party official appointing him, instead of allocating funds (which are being monopolized by the expense of the upcoming election), arms Juan with a giant book of federal and state laws, to squeeze fees and taxes out of the poor, and a gun, to buttress his authority. When the madam of the local brothel resists his attempt to extort money from her, he shoots her and her bodyguard dead and moves to frame a doctor who has threatened to have him removed from office. It is in this vein that Estrada's film continues, frequently hilariously. Vargas ends up becoming a wife-beater, killing his mentor and publicly announcing the Party's determination to stay in power forever: *business as usual.*

Some have complained about the film's broadness and bluntness; farcical satire isn't the worse for being unsubtle, un-Shavian.

The accumulation of plot twists and turns suggests the depth of political corruption and social inattention during so many decades of entrenched PRI rule. Estrada overlooks little; for instance, *La ley de Herodes* is withering on the subject of the contribution made by Mexico's gringo northern neighbor to the host of woes routinely visited on Mexico's poor.

Films of the new millennium

Chicago-born Jon Jost is among those filmmakers who have made the move to digital video. His *Passages* unfolds in a young child's world of Nature, visual wonder, and a father's implicit protection, companionship and love. In a written prologue, Jost explains that much of the film's material was shot while his young daughter, Clara, was by his side, beginning in 1997. I flip such statements for a fuller view; Clara's being by his side means also that Jost was by *her* side, applying protective care without her being objectively aware of it (to which fact Jost's, for now, invisibility becomes, for us, correlative). For once, normality and the romance of an idyllic state coincide. Here are father and daughter before a terrible fall; for the written prologue proceeds to summarize unfortunate subsequent history. Jost's legal rights regarding his daughter were severed by Portuguese courts on petition by the child's mother, who, defying the custody ruling of a Roman court, had kidnapped Clara from their Rome apartment in 2002, following the breakup of their (non-marital) union. Kierkegaard once wrote that we deduce innocence from its subsequent loss; Jost, as a result of the malicious actions of the mother of his treasure and the lack of responsiveness to a child's needs by Portugal's legal system, is left to deduce the existence of Paradise from his subsequent loss of it. *Passages* has thus become what its material was not initially meant to be: a means by which Jost can spiritually reconnect with his daughter, to ease his side of their physical separation, and a monument to his love for her that someday Clara herself might visit, to ease the perplexing pain and anguish of lost time together that others have inflicted on her. What might have been merely a delightful work has deepened into a passionate reflection on the ties that bind and life's unpredictability. Jost has subtitled the piece "a meditation for Clara."

The video itself is a thing of Monetic/Turneresque beauty, of gorgeous imagery, processed in-camera, in perpetual transformation—a measured, almost entirely silent kaleidoscopic work that lives up to its title. However, *Passages* begins with three stills and two screens of the written introduction. The first bit of motion follows: letters of the title moving, in order, across the bottom of a blank screen, right to left—a scrolling reversal of which Jost is fond, perhaps to proclaim his independence from cultural norms. In any case, the delayed introduction of movement of any kind projects a magical aura, as though the invocation that the title represents has set the thing in motion. As the letters of the title are about to disappear off-screen left, the first image in motion appears, filling up the screen. Language has been replaced by something more elemental, primitive, enchanting. From its understandably embittered written prologue, *Passages* has found its way back to innocence.

Of what does this monochromatic opening image-in-motion consist? Well, that's hard to say; and those deficient in Keatsian negative capability, who insist on knowing what literally the camera had in view, which now appears in a mysterious visual form, rather than allowing themselves to enjoy the sheer beauty of the image, may have a problem with the video's opening movement—a problem, of course, of their own making. But a friend to whom I showed the video made a persuasive suggestion: hair; perhaps a child's hair. However, abetted by the fact that the last of the opening stills, which comes from the film, consists of tall trees in a darkened forest, a viewer may as easily interpret the image as being a forest or some other form of plant growth. The result, in any case, is suggestive of the waving wheat at the beginning of Aleksandr Dovzhenko's silent *Earth* (1930). A seemingly infinite number of vertical strands fluctuate, creating a dance of dark and shimmering light in a field, or sea, of grays. It is an image of heart-catching loveliness and pure enchantment; but as the fluctuation, after a spell, gives the appearance of slowing down because of the introduction of color (that is the effect color always has, at least to me), slightly rigidifying the image, at least impeding its luxuriant flow, a suggestion of trouble, or danger, enters in, and the image begins to resemble a forest more clearly—the kind in which children lose their way in fairy tales. Or perhaps the light green color suggests a field of blades of grass. In any case, we are not looking at whatever it is from a distance; we are in the thick of it, and the slightly suffocating quality now makes each inflection of light seem all the more precious, as though it were an opening that's letting in sunlit air.

Indeed, the clarification of the image suggests the perception, or the sharpening of perception, that accompanies the coming into being of someone from the oceanic "feel," or sensitivity, of prenatal existence. Along with this, the fixed or static camera springs into life, moving screen-leftward, as the title had earlier done, only much more quickly. Layered in superimpositions, the forest sprints past. As viewer, we no longer are in the thick of something indeterminate; we are watching something apart from us, and this separation strikes us as correlative to the sharpening objectivity of an emerging consciousness. At the same time, memories of prenatal existence merge with the newer cluster of perceptions accompanied by a rapid static-like thumping on the soundtrack that can be interpreted as a heartbeat. The camera is again stationary. Dividing the forest are, first, one and then two vertical trunk-like outlines, one light and the other dark, that appear to contain the sea in motion, although in each case the sea moves up and down rather than laterally, as if the images had been cranked from their base line by 90°. This suggests a degree of unnaturalness in contradistinction to the "naturalness" of the oceanic existence that preceded it, traces of which persist. Concomitantly, a suggestion of exposure and vulnerability asserts itself. The image is dynamic; the surrounding forest disappears into blackness, the side-by-side trunk-like formations multiply, each containing its bit of ocean, the "heartbeat" persists, and we realize that we at some point have passed the image has gone from color back to black and white. The further multiplication of the sea-containing trunk-like outlines results in a new forest, an abstract, symbolical one wherein the unnatural direction of flowing water implies further divisions between world and self, further self-divisions, further vulnerability and danger. The imagery becomes more and more abstract as the differently textured streams of water seemingly flow vertically upwards and, increasingly appearing as merging streams of dots, become less something than a sense or impression of something—an ironical reversal of the movement from abstraction to clarity that preceded it. For me, the ideas of our original oceanic existence (cosmic as well as prenatal), bloodstream, and the "stream of life" all merge here. This stunning passage culminates in another kind of reversal: the camera zips past clearly defined forest, only this time moving screen-right, and now in color, specifically, woodsy greens and browns. The sum of the camera movement left and now right prompts the ironical suggestion of stasis (mathematically, zero), as though the entire passage were illuminating a single split-second of time, being, consciousness. The rapidity of the motion, accompanied by the "heartbeat," besides suggesting pulse, creates the illusion that the trees themselves have taken flight and are in motion, conflating the grounded and the airborne, definition and abstraction, perception and feeling, time and timelessness, naturalness and unnaturalness. It is an evocation of life itself, with a nod to the oceanic existence that preceded it and dangers that lurk ahead. Jost's retrospective "meditation for Clara" is also a meditation *about* his daughter.

Several passages later, by which time the imagery has moved back into black and white, the camera turns to put the sea back to the horizontal way that we normally perceive it. The water seems primordial, oozing with reptiles; as it degenerates into dots, sea could pass for forest or fields of grasses. Serpents, or gigantic sea-worms, appear in water that could be land or land that could be water. Sharp, jaggedy forms resembling gray glass and metal blades enter the frame, accompanied by a shrill noise like a drill—a threat. We glimpse behind this visual rendering of unnatural danger, and through it since the invading objects include transparent areas, rolling waves. As if by magic, the invaders withdraw and the shrill sound fades and is replaced by the lapping sound of the water. A child appears in the water—Clara, here perhaps five or six years old. Her blue bathing suit punctuates her gradual transformation from almost cartoonish abstraction to vibrant reality. Clara is under her father's watchful eye. She speaks to her father: "Daddy, come swim." Her importance is indicated by the blue of the suit (nothing else blue has appeared in the video), her removal of Jost from the realm of anonymity by her addressing him and, of course, her speech itself—the only words uttered in *Passages*.

Now the glass and metallic invaders re-enter the frame, this time targeting and closing in on Clara. It is one of the most striking moments when they withdraw from her, leaving the frame along with their shrill sound, leaving the happy child oblivious to all harm or threat of harm to her. What pressures danger's withdrawal? A father's *will*. Here is an expression of Jost's parental desire to protect his daughter.

Given the associative logic of the heart, this desire of Jost's leads him to a consideration of Clara's birth—perhaps the work's most brilliant, most piercing passage. Water has appeared so often in this film, how can Jost possibly signal that its next appearance is meant to evoke the cosmic ocean from which Clara, like the rest of us, sprung? In a passage of Warholian steadfastness and intentness, a gently rocking gray ocean, with hypnotic rolling patches of light, fills the screen. Jost holds this image a very long time, and, unless we foolishly resist this rhythmic expression of Clara's (and our own) pre-conscious existence, this allows our own consciousness to be subsumed in it—at the least, imaginatively; possibly, even actually. But far more to the point is that his own entrance into this imagery allows Jost to reconnect spiritually with the daughter who has been taken away from him. At the least, in her absence he is able to reaffirm their bond. The video passes from closeup to long-shot (or, at least, to an image that gives the appearance of greater distance), and bits and threads of red enter the image of water: the blood of Clara's birth; the blood of life. This image is so moving because it is painfully divided. What appears to reunite father and daughter, spiritually, imaginatively, at the same time underscores their separation. The blood of birth is also the mother's blood, and it's the mother here who has separated parent and child. Any attempt to reimagine a child's birth as the father's (spiritual, imaginative, whatever) birthing process highlights the biological reality that is being imaginatively worked on, trumped and reversed. The blood of life, moreover, coincides with humanity's mortal condition, so Jost's endeavors to compensate for his and his daughter's separation ironically underscore the possibility that the end of one or the other will intervene, imposing, at least on earth, a permanent separation. Pulse signifies the birth of life but also the gradual losing of it, and in Jost's image—it is the most exquisite one in *Passages*—the red flows from left to right, not towards the camera, not towards either Jost or us. It signifies the connection he seeks while at the same time implying a spectacle that one is helplessly left to watch (again, the seemingly more distant image of water contributes to this outcome), like the legal ordeal that Jost has undergone. Clara's blood is *his* blood, made so by paternity and love, and in the image in question we along with Jost must sit and watch it pass away. There is the ultimate irony that Clara is probably as oblivious to Jost's efforts to reconnect with her through *Passages* as she was to the danger from which Jost sought to protect her in the earlier scene—danger that, in the form of her mother's stealing her away from her father, has come to pass. Accompanying the shot of ruby-tinged water isn't the "heartbeat" we have heard but another repetitive, more jarring sound.

These dark undercurrents render more complex the water imagery itself, even apart from the ambiguity of the blood. Everywhere the water conveys the sense of absence that both father and daughter are suffering on his or her side of the enforced separation. One can't hold on to water; it slips away, through one's grip and grasp. (I recall an image in which water eludes the hand attempting to catch it in Jost's 1987 *Plain Talk & Common Sense (Uncommon Senses)*.) *Passages* is a poem of absence seeking an impossible alchemy to transform this into presence and reunion. One cannot say how much of this darker material is conscious on Jost's part, but it enriches his prayer for his daughter, which conclusively becomes that she should be graced with love. Even this written declaration at the end of *Passages*, however, is riddled with ambiguity and a sense of loss and helplessness; for although Jost is ostensibly wishing for love to come to and protect Clara from a multitude of sources, to compensate for his enforced absence in his daughter's life, Jost is also praying that Clara receive his love, somehow, from close-up rather than afar. Every hope in *Passages* implies the absence or loss that requires hopefulness as compensation. This helps make everything that is seemingly simple in it emotionally complex and terribly moving.

The image of the stream of life baptized in blood turns out to be, like every other image in *Passages*, a bridge to something else, a transformation, a *passage*—only more so. A whirling image implying creation—the video has summoned similar motifs before—moves the piece into another sustained dimension. Favoring pale, luminous yellow, pink and pink-violet, this long passage is as pure an expression of original awakening as I have seen. It is like a series of constantly, kaleidoscopically changing Turner watercolors—all that light, sunlit color, transparency, evanescence. We scarcely know how to explain to young people nowadays how decades of deepening pollution have robbed flowers and fruits in the United States of the richness of their perfumes and sweetness; but for those of us who cherish trace memories of the past richness, this passage in Jost's piece has the capacity to restore our sensory delight to the imaginative full. That is how perfectly beautiful it is.

This "fall" into innocence culminates in a closeup of (I presume) Clara in the fullness of her glowing infancy. Not since Chris Marker's *La jetée* (1962) has a closeup of someone's sleeping eyes drawn such total attention. The baby is bathed in light. Imaginatively, spiritually, heartrendingly, Jost has worked his way back to a moment when he was there at his daughter's side and their whole life together lay before them. The end of *Passages* is in search of a new beginning.

The title has at least a double meaning, referring not only to the transformations that images in the video seem to undergo but also to the state of visual form at a given point along that transformational journey—taken together, "passages" in the sense of parts, like passages in a piece of writing, or chapters of a book. However, it is the transformational implication of the title that most deeply engages my interest. In its course *Passages* moves back and forth between black and white and color, vast silence and some sound, mysteriously indeterminate imagery and clear-cut live action (Clara at play), the prenatal suggestion that this "mysteriously indeterminate," oceanic imagery conjures and the live suggestion of the child's soon-after-birth, a fixed camera and one in quick lateral motion. At any given point the imagery is in motion, fluctuating; but there is also this movement from one category of images to another, creating an impression of powerful cycles of movement inside larger powerful cycles of movement. Jost is thus able to evoke, amazingly, some sense of the force of life.

Like *Passages*, *Alexei and the Spring* (*Alexei to izumi*) is one of the most beautiful films of the past decade.

An unpopular war in Afghanistan, the economic drain imposed by a long "cold war" not of its making, the whetted appetite for freedom that liberalization, ironically, had wrought: there are all sorts of explanations for the collapse of the Soviet Union, the enormous fallout from which includes the world's current crises deriving from an unchecked United States of unbridled and vicious power. In truth, these and other causes contributed to the end of a superpower both directly and by interacting with one another—what, in another context, Freud described as *overdetermination*. It was in 1985 that Soviet Premier Mikhail Gorbachev instituted *perestroika* and *glasnost*, the twin pillars of his policy of liberalization. *Perestroika* was the economic pillar; in retrospect, Gorbachev's holding agriculture exempt from this economic restructuring, partly because of nostalgia he couldn't muster the will to curb, proved troublesome. *Glasnost*, the political pillar that brought much greater freedom of speech to the Soviet people, as well as encouraging (really, for the first time) national self-examination on a broad scale, needed *perestroika* to succeed if the Soviet state was to continue. Without this success, state erosion was bound to proceed. Moreover, the downward spiral was speeded up by the Chernobyl nuclear plant calamity, on April 26, 1986, that gave the state (at least) the appearance of incompetence and of wanton disregard for the welfare of its citizenry. The fall of the Berlin Wall, in 1989, also contributed to the outcome. By the end of 1991 the Union of Soviet Socialist Republics had disintegrated.

The documentary *Alexei and the Spring* was made in the shadow of Chernobyl. The filmmaker, Motohashi Seiichi, is Japanese. The film, however, is in Russian, the language of those whose daily lives it explores. The setting is Budische, in Belarus, a rural farm village emptied of nearly all of its 600-some residents by the Chernobyl disaster in the Ukraine that, the result of a flawed reactor design and lax, unskilled operation, produced a steam explosion and fire that released into the atmosphere and downwind a small percentage of the radioactive reactor core. Defying the government order to evacuate, fewer than sixty residents remained in Budische, all of them older folk, except for Alexei, a gentle boy in his mid-thirties. The younger residents who left return periodically to help parents and grandparents with planting and with harvest. Sustaining the villagers, both physically and spiritually, is the local spring; one hundred years old at least, its waters remain uncontaminated, as though sanctified by Nature, which will not abandon the villagers no matter what.

The deaths of the villagers will mean the death of the village. In the meantime, the place is full of life—the daily life of work, talk, routines. Seiichi's film is infused with irony; life continues and continues while inching toward its end. *Alexei and the Spring* thus admits a certain affinity with documentaries by Robert J. Flaherty and with Werner Herzog's *Herdsmen of the Sun* (1988), which documents a Saharan tribe's nomadic, fragile existence. But the irony of the downsized Belarussian village's ongoing stability keeps pulling Seiichi's film back from the brink of elegy even as his portrait of the hauntingly beauteous Nature amidst which the villagers draw seemingly pristine breaths poises everything we watch in the direction of elegy. The result is an emotionally and spiritually complex work of art that accumulates into a meditation on what constitutes life and the degree to which its upcoming finish informs the definition of life. Along with this, the film measures the finitude of Budische, as a function of the inevitable attrition of the human life inhabiting it, against the eternal idea of the village as it has developed through generations of habitude. This, in turn, implies a similar measurement for the existence of the U.S.S.R. Ultimately, *Alexei and the Spring* becomes an elegy—if you will, a delayed elegy waiting upon the end of Budische— for the Soviet Union, wherein Nature and, implicitly, human nature are repositories for the defunct state's continued spiritual existence. In a way, then, the film with which *Alexei and the Spring* claims the greatest affinity is perhaps the greatest film ever made: Aleksandr Dovzhenko's illimitable *Earth* (1930), whose look ahead, invested with images of spiritual continuity (for instance, oceanic waves of wheat, huge sunflowers, human faces), has now become a look back—and in color yet.

Seiichi's film opens with printed background information that yields to an evocative forward traveling shot on a road penetrating woods. We are approaching Budische, but the shot, metaphoric as well as topographic, is correlative to memory's penetration of the fogs of time which has passed, in this case, fourteen years' worth. A disembodied voice reminisces about that April 1986 evening when, while planting potatoes, the man to whom the voice belongs saw the sky turn orange suddenly. Dust arose; wind rattled the fence. The Chernobyl disaster had just occurred, although no one knew that at the time. It is as if a wraith had descended, setting the peaceful place into dark and sinister motion. A light rain fell and then abruptly stopped, the voice tells us. We infer the irony: there is no way to determine which events belonged coincidentally to Nature rather than to human activity in Chernobyl. Some of the blur is beyond the scope of memory to clarify. This partial knowledge, as it were, reflects back on the human failings that wrought the Chernobyl disaster in the first place. Thus while the camera (strapped to the vehicle being driven by the man whose voice we hear) penetrates the forest, a circularity of associations accompanies the camera's single forward movement, creating a sense of recollection as navigating and intellectually embodying clarity and confusion, certainty and uncertainty, knowledge and ignorance. This opening, which goes in different directions at once, also implicitly conjoins activity and passivity; the speaker reaches for memory, but he must also rely on the fact that memories will come to him—and when they do, even if they are perfect (which they are not), they are inadequate to the task of coping with the enormity of the event. Compare this rich, dense opening to the kind of thin, literal, connect-the-dots work made familiar to us during the last few decades by American pop filmmakers.

The colors in this part of the opening movement are sober and subdued. However, even greater desaturation characterizes the shots that introduce the village. Moreover, this introduction consists of one static shot after another (at one point only the camera moves)—wintry long-shots in which the faint flutter of tree leaves or of sparse falling snow on blankets of snow constitute the only motion. They very nearly appear to be black-and-white photographs consisting of mostly white and grays (Seiichi's superb cinematographer is Masafumi Ichinose), and the voiceover resumes, noting that the spring is the reason the inhabitants will give, if asked, why they have remained. This subtly implies that the spring isn't the real, or at least the whole, reason; the older folk may have remained in order to hold on to their familiar lives—lives with which they are comfortable—for the rest of their lives. Therefore, Seiichi is conjoining the fact of continuing human life and cold, bleak, peopleless images of death, creating an image of the nothing that Budische will become once its inhabitants die out. It is at once an image of continuity and disruption on material and metaphorical levels, and it refers to the past—both Chernobyl and the Soviet Union—and the future, that is, the ultimate consequences of the nuclear plant disaster and of the end of the Soviet Union. What we see is a wasteland of trees, seemingly abandoned huts and unending snow. (The only human thus far introduced is the one to whom the voiceover belongs, but as yet this could as easily belong to a ghost that is surveying a long-ago past.) Now Seiichi achieves one of the film's most phenomenal images, a chilling, immemorially sad, haunting overhead shot of the percolating spring, all white with snow, into which new snow falls: an epiphany of the mystery of Nature and of existence—another conjoining of Nature and humanity made all the more ironic for the absence of humanity in our current view. (I am reminded of the mysterious shot of the percolating volcano in Roberto Rossellini's 1953 *Voyage in Italy*.) But the connection to humanity is the fact that this spring is why, people would say, according to the speaker (whom we believe), that they have remained in Budische; and, at the same time, the vast mystery of the image of the spring suggests the unfathomable nature of human motivation as well as the unfathomability of everything to do with Nature and with human existence. This second part of the film's opening movement—the title of the film now finally appears—provides a ghostly elastic framework for a film that will principally show the villagers at work inside and outside their homes, preparing food for the pigs, farming, buying and selling, and so forth. In this beautiful film, spirituality bathes and, in a sense, animates the materiality of human existence, suggesting an eternal reality beyond mortal limits and, by implication, extending this to the Soviet Union that has disappeared much as the inhabitants of Budische will—a circumstance that the delay of humanity's materialization in the film timelessly evokes. Seiichi's opening movement takes one's breath away.

After an additional shot of the spring, the disembodied voice is finally given a body; Alexei appears, carrying two buckets of water, joined by a pole, from the spring toward the house. (This came as a mild shock to me. I wasn't expecting the voice to belong to so young a person.) Indoors, a closeup of the virulent fire in the fireplace, emphasizing the cold weather outdoors that Alexei has vacated, introduces the first vivid patch of color in the film. "In this village," the boy explains, "to work is to eat." Alexei is reading; his mother, wearing a red kerchief, is softly singing while sewing an exceptionally pretty tablecloth (I think that's what it is); his father is silently weaving a basket. Alexei speaks to the camera, and, throughout the film, he will go back and forth between doing this and providing voiceover. Alexei notes that those who have left the village for the city retain the center of their consciousness in Budische. By implication, the spring remains the spiritual source of their humanity despite the distance now between them and the village. By dint of the film's complex of associations, this means as well that the spiritual source of their humanity remains those they have left behind, to whom they return to help with the farm work. It takes little effort to glean from all this a complex of associations comprising Nature, humanity, family, community, farming, socialism—the same complex of associations (if we get passed the brutality of Stalin's actual collectivist policies) that we identify with Dovzhenko's *Earth*.

The film shifts time from winter to summer. The colors are a bit stronger—green of grass, brown of wood, trees in the distance auburn in the glow of rising sun—but still very much subdued, as in, say, Andrei Tarkovsky's *Stalker* (1979). We're not in The Zone here, though, but on the farm. Or, rather, on different farms, as, in addition to Alexei's household (his older brother and younger sister visit in order to help), neighboring families start planting once sons and daughters revisit to help out. Shots show this labor—both medium shots and closeups, and Alexei contributes one of the finest utterances about farming I have heard on film: "When you are planting potatoes, you dig with your whole body"—a remark to whose accuracy the accompanying images of people at work attest. (No one is credited with a script, but something tells me that Seiichi gave Alexei some, if not all, of his monologues. I have no purist's problem with this; although a documentary, this is Seiichi's film.) Alexei also explains that the planting in summer is necessary for each family to have sufficient food for themselves and their animals throughout the year. Both these utterances are holistic and speak to one of the film's principal themes: the mystery of existence as it mutually implicates humanity and Nature. This, in turn, implies the Soviet system that, at least as Soviet mythology would have it, translated all this into sociopolitical reality and celebrated the idea of people on their knees, instead of praying to a nonexistent God, working. There is something infinitely touching about another remark that Alexei makes, regarding all the familial visitors in summer: "This is the liveliest time of the year."

On the other hand, this is a film about farming, not agriculture—the latter the academic term that better suits Soviet aspirations of modernity and technical accomplishment. The farmers in *Alexei and the Spring* haven't learned about what they do from either schools or the state; their "teachers" have been ancestors, one another, and the practice of farming itself. Throughout, Seiichi implies a difference between Soviet practice and Soviet reality. In line with this, Alexei notes how Soviet tractors and other equipment, purchased from communes, is perpetually in a state of breaking down, frustrating the determination of farmers to get on with their work. Is *Alexei and the Spring*, therefore, turning *Earth* on its head and reflecting back on Stalin, the Soviet dictator at the time of *Earth*, questioning his contribution to the Soviet state and, mindful of the fact that glasnost targeted him for reconsideration even beyond, earlier, Soviet Premier Nikita Khrushchev's program of deStalinization, weighing his imprint on the fortunes of Soviet progress? This film so reverberates that one must gather up —*harvest*—its riches.

Indeed, the centrality of wheat to the poetic imagery of *Earth* resonates through the passage in *Alexei* where, after Alexei's voiceover announces the importance to Budische farmers of even the old equipment that they are able to muster, shot after shot appears—long shot, middle shot, closeup—of the threshing of wheat. Context is a peculiar thing; it releases meaning that otherwise wouldn't see the light of day. On the surface, the sequence is one of work process, in line with the fact that so much of Seiichi's film is devoted to showing people at work. But we don't really see those who are operating the combines in these shots; either the distance is too great, or the people involved aren't included in the frames. Yet the human element is paramount, because the context that Alexei's voiceover supplies implies Seiichi's thematic interest here: human adaptability. The villagers, making do without the best of equipment, are getting the job at hand done, and, suddenly, the threshing activity we watch, engrossed, rushes into the visual form of a metaphor for human adaptability during the lean and economically trying years of Soviet governments. (Nor are conditions any better now.) Nor should we forget, especially given the nationality of the filmmaker and the stark and indelible images of a radioactive wasteland with which Seiichi introduces Budische (the association is the atomic bombing with which the U.S. resolved the Pacific War), that the failure of the Soviet Union was not only the result of its own considerable mismanagement and brutality but also of the screws turned on it by relentless U.S. propaganda and by the Cold War that the U.S. inflicted upon it, battling which drained the nation's resources. The irritant irony at the core of this pearl of associations is, of course, the fact that Chernobyl's very existence derived from the demands of the Cold War and of the felt need by the Soviet Union to keep up with that other superpower, the United States.

A sense of community is very strong among the villagers in Budische. However, the sense is elastic, and we watch Alexei prepare to answer the call for help from a neighboring village. Curiously, and very movingly, this is immediately followed by his observation that his father and mother have lately been looking back, as never before, to the time when they were young. Seated together outdoors, and facing the camera, the couple reminisce about their courtship, about how their mutual poverty, parental objections, and the interference of war made their marriage difficult. Having established its thematic coordinates, the film can't show us or permit us to hear anything that doesn't instantly flow into metaphor; but it is the nature of this humane and humanistic film that it never loses grip of humanity. As we watch and listen to the elderly couple imaginatively go back in time, we certainly follow, but a part of us remains in the present, thinking about who these two persons are, and who they are in relation to Alexei and his siblings. And, again, all this resonates on a level of broader, less local inference. We are taken aback when Alexei's mother's thoughts jump from the past to the near-total abandonment of the village in the present. The connection is one of hardship and struggle—if you will, one of the two persistent chords in the couple's life, the other being love: love of one another, love of their children, love of community, love of life. (In a later scene, Alexei's father, after hugging her, thanks his wife for marrying him; it's a poignant moment whose heartiness, we nonetheless feel, is somewhat induced by the camera, and the woman counters by touting her fidelity and recalling her spouse's long-ago infidelity.) Alexei's mild retardation only compounds our sense of the preciousness of everything that the elderly couple are now perpetually poised to lose. Perhaps Seiichi's highest attainment is that he retains the full measure of everything human that he shows us while pursuing his method of associations. Every loss and potential loss in his film echoes the loss of the Soviet Union.

There are two "holy men" in the film. One is a villager, a primitive "holy man" who is close to Nature, a wee bit batty, and authentic in his moral prescriptions. He identifies as evil three things: war, the Mafia, radioactivity. (Whatever "Mafia" means for the villager, for Seiichi it is likely code for the forces, unleashed by capitalism, that wield power in post-Soviet urban society.) The other "holy man" is an itinerant Orthodox priest. In one of the film's most extraordinary passages, this man's holy-day visit discloses how judicious a filmmaker Seiichi can be; for, in Soviet fashion, he skewers this priest with ridicule (*Eisenstein lives!*), but at the same time spares the villagers, whose religious devotion Seiichi must feel they are entitled to on the basis of the hardship of their lives. In one of the film's surreal moments, the priest encourages the villagers to kiss the portable icon that he identifies as "Our Lady of Chernobyl." (See how up-to-date the Church can be?!) Discretion can be the better part of filmmaking; perhaps villagers did kiss this cheesy-looking icon, but Seiichi doesn't show them doing so. At the same time he doesn't shortchange the seriousness of their devotion. In another passage, the villagers bless their homes with handmade wooden crosses dipped into the waters of the village spring. And Seiichi again skewers the itinerant priest, who reappears and fatuously thanks the villagers for this activity of theirs. This control of tone, going back and forth between religious villagers and religious priest, sparing the former ridicule and inflicting it upon the latter, testifies to Seiichi's focus, flexibility, and high degree of skill.

In another episode, Alexei's grandparents take a bus to visit their children and grandchildren in town, bringing cooked chicken. Two brilliant images follow: fish out of water, Grandpa and Grandma set against the high-rise apartment buildings in the background; at table indoors, Grandma in her babushka—a babushka *wearing* a babushka. The fact that she is so short adds comical zest to one of the film's most endearing images.

The colors become richer as the film proceeds, perhaps correlative to our admittance into the life of the village, and there are vistas at dawn of the most powerful and delicate beauty. The film shifts in time, for instance, to the Apple Festival in August, with Alexei's reliable voiceover threading the film's continuity. (One shot of fruit during the festival brings back another draught of *Earth*.) And the film returns to winter; and just when we feel it is to be bookended by winter snow, it returns to spring. But then the film does return again to winter. This refusal to straightjacket the film into a single, chronological seasonal cycle is yet another of Seiichi's strategies for avoiding the reductive and the schematic. It becomes another means for making the life of the village and the villagers paramount.

It isn't many documentaries that holistically envelop us, but this is one. Steeped in the life of the village (and, therefore, indirectly, in the death of the village), we become part of the film. We breathe to its measure; our spirits merge with the spirit of the film. Additionally, the film conveys a love for animals unsurpassed in cinema, and there's a humble, ennobling sense throughout of humanity's connection to Nature—this, in addition to the film's sense of humanity's connection to humanity, of people helping out one another whenever they can. And *work*—the film is steeped in work: cooking, mushroom gathering, washing clothes, fishing, felling trees, hauling logs, building, and so forth. And vodka—men drinking together to celebrate the project they have (well, almost!) completed.

The film ends as a circle that has been completed. We see Alexei cutting timber in the forest and hauling it, and we realize that the objective shot of his returning home matches the activity that, at the beginning of the film, is presented subjectively, as a traveling shot from Alexei's point of view. Ensuring our understanding, Seiichi has Alexei again drawing buckets of water and carrying them to the house. Why Alexei remained in Budische, we learn, is a mystery even to him. Perhaps the spring kept him there—that, and all the mysterious familial and communal connections it embodies.

Alexei and the Spring won Seiichi two prizes at Berlin.

The list:

2000

LA COMMUNE (PARIS 1871) (France). Fiction yielding to documentary; documentary, to fiction: British filmmaker Peter Watkins, on this occasion working in French, achieves an exhilaratingly elastic result with his ten-hour *La Commune (Paris 1871)*, of which only a version shortened by four hours has been exhibited outside France.

In this film about the doomed Parisian commune that popularly arose during the last gasps of the Franco-Prussian War, a huge cast of nonprofessionals playing the communards slip out of their historical roles to reflect on the state of France and of the current world, engaging in citizen discussions—in their period costumes!—that (like so much else in the film) stress the connections between past and present. Frames interrupting the action provide, moreover, a wealth of relevant written information, not to mention shafts of irony, as the past and the present each becomes a lens through which we apprehend the other. Watkins, then, has fashioned an eclectic work that captivates by capturing a number of levels of flux, interaction, analysis, self-reflexivity.

Although he is scarcely known for merriment, Watkins wrings wry humor from his present-tense disclosure of the past by interjecting into it modern televised media coverage of the unfolding events, thereby comparing accounts that differ according to the reporters and commentators involved—that is, according to their independence or allegiance to the state.

Shot in thirteen days, in and about an abandoned warehouse, using visually rich, black-and-white Beta Digital videotape, this film allows viewers to feel that they are entering history, which here has an immediacy that makes the tragic end of the Paris Commune devastating to watch.

This *people's* film reflects the feelings of working-class men and women who want to better their own and their children's lives, and details the reactionary forces arrayed against their hopes.

DEVILS ON THE DOORSTEP (China). In stark black and white (until the blood-red finish), Wen Jiang's *Guizi lai le* (*The Nips Are Here*) may be the most staggering vision ever devised of the absurdity of war. The Japanese occupy China during the last gasps of the Second World War. In a northern village near the Great Wall, peasants Ma Dasan and his mistress suffer *coitus interruptus* when a knock at the door dumps two sacks on their doorstep. Filling one is a Japanese prisoner, who eventually moderates as a result of Chinese humanity; the other is his Chinese interpreter, who will do anything to survive, including mistranslating the prisoner's more bellicose remarks. Jiang's black comedy suggests a fusion of Ichikawa's *Nobi* (1959), Imamura's *Pornographers* (1966) and Emir Kusturica's *Underground* (1996)— anything but something *Chinese!* With various communal pressures making their mark on him, Dasan must decide whether to pickle or preserve his "guests." In war, it seems, the trick is to keep from killing while managing to stay alive. A plan emerges to exchange the hostages for grain. This leads to a feast, which in turn leads to an event with ancient mythological and literary echoes: the *failed feast*: here, a bloodbath that the Japanese commander commandeers (he even burns the grain), during which the news of Emperor Hirohito's surrender arrives. War is constant *interruption*.

One might think that the restoration of Chinese authority in the village would be beneficent. But the pressure that Dasan has endured takes its toll; he implodes, goes on a rampage, killing Japanese. He is beheaded by a Japanese at Chinese instruction. His head descends through space, observing the "civilized" aftermath of war's carnage; it lands upright on the ground, eyes still alert, taking too much in. Past is prologue.

Jiang himself plays Dasan.

IN VANDA'S ROOM (Portugal, Germany, Switzerland, Italy). "The real torture was knowing that other people could smoke [smack]."

Having viewed the films out of order, I must fix this in my head, because Vanda Duarte, the heroin-addicted woman with a racking cough in *No Quarto da Vanda*, the tremendous three-hour middle film, is a through-character in Portuguese writer-director Pedro Costa's *Fountaínhas trilogy*. The same Cape Verde slum outside Lisbon where *Ossos* (1997) was set is now in the early stages of being gradually demolished. This process is further along in *Juventude Em Marcha* (2006), by which time former inhabitants have been relocated. Vanda, who began as Tina's hardworking, spirited chum, now shares affectionate, nostalgic scenes, and drugs, with her sister, Zita; their bickering usually resolves itself in laughter. In the last part, Zita dies; Vanda still coughs but is in recovery; alone, she is a television-viewing zombie. Ironically, in *No Quarto da Vanda*, her TV set is on without her paying notice.

Visually intricate, astonishing (Costa digitally-videographed), Costa fixes his camera for long takes inside various apartments; but another passage detailing Vanda's neighbors consists of short, rapid shots. Costa's fixed camera attempts to impose stability amidst the dismantling of homes and lives. Relatedly, a man nails something to the wall with a hammer. Life goes on until it's sent packing.

All films exist on a continuum whose poles are documentary and fiction. Costa's fiction is extremely close to documentary; like Robert J. Flaherty in *Nanook of the North* (1922), Costa has his nonprofessional "actors" play themselves doing what they otherwise would. *No Quarto da Vanda* took the prize of international critics at the Yamagata International Documentary Film Festival "for presenting life in its near-original form."

I was premature in declaring *Juventude Em Marcha* Portugal's greatest film. This may be it instead.

LES GLANEURS ET LA GLANEUSE (France). Armed with a digital camera, Agnès Varda has made what she calls "a wandering-road documentary." *Les glaneurs et la glaneuse*, about those who pick up leftovers from fields following a harvest, finds Varda "gleaning" *images*. She draws sustenance from the men and women gleaners she watches and interviews and from the tradition of the female gleaner to which she herself belongs. It's a delicious sense of gender communion—the essence of the feminist mindset.

We hear Varda's voice: "In the beginning, only women were gleaners." This implies that the activity, close to the earth, is somehow essentially, innately female; the gleaners we see in Jean-François Millet's painting *The Gleaners* (1857) are metaphorically giving birth to what they glean, for they are giving the "new life" of utility to what would otherwise be left to rot. Moreover, in this case "utility" denotes the nurturing and sustenance of human life. Humans need food to live, and Millet's painting captures a scene of dire poverty besides, where gleaning isn't simply useful but necessary to avert starvation. Millet also imparts a glow to his image that suggests a spiritual as well as material activity—and this aura, ironically, reminds us how close to death, to burial, are these women and the families they represent.

Gleaning as snatching morsels of life from the hovering mortal shadow: to suggest the rush of time, Varda speeds up the motion of (mostly young) museum patrons viewing the Millet painting. Varda's odd handless clock has symbolical hands: Varda's own wrinkled ones, which she shows in closeup throughout the film.

Grapes are left for ruin because Burgundy winegrowers prohibit gleaning; moreover, wine production is strategically limited to increase its financial value, ensuring *more* wasted grapes: *capitalism*.

For Varda, gleaning recycles, converting waste to use.

WERCKMEISTER HARMONIES (Hungary, Italy, Germany, France). From László Krasznahorkai's novel *The Melancholy of Resistance*, Béla Tarr and wife Ágnes Hranitzky's *Werckmeister harmóniák* opens in a bar, at closing time, in a forlorn, wintry provincial town. János Valuska leads patrons in a representation-in-motion of a lunar eclipse. Afterwards, when the boy walks home, alone, in streetlamped darkness, his intrusion into space within the frame extends the idea of the disruption of cosmological order. Tarr and Hranitzky have in mind Hungarian communism, but also the absence of God and, the result of both, humanity's loose-endedness. Evidence of all this: families are disappearing—"not natural," someone remarks.

That same night, down the same street that János walked, a huge truck moves, the low churn of its engine intruding into the silence. In the foreground, János faces the truck, watching; and, although he is standing still, the truck's movement—we now see its striated metal siding: an image of imprisonment—makes it appear as though the boy is in motion. The truck brings a circus whose advertised centerpiece is a gigantic stuffed whale, the implication being it is humans who disrupt the natural order; some exploit the captured beast, while others gawk at it. An ominous figure known as The Prince, who prefers to remain hidden, will oversee the show that will attract people from all around. Does the whale hold up a mirror to them?

János cares for his ailing uncle (Peter Fitz, brilliant), who is obsessed with the unnaturalness of Andreas Werckmeister's 17th-century theory of tonalities, which he believes has undone humanity by undermining people's faith. The recluse's ex-wife (Hanna Schygulla, excellent), meanwhile, involves János in a questionable underground political movement.

The bleak, languid black-and-white landscape of this poetic film erupts into apocalypse— not the world's literal end, but a metaphor for upheaved order.

THE CIRCLE (Iran, Italy, Switzerland). Jafar Panahi's *Dayereh* is about the oppression of women in patriarchal Iran. It begins by showing one female character, then, leaving her behind, jumps to a pair of other female characters, then follows one of these, then jumps to another woman entirely, then another, and so on. Each character reveals something more about the social, economic and political state of women in the Islamic Republic. As the circle closes and the theme becomes more firmly set, the formerly handheld camera settles into a fixed state, by which time we ourselves have interiorized the anxiety of the camera's earlier incarnation.

But at the very start the camera is fixed. Not in Kambuzia Partovi's inspired script; the scene is of Panahi's own devising: "[t]he rest of the film," Panahi has said, "explains that first shot"—a long take. In a hospital waiting room, a woman is informed through a small window that her daughter has given birth to a girl. In the head-to-toe black outer garment prescribed by *hejab* (the Iranian dress code for females), the woman has her back to us. (In *Dayereh*, women often are shot from behind. This visually underscores both the oppression to which women are subject and their constant fear of legal retribution.) The window is slid shut; the woman doesn't budge, instead knocking at the window, to speak to the nurse again, in hope that the just-born infant is actually a boy. The new grandmother mutters, "My poor daughter," and the nurse slides the window shut again with alarming finality. Distressed, the woman lies to the in-laws; and, as one of them approaches the window to inquire, she takes off down a narrow, circular stairway to the street. Again: "My poor daughter!" The camera, at her back, erupts into agitation during this black-robed descent.

FAAT KINÉ (Senegal). Ousmane Sembène has fashioned a brilliant social comedy about three generations. Kiné (Venus Seye, spirited, poised) operates a gas station; tough at business, she is nobody's fool. Her daughter and son have just graduated high school and, because of her sacrifices, will proceed to college, unlike her. (Kiné had wanted to be a lawyer.) Neither child's father married Kiné, and neither helped. Indeed, one of them, Kiné's teacher, impregnated her and then had her expelled just weeks before graduation. Disgraced, Kiné's father attempted to burn her, but Kiné's mother interceded, as a result of which Mommy's scorched back became "stiff as a dead tree." Kiné supported her family on her own, her independence a reflection of Senegal's independence.

There is witty, sometimes hilarious conversation amongst Kiné and two peers. (Kiné, about forty, was born about the time that Senegal became independent from France.) But always there is a serious undertone to the women's talk. For instance, Kiné advises her friend whose spouse has multiple wives to assert herself in the bedroom by enrobing the man's organ in a condom—this, on a continent that is ravaged by AIDS. While the film is contemporary, it is riddled with Kiné's flashbacks. We see the event in which Mommy is burned, and in the present we constantly see Mommy's unbending back. At a red light, a procession of traditionally garbed women, holding up baskets, walk in front of Kiné's car after Kiné has dropped off her jean-clad daughter at school and is herself proceeding to the office. *Progress:* a car radio announces that national school test results are higher than ever.

Jubilantly optimistic, the film romantically couples Kiné with a man who is not Muslim, but Catholic. They will not marry in a mosque or a church, but at City Hall.

Chronology of World Cinema

2000

KIPPUR (Israel, France). Amos Gitaï, Israel's premier filmmaker, based *Kippur* on his own combat experience in the 1973 Yom Kippur War that reshaped the Israeli mindset.

In the film's opening movement, a town is deserted. None of the few parked cars are in motion to interrupt the eerie silence. Weinraub, in his mid-twenties, is walking the street towards the camera, unhurried in a seeming stoppage of time. Indoors, a white sheet appears. It becomes a canvas for smeared paint: blue, green, prussian blue, red, yellow. Weinraub and his girlfriend make love on the sheet, their bodies tattooed by the paint: the essential beauty of sexual intimacy—the in-the-momentness of love and of existential life. When at the film's conclusion the pair again have their passion amidst the paints, after Weinraub has barely held onto his life at the Syrian front to which he will soon have to return, the creativity of love, buttressing the soul against war's uncreating—killing—nature, will release a piercing store of poignancy. *Kippur* ends where it began, but in a different Israel, a different world.

In one passage, Lt. Ruso's unit, to which Sergeant Weinraub belongs, attempts to carry a badly wounded soldier to the evacuating helicopter. The rescuers are trudging through mud that's like quicksand. Several times during this agonizingly slow ordeal the men lose their footing, stumble, drop the wounded boy's body and struggle to replace him on the stretcher. After all that effort, he turns out to be dead. Some of the soldiers are reluctant to leave the corpse behind, as they must do with the dead, unable to grasp, it seems, that he *is* dead. They have exhausted themselves in hopes of a redeeming conclusion that war's reality has thwarted at the last moment.

At home, Weinraub's hands ooze with red paint.

THE BIG ANIMAL (Poland). From the short story "Wielbłąd" by Kazimierz Orłos, *Duże zwierzę* was adapted in the 1970s by Krzysztof Kieślowski, who did not film it in Communist Poland presumably for political reasons. Following Kieślowski's death in 1996, Jerzy Stuhr filmed it (rightly) in black and white—Paweł Edelman cinematographed—and cast himself in the lead role of a small-town bank clerk who adopts an orphaned double-humped camel that an itinerant circus abandoned. Zygmunt and Marysia, childless, grow to love the animal, which endearingly sings along when Zygmunt plays the clarinet. Zygmunt evidences pride when he walks his pet; the animal suggests freedom (albeit on a leash), individualism, a spark of warm poetry amidst a prosaic existence. However, neighbors, consumed by fear, their own unhappiness and petty jealousy, turn on the couple and their camel. The local bureaucracy officially declares the "culturally foreign" creature "useless and unnecessary," as though living beauty and elegance, because of the joy these engender, do not constitute a form of utility. "Indignant residents" demand "law and order"; Zygmunt is advised to have the animal institutionalized and "put to work." He should have been content, he is told, with "normal human animals." Devastating: the scene where the camel no longer pipes in when Zygmunt plays the clarinet.

Stupendously funny (reaction shots of the camel, often while munching, figure prominently here), Stuhr's satirical comedy assumes a darker complexion as the couple are increasingly harassed, are robbed of their pet (which is likely liquidated) and left bereft. A boy's hidden sculpted camel suggests his secret appetite for the political freedom that is lying in wait. The film ends tremendously, with Zygmunt and Marysia affectionately interacting with three camels.

Indeed, the entire film, with its brilliant visual humor followed by growing melancholy, is wonderful and sharp.

DOFKA NAI MEUMAN (Thailand). French poet André Breton founded Surrealism in the mid-1920s, inventing the parlor game *cadavres exquis*, in which members of a gathered group each contributes the next sequential part of a made-up story as a means of unearthing group unconsciousness, thus affirming group consciousness. This "pure psychic automatism," as Breton called it, could generate fantastic, unexpected images that social strictures would otherwise suppress.

Educated at the School of the Art Institute in Chicago, Thai filmmaker Apichatpong Weerasethakul has adopted Breton's "Exquisite Corpses" to create an ebullient documentary. Weerasethakul traveled throughout rural and urban Thailand interviewing ordinary people, each of whom contributed a line, an episode, whatever, to a continuous piece of make-believe about a handicapped child and his teacher, Dogfar. Some of the shown interviewees are making up their contribution; others, plainly, are drawing upon their own experiences. The result that Weerasethakul fashions, in ravishing black and white, is a seamless, breathing fabric of people at work and in their daily routines, each in their different environment, interwoven with whatever each soul contributes to the ongoing "story," as well as Weerasethakul's visual imaginings—dramatic enactments—of these contributions. A good deal of Keatsian negative capability is needed to navigate this eclectic, unsignposted movie.

Weerasethakul has said he is "interested in the possibilities of involving both fact and fiction in the same film." His method sounds out the space where reality and imagination intersect and interact. Although this isn't a lyrical film, the outcome resembles Vertov's *Three Songs of Lenin* (1934), whose sum is a composite national portrait. Weerasethakul's hymn to humanity, moreover, bursts with sounds of children at play.

Incidentally, the title *Dokfa nai meuman* translates literally as *Dogfar (or Heavenly Flowers) in the Hands of Devils*. Here, it is called *Mysterious Object at Noon*. Close enough.

BLACKBOARDS (Iran, Italy, Japan). Samira Makhmalbaf's stunning *Takhté siah*, made when she was 19, follows her achingly humane debut, *The Apple* (*Sib*, 1997), in which a real-life situation is reenacted by the very persons who very recently were actually involved in it, including two 11-year-old girls, who, locked up in their home by their parents, are released by social services into an adventure of new freedom. Both films were written by Makhmalbaf and her father, Mohsen Makhmalbaf.

The human landscape of war, in the landmine-booby trapped mountains near the Iran-Iraq border: *Blackboards* is about itinerant Kurdish schoolteachers searching for pupils—children as dispossessed as they—in order to ply their trade. It is a desperate, futile attempt to enforce a semblance of normalcy on an abnormal situation. Right now, survival overwhelms other considerations, including education. The would-be-again teachers are burdened by the reality they are trying to accommodate and modify; each carries his huge slate on his back—images of which recall the door-toting in "The Door," a short film that Mohsen Makhmalbaf contributed in *Ghessé hayé kish* (1999).

The film follows two of the teachers, Saïd and Reeboir, whose boards rarely get used for the intended purpose. Along the way, the children and adults they meet require other uses for the slates. One of the boards becomes a cot for carrying a dying old man, whose daughter Saïd marries, who ends up with Saïd's board when they divorce and she crosses the border; the other is hacked apart altogether, to provide a splint for an injured child. We watch uprooted, nomadic lives.

The film's haunting visual beauty is painfully ironic: a metaphor for all the good things in life—love; safety; comfort; food and shelter—that these refugees from inescapable conflict, amidst fire on the ground and from above, must do without.

THE LEGEND OF RITA (Germany). Brilliantly co-written by Wolfgang Kohlhaase and the director, Volker Schlöndorff's *Die Stille nach dem Schuß* meditates afresh on the division and reunification of Germany. Rita Vogt, its protagonist, is a West German radical whose group commits robberies and murders to destabilize an unfair capitalistic society. Rita herself has killed a policeman. East Germany gives her a new identity as a textile factory worker, but her fear of discovery continues unabated, and German reunification leads to her capture. Among other things, the fall of the Berlin Wall provides a metaphor for the collapse of political idealism.

Sober and analytical rather than "exciting entertainment," the film is also sufficiently nonpartisan to have drawn protests from both Left and Right. This is how I would describe its political viewpoint: *Only the Left had any moral standing to lose.* The film's worn, weary tenor encapsulates not only exhaustion from a life on the lam but also disillusionment. Upon her entrance into East Germany, Rita is allowed to keep her gun but not bullets. We tend to think of Germany as having been divided between East and West, but Kohlhaase and Schlöndorff compel us to think of each side as being self-divided.

Rita's decency is plain. However, her personality is as self-divided as either Germany. She continues to be, in some sense, who she no longer is; and the decency of her nature may reflect past political motives rather than past political acts. Kohlhaase and Schlöndorff provide a complex, ambiguous human portrait. In a way, neither East nor West will permit Rita's departure from her political past.

German reunification: an unassailably wonderful thing? Once the sentimental dust settles (the fact that fractured families could become, at least superficially, whole), there remain national/political problems that, instead of being resolved, have been driven underground.

BRAVE NEW LAND (Brazil, Portugal). The principal woman participant in Brazil's *cinema nôvo*, and a journalist and human rights activist, Lúcia Murat was imprisoned and tortured in the 1970s, by Brazil's military dictatorship, for guerrilla activities.

Her *Brava Gente Brasileira*—literally, *Brave Brazilian People*—reaches back to 1778, approximately 245 years after Portugal first colonized Brazil. The protagonist is Diogo de Castro e Albuquerque, a Portuguese cartographer attempting to discover thus far uncharted Brazilian locations. After sketching her, Diogo falls in love with Ánote, a Guaicuru Indian. (In a collapse of times more than two hundred years apart, and a blend of fiction and documentary over time, a surviving Kadiwéu community enacts the Guaicuru tribe.) Murat's film opens with Ánote's experiencing her first period, her announcement of this to her mother, and the initiating ritual that attends the event. The film, then, opens with a discharge of blood that's natural; it is headed for bloodshed only the presumptuousness of European colonizers have deluded themselves into believing is natural. An early closeup of two large tortoises that a "white boy"—his father, a Christian fanatic, is determined that he be officially declared white—stacks one on top of the other conveys a passive way of life that has been overpowered by invaders.

The captain leading the military contingent accompanying him (and the boy's father) tells Diogo, "A man always has to prove himself." Narrowly, the remark refers to sex, but it also suggests a motivating factor for colonizing by European countries. Indeed, the "civilized" Portuguese men have a rape party with young natives, whose corpses—the victims are summarily shot—they casually toss into the river as the camera, positioned low, looks up. Their coldness is contrasted with a mother's grief.

Natives revolt.

Memorable shot: Diogo washing his painted face.

THE STARS' CARAVAN (Czech Republic, Denmark, Belgium, Finland). Finnish writer-director Arto Halonen made *Taivasta vasten* for Czech television in Kyrgyzstani and Russian. This documentary is set in the town of Naryn, in the former Soviet republic of Kyrgyzstan, which is preparing to celebrate the millennial anniversary of national hero Manas. One of the protagonists is Zarylbek, an itinerant film projectionist since Soviet days; "I am a Communist, but I am a Muslim," he says, recalling the Soviet inhospitality to religious worship. Myrat, a much younger film enthusiast, has grown up in the post-Soviet era. He loves American rather than Soviet films. Both men's voiceovers reflect on the old and the new.

A man out of time on horseback sends his eagle to the skies at the opening of *The Stars' Caravan*; at the close, the eagle returns and the two, their backs to the camera, ride off. Or is that *precisely* what happens? Actually, the film opens with the eagle's return before the bird is sent back into flight. What we see at the finish: is it a new return, or the very one we witnessed at the outset? What is perhaps most haunting is that the bird returns twice empty clawed. Kyrgyzstan is in the throes of economic trials, and Zarylbek's mission—"It was an honor to bring culture to the nomads," he remarks—persists despite the evaporation of funding for the arts, which Halonen relates to the independent nation's chaotic state.

Chaotic indeed. Periodically we hear radio reports about invading Islamic fanatics, setting Kyrgyzstan on the verge of war. How long can Zarylbek continue? Or Kyrgyzstan stand? Periodically we see moments from an epic film about Manas—imagine *Alexander Nevsky* (1938) in beauteous color: the more distant past than Communism that unites Kyrgyzstan's people. A folk legend; a dream.

2001

IN PRAISE OF LOVE (France, Switzerland). The former *enfant terrible* of the *nouvelle vague*, Jean-Luc Godard has made more brilliant films than anyone else. At seventy, he achieved his masterpiece: *Éloge de l'amour*.

The film is divided into two parts. The first centers on a filmmaker's project about a love affair. It is filmed in luxuriant black and white (cinema past). Shifting to two years earlier, the second part is videographed in saturated color (cinema future). The order is accurate; past follows present here because it is the filmmaker's memory, in this instance triggered by the suicide of a young woman whose grandparents also are suicides.

The French intriguingly investigate memory as part of people's intelligent lives. Italians, by contrast, mine the nostalgic—the emotional—properties of memory.

Reflections from the first part: History has been replaced by technology; politics, by gospel. "There can be no resistance without memory of universalism." In the second part, the grandmother, a Resistance fighter during the Second World War, recalls that money then was a means, not an end. Her and her husband's story is now being bought by Hollywood. Because they have no memories of their own, Godard reminds us, Americans buy the memories of others.

Haunted shot after haunted shot encapsulates the idea of memory. Scenes of nighttime Paris, besides evoking memories of futuristic ones in Godard's earlier *Alphaville* (1965), seem to enter the dominion of memory. Here is a film saturated in memory—memory as a force that participates in inventing current reality. Here is a film in which the tone of a woman's voice "brought ideas to life."

Memory is omnipresent. "You can think of something only if you think about something else," something familiar.

We're creatures of habit—creatures of habitual memory.

MULHOLLAND DR. (France, U.S.). Spectral, deeply mysterious, writer-director David Lynch's *Mulholland Dr.* charts the consumption of hopeful innocence by experience and betrayal in a shifting dream landscape that measures each disappointment against an atmosphere of perpetual possibility, which deepens the disappointment. Dream eventually becomes harrowing nightmare. The dreamer commits suicide, and *still* the nightmare continues. Fluent and terrifying, *Mulholland Dr.*, like Carl Theodor Dreyer's *Vampyr* (1931), is a work of sinister enchantment.

All but one of the lead characters shift identities. One of these, Diane (Naomi Watts, phenomenal), has come to L.A. as Betty in search of stardom. Girls and boys in two speeding cars careen down Mulholland Drive and smash into another car, killing the children and ejecting from the third car a woman, setting her off on an amnesiac adventure that crosses her path with Diane/Betty's—until, that is, it turns out that their paths had already long since meshed into a single path across which their identities have exchanged.

Lynch intuitively addresses one of the core issues of our time: given our heightened self-awareness, the problem of identity. Moreover, he pursues it in a context that suggests its lack of possible solution; for life has become a replaying tape, an illusion, he flat-out declares at the Club Silencio, a theatrical club where musicians play and a singer sings her heart out—only, all the music is prerecorded: a poignant, fatalistic touch. Identity, *too*, is an illusion; at any moment our identities may shift, or seem to shift, poising us in the direction of our becoming strangers to ourselves and each other over and over.

Mulholland Dr. recalls August Strindberg's late Expressionism and Luigi Pirandello, and resembles a darker version of Jacques Rivette's intricate, magical film *Celine and Julie Go Boating* (1974). It is also unlike anything else.

THE PROFESSION OF ARMS (Italy, France, Germany, Bulgaria). Austere, sad, overwhelming, Ermanno Olmi's *Il mestiere delle armi* is one of the great war films. Revolving around Giovanni de Medici, who led papal troops in Charles V's early sixteenth-century war against the Pope, it owes something to Roberto Rossellini's present-day histories and the cinema of Peter Watkins. The practice of war has shifted, from bayonets to firepower. Captain de Medici himself was taken down by the newfangled artillery and died at 28. The film ends on an historical note: the plea that cannons should be outlawed for wartime use. But, as we know, even worse weaponry followed.

The opening long-held shot is brilliant: a head shot where we cannot see the human being underneath his metal face mask—alien, estranged, unnatural: emblematic of war itself. Later, the process of making cannonballs is patiently shown, powerfully reiterating the message. But by far the film's most compelling aspect consists of its gray, fog-entrenched, melancholy landscapes, the battlefields of lost souls whom combat divides from their humanity. Olmi's son, Fabio, contributes haunting color cinematography.

An already fractious Italy is ripe for the invasion of mercenary German troops; but war's agony supercedes political considerations. The aim is victory, which is to say, clarity; but war extends ambiguity. Here is a film that exemplifies "the fog of war." Soldiers have chosen their jobs or roles; they haven't been impressed into service. Yet does anyone really *choose* such an unfathomable and unexpectedly shifting workplace or its inconceivably horrific activities, and its deaths?

Indeed, the film begins at the end, with Giovanni de Medici's death, which it unravels, deconstructs. The implication is that this outcome was inevitable. The condottiere's fate could not be diverted by his status of hero. War devours heroes for the sake of its own myth.

OLD BELIEVERS (Czech Republic). In the seventeenth century a schism occurred in the Russian Orthodox Church as a result of its attempt to reconcile with the Greek Orthodox Church by altering or eliminating certain dogmas and practices. "Old Believers" are descendants of those who left the Church and formed Christian communities adhering to the old ways. Targets of Church and State, they scattered across the Earth.

Jana Sevcikova's stunning *Staroverci* documents current Old Believers who live a medieval existence in the Danube Delta region. The gorgeous black-and-white film opens and closes with tracking shots of bare, twisted trees, their branches shooting off in every direction as if to cull every bit of oxygen from the air. By contrast, the Old Believers interviewed stand upright in the cold while a fixed camera records their thoughts and responses. One massive tree, its thick tentacle-like roots exposed, seems to embody their life and faith.

Older people, especially devout, are nonetheless mentally agile, curious, questioning. One practical young man presages either the community's continuation or demise. Refusing to grow a beard (as is prescribed for grown males), he will do so when he is old, and will go to church twice as often to repent the sins he is now committing!

Tracking shots along the river capture gleaming reflections of trees in the water, suggesting the natural basis for belief in the hereafter. Indeed, the primitive landscape and the people each appear to extend the other. But Sevciková undercuts the impression of utter strength and calm in a number of ways. A classroom scene is out of tune. A bellringer exhausts himself pulling cords to ring two bells simultaneously at different paces. At a barbaric baptismal ritual, an infant, screaming and crying, is immersed three times—for the Father, Son and Holy Ghost.

BUÑUEL AND KING SOLOMON'S TABLE (Spain, Mexico, Germany). They were countrymen, both from Aragón; Carlos Saura considers himself Luis Buñuel's disciple. Perhaps Saura's masterpiece, *Buñuel y la mesa del rey Salomón*, which Saura wrote with Agustín Sánchez Vidal, whose documentary *A propósito de Buñuel* (2000) had investigated Buñuel's Surrealism and atheism, is an attempt to imagine Buñuel alive again (nearly twenty years after his death) and inside his head as Buñuel contemplates making another film. It opposes time as well by imagining as Buñuel's cohorts in the adventure at the heart of this impossible film of Bunuel's dreams inside Saura's dreams two other deceased Spaniards: Catalonian Surrealist painter Salvador Dalí, who had died, conventionally, in the arms of the Church about a half-dozen years after Buñuel; Andalusian poet/playwright Federico García Lorca, whom a band of fascists murdered in 1936 at the advent of the Spanish Civil War. In reality, the three young men had been eternal friends (for a time), Dalí and García Lorca lovers—before Gala intervened and Dalí married her. In Saura's achingly dark, mysterious, beautiful film, the three search through fantastic corridors and catacombs in Toledo for the lustrous magical table of King Solomon, which permits one a view of past, present and future.

Saura's film cuts between the "present" that Saura imagines, in which Buñuel imagines the never-was film, and the world of this imagined film—a region (depending on your point of view) that dips below or rises above the surface of reality to confront phantoms of the past, the hereafter, the nothing-after.

There is an image that owes its visionary style to Dalí: while Buñuel as a young boy watches, a young girl on the beach lifts up the ocean, a rubbery sheet of water, and espies the horrors underneath: against Nature, Franco's Spain.

A.B.C. AFRICA (Iran). As joyous as it is heartrending, as hallucinatory as it is real, *A.B.C. Africa* is by Abbas Kiarostami. The Iranian film was shot in Uganda, using two digital cameras, over the course of ten days. It documents both children who have been orphaned by the AIDS epidemic and the Ugandan women who have assumed their care. In addition to its struggle with HIV-AIDS, Uganda has been beset with civil war for two decades now. The AIDS crisis has left 1.6 million children without one or both parents. (While wreaking havoc in Iraq, the United States joined Russia and China in keeping the Ugandan crisis off the United Nations Security Council agenda.)

The film opens with the sound of the arrival of a fax, followed by the fax itself, to Kiarostami, from the International Fund for Agricultural Development, thanking him in advance for the attention that his trip will bring to the Ugandan crisis. This "outgoing fax" is being received: a symbolical reciprocation between Kiarostami's familiar world and the unfamiliar one he enters, which the film documents.

The first caregiver we meet is an elderly woman who works to support herself and the 35 children under her care, most of them relations. All eleven of her own offspring are dead from AIDS.

Much of the film, however, simply observes the children. The younger boys interrupt their play to mug for the camera; they shout, dance and gesticulate. Teenagers, though, seem to penetrate the camera with a sullen gaze. Later, all dressed in yellow, kids clap and sing.

A brilliant shot traverses a wire fence on which colorful clothes hang, drying. The camera stops. Through the fence, we see a woman folding laundry on the lawn. The camera's approach is stopped by the fence. So close; so far away.

MAIDS (Brazil). From Renata Melo's play and filmmaker interviews, *Domésticas* focuses on five domestics in São Paulo. (There are three million in Brazil.) Following a pseudo-documentary prologue suggesting it's better not to have been born than to be a domestic, an upbeat montage shows different maids performing various chores. (One is atop a sloped roof adjusting a TV antenna.) One of these is Quitéria, whom Zefa constantly refers to new jobs because Quitéria keeps getting fired. The vase slipped out of her hands, she explains; but a quick insert shows that she smashed the thing. Why? Quitéria owns no such family heirloom; her family history does, however, include slavery, which her employment echoes. Quitéria shrugs as she explains the loss of another job: "The vacuum cleaner got stuck on the dog's nose." This seemingly cheerful young woman is seething with revolt. At film's end, a(n actual?) domestic rages over all she has endured from employers, giving vent to feelings most domestics suppress. Early on, though, Quitéria seems to belong to a lighthearted comedy. Spirited co-directors Fernando Meirelles and Nando Olival never show an employer.

The black-and-white prologue introduces Quitéria. It consists of an overhead shot of her looking up—an ironical posture—and talking directly into the camera. Thereafter, similar black-and-white inserts of housemaids punctuate the film, encapsulating a more reflective mood than her busy life otherwise affords each woman. We also see the women at home. Each one harbors a dream; all hope for a better life. Their lives cross in employer kitchens and on the bus taking them from and to work—motion without progress. Relevant: Quitéria's mother was also a domestic.

There is a stunning montage of domestic complaints ("They think we are all thieves") and another of actual domestics, smiling, each doubtless making the best of things.

BOLIVIA (Argentina, Netherlands). In grainy black and white, its style journalistic-*cinéma-vérité*, Adrián Caetano's nonprofessionally cast *Bolivia* is sharply observant, finely expressive. It follows Freddy, a Bolivian father of four, who has separated from wife and family to work in Buenos Aires. He is a short order cook in a cheap restaurant. His pay is commensurate with the illegal status of his labor, and he must contend with Argentine bigotry at a foreign interloper. With Argentina reeling from its own economic recession, Freddy is seen as belonging to an army of "niggers" who are taking away jobs from locals. He is in fact keeping prices on the menu affordable.

Freddy had had a job at home, as a field worker, but, in its war on drugs, the U.S. scorched Bolivia's fields indiscriminately, casting adrift the already impoverished in even worse poverty. Once hungry, Freddy's family is now starving. Meanwhile, at night, the police stop and harass Freddy on the street, he is treated with contempt by everyone except Rosa, the waitress from Paraguay, and Enrique (Enrique Liporache, superb), the frazzled restaurant owner who is exploiting them, and it's impossible to see how Freddy's meager pay and tips allow for anything to be sent home. Poverty isn't sentimentalized here, nor is it ignored to wax lyrical over the dignity to which the poor rise. *Bolivia* is about an ordinary human being who is simply doing his best. It recalls a fine West German film also set in a restaurant: Jan Schütte's *Dragon Chow* (*Drachenfutter*, 1987), about an illegal Pakistani immigrant in Hamburg.

Freddy epitomizes the plight of his poor country, which is under the seige of globalization. Bolivia's current fate also predicts that of the marginally better-off Argentina. Caetano's film functions as a companion-piece to an Argentinean one: Pablo Trapero's *Mundo grúa* (1999).

THE NAVIGATORS (UK, Germany, Spain). A robust, humane, sometimes hilarious comedy, Ken Loach's typically sociopolitically committed *The Navigators* is set in 1995, when parts of Britain's railway industry were being privatized as one of the last acts of Thatcherism conducted by Prime Minister John Major.

About a small, tightly knit group of Sheffield railway workers, the film proceeds inexorably, like a train, to a harsh conclusion that dramatizes the cruelty and chaos of privatization.

The men are alotted a maximum of two deaths a year—out of concern for the company's reputation since a bad rep would limit the company's ability to bid successfully for railway projects. This twisted logic reaches its logical conclusion, where the actual safety of workers is brutally sacrificed for an abstract idea of worker safety. At the last, even workers prove undone in their humanity; they become accomplices to ownership/management logic.

Already financially strapped laborers have been plunged into a cauldron of competition, where they scramble to nab each piecemeal job. Moreover, all the benefits that their trade unions have negotiated and "secured" on their behalf no longer apply vis-à-vis the privately owned companies for which they now tenuously work: "The slate has been wiped clean." Now they have to pay for child care out of pocket. No more sick pay, either.

When Paul brings a bouquet to his separated-from wife, he is firmly refused entrance. *Pass the bouquet through the mail slot*, he is told! He complies, only to see his hard-bought gift of roses decapitated—a private incident clarifying the humiliation that Paul endures at work.

Loach's *mise-en-scène*, vibrant, "uncomposed," overflowing with life, correlates to how the men work together prior to privatization: seemingly *loosely*. Their remarkable safety record helps us realize that this apparent "looseness" is actually experience, competence and confidence thoroughly relaxed into.

NADA (Cuba, Spain, France, Italy). Carla Pérez is lonely in Havana. A postal worker, Carla contests the doldrums and habitual power outages at home by appropriating scores of letters, and reading and revising them before sending them on their way, to help out, she maintains, the people involved. (What Carla reads, we see imagined in priceless vignettes.) The bane of her existence is her supervisor, who suspects something is going on. This woman cuts the difference between terrorist and by-the-book bureaucrat.

Juan Carlos Cremata Malberti's *Nada*—the U.S. has adopted the title that Spain has given the Cuban film—is fresh, exhilarating and full of visual invention, in the manner of Buster Keaton's 1924 *Sherlock Jr.* (to which Carla's boyfriend's flight from trouble on a bicycle in traffic pays homage) and Věra Chytilová's *Daisies* (1966). Its black-and-white images are sparked by bits of color (an orange pencil, a yellow flower, etc.) until one late, full-color shot stuns with sudden richness and beauty. Bits of animation also (delightfully) figure in, as well as speed-motion and unexpected sounds in lieu of certain voices, but the actors themselves, along with Malberti, supply most of the film's slapstick comedy. Satirizing bureaucracy, *Nothing* (or *Nothing More*) variously makes us laugh hard and thoughtfully chuckle.

Carla and a younger co-worker become girlfriend and boyfriend some time into the film. Life is looking up! However, Carla's Castrotted parents, exiles in Miami (where else?), have entered her name into the lottery for an exit visa, and Carla eventually must decide whether to remain in Cuba or leave. She explains to her boyfiend, "I've never won anything before." Malberti toys with our heart a bit (a minor lapse), but when Carla makes the right decision, choosing love, solidarity and some measure of self-determination over the alternatives, whatever your politics you cheer.

I hope!

GOSFORD PARK (UK, U.S., Italy). Robert Altman is identified with distinctly American works with American themes. But *Gosford Park* takes place in England, where it was filmed, in 1932, months before Adolf Hitler became Germany's chancellor. At a posh country estate, the persistence of Britain's rigid class system seems a kind of social/moral blindness, especially given the tumult Europe is on the brink of enduring. Guests have gathered for a weekend shooting party; the host is murdered. Altman has described the film as "[Jean Renoir's 1939] *Rules of the Game* meets [Agatha Christie's] *10 Little Indians*."

The mystery is see-through. The bumbling police detective assigned to the case investigates only upstairs; what, after all, could anyone *downstairs* have to do with the wealthy victim? Indeed; just as sex between races provides the key for unlocking Altman's *Cookie's Fortune* (1999), exploitive sex between classes provides the key here.

One of the guests, a bourgeois American Jew brought along by an invited guest, provides Altman the opportunity to investigate how European classism often politely masks virulent anti-Semitism, and the hunt itself, in this context, evolves into an image of the Holocaust a decade away. It also provides a metaphor for war, showing its participants in a kind of limbo between world wars. Altman evokes a world of cocooned leisure poised to dissolve under the weight of war.

Formally, *Gosford Park* is finely realized, with exquisite use made of long-shots and slight, persistent camera movements which cumulatively suggest a world passing and being lost, unnoticed, to time.

Except for Maggie Smith, who mugs, the film is beautifully acted; but warranting especial praise, playing servants haunted by their pasts, are Alan Bates and Helen Mirren, who is shattering.

BEIJING BICYCLE (China, Taiwan, France). Wang Xiaoshuais's *Shiqi sui de dan che* deconstructs ideas of property and ownership to expose savage, antisocial impulses underneath.

Each of two teenaged boys lays claim of ownership to the same bicycle. Jian is a student from Beijing; hoping to advance, Guei has moved from rural poverty to the city. Jian wants to fit in with his bike-obsessed peer group; for his job as a courier, Guei is requisitioned the bicycle that Jian covets. Guei's pay installments are deducted from his earnings, which are decided on a piecemeal basis per delivery, 80% of which is retained by the company for which he works. When the bicycle is stolen, Guei attempts to steal another to keep his job. Jian buys the bike; it's *his*. However, Guei just as stubbornly insists that the bicycle is *his*.

Each boy steals back the bicycle. Transformed into a ruthless gang, Jian's friends assault Guei to retrieve the bicycle, which is flat down on the ground as Guei, bloodied, clings to it while hysterically crying, screaming. Eventually the two "owners" strike a deal by whose terms they alternate possession; but, when Jian uses the bicycle in assaulting a romantic rival, whose head he bloodies with a stray slab (a sign of the construction that Beijing is undergoing now that foreign capital is pouring in), the gang targets both Jian and Guei, who is with Jian for their routine bicycle exchange. The bicycle has reduced the two "co-owners" to a single identity; beating up one now requires beating up the other. The bicycle, once their bone of contention, is destroyed in the fracas. Guei, the gentle country boy, picks up a slab and bludgeons one of the gang members before retrieving "his" bicycle, whose bent, broken carcass he carries through the streets.

UNDER THE SKIN OF THE CITY (Iran). *Zir-e poost-e shahr* unfolds against the background of Iran's 1997 parliamentary elections. It is a turbulent time when Islamic fundamentalism is being bravely challenged by elements of an oppressed citizenry.

Rakhshan Bani-Etemad focuses on a single family, all but one of whom live in the cramped quarters that the parents own in a Tehran suburb. Mahmoud Rahmat-Abdi, who is lame and doesn't work, is the titular head, but Tuba, his wife (Golab Adineh, wonderful), wields some authority. Besides earning the family's keep, Tuba is pursuing a basic education after work—and, of the two, she is the one who votes. Her work, though, has contaminated her lungs.

Shots at Tuba's textile/paper factory stress the harsh labor as each worker, on her feet, womans her gigantic machine; one angled overhead shot discloses rows and rows of faceless laboring women as far as eye can see, their discomfort increased by their traditional heavy garb. During breaks, however, the women congregate in small groups, sharing home problems, and supporting one another in their shared travail. Tuba leads her group effortlessly.

Tuba and Mahmoud's elder daughter, married, continually returns home, seeking refuge each time her husband beats her. Her pregnancy doubtless has intensified her debt-ridden husband's sense of irresolvable economic burden. This offscreen spouse delivered the punch whose bruising result we see, linking him to the offscreen managerial male voice that ends the workers' lunch break. Hamideh's victimization mimics her father's depressing passivity; her bruised face, her mother's lungs. Her lack of authority in a patriarchal culture and nation mirror-images Mahmoud's undermined authority, underscoring Bani-Etemad's implicit point that Iran is pretty much failing *everyone*. Those dividing themselves from others on various grounds (age, gender, economic status) miss the point they all precariously exist in the same boat.

LIKE FATHER (UK). Brilliant and heartrending, *Like Father* is the middle work of the Amber Collective's East Durham trilogy in the wake of the closing of the coal mines. Arthur Elliott, 70, and son Joe, 40, are both former miners. Arthur is among the pigeon fanciers whose eviction is imminent as the coastal area undergoes redevelopment; Joe's old-time schoolmate, slime-bucket David Hylton, heads the redevelopment charge. But Arthur isn't about to budge. Meanwhile, Joe is holding down so many jobs, all having to do with teaching, playing and composing music, that he has squeezed the time out of his marriage to Carol, whom he is barely able to support despite his endless hours of work. Carol, who sews costumes for a party shop, one night tells Joe she no longer loves him and demands that he leave as their 12-year-old son, Michael, listens in. For leverage to rid themselves of Arthur, Hylton arranges for Joe to be awarded a commission to compose an original piece commemorating the redevelopment. To Arthur, this makes his son a "scab"; but Joe arrives independently at the same moral conclusion even before Hylton arranges for the slaughter of Arthur's birds. Meanwhile, Michael learns of some family history that helps explain the harsh relationship between his father and grandfather, but also tears at his fragile sense of identity.

Extreme long-shots show the sky filled with birds: powerful images of loss (birds released against the fanciers' will), the passing of a way of life, but images also encapsulating residual hope for the future.

Intricately edited quick shots or short scenes compose a portrait of social and familial fragmentation and interrelatedness. All three lead roles, representing three generations of Elliotts, are enacted by nonprofessional locals drawing upon their own experience and that of regional neighbors.

LIFE AND DEBT (U.S.). *Life and Debt* is a tale of two Jamaicas. There is the bright, shiny Jamaica that caters to tourists. The other Jamaica consists of struggling Jamaicans. With narration by Jamaica Kincaid, based on her book *A Small Place* (actually, about Antigua), Stephanie Black's documentary takes a look at the tiny nation that gained its independence from Great Britain in 1962, its economic difficulties ever deepened by the ruthless manipulation of its economy by outside corporations and financial institutions.

A focus is the relationship between Jamaica and the International Monetary Fund as, beginning with the 1970s world economic crisis, Jamaica borrowed heavily, at exhorbitant interest, in order to stay afloat after other banks refused to help. The film reminds us that the I.M.F., set up by Allied nations anticipating victory in 1944, was intended to rebuild Europe, not help the Third World, which came into existence later as states gained independence from colonial empires. Like the separate World Bank, the I.M.F. additionally imposed economic restrictions, all to local detriment, in exchange for absolutely necessary financial assistance.

One segment addresses Jamaica's once growing dairy industry, which is being squeezed out of existence in compliance with U.S. demands through the agency of the Inter-American Development Bank. The ideology of an "integrated global economy" will not permit Jamaican farming, including dairy farming, to feed Jamaicans and sustain local farmers. "Lower trade barriers," this tiny country is instructed by the Megabeast; "compete with us on a level playing field." Cheap imported powdered milk, subsidized 130% by the U.S. government (as one farmer puts it, "Nobody can compete with *that*"), has replaced actual milk in Jamaica. Recurrent images of wholesome milk in streams, discarded by mandate, are heartrending; or is it the fact behind them, that children are drinking powder & water instead?

2002

SUPPLEMENT (Poland). One of the most moving films ever made, *Supplement* is writer-director Krzysztof Zanussi's deepening of *Life as a Fatal Sexually Transmitted Disease* (2000). Recycling the three most important characters, it covers the same period, hits several of the same scenes from the lives of these characters, including Dr. Tomasz Berg's death, but opens up, with new disclosures in some cases and in much greater detail in others, two aspects: medical student Filip's interior struggle to know the will of his God, and the course of his romantic relationship with Hanka. *Supplement*—or *Suplement*—also adds Filip's relationship with an annoying though loving brother and closes on an overwhelming scene of lovemaking on a mountain ledge.

Filip's monastic retreat hasn't helped him decide whether God wants him to serve Him directly, as a priest, or indirectly, as a medical doctor. Deeply religious, Filip feels he must resolve this matter, which means putting his relationship with Hanka at least on hold. If he chooses a life of devotion, of course, Hanka will be permanently dropped from the queue of his concerns, along with other people. Frustrated, Filip becomes a solitary wanderer up a mountain, a haunt to which his brother has introduced him. It is his brother who retrieves Filip, whose end might otherwise have come about. Filip decides that "plain ordinary living is the most important thing." His crisis of confusion and ambivalence resolved, he must again win over Hanka, who feels she has already waited too long for him.

Darkness often bathes the characters, but we find them by their light and ours. Zanussi explores how we differently balance spiritual, practical and other claims on us, showing again, in a different context, the sparkling friendship between old Tomasz and young Filip, the atheist and the believer.

SHADOW KILL (India, France, Netherlands, Switzerland). In early-1940s Travancore, Kaliyappan is the Maharajah's hangman—considered holy, often deep in prayer (to Kali, Mother Goddess of creation/destruction), the ashes from burned portions of whose used ropes (which hang from a miniature noose) presumably cure the sick. Kaliyappan lives, secluded, with his affectionate family: wife Marakatam, son Muthu, 13-year-old daughter Mallika. An older daughter, married, lives nearby. Someone he executed Kaliyappan knows was innocent. Could hanging an innocent man be blamed on the executioner?

An execution awaits. Sick with dread and alcohol, Kaliyappan tries begging out; but the State won't budge. Journeying to the appointed place, Kaliyappan enters the dark night of his soul. "The condemned man cannot sleep [the night before the execution]," one of those accompanying him remarks, "so neither should the hangman."

A story now told Kaliyappan, which we see as he envisions it, takes on a postmodern twist, casting Mallika as a rape-murder victim, Kaliyappan's son-in-law as the predator, but Mallika's gentle boyfriend as the one who pays. Tomorrow morning Kaliyappan will hang the boy, the storyteller explains, thus conflating both unjust hangings. Kaliyappan, overcome, collapses; Muthu is ordered to fill in—which he does, although, a Gandhian, he is non-violent. As with Prince Hal upon becoming Henry V, Muthu must complete his father's work.

Writer-director Adoor Gopalakrishnan's *Nizhalkkuthu* indicts the pernicious ethos of individual responsibility, arguing instead for *social* responsibility, community, shared identity. (There is no moral "division of labor.") It is a film of rituals, such as that marking Mallika's entry into womanhood after her first menstruation. Gopalakrishnan finds humans resorting to religious faith to unburden themselves of the weight of personal responsibility that power structures have foisted upon them. The film distinguishes between authentic and illusory

2002

freedom, between dependency and independence, including national independence.

Final Segment, *11'09"01* (Japan, France). For *11'09"01* (the U.S. DVD is titled *September 11*), eleven filmmakers, each from a different country, were invited to contribute an eleven-minute film responding to the 2001 attack on the U.S. Shohei Imamura's Japanese contribution is brilliant.

World War II continues. Outdoors, a snake is slithering on the ground. On the floor of a family hut, a man wearing an army cap is also slithering. Not using his hands, he drinks water out of a container on the floor. "He fought for his country," a relation notes. In addition to compassion, Yukichi's family feels disgust. In becoming a snake, Yukichi has shed his human skin; humanity now, for him, is identified with war's inhumanity. But it is precisely for field combat that Yukichi was trained to crawl on his belly.

He devours a large rat, head first. Yukichi's blank eye shows he is dissociated from the act, much as he attempted to dissociate himself from what was happening while in combat; but dissociation from his home environment, ironically, implies Yukichi's entrenchment in memories of war.

Imminent humiliating defeat has transformed the villagers' impression of the war. Yukichi's reduced state now reminds them of *their* reduced state. Driven out of his home, Yukichi is hunted as a criminal—a scene out of Imamura's beautiful *Ballad of Narayama* (1993).

"What does the Holy War mean to you?" Yukichi asks a comrade-in-arms in a flashback. An image of humility because he is close to the ground, Yukichi now seems human, sacred. We see a pristine waterfall in the moonlight and trees animated by wind. Yukichi crawls into the river.

Is it Imamura's voice we hear reading aloud the script that appears on the left side of the screen? *There is no such thing as a Holy War.*

MONDAY MORNING (France, Italy). Gently satirical, Georgian/Soviet-born Otar Iosseliani's *Lundi matin* is a great French comedy.

Vincent, Iosseliani's Everyman, is a welder at a chemical plant, where he endures voluminous industrial smoke daily. At home, he is a creature of habit; after home repairs, he paints landscapes. One day Vincent doesn't pass through the gate into the factory. He pauses long enough to turn around and spend the day instead on a grassy hill in deep contemplation of things. He decides on a vacation, an adventure, leaving behind wife, kids, home, job. Others may negotiate a mid-life crisis by having an extramarital affair; he will simply take off for a bit. His gravely ill father donates his life's savings to give his son the means. Venice, Cairo, Constantinople: the itinerary is set. Without word to anyone else, Vincent is gone.

Pickpocketed, Vincent gets no farther than Venice—although he creates the illusion of wider travels by sending various postcards home, all of which his miffed wife rips up without reading. (Her mother-in-law must break into her backyard-buried pot to get at her savings so that the family may continue during her son's absence.) In Venice, Vincent escapes his routines; ironically, though, his excursion crosses the circle of *other* people's routines.

This isn't a film that connects narrative dots. We must therefore bring our Keatsian negative capability to it. The movie's elliptical, elusive quality accumulates into a wondrous metaphor for the thread of his life that Vincent feels has slipped out of his grasp. Once back at work, Vincent cannot see what *we* see, though doubtless he feels its effect: a stunning long-shot of the fume-belching factory.

Iosseliani's moving, roving camera is exactly correlative to the riches of life—and humanity's appetite for these—with which his life-affirming masterpiece abounds.

ALEXEI AND THE SPRING (Japan). *See above.*

FRIDAY NIGHT (France). *Vendredi soir* opens ambiguously; is it a rose of dusk or dawn that blossoms in the sky? In the wide-angle shot of Paris only the distant Eiffel Tower seems to be dissolving into fog. Vacating her apartment, Laure is planning this Friday night on dinner with friends before moving into her lover's place. But François is remote, indistinct, represented by a brief note Laure leaves behind and a message tape when she phones.

Paris is at a near standstill, its dense traffic generated by a public transport strike. A voice on the radio urges Parisians to be "charitable" by offering rides to others; people are stepping outside themselves to let strangers in. Jean knocks at Laure's car window; these ordinary two will end up spending the night together—a "one-night stand": the fleeting experience of a lifetime. At dawn, Laure will resume the course of her life as Jean sleeps, her leaps to her parked car, along with her wide smile, recorded in slow motion. It's off to François, without a care—except, we recall, the glove Laure dropped onto the pavement amidst her first kiss with Jean en route to the hotel. It is the something of herself that she has forever left behind.

Written by Emmanuèle Bernheim, from her novel, and the director, Claire Denis, this is a film of tender, intimate feelings shared by two strangers in something of a dream. It is a quiet film of hugs and caresses, closeups of silently moving hands and bare feet, sparse dialogue, and a rapturous instance of lovemaking, with the camera's eye in the folds of seemingly effortless flesh.

Stasis yields to transience, and in the hotel room, magically, a red lampshade has drifted onto a bulb.

Denis's finest film stills our breath.

JAPÓN (Mexico, Germany, Netherlands, Spain). The protagonist of Carlos Reygadas's nonprofessionally cast film has forsaken his home in Mexico City to venture into Mexico's remote rural interior: a mountainously walled canyon. A painter in his fifties and lame, "El Hombre"—the Man—plans on committing suicide.

Reygadas erases sound to create a dreamlike silence and to emphasize the man's inwardness, his romance with death. At times the film is agonizingly slow. Near the end it achieves a perfect stasis: bereft of onward movement, a scene of huddled humanity—a "dead" spot that ironically signals the man's rebirth. He has had sex with a very old, humane person, Ascencion, whose naked body, like his, is long past the firmness and suppleness of youth. This sexual intercourse that renews the man's appetite for life represents the impact made on him by *all* the villagers. Mired in abstraction (the devil of our time, Reygadas feels), the painter had forgotten to take into account the antidote to his pessimism and despair, humanity, which therefore catches him unawares.

But at a terrible price. The film's completion is a stunning traveling shot that records an inevitable yet unexpected catastrophe. Down from the mountains a cart carries a slew of villagers while the reborn stranger remains above. The death he brought with him is now projected onto people who combinately helped rescue him. Reygadas's 16mm camera, achieving an awesome sense of gravity correlative to humankind's burden of mortal awareness, bears down on pebbled railroad tracks at lightning speed. Again and again it swoops around 360°, picking up on or off the tracks this villager's corpse or that: the upshot of both the stranger's suicidal self-involvement and humanity's interconnectedness, for even rural Mexico is not immune to the currents of discontent the cosmopolitan stranger represents. Hence the title: *Japan.*

WAITING FOR HAPPINESS (France, Mauritania). Abderrahmane Sissako's gorgeous *Heremakono* is set in the coastal village of Nouadhibou, where the Sahara Desert and the Atlantic Ocean meet. Seventeen-year-old Abdallah, visiting en route to Russia, is based on Sissako, who was born in Mauritania, grew up in Mali, lived for ten years in Moscow, where he studied film, and now lives in Paris. The housing in Nouadhibou is makeshift, as in Mali, where it is called *heremakono*, meaning, *waiting for happiness*. Theoretically, everyone there is in transit, en route to a happier life.

Happiness sometimes never comes. The film details a tragic emigration. Maata, an older villager, long ago rejected the one opportunity he had to leave Nouadhibou with a friend. His mysterious death in the dunes ends a repressed, bitterly regretful life. Another man has been found dead, perhaps washed up on shore—perhaps someone, like Abdallah, bound for Europe. Meanwhile, Paris-educated Abdallah cannot even speak Hassaniya, the language of his homeland.

Melancholy: the ocean's persistent lapping sound that surrounds the isolated village. *Backwardness:* the momentousness of Maata's purchase of an electric light bulb, which he tries mightily to wire up so that it works. For all this, there is something admirable about the villagers' simple, largely uncomplaining lives.

A woman plays the *kora*, a lute-like West African folk instrument; a young girl listens and mimics. Such traditional education will likely limit the child's prospects to the village; at the same time, it implicitly protests the invading karaoke music and, beyond that, the intrusion of French influence that, more than forty years after Mauritania's independence from French West Africa, globalization has revived.

Abdallah's experience at travel, hence exile, is shown by the proficiency with which he packs his suitcase before leaving his mother, with exceptionally little fuss from either of them.

THE FIRST MONSOON DAY (India). A beauty from India, Bengali writer-director Rituparno Ghosh's *Titli* takes its title from the 17-year-old girl whose home in Darjeeling includes a huge blowup of Rohit Roy, the Bollywood star Titli would *marry* even. Much of the film eyes the close relationship between Titli and her mother, and from the start there's an elusive something about Urmila's Mona Lisa-smile as her daughter enthuses about the dreamy star. What is it with Urmila?

Mother and daughter are off to the airport to pick up Amar, their husband and father. (He is a tea planter.) A road accident delivers them another airport-headed passenger. It is Rohit Roy! As Titli goes off to buy cigarettes for her idol, Urmila and "Rona"—former lovers—reminisce. They would have married once, but he had no certain future, so Urmila's parents interceded and struck a practical match. Rona never married—except his career. Returning, cloaked in the heavy mist, Titli hears the truth and finds her adolescent world gently though irreversibly ripped.

Why did you never tell me about you and Rohit? Would you marry Rohit now? Urmila tells Titli, had she married Rona instead of Titli's father, then she would be *their* daughter. That isn't so—a different father would have made a different daughter; ah, but Titli's obsession with Rohit Roy surely must have made Urmila *dream* that Titli *was* their child! Urmila's loveless (although amicable) marriage has her looking backward with regret; Titli, her crush crushed, can now look forward to the reality of love. Rona? Believing her marriage happy, he writes Urmila to tell her that he, too, is about to marry, deepening further Urmila's regret.

Aparna Sen, superb, and Konkona Sen Sharma, excellent, play mother and daughter—and in reality are mother and daughter.

OUI NON (Italy). The visual countdown prior to the beginning of a movie: these numbers are distributed throughout American-in-Paris Jon Jost's *Oui non*, with a flurry of seasonally titled vignettes toward the end that culminates in a surprising, tragic, funny resolution: the death of a young acrobat. It is the slapped-on commercial "happy ending"—only here, if taken literally, a most unhappy one. An "improvised love story," *Oui non* attends to a boy and a girl, James and Hélène, the circus acrobat and a musically inclined aspiring actress, as the two actually fall in and out and possibly back in love in front of Jost's indefatigable video camera, although the final phase, before the boy's fall to his death while celebrating (in dance) his amorous joy, is riotously suspect. (In the fictional film-within-the-documentary film, James is called Jérôme.) How the girl howls and cries as the boy takes his offscreen tumble. Adding to the confusion—conflation?—of reality and cinema, James Thiérrée really did take a debilitating spill during the course of shooting, resulting in the loss of six months' worth of work and pay. One assumes this isn't being passed off as the character's fatal fall; here and there, Jost's film is as playful and mischievous as another Pirandellian work: Jacques Rivette's *Celine and Julie Go Boating* (1974).

The film opens in the Paris of another world: a montage of early twentieth-century black-and-white photographs: elegant, unadorned, humanistic glimpses of time. The outdoor photographs, by Eugene Atget, reflect the loss of this older Paris to time: here people once walked; this, there, they once saw. We "create reality from fiction" in order to keep it from dissolving before our eyes.

Jost's exquisite film segues from Paris Past to Paris Present. It distills Wordsworth's "still, sad music of humanity."

IN THIS WORLD (UK). Michael Winterbottom's *In This World* follows two Afghan refugees, 16-year-old Jamal and older cousin Enayatullah, on their trek from Pakistan to England in search of freedom and a better life. The two leads play, or just *are*, themselves.

The film's nature is unclear. Is it documentary, or faux-documentary into which real events are interwoven? Regardless, Winterbottom's use of digital cameras and in-the-moment technique achieve a sense of unfolding reality. The film also is an epic, taking up in the middle of things two adventurers who represent the aspirations of their war-shattered community. Instead of going home, though, the homeless pair are "returning" to where they have never been. Post-*Marienbad*, this becomes a metaphor for their wrenched, discombobulated lives.

Early on, a narrator provides statistics pertaining to the human displacement that began with the Soviet war against Afghanistan and whose last wave of refugees the 2001 U.S. bombing generated. The film opens in the Shamshatoo refugee camp, where Jamal, an orphan, was born; earning a dollar a day at a local brick factory, he lives with his brothers and sisters. (About 58,000 refugees occupy this camp.) The "plot"—Enayat and Jamal's westward journey—immerses them in the people-smuggling business: a representation of all the forces that conspire to exploit the misery of refugees.

In This World is on-the-run through many transports through many cities, including Istanbul, Trieste and Paris. Along the way, Bressonian issues of risk and trust arise; so do stints in a sweatshop—rare sit-down scenes in an agitated film almost constantly on the move. The film's most brilliant passage is nearly bereft of light; the image is degenerated to dots as a group of refugees, including Jamal and Enayat, scurry across hills as rounds of bullets are shot at them.

FROM THE OTHER SIDE (France, Belgium, Australia, Finland). Chantal Äkerman's documentary *De l'autre côté* opens in Agua Prieta with interviews of Mexicans still mourning the loss of loved ones who managed to get across *la frontera* only to perish in the States. A coin toss determined which twin brother would cross the Mexico-U.S. border; now the burden of one boy's life is his brother's death. He recounts the fate of a group of undocumented aliens, all freezing and starving in the Arizona desert into which the design of impenetrable fences had forced them, each of whom died—part of a scattered, cumulative holocaust.

Äkerman's Mexican border towns are parched, hazily sunlit, largely inert. Fixed, level long-shots create placid scenes of dusty road and still sky. Sparse activity is correlative to the socioeconomic doldrums, the listless poverty that provokes illegal immigration across the border despite the risk.

Repeated shots of the seemingly endless tall, striated metal fence prohibiting Mexican flight along that stretch find deceptive beauty. Behind this appearance, though, lurks an

attitude of hostility, racism, and a casual U.S. disregard for human life.
Arizona ranchers have put up a sign: "Stop the Crime Wave. Our Property and Environment [I]s Being Trashed by Invaders." With rifles and magnums, these vigilantes hunt down Mexican immigrants and transport them to the Mexican side of the border. "At times," Äkerman has explained, "the ranchers have held more than four hundred people on their land, treating them like prisoners of war."

The ranchers identify the Mexicans with "filth." This fear of impurity and contagion bears for Äkerman, a Jewish European, a terrible echo.

The film is difficult. We end up investigating its silences and landscapes to glean shards of truth. Because Äkerman's film never manipulates us, its constant accompaniment is our beating human heart.

AMEN (France, Germany, Romania, U.S.). During World War II, German chemical engineer Kurt Gerstein risked his life by warning visiting diplomatic authorities, including ones from the U.S., and religious leaders about Hitler's program of exterminating Jews. It is he whose work with zyklon B, aimed at purifying typhus-infected water for troops, was used for gassing Jews and others. Gerstein is the central figure in Rolf Hochhuth's play *The Deputy* (*Der Stellvertreter*), which devastated Pope Pius XII's reputation by suggesting, at worst, by withholding the full weight of his moral authority the Pope was accomplice to the Holocaust. Working from a clear, intelligent script by himself and Jean-Claude Grumberg, the politically minded Constantinos Costa-Gavras made the decades-delayed film version, rechristened *Amen*. Because it doesn't enter Gerstein's mind, where the principal drama occurs, it is superficial, like all Costa-Gavros films; but it is patient, measured, immensely convincing.

With immaculate humor, Costa-Gavras punctuates his film with long-shots of the unflappable pope at the head of a huge, orderly flock of apostles moving silently down and across Vatican corridors. Combined with the camera distance, this *mise-en-scène* is potent; while innocent civilians suffer and die outside (eventually) in the millions, in his insular world the pontiff pompously leads an idolatrous troop of scouts.

Riccardo Fontana, a young Jesuit cleric, joins Gerstein in raising alarms. This fictional character represents activist clergy, including Bernhard Lichtenberg, Cathedral Provost of Berlin, and Maximilian Kolbe, a Polish Franciscan priest, who decried the deportation of Jews to death camps, ultimately choosing to die in Dachau and Auschwitz. Failing to move the Pope, Fontana likewise joins deported Jews. Mathieu Kassovitz's familiar, recognizably Jewish face in this role creates an epiphany as we, projecting his image back in time, realize what would have been *his*—Kassovitz's—fate had he lived in the 1940s.

NDEYSAAN (Senegal, France). According to Senegalese filmmaker Mansour Sora Wade, *Ndeysaan* reflects his position that "belief [in the supernatural] and pragmatism co-exist naturally." Contemporary Africa will drown if it drifts too far from its tribal past.

In a pre-colonial coastal village, waves of fog roll in, keeping fishermen out of the water and thus imperiling the village's existence. Two best friends love the same woman, beauteous, dignified Maxoye, who loves only Mbanick. Mbanick is the son of the village marabount. In a trance, Mbanick fells the tree under which his father is buried, carving a canoe from the trunk, taking it to sea, disappearing into the heart of the fog. When he emerges, it is with treasure: the countless fish that he caught. Mbanick now not only has Maxoye but everyone's respect and gratitude for conquering the fog and saving the village. One night, at sea, Yatma, jealous, kills his friend, whose dying vow promises revenge. Maxoye, pregnant with Mbanick's son, marries Yatma, knowing he murdered her beloved. The "price of forgiveness" is that theirs will be an unconsummated union and Yatma will have to raise his victim's son, also named Mbanick. While Maxoye eventually relents and the couple have a child of their own, the sea exacts its own price. In effect, the sea's forgiveness requires the forfeit of all our lives—and the tale's survival.

As the tree falls in slow motion, villagers appear as a procession of phantoms—ghosts of the past, but also the ghosts the villagers will one day be.

Analytical and gorgeous, rigorous and haunting, *Ndeysaan* is narrated by an old man, the son of a griot. He prophesies the end of the African oral folk tradition. At the same time, the film itself underscores cinema's capacity to keep the past, tradition, and hope alive.

WAR AND PEACE (India). *Jang Aur Aman* studies the nuclear arms race between India and Pakistan. Documentarian Anand Patwardhan is a Gandhian pacifist.

Against black-and-white archival material illustrating atomic tests and destruction, Patwardhan notes the nuclear advances that neutered each vestige of pacifism on the world stage: "Paranoia that the atom bomb [the United States] had dropped on . . . [Japan] would someday come back to strike home ensured a permanent quest for nuclear superiority." The Soviet Union, Britain, France and China "joined the nuclear club." By the 1980s, "there were enough bombs to destroy the world fifty times," and "radioactive waste from mining and processing, along with thousands of atmospheric and underground tests, polluted sections of the globe for eternity." In 1974, India joined the club; "the Soviet Union eventually collapsed under the weight of the arms race, but America, hostage to a privatized defence industry, refused to disarm. In India, the collapse of socialism saw a revival of bigotry. . . . Nuclear nationalism was in the air"—like radioactive fallout.

India's nuclear test triggered a nuclear arms race with Pakistan. Patwardhan examines India's domestic campaign of deception to manipulate the electorate. In a Pakistani schoolroom, girls present speeches, some in favor of Pakistan's nuclear tests, some opposed. One pupil: "Our atomic tests brought honor and relief . . . to Pakistan . . . [and] other Muslim nations." Afterwards, she calls senseless the killing on both sides of the India-Pakistan conflict. Patwardhan therefore asks about her contrary speech. The student replies, "We chose the stand that will . . . [inflame] passions and make our side in the debate win." "Our politicians think the same way," Patwardhan tells her. "They advocate positions that instigate passions so that they can win [elections]."

And the people lose.

TRILOGY (France, Belgium). The experimental narrative form of Lucas Belvaux's *Trilogy* may be described as three overlapping circles of plot. The same event that's central in one film may be peripheral in another; a character who is major here may be "supporting" there.

The recycled cast of characters includes three schoolteachers: Cécile, who is married to hypochondriac Alain; Jeanne, who used to be the lover and sister radical of Bruno, the terrorist who has just escaped from prison after 15 years; Agnès, a morphine addict whose husband, Pascal, is a cop who, hunting down Bruno, must decide whether to kill him to keep a supply of morphine flowing from the crime boss who used to be Bruno's ally. The first film, a comedy, is titled "Un couple épatant"; the second, "Cavale," is a thriller; the last, "Après la vie," a melodrama. Writer-director Belvaux has said that the three films, which don't constitute a chronological series, can be viewed in any order.

Each film is about what their marriage means to its participants. Noticing that on a specific Saturday Alain's behavior changes and thus suspecting infidelity, Cécile asks co-worker Agnès's spouse to check things out. Jeanne's settled life, including spouse and kids, is her barrier against political disillusionment that Bruno's escape threatens to crash. Morphine is the glue of Pascal and Agnès's relationship; when Pascal can no longer express his love for her by providing it, because of the crime boss's interference, Agnès takes to the streets in search of a fix; there, Bruno becomes her protector, and she his.

Trilogy contests the stereotypical narrative tyranny that assigns certain characters greater importance and other characters lesser importance. Correlative to this, Belvaux argues for the equal importance of all our lives, each of which intersects the equally important lives of others.

Chronology of World Cinema

2002

BUS 174 (Brazil). Sandro do Nascimento never met his father. When he was six, robbers stabbed his hardworking mother to death before his eyes. On his own, Sandro survived the "unsolved" Candelária Massacre, in which probably off-duty police officers opened fire on homeless children in a makeshift outdoor shelter in front of a church. Thus Sandro lost a number of friends—another family. He robbed, to survive and to support a cocaine habit. Imprisoned in a filthy, teemingly overcrowded juvenile detention facility, the adolescent boy was starved and beaten. On June 12, 2000, armed with a gun loaded with a few bullets, Sandro hijacked a city bus and held its passengers hostage. At 18, he was one homeless youth who would be "invisible" no longer. Televised, the standoff between him and the police became a ratings hit, lasting a few hours. In camera view, Sandro's life was foolproof against police assassination. Eventually, though, he left his safety zone, with one hostage in tow. Out of camera range, intending to shoot Sandro, the police are likely the ones who shot and killed his young hostage instead. The police had done what they were supposed to do: catch Sandro do Nascimento alive. However, in the police wagon en route to the station, they suffocated him. Rio de Janeiro rejoiced when Sandro's murderers were acquitted at trial.

José Padilha and Felipe Lacerda's Brazilian documentary begins with an aerial shot traversing water, shore, moneyed mansions and, on the other side of a hill, Rocinha, a teemingly overcrowded, vast *favela*—the juxtaposition of rich and poor, in a single sweeping shot. The bus footage is woven into contextualizing interviews, including the film's zenith, in photographic negative a passage about other detainees in Sandro's prison—a "hell-hole," one guard calls it.

Ônibus 174 makes the invisible visible.

METAMORPHOSIS (Russia). "As Gregor Samsa awoke one morning from disquieting dreams he found himself transformed in his bed into a gigantic insect."

Written in German, Czech author Franz Kafka's satirical 1912 *The Metamorphosis* (*Die Verwandlung*) weighs the sense of isolation and alienation that has overtaken a traveling salesman. Gregor's "disquieting dreams" reflect his waking life, which, except that Kafka's was at a desk, mirror Kafka's humdrum clerical work. By his dreams Gregor imagines his own death.

Valerij Fokin's *Prevrashcheniye* is mesmerizing—and painfully hilarious. Now a period piece, it's part of our dream of the modern past. During opening credits a sepia photograph of a corner of Gregor's bed appears, joined by the trace sound of lapping water, suggesting the unconscious. The film proper begins, surely, as a black-and-white dream (except for a disquieting patch of pink), where the sound has materialized as falling rain. The camera glides to reveal a train silently pulling in at the Prague station. (The muffled measured drumbeat could be the dreamer's heartbeat.) Passengers exit. "Mother, father, it's Gregor!" we hear, as the camera withdraws from a solemnly dressed man standing on the platform; Gregor *imagines* the greeting, for he walks alone a long way home, shielding himself from the rain with his suitcase. More and more color slips into view; by rote, Gregor leans in at the dinner table so that Mother can dab clean a corner of his mouth. That night, Gregor dreams of yet another train departure; the conductor is his indifferent father, drawing from Gregor a quizzical look.

Next morning, Gregor cannot get off his back and out of bed—until he falls onto the floor, anxiously flexing hands and feet. Yevgeni Mironov's performance is phenomenal. Through body movements, contortions and noises, he expresses how Gregor feels—what Gregor has turned into.

2003

FIVE LONG TAKES DEDICATED TO YASUJIRO OZU (Iran, Japan, France). Iran's Abbas Kiarostami's tribute to Japan's Yasujiro Ozu engages such Ozuvian themes as separation, longing and acceptance while arranging Nature, behind the guise of purely objective documentary videography, the better for us to perceive it with fresh eyes, fresh ears.

The film consists of five shoreside segments, ostensibly shot in the course a single darkening day. A piece of driftwood is on the beach. Under a cloudy sky, waves advancing and withdrawing provide the only sound. Each advance towards the camera seems another attempt by the sea to gather up the piece of driftwood and carry it off. Eventually the sea's force breaks off a fragment and carries off the main piece. All the sea's attempts to gather up the fragment, however, fail.

In the second segment, people walk in either direction on a railed boardwalk, oblivious to the sea just beyond. In the third, distinctions between hazy sky and sea disappear and the image becomes progressively more abstract. There is a whiting out, although a remnant of the motion of waves remains. The third segment is hilarious, as a stream of ducks make their way screen-right before reversing course and stampeding screen-left. It is dusk.

The final, perhaps black-and-white segment brings the film to dark, mysterious fruition. It is nighttime, and we hear a storm brewing. A full moon becomes visible—not in the sky, though; rather, we see its wavering reflection on the water's surface. Amidst a cacophony of animal sounds, the reflected moon vanishes behind clouds and reappears. The image grows abstract and segmented—another image of separation. Flashes of lightning; the screen bursts with a thousand flickers of rain. Darkness yields to dawn. Reflections of birds fly across the reflected sky—trains of transience. The Spirit of Ozu is everywhere.

ELEPHANT (U.S.). Populated by actual Portland, Oregon, highschoolers, *Elephant* shows a day at a typical American high school. Today, however, the school falls seige to a Columbine-type rampage by two disaffected, gun-toting pupils. Gus Van Sant has written, directed and edited his most powerful, most haunting film.

At the outset, when John returns to school late from lunch with his drunken father, we have no idea whether he will be one of the student killers or victims, or what. Any of the boys at the school, and even some girls, might have turned into the unhappy killers Alex and Eric have turned into. We glimpse the pair's harassment and humiliation by fellow students in class, as the teacher either misses what's going on or turns a blind eye, and we wonder: When will *anybody*, especially a largely defenseless adolescent, snap? John also has his hands full —with his father, whom *he* must father. Van Sant's patient, associative, cumulative work has begun to weave its rich, breathing fabric.

There is a precise sense of loss as kids are coldly shot down, one after the other. Van Sant doesn't detail the teenagers' lives but shows us enough so we want to know more. When each death cancels this possibility, we are left with an awful sense of the incompletion of the victim's life.

Long, bewitching tracking shots follow students in and out of the school and down its long hallways. Inspired by Béla Tarr's Hungarian masterpiece, *Sátántangó* (1994), an unbroken tracking shot in *Elephant* may bend chronology around, seamlessly coming across the same action, this time shown from a different perspective. This convoluted method correlates to the fomenting violence that will shatter the innocence of a seemingly safe, placid, glass-encased world.

One thing more: Van Sant's signature time-lapsed skies have never been more heartachingly poetic.

CAFE LUMIERE (Japan, Taiwan). Marking the occasion of the centennial of Yasujiro Ozu's birth, Hou Hsiao-hsien's calm, quiet *Kôhî jikô* shows Yoko's back as she hangs wash inside her small Tokyo apartment. A part-time journalist, Yoko wanders the city taking photographs and riding trains, drops in on her friend Hajime in his used bookstore, drinks coffee in cafés —this, a sign of her contemporaneity. Most of the film, plotless, is taken up by her wanderings—and Hajime's, as he goes from one train to another recording their sounds.

Yoko is nonchalant about being pregnant, determined not to marry the father (her boyfriend in Taiwan), and disinclined to have her settled life interrupted in any way by her condition. Easier said than done. When she visits Father and Stepmother (Nenji Kobayashi and Kimiko Yo, both wonderful), why does her father keep mum about the disclosure? For one thing, we have Ozu as a reference for the postwar displacement of fathers from a confident position of authority in the family unit. Moreover, the father's greeting upon Yoko's arrival at the train depot personalizes this generalization: "Thank you for coming." This man doesn't quite know what place he occupies in his daughter's life and heart—this, a reflection of family history. (When she was abandoned by her mother at an early age, Yoko was raised by an uncle.) Later, in a superlative shot in Yoko's apartment, with father and daughter seated on mats, both *mise-en-scène* and lighting emphasize the father, providing a stunning portrait of his silent agony over the matter of Yoko's pregnancy outside of marriage, including his sense that she has rejected him and his traditional values.

The unsteady nature of Yoko's girlfriend-boyfriend relationship joins with the moving trains, Hajime's used bookstore, and assorted cafés to convey flux and impermanence. Updated, Ozu's world continues.

HERE AND PERHAPS ELSEWHERE (?). Born in Beirut, Lamia Joreige returned there from France, where she has lived for twenty years, for her documentary inquiry *Houna wa roubbama hounak*, which takes its title from a 1976 Godard film, but which draws inspiration also from Chris Marker's *Chronicle of a Summer* (1961), in which Parisian passers-by are asked, "Are you happy?" Joreige's question refers to Lebanon's civil war (roughly, 1975-90), challenging her birth nation's official amnesia on the topic (despite a loss of 150,000 lives, its history isn't taught in Lebanese schools): "Do you know of anyone who was kidnapped from around here during the war?" Joreige travels the old line of demarcation between Muslim West Beirut and Christian East Beirut, prodding memories with her question. At each crossing or checkpoint, a freeze frame implies a residual impasse, war's ongoing legacy. Late in the film Joreige reveals her own family's stake in her inquiry into wartime disappearances at the hands of militias.

About faces, fears and the heartache of survivors, hers is one of the most intensely moving films I have seen. Some interviewees recall the abduction and disappearance of neighbors; others, of loved ones. Some open up, responding with a torrent of recollection; others, wary, hesitate or even stonewall the question, some defiantly, others apologetically. The psychological scars of war achieve a heartrending metaphor when a man reveals the scar from his open-heart surgery following a medical condition that he attributes to the loss of a son in the war.

Occasionally from the periphery of the gaze of Joreige's handheld video camera we see young children. François Truffaut once wrote that children should appear in films only if love is expressed for them. Never have I seen a film whose love for children is deeper than *Here and Perhaps Elsewhere*'s.

THE FLOWER OF EVIL (France). With its Baudelairean title, Claude Chabrol's *La fleur du mal* is precise, catlike. It is about the impact of past on present for a family—and for a nation. The marriage of Anne and Gérard, both Vasseurs, came about after their spouses, lovers, died together in an automobile accident that Gérard may have engineered. Now their young offspring, stepsibling/cousins, the children of their first marriages, are also lovers. Michèline (Suzanne Flon, brilliant)—"Aunt Line"—took over Anne's care after Anne's parents died in a plane crash; Michèline had had sexual relations with her older brother, a Resistance fighter during the Second World War, whom her father, Pierre Charpin, a collaborationist, murdered on D-Day. Killing her father, Michèline exacted both familial and patriotic revenge.

Charpin, according to Chabrol (who along with Caroline Eliacheff and Louise L. Lambrichs wrote the superb script), suggests Maurice Papon, who, as an official in the Vichy government, in the years 1942-1944 directed the deportation of over 1500 French Jews from

Bordeaux to Auschwitz. French anti-Semitism has been a recurrent theme in Chabrol's films. Memory haunts—as indicated by the first shot, among Chabrol's greatest. It is night. The camera, as though floating in a dream, moves through leafy trees and approaches the Vasseur mansion in Bordeaux. Chabrol's camera enters the darkened house and floats up a staircase and through a hallway, catching glimpses, in turn, of two different rooms: in one, a young woman is sitting on the floor, her head down; in the next room, a man lies face-up on the floor, dead. We instantly realize that one has murdered the other. We later learn that Gérard attempted to rape his stepdaughter.

Aunt Line : "I feel I'm doing things backwards. . . . Time doesn't exist. Life is one perpetual present."

GOOD MORNING, NIGHT (Italy). In 1978, a Red Brigade kidnapped and executed/assassinated Italy's presumed next president, Aldo Moro, 61, president of the Christian Democrats, which sought to strike a compromise with the Italian Communist Party: a bourgeois appropriation of the Left that threatened to shift ground beneath class struggle. The revolutionaries aimed to keep alive a Marxist dream of social and economic justice.

But the ill-conceived event required killing five bodyguards before Moro himself was snatched. The abductors announced Moro would be tried by them. Parliament replaced Moro with Giulio Andreotti, whose coalition government, including Communists for the first time in Italy's history, orchestrated a virulent crackdown on terrorism.

Buongiorno, notte, writer-director Marco Bellocchio's brilliant satire, parallels rather than reproduces the original event. It discloses the "inside" view of 23-year-old Chiara (Maya Sansa, superb)—a changing viewpoint, it turns out, as she takes in the television news coverage, and alternates between her workaday life as university librarian and her hidden life as a revolutionary.

In the film's first half, Red Brigade members rent and set up the apartment and establish their relationships with Moro, whom they confront with their intentions and motives. In the second half, Bellocchio seamlessly interweaves actual action and surrealism that is keyed to the dreams and, perhaps, only the thoughts of characters, especially Chiara's. It is riotously funny how the Pope and Moro's fellow politicians seek public ways to appropriate Moro's misfortune for their own benefit. Bellocchio suggests that the state pursued Moro's end by thwarting any possible exchange of Moro for imprisoned Leftists. Ultimately, Moro's family opts not to participate in the media event that the public funeral for Moro becomes. Meanwhile, we see Moro in the flesh, jauntily walking, safe and sound, down city streets—whose wish fulfillment this, we can never be sure.

THE REVOLUTION WILL NOT BE TELEVISED (Ireland, Netherlands, U.S., Germany, Finland, UK). Hugo Chávez was elected Venezuela's president in 1998, his support largely coming from the poor—80% of the population. In 2002, a coup very briefly deposed him. At the time, Irish filmmakers Kim Bartley and Donnacha O'Briain were in Caracas, shooting a documentary about Chávez for British television. Their film deconstructs the coup and its aftermath—and electrifyingly records history unfolding on-the-spot, outside and inside the presidential palace.

Chávez aimed to free Venezuela from free-market policies imposed on it by the U.S. He did not, however, nationalize Venezuela's oil. This industry already was state-owned, but run for private benefit by executives Chávez would replace. The poor had gotten nothing by Venezuela's being the world's fourth largest oil supplier.

Six private TV stations opposed the state-run one, questioning Chávez's motives, sanity, sexual orientation. Once in power, "re-establishing democracy," the opposition silenced the state-run station and dissolved the National Electoral Board, Supreme Court, National Assembly. With his presidential return following the coup's collapse, Chávez addressed opponents: "Oppose me: fine! But you must not oppose the Constitution."

Moneyed interests, backed by military elite (at least encouraged by the U.S.), organized a citizens' march on the presidential palace to effect the coup. Snipers shot at Chávez supporters, but private media edited footage so it appeared that return fire was aimed at the opposition march that in fact had been safely diverted. Police went on a shooting rampage against Chávez supporters, further bloodying the streets.

Chávez, held captive, refused to resign; but the media/government lied, saying he had resigned. Chávez cabinet members communicated the truth to the international community, which got the message back to Venezuela by cable TV. The people rose up, pressuring the return of the president they had elected, whom only a referendum could constitutionally replace.

AT FIVE IN THE AFTERNOON (Iran, France). Written by Mohsen Makhmalbaf and daughter Samira, *Panj é asr* is a compassionate film about post-Taliban Afghanistan that appreciates both religious elders and the young who yearn for self-determination, and a visionary film, a circular "road picture" that keeps returning to the school where girls are encouraged to think about national affairs and how they may contribute to their country's forward journey, and not just about housework and raising children. Samira Makhmalbaf was in her mid-twenties when she made this film; Nogreh, her protagonist, is three years younger.

Inspired by the example of Pakistan's Benazir Bhutto, Nogreh dreams of someday being Afghanistan's president; but she cannot share this dream with her father, nor lift the veil of her burqa, nor wear her high-heeled shoes, in front of him. Nor may her dream survive the reactionary social and cultural forces arrayed against it.

Leylomah, Nogreh's sister-in-law, and her sick baby have been abandoned by their husband and father, Nogreh's brother: an illustration of misguided male prerogatives. Leylomah has run out of milk and options, but Makhmalbaf keeps symbolism simmering rather than allowing it to take over and abstract the pain of ordinary human lives. Nogreh could be Leylomah if she loses her grasp on her progressive dream. The search for Leylomah's spouse is part of the movie's "road" aspect.

Assisted by her superb cinematographer, Ebrahim Ghafuri, Makhmalbaf creates exceptionally hard-edged images that appear to have little space for dreams. The film's bravura opening shows Nogreh stealing to the outdoor school by passing through enveloping structures of darkness; her walk back home, also towards the camera, finds her face darkened as well.

By stark contrast, shot from behind, the pupils at school, in long-shot a field of white head scarves, encapsulate some progress, hope.

CRIMSON GOLD (Iran). "Why are you doing this?!"

This is the question that an upscale jeweler, at gunpoint, asks the thief who has pushed his way into the man's shop in the early hours. The thief kills the owner before committing suicide. (When the thief puts the gun to his head, the camera quickly rises.) An extended flashback that loops back to the opening answers the jeweler's question in *Talaye sorkh*; Jafar Panahi directed from a script by mentor Abbas Kiarostami, who consulted an actual crime reported in the daily newspaper. Theirs is a major work about class collision.

Hussein, we learn, was a hero during the Iran-Iraq War that ended fifteen years earlier. He is a quiet, unassuming, considerate man, but the evenness of his affect may be partly due to drugs that numb war injuries and war memories; his bloated appearance, he notes, is the result of cortisone treatments. Hussein subsists on what he earns as a motorbike pizza deliveryman. He is in the lower social stratum.

What brings Hussein to a point of monstrous criminality? A series of events inaugurated by a chanced-upon purse in which Hussein and friend Ali discover a receipt, for a necklace from the jewelry shop, in an amount high beyond their imaginings. Their interest piqued, they go to the shop to check out the necklace, whereupon the jeweler treats them with disdain and dismissal. This and another confrontation encapsulate a Tehran of two incompatible worlds, suggesting a nation beset by social inequity.

The factual receipt inspires Hussein and Ali to pursue a fiction, their belonging to another, higher social world so that, hopefully by viewing the exotic necklace (which is all, initially, they intend to do), their drab, workday lives will be, however briefly, brilliantly transformed. Reality, though, dictates a different conclusion.

2004

MOOLAADÉ (Senegal, Burkina Faso). "The father of African cinema," Senegal's Ousmane Sembène, was 81 when he made *Moolaadé*, a movie both elegant and incendiary. Its topic is tribal female circumcision; its theme, tradition clung to in order to maintain the status quo, in this instance, male supremacy. The action takes place in Djerisso, a tiny, impoverished village in Burkina Faso, in East Africa. Female circumcision, however, is practiced throughout Africa, in thirty-eight countries. A marker of the village is its bizarre, irregular mosque, which is patterned after the adjacent termite hill. Showing male elders emerging through its arched doorways, dark, irregular gaping holes, Sembène applies a satirical spin to their humorless demeanor and reactionary activities.

The protagonist is the village chief's wife, Collé Ardo, who refused to have their daughter, Amsatou, cut because her own genital mutilation cost her two babies in childbirth. Collé is publicly whipped by her husband for her declaration of Moolaadé, that is, "Protection," for four girls who have fled their parents and taken refuge with Collé rather than be cut. During Collé's beating, one of the mothers kidnaps her daughter from the protected compound, thereby ending the Moolaadé, and has her daughter cut. The girl dies as a result. Now radicalized, the mother joins Collé in opposing the practice of female cutting and in confiscating the circumcision knives from the women elders who use them.

Sembène's finely judged distancing techniques gradually dissolve; their disappearance following their use makes all the more powerful the representation of reality that remains. Intended as the middle part of a trilogy begun with *Faat Kiné* (2000) and not completed, and now, because of Sembène's death in 2007, never to be, *Moolaadé* is stark, humane and radical, as befits an artist who studied under Mark Donskoi (the Maxim Gorky trilogy, 1938-40; *The Rainbow*, 1944), no less, in Moscow.

DARWIN'S NIGHTMARE (Austria). Hubert Sauper's documentary provides an inside-out view of globalization, focusing on a fishing community in the East African nation of Tanzania. Mwanza depends for its livelihood on Lake Victoria, the origin of the Nile River. The lake once sustained the Bantu inhabitants with its flourishing fish, but its ecological system was destroyed by the introduction into it of a predatory fish as a "scientific" experiment in the 1960s. Today, Mwanza's industries are catching, processing and packaging the predators so that boxfuls of cans can be flown to Europe and Japan, where they inexpensively appear on supermarket shelves. Sauper's film documents the cost to locals; Lake Victoria identifies the new global economy with earlier forms of European colonization of Africa as effortlessly as the Nile perch, which eats other fish and its own, exemplifies Darwin's "survival of the fittest." Sauper's bold images are as hallucinatory as they are indisputably real.

Famine is widespread. Locals make do with scraps of fish that the plant discards. We see a "killing field" of these scraps: heads and eyes, tails, bits of flesh stuck to skeletons—an expanse of waste swarming with maggots.

In exchange for the fish, the West exports arms to Africa, helping to keep the continent embroiled in national and regional conflicts.

Meanwhile, local workers are paid sub-subsistence wages, but the Europeans there to manage and secure the processing plant and to direct the arms/fish exchange have endowed another industry: prostitution. Exploitation having undermined and undone the local social

structure, sexual promiscuity abounds, and AIDS and H.I.V. are rampant. With only fish scraps to eat and nothing else to do, boys knock themselves out outdoors by melting the plant's discarded boxes and sniffing the resultant chemical glue: children ripe for sodomization.
And this is only part of the nightmare.

MICHELANGELO'S GAZE (Italy). Text introduces this fifteen-minute film: "In 1985 Antonioni suffered a stroke and was confined to a wheelchair. In 2004, through the magic of cinema, he made this visit to San Pietro in Vincoli." This visit, then, enables the artist to transcend imaginatively his limitations. We're about to witness an illusion.
Light, then his shadow, precede Antonioni as he enters the immense structure through an outside door. The angled overhead long-shot establishes his small place in the universe. He is Everyone. As he enters another part of the hall, again his shadow precedes him. The sound of his footsteps confirms his materiality. (Later, he coughs.) Sacred music is heard toward the end, but mostly this is a silent—the dream that is cinema.
Michelangelo Antonioni, bespectacled, looks up at the other Michelangelo's *Moses*. Closeup of Moses's head; tighter closeup; Moses's eyes; upward pans; Antonioni gazing; closeups of Moses's impassive eyes; Antonioni searchingly gazing. The camera views Moses from a myriad of perspectives.
Antonioni's hand feels the sensuous folds of marble. A closeup of the human hand as it moves forward (in hauntingly subtle slow motion) collapses the identities of both Michelangelos; for isn't the sculptor reaching through eternity to the creativity he left behind, and isn't the statue the film that Antonioni is creating? The sixteenth century; now; eternity: time itself collapses.
Motion and the illusion of motion: dissolves; the camera, panning across features (such as the flowing beard), seems to animate the statue, releasing it to the flux of the artist's own mortal condition. Before exiting the hall, Antonioni pauses for a backward glance and passes through a shaft of blue light to the outdoors. The camera does not follow. It remains in the dream.
Antonioni won't give up art a moment sooner than necessary.

ROLLING FAMILY (Argentina). *Familia rodante*, one of the most brilliant films of the new century, finds Argentinean writer-director Pablo Trapero (*Mundo grúa*, 1999; *Leonera*, 2008) invisibly along for the ride on a family trip in a camper van. Four generations cram the van, ranging from an infant to Emilia, the infant's 84-year-old great-grandmother. At her birthday celebration in a rural part of Buenos Aires, her sister telephones from Misiones, inviting her to a family wedding in her hometown. This sets up the trip, with the entire Buenos Aires part of the family participating at Emilia's command, but Trapero's virtually plotless film homes in on the transport, with a payoff at the end that is both emotionally sweeping and witheringly ironical. Trapero captures a rhythm of life and a bounty of familial disappointment—the predictability/unpredictability of life. In his early thirties, Trapero has created a masterpiece, richly deserving the prizes he won for it: best director, Gijón; prize of the international film critics, Guadalajara.
What then does Trapero give us in lieu of plot? Various activities along the way, including washing a family dog, the preparation of a meal, work on the vehicle after it breaks down, and so forth. One soul's dental emergency accounts for a necessary detour; where at night is everyone going to sleep? We are also given, pressured by the vehicle's mechanical problems, eruptions of ancient quarrels, and of old and new romantic realignments, one of which, igniting jealousy, sends a trip member into ignominious exile. Emilia herself, once the Buenos-Aires crowd makes it to Misiones, sees again an old boyfriend whose name she no longer quite recalls.
Trapero's fiction, then, gravitates toward a dramatically heightened documentary-style presentation. At its center is a touching performance by a nonprofessional: Graciana Chironi

as Emilia (best actress, Gijón).

SUD PRALAD (Thailand). The film called in the States *Tropical Malady* is divided into two parts. The first depicts the romance between two boys, Keng, an army reservist stationed in Thailand's rural north, and Tong, a local worker. Prior to this, we see Keng cheesily posing with troop members around the dead body of a civilian who was mauled by a tiger—a marriage of *machismo* and the jaunty disregard of life and death. (Whistling in the dark?) This in turn is preceded by a quotation from novelist Ton Nakajima: "All of us are by nature wild beasts. Our human duty is to keep our animal in check and even teach it to perform tasks alien to its bestiality." The soldiers, George W. Bush might say, are doing a heckuva job.

Nakajima's words govern the second part, which otherwise might seem to belong to another movie, leaving the first one brusquely abandoned. Now Keng, toting his weapon, is alone in the forest, proceeding stealthily through a lush landscape rife with danger. A tiger embodies this danger. But this is no ordinary tiger. It is a legendary shadow-creature that shifts shape, like the beast in *Predator* (John McTiernan, 1987). The stuff of a shaman legend (the first part touches on other mythical material), the tiger that Keng hunts is also a transformed version of Tong. *Sud pralad* takes us through the looking-glass of a man's soul.

Writer-director Apichatpong Weerasethakul relates romantic love to issues of self-mastery and cultural identity, traditional myth and in-the-momentness. When it may seem to have turned from the subjectivity of romance to the objectivity of a soldier's jungle mission, his film, in fact, draws us ever more deeply into his protagonist and into ourselves. It is a journey into the heart of darkness and many kinds of light.

TROPIC OF CANCER (Mexico). A stark examination of post-NAFTA Mexico, *Tropico de cancer* considers how hard some people must work just to survive.

Charco Cercado is a small village. The parched region may once have yielded silver and gold, but the mines have long since been exhausted. Villagers illegally trap animals, including canaries, and sell them at roadside to tourists, who stuff them deep into trunks of cars to escape customs detection. These affluent passers-through pay little for a hideous amount of work. Meanwhile, the adjacent road is busy with commercial trucks: ironic counterpoint to the struggling black market—legal sales that will eventually fill corporate pockets with inexhaustible silver and gold.

The process of the capture and bagging of snakes is meticulously observed. At home a trapper's wife skins a snake and dries the skin. Racks of skins will be part of the makeshift roadside bazaar at film's end. In Mexico, incidentally, selling protected animals is punishable by up to nine years in prison and a $200,000 fine.

Earsplittlingly cacophonous birds are released into the desert. Who would buy such noisy creatures?

Children check countless traps—monotonous, necessary work. Father and son go off together in the afternoon, passing under a barb-wire fence to hunt rodents. The boy's slingshot fells a rat. Cut to the big outdoor pot in which the mother cooks and seasons that night's dinner: rat stew.

The suspenseful closing long-shot, at roadside, encapsulates the precariousness of these people's lives, how survival may depend on a sale. A car slows down; as the seller approaches the driver, the car speeds up and drives off. And the trucks keep rolling by.

Eugenio Polgovsky wrote, directed, digitally videographed, and edited this powerful documentary. A kid in his twenties born in Mexico City, Polgovsky is the future of cinema.

THE NIGHT OF TRUTH (Burkina Faso). "We are of the same clay. We have endured the same nightmare. . . . Your pain is my pain."

Burkina Faso's first feature by a woman, Fanta Régina Nacro's *La nuit de la vérité* is a fable of the attempted reconciliation between opposing sides in a fictitious just-ended ten years' West African civil war. A nighttime celebration shared by government Nayaks and Bonande rebels instances the classical motif of the "failed feast"; burdened by memories of the conflict, including of war atrocities, "war" erupts anew. Confessing an atrocity he committed against the President's child, the rebel leader explains, "War opens up our souls, and demons drive their way in." Tied above an open pit, the man is roasted to a crisp. *More demons*—more evidence that a peace treaty can punctuate a war but not erase it.

Nacro employs an artillery of Brechtian distancing techniques that at first gives the film a stilted, stagy appearance. Nacro doesn't want her film to wash over us; we are snapped to analytic attention. By degrees, however, the film adds emotional force to its brilliant intellectual clarity as Nacro draws her material out of its distanced domain into a startling naturalism. Nacro's first procedure encourages our thoughtful understanding; her second, our humane engagement.

Nacro is an ironist. The film's opening long-shot tweaks Monet; but it is a procession of souls—presumably enjoined Bonandes and Nayaks—whose reflection we see in the water below rather than the Impressionist's luxuriant Nature. But are these reconciled beings or ghosts of the war dead? The President later gets over his wife's murder disconcertingly easily; is there more blood to pay? There's a "happy" schoolroom conclusion that relegates the war to the nation's past; but isn't this punctured by the film's ironical procedure?

PERSONA NON GRATA (Poland). The end of the Cold War that the U.S. had launched to the detriment of the world after the Second World War has left the world changed in some ways and intact in others. Writer-director Krzysztof Zanussi's *Persona non grata* revolves around Wiktor (Zbigniew Zapasiewicz, superb yet again), Poland's ageing Ambassador to Uruguay, where he finds his nation competing with the Russians for a helicopter contract, suspects Russian spying, quarrels with fellow Polish diplomats, and quarrels with his own past. His anti-Sovietism has finally prevailed, but Wiktor still suspects old friend Oleg (fascistic filmmaker Nikita Mikhalkov giving a marvelous performance) of having bedded with his deceased wife, Helena.

The film opens with haunting snapshots of Helena. If I am to believe reviewers I have read over the past few years, Helena and Wiktor had a serenely happy marriage, the loss of which, executed by her death, has been tragic for her widower. Really? Yet Wiktor must go to Poland to attend her funeral, implying that they were probably estranged (it is possible she was on holiday, I suppose), and Wiktor's confrontation with Oleg over possible long-ago adultery suggests the suspiciousness with which the marriage had become infected, perhaps explaining the estrangement. Once back in Montevideo, Wiktor tries enlisting a priest to safeguard Helena's ashes, and he interestingly remarks how Helena's unexpected death left important matters unresolved between them. Am I alone in thinking theirs was *not* the happiest of marriages?

Ironically, Wiktor is viewed by peers and superiors as a Cold War relic. The only "person" he seems to trust is his old, faithful dog, Hippolyt. He drinks to excess to assuage his loneliness.

He earns my affection, however, when he refers to lyric LXVIII of poet Alfred Tennyson's *In Memoriam* ("Sleep, Death's twin-brother ...").

THE KEYS TO THE HOUSE (Italy). "Prepare yourself for great suffering if you remain close to your son."

Nicole (Charlotte Rampling, superb), the mother of a daughter with muscular dystrophy, tells Gianni this (Kim Rossi Stuart, endearing, sensitive), the young father of a severely disabled 15-year-old boy, Paolo, in Gianni Amelio's massively moving *Le Chiavi di casa*. Gianni, whose wife and eight-month-old son are back home in Milan, meets Nicole at a Berlin hospital to which he has accompanied Paolo for tests and therapy. This is the first time

Gianni and Paolo have met; Gianni's teenaged girlfriend died giving birth to Paolo. The film chronicles the bond that now, with great difficulty, develops between Paolo and Gianni.

Amelio devises point-of-view shots to disclose the depths of Paolo's dissatisfaction with his crippled, brain-damaged life. In one, kids running and playing normally reveal the envy that Paolo doesn't give voice to.

"How can you be so serene?" Gianni admiringly asks Nicole. In the film's most stunning shot, in which Gianni joins Nicole as she waits for a subway train, we see that Nicole's "serenity" masks hardship, envy, exhaustion, regret.

Gianni is trying to make peace with a ruptured past. Suddenly there are so many new things Gianni must learn how to do and, frequently in over his head, he keeps making mistakes for which his patient son must reprimand him. For instance, Gianni keeps forgetting which arm of Paolo's he is to put into a shirt or jacket sleeve first, and which one he is to take out of the sleeve first, so as not to hurt the boy when dressing or undressing him. At one point, overwhelmed, Gianni dissolves into tears, and it is Paolo who comforts him—and chides him: "You shouldn't cry. Fathers don't cry."

Children have no idea.

THE WAYWARD CLOUD (Taiwan). Tsai Ming-liang's *Tian Bian Yi Duo Yun* is a sequel to his 2001 *What Time Is It There?* (*Ni neibian jidian*), the "there" being Paris, from which Shiang-chyi has returned to Taipei. On a pedestrian overpass she runs into former street vendor and boyfriend Hsiao-kang. "Do you still sell watches?" she asks. Hsiao-kang's reply: "No."

Hsiao-kang makes a living now as a porno actor; his current shoot, coincidentally, is in Shiang-chyi's apartment building. Tsai's film opens with a long-held shot of a pedestrian underpass whose vacancy is interrupted by two young women crossing paths: Shiang-chyi and her porno film counterpart, Hsiao-kang's co-star. The camera view of the structure suggests a gigantic vagina. In bed for the shoot, the camera here as invisible as in the outer film, the actress has half a watermelon between her legs; Hsiao-kang cuts the fruit with his indefatigable pecker, feeds his co-star, and licks running juice off her body with a darting tongue. Now Hsiao-kang is wearing the hollowed-out melon as a helmet. The city is experiencing a terrible drought, and the demand for wet watermelon has skyrocketed.

Malaysian-born Taiwanese filmmaker Tsai punctuates his deadpan comedy with playback musical numbers. A plethora of umbrella-clad people in an overhead shot suggests the wishfulfilling tendency of these fantasies. The water released when Hsiao-kang digs out Shiang-chyi's key from a tarseal suggests how fluent are some of Tsai's transitions from reality to dream. The musical numbers themselves, in one of which Hsiao-kang appears as a dancing penis, are exhilarating and hilarious—like a draught of cool water in the midst of drought.

Tsai's theme of urban dryness, alienation, disenchantment and loneliness achieves a powerful consummation when Hsiao-kang tears himself away from movie sex with a comatose partner to Shiang-chyi, who has been silently looking on.

HARVEST TIME (Ukraine). Ukraine, 1950. Gennady, who lost both legs in the war, his wife Antonina, and their two small sons live in a farm shack only one wall of which is wallpapered; the boys have one toy, a wooden truck, in addition to their father's wheel board, which his increasing drunkenness makes available for the younger one's use. Gena explains to the latter that the soldiers in his photographs are all dead. "I will never die," the boy says. With aching tenderness, Gena responds, "No, *you* will not die." Decades hence, this son narrates. Father, mother and brother are all dead, and so is he—a casualty of the Soviet war in Afghanistan. As our guide, the narrator is a bit lost, confessing, "I don't remember anybody," when the film shows a series of old photographs. The narrator recalls when his mother won the Red Banner as her region's best combine operator. She would have preferred a length of calico, to make drapes, but her prize is embossed with likenesses of Soviet political heroes. Mice are at her prize, though, so when not at work Antonina must cut and repair until nothing is left but "a red velvet rag." Lack of sexual intimacy as a result of Gena's war injuries has undercut the fabric of her marriage. Narrator: "Years later, I realized that Father could live without legs, but not without love. And Mother no longer had strength left to love [my brother and me]." The film's color scheme leans to sepia, like old photographs, making each dab of color—usually desaturated green or drab red—precious. A spiritual assessment of the Stalinist Soviet Union pitched between recollection and legend, Marina Razbezhkina's *Vremya zhatvy* is about the tattering of political and religious faith, the bankruptcy of people's hopes and dreams.

THE INTRUDER (France). Inspired by Jean-Luc Nancy's novel *L'Intrus*, Claire Denis's same-titled film includes two of her most moving moments. One shows Sidney Trebor (Grégoire Colin, wonderful), a young father carrying his infant, Louis, in a sling-harness against his heart. Louis looks up at his father's face. Slowly the child smiles, and we understand, even though Sidney's face is outside the frame, that the infant is following his father's lead in expressing love. Sidney's father, Louis, from whom Sidney is estranged, later buys a heart on the post-Soviet Russian black market as a surgical replacement for his own. After intermediate stops, Louis ends up in Tahiti looking for another son. A village panel indulges Louis's fantasy of leaving a wad of bills to whomever and conducts interviews to select a fitting "son" for him. (The scene parodies a casting session!) Before he expires (or, given the film's dream fabric, perhaps *when* or *after*), Louis imagines seeing Sidney cold dead in a Tahitian morgue. Sidney's chest shows the surgical scar that by now has faded from Louis's own body. How does one enter into the mystery of this moment without dissolving into tears?

The woman who arranged for Louis's heart shadows him; perhaps she is his guilty conscience. On a dark street Louis cries out at her to leave him alone. "I have a sick heart!" She shoots back: "Not anymore! Your heart is just empty."

Or so full, it needs emptying out.

Denis's film, strange, elusive, very quiet, dreamlike, begins at the border between France and Switzerland but mostly navigates the border between the love one feels and the love one cannot express. Louis's journey home in a coffin, the sea rolling underneath an immense gray and charcoal sky (except for a patch of eerie light), catches a remarkable chill.

2005

LA SIERRA (U.S.). "We're in the hands of kids with guns."

Scott Dalton and Margarita Martinez's documentary about the armed struggle between Colombian Leftist guerrillas and right-wing paramilitaries for control of Medellín's hillside barrio of La Sierra contemplates the contorted relations among youth, poverty, desperation, violence. Shortly after opening pages of script ("In the past decade, over 35,000 people have been killed in Colombia's bloody civil conflict"), we see a shot-dead youth on the ground, his bloody corpse a magnet for flies. His girlfriend is beside herself. This will be a film in which other teenaged girls are stricken with identical grief over the loss of their children's young fathers.

One member of the paramilitary group Bloque Metro notes that he worries not about harm coming to him but to his family. We think: Your being killed—*that* will harm your family.

Dalton and Martinez focus on three persons: Edison Flores, the 22-year-old commander of Bloque Metro, who has six offspring with six different girls; Cielo, the 17-year-old girlfriend of an incarcerated Bloque Metro member; 19-year-old Jesús, who is under Edison's command and who has lost a hand to his own grenade: a natural metaphor that plays out through the film, encapsulating the self-destructive nature of gangland violence. "I'm one of the good guys," Jesús professes; "I'm only bad to bad people." Offscreen, Martinez asks him, "Do you think you will die young?" Jesús: "Of course."

By joining forces with another paramilitary group, Bloque Metro is finally able to defeat the local guerrillas, at which point war erupts afresh as the other group seeks total control of La Sierra. Government forces shoot dead Edison; we watch a small neighborhood boy ignite a legend about the fallen commander.

Reality is a rock upon which the human heart breaks of its own accord.

SOLNTSE (Russia). Aleksandr Sokurov's film about Emperor Hirohito (Issei Ogata, brilliant), Japanese emperor, during the time of his surrender to General MacArthur, is his most exquisite piece of work. *The Sun* proceeds along two tracks. One is Japanese defeat and humiliation as a result of the outcome of the Second World War. During an automobile ride taking the emperor to a meeting with the Allied commander, a tracking shot records Japan's devastation; the sound engineer assigned to Hirohito's announcement of defeat to the Japanese public, we learn, ritually disembowels himself immediately afterwards.

The other track is ironical. Defeat means freedom for Hirohito. He renounces his status as deity. At the last he and the empress (Kaori Mamoi, superb) are shown running to their children, a couple with family straining to behave normally, but without practice or a road map.

Working as his own cinematographer, Sokurov leans on grays and browns in his mostly medium long-shots. Both the colors and camera distance undercut Hirohito's exalted public status; rather, they imply his release into earthly humanity. When we finally see the sun, a blur in the sky, it is the abstraction from which Hirohito has been released.

One of the film's amazing shots follows Hirohito from his rooms to his office. It is a subterranean trek, with the unkempt passageways resembling a space ship. The imagery here impresses upon us the emperor's insularity—and more: the unnaturalness of his station and existence.

There is, actually, a third track: the obscene arrogance of the conquering and occupying Americans. Douglas MacArthur is portrayed as a boor, a monster. At one point he ridicules Hirohito for his alliance with Hitler. Hirohito's ironic response: "We had only 50 out of 100 chances to win the war, but Germany had 100 out of 100 chances to win."

FREE ZONE (Israel, France, Belgium, Spain). The first Israeli film to be shot in an Arab country, Jordan, *Free Zone* may be Amos Gitaï's masterpiece. East of Jordan, the "Free Zone" lies between the borders of Syria and Iraq; cars are bought and sold there, tax-free.

Hanna (Hana Laszlo, wonderful—best actress, Cannes) drives her husband's taxi cab from Tel Aviv to the Free Zone to collect money they are owed for armored vehicles they have sold to Arabs. Two Intifadas have ruined their prior businesses. Hana explains to Rebecca, a U.S. passenger: "We've got to make a living. Everyone wants to survive."

Upon learning that he raped a Palestinian woman in a refugee camp, Rebecca has just ended her engagement to an Israeli citizen. The film opens with a very long, claustrophobic take of Rebecca (in profile) in the back seat of the cab, crying, as a children's song, "Had Gadia," is heard, its lyric detailing—these are Gitaï's words—"a chain of oppressive actions." We also hear a call to prayer in Arabic. Much of the film unfolds inside the cab.

Crossing the border into Jordan, both women are now in the front seat. The "long journey" to the Free Zone, which takes eight hours, is dazzlingly experimental. Layered superimpositions show the road ahead, the sights through a side window, the two women conversing or, at times, silent, and flashbacks showing in turn what has brought each woman to this journey. In the Free Zone, Samir, from whom Hana is supposed to collect the debt, has already left, and his partner, Leila (Hiam Abbass, excellent), agrees to drive the women to him. Hana follows her and Rebecca. En route, Leila, who is Palestinian, explains after speaking some Hebrew, "I think it's really important to learn the language of your enemy." She further opines that, if Israelis learned Arabic to the extent that Occupied Arabs are

compelled by circumstance to learn Hebrew, "things might change."
Leila's village is in flames, torched by Samir's son, who hates Leila. Leila: "I had plans to change the past. I will do it!"
The film ends hilariously, with Leila and Hana bickering in the front seat about the uncollected $30,000. This is the second explosion of irresistible humor; the first, back at the office, consists of dueling phone calls by Hana and Leila to their respective partners.
A truly liberating film, this.

THE FORSAKEN LAND (Sri Lanka). Recurrent civil war since 1983 in Sri Lanka has had a devastating effect on the land and its people. Writer-director Vimukthi Jayasundara was both rewarded and censured for his *Sulanga Enu Pinisa*, winning the Caméra d'Or (for best first feature) at Cannes and being warned by his government to make films praising the national military rather than criticizing it. In 2009, another film by Jayasundara, *Ahasin Wetei* was released.
Embedded in the opening credits is a long-shot of an armed soldier at night in a vast barren landscape. In a bravura long-shot the next day, a woman and a girl both aim to board a bus. The woman is walking leisurely across a field to the bus stop; the girl is on the road, running fast to reach the stop and not be left behind. She makes it; the woman gives her a lift up. Like most of Jayasundara's images, this one is poetic, ambiguous and emotionally sweeping. We see the shared experience of two anonymous characters and something more elusive: the possibility that both are the same character, at different stages of her life, doubly inhabiting the same haunted frame. We eventually learn that the two are aunt and niece. In another long-shot a stripped-naked man is tossed into the river by fellow soldiers; a solitary bird perches on the branch of a bare, solitary tree. The bird flies off, but either another bird or the same one lands on the tree. Odd-man-out; two birds or one: both aspects of the *mise-en-scène* strangely connect. Both niece and aunt, the soldier's daughter and sister, are subsequently referred to as "Little Bird."
Episodic, elliptical, minimalist, powerful, Jayasundara's near-speechless film includes marital infidelity, unwanted sexual attentions, two suicides, a graphic scene of torture, a grotesque military murder.

MATCH POINT (UK, U.S., Ireland, Russia). Writer-director Woody Allen's *Match Point* is all about luck. Set in London, it is a witty, almost unendurably suspenseful exploration of class meldings and collisions. The egotistical shenanigans of (nonetheless) incredibly likeable Chris Wilton (Jonathan Rhys Meyers, terrific) include two cold-blooded murders with a shotgun, one at nearly point-blank range.
Chris was born poor. Selling tennis lessons at an exclusive club, he befriends rich boy Tom Hewett, and dates and weds Tom's sister, Chloe—and has an affair with Tom's fiancée, Nola, whom Tom, quitting slumming, eventually dumps.
One doesn't choose one's class; it's *purely* a matter of luck. When she becomes pregnant, jeopardizing his marriage to Chloe and the lifestyle and work opportunity that are attached to it (Chris has a responsible position in his father-in-law's company), Nola must be gotten rid of. Chris commits a first murder in anticipation of covering up this second murder; making his own luck, Chris must murder to save his marriage.
Accompanied by Chris's voiceover weighing luck and goodness, and preferring luck, the opening shows a tennis net running in angled depth through the frame. The ball that has been going back and forth in slow motion strikes the top of the net and stays suspended in air over the net. Wickedly, Allen never releases the freeze frame, dissolving instead to the narrative proper. Chris's whole life is one of suspense. Later, Chris tosses a ring he has stolen to cover up a murder, expecting it to be washed away in the Thames; instead, unbeknownst to him, it hits the top of the guard rail and falls down landside. Will Chris be caught? Or haunted by guilt? Allen cuts in half the difference between the two alternatives—the *narrative* translation of the earlier freeze frame. Brilliant!

REGULAR LOVERS (France). A response to Bernardo Bertolucci's crass, sentimental *The Dreamers* (2003), Philippe Garrel's tremendous *Les amants réguliers* could be called *After the Revolution*—or, *After the Hoped-for Revolution*.

Louis Garrel, Philippe's son, plays François Dervieux, a 20-year-old poet who joins comrades (one of whom is a Léaud-lookalike), some of them Communists, others anarchists, in violent street activism in 1968 Paris. Factory strikes fold into "the movement," which disintegrates, provoking François to muse (I do not know whom he is quoting), "Can we make the revolution for the working class *despite* the working class?" It appears that labor wants more money only.

In shimmering black and white (William Lubtchansky is his inspired cinematographer), Garrel takes to the nighttime streets not just for car burnings and confrontations with the police but also for walks shared by François and Lilie (Clotilde Hesme, wonderful), the essence of youthful romance. (Lilie is a sculptor; another character, a painter.) Garrel's style could be described as consisting of snatches of real time. Long, fluid takes in the dark, outdoors or in, create a delicate dreaminess that Garrel punctuates with snippets of François's actual dreams. Garrel loves to suspend time, to hold the hopefulness of the sixties in his mind, but he also cuts to shots of intricate activity to provide surprising outbursts of in-the-momentness.

The romance of François and Lilie—although lovers, they aren't ever shown making love—reflects on François's revolutionary idealism. It, too, dissolves—not for want of love on either soul's part but for what Lilie regards as practical necessity. Left with neither a new France nor the love of his life, François dies dreaming in his sleep.

For some of us of the sixties, life has struggled in the shadow of the French Revolution that was not to be.

FATELESS (Hungary). From Nobel Laureate Imre Kertész's autobiographical novel, *Sorstalanság* (literally, *Fatelessness*) is about a Jewish boy, living with his father and stepmother in Budapest, who, beginning in 1944, is sent to a series of concentration camps. This was routine, but the ultimate destination was usually a death camp; 14-year-old György ("Gyuri") Köve moves instead from a death camp to one without gas chambers. His ordeal is nonetheless horrific (he nearly loses a leg after it becomes infected), but it appears he isn't "fated" for extinction like the Six Million.

However, Gyuri's fate isn't entirely out of his hands. At the first stop, Auschwitz, his lie that he is sixteen spares Gyuri immediate extermination. Surrounded by torture and death, the boy embraces this article of understanding: "I could be *killed*—anywhere, anytime." This acceptance frees him to live in unlivable circumstances, becoming his mental, spiritual, existential "edge." In addition, he is lucky; because he is inexplicably alive, he draws the help of others who want to help keep him alive.

After being liberated and choosing to go home, Gyuri finds "hatred" being aimed at him. Neighbors want him, and the war memories for them that he embodies, to disappear. He misses Buchenwald, the last camp, which, after all, was his home, and was a place of kindness as well as cruelty. His father has died in a camp; but a pair of family friends, hilarious, also introduce an unexpected note—Jewish joy: hatred's defeat.

Celebrated cinematographer, first time-director Lajos Koltai mostly confines his palette to white, yellows and browns, but the intense golds of the opening movement turn dull in the camps. Koltai's impressionistic style—numerous short scenes fading out—suggests mental snapshots of Gyuri's sharp observation and subsequent memories.

Fateless is one of the freshest fictional movies about the Holocaust.

NINA'S JOURNEY (Sweden). Nina Rajmic, filmmaker Lena Einhorn's mother, is a teenager when her mother, Fania, moves her from Lódź to Warsaw in an attempt to elude ghettoization. The Nazis follow. Fania and Nina, helped by Rudek, their son and elder brother, escape the Warsaw Ghetto and go into hiding. Artur, their spouse and father, is deported to a death camp.

We do not have to wonder whether Nina survives the war. We see and hear the actual Nina 55 years later, and hear her voiceover. After the war, Nina went to medical school in Denmark, met there and married Einhorn's father, and settled in Sweden.

Massively moving and humane, *Ninas resa* recounts a particular, vivid Jewish family history. Einhorn has combined, along with her mother's own oral history, both fiction and documentary. The "fiction," in color, consists of dramatic re-enactments of what occurred to the Rajmics and extended family members; the "documentary," in black and white, consists of archival newsreel snips and photographs. However, the old film elements do not appear as inserts interrupting the flow of the family narrative; rather, these elements are selected and combined with the other elements so that a single narrative stream, all moving in one direction, is the remarkable result. Moreover, Einhorn achieves a fine flexibility with her various materials, creating a harmony of chords like a virtuoso's bow across the strings of a violin. At one point, sound from one kind of element continues on into the next, different element; and, at one amazing point, Fania, that is to say, the actress playing her, appears in a black-and-white snippet of faux-newsreel: one kind of element sliding into another. In retrospect, we may even wonder if some of the other archival contributions were in fact devised for the film.

CHETYRE (Russia). Ilya Khrjanovsky's *4*, from Vladimir Sorokin's script, suggests that post-Soviet life in Russia is bleak. It opens stunningly, on a desolate, deserted city street in darkness. A quartet of wild dogs lie expectantly, their homelessness correlative to the post-Soviet problem of *human* homelessness. Into the frame four monstrous legs descend onto the street, the whatever to which these legs belong having already sent the dogs screeching and fleeing.

Inside a city bar in the wee hours, three customers, strangers, sit, drink, talk. Their success comes at the expense of fellow citizens, which is to say, themselves. Hoping to remain "successful," they must secretly fear that monstrous legs will descend out of nowhere to stomp them out. They lie, hoping to secure their advantageous position while hiding their vulnerability. One, a piano tuner, claims he is a technician who knows about 1930s Soviet cloning experiments. There are, he says, countless clones among the current Russian population: *whole villages*—a totalitarian nightmare; places to take care of the infirm ones—a socialist dream. The sole female customer is likely a prostitute; but she says she sells a Japanese machine that increases worker productivity. This woman, we learn, is one of the clones!

The film's second part, exceedingly strange, follows the prostitute to her remote home village, most of whose inhabitants are old crones who provide a grotesque parody of marketplace self-sufficiency by producing folk dolls out of over-chewed bread—a gross communal activity. The hags negotiate the unpleasant process with drunkenness. They also undress and pinch one another's withered breasts. Khrjanovsky splendidly portrays the insularity, the inwardness, of this rural community—the degree to which these women rely on one another for what sense of identity they possess. All these women do whatever they must in order to survive.

Unshakeable.

THREE TIMES (Taiwan). Written by Chu Tien-wen and the director, Hou Hsiao-hsien's *Zui hao de shi guang* consists of three segments, each superbly acted by the same young leads (Shu Qui, Chang Chen), each set at a different time (1966, 1911, 2005) in a different Taiwanese location. Each segment, in its way a romance, ends in a suspended state, unresolved.

"A Time for Love" revolves around a soldier whose heart is taken up by a snooker parlor hostess. They wait together for the morning bus to take him back to base. Punctuated by Taiwanese and American tunes, and one by the Beatles, this first segment suggests the shyness of a generation that must express their feelings through popular songs.

The second segment's reddish hue, replacing the first one's dim, possibly fertile greenishness, suggests alluring femininity and spilt, dispersed blood. It is set in a brothel, the projection of patriarchy, during a time of Japanese occupation: one prison inside another. Accompanied by delicately mournful piano music, this segment is silent, for the girl whom Shu now plays, one of the prostitutes, is culturally and politically bereft of a voice. Her silent heart has especially responded to one particular client.

In the present-day final segment, which balances greenish and reddish hues, the girl now is near-blind in one eye and epileptic. She is a pop singer; the boy, a photographer whose complacently obsessive attentions interrupt and confound her current lesbian relationship. The last we see of her she is sitting right behind him as his motorcycle takes off into an indeterminate future of numbed emotions.

This segment implies that the contemporary gadgetry and communications with which it is overloaded help drain youth of spirit and humanity. It unfolds also in the shadow of China's threats against the independent existence of Taiwan.

LAST DAYS (U.S.). Blake, the protagonist of *Last Days*, suggests Kurt Cobain, guitarist, lead singer, composer and lyricist for the 1990s grunge band Nirvana. Cobain became addicted to heroin, which helped him cope with pain from stomach ulcers. He committed suicide at 27. The conclusion of a marvelous trilogy (*Gerry*, 2002; *Elephant*, 2003) following a commercial-go that writer-director Gus Van Sant has since repudiated depicts in both a highly particular and nearly abstract way the last two days or so of Blake's life.

Besides Cobain, Blake suggests another Pacific Northwesterner (from Madras, Oregon) and a contemporary of Cobain's, whom Van Sant befriended when he directed him in a legendary performance in *My Own Private Idaho* (1991): River Phoenix, whose inadvertent drug overdose triggered a fatal heart attack, at 24, that left Van Sant grief-stricken. His 1997 novel, *Pink*, was written in hopes of working his way through his grief.

While the film is largely composed of Blake's seemingly random, haphazard actions and activities, including eating a bowl of cereal and making macaroni and cheese, it is bookended by music: the King Sisters' gorgeous rendition of "La Guerre," a sixteenth-century choral piece that imparts an otherworldly "feel" to a film largely bound up in cut-and-dried realistic matter and minutia. The film thus attends to both Blake's last days and the eternity to follow.

In a stupendous Bressonian shot, Blake walks past a tree upon which the camera remains fixed with Blake out of frame. Van Sant is juxtaposing Blake's transience, his restless, anxious spirit, and the tree's sturdiness, permanence (its *treeness*), extracting from its materiality the spiritual store its integrity implies.

Also like Bresson, *Last Days* is very pure, nondramatic, unaffected. Blake's death occurs offscreen, unimpeding hopefulness in the camera's mysterious ascension of an outdoor ladder as Blake's spirit approaches nirvana.

THE BLUE UMBRELLA (India). Himachal Pradesh, located in northwest India, literally means "region of snowy mountains." It is also called Deva Bhoomi, "land of the gods." There, Biniya, who is nine, trades her bear-claw necklace for a Japanese tourist's blue umbrella. This umbrella excites the envy of shopowner Nandakishore, who gains the sympathy of the village when Biniya accuses him of having stolen her umbrella and the police, ransacking his home/shop, find nothing. A red Japanese umbrella arrives as Nandakishore's proof he doesn't need to steal the item. But when Biniya closes it for him, her sense of touch identifies this umbrella as her own. Biniya sleuths out the truth: Nandakishore had her umbrella dyed to conceal his theft; now the dye is dissolving in the rain. The village decides not to patronize Nandakishore's shop, sending him into poverty. Biniya, maturing, transcends her possessiveness and, realizing the enormous price that the old man has had to pay for his, gives him the umbrella, explaining, as he tries to return it, it doesn't belong to her. She might as easily have said that she doesn't belong to it.

Earlier, a village boy had asked Nandakishore what use the blue umbrella he coveted was. "What use is the rainbow in the sky?" he replied. "One cannot put a price on a peaceful soul."

From Ruskin Bond's novella, Vishal Bharadwaj's Hindi *Chatri Chor* locates an emotional space where everyday humanity brushes against the hem of spirituality. For the Japanese tourist, it is the necklace that promises access to spirit; for the child, it is the gorgeous umbrella, which seems to bring the surrounding sky within reach. For us, it is the pure enchantment of long-shots—the color cinematographer is Sachin K. Krishn—where we sense a spiritual presence: the essence, the air, of Nature.

2006

PASSAGES (U.S.). *See above.*

THE WIND THAT SHAKES THE BARLEY (Ireland, UK, Germany, Italy, Spain, France). "I tried not to get into this war, and did; and now try to get out, and can't." — Damien O'Donovan

Beautifully written by Paul Laverty, the most massively moving film about brothers I've seen won Ken Loach the Palme d'Or at Cannes. Glimpsing the infancy of the Irish Republican Army, it encompasses both post-World War I periods of conflict in Ireland, England's oldest colony, the first (1919-1921) when Irish rebels sought freedom from British rule, culminating in the 1921 settlement establishing the so-called Irish Free State, and the second (1922-23) when Irish rebel holdouts contested this settlement for its compromises, leading to bloodshed between both Irish factions.

1920. Blacks and Tans terrorize locals, murdering one boy for giving his name in Irish Gaelic.

Loach's film is primarily about two brothers, Teddy and Damien O'Donovan (Cillian Murphy, unforgettable), who are on the same side against the British but, later, post-treaty, on opposing sides. Once Damien is captured, Teddy, now an officer in the Irish Free State Army, pleads with his brother to betray the rebels; Damien refuses, and Teddy, steeling himself past overwhelming regret, has him executed.

Damien is a medical doctor. What seals his determination not to compromise is that he drew the lot that required his dispatching a boy who had given information to the enemy. The long-shot of Damien walking away after the execution, the fixed camera toward his back, shoulders seized by a quick shudder, bares the torn heart of a healer who has just killed. Teddy pleads they will tear up the treaty with the British once they are strong enough; Damien cannot give in. Doing so would cast his killing act to the senseless winds and break faith with all the Irish dead.

BAMAKO (Mali). "They take our money; they take our minds, too."

Abderrahmane Sissako's masterpiece begins at dawn; the village of Bamako is waking up. Among intercut actions: daily activities; an impoverished couple quarrel as their ill daughter sleeps; a man scrounges a living videographing weddings and funerals; a trial in a courtyard, where the West's financial and economic forces bleeding Africa—the World Bank, International Monetary Fund, World Trade Organization, the G8—face charges in absentia.

A western film-within-the-film encapsulates African frustration, anger—for many, repressed feelings. "The trial's becoming annoying," one villager opines.

It fascinates us, however. "Pay or die," an attorney for the plaintiff, black Africa, declares. "That's the West's lesson."

Africa finds itself trapped in a "vicious circle" of debt, owed to the World Bank and the

I.M.F.; while 10% of a nation's annual budget may be directed to social services, education, infrastructure, etc., at least 40% goes to debt repayment—because of interest, an infinite amount. The borrowed money, we learn, wasn't invested in creating jobs. The world is "open" for whites, not African blacks, who are sent back home when they try emigrating to find work. Barely living under "imposed destitution" (life expectancy is 46), they find multinational corporations seizing whatever a nation needs to be sovereign. Colonialism "took everything away"; this new form of colonialism keeps taking. The World Bank threatened to withdraw financial support if the transport system wasn't privatized. Victims of "unchained capitalism," people have had their public institutions and social services sold off. While two-thirds of their children are illiterate, now they must pay for education.

Hilariously, the judges settle uneasily into their robes. A dog that earlier appeared dead may have sprung back to life, but only to sniff at the corpse of a suicide.

COLOSSAL YOUTH (Portugal, France, Switzerland). Reminiscent of Elem Klimov's *Farewell* (1981), Portuguese writer-director Pedro Costa's *Juventude Em Marcha* completes his Fountaínhas trilogy. The Cape Verdean shantytown is being demolished, its inhabitants relocated northward to a housing project in a Lisbon suburb. The film begins with the voices of indeterminate people and ends with the sound of an infant's contentment.

Apparently, 75-year-old communal patriarch Ventura (Ventura, dignified, without false nobility, part of the nonprofessional casting) has lost one home but has yet to be deposited in another. Thus the somber film largely consists of his homeless wanderings and drop-ins here and there, including on a daughter or, possibly, surrogate daughter. One character may be a ghost; other ambiguous elements set reality on the border of memory and myth.

This thoroughly absorbing work, besides providing an unwincing portrait of poverty, casts Ventura amidst the "new" environment; early on, a low camera finds the tall, gracious man "outgunned" by the sterile white buildings towering him. Their juxtaposition is correlative to the battle that the old man embodies. Uprooted, the Creole souls, having already suffered more than their historical share (colonization, slavery), now must face the lonely prospect of losing their culture; their memories and collective memory are being "whited out."

In some ways Costa made an unannounced, uncertified Dogme 95 film. (The purist movement had already run its course.) Certainly his (gorgeous) use of natural light—he and Leonardo Simões digitally videographed, transferring the result to 35mm—suggests this; his dim, luxuriantly dark interiors on occasion evoke Rembrandt. Costa fills much space with nothingness—a projection of both current feelings of the characters and their worried-after destiny.

Costa may cut from one doorway to another or include in the same shot two doorways, one canceling the other. There's no place to go.

Staggering.

TEN NIGHTS OF DREAM (Japan). Ten different Japanese filmmakers contribute short films to *Yume jû-ya*. One of them is Kon Ichikawa, whose contribution is his penultimate piece of work. The "second night of dream" is a miniature marvel—more evidence that Ichikawa is one of Japan's very greatest filmmakers.

There are two male characters, one of whom is middle-aged, the other perhaps a quarter-century older. The "characters" may in fact be figures, for it is ambiguous whether they represent two different persons; perhaps they represent the same person at two different stages of life. It is also ambiguous which is the dreamer.

The filmlet conjures the world of a dream. Except for sparse sounds, but not the sounds of speech, it is a silent world; titles convey words that the characters or figures apparently are dream-saying or thinking. Somehow suiting this mysterious muteness is the grayness of the filmlet's ghostly appearance; there are also traces of eerie light.

The filmlet opens with the younger man walking down a narrow corridor to a room that he enters in order to meditate. He sits on the floor. Seeking enlightenment, he thinks, "You must awaken to emptiness." The word "awaken" is charged with double meaning, referring to waking up from sleep and awakening to a higher level of consciousness. The older man stands over the younger one, expressing doubt that he will attain enlightenment and even hostility toward him. Indeed, the younger man feels himself a total failure. Again and again he tries suicide with an unsheafed blade, failing each time: "I cannot even pierce my flesh." He hangs his head in shame. The older man "speaks": "Enlightenment is upon you."

Dreams rarely, if ever, reach completion; the dreamer's awakening interrupts, ending the dream: a final touch, here, of mystery and ambiguity.

CŒURS (France). One of Alain Resnais's loveliest films, *Cœurs*, based on Alan Ayckbourn's play *Private Fears in Public Places*, is an upclose meditation on six crisscrossing lives in Paris. Its leitmotif is sparse falling snow that appears outdoors and in, conflating the emotional distance between venues, and evoking the fragile nature of feeling and the transience of life. Snow falling outside is extended indoors by way of superimpositions, and when this expressionistic technique is erased we still see snow falling outdoors, through an open door, perhaps, converting Expressionism to naturalism and leaving us a little haunted. Resnais is always humane; here, more intimately so.

The main characters: a real estate agent; his co-worker; Lionel, a bartender at a hotel whose father is in his son's care and is dying; the father (Claude Rich, hilariously libidinous in an offscreen performance); Lionel's most committed barfly, whose partner had been the agent's client in search of a new apartment—a new life—for the both of them; the barfly's new girlfriend, the agent's sister.

Charlotte, real estate agent Thierry's devout Catholic co-worker, keeps giving shy Thierry tapes of a TV program, *Songs That Changed My Life*, but with an add-on: herself in strutting sexual get-up. Following her cue, one day at work he steals a kiss, only to be greeted by incensed virtue; impelled by worries of charges of sexual harassment, he proffers profuse apologies. In truth, if only he could see it, the one he ought to be pursuing is client Nicole (Laura Morante, wonderful), but Thierry doesn't know that Nicole has parted ways with her barfly-boyfriend. But one is always inside and outside one's own life, like the snow, and loneliness seems to be what one can settle on.

The TV show provides pseudo-documentary excerpts inside Resnais's melancholy dream.

FOREVER (Netherlands). Dutch documentarian Heddy Honigmann's *Forever* wittily opens with the camera's descent from heaven to view a patch of gravestones. The faded blue of a gravedigger's jeans blends in with the predominant grays; *but wait!* An older couple, walking away from the camera, silently enters the frame. The woman is dressed in flaming red: "I am alive!" Later, there's a black-and-white clip of Maria Callas, one of the luminaries eternally resting at Père-Lachaise, singing an aria. Perhaps we connect that enchanting voice, her (at that point) delicate, fragile face, and the red outfit of the anonymous woman whose face will forever be a mystery to us. This is a magical film.

One of the other luminaries buried in the Paris cemetery is Georges Méliès, cinema's original magician, whose grave is marked by an imposing statue. Now he is alive, in an amazing clip from one of his black-and-white silent films. Méliès keeps taking off his reappearing head, setting it on either of the tables flanking him. At one point there are four smiling Méliès-heads in the frame, including one on his neck, all this tweaking the sturdy dignity of the sculpted face at Père-Lachaise.

Chopin is also buried there. Honigmann, who remains offscreen throughout the film, interviews a young Japanese pianist, Yoshino Kimura, who is rehearsing a Chopin piece for public performance. The film periodically returns to her, including, eventually, to part of the performance. Several people are interviewed throughout; these include mostly visitors to graves of both the famous and (but for the visitors) the anonymous, as well as people who

work at Père-Lachaise. They clean stones, water flowers, pay respect—to a cherished father; Proust; Modigliani. Only one mourns: a woman who loved a boy with all her heart. He died from a bee-sting.
Life.

TIMES AND WINDS (Turkey). Five times a day, from the minaret of the mosque in this poor Turkish village, the imam delivers the call to prayer, combinately a daily summation of the essential beliefs of Islam as given in the Quran. This structures the everyday life of the village but also breaks the monotony of labor, giving the prayerful faithful a taste of heaven in the midst of their encounter with a largely intransigent earth. Ömer, who is perhaps 12, knows the call to prayer by heart. He has learned it by listening to his imam father. Only, now, his father is sick; he asks Ömer, his elder son, to fetch the neighbor who substitutes for him on these occasions. Perhaps Ömer wishes that his father would ask *him* to deliver the call.

Ömer hates his father, who treats him cruelly and openly favors Ömer's younger brother. One night, Ömer passes by his brother's bed and leans over. Is he going to harm his brother? To protect him from the cold, Ömer pulls up the child's blanket carefully, so as not to wake him, sneaks into his parents' bedroom and opens the window above his sleeping father, whose doctor has warned him to keep his chest warm.

Much later, Ömer loosens his hand from his father's dying grip, ascends a cliff, sits, breaks into tears of shame, love, regret.

Writer-director Reha Erdem's powerful, unsentimental, beauteous *Beş vakit* follows Ömer and two classmates, Yakup and Yildiz, each of whom is embedded in a hard life. (Yildiz, for instance, is her mother's slave.) Erdem often positions the camera at a child's invisibly burdened back and follows and follows him or her, straight or windingly, on some paced or rushed task: the boundless motion of young life headed into parental shadow.

DREAMS OF DUST (France, Canada, Burkina Faso). French writer-director Laurent Salgues's *Rêves de poussière* is a vivid depiction of hard labor, sustained by hopes for a better future, and poverty. Mocktar, a Nigerian farmer, has just lost his youngest daughter. Burdened by guilt for inadequately providing for wife and family, he travels to northeast Burkina Faso to work in the gold mines. An official explains, "The gold rush is over." His response gets Mocktar hired: "I'm just looking for a job."

The film opens with an extreme long-shot of sand being blown by wind screen-right across the landscape. A human figure enters the frame and proceeds, by foot, screen-left—in the face of the wind. This is Mocktar symbolically braving life's misfortunes. Neocolonialist exploitation of African resources and peasants contributes to African poverty. "The gold we risk our lives for," Mocktar himself notes later on, "is for white people." At the camp, Mocktar is attracted to Coumba, who has lost family members in a shaft collapse there, and whose young daughter Mocktar helps with his pay, redeeming himself from guilt over his own recent loss. At the last, in an extreme long-shot, he is shown journeying home.

Much of the film is given over to showing, in documentary fashion, the harsh, dangerous labor involved in different facets of the mining. (Mocktar, his first day, suffers a horrible accident.) We also see Mocktar's after-work interactions with an older miner who takes Mocktar under his wing; but when this gentleman replaces the bullying, uncaring boss, we see the start of his transformation into a facsimile of that boss—black against black at the behest of white interests: an appropriation of available limited power.

Cinematographed by Crystel Fournier, images are hauntingly dreamlike. Wind-swept dust is a recurrent motif.

FLANDERS (Belgium, France). I detest Pier Paolo Pasolini's last film, *Salò, or the 120 Days of Sodom* (1975), which assaults us with its grotesque cruelties however much it meant for this to reflect on the barbarism of Nazis and Nazism. Alas, I postponed seeing Bruno Dumont's *Flandres*, despite its winning the Grand Prix at Cannes, because American reviewers had described this war film as though it also catalogues horrors rather than apply the rigor, discipline and distancing of genuine art. These reviewers are wrong, however—why, I'm unsure. Some are probably fabricating; others may have experienced the film so powerfully that they are convinced they witnessed in it sights that in fact Dumont left to the imagination. One of the most horrific events—probably the *most* horrific—occurs offscreen, with a soldier's howls of torment evoking it.

Wintry, austere, somber, measured and brilliantly soul-battering, *Flandres* is principally about two young persons: André Demester, a Belgian farmer who, along with neighbors, receives his letter to report for military service at a time of war in Africa; Barbe, the girl left behind—*André's* girl (the pair have joyless farewell sex that one gleans is routine for them), but who has sex with another boy who also goes off to war. In Africa, atrocities are committed by both sides. Back home, Barbe has an abortion, a mental breakdown.

The film, which is set in the present, is extraordinary in two regards: showing how a bleak, hard existence helps make wartime experience a segue, not a rupture; showing an instance of stressful connection between war zone and homefront. The war she never sees magnifies the loose ends and guilt that dominate Barbe's life. In both places, audible heavy breaths and sighs poise life on the cusp of death.

Superbly cinematographed by Yves Cape.

MADEINUSA (Peru). In fictional Manataycuna, "the town that no one can enter," young geologist Salvador, from Lima, has hitched a ride in during "Holy Time," when the native Peruvian residents celebrate God's being temporarily blind and mute, releasing them from moral scrutiny. The three-day carnival mixes pagan and Christian rituals and icons, and intruder Salvador's Spanish ancestry hints an allegory of Peru's sixteenth-century conquest by Spain. Cayo, the town's mayor, puts the stranger to work before locking him up, a redress of history and a response to one daughter's attraction to Salvador, which threatens Cayo's control of his family. Cayo's attic is a storeroom of artifacts from Holy Times past.

This daughter is Madeinusa (pronounced Mad-ay-NOO-sa, but a play on "Made in U.S.A.," suggesting neocolonial exploitation). We are introduced to the teenager as she spreads rat poison around the house, along the way picking up a large dead rat and flinging it aside, her hands protected by plastic bags—makeshift gloves that suggest how resourceful some people have to be just to survive. Later, Cayo impresses Madeinusa into incest in the bed that she and sister Chale share. The girls' mother, the family legend goes, ran off to Lima years earlier. Madeinusa hopes to do the same, and Salvador may be the means; but Salvador is monstrously unfeeling regarding this sustaining dream. He is blasé about taking her; "Why not?" he says.

But Salvador's own leavetaking is thwarted—in a spontaneous ritual, he is scapegoated for Madeinusa's own crime—and Madeinusa takes his place as the hitcher.

Claudia Llosa raw, vulgar, visually dazzling film includes eye-opening closeups, of hands at work as well as faces. It shows people's lives under the thumb of history and of social and economic forces not of their making or choosing, and beyond their control.

IRAQ IN FRAGMENTS (U.S.). James Longley started shooting his impressionistic, dynamic documentary before the U.S. invasion. (The digital video has been transferred to film.) Unscripted, brilliantly edited (by Longley, Fiona Otway, Billy McMillin) from more than 300 hours of material, *Iraq in Fragments* shows Iraq from different perspectives, all Iraqi. The "fragments" refer to people's lives in disparate territories and to conflicts among different Iraqi peoples, Sunni, Shia, Kurds.

The first segment unfolds in Old Baghdad, from the perspective of Mohammed, an orphaned 11-year-old Sunni boy (in a mixed neighborhood) who is apprenticed to an auto mechanic. To this portrait of poverty and scant hope, Mohammed lends haunting voiceover, an untutored record of his bleak, fractured existence. An elderly man refers to the United States: "Why don't they just take [the oil] and leave us alone?"

The second, pulsating segment, set in Naserijah and the holy city of Najaf in southern Iraq, is more political. With fortuitously gained access, it records the rise of Moqtada al-Sadr, the fundamentalist Islamic cleric who rallies crowds and consolidates his own political power by exploiting Iraqi history, including the U.S. invasion and occupation.

This is a film about fathers and their disappearance. (One can add Saddam Hussein, the nation's deposed, now hanged father, to the list.) In Part I, Mohammed's anonymous father is missing; in Part II, Moqtada al-Sadr's murdered father contributes to his son's rise to power. In Part III, which is set in Iraq's Kurdish rural north near Arbil, an elderly farmer, approaching his own end, worries about Kuridsh freedom, his faith, his farming community, his legacy and the future of his teenaged boy. This, the most lyrical and traditional segment, then, is primarily communal and familial, and set among those Iraqis who are, as a group, glad for the U.S. invasion.

IT'S WINTER (Iran, France). Writer-director Rafi Pitts (New Voices/New Visions prize, Palm Springs) has turned Mahmoud Dowlatabadi's story "Safar" into an assured piece of visionary cinema—one that captures both a rhythm of life and the depth of despair and alienation in one segment of today's Iran, an economically stressed industrial suburb. Its joint protagonists, one who has left town to find desperately needed work and another who has come to the same town in a desperate attempt to find work, are each identified with the other on another score: Mokhtar has temporarily abandoned his younger wife, Khatoun, and their little girl for his offscreen pursuit of employment and wages; Marhab, a clumsy worker who nonetheless boasts he can "fix anything," is attracted to Khatoun. When Mokhtar leaves, it is bleak winter; when he returns, it is the next winter, he is missing a leg, and he cannot return home, still having no money, and Marhab now having "taken" Khatoun. Pride prevents Mokhtar's even seeing his daughter. One thing more must be noted: it is Khatoun, we learn, who insisted that they build their house rather than—Mokhtar's preference—invest their money. Mokhtar feels doubly left out in the cold.

Zemestan is a mournful, unsentimental portrait of an undone family. Nor can another family replace it, for Marhab's prospects scarcely exceed what Mokhtar's were. Youth bestows on Marhab little more than pluck and edgy expectations. One would not be going too far to glean from the believability of Pitts's film that Iran, as it is now constituted, is a doomed nation. Wedded to her sewing machine and her work ethic, only Khatoun, as well as her daughter, seems to have a future—in an Iran yet to be.

Mohammad Davudi's fine color cinematography took prizes at Valladolid and Fajr.

12:08 EAST OF BUCHAREST (Romania). Wryly written and directed by Corneliu Porumboiu, who was 14 when Nicolae Ceauşescu's regime, and along with it Communism, collapsed in Romania in 1989, *A fost sau n-a fost?* questions the weight of this event—recent past for some; ancient for others—on Romania's present. The setting is a small, sleepy town, Vaslui. Jderescu, the owner of a local television station, moderates a news-interview show; Manescu is an alcoholic, debt-ridden history teacher; Piscoci, a retiree and one-time Christmastime Santa Claus. Flanking him, the last two are Jderescu's TV guests on December 22, the anniversary of the "revolution." Behind the trio is a blown-up photograph of the Vaslui town square, where there either was or wasn't a protest against Ceauşescu on that fateful day sixteen years ago before the dictator helicoptered his way out of Bucharest. Everyone agrees that once Ceauşescu fled for his life townsfolk flooded the square.

Pompously assuring viewers that he is a journalist committed to discovering the truth, Jderescu relentlessly interrogates Manescu, who (convincingly) claims to have been one of four teachers to have participated in the protest prior to Ceauşescu's hasty departure from power. (Two of Manescu's compatriots are dead; the other now lives in Canada.) Call-in viewers assist Jderescu in his attack, claiming to have seen no such morning protest as Manescu describes and branding him a liar. But their accounts are riddled with inconsistencies, not to mention pro-Ceaușescu bias, that Jderescu declines to take on. When a Chinese-born caller defends Manescu, Jderescu proves himself a chauvinist. The final caller says that the moderator and guests should go outside and enjoy falling snow before the ground turns to mud.

Except for the flat program set, interiors seem dreary leftovers from the days of Soviet domination.

Exteriors are gorgeous.

LIGHTS IN THE DUSK (Finland, Germany, France). Concluding a trilogy begun with *Drifting Clouds* (1996) and *The Man Without a Past* (2002), but in this case characterized by only ontological humor, Aki Kaurismäki's quietly lovely, intense *Laitakaupungin valot* essays a nighttime security guard whose location sums up his existence: the nearby harbor, his loneliness and aspiration; the patch of businesses he guards, including a high-end jeweler's, his reality: a constant reminder that Helsinki has more or less left him behind. Koistinen's nemesis is a businessman who hates him for being a "loser" and targets him, in a complicated scheme of hoodwinking that involves a kept blonde femme fatale, to take the fall for the theft of the jewels that he engineers. This malicious individual is a cosmic force executing the unfairness of capitalism.

Koistinen is the only character to appear in full; the businessman and the blonde lack depth, are various shades of colorlessness. A sign of some universal concern is a black boy who adopts an abused, abandoned dog and sympathetically watches over Koistinen. His eyes tell us he knows the score despite his youth. A woman who operates a coffee stand represents a possible future of assuaged loneliness for our hero. The film ends in a closeup of their joined hands.

Kaurismäki's most Bressonian film, with a touch of Dreyer and Cocteau besides, conjoins Koistinen's immense loneliness with an accounting of silence punctuated by enhanced material sounds. Although he is kept from being a killer by his too-weak arm and knife, Koistinen reminded me of the young man at the center of Bresson's *L'argent* (1983).

A wonderful shot shows wind animating the ground, immediately followed, in prison, of our first glimpse of a sociable Koistinen.

What courage and nobility are often called upon to keep hope alive!

IN THE PIT (Mexico). The occasion for Juan Carlos Rulfo's *En el hoyo* is the construction, 2003-05, of the second deck of the Periférico Freeway in Mexico City. Largely comprising interviews of construction workers involved in the project, it is an ironical documentary.

Rulfo signals an almost mocking intent from the get-go, with the first bit of voiceover announcing a fairy tale or fable ("Once upon a time . . ."), a genre at odds with a chronicle of productive labor. The film leaves the expansion unfinished, ironically withholding from the material the salutary effect of the seemingly obligatory shot of its completion; a long aerial shot begins with the completed part but then passes into the disarray of unfinished construction—with its rapid roller-coaster effect (for us the audience), a shot of devastating wit. Along the way, one of the interviewed workers remarks that one can get used to anything, except work. Rulfo's film is full of surprises and reversals of expectation.

Numerous shots facing downwards, with a gaping depth of space below the men at work, reiterate the constant danger. "Aren't you afraid?" at one point Rulfo asks, and a worker responds, "I am more afraid of not eating on Saturday." Opening and nearly closing the film are headlong shots into the ground-level construction pit, into which, at the last, a worker has fallen, perhaps one of the project's "inevitable" fatalities, suggesting a linkage of "sacrifices" over time. The 330-second aerial shot of the finished and unfinished parts of the construction, because of the anonymous workers we see being rapidly passed by, reminds us that the project's completion will mean an end of some duration to these people's paid work. This returns us to the nature of that work. Few would choose such dangerous work if there were alternatives.

A SCANNER DARKLY (U.S.). Richard Linklater's unexpectedly heartrending *A Scanner Darkly*, from the futuristic novel by Philip K. Dick, challenges familiar social interpretations of habitual drug use and the status quo by presenting a holistic view in which users, entities that manufacture the substances and move them illicitly into society, and law enforcement (the "war on drugs") all work to reinforce one another in what can be described as an unwitting conspiracy. The protagonist is an undercover law enforcement officer—"Fred"—who has become part of a cell of druggies, one of whose members is the subject of official investigation. In reality, the ultimate target is the agricultural/manufacturing concern that has introduced "Substance D"—"Death"—onto U.S. streets. The operative is himself unaware of the farthest reaches of the plot, which includes, ultimately, his being sacrificed. The film exposes the nurturing of demand, bureaucracy's requirement to perpetuate itself, and the criminal scapegoating of "criminals."

As was part of Linklater's *Waking Life* (2001), this entire film is "rotoscoped." Richard Baimbridge has thus summarized the process: "animators trace over life-action [digital video] footage." Here, the divide between the rotoscoped representation of reality and a traditional one serves as a constant metaphor for the drug-induced division between users and "reality," including one another, and another sort of "division": official duplicity that manipulates people's lives, undercutting their capacity for self-determination. Rotoscoping, then, is an essential part of this film's thematic unity.

The principal source of the film's power and humanity is Keanu Reeves's performance as "Fred," whose undercover identity is Bob Arctor. His brain discombobulated, Fred/Bob has come to accept as reality the "past" he may have been given only to mask his identity: the wife and two daughters he is supposed to have abandoned. Perpetually lost to himself, Fred/Bob eventually freefalls into nothingness.

2007

ALEKSANDRA (Russia, France). Aleksandra, an elderly Russian woman (Galina Vishnevskaya, magnificent), rarely admits to frailty or weakness. When she is asked if she is tired, right before nodding off she emphatically states, "No."

Widowed, estranged from her daughter, who finds her domineering, Aleksandra takes an arduous trip to an army camp in Chechnya, where her grandson, Denis, is an officer. Feeling close to death, she wishes to see the boy again. However young is he, and younger still those who are under his command, Aleksandra may outlive them. Indeed, ethereal lighting and other elements suggest the possibility that we are witnessing either Aleksandra's or Denis's dream—and, if the latter, possibly the dream of a dead man.

Writer-director Aleksandr Sokurov's wondrous *Aleksandra* treads a fine line where fiction seems to translate into documentary. Aleksandra keeps losing her way around the camp—a projection of how lost the young draftees feel away from home. (Many seem to have adopted Aleksandra as their grandmother because she represents a bit of home.) She wanders about, in effect interviewing the boys (Aleksandra = Aleksandr?), who share their feelings and reveal raw youth. One shows off by playing with his gun as if it were a toy. He may be wishing it were.

Aleksandra exits to bring back cigarettes and cookies for the boys. At market, she befriends an elderly Chechen who invites her home for tea. Malika enlists a teenaged neighbor to walk Aleksandra back to camp. The boy, though respectful, asks: "I know it isn't up to you, but can't you leave us so we can be free?"

Tenderly, Denis braids Aleksandra's hair—and deftly, as though benefiting from prior experience. One is reminded of Sokurov's *Mother and Son* (1997). In both films the son or grandson carries the older woman effortlessly.

THE MAN FROM LONDON (Hungary, France, Germany). "[W]e don't translate literature into film; rather, we translate literature back into life." — Béla Tarr, discussing his film from Georges Simenon's *L'homme de Londres*
A londoni férfi, in French and English, involves a wee-hours fight between two men on a dock that ends in a drowning death—and the loss of the case in which stolen money is stacked. Long-shots correspond to switchman Maloin's view from his office in the railway station tower. Maloin retrieves the case from the water; the dreamily indefinite scene of docked ferry, dock, tracks and train in darkness yields to the specificity of the British notes, each of which Maloin dries once he is back inside.

Brilliantly directed by Hungary's Béla Tarr, with editor and life-partner Ágnes Hranitzky credited as co-director, the black-and-white film opens with one of Tarr's amazing shots; the camera very slowly scales the ferry, beginning at the hull, through the window that provides Maloin with his godlike view; intermittently, strips of black—lattice—interrupt this view. The camera's ascent ironically correlates to a descent into the waters of Maloin's corruptible soul.

Maloin, beautifully acted by Miroslav Krobot, is a complex, sympathetic figure—a proud man long shoehorned into an unhappy, humiliating life; he now grapples with his guilt. Atypically, inexplicably, he starts to rage against wife and daughter.

Initially, the camera perspective forges an identification between us and Maloin; as we watch his return with the case, from the vantage of his office, however, we separate from him. Those calling the film a *noir* mistake style for genre; *noirs* explore an amoral or immoral world, but the one here is hardly that. Past the point of identifying with Maloin, we bring moral consideration to his world—Maloin's own latent morality, which eventually surfaces.

FADOS (Portugal, Spain). Since the nineteenth century, the wistful, melancholy *fados* of Portugal have been a tradition of music—sung, danced, performed by instrumental groups—that bespeaks the sense of separation of those who moved to Lisbon from rural Portugal and from Portuguese colonies in Africa and from Brazil, which Portugal likewise colonized. Separation: separation of present from past, of place to place, "the memory of those departed like the wind." One sings of "my old Lisbon of another era." Another: "The wind blows too hard for me to rest."

One of the three or four most brilliant musical films ever, Spain's Carlos Saura's *Fados*, filmed on a Madrid soundstage, records the ache of separation that is the fado's soul, but also combines past and present to ease the ache, as when contemporary dancers make their moves in front of a huge screen on which is projected a *fadista* from the past in performance. The film's opening movement, as the credits appear, suggests the heart of Saura's method: A black screen moves steadily screen-left, revealing a huge screen on which is projected images of Lisbonians in the street walking towards an invisible camera, separated from dancers dancing in front of the screen in haunting silhouette, in effect, ghosts separated from their own substance. Throughout, Saura orchestrates performers in the flesh (sometimes, their faces move in and out of shadows), silhouettes, mirror images, multiple exposures and back projection to indicate layers of separation. Love is uncertain in some *fados*; in one, the singer pleads against the possibility of romantic rejection, while in another another singer has already been rejected: all this, another elusive embodiment of separation.

The ultimate *fado* that Saura shows performed is the most stirring, aching lament imaginable. It is the soul in full in its divided state.

LONG LIVE THE WHALE! (France). In the 2007 English-language update of Mario Ruspoli and Chris Marker's 1972 *Vive la baleine*, voiceovers compete: the masculine "master," disseminating facts about whales and whaling, and the feminine "interior voice," expressing feelings ("Whales, I love you"), questions, surmises, wonder. Marker, who wrote and edited this masterpiece, synopsizes the history of whaling against a backdrop of engravings, paintings, photographs. A film snippet glimpses the modern practice of whaling; but, towards the end, such film graphically overtakes the visual content, much as the "interior voice" has overtaken the "master voice."

Marker discredits the Japanese with turning the whale into industry, but—keep in mind this film was made during its Southeast Asian war—he reserves equal contempt for the United States: ". . . at the end of the nineteenth century the birth of the biggest modern empire was accompanied by the birth of a powerful whaling fleet. The Americans helped themselves to all the resources needed for beginning their industry, and you[, whales,] were no exception. Your oil would make machines run and lights burn softly. . . ." The havoc that America is willing to wreak in its quest for oil (and other resources) has found, since, other targets.

Marker: "Americans reduced you[, whales,] to a commodity on the Stock Exchange." But it is a Norwegian who invented the "exploding" harpoon-gun that moved whaling from a small-scale practice to "industrial extermination" conducted "aboard factory ships." Yet this vicious weapon becomes American-by-association when Marker likens it to an "atomic bomb." Marker: "Every whale that dies hands down to us, like a prophecy, the image of our own death."

The zip of the harpoon-gun; the unearthly moans of the struck whale; the blood: not since Georges Franju's *Blood of the Beasts* (1949) has there been a documentary like this.

OVER HERE (U.S.). For a decade now Jon Jost has been working in digital video. *Over Here* is "a kind of companion-piece," according to Jost, to his wonderful *Homecoming* (2004); both revolve around W's war in Iraq, from the vantage of the homefront. In *Homecoming*, a soldier has been sent home for burial following his absurd drowning death; the returning veteran is alive in *Over Here*, but shattered, possibly beyond repair. Jason (Ryan Harper Gray, deeply affecting) ends up homeless, living with a companion under a bridge. His silent tenderness toward her—he caresses her head, gently awakening her to a new day—suggests the waste of his humanity that a mendacious, oil-mad administration has wrought.

The pre-credit opening: a long-held tight closeup of Jason—a degenerative image, a blowup appearing as a dark sea of dots; its aural accompaniment, electronic discordance, science-fiction chords. The image is mute. Jason speaks; but his ordeal "over there," which has rearranged his psyche, dissolving his connections to reality, he finds himself at a loss to communicate. He covers his face with his hands. Jason has brought "over there" back home with him. It has taken over him.

In a deeply moving passage, Jason visits his parents. With darkness at the top and bottom of the screen, the face of each of the three characters occupies his or her own square in a row across the screen. Mother and Father flank Jason. There is much silence and pain as Jason dissolves into sadness; what talk is there is inaudible. It is impossible for Jason to unburden himself. Everyone is helpless. Jost manipulates the screens-within-the-screen, changing their appearance and relationships, to suggest the interiority of the three characters. Despite parental pleas, Jason must leave. He is as lost to America as America is to him.

ASSEMBLY (China). Written by Liu Heng, Feng Xiaogang's *Ji jie hao* opens with a shot of a bugle in official repose. Its silence here couldn't be more apt. During the Chinese Civil War, Captain Gu Zidi (Zhang Hanyu, tremendous), leading Ninth Company, 139th Regiment, 3rd Battalion of the Liberation Army, is charged with defending a mine against the enemy, the Nationalist Kuomintang, until the blow of the bugle instructs retreat to assembly.

Gu persists in the suicide mission although others in the company believe that the bugle sounded; Gu, it turns out, is the sole survivor. Yet instead of his soldiers being regarded as heroes, they are officially declared "missing in action." After the war, and the Korean War as well in which he enlists, Gu assumes a peacetime mission: to locate the bodies of his fallen brethren and have the 46 soldiers declared heroes. It is an insult to this brilliant film to compare it to Steven Spielberg's silly, sentimental *Saving Private Ryan* (1998), except that its first part is unusually gripping in its grim, bloody portrait of combat. Rather, Feng's film reminds me much more of the great Polish film *Eroica* (1957). Like that film, which was written by Jerzy Stefan Stawiński and directed by Andrzej Munk, Feng's *Ji jie hao* pricks the whole notion of war heroism, and it does so on two fronts: in order for the Forty-Six to be heroic, it becomes necessary for Gu to have them officially declared so—an indication that heroism isn't bound up in actions or behavior but in official acknowledgment and political advertising; moreover, the driving force behind Gu's allegiance to this cause of his is not what the Forty-Six did, or how they behaved, but rather his own enormous guilt over their deaths.

THE SECRET OF THE GRAIN (France). Dedicated to his deceased father, memory of whom presumably informs his ageing, taciturn protagonist, Slimane Beiji, Tunisian-born writer-director Abdellatif Kechiche's *La graine et le mulet* revolves around family and extended family in France's Mediterranean coastal Sète, where Slimane is discharged after 35 years as a shipyard laborer. Juggling a proud ex-wife, Souad, and a current partner, hotel-owner Latifa, he hopes to open a fish couscous restaurant with Souad as cook. But family difficulties match his other difficulties: financial; municipal reluctance to grant approval. (One official interviewing Slimane repeats over and over that his place would have to pass a health inspection as if she cannot conceive of his attachment to cleanliness, although there he is right in front of her, immaculately clean, neat, well-groomed.) Slimane decides to invite every official whose approval he must secure to a free dinner at his prospective restaurant, hoping for the best; but it appears that his womanizing married son has accidentally taken off with the huge container of cooked couscous. Is there even time for Souad to cook another batch of her celebrated recipe?

Making assured use of handheld camera, this glorious tragicomedy has two great set-pieces, a Sunday meal and the restaurant's climactic trial-run, where officials are fidgeting and hungry as the couscous keeps not coming and the wine being served expands their frustrated appetites. Latifa's 19-year-old daughter, Rym, who adores her stepfather, comes to what she hopes will be the rescue by giving everyone something else to attend to: a sustained, accomplished belly dance. It is spectacular, although Rym's intense sweat underscores the irony of her tailoring her effort to stereotypical expectations.

Best film: Prix Louis Delluc; French critics; Étoiles d'Or; César. Prizes for Kechiche's writing, direction. International Critics' prizes: Venice; European Film Awards.

SILENT LIGHT (Mexico, France, Netherlands, Germany). In Plautdietsch, not Spanish, because it deals with Mennonites, *Stellet licht* is as mysterious as either cosmos or humanity. Its title refers to dawn, but also to cinema, and writer-director Carlos Reygadas draws upon Dreyer, Bergman (note the clock), Tarkovsky (note the wet), others. Recalling Sokurov's *Spiritual Voices* (1996), the opening shot is a long time-lapsed observance of dawn's light replacing darkness at a farm outside Chihuahua. (Animal noises, both savage and domestic, abound.) Thus Reygadas introduces a central theme: transformations that seem like ruptures actually occur gradually, cumulatively. The film ends with a garish sunset passing into darkness.

Esther (Miriam Toews, gut-wrenching) and Johan are a Mennonite couple with six children. Much of the film details the family at farm work and play. Johan is having an affair with Marianne; he has confided his infidelity to Esther but (with her knowledge) continues it. Marianne, torn between flesh and decency, ends the affair, telling Johan, "Peace is stronger than love"; but, believing Marianne is his soul-mate, Johan presses her back into the affair. How does all this affect Esther? She is mostly a "silent light"; her forbearance seems admirable, resolute. However, she confesses being shattered by the betrayal: "I have lost my place in the world." Eventually a massive heart attack kills her and Johan finds his guilt and sorrow compounded. Marianne comes to the funeral service and kisses the corpse on the lips. Esther's eyes open; Esther says, "Poor Johan." *Love* is stronger than *peace*.

Throughout, the camera enters or nearly enters dark spaces, such as the shed where we not-quite-see Marianne's bare ass as Marianne and Johan have stand-up sex. At the funeral, through a window the figures indoors around Esther's laid-out body, including Johan, are diaphanous reflections—*ghosts*.

PROFIT MOTIVE AND THE WHISPERING WIND (U.S.). Inspired by Howard Zinn's book *A People's History of the United States*, John Gianvito's meditative *Profit Motive and the Whispering Wind* catches the continuing breeze of American political enlightenment as it animates trees, grasses, wildflowers and people's souls. The seeming serenity of this documentary is a kind of stillness enjoining a long line of tragic failures, perhaps leading up ahead to where we want to take America, and the persistent hopefulness that drives us on. Considering the bleeding nature of the material that it engages, this film merits high praise for avoiding so much as one sentimental moment or gesture. It took the Human Rights Award at Buenos Aires and the prize as best experimental film from the National Society of Film Critics.

The film is quiet, absent rhetoric, or any talking heads or voiceover narration. Rather, it observes Nature's green in wind as breathing metaphor, along with tombstones, historic statues and plaques marking people who have benefited us: Revolutionary pamphleteer Thomas Paine, Seneca chief "Red Jacket," Sa-co-ye-wat-ha ("My heart fails me when I think of my people, so soon to be scattered and forgotten"), Uriah Smith Stephens, who co-founded and led the first national U.S. labor union, abolitionist and women's rights advocate Sojourner Truth, antiwar activist Philip Francis Berrigan—*and all the others*.

And events as well as people: the Haymarket, Morewood and Matewan massacres, and the Battle of Homestead between striking workers and the Carnegie Steel Company. Sa-co-ye-wat-ha again: "When I am gone, and my warnings are no longer heeded, the craft and avarice of the white man will prevail." A montage toward the close of the film consists of news clips of recent citizen protests and demonstrations.

High schools and colleges could base classes on this wonderful film.

DON'T TOUCH THE AXE (France, Italy). "The Duchess of Langeais is my mistress!" Armand, the Marquis of Montriveau, is being premature when he announces this in solitude to whatever is keeping score. Indeed, he will never have Antoinette, who is married, and whose future cloistered marriage will be with Jesus Christ. Beginning in 1823, Armand is obsessed; for him, the consummation of the affair might provide an antidote to his battlefield experience. He is a national hero; he needs to be at peace and feel he is a man.

Drawn from Honoré de Balzac's 1834 novella *La duchesse de Langeais*, Jacques Rivette's *Ne touchez pas la hache* is careful, deliberate, poised, elegant; form expresses content as the film itself constantly seems anticipatory of consummation. Rivette, at 80, knows what he is doing. Every bit of his remarkably patient and cumulative film exudes the redress for war, for national service, that Armand psychically and emotionally requires—all that he will not get. This film will be (except historically) irrelevant when war is obsolete.

Its signature, unmistakable, surprises. Throughout, we do not think "Rivette"; we think "Rohmer," Rivette's long-ago fellow cinéaste. It is their friendship that brought Rivette to Bazin's *Cahiers du cinéma*, the legendary (and still existant) film journal. What makes Rivette's film so personal is its sense of his never having adequately discharged the debt he feels he owes to Rohmer. Rivette, one might say, has never consummated the expression of gratitude he feels. That is what this film is meant to do.

Both Rohmer and Rivette were part of the *nouvelle vague*, cinema's most important movement. With his Roman Catholic determinism, Rohmer never seemed a perfect fit. Is *Ne touchez pas la hache* Rivette's apology for *La religieuse* (1966)—not to God, not to the Church, but to Eric Rohmer?

THE BAND'S VISIT (Israel, France, U.S.). Droll, humane, sensitively composed, exquisitely paced, *Bikur Ha-Tizmoret* is Israeli writer-director Eran Kolirin's first feature. This beautiful comedy swept the Israeli Film Academy Awards, winning in eight categories including best film, director, screenplay, actor (Sasson Gabai) and actress (Ronit Elkabetz). It also won three prizes at Cannes for young Kolirin.

The eight-member Alexandria Ceremonial Police Orchestra has arrived in Israel for the opening of an Arab arts center in Petah Tiqva the next night. Lost, they've ended up instead in the sleepy town of Beit Hatikva—and they've missed the last bus out. Moreover, there is no hotel. Dina, who runs a small restaurant, takes in a couple of the Egyptian musicians and arranges lodging for the rest. During their one night together, the Arabs and Jews become part of one another's lives. Indeed, for all of Dina's wry, crackling, sophisticated personality and the wit generated by the cuts from one shot to the next, this is a soulful film from start to finish. Across the Arab-Israeli divide, characters respond to the kindness and loneliness of strangers.

Solemn orchestra leader Tawfiq Zacharaya discloses to Dina a tragic stretch of personal history for which he blames himself; after their son, who "was fragile, like his mother," committed suicide, Tawfig's wife either also committed suicide or, grief-stricken, became fatally ill. Tawfig can tell Dina all this, opening and unburdening at least a portion of his heart, precisely because they will part the next day and never see each other again. Deft, light, unsentimental, Kolirin lets his comedy remain a comedy, but one admitting fine touches of rue and barely concealed unhappiness.

Because half the dialogue is in English, a language that all the characters share, Kolirin's film was barred from Oscar consideration in the foreign-language category.

2008

24 CITY (China). Once the industrial centerpiece in Chengdu, a munitions plant is being dismantled to make room for a hotel as well as residential and commercial space. Jia Zhang-Ke interviewed more than a hundred workers, some of whom appear as themselves while the experiences of others are combined for roles played by actors. The result is a blend of documentary and quasi-documentary, a national epic about China's journey from a planned economy, with all the dislocations and sacrifices that letting in private enterprise has inflicted, and a vision of aging, mortality. *Er shi si cheng ji*, Jia's most ambitious work, includes text from Chinese and other poems (including two by Yeats) as well as songs (including "The Internationale," sung by zombies of the past). It is at once caustic about factories and celebratory about those who worked in them. The final interview is of a young woman who recounts entering the plant for the first time to see her mother and having to search soul by soul because all the workers were dressed in the same blue uniform. For the first time she saw the backbreaking work her mother did to put food on the table. Now she wants to make a lot of money—this is all she thinks about—to give her parents a comfortable home.

Scenes of factory labor yield to the hauntingly abandoned, then demolished, structure.

Joan Chen plays someone who (she has been told) resembles Joan Chen. Indoors, she faces her offscreen interviewer, presumably Jia, with an angled mirror behind her having her reflection face an open door to the outside. Within the same frame she speaks both of the past and to it—truly inspired *mise-en-scène*.

The final high wide-angle shot of the overdeveloped gray city—a graveyard—is embittered, powerful.

THE VANISHED EMPIRE (Russia). Written by Sergei Rokotov and Evgeny Nikishov, and brilliantly directed by Karen Shakhnazarov, *Ischeznuvshaya imperiya* may be a masterpiece. In mid-1970s Moscow, 18-year-old Sergei has begun university. He is immersed in a social life that involves vodka-fueled comradery, the purchase of Western rock albums on a floating black market, and his romancing Lyuda Beletskaya, the volatility of their relationship largely the result of competing claims on his attention and his irresponsibility. When she becomes sick, his mother makes Sergei promise not to abandon his younger brother and elderly grandfather. At hospital, as Sergei leaves down a forlornly lit corridor, his mother calls out to him, but when he turns around she catches herself. "Later," she says; but there *is* no later. Shakhnazarov creates a haunting vision where all loose ends turn out to be dead ends.

Pressing lightly, the director of *The Rider Named Death* (*Vsadnik po imeni Smert*, 2004) creates a vision where such "ends" prefigure the disappearance of the Soviet Union. The last meeting we see between Sergei and Lyuda—pregnant, she is poised to marry the baby's father—plays out outside her apartment building, with a parked car, completely covered in cloth, in the background: a stunning metaphor for private and national worlds going nowhere, without a future. His grandfather has told Sergei about the "Ozymandias"-type ruin that now exists where the ancient Khorezm civilization had once held sway. In a final, hauntingly Antonionian movement, Sergei even visits this "City of the Winds" into which so much is passing.

An offhanded 30-year-later coda finds Sergei, whom we only hear as a voice, and his long-ago romantic rival meeting by chance in an airport waiting room. Sergei translates Farsi for a living, and the other man's marriage to Lyuda lasted a year.

THE WAY WE ARE (Hong Kong). Hong Kong writer-director Ann Hui's *Tin shui wai dik yat yu ye*—literally, *Days and Nights of Tin Shui Wai*, but called in the U.S. *The Way We Are* —opens with a series of archæological black-and-white images. The first two photographs are of a butterfly, Nature's flitting soul of evanescence. But here the butterfly is without motion, and the circumstance is incongruous, unsettling. Another snapshot, of a marsh or swamp, dissolves into a color shot of a field. A train introduces motion. The camera crosses the field to enter an apartment: part of the urban present that has replaced the past. On this summer morning, a woman leaves the apartment. We see a closeup of a sleeping teenager: an exquisitely pretty girl, an earring sparkling in her visible ear. This is On. She is not the woman's daughter; he, it turns out, is the woman's son. The woman, Kwai, is a widow (Paw Hee Ching, magnificent); On refers to himself by his full name, Cheung Ka On, as a way of holding onto his father's memory.

On, loving and amiably helpful to family, is in a holding pattern. He has just graduated high school and is awaiting his final exam grade, which will determine whether he proceeds to higher education or a job. Meanwhile, Kwai works in the produce department of a supermarket. She supports herself and On and has helped pay for the education abroad of her brothers. She also does what she can to alleviate the hardship and poverty of an older co-worker, "Granny."

With documentary detail, Hui's film seems to observe human lives and make emotional disclosures patiently, gradually. Hui's characters in the City of Sadness are kind, decent, caring.

Best film, director and actress from the Hong Kong critics.

35 SHOTS OF RUM (France, Germany). "Don't feel I need looking after," Lionel tells daughter Joséphine, but he does need this and might never be prepared to set her free, although he knows he must accept that Jo will set herself free, and soon. Since the death of his wife, Jo's German mother, Lionel and Jo have developed a life together of unusually tender intimacy betwixt father-and-daughter and their being some sort of couple. (We see Lionel's jealousy when Jo dances at a café with someone else.) Lionel is a train conductor;

the film's overture consists of many passing trains: transience; things "moving on."

35 rhums, one of her greatest works, is Claire Denis's *hommage* to Yasujiro Ozu, especially *Late Spring* (1949), where a father presses for his daughter's leaving him for marriage when all she wants to do is stay on the same track in life and take care of him. Sometimes, the gentle pace and rhythms of Denis's elliptical film suggest not only Ozu but Hou Hsiao-hsien's *hommage* to Ozu, *Café Lumière* (2003). But train's-eye views-in-motion insinuate also Jean Renoir's *La bête humaine* (1938), from Zola. There is no murder in Denis's film—unless we count the suicide of René, Lionel's co-worker who cannot cope with forced retirement and has Lionel unknowingly run him over and find his body, perhaps as a reproach.

"Moving on": Lionel is a black African immigrant; France itself has had to leave its African colonies; neighbor Gabrielle and Lionel no longer are romantically involved. Noé (Grégoire Colin, brilliant), another neighbor in their low-district apartment building in the outskirts of Paris, desires Jo. (All four: "a family," Gabrielle at one point says.) Since the deaths of his parents, Noé has been a shattered soul; when his cat dies, he *still* can't move on.

LORNA'S SILENCE (Belgium, France). *Le silence de Lorna* is the best thing that Belgium's writing-directing Dardenne brothers, Luc and Jean-Pierre, have done (best screenplay, Cannes). Like other Dardenne films, it is about immigrants in Belgium. Lorna and lover Sokol are Albanians who hope to start up a snack bar. Fabio, an Italian taxi cab driver, connives to get Lorna permanent residential status by convincing Claudy, a drug addict, to marry her so that, once Claudy is eliminated (either by overdose or whatever other necessary means), Lorna can marry Andrei, a stinking rich Russian smuggler who wants a European Union passport. Andrei will generously pay everyone. But a hitch comes into play: Claudy's intense effort to clean up his act touches Lorna's heart. She will pay dearly for her silence in not letting Claudy know about the current plan for him to be killed.

Actually, the "silence" of the title refers to several things; but the vision that the Dardennes fashion—and, unlike their other films, this one *is* visionary—is as much about talk as about silence: the schemes and dreams of immigrants in an undone, upside-down, shaken-loose Europe. A culminating metaphor for current European uncertainty is that Lorna may be pregnant by Claudy, who has "left the scene": one doctor says she is pregnant, but another says she is not. Believing herself to be, ironically, steels Lorna's determination to keep herself and the fetus alive when Fabio's henchman, she believes, is trying to kill her for screwing up Fabio's elaborate plot. She ends up alone in a dark fairy-tale forest cabin—alone, talking to Claudy's possibly nonexistent son or daughter, whom she will not betray as she did the father.

Arta Dobroshi beautifully plays Lorna, whose moral sense belatedly kicks into high gear; Jérémie Renier is brilliant as Claudy.

GOMORRA (Italy). The Camorra is an actual criminal mob whose base of operations is Naples, Italy. Matteo Garrone's sober, unblinking, coolly observant *Gomorra* is pulsatingly contemporary, riveting, unsentimental and, cumulatively, massively moving. It is based on the 2006 book by 26-year-old journalist Roberto Saviano; since its publication Saviano has needed constant police protection. We learn at film's end that the Camorra, a money-making colossus, has invested in the rebuilding of New York's World Trade Center.

The film juggles five plot-lines, two of which remain unresolved, the others testifying to gangland's decisive spirit of retribution. In the latter group is a haunting, powerful plot-line revolving around 13-year-old Totò, a grocery store delivery boy whose acceptance into the Camorra leads to disaster: first, one-time playmate Simone's becoming his "enemy" after Simone joins a rival gang; secondly, after a street killing, his reluctant set-up for Maria, his customer and Simone's mother, for a response-kill. Yet even here there's a loose end: Totò's immediate group has acted thusly without official instruction.

The Camorra "manages" industrial toxic waste by illegally dumping it. Franco, the gang's agent, bullies educated Roberto, his increasingly distressed young apprentice. When some of the waste spills on one of the transportation crew, Franco refuses to call an ambulance and the men in turn refuse to work. Franco exits the scene, leaving Roberto in charge; when he returns, he brings with him the new crew: children. Roberto's conscience churns.

Whereas Totò turns in to the gang drugs and gun dropped by dealers in a police pursuit, two reckless older teenagers horde a stash of arms and are dealt a death sentence.

Garrone's camera moves deliberately, often very briefly. No violence titillates here; it is all dreadful.

Grand Prix, Cannes; best film, director, script, European Film Awards, David di Donatello Awards.

TULPAN (Kazakhstan, Russia). All films exist on a continuum whose opposite poles are documentary and fiction, and former documentarian Sergei Dvortsevoy's *Tulpan* is closer to the documentary pole than any other fictional film I can think of. It is set in the windy, sandy, frigid steppes of Kazakhstan; Dvortsevoy himself was born in Kazakhstan. In Kazakh and Russian, this brilliant tragicomedy is like no other movie I've seen (best film, Tokyo, Montréal, International Film Festival of India).

After a stint in the Russian navy, Asa wants to realize his dream: a flock of sheep to tend, his own yurt (with solar panels, for electricity!), and a wife to share it with. Because she is the only unmarried girl around, Asa convinces himself he is in love with Tulpan (Dvortsevoy implies this mental process by keeping Tulpan always from our view, thus making her the void that Asa accordingly fills); but she turns him down, ostensibly because his ears are too big. (They aren't, but like Clark Gable's they protrude.) In reality, Tulpan has no desire to stick around; she has her sights on an urban college education.

Young Asa finds himself in a rut: without a wife, he will be given no flock. Asa's resultant stasis, along with the absence of almost any narrative advancement, is formally embodied in Asa's continual return to Tulpan, to plead his marital case, no matter how often she rejects him. Eventually Asa earns his flock, by delivering a living lamb amidst a rash of stillborns. One last time, now, he petitions the girl of his dreams. But she is in pursuit of her own dream.

The final image, of the flock materializing from the kicked-up dust, haunts, moves and astounds. Jolanta Dylewska's contribution here (best cinematography, Asian Film Awards), as elsewhere, is essential.

ONE DAY YOU'LL UNDERSTAND (France, Israel). From Jérôme Clément's 2005 autobiographical novel, *Plus tard, tu comprendras*, Israeli filmmaker Amos Gitaï has made a delicate, sensitive, dearly ironical work: *Plus tard*—literally, poignantly, *Later*. In 1987 Paris, elderly Rivka (Jeanne Moreau, astounding—Garbo's equal now) hides things, among them, from son Victor, the fate of her parents.

Hushed, dimly lit, *Plus tard* is an interior piece—a film lost in mental corridors, including for a nation. Victor's children, like Victor, has been raised Catholic; but on Yom Kippur, Rivka takes her grandchildren to synagogue, mentions her Russian Jewish mother, hands her grandson the cloth Star of David she had once been forced to wear, and draws a promise for undimmed memory.

Two great passages after this climax involve a monetary reckoning. At a pre-gravesite gathering in Rivka's apartment, an antiques dealer appraises—aloud—each nick-knack, piece of furniture and art treasure: the deceased Rivka's bald worth. Flashforward: in 1995, Chirac became the first French president to acknowledge national responsibility for the wartime deportation of French Jews to death camps; thus in 1999, the process of fixing "symbolic" restitution is underway. Two bureaucratic women lead Victor down an exceedingly long hallway in the bowels of some official building in order to interview him in a small, seemingly secret room, passing the experience of his maternal grandparents through a series of dispositive criteria to determine the appropriate sum the surviving family members are due. Overwhelmed, Victor flees, the camera following him back down the hallway to a window revealing, outside, a patch of the real, familiar, digestible: the Eiffel Tower. In a stunning reverse motion, the camera then withdraws down the now vacant hallway in an expression of the pull of the past and the burden of French shame that has accrued to it.

THE SONG OF SPARROWS (Iran). *Avaze Gonjeshk-ha* is, by far, Majid Majidi's finest achievement to date (best director, Fajr). The protagonist is Karim (Mohammad Amir Naji, best actor, Berlin, Asia-Pacific), who loses his job after one of the birds gets loose at the ostrich ranch where he works because he left the corral to retrieve daughter Haniyeh's hearing aid, which had fallen down an unused, muck-filled well. The hearing aid now no longer works. The film thus begins with a quadruple loss, and indeed life as a series of losses is a principal theme here. Encasing these losses is Karim's loss of his quiet rural existence; he finds a job when a stranger hops onto his moped—Karim is in Tehran to replace Haniyeh's hearing aid, which it turns out he cannot afford to do—after someone mistakes him for a motorcycle taxi driver.

Karim has embarked on a humbling odyssey that takes him from what in retrospect seems Paradise to a more complex place; for example, especially after he breaks a leg, he must cope with the shame of having his young children work to support him and their mother. His existence moves from being experiential to being, also, contemplative, and with very brief forward movements of the camera, whether towards Karim or an outdoor storage space, Majidi evokes the spiritual dimension of Karim's odyssey.

Patches of blue, the color of spirit here, crop up, such as when Karim carries by hand a blue-painted door that he has promised someone; a shot of him underneath it emphasizes life's burdens, while an overhead long-shot dissolves the burdensomeness, suggesting Karim's capacity to transport a bit of sky. Another overhead shot appears to be the star-dappled nighttime sky; the camera pulls up, revealing women's hands at work on sequined fabric.

SERAPHINE (France). "When she wasn't mopping the floor, she was painting."

A great film about the creative impulse and forces either supporting or arrayed against it, Martin Provost's *Séraphine* is about Séraphine Louis, the modern primitive painter later known as Séraphine de Senlis, after the town, outside Paris, where she worked as a domestic. Nearing fifty, Séraphine is a quiet, intense woman who goes off by herself and sings aloud; a wonderful shot showing her sitting in a tree, her hefty legs dangling, suggests her holistic intimacy with Nature. In 1914, gay German art collector and dealer Wilhelm Uhde discovers Séraphine's promising artwork and encourages its development. After the First World War, Uhde rediscovers Séraphine and, finding that her gorgeous painting has immeasurably progressed, becomes her patron. The misconception that her fame and fortune were now assured implodes when the worldwide depression slashes Uhde's resources, compelling him to withdraw support and sending Séraphine, once an object of ridicule, into a downward spiral of mental illness that leads to her institutionalization at Clermont Asylum, where her obsession with her artwork departs. "Painting," she now says, "has gone in the night."

The film's exquisite Old Masters lighting—the César-winning color cinematography is by Laurent Brunet—is ironic; it may seem out of sync with Séraphine's own time and her richly colored paintings of (somehow) fluid fruits and flowers, but it becomes correlative to the darkness that increasingly overtakes her faculties and art, bringing to fruition the "dark" and dangerous element in her work that she confesses early on terrifies even her.

Yolande Moreau won her second best actress César Award for her superlative work as Séraphine; in all, *Séraphine* won seven Césars, including best film. Moreau, best actress: Lumiere Award, Étoiles d'Or, National Society of Film Critics, Los Angeles critics.

2009

(as of this date, I have seen very few 2009 films.)

THE WIND JOURNEYS (Colombia, Germany, Netherlands, Argentina). Competing claims, on a former itinerant accordian player, of past and future: in *Los viajes del viento* Colombian writer-director Ciro Guerra stakes out an epic theme, for Ignacio Carrillo's predicament reflects that of fellow Colombians and the country they share. This tremendous film assumes the form of a quest—with early forward movements of the camera, wispy and delicate, suggesting the interior journey that is suited to the exterior one: a soul's progress.

Ignacio's wife, for whom he had given up his nomadic existence, has died. On Ash Wednesday he embarks on an odyssey to return his accordian, which is rumored cursed, to the master (named, interestingly, Guerra) who taught him to play. It is easier to recognize others' superstitiousness than one's own. Ignacio thus refers to "ignorant" people who "believe that if today they kill a certain bird they will become drummers overnight." In Ignacio's case, selfconsciousness must give way to self-knowledge.

The long journey by burro takes Ignacio northward from one place to another. Guerra's film is in native languages—Ikun, Palenquero, Wayuunaiki—as well as Spanish and encompasses sun-baked earth and snowy mountains.

Ignacio, solitudinous, is nonetheless accompanied by Fermín Morales, a teenaged drummer who idolizes Ignacio and wishes to learn from him. (Fermín's complexion suggests both Indian and Spanish parentage.) When Ignacio's accordian is stolen, Fermín risks death to retrieve it.

Death indeed hovers throughout the film; hauntingly, Guerra sometimes images people as light shadows. Ignacio is impressed into accompanying with his music a knife-fight between two men on a bridge; Guerra films the event largely as upside-down reflections in the water below.

A Shakespearean conclusion provides Ignacio with a new, unexpected future, and in long-shot Fermín pursues his own destiny.

Best film, best direction, Bogota; best film, Cartagena

PROTECTOR (Czech Republic, Germany). Marriage is a complicated thing; add to it the tumult of history and you have material so potentially rich as to cry out for the kind of rigor, formal beauty, and close, penetrating attention it receives in *Protektor*. Beautifully written by Robert Geisler, Benjamin Tuček and Marek Najbrt, and directed for the ages by Najbrt, it is a devastating film, at least as wonderful as the Hungarian *Bizalom* (*Confidence*, 1980), by István Szabó, on the subject of foreign occupation, whose dreadful atmosphere it, too, evokes brilliantly. Najbrt's film is essential.

The title is cunningly ironic. The film opens on a Prague street in 1942, with a man, journalist Emil Vrbata, bicycling home furiously; it is the day that the Butcher of Prague, Reinhard Heydrich, Reichsprotektor of Czechoslovakia, has been assassinated. The film flashes back to the late 1930s, showing us Emil and his wife (Marek Daniel and Jana Plodková, both superb), popular movie star Hana Vrbatová, whose greater success tries her husband's professional self-esteem; he becomes her "protector" for real, however, when to spare her reprisals, and to court success for himself, he joins a radio station and propagandizes on-air for the Third Reich. Hana is Jewish. Emil's compromises to protect the love of his life generate horrible results. Now he is ordered to divorce and denounce his wife. Proceeding ahead in time, even beyond the (now comprehensible) 1942 starting-point, the loop-around structure, suggesting a noose, pulls tight. Drawing on the closing shot of Pabst's *Die Dreigroschenoper* (1931), *Protektor* ends with a hauntingly out-of-focus evocation of the Holocaust.

Indeed, one of the film's many ironies is that, although in color (the murky cinematography is a liability), it marshals silent-film techniques of German Expressionism—

at first, intriguingly; ultimately, piercingly.

AJAMI (Israel, Germany). A beneficiary of the legacy of Roberto Rossellini's and Krzysztof Kieślowski's narrative strategies unhinging linear plot (think *Paisà*, 1946, *Dekalog*, 1988), *Ajami* is an Israeli masterpiece. Set in Ajami, Jaffa, south of Tel Aviv, where Jews, Arabs, including Palestinians, and Christians live together in an atmosphere fraught with tension, luridly gripped by criminal elements and blood-vengeance vendettas, its five chapters recycle characters and bits of plot, expanding our understanding of what we have already seen and achieving a terribly, almost intolerably moving finale. Co-written, -directed and -edited by an Israeli Arab and an Israeli Jew, Scandar Copti and Yaron Shani, the film claims an actual incident as its springboard.

There has been little reconstruction in Jaffa since Israel, responding to protests, ceased demolishing the old Arab neighborhood in the 1950s. With deep unemployment, it is an environment that no one, in its current state, should have to call *home*. Young inhabitants all bear burdens beyond their means to shoulder: 19-year-old Omar, the intended target of a hit, because of a killing that he individually had nothing to do with (his uncle perpetrated it), that mistakenly takes down someone else, absurdly, anyhow; Nasri, Omar's 13-year-old brother, who adores Omar, who adores him; 16-year-old Malek, who works in a crime boss's establishment to earn money to keep his dying mother alive at hospital; others. Speaking specifically, someone lights on a widely applicable generalization: "Money is the only solution."

Boaz Yehonatan Yacov's hauntingly underlit color cinematography leans on gold, suggesting the money so many are after, flickering amidst browns of burial-earth. Some have complained about its murkiness, but they are dead-wrong. Copti, Shani and Yacov achieve supernal clarity, showing us the moral and sociopolitical murkiness that *is*.

Exhaustively humane.

Best film, direction, script, editing, Israeli Film Academy.

VINCERE (Italy). A Pirandellian air permeates *Vincere*, which means *to win, to overcome*, written (along with Daniela Ceselli) and directed by the maker of *Enrico IV* (1984), Marco Bellocchio. Mockingly aping his father, dictator Benito Mussolini, after one of Mussolini's exaggerated speeches, Mussolini's son, also named Benito (Filippo Timi plays both characters), goes insane under a combinate burden: his mother's incarceration in an insane asylum for insisting that Mussolini, who has married since, is *her* legal husband and that her son, "Benitino," is also *his* son; his father's having nothing to do with him; his father's being both beast and buffoon on national and international stages. However, it is the boy's mother, Ida Delser, who is the protagonist of Bellocchio's brilliant film. The existence of Mussolini's first wife and son became widely "known" only in 2005.

Covering nearly forty years of twentieth-century Italian history, *Vincere* charts Mussolini's rise from impoverished socialist-activist to Fascist dictator through two agencies: rabble-rousing exploitation of class division and anti-clerical sentiment (Mussolini ultimately uses the Church to legitimize his rule); his own newspaper, *Il Popolo d'Italia*, which bourgeois Ida bankrolls—this, despite their (presumably) marrying, the sum of Mussolini's own use for her. Ida is unable to "move on." Along the way, she is advised to "play a different role," that of an obedient, submissive, domestically inclined woman rather than an enraged, agitated irritant. This is what Mussolini himself has done in becoming Il Duce: he has found *another role* to play. For Mussolini, power means hiding from view–his own and others'–the trauma of his initial poverty.

Favoring browns and dimly lit, the first movement suggests buried lives and buried truth. Bellocchio strikingly weaves fictional and archival materials as time, proceeding, locks Ida and son into hopeless lives and, finally, common graves.

TETRO (U.S., Italy, Spain, Argentina). Writer-director Francis Ford Coppola's *Tetro* is a great, highly imaginative work—and, at the same time, Coppola's most heartfelt, bleedingly personal film. It is (like *The Godfather* trilogy, 1972-1990) a family saga, this one about a blended Argentine and Italian family, like Coppola's own. It is a film about brothers, about fathers and sons, about lost mothers and a lost love—and about a family betrayal.

Vincent Gallo, a fine American filmmaker and fine actor, gives the performance of a lifetime as Angelo Tetrocinni, a once-promising writer who is estranged from his father and now calls himself Tetro, and lives with his girlfriend, Miranda (Maribel Verdú, excellent), in Buenos Aires. His broken leg in a cast, Bennie, Tetro's 17-year-old brother, who hasn't seen Tetro in ten years, visits and eventually completes, on the sly, one of Tetro's old plays and arranges for its public performance. "I don't want Bennie to save me," Tetro tells Miranda. "I don't want anybody to save me. . . . I understand this is your way of showing love."

Tetro is almost entirely in black and white, almost all of which is in exceedingly dim black and white—but without the optical torture that *The Godfather*, in color, imposes on the viewer. (Color, generally, is harder on the eyes.) Much about the Tetrocinni family, about its relationships, is hidden, and the film's dark images correlate to this. At night, the parting of headlighted heavy traffic as Bennie wanders into it in his suicidal determination contrasts sharply with this. Moreover, bursts of rich color, mostly in flashbacks, also punctuate the dimness.

In all likelihood, you will suspect (as did I) how Tetro and Bennie are really related. What family doesn't have its secrets? What can be more difficult, sometimes, than giving or receiving love?

SAVIORS IN THE NIGHT (Germany, France). Based on Marga Spiegel's memoir, published in 1965, *Unter Bauern: Retter in der Nacht* examines the lives-in-hiding of the three actual surviving German Jews out of the hundreds who resided in a rural town in Westphalia during the Second World War: Marga, her husband, Siegmund, nicknamed Menne, and their young daughter, Karin. With the help of non-Jewish farmers, whose courage and humanity are honored at the Yad Vashem memorial in Israel, this family escaped deportation. A riveting chronicle rich in detail and bereft of melodrama, the film ends with a heart-piercing coda: the actual Marga and Maria Aschoff, the farmer's wife who opened her home to Marga and Karin, both now well into their nineties, sitting side-by-side. The camera dips to reveal that the two women are holding hands—a bridge of memory over time. The moment is sent into warm-hearted hilarity when one asks the other something; see for yourselves.

Ludi Boeken has beautifully directed from a beautifully crafted script showing the conflicted humanity of real people. Heinrich, Maria's husband, a First World War comrade of Menne's (the film opens with Menne's voiced-over ironical remark that the nation that had awarded him the Iron Cross now wanted to kill him), tells Menne that he will take in Menne's wife and daughter, but not him, since the horse seller's face is so well-known in the area; risk has its limits, and Menne spends 1943-45 hiding here, there, everywhere. Maria must juggle her sympathy for the Jewish Spiegels and her constant worry over her son, Klemens, a soldier at the front. A neighboring Hitler Youth, smitten with the Aschoffs' daughter, is horribly conflicted over how to behave in a world where Hitler claims the most commanding voice.

Superbly acted; brilliant editing by Suzanne Fenn.

INDEX

Alphabetical index of film titles and directors names

11'09"01..480
12 O'CLOCK HIGH................................133
12:08 EAST OF BUCHAREST.............507
1860...68
24 CITY...514
35 SHOTS OF RUM...............................516

A

A BOUT DE SOUFFLE..........148, 150-152, 198, 262, 294, 310
A DAY IN THE COUNTRY.....................76
A DEADLY INVENTION.......................194
A DOG'S LIFE..12
A FISH PROCESSING FACTORY IN ASTRAKHAN...8
A HEN IN THE WIND...........................130
A MAN ESCAPED.................................181
A MAN THERE WAS...............................11
A PEBBLE BY THE WAYSIDE...............82
A PROPOS DE NICE................................38
A REPORT ON THE PARTY AND THE GUESTS 266
A SCANNER DARKLY.........................509
A SPECIAL DAY....................................337
A STORY OF FLOATING WEEDS.........69
A STORY OF WOMEN 386
A SUMMER AT GRANDPA'S...............366

A TALE OF THE WIND........................384
A TALE OF WINTER.............................418
A TASTE OF CHERRY.........394, 397, 443
A TIME TO LIVE, A TIME TO DIE.....370
A VALPARAÍSO....................................239
A.B.C. AFRICA......................................474
Abschied von gestern—(Anita G,).........263
ACCATTONE...235
ACCIDENT...273
ACE IN THE HOLE...............................160
ADWA..450
AEROGRAD...74
Agostino d'Ippona.................................308
AGUIRRE, THE WRATH OF GOD.....309
AIMÉE & JAGUAR...............................455
AJAANTRIK..193
AJAMI..520
Äkerman, Chantal.................234, 325, 333, 340, 360, 361, 400-402, 484, 485
Alea, Tomás Gutiérrez.....................335, 364
ALEKSANDRA.....................................509
ALEXANDER NEVSKY........................81
ALEXEI AND THE SPRING................461
Alexei to izumi..461
All Night Long.......................................360
All That Heaven Allows........................322
ALL THE MEMORY OF THE WORLD 184
Allen, Woody...................333, 346, 364, 499
ALONE ON THE PACIFIC...................239

Alphabetical index

ALPHAVILLE..256
Altman, Robert......107, 291, 316, 326, 477, 478
AMADA..364
Amaral, Suzana....................................374
Amber Collective.................................479
Amelio, Gianni............... 228, 300, 322, 407, 408, 428, 495
AMEN..484
AMERICAN MADNESS........................63
AMONG PEOPLE..................................83
AN AMERICAN TRAGEDY..................60
AN INN IN TOKYO...............................73
ANATOMY OF A MURDER................201
AND THE SHIP SAILS ON.................363
Anderson, Lindsay.......... 279, 280, 305, 359
ANDREI RUBLEV...............................260
Andres, Jo..435
ANGANO... ANGANO...................391
ANGEL..81
Angelopoulos, Theodoros..............433, 447
Antoine, André......................................19
ANTÔNIO DAS MORTES...................289
ANTONIO GAUDÍ...............................370
Antonioni, Michelangelo.......112, 127, 177, 190, 205-210, 249, 267, 274, 285, 308, 323, 359, 379, 394, 397, 416, 431, 432, 450, 493, 516
APARAJITO...188
Apur Sansar...198
ARIEL..382
ARISTOTLE'S PLOT...........................433
Armendáriz, Montxo............................409
ARMY OF THE SHADOWS.................285
Arrière-saison......................................156
ARSENAL..37

ARTISTS AT THE TOP OF THE BIG TOP: DISORIENTED...........................279
ASCENSEUR POUR L'ECHAFAUD ..190
ASCENT..328
ASHES AND DIAMONDS...................196
ASHIK KERIB.....................................385
Askoldov, Aleksandr............................387
Assayas, Olivier.............................10, 448
ASSEMBLY...511
AT FIVE IN THE AFTERNOON.........490
AU HASARD, BALTHAZAR..............261
August, Bille................................369, 438
AUGUSTINE OF HIPPO.....................308

B

BACKWARD SEASON.......................156
BAD LUCK...200
BAMAKO..502
Bani-Etemad, Rakhshan......................478
Barnet, Boris...67
BARREN LIVES.................................243
Bartabas..440
Bartley, Kim..490
BATTLESHIP POTEMKIN...................25
Baum, L. Frank.....................................10
BEAU TRAVAIL.................................455
BEAUTY AND THE BEAST........119, 341
Becker, Jacques.....................77, 165, 168
BEFORE THE REVOLUTION............252
BEIJING BICYCLE.............................477
Bekolo, Jean-Pierre.....................422, 434
BELFAST, MAINE..............................453
BELLISSIMA......................................158

Bellocchio, Marco..........*257, 273, 299, 305,*
306, 375, 441, 442, 490, 521
BELLS FROM THE DEEP...................424
Belvaux, Lucas...*486*
Bergman, Ingmar.....................*19, 111, 138,*
178, 182, 202, 205, 207, 210-214, 248,
262, 274, 275, 289, 311, 337, 358, 366,
369, 377, 390, 395, 423, 438, 447, 513
BERLIN..116
BERLIN ALEXANDERPLATZ............350
BERLIN-JERUSALEM.........................389
BERLIN: SYMPHONY OF A GREAT CITY..30
Bernard, Raymond............................*28, 63*
Bertolucci, Bernardo.....*252, 262, 298, 379, 380, 500*
BEWARE OF A HOLY WHORE...........299
BEYOND THE CLOUDS......................430
BEZHIN MEADOW................................80
Bharadwaj, Vishal...................................*503*
Biberman, Herbert J...............................*174*
BICYCLE THIEVES.............................127
Birth of a Nation..7
Biruma no Tategoto................................180
BLACK GOD, WHITE DEVIL.............250
BLACK KITES.......................................434
Black, Stephanie....................................*479*
BLACKBOARDS...................................470
BLACKMAIL...40
Blade af Satans Bog..................................13
BLAISE PASCALE...............................304
Blasetti, Alessandro.................................*68*
BLIND DATE...197
BLOOD OF THE BEASTS...................132
BLOOD WEDDING..............................354
BLOWUP..267

BLUE PLANET.....................................353
BLUEBEARD...115
BOATMAN...426
Bodrov, Sergei...*439*
Boeken, Ludi...*522*
BOLIVIA...475
BOOMERANG.......................................126
BORDER STREET................................130
BORINAGE..70
Böttcher, Jürgen............................*233, 407*
Boudu sauvé des eaux...............................62
BOUDU SAVED FROM DROWNING..62
Boulting, Roy and John.........................*155*
BOY..289
BRAVE NEW LAND.............................471
Bread and Flower...................................436
Breathless...148
Bresson, Robert..........*73, 80, 117, 153, 181,*
187, 198, 199, 221-224, 238, 261, 274,
292, 322, 362, 363, 437, 484, 509
BRIEF ENCOUNTER...........................118
BRIGANDS, CHAPTER VII................434
BRINGING UP BABY............................84
BRITANNIA HOSPITAL......................359
Brutalität in Stein..................................*233*
BRUTALITY IN STONE......................233
BULLET BALLET................................448
BUÑUEL AND KING SOLOMON'S TABLE...474
Buñuel, Luis.........................*10, 34, 49, 55,*
61, 73, 162, 163, 167, 192, 224, 230, 238,
239, 255, 272, 284, 285, 288, 293, 306,
312, 325, 435, 475
BUS 174...486

C

CABEZA DE VACA..............................414
Caetano, Adrián....................................476
CAFE LUMIERE..................................487
Caiozzi, Silvio...335
CAMILLE...75
CAMMINA CAMMINA.......................357
CAMOUFLAGE....................................334
Camus, Mario..........................252, 271, 369
Capra, Frank...............63, 64, 71, 161, 282
Carné, Marcel...10, 41, 72, 83, 86, 111, 342
CARTESIO..318
CASQUE D'OR.....................................165
Cassenti, Frank.......................................343
Cavalier, Alain..376
CEDDO..334
CELINE AND JULIE GO BOATING...323
Chabrol, Claude............66, 100, 148, 161, 196, 217, 226, 254, 278, 279, 286, 287, 291, 386, 454, 489, 490
Chapaev...76
Chaplin, Charles........12, 13, 21, 26, 55, 60, 64, 75, 104, 123, 124, 134, 144, 154, 156, 161, 164, 167, 199, 259, 269, 327, 337
CHARULATA..251
CHELSEA GIRLS.................................268
CHETYRE..500
CHIKAMATSU MONOGATARI..........174
Chimes at Midnight.........................260, 417
CHIMES AT MIDNIGHT......................260
CHINA IS NEAR...................................273
CHRIST STOPPED AT EBOLI.............343
CHRONICLE OF ANNA MAGDALENA BACH..269
Chytilová, Věra.......266, 288, 323, 346, 477
Cissé, Soulaymane..................................381

CITIZEN KANE......................................89
CITY LIGHTS...55
CITY STREETCLEANERS..................127
Clair, René....8, 21, 25, 31, 59, 60, 66, 161, 179
CLAIRE'S KNEE..................................302
CLASS RELATIONS............................366
Clément, René..........................37, 120, 185
CLEO FROM 5 TO 7............................236
Close Encounters of the Third Kind.......297
CLOUDS OF MAY...............................451
Clouzot, Henri-Georges..........169, 174, 305
Cocteau, Jean......................57, 117, 119, 120, 131, 132, 189, 240, 306, 341, 370, 379, 384, 430, 509
CŒURS..504
COLOSSAL YOUTH............................503
COME AND SEE..................................372
COMMENT ÇA VA?............................330
COMMISSAR.......................................387
CONFIDENCE......................................351
Conte d'hiver..419
CONVERSATION PIECE.....................319
Cooper, Merian C.....................................68
Coppola, Francis Ford............32, 340, 521
Copti, Scandar..520
Costa-Gavras, Constantinos..348, 425, 485
Costa, Pedro....................................467, 504
CRASH..437
CRÍA CUERVOS 327
Cries and Whispers 311
CRIES AND WHISPERS 311
CRIMSON GOLD.................................490
Cronenberg, David.................................438
CUL-DE-SAC.......................................264
CULLODEN..252

D

D'EST 400
DAISIES 265
Dalton, Scott *497*
DAMNATION 378
Danquart, Didi *450*
DANZÓN 415
Dardenne, Luc & Jean-Pierre *517*
DARWIN'S NIGHTMARE 491
Dassin, Jules *54, 191, 194, 197*
DAY OF WRATH 111
DAYS AND NIGHTS IN THE FOREST
.... 285
DAYS OF ECLIPSE 384
de Oliveira, Manoel *445*
De Santis, Giuseppe *163*
De Sica, Vittorio *73, 100, 101, 116, 127, 128, 140-144, 147, 303, 341, 364, 385*
DEAR EMMA, SWEET BÖBE 421
DEATH BY HANGING 281
Debord, Guy *315, 342*
DEKALOG 383
Delannoy, Jean *122*
Denis, Claire *456, 482, 497, 517*
Der letzte Mann 16
Der Müde Tod 19
des Pallières, Arnaud *444*
DESERTER 65
DESTINY 19
Deus e o Diabo na Terra do Sol, ... 250
DEVI 225
DEVIL IN THE FLESH 375
Deville, Michel *156, 340, 402*
DEVILS ON THE DOORSTEP 466
DIAMONDS OF THE NIGHT 249
DIARY FOR MY CHILDREN 353

DIARY OF A COUNTRY PRIEST 153
Die Abenteuer des Prinzen Achmed 27
Die Angst des Tormanns beim Elfmeter
.... 308
Die Blechtrommel 347
DIE DREIGROSCHENOPER 58
Die Freudlose Gasse 26
DIE HALBSTARKEN 185
Die Mauer 407
DIE NIBELUNGEN 24
Die Straße 21
Disney, Walt *64*
DISTANT THUNDER 314
DO YOU REMEMBER DOLLY BELL?
.... 354
DÔDESUKADEN 299
DOFKA NAI MEUMAN 469
Domésticas 476
DON QUIJOTE 416
DON QUIXOTE 66
DON'T TOUCH THE AXE 513
Donskoi, Mark *28, 82-84, 86, 334, 492*
dos Santos, Nelson Pereira *243, 367*
DOSSIER 51 340
DOUBLE INDEMNITY 114
Dovzhenko, Aleksandr *34, 37, 38, 43, 44, 61, 62, 74, 80, 117, 245, 260, 264, 288, 321, 329, 384, 390, 448, 458, 462, 464*
DRANCY AVENIR 443
Drankov, Aleksandr *9*
DREAM OF LIGHT 417
DREAMS 407
DREAMS OF DUST 505
Dreyer, Carl Theodor *10, 13, 17, 18, 26, 37, 38, 44, 45, 70, 101, 111, 112, 126, 170, 186, 210, 238, 243, 248, 250, 369, 380,*

383, 473, 509, 513
DRIFTING CLOUDS...........................436
DRUGSTORE COWBOY.....................391
DUCK SOUP..67
Dudow, Slatan..62
Dumont, Bruno...............................451, 507
DUST IN THE WIND.............................374
Dzigan, Efim...77

E

E la nave va..363
EARLY SUMMER.................................157
EARTH..43
EASTERN ELEGY.................................439
Ecaré, Désiré..371
Echevarría, Nicolás..................................415
EDVARD MUNCH..................................321
Edzard, Christine............................387, 413
EFFI BRIEST..321
Einhorn, Lena..................................500, 501
Eisenstein, Sergei M.............22, 23, 25, 27, 29-31, 38, 39, 40, 43, 46-51, 65, 69, 80-82, 107, 113, 114, 119, 148, 179, 251, 254, 262, 296, 347, 352, 465
ÉL..162
El ángel exterminador...........................238
EL JARDÍN DEL EDÉN........................429
ELEKTRA, MY LOVE...........................320
ELEPHANT...487
Elevator to the Gallows..........................190
ELISA, MY LIFE....................................337
Éloge de l'amour......................................473
Engel, Erich...129

ENJO...193
ENTR'ACTE...25
EPIDEMIC..383
Epstein, Jean..39
EQUINOX FLOWER.............................192
Erdem, Reha..506
Erice, Victor....................................317, 418
EROICA..189
Estrada, Luis..457
ETERNITY AND A DAY 4465
EUROPA...413
EUROPA '51...158
Europa Europa...............................403, 406
Eustache, Jean...315
EVEN DWARFS STARTED SMALL...287
EVERY MAN FOR HIMSELF AND GOD AGAINST ALL.......................................320
EXITING THE FACTORY........................8
EYES WITHOUT A FACE....................201

F

F FOR FAKE..326
FAAT KINÉ..468
FACES OF WOMEN..............................371
FADOS..510
FAMILY DIARY....................................242
FANNY AND ALEXANDER................358
Färberböck, Max......................................456
FAREWELL..356
Farocki, Harun...............................176, 388
Fassbinder, Rainer Werner..........291, 299, 302, 321, 322, 345, 348, 350
FATA MORGANA 284

FATELESS..499
FATHER OF A SOLDIER......................250
FAUST..27
Faver, Héctor..................................176, 419
FEAR...173
FEAR EATS THE SOUL......................322
Fehér, György........................110, 409, 446
Fei, Mu 128, 374
FELLINI SATYRICON.........................287
Fellini, Federico............152, 156, 157, 167, 171, 172, 177, 178, 183, 192, 199, 205, 226, 248, 269, 287, 300, 328, 363, 376, 378, 398
Feng, Xiaogang......291, 374, 375, 425, 512
Feuillade, Louis............................10, 12, 16
FINIS TERRÆ...39
FIRES ON THE PLAIN........................200
FISTS IN THE POCKET.......................257
FIVE LONG TAKES DEDICATED TO YASUJIRO OZU....................................486
Flaherty, Robert J...............19, 20, 26, 60, 69, 112, 374, 386, 462, 468
FLANDERS...505
Fleming, Victor.........39, 172, 199, 282, 408
FLIGHT OF THE EAGLE 361
FLOWERS OF SHANGHAI.................444
FLOWING...185
Fokin, Valerij..487
Ford, Aleksander...................................130
Ford, John..............15, 21, 51, 74, 85, 96, 103, 104, 108, 113, 117, 125, 126, 138, 153, 171, 181, 182, 195, 197, 237, 248, 274, 290, 291, 298, 344, 367, 440
FOREVER..504
FORTY GUNS......................................191
FOUR MEN ON A RAFT......................110

FRANCESCO, GIULLARE DI DIO.....152
Franju, Georges....132, 133, 159, 201, 209, 243, 316, 512
FREE ZONE..497
FREEZE, DIE, RISE! 390
FRENCH CANCAN.............................172
FRENZY..311
FRIDAY NIGHT...................................481
Friedrich, Su............32, 316, 330, 372, 411
From the East..400
FROM THE OTHER SIDE...................483
Fuller, Samuel........................137, 191, 291

G

Gance, Abel..............................14, 32, 37
Garrel, Philippe.....................299, 424, 500
Garrone, Matteo....................................517
GATE OF HELL....................................170
Gatlif, Tony...427
GENESIS...452
Gerima, Haile.......................324, 426, 451
GERMANY YEAR NINE ZERO.........413
GERMANY, YEAR ZERO.....................99
GERTRUD...248
GERVAISE..184
Ghatak, Ritwik..............163, 194, 230, 258
Ghosh, Rituparno...................259, 455, 483
GHOST DOG: THE WAY OF THE SAMURAI..456
GHOSTS BEFORE BREAKFAST..........36
GINGER AND FRED...........................376
Giral, Sergio..347
Gitaï, Amos............352, 389, 470, 498, 518

Godard, Jean-Luc......................*19, 38, 60,*
78, 148-152, 205, 215-220, 230, 244, 245,
251, 252, 255-257, 262-264, 268, 269, 276,
279-281, 288, 290, 294-298, 300-302, 310,
316, 330, 348, 385, 388, 394, 410, 411,
414, 424, 434, 473, 489
Godzilla...175
GOJIRA..175
GOLDEN RIVER.................................258
Gomes, Flora................................382, 421
GOMORRA..516
GOOD MEN, GOOD WOMEN.............431
GOOD MORNING, NIGHT..................489
GOODBYE SOUTH, GOODBYE........434
Gopalakrishnan, Adoor.........................480
Gorima, Haile..335
GOSFORD PARK..................................476
Gostev, Igor..425
Gothár, Péter...362
GREED..23
Greenaway, Peter..................................436
Gribov, Efim..421
Grierson, John..72
Griffith, David Wark....................7, 16, 111
GRIN WITHOUT A CAT......................335
Grune, Karl......................................16, 20
Gruppo di famiglia in un interno............319
GUELWAAR..418
GUERNICA..152
Guerra, Ciro..520
Guzmán, Patricio...................239, 325, 334

H

HALLELUJAH!......................................39
Halonen, Arto..472
Hamer, Robert.......................................134
HANDS OVER THE CITY...................247
Hanson, John................................339, 343
Hara, Kazuo..381
HARVEST 3,000 YEARS......................324
HARVEST TIME...................................495
Has, Wojciech J.....................................317
Hawks, Howard.......................71, 84, 135,
160, 164, 199, 291
HE WHO MUST DIE 191
HENRY V..113
HERDSMEN OF THE SUN 386
HERE AND PERHAPS ELSEWHERE.488
HEROD'S LAW.....................................456
Herz, Juraj.....................................281, 341
Herzog, Werner......................284, 287, 305,
309, 320, 328, 386, 424, 440, 461
HIGH SCHOOL.....................................290
HIROSHIMA, MON AMOUR..............203
Hirszman, Leon.....................................356
HIS MAJESTY, THE SCARECROW OF
OZ...10
HISTOIRE(S) DU CINEMA 388
Hitchcock, Alfred......10, 19, 40, 74, 75, 79,
112, 113, 120, 156, 162, 163, 175, 178,
182, 194, 195, 202, 203, 225, 238, 257,
268, 282, 293, 311, 312, 326, 350, 388
Hitler—ein Film aus Deutschland 337
Holland, Agnieszka.......................339, 340,
403-407, 413, 473, 474
Honda, Ishirô................................175, 408
Honigmann, Heddy...............................505

Alphabetical index

HORSE THIEF..........................374
HOTEL DES INVALIDES...................159
Hou Hsiao-Hsien...........423, 432, 435, 445
HOUR OF THE STAR.....................373
HOUR OF THE WOLF........................274
HOUSE......................................352
Hui, Ann.......................... 411, 516
Huillet, Danièle....................269, 366
HUMANITY...........................450
HUNGER..............................261
Huston, John..................83, 106, 115, 125, 169, 186, 194, 253, 291, 345, 378
HYENAS..............................420
HYPOTHESIS OF THE STOLEN PAINTING...............................338

I

(I EVEN MET) HAPPY GYPSIES........273
I fidanzati...............................237
I VITELLONI........................167
I WAS A FIREMAN..............................110
I WAS A MALE WAR BRIDE..............135
I WAS BORN, BUT.........................61
I WAS NINETEEN..............................269
ICE..303
Ichikawa, Kon........180, 181, 193, 200, 203, 239, 246, 381, 467, 504
IDENTIFICATION OF A WOMAN......358
IF 279
IKIRU.....................................161
IL BIDONE.............................177
IL CONFORMISTI 298
IL DESERTO ROSSO.........................249
IL GATTOPARDO.............................244
IL GRIDO................................190
Il mestiere delle armi.............................474
IL POSTO.................................235
IL VANGELO SECONDO MATTEO...250
ILLUMINATION......................312
ILLUSION TRAVELS BY STREETCAR 167
ILLUSTRIOUS CORPSES.................331
IMAGES OF THE WORLD AND THE INSCRIPTION OF WAR.......................388
Imamura, Shohei...253, 263, 283, 363, 381, 394, 443, 467, 481
IN PRAISE OF LOVE.........................472
IN THE COURSE OF TIME.................328
IN THE NAME OF THE FATHER.......305
IN THE PIT............................508
IN THE REALM OF PASSION............338
IN THIS WORLD..............................483
IN VANDA'S ROOM.............................466
INDONESIA CALLING.......................121
INGEBORG HOLM................................9
Ingenjör Andrées luftfärd......................362
INNOCENCE UNPROTECTED..........276
INTENTIONS OF MURDER...............253
Intolerance...................................7
Iosseliani, Otar......................329, 435, 481
IRAQ IN FRAGMENTS.......................506
IT'S WINTER...............................507
IVAN..61
IVAN THE TERRIBLE, PART ONE.....113
IVAN THE TERRIBLE, PART TWO....119
Ivens, Joris....37, 38, 60, 64, 65, 70, 71, 80, 81, 86, 105, 121, 187, 188, 239, 283, 324, 384

Alphabetical index

J

J'ACCUSE!..14
Jablonski, Dariusz.........................176, 447
JAGUAR..270
JANA ARANYA....................................329
Jancsó, Miklós..............254, 255, 270, 274, 290, 309, 320, 331, 353
JAPÓN...481
Jarmusch, Jim.........................291, 402, 457
Jayasundara, Vimukthi..........................499
JE T'AIME, JE T'AIME.......................282
JEANNE DIELMAN, 23 QUAI DU COMMERCE, 1080 BRUXELLES........325
Jennings, Humphrey...............................110
JEW-BOY LEVI 448
Jia, Zhang-Ke...515
Jiang, Wen...467
JOAN OF ARC AT THE STAKE...........172
JOAN THE MAID................................429
Joreige, Lamia.......................................489
Jost, Jon...........3, 234, 336, 380, 402, 412, 424, 458-461, 483, 484, 512
Journal d'un curé de campagne..............153
JOURNEY TO THE SUN......................452
JUDEX..12
JULES AND JIM..................................231
JULIO BEGINS IN JULY......................335
Jungfrukällan...202

K

Kabore, Gaston...360
KAGI..203
KAIDAN...253
KAMERADSCHAFT..............................57
KANCHENJUNGHA............................240
Kanevski, Vitaly....................................390
KARIN'S FACE....................................369
KARL MAY..319
Kaurismäki, Aki.............382, 410, 437, 509
Kazan, Elia.....................113, 126, 127, 191
Keaton, Buster......23, 26, 36, 164, 266, 477
Kechiche, Abdellatif..............................513
Keene, Nietzchka...................................390
Khrjanovsky, Ilya...........................129, 501
Kiarostami, Abbas.........394-397, 400, 418, 429, 436, 445, 450, 452, 475, 487, 491
Kieślowski, Krzysztof.............383, 403, 470
KIND HEARTS AND CORONETS......134
KING KONG...68
King of Songs.......................................277
King, Henry...............................99, 133, 159
KINO-EYE...24
Kinugasa, Teinosuke......................170, 246
KIPPUR...469
Kirsanoff, Dimitri............................28, 156
Klimov, Elem..........264, 328, 356, 372, 504
KNIFE IN THE WATER......................238
Koch, Ulrike...440
KOKORO...180
Kolirin, Eran...515
Koltai, Lajos..................351, 362, 423, 500
KORCZAK..412
Körkarlen...18
Kozintsev, Grigori..................................40
Kramer, Robert.....................................303
Krylya..264
KUHLE WAMPE...................................62
Kurosawa, Akira...............51, 129, 157, 161, 162, 171, 187, 193, 202, 248, 260,

299, 300, 408, 449
Kusturica, Emir......354, 427, 432, 433, 467

L

L'albero degli zoccoli............................341
L'Age d'Or..55
L'ARGENT..36
L'ARGENT (1983)...................................362
L'AVVENTURA......................................205
L'ECLISSE..205
L'étoile de mer...35
L'Herbier, Marcel....................................36
L'IMMORTELLE....................................245
La Belle et la Bête..................................119
LA CHANSON DE ROLAND 343
LA CHIENNE..59
LA COMMUNE (PARIS 1871)..............465
La femme infidèle...................................278
LA GRANDE ILLUSION.........................79
La leggenda del santo bevitore...............384
LA NOTTE...205
La notti di Cabiria..................................183
La nuit américaine..................................298
LA PETITE VENDEUSE DE SOLEIL. 397
LA RÉGION CENTRALE......................306
La règle du jeu...84
LA RONDE..155
LA SIERRA..496
La sortie des usines Lumière.....................8
LA STRADA..171
LA SYMPHONIE PASTORALE............122
LA TERRA TREMA................................128
LA TERRE...19
LA VIE EST A NOUS..............................77

LaCava, Gregory..........................105, 235
LADY OYÛ..160
LAMERICA...427
LANCELOT OF THE LAKE.................322
LAND IN ANGUISH 272
LAND OF SILENCE AND DARKNESS
....305
Landri di biciclette.................................127
Lang, Fritz.......................10, 17, 19, 24,
27, 29, 45, 58, 60, 82, 97, 109, 115, 122,
130, 135, 137, 140, 194, 307, 338
LAS HURDES...61
LAST CHANTS FOR A SLOW DANCE
....336
LAST DAYS..501
LAST YEAR AT MARIENBAD...........230
LATCHO DROM....................................426
LATE AUGUST, EARLY SEPTEMBER
....447
LATE AUTUMN....................................226
LATE SPRING.......................................132
Lattuada, Alberto....................................156
LE AMICHE..177
LE BEAU MARIAGE............................355
LE BOUCHER 291
Le complot d'Aristote.............................434
Le diable noir,...8
LE DOULOS...241
Le fond de l'air est rouge.......................335
LE GAI SAVOIR....................................280
Le genou de Claire.................................302
Le gros et le maigre................................234
LE JOLI MAI..246
LE JOUR SE LEVE..................................86
Le mani sulla città..................................247
LE MILLION..59

Le retour à la raison..................22
Le salaire de la peur...................169
LE SAMOURAI............................271
Le sang d'un poète.....................57
Le sang des bêtes......................132
Le thé a la menthe.....................234
Lean, David..............54, 118, 285
LEAVES FROM SATAN'S BOOK.........13
LEMONADE JOE.........................254
LES BONNES FEMMES..................226
LES CARABINIERS......................244
Les croix de bois........................63
LES DAMES DU BOIS DE BOULOGNE
....117
LES DIABOLIQUES......................174
LES GLANEURS ET LA GLANEUSE 467
LES MISTONS............................189
Les parapluies de Cherbourg...........251
LES PARENTS TERRIBLES.............131
Les quatre cents coups.................199
LES RENDEZ-VOUS D'ANNA...........340
LES VAMPIRES...........................10
Les visiteurs du soir....................111
Les yeux sans visage...................201
LETTER FROM AN UNKNOWN
WOMAN......................................91
LETTERS FROM ALOU..................408
LIFE AND DEBT..........................478
Life and Nothing More...........397, 429
LIFE AND NOTHING MORE............417
LIFE ON EARTH..........................446
LIGHTS IN THE DUSK..................508
LIKE FATHER.............................478
LIMELIGHT................................164
Linklater, Richard......................510
LITTLE DORRIT..........................387

Llosa, Claudia..........................507
Loach, Ken...............355, 476, 477, 503
LOLA..229
LOLA MONTES...........................177
LONG LIVE THE LADY!.................378
LONG LIVE THE WHALE!..............510
Longley, James........................507
LOOKS AND SMILES....................355
Lorentz, Pare......................77, 81
LORNA'S SILENCE......................516
Losey, Joseph...........197, 207, 232, 233, 267, 273, 313
LOST HIGHWAY.........................441
LOVE.......................................304
LOVE AFFAIR, OR THE CASE OF THE
MISSING SWITCHBOARD OPERATOR
....275
Lubitsch, Ernst........75, 81, 92, 95, 105, 149
LUCÍA......................................282
Lumière, Louis & Auguste..............7, 8
Lunga vita alla signora................378
Lutsik, Pyotr............................448
Lynch, David...............287, 366, 367, 408, 412, 417, 442, 457, 473

M

M...58
M'mbugu-Schelling, Flora............420
MACBETH.................................129
Mackendrick, Alexander..............161
MADAME BOVARY......................66
MADAME de 144
MADE IN U.S.A..........................263

MADEINUSA...........................506
MAHAPURISH................................259
MAIDS.................................475
Majidi, Majid..........................519
Makhmalbaf, Mohsen..............436, 471, 491
MALA NOCHE....................373
MALAISE...............................454
Malaparte, Curzio................................154
Malberti, Juan Carlos Cremata............477
Malle, Louis......................65, 190, 252, 398
MALUALA..............................347
Mambéty, Djibril Diop....316, 397-400, 421
MAN IS NOT A BIRD..........................257
MAN OF ARAN.........................69
MAN OF IRON............................354
MAN ON THE TRACKS...................183
MANDABI................................277
MANHATTAN..........................346
Mankiewicz, Herman J..............89, 99, 156
Marcovich, Carlos...................443
Mariage, Benoît........................355, 452
Marker, Chris..53, 168, 171, 220, 233, 239, 240, 246, 247, 256, 262, 306, 325, 335, 336, 342, 372, 461, 489, 492, 511, 512
Martinez, Margarita...........................497
MASCULIN-FÉMININ........................215
MATCH POINT...........................498
Mayo, Archie............................79
Maysles, Albert and David.....................293
McCarey, Leo..............................67
MEDEA............................292, 380
MEET ME IN ST. LOUIS.....................114
Meirelles, Fernando...........................476
Méliès, Georges...........7, 8, 10, 13, 384, 505
MELO...................................377
Melville, Jean-Pierre....124, 139, 194, 195,

241, 271, 285, 442, 454, 456
MEMORIES OF MY MOTHER..........241
MEMORIES OF PRISON....................367
MEN ON THE MOUNTAIN.................111
MENILMONTANT.............................28
MESSIDOR.............................343
Mészáros, Márta..............................353
METAMORPHOSIS............................486
Metropolis...............................17
MEXICO: THE FROZEN REVOLUTION
....304
Meyers, Sidney.........................131
MICHELANGELO'S GAZE.................492
MICKEY'S GOOD DEED.....................64
Minnelli, Vincente....................66, 114, 169
MINT TEA...............................234
MIRROR................................318
Misty Stars of the Great Bear.................256
Mizoguchi, Kenji............78, 87, 130, 160, 162, 166, 171, 174, 179, 185, 193
MODERN TIMES....................................75
MODESTY BLAISE.................................267
Mon oncle d'Amérique..........................352
MONDAY MORNING..........................481
Monicelli, Mario....................121, 197, 248
MONKEY BUSINESS..........................164
MONSIEUR VERDOUX......................123
MOOLAADÉ.............................491
MOONLIGHTING................................361
Moorhouse, Jocelyn.............................415
Morris, Errol.............................385
MORTU NEGA.............................382
MOTHER...........................16, 27
MOTHER AND SON............................440
MOTHER OF KINGS....................331
MOUCHETTE..............................221

MULHOLLAND DR............................472
MUNDO GRÚA...................................454
Munk, Andrzej *183, 189, 200, 245, 512*
Murat, Lúcia................................*439, 472*
MURDERERS ARE AMONG US.........122
MURIEL OR THE TIME OF A RETURN
....247
Muriel ou Le temps d'un retour.............247
Murnau, Friedrich Wilhelm........*15, 16, 20, 27, 28, 30, 32*
MY AMERICAN UNCLE.....................352
MY DARLING CLEMENTINE..............96
MY NIGHT AT MAUD'S.....................286
MY OWN PRIVATE IDAHO................415
MY UNIVERSITIES..............................86

NIGHT AND FOG IN JAPAN...............224
Nilsson, Leopoldo Torre........................*188*
Nilsson, Rob..*339*
NINA'S JOURNEY...............................499
NINE DAYS OF ONE YEAR...............232
NORTH BY NORTHWEST..................202
NORTHERN LIGHTS..........................339
NOSFERATU..20
NOSTOS: THE RETURN....................389
NOTORIOUS..120
NOUVELLE VAGUE..........................409
Novaro, María...............................*416, 430*
Nóz w wodzie..238
Nuit et brouillard...................................176
NUMÉRO DEUX..................................294
NUN VA GOLDOON 435

N

Nabili, Marva..*332*
Nacro, Fanta Régina.............................*494*
NADA..476
Nagarik..163
Nair, Murali..*450*
Najbrt, Marek..*520*
NANOOK OF THE NORTH..................19
NAPOLEON..32
Naruse, Mikio...............................*185, 229*
NASHVILLE...326
Nattvardsgästerna..................................211
NAZARÍN..192
NDEYSAAN..484
NEW EARTH..64
NEWS FROM HOME..........................333
NIGHT AND FOG................................176

O

O'Briain, Donnacha..............................*490*
OBSESSION...109
OCTOBER...29
ODD MAN OUT...................................125
Offret...377
OKRAINA...67
OLD BELIEVERS................................473
Olival, Nando..*476*
Olivier, Laurence....*103, 113, 124, 178, 354*
OLIVIER, OLIVIER.............................402
Olmi, Ermanno............*235, 237, 341, 357, 378, 385, 474*
ON THE BOWERY..............................186
ONE DAY YOU'LL UNDERSTAND...517
ONE, TWO, THREE.............................234

OPEN DOORS..406
*Ophüls, Max........91-95, 144-147, 155, 177,
179, 331*
ORATORIO FOR PRAGUE..................283
ORDET...170
OSAKA ELEGY..78
*Oshima, Nagisa............................224, 243,
281, 289, 301, 308, 338*
Ossessione..109
Ouédraogo, Idrissa........................392, 412
OUI NON..482
OUR HITLER...337
OUT 1: SPECTRE.................................310
OUTSKIRTS..447
OVER HERE..511
Oyû-sama...160
*Ozu, Yasujiro.....................56, 61, 65, 69,
73, 123, 130, 132, 157, 165, 186, 192, 226,
263, 401, 486, 487, 516*

P

*Pabst, Georg Wilhelm............26, 35, 56-58,
62, 63, 66, 75, 78, 226, 520*
PADRE PADRONE................................336
Paes, César..391
PAISÀ..120
Panahi, Jafar...................................469, 491
PANDORA'S BOX..................................35
Panh, Rithy...429
Parajanov, Sergei............................277, 385
PARIS NOUS APPARTIENT................228
PARIS QUI DORT..................................21
PARIS, TEXAS......................................367

*Pasolini, Pier Paolo................13, 235,
250, 265, 280, 292, 299, 341, 380, 506*
PASSAGES..458
PASSENGER...245
PASSING FANCY...................................65
PASSION..445
PASTORALI...329
PATHER PANCHALI..........................176
Patwardhan, Anand..............................486
Peck, Raoul..426
PEOPLE OF THE PO VALLEY...........112
PEOPLE ON SUNDAY..........................41
PERCEVAL...342
PERFORMANCE..................................301
PERSONA NON GRATA.....................494
Petrov, Vladimir....................................134
PHILIPS-RADIO....................................60
PHOTOGRAPHER...............................446
Piavoli, Franco..............................353, 389
PICKPOCKET......................................198
PIEMULE..368
PIERROT LE FOU................................255
Pitts, Rafi...508
PLAIN TALK & COMMON SENSE....380
PLAYTIME...269
*Polanski, Roman................129, 202,
234, 238, 264, 332, 361*
Polgovsky, Eugenio..............................494
PORT OF SHADOWS............................83
Porumboiu, Corneliu............................508
Potter, Sally...442
POWER AND THE LAND...................105
Prästänkan..18
Preminger, Otto....................................201
Prima della rivoluzione........................252
PRIMROSE PATH................................105

PRISONER OF THE MOUNTAINS.....438
PRIVATE CONFESSIONS...................437
PRIVATE VICES, PUBLIC VIRTUES..330
PROFIT MOTIVE AND THE
WHISPERING WIND..........................513
PROOF...414
Prospero's Books....................................436
PROTECTOR..519
PROVINCIAL ACTORS........................339
Provost, Martin.......................*273, 485, 519*
PSYCHO..225
Pudovkin, Vsevolod I.......16, 26, 29, 33, 65, 178, 208, 303
Puenzo, Luis...*373*

Q

Quai des brûmes.......................................83
QUARTIER MOZART..........................421
QUATORZE JUILLET............................66
QUE LA BETE MEURE.......................286
QUÉ VIVA MÉXICO...............................46

R

Rain..37
RAISE THE RED LANTERN...............414
Raizman, Yuli..*116*
RAMPARTS OF CLAY........................278
RANCHO NOTORIOUS......................137
Ray, Man..*22, 35*
Ray, Satyajit....98, 163, 176, 188, 195, 198, 225, 240, 251, 259, 285, 314, 329, 334, 365, 455
Razbezhkina, Marina.............................*497*
REAR WINDOW...................................175
RECORD OF A TENEMENT
GENTLEMAN..123
RED PSALM..309
Reed, Carol...........................*125, 164, 369*
REGEN..37
REGULAR LOVERS............................499
Reiniger, Lotte..*27*
Renoir, Jean........43, 59, 62, 66, 70, 72, 76, 77, 78, 79, 80, 85, 99, 100, 109, 110, 117, 148, 150, 158, 165, 172, 173, 176, 178, 179, 205, 225, 231, 240, 251, 254, 285, 477, 517
Resnais, Alain.......153, 168, 176, 184, 203, 204, 224, 230, 231, 233, 247, 248, 252, 271, 273, 282, 352, 377, 397, 444, 505
REVENGE OF A KABUKI ACTOR.....246
Reygadas, Carlos..........................*482, 513*
RICE PEOPLE.......................................428
RICHARD III...178
Richards, Richard..................................*313*
Richter, Hans...*36*
RIO BRAVO..199
Rivette, Jacques............228, 310, 323, 430, 442, 474, 484, 514
ROCCO AND HIS BROTHERS...........228
Rogosin, Lionel.....................................*186*
Rohmer, Eric.........286, 302, 330, 342, 355, 419, 514
ROLLING FAMILY..............................492
Roma, Città aperta.................................116
ROME, 11 O'CLOCK...........................163
ROME, OPEN CITY.............................116

ROSA LUXEMBURG...........................375
Rosi, Francesco... *228, 231, 232, 247, 259,
272, 290, 310, 311, 331, 343, 344, 351*
Rosi, Gianfranco......................................427
Rossellini, Roberto....*68, 99, 100, 102, 103,
107, 115, 116, 120, 133, 143, 148, 152,
159, 166, 172, 173, 177, 190, 231, 233,
238, 244, 245, 250, 262, 269, 304, 305,
308, 314, 318, 341, 380, 390, 408, 414,
463, 474*
ROSTOV-LUANDA.............................443
Ruiz, Raúl........................*338, 357, 437, 438*
Rulfo, Juan Carlos..................................*509*
Ruttmann, Walther.....................*27, 30, 127*

S

SALESMAN...293
Saless, Sohrab Shahid............................*319*
Salgues, Laurent.....................................*506*
SALT OF THE EARTH........................173
SALVATORE GIULIANO....................231
SAN PIETRO...115
SANKOFA..425
Sanshô dayû..*171*
SANSHO, THE BAILIFF......................170
SÁTÁNTANGÓ.....................................427
Sauper, Hubert..*492*
Saura, Carlos............................*174, 266,
267, 327, 337, 354, 364, 475, 511*
SAVIORS IN THE NIGHT...................521
SAYAT-NOVA.......................................277
Schindler's List..*297*
Schlöndorff, Volker...................*327, 347, 471*

Schoedsack, Ernest B...............................68
Scola, Ettore..337
Scorsese, Martin.....................................332
Sellars, Peter...417
Sembène, Ousmane...................... *277, 325,
326, 334, 419, 469, 492*
September 11..481
SERAPHINE..518
Sevciková, Jana.............................*368, 474*
SEVEN DAYS TO NOON....................155
Seven Samurai...*51*
SEVEN SAMURAI...............................171
SHADOW KILL....................................479
SHADOW OF A DOUBT.....................112
Shakhnazarov, Karen..............................*516*
SHAMAN...439
Shani, Yaron...*520*
SHEER MADNESS..............................358
Shepitko, Larisa......*264, 265, 328, 329, 356*
SHERLOCK JR..23
SHIRO OF AMAKUSA, REBEL.........242
SHOOT THE PIANO PLAYER...........227
Shub, Esfir..*31, 328*
SILENCE AND CRY............................274
SILENT LIGHT.....................................512
SIMON OF THE DESERT...................255
SINK OR SWIM....................................410
Siodmak, Curt..*41*
Sirk, Douglas..*322*
Sissako, Abderrahmane...............*444, 445,
447, 482, 503*
Sissoko, Cheick Oumar..........................*453*
Sjöström, Victor *7, 9, 11, 12, 18, 30*
Skolimowski, Jerzy........................*238, 361*
SMILES OF A SUMMER NIGHT........178
Snow, Michael.......................................*306*

Sokurov, Aleksandr....................384, 423,
433, 440, 441, 498, 510, 511, 513
SOLARIS.................................309
Solás, Humberto....................282, 364, 365
SOLNTSE...............................497
Solomun, Zoran.........................436
SOMERSAULT IN A COFFIN..............438
SONG OF CEYLON..............................72
SONG OF THE EXILE.........................410
Spielberg, Steven....................297, 394,
413, 438, 448, 513
SPIRITUAL VOICES: FROM THE
DIARIES OF WAR..............................432
SPRING IN A SMALL TOWN 128
Stachka...22
STAGECOACH.................................85
STALKER.......................................344
Starewicz, Władysław.........................9
STATUES ALSO DIE..........................168
STEAMBOAT BILL JR. 36
Steklý, Karel....................................126
Sternberg, Josef von........16, 31, 44, 46, 56,
60, 73, 74, 78, 83, 113, 144, 152, 229, 282
Stevens, George...........................60, 79
STILL LIFE 319
STORM OVER ASIA............................33
STORY OF THE LAST
CHRYSANTHEMUM..........................87
Straub, Jean-Marie.................237, 269, 366
STRIKE......................................22
Stroheim, Erich von.........23, 109, 144, 155
STROMBOLI.................................133
Stuhr, Jerzy....................................470
Sturges, Preston...............................107
SUD PRALAD................................493
SULLIVAN'S TRAVELS......................107

SUN SEEKERS................................197
SUNRISE.....................................32
SUNSET BOULEVARD.......................154
SUPPLEMENT................................479
SURE FIRE 411
Švankmajer, Jan.........................365
SWING TIME................................78
Syberberg, Hans-Jürgen.............320, 337
Szabó, István...................351, 422, 520
Szász, János..................................431
Szöts, István..................................111

T

Tales of the Pale and Mysterious Moon
After the Rain...........................166
TALES OF THE TAIRA CLAN............179
Tanner, Alain................................317, 343
Tarkovsky, Andrei.............260, 261, 282,
309, 310, 318, 319, 344, 350, 377, 380,
384, 385, 434, 449, 464, 513
Tarr, Béla.......360, 379, 428, 446, 468, 488,
511, 513
Tasaka, Tomotaka.............................82
Taviani, Paolo and Vittorio....................336
TEN NIGHTS OF DREAM..................503
TEOREMA...................................280
Teshigahara, Hiroshi..........................370
TETRO......................................521
THAT NIGHT'S WIFE........................56
THE 17TH PARALLEL: THE PEOPLE'S
WAR 283
THE 39 STEPS...............................74
THE 400 BLOWS............................199

Alphabetical index

THE 400 MILLION....................86
THE ADVENTURES OF PRINCE ACHMED................................27
THE AGE OF COSIMO DE MEDICI...314
THE AMERICAN SOLDIER................302
THE ASSASSINATION OF TROTSKY 313
THE BALLAD OF NARAYAMA.........363
THE BAND WAGON............................169
THE BAND'S VISIT..............................514
THE BATTLE OF ALGIERS.................259
THE BATTLE OF CHILE: THE STRUGGLE OF AN UNARMED PEOPLE................................324
THE BATTLE OF CHILE: THE STRUGGLE OF AN UNARMED PEOPLE, PART II...................333
THE BATTLE OF STALINGRAD........134
THE BED YOU SLEEP IN....................423
THE BEST YEARS OF OUR LIVES...121
THE BIG ANIMAL................................469
THE BIRTH OF LOVE..........................423
THE BLACK CAT...................................71
THE BLACK DEVIL...................................8
THE BLOOD OF A POET 57
THE BLUE ANGEL................................55
THE BLUE EYES OF YONTA............419
THE BLUE KITE..................................424
THE BLUE UMBRELLA....................501
THE BLUM AFFAIR 129
The Bride Wore Black........................231
THE BURMESE HARP.......................180
THE CABINET OF DR. CALIGARI......13
THE CABINET OF DR. RAMIREZ.....416
THE CAMERAMAN'S REVENGE.........9
THE CARRIERS ARE WAITING 451

THE CEREMONY 308
THE CHESS PLAYER...........................28
THE CHILDHOOD OF MAXIM GORKY 82
THE CIRCLE..468
THE CITADEL.......................................84
THE CITIZEN......................................163
THE CLOUD-CAPPED STAR..............229
THE CLOWNS....................................300
THE COLOR OF LIES.........................453
THE CONSTANT FACTOR.................350
The Conversation...................................340
THE COUSINS....................................196
The Crazy Ray...21
THE CREMATOR................................281
THE CRIME OF MONSIEUR LANGE..72
THE CULPEPPER CATTLE CO..........313
THE DAMNED (1969)..........................288
THE DEAD..378
THE DECAMERON.............................299
THE DEEP DESIRE OF THE GODS...283
THE DEVIL IS A WOMAN....................73
THE DEVIL'S ENVOY 111
THE DISCREET CHARM OF THE BOURGEOISIE......................................312
THE DYING SWAN................................11
THE EEL...442
THE ELEMENT OF CRIME.................368
THE EMPEROR'S NAKED ARMY MARCHES ON......................................381
THE END OF ST. PETERSBURG..........29
THE EXILES..233
THE EXTERMINATING ANGEL........238
THE FALL OF THE ROMANOV DYNASTY...31
THE FAT AND THE LEAN................234

Alphabetical index

THE FIANCÉS...................................237	THE IRON HORSE...........................15, 25
THE FIFTH HORSEMAN IS FEAR.....275	THE ITALIAN STRAW HAT.................31
THE FIRST MONSOON DAY..............482	THE JOYLESS STREET.........................26
THE FLOWER OF EVIL.......................488	THE JUNIPER TREE...........................390
THE FOOL...412	THE KEYS TO THE HOUSE...............494
THE FORBIDDEN CHRIST.................154	THE KILLING OF A CHINESE BOOKIE
THE FORSAKEN LAND......................498	332
THE FRUIT OF PARADISE.................288	THE LADY EVE...................................108
THE FUGITIVE....................................125	THE LADY FROM SHANGHAI.........124
THE GARDEN OF THE FINZI-CONTINIS 303	THE LADY WITH THE LITTLE DOG 227
	THE LAMP..202
THE GENERAL......................................26	THE LAST EMPEROR........................379
THE GENERAL LINE............................38	The Last Laugh......................................16
THE GOALIE'S ANXIETY AT THE PENALTY KICK..................................307	THE LAST LAUGH................................25
	THE LEGEND OF RITA......................470
The Goddess..225	THE LEGEND OF THE HOLY DRINKER
THE GOLD RUSH..................................26	384
THE GOLDEN AGE...............................55	The Leopard..244
The Gospel According to St. Matthew...250	THE LETTER.......................................106
THE GRAND MANEUVERS...............179	THE LIFE OF OHARU........................162
THE GRAPES OF WRATH..................104	THE LIGHT AHEAD.............................87
THE GREAT DICTATOR.....................104	THE LION HUNTERS........................257
THE GREY WOLVES..........................424	The Little Girl Who Sold the Sun..........397
THE HAWKS AND THE SPARROWS 265	THE LONG GOODBYE......................316
THE HOLY INNOCENTS....................369	THE LONG VOYAGE HOME.............103
The Holy Man..259	THE LOST HONOR OF KATHARINA BLUM..327
THE HOME AND THE WORLD.........365	
THE HOUR OF THE FURNACES.......276	THE LOST PATROL..............................51
THE HOURGLASS SANATORIUM....316	THE LOVERS OF TERUEL.................240
THE HOUSE OF THE ANGEL.............188	THE MAGNIFICENT AMBERSONS. .109
THE HUNT...266	THE MALTESE FALCON....................106
THE IDIOT...157	THE MAN BY THE SHORE................425
THE IDIOTS..445	THE MAN FROM LONDON................510
THE IMMORTAL STORY 278	THE MAN IN THE WHITE SUIT........160
THE INFORMER...................................74	THE MAN WHO HAD HIS HAIR CUT SHORT..258
THE INTRUDER..................................496	

Alphabetical index

THE MAN WHO SHOT LIBERTY VALANCE...237	THE PREFAB PEOPLE 360
THE MAN WITH A MOVIE CAMERA.33	THE PREFAB STORY...........................346
THE MARQUISE OF O 330	THE PRINCE OF HOMBURG.............440
THE MARRIAGE OF MARIA BRAUN 345	THE PROFESSION OF ARMS.............473
THE MATCH FACTORY GIRL 409	THE PUPPETMASTER........................422
THE MATTEI AFFAIR...........................310	THE QUIET ONE..................................131
THE MEMORY OF WATER 418	THE RED AND THE WHITE 270
THE MIDDLE OF THE WORLD.........317	The Red Desert......................................249
THE MILKY WAY.................................284	THE RETURN OF REASON..................22
THE MOTHER AND THE WHORE....315	THE REVOLUTION WILL NOT BE TELEVISED..489
THE MUSIC ROOM..............................195	THE RISE TO POWER OF LOUIS XIV 262
THE NAVIGATORS 475	THE RISING OF THE MOON..............182
THE NEW BABYLON.............................40	THE RIVER....................................81, 158
THE NIGHT OF TRUTH......................493	THE ROAD HOME 451
THE NIGHTS OF CABIRIA..................183	THE ROUND-UP..................................254
THE OFFICIAL STORY.......................373	THE RULES OF THE GAME.................85
THE OLD AND THE NEW.....................38	THE SACRIFICE...................................377
THE ORGANIZER................................248	THE SALTMEN OF TIBET..................439
THE OUTLAW AND HIS WIFE..............7	THE SEALED SOIL..............................332
THE PARSON'S WIDOW......................18	THE SEARCHERS................................181
THE PASSENGER.................................323	THE SECRET OF THE GRAIN............512
THE PASSION OF JOAN OF ARC........17	THE SEINE MEETS PARIS..................187
THE PASSION OF JOAN OF ARC 33	THE SEVENTH SEAL..........................182
THE PETRIFIED FOREST 79	THE SHOP AROUND THE CORNER. 105
THE PHANTOM CARRIAGE.................18	THE SILENCE..212
THE PHARMACY.................................324	THE SILENCE OF THE SEA...............124
THE PILGRIM 21	THE SILENCES OF THE PALACE.....429
THE PIT, THE PENDULUM AND HOPE 365	THE SOCIETY OF THE SPECTACLE 315
THE PLOW THAT BROKE THE PLAINS 77	THE SONG OF SPARROWS................518
	THE SOUTHERNER.............................117
THE PORNOGRAPHERS: INTRODUCTION TO ANTHROPOLOGY 263	THE SPANISH EARTH..........................80
	THE SPIRIT OF THE BEEHIVE..........317
	THE STARFISH......................................35
	THE STARS' CARAVAN......................471

Alphabetical index

THE STORY OF G.I. JOE.......................118	THE WIND WILL CARRY US..............449
THE STRANGER....................271	The Wizard of Oz.....................39, 199, 408
THE STRANGER'S HAND.................164	THE WORKING CLASS GOES TO HEAVEN.................307
THE STREET.........................20	THE WORLD OF APU..........................198
THE STRIKE..........................126	THE WRONG MAN.............................182
THE STRUCTURE OF CRYSTALS.....289	THERESE................376
THE TANGO LESSON 441	THERESE DESQUEYROUX...............243
THE THIN BLUE LINE........................385	(THESE ARE) THE DAMNED.............232
THE THING FROM ANOTHER WORLD 159	THESE HANDS........................419
THE THIRD GENERATION..................348	THEY DON'T WEAR BLACK-TIE.....356
The Threepenny Opera..............................58	THEY WERE EXPENDABLE..............116
THE TIES THAT BIND.........................372	THREE BROTHERS......................351
THE TIN DRUM 347	THREE LIVES AND ONLY ONE DEATH 436
THE TRAIN ROLLS ON......................306	THREE SONGS OF LENIN..................70
THE TREE OF WOODEN CLOGS.......341	THREE TIMES......................500
THE TRIAL...........................236	THRONE OF BLOOD.........................187
THE TRIAL OF JOAN OF ARC...........238	THRONE OF DEATH 449
THE UMBRELLAS OF CHERBOURG 251	Through a Glass Darkly........................210
THE UNFAITHFUL WIFE.........................278	THROUGH THE OLIVE TREES.........428
THE USUAL UNIDENTIFIED THIEVES 197	TILAÏ.......................411
THE VANISHED EMPIRE....................515	TIME STANDS STILL.......................362
The Virgin Spring.................................210	TIMES AND WINDS..........................505
THE VIRGIN SPRING.........................202	TIRED COMPANIONS: FIVE STORIES FROM THE WAR................................435
THE WAGES OF FEAR........................169	Tirez sur le pianiste...............................227
THE WALL.......................406	*Tlatli, Moufida..........................430*
THE WAY WE ARE.........................515	TO LIVE IN PEACE..............................121
THE WAYWARD CLOUD..................495	TOBACCO ROAD...............................108
THE WHITE SHIP................................107	Tokyo boshoku.........................186
THE WILD BUNCH..........................290	Tokyo monogatari.........................165
THE WIND..........................30	TOKYO SENSO SENGO HIWA..........301
THE WIND JOURNEYS......................519	TOKYO STORY........................165
THE WIND THAT SHAKES THE BARLEY........................502	TOKYO TWILIGHT.........................186
	TONI.................70

Alphabetical index

TOP OF THE WHALE.........................357
TOUCH OF EVIL.................................192
TOUCHEZ PAS AU GRISBI................168
TOUKI-BOUKI 315
TOUTE UNE NUIT...............................360
TRANSPORT FROM PARADISE........241
Trapero, Pablo...............455, 456, 476, 493
Trauberg, Leonid 40
TREASURE OF THE SIERRA MADRE
....125
Tressler, Georg..185
Trier, Lars von 369, 380, 381, 383, 414, 446
TRILOGY..485
Troëll, Jan...361
TROPIC OF CANCER..........................493
Trotta, Margarethe von. .327, 358, 375, 414
Truffaut, François...........56, 103, 152, 189, 199, 217, 220, 227, 228, 231, 251, 264, 296, 297, 299, 316, 350, 388, 489
Tsai, Ming-liang...................................496
Tsukamoto, Shinya...............................449
TULPAN..517
Turin, Victor...15
TURKSIB..15, 40
TWENTIETH CENTURY......................71
TWILIGHT...408
TWO MEN IN MANHATTAN.............194
Tystnaden..212

U

Uccellacci e uccellini 265
UGETSU MONOGATARI....................166
Ulica Graniczna....................................130

Ullmann, Liv..................................369, 438
Ulmer, Edgar G...................41, 71, 87, 115
ULYSSES' GAZE.................................432
UMBERTO D..140
Un chapeau de paille d'Italie...................31
UN CHIEN ANDALOU..........................34
Un condamné à mort s'est échappé........181
UNDER THE SKIN OF THE CITY......477
UNDERGROUND................................431
UNDERWORLD.....................................31
UNE FEMME DOUCE.........................292
Une histoire de vent..............................384
Une partie de campagne.........................76
UP TO A CERTAIN POINT..................364
Ustaoglu, Yesim....................................453

V

VAGABOND...371
VAGHE STELLE DELL'ORSO............256
Vajda, Ladislao 409
VAMPYR...44
Van Sant, Gus.........257, 373, 391, 412, 416, 417, 488, 502
Varda, Agnès..........236, 371, 372, 416, 468
VARIETY LIGHTS...............................156
Vasiliev, Sergei and Georgy....................76
Vérités et mensonges............................326
VERTIGO..195
Vertov, Dziga............24, 27, 30, 33, 37, 38, 60, 70, 100, 148, 152, 301, 400, 471
Vidas Secas...243
Vidor, King........................39, 84, 199, 408
Vigo, Jean.............38, 73, 78, 112, 199, 305

VINCERE..520
VIRIDIANA...230
Visconti, Luchino 24, 68, 70, 99, 100,
101, 109, 110, 112, 128, 129, 133, 158,
187, 192, 205, 228, 231, 244, 248, 256,
271, 272, 288, 308, 319, 335, 425, 453
VLADIMIR AND ROSA 300
VOYAGE IN ITALY..............................166
VOYAGE TO THE BEGINNING OF THE
WORLD..444
Vredens Dag..111

W

Wade, Mansour Sora......135, 147, 365, 485
WAGON MASTER................................153
WAITING FOR HAPPINESS................481
Wajda, Andrzej.......196, 335, 354, 355, 413
Walsh, Raoul...................................135, 137
Wang, Xiaoshuais...........370, 371, 445, 478
WAR AND PEACE...............................485
Watkins, Peter. 40, 156,
252, 321, 465, 473
WAVELENGTH....................................262
WAYS IN THE NIGHT.........................344
WE ARE GOING TO AMERICA.........420
WE SPIN AROUND THE NIGHT AND
ARE CONSUMED BY FIRE 342
WE STILL KILL THE OLD WAY 272
WE, FROM KRONSTADT.....................76
WEEKEND..268
WEEKEND STORIES...........................433
Weerasethakul, Apichatpong..........471, 494
Welles, Orson......89-91, 109, 110, 123-125,

128-130, 147, 192, 236, 237, 260, 278,
311, 326, 327, 350, 364, 384, 385, 395,
414, 417, 418
Wellman, William A. 32, 118, 131
WÊND KÛUNI 359
Wenders, Wim.........307, 328, 367, 379, 431
WERCKMEISTER HARMONIES.......467
WESTFRONT 1918.................................56
WHEN A WOMAN ASCENDS THE
STAIRS..229
WHISPERING PAGES.........................422
WHITE HEAT 135
WHITE NIGHTS...................................187
WHO THE HELL IS JULIETTE?.........442
WHY DOES HERR R. RUN AMOK?. .291
WHY HAS BODHI-DHARMA LEFT FOR
THE EAST?...389
Wiene, Robert...................................13, 416
WILD AT HEART................................407
Wilder, Billy 41, 114, 154, 161, 234, 302,
442
WINGS..264
WINGS OF DESIRE.............................379
WINTER LIGHT..................................211
Winterbottom, Michael..................291, 484
WISE BLOOD 345
Wiseman, Frederick..............290, 454, 455
Wolf, Konrad..................................198, 269
WOODEN CROSSES............................63
WOYZECK...430
Wright, Basil...72
Wyler, William..................64, 106, 121, 122

X

XALA..325

Y

YAABA..392
YEELEN..381
YELLOW EARTH................................368
YELLOW SKY......................................131
YESTERDAY GIRL 263
Yimou, Zhang........................*368, 415, 452*
Yong-Kyun, Bae.....................................*389*

Z

Zaim, Dervis..*438*
Zampa, Luigi..*121*
Zanussi, Krzysztof................................*289,*
312, 334, 344, 350, 433, 479, 494
Zaorski, Janusz......................................*331*
ZELIG..364
Zéro de conduite.......................78, 199, 305
Zhuangzhuang, Tian......................*374, 425*
ZVENIGORA..34